OXFORD WORLD'S CLASSICS

JAMES JOYCE

Ulysses

Edited with an Introduction and Notes by
JERI JOHNSON

OXFORD
UNIVERSITY PRESS

OXFORD
UNIVERSITY PRESS

Great Clarendon Street, Oxford OX2 6DP

Oxford University Press is a department of the University of Oxford.
It furthers the University's objective of excellence in research, scholarship,
and education by publishing worldwide in

Oxford New York

Athens Auckland Bangkok Bogotá Buenos Aires Cape Town
Chennai Dar es Salaam Delhi Florence Hong Kong Istanbul Karachi
Kolkata Kuala Lumpur Madrid Melbourne Mexico City Mumbai Nairobi
Paris São Paulo Shanghai Singapore Taipei Tokyo Toronto Warsaw

with associated companies in Berlin Ibadan

Oxford is a registered trade mark of Oxford University Press
in the UK and in certain other countries

Published in the United States
by Oxford University Press Inc., New York

First published 1922. This edition reproduced
from copy no. 785 in the Bodleian Library, shelfmark Arch.Dd.50.
First published as a World's Classics paperback 1993
Reissued as an Oxford World's Classics paperback 1998

British Library Cataloguing in Publication Data
Data available

Library of Congress Cataloging in Publication Data
Data available

ISBN–13: 978–0–19–283464–5

11

Printed in Great Britain by
Clays Ltd, St Ives plc

CONTENTS

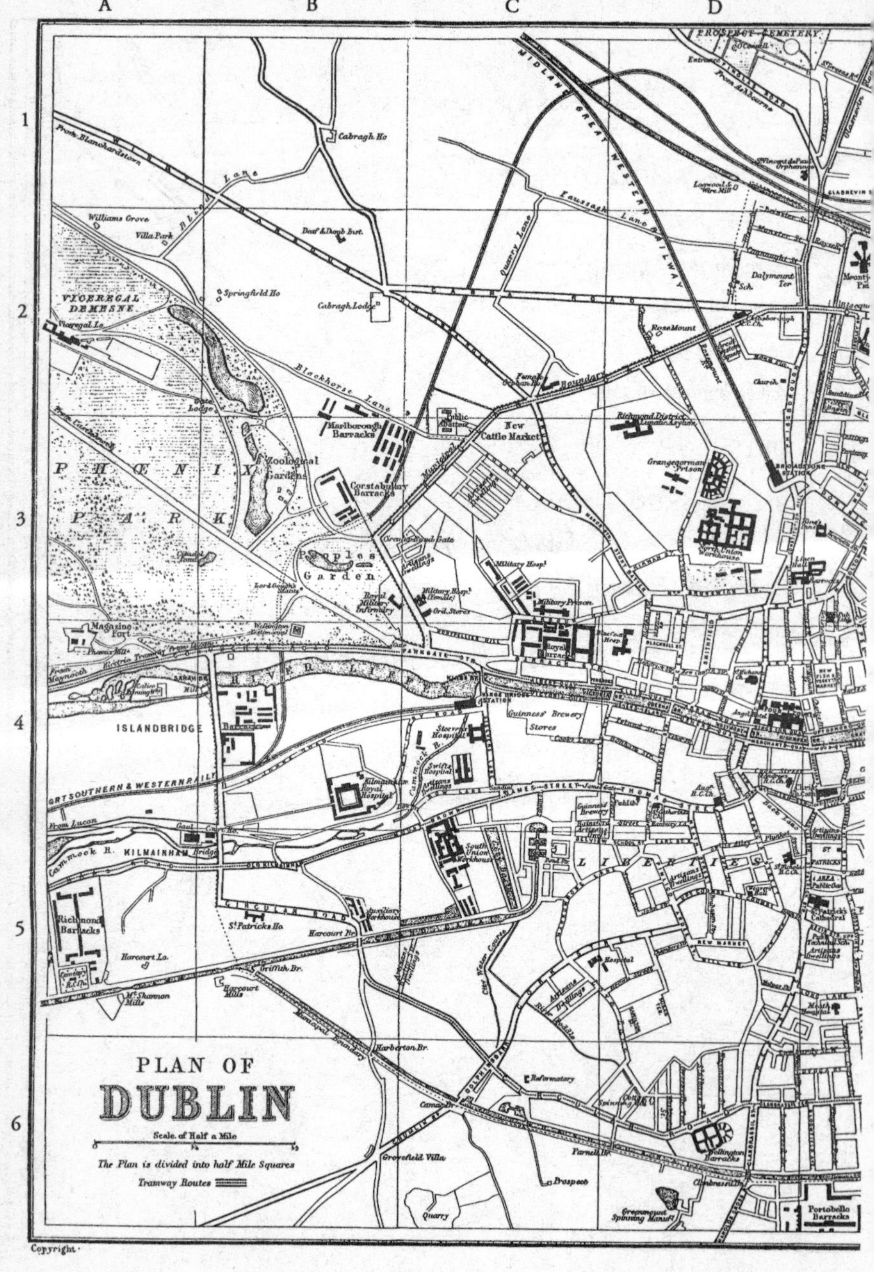
A
B
C
D
1
2
3
4
5
6
PLAN OF
DUBLIN
Scale of Half a Mile
The Plan is divided into half Mile Squares
Tramway Routes
PHŒNIX PARK
VICEREGAL DEMESNE
Viceregal Lo.
Williams Grove
Villa Park
Springfield Ho
Cabragh Ho
Cabragh Lodge
Deaf & Dumb Inst.
Blackhorse Lane
Marlborough Barracks
Zoological Gardens
Constabulary Barracks
Peoples Garden
Magazine Fort
ISLANDBRIDGE
KILMAINHAM
Richmond Barracks
St. Patricks Ho.
Harcourt Br.
Harcourt Lo.
Griffith Br.
Harberton Br.
New Cattle Market
Military Prison
Royal Barracks
Guinness' Brewery Stores
South Union Workhouse
LIBERTIES
Richmond District Lunatic Asylum
Grangegorman Prison
North Union Workhouse
Broadstone Station
PROSPECT CEMETERY
Dalymount Ter.
Rose Mount
Wellington Barracks
Portobello Barracks
Groveneld Villa
Quarry
Prospect
Parnell Br.
GRT SOUTHERN & WESTERN RAIL
MIDLAND GREAT WESTERN RAILWAY
From Lucan
From Blanchardstown
Copyright

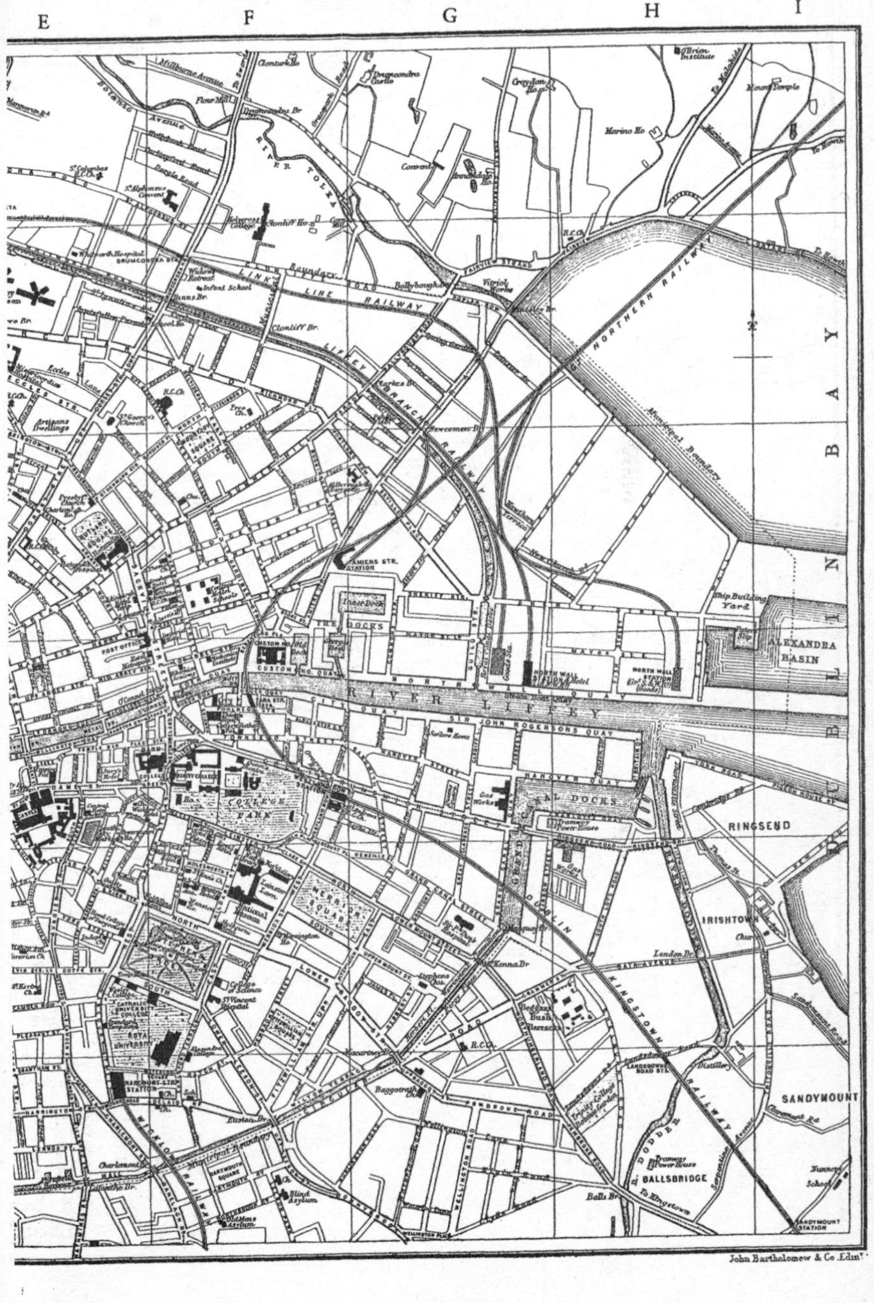

E
F
G
H
I
RIVER TOLKA
Drumcondra Castle
Marino Ho
Mount Temple
O'Brien Institute
Convent
Clonliff Ho
Holycross College
Flour Mill
Drumcondra Br
Millbourne Avenue
Botanic Avenue
Dargle Road
Whitworth Hospital
Drumcondra Sta.
Infant School
Binns Br.
Clonliff Br.
Ballybough Br.
Vitriol Works
Fairview Strand
R.C.Ch.
Annesley Br.
Newcomen Br.
Municipal Boundary
LINK LINE RAILWAY
LIFFEY BRANCH RAILWAY
G. NORTHERN RAILWAY
Eccles Lane
Artizans Dwellings
St. George's Church
Free Ch.
Rotunda Hospital
AMIENS STR. STATION
Inner Dock
THE DOCKS
Mayor St.
Goods Sta.
NORTH WALL STATION & Hotel
NORTH WALL STATION
Ship Building Yard
ALEXANDRA BASIN
POST OFFICE
CUSTOM HO.
CUSTOM HO. QUAY
NORTH WALL QUAY
RIVER LIFFEY
CITY QUAY
SIR JOHN ROGERSONS QUAY
Sailors Home
Steam Boat Quay
HANOVER QUAY
Hanover Street
Gas Works
GRAND CANAL DOCKS
Tramway Power House
RINGSEND
York Road
Pigeon House Rd.
Thorncastle Street
Thomas St.
IRISHTOWN
Church
London Br.
Bath Avenue
Sandymount Road
SANDYMOUNT
Claremont Rd.
Distillery
Lansdowne Road Sta.
Trinity College Botanic Garden
R. DODDER
Tramway Power House
BALLSBRIDGE
To Kingstown
Balls Br.
SANDYMOUNT STATION
KINGSTOWN RAILWAY
Dame St.
Trinity College
COLLEGE PARK
Leinster Lawn
National Museum
MERRION SQUARE
Fitzwilliam Square
Grand Canal Street
Sir P. Dun's Hospital
Macquay Br.
McKenna Br.
Beggars Bush Barracks
College of Science
St. Vincent Hospital
ROYAL UNIVERSITY
CATHOLIC UNIVERSITY
HARCOURT STR. STATION
Alexandra College
R.C.Ch.
Baggotrath Ch.
Pembroke Road
Wellington Road
Eustace Br.
Municipal Boundary
Charlemont Br.
Dartmouth Square
Blind Asylum
Old Men's Asylum
Wellington Place
B A Y
John Bartholomew & Co. Edin.

ABBREVIATIONS

G	*'Ulysses': A Critical and Synoptic Edition*, ed. Hans Walter Gabler with Wolfhard Steppe and Claus Melchior, with an Afterword by Hans Walter Gabler, 3 vols. (New York and London: Garland, 1984 and rev. pbk. edn. 1986)
JJ	Richard Ellmann, *James Joyce* (1959; rev. edn. 1982; corr. New York: Oxford University Press, 1983)
JJA	*The James Joyce Archive*, ed. Michael Groden, 63 vols. (New York and London: Garland, 1977–80), vols. xii–xxvii: *Ulysses* manuscripts
LI, LII, LIII	*Letters of James Joyce*, 3 vols.: vol. i, ed. Stuart Gilbert; vols. ii and iii, ed. Richard Ellmann (New York: Viking, 1957, 1966)
P/J	Ezra Pound, *Pound/Joyce: The Letters of Ezra Pound to James Joyce, with Pound's Essays on Joyce*, ed. Forrest Read (1967; repr. London: Faber & Faber, 1968)
SL	*Selected Letters of James Joyce*, ed. Richard Ellmann (New York: Viking, 1975)

INTRODUCTION

'Worst is beginning'

'WHERE do you begin in this?' (25) Stephen Dedalus asks his Dalkey schoolboys, 'this' being the book before them. The question returns with each new reader approaching *Ulysses* for the first time. The commonplace response of the contemporary Joyce critic is itself Joycean: of course, there is no possibility of beginning *Ulysses*, much less of finishing (with) it. Joyce's book has so colonized twentieth-century Anglophone culture that we can never now enter it for the first time. Instead, we most resemble members of that parade of guests Bloom imagines both preceding and succeeding him into Molly's bed: 'he is always the last term of a preceding series even if the first term of a succeeding one, each imagining himself to be first, last, only and alone whereas he is neither first nor last nor only nor alone in a series originating in and repeated to infinity'. (683)

There is more seriousness in this contention than first meets the eye. While every new reader faced with *this* book addresses it new, this newness is modified by the generations of readers who have come before and whose disseminations of it have seeped into virtually every aspect of high and popular culture. Approach must now be made through an air thick with rumours about the book and from a position inside a culture saturated with the effects of its influence. In 1941 Harry Levin declared *Ulysses* 'a novel to end all novels'.[1] In saying so, he credited it with being the culmination of one tradition (say, the nineteenth-century realist novel) while setting out the questions to be debated in the next (next two, perhaps, Modernism and postmodernism). If, after Joyce, everything suggested itself only as repetition, many found the repetition fruitful, not least Joyce's immediate contemporaries Ezra Pound, T. S. Eliot, and Virginia Woolf. Later (to name but a few of Joyce's more obvious beneficiaries), Samuel Beckett and Dylan Thomas, later still Anthony Burgess, B. S. Johnson, Martin (if not Kingsley) Amis, A. S. Byatt, and Salman Rushdie all bear the mark of his influence, as, in the wider sphere, do Jorge Luis Borges, Italo Calvino, Gabriel García Márquez, Umberto Eco, and a whole generation of American novelists. And this is to stay within the realm of 'high' culture. The impact is no less felt on television, film, popular music, and Bloom's own profession, advertising, in their use of montage, open-ended narrative, pastiche, parody, multiple viewpoint, neologism.

[1] Harry Levin, *James Joyce: A Critical Introduction* (1941; rev. edn. New York: New Directions, 1960), 207.

While this may be incontestable, it is as likely to leave the novice reader as much bemused and intimidated as enlightened and encouraged. Often rumours create more static than clear signal. A small example. *Ulysses*, the title, utterly flummoxed many early readers. To them it conjured up classical associations: the Roman name of the Greek hero Odysseus. Expecting perhaps a modern novelization of Homer's epic, they opened the book only to discover themselves thrown into the middle of a narrative (*in medias res*—in the midst of things—the way all good epics begin) featuring 'Stately plump Buck Mulligan' (hardly a Greek or Roman name), then a 'displeased and sleepy' Stephen Dedalus (here, at least, was a Greek name), then Haines, a 'ponderous Saxon'. Where was Ulysses?[2] Most modern readers don't face *this* dilemma because by now the title has virtually lost its ability to refer to the Roman name of a Greek hero. Now it simply means 'That Book By James Joyce'. If today we are to recognize both the significance and the force of the title, we may need to make it strange again, to untie the knot binding it to its creator. Jennifer Levine suggests imagining that this book is called *Hamlet* to 'regain a sense of it as a text brought into deliberate collision with a powerful predecessor'.[3] That's the kind of 'making strange' required.

There is a further related problem. If Joyce has spawned generations of writers, he has no less stimulated whole libraries of criticism. What may have appeared at the time as enormous egoism—Joyce's claim, 'I've put in so many enigmas and puzzles that it will keep the professors busy for centuries arguing over what I meant, and that's the only way of insuring one's immortality' (*JJ* 521)—begins to seem modest seventy years on. More to the point, virtually every Joyce critic these days expects one to know already things about the book which aren't to be found within it: the episode titles, for example, or the history of Joyce's personal campaign to create a critical context for the book. What is a new reader to do?

In what follows, that question (or its twin, what do you need to know to read *Ulysses*?) focuses my discussion. This is by no means to suggest that anything can substitute for the vertiginous experience of actually reading the

[2] The fact that 'Ulysses' does not appear until episode 4, and then under the guise of 'Mr Leopold Bloom', bourgeois advertising canvasser, confused at least one hapless critic. As Joyce took delight in relating to Harriet Weaver: 'Another American "critic" who wanted to interview me (I declined) told me he had read the book with great interest but that he could not understand why Bloom came into it. I explained to him why and he [was] surprised and disappointed for he thought Stephen was Ulysses. He heard some talk of Penelope and asked me who she was. This also I told him but did not convince him entirely because he said rather doubtfully "But is Penelope a really Irish name?"' (*LI* 184)

[3] Jennifer Levine, '*Ulysses*', in Derek Attridge, ed., *The Cambridge Companion to James Joyce* (Cambridge: Cambridge University Press, 1990), 131–2.

book, nor that a preface of this sort does not run the risk of creating its own static. My hope is of kindling curiosity rather than dampening it, and of opening just enough doors that the reader will want to walk through.

'I wonder what kind is that book he brought me'

The large majority of *Ulysses*'s first readers were clearly baffled and outraged. The popular press (the *Sporting Times*!) opined that the book 'appears to have been written by a perverted lunatic who has made a speciality of the literature of the latrine.... [It's] enough to make a Hottentot sick.'[4] When it wasn't being decried as pornography (hadn't the American courts already proved it was?),[5] it was being compared, repeatedly, to a telephone directory (which became one of Joyce's favourite euphemisms for it). At its most extreme, this criticism announced: 'As a whole, the book must remain impossible to read.... [It is] literary Bolshevism. It is experimental, anti-conventional, anti-Christian, chaotic, totally unmoral.'[6] Other reviewers were more prosaic: '*Ulysses* is many things: it is very big, it is hard to read, difficult to procure, unlike any other book that has been written.'[7] Perhaps the oddest thing about this proliferation of 'critical opinion' is that reviewers were addressing an audience about a book which they hadn't a chance of obtaining for at least another twelve or fourteen years, when the first unlimited editions were published (in the USA and England, respectively). Still, the book's appearance was considered a literary event of such magnitude and a publication so threatening ('literary Bolshevism') that every respectable journal or '**DAILY ORGAN**' (114) had to respond. H. G. Wells is reputed to have said that when he put the book down, having finished reading, he felt as though he had suppressed a revolution.

What was it about *Ulysses* that struck Joyce's contemporaries with such tremendous force? The vast majority of them could make neither head nor tail of the prose: 'Two-thirds of it is incoherent'; '*Ulysses* is a chaos'; 'inspissated obscurities'.[8] While even these critics inevitably praised Joyce's stylistic facility—when he set his mind to it—rudimentary comprehension of large

[4] 'Aramis', 'The Scandal of *Ulysses*', *Sporting Times* (1 Apr. 1922), repr. in Robert H. Deming, ed., *James Joyce: The Critical Heritage*, 2 vols. (London: Routledge & Kegan Paul, 1970), i. 192, 193.

[5] See 'Composition and Publication History'.

[6] Shane Leslie, '*Ulysses*', *Quarterly Review* (Oct. 1922), repr. in Deming, ed., *Critical Heritage*, i. 207.

[7] J. M. Murry, review of *Ulysses*, *Nation & Athenæum* (22 Apr. 1922), repr. in ibid. 195.

[8] 'Aramis' in ibid. 192; Holbrook Jackson, 'Ulysses à la Joyce', *To-Day* (June 1922), repr. in ibid. 199; Murry in ibid. 197.

sections of the book lay beyond the grasp of its first readers. What *could* be understood deserved pruning, they thought. The book was ill-disciplined, its author perverse. As Holbrook Jackson stated the case most dispassionately, 'Everything that is never done or never mentioned is done and said by him.'[9] Of course, Jackson really means 'never done or never mentioned' in Proper Literature. Precisely. *Ulysses* assaulted propriety.

For Joyce's co-Modernists, his social improprieties (which they met with varying degrees of tolerance) were a small price to pay for the stylistic possibilities opened up by his literary 'improprieties'. For T. S. Eliot, Joyce's *Ulysses* took a major 'step toward making the modern world possible for art'.[10] Ezra Pound praised Joyce's stylistic veracity and compression: 'Joyce's characters not only speak their own language, but they think their own language.'[11] '[There is] not a line, not a half-line which does not receive an intellectual intensity incomparable in a work of so long a span.'[12] Virginia Woolf found the 'indecency' less tolerable, but eventually admitted to having read it 'with spasms of wonder, of discovery'.[13] If the populace was being warned that Joyce was scandalous, incomprehensible, a 'frustrated Titan . . . splutter[ing] hopelessly under the flood of his own vomit',[14] the literati were being given notice that this writer could not be ignored. '"Unite to give praise to Ulysses,"' declared Pound; 'those who will not, may content themselves with a place in the lower intellectual orders.'[15]

Sufficient numbers even of those who praised the book found it so disconcertingly unreadable, at least in part, to prompt the question 'why?' The charge of incomprehensibility may be laid fairly at the door of the book's uncanny likeness to, and utter difference from, novels which had preceded it. As Hugh Kenner argues, 'printed words on a page—any words, any page—are so ambiguously related to each other that we collect sense only with the

[9] Jackson in Deming, ed., *Critical Heritage*, i. 198.

[10] T. S. Eliot, '*Ulysses*, Order, and Myth', *The Dial* (Nov. 1922), repr. in Frank Kermode, ed., *Selected Prose of T. S. Eliot* (London: Faber & Faber, 1975), 178.

[11] Ezra Pound, 'Paris Letter', *The Dial* (June 1922), repr. in *P/J* 195.

[12] Pound, '*James Joyce et Pécuchet*', *Mercure de France* (June 1922), trans. and repr. in Deming, ed., *Critical Heritage*, i. 266.

[13] And 'then again with long lapses of intense boredom'. From Woolf's diary entry of 15 Jan. 1941, on hearing of Joyce's death (*The Diary of Virginia Woolf*, ed. Anne Olivier Bell and Andrew McNeillie, 5 vols. (1984; repr. Harmondsworth: Penguin, 1985), vol. v, *1936–1941*, p. 353). 'Indecency' is Woolf's word: 'the pages reeled with indecency'. The effect of what Woolf might have 'discovered' on first reading *Ulysses* in 1922 can perhaps be seen in her own evocation of a single day in June, *Mrs Dalloway*, published in 1925.

[14] 'Domini Canis' (Shane Leslie), '*Ulysses*', *Dublin Review* (Sept. 1922), repr. in Deming, ed., *Critical Heritage*, i. 203.

[15] Pound, 'Paris Letter', in *P/J* 194.

aid of a tradition: this means, helped by prior experience with a genre, and entails our knowing which genre is applicable.'[16] *Ulysses* looked like a novel, but it also looked like drama, or catechism, or poetry, or music depending on which page one happened to open. If the book had played a little more fair—had it, say, used quotation marks to identify the speakers of dialogue and to make that dialogue more readily distinguishable from the circumambient prose, or had it provided a leisurely preamble setting the scene and gently leading the reader toward a first encounter with Buck Mulligan and Stephen Dedalus, had there been less neologistic word-play of the sort more usually found in poetry, or less psychological verisimilitude, less parody, pastiche, or stylistic extravagance—it might have been recognized as a novel. That it wasn't is simply because it isn't—a novel, that is. Not quite. Or rather, it contains within itself at least one novel (a point to which we will return), but it also challenges, expands, even explodes that genre's previously established conventions. Joyce himself began by calling it a novel, soon abandoned this for 'epic', 'encyclopaedia', or even *maledettisimo romanzaccione*,[17] and finally settled simply for 'book'.

From the outset, Joyce recognized that his audience, whether popular or literary, was going to be nonplussed. As early as *Ulysses*'s initial appearance in the *Little Review* (where it was serialized between 1918 and 1920),[18] Joyce began filling his letters to loyal friends with explanations and exegeses. If *Ulysses* were to find an informed, appreciative audience, its author would have to create one.

'preparation should be with importance commensurate'

For at least fifty years after *Ulysses*'s publication, criticism of the book fell into two principal, though not always competing, groups. One group formed of those interested in the book as novel (with that genre's preoccupation with identifiably 'human' characters inhabiting a recognizably 'real' version of this world and engaged in plotted actions). Here we find lovers of realism, of facts, of social and political history, of humane acts, of psychological verisimilitude, of fictions which mask their fictiveness. The other group preferred patterns,

[16] Hugh Kenner, *Ulysses* (1980; rev. edn. Baltimore and London: Johns Hopkins University Press, 1987), 3.

[17] 'Bastard' Italian for, roughly, 'damnedest monstrously big novel'. These three euphemisms all occur in Joyce's letter of 21 Sept. 1920 to Carlo Linati (*SL* 270). For a discussion of the book's defiance of generic classification, see A. Walton Litz, 'The Genre of *Ulysses*', in John Halperin, ed., *The Theory of the Novel: New Essays* (New York: Oxford University Press, 1974), 109–20.

[18] See 'Composition and Publication History'.

parallels, systems, symbols, myths, literature which proudly declared its 'literariness'. Of course, *Ulysses* was book enough for both. But, in the beginning, Joyce had to draw attention to some of the ways in which it was so.

In December 1921, two months before *Ulysses* was published, the French novelist, poet, and critic Valéry Larbaud presented the book to an enthusiastic audience gathered in Adrienne Monnier's Paris bookshop, *La Maison des Amis des Livres*. Larbaud, who had read the book in its *Little Review* form, declared it as 'great and comprehensive and human as Rabelais' (*LIII* 40). Joyce approved. When Larbaud suggested a conference to introduce *Ulysses* to the public, Joyce graciously acceded and promptly provided him with typescripts, proofs, suggested portions for reading at the '*séance*', then critical hints, including a 'plan' of the book, versions of which he had been circulating to select friends since at least a year earlier. In Larbaud's lecture we can see the seeds Joyce has planted beginning to sprout. Here we first glimpse the arguments which will determine the shape of future critical debates.

What did Larbaud, nudged by Joyce, think readers ought to know about the book confronting them?[19] 'Preparatory to anything else' (569), the ways in which it *was* a novel. Larbaud stressed that the narrative consisted of eighteen discrete episodes though it is rendered coherent by the continuing presence of one or more of the three principal characters: Stephen Dedalus (late of *A Portrait of the Artist as a Young Man*), Leopold and Molly Bloom. The setting: Dublin. The time: a single day in June (16 June 1904 to be precise). Further, the narrative made frequent use of *monologue intérieur*, the unmediated, first-person rendering of the characters' private thoughts in their own idiom and the registering in those thoughts of external events, conversations, physical surroundings, sensations. Much of the action is thus related through the consciousness of these three characters. By attending to these aspects of *Ulysses*, one could see, as Larbaud stressed, that 'in this book . . . the illusion of life, of the thing in the act, is complete'.[20]

If *Ulysses* was novelistic triumph, though, it had another, more discomfiting side and that was its relation to its epic precursor, *The Odyssey*. It is hard to imagine any reader stumbling on to this relation on her or his own. True, there is that title. A little cogitation might take one as far as Homer's hero (by way of his Roman descendant), but had Joyce left only the title, chances are that that is where one would come to a halt. Should anyone later have suggested that the book was, at least in part, an extravagant contemporary

[19] Valéry Larbaud, 'James Joyce', *Nouvelle Revue Française*, 18 (Apr. 1922), 385–407. This is an expanded version of Larbaud's original lecture. A translated lengthy excerpt of this article is reprinted in Deming, ed., *Critical Heritage*, i. 252–62.

[20] Larbaud in ibid. 259.

rewriting of Homer, they would probably have been laughed out of the academy. But, on this matter, Joyce was taking no chances.

From the time that *Ulysses* was sufficiently complete for its publication to be seriously discussed, Joyce began to refer in his letters to sections of it as bearing Odyssean titles. Any published edition of the final book contains only three clearly numbered divisions: I (the first three episodes), II (the next twelve), and III (the final three). These Joyce alluded to with Homeric inflection as the *Telemachia*, the *Odyssey*, and the *Nostos* (or 'Return Home') (*LI* 113). Further, each of the eighteen episodes contained within these three Homeric divisions had titles gleaned from Odysseus's adventures. These Joyce released in dribs and drabs until in 1920 he sent to Carlo Linati, proposed translator of *Exiles*, what he described as 'a sort of summary—key—skeleton—schema' of the entire book '(for home use only)' (*SL* 270). Unfortunately, Linati took Joyce at his word and held on to the schema, so that when it came time for Larbaud to deliver his lecture, Joyce had to provide him with another plan of the book. This plan differed considerably from the first in detail, but the essential features were the same.[21] The title of each episode was given: the *Telemachia* comprised 'Telemachus', 'Nestor', 'Proteus'; the *Odyssey*: 'Calypso', 'Lotus Eaters', 'Hades', 'Aeolus', 'Lestrygonians', 'Scylla and Charybdis', 'Wandering Rocks', 'Sirens', 'Cyclops', 'Nausicaa', 'Oxen of the Sun', 'Circe'; and the *Nostos*: 'Eumaeus', 'Ithaca', and 'Penelope'.[22] In addition, it seemed, Joyce employed correspondences between Homeric characters and his own: obviously Stephen was Telemachus (son of Odysseus/Ulysses); Bloom, Ulysses; Molly, Penelope (his faithful, weaving wife); but, too, Mulligan was Antinous; the barmaids, Miss Lydia Douce and Miss Mina Kennedy, were the Sirens; Bella the brothel keeper was Circe, and so on.[23] Further, Homeric places were translated as Joycean themes: Scylla the Rock became Dogma, while Charybdis the

[21] A version of this second plan was first published in Stuart Gilbert's *James Joyce's 'Ulysses'* (1930)—the first substantial book of *Ulysses* criticism, written again with Joyce's approval and with the benefit of his guidance. Both the Linati and Gilbert schemata are reproduced in Appendix A, below. The Linati schema has also been published, in both Italian and a different translation, in Richard Ellmann, *Ulysses on the Liffey* (London: Faber & Faber, 1974).

[22] The episodes can be located in this edition on the following pages: 'Telemachus' (3–23), 'Nestor' (24–36), 'Proteus' (37–50), 'Calypso' (53–67), 'Lotus Eaters' (68–83), 'Hades' (84–111), 'Aeolus' (112–43), 'Lestrygonians' (144–75), 'Scylla and Charybdis' (176–209), 'Wandering Rocks' (210–44), 'Sirens' (245–79), 'Cyclops' (280–330), 'Nausicaa' (331–65), 'Oxen of the Sun' (366–407), 'Circe' (408–565), 'Eumaeus' (569–618), 'Ithaca' (619–89), and 'Penelope' (690–732).

[23] See the Notes for Homeric glosses.

Whirlpool became Mysticism; or Helios's sacred Oxen became Fertility or Penelope's Suitors, Scruples. Joyce had an infinitely adaptable creative mind which thrived on noticing the ways in which one thing (a Dublin conversation, say) both was and was not like another (a battle between a Greek warrior trying to get home and the immediate opponent who stood in his way). It is these not-quite-samenesses which Joyce exploits in his connecting *Ulysses* and *The Odyssey*.

Beyond the strictly Homeric parallels, each episode had its own particular setting, hour, bodily organ, art, colour, symbol, technique (and earlier, in the Linati schema, its own 'Meaning'). As Joyce explained this elaborate system to Linati:

> [*Ulysses*] is the epic of two races (Israel–Ireland) and at the same time the cycle of the human body as well as a little story of a day (life). . . . It is also a kind of encyclopaedia. My intention is not only to render the myth *sub specie temporis nostri* but also to allow each adventure (that is, every hour, every organ, every art being interconnected and interrelated in the somatic scheme of the whole) to condition and even to create its own technique. Each adventure is so to speak one person although it is composed of persons—as Aquinas relates of the heavenly hosts. (*SL* 271)

Now this was a novel with a difference. Larbaud might stress that 'the plan, which cannot be detached from the book, because it is the very web of it' was actually subordinate to 'man, the creature of flesh, living out his day',[24] but the extraordinarily intricate and elaborate symbolic systems carry it away from the domain of more conventional fiction and toward something which, for lack of a better name, we might call the 'hyperliterary'. For this is literature which draws attention to itself *as literature*, as artefact constructed out of words and symbols and correspondences and systems which we take pleasure in precisely because of (rather than despite) their craftedness, precisely because they draw our attention to word *as* word, symbol *as* symbol, system *as* system, rather than simply urging us to see through this artifice toward some meaning residing within. If we have been trained to read novels in such a way as to discover the correlation between the novel and life, or to provide a paraphrase of its 'meaning', or to explicate the moral dilemma, this foregrounding of word, symbol, system, correspondence, frustrates that training. What possible 'moral' can be drawn from the proliferation of flower names in the 'Lotus Eaters' episode? or from the fact that 'Calypso's' colour is orange? or that 'Ithaca's' symbol is 'Comets'? *Ulysses* in this mode will *not* play that game.

[24] Larbaud in Deming, ed., *Critical Heritage*, i. 261.

It is probably time to attempt the formulation of a rule about *Ulysses*, a rule which emerges as the logical conclusion of Joyce's having drawn Larbaud's attention simultaneously to two different (both independently verifiable) aspects of the book. The rule: A salient, if not the quintessential, characteristic of *Ulysses* is that it is allotropic.[25] That is, it is capable of existing, and indeed does exist, in at least two distinct, and distinctively different, forms at one and the same time: in this case, 'distilled essence of novel' and 'extravagant, symbolically supersaturated anti-novel'.

The two strains had been alive in Joyce's mind at least since 1912 when he delivered two lectures at the Università Popolare in Trieste under the series title 'Verismo ed idealismo nella letterature inglese (Daniele De Foe–William Blake)'.[26] To any reader of *Ulysses*, the combination of Defoe and Blake comes as no surprise. Joyce's Defoe is the master of 'matter-of-fact realism' and prophetic creator of characters who embody the coming 'Anglo-Saxon spirit': 'English feminism and English imperialism already lurk in these souls.'[27] In other words, his Crusoe is both particular and typical. Joyce's Blake is a sensitive, practical idealist—practical in that he practised in his life what he preached in his art—visionary seer, the 'humble' through whose mouth the 'Eternal' spoke. What Joyce found in his art was 'the innate sense of form [and] the coordinating force of the intellect'.[28] Joyce stresses not Blake's mystical visions but his capacity for, and attendance to, the artistic matters of form and correspondence. *Verismo* and *idealismo*, Defoe and Blake, become in *Ulysses* the two competing yet co-ordinated strains we have already identified.

These two allotropes or 'modes' each inevitably produced its own school of *Ulysses* criticism. The two contrasting critical positions ('it's a novel'; 'it's a symbolic system') were adopted respectively by two of the book's most ardent admirers, Ezra Pound and T. S. Eliot. Pound, who had been intimately involved with the book's serialization, preferred to ignore the Homeric correspondences and to focus instead on its huge humane expansiveness and its stylistic fidelity to nuances of character. In fact, Pound bears responsibility for generations of Joyceans approaching the systems and symbols with embarrassment, for in an early review he announced, 'These correspondences

[25] 'Allotropy': from chemistry, the property of certain elements to exist in two or more distinct forms: e.g. carbon exists within nature as graphite and diamond.

[26] The two lectures have been published as 'Daniel Defoe by James Joyce', ed. and trans. Joseph Prescott, *Buffalo Studies* 1/1 (Dec. 1964), 1–27; and James Joyce, 'William Blake', ed. Ellsworth Mason, *Criticism*, 1 (Summer 1959), 181–9; trans. and repr. in *The Critical Writings of James Joyce*, ed. Ellsworth Mason and Richard Ellmann (New York: Viking, 1959), 214–22.

[27] Joyce, 'Daniel Defoe', 12, 24, 23.

[28] Joyce, 'William Blake', 218, 221.

are part of Joyce's mediaevalism and are chiefly his own affair, a scaffold, a means of construction, justified by the result, and justifiable by it only.' Instead, he pronounced the book a 'super-novel'.[29] Eliot, who never demonstrated any particular affection for fiction, was antithetically disposed. In his influential review, '*Ulysses*, Order, and Myth', he declared,

> Mr Joyce's parallel use of the *Odyssey* has ... the importance of a scientific discovery. No one else has built a novel upon such a foundation before. ... I am not begging the question in calling *Ulysses* a 'novel'; and if you call it an epic it will not matter. If it is not a novel, that is simply because the novel is a form which will no longer serve. ... In using the myth, in manipulating a continuous parallel between contemporaneity and antiquity, Mr Joyce [has discovered] a way of controlling, of ordering, of giving a shape and a significance to the immense panorama of futility and anarchy which is contemporary history. ... Instead of narrative method, we may now use the mythical method.[30]

One might be forgiven for thinking that Eliot's oration has perhaps more to do with his own 1922 'mythic parallelism' *The Waste Land* than with *Ulysses*, but it served as his declaration both of how Joyce's book should be conceived and of what Modernism might mean. Henceforth Joyce critics would steer a course between the Scylla of novelistic realism and hard facts and the Charybdis of myth, symbol, and form for its own sake.[31] The first major critical book on *Ulysses*, Stuart Gilbert's *James Joyce's 'Ulysses'* (1930), emphasized, through constant reference to the schema with which Joyce had previously provided Larbaud, the elaborate systems, correspondences, and significances of the book. Balancing this four years later was Frank Budgen's *James Joyce and the Making of 'Ulysses'*, which placed Bloom, bourgeois everyman, at the centre of the 'novel' and asserted the comic spirit of the whole. Both books were written with Joyce's knowledge, encouragement, and occasional advice. A generation later Richard Ellmann (with his *Ulysses on the Liffey*) and Hugh Kenner (with *Dublin's Joyce*, *Joyce's Voices*, and *Ulysses*) took up (respectively) the Gilbert and Budgen, Eliot and Pound, lines once again. However, by the time of the arrival of this second generation of Joyceans, readers had begun to attend very carefully to the book's language, to its predisposition not only to fulfil conventions but to push them to the

[29] Pound, 'Paris Letter', in *P/J* 197.

[30] Eliot, '*Ulysses*, Order, and Myth', 177–8.

[31] A. Walton Litz argues similarly that Eliot and Pound set the terms for the succeeding critical debate. I would disagree only in so far as to claim that the Master Builder was Joyce himself. A. Walton Litz, 'Pound and Eliot on *Ulysses*: The Critical Tradition', in Thomas F. Staley, ed., *'Ulysses': Fifty Years* (1972; repr. Bloomington: Indiana University Press, 1974), 5–18.

bursting point, to its seeming self-conscious awareness of itself as a written yet material artefact, to the way in which it seemed not only to say things but to do them. In short, readers became aware of *Ulysses* as, in Roland Barthes's use of the term, a 'Text': an actively productive, literally paradoxical, non-closed, irreducibly plural, playful, self-pleasuring writing.[32]

Ironically, something of *Ulysses*'s *textual* nature had been detected as early as 1927, by another of Joyce's co-Modernists, Wyndham Lewis. Where recent readers have leapt on this discovery with enthusiasm and delight, Lewis deplored it. In his *Time and Western Man*, he excoriated 'The Mind of James Joyce'.[33] Here he puts succinctly—he intended it to sting—what many another Joyce critic missed: 'what stimulates [Joyce] is *ways of doing things*, and technical processes, and not *things to be done*'.[34] Of course, Joyce himself was well aware of his predilection. He once boasted to Samuel Beckett, 'I have discovered that I can do anything with language I want' (*JJ* 702). Notice that he does not say, 'I can *say* anything I want with language.' For Joyce, language was for doing, not saying. If the first fifty years of *Ulysses* criticism were spent in a tug-of-war between the critical offspring of Eliot and Pound, the last twenty have brought Lewis's (unintended) progeny to the fore. But all have in one way or another been Joyce's posterity. A closer look at *Ulysses*, as novel and as symbolic/stylistic system, but with one eye always open to its 'textuality', reveals much about why it might be considered, as it refers to itself, as a 'chaffering allincluding most farraginous chronicle'. (402)

'write a book out of it the works of Master Poldy'

When Joyce dropped to Larbaud the phrase *monologue intérieur*, he was steering him ever so gently in the direction of recognizing the book as a novel.

[32] Roland Barthes, 'From Work to Text' (1971), repr. in Stephen Heath, ed. and trans., *Image Music Text* (1977; repr. London: Fontana, 1984), 155–64. Though note that Barthes uses the term 'play' in the various senses of 'like a door, like a machine with play', 'playing the Text as one plays a game', and 'playing the Text in the musical sense of the term' (p. 162). See, too, Levine's description of *Ulysses*'s 'textual' aspect in her discussion of 'Oxen of the Sun' (Levine, 'Ulysses', 146–58).

[33] Wyndham Lewis, 'An Analysis of the Mind of James Joyce', in *Time and Western Man* (London: Chatto & Windus, 1927), 91–130. Lewis's criticism is mainly known to Joyce scholars through Kenner's use of him as the buffoon who clumsily misreads Joyce's style. Kenner was one of the earliest critics to attend to the 'productive' aspect of the book which Lewis so deplored. See Kenner, *Joyce's Voices* (Berkeley and Los Angeles: University of California Press, 1978), 16–17, 23, 69–70.

[34] Lewis, 'Analysis', 106–7; emphasis in original. See, too, Derek Attridge and Daniel Ferrer, 'Introduction', in Attridge and Ferrer, eds., *Post-Structuralist Joyce: Essays from the French* (Cambridge: Cambridge University Press, 1984), 5–6.

Here was a literary technique capable of presenting directly without aid of an intrusive omniscient narrator the most intimate, often half-formed, only half-verbalized, thoughts of a character, and in so doing, if one were as stylistically dextrous as Joyce, deftly and economically drawing the curve of a personality.

Watch the technique in action, how within a few words Joyce is able to convey intimacy, immediacy, and ineradicable distinctions of character: Mr Leopold Bloom, Jewish Dubliner, inside/outsider, idiosyncratic everyman, homegrown philosopher, as he ponders in passing Saint Joseph's, National school, on his way to buy a pork kidney for his breakfast: 'Brats' clamour. Windows open. Fresh air helps memory. Or a lilt. Ahbeesee defeegee kelomen opeecue rustyouvee double you. Boys are they? Yes. Inishturk. Inishark. Inishboffin. At their joggerfry. Mine. Slieve Bloom' (56). Or as he frantically searches through his pockets in a desperate attempt to look nonchalant with 'the wife's admirer' bearing down on him: 'I am looking for that. Yes, that. Try all pockets. Handker. *Freeman*. Where did I? Ah, yes. Trousers. Purse. Potato. Where did I?' (175). Or Stephen Dedalus, self-styled, self-serious philosopher poet, as he meditates during his morning stroll along Sandymount Strand: 'Signatures of all things I am here to read, seaspawn and seawrack, the nearing tide, that rusty boot. Snotgreen, bluesilver, rust: coloured signs' (37). Or in a different mourning mood, as he painfully, fearfully, recalls his mother's death:

> Her glazing eyes, staring out of death, to shake and bend my soul. On me alone. The ghostcandle to light her agony. Ghostly light on the tortured face. Her hoarse loud breath rattling in horror, while all prayed on their knees. Her eyes on me to strike me down. (10)

Or Mrs Marion Tweedy, alias Molly Bloom, as she ruminates, remembering a day out with Poldy (or Bloom as we know him):

> something always happens with him the time going to the Mallow Concert at Maryborough ordering boiling soup for the two of us then the bell rang out he walks down the platform with the soup splashing about taking spoonfuls of it hadnt he the nerve and the waiter after him making a holy show of us screeching and confusion for the engine to start but he wouldnt pay till he finished it the two gentlemen in the 3rd class carriage said he was quite right so he was too hes so pigheaded sometimes when he gets a thing into his head a good job he was able to open the carriage door with his knife or theyd have taken us to Cork. (699)

Knowing that these passages are interior monologue,[35] and not simply

[35] Interior monologue should not be confused with 'stream-of-consciousness'. The latter term is borrowed from philosophy, specifically from William James, philosopher brother of

unattributable mumbo-jumbo, allows us to recognize the book as a novel, at least in part, and as a novel which lovingly attends to the most delicate nuances and subtle shades of character. Bloom's mind is replete with the detritus of popular culture—clichés, aphorisms, advertising slogans, half-remembered bits of knowledge acquired at school or on Dublin's streets or from his eclectic reading—and he calls on it constantly in his humble attempts to make sense of the world around him. In the first quoted passage, for example, he hears the children's voices, [wonders why,] notices that the window is open, [wonders why,] thinks that fresh air helps the memory, [and this is why,] thinks that lilts also help the memory, recalls an alphabetic lilt, wonders if they're boys' voices, yes, hears [or recalls?] another [geographic] lilt about the islands off the west coast of Ireland, [identifies a geography lesson,] names it in boyish mispronunciation, [places himself within his country as he] identifies with the mountain range in central Ireland which shares his name (Slieve Bloom). Those whys and identifications and namings and placings typify Bloom the Curious. With an economy and precision unavailable in third-person narrative description, Joyce reveals Bloom's character, or, rather, allows Bloom himself to reveal it. For one powerful effect of this method, when exercised so deftly, is that it creates (at least the illusion of) an integrity of character virtually unattainable in more conventionally narrated fictions.

Though, too, we are constantly reminded of the very textuality of these individuals: character here is style, or, as Joyce phrased it much earlier, an 'individuating rhythm, the first or formal relation of their parts'.[36] Bloom's

the novelist Henry, who used it to describe the workings of consciousness as experienced by the individual. When applied to literature, it remains descriptive only of fictions which share a preoccupation with representing character through pre-verbal or unspoken 'thoughts'. It is thus a generic grouping, not a technique. The term will tell us nothing about how the aim of 'representing thoughts' is accomplished. Thus, Virginia Woolf's *Mrs Dalloway*, which arguably contains not one line of interior monologue (being written instead as dialogue, third-person narrative, and free indirect discourse), has as great a claim to the stream-of-consciousness trademark as has *Ulysses*. And if the latter can be called stream-of-consciousness at all, it is so only in part. See William James, *Principles of Psychology* (New York: Henry Holt, 1890), i. 239; Robert Hurley, *Stream of Consciousness in the Modern Novel* (Berkeley and Los Angeles: University of California Press, 1954); and, for 'free indirect discourse', see Mieke Bal, *Narratology: Introduction to the Theory of Narrative* (1980), trans. Christine van Boheemen (Toronto: University of Toronto Press,1985), 140–2; or Seymour Chatman, *Story and Discourse: Narrative Structure in Fiction and Film* (Ithaca, NY, and London: Cornell University Press, 1978).

[36] James Joyce, 'A Portrait of the Artist' (1904), repr. in *Poems and Shorter Writings*, ed. Richard Ellmann, A. Walton Litz, and John Whittier-Ferguson (London: Faber & Faber, 1991), 211.

staccato, Stephen's polished periods, Molly's one-thing-after-another-in-continuous-uninterruptible-sequence, each draws a stylistic curve. Further, interior monologue is a device of memory, but what is 'remembered' is textual: Bloom's clichés, slogans, even his literalized rendering of the alphabet—'rustyouvee'; Stephen's philosophers' and writers' and heretics' words; Molly's stories and materially graphic signs ('3rd' not 'third'). In fact, character here is a carefully styled, specifically delimited, intertextual field.

The fact that Joyce's characters' 'thoughts' were unspoken, internal, often seemingly only half conscious, led critics to speculate that he had been influenced by Freud's discovery of the 'unconscious mind'. Joyce admitted only a literary antecedent, Édouard Dujardin, author of *Les Lauriers sont coupés* (1887) and, according to Joyce, inventor of the technique.[37] Later, however, he surreptitiously justified his use of such an interiorized method by asserting,

> the modern mind ... is interested above all in subtleties, equivocations and the subterranean complexities which dominate the average man and compose his life. ... modern literature is concerned with the twilight, the passive rather than the active mind ... those undercurrents which flow beneath the apparently firm surface.[38]

The interior monologue allowed Joyce to explore and reveal 'subterranean complexities' and 'undercurrents' without having to resort to the kind of authorial philosophizing practised by, for example, George Eliot.

If interior monologue establishes character with no little degree of psychological verisimilitude, Joyce's handling of characters' situations is no less truthful. If, in the midst of all its textual exuberance, we occasionally lose sight of the humanity of the book, we are soon reminded. Note the poignancy prompted in the account of Master Patrick Aloysius Dignam, son of the late Paddy, as he dawdles home from the butcher's and pauses to stare in the shopwindow of Madame Doyle, courtdress milliner:

> From the sidemirrors two mourning Masters Dignam gaped silently. ... Master Dignam on his left turned as he turned. That's me in mourning. ... He turned to the right and on his right Master Dignam turned, his cap awry, his collar sticking up. ...
>
> Master Dignam got his collar down and dawdled on. ...

[37] Joyce always said that he discovered the method on reading Dujardin's book, which he picked up at a railway kiosk on his first trip to Paris in 1903. See *JJ* 126, 358, and 519–20. Later Joyce persuaded Stuart Gilbert to translate the book (which he did with Joyce's help; published as *We'll to the Woods No More* in 1938) (*JJ* 665). A new English translation by Anthony Suter, *The Bays are Sere*, appeared in 1991 (London: Libris).

[38] Joyce to Arthur Power, quoted in Arthur Power, *Conversations with James Joyce*, ed. Clive Hart (1974; repr. Chicago: University of Chicago Press, 1982), 74.

Master Dignam walked along Nassau street, shifted the porksteaks to his other hand. His collar sprang up again and he tugged it down. The blooming stud was too small for the buttonhole of the shirt, blooming end to it. . . . He met other schoolboys. Do they notice I'm in mourning? Uncle Barney said he'd get it into the paper tonight. Then they'll all see it in the paper and read my name printed and pa's name.

His face got all grey instead of being red like it was and there was a fly walking over it up to his eye. The scrunch that was when they were screwing the screws into the coffin: and the bumps when they were bringing it downstairs. (241)

This is no scene of a 'pet-lamb in a sentimental farce'.[39] The details of the collar, the porksteaks, the boyish wondering whether others will notice his 'special' status, but more, the change of colour from red to grey, the fly, the 'scrunch' of the coffin screws, and the bumping coffin all bring it back from the brink of sentimentality with which it flirts. If it's painful, that is because it captures the humour and the brute reality at one and the same time. Just as they are captured in the scene in the Dedalus house as Katey, Boody, and Maggy (just back from trying unsuccessfully to sell Stephen's books so the rest of the family will have money for food) sit down to peasoup provided by Sister Mary Patrick (217–18). Or when Dilly, another sister, prods her father to part with some money so she too can eat (228–9), and then, taking after her elder brother, spends some of it on Chardenal's French primer (233). Sentimentality distorts, corrodes, lies. 'Life' is not like that, nor is *Ulysses*. As Joyce remarked to Arthur Power,

that is now what interests me most, to get down to the residuum of truth about life . . . in *Ulysses* I have tried to see life clearly, I think, and as a whole . . . it has taken me half a lifetime to reach the necessary equilibrium to express it, for my youth was exceptionally violent; painful and violent.[40]

Pain, violence, but also equilibrium bought with vast quantities of affection and humour. (Joyce was to complain to Ezra Pound of the contemporary responses to *Ulysses*, 'If only someone would say the book was so damn' funny.'[41]) The combination may have left the first readers of *Ulysses* reeling, but it is what makes the book so lastingly and honestly humane.

If *Ulysses* is unsentimental, no less is it anti-romantic. As Joyce proclaimed his views, again to Power:

in realism you are down to facts on which the world is based: that sudden reality which smashes romanticism into a pulp. What makes most people's lives

[39] John Keats, 'Ode on Indolence', l. 54.
[40] Joyce to Power, in Power, *Conversations*, 36–7.
[41] Quoted in Kenner, '*Ulysses*', 169.

unhappy is some disappointed romanticism, some unrealizable or misconceived ideal. In fact you may say that idealism is the ruin of man, and if we lived down to fact, as primitive man had to do, we would be better off. That is what we were made for. Nature is quite unromantic. It is we who put romance into her, which is a false attitude, an egotism, absurd like all egotisms. In *Ulysses* I tried to keep close to fact.[42]

Joyce's loathing of sentimentality and his insistence on an anti-romantic living 'down to facts' have technical as well as thematic significance in his work. Further, if adherence to fact is a fundamental tenet of *Ulysses*, Joyce's conception of fact is not without its attendant complexities. To examine these propositions, we might usefully start by looking at how carefully the book situates itself within the 'real' world.

If *Ulysses*'s first commitment is to the creation of realistic character (bearing in mind the very textuality of such characters), its second is to the accurate re-creation of a particular setting within a precise moment in history. That precise moment is the single day of 16 June 1904, as we discover by looking over the shoulder of Miss Dunne, secretary to Blazes Boylan, as she absent-mindedly clicks away on the typewriter. It is a day undistinguished except that its very ordinariness makes it remarkable within fiction; fictional days are more likely to be distinctly unusual. Arnold Bennett, a writer who knew the quotidian when he saw it, thought he detected a Joycean 'sardonic temper' lurking behind this day's selection: 'I expect that he found malicious pleasure in picking up the first common day that came to hand. It happened to be nearly the dailiest day possible.'[43] What Bennett means, of course, is that nothing much happened on this day in Dublin and nothing much happens in *Ulysses*, a novel in which the word 'plot' is more likely to refer to Paddy Dignam's resting place than to the machinations of fiction. Dignam's funeral is a 'major' event of the day, as are Master Mortimer Edward Purefoy's birth, Molly's adultery, Stephen and Bloom's meeting, their sharing of a cup of Epps's cocoa. Already we begin to descend to the mundane. Mostly in *Ulysses* people talk, or think, or remember, or drink, or argue, or gossip. The rest of the time they walk, read, eat, bathe, defecate, urinate, fall asleep. Not much really to write home about. But they do it within a world so acutely, minutely, and particularly rendered that Wyndham Lewis, a Modernist who preferred his art abstract and classical, could accuse the book of being a 'sardonic catafalque of the victorian world'.[44] What he meant, as he makes

[42] Joyce to Power, in Power, *Conversations*, 98.

[43] Arnold Bennett, 'James Joyce's *Ulysses*', *Outlook* (London) (29 Apr. 1922), repr. in Deming, ed., *Critical Heritage*, i. 220.

[44] Lewis, 'Analysis', 109.

quite clear, is that in his fidelity to the 'real world', a fidelity that Lewis calls a 'fanatic naturalism', Joyce minutely details all the detritus and ephemera, all the junk of the daily life of 1904. Joyce preserved the 'rubbish'. When we remember that in *Finnegans Wake*, it is in the dung or rubbish heap that Biddy the Hen scratches for the crucial letter which may or may not exonerate HCE, or that Stephen Dedalus compares the rubbish-strewn sands of Sandymount to 'language tide and wind have silted here' (44), we might recognize that the rubbish heap was Joyce's desired site for the erecting of his House of Fiction—a far more promising location for him than Pound and Eliot's purified Dialect of the Tribe.[45]

If *Ulysses* is a 'victorian catafalque', it is an accurately rendered one. Joyce's claim to Frank Budgen concerning his intention to re-create Dublin meticulously is, by now, infamous: 'I want to give a picture of Dublin so complete that if the city one day suddenly disappeared from the earth it could be reconstructed out of my book.'[46] And while this smacks of typical Joycean hyperbole, his Dublin is drawn with more precise physical specificity than any other city in literature before or since. Every Joycean who has ever visited Dublin *after* having made an intimate acquaintance with *Ulysses* knows the uncanny frisson prompted by walking into the D.B.C. (Dublin Bakery Company) tearoom or past Hodges Figgis bookshop, places which had until then existed only in the imagination—much as Middlemarch village does for the reader of George Eliot. (Though Dublin has changed a great deal since 1904, and some places which had disappeared in the interim have reappeared of late in the wake of Dubliners' recognition that *Joyce's* Dublin, like Dickens's London, draws the tourists.)

In fact, *Ulysses*'s fidelity to an actual place, Dublin, at a specific time, 16 June 1904, is so exacting as to raise questions about the nature of the relation between fiction and 'reality'. Stephen Dedalus and Leopold Bloom, two fictional characters, walk across actual Dublin bridges, through actual Dublin streets filled with actual Dublin shops, museums, libraries, pubs, cemeteries, schools, churches, breweries, tearooms, turkish baths, bookshops, all accurately and precisely placed by Joyce with, as a diligent Joyce critic was to discover, the aid of *Thom's Official [Dublin] Directory*.[47] They reside in actual

[45] See Pound on Imagism or the Chinese Ideogram, or Eliot in his stealing of Mallarmé's phrase from 'Le Tombeau d'Edgar Poe': 'to purify the dialect of the tribe' (*Four Quartets*, 'Little Gidding', II. 74).

[46] Joyce to Frank Budgen, quoted in Frank Budgen, *James Joyce and the Making of 'Ulysses'* (1934; repr. Bloomington: Indiana University Press, 1960), 67–8.

[47] Actually, *Thom's Official Directory of the United Kingdom of Great Britain and Ireland*, 1904 edition, Dublin section. Richard M. Kain was the first to think to use such a guide and discovered that Joyce too must have consulted it (*Fabulous Voyager: James Joyce's 'Ulysses'* (1947; repr. New York: Viking, 1959)).

Dublin houses (at least one of which, Bloom's residence, 7 Eccles Street, was conveniently uninhabited on 16 June 1904). They read actual Dublin newspapers (and visit their offices to place letters or advertisements) and converse with actual Dubliners. In 'Scylla and Charybdis', for example, Stephen talks with George Russell, author; Mr Best, assistant director of, and Mr Lyster, librarian of, the National Library; and William Patrick Magee (masquerading as John Eglinton, his pseudonym); all of whom are actual historical figures. They bet on actual horseraces (the Ascot Gold Cup) and discuss actual current events (a meeting of the Dublin City Council, for example, or the disastrous burning of a New York steamer called the *General Slocum*).

Joyce is committed not only to getting it right but to getting it *exactly* right. 'Is it possible for an ordinary person to climb over the area railings of no 7 Eccles street, either from the path or the steps, lower himself from the lowest part of the railings till his feet are within 2 feet or 3 of the ground and drop unhurt. I saw it done myself but by a man of rather athletic build', Joyce wrote to his Aunt Josephine on 2 November 1921, checking a 'fact' about Bloom he had included in 'Ithaca', the episode he had completed only a few days earlier (*LI* 175).[48] Indeed, fact and fiction are so intimately commingled in *Ulysses* that we find ourselves drawn to some discomfiting questions. Who is more 'real' in this fiction, Stephen Dedalus or George Russell? If one could step into H. G. Wells's time machine and travel back to Dublin, 16 June 1904, who would one find in Barney Kiernan's pub at 5 p.m.? And would they be talking about athletics and horseraces and Irish nationalism? Who is M'Intosh?[49] And is this fiction?

If novels pretend to gesture toward the 'real' world, *Ulysses* gestures more emphatically than others, and in that process challenges our very understanding of the 'real'. We soon come to realize not only how real this text is, but how very textual reality is. We might at this point posit another rule about the book: every literary convention it performs (in this case, 'realism') it performs so completely that it appears to exhaust the convention and so to draw attention to the status of the convention as merely conventional. We are thus pressed to ask what it might mean for a text to perform and exhaust literary

[48] This is not the only 'fact' Joyce checked with his long-suffering aunt: he also wanted to know 'whether there are trees (and of what kind) behind the Star of the Sea church in Sandymount visible from the shore and also whether there are steps leading down at the side of it from Leahy's terrace' (*LI* 135). In 'Nausicaa', there are trees behind the church and laurel hedges at Leahy's terrace (though in the manuscript they were elms (*JJA* xiii. 237)) but no steps. (The 'steps from Leahy's terrace' are in 'Proteus' (38) instead.) See also *LI* 136, 174, 175; *SL* 285.

[49] One of *Ulysses*'s more playful preoccupations. See 105–8, 244, 319, 358, 458, 602, 681.

conventions. ('What does it mean to exhaust "realism" by fulfilling it so completely?') It is this move through definitive accomplishment to expansion and exhaustion and thence to the questions that these moves provoke that makes *Ulysses* not only text, but its own meta-text. That is, it seems to show a self-conscious awareness of its own status as a text. *Ulysses* moves from work to text to meta-text with exuberance and panache; it flaunts its ability to prompt questions about the very processes of making meanings. Many have asserted that this is what makes it 'Modern'. If this is a characteristic of Modernism, we are tempted to suggest that *Ulysses* is the defining and consummate member of that movement.

Let us return for a moment to Joyce's insistence on the factual, for we have not yet exhausted an examination of its effects within his fiction. From very early in his career, Joyce insisted that fiction stay strictly within the realm of the actual or plausibly possible. In 1904 he had written a letter to his brother Stanislaus complaining about a 'Damned stupid!' story by George Moore:

> A lady who has been living for three years on the line between Bray and Dublin is told by her husband that there is a meeting in Dublin at which he must be present. She looks up the table to see the hours of the trains. This on D[ublin] W[icklow] and W[exford] R[ailway] where the trains go regularly: this after three years. (*SL* 44)

Joyce's point is a simple one but it had profound consequences for his writing. His fundamental rule, one which he clearly believed every writer of fiction ought to follow, was absolute fidelity to what really would have occurred. It is inconceivable that the 'lady' would not know what time the trains ran. George Moore didn't know, but she would have. This rule, and its corollary—admit nothing into the ambit of the characters' consciousness which would not reasonably have been there—accounts for both the authenticity of *Ulysses* and much of its ability to stymie its readers.[50] Not telling us what we wouldn't need to know were we there at the time means that we get no narratorial preface. We arrive on the scene with Buck Mulligan and see and hear what he does and says (though of course through words delicately arranged by another). So it is only gradually that we begin to piece together the fragments and discover that the stairhead opens out on to the top of a tower, situated near Dublin bay, somewhere near Kingstown harbour. With each new episode, we begin again. Where are we? Who is present? What is happening? And over the course of the book we gain much

[50] Hugh Kenner is the critic who takes most delight in teasing out the implications of this rule. See especially his '*Ulysses*', virtually every page of which reveals a juicy morsel derived by careful and sustained attention to the book's ellipses and its delight in fact.

information which allows us to make sense of the past. Of course, the rule also means that we aren't told what a character does not know or has no need to think about or say. 'Omissions are not accidents', as Marianne Moore once wrote in an entirely different context,[51] but they can cause no end of confusion. A single, perhaps the most famous, example must suffice.

At approximately 5.30 p.m., Lenehan arrives at Barney Kiernan's pub:

—What's up with you, says I to Lenehan. You look like a fellow that had lost a bob and found a tanner.

—Gold cup, says he.

—Who won, Mr Lenehan? says Terry.

—*Throwaway*, says he, at twenty to one. A rank outsider. And the rest nowhere. (312)

Slightly later, Bloom—who has been arguing with the assembled company about nationalism, the unnecessary use of force, and 'Love. I mean the opposite of hatred'—slips out on an errand of brotherly love. Lenehan, a page later, suddenly bursts out:

—I know where he's gone, says Lenehan, cracking his fingers.

—Who? says I.

—Bloom, says he, the courthouse is a blind. He had a few bob on *Throwaway* and he's gone to gather in the shekels. . . . I met Bantam Lyons going to back that horse only I put him off it and he told me Bloom gave him the tip. (320–1)

When Bloom returns to Kiernan's pub and doesn't stand a round of drinks to the house, the animosity towards him grows until finally the citizen, shouting obscenities, hurls a Jacob's biscuit tin at him. Now we've spent the day with Bloom (or most of it) and we know he didn't place a bet while we were there. Did he slip out on us? Is he holding out on us? Nor did he give Bantam Lyons a tip. Or are we simply misremembering? If we turn back to Lyons's encounter with Bloom some 230 pages and seven hours earlier, we find this:

—I want to see about that French horse that's running today, Bantam Lyons said. Where the bugger is it?

He rustled the pleated pages, jerking his chin on his high collar. Barber's itch. Tight collar he'll lose his hair. Better leave him the paper and get shut of him.

—You can keep it, Mr Bloom said.

—Ascot. Gold cup. Wait, Bantam Lyons muttered. Half a mo. Maximum the second.

—I was just going to throw it away, Mr Bloom said.

Bantam Lyons raised his eyes suddenly and leered weakly.

[51] Marianne Moore, authorial note prefacing *The Complete Poems of Marianne Moore* (1967; repr. Harmondsworth: Penguin, 1982), p. [vii].

—What's that? his sharp voice said.

—I said you can keep it, Mr Bloom answered. I was going to throw it away that moment.

Bantam Lyons doubted an instant, leering: then thrust the outspread sheets back on Mr Bloom's arms.

—I'll risk it, he said. Here, thanks.

He sped off towards Conway's corner. God speed scut. (82)

Bloom's throwaway line: 'I was just going to throw it away', repeated for emphasis, is lost on us. We do not know what Bantam Lyons assumes he's heard until we come back to read again armed with more information. In the realm of the 'real', 'the unfacts, did we possess them, are too imprecisely few to warrant our certitude', as *Finnegans Wake* admonishes.[52] In the realm of fiction, at least, we can go back and reread until we get it right.

Though getting it right is never easy in *Ulysses*, a book riddled with error.[53] If we rely on the book's newspaper account of those attending Paddy Dignam's funeral, for example, we will get it wrong—and miss a point central to the book. In 'Eumaeus', Bloom reads from (and construes) the 'pink edition, extra sporting, of the *Telegraph*, tell a graphic lie' (601):

The mourners included: Patk. Dignam (son), Bernard Corrigan (brother-in-law), John Henry Menton, solr. Martin Cunningham, John Power eatondph 1/8 ador dorador douradora (must be where he called Monks the dayfather about Keyes's ad.) *Thomas Kernan, Simon Dedalus, Stephen Dedalus B.A., Edward J. Lambert, Cornelius Kelleher, Joseph M'C. Hynes, L. Boom, C. P. M'Coy — M'Intosh, and several others*. (602)[54]

Neither Stephen Dedalus nor M'Coy were present, as 'L. Boom' himself notes, 'nettled not a little' by his new misnomer. 'To say nothing of M'Intosh' who is not even a character in any ordinary sense, the missing name of this unknown man having been supplied by Hynes, the reporter, by metonymic substitution of the article of clothing he happened to be wearing (107–8). *Ulysses* takes lines 'of bitched type' (as the non-newspaper narrator of 'Eumaeus' calls it) and 'the usual crop of nonsensical howlers of misprints' (602) quite seriously. Since Bloom is a textual being, he legitimately becomes 'Boom (to give him for the nonce his new misnomer)' (602).

[52] James Joyce, *Finnegans Wake* (1939; repr. Harmondsworth: Penguin, 1976), 57.16–17.

[53] For an understanding of how this statement refers not simply to the book's treatment of error but to the materiality of error in its published forms, see 'Composition and Publication History'.

[54] The actual French printers mistakenly 'corrected' the fictive Dublin typesetter's misset 'L. Boom', just as they mistakenly deleted the mistakenly reported 'Stephen Dedalus'. Joyce correctly reinstated these errors in the Errata lists. See Appendix C, below.

When earlier in the day, Bloom (this time in the guise, not of L. Boom, but of Henry Flower) reads Martha Clifford's billet-doux, he encounters more 'bitched type': 'I called you naughty boy because I do not like that other world. . . . So now you know what I will do to you, you naughty boy, if you do not wrote' (74–5). Her substitution of 'world' for 'word' teases the imagination: we notice, perhaps for the first time, that 'world' contains 'word' (plus a floating 'l'—the one gone missing from 'Boom'?), the two being inextricably conjoined in this book. Her second mistyping, 'if you do not wrote', floats into Bloom's mind a paragraph later: 'I wonder did she wrote it' (75). The odd thing about this mistake is that Joyce the author wrote 'write'. It was either the typist or the typesetter who 'wrote' 'wrote'. Joyce did not notice it until several proofs of this episode had been pulled and had repeatedly repeated 'wrote'. When he did notice it, Joyce the writer wrote Bloom's 'I wonder did she wrote it', thus opening wide his authorial arms to embrace the typesetter's mistake. As Stephen Dedalus says later: 'A man of genius makes no mistakes. His errors are volitional and are the portals of discovery' (182). Errors, it seems, are volitional even when made by someone else.

What do we learn from all this? As Fritz Senn remarks, 'After half a century of *Ulysses*, we have learned to regard any information provided within the novel with skeptical, in fact Bloomian reserve. On the other hand, we invest the words of the text with unusual trust.'[55] We trust, that is, that despite their erroneous status 'L. Boom', 'world', and 'wrote' communicate meanings that lie outside the scope of narrow rectitude. *Ulysses* repeatedly reminds us that certitude aligns itself with bigotry, racial hatred, blind nationalism, egotism, violence. ('Cyclops' distils this alliance.) Joyce's alternative authority is one which recognizes the inevitability of error, exercises a healthy scepticism, and yet happily embraces the new world occasioned by the fall, the lapses. (See *Finnegans Wake*!) It is thus that Joyce retells the tale of the *felix culpa*.

'One thinks of Homer'

But these novelistic qualities of *Ulysses* are only part of the story, no matter how much we recognize the 'textual' quality of that novel. Beyond this there lies the haunting symbolic and stylistic 'system' to which Joyce repeatedly directed his friends. When A. Walton Litz first carefully examined the composition process of *Ulysses* in the late 1950s,[56] he discovered that a good

[55] Fritz Senn, 'Book of Many Turns', in Staley, ed., *'Ulysses': Fifty Years*, 44.

[56] A. Walton Litz, *The Art of James Joyce: Method and Design in 'Ulysses' and 'Finnegans Wake'* (1961; rev. edn. New York: Oxford University Press, 1964).

deal of the 'incidental symbolism' was added by Joyce to late proofs. This, combined with Pound's early dismissal of the correspondences as mere 'scaffolding', led many critics to regard these elements as extraneous flourish, not central to the main business of the book, as though only Joyce's initial ideas for it merit legitimate enquiry.[57] This notion—that only the first draft of a book should concern the reader—is surely extraordinary. True, Joyce did expand his understanding and vision of the book as the long composition progressed, but in this we see another aspect of the book's textuality and the extent to which Joyce was both author and first reader. As Henry James maintained, 'To revise is to see, or to look over, again—which means in the case of a written thing neither more nor less than to re-read it.'[58] Reading as active engagement (as 'writing') rather than static consumption led Joyce to expand and thicken the text. Much of the lasting effect on the reader of feeling that the book must be held in the head all in one moment in order to be able to detect the connections between one element 'thrown away' in an early episode and its appearance many pages later derives from Joyce's being able to move back and forth between episodes as he reread and revised and rewrote it.[59]

More relevant to our considerations here is that each rereading appears to have prompted Joyce to reassess the implications of his 'plan' for the book as he announced it to, among others, Carlo Linati. Let us reread those expressed designs:

[*Ulysses*] is the epic of two races (Israel–Ireland) and at the same time the cycle of the human body as well as a little story of a day (life). . . . It is also a kind of encyclopaedia. My intention is not only to render the myth *sub specie temporis nostri* but also to allow each adventure (that is, every hour, every organ, every art being interconnected and interrelated in the somatic scheme of the whole) to condition and even to create its own technique. Each adventure is so to speak one

[57] See e.g. Kenner: 'That the schema was not Joyce's working blueprint but a *post facto* orthogonality, that many of its details . . . are casual and funny, not central and portentous, did not get clarified till Walton Litz (1961) showed how very late Joyce inserted many such touches.' Though Kenner also argues that the Homeric correspondences 'deserve' 'centrality' (Kenner, '*Ulysses*', 170).

[58] Henry James, 'Preface to *The Golden Bowl*', in *The Art of the Novel: Critical Prefaces* (1934; repr. Boston: Northeastern University Press, 1984), 338–9.

[59] This demand of the book, that we treat it at times like a huge poem in which we can move freely upwards and backwards, from line to line in any order, rather than as a linear narrative, was initially addressed by Joseph Frank in his theorizing of the book in terms of 'spatial form'. Joseph Frank, 'Spatial Form in Modern Literature' (1945), in *The Widening Gyre: Crisis and Mastery in Modern Literature* (New Brunswick, NJ: Rutgers University Press, 1963), 3–62.

person although it is composed of persons—as Aquinas relates of the heavenly hosts. (*SL* 271)

To take only three aspects of this plan, what might it mean for the book to be an encyclopaedia, for 'each adventure . . . to condition and even to create its own technique', for a text to be an epic 'body' with episodes comprising somatically interrelated and interconnected arts, organs, and hours?

The first of these is the most easily addressed. The encyclopaedic aspect of *Ulysses* has already been noted in its collecting and preserving like a fly in amber the stuff and junk, the commodities consumed by ordinary Dubliners in 1904. Beyond this, though, the book is also an encyclopaedia of rhetorical devices. In 'Aeolus', the episode in the newspaper office, the art of which, as the schemata tell us, is Rhetoric, we find 95 different rhetorical figures, at least as Stuart Gilbert counts. In 'Lotus Eaters' the book becomes a virtual gardener's catalogue of flower names. 'Cyclops' flaunts its ability to itemize (parodically, irreverently, erroneously): trees; Irish heroes; Irish livestock and produce; Irish crafts; Irish harbours; Irish mountains; Irish scenes of 'ancient duns and raths and cromlechs and grianauns and seats of learning and maledictive stones'; 'saints' come to bless Barney Kiernan's pub bringing with them their attendant miracles and symbols; members of foreign delegations; cheers; 'clergymen' present at a discussion of 'the revival of ancient Gaelic sports and the importance of physical culture'; the 'high sinhedrim of the twelve tribes of Iar'; the honorific titles of 'sir Hercules Hannibal Habeas Corpus Anderson'. The entire episode 'Oxen of the Sun', written as it is as a parodic gestation of the English language, could stand as a handbook of the history of English style (which indeed is what Joyce appears to have consulted in drafting it).[60] 'Ithaca' delights in an ostensibly precise, nominative language worthy of the most abstruse encyclopaedic entries. This is *Ulysses* in high spirits, each list or parody spawning further more furiously expansive ironic inventories. On writing to Frank Budgen of 'Oxen', Joyce detailed its gestative parallels (the foetus and the language) and then gleefully cracked, 'How's that for high?' (*SL* 251–2). If we remind ourselves that 'high' means not only lofty or exalted (as in 'high culture'), but also intoxicated,

[60] Stanislaus Joyce commented to Richard Ellmann that in writing 'Oxen' Joyce 'studied Saintsbury's *A History of English Prose Rhythm*' (*JJ* 475). As J. S. Atherton discovered, Joyce seems also to have used William Peacock's *English Prose from Mandeville to Ruskin*. George Saintsbury, *A History of English Prose Rhythm* (London: Macmillan, 1912); William Peacock, *English Prose from Mandeville to Ruskin* (London: Oxford University Press, 1903); J. S. Atherton, 'The Peacock in the Oxen', *A Wake Newslitter*, 7 (Oct. 1970), 77–8; Roberto Janusko, *The Sources and Structures of James Joyce's 'Oxen'* (Ann Arbor, Mich.: UMI Research Press, 1983).

elated, and (as with game) beginning to decompose, we capture the 'height' of *Ulysses*'s encyclopaedic character as it goes 'over the top'.

Similar fun is had by *Ulysses* in its exploitation of the mandate that 'each adventure . . . condition and even . . . create its own technique'. Almost any aspect of an episode can prompt its technique. In 'Aeolus', for example, it is the setting and the art, both perhaps derived from the Homeric episode where Aeolus, god of winds, gives Odysseus a bag of wind to help his becalmed ship. Bag of wind? Windbag? Setting: the offices of the *Freeman's Journal*, Dublin '**DAILY ORGAN**'. Art: Rhetoric. We have already noted the stylistic proliferation of 'windy' rhetorical devices, but the technique also, and perhaps more obviously, derives from its setting: a newspaper office produces a newspaper layout. Headlines punctuate the text as though laid in by some demonic editor scanning copy: '**IN THE HEART OF THE HIBERNIAN METROPOLIS**'; '**HOUSE OF KEY(E)S**'; '**? ? ?**'; '**DEAR DIRTY DUBLIN**'; '**K.M.R.I.A.**'; '**SOPHIST WALLOPS HAUGHTY HELEN SQUARE ON PROBOSCIS. SPARTANS GNASH MOLARS. ITHACANS VOW PEN IS CHAMP.**' The very appearance of these headlines seems to generically displace *Ulysses* from novel to newspaper and calls into question many of our most closely held illusions about fiction. Like the narrator, for instance. Here we have not a narrator but an editor, or an Arranger, as David Hayman called 'him'.[61] Unlike a narrator, the Arranger participates in and actively shapes and manipulates the text as though it were the physical object of paper and ink we too frequently ignore. No passive narrator, not even a Brontëan 'unreliable' Nelly Dean, the Arranger is more interested in playfully disrupting, reiterating, cajoling, and his eye is always on the text as text. Think of the 'symphonic prelude' to 'Sirens' (245–6), for example. It is as though the conductor of the orchestral piece which is the episode quickly flips through the score before tapping his baton to 'Begin!' That's the Arranger. If in 'Aeolus' he is an editor, in 'Sirens' a conductor, he is far more frequently simply an 'it': a subversive textual force always drawing our attention back to *Ulysses* as a field in which meanings are produced, countered, remade, and undone. In fact, the process of deriving meaning from *Ulysses* is

[61] David Hayman, '*Ulysses*': *The Mechanics of Meaning* (1970; rev. edn. Madison: University of Wisconsin Press, 1982). In his added 'Ten Years After Thoughts', Hayman suggests that 'the arranger should be seen as something between a persona and a function, somewhere between the narrator and the implied author. One is tempted to think of "him" as an "it," . . . but we are also tempted to think of a behind-the-scenes persona like the shaper of pantomimes, also called the arranger. Perhaps it would be best to see the arranger as a significant, felt absence in the text, an unstated but inescapable source of control' (pp. 122–3). Hence Hayman's Arranger is very like Barthes's 'Textuality'. Given recent feminist textual theories which link such subversive elements within writing to the 'feminine', 'he' ought perhaps to

very like the strategy Penelope employed with her tapestry when faced with her suitors' pressing suits. Having announced that she would select a husband from among those competing for her hand once she had finished her weaving, she maintained her fidelity to Odysseus by weaving during the day only to unweave at night. Her textile became thus not product but process. Fittingly, *text* and *textile* share the same etymological root. Both derive from *texere*, to weave. Often in reading *Ulysses* we find ourselves weaving one pattern, only to unravel this and begin another in the face of new information or expanding awareness of what is possible within this text.

In much this way, when we encounter the manipulated, derived newspaper-copy style of 'Aeolus', the pattern we have come to depend upon—that this is a 'novel'—dissolves. For this episode dramatically transforms the book from 'novel' to 'text'. As Karen Lawrence demonstrates, the breaking up of the continuous linear prose unsettles our belief in a stable narrative voice and in plot as progressive development.[62] The headlines' authorship is contentious (hence our derived Arranger); their style is that of anonymous, public discourse; their effect is to 'advertise the fact that [they are] "written"'.[63] This unsettling of narrative expectations happens with increasing frequency as we move through *Ulysses*. 'Aeolus' is the first glaring example of the disruptive consequences of taking seriously the challenge that each Homerically entitled episode condition its own style. But once the book passes through what Joyce referred to as 'the initial style'[64] (roughly equivalent to the style of the first nine episodes, with the obvious exceptions of 'Aeolus' and a few Shakespearian eccentricities in 'Scylla and Charybdis'), every episode performs this dictum. In 'Cyclops', the one-eyed giant is metamorphosed into two monocular styles: the first, the grizzly 'I' (pun intended you may rest assured), the second the flamboyant, parodic, inflated (read 'gigantic'), very-much-written style of the lists. In 'Circe', the effects of Madame Circe's transformation of men into swine register in the hallucinatory drama of the visit to Bella Cohen's brothel. The

be seen as a 'she'. (See Julia Kristeva, *Revolution in Poetic Language* (1974), trans. Margaret Walker (New York: Columbia University Press, 1984), or Hélène Cixous, 'Laugh of the Medusa' (1975), trans. Keith Cohen and Paula Cohen, *Signs*, 1/4 (Summer 1976), 875–93.

[62] Karen Lawrence, *The Odyssey of Style in 'Ulysses'* (Princeton, NJ: Princeton University Press, 1981), 60–1.

[63] Ibid. 62.

[64] Joyce's description to Harriet Weaver: 'I understand that you may begin to regard the various styles of the episodes with dismay and prefer the initial style much as the wanderer did who longed for the rock of Ithaca. But in the compass of one day to compress all these wanderings and clothe them in the form of this day is for me only possible by such variation which, I beg you to believe, is not capricious' (*LI* 129). See also Michael Groden, *'Ulysses' in Progress* (Princeton, NJ: Princeton University Press, 1977), 15 and *passim*.

rock of Ithaca to which Odysseus longs to return becomes stylistically 'Ithaca's' 'hard facts', its scientific catechistical method, or, as Joyce claimed, 'all geometry, algebra, and mathematics' (*LIII* 45–6).

No less does the body condition the technique. If each episode has its Homeric parallel, so too it is assigned a bodily organ.[65] Clearly 'Sirens'' 'ear' promotes its musical style, music being the most aural art. Everything sounds its own note in this episode, from Bloom's elastic band ('Twang') to Blazes Boylan as he crosses Dublin to Molly's 'loose brass quoit[ed]' bed ('Jingle a tinkle jaunted'). The most extravagant (yet least rigidly maintained) correspondence is between the gestating foetus in 'Oxen's' 'womb' and the growth of the English language. More disorienting in its effects, though less flamboyant in its execution, is the exhausted style of 'Eumaeus' with its redundancies, clichés, and infelicitous dislocutions. If the episode's organ is the 'nerves', its style is more enervated than nervous:

Between this point and the high, at present unlit, warehouses of Beresford Place Stephen thought to think of Ibsen, associated with Baird's, the stonecutter's in his mind somehow in Talbot Place, first turning on the right, while the other, who was acting as his *fidus Achates* inhaled with internal satisfaction the smell of James Rourke's city bakery, situated quite close to where they were, the very palatable odour indeed of our daily bread, of all commodities of the public the primary and most indispensable. Bread, the staff of life, earn your bread, O tell me where is fancy bread? At Rourke's the baker's, it is said. (570)

Art ('Narrative (old)'), organ ('Nerves') and hour ('1 a.m.') substantiate the textual body of 'Eumaeus'; the three are so interconnected that determining which one prompted the others, which one originated the textual corpus, is impossible.

Of course, the infamous 'body' in *Ulysses* is Molly's, 'Penelope' being her textual incarnation. Joyce's exegesis of her is, by now, notorious:

Penelope is the clou of the book. The first sentence contains 2500 words. There are eight sentences in the episode. It begins and ends with the female word *yes*. It turns like the huge earth ball slowly surely and evenly round and round spinning, its four cardinal points being the female breasts, arse, womb and cunt expressed by the words *because*, *bottom* (in all senses bottom button, bottom of the class, bottom of the sea, bottom of his heart), *woman*, *yes*. Though probably more obscene than any preceding episode it seems to me to be perfectly sane full

[65] The Linati (L) and Gilbert (G) schemata by and large agree on organic distribution. Only to 'Lotus Eaters' (L: skin; G: genitals), 'Ithaca' (L: juices; G: skeleton) and 'Penelope' (L: fat; G: flesh) do they actually assign entirely different organs. In the case of two further episodes, the assignments have been pared down from L to G: 'Cyclops' (L: muscles and bone; G: muscle) and 'Circe' (L: locomotor apparatus, skeleton; G: locomotor apparatus).

amoral fertilisable untrustworthy engaging shrewd limited prudent indifferent *Weib. Ich bin der* [*sic*] *Fleisch der stets bejaht.* (*SL* 285)[66]

Obscene and full-bodied, 'Penelope' weaves her tapestry. No episode has given critics more grief, nor have critical comments ever revealed so little about an episode and so much about the critics who have made them.[67]

Partly perhaps because Penelope (after whom 'Penelope' is named) and Molly are female, the episode is assumed to be more bodily, less textual than the others, for it is traditionally woman's plight to be seen as body against man's mind. (Stephen thinks like this, for example.) But read again Joyce's description and see how textual it is: words, sentences, expressions, punning associations, intertextual allusions. 'Penelope' might more profitably be considered as a somatic text of the feminine gender, opposite number to 'Nausicaa' the technique of which is 'Tumescence/Detumescence'. In keeping with this masculine libidinal economy, 'Nausicaa's' narrative trajectory approximates the 'rising action' of Bloom's arousing fantasy of Gerty McDowell ('lovely seaside girl'), the ejaculatory climax complete with exploding rockets and the 'falling action' of Bloom's slow decline into lethargy. (Notice, too, just how much Gerty is a fantasy creature: she is not evinced through interior monologue—'she' is the object of the discourse not its subject—unlike Bloom, who is granted first-person subjectivity.) If, however, the language of 'Penelope' 'flows' (in some feminine libidinal approximation), this is because it corresponds as much to Penelope's relentless weaving and unweaving as to Molly's menstrual flow. The episode's discursive manœuvres are textual strategies closely aligned with Penelope's weaving wiles. For example, in the course of eight unpunctuated 'sentences', Molly/'Penelope' considers and dismisses her stream of undifferentiated suitors (all referred to indiscriminately as 'he'); one is woven only to be unravelled and replaced by the next. Further, as Vicki Mahaffey argues, Molly is a woman of letters (as, even more literally, I would argue, is 'Penelope'): 'obsessed with letter writing as a form of lovemaking, liberal with letters in her mental orthography, and literal in her approach to foreign words'.[68]

[66] The German phrase: 'woman. I am the flesh that always affirms.' Joyce inverts Goethe's description of Mephistopheles in *Faust*, I, '*Studienzimmer*': '*Ich bin der Geist, der stets verneint*' ('I am the spirit that always denies') (*SL* 285 n. 2). Note that in assigning Flesh to woman, Joyce's pen slipped and misassigned the masculine gender to the neuter noun. A 'textual error' unweaves Joyce's alliance of Flesh and the Female in the very moment of its inscription, tying Flesh instead to masculinity.

[67] For an excellent summary of 'Penelope's' critics, see Vicki Mahaffey, *Reauthorizing Joyce* (Cambridge: Cambridge University Press, 1988), 138–40.

[68] Ibid. 175.

In short, we will go astray if we read Molly as either a positive or a negative representation of woman (something we are likely to do if we read her as more 'fleshed-out' than Bloom). For 'Penelope' is no more, and no less, bodily than *Ulysses*, the entire book constituting one gigantic textual body, a textual body which embraces and exults in the libidinal. In this it most resembles its younger sibling *Finnegans Wake*, in which the text composes and decomposes the body of the sleeping mythical giant Fionn MacCumhail (at least in one of its configurations). It is in this sense that *Ulysses* is an epic 'body' whose episodes (and within whose episodes) are the somatically interrelated and interconnected arts, organs, and hours. Instead of praising or blaming Molly as a representation of a woman, we might more profitably recognize the extent to which 'Penelope's' *textual* strategies point the way back to a necessarily endless and endlessly rewarding rereading of *Ulysses* and forward to the infinite, and definitely material, play of *Finnegans Wake*.

More remains to be said, of course, for *Ulysses*, like all texts, is infinitely inexhaustible. Stephen as Son and Bloom as Father, a favourite subject of early readers, goes unremarked, for example. (Though if one examines the topos from a slightly different angle as a question of how character functions symbolically in this book, I hope one will find in the foregoing hints to follow.) Similarly, the fundamentally significant issue of politics has only been touched upon. It is no coincidence that this irreverent, error-embracing, anti-authoritarian text emerged from Ireland (punningly regarded in the *Wake* as 'Errorland'[69]) by way of Europe just as the sun began to set on the British Empire. Nor is it surprising that *Ulysses* has found itself at the centre of critical debates about feminism and Modernism. Sadly, too, no more than a tiny glimpse has been given of the seriously playful quality of *Ulysses*'s language or of the readerly engagement it necessarily elicits. All these have been explored elsewhere. The pleasure lies ahead in reading. When reviewing *Ulysses* in 1922, J. M. Murry remarked: 'It may be said that our negative judgments are only provisional, and that fuller illumination would make the dark places clear. Possibly. But we cannot spend our life with *Ulysses*.'[70]

Oh yes we can. Or as the Arranger put it, 'Begin!'

[69] Joyce, *Finnegans Wake*, 62. 25.

[70] Murry, in Deming, ed., *Critical Heritage*, i. 197.

COMPOSITION AND PUBLICATION HISTORY

The composition and publication histories of *Ulysses* are nearly as complex as the novel itself.[1] As a schoolboy studying the Trojan War, Joyce read Charles Lamb's *Adventures of Ulysses*,[2] the second of Lamb's adaptations of the *Odyssey* for children. His treatment of the Homeric legend extracts from the 'prolixity' of the original the underlying story and recasts it in contemporary language, while preserving its 'picture . . . of a brave man struggling with adversity; by a wise use of events, and with an inimitable presence of mind under difficulties, forcing out a way for himself'.[3] Lamb's Ulysses is a nineteenth-century Everyman, exemplar of the advantages of the application of wit to the obstacles presented by a wily world. He bears a striking resemblance to that Ulysses described by Joyce to Frank Budgen as the only 'complete all-round character presented by any writer . . . a complete man . . . a good man'.[4] Clearly this 'complete' Ulysses appealed to the young Joyce, for, as he told his first biographer Herbert Gorman, while at Belvedere College he wrote an essay on Ulysses as his 'Favourite Hero'.[5] Years later, when Joyce came to write *Dubliners*, Ulysses returned.

From Rome in September 1906, Joyce wrote to his brother Stanislaus: 'I have a new story for *Dubliners* in my head. It deals with Mr. Hunter' (*LII* 168),[6] and two months later he named the tale: 'I thought of beginning my

[1] For fuller histories of the composition of *Ulysses*, see Michael Groden, *'Ulysses' in Progress* (Princeton, NJ: Princeton University Press, 1977); A. Walton Litz, *The Art of James Joyce: Method and Design in 'Ulysses' and 'Finnegans Wake'* (1961; rev. edn. New York: Oxford University Press, 1964); and Rodney Wilson Owen, *James Joyce and the Beginnings of 'Ulysses'* (Ann Arbor, Mich.: UMI Research Press, 1983).

[2] W. B. Stanford, *The Ulysses Theme: A Study in the Adaptability of a Traditional Hero* (1954; 2nd edn. rev. Oxford: Basil Blackwell, 1968), 186–7. For a discussion of the significance of Lamb's *Adventures* to *Ulysses*, see Litz, *Art of James Joyce*, 1–2.

[3] Charles Lamb, 'Preface', *The Adventures of Ulysses* (1808), in William McDonald, ed., *The Works of Charles Lamb*, vol. vii: *Stories for Children* (London: Dent, 1903), 115. 'Prolixity' is Lamb's word.

[4] Quoted in Frank Budgen, *James Joyce and the Making of 'Ulysses'* (1934; repr. Bloomington: Indiana University Press, 1960), 15, 17.

[5] Herbert Gorman, *James Joyce: A Definitive Biography* (1939; repr. London: John Lane and Bodley Head, 1941), 45; see p. 638 below.

[6] Mr Hunter was, Ellmann speculates, Alfred H. Hunter, a Jewish Dubliner with an unfaithful wife. Hunter supposedly rescued the young James after a brief skirmish resulting from his having approached, one evening in St Stephen's Green, a young woman he mis-

story *Ulysses*: but I have too many cares at present' (*LII* 190). By February of the next year, he had to concede that '*Ulysses* never got any forrader than the title' (*LII* 209).[7] Joyce was later to tell Georges Borach that it was while writing *A Portrait of the Artist as a Young Man* in 1906 or 1907 that he felt the need to move on from Daedalus to Ulysses:

I was twelve years old when we dealt with the Trojan War at school; only the *Odyssey* stuck in my memory.... When I was writing *Dubliners*, I first wished to choose the title *Ulysses in Dublin*, but gave up the idea. In Rome, when I had finished about half of the *Portrait*, I realized that the Odyssey had to be the sequel, and I began to write *Ulysses*.[8]

It seems unlikely that Joyce actually 'began' *Ulysses* in 1907, but Stanislaus's diary entry of 10 November that year at least confirms that the 'story' was growing too big for *Dubliners*: 'Jim told me he is going to expand his story "Ulysses" into a short book and make a Dublin "Peer Gynt" of it' (quoted in *JJ* 265). Just how far the 'sequel' progressed at this stage is unclear. Between 1907 and 1914, Joyce was preoccupied with other matters: rheumatic fever, the first of what would be recurrent eye troubles, family and financial pressures, the birth of a second child, a failed business venture (opening the first cinema in Dublin), not to mention the revision of *Dubliners* (and continuing wrangles with publishers over its promised publication), the scrapping of 26 chapters of *Stephen Hero* and its recasting as *A Portrait of the Artist as a Young Man*, or the delivery of twelve lectures on *Hamlet* at the university in Trieste.

In December 1913 Joyce received a letter from Ezra Pound, then literary editor of the *Egoist*,[9] who had written at Yeats's suggestion. Had Joyce

takenly assumed was 'unaccompanied'. Her escort physically disabused Joyce of the notion. Mr Hunter, it is claimed, showed kindness to Joyce by taking him home and fixing him up (*JJ* 161–2).

[7] Critics have suggested that these *Dubliners* beginnings can be seen in the shape and significance of the initial Bloom sequence of episodes or in the subject matter of the final episodes where Bloom rescues Stephen from the police and takes him home to a cup of cocoa. See e.g. Hugh Kenner, *'Ulysses'* (1980; rev. edn. London and Baltimore: Johns Hopkins University Press, 1987), 61.

[8] Georges Borach, 'Conversations with James Joyce', trans. Joseph Prescott, *College English*, 15 (Mar. 1954), 325.

[9] The *Egoist* had begun life in 1911 as the *Freewoman*, founded and edited by Dora Marsden, feminist and member of the Women's Social and Political Union. Two years later, in June 1913, the *Freewoman* was relaunched as the *New Freewoman* with Marsden as editor and Rebecca West as assistant editor. Pound took over as literary editor when West left after two issues and, in December, suggested (with various other male contributors) that the name be changed to something more appropriate to 'an organ of individualists of both sexes' (quoted in *JJ* 352). The *Egoist* was born. When, in June 1914, Harriet Shaw Weaver, previously business manager, assumed the editorship, what was to be the most 'profitable' and

anything he might like published? (*P/J* 17–18). Joyce sent him *Dubliners* (which Grant Richards was reconsidering and eventually published on 15 June 1914) and the first chapter of *Portrait*. Pound was delighted with the novel, and the *Egoist* began serializing it on 2 February. As it would later with *Ulysses*, serialization pushed Joyce to complete the book. With *Dubliners* now placed and *Portrait* being issued, Joyce began other projects: he drafted the notes for *Exiles*, wrote *Giacomo Joyce*, and settled down to serious work on *Ulysses*. It is in *Giacomo Joyce* (probably written in July or August 1914) that *Ulysses* as we know it is first mentioned. Here Joyce records a dream: 'Gogarty came yesterday to be introduced. *Ulysses* is the reason.'[10]

The outbreak of the First World War meant that the Joyce family had to leave Trieste (where they had lived since 1904 except for a brief stay in Rome between 1906 and 1907). In exchange for a pledge of neutrality, Joyce was permitted to move to neutral Zurich. By the time he left Trieste in June 1915, Joyce had advanced *Ulysses* sufficiently to be able to write to Stanislaus: 'The first episode of my new novel *Ulysses* is written. The first part, the Telemachia, consists of four episodes: the second of fifteen, that is, Ulysses's wanderings: and the third, Ulysses's return home, of three more episodes' (*SL* 209).[11] In Zurich composition continued slowly, but by August 1917 Joyce felt confident enough of the book's eventual completion to write to Pound, 'I am prepared to consign it serially from 1 January next, instalments of about 6000 words' (*SL* 227). Harriet Shaw Weaver, editor of the *Egoist*, contracted for English publication (for £50). Meanwhile Pound pressed for the *Little Review* (an American journal edited by Margaret Anderson and Jane Heap; Pound was the European editor) to bring it out simultaneously in the United States.

enduring relationship of Joyce's creative life began. From this point until Joyce's death, Weaver was to act by turns the roles of editor, patron (becoming, in 1917, his anonymous benefactor), family friend, and Joyce's most loyal (and long-suffering) supporter.

[10] James Joyce, *Giacomo Joyce*, ed. Richard Ellmann (London: Faber & Faber, 1968), 15. Ellmann maintains that 'the likeliest time . . . for the final version of *Giacomo Joyce* is July or August 1914' (p. xvi). 'Gogarty' is Oliver St John Gogarty, Dublin physician, writer of scurrilous verse, and original of Buck Mulligan. Joyce met him in 1903 while home from Paris for Christmas. They shared lodgings in the Martello Tower, Sandycove, in Sept. 1904.

[11] The book had clearly not assumed its final shape (the published version has 3 sections: 3/12/3, not 4/15/3 as he says here), though Joyce had its main outlines in mind. In fact, as late as May 1918, i.e. after the *Little Review* had begun serial publication (which ran from Mar. 1918 until Dec. 1920), Joyce seems still not to have settled on the final pattern of the book, for he stated in a letter to Harriet Weaver that it would consist of 17 episodes in the arrangement: 3/11/3 (*LI* 113). In 1917 Joyce had written to Pound, 'As regards *Ulysses* I write and think and write and think all day and part of the night. . . . But the ingredients will not fuse until they have reached a certain temperature.' Clearly this continued to be the case until the end. (Unpublished letter to Ezra Pound, 24 July 1917, quoted in *JJ* 416.)

By December, Joyce was able to send Pound the first episode, 'Telemachus'. Pound's response was typical: 'Wall, Mr. Joice, I recon your a damn fine writer, that's what I recon'. An' I recon' this here work o' yourn is some concarn'd litterchure. You can take it from me, an' I'm a jedge.'[12] The *Little Review* began serialization of *Ulysses* with its March 1918 issue.

From the beginning, Pound worried that *Ulysses* might be unpalatable to the American public: 'I suppose we'll be damn well suppressed if we print the text as it stands. BUT it is damn wellworth it' (*P/J* 129). In London, where printers could themselves be jailed for setting obscene type, Harriet Weaver was having difficulty finding an English printer willing to print it (*P/J* 131). In what he claimed was merely an attempt to circumvent suppression, Pound cut numerous passages from the text before sending the typescripts on to the *Little Review*. Most drastically, he excised from 'Calypso' all references to Bloom's defecation.[13] Perhaps unfortunately, his blue pencil was insufficiently exercised: by January 1919 the *Little Review* had reached the first part of 'Lestrygonians', and the US Postal Authorities were not amused; they stopped the mailing. May 1919 brought the serialization as far as the second half of 'Scylla and Charybdis'; the Postal Authorities again intervened. The January 1920 (second half of 'Cyclops') and the July–August (second half of 'Nausicaa') issues were again suppressed, confiscated, and burned. Nor did the indignity end here. 'Nausicaa' fell into the hands of one John S. Sumner, secretary of the New York Society for the Suppression of Vice, who, on 21 October, swore out a complaint against Margaret Anderson and Jane Heap as publishers of 'obscenity'. Citing virtually every page of 'Nausicaa', the complaint charged that it was 'obscene, lewd, lascivious, filthy, indecent and disgusting'.[14] When the case came to trial on 14 February 1921, Anderson and Heap were found guilty, fined $100, and fingerprinted. All publication stopped. By this point, *Ulysses* had progressed only part-way through 'Oxen of the Sun' (in the September–December 1920 issue).[15] For Joyce, the loss of the case also meant the loss of any possibility of *Ulysses* appearing in book form in the United States. Indeed, B. W. Huebsch, who had been negotiating with the author over publication, withdrew his offer when it became clear

[12] Ezra Pound to James Joyce, 19 Dec. 1917, *P/J* 129.

[13] For a full account of all Pound's excisions, see Clive Driver, 'Bibliographical Preface', in James Joyce, *'Ulysses': A Facsimile of the Manuscript*, 3 vols. (London: Faber & Faber; Philadelphia: Rosenbach Foundation, 1975), i. 19–21. See also the *Little Review*, 5/2 (June 1918), 39–52; *LI* 116, 117; and *P/J* 131.

[14] Complaint sworn before the New York City Magistrate, 21 Oct. 1920, by John S. Sumner, Agent of the New York Society for the Suppression of Vice, quoted in full in Gorman, *James Joyce*, 274–5.

[15] For the full history of *Ulysses*'s *Little Review* serialization, see Appendix B, below.

that Joyce insisted on a full, unexpurgated edition (including Pound's excisions) or none at all (*LIII* 17).

In London, Harriet Weaver had found a willing printer but had none the less only been able to publish heavily edited versions of four of the 'milder' episodes ('Nestor', 'Proteus', 'Hades', and 'Wandering Rocks').[16] With the US ruling, no one in the English-speaking world could now publish *Ulysses* without fear of further prosecution. Paris, however, was a different matter. Shortly after arriving in Paris in July 1920, Joyce met Sylvia Beach, proprietor of the Shakespeare and Company bookshop and friend to modern writers. On 8 April 1921, immediately on hearing of the collapse of Joyce's hopes of US or English publication of *Ulysses*, Sylvia Beach offered to publish the book under the auspices of Shakespeare and Company, to have it printed in Dijon by Maurice Darantiere, and to finance it by advance subscription. Joyce agreed at once. Printing was to begin as soon as subscriptions provided funds sufficient to the cost. But publication was still nearly a year away.

When Harriet Weaver agreed in 1917 to publish *Ulysses* in the *Egoist*, Joyce had settled down to complete the novel to schedule. At that point he had written steadily, producing about one episode every three months. As the episodes grew in complexity, however, Joyce found it increasingly difficult to meet deadlines. The text grew so much in his mind, even apparently retrospectively, that, by the end of 1919 and his work on 'Cyclops', he repeatedly stressed that the text as represented by the *Little Review* was not complete. Not only must any published edition of the complete book reinstate those passages omitted by the editors of the *Little Review*, it must also include numerous addenda which he had been unable to transfer from his notes to the drafts during composition because of the pressure of time and the unavailability of notes he had previously drafted for various episodes, notes which he had been forced to leave behind when he left Trieste (*LI* 116, 117; *LII* 456; and see *LIII* 30–1).

In 1920 the *Little Review* had stopped publishing monthly issues. (Seven numbers were published that year; only three episodes—'Cyclops', 'Nausicaa', and 'Oxen of the Sun'—were printed.) Joyce was sufficiently ahead of schedule with his submissions ('Oxen' was sent to the typist by 12 May (*LII* 464)) that a time lag developed. Almost in response to the lifting of pressure, 'Circe', the next episode to be drafted, took over six months to complete (*LIII* 34).[17] The work clearly expanded to fill the time available. When Sylvia Beach

[16] The *Egoist* printed the four episodes in its Jan.–Feb., Mar.–Apr., July, Sept., and Dec. 1919 issues. Only the first third of 'Wandering Rocks' appeared.

[17] See Michael Groden's discussion of the complex changes Joyce wrought in 'Circe' during those six months (*'Ulysses' in Progress*, 168–78).

agreed not only to publish *Ulysses* but to finance multiple proof pullings so that Joyce could augment earlier episodes, he was again freed—this time to expand his book in both directions. The first six episodes were set in type by early June of 1921, while Joyce was still writing 'Ithaca' and 'Penelope'. From this point on, Joyce corrected, and added to, all of the previously published episodes and 'completed', then continually enlarged, the remaining four. It is not surprising that publication was still eight months away.

The delay in bringing the entire work to completion was due in large part to Joyce himself, whose complicated composition methods are now famous. He had for years been jotting down notes—from whatever source caught his fancy—either in notebooks by episode or on little tablets, themselves gathered together by episode in large envelopes.[18] When it came time to write an episode, he would (probably) write a first draft, then compile all the notes on to large sheets by episode, then systematically emend and augment the drafts with use of the notes, carefully crossing through a note in crayon when he had inserted it in its apparently predestined place in the draft.[19] A final working draft would be written out in careful longhand. This final working

[18] For a colourful description of this process, see Frank Budgen's account: 'in Zurich Joyce was never without . . . little writing blocks specially made for the waistcoat pocket. At intervals, alone or in conversation, seated or walking, one of these tablets was produced, and a word or two scribbled on it at lightning speed as ear or memory served his turn. . . . from time to time in Joyce's flat one caught glimpses of a few of those big orange-coloured envelopes that are one of the glories of Switzerland, and these I always took to be storehouses of building material' (*Making of 'Ulysses'*, 172).

[19] This is slightly misleading. What I have described is probably true only for the later composition stage. Joyce must have used notes during his early composition, but virtually none of these survive. Only a very early 'Alphabetical notebook' of material used both for *Portrait* and *Ulysses*, a second notebook of 'Shakespeare dates' for 'Scylla and Charybdis', and a third of jottings from Joyce's reading of Bérard, Otway, a seventeenth-century French translation of Aristotle, and a German dictionary of Greek and Roman mythology are extant (the first as Cornell MS 25, the second as Buffalo MS V.A.4, the third as Buffalo MS VIII.A.5; the latter two are edited by Philip Herring in his *Joyce's Notes and Early Drafts for 'Ulysses'* (Charlottesville: University Press of Virginia, 1978)). These are very different from the later surviving notes which all take the form of words or phrases collected together on pages by episode, with individual entries crossed through in different coloured pencil seemingly as the notes found their place in the episodes at a stage of either composition or augmentation. The 1919–1921 British Library Notesheets (British Library Add. MS 49975) and a 1921 notebook (Buffalo MS V.A.2) take this form. It is probable, therefore, that it was only as the episodes became more complex that the elaborate note system represented most dramatically in the British Library Notesheets became necessary. (See Groden, *'Ulysses' in Progress*, 43, 43 n. 17, 139, *passim*, and Litz, *Art of James Joyce*, 9–27, and Appendix A, below.) All of these notes are reproduced in facsimile in *JJA* vii. 109–56; xii. 323–48, 129–66, 2–95, 97–125.

draft would then be sent to the typist, who would type three copies (one original and two carbons). (The 'draft' from which the typist worked was, for just over half the episodes, the *Rosenbach Manuscript*; for the remainder, it was another document now lost.)[20] Joyce in turn would make additions and corrections on the copies (usually on only one or two, seldom on all three) and would send two copies off to Pound (one for the *Little Review* and one for Harriet Weaver for the *Egoist*).[21]

When it came time to send copy to the French printers for typesetting, Joyce apparently dug out his copy of the typescript (one which he had previously marked, though not necessarily identically to those dispatched earlier), made further corrections and additions beyond those made on the *Little Review* typescript, and sent it to Darantiere. Joyce received back, first, *placards* (*épreuves en placard*, the French equivalent of galleys: very large sheets with 8 pages printed on one side, 2 below 1, 4 below 3, etc.), and, later, page proofs, on virtually all of which he marked corrections and further additions.

At any given moment from this point on, Joyce would be correcting, adding to, or revising proofs for one or more early episodes while simultaneously composing a draft of a late chapter. For example, in mid-August 1921, Joyce was making final corrections to the *placards* of 'Telemachus', 'Nestor', 'Proteus', 'Calypso', and 'Lotus Eaters'; making initial revisions and additions to the *placards* of 'Hades', 'Lestrygonians', 'Scylla and Charybdis', and 'Wandering Rocks'; writing 'Ithaca' with his right hand and 'Penelope' with his left.[22]

[20] For episodes 1–4, (?)5, 10, 12, 15–18, the *Rosenbach Manuscript* (or another document virtually identical to it) is the direct antecedent of the typescript. For episodes (?)5, 6–9, 11, 13–14, another document (not the *Rosenbach*) is the direct antecedent of the typescript (i.e. the *Rosenbach* lies outside the direct line of transmission for these episodes). The *Rosenbach Manuscript* itself is not what one might ordinarily think of as a fair copy manuscript. Rather, it is a non-continuous holograph: a handwritten manuscript of eighteen discrete episodes (each developed to a roughly equivalent stage of textual achievement), collected together. As Hans Walter Gabler argues, 'It comprises the novel by individual episodes as written out over a period of four years' (Hans Walter Gabler, 'Afterword', in James Joyce, *Ulysses: A Critical and Synoptic Edition*, prepared by Hans Walter Gabler with Wolfhard Steppe and Claus Melchior, 3 vols. (New York and London: Garland, 1984), iii. 1868, 1876–7. It was sold by Joyce to John Quinn, a New York lawyer (the one who defended the *Little Review* editors), who later sold it at auction to Dr A. S. W. Rosenbach. It has been published in facsimile in Driver, ed., James Joyce, *'Ulysses': A Facsimile of the Manuscript*.

[21] For a fuller description of this process, see Groden, *'Ulysses' in Progress*, 6.

[22] My reconstruction is derived from the following evidence: *Placard* I, Version 1 ('Telemachus') through *Placard* X, Version 1 ('Lotus Eaters') were pulled by Darantiere on 18 Aug. 1921 (*JJA* xvii. 96); these were the penultimate proof pullings of these episodes on which very few changes were entered. *Placard* 11, Version 1 ('Hades') through *Placard* 27,

From the time that the first *placards* were pulled (11 June 1921) until the published book was in his hands, Joyce added as interlineations and marginal additions what constitutes about 30 per cent of the present text. He continued to write and correct until three days before the official publication date, his fortieth birthday, 2 February 1922.

Even as the book was being serialized, Joyce complained about the rough treatment it was getting at the hands of the printers. Initially his concern was more for the passages deleted than for the misprints in what remained. Later, as he struggled to correct Darantiere's proofs before publication, he complained to Harriet Weaver, 'I am extremely irritated by all those printer's errors. Working as I do amid piles of notes at a table in a hotel I cannot possibly do this mechanical part with my wretched eye and a half' (*LI* 176). When the book was published, his gratitude to Sylvia Beach and Darantiere for their Herculean efforts in bringing the book to completion seems initially to have prevented him complaining too loudly about the errors it contained. However, when Weaver floated the possibility of an 'English edition' to be published in France and imported into England, Joyce immediately voiced dissatisfaction with the state of the text in the first edition: 'In a second edition the mistakes must be corrected' (*LI* 183).

The places for errors to have entered the text of the first edition are numerous: typists, Joyce himself (should he fail to transfer a change from one draft on to the next or changes he had made on one typescript to another, or fail to pick up a misprint or omission in his proofreading but nevertheless add new text at the same site at a later proof stage), Darantiere or his foreman, Hirchwald (whose 'corrections' into 'proper English' of Joyce's dislocutions have become notorious),[23] and inevitably those French typesetters who were having to set by hand what was perhaps the most linguistically complex work of English literature yet written (only to be supplanted by *Finnegans Wake*) in a language they did not know, from handwriting which is, at the best of times, difficult to decipher, on proofs which were often dense with addenda. And so mistakes there were. Exactly how many (or even what they might be) has

Version 1 ('Wandering Rocks') were pulled on various dates between 10 Aug. and 26 Aug. 1921 (*JJA* xvii. 220, 246; xviii. 34, 140, 176, 266); these were the first *placards* pulled for these episodes to which Joyce made numerous corrections and additions. He wrote to Harriet Weaver on 7 Aug. 1921 that he was in the midst of 'Ithaca' and had begun 'Penelope' (*LI* 168).

[23] See Jack P. Dalton's early and highly amusing account (which nevertheless makes a very serious point about the successively more corrupt editions of *Ulysses*) in his 'The Text of *Ulysses*', in Fritz Senn, ed., *New Light on Joyce from the Dublin Symposium* (Bloomington and London: Indiana University Press, 1972), 99–119, esp. 108.

become a huge bone of contention in the last few years—a point to which we will return.

As an initial remedy for this sad state of affairs, Joyce himself began compiling lists of errata. When Weaver's 'English edition' was published (in October 1922),[24] a first printed list of 'ERRATA' was laid in. A second 'English edition' (for which the plates were corrected from the 'ERRATA' list)[25] came out three months later. Still unhappy, Joyce began a second errata list from a careful reading through of Weaver's first 'English edition'. However, he had suffered severe eye troubles in the early summer of 1922 which, having abated sufficiently for him to begin reading, recurred in late October. Apparently, he abandoned attempts at a full gleaning of errors at this point (his autograph errata list stops with an entry for page 258) and never seriously returned to it. The list was fleshed out with misprints discovered by Harriet Weaver and was eventually printed and bound with the fourth impression a year later.[26] Unfortunately, even at the earliest stages of reprinting, attempts to correct the text fell to the ubiquity and tenacity of error. The second printing contained errors not present in the first, errors which remained even after and despite the corrections to the plates for the third impression. This pattern appears to have been repeated again and again over the entire publishing history of the book. 'Eradication' went hand in hand with proliferation.[27] (A bibliography of *Ulysses*'s printing history is given in Appendix B below, while a full account of these discovered misprints and a collation of the lists themselves appears in Appendix C.)

By March 1923 Joyce's interest in the text of *Ulysses* had dropped away.

[24] This was actually a second impression of the first edition, printed from the Shakespeare and Company plates, issued with the imprint 'Published for the Egoist Press, London by John Rodker, Paris' on 12 Oct. 1922. See Appendix B, below.

[25] Again, really a third impression of the first edition, published (again with the 'Egoist Press' imprint) in late Jan. 1923. I have assumed that John Kidd is correct in his claim that the two copies of this printing now at Yale show the corrections to have been made. More precisely, Kidd claims that one copy 'has the errata changes throughout and the other only in the first two gatherings, the remainder of the book being made up of October 1922 gatherings'. This would mean, of course, that the changes were worked into the plates over the course of the print run. (John Kidd, 'An Inquiry into *Ulysses: The Corrected Text*', *PBSA* 82 (Dec. 1988), 509.) See Appendix B, below.

[26] This printing returned to the Shakespeare and Company imprint and was issued in Jan. 1924. See Appendix B, below.

[27] Which, if you are Jack Dalton or Fredson Bowers, is a virtually inevitable state of affairs. Dalton quotes Bowers, who speaks of 'the remorseless corrupting influence that eats away at a text during the course of its transmission' (Dalton, 'Text of *Ulysses*', 107, quoting Fredson Bowers, *Textual and Literary Criticism* (Cambridge: Cambridge University Press, 1959), 8).

Instead, as he wrote to Harriet Weaver, his attention was drawn again to creation: 'Yesterday I wrote two pages—the first I have written since the final *Yes* of *Ulysses*. Having found a pen, with some difficulty I copied them out in a large handwriting on a double sheet of foolscap so that I could read them. *Il lupo perde il pelo ma non il vizio*, the Italians say. The wolf may lose his skin but not his vice or the leopard cannot change his spots' (*LI* 202). *Finnegans Wake* was born. *Ulysses* was not entirely left to fend for itself, but its place at the centre of Joyce's attention was usurped.

Ulysses's publishing history continues nearly as curiously as it began. Shakespeare and Company brought out a second edition in 1926.[28] Three years later, the shady but enterprising American publisher Samuel Roth published a pirated version in New York under the false imprint of Shakespeare and Company.[29] *Ulysses*, having been found obscene in the States, could not be legitimately published there. Nor, of course, had it any protected copyright status. Roth, a magazine publisher with an eye for a good deal, had earlier taken advantage of this situation and published unauthorized (and bowdlerized) versions of fourteen episodes of *Ulysses* in his *Two Worlds Monthly*. An outraged Joyce sought legal redress and prompted an International Protest letter signed by 167 world authors. Roth ceased publication in October 1927, but was not enjoined by law from doing so until a year later (*JJ* 585–7). Cut off from this avenue of extracting illicit funds from Joyce's 'Blue Book',[30] Roth turned to a second piracy—the false imprint in 1929. When the ban on publication of *Ulysses* was finally lifted by the landmark decision of the Hon. John M. Woolsey of the US District Court on 6 December 1933, Bennett Cerf of Random House rushed the book into print (25 January 1934).[31] Ironically, the text from which this first Random House edition was set (which remained the standard American edition until 1961) was that of the corrupt Roth piracy.

When, after the fourth printing of the second Shakespeare and Company

[28] That is, the plates were entirely reset. See Appendix B, below.

[29] This is the third edition, the text having been set from the second (1927) impression of the second (Shakespeare and Company) edition of 1926. Issued with the (false) imprint: 'Shakespeare and Company[,] ... Paris[,] 1927'. See Appendix B, below.

[30] In *Finnegans Wake*, Joyce punningly refers to *Ulysses* as his 'usylessly unreadable Blue Book of Eccles'—'Blue' combining both its 'obscene' nature and its original blue paper covers (Joyce having requested that it be bound in the colours of the Greek flag—blue and white; the lettering was white). James Joyce, *Finnegans Wake* (London: Faber & Faber; New York: Viking, 1939), 179. 26–7.

[31] The Random House edition of 1934 was the fifth edition, set from the third. See Appendix B, below.

edition,[32] Sylvia Beach showed little interest in reprinting *Ulysses* again, Joyce contracted with the Albatross Press, based in Hamburg, to take over publication. Stuart Gilbert, Joyce's friend and author of the first substantial critical book on *Ulysses*,[33] was to 'revise' the text. This 'revised' text, published under the imprint of The Odyssey Press in 1932,[34] is generally agreed to be the most accurate text of *Ulysses*. Some have challenged this, citing Gilbert's admission that he had not really done all that much.[35] It is at least interesting to note that a few errors not present in the first edition managed to creep into this 'definitive' text.[36]

Various negotiations proceeded in England for full English publication, but there continued to be some worry that the book might yet again be prosecuted for obscenity. In 1932 T. S. Eliot, by now director of Faber & Faber, approached Joyce about publishing a series of episodes in the *Criterion Miscellany*. With his usual vehemence, Joyce refused. To publish only part of the book would be wrong: 'it implies that I have recognised the right of any authorities in either of Bull's islands to dictate to me what and how I am to write. I never did and never will. . . . *Ulysses* is a book with a beginning, middle and an end and should be presented as such' (*LI* 315). But by November Joyce had discovered that a decision had been taken not to prosecute, and negoti-

[32] Issued in May 1930. The book describes itself as the '11th printing', but it is actually the fourth impression of the second edition. See Appendix B, below.

[33] Stuart Gilbert, *James Joyce's 'Ulysses': A Study* (1930; 2nd edn. London: Faber & Faber, 1952).

[34] The first and second impressions of the Odyssey Press edition carry the statement: 'The present edition may be regarded as the definitive standard edition, as it has been specially revised, at the author's request, by *Stuart Gilbert*' (James Joyce, *Ulysses* (1922; Hamburg: The Odyssey Press, 1932), title-page verso). This edition—the fourth, set from the second—was eventually issued in four impressions with progressive corrections being made over subsequent impressions. See James F. Spoerri, 'The Odyssey Press Edition of James Joyce's *Ulysses*', *PBSA* 50 (1956), 195–8. See also Appendix B, below.

[35] I quote Hugh Kenner: 'The student will . . . encounter references to the "definitive standard edition" issued in two volumes by the Odyssey Press, Hamburg, in 1932. This has derived a spurious authority from the claim that it was "specially revised, at the author's request, by Stuart Gilbert"' (Kenner, *'Ulysses'*, 174). Kenner's suspicions themselves derive from Jack Dalton: 'Joyceans have . . . seriously imagin[ed] Mr Gilbert to have collated manuscripts and otherwise filled the office of professional scholar. Mr Gilbert himself suffered under no such delusions' (Dalton, 'Text of *Ulysses*', 115). He then quotes Gilbert (in a letter to Dalton) at length, whose account does make it sound, as Kenner claims, that 'he had not in fact done all that much' (Kenner, *'Ulysses'*, 174).

[36] Spoerri cites four errors noted by Gilbert (and added by him as marginalia in a copy of the book). None of these were errors in the first edition. (Spoerri, 'Odyssey Press Edition', 196.) My personal favourite is the 'Aeolus' headline: 'LINKS TH BYGONE DAYS OF YOREWI' (143).

ations began anew (*JJ* 653). The real 'first English edition' was published by John Lane at Bodley Head in 1936.[37] As the Limited Editions Club in the USA had published a special edition with illustrations by Henri Matisse the previous year,[38] *Ulysses* had now seen one unauthorized and six authorized editions—all that it would see in its author's lifetime.

Bodley Head, Random House, and Penguin all brought out new editions in the 1960s.[39] Each was set from a previous edition. Each attempted to correct the text. Varying degrees of success were achieved. Despite attempts to control this unruly text, every new printing and every new attempt to correct old errors seemed instead to spawn a new generation of blunders. It was not until the late 1970s that a serious attempt at a critical edition was made. Paradoxically (or perhaps we should say inevitably), this created a furore nearly as loud (and which certainly threatens to be as voluble) as that which greeted the book's initial publication.

For years Joyce critics had been loudly denouncing the corrupt state of the text of *Ulysses*. When the 1961 Random House edition appeared with its dust-jacket declaration that the text had been 'scrupulously corrected', there was general rejoicing; rejoicing, that is, until the text had been 'scrupulously examined'. Jack Dalton was only the loudest and most vehement in his indictment: 'It was the kind of book you could use only a few minutes in a chemistry lab before blowing the place up.' He claimed to have discovered 'some 4,000 corruptions' in this edition.[40] Prompted by his claims, Random House contracted with him for a new, full critical edition, but it was never completed.

In the late 1970s Hans Walter Gabler, a German textual critic and English professor, began the mammoth project of producing a new, 'corrected text'.[41] When the work appeared in 1984, it was greeted first with loud acclaim, then with muted uncertainty, then with cries of 'Scandal!' To understand just what had happened to cause such a stir, it is necessary first to understand at least the rudiments of traditional Anglo-American textual theory. This theory, as

[37] The seventh edition, set from the fourth. See Appendix B, below.

[38] The sixth edition, set from the fourth. See Appendix B, below.

[39] Kidd's case that the Bodley Head 1960 edition, the eighth, was set from the 1958 (eighth) impression of the seventh edition (the 1936 Bodley Head) is persuasive ('An Inquiry', 512). The Random House 1961 edition, the ninth, was set from the eighth, as was the 1968 Penguin (tenth) edition. See Appendix B, below.

[40] Dalton, 'Text of *Ulysses*', 102.

[41] The phrase 'corrected text' has significance in the ensuing debate beyond its literal meaning. When the Random House, Bodley Head, and Penguin trade editions (taken from the Gabler text) were issued in 1986, they appeared with the title *Ulysses: The Corrected Text*. It is this assertion of 'correction' with which Kidd contends.

developed by W. W. Greg, Fredson Bowers, and, most recently, G. Thomas Tanselle, basically maintains that, in the establishment of a critical edition, a 'copy-text' is nominated from among extant texts (ideally, the text closest to the author's text, whether a first edition or a complete 'authorized' pre-publication manuscript) which is then edited (by reference to later published texts) to arrive at a 'corrected' text, i.e. a text from which as many 'corruptions' (non-authorial changes) as possible have been removed. The goal of such a procedure is to arrive at a text as close to an 'authorized' text as possible, as near, that is, to the author's intentions for his published text as can feasibly be achieved.[42]

For *Ulysses* arguably two 'texts' compete for the right to be chosen copy-text: the 1922 first edition and Joyce's manuscript. Of course, choosing the former has distinct advantages, most obviously the fact that the latter does not exist—at least not within a single document. If one chose the 1922 text as copy-text, one would then edit and emend it by reference to all available manuscript evidence (including author's instructions contained on correspondence) and a full collation of all printings published in (and within a reasonable period after) Joyce's lifetime. The status of the 1922 edition as copy-text would be that it would have, in Tanselle's words, 'presumptive authority' in cases of indifferent variants,[43] but substantial variants in Joyce's hand, or in other printings which could be argued to have Joyce's authority, would take precedence over those in the 1922 edition. Such a critical edition could—and now inevitably will—be produced, but Gabler chose quite specifically not to do it. Instead, he plumped for the option of the 'manuscript text' as copy-text.

Maintaining that 'an edition of *Ulysses* based on the first edition would not in a full sense attain the quality or scope of a critical edition' (the 1922 text is too 'corrupt' to correct), Gabler argued instead that 'the text of highest overall authority on which to base a critical edition of *Ulysses* resides in

[42] This is a gross oversimplification, but further detail is unnecessary for the argument here. For a cogent summary of Greg's, Bowers's, and Tanselle's theories, see Michael Groden, 'Contemporary Textual and Literary Theory', in George Bornstein, ed., *Representing Modernist Texts: Editing as Interpretation* (Ann Arbor: University of Michigan Press, 1991), 259–86. Greg's theory and its elaboration can be reconstructed from the following: W. W. Greg, 'The Rationale of Copy-Text', *Studies in Bibliography*, 3 (1950–1), 19–36; Fredson Bowers, *Textual and Literary Criticism* (Cambridge: Cambridge University Press, 1959) and *Essays in Bibliography, Text, and Editing* (Charlottesville: University Press of Virginia, 1975); G. Thomas Tanselle, *A Rationale of Textual Criticism* (Philadelphia: University of Pennsylvania Press, 1989) and *Textual Criticism since Greg: A Chronicle, 1950-1985* (Charlottesville: University Press of Virginia, 1987).

[43] Tanselle, *Textual Criticism since Greg*, 106.

Joyce's autograph notation' (G 1895). Unfortunately, as we have seen, this 'autograph notation' does not exist as 'a unified holograph manuscript at the state of development corresponding to the first-edition text' (G 1895), but rather exists on a series of pre-publication documents: the *Rosenbach Manuscript*, autograph notations to typescripts, *placards*, and page proofs.[44] Still, Gabler argues, 'one may define a continuous manuscript text for *Ulysses*, extending over a sequence of actual documents. It is this continuous manuscript text that the critical edition assembles and declares as its copytext' (G 1895).

Joyce's method of composition was almost entirely accretive. That is, he virtually never deleted a line—at least once he reached a certain stage of composition. Instead, he added layer upon layer of text as interlineations and marginal addenda to one proof after another. Given this fact, Gabler's aim was to go back to a base text (roughly equivalent to the (now lost) final working draft) and add layer upon layer of Joyce's autograph additions until he arrived at the complete text as Joyce wrote it. This reconstruction, which he labels the 'continuous manuscript text', serves as his copy-text. It is this 'continuous manuscript [copy-]text' which he then edits to produce his 'critical edition'.

Given the fact of his having rebuilt the text that Joyce wrote, he could include the *edited* version of this dynamic text in his new edition. That is, he was able to include what he called a 'synoptic' text: a critically edited version of *Ulysses* in progress or, as he puts it, 'in compositional development' from a base text amended with Joyce's notational addition, 'displayed synoptically by a system of diacritics to analyze its layers of growth' (G 1901). This 'synoptic' text was printed on the versos of the 1984 edition. The 'critical' or 'continuous reading text', displayed on the rectos, 'results as the extrapolation without diacritics of the edition text, i.e., the emended continuous manuscript text at its ultimate level of compositional development' (G 1903). It is this 'continuous reading text' which was reprinted by Random House, Bodley Head, and Penguin in 1986 as the new 'Corrected Text' of *Ulysses*.

Gabler's edition represents an innovation in textual editing on at least two counts. First, Gabler expanded the category of copy-text: no longer necessarily a single extant document (whether published or holograph), it could be (and is in his new edition) rather a reconstructed theoretical ideal which in so far as it is extant is spread over multiple documents. Secondly, in including a 'synoptic' text in his critical edition, Gabler foregrounded the unstable,

[44] The bulk of these documents has been photoreproduced and published: *Rosenbach Manuscript* in Driver, ed., *'Ulysses': A Facsimile of the Manuscript*, vols. i, ii; pre-*Rosenbach* manuscripts, as well as typescripts, *placards*, and page proofs in *JJA* xii–xxvii.

fluctuating character of *Ulysses* as written. No longer a fixed, final word, this text is, as Jerome McGann pointed out, 'a concrete and particular presentation ... of a self-deconstructing and unstable text'.[45] In going back to the composition documents rather than 'correcting' the *Ulysses* that Joyce *published*, Gabler attempted to reconstruct the *Ulysses* that Joyce *wrote*. In presenting an edited representation of the thickening, growing text, Gabler captured something in the nature of *Ulysses* itself: its multiplicity and dynamism.[46]

When the 1984 text was released, the response in the popular press was extraordinary: 'The sacred text has changed', declared *The Economist*; 'New Edition Fixes 5,000 Errors in *Ulysses*', announced the headline of the *New York Times*.[47] Hurrahs and acclaim all around. Within the year, however, the American academic John Kidd was to claim in relation to the new edition, 'I think what I have to say is going to blow the whole Joyce establishment wide open.'[48] What he said has certainly produced shockwaves. His first argued presentation came in his paper, 'Errors of Execution in the 1984 *Ulysses*', delivered to the Society for Textual Scholarship in New York on 26 April 1985.[49] Later in 1985, a conference devoted to a reassessment of the Gabler edition was held in Monaco with such well-known Joyce scholars as Richard Ellmann, Bernard Benstock, Clive Hart, David Hayman, Richard M. Kain, Charles Peake, and Fritz Senn all voicing in different ways some rising disquiet about one element or another of the new edition.[50] Kidd's second major salvo was launched in June 1988 with his article in the *New York Review of Books*, 'The Scandal of *Ulysses*'.[51] This was followed by vociferous debates

[45] Jerome J. McGann, '*Ulysses* as a Postmodern Text: The Gabler Edition', *Criticism*, 27/3 (Summer 1985), 299.

[46] For examples of criticism which develop this argument, see Patrick McGee, 'The Error of Theory', *Studies in the Novel*, 22/2 (Summer 1990), 148–62; and Vicki Mahaffey, 'Intentional Error: The Paradox of Editing Joyce's *Ulysses*', in Bornstein, ed., *Representing Modernist Texts*, 171–91.

[47] 'The New *Ulysses*', *The Economist* (23 June 1984), 85; *New York Times* (7 June 1984), 1.

[48] Caption to a photograph of John Kidd included in David Remnick, 'The War over "Ulysses"', *Washington Post* (2 Apr. 1985), B1–4.

[49] Published, with Gabler's reply, in *Studies in the Novel*, 22/2 (Summer 1990), 243–9 and 250–6. This 'Special Issue on Editing *Ulysses*', edited by Charles Rossman, contains an annotated bibliography of articles published on the Gabler edition as well as numerous articles contextualizing, as well as continuing, the debate.

[50] The proceedings of this conference are collected in C. George Sandulescu and Clive Hart, eds., *Assessing the 1984 'Ulysses'* (Gerrards Cross: Colin Smythe, 1986).

[51] Kidd, *New York Review of Books*, 35 (30 June 1988), 32–9. In the autumn of 1985, Kidd also published an article 'Gaelic in the New *Ulysses*' in the *Irish Literary Supplement*, 4 (Fall 1985), 41–2.

conducted between Kidd, Gabler, and their respective supporters in the letters columns of both the *Times Literary Supplement* and the *New York Review*.[52] Seemingly in response to the uproar, in June 1988, Random House (publishers of *Ulysses* in the USA) established a committee, headed by G. Thomas Tanselle, to investigate the claims raised by Kidd and others. Was the new text of *Ulysses* really what it claimed to be or was Kidd right? In 1989 Kidd published his long-awaited scholarly response to the Gabler edition, 'An Inquiry into *Ulysses: The Corrected Text*' in *Papers of the Bibliographical Society of America*.[53] Then, oddly, almost silently, Jacob Epstein, director of Random House and convenor of their investigative committee, withdrew from the committee of inquiry, which then dissolved having made no recommendations one way or the other. True, in 1990 Random House also almost silently put the 1961 text back into print, thus providing readers with two texts of *Ulysses* to choose from.

What was all the noise about? Kidd charges that Gabler's editing methods are too elaborate, based on a misunderstanding of Joyce's composition procedures, and violate the well-established methods and standards of Anglo-American textual editing. Further, he accuses Gabler of relying on facsimiles rather than manuscript originals, of failing to research adequately the archives of Joyce's publishers or Joyce collections in libraries (and so missing vital documents containing his instructions for corrections to the text), and of not fully collating all printings of *Ulysses* published in Joyce's lifetime. Further still, he decries what he maintains are Gabler's erratic and inconsistently applied rules of emendation: for example, Kidd says, at times Gabler emends a spelling in Joyce's hand to make it historically correct, while at others he misreads the manuscript evidence and produces a name which is historically incorrect. His two most famous examples are Gabler's emendation of the names of H. Thrift (to H. Shrift) and Captain Buller (to Captain Culler). Both Thrift and Buller were real Dubliners; Shrift and Culler are Gabler's emendations apparently based on manuscript evidence.[54]

[52] See *Times Literary Supplement*, 1–7 July 1988 (733), 8–14 July 1988 (755), 22–8 July 1988 (805, 818), 12–18 Aug. 1988 (883), 19–25 Aug. 1988 (907), 2–8 Sept. 1988 (963), 9–15 Sept. 1988 (989), 7–13 Oct. 1988 (1109, 1132), 21–7 Oct. 1988 (1175), 4–10 Nov. 1988 (1227) and 16–22 Dec. 1988 (1395); and *New York Review of Books*, 18 Aug. 1988 (63–5), 29 Sept. 1988 (80–3), 27 Oct. 1988 (100–1), 8 Dec. 1988 (53–8), 19 Jan. 1989 (58–9), 30 Mar. 1989 (43–5) and 1 June 1989 (40–1).

[53] *PBSA* 82 (Dec. 1988), 411–584; though this issue is dated 'December 1988' it was actually published in 1989.

[54] These two 'emendations' really do appear to be blunders on Gabler's part: the first the result of misreading Frank Budgen's handwriting on the *Rosenbach Manuscript* (for the final section of 'Aeolus' Budgen acted as Joyce's amanuensis), the second of mistaking a printer's

What is one to make of the accusations? As to the first charge—Gabler's methods—Kidd clearly disagrees with Gabler's radical procedures, but he has yet to demonstrate more than this. True, Gabler's explanation of his editorial procedures in his 'Afterword' could have been clearer, but he can hardly be hanged for his prose style. The overwhelming majority of Kidd's individually cited examples arise not from faulty procedures but from editorial decisions. Kidd may have taken a different decision, but this does not render the edition faulty *per se*. Point (probably) to Gabler.

As to the second charge, that Gabler used facsimiles, not originals, Gabler has admitted that he read through the originals, transcribed the facsimiles noting problems to check against the originals, then rechecked these transcriptions against the originals.[55] This probably was not enough for an edition which maintains that its copy-text comprises the reassembled originals. And, while the pragmatic argument that not fully transcribing the originals only produced two real blunders ('Shrift' and 'Culler') may have the weight of common sense on its side, it does not outweigh virtue or the necessity of scholarly thoroughness. Point to Kidd. As to the second part of this charge, that Gabler did not sufficiently research the archives, Gabler should certainly have scoured the archives. That he did not has not been shown. What Kidd's own scourings produced were two instances of instructions to alter text, and evidence that Joyce had a hand in the 1935 Matisse edition. Gabler should have found the instructions; he says he found one (and that it did not affect his text), but admits to not finding the other; his failure may be either delinquency or bad luck. Gabler's argument on this charge generally is that almost invariably these stray instructions merely return the incorrectly typed (or typeset) text to its state of manuscript 'correctness'. The Matisse matter is by the by: Gabler's refusal to collate the Matisse does not affect his edition at all, merely the historical collation list. This is because Gabler's edition is produced from *pre-publication* documents: that is, all the text Joyce wrote up to—but excluding—its final published form in 1922. Changes after that point are only admitted if they can be shown clearly to be Joyce's own changes. Published texts are collated to show published variants. This answers the final part of this charge: the failure to collate all printings of

mark for an authorial emendation on the first *placard* pulled for 'Lotus Eaters' (*Rosenbach Manuscript*, 'Aeolus' (episode 10), fo. 47; *JJA* xvii. 93). See Kidd, 'Scandal', 32–3. Just for the record, the fact that Thrift and Buller were real Dubliners is utterly irrelevant. The only thing that matters is what Joyce wrote.

55 Hans Walter Gabler, 'Position Statement', *James Joyce Literary Supplement*, 3 (Fall 1989), 3. This entire issue is devoted to the controversy over the 1984 *Ulysses*, being in large part the 'edited' proceedings of the Third Annual Miami J'yce Conference.

Ulysses published in Joyce's lifetime. Half a point to Kidd, one point to Gabler.

Finally, Gabler is charged with inconsistently applying rules of emendation and failing to delineate those rules. Kidd arrives at this conclusion from the gleaning of hundreds, nay thousands, of specific examples. He deplores inconsistency, though Gabler clearly states that his editorial policy will leave inconsistencies.[56] Here, Kidd cannot legitimately be said to be pointing out 'errors of execution', but rather must be content with citing points of disagreement or, at most, calling into question editorial judgement. Producing a critical edition, even under the conservative aims of traditional Anglo-American textual bibliography, will not produce the text either as the author wished he had written it (letter perfect) or as he intended it to be read (letter perfect). The perfect text is a mythical beast. At the risk of being tautologous, it bears saying that 'critical' editions result from editorial decisions. Kidd has contracted to produce a 1922-copy-text *Ulysses* (perhaps by the time this book is in your hands he will already have done so). Of course it will be different from Gabler's: it will start from utterly different premisses. But it will be no more 'correct'. He too will have to make editorial decisions which will themselves be subject to scrutiny and open to dispute. Perhaps the awarding of points on this round should wait until that time.

The final result? The balance tips in Gabler's favour. In my opinion, the production of the 'synoptic' text itself justifies the entire undertaking. It is the text most in tune with Joyce's own themes and procedures. One can imagine Joyce picking up any edition of *Ulysses* ever produced and finding himself incapable of resisting the urge to tinker and expand. Were he not quite so superstitious (and so insistent on publishing his *magnum opus* on his fortieth birthday), we might now have a *Ulysses* 'as thick as the *Post Office Directory* and as closely printed as the law notices in the newspaper',[57] as the master says in a different context. It is this Joyce that the 'synoptic' text allows us to find.

While all of the kerfuffle over the 1984 *Ulysses* has had the enormously beneficial result of causing an entire generation of Joyceans to attend a little more carefully to the implications of textual bibliography, it has also unfortunately distracted attention from this multiplicitous Joyce. Little has followed on from Jerome J. McGann's suggestion, as early as 1985, that the 'synoptic' text

be a required object of study for every scholar working in English literature. Nor do I have in mind here only textual scholars or editors. More clearly and

[56] 'On the whole, this results in an unstandardised and unmodernised text. Inconsistencies of usage and orthography, unconventional spellings, obsolescent word forms and of course the idiosyncrasies of Joyce's punctuation are largely left standing' (G 1898).

[57] James Joyce, 'The Sisters', *Dubliners* (1914; repr. Harmondsworth: Penguin, 1992), 5.

practically than any of the recent spate of theoretical work in criticism and hermeneutics, this edition raises up all the central questions that have brought such a fruitful crisis to literary work in the postmodern period.[58]

Perhaps now is the time to attend to such a study.

Finally the question arises, why reprint the 1922 first edition? The first response to this is that it is a historically significant document in its own right. Every Joycean knows by heart the tale of its making. Up to now, it has been readily available only in the reduced facsimile (marked up by Clive Driver to show departures from the *Little Review* and *Rosenbach*). Further, it is still the text closest to Joyce in time. Yes, it is full of errors (and those errors have been left to stand 'uncorrected'), but just how error-ridden it is, is itself a matter of dispute. Jack Dalton maintained that the 1922 text contains over 2,000 errors, but that it is also the least faulty text. Additional errors accumulated rather than diminished over the course of the publication history.[59] Philip Gaskell, himself an adviser to the Gabler edition, states that 'no later edition improved on or even matched the first for accuracy, for each one both accumulated the errors of its predecessors and introduced new errors of its own.... The later editions of *Ulysses* are of little textual interest except as a classic case of textual deterioration.'[60] Finally, though botched and faulty, it remains Joyce's published *Ulysses*, his own 'usylessly unreadable Blue Book of Eccles'.

An ultimate admission: one kind of 'emendation' has been performed. The worst examples of broken type have been repaired for the sake of readability. No other corrections have been made; even when the broken letters have occurred in misspelled words, the misspelling has been retained. Joyce's 'misses in prints'[61] are now yours.

58 McGann, '*Ulysses* as a Postmodern Text', 284.

59 Dalton, 'Text of *Ulysses*', 113, 102.

60 Philip Gaskell, *From Writer to Reader: Studies in Editorial Method* (Oxford: Clarendon Press, 1978), 219 and 219 n. 23.

61 *Finnegans Wake*, 20. 11.

SELECT BIBLIOGRAPHY

Bibliography

Cohn, Alan M., and Kain, Richard M., comps., 'Supplemental James Joyce Checklist' (now 'Current James Joyce Checklist'), *James Joyce Quarterly*, 1– (1964–).

Deming, Robert H., ed., *A Bibliography of James Joyce Studies* (1964; 2nd edn., Boston: Hall, 1977).

Gabler, Hans Walter, 'Bibliography[:] Editions', *Ulysses: A Critical and Synoptic Edition*. Prepared by Hans Walter Gabler with Wolfhard Steppe and Claus Melchior (New York and London: Garland, 1984), 1855–6.

Gaskell, Philip, 'Example 11: Joyce, *Ulysses*, 1922', in *From Writer to Reader: Studies in Editorial Method* (Oxford: Clarendon Press, 1978), 213–44.

Hettche, Walter, and Melchior, Claus, 'A Famous Fighter and Mairy's Drawers: Joyce's Corrections for the 1936 John Lane Edition of *Ulysses*', *James Joyce Quarterly*, 21/2 (Winter 1984), 165–9.

Kidd, John, 'An Inquiry into *Ulysses: The Corrected Text*', *Papers of the Bibliographical Society of America*, 82 (Dec. 1988), 411–585 (pub. 1989).

Owen, Rodney Wilson, *James Joyce and the Beginnings of 'Ulysses'* (Ann Arbor, Mich.: UMI Research Press, 1983).

Rice, Thomas Jackson, *James Joyce: A Guide to Research* (New York and London: Garland, 1982).

Roberts, R. F., 'Bibliographical Notes on James Joyce's *Ulysses*', *The Colophon*, NS 1/4 (Spring 1936), 565–79.

Slocum, John J., and Cahoon, Herbert, *A Bibliography of James Joyce (1882-1941)* (1953: repr. Westport, Conn.: Greenwood Press, 1971).

Spoerri, James F., 'The Odyssey Press Edition of James Joyce's *Ulysses*', *Papers of the Bibliographical Society of America*, 50 (1956), 195–8.

Biography

Ellmann, Richard, *James Joyce* (1959; rev. edn. 1982; corr. New York: Oxford University Press, 1983). (This is *the* landmark biography, though it can usefully be supplemented by the other works in the following list.)

Banta, Melissa, and Silverman, Oscar, eds., *James Joyce's Letters to Sylvia Beach* (Bloomington, Ind.: Indiana University Press, 1987).

Beach, Sylvia, *Shakespeare and Company* (1959; repr. London: Plantin, 1987).

Gorman, Herbert, *James Joyce: A Definitive Biography* (1939; repr. London: John Lane and Bodley Head, 1941).

Joyce, Stanislaus, *The Complete Dublin Diary of Stanislaus Joyce* (Ithaca, NY: Cornell University Press, 1971).

Joyce, Stanislaus, *My Brother's Keeper: James Joyce's Early Years*, ed. Richard Ellmann (London: Faber & Faber, 1958).

Lidderdale, Jane, and Nicholson, Mary, *Dear Miss Weaver: Harriet Shaw Weaver, 1876-1961* (New York: Viking, 1970).

Maddox, Brenda, *Nora: A Biography of Nora Joyce* (London: Hamish Hamilton, 1988).

Potts, Willard, ed., *Portraits of the Artist in Exile: Recollections of James Joyce by Europeans* (1979; repr. New York: Harcourt Brace, 1986).

Pound, Ezra, *Pound/Joyce: The Letters of Ezra Pound to James Joyce, with Pound's Essays on Joyce*, ed. Forrest Read (1967; repr. London: Faber & Faber, 1968).

Power, Arthur, *Conversations with James Joyce*, ed. Clive Hart (1974; repr. Chicago: University of Chicago Press, 1982).

Editions and Other Works

James Joyce: Poems and Shorter Writings, ed. Richard Ellmann, A. Walton Litz, and John Whittier-Ferguson (London: Faber & Faber, 1991), especially 'A Portrait of the Artist' (1904), 211–18.

Letters of James Joyce, vol. i: ed. Stuart Gilbert; vols. ii and iii: ed. Richard Ellmann (3 vols.; New York: Viking, 1957, 1966).

Selected Letters of James Joyce, ed. Richard Ellmann (New York: Viking, 1975).

The Critical Writings of James Joyce, ed. Ellsworth Mason and Richard Ellmann (New York: Viking, 1959).

The James Joyce Archive, ed. Michael Groden (63 vols.; New York and London: Garland, 1977–80), vols. xii–xxvii: *Ulysses* manuscripts, *placards*, and proofs.

Groden, Michael, ed., *James Joyce's Manuscripts: An Index to the James Joyce Archive* (New York and London: Garland, 1980).

'Ulysses': A Facsimile of the Manuscript, ed. Clive Driver (3 vols.; London: Faber & Faber; Philadelphia: Rosenbach Foundation, 1975); vols. i and ii: facsimile of the Rosenbach holograph, vol. iii: facsimile of 1922 first edition.

'Ulysses': A Critical and Synoptic Edition, ed. Hans Walter Gabler with Wolfhard Steppe and Claus Melchior (3 vols.; New York and London: Garland, 1984, and rev. pbk. edn., 1986).

General Criticism

Attridge, Derek, *Peculiar Language: Literature as Difference from the Renaissance to James Joyce* (London: Methuen, 1988).

— ed., *The Cambridge Companion to James Joyce* (Cambridge: Cambridge University Press, 1990).

— and Ferrer, Daniel, eds., *Post-Structuralist Joyce: Essays from the French* (Cambridge: Cambridge University Press, 1984).

Beja, Morris, *et al.*, eds., *James Joyce: The Centennial Symposium* (Urbana and Chicago: University of Illinois Press, 1986).

Borach, Georges, 'Conversations with James Joyce', trans. and ed. Joseph Prescott, *College English*, 15 (Mar. 1954), 325–7.

Bowen, Zack, and Carens, James F., eds., *A Companion to Joyce Studies* (Westport, Conn., and London: Greenwood Press, 1984).

Brown, Richard, *James Joyce and Sexuality* (Cambridge: Cambridge University Press, 1985).

Cixous, Hélène, *The Exile of James Joyce* (1968), trans. Sally A. J. Purcell (New York: David Lewis, 1972).

Deming, Robert H., ed., *James Joyce: The Critical Heritage* (2 vols.; London: Routledge & Kegan Paul, 1970).

Goldman, Arnold, *The Joyce Paradox: Form and Freedom in his Fiction* (London: Routledge & Kegan Paul, 1966).

Herr, Cheryl, *Joyce's Anatomy of Culture* (Urbana and Chicago: University of Illinois Press, 1986).

Kenner, Hugh, *Dublin's Joyce* (1956; repr. New York: Columbia University Press, 1987).

—— *Joyce's Voices* (Berkeley and Los Angeles: University of California Press, 1978).

Levin, Harry, *James Joyce: A Critical Introduction* (1941; rev. edn. New York: New Directions, 1960).

MacCabe, Colin, *James Joyce and the Revolution of the Word* (London: Macmillan, 1978).

—— ed., *James Joyce: New Perspectives* (Brighton: Harvester Press, 1982).

Manganiello, Dominic, *Joyce's Politics* (London: Routledge & Kegan Paul, 1980).

Parrinder, Patrick, *James Joyce* (Cambridge: Cambridge University Press, 1984).

Peake, C. H., *James Joyce: The Citizen and the Artist* (London: Edward Arnold, 1977).

Rabaté, Jean-Michel, *Joyce Upon the Void: The Genesis of Doubt* (New York: St Martin's Press, 1991).

Riquelme, John Paul, *Teller and Tale in Joyce's Fiction: Oscillating Perspectives* (Baltimore and London: Johns Hopkins University Press, 1983).

Scott, Bonnie Kime, *Joyce and Feminism* (Brighton: Harvester, 1984).

Senn, Fritz, *Nichts Gegen Joyce: Joyce Against Nothing*, ed. Franz Cavigelli (Zurich: Haffmans Verlag, 1983).

—— *Joyce's Dislocations: Essays on Reading as Translation*, ed. John Paul Riquelme (Baltimore and London: Johns Hopkins University Press, 1984).

On *Ulysses*

Adams, Robert M., *Surface and Symbol: The Consistency of James Joyce's 'Ulysses'* (1962; rev. edn. New York: Oxford University Press, 1967).

Beebe, Maurice, '*Ulysses* and the Age of Modernism', in Thomas F. Staley, ed., *'Ulysses': Fifty Years* (1972; repr. Bloomington: Indiana University Press, 1974), 172–88.

Bérard, Victor, *Les Phéniciens et l'Odyssée* (2 vols.; Paris: Armand Colin, 1902).

Bonnerot, Louis, ed., *'Ulysses': Cinquante ans après* (Paris: Didier, 1974).

Budgen, Frank, *James Joyce and the Making of 'Ulysses'* (1934; reissued London: Oxford University Press, 1972).

Dalton, Jack P., 'The Text of *Ulysses*', in Fritz Senn, ed., *New Light on Joyce from the Dublin Symposium* (Bloomington and London: Indiana University Press, 1972), 99–119.

Derrida, Jacques, '*Ulysses* Gramophone: Hear Say Yes in Joyce', trans. Tina Kendall, in Bernard Benstock, ed., *James Joyce: The Augmented Ninth* (Syracuse, NY: Syracuse University Press, 1988), 27–75.

Devlin, Kimberly, 'The Romance Heroine Exposed: "Nausicaa" and *The Lamplighter*', *James Joyce Quarterly*, 22/4 (1985), 383–96.

Eliot, T. S., 'Lettre d'Angleterre: Le Style dans la prose anglaise contemporaine', *Nouvelle Revue Française*, 19 (July–Dec. 1922), 751–6.

—— '*Ulysses*, Order and Myth', *The Dial* (Nov. 1923), repr. in Frank Kermode, ed., *Selected Prose of T. S. Eliot* (London: Faber & Faber, 1975), 175–8.

Ellmann, Maud, 'The Ghosts of *Ulysses*', in Augustine Martin, ed., *James Joyce: The Artist and the Labyrinth* (London: Ryan, 1990), 193–228.

Ellmann, Richard, *'Ulysses' on the Liffey* (1972; corr. London: Faber & Faber, 1974).

Empson, William, 'The Theme of *Ulysses*', in Marvin Magalaner, ed., *A James Joyce Miscellany, Third Series* (Carbondale: Southern Illinois University Press, 1962).

Frank, Joseph, 'Spatial Form in Modern Literature' (1945), in *The Widening Gyre: Crisis and Mastery in Modern Literature* (New Brunswick, NJ: Rutgers University Press, 1963), 3–62.

Gifford, Don, with Seidman, Robert J., *'Ulysses' Annotated: Notes for James Joyce's 'Ulysses'* (2nd edn. Berkeley and Los Angeles: University of California Press, 1988).

Gilbert, Stuart, *James Joyce's 'Ulysses': A Study* (1930; 2nd edn. London: Faber & Faber, 1952).

Goldberg, S. L., *The Classical Temper: A Study of James Joyce's 'Ulysses'* (London: Chatto & Windus, 1961).

Groden, Michael, *'Ulysses' in Progress* (Princeton, NJ: Princeton University Press, 1977).

Hart, Clive, and Hayman, David, eds., *James Joyce's 'Ulysses': Critical Essays* (Berkeley and Los Angeles: University of California Press, 1974).

Hayman, David, *'Ulysses': The Mechanics of Meaning* (1970; rev. edn. Madison: University of Wisconsin Press, 1982).

Herring, Philip, *Joyce's Notes and Early Drafts for 'Ulysses': Selections from the Buffalo Collection* (Charlottesville: University Press of Virginia, 1977).

—— *Joyce's 'Ulysses' Notesheets in the British Museum* (Charlottesville: University Press of Virginia, 1972).

Homer, *The Odyssey*, trans. S. H. Butcher and Andrew Lang (London: Macmillan, 1879).

Iser, Wolfgang, 'Patterns of Communication in Joyce's *Ulysses*', in *The Implied Reader: Patterns of Communication in Prose Fiction from Bunyan to Beckett* (Baltimore and London: Johns Hopkins University Press, 1974), 196–233.

Jacquet, Claude, 'Les Plans de Joyce pour *Ulysses*', in Louis Bonnerot, ed., *'Ulysses': Cinquante ans après* (Paris: Didier, 1974), 45–82.

Jameson, Fredric, '*Ulysses* in History', in W. J. McCormack and Alistair Stead, eds., *James Joyce and Modern Literature* (London: Routledge & Kegan Paul, 1982), 126–41.

Kenner, Hugh, *'Ulysses'* (1980; rev. edn. Baltimore and London: Johns Hopkins University Press, 1987).

Kristeva, Julia, 'Joyce "The Gracehoper" or The Return of Orpheus', trans. Louise Burchill, rev. trans. Jacques Aubert and Shari Benstock, in Bernard Benstock, ed., *James Joyce: The Augmented Ninth* (Syracuse, NY: Syracuse University Press, 1988), 167–80.

Lamb, Charles, 'The Adventures of Ulysses' (1808), in William McDonald, ed., *The Works of Charles Lamb*, vol. vii: *Stories for Children* (London: Dent, 1903), 113–230.

Larbaud, Valery, 'James Joyce', *Nouvelle Revue Française*, 18 (Apr. 1922), 385–407.

— 'The *Ulysses* of James Joyce', *Criterion*, 1 (1922), 94–103.

Lawrence, Karen, *The Odyssey of Style in 'Ulysses'* (Princeton, NJ: Princeton University Press, 1981).

Levine, Jennifer Schiffer, 'Originality and Repetition in *Finnegans Wake* and *Ulysses*', *PMLA* 94/1 (1979), 106–20.

— *'Ulysses'*, in Derek Attridge, ed., *The Cambridge Companion to James Joyce* (Cambridge: Cambridge University Press, 1990), 131–59.

Lewis, Wyndham, 'An Analysis of the Mind of James Joyce', *Time and Western Man* (London: Chatto & Windus, 1927), 91–130.

Litz, A. Walton, *The Art of James Joyce: Method and Design in 'Ulysses' and 'Finnegans Wake'* (1961; rev. edn. New York: Oxford University Press, 1964).

— 'The Genre of *Ulysses*', in John Halperin, ed., *The Theory of the Novel: New Essays* (New York: Oxford University Press, 1974), 109–20.

— 'Pound and Eliot on *Ulysses*: The Critical Tradition', in Thomas F. Staley, ed., *'Ulysses': Fifty Years* (1972; repr. Bloomington: Indiana University Press, 1974), 5–18.

McGann, Jerome J., '*Ulysses* as a Postmodern Text: The Gabler Edition', *Criticism* 27/3 (Summer 1985), 283–306.

McGee, Patrick, *Paperspace: Style as Ideology in Joyce* (Lincoln and London: University of Nebraska Press, 1988).

Maddox, James H., *Joyce's 'Ulysses' and the Assault upon Character* (Brighton: Harvester, 1978).

Mahaffey, Vicki, *Reauthorizing Joyce* (Cambridge: Cambridge University Press, 1988).

Moretti, Franco, 'The Long Goodbye: *Ulysses* and the End of Liberal Capitalism', in *Signs Taken for Wonders: Essays in the Sociology of Literary Forms*, trans. Susan Fischer, David Forgacs, and David Miller (1983; rev. edn. London: Verso, 1988), 182–208.

Rabaté, Jean-Michel, *James Joyce, Authorized Reader* (Baltimore and London: Johns Hopkins University Press, 1991)

Restuccia, Frances, *Joyce and the Law of the Father* (New Haven, Conn., and London: Yale University Press, 1989).

Seidel, Michael, *Epic Geography: James Joyce's 'Ulysses'* (Princeton, NJ: Princeton University Press, 1976).

Senn, Fritz, 'Book of Many Turns', in Thomas F. Staley, ed., *'Ulysses': Fifty Years* (1972; repr. Bloomington: Indiana University Press, 1974), 29–45.

—— 'Seven Against *Ulysses*', *James Joyce Quarterly*, 4/3 (Spring 1967), 170–93.

Stanford, W. B., *The Ulysses Theme: A Study in the Adaptability of a Traditional Hero* (1954; 2nd edn. rev. Oxford: Basil Blackwell, 1968).

van Boheemen, Christine, 'The Difference of *Ulysses* and the Tautology of Mimesis' and 'The Syntax of Return: "Still an Idea Behind It"', in *The Novel as Family Romance: Language, Gender and Authority from Fielding to Joyce* (Ithaca, NY, and London: Cornell University Press, 1987), 132–69, 170–93.

A CHRONOLOGY OF JAMES JOYCE

1882 (2 Feb.) Born James Augustine Joyce, eldest surviving son of John Stanislaus Joyce ('John'), a Collector of Rates, and Mary Jane ('May') Joyce née Murray, at 41 Brighton Square West, Rathgar, Dublin. (May) Phoenix Park murders.

1884 First of many family moves, to 23 Castlewood Avenue, Rathmines, Dublin. (17 Dec.) John Stanislaus Joyce ('Stanislaus') born.

1886 Gladstone's Home Rule bill defeated.

1887 Family (now four children: three boys, one girl) moves to 1 Martello Terrace, Bray, south of Kingstown (now Dun Laoghaire). JJ's uncle, William O'Connell, moves in with family, as does Mrs 'Dante' Hearn Conway, who is to act as a governess.

1888 (1 Sept.) JJ enrolls at Clongowes Wood College, near Sallins, County Kildare, a Jesuit boys' school.

1889 After his first communion, JJ becomes altar boy. (At his later confirmation, also at Clongowes, JJ takes 'Aloysius' as his saint's name.) Given four strikes on the back of the hand with a pandybat for use of 'vulgar language'. (24 Dec.) Captain O'Shea files for divorce from Katherine ('Kitty') O'Shea on grounds of her adultery with Charles Stewart Parnell, MP, leader of the Irish Home Rule Party.

1890 Parnell ousted as leader of Home Rule Party.

1891 (June) JJ removed from Clongowes as family finances fade. John Joyce loses job as Rates Collector (pensioned off at age of 42). (6 Oct.) Parnell dies. JJ writes 'Et Tu, Healy', identifying Tim Healy, Parnell's lieutenant, with Brutus and indicting Ireland's rejection of Parnell as treachery.

1892 Family (now eight children: four boys, four girls) moves to Blackrock, then into central Dublin. Children sent to the Christian Brothers School on North Richmond Street.

1893 (6 Apr.) JJ and his brothers enter Belvedere College, Jesuit boys' day-school, fees having been waived. Last Joyce child born (family now four boys, six girls). Gaelic League founded.

1894 JJ travels to Cork with John Joyce, who is disposing of the last of the family's Cork properties. Family moves to Drumcondra. JJ wins first of many Exhibitions for excellence in state examinations. (Summer) Trip to Glasgow with John Joyce. Family moves again, to North Richmond Street.

JJ reads Lamb's *Adventures of Ulysses* and writes theme on Ulysses as 'My Favourite Hero'.

1895 JJ enters the Sodality of the Blessed Virgin Mary.

1896 JJ chosen prefect of the Sodality, attends retreat, later claims to have begun his 'sexual life' in this, his fourteenth year.

1897 JJ wins prize for best English composition in Ireland for his age group.

1898 JJ begins to read Ibsen, attends and reviews plays. Leaves Belvedere. (Sept.) Enters Royal University (now University College, Dublin). Family continues to move from house to house.

1899 (8 May) JJ attends première of Yeats's *The Countess Cathleen*, refuses to sign students' letter of protest to the *Freeman's Journal* against the play.

1900 (20 Jan.) JJ delivers paper 'Drama and Life' before the university Literary and Historical Society, defending the attention paid to mundane life in contemporary drama (especially Ibsen's); outraged protest from students. (1 Apr.) JJ's review of Ibsen's *When We Dead Awaken*, 'Ibsen's New Drama', published in *Fortnightly Review*. Ibsen responds with pleasure. JJ visits London, attends Music Hall, writes prose and verse plays, poems, begins to keep 'epiphany' notebook.

1901 JJ writes 'The Day of the Rabblement', an attack on the Irish Literary Theatre and its narrow nationalism, and publishes it privately in a pamphlet with Francis Skeffington's essay arguing for equality for women.

1902 (1 Feb.) JJ delivers paper to Literary and Historical Society praising the Irish poet James Clarence Mangan and advocating literature as 'the continual affirmation of the spirit'. (Mar.) JJ's brother George dies. JJ leaves university and registers for the Royal University Medical School. (Oct.) Meets Yeats and, later, Lady Gregory. Leaves Medical School and (1 Dec.) departs for Paris, ostensibly to study medicine. Passes through London where Yeats introduces him to Arthur Symons. Reviews books for Dublin *Daily Express*. Returns to Dublin for Christmas.

1903 JJ meets Oliver St John Gogarty. (17 Jan.) Returns to Paris by way of London. Giving up on medical school, spends days in Bibliothèque Nationale, nights in Bibliothèque Sainte-Geneviève. (Mar.) Meets Synge. (Apr.) Returns to Dublin due to mother's illness; she dies (13 Aug.). JJ continues to write reviews.

1904 JJ writes essay 'A Portrait of the Artist', first seeds of later novel *A Portrait of the Artist as a Young Man*. Begins writing stories, which will become *Dubliners*, and publishes three in the *Irish Homestead*. Begins work on *Stephen Hero*. Writes and publishes poems which will be collected later as *Chamber Music*. Leaves the family home, takes rooms in Dublin, teaches at Clifton School, Dalkey. Joins Gogarty (for one week) in the Martello

Tower, Sandycove. Writes 'The Holy Office', a satirical poem about the contemporary Dublin literary scene. (10 June) Meets Nora Barnacle and on 16 June first goes out with her. (8 Oct.) JJ and Nora leave together for the Continent, first to Zurich, then to job with the Berlitz School in Pola where JJ will teach English.

1905 JJ and Nora move to Trieste, where JJ teaches English for Berlitz School. (27 July) Son, Giorgio, born. *Chamber Music* submitted to (and refused by) four publishers in Dublin and London. First version of *Dubliners* submitted to Grant Richards, Dublin publisher, who contracts to publish it, but later withdraws. Stanislaus moves to Trieste (where he stays until his death in 1955).

1906 (July) Family moves to Rome where JJ accepts abortive job in bank. (30 Sept.) JJ writes to Stanislaus, 'I have a new story for Dubliners in my head. It deals with Mr. Hunter'; later (13 Nov.) identifies it: 'I thought of beginning my story *Ulysses*.' Begins 'The Dead' instead.

1907 (Jan.) Riots at the Abbey Theatre over J. M. Synge's *The Playboy of the Western World*. (7 Feb.) JJ writes to Stanislaus: '*Ulysses* never got any forrader than the title.' (Mar.) Family returns to Trieste. JJ writes three articles for *Il Piccolo della Sera* on Ireland. (Apr.) Lectures on 'Ireland, Island of Saints and Sages', at the Università del Popolo in Trieste. (May) Elkin Matthews (London) publishes *Chamber Music*. (July) JJ contracts rheumatic fever and is hospitalized; beginnings of his eye troubles. (26 July) Daughter, Lucia, born. Scraps the 26 chapters of *Stephen Hero* and begins to rework entirely as *Portrait*. (Nov.) JJ tells Stanislaus that he will 'expand his story "Ulysses" into a short book and make a Dublin "Peer Gynt" of it'. Completes 'The Dead'.

1908 JJ completes first three chapters of *Portrait*, but then sets them aside. Family troubles and continued poverty.

1909 Friendship with Ettore Schmitz (Italian author 'Italo Svevo'), whose high opinion of *Portrait* fragments spurred JJ to revise and continue. (Mar.) JJ writes article on Oscar Wilde for *Piccolo della Sera*. (Apr.) Revised *Dubliners* sent to Maunsel & Co. in Dublin. (July) JJ and Giorgio go to Dublin and Galway. JJ signs contract with Maunsel & Co. and meets old acquaintances. One, Vincent Cosgrave, who had also wooed Nora, claimed that she had been unfaithful to JJ with him. JJ's '1909 Letters' to Nora written as result, first, of his doubting and, later, of his reconcilation with, her. (Sept.) JJ, Giorgio, and JJ's sister Eva return to Trieste. (Oct.) JJ returns to Dublin as agent for Triestine consortium to open first cinema in Dublin. (20 Dec.) The 'Volta' cinema opens.

1910 (2 Jan.) JJ returns to Trieste with another sister, Eileen. 'Volta' fails. Publication of *Dubliners* delayed.

1911 Continuing delay of *Dubliners*. JJ writes open letter, published in Arthur Griffiths's *Sinn Féin*, complaining of his mistreatment at the hands of his publishers. Home Rule bill passed in House of Commons, defeated in Lords.

1912 JJ lectures on Blake and Defoe at the Università, writes article '*L'Ombra di Parnell*' for *Piccolo della Sera*, sits Italian state examinations to become a teacher. Nora and Lucia travel to Ireland, followed quickly by JJ and Giorgio. (JJ's last trip to Ireland.) Negotiations with Maunsel & Co. finally fail; proofs destroyed. JJ writes broadside 'Gas from a Burner' in response and publishes it on his return to Trieste (15 Sept.). JJ begins his (twelve) *Hamlet* lectures at the Università. Begins writing poetry again.

1913 JJ continues *Hamlet* lectures. Grant Richards again shows interest in *Dubliners*. Ezra Pound writes (having been told by Yeats of JJ).

1914 JJ revises *Portrait*, sends first chapter and *Dubliners* to Pound. Pound asks to publish poem ('I Hear an Army') in Imagist anthology in USA, and begins serialization of *Portrait* (beginning 2 Feb.) in the *Egoist* (originally called the *New Freewoman* and edited by Dora Marsden and Rebecca West). Under demand of publishing, JJ finishes last two chapters. (June) Harriet Shaw Weaver takes over editorship of *Egoist*. (15 June) Grant Richards publishes *Dubliners*. (Aug.) World War I begins. JJ writes *Giacomo Joyce*. (Nov.) JJ drafts notes for *Exiles*. Begins *Ulysses*.

1915 (9 Jan.) Stanislaus arrested, interned in Austrian detention centre for remainder of war. *Exiles* completed. (15 May) Italy enters war. (June) In return for a pledge of neutrality, Joyce family allowed to leave Austrian Trieste and move to neutral Swiss Zurich. Through the intercession of Yeats and Pound, JJ awarded a grant (£75) from the Royal Literary Fund. *Ulysses* in progress.

1916 Easter Rising in Dublin. (Aug.) JJ granted £100 from the British Civil List (again at Pound's instigation). (Dec.) B. W. Heubsch (New York) publishes *Dubliners* and *Portrait*. JJ writes 'A Notebook of Dreams'—'record' of Nora's dreams with JJ's interpretations.

1917 (Feb.) English edition of *Portrait* published by Egoist Press. JJ suffers eye troubles which lead to his first eye operation (Aug.). (Feb.) Harriet Shaw Weaver begins anonymous benefaction to JJ; her financial support will continue until (and beyond) JJ's death (when she pays for his funeral). (Oct.) Family goes to Locarno for winter. *Ulysses* continues; first three chapters ('Telemachia') written and sent to Pound. JJ contracts with Weaver to publish *Ulysses* serially in the *Egoist*.

1918 (Jan.) Family returns to Zurich. Pound sends 'Telemachia' to Jane Heap and Margaret Anderson, editors of the *Little Review*. Serial publication begins with March issue. Under pressure of serialization, JJ continues writing. (May) *Exiles* published by Grant Richards. JJ receives financial gift from Mrs Harold McCormick. JJ forms theatrical group, the English Players, with Claud Sykes. First performance: *The Importance of Being Earnest*. JJ meets Frank Budgen. Further eye troubles. (11 Nov.) Armistice signed. By New Year's Eve, *Ulysses* drafted through episode 9, 'Scylla and Charybdis'.

1919 (Jan.) Irish War of Independence begins. Publication of *Ulysses* continues in *Little Review*. January (first part of 'Lestrygonians') and May (first half of 'Scylla and Charybdis') issues confiscated and burned by US Postal Authorities. *Egoist* publishes edited versions of four episodes (2, 3, 6, and 10). (7 Aug.) *Exiles* performed (unsuccessfully) in Munich. Mrs McCormick discontinues financial support, ostensibly because JJ refused to be psychoanalysed by her analyst, Carl Jung. (Oct.) Family returns to Trieste.

1920 (June) JJ and Pound meet for the first time. (July) Family moves to Paris. JJ meets Adrienne Monnier and Sylvia Beach, later T. S. Eliot and Wyndham Lewis and, later still, Valery Larbaud. (Sept.) JJ sends first *Ulysses* 'schema' to Carlo Linati. *Ulysses* composition and serialization continue. January (second half of 'Cyclops') and July–August (second half of 'Nausicaa') issues of the *Little Review* confiscated by US Postal Authorities. (20 Sept.) Complaint lodged by the New York Society for the Suppression of Vice, specifically citing 'Nausicaa' issue. What was to be the final *Little Review* instalment of *Ulysses* (first part of 'Oxen of the Sun') published in Sept.–Dec. issue.

1921 (Feb.) Editors of *Little Review* convicted of publishing obscenity; publication ceases. Sylvia Beach offers to publish *Ulysses* under the imprint of Shakespeare and Company (her Paris bookshop), to be printed in Dijon by Maurice Darantière, to be funded by advance subscription. JJ agrees. Episodes sent seriatim to printers; JJ continues to compose while also adding to and correcting returned proofs. Manuscript of episode 15, 'Circe', thrown in fire by typist's outraged husband. (29 Oct.) JJ 'completes' 'Ithaca' (last episode to be drafted), continues correction and addition. (7 Dec.) Valery Larbaud delivers lecture on *Ulysses* at Shakespeare and Company; uses another 'schema' of the book provided by Joyce (the 'Gilbert schema'). (Dec.) Treaty granting southern Ireland dominion status signed, the war having ended in July.

1922 (2 Feb.) First two copies of *Ulysses* delivered by express train from Dijon in time for celebration of JJ's fortieth birthday. Irish Civil War. (1 Apr.) Nora and children visit Ireland where their train is fired upon by troops. Return to Paris. JJ's eye troubles recur. (Aug.) Family travels to England where JJ meets Harriet Weaver for the first time. (Sept.) Return to Paris and trip to Côte d'Azure.

1923 (Mar.) JJ begins *Work in Progress* (working title of *Finnegans Wake*). (May) Irish Civil War ends.

1924 (Apr.) First fragments from *Work in Progress* published in *transatlantic review*. French translation of *Portrait* published.

1927 (June) Instalments of *Work in Progress* begin to be published in Eugene Jolas's *transition*. (July) *Pomes Penyeach* published by Shakespeare and Company.

1928 *Anna Livia Plurabelle* published in New York.

1929 (Feb.) French translation of *Ulysses* published by Adrienne Monnier's *La Maison des Amis des Livres*. Samuel Beckett *et al.* publish *Our Exagmination Round his Factification ...* as *aide d'explication* and defence of *Work in Progress*. *Tales Told of Shem and Shaun* published in Paris. Roth's pirated edition of *Ulysses* published in New York.

1930 Publication of Stuart Gilbert's *James Joyce's 'Ulysses'*, critical study of *Ulysses*, written with JJ's assistance. *Haveth Childers Everywhere* published in Paris and New York.

1931 (May) French translation (completed with JJ's assistance) of *Anna Livia Plurabelle* published in *Nouvelle Revue*. (4 July) JJ and Nora Barnacle married in London to ensure the inheritance of their children. (29 Dec.) John Joyce dies.

1932 (15 Feb.) Son, Stephen James Joyce, born to Giorgio and Helen Joyce. JJ writes 'Ecce Puer'. Lucia's first breakdown and stay in Maillard clinic. The Odyssey Press edition of *Ulysses*, 'specially revised ... by Stuart Gilbert', published in Hamburg.

1933 Lucia's initial hospitalization in Nyon near Zurich. (6 Dec.) Judge John M. Woolsey, US District Court, delivers opinion that *Ulysses* is not obscene and can be published in the USA.

1934 Random House publishes US edition of *Ulysses*. Lucia again hospitalized. JJ returns to *Work in Progress. The Mime of Mick Nick and the Maggies*, published in The Hague. Frank Budgen's *James Joyce and the Making of 'Ulysses'* (written with JJ's assistance) published in London. Lucia under the care of Carl Jung.

1935 Publication of Limited Editions Club edition of *Ulysses* with illustrations by Henri Matisse.

1936 (Oct.) Bodley Head publishes *Ulysses* in London. (Dec.) *Collected Poems* published in New York.

1937 (Oct.) *Storiella She is Syung* published in London.

1938 (13 Nov.) Finishes *Finnegans Wake*. Douglas Hyde becomes Eire's first president.

1939 (Jan.) Yeats dies. (4 May) *Finnegans Wake* is published in London and New York, though advance copy reaches JJ in time for his 57th birthday on 2 Feb. (1 Sept.) Germany invades Poland; two days later France and Great Britain declare war on Germany. Family leaves Paris for St Gérard-le-Puy, near Vichy. Herbert Gorman's biography, commissioned and abetted by JJ, published in New York.

1940 France falls to the Nazis. Family moves to Zurich.

1941 (13 Jan.) JJ dies after surgery on a perforated ulcer, buried in Fluntern cemetery, Zurich, without the last rites of the Catholic Church. Nora dies in 1951, buried separately in Fluntern, though both bodies were reburied together in 1966.

ULYSSES

ULYSSES

by

JAMES JOYCE

SHAKESPEARE AND COMPANY
12, Rue de l'Odéon, 12
PARIS
1922

THIS EDITION IS LIMITED TO 1000 COPIES: 100 COPIES (SIGNED) ON DUTCH HANDMADE PAPER NUMBERED FROM 1 TO 100; 150 COPIES ON VERGÉ D'ARCHES NUMBERED FROM 101 TO 250; 750 COPIES ON HANDMADE PAPER NUMBERED FROM 251 TO 1000.

Nº 785

The publisher asks the reader's indulgence for typographical errors unavoidable in the exceptional circumstances.

S. B.

I

Stately, plump Buck Mulligan came from the stairhead, bearing a bowl of lather on which a mirror and a razor lay crossed. A yellow dressinggown, ungirdled, was sustained gently behind him by the mild morning air. He held the bowl aloft and intoned :

— *Introibo ad altare Dei.*

Halted, he peered down the dark winding stairs and called up coarsely :

— Come up, Kinch. Come up, you fearful Jesuit.

Solemnly he came forward and mounted the round gunrest. He faced about and blessed gravely thrice the tower, the surrounding country and the awaking mountains. Then, catching sight of Stephen Dedalus, he bent towards him and made rapid crosses in the air, gurgling in his throat and shaking his head. Stephen Dedalus, displeased and sleepy, leaned his arms on the top of the staircase and looked coldly at the shaking gurgling face that blessed him, equine in its length, and at the light untonsured hair, grained and hued like pale oak.

Buck Mulligan peeped an instant under the mirror and then covered the bowl smartly.

— Back to barracks, he said sternly.

He added in a preacher's tone :

— For this, O dearly beloved, is the genuine Christine : body and soul and blood and ouns. Slow music, please. Shut your eyes, gents. One moment. A little trouble about those white corpuscles. Silence, all.

He peered sideways up and gave a long low whistle of call then paused awhile in rapt attention, his even white teeth glistening here and there with gold points. Chrysostomos. Two strong shrill whistles answered through the calm.

— Thanks, old chap, he cried briskly. That will do nicely. Switch off the current, will you ?

He skipped off the gunrest and looked gravely at his watcher, gathering about his legs the loose folds of his gown. The plump shadowed face and sullen oval jowl recalled a prelate, patron of arts in the middle ages. A pleasant smile broke quietly over his lips.

— The mockery of it, he said gaily. Your absurd name, an ancient Greek.

He pointed his finger in friendly jest and went over to the parapet, laughing to himself. Stephen Dedalus stepped up, followed him wearily halfway and sat down on the edge of the gunrest, watching him still as he propped his mirror on the parapet, dipped the brush in the bowl and lathered cheeks and neck.

Buck Mulligan's gay voice went on.

— My name is absurd too : Malachi Mulligan, two dactyls. But it has a Hellenic ring, hasn't it? Tripping and sunny like the buck himself. We must go to Athens. Will you come if I can get the aunt to fork out twenty quid?

He laid the brush aside and, laughing with delight, cried :

— Will he come? The jejune jesuit.

Ceasing, he began to shave with care.

— Tell me, Mulligan, Stephen said quietly.

— Yes, my love?

— How long is Haines going to stay in this tower?

Buck Mulligan showed a shaven cheek over his right shoulder.

— God, isn't he dreadful? he said frankly. A ponderous Saxon. He thinks you're not a gentleman. God, these bloody English. Bursting with money and indigestion. Because he comes from Oxford. You know, Dedalus, you have the real Oxford manner. He can't make you out. O, my name for you is the best : Kinch, the knifeblade.

He shaved warily over his chin.

— He was raving all night about a black panther, Stephen said. Where is his guncase?

— A woful lunatic, Mulligan said. Were you in a funk?

— I was, Stephen said with energy and growing fear. Out here in the dark with a man I don't know raving and moaning to himself about shooting a black panther. You saved men from drowning. I'm not a hero, however. If he stays on here I am off.

Buck Mulligan frowned at the lather on his razor blade. He hopped down from his perch and began to search his trouser pockets hastily.

— Scutter, he cried thickly.

He came over to the gunrest and, thrusting a hand into Stephen's upper pocket, said :

— Lend us a loan of your noserag to wipe my razor.

Stephen suffered him to pull out and hold up on show by its corner a dirty crumpled handkerchief. Buck Mulligan wiped the razorblade neatly. Then, gazing over the handkerchief, he said :

— The bard's noserag. A new art colour for our Irish poets : snotgreen. You can almost taste it, can't you ?

He mounted to the parapet again and gazed out over Dublin bay, his fair oakpale hair stirring slightly.

— God, he said quietly. Isn't the sea what Algy calls it : a great sweet mother? The snotgreen sea. The scrotumtightening sea. *Epi oinopa ponton.* Ah, Dedalus, the Greeks. I must teach you. You must read them in the original. *Thalatta! Thalatta!* She is our great sweet mother. Come and look.

Stephen stood up and went over to the parapet. Leaning on it he looked down on the water and on the mailboat clearing the harbour mouth of Kingstown.

— Our mighty mother, Buck Mulligan said.

He turned abruptly his great searching eyes from the sea to Stephen's face.

— The aunt thinks you killed your mother, he said. That's why she won't let me have anything to do with you.

— Someone killed her, Stephen said gloomily.

— You could have knelt down, damn it, Kinch, when your dying mother asked you, Buck Mulligan said. I'm hyperborean as much as you. But to think of your mother begging you with her last breath to kneel down and pray for her. And you refused. There is something sinister in you...

He broke off and lathered again lightly his farther cheek. A tolerant smile curled his lips.

— But a lovely mummer, he murmured to himself. Kinch, the loveliest mummer of them all.

He shaved evenly and with care, in silence, seriously.

Stephen, an elbow rested on the jagged granite, leaned his palm against his brow and gazed at the fraying edge of his shiny black coatsleeve. Pain, that was not yet the pain of love, fretted his heart. Silently, in a dream she had come to him after her death, her wasted body within its loose brown graveclothes giving off an odour of wax and rosewood, her breath, that had bent upon him, mute, reproachful, a faint odour of wetted ashes. Across the threadbare cuffedge he saw the sea hailed as a great sweet mother by the wellfed voice beside him. The ring of bay and skyline held a dull green mass of liquid. A bowl of white china had stood beside her deathbed holding the green sluggish bile which she had torn up from her rotting liver by fits of loud groaning vomiting.

Buck Mulligan wiped again his razorblade.

— Ah, poor dogsbody, he said in a kind voice. I must give you a shirt and a few noserags. How are the secondhand breeks?

— They fit well enough, Stephen answered.

Buck Mulligan attacked the hollow beneath his underlip.

— The mockery of it, he said contentedly, secondleg they should be. God knows what poxy bowsy left them off. I have a lovely pair with a hair stripe, grey. You'll look spiffing in them. I'm not joking, Kinch. You look damn well when you're dressed.

— Thanks, Stephen said. I can't wear them if they are grey.

— He can't wear them, Buck Mulligan told his face in the mirror. Etiquette is etiquette. He kills his mother but he can't wear grey trousers.

He folded his razor neatly and with stroking palps of fingers felt the smooth skin.

Stephen turned his gaze from the sea and to the plump face with its smokeblue mobile eyes.

— That fellow I was with in the Ship last night, said Buck Mulligan says you have g. p. i. He's up in Dottyville with Conolly Norman. Genera paralysis of the insane.

He swept the mirror a half circle in the air to flash the tidings abroad in sunlight now radiant on the sea. His curling shaven lips laughed and the edges of his white glittering teeth. Laughter seized all his strong wellknit trunk.

— Look at yourself, he said, you dreadful bard.

Stephen bent forward and peered at the mirror held out to him, cleft by a crooked crack, hair on end. As he and others see me. Who chose this face for me? This dogsbody to rid of vermin. It asks me too.

— I pinched it out of the skivvy's room, Buck Mulligan said. It does her all right. The aunt always keeps plainlooking servants for Malachi. Lead him not into temptation. And her name is Ursula.

Laughing again, he brought the mirror away from Stephen's peering eyes.

— The rage of Caliban at not seeing his face in a mirror, he said. If Wilde were only alive to see you.

Drawing back and pointing, Stephen said with bitterness :

— It is a symbol of Irish art. The cracked lookingglass of a servant.

Buck Mulligan suddenly linked his arm in Stephen's and walked with him round the tower, his razor and mirror clacking in the pocket where he had thrust them.

— It's not fair to tease you like that, Kinch, is it? he said kindly. God knows you have more spirit than any of them.

Parried again. He fears the lancet of my art as I fear that of his. The cold steel pen.

— Cracked lookingglass of a servant. Tell that to the oxy chap downstairs and touch him for a guinea. He's stinking with money and thinks you're not a gentleman. His old fellow made his tin by selling jalap to Zulus or some bloody swindle or other. God, Kinch, if you and I could only work together we might do something for the island. Hellenise it.

Cranly's arm. His arm.

— And to think of your having to beg from these swine. I'm the only one that knows what you are. Why don't you trust me more? What have you up your nose against me? Is it Haines? If he makes any noise here I'll bring down Seymour and we'll give him a ragging worse than they gave Clive Kempthorpe.

Young shouts of moneyed voices in Clive Kempthorpe's rooms. Palefaces : they hold their ribs with laughter, one clasping another, O, I shall expire! Break the news to her gently, Aubrey! I shall die! With slit ribbons of his shirt whipping the air he hops and hobbles round the table, with trousers down at heels, chased by Ades of Magdalen with the tailor's shears. A scared calf's face gilded with marmalade. I don't want to be debagged! Don't you play the giddy ox with me!

Shouts from the open window startling evening in the quadrangle. A deaf gardener, aproned, masked with Matthew Arnold's face, pushes his mower on the sombre lawn watching narrowly the dancing motes of grasshalms.

To ourselves... new paganism... omphalos.

— Let him stay, Stephen said. There's nothing wrong with him except at night.

— Then what is it? Buck Mulligan asked impatiently. Cough it up. I'm quite frank with you. What have you against me now?

They halted, looking towards the blunt cape of Bray Head that lay on the water like the snout of a sleeping whale. Stephen freed his arm quietly.

— Do you wish me to tell you ? he asked.

— Yes, what is it ? Buck Mulligan answered. I don't remember anything.

He looked in Stephen's face as he spoke. A light wind passed his brow, fanning softly his fair uncombed hair and stirring silver points of anxiety in his eyes.

Stephen, depressed by his own voice, said :

— Do you remember the first day I went to your house after my mother's death ?

Buck Mulligan frowned quickly and said :

— What ? Where ? I can't remember anything. I remember only ideas and sensations. Why ? What happened in the name of God ?

— You were making tea, Stephen said, and I went across the landing to get more hot water. Your mother and some visitor came out of the drawing room. She asked you who was in your room.

— Yes ? Buck Mulligan said. What did I say ? I forget.

— You said, Stephen answered, *O, it's only Dedalus whose mother is beastly dead.*

A flush which made him seem younger and more engaging rose to Buck Mulligan's cheek.

— Did I say that ? he asked. Well ? What harm is that ?

He shook his constraint from him nervously.

— And what is death, he asked, your mother's or yours or my own ? You saw only your mother die. I see them pop off every day in the Mater and Richmond and cut up into tripes in the dissecting room. It's a beastly thing and nothing else. It simply doesn't matter. You wouldn't kneel down to pray for your mother on her deathbed when she asked you. Why ? Because you have the cursed jesuit strain in you, only it's injected the wrong way. To me it's all a mockery and beastly. Her cerebral lobes are not functioning. She calls the doctor Sir Peter Teazle and picks buttercups off the quilt. Humour her till it's over. You crossed her last wish in death and yet you sulk with me because I don't whinge like some hired mute from Lalouette's. Absurd ! I suppose I did say it. I didn't mean to offend the memory of your mother.

He had spoken himself into boldness. Stephen, shielding the gaping wounds which the words had left in his heart, said very coldly :

— I am not thinking of the offence to my mother.

— Of what, then ? Buck Mulligan asked.

— Of the offence to me, Stephen answered.

Buck Mulligan swung round on his heel.

— O, an impossible person! he exclaimed.

He walked off quickly round the parapet. Stephen stood at his post, gazing over the calm sea towards the headland. Sea and headland now grew dim. Pulses were beating in his eyes, veiling their sight, and he felt the fever of his cheeks.

A voice within the tower called loudly:

— Are you up there, Mulligan?

— I'm coming, Buck Mulligan answered.

He turned towards Stephen and said:

— Look at the sea. What does it care about offences? Chuck Loyola, Kinch, and come on down. The Sassenach wants his morning rashers.

His head halted again for a moment at the top of the staircase, level with the roof:

— Don't mope over it all day, he said. I 'm inconsequent. Give up the moody brooding.

His head vanished but the drone of his descending voice boomed out or the stairhead:

And no more turn aside and brood
Upon love's bitter mystery
For Fergus rules the brazen cars.

Woodshadows floated silently by through the morning peace from the stairhead seaward where he gazed. Inshore and farther out the mirror of water whitened, spurned by lightshod hurrying feet. White breast of the dim sea. The twining stresses, two by two. A hand plucking the harpstrings merging their twining chords. Wavewhite wedded words shimmering on the dim tide.

A cloud began to cover the sun slowly, shadowing the bay in deeper green. It lay behind him, a bowl of bitter waters. Fergus' song: I sang it above in the house, holding down the long dark chords. Her door was open: she wanted to hear my music. Silent with awe and pity I went to her bedside. She was crying in her wretched bed. For those words, Stephen: love's bitter mystery.

Where now?

Her secrets : old feather fans, tassled dancecards, powdered with musk, a gaud of amber beads in her locked drawer. A birdcage hung in the sunny window of her house when she was a girl. She heard old Royce sing in the pantomine of Turko the terrible and laughed with others when he sang :

I am the boy
That can enjoy
Invisibility.

Phantasmal mirth, folded away : muskperfumed.

And no more turn aside and brood.

Folded away in the memory of nature with her toys. Memories beset his brooding brain. Her glass of water from the kitchen tap when she had approached the sacrament. A cored apple, filled with brown sugar, roasting for her at the hob on a dark autumn evening. Her shapely fingernails reddened by the blood of squashed lice from the children's shirts.

In a dream, silently, she had come to him, her wasted body within its loose graveclothes giving off an odour of wax and rosewood, her breath bent over him with mute secret words, a faint odour of wetted ashes.

Her glazing eyes, staring out of death, to shake and bend my soul. On me alone. The ghostcandle to light her agony. Ghostly light on the tortured face. Her hoarse loud breath rattling in horror, while all prayed on their knees. Her eyes on me to strike me down. *Liliata rutilantium te confessorum turma circumdet : iubilantium te virginum chorus excipiat.*

Ghoul ! Chewer of corpses !

No, mother. Let me be and let me live.

— Kinch ahoy !

Buck Mulligan's voice sang from within the tower. It came nearer up the staircase, calling again. Stephen, still trembling at his soul's cry, heard warm running sunlight and in the air behind him friendly words.

— Dedalus, come down, like a good mosey. Breakfast is ready. Haines is apologising for waking us last night. It's all right.

— I'm coming, Stephen said, turning.

— Do, for Jesus' sake, Buck Mulligan said. For my sake and for all our sakes.

His head disappeared and reappeared.

— I told him your symbol of Irish art. He says it's very clever. Touch him for a quid, will you? A guinea, I mean.

— I get paid this morning, Stephen said.

— The school kip? Buck Mulligan said. How much? Four quid? Lend us one.

— If you want it, Stephen said.

— Four shining sovereigns, Buck Mulligan cried with delight. We'll have a glorious drunk to astonish the druidy druids. Four omnipotent sovereigns.

He flung up his hands and tramped down the stone stairs, singing out of tune with a Cockney accent:

O, won't we have a merry time,
Drinking whisky, beer and wine,
On coronation
Coronation day?
O, won't we have a merry time
On coronation day?

Warm sunshine merrying over the sea. The nickel shavingbowl shone, forgotten, on the parapet. Why should I bring it down? Or leave it there all day, forgotten friendship?

He went over to it, held it in his hands awhile, feeling its coolness, smelling the clammy slaver of the lather in which the brush was stuck. So I carried the boat of incense then at Clongowes. I am another now and yet the same. A servant too. A server of a servant.

In the gloomy domed livingroom of the tower Buck Mulligan's gowned form moved briskly about the hearth to and fro, hiding and revealing its yellow glow. Two shafts of soft daylight fell across the flagged floor from the high barbacans: and at the meeting of their rays a cloud of coalsmoke and fumes of fried grease floated, turning.

— We'll be choked, Buck Mulligan said. Haines, open that door, will you?

Stephen laid the shavingbowl on the locker. A tall figure rose from the hammock where it had been sitting, went to the doorway and pulled open the inner doors.

— Have you the key? a voice asked.

— Dedalus has it, Buck Mulligan said. Janey Mack, I'm choked.

He howled without looking up from the fire :

— Kinch !

— It's in the lock, Stephen said, coming forward.

The key scraped round harshly twice and, when the heavy door had been set ajar, welcome light and bright air entered. Haines stood at the doorway, looking out. Stephen haled his upended valise to the table and sat down to wait. Buck Mulligan tossed the fry on to the dish beside him. Then he carried the dish and a large teapot over to the table, set them down heavily and sighed with relief.

— I'm melting, he said, as the candle remarked when... But hush. Not a word more on that subject. Kinch, wake up. Bread, butter, honey. Haines, come in. The grub is ready. Bless us, O Lord, and these thy gifts. Where's the sugar? O, jay, there's no milk.

Stephen fetched the loaf and the pot of honey and the buttercooler from the locker. Buck Mulligan sat down in a sudden pet.

— What sort of a kip is this ? he said. I told her to come after eight.

— We can drink it black, Stephen said. There's a lemon in the locker.

— O, damn you and your Paris fads, Buck Mulligan said. I want Sandycove milk.

Haines came in from the doorway and said quietly :

— That woman is coming up with the milk.

— The blessings of God on you, Buck Mulligan cried, jumping up from his chair. Sit down. Pour out the tea there. The sugar is in the bag. Here, I can't go fumbling at the damned eggs. He hacked through the fry on the dish and slapped it out on three plates, saying :

— *In nomine Patris et Filii et Spiritus Sancti.*

Haines sat down to pour out the tea.

— I'm giving you two lumps each, he said. But, I say, Mulligan, you do make strong tea, don't you ?

Buck Mulligan, hewing thick slices from the loaf said in an old woman's wheedling voice :

— When I makes tea I makes tea, as old mother Grogan said. And when I makes water I makes water.

— By Jove, it is tea, Haines said.

Buck Mulligan went on hewing and wheedling :

— *So I do, Mrs Cahill,* says she. *Begob, ma'am,* says Mrs Cahill, *God send you don't make them in the one pot.*

He lunged towards his messmates in turn a thick slice of bread, impaled on his knife.

— That's folk, he said very earnestly, for your book, Haines. Five lines of text and ten pages of notes about the folk and the fishgods of Dundrum. Printed by the weird sisters in the year of the big wind.

He turned to Stephen and asked in a fine puzzled voice, lifting his brows :

— Can you recall, brother, is mother Grogan's tea and water pot spoken of in the Mabinogion or is it in the Upanishads ?

— I doubt it, said Stephen gravely.

— Do you now ? Buck Mulligan said in the same tone. Your reasons, pray ?

— I fancy, Stephen said as he ate, it did not exist in or out of the Mabinogion. Mother Grogan was, one imagines, a kinswoman of Mary Ann.

Buck Mulligan's face smiled with delight.

— Charming, he said in a finical sweet voice, showing his white teeth and blinking his eyes pleasantly. Do you think she was ? Quite charming.

Then, suddenly overclouding all his features, he growled in a hoarsened rasping voice as he hewed again vigorously at the loaf :

— *For old Mary Ann*
She doesn't care a damn.
But, hising up her petticoats...

The doorway was darkened by an entering form.

— The milk, sir.

— Come in, ma'am, Mulligan said, Kinch, get the jug.

An old woman came forward and stood by Stephen's elbow.

— That's a lovely morning, sir, she said. Glory be to God.

— To whom ? Mulligan said, glancing at her. Ah, to be sure.

Stephen reached back and took the milkjug from the locker.

The islanders, Mulligan said to Haines casually, speak frequently of the collector of prepuces.

— How much, sir ? asked the old woman.

— A quart, Stephen said.

He watched her pour into the measure and thence into the jug rich white milk, not hers. Old shrunken paps. She poured again a measureful and a tilly. Old and secret she had entered from a morning world, maybe a messenger. She praised the goodness of the milk, pouring it out. Crouching by a patient cow at daybreak in the lush field, a witch on her toadstool, her wrinkled fingers quick at the squirting dugs. They lowed about her whom they knew, dewsilky cattle. Silk of the kine and poor old woman, names given her in old times. A wandering crone, lowly form of an immortal serving her conqueror and her gay betrayer, their common cuckquean, a messenger from the secret morning. To serve or to upbraid, whether he could not tell : but scorned to beg her favour.

— It is indeed, ma'am, Buck Mulligan said, pouring milk into their cups.

— Taste it, sir, she said.

He drank at her bidding.

— If we could only live on good food like that, he said to her somewhat loudly, we wouldn't have the country full of rotten teeth and rotten guts. Living in a bogswamp, eating cheap food and the streets paved with dust, horsedung and consumptives' spits.

— Are you a medical student, sir ? the old woman asked.

— I am, ma'am, Buck Mulligan answered.

Stephen listened in scornful silence. She bows her old head to a voice that speaks to her loudly, her bonesetter, her medicineman : me she slights. To the voice that will shrive and oil for the grave all there is of her but her woman's unclean loins, of man's flesh made not in God's likeness the serpent's prey. And to the loud voice that now bids her be silent with wondering unsteady eyes.

— Do you understand what he says ? Stephen asked her.

— Is it French you are talking, sir ? the old woman said to Haines.

Haines spoke to her again a longer speech, confidently.

— Irish, Buck Mulligan said. Is there Gaelic on you ?

— I thought it was Irish, she said, by the sound of it. Are you from west, sir ?

— I am an Englishman, Haines answered.

— He's English, Buck Mulligan said, and he thinks we ought to speak Irish in Ireland.

— Sure we ought to, the old woman said, and I'm ashamed I don't speak the language myself. I'm told it's a grand language by them that knows.

— Grand is no name for it, said Buck Mulligan. Wonderful entirely. Fill us out some more tea, Kinch. Would you like a cup, ma'am ?

— No, thank you, sir, the old woman said, slipping the ring of the milkcan on her forearm and about to go.

Haines said to her :

— Have you your bill ? We had better pay her, Mulligan, hadn't we ?

Stephen filled again the three cups.

— Bill, sir ? she said, halting. Well, it's seven mornings a pint at two pence is seven twos is a shilling and twopence over and these three mornings a quart at fourpence is three quarts is a shilling and one and two is two and two, sir.

Buck Mulligan sighed and having filled his mouth with a crust thickly buttered on both sides, stretched forth his legs and began to search his trouser pockets.

— Pay up and look pleasant, Haines said to him smiling.

Stephen filled a third cup, a spoonful of tea colouring faintly the thick rich milk. Buck Mulligan brought up a florin, twisted it round in his fingers and cried :

— A miracle !

He passed it along the table towards the old woman, saying :

— Ask nothing more of me, sweet. All I can give you I give.

Stephen laid the coin in her uneager hand.

— We'll owe twopence, he said.

— Time enough, sir, she said, taking the coin. Time enough. Good morning, sir.

She curtseyed and went out, followed by Buck Mulligan's tender chant :

— *Heart of my heart, were it more,*
More would be laid at your feet.

He turned to Stephen and said :

— Seriously, Dedalus. I'm stony. Hurry out to your school kip and bring us back some money. Today the bards must drink and junket. Ireland expects that every man this day will do his duty.

— That reminds me, Haines said, rising, that I have to visit your national library today.

— Our swim first, Buck Mulligan said.

He turned to Stephen and asked blandly :

— Is this the day for your monthly wash, Kinch ?

Then he said to Haines :

— The unclean bard makes a point of washing once a month.

— All Ireland is washed by the gulfstream, Stephen said as he let honey trickle over a slice of the loaf.

Haines from the corner where he was knotting easily a scarf about the loose collar of his tennis shirt spoke :

— I intend to make a collection of your sayings if you will let me.

Speaking to me. They wash and tub and scrub. Agenbite of inwit. Conscience. Yet here's a spot.

— That one about the cracked lookingglass of a servant being the symbol of Irish art is deuced good.

Buck Mulligan kicked Stephen's foot under the table and said with warmth of tone :

— Wait till you hear him on Hamlet, Haines.

— Well, I mean it, Haines said, still speaking to Stephen. I was just thinking of it when that poor old creature came in.

— Would I make money by it ? Stephen asked.

Haines laughed and, as he took his soft grey hat from the holdfast of the hammock, said :

— I don't know, I'm sure.

He strolled out to the doorway. Buck Mulligan bent across to Stephen and said with coarse vigour :

— You put your hoof in it now. What did you say that for ?

— Well ? Stephen said. The problem is to get money. From whom ? From the milkwoman or from him. It's a toss up, I think.

— I blow him out about you, Buck Mulligan said, and then you come along with your lousy leer and your gloomy jesuit jibes.

— I see little hope, Stephen said, from her or from him.

Buck Mulligan sighed tragically and laid his hand on Stephen's arm.

— From me, Kinch, he said.

In a suddenly changed tone he added :

— To tell you the God's truth I think you're right. Damn all else they are good for. Why don't you play them as I do ? To hell with them all. Let us get out of the kip.

He stood up, gravely ungirdled and disrobed himself of his gown, saying resignedly :

— Mulligan is stripped of his garments.

He emptied his pockets on to the table.

— There's your snotrag, he said.

And putting on his stiff collar and rebellious tie, he spoke to them, chiding them, and to his dangling watchchain. His hands plunged and rummaged in his trunk while he called for a clean handkerchief. Agenbite of inwit. God, we'll simply have to dress the character. I want puce gloves and green boots. Contradiction. Do I contradict myself? Very well then, I contradict myself. Mercurial Malachi. A limp black missile flew out of his talking hands.

— And there's your Latin quarter hat, he said.

Stephen picked it up and put it on. Haines called to them from the doorway :

— Are you coming, you fellows ?

— I'm ready, Buck Mulligan answered, going towards the door. Come out, Kinch. You have eaten all we left, I suppose. Resigned he passed out with grave words and gait, saying, wellnigh with sorrow :

— And going forth he met Butterly.

Stephen, taking his ashplant from its leaningplace, followed them out and, as they went down the ladder, pulled to the slow iron door and locked it. He put the huge key in his inner pocket.

At the foot of the ladder Buck Mulligan asked :

— Did you bring the key ?

— I have it, Stephen said, preceding them.

He walked on. Behind him he heard Buck Mulligan club with his heavy bathtowel the leader shoots of ferns or grasses.

— Down, sir. How dare you, sir.

Haines asked :

— Do you pay rent for this tower ?

— Twelve quid, Buck Mulligan said.

— To the secretary of state for war, Stephen added over his shoulder.

They halted while Haines surveyed the tower and said at last :

— Rather bleak in wintertime, I should say. Martello you call it ?

— Billy Pitt had them built, Buck Mulligan said, when the French were on the sea. But ours is the *omphalos*.

— What is your idea of Hamlet ? Haines asked Stephen.

— No, no, Buck Mulligan shouted in pain. I'm not equal to Thomas Aquinas and the fiftyfive reasons he has made to prop it up. Wait till I have a few pints in me first.

He turned to Stephen, saying as he pulled down neatly the peaks of his primrose waistcoat :

— You couldn't manage it under three pints, Kinch, could you?

— It has waited so long, Stephen said listlessly, it can wait longer.

— You pique my curiosity, Haines said aimiably. Is it some paradox?

— Pooh! Buck Mulligan said. We have grown out of Wilde and paradoxes. It's quite simple. He proves by algebra that Hamlet's grandson is Shakespeare's grandfather and that he himself is the ghost of his own father.

— What? Haines said, beginning to point at Stephen. He himself?

Buck Mulligan slung his towel stolewise round his neck and, bending in loose laughter, said to Stephen's ear:

— O, shade of Kinch the elder! Japhet in search of a father!

— We're always tired in the morning, Stephen said to Haines. And it is rather long to tell.

Buck Mulligan, walking forward again, raised his hands.

— The sacred pint alone can unbind the tongue of Dedalus, he said.

— I mean to say, Haines explained to Stephen as they followed, this tower and these cliffs here remind me somehow of Elsinore. *That beetles o'er his base into the sea,* isn't it?

Buck Mulligan turned suddenly for an instant towards Stephen but did not speak. In the bright silent instant Stephen saw his own image in cheap dusty mourning between their gay attires.

— It's a wonderful tale, Haines said, bringing them to halt again.

Eyes, pale as the sea the wind had freshened, paler, firm and prudent. The seas' ruler, he gazed southward over the bay, empty save for the smokeplume of the mailboat, vague on the bright skyline, and a sail tacking by the Muglins.

— I read a theological interpretation of it somewhere, he said bemused. The Father and the Son idea. The Son striving to be atoned with the Father.

Buck Mulligan at once put on a blithe broadly smiling face. He looked at them, his wellshaped mouth open happily, his eyes, from which he had suddenly withrawn all shrewd sense, blinking with mad gaiety. He moved a doll's head to and fro, the brims of his Panama hat quivering, and began to chant in a quiet happy foolish voice:

— *I'm the queerest young fellow that ever you heard.*
My mother's a jew, my father's a bird.
With Joseph the joiner I cannot agree,
So here's to disciples and Calvary.

He held up a forefinger of warning.

— *If anyone thinks that I amn't divine*
He'll get no free drinks when I'm making the wine
But have to drink water and wish it were plain
That I make when the wine becomes water again.

He tugged swiftly at Stephen's ashplant in farewell and, running forward to a brow of the cliff, fluttered his hands at his sides like fins or wings of one about to rise in the air, and chanted :

— *Goodbye, now, goodbye. Write down all I said*
And tell Tom, Dick and Harry I rose from the dead.
What's bred in the bone cannot fail me to fly
And Olivet's breezy... Goodbye, now, goodbye.

He capered before them down towards the fortyfoot hole, fluttering his winglike hands, leaping nimbly, Mercury's hat quivering in the fresh wind that bore back to them his brief birdlike cries.

Haines, who had been laughing guardedly, walked on beside Stephen and said :

— We oughtn't to laugh, I suppose. He's rather blasphemous. I'm not a believer myself, that is to say. Still his gaiety takes the harm out of it somehow, doesn't it? What did he call it? Joseph the Joiner?

— The ballad of Joking Jesus, Stephen answered.

— O, Haines said, you have heard it before?

— Three times a day, after meals, Stephen said drily.

— You're not a believer, are you? Haines asked. I mean, a believer in the narrow sense of the word. Creation from nothing and miracles and a personal God.

— There's only one sense of the word, it seems to me, Stephen said.

Haines stopped to take out a smooth silver case in which twinkled a green stone. He sprang it open with his thumb and offered it.

— Thank you, Stephen said, taking a cigarette.

Haines helped himself and snapped the case to. He put it back in his sidepocket and took from his waistcoatpocket a nickel tinderbox, sprang it open too, and, having lit his cigarette, held the flaming spunk towards Stephen in the shell of his hands.

— Yes, of course, he said, as they went on again. Either you believe or you don't, isn't it? Personally I couldn't stomach that idea of a personal God. You don't stand for that, I suppose?

— You behold in me, Stephen said with grim displeasure, a horrible example of free thought.

He walked on, waiting to be spoken to, trailing his ashplant by his side. Its ferrule followed lightly on the path, squealing at his heels. My familiar, after me, calling Steeeeeeeeeeeephen. A wavering line along the path. They will walk on it tonight, coming here in the dark. He wants that key. It is mine, I paid the rent. Now I eat his salt bread. Give him the key too. All. He will ask for it. That was in his eyes.

— After all, Haines began...

Stephen turned and saw that the cold gaze which had measured him was not all unkind.

— After all, I should think you are able to free yourself. You are your own master, it seems to me.

— I am the servant of two masters, Stephen said, an English and an Italian.

— Italian? Haines said.

A crazy queen, old and jealous. Kneel down before me.

— And a third, Stephen said, there is who wants me for odd jobs.

— Italian? Haines said again. What do you mean?

— The imperial British state, Stephen answered, his colour rising, and the holy Roman catholic and apostolic church.

Haines detached from his underlip some fibres of tobacco before he spoke.

— I can quite understand that, he said calmly. An Irishman must think like that, I daresay. We feel in England that we have treated you rather unfairly. It seems history is to blame.

The proud potent titles clanged over Stephen's memory the triumph of their brazen bells : *et unam sanctam catholicam et apostolicam ecclesiam* : the slow growth and change of rite and dogma like his own rare thoughts, a chemistry of stars. Symbol of the apostles in the mass for pope Marcellus, the voices blended, singing alone loud in affirmation : and behind their chant the vigilant angel of the church militant disarmed and menaced her heresiarchs. A horde of heresies fleeing with mitres awry : Photius and the brood of mockers of whom Mulligan was one, and Arius, warring his life long upon the consubstantiality of the Son with the Father, and Valentine, spurning Christ's terrene body, and the subtle African heresiarch Sabellius who held that the Father was Himself His own Son. Words Mulligan had spoken a moment since in mockery to the stranger. Idle mockery. The void awaits surely all them that weave the wind: a menace, a disarming and a worsting from those embattled angels of the church, Michael's host, who defend her ever in the hour of conflict with their lances and their shields.

Hear, hear. Prolonged applause. *Zut! Nom de Dieu!*

— Of course I'm a Britisher, Haine's voice said, and I feel as one. I don't want to see my country fall into the hands of German jews either. That's our national problem, I'm afraid, just now.

Two men stood at the verge of the cliff, watching: businessman, boatman.

— She's making for Bullock harbour.

The boatman nodded towards the north of the bay with some disdain.

— There's five fathoms out there, he said. It'll be swept up that way when the tide comes in about one. It's nine days today.

The man that was drowned. A sail veering about the blank bay waiting for a swollen bundle to bob up, roll over to the sun a puffy face, salt white. Here I am.

They followed the winding path down to the creek. Buck Mulligan stood on a stone, in shirtsleeves, his unclipped tie rippling over his shoulder. A young man clinging to a spur of rock near him, moved slowly frogwise his green legs in the deep jelly of the water.

— Is the brother with you, Malachi?

— Down in Westmeath. With the Bannons.

— Still there? I got a card from Bannon. Says he found a sweet young thing down there. Photo girl he calls her.

— Shapshot, eh? Brief exposure.

Buck Mulligan sat down to unlace his boots. An elderly man shot up near the spur of rock a blowing red face. He scrambled up by the stones, water glistening on his pate and on its garland of grey hair, water rilling over his chest and paunch and spilling jets out of his black sagging loincloth.

Buck Mulligan made way for him to scramble past and, glancing at Haines and Stephen, crossed himself piously with his thumbnail at brow and breastbone.

— Seymour's back in town, the young man said, grasping again his spur of rock. Chucked medicine and going in for the army.

— Ah, go to God, Buck Mulligan said.

— Going over next week to stew. You know that red Carlisle girl, Lily?

— Yes.

— Spooning with him last night on the pier. The father is rotten with money.

— Is she up the pole?

— Better ask Seymour that.

— Seymour a bleeding officer, Buck Mulligan said.

He nodded to himself as he drew off his trousers and stood up, saying tritely:

— Redheaded women buck like goats.

He broke off in alarm, feeling his side under his flapping shirt.

— My twelfth rib is gone, he cried. I'm the *Uebermensch*. Toothless Kinch and I, the supermen.

He struggled out of his shirt and flung it behind him to where his clothes lay.

— Are you going in here, Malachi?

— Yes. Make room in the bed.

The young man shoved himself backward through the water and reached the middle of the creek in two long clean strokes. Haines sat down on a stone, smoking.

— Are you not coming in, Buck Mulligan asked.

— Later on, Haines said. Not on my breakfast.

Stephen turned away.

— I'm going, Mulligan, he said.

— Give us that key, Kinch, Buck Mulligan said, to keep my chemise flat.

Stephen handed him the key. Buck Mulligan laid it across his heaped clothes.

— And twopence, he said, for a pint. Throw it there.

Stephen threw two pennies on the soft heap. Dressing, undressing. Buck Mulligan erect, with joined hands before him, said solemnly:

— He who stealeth from the poor lendeth to the Lord. Thus spake Zarathustra.

His plump body plunged.

— We'll see you again, Haines said, turning as Stephen walked up the path and smiling at wild Irish.

Horn of a bull, hoof of a horse, smile of a Saxon.

— The Ship, Buck Mulligan cried. Half twelve.

— Good, Stephen said.

He walked along the upwardcurving path.

Liliata rutilantium.
Turma circumdet.
Jubilantium te virginum.

The priest's grey nimbus in a niche where he dressed discreetly. I will not sleep here tonight. Home also I cannot go.

A voice, sweettoned and sustained, called to him from the sea. Turning the curve he waved his hand. It called again. A sleek brown head, a seal's, far out on the water, round.

Usurper.

— You, Cochrane, what city sent for him?

— Tarentum, sir.

— Very good, Well?

— There was a battle, sir.

— Very good. Where?

The boy's blank face asked the blank window.

Fabled by the daughters of memory. And yet it was in some way it not as memory fabled it. A phrase, then, of impatience, thud of Blake's wings of excess. I hear the ruin of all space, shattered glass and toppling masonry, and time one livid final flame. What's left us then?

— I forget the place, sir. 279 B. C.

— Asculum, Stephen said, glancing at the name and date in the gorescarred book.

— Yes, sir. And he said : *Another victory like that and we are done for.*

That phrase the world had remembered. A dull ease of the mind. From a hill above a corpsestrewn plain a general speaking to his officers, leaned upon his spear. Any general to any officers. They lend ear.

— You, Armstrong, Stephen said. What was the end of Pyrrhus?

— End of Pyrrhus, sir?

— I know, sir. Ask me, sir, Comyn said.

— Wait. You, Armstrong. Do you know anything about Pyrrhus?

A bag of figrolls lay snugly in Armstrong's satchel. He curled them between his palms at whiles and swallowed them softly. Crumbs adhered to the tissues of his lips. A sweetened boy's breath. Welloff people, proud that their eldest son was in the navy. Vico Road, Dalkey.

— Pyrrhus, sir? Pyrrhus, a pier.

All laughed. Mirthless high malicious laughter. Armstrong looked round at his classmates, silly glee in profile. In a moment they will laugh more loudly, aware of my lack of rule and of the fees their papas pay.

— Tell me now, Stephen said, poking the boy's shoulder with the book, what is a pier.

— A pier, sir, Armstrong said. A thing out in the waves. A kind of bridge. Kingstown pier, sir.

Some laughed again : mirthless but with meaning. Two in the back bench whispered. Yes. They knew : had never learned nor ever been innocent. All. With envy he watched their faces. Edith, Ethel, Gerty, Lily. Their likes : their breaths, too, sweetened with tea and jam, their bracelets tittering in the struggle.

— Kingstown pier, Stephen said. Yes, a disappointed bridge.

The words troubled their gaze.

— How, sir? Comyn asked. A bridge is across a river.

For Haines's chapbook. No-one here to hear. Tonight deftly amid wild drink and talk, to pierce the polished mail of his mind. What then? A jester at the court of his master, indulged and disesteemed, winning a clement master's praise. Why had they chosen all that part? Not wholly for the smooth caress. For them too history was a tale like any other too often heard, their land a pawnshop.

Had Pyrrhus not fallen by a beldam's hand in Argos or Julius Caesar not been knifed to death. They are not to be thought away. Time has branded them and fettered they are lodged in the room of the infinite possibilities they have ousted. But can those have been possible seeing that they never were? Or was that only possible which came to pass? Weave, weaver of the wind.

— Tell us a story, sir.

— Oh, do, sir. A ghoststory.

— Where do you begin in this? Stephen asked, opening another book.

— *Weep no more,* Comyn said.

— Go on then, Talbot.

— And the history, sir?

— After, Stephen said. Go on, Talbot.

A swarthy boy opened a book and propped it nimbly under the breastwork of his satchel. He recited jerks of verse with odd glances at the text :

— *Weep no more, woful shepherd, weep no more*
For Lycidas, your sorrow, is not dead,
Sunk though he be beneath the watery floor...

It must be a movement then, an actuality of the possible as possible. Aristotle's phrase formed itself within the gabbled verses and floated out into the studious silence of the library of Saint Genevieve where he had read, sheltered from the sin of Paris, night by night. By his elbow a delicate Siamese conned a handbook of strategy. Fed and feeding brains about me : under glowlamps, impaled, with faintly beating feelers : and in my mind's darkness a sloth ot the underworld, reluctant, shy of brightness, shifting her dragon scaly folds. Thought is the thought of thought. Tranquil brightness. The soul is in a manner all that is : the soul is the form of forms. Tranquillity sudden, vast, candescent : form of forms.

Talbot repeated :

— *Through the dear might of Him that walked the waves,*
Through the dear might...

— Turn over, Stephen said quietly. I don't see anything.

— What, sir? Talbot asked simply, bending forward.

His hand turned the page over. He leaned back and went on again having just remembered. Of him that walked the waves. Here also over these craven hearts his shadow lies and on the scoffer's heart and lips and on mine. It lies upon their eager faces who offered him a coin of the tribute. To Caesar what is Caesar's, to God what is God's. A long look from dark eyes, a riddling sentence to be woven and woven on the church's looms. Ay.

Riddle me, riddle me, randy ro.
My father gave me seeds to sow.

Talbot slid his closed book into his satchel.

— Have I heard all? Stephen asked.

— Yes, sir. Hockey at ten, sir.

— Half day, sir. Thursday.

— Who can answer a riddle? Stephen asked.

They bundled their books away, pencils clacking, pages rustling. Crowding together they strapped and buckled their satchels, all gabbling gaily :

— A riddle, sir. Ask me, sir.
— O, ask me, sir.
— A hard one, sir.
— This is the riddle, Stephen said :

The cock crew
The sky was blue :
The bells in heaven
Were striking eleven.
'Tis time for this poor soul
To go to heaven.

What is that?
— What, sir?
— Again, sir. We didn't hear.

Their eyes grew bigger as the lines were repeated. After a silence Cochrane said :

— What is it, sir? We give it up.

Stephen, his throat itching, answered :

— The fox burying his grandmother under a hollybush.

He stood up and gave a shout of nervous laughter to which their cries echoed dismay.

A stick struck the door and a voice in the corridor called :

— Hockey!

They broke asunder, sidling out of their benches, leaping them. Quickly they were gone and from the lumberroom came the rattle of sticks and clamour of their boots and tongues.

Sargent who alone had lingered came forward slowly, showing an open copybook. His tangled hair and scraggy neck gave witness of unreadiness and through his misty glasses weak eyes looked up pleading. On his cheek, dull and bloodless, a soft stain of ink lay, dateshaped, recent and damp as a snail's bed.

He held out his copybook. The word *Sums* was written on the headline. Beneath were sloping figures and at the foot a crooked signature with blind loops and a blot. Cyril Sargent : his name and seal.

— Mr Deasy told me to write them out all again, he said, and show them to you, sir.

Stephen touched the edges of the book. Futility.

— Do you understand how to do them now? he asked.

— Numbers eleven to fifteen, Sargent answered. Mr Deasy said I was to copy them off the board, sir.

— Can you do them yourself? Stephen asked.

— No, sir.

Ugly and futile : lean neck and tangled hair and a stain of ink, a snail's bed. Yet someone had loved him, borne him in her arms and in her heart. But for her the race of the world would have trampled him under foot, a squashed boneless snail. She had loved his weak watery blood drained from her own. Was that then real? The only true thing in life? His mother's prostrate body the fiery Columbanus in holy zeal bestrode. She was no more : the trembling skeleton of a twig burnt in the fire, an odour of rosewood and wetted ashes. She had saved him from being trampled under foot and had gone, scarcely having been. A poor soul gone to heaven : and on a heath beneath winking stars a fox, red reek of rapine in his fur, with merciless bright eyes scraped in the earth, listened, scraped up the earth, listened, scraped and scraped.

Sitting at his side Stephen solved out the problem. He proves by algebra that Shakespeare's ghost is Hamlet's grandfather. Sargent peered askance through his slanted glasses. Hockeysticks rattled in the lumberroom : the hollow knock of a ball and calls from the field.

Across the page the symbols moved in grave morrice, in the mummery of their letters, wearing quaint caps of squares and cubes. Give hands, traverse, bow to partner : so : imps of fancy of the Moors. Gone too from the world, Averroes and Moses Maimonides, dark men in mien and movement, flashing in their mocking mirrors the obscure soul of the world, a darkness shining in brightness which brightness could not comprehend.

— Do you understand now? Can you work the second for yourself?

— Yes, sir.

In long shaky strokes Sargent copied the data. Waiting always for a word of help his hand moved faithfully the unsteady symbols, a faint hue of shame flickering behind his dull skin. *Amor matris* : subjective and objective genitive. With her weak blood and wheysour milk she had fed him and hid from sight of others his swaddling bands.

Like him was I, these sloping shoulders, this gracelessness. My childhood bends beside me. Too far for me to lay a hand there once or lightly. Mine is far and his secret as our eyes. Secrets, silent, stony sit in the dark palaces of both our hearts : secrets weary of their tyranny : tyrants willing to be dethroned.

The sum was done.

— It is very simple, Stephen said as he stood up.

— Yes, sir. Thanks, Sargent answered.

He dried the page with a sheet of thin blottingpaper and carried his copybook back to his desk.

— You had better get your stick and go out to the others, Stephen said as he followed towards the door the boy's graceless form.

— Yes, sir.

In the corridor his name was heard, called from the playfield.

— Sargent!

— Run on, Stephen said. Mr Deasy is calling you.

He stood in the porch and watched the laggard hurry towards the scrappy field where sharp voices were in strife. They were sorted in teams and Mr Deasy came stepping over wisps of grass with gaitered feet. When he had reached the schoolhouse voices again contending called to him. He turned his angry white moustache.

— What is it now? he cried continually without listening.

— Cochrane and Halliday are on the same side, sir, Stephen cried.

— Will you wait in my study for a moment, Mr Deasy said, till I restore order here.

And as he stepped fussily back across the field his old man's voice cried sternly :

— What is the matter? What is it now?

Their sharp voices cried about him on all sides : their many forms closed round him, the garish sushine bleaching the honey of his illdyed head.

Stale smoky air hung in the study with the smell of drab abraded leather of its chairs. As on the first day he bargained with me here. As it was in the beginning, is now. On the sideboard the tray of Stuart coins, base treasure of a bog : and ever shall be. And snug in their spooncase of purple plush, faded, the twelve apostles having preached to all the gentiles : world without end.

A hasty step over the stone porch and in the corridor. Blowing out his rare moustache Mr Deasy halted at the table.

— First, our little financial settlement, he said.

He brought out of his coat a pocketbook bound by a leather thong. It slapped open and he took from it two notes, one of joined halves, and laid them carefully on the table strapping and

— Two, he said, strapping and stowing his pocketbook away.

And now his strongroom for the gold. Stephen's embarrassed hand moved over the shells heaped in the cold stone mortar : whelks and money cowries and leopard shells : and this, whorled as an emir's turban, and this, the scallop of Saint James. An old pilgrim's hoard, dead treasure, hollow shells.

A sovereign fell, bright and new, on the soft pile of the tablecloth.

— Three, Mr Deasy said, turning his little savingsbox about in his hand. These are handy things to have. See. This is for sovereigns. This is for shillings, sixpences, halfcrowns. And here crowns. See.

He shot from it two crowns and two shillings.

— Three twelve, he said. I think you'll find that's right.

— Thank you, sir, Stephen said, gathering the money together with shy haste and putting it all in a pocket of his trousers.

— No thanks at all, Mr Deasy said. You have earned it.

Stephen's hand, free again, went back to the hollow shells. Symbols too of beauty and of power. A lump in my pocket. Symbols soiled by greed and misery.

— Don't carry it like that, Mr Deasy said. You'll pull it out somewhere and lose it. You just buy one of these machines. You'll find them very handy.

Answer something.

— Mine would be often empty, Stephen said.

The same room and hour, the same wisdom : and I the same. Three times now. Three nooses round me here. Well. I can break them in this instant if I will.

— Because you don't save, Mr Deasy said, pointing his finger. You don't know yet what money is. Money is power, when you have lived as long as I have. I know, I know. If youth but knew. But what does Shakespeare say ? *Put but money in thy purse.*

— Iago, Stephen murmured.

He lifted his gaze from the idle shells to the old man's stare.

— He knew what money was, Mr Deasy said. He made money. A poet. but an Englishman too. Do you know what is the pride of the English ? Do you know what is the proudest word you will ever hear from an Englishman's mouth ?

The seas' ruler. His seacold eyes looked on the empty bay : history is to blame : on me and on my words, unhating.

— That on his empire, Stephen said, the sun never sets.

— Ba! Mr Deasy cried. That's not English. A French Celt said that. He tapped his savingsbox against his thumbnail.

— I will tell you, he said solemnly, what is his proudest boast. *I paid my way.*

Goood man, good man.

— *I paid my way. I never borrowed a shilling in my life.* Can you feel that? *I owe nothing.* Can you?

Mulligan, nine pounds, three pairs of socks, one pair brogues, ties. Curran, ten guineas. McCann, one guinea. Fred Ryan, two shillings. Temple, two lunches. Russell, one guinea, Cousins, ten shillings, Bob Reynolds, half a guinea, Köhler, three guineas, Mrs McKernan, five weeks' borard. The lump I have is useless.

— For the moment, no, Stephen answered.

Mr Deasy laughed with rich delight, putting back his savingsbox.

— I knew you couldn't, he said joyously. But one day you must feel it. We are a generous people but we must also be just.

— I fear those big words, Stephen said, which make us so unhappy.

Mr Deasy stared sternly for some moments over the mantelpiece at the shapely bulk of a man in tartan fillibegs: Albert Edward, Prince of Wales.

— You think me an old fogey and an old tory, his thoughtful voice said. I saw three generations since O'Connell's time. I remember the famine. Do you know that the orange lodges agitated for repeal of the union twenty years before O'Connell did or before the prelates of your communion denounced him as a demagogue? You fenians forget some things.

Glorious, pious and immortal memory. The lodge of Diamond in Armagh the splendid behung with corpses of papishes. Hoarse, masked and armed, the planters covenant. The black north and true blue bible. Croppies lie down.

Stephen sketched a brief gesture.

— I have rebel blood in me too, Mr Deasy said. On the spindle side. But I am descended from sir John Blackwood who voted for the union. We are all Irish, all kings' sons.

— Alas, Stephen said.

— *Per vias rectas*, Mr Deasy said firmly, was his motto. He voted for it and put on his topboots to ride to Dublin from the Ards of Down to do so.

Lal the ral the ra
The rocky road to Dublin.

A gruff squire on horseback with shiny topboots. Soft day, sir John. Soft, day, your honour... Day... Day... Two topboots jog dangling on to Dublin. Lal the ral the ra, lal the ral the raddy.

— That reminds me, Mr Deasy said. You can do me a favour, Mr Dedalus, with some of your literary friends. I have a letter here for the press. Sit down a moment. I have just to copy the end.

He went to the desk near the window, pulled in his chair twice and read off some words from the sheet on the drum of his typewriter.

— Sit down. Excuse me, he said over his shoulder, *the dictates of common sense.* Just a moment.

He peered from under his shaggy brows at the manuscript by his elbow and, muttering, began to prod the stiff buttons of the keyboard slowly, some times blowing as he screwed up the drum to erase an error.

Stephen seated himself noiselessly before the princely presence. Framed around the walls images of vanished horses stood in homage, their meek heads poised in air : lord Hastings' Repulse, the duke of Westminster's Shotover, the duke of Beaufort's Ceylon, *prix de Paris,* 1866. Elfin riders sat them, watchful of a sign. He saw their speeds, backing king's colours, and shouted with the shouts of vanished crowds.

— Full stop, Mr Deasy bade his keys. But prompt ventilation of this important question...

Where Cranly led me to get rich quick, hunting his winners among the mudsplashed brakes, amid the bawls of bookies on their pitches and reek of the canteen, over the motley slush. Even money Fair Rebel : ten to one the field. Dicers and thimbleriggers we hurried by after the hoofs, the vying caps and jackets and past the meatfaced woman, a butcher's dame, nuzzling thirstily her clove of orange.

Shouts rang shrill from the boys' playfield and a whirring whistle.

Again : a goal. I am among them, among their battling bodies in a medley, the joust of life. You mean that knockkneed mother's darling who seems to be slightly crawsick ? Jousts. Time shocked rebounds, shock by shock. Jousts, slush and uproar of battles, the frozen deathspew of the slain, a shout of spear spikes baited with men's bloodied guts.

— Now then, Mr Deasy said, rising.

He came to the table, pinning together his sheets. Stephen stood up.

— I have put the matter into a nutshell, Mr Deasy said. It's about the foot and mouth disease. Just look through it. There can be no two opinions on the matter.

May I trespass on your valuable space. That doctrine of *laissez faire* which so often in our history. Our cattle trade. The way of all our old industries. Liverpool ring which jockeyed the Galway harbour scheme. European conflagration. Grain supplies through the narrow waters of the channel. The pluterperfect imperturbability of the department of agriculture. Pardoned a classical allusion. Cassandra. By a woman who was no better than she should be. To come to the point at issue.

— I don't mince words, do I? Mr Deasy asked as Stephen read on.

Foot and mouth disease. Known as Koch's preparation. Serum and virus. Percentage of salted horses. Rinderpest. Emperor's horses at Mürzsteg, lower Austria. Veterinary surgeons. Mr Henry Blackwood Price. Courteous offer a fair trial. Dictates of common sense. Allimportant question. In every sense of the word take the bull by the horns. Thanking you for the hospitality of your columns.

— I want that to be printed and read, Mr Deasy said. You will see at the next outbreak they will put an embargo on Irish cattle. And it can be cured. It is cured. My cousin, Blackwood Price, writes to me it is regularly treated and cured in Austria by cattledoctors there. They offer to come over here. I am trying to work up influence with the department. Now I'm going to try publicity. I am surrounded by difficulties, by... intrigues by... backstairs influence by...

He raised his forefinger and beat the air oldly before his voice spoke.

— Mark my words, Mr Dedalus, he said. England is in the hands of the jews. In all the highest places: her finance, her press. And they are the signs of a nation's decay. Wherever they gather they eat up the nation's vital strength. I have seen it coming these years. As sure as we are standing here the jew merchants are already at their work of destruction. Old England is dying.

He stepped swiftly off, his eyes coming to blue life as they passed a broad sunbeam. He faced about and back again.

— Dying, he said, if not dead by now.

The harlot's cry from street to street
Shall weave old England's winding sheet.

His eyes open wide in vision stared sternly across the sunbeam in which he halted.

— A merchant, Stephen said, is one who buys cheap and sells dear, jew or gentile, is he not?

— They sinned against the light, Mr Deasy said gravely. And you can see the darkness in their eyes. And that is why they are wanderers on the earth to this day.

On the steps of the Paris Stock Exchange the goldskinned men quoting prices on their gemmed fingers. Gabble of geese. They swarmed loud, uncouth about the temple, their heads thickplotting under maladroit silk hats. Not theirs: these clothes, this speech, these gestures. Their full slow eyes bellied the words, the gestures eager and unoffending, but knew the rancours massed about them and knew their zeal was vain. Vain patience to heap and hoard. Time surely would scatter all. A hoard heaped by the roadside: plundered and passing on. Their eyes knew the years of wandering and, patient, knew the dishonours of their flesh.

— Who has not? Stephen said.

— What do you mean? Mr Deasy asked.

He came forward a pace and stood by the table. His underjaw fell sideways open uncertainly. Is this old wisdom? He waits to hear from me.

— History, Stephen said, is a nightmare from which I am trying to awake.

From the playfield the boys raised a shout. A whirring whistle: goal. What if that nightmare gave a you a back kick?

— The ways of the Creator are not our ways, Mr Deasy said. All history moves towards one great goal, the manifestation of God.

Stephen jerked his thumb towards the window, saying:

— That is God.

Hooray! Ay! Whrrwhee!

— What? Mr Deasy asked.

— A shout in the street, Stephen answered, shrugging his shoulders.

Mr Deasy looked down and held for a while the wings of his nose tweaked between his fingers. Looking up again he set them free.

— I am happier than you are, he said. We have committed many errors and many sins. A woman brought sin into the world. For a woman who was no better than she should be, Helen, the runaway wife of Menelaus, ten years the Greeks made war on Troy. A faithless wife first brought the strangers to our shore here, MacMurrough's wife and her leman O'Rourke, prince ot Breffni. A woman too brought Parnell low. Many errors, many failures but not the one sin. I am a struggler now at the end of my days. But I will fight for the right till the end.

For Ulster will fight
And Ulster will be right.

Stephen raised the sheets in his hand.

— Well, sir, he began.

— I foresee, Mr Deasy said, that you will not remain here very long at this work. You were not born to be a teacher, I think. Perhaps I am wrong.

— A learner rather, Stephen said.

— And here what will you learn more?

Mr Deasy shook his head.

— Who knows? he said. To learn one must be humble. But life is the great teacher.

Stephen rustled the sheets again.

— As regards these, he began.

— Yes, Mr Deasy said. You have two copies there. If you can have them published at once.

Telegraph. Irish Homestead.

— I will try, Stephen said, and let you know tomorrow. I know two editors slightly.

— That will do, Mr Deasy said briskly. I wrote last night to Mr Field, M. P. There is a meeting of the cattletraders' association today at the City Arms Hotel. I asked him to lay my letter before the meeting. You see if you can get it into your two papers. What are they?

— *The Evening Telegraph...*

— That will do, Mr Deasy said. There is no time to lose. Now I have to answer that letter from my cousin.

— Good morning, sir, Stephen said, putting the sheets in his pocket. Thank you.

— Not at all, Mr Deasy said as he searched the papers on his desk. I like to break a lance with you, old as I am.

— Good morning, sir, Stephen said again, bowing to his bent back.

He went out by the open porch and down the gravel path under the trees, hearing the cries of voices and crack of sticks from the playfield. The lions couchant on the pillars as he passed out through the gate; toothless terrors. Still I will help him in his fight. Mulligan will dub me a new name : the bullockbefriending bard.

— Mr Dedalus!

Running after me. No more letters, I hope.

— Just one moment.

— Yes, sir, Stephen said, turning back at the gate.

Mr Deasy halted, breathing hard and swallowing his breath.

— I just wanted to say, he said. Ireland, they say, has the honour of being the only country which never persecuted the jews. Do you know that? No. And do you know why?

He frowned sternly on the bright air.

— Why, sir, Stephen asked, beginning to smile.

— Because she never let them in, Mr Deasy said solemnly.

A coughball of laughter leaped from his throat dragging after it a rattling chain of phlegm. He turned back quickly, coughing, laughing, his lifted arms waving to the air.

— She never let them in, he cried again through his laughter as he stamped on gaitered feet over the gravel of the path. That's why.

On his wise shoulders through the checkerwork of leaves the sun flung spangles, dancing coins.

3

Ineluctable modality of the visible : at least that if no more, thought through my eyes. Signatures of all things I am here to read, seaspawn and seawrack, the nearing tide, that rusty boot. Snotgreen, bluesilver, rust : coloured signs. Limits of the diaphane But he adds : in bodies. Then he was aware of them bodies before of them coloured. How ? By knocking his sconce against them, sure. Go easy. Bald he was and a millionaire, *maestro di color che sanno*. Limit of the diaphane in. Why in ? Diaphane, adiaphane. If you can put your five fingers throught it, it is a gate, if not a door. Shut your eyes and see.

Stephen closed his eyes to hear his boots crush crackling wrack and shells. You are walking through it howsomever. I am, a stride at a time. A very short space of time through very short times of space. Five, six : the *nacheinander*. Exactly : and that is the ineluctable modality of the audible. Open your eyes. No. Jesus ! If I fell over a cliff that beetles o'er his base, fell through the *nebeneinander* ineluctably. I am getting on nicely in the dark. My ash sword hangs at my side. Tap with it : they do. My two feet in his boots are at the end of his legs, *nebeneinander*. Sounds solid : made by the mallet of *Los Demiurgos*. Am I walking into eternity along Sandymount strand ? Crush, crack, crick, crick. Wild sea money. Dominic Deasy kens them a'.

Won't you come to Sandymount,
Madeline the mare ?

Rhythm begins, you see. I hear. A catalectic tetrameter of iambs march ing. No, agallop : *deline the mare*.

Open your eyes now. I will. One moment. Has all vanished since? If I open and am for ever in the black adiaphane. *Basta!* I will see if I can see.

See now. There all the time without you: and ever shall be, world without end.

They came down the steps from Leahy's terrace prudently, *Frauenzimmer*: and down the shelving shore flabbily their splayed feet sinking in the silted sand. Like me, like Algy, coming down to our mighty mother. Number one swung lourdily her midwife's bag, the other's gamp poked in the beach. From the liberties, out for the day. Mrs Florence Mac Cabe, relict of the late Patk MacCabe, deeply lamented, of Bride Street. One of her sisterhood lugged me squealing into life. Creation from nothing. What has she in the bag? A misbirth with a trailing navelcord, hushed in ruddy wool. The cords of all link back, strandentwining cable of all flesh. That is why mystic monks. Will you be as gods? Gaze in your omphalos. Hello. Kinch here. Put me on to Edenville. Aleph, alpha: nought, nought, one.

Spouse and helpmate of Adam Kadmon: Heva, naked Eve. She had no navel. Gaze. Belly without blemish, bulging big, a buckler of taut vellum, no, whiteheaped corn, orient and immortal, standing from everlasting to everlasting Womb of sin.

Wombed in sin darkness I was too. made not begotten. By them, the man with my voice and my eyes and a ghostwoman with ashes on her breath. They clasped and sundered, did the coupler's will. From before the ages He willed me and now may not will me away or ever. A *lex eterna* stays about Him. Is that then the divine substance wherein Father and Son are consubstantial? Where is poor dear Arius to try conclusions? Warring his life long on the contransmagnificandjewbangtantiality. Illstarred heresiarch. In a Greek watercloset he breathed his last: euthanasia. With beaded mitre and with crozier, stalled upon his throne, widower of a widowed see, with upstiffed omophorion, with clotted hinderparts.

Airs romped around him, nipping and eager airs. They are coming, waves. The whitemaned seahorses, champing, brightwindbridled, the steeds of Mananaan.

I mustn't forget his letter for the press. And after? The Ship, half twelve. By the way go easy with that money like a good young imbecile. Yes, I must.

His pace slackened. Here. Am I going to Aunt Sara's or not? My consubstantial father's voice. Did you see anything of your artist brother

Stephen lately? No? Sure he's not down in Strasburg terrace with his aunt Sally? Couldn't he fly a bit higher than that, eh? And and and and tell us Stephen, how is uncle Si? O weeping God, the things I married into. De boys up in de hayloft. The drunken little costdrawer and his brother, the cornet player. Highly respectable gondoliers. And skeweyed Walter sirring his father, no less. Sir. Yes, sir. No, sir. Jesus wept: and no wonder, by Christ.

I pull the wheezy bell of their shuttered cottage: and wait. They take me for a dun, peer out from a coign of vantage.

— It's Stephen, sir.

— Let him in. Let Stephen in.

A bolt drawn back and Walter welcomes me.

— We thought you were someone else.

In his broad bed nuncle Richie, pillowed and blanketed, extends over the hillock of his knees a sturdy forearm. Cleanchested. He has washed the upper moiety.

— Morrow, nephew.

He lays aside the lapboard whereon he drafts his bills of costs for the eyes of Master Goff and Master Shapland Tandy, filing consents and common searches and a writ of *Duces Tecum*. A bogoak frame over his bald head: Wilde's *Requiescat*. The drone of his misleading whistle brings Walter back.

— Yes, sir?

— Malt for Richie and Stephen, tell mother. Where is she?

— Bathing Crissie, sir.

Papa's little bedpal. Lump of love.

— No, uncle Richie...

— Call me Richie. Damn your lithia water. It lowers. Whusky!

— Uncle Richie, really...

— Sit down or by the law. Harry I'll knock you down.

Walter squints vainly for a chair.

— He has nothing to sit down on, sir.

— He has nowhere put toit, you mug. Bring in our Chippendale chair. Would you like a bite of something? None of your damned lawdeedaw airs here; the rich of a rasher fried with a herring? Sure? So much the better. We have nothing in the house but backache pills.

All'erta!

He drones bars of Ferrando's *aria di sortita*. The grandest number, Stephen, in the whole opera. Listen.

His tuneful whistle sounds again, finely shaded, with rushes of the air, his fists bigdrumming on his padded knees.

This wind is sweeter.

Houses of decay, mine, his and all. You told the Clongowes gentry you had an uncle a judge and an uncle a general in the army. Come out of them, Stephen. Beauty is not there. Nor in the stagnant bay, of Marsh's library where you read the fading prophecies of Joachim Abbas. For whom? The hundredheaded rabble of the cathedral close. A hater of his kind ran from them to the wood of madness, his mane foaming in the moon, his eyeballs stars. Houyhnhnm, horsenostrilled. The oval equine faces, Temple, Buck Mulligan, Foxy Campbell, Lantern jaws. Abbas father, furious dean what offence laid fire to their brains? Paff! *Descende, calve, ut ne nimium decalveris.* A garland of grey hair on his comminated head see him me clambering down to the footpace *(descende)*, clutching a monstrance, basliskeyed. Get down, bald poll! A choir gives back menace and echo, assisting about the altar's horns, the snorted Latin of jackpriests moving burly in their albs, tonsured and oiled and gelded, fat with the fat of kidneys of wheat.

And at the same instant perhaps a priest round the corner is elevating it. Dringdring! And two streets off another locking it into a pyx. Dringadring! And in a ladychapel another taking housel all to his own cheek. Dringdring! Down, up, forward, back. Dan Occam thought of that, invincible doctor. A misty English morning the imp hypostasis tickled his brain. Bringing his host down and kneeling he heard twine with his second bell the first bell in the transept (he is lifting his) and, rising, heard (now I am lifting) their two bells (he is kneeling) twang in diphthong.

Cousin Stephen, you will never be a saint. Isle of saints. You were awfully holy, weren't you? You prayed to the Blessed Virgin that you might not have a red nose. You prayed to the devil in Serpentine avenue that the fubsy widow in front might lift her clothes still more from the wet street. *O si, certo!* Sell your soul for that, do, dyed rags pinned round a squaw. More tell me, more still! On the top of the Howth tram alone crying to the rain: *naked women!* What about that, eh?

What about what? what else were they invented for?

Reading two pages apiece of seven books every night, eh? I was young. You bowed to yourself in the mirror, stepping forward to applause earnestly, striking face. Hurray for the Goddamned idiot! Hray! No-one saw: tell no-one. Books you were going to write with letters for titles. Have you read his

F? O yes, but I prefer Q. Yes, but W is wonderful. O yes, W. Remember your epiphanies on green oval leaves, deeeply deep, copies to be sent if you died to all the great libraries of the world, including Alexandria? Someone was to read them there after a few thousand years, a mahamanvantara. Pico della Mirandola like. Ay, very like a whale. When one reads these strange pages of one long gone one feels that one is at one with one who once...

The grainy sand had gone from under his feet. His boots trod again a damp crackling mast, razorshells, squeaking pebbles, that on the unnumbered pebbles beats, wood sieved by the shipworm, lost Armada. Unwholesome sandflats waited to suck his treading soles, breathing upward sewage breath. He coasted them, walking warily. A porterbottle stood up, stogged to its waist, in the cakey sand dough. A sentinel : isle of dreadful thirst. Broken hoops on the shore; at the land a maze of dark cunning nets; farther away chalkscrawled backdoors and on the higher beach a dryingline with two crucified shirts. Ringsend : wigwams of brown steersmen and master mariners. Human shells.

He halted. I have passed the way to aunt Sara's. Am I not going there? Seems not. No-one about. He turned northeast and crossed the firmer sand towards the Pigeonhouse.

— *Qui vous a mis dans cette fichue position?*

— *C'est le pigeon, Joseph.*

Patrice, home on furlough, lapped warm milk with me in the bar MacMahon. Son of the wild goose, Kevin Egan of Paris. My father's a bird, he lapped the sweet *lait chaud* with pink young tongue, plump bunny's face. Lap, *lapin*. He hopes to win in the *gros lots*. About the nature of women he read in Michelet. But he must send me *La Vie de Jésus* by M. Léo Taxil. Lent it to his friend.

— *C'est tordant, vous savez. Moi je suis socialiste. Je ne crois pas en l'existence de Dieu. Faut pas le dire à mon père.*

— *Il croit?*

— *Mon père, oui.*

Schluss. He laps.

My Latin quarter hat. God, we simply must dress the character. I want puce gloves. You were a student, weren't you? Of what in the other devil's name? Paysayenn. P. C. N., you know : *physiques, chimiques et naturelles*. Aha. Eating your groatsworth of *mou en civet,* fleshpots of Egypt, elbowed by belching cabmen. Just say in the most natural tone : when I was in Paris, *boul'Mich',* I used to. Yes, used to carry punched tickets to prove an alibi if they arrested you for murder somewhere. Justice. On the night of the seventeenth of February 1904 the prisoner was seen by two witnesses. Other fellow did it : other me. Hat, tie, overcoat, nose. *Lui, c'est moi*. You seem to have enjoyed yourself.

Proudly walking. Whom were you trying to walk like? Forget : a dispossessed. With mother's money order, eight shillings, the banging door of the post office slammed in your face by the usher. Hunger toothache. *Encore deux minutes.* Look clock. Must get. *Fermé.* Hired dog! Shoot him to bloody bits with a bang shotgun, bits man spattered walls all brass buttons. Bits all khrrrrklak in place clack back. Not hurt? O, that's all right. Shake hands. See what I meant, see? O, that's all right. Shake a shake. O, that's all only all right.

You were going to do wonders, what? Missionary to Europe after fiery Columbanus. Fiacre and Scotus on their creepystools in heaven spilt from their pintpots, loudlatinlaughing : *Euge! Euge!* Pretending to speak broken English as you dragged your valise, porter threepence, across the slimy pier at Newhaven. *Comment?* Rich booty you brought back; *Le Tutu,* five tattered numbers of *Pantalon Blanc et Culotte Rouge,* a blue French telegram, curiosity to show :

— Mother dying come home father.

The aunt thinks you killed your mother. That's why she won't.

Then here's a health to Mulligan's aunt
And I'll tell you the reason why.
She always kept things decent in
The Hannigan famileye.

His feet marched in sudden proud rhythm over the sand furrows, along by the boulders of the south wall. He stared at them proudly, piled stone mammoth skulls. Gold light on sea, on sand, on boulders. The sun is there, the slender trees, the lemon houses.

Paris rawly waking, crude sunlight on her lemon streets. Moist pith of farls of bread, the froggreen wormwood, her matin incense, court the air. Belluomo rises from the bed of his wife's lover's wife, the kerchiefed housewife is astir, a saucer of acetic acid in her hands. In Rodot's Yvonne and Madeleine newmake there tumbled beauties, shattering with gold teeth *chaussons* of pastry, their mouths yellowed with the *pus* of *flan bréton.* Faces of Paris men go by, their well pleased pleasers, curled conquistadores.

Noon slumbers. Kevin Egan rolls gunpowder cigarettes through fingers smeared with printer's ink, sipping his green fairy as Patrice his white. About us gobblers fork spiced beans down their gullets. *Un demi sétier* ! A jet of coffee steam from the burnished caldron. She serves me at his beck. *Il est Irlandais. Hollandais? Non fromage. Deux Irlandais, nous, Irlande, vous savez? Ah, oui!* She thought you wanted a cheese *hollandais*. Your postprandial, do you know that word? Postprandial. There was a fellow I knew once in Barcelona, queer fellow, used to call it his postprandial. Well : *slainte !* Around the slabbed tables the tangle of wined breaths and grumbling gorges. His breath hangs over our saucestained plates, the green fairy's fang thrusting between his lips. Of Ireland, the Dalcassians, of hopes, conspiracies, of Arthur Griffith now. To yoke me as his yokefellow, our crimes our common cause. You're your father's son. I know the voice. His fustian shirt, sanguineflowered, trembles its Spanish tassels at his secrets. M. Drumont, famous journalist, Drumont, know what he called queen Victoria? Old hag with the yellow teeth. *Vieille ogresse* with the *dents jaunes*. Maud Gonne, beautiful woman, *La Patrie,* M. Millevoye, Félix Faure, know how he died? Licentious men. The froeken, *bonne à tout faire,* who rubs male nakedness in the bath at Upsala. *Moi faire,* she said. *Tous les messieurs* not this *Monsieur*, I said. Most licentious custom. Bath a most private thing. I wouldn't let my brother, not even my own brother, most lascivious thing. Green eyes, I see you. Fang, I feel. Lascivious people.

The blue fuse burns deadly between hands and burns clear. Loose tobacco shreds catch fire : a flame and acrid smoke light our corner. Raw facebones under his peep of day boy's hat. How the head centre got away, authentic version. Got up as a young bride, man, veil orangeblossoms, drove out the road to Malahide. Did, faith. Of lost leaders, the betrayed, wild escapes. Disguises, clutched at, gone, not here.

Spurned lover. I was a strapping young gossoon at that time, I tell you, I'll show you my likeness one day. I was, faith. Lover, for her love he prowled with colonel Richard Burke, tanist of his sept, under the walls of Clerkenwell and, crouching, saw a flame of vengeance hurl them upward in the fog. Shattered glass and toppling masonry. In gay Paree he hides, Egan of Paris, unsought by any save by me. Making his day's stations, the dingy printingcase, his three taverns, the Montmartre lair he sleeps short night in, rue de la Goutte-d'Or, damascened with flyblown faces of the gone. Loveless, landless, wifeless. She is quite nicey comfy without her outcast man, madame, in rue Git-le-Cœur, canary and two buck lodgers. Peachy cheeks, a zebra skirt, frisky as a young thing's. Spurned and undespairing. Tell Pat you saw me, won't you? I wanted to get poor Pat a job one time. *Mon fils,* soldier of France. I taught him to sing. *The boys of Kilkenny are stout roaring blades.* Know that old lay? I taught Patrice that. Old Kilkenny : saint Canice, Strongbow's castle on the Nore. Goes like this. *O, O.* He takes me, Napper Tandy, by the hand.

O, O the boys of
Kilkenny...

Weak wasting hand on mine. They have forgotten Kevin Egan, not he them. Remembering thee, O Sion.

He had come nearer the edge of the sea and wet sand slapped his boots. The new air greeted him, harping in wild nerves, wind of wild air of seeds or brightness. Here, I am not walking out to the Kish lightship, am I? He stood suddenly, his feet beginning to sink slowly in the quaking soil. Turn back.

Turning, he scanned the shore south, his feet sinking again slowly in new sockets. The cold domed room of the tower waits. Through the barbacans the shafts of light are moving ever, slowly ever as my feet are sinking, creeping duskward over the dial floor. Blue dusk, nightfall, deep blue night. In the darkness of the dome they wait, their pushedback chairs, my obelisk valise, around a board of abandoned platters. Who to clear it? He has the key. I will not sleep there when this night comes. A shut door of a silent tower entombing their blind bodies, the panthersahib and his pointer. Call : no answer. He lifted his feet up from the suck and turned back by the mole of boulders. Take all, keep all. My soul walks with me, form of forms. So in the moon's midwatches I pace the path above the rocks, in sable silvered, hearing Elsinore's tempting flood.

The flood is following me. I can watch it flow past from here. Get back then by the Poolbeg road to the strand there. He climbed over the sedge and eely oarweeds and sat on a stool of rock, resting his ashplant in a grike.

A bloated carcase of a dog lay lolled on bladderwrack. Before him the gunwale of a boat, sunk in sand. *Un coche ensablé,* Louis Veuillot called Gautier's prose. These heavy sands are language tide and wind have silted here. And there, the stoneheaps of dead builders, a warren of weasel rats. Hide gold there. Try it You have some. Sands and stones. Heavy of the past. Sir Lout's toys. Mind you don't get one bang on the ear. I'm the bloody well gigant rolls all them bloody well boulders, bones for my steppingstones. Feefawfum. I zmellz de bloodz odz an Iridzman.

A point, live dog, grew into sight running across the sweep of sand. Lord, is he going to attack me? Respect his liberty. You will not be master of others or their slave. I have my stick. Sit tight. From farther away, walking shoreward across from the crested tide, figures, two. The two maries. They have tucked it safe mong the bulrushes. Peekaboo. I see you. No, the dog. He is running back to them. Who?

Galleys of the Lochlanns ran here to beach, in quest of prey, their bloodbeaked prows riding low on a molten pewter surf. Dane vikings, torcs of tomahawks aglitter on their breasts when Malachi wore the collar of gold. A school of turlehide whales stranded in hot noon, spouting, hobbling in the shallows. Then from the starving cagework city a horde of jerkined dwarfs, my people, with flayers' knives, running, scaling, hacking in green blubbery whalemeat. Famine, plague and slaughters. Their blood is in me, their lusts my waves. I moved among them on the frozen Liffey, that I, a changeling, among the spluttering resin fires. I spoke to no-one: none to me.

The dog's bark ran towards him, stopped, ran back. Dog of my enemy. I just simply stood pale, silent, bayed about. *Terribilia meditans.* A primrose doublet, fortune's knave, smiled on my fear. For that are you pining, the bark of their applause? Pretenders: live their lives. The Bruce's brother, Thomas Fitzgerald, silken knight, Perkin Warbeck, York's false scion, in breeches of silk of whiterose ivory, wonder of a day, and Lambert Simnel, with a tail of nans and sutlers, a scullion crowned. All kings' sons. Paradise of pretenders then and now. He saved men from drowning and you shake at a cur's yelping. But the courtiers who mocked Guido in Or san Michele were in their own house. House of... We don't want any of your medieval abstrusiosities. Would you do what he did? A boat would be near, a lifebuoy. *Natürlich,* put there for you. Would you or would you not? The man that was drowned nine days ago off Maiden's rock. They are waiting for him now. The truth, spit it out. I would want to. I would try. I am not a strong swimmer. Water cold soft. When I put my face into it in the basin at Clongowes. Can't see! who's behind me? Out quickly, quickly! Do you see the tide flowing quickly in on all sides, sheeting the lows of sands quickly, shellcocoacoloured? If I had land under my feet I want his life still to be his, mine to be mine. A drowning man. His human eyes scream to me out of horror of his death. I... With him together down... I could not save her. Waters: bitter death: lost.

A woman and a man. I see her skirties. Pinned up, I bet.

Their dog ambled about a bank of dwindling sand, trotting, sniffing on all sides. Looking for something lost in a past life. Suddenly he made off like a bounding hare, ears flung back, chasing the shadow of a lowskimming gull. The man's shrieked whistle struck his limp ears. He turned, bounded back, came nearer, trotted on twinkling shanks. On a field tenney a buck, trippant, proper, unattired. At the lacefringe of the tide he halted with stiff forehoofs, seawardpointed ears. His snout lifted barked at the wavenoise, herds of seamorse. They serpented towards his feet, curling, unfurling many crests, every ninth, breaking, plashing, from far, from farther out, waves and waves.

Cocklepickers. They waded a little way in the water and, stooping, soused their bags, and, lifting them again, waded out. The dog yelped running to them, reared up and pawed them, dropping on all fours, again reared up at them with mute bearish fawning. Unheeded he kept by them as they came towards the drier sand, a rag of wolf's tongue redpanting from his jaws. His speckled body ambled ahead of them and then loped off at a calf's gallop. The carcase lay on his path. He stopped, sniffed, stalked round it, brother, nosing closer, went round it, sniffling rapidly like a dog all over the dead dog's bedraggled fell. Dogskull, dogsniff, eyes on the ground, moves to one great goal. Ah, poor dogsbody. Here lies poor dogsbody's body.

— Tatters! Out of that, you mongrel.

The cry brought him skulking back to his master and a blunt bootless kick sent him unscathed across a spit of sand, crouched in flight. He slunk back in a curve. Doesn't see me. Along by the edge of the mole he lolloped, dawdled, smelt a rock and from under a cocked hindleg pissed against it. He trotted forward and, lifting his hindleg, pissed quick short at an unsmelt rock The simple pleasures of the poor. His hindpaws then scattered sand : then his forepaws dabbled and delved. Something he buried there, his grandmother. He rooted in the sand, dabbling, delving and stopped to listen to the air, scraped up the sand again with a fury of his claws, soon ceasing, a pard, a panther, got in spousebreach, vulturing the dead.

After he woke me up last night same dream or was it? Wait. Open hallway. Street of harlots. Remember. Haroun al Raschid. I am almosting it. That man led me, spoke. I was not afraid. The melon he had he held against my face. Smiled : creamfruit smell. That was the rule, said. In. Come. Red carpet spread. You will see who.

Shouldering their bags they trudged, the red Egyptians. His blued feet out of turnedup trousers slapped the clammy sand, a dull brick muffler strangling his unshaven neck. With woman steps she followed : the ruffian and his strolling mort. Spoils slung at her back. Loose sand and shellgrit crusted her bare feet. A bout her windraw face her hair trailed. Behind her lord his helpmate, bing awast, to Romeville. When night hides her body's flaws calling under her brown shawl from an archway where dogs have mired. Her fancyman is treating two Royal Dublins in O'Loughlin's of Blackpitts. Buss her, wap in rogue's rum lingo, for, O, my dimber wapping dell. A shefiend's whiteness under her rancid rags. Fumbally's lane that night : the tanyard smells.

White thy fambles, red thy gan
And thy quarrons dainty is.
Couch a hogshead with me then.
In the darkmans clip and kiss.

Morose delectation Aquinas tunbelly calls this, *frate porcospino*. Unfallen Adam rode and not rutted. Call away let him : *thy quarrons dainty is*. Language no whit worse than his. Monkwords, marybeads jabber on their girdles : roguewords, tough nuggets patter in their pockets.

Passing now.

A side-eye at my Hamlet hat. If I were suddenly naked here as I sit ? I am not. Across the sands of all the world, followed by the sun's flaming sword, to the west, trekking to evening lands. She trudges, schlepps, trains, drags, trascines her load. A tide westering, moondrawn, in her wake. Tides, myriadislanded, within her, blood not mine, *oinopa ponton*, a winedark sea. Behold the handmaid of the moon. In sleep the wet sign calls her hour, bids her rise. Bridebed, childbed, bed of death, ghostcandled. *Omnis caro ad te veniet*. He comes, pale vampire, through storm his eyes, his bat sails bloodying the sea, mouth to her mouth's kiss.

Here. Put a pin in that chap, will you ? My tablets. Mouth to her kiss. No. Must be two of em. Glue em well. Mouth to her mouth's kiss.

His lips lipped and mouthed fleshless lips of air : mouth to her womb. Oomb, allwombing tomb His mouth moulded issuing breath, unspeeched : ooeeehah : roar of cataractic planets, globed, blazing, roaring wayawayawayawayawayawayaway. Paper. The banknotes, blast them. Old Deasy's letter. Here. Thanking you for hospitality tear the blank end off. Turning his back to the sun he bent over far to a table of rock and scribbled words. That's twice I forgot to take slips from the library counter.

His shadow lay over the rocks as he bent, ending. Why not endless till the farthest star? Darkly they are there behind this light, darkness shining in the brightness, delta of Cassiopeia, worlds. Me sits there with his augur's rod of ash, in borrowed sandals, by day beside a livid sea, unbeheld, in violet night walking beneath a reign of uncouth stars. I throw this ended shadow from me, manshape ineluctable, call it back. Endless, would it be mine, form of my form? Who watches me here? Who ever anywhere will read these written words? Signs on a white field. Somewhere to someone in your flutiest voice. The good bishop of Cloyne took the veil of the temple out of his shovel hat : veil of space with coloured emblems hatched on its field. Hold hard. Coloured on a flat : yes, that's right. Flat I see, then think distance, near, far, flat I see, east, back. Ah, see now : Falls back suddenly, frozen in stereoscope. Click does the trick. You find my words dark. Darkness is in our souls, do you not think? Flutier. Our souls, shamewounded by our sins, cling to us yet more, a woman to her lover clinging, the more the more.

She trusts me, her hand gentle, the longlashed eyes. Now where the blue hell am I bringing her beyond the veil? Into the ineluctable modality of the ineluctable visuality. She, she, she. What she? The virgin at Hodges Figgis' window on Monday looking in for one of the alphabet books you were going to write. Keen glance you gave her. Wrist through the braided jesse of her sunshade. She lives in Leeson park, with a grief and kickshaws, a lady of letters. Talk that to some one else, Stevie : a pickmeup. Bet she wears those curse of God stays suspenders and yellow stockings, darned with lumpy wool. Talk about apple dumplings, *piuttosto*. Where are your wits?

Touch me. Soft eyes. Soft soft soft hand. I am lonely here. O, touch me soon, now. What is that word known to all men? I am quiet here alone. Sad too. Touch, touch me.

He lay back at full stretch over the sharp rocks, cramming the scribbled note and pencil into a pocket, his hat tilted down on his eyes. That is Kevin Egan's movement I made nodding for his nap, sabbath sleep. *Et vidit Deus. Et erant valde bona.* Alo! *Bonjour,* welcome as the flowers in May. Under its leaf he watched through peacocktwittering lashes the southing sun. I am caught in this burning scene. Pan's hour, the faunal noon. Among gumheavy serpentplants, milkoozing fruits, where on the tawny waters leaves lie wide. Pain is far.

And no more turn aside and brood.

His gaze brooded on his broadtoed boots, a buck's castoffs *nebeneinander.* He counted the creases of rucked leather wherein another's foot had nested warm. The foot that beat the ground in tripudium, foot I dislove. But you were delighted when Esther Osvalt's shoe went on you : girl I knew in Paris. *Tiens, quel petit pied!* Staunch friend, a brother soul : Wilde's love that dare not speak its name. He now will leave me. And the blame? As I am. As I am. All or not at all.

In long lassoes from the Cock lake the water flowed full, covering greengoldenly lagoons of sand, rising, flowing. My ashplant will float away. I shall wait. No, they will pass on, passing chafing against the low rocks, swirling, passing. Better get this job over quick. Listen : a fourworded wavespeech : seesoo, hrss, rsseeiss ooos. Vehement breath of waters amid seasnakes, rearing horses, rocks. In cups of rocks it slops : flop, slop, slap : bounded in barrels. And, spent, its speech ceases. It flows purling, widely flowing, floating foampool, flower unfurling.

Under the upswelling tide he saw the writhing weeds lift languidly and sway reluctant arms, hising up their petticoats, in whispering water swaying and upturning coy silver fronds. Day by day : night by night : lifted, flooded and let fall. Lord, they are weary : and, whispered to, they sigh. Saint Ambrose heard it, sigh of leaves and waves, waiting, awaiting the fullness of their times, *diebus ac noctibus iniurias patiens ingemiscit.* To no end gathered : vainly then released, forth flowing, wending back : loom of the moon. Weary too in sight of lovers, lascivious men, a naked woman shining in her courts, she draws a toil of waters.

Five fathoms out there. Full fathom five thy father lies. At one he said. Found drowned. High water at Dublin bar. Driving before it a loose drift of rubble, fanshoals of fishes, silly shells. A corpse rising saltwhite from the undertow, bobbing landward, a pace a pace a porpoise. There he is. Hook it quick. Sunk though he be beneath the watery floor. We have him. Easy now.

Bag of corpsegas sopping in foul brine. A quiver of minnows, fat of a spongy titbit, flash through the slits of his buttoned trouserfly. God becomes man becomes fish becomes barnacle goose becomes featherbed mountain. Dead breaths I living breathe, tread dead dust, devour a urinous offal from all dead. Hauled stark over the gunwale he breathes upward the stench of his green grave, his leprous nosehole snoring to the sun.

A seachange this, brown eyes saltblue. Seadeath, mildest of all deaths known to man. Old Father Ocean. *Prix de Paris :* beware of imitations. Just you give it a fair trial. We enjoyed ourselves immensely.

Come. I thirst. Clouding over. No black clouds anywhere, are there? Thunderstorm. Allbright he falls, proud lightning of the intellect, *Lucifer, dico, qui nescit occasum.* No. My cockle hat and staff and hismy sandal shoon. Where? To evening lands. Evening will find itself.

He took the hilt of his ashplant, lunging with it softly, dallying still. Yes, evening will find itself in me, without me. All days make their end. By the way next when is it? Tuesday will be the longest day. Of all the glad new year, mother, the rum tum tiddledy tum. Lawn Tennyson, gentleman poet. *Già.* For the old hag with the yellow teeth. And Monsieur Drumont, gentleman journalist. *Già.* My teeth are very bad. Why, I wonder? Feel. That one is going too. Shells. Ought I go to a dentist, I wonder, with that money? That one. Toothless Kinch, the superman. Why is that, I wonder, or does it mean something perhaps?

My handkerchief. He threw it. I remember. Did I not take it up?

His hand groped vainly in his pockets. No, I didn't. Better buy one.

He laid the dry snot picked from his nostril on a ledge of rock, carefully. For the rest let look who will.

Behind. Perhaps there is someone.

He turned his face over a shoulder, rere regardant. Moving through the air high spars of a threemaster, her sails brailed up on the crosstrees, homing, upstream, silently moving, a silent ship.

II

Mr Leopold Bloom ate with relish the inner organs of beasts and fowls. He liked thick giblet soup, nutty gizzards, a stuffed roast heart, liver slices fried with crustcrumbs, fried hencods' roes. Most of all he liked grilled mutton kidneys which gave to his palate a fine tang of faintly scented urine.

Kidneys were in his mind as he moved about the kitchen softly, righting her breakfast things on the humpy tray. Gelid light and air were in the kitchen but out of doors gentle summer morning everywhere. Made him feel a bit peckish.

The coals were reddening.

Another slice of bread and butter : three, four : right. She didn't like her plate full. Right. He turned from the tray, lifted the kettle off the hob and set it sideways on the fire. It sat there, dull and squat, its spout stuck out. Cup of tea soon. Good. Mouth dry. The cat walked stiffly round a leg of the table with tail on high.

— Mkgnao!

— O, there you are, Mr Bloom said, turning from the fire.

The cat mewed in answer and stalked again stiffly round a leg of the table, mewing. Just how she stalks over my writingtable. Prr. Scratch my head. Prr.

Mr Bloom watched curiously, kindly, the lithe black form. Clean to see : the gloss of her sleek hide, the white button under the butt of her tail, the green flashing eyes. He bent down to her, his hands on his knees.

— Milk for the pussens, he said.

— Mrkgnao! the cat cried.

They call them stupid. They understand what we say better than we understand them. She understands all she wants to. Vindictive too. Wonder what I look like to her. Height of a tower? No, she can jump me.

— Afraid of the chickens she is, he said mockingly. Afraid of the chookchooks. I never saw such a stupid pussens as the pussens.

Cruel. Her nature. Curious mice never squeal. Seem to like it.

— Mrkrgnao! the cat said loudly.

She blinked up out of her avid shameclosing eyes, mewing plaintively and long, showing him her milkwhite teeth. He watched the dark eyeslits narrowing with greed till her eyes were green stones. Then he went to the dresser took the jug Hanlon's milkman had just filled for him, poured warmbubbled milk on a saucer and set it slowly on the floor.

— Gurrhr! she cried, running to lap.

He watched the bristles shining wirily in the weak light as she tipped three times and licked lightly. Wonder is it true if you clip them they can't mouse after. Why? They shine in the dark, perhaps, the tips. Or kind of feelers in the dark, perhaps.

He listened to her licking lap. Ham and eggs, no. No good eggs with this drouth. Want pure fresh water. Thursday : not a good day either for a mutton kidney at Buckley's. Fried with butter, a shake of pepper. Better a pork kidney at Dlugacz's. While the kettle is boiling. She lapped slower, then licking the saucer clean. Why are their tongues so rough? To lap better, all porous holes. Nothing she can eat? He glanced round him. No.

On quietly creaky boots he went up the staircase to the hall, paused by the bedroom door. She might like something tasty. Thin bread and butter she likes in the morning. Still perhaps : once in a way.

He said softly in the bare hall :

— I am going round the corner. Be back in a minute.

And when he had heard his voice say it he added :

— You don't want anything for breakfast?

A sleepy soft grunt answered :

— Mn.

No. She did not want anything. He heard then a warm heavy sigh, softer, as she turned over and the loose brass quoits of the bedstead jingled. Must get those settled really. Pity. All the way from Gibraltar. Forgotten any little Spanish she knew. Wonder what her father gave for it. Old style. Ah yes, of course. Bought it at the governor's auction. Got a short knock. Hard as nails at a bargain, old Tweedy. Yes, sir. At Plevna that was. I rose from the ranks, sir, and I' m proud of it. Still he had brains enough to make that corner in stamps. Now that was farseeing.

His hand took his hat from the peg over his initialled heavy overcoat and his lost property office secondhand waterproof. Stamps : stickyback pictures. Daresay lots of officers are in the swim too. Course they do. The sweated legend in the crown of his hat told him mutely : Plasto's high grade ha. He peeped quickly inside the leather headband. White slip of paper. Quite safe.

On the doorstep he felt in his hip pocket for the latchkey. Not there. In the trousers I left off must get it. Potato I have. Creaky wardrobe. No use disturbing her. She turned over sleepily that time. He pulled the halldoor to after him very quietly, more, till the footleaf dropped gently over rhe threshhold, a limp lid. Looked shut. All right till I come back anyhow.

He crossed to the bright side, avoiding the loose cellarflap of number seventyfive. The sun was nearing the steeple of George's church. Be a warm day I fancy. Specially in these black clothes feel it more. Black conducts, reflects (refracts is it ?), the heat. But I couldn't go in that light suit. Make a picnic of it. His eyelids sank quietly often as he walked in happy warmth. Boland's breadvan delivering with trays our daily but she prefers yesterday's loaves turnovers crisp crowns hot. Makes you feel young. Somewhere in the east : early morning : set off at dawn, travel round in front of the sun steal a day's march on him. Keep it up for ever never grow a day older technically. Walk along a strand, strange land, come to a city gate, sentry there, old ranker too, old Tweedy's big moustaches leaning on a long kind of a spear. Wander through awned streets. Turbaned faces going by. Dark caves of carpet shops, big man, Turko the terrible, seated crosslegged smoking a coiled pipe. Cries of sellers in the streets. Drink water scented with fennel, sherbet. Wander along all day. Might meet a robber or two. Well, meet him. Getting on to sundown. The shadows of the mosques along the pillars : priest with a scroll rolled up. A shiver of the trees, signal, the evening wind. I pass on. Fading gold sky. A mother watches from her doorway. She calls her children home in their dark language. High wall : beyond strings twanged. Night sky moon, violet, colour of Molly's new garters. Strings. Listen. A girl playing one of those instruments what do you call them : dulcimers. I pass.

Probably not a bit like it really. Kind of stuff you read : in the track of the sun. Sunburst on the titlepage. He smiled, pleasing himself. What Arthur Griffith said about the headpiece over the *Freeman* leader : a homerule sun rising up in the northwest from the laneway behind the bank of Ireland. He prolonged his pleased smile. Ikey touch that : homerule sun rising up in the northwest.

He approached Larry O'Rourke's. From the cellar grating floated up the flabby gush of porter. Through the open doorway the bar squirted out whiffs of ginger, teadust, biscuitmush. Good house, however : just the end of the city traffic. For instance M'Auley's down there : n. g. as position. Of course if they ran a tramline along the North Circular from the cattle market to the quays value would go up like a shot.

Bald head over the blind. Cute old codger. No use canvassing him for an ad. Still he knows his own business best. There he is, sure enough, my bold Larry, leaning against the sugarbin in his shirtsleeves watching the aproned curate swab up with mop and bucket. Simon Dedalus takes him off to a tee with his eyes screwed up. Do you know what I'm going to tell you? What's that, Mr O'Rourke? Do you know what? The Russians, they 'd only be an eight o' clock breakfast for the Japanese.

Stop and say a word : about the funeral perhaps. Sad thing about poor Dignam, Mr O' Rourke.

Turning into Dorset street he said freshly in greeting through the doorway :

— Good day, Mr O'Rourke.

— Good day to you.

— Lovely weather, sir.

— 'Tis all that.

Where do they get the money? Coming up redheaded curates from the country Leitrim, rinsing empties and old man in the cellar. Then, lo and behold, they blossom out as Adam Findlaters or Dan Tallons. Then think of the competition. General thirst. Good puzzle would be cross Dublin without passing a pub. Save it they can't. Off the drunks perhaps. Put down three and carry five. What is that? A bob here and there, dribs and drabs. On the wholesale orders perhaps. Doing a double shuffle with the town travellers. Square it with the boss and we'll split the job, see?

How much would that tot to off the porter in the month? Say ten barrels of stuff. Say he got ten per cent off. O more. Ten. Fifteen. He passed Saint Joseph's, National school. Brats' clamour. Windows open. Fresh air helps memory. Or a lilt. Ahbeesee defeegee kelomen opeecue rustyouvee double you. Boys are they? Yes. Inishturk. Inishark. Inishboffin. At their joggerfry. Mine. Slieve Bloom.

He halted before Dlugacz's window, staring at the hanks of sausages, polonies, black and white. Fifty multiplied by. The figures whitened in his mind unsolved : displeased, he let them fade. The shiny links packed with forcemeat fed his gaze and he breathed in tranquilly the lukewarm breath of cooked spicy pig's blood.

A kidney oozed bloodgouts on the willowpatterned dish : the last. He stood by the nextdoor girl at the counter. Would she buy it too, calling the items from a slip in her hand. Chapped : washing soda. And a pound and a half of Denny's sausages. His eyes rested on her vigorous hips. Woods his name is. Wonder what he does. Wife is oldish. New blood. No followers allowed. Strong pair of arms. Whacking a carpet on the clothesline. She does whack it, by George. The way her crooked skirt swings at each whack.

The ferreteyed porkbutcher folded the sausages he had snipped off with blotchy fingers, sausagepink. Sound meat there like a stallfed heifer.

He took up a page from the pile of cut sheets. The model farm at Kinnereth on the lakeshore of Tiberias. Can become ideal winter sanatorium. Moses Montefiore. I thought he was. Farmhouse, wall round it, blurred cattle cropping. He held the page from him : interesting : read it nearer, the title, the blurred cropping cattle, the page rustling. A young white heifer. Those mornings in the cattlemarket the beasts lowing in their pens, branded sheep, flop and fall of dung, the breeders in hobnailed boots trudging through the litter, slapping a palm on a ripemeated hindquarter, there's a prime one, unpeeled switches in their hands. He held the page aslant patiently, bending his senses and his will, his soft subject gaze at rest. The crooked skirt swinging whack by whack by whack.

The porkbutcher snapped two sheets from the pile, wrapped up her prime sausages and made a red grimace.

— Now, my miss, he said.

She tendered a coin, smiling boldly, holding her thick wrist out.

—Thank you, my miss. And one shilling threepence change. For you, please ?

Mr Bloom pointed quickly. To catch up and walk behind her if she went slowly, behind her moving hams. Pleasant to see first thing in the morning. Hurry up, damn it. Make hay while the sun shines. She stood outside the shop in sunlight and sauntered lazily to the right. He sighed down his nose : they never understand. Sodachapped hands. Crusted toenails too. Brown scapulars in tatters, defending her both ways. The sting of disregard glowed to weak pleasure within his breast. For another : a constable off duty cuddled her in Eccles' Lane. They like them sizeable. Prime sausage. O please, Mr Policeman, I'm lost in the wood.

— Threepence, please.

His hand accepted the moist tender gland and slid it into a sidepocket. Then it fetched up three coins from his trousers' pocket and laid them on the rubber prickles. They lay, were read quickly and quickly slid, disc by disc, into the till.

— Thank you, sir. Another time.

A speck of eager fire from foxeyes thanked him. He withdrew his gaze after an instant. No : better not : another time.

— Good morning, he said, moving away.

— Good morning, sir.

No sign. Gone. What matter ?

He walked back along Dorset street, reading gravely. Agendath Netaim : planters' company. To purchase waste sandy tracts from Turkish government and plant with eucalyptus trees. Excellent for shade, fuel and construction. Orangegroves and immense melonfields north of Jaffa. You pay eight marks and they plant a dunam of land for you with olives, oranges, almonds or citrons. Olives cheaper : oranges need artificial irrigation. Every year you get a sending of the crop. Your name entered for life as owner in the book of the union. Can pay ten down and the balance in yearly instalments. Bleibtreustrasse 34, Berlin, W, 15.

Nothing doing. Still an idea behind it.

He looked at the cattle, blurred in silver heat. Silvered powdered olivetrees. Quiet long days : pruning ripening. Olives are packed in jars, eh ? I have a few left from Andrews. Molly spitting them out. Knows the taste of them now. Oranges in tissue paper packed in crates. Citrons too. Wonder is poor Citron still alive in Saint Kevin's parade. And Mastiansky with the old cither. Pleasant evenings we had then. Molly in Citron's basketchair. Nice to hold, cool waxen fruit, hold in the hand, lift it to the nostrils and smell the perfume. Like that, heavy, sweet, wild perfume. Always the same, year after year. They fetched high prices too Moisel told me. Arbutus place : Pleasants street : pleasant old times. Must be without a flaw, he said. Coming all that way : Spain, Gibraltar, Mediterranean, the Levant. Crates lined up on the quayside at Jaffa, chap ticking them off in a book, navvies handling them in soiled dungarees. There's whatdoyoucallhim out of. How do you ? Doesn't see. Chap you know just to salute bit of a bore. His back is like that Norwegian captain's. Wonder if I'll meet him today. Watering cart. To provoke the rain. On earth as it is in heaven.

A cloud began to cover the sun wholly slowly wholly. Grey. Far.

No, not like that. A barren land, bare waste. Vulcanic lake, the dead sea : no fish, weedless, sunk deep in the earth. No wind would lift those waves, grey metal, poisonous foggy waters. Brimstone they called it raining down : the cities of the plain : Sodom, Gommorah, Edom. All dead names. A dead sea in a dead land, grey and old. Old now. It bore the oldest, the first race. A bent hag crossed from Cassidy's clutching a naggin bottle by the neck. The oldest people. Wandered far away over all the earth, captivity to captivity, multiplying, dying, being born everywhere. It lay there now. Now it could bear no more. Dead : an old woman's : the grey sunken cunt of the world.

Desolation.

Grey horror seared his flesh. Folding the page into his pocket he turned into Eccles' Street, hurrying homeward. Cold oils slid along his veins, chilling his blood : age crusting him with a salt cloak. Well, I am here now. Morning mouth bad images. Got up wrong side of the bed. Must begin again those Sandow's exercises. On the hands down. Blotchy brown brick houses. Number eighty still unlet. Why is that? Valuation is only twentyeight. Towers, Battersby, North, MacArthur : parlour windows plastered with bills. Plasters on a sore eye. To smell the gentle smoke of tea, fume of the pan, sizzling butter. Be near her ample bedwarmed flesh. Yes, yes.

Quick warm sunlight came running from Berkeley Road, swiftly, in slim sandals, along the brightening footpath. Runs, she runs to meet me, a girl with gold hair on the wind.

Two letters and a card lay on ihe hallfloor. He stooped and gathered them. Mrs Marion Bloom. His quick heart slowed at once. Bold hand. Mrs Marion.

— Poldy!

Entering the bedroom he halfclosed his eyes and walked through warm yellow twilight towards her tousled head.

— Who are the letters for?

He looked at them. Mullingar. Milly.

— A letter for me from Milly, he said carefully, and a card to you. And a letter for you.

He laid her card and letter on the twill bedspread near the curve of her knees.

— Do you want the blind up?

Letting the blind up by gentle tugs halfway his backward eye saw her glance at the letter and tuck it under her pillow.

— That do? he asked, turning.

She was reading the card, propped on her elbow.

— She got the things, she said.

He waited till she had laid the card aside and curled herself back slowly with a snug sigh.

— Hurry up with that tea, she said.I'm parched.

— The kettle is boiling, he said.

But he delayed to clear the chair : her striped petticoat, tossed soiled linen : and lifted all in an armful on to the foot of the bed.

As he went down the kitchen stairs she called :

— Poldy!

— What?

— Scald the teapot.

On the boil sure enough : a plume of steam from the spout. He scalded and rinsed out the teapot and put in four full spoons of tea, tilting the kettle then to let water flow in. Having set it to draw, he took off the kettle and crushed the pan flat on the live coals and watched the lump of butter slide and melt. While he unwrapped the kidney the cat mewed hungrily against him. Give her too much meat she won't mouse. Say they won't eat pork. Kosher. Here. He let the bloodsmeared paper fall to her and dropped the kidney amid the sizzling butter sauce. Pepper. He sprinkled it through his fingers, ringwise, from the chipped eggcup.

Then he slit open his letter, glancing down the page and over. Thanks : new tam : Mr Coghlan : lough Owel picnic : young student : Blazes Boylan's seaside girls.

The tea was drawn. He filled his own moustachecup, sham crown Derby, smiling. Silly Milly's birthday gift. Only five she was then. No, wait : four. I gave her the amberoid necklace she broke. Putting pieces of folded brown paper in the letterbox for her. He smiled, pouring.

O, Milly Bloom, you are my darling.
You are my looking glass from night to morning.
I'd rather have you without a farthing
Than Katey Keogh with her ass and garden.

Poor old professor Goodwin. Dreadful old case. Still he was a courteous old chap. Oldfashioned way he used to bow Molly off the platform. And the little mirror in his silk hat. The night Milly brought it into the parlour. O, look what I found in professor Goodwin's hat! All we laughed. Sex breaking out even then. Pert little piece she was.

He prodded a fork into the kidney and slapped it over: then fitted the teapot on the tray. Its hump bumped as he took it up. Everything on it? Bread and butter, four, sugar, spoon, her cream. Yes. He carried it upstairs, his thumb hooked in the teapot handle.

Nudging the door open with his knee he carried the tray in and set it on the chair by the bedhead.

— What a time you were? she said.

She set the brasses jingling as she raised herself briskly, an elbow on the pillow. He looked calmly down on her bulk and between her large soft bubs, sloping within her nightdress like a shegoat's udder. The warmth of her couched body rose on the air, mingling with the fragrance of the tea she poured.

A strip of torn envelope peeped from under the dimpled pillow. In the act of going he stayed to straighten the bedspread.

— Who was the letter from? he asked.

Bold hand. Marion.

— O, Boylan, she said. He's bringing the programme.

— What are you singing?

— *Là ci darem* with J. C. Doyle, she said, and *Love's Old Sweet Song.*

Her full lips, drinking, smiled. Rather stale smell that incense leaves next day. Like foul flowerwater.

— Would you like the window open a little?

She doubled a slice of bread into her mouth, asking:

— What time is the funeral?

— Eleven, I think, he answered. I didn't see the paper.

Following the pointing of her finger he took up a leg of her soiled drawers from the bed. No? Then, a twisted grey garter looped round a stocking: rumpled, shiny sole.

— No: that book.

Other stocking. Her petticoat.

— It must have fell down, she said.

He felt here and there. *Voglio e non vorrei.* Wonder if she pronounces that right: *voglio.* Not in the bed. Must have slid down. He stooped and lifted the valance. The book, fallen, sprawled against the bulge of the orangekeyed chamberpot.

— Show here, she said. I put a mark in it. There's a word I wanted to ask you.

She swallowed a draught of tea from her cup held by nothandle and, having wiped her fingertips smartly on the blanket, began to search the text with the hairpin till she reached the word.

— Met him what? he asked.

— Here, she said. What does that mean?

He leaned downward and read near her polished thumbnail.

— Metempsychosis?

— Yes. Who's he when he's at home?

— Metempsychosis, he said, frowning. It's Greek : from the Greek. That means the transmigration of souls.

— O, rocks! she said. Tell us in plain words.

He smiled, glancing askance at her mocking eye. The same young eyes. The first night after the charades. Dolphin's Barn. He turned over the smudged pages. *Ruby : the Pride of the Ring.* Hello. Illustration. Fierce Italian with carriagewhip. Must be Ruby pride of the on the floor naked. Sheet kindly lent. *The monster Maffei desisted and flung his victim from him with an oath.* Cruelty behind it all. Doped animals. Trapeze at Hengler's. Had to look the other way. Mob gaping. Break your neck and we'll break our sides. Families of them. Bone them young so they metamspychosis. That we live after death. Our souls. That a man's soul after he dies. Dignam's soul...

— Did you finish it? he asked.

— Yes, she said. There's nothing smutty in it. Is she in love with the first fellow all the time?

— Never read it. Do you want another?

— Yes. Get another of Paul de Kock's. Nice name he has.

She poured more tea into her cup, watching its flow sideways.

Must get that Capel street library book renewed or they'll write to Kearney, my garantor. Reincarnation : that's the word.

— Some people believe, he said, that we go on on living in another body after death, that we lived before. They call it reincarnation. That we all lived before on the earth thousands of years ago or some other planet. They say we have forgotten it. Some say they remember their past lives.

The sluggish cream wound curdling spirals through her tea. Better remind her of the word : metempsychosis. An example would be better. An example?

The *Bath of the Nymph* over the bed. Given away with the Easter number of *Photo Bits* : Splendid masterpiece in art colours. Tea before you put milk in. Not unlike her with her hair down : slimmer. Three and six I gave for the frame. She said it would look nice over the bed. Naked nymphs : Greece : and for instance all the people that lived then.

He turned the pages back.

— Metempsychosis, he said, is what the ancient Greeks called it. They used to believe you could be changed into an animal or a tree, for instance. What they called nymphs, for example.

Her spoon ceased to stir up the sugar. She gazed straight before her, inhaling through her arched nostrils.

— There's a smell of burn, she said. Did you leave anything on the fire?

— The kidney! he cried suddenly.

He fitted the book roughly into his inner pocket and, stubbing his toes against the broken commode, hurried out towards the smell, stepping hastily down the stairs with a flurried stork's legs. Pungent smoke shot up in an angry jet from a side of the pan. By prodding a prong of the fork under the kidney he detached it and turned it turtle on its back. Only a little burned. He tossed it off the pan on to a plate and let the scanty brown gravy trickle over it.

Cup of tea now. He sat down, cut and buttered a slice of the loaf. He shore away the burnt flesh and flung it to the cat. Then he put a forkful into his mouth, chewing with discernment the toothsome pliant meat. Done to a turn. A mouthful of tea. Then he cut away dies of bread, sopped one in the gravy and put it in his mouth. What was that about some young student and a picnic? He creased out the letter at his side, reading it slowly as he chewed, sopping another die of bread in the gravy and raising it to his mouth.

Dearest Papli,

Thanks ever so much for the lovely birthday present. It suits me splendid. Everyone says I'm quite the belle in my new tam. I got mummy's lovely box of creams and am writing, They are lovely. I am getting on swimming in the photo business now. Mr Coghlan took one of me and Mrs will send when developed. We did great biz yesterday. Fair day and all the beef to the heels were in. We are going to lough Owel on Monday with a few friends to make a scrap picnic. Give my love to mummy and to yourself a big kiss and thanks. I hear them at the piano downstairs. There is to be a concert in the

Greville Arms on Saturday. There is a young student comes here some evenings named Bannon his cousins or something are big swells he sings Boylan's (I was on the pop of writing Blazes Boylan's) song about those seaside girls. Tell him silly Milly sends my best respects. Must now close with fondest love.

Your fond daughter,

MILLY.

P. S. Excuse bad writing, am in a hurry. Byby.

M.

Fifteen yesterday. Curious, fifteenth of the month too. Her first birthday away from home. Separation. Remember the summer morning she was born, running to knock up Mrs Thornton in Denzille street. Jolly old woman. Lots of babies she must have helped into the world. She knew from the first poor little Rudy wouldn't live. Well, God is good, sir. She knew at once. He would be eleven now if he had lived.

His vacant face stared pitying at the postscript. Excuse bad writing. Hurry. Piano downstairs. Coming out of her shell. Row with her in the XL Café about the bracelet. Wouldn't eat her cakes or speak or look. Saucebox. He sopped other dies of bread in the gravy and ate piece after piece of kidney. Twelve and six a week. Not much. Still, she might do worse. Music hall stage. Young student. He drank a draught of cooler tea to wash down his meal. Then he read the letter again : twice.

O well : she knows how to mind herself. But if not? No, nothing has happened. Of course it might. Wait in any case till it does. A wild piece of goods. Her slim legs running up the staircase. Destiny. Ripening now. Vain : very.

He smiled with troubled affection at the kitchen window. Day I caught her in the street pinching her cheeks to make them red. Anemic a little. Was given milk too long. On the *Erin's King* that day round the Kish. Damned old tub pitching about. Not a bit funky. Her pale blue scarf loose in the wind with her hair.

All dimpled cheeks and curls,
Your head it simply swirls.

Seaside girls. Torn envelope. Hands stuck in his trousers' pockets, jarvey off for the day, singing. Friend of the family. Swurls, he says. Pier with lamps, summer evening, band,

Those girls, those girls,
Those lovely seaside girls.

Milly too. Young kisses : the first. Far away now past. Mrs Marion. Reading lying back now, counting the strands of her hair, smiling, braiding.

A soft qualm regret, flowed down his backbone, increasing. Will happen, yes. Prevent. Useless : can't move. Girl's sweet light lips. Will happen too. He felt the flowing qualm spread over him. Useless to move now. Lips kissed, kissing kissed. Full gluey woman's lips.

Better where she is down there : away. Occupy her. Wanted a dog to pass the time. Might take a trip down there. August bank holiday, only two and six return. Six weeks off however. Might work a press pass. Or through M'Coy.

The cat, having cleaned all her fur, returned to the meatstained paper, nosed at it and stalked to the door. She looked back at him, mewing. Wants to go out. Wait before a door sometime it will open. Let her wait. Has the fidgets. Electric. Thunder in the air. Was washing at her ear with her back to the fire too.

He felt heavy, full : then a gentle loosening of his bowels. He stood up, undoing the waistband of his trousers. The cat mewed to him.

— Miaow! he said in answer. Wait till I'm ready.

Heaviness : hot day coming. Too much trouble to fag up the stairs to the landing.

A paper. He liked to read at stool. Hope no ape comes knocking just as I'm.

In the table drawer he found an old number of *Titbits*. He folded it under his armpit, went to the door and opened it. The cat went up in soft bounds. Ah, wanted to go upstairs, curl up in a ball on the bed.

Listening, he heard her voice :

— Come, come, pussy. Come.

He went out through the backdoor into the garden : stood to listen towards the next garden. No sound. Perhaps hanging clothes out to dry. The maid was in the garden. Fine morning.

He bent down to regard a lean file of spearmint growing by the wall. Make a summerhouse here. Scarlet runners. Virginia creepers. Want to manure the whole place over, scabby soil. A coat of liver of sulphur. All soil like that without dung. Household slops. Loam, what is this that is? The hens in the next garden : their droppings are very good top dressing. Best of all though are the cattle, especially when they are fed on those oilcakes. Mulch of dung. Best thing to clean ladies' kid gloves. Dirty cleans. Ashes too. Reclaim the whole place. Grow peas in that corner there. Lettuce. Always have fresh greens then. Still gardens have their drawbacks. That bee or bluebottle here Whitmonday.

He walked on. Where is my hat, by the way? Must have put it back on the peg. Or hanging up on the floor. Funny, I don't remember that. Hallstand too full. Four umbrellas, her raincloak. Picking up the letters. Drago's shopbell ringing. Queer I was just thinking that moment. Brown brillantined hair over his collar. Just had a wash and brushup. Wonder have I time for a bath this morning. Tara street. Chap in the paybox there got away James Stephens they say. O'Brien.

Deep voice that fellow Dlugacz has. Agenda what is it? Now, my miss. Enthusiast.

He kicked open the crazy door of the jakes. Better be careful not to get these trousers dirty for the funeral. He went in, bowing his head under the low lintel. Leaving the door ajar, amid the stench of mouldy limewash and stale cobwebs he undid his braces. Before sitting down he peered through a chink up at the nextdoor window. The king was in his countinghouse. Nobody.

Asquat on the cuckstool he folded out his paper turning its pages over on his bared knees. Something new and easy. No great hurry. Keep it a bit. Our prize titbit. *Matcham's Masterstroke.* Written by Mr Philip Beaufoy, Playgoers' club, London. Payment at the rate of one guinea a column has been made to the writer. Three and a half. Three pounds three. Three pounds thirteen and six.

Quietly he read, restraining himself, the first column and, yielding but resisting, began the second. Midway, his last resistance yielding, he allowed his bowels to ease themselves quietly as he read, reading still patiently that slight constipation of yesterday quite gone. Hope it's not too big bring on piles again. No, just right. So. Ah! Costive one tabloid of cascara sagrada. Life might be so. It did not move or touch him but it was something quick and neat. Print anything now. Silly season. He read on, seated calm above his own rising smell. Neat certainly. *Matcham often thinks of the masterstroke by which he won the laughing Witch Who now.* Begins and ends morally. *Hand in hand.* Smart. He glanced back through what he had read and, while feeling his water flow quietly, he envied kindly Mr Beaufoy who had written it and received payment of three pounds thirteen and six.

Might manage a sketch. By Mr and Mrs L. M. Bloom. Invent a story for some proverb which? Time I used to try jotting down on my cuff what she said dressing. Dislike dressing together. Nicked myself shaving. Biting her nether lip, hooking the placket of her skirt. Timing her. 9.15. Did Roberts pay you yet? 9.20. What had Gretta Conroy on? 9.23. What possessed me to buy this comb? 9.24. I'm swelled after that cabbage. A speck of dust on the patent leather of her boot.

Rubbing smartly in turn each welt against her stocking calf. Morning after the bazaar dance when May's band played Ponchielli's dance of the hours. Explain that morning hours, noon, then evening coming on, then night hours. Washing her teeth. That was the first night. Her head dancing. Her fansticks clicking. Is that Boylan well off? He has money. Why? I noticed he had a good smell off his breath dancing. No use humming then. Allude to it. Strange kind of music that last night. The mirror was in shadow. She rubbed her handglass briskly on her woollen vest against her full wagging bub. Peering into it. Lines in her eyes. It wouldn't pan out somehow.

Evening hours, girls in grey gauze. Night hours then black with daggers and eyemasks. Poetical idea pink, then golden, then grey, then black. Still true to life also. Day, then the night.

He tore away half the prize story sharply and wiped himself with it. Then he girded up his trousers, braced and buttoned himself. He pulled back the jerky shaky door of the jakes and came forth from the gloom into the air.

In the bright light, lightened and cooled in limb, he eyed carefully his black trousers, the ends, the knees, the houghs of the knees. What time is the funeral? Better find out in the paper.

A creak and a dark whirr in the air high up. The bells of George's church. They tolled the hour: loud dark iron.

Heigho! Heigho!
Heigho! Heigho!
Heigho! Heigho!

Quarter to. There again: the overtone following through the air. A third.

Poor Dignam!

5 - LOTUS EATERS

By lorries along sir John Rogerson's quay Mr Bloom walked soberly, past Windmill lane, Leask's the linseed crusher's, the postal telegraph office. Could have given that address too. And past the sailors' home. He turned from the morning noises of the quayside and walked through Lime street. By Brady's cottages a boy for the skins lolled, his bucket of offal linked, smoking a chewed fagbutt. A smaller girl with scars of eczema on her forehead eyed him, listlessly holding her battered caskhoop. Tell him if he smokes he won't grow. O let him! His life isn't such a bed of roses! Waiting outside pubs to bring da home. Come home to ma, da. Slack hour : won't be many there. He crossed Townsend street, passed the frowning face of Bethel. El, yes : house of : Aleph, Beth. And past Nichols' the undertaker's. At eleven it is. Time enough. Daresay Corny Kelleher bagged that job for O' Neill's. Singing with his eyes shut. Corny. Met her once in the park. In the dark. What a lark. Police tout. Her name and address she then told with my tooraloom tooraloom tay. O, surely he bagged it. Bury him cheap in a whatyoumay call. With my tooraloom, tooraloom, tooraloom, tooraloom.

In Westland row he halted before the window of the Belfast and Oriental Tea Company and read the legends of leadpapered packets : choice blend, finest quality, family tea. Rather warm. Tea. Must get some from Tom Kernan. Couldn't ask him at a funeral, though. While his eyes still read blandly he took off his hat quietly inhaling his hairoil and sent his right hand with slow grace over his brow and hair. Very warm morning. Under their dropped lids his eyes found the tiny bow of the leather headband inside his high grade ha. Just there. His right hand came down into the bowl of his hat. His fingers found quickly a card behind the headband and transferred it to his waistcoat pocket.

So warm. His right hand once more more slowly went over again : choice blend, made of the finest Ceylon brands. The far east. Lovely spot it must be : the garden of the world, big lazy leaves to float about on, cactuses, flowery meads, snaky lianas they call them. Wonder is it like that. Those Cinghalese lobbing around in the sun, in *dolce far niente.* Not doing a hand's turn all day. Sleep six months out of twelve. Too hot to quarrel. Influence of the climate. Lethargy. Flowers of idleness. The air feeds most. Azotes. Hothouse in Botanic gardens. Sensitive plants. Waterlilies. Petals too tired to. Sleeping sickness in the air. Walk on roseleaves. Imagine trying to eat tripe and cowheel. Where was the chap I saw in that picture somewhere ? Ah, in the dead sea, floating on his back, reading a book with a parasol open. Couldn't sink if you tried : so thick with salt. Because the weight of the water, no, the weight of the body in the water is equal to the weight of the. Or is it the volume is equal to the weight ? It's a law something like that. Vance in High school cracking his fingerjoints, teaching. The college curriculum. Cracking curriculum. What is weight really when you say the weight? Thirtytwo feet per second, per second. Law of falling bodies : per second, per second. They all fall to the ground. The earth. It's the force of gravity of the earth is the weight.

He turned away and sauntered across the road. How did she walk with her sausages ? Like that something. As he walked he took the folded *Freeman* from his sidepocket, unfolded it, rolled it lengthwise in a baton and tapped it at each sauntering step against his trouserleg. Careless air : just drop in to see. Per second, per second. Per second for every second it means. From the curbstone he darted a keen glance through the door of the postoffice. Too late box. Post here. No-one. In.

He handed the card through the brass grill.

— Are there any letters for me ? he asked.

While the postmistress searched a pigeonhole he gazed at the recruiting poster with soldiers of all arms on parade : and held the tip of his baton against his nostrils, smelling freshprinted rag paper. No answer probably. Went too far last time.

The postmistress handed him back through the grill his card with a letter. He thanked and glanced rapidly at the typed envelope.

Henry Flower, Esq,

c/o P. O. Westland Row,

City.

Answered anyhow. He slipped card and letter into his sidepocket, reviewing again the soldiers on parade. Where's old Tweedy's regiment? Castoff soldier. There: bearskin cap and hackle plume. No, he's a grenadier. Pointed cuffs. There he is: royal Dublin fusiliers. Redcoats. Too showy. That must be why the women go after them. Uniform. Easier to enlist and drill. Maud Gonne's letter about taking them off O'Connell street at night: disgrace to our Irish capital. Griffith's paper is on the same tack now: an army rotten with venereal disease: overseas or halfseasover empire. Half baked they look: hypnotised like. Eyes front. Mark time. Table: able. Bed: ed. The King's own. Never see him dressed up as a fireman or a bobby. A mason, yes.

He strolled out of the postoffice and turned to the right. Talk: as if that would mend matters. His hand went into his pocket and a forefinger felt its way under the flap of the envelope, ripping it open in jerks. Women will pay a lot of heed, I don't think. His fingers drew forth the letter and crumpled the envelope in his pocket. Something pinned on: photo perhaps. Hair? No.

M'Coy. Get rid of him quickly. Take me out of my way. Hate company when you.

— Hello, Bloom. Where are you off to?

— Hello, M'Coy. Nowhere in particular.

— How's the body?

— Fine. How are you?

— Just keeping alive, M'Coy said.

His eyes on the black tie and clothes he asked with low respect:

— Is there any... no trouble I hope? I see you're...

— O no, Mr Bloom said. Poor Dignam, you know. The funeral is today.

— To be sure, poor fellow. So it is. What time?

A photo it isn't. A badge maybe

— E...eleven, Mr Bloom answered.

— I must try to get out there, M'Coy said. Eleven, is it? I only heard it last night. Who was telling me? Holohan. You know Hoppy?

— I know.

Mr Bloom gazed across the road at the outsider drawn up before the door of the Grosvenor. The porter hoisted the valise up on the well. She stood still, waiting, while the man, husband, brother, like her, searched his pockets for change. Stylish kind of coat with that roll collar, warm for a day like this, looks like blanketcloth. Careless stand of her with her hands in those patch pockets. Like that haughty creature at the polo match. Women all for caste till you touch the spot. Handsome is and handsome does. Reserved about to yield. The honourable Mrs and Brutus is an honourable man. Possess her once take the starch out of her.

— I was with Bob Doran, he's on one of his periodical bends, and what do you call him Bantam Lyons. Just down there in Conway's we were.

Doran, Lyons in Conway's. She raised a gloved hand to her hair. In came Hoppy. Having a wet. Drawing back his head and gazing far from beneath his vailed eyelids he saw the bright fawn skin shine in the glare, the braided drums. Clearly I can see today. Moisture about gives long sight perhaps. Talking of one thing or another. Lady's hand. Which side will she get up?

— And he said : *Sad thing about our poor friend Paddy! What Paddy?* I said. *Poor little Paddy Dignam,* he said.

Off to the country : Broadstone probably. High brown boots with laces dangling. Wellturned foot. What is he fostering over that change for? Sees me looking. Eye out for other fellow always. Good fallback. Two strings to her bow.

— *Why?* I said. *What's wrong with him?* I said.

Proud : rich : silk stockings.

— Yes, Mr Bloom said.

He moved a little to the side of M'Coy's talking head. Getting up in a minute.

— *What's wrong with him,* he said. *He's dead,* he said. And, faith, he filled up. *Is it Paddy Dignam?* I said. I couldn't believe it when I heard it. I was with him no later than Friday last or Thursday was it in the Arch. *Yes,* he said. *He's gone. He died on Monday, poor fellow.*

Watch! Watch! Silk flash rich stockings white. Watch!

A heavy tramcar honking its gong slewed between.

Lost it. Curse your noisy pugnose. Feels locked out of it. Paradise and the peri. Always happening like that. The very moment. Girl in Eustace street hallway Monday was it settling her garter. Her friend covering the display of. *Esprit de corps.* Well, what are you gaping at?

— Yes, yes, Mr Bloom said after a dull sigh. Another gone.

— One of the best, M'Coy said.

The tram passed. They drove off towards the Loop Line bridge, her rich gloved hand on the steel grip. Flicker, flicker : the laceflare of her hat in the sun : flicker, flick.

— Wife well, I suppose? M'Coy's changed voice said.

— O yes, Mr Bloom said. Tiptop, thanks.

He unrolled the newspaper baton idly and read idly:

What is home without
Plumtree's Potted Meat?
Incomplete.
With it an abode of bliss.

— My missus has just got an engagement. At least it's not settled yet.

Valise tack again. By the way no harm. I'm off that, thanks.

Mr Bloom turned his largelidded eyes with unhasty friendliness:

— My wife too, he said. She's going to sing at a swagger affair in the Ulster hall, Belfast, on the twentyfifth.

— That so? M'Coy said. Glad to hear that, old man. Who's getting it up?

Mrs Marion Bloom. Not up yet. Queen was in her bedroom eating bread and. No book. Blackened court cards laid along her thigh by sevens. Dark lady and fair man. Cat furry black ball. Torn strip of envelope.

Love's
Old
Sweet
Song
Comes lo-ve's old...

— It's a kind of a tour, don't you see? Mr Bloom said thoughtfully. *Sweeeet song*. There's a committee formed. Part shares and part profits.

M'Coy nodded, picking at his moustache stubble.

— O well, he said. That's good news.

He moved to go.

— Well, glad to see you looking fit, he said. Meet you knocking around.

— Yes, Mr Bloom said.

— Tell you what, M'Coy said. You might put down my name at the funeral, will you? I'd like to go but I mightn't be able, you see. There's a drowning case at Sandycove may turn up and then the coroner and myself would have to go down if the body is found. You just shove in my name if I'm not there, will you?

— I'll do that, Mr Bloom said, moving to get off. That'll be all right.

— Right, M'Coy said brightly. Thanks, old man. I'd go if I possibly could. Well, tolloll. Just C. P. M'Coy will do.

— That will be done, Mr Bloom answered firmly.

Didn't catch me napping that wheeze. The quick touch. Soft mark. I'd like my job. Valise I have a particular fancy for. Leather. Capped corners, rivetted edges, double action lever lock. Bob Cowley lent him his for the Wicklow regatta concert last year and never heard tidings of it from that good day to this.

Mr Bloom, strolling towards Brunswick street, smiled. My missus has just got an. Reedy freckled soprano. Cheeseparing nose. Nice enough in its way : for a little ballad. No guts in it. You and me, don't you know? In the same boat. Softsoaping. Give you the needle that would. Can't he hear the difference? Think he's that way inclined a bit. Against my grain somehow. Thought that Belfast would fetch him. I hope that smallpox up there doesn't get worse. Suppose she wouldn't let herself be vaccinated again. Your wife and my wife.

Wonder is he pimping after me?

Mr Bloom stood at the corner, his eyes wandering over the multicoloured hoardings. Cantrell and Cochrane's Ginger Ale (Aromatic). Clery's summer sale. No, he's going on straight. Hello. *Leah* tonight : Mrs Bandman Palmer. Like to see her in that again. *Hamlet* she played last night. Male impersonator. Perhaps he was a woman. Why Ophelia committed suicide? Poor papa! How he used to talk about Kate Bateman in that! Outside the Adelphi in London waited all the afternoon to get in. Year before I was born that was : sixtyfive. And Ristori in Vienna. What is this the right name is? By Mosenthal it is. Rachel, is it? No. The scene he was always talking about where the old blind Abraham recognises the voice and puts his fingers on his face.

— Nathan's voice! His son's voice! I hear the voice of Nathan who left his father to die of grief and misery in my arms, who left the house of his father and left the God of his father.

Every word is so deep, Leopold.

Poor papa! Poor man! I'm glad. I didn't go into the room to look at his face. That day! O dear! O dear! Ffoo! Well, perhaps it was the best for him.

Mr Bloom went round the corner and passed the drooping nags of the hazard. No use thinking of it any more. Nosebag time. Wish I hadn't met that M'Coy fellow.

He came nearer and heard a crunching of gilded oats, the gently champing teeth. Their full buck eyes regarded him as he went by, amid the sweet oaten reek of horsepiss. Their Eldorado. Poor jugginses! Damn all they know or care about anything with their long noses stuck in nosebags. Too full for words. Still they get their feed all right and their doss. Gelded too : a stump of black guttapercha wagging limp between their haunches. Might be happy all the same that way. Good poor brutes they look. Still their neigh can be very irritating.

He drew the letter from his pocket and folded it into the newspaper he carried. Might just walk into her here. The lane is safer.

He passed the cabman's shelter. Curious the life of drifting cabbies, all weathers, all places, time or setdown, no will of their own. *Voglio e non.* Like to give them an odd cigarette. Sociable. Shout a few flying syllables as they pass. He hummed :

Là ci darem la mano
La la lala la la.

He turned into Cumberland street and, going on some paces, halted in the lee of the station wall. No-one. Meade's timberyard. Piled balks. Ruins and tenements. With careful tread he passed over a hopscotch court with its forgotten pickeystone. Not a sinner. Near the timberyard a squatted child at marbles, alone, shooting the taw with a cunnythumb. A wise tabby, a blinking sphinx, watched from her warm sill. Pity to disturb them. Mohammed cut a piece out of his mantle not to wake her. Open it. And once I played marbles when I went to that old dame's school. She liked mignonette. Mrs Ellis's. And Mr? He opened the letter within the newspaper.

A flower. I think it's a. A yellow flower with flattened petals. Not annoyed then? What does she say?

Dear Henry,

I got your last letter to me and thank you very much for it. I am sorry you did not like my last letter. Why did you enclose the stamps? I am awfully angry with you. I do wish I could punish you for that. I called you naughty boy because I do not like that other world. Please tell me what is the real meaning of that word. Are you not happy in your home you poor little naughty boy? I do wish I could do something for you. Please tell me what you think of poor me. I often think of the beautiful name you have. Dear Henry, when will we meet? I think of you so often you have no idea. I have never felt myself so much drawn to a man as you. I feel so bad about. Please write me a long letter and tell me more. Remember if you do not I will punish you. So now you know what I will do to you, you naughty boy, if you do not wrote. O how I long to meet you. Henry dear, do not deny my request before my patience are exhausted. Then I will tell you all. Goodbye now, naughty darling. I have such a bad headache today and write *by return* to your longing

MARTHA.

P. S. Do tell me what kind of perfume does your wife use. I want to know.

He tore the flower gravely from its pinhold smelt its almost no smell and placed it in his heart pocket. Language of flowers. They like it because no-one can hear. Or a poison bouquet to strike him down. Then, walking slowly forward, he read the letter again, murmuring here and there a word. Angry tulips with you darling manflower punish your cactus if you don't please poor forgetmenot how I long violets to dear roses when we soon anemone meet all naughty nightstalk wife Martha's perfume. Having read it all he took it from the newspaper and put it back in his sidepocket.

Weak joy opened his lips. Changed since the first letter. Wonder did she wrote it herself. Doing the indignant : a girl of good family like me, respectable character. Could meet one Sunday after the rosary. Thank you : not having any. Usual love scrimmage. Then running round corners. Bad as a row with Molly. Cigar has a cooling effect. Narcotic. Go further next time. Naughty boy : punish : afraid of words, of course. Brutal, why not ? Try it anyhow. A bit at a time.

Fingering still the letter in his pocket he drew the pin out of it. Common pin, eh ? He threw it on the road. Out of her clothes somewhere : pinned together. Queer the number of pins they always have. No roses without thorns.

Flat Dublin voices bawled in his head. Those two sluts that night in the Coombe, linked together in the rain.

O, Mairy lost the pin of her drawers.
She didn't know what to do
To keep it up
To keep it up.

It ? Them. Such a bad headache. Has her roses probably. Or sitting all day typing. Eyefocus bad for stomach nerves. What perfume does your wife use ? Now could you make out a thing like that.

To keep it up.

Martha, Mary. I saw that picture somewhere I forget now old master or faked for money. He is sitting in their house, talking. Mysterious. Also the two sluts in the Coombe would listen.

To keep it up.

Nice kind of evening feeling. No more wandering about. Just loll there : quiet dusk : let everything rip. Forget. Tell about places you have been, strange customs. The other one, jar on her head, was getting the supper : fruit, olives, lovely cool water out of the well stonecold like the hole in the wall at Ashtown. Must carry a paper goblet next time I go to the trottingmatches. She listens with big dark soft eyes. Tell her : more and more : all. Then a sigh : silence. Long long long rest.

Going under the railway arch he took out the envelope, tore it swiftly in shreds and scattered them towards the road. The shreds fluttered away, sank in the dank air : a white flutter then all sank.

Henry Flower. You could tear up a cheque for a hundred pounds in the same way. Simple bit of paper. Lord Iveagh once cashed a sevenfigure cheque for a million in the bank of Ireland. Shows you the money to be made out or porter. Still the other brother lord Ardilaun has to change his shirt four times a day, they say. Skin breeds lice or vermin. A million pounds, wait a moment. Twopence a pint, fourpence a quart, eightpence a gallon of porter, no, one and fourpence a gallon of porter. One and four into twenty : fifteen about. Yes, exactly. Fifteen millions of barrels of porter.

What am I saying barrels ? Gallons. About a million barrels all the same.

An incoming train clanked heavily above his head, coach after coach. Barrels bumped in his head : dull porter slopped and churned inside. The bungholes sprang open and a huge dull flood leaked out, flowing together, winding through mudflats all over the level land, a lazy pooling swirl of liquor bearing along wideleaved flowers of its froth.

He had reached the open backdoor oı All Hallows. Stepping into the porch he doffed his hat, took the card from his pocket and tucked it again behind the leather headband. Damn it. I might have tried to work M'Coy for a pass to Mullingar.

Same notice on the door. Sermon by the very reverend John Conmee S. J. on saint Peter Claver and the African mission Save China's millions. Wonder how they explain it to the heathen Chinee. Prefer an ounce of opium. Celestials. Rank heresy for them. Prayers for the conversion of Gladstone they had too when he was almost unconscious. The protestants the same. Convert Dr William. J. Walsh D. D. to the true religion. Buddha their god lying on his side in the museum. Taking it easy with hand under his cheek. Jossticks burning. Not like Ecce Home. Crown of thorns and cross. Clever idea Saint Patrick the shamrock. Chopsticks ? Conmee : Martin Cunningham knows him : distinguished looking. Sorry I didn't work him about getting Molly into the choir instead of that Father Farley who looked a fool but wasn't. They're taught that. He's not going out in bluey specs whit the sweat rolling off him to baptise blacks, is he ? The glasses would take their fancy, flashing. Like to see them sitting round in a ring with blub lips, entranced, listening. Still life. Lap it up like milk, I suppose.

The cold smell of sacred stone called him. He trod the worn steps, pushed the swingdoor and entered softly by the rere.

Something going on : some sodality. Pity so empty. Nice discreet place to be next some girl. Who is my neighbour ? Jammed by the hour to slow music. That woman at midnight mass. Seventh heaven. Women knelt in the benches with crimson halters round their necks, heads bowed. A batch knelt at the altar rails. The priest went along by them, murmuring, holding the thing in his hands. He stopped at each, took out a communion, shook a drop or two (are they in water ?) off it and put it neatly into her mouth. Her hat and head sank. Then the next one : a small old woman. The priest bent down to put it into her mouth, murmuring all the time. Latin. The next one. Shut your eyes and open your mouth. What ? *Corpus*. Body. Corpse. Good idea the Latin. Stupefies them first. Hospice for the dying. They don't seem to chew it : only swallow it down. Rum idea : eating bits of a corpse why the cannibals cotton to it.

He stood aside watching their blind masks pass down the aisle, one by one, and seek their places. He approached a bench and seated himself in its corner, nursing his hat and newspaper. These pots we have to wear. We ought to have hats modelled on our heads. They were about him here and there, with heads still bowed in their crimson halters, waiting for it to melt in their stomachs. Something like those mazzoth : it's that sort of bread : unleavened shewbread. Look at them. Now I bet it makes them feel happy. Lollipop. It does. Yes, bread of angels it's called. There's a big idea behind it, kind of kingdom of God is within you feel. First communicants. Hokypoky penny a lump. Then feel all like one family party, same in the theatre, all in the same swim. They do. I'm sure of that. Not so lonely. In our confraternity. Then come out a bit spreeish. Let off steam. Thing is if you really believe in it. Lourdes cure, waters of oblivion, and the Knock apparition, statues bleeding. Old fellow asleep near that confessionbox. Hence those snores. Blind faith. Safe in the arms of kingdom come. Lulls all pain. Wake this time next year.

He saw the priest stow the communion cup away, well in, and kneel an instant before it, showing a large grey bootsole from under the lace affair he had on. Suppose he lost the pin of his. He wouldn't know what to do to. Bald spot behind. Letters on his back I. N. R. I? No : I. H. S. Molly told me one time I asked her. I have sinned : or no : I have suffered, it is. And the other one? Iron nails ran in.

Meet one Sunday after the rosary. Do not deny my request. Turn up with a veil and black bag. Dusk and the light behind her. She might be here with a ribbon round her neck and do the other thing all the same on the sly. Their character. That fellow that turned queen's evidence on the invincibles he used to receive the, Carey was his name, the communion every morning. This very church. Peter Carey. No, Peter Claver I am thinking of. Denis Carey. And just imagine that. Wife and six children at home. And plotting that murder all the time. Those crawthumpers, now that's a good name for them, there's always something shiftylooking about them. They're not straight men of business either. O no she's not here : the flower : no, no. By the way did I tear up that envelope? Yes : under the bridge.

The priest was rinsing out the chalice : then he tossed off the dregs smartly. Wine. Makes it more aristocratic than for example if he drank what they are used to Guinness's porter or some temperance beverage Wheatley's Dublin hop bitters or Cantrell and Cochrane's ginger ale (aromatic). Doesn't give them any of it : show wine : only the other. Cold comfort. Pious fraud but quite right : otherwise they' d have one old booser worse than another coming along, cadging for a drink. Queer the whole atmosphere of the. Quite right. Perfectly right that is.

Mr Bloom looked back towards the choir. Not going to be any music. Pity. Who has the organ here I wonder? Old Glynn he knew how to make that instrument talk, the *vibrato*: fifty pounds a year they say he had in Gardiner street. Molly was in fine voice that day, the *Stabat Mater* of Rossini. Father Bernard Vaughan's sermon first. Christ or Pilate? Christ, but don't keep us all night over it. Music they wanted. Footdrill stopped. Could hear a pin drop. I told her to pitch her voice against that corner. I could feel the thrill in the air, the full, the people looking up:

Quis est homo?

Some of that old sacred music is splendid. Mercadante: seven last words. Mozart's twelfth mass: the *Gloria* in that. Those old popes were keen on music, on art and statues and pictures of all kinds. Palestrina for example too. They had a gay old time while it lasted. Healthy too chanting, regular hours, then brew liqueurs. Benedictine. Green Chartreuse. Still, having eunuchs in their choir that was coming it a bit thick. What kind of voice is it? Must be curious to hear after their own strong basses. Connoisseurs. Suppose they wouldn't feel anything after. Kind of a placid. No worry. Fall into flesh don't they? Gluttons, tall, long legs. Who knows? Eunuch. One way out of it.

He saw the priest bend down and kiss the altar and then face about and bless all the people. All crossed themselves and stood up. Mr Bloom glanced about him and then stood up, looking over the risen hats. Stand up at the gospel of course. Then all settled down on their knees again and he sat back quietly in his bench. The priest came down from the altar, holding the thing out from him, and he and the massboy answered each other in Latin. Then the priest knelt down and began to read off a card:

— O God, our refuge and our strength...

Mr Bloom put his face forward to catch the words. English. Throw them the bone. I remember slightly. How long since your last mass? Gloria and immaculate virgin Joseph her spouse. Peter and Paul. More interesting if you understood what it was all about. Wonderful organisation certainly, goes like clockwork. Confession. Everyone wants to. Then I will tell you all. Penance. Punish me, please. Great weapon in their hands. More than doctor or solicitor. Woman dying to. And I schschschschschsch. And did you chachachachacha? And why did you? Look down at her ring to find an excuse. Whispering gallery walls have ears. Husband learn to his surprise. God's little joke. Then out she comes. Repentance skindeep. Lovely shame. Pray at an altar.

Hail Mary and Holy Mary. Flowers, incense, candles melting. Hide her blushes. Salvation army blatant imitation. Reformed prostitute will address the meeting. How I found the Lord. Squareheaded chaps those must be in Rome : they work the whole show. And don't they rake in the money too? Bequests also: to the P. P. for the time being in his absolute discretion. Masses for the repose of my soul to be said publicly with open doors. Monasteries and convents. The priest in the Fermanagh will case in the witness box. No browbeating him. He had his answer pat for everything. Liberty and exaltation of our holy mother the church. The doctors of the church : they mapped out the whole theology of it.

The priest prayed :

— Blessed Michael, archangel, defend us in the hour of conflict. Be our safeguard against the wickedness and snares of the devil (may God restrain him, we humbly pray) : and do thou, O prince of the heavenly host, by the power of God thrust Satan down to hell and with him those other wicked spirits who wander through the world for the ruin of souls.

The priest and the massboy stood up and walked off. All over. The women remained behind : thanksgiving.

Better be shoving along. Brother Buzz. Come around with the plate perhaps. Pay your Easter duty.

He stood up. Hello. Were those two buttons of my waistcoat open all the time. Woman enjoy it. Annoyed if you don't. Why didn't you tell me before. Never tell you. But we. Excuse, miss, there's a (whh!) just a (whh!) fluff. Or their skirt behind, placket unhooked. Glimpses of the moon. Still like you better untidy. Good job it wasn't farther south. He passed, discreetly buttoning, down the aisle and out through the main door into rhe light. He stood a moment unseeing by the cold black marble bowl while before him and behind two worshippers dipped furtive hands in the low tide of holy water. Trams : a car of Prescott's dyeworks : a widow in her weeds. Notice because I'm in mourning myself. He covered himself. How goes the time? Quarter past. Time enough yet. Better get that lotion made up. Where is this? Ah yes, the last time. Sweny's in Lincoln place. Chemists rarely move. Their green and gold beaconjars too heavy to stir. Hamilton Long's, founded in the year of the flood. Huguenot churchyard near there. Visit some day.

He walked southward along Westland row. But the recipe is in the other trousers. O, and I forgot that latchkey too. Bore this funeral affair. O well, poor fellow, it's not his fault When was it I got it made up last? Wait.

I changed a sovereign I remember. First ot the month it must have been or the second. O he can look it up in the prescriptions book.

The chemist turned back page after page. Sandy shrivelled smell he seems to have, Shrunken skull. And old. Quest for the philosopher's stone. The alchemists. Drugs age you after mental excitement. Lethargy then. Why? Reaction. A lifetime in a night. Gradually changes your character. Living all the day among herbs, ointments, disinfectants. All his alabaster lilypots. Mortar and pestle. Aq. Dist. Fol. Laur. Te Virid. Smell almost cure you like the dentist's doorbell. Doctor whack. He ought to physic himself a bit. Electuary or emulsion. The first fellow that picked an herb to cure himselt had a bit of pluck. Simples. Want to be careful. Enough stuff here to chloroform you. Test : turns blue litmus paper red. Chloroform. Overdose of laudanum. Sleeping draughts. Lovephiltres. Paragoric poppysyrup bad for cough. Clogs the pores or the phlegm. Poisons the only cures. Remedy where you least expect it. Clever of nature.

— About a fortnight ago, sir?

— Yes, Mr Bloom said.

He waited by the counter, inhaling the keen reek of drugs, the dusty dry smell of sponges and loofahs. Lot of time taken up telling your aches and pains.

— Sweet almond oil and tincture of benzoin, Mr Bloom said, and then orangeflower water...

It certainly did make her skin so delicate white like wax.

— And white wax also, he said.

Brings out the darkness of her eyes. Looking at me, the sheet up to her eyes, Spanish, smelling herself, when I was fixing the links in my cuffs. Those homely recipes are often the best : strawberries for the teeth : nettles and rainwater : oatmeal they say steeped in buttermilk. Skinfood. One of the old queen's sons, duke of Albany was it ? had only one skin. Leopold, yes. Three we have. Warts, bunions and pimples to make it worse. But you want a perfume too. What perfume does your? *Peau d'Espagne*. That orange-flower. Pure curd soap. Water is so fresh. Nice smell these soaps have. Time to get a bath round the corner. Hammam. Turkish. Massage. Dirt gets rolled up in your navel. Nicer if a nice girl did it. Also I think I. Yes I. Do it in the bath. Curious longing I. Water to water. Combine business with pleasure. Pity no time for massage. Feel fresh then all day. Funeral be rather glum.

— Yes, sir, the chemist said. That was two and nine. Have you brought a bottle?

— No, Mr Bloom said. Make it up, please. I'll call later in the day and I'll take one of those soaps. How much are they?

— Fourpence, sir.

Mr Bloom raised a cake to his nostrils. Sweet lemony wax.

— I'll take this one, he said. That makes three and a penny.

— Yes, sir, the chemist said. You can pay all together, sir, when you come back.

— Good, Mr Bloom said.

He strolled out of the shop, the newspaper baton under his armpit, the coolwrappered soap in his left hand.

At his armpit Bantam Lyons' voice and hand said:

— Hello, Bloom, what's the best news? Is that today's? Show us a minute.

Shaved off his moustache again, by Jove! Long cold upper lip. To look younger. He does look balmy. Younger than I am.

Bantam Lyons' yellow blacknailed fingers unrolled the baton. Wants a wash too. Take off the rough dirt. Good morning, have you used Pears' soap. Dandruff on his shoulders. Scalp wants oiling.

— I want to see about that French horse that's running today, Bantam Lyons' said. Where the bugger is it?

He rustled the pleated pages, jerking his chin on his high collar. Barber's itch. Tight collar he'll lose his hair. Better leave him the paper and get shut of him.

— You can keep it, Mr Bloom said.

— Ascot. Gold cup. Wait, Bantam Lyons muttered. Half a mo. Maximum the second.

— I was just going to throw it away, Mr Bloom said.

Bantam Lyons raised his eyes suddenly and leered weakly.

— What's that? his sharp voice said.

— I say you can keep it, Mr Bloom answered. I was going to throw it away that moment.

Bantam Lyons doubted an instant, leering: then thrust the outspread sheets back on Mr Bloom's arms.

— I'll risk it, he said. Here, thanks.

He sped off towards Conway's corner. God speed scut.

Mr Bloom folded the sheets again to a neat square and lodged the soap in it, smiling. Silly lips of that chap. Betting. Regular hotbed of it lately. Messenger boys stealing to put on sixpence. Raffle for large tender turkey.

Your Christmas dinner for threepence. Jack Fleming embezzling to gamble then smuggled off to America. Keeps a hotel now. They never come back. Fleshpots of Egypt.

He walked cheerfully towards the mosque of the baths. Remind you of a mosque redbaked bricks, the minarets. College sports today I see. He eyed the horseshoe poster over the gate of college park : cyclist doubled up like a cod in a pot. Damn bad ad. Now if they had made it round like a wheel. Then the spokes : sports, sports, sports : and the hub big : college. Something to catch the eye.

There's Hornblower standing at the porter's lodge. Keep him on hands : might take a turn in there on the nod. How do you do, Mr Hornblower? How do you do, sir?

Heavenly weather really. If life was always like that. Cricket weather. Sit around under sunshades. Over after over. Out. They can't play it here. Duck for six wickets. Still Captain Buller broke a window in the Kildare street club with a slog to square leg. Donnybrook fair more in their line. And the skulls we were acracking when M'Carthy took the floor. Heatwave. Won't last. Always passing, the stream of life, which in the stream of life we trace is dearer than them all.

Enjoy a bath now : clean trough of water, cool enamel, the gentle tepid stream. This is my body.

He foresaw his pale body reclined in it at full, naked, in a womb of warmth, oiled by scented melting soap, softly laved. He saw his trunk and limbs riprippled over and sustained, buoyed lightly upward, lemonyellow : his navel, bud of flesh : and saw the dark tangled curls of his bush floating, floating hair of the stream around the limp father of thousands, a languid floating flower.

6 - HADES

Martin Cunningham, first, poked his silkhatted head into the creaking carriage and, entering deftly, seated himself. Mr Power stepped in after him, curving his height with care.

— Come on, Simon.

— After you, Mr Bloom said.

Mr Dedalus covered himself quickly and got in, saying :

— Yes, yes.

— Are we all here now? Martin Cunningham asked. Come along, Bloom.

Mr Bloom entered and sat in the vacant place. He pulled the door to after him and slammed it tight till it shut tight. He passed an arm through the armstrap and looked seriously from the open carriage window at the lowered blinds of the avenue. One dragged aside : an old woman peeping. Nose white-flattened against the pane. Thanking her stars she was passed over. Extraordinary the interest they take in a corpse. Glad to see us go we give them such trouble coming. Job seems to suit them. Huggermugger in corners. Slop about in slipperslappers for fear he'd wake. Then getting it ready. Laying it out. Molly and Mrs Fleming making the bed. Pull it more to your side. Our windingsheet. Never know who will touch you dead. Wash and shampoo. I believe they clip the nails and the hair. Keep a bit in an envelope. Grow all the same after. Unclean job.

All waited. Nothing was said. Stowing in the wreaths probably. I am sitting on something hard. Ah, that soap in my hip pocket. Better shift it out of that. Wait for an opportunity.

All waited. Then wheels were heard from in front, turning : then nearer : then horses' hoofs. A jolt. Their carriage began to move, creaking and swaying.

Other hoofs and creaking wheels started behind. The blinds ot the avenue passed and number ten with its craped knocker, door ajar. At walking pace.

They waited still, their knees jogging, till they had turned and were passing along the tramtracks. Tritonville road. Quicker. The wheels rattled rolling over the cobbled causeway and the crazy glasses shook rattling in the doorframes.

— What way is he taking us? Mr Power asked through both windows.

— Irishtown, Martin Cunningham said. Ringsend. Brunswick street.

Mr Dedalus nodded, looking out.

— That's a fine old custom, he said. I am glad to see it has not died out.

All watched awhile through their windows caps and hats lifted by passers. Respect. The carriage swerved from the tramtrack to the smoother road past Watery lane. Mr Bloom at gaze saw a lithe young man, clad in mourning, a wide hat.

— There's a friend of yours gone by, Dedalus, he said.

— Who is that?

— Your son and heir.

— Where is he? Mr Dedalus said, stretching over, across.

The carriage, passing the open drains and mounds of rippedup roadway before the tenement houses, lurched round the corner and, swerving back to the tramtrack, rolled on noisily with chattering wheels. Mr Dedalus fell back, aying:

— Was that Mulligan cad with him? His *fidus Achates!*

— No, Mr Bloom said. He was alone.

— Down with his aunt Sally, I suppose, Mr Dedalus said, the Goulding faction, the drunken little costdrawer and Crissie, papa's little lump of dung, the wise child that knows her own father.

Mr Bloom smiled joylessly on Ringsend road. Wallace Bros the bottleworks. Dodder bridge.

Richie Goulding and the legal bag. Goulding, Collis and Ward he calls the firm. His jokes are getting a bit damp. Great card he was. Waltzing in Stamer street with Ignatius Gallaher on a Sunday morning, the landlady's two hats pinned on his head. Out on the rampage all night. Beginning to tell on him now: that backache of his, I fear. Wife ironing his back. Thinks he'll cure it with pills. All breadcrumbs they are. About six hundred per cent profit.

— He's in with a lowdown crowd, Mr Dedalus snarled. That Mulligan is a contaminated bloody doubledyed ruffian by all accounts. His name stinks all over Dublin. But with the help of God and His blessed mother I'll make it my business to write a letter one of those days to his mother or his aunt or whatever she is that will open her eye as wide as a gate. I'll tickle his catastrophe, believe you me.

He cried above the clatter of the wheels.

— I won't have her bastard of a nephew ruin my son. A counterjumper's son. Selling tapes in my cousin, Peter Paul M'Swiney's. Not likely.

He ceased. Mr Bloom glanced from his angry moustache to Mr Power's mild face and Martin Cunningham's eyes and beard, gravely shaking. Noisy selfwilled man. Full of his son. He is right. Something to hand on. If little Rudy had lived. See him grow up. Hear his voice in the house. Walking beside Molly in an Eton suit. My son. Me in his eyes. Strange feeling it would be. From me. Just a chance. Must have been that morning in Raymond terrace she was at the window, watching the two dogs at it by the wall of the cease to do evil. And the sergeant grinning up. She had that cream gown on with the rip she never stitched. Give us a touch, Poldy. God, I'm dying for it. How life begins.

Got big then. Had to refuse the Greystones concert. My son inside her. I could have helped him on in life. I could. Make him independent. Learn German too.

— Are we late? Mr Power asked.

— Ten minutes, Martin Cunningham said, looking at his watch.

Molly. Milly. Same thing watered down. Her tomboy oaths. O jumping Jupiter! Ye gods and little fishes! Still, she's a dear girl. Soon be a woman. Mullingar. Dearest Papli. Young student. Yes, yes: a woman too. Life. Life.

The carriage heeled over and back, their four trunks swaying.

— Corny might have given us a more commodious yoke, Mr Power said.

— He might, Mr Dedalus said, if he hadn't that squint troubling him. Do you follow me?

He closed his left eye. Martin Cunningham began to brush away crustcrumbs from under his thighs.

— What is this? he said, in the name of God? Crumbs?

— Someone seems to have been making a picnic party here lately, Mr Power said.

All raised their thighs, eyed with disfavour the mildewed buttonless leather of the seats. Mr Dedalus, twisting his nose, frowned downward and said:

— Unless I'm greatly mistaken. What do you think, Martin?

— It struck me too, Martin Cunningham said.

Mr Bloom set his thigh down. Glad I took that bath. Feel my feet quite clean. But I wish Mrs Fleming had darned these socks better.

Mr Dedalus sighed resignedly.

— After all, he said, it's the most natural thing in the world.

— Did Tom Kernan turn up? Martin Cunningham asked, twirling the peak of his beard gently.

— Yes, Mr Bloom answered. He's behind with Ned Lambert and Hynes.

— And Corny Kelleher himself? Mr Power asked.

— At the cemetery, Martin Cunningham said.

— I met M'Coy this morning, Mr Bloom said. He said he'd try to come.

The carriage halted short.

— What's wrong?

— We're stopped.

— Where are we?

Mr Bloom put his head out of the window.

— The grand canal, he said.

Gasworks. Whooping cough they say it cures. Good job Milly never got it. Poor children! Doubles then up black and blue in convulsions. Shame really. Got off lightly with illnesses compared. Only measles. Flaxseed tea. Scarlatina, influenza epidemics. Canvassing for death. Don't miss this chance. Dogs' home over there. Poor old Athos! Be good to Athos, Leopold, is my last wish. Thy will be done. We obey them in the grave. A dying scrawl. He took it to heart, pined away. Quiet brute. Old men's dogs usually are.

A raindrop spat on his hat. He drew back and saw an instant of shower spray dots over the grey flags. Apart. Curious. Like through a colander. I thought it would. My boots were creaking I remember now.

— The weather is changing, he said quietly.

— A pity it did not keep up fine, Martin Cunningham said.

— Wanted for the country, Mr Power said. There's the sun again coming out.

Mr Dedalus, peering through his glasses towards the veiled sun, hurled a mute curse at the sky.

— It's as uncertain as a child's bottom, he said.

— We're off again.

The carriage turned again its stiff wheels and their trunks swayed gently. Martin Cunningham twirled more quickly the peak of his beard.

— Tom Kernan was immense last night, he said. And Paddy Leonard taking him off to his face.

— O draw him out, Martin, Mr Power said eagerly. Wait till you hear him, Simon, on Ben Dollard's singing of *The Croppy Boy*.

— Immense, Martin Cunningham said pompously. *His singing of that simple ballad, Martin, is the most trenchant rendering I ever heard in the whole course of my experience.*

— Trenchant, Mr Power said laughing. He's dead nuts on that. And the retrospective arrangement.

— Did you read Dan Dawson's speech? Martin Cunningham asked.

— I did not then, Mr Dedalus said. Where is it?

— In the paper this morning.

Mr Bloom took the paper from his inside pocket. That book I must change for her.

— No, no, Mr Dedalus said quickly. Later on, please.

Mr Bloom's glance travelled down the edge of the paper, scanning the deaths. Callan, Coleman, Dignam, Fawcett, Lowry, Naumann, Peake, what Peake is that? is it the chap was in Crosbie and Alleyne's? no, Sexton, Urbright. Inked characters fast fading on the frayed breaking paper. Thanks to the Little Flower. Sadly missed. To the inexpressible grief of his. Aged 88 after a long and tedious illness. Month's mind Quinlan. On whose soul Sweet Jesus have mercy.

It is now a month since dear Henry fled
To his home up above in the sky
While his family weeps and mourns his loss
Hoping some day to meet him on high.

I tore up the envelope? Yes. Where did I put her letter after I read it in the bath? He patted his waistcoat pocket. There all right. Dear Henry fled. Before my patience are exhausted.

National school. Meade's yard. The hazard. Only two there now. Nodding. Full as a tick. Too much bone in their skulls. The other trotting round with a fare. An hour ago I was passing there. The jarvies raised their hats.

A pointsman's back straightened itself upright suddenly against a tramway standard by Mr Bloom's window. Couldn't they invent something automatic so that the wheel itself much handier? Well but that fellow would lose his job then? Well but then another fellow would get a job making the new invention?

Antient concert rooms. Nothing on there. A man in a buff suit with a crape armlet. Not much grief there. Quarter mourning. People in law, perhaps.

They went past the bleak pulpit of Saint Mark's, under the railway bridge, past the Queen's theatre : in silence. Hoardings. Eugene Stratton. Mrs Bandmann Palmer. Could I go to see *Leah* tonight, I wonder. I said I. Or the *Lily of Killarney?* Elster Grimes Opera company. Big powerful change. Wet bright bills for next week. *Fun on the Bristol.* Martin Cunningham could work a pass for the Gaiety. Have to stand a drink or two. As broad as it's long.

He's coming in the afternoon. Her songs.

Plasto's. Sir Philip Crampton's memorial fountain bust. Who was he?

— How do you do? Martin Cunningham said, raising his palm to his brow in salute.

— He doesn't see us, Mr Power said. Yes, he does. How do you do?

— Who? Mr Dedalus asked.

— Blazes Boylan, Mr Power said. There he is airing his quiff.

Just that moment I was thinking.

Mr Dedalus bent across to salute. From the door of the Red Bank the white disc of a straw hat flashed reply : passed.

Mr Bloom reviewed the nails of his left hand, then those of his right hand. The nails, yes. Is there anything more in him that they she sees? Fascination. Worst man in Dublin. That keeps him alive. They sometimes feel what a person is. Instinct. But a type like that. My nails. I am just looking at them : well pared. And after : thinking alone. Body getting a bit softy. I would notice that from remembering. What causes that I suppose the skin can't contract quickly enough when the flesh falls off. But the shape is there. The shape is there still. Shoulders. Hips. Plump. Night of the dance dressing. Shift stuck between the cheeks behind.

He clasped his hands between his knees and, satisfied, sent his vacant glance over their faces.

Mr Power asked :

— How is the concert tour getting on, Bloom?

— O very well, Mr Bloom said. I hear great accounts of it. It's a good idea, you see...

— Are you going yourself?

— Well no, Mr Bloom said. In point of fact I have to go down to the county Clare on some private business. You see the idea is to tour the chiei towns. What you lose on one you can make up on the other.

— Quite so, Martin Cunningham said. Mary Anderson is up there now.

— Have you good artists?

— Louis Werner is touring her, Mr Bloom said. O yes, we'll have all topnobbers. J. C. Doyle and John MacCormack I hope and. The best, in fact.

— And *Madame*, Mr Power said, smiling. Last but not least.

Mr Bloom unclasped his hands in a gesture of soft politeness and clasped them. Smith O'Brien. Someone has laid a bunch of flowers there. Woman. Must be his deathday. For many happy returns. The carriage wheeling by Farrell's statue united noiselessly their unresisting knees.

Oot : a dullgarbed old man from the curbstone tendered his wares, his mouth opening : oot.

— Four bootlaces for a penny.

Wonder why he was struck off the rolls. Had his office in Hume street. Same house as Molly's namesake. Tweedy, crown solicitor for Waterford. Has that silk hat ever since. Relics of old decency. Mourning too. Terrible comedown, poor wretch! Kicked about like snuff at a wake. O'Callaghan on his last legs.

And *Madame*. Twenty past eleven. Up. Mrs Fleming is in to clean. Doing her hair, humming : *voglio e non vorrei*. No : *vorrei e non*. Looking at the tips of her hairs to see if they are split. *Mi trema un poco il*. Beautiful on that *tre* her voice is : weeping tone. A thrush. A throstle. There is a word throstle that expresses that.

His eyes passed lightly over Mr Power's goodlooking face. Greyish over the ears. *Madame* : smiling. I smiled back. A smile goes a long way. Only politeness perhaps. Nice fellow. Who knows is that true about the woman he keeps? Not pleasant for the wife. Yet they say, who was it told me, there is no carnal. You would imagine that would get played out pretty quick. Yes, it was Crofton met him one evening bringing her a pound of rumpsteak. What is this she was? Barmaid in Jury's. Or the Moira, was it?

They passed under the hugecloaked Liberator's form.

Martin Cunningham nudged Mr Power.

— Of the tribe of Reuben, he said.

A tall blackbearded figure, bent on a stick, stumping round the corner oi Elvery's elephant house showed them a curved hand open on his spine.

— In all his pristine beauty, Mr Power said.

Mr Dedalus looked after the stumping figure and said mildly:

— The devil break the hasp of your back!

Mr Power, collapsing in laughter, shaded his face from the window as the carriage passed Gray's statue.

— We have all been there, Martin Cunningham said broadly.

His eyes met Mr Bloom's eyes. He caressed his beard, adding:

— Well, nearly all of us.

Mr Bloom began to speak with sudden eagerness to his companions' faces.

— That's an awfully good one that's going the rounds about Reuben J. and the son.

— About the boatman? Mr Power asked.

— Yes. Isn't it awfully good?

— What is that? Mr Dedalus asked, I didn't hear it.

— There was a girl in the case, Mr Bloom began, and he determined to send him to the isle of Man out of harm's way but when they were both.....

— What? Mr Dedalus asked. That confirmed bloody hobbledehoy is it?

— Yes, Mr Bloom said. They were both on the way to the boat and he tried to drown.....

— Drown Barabbas! Mr Dedalus cried. I wish to Christ he did!

Mr Power sent a long laugh down his shaded nostrils.

— No, Mr Bloom said, the son himself.....

Martin Cunningham thwarted his speech rudely.

— Reuben J. and the son were piking it down the quay next the river on their way to the isle of Man boat and the young chiseller suddenly got loose and over the wall with him into the Liffey.

— For God' sake! Mr Dedalus exclaimed in fright. Is he dead?

— Dead! Martin Cunningham cried. Not he! A boatman got a pole and fished him out by the slack of the breeches and he was landed up to the father on the quay. More dead than alive. Half the town was there.

— Yes, Mr Bloom said. But the funny part is.....

— And Reuben J., Martin Cunningham said, gave the boatman a florin for saving his son's life.

A stifled sigh came from under Mr Power's hand.

— O, he did, Martin Cunningham affirmed. Like a hero. A silver florin.

— Isn't it awfully good? Mr Bloom said eagerly.

— One and eightpence too much, Mr Dedalus said drily.

Mr Power's choked laugh burst quietly in the carriage.

Nelson's pillar.

— Eight plums a penny! Eight for a penny!

— We had better look a little serious, Martin Cunningham said.

Mr Dedalus sighed.

— Ah then indeed, he said, poor little Paddy wouldn't grudge us a laugh. Many a good one he told himself.

— The Lord forgive me! Mr Power said, wiping his wet eyes with his fingers. Poor Paddy! I little thought a week ago when I saw him last and he was in his usual health that I'd be driving after him like this. He's gone from us.

— As decent a little man as ever wore a hat, Mr Dedalus said. He went very suddenly.

— Breakdown, Martin Cunningham said. Heart.

He tapped his chest sadly.

Blazing face: redhot. Too much John Barleycorn. Cure for a red nose. Drink like the devil till it turns adelite. A lot of money he spent colouring it.

Mr Power gazed at the passing houses with rueful apprehension.

— He had a sudden death, poor fellow, he said.

— The best death, Mr Bloom said.

Their wide open eyes looked at him.

— No suffering, he said. A moment and all is over. Like dying in sleep.

No-one spoke.

Dead side of the street this. Dull business by day, land agents, temperance hotel, Falconer's railway guide, civil service college, Gill's, catholic club, the industrious blind. Why? Some reason. Sun or wind. At night too. Chummies and slaveys. Under the patronage of the late Father Matew. Foundation stone for Parnell. Breakdown. Heart.

White horses with white frontlet plumes came round the Rotunda corner, galloping. A tinycoffin flashed by. In a hurry to bury. A mourning coach. Unmarried. Black for the married. Piebald for bachelors. Dun for a nun.

— Sad, Martin Cunningham said. A child.

A dwarf's face mauve and wrinkled like little Rudy's was. Dwarf's body, weak as putty, in a whitelined deal box. Burial friendly society pays. Penny a week for a sod of turf. Our. Little. Beggar. Baby. Meant nothing. Mistake of nature. If it's healthy it's from the mother. If not the man. Better luck next time.

— Poor little thing, Mr Dedalus said. It's well out of it.

The carriage climbed more slowly the hill of Rutland square. Rattle his bones. Over the stones. Only a pauper. Nobody owns.

— In the midst of life, Martin Cunningham said.

— But the worst of all, Mr Power said, is the man who takes his own life.

Martin Cunningham drew out his watch briskly, coughed and put it back.

— The greatest disgrace to have in the family, Mr Power added.

— Temporary insanity, of course, Martin Cunningham said decisively. We must take a charitable view of it.

— They say a man who does it is a coward, Mr Dedalus said.

— It is not for us to judge, Martin Cunningham said.

Mr Bloom, about to speak, closed his lips again. Martin Cunningham's large eyes. Looking away now. Sympathetic human man he is. Intelligent. Like Shakespeare's face. Always a good word to say. They have no mercy on that here or infanticide. Refuse christian burial. They used to drive a stake of wood through his heart in the grave. As if it wasn't broken already. Yet sometimes they repent too late. Found in the riverbed clutching rushes. He looked at me. And that awful drunkard of a wife of his. Setting up house for her time after time and then pawning the furniture on him every Saturday almost. Leading him the life of the damned. Wear the heart out of a stone, that. Monday morning start afresh. Shoulder to the wheel. Lord, she must have looked a sight that night, Dedalus told me he was in there. Drunk about the place and capering with Martin's umbrella :

— *And they call me the jewel of Asia,*
Of Asia,
The geisha.

He looked away from me. He knows. Rattle his bones.

That afternoon of the inquest. The redlabelled bottle on the table. The room in the hotel with hunting pictures. Stuffy it was. Sunlight through the slats of the Venetian blinds. The coroner's ears, big and hairy. Boots giving evidence. Thought he was asleep first. Then saw like yellow streaks on his face. Had slipped down to the foot of the bed. Verdict : overdose. Death by misadventure. The letter. For my son Leopold.

No more pain. Wake no more. Nobody owns.

The carriage rattled swiftly along Blessington street. Over the stones.

— We are going the pace, I think, Martin Cunningham said.

— God grant he doesn't upset us on the road, Mr Power said.

— I hope not, Martin Cunningham said. That will be a great race tomorrow in Germany. The Gordon Bennett.

— Yes, by Jove, Mr Dedalus said. That will be worth seeing, faith.

As they turned into Berkeley street a streetorgan near the Basin sent over and after them a rollicking rattling song of the halls. Has anybody here seen Kelly? Kay ee double ell wy. Dead march from *Saul*. He's as bad as old Antonio. He left me on my ownio. Pirouette! The *Mater Misericordiæ*. Eccles street. My house down there. Big place. Ward for incurables there. Very encouraging. Our Lady's Hospice for the dying. Deadhouse handy underneath. Where old Mrs Riordan died. They look terrible the women. Her feeding cup and rubbing her mouth with the spoon. Then the screen round her bed for her to die. Nice young student that was dressed that bite the bee gave me. He's gone over to the lying-in hospital they told me. From one extreme to the other.

The carriage galloped round a corner: stopped.

— What's wrong now?

A divided drove of branded cattle passed the windows, lowing, slouching by on padded hoofs, whisking their tails slowly on their clotted bony croups. Outside them and through them ran raddled sheep bleating their fear.

— Emigrants, Mr Power said.

— Huuuh! the drover's voice cried, his switch sounding on their flanks. Huuuh! out of that!

Thursday of course. Tomorrow is killing day. Springers. Cuffe sold them about twentyseven quid each. For Liverpool probably. Roast beef for old England. They buy up all the juicy ones. And then the fifth quarter is lost: all that raw stuff, hide, hair, horns. Comes to a big thing in a year. Dead meat trade. Byproducts of the slaughterhouses for tanneries, soap, margarine. Wonder if that dodge works now getting dicky meat off the train at Clonsilla.

The carriage moved on through the drove.

— I can't make out why the corporation doesn't run a tramline from the parkgate to the quays, Mr Bloom said. All those animals could be taken in trucks down to the boats.

— Instead of blocking up the thoroughfare, Martin Cunningham said. Quite right. They ought to.

— Yes, Mr Bloom said, and another thing I often thought is to have municipal funeral trams like they have in Milan, you know. Run the line out to the cemetery gates and have special trams, hearse and carriage and all. Don't you see what I mean ?

— O that be damned for a story, Mr Dedalus said. Pullman car and saloon diningroom.

— A poor lookout for Corny, Mr Power added.

— Why ? Mr Bloom asked, turning to Mr Dedalus. Wouldn't it be more decent than galloping two abreast ?

— Well, there's something in that, Mr Dedalus granted.

— And, Martin Cunningham said, we wouldn't have scenes like that when the hearse capsized round Dunphy's and upset the coffin on to the road.

— That was terrible, Mr Power's shocked face said, and the corpse fell about the road. Terrible !

— First round Dunphy's, Mr Dedalus said, nodding. Gordon Bennett cup.

— Praises be to God ! Martin Cunningham said piously.

Bom ! Upset. A coffin bumped out on to the road. Burst open. Paddy Dignam shot out and rolling over stiff in the dust in a brown habit too large for him. Red face : grey now. Mouth fallen open. Asking what's up now. Quite right to close it. Looks horrid open. Then the insides decompose quickly. Much better to close up all the orifices. Yes, also. With wax. The sphincter loose. Seal up all.

— Dunphy's, Mr Power announced as the carriage turned right.

Dunphy's corner. Mourning coaches drawn up drowning their grief. A panse by the wayside. Tiptop position for a pub. Expect we'll pull up here on the way back to drink his health. Pass round the consolation. Elixir of life.

But suppose now it did happen. Would he bleed if a nail say cut him in the knocking about ? He would and he wouldn't, I suppose. Depends on where. The circulation stops. Still some might ooze out of an artery. It would be better to bury them in red : a dark red.

In silence they drove along Phibsborough road. An empty hearse trotted by, coming from the cemetery : looks relieved.

Crossguns bridge : the royal canal.

Water rushed roaring through the sluices. A man stood on his dropping barge between clamps of turf. On the towpath by the lock a slacktethered horse. Aboard of the *Bugabu*.

Their eyes watched him. On the slow weedy waterway he had floated on his raft coastward over Ireland drawn by a haulage rope past beds of reeds, over slime, mudchoked bottles, carrion dogs. Athlone, Mullingar, Moyvalley, I could make a walking tour to see Milly by the canal. Or cycle down. Hire some old crock, safety. Wren had one the other day at the auction but a lady's. Developing waterways. James M'Cann's hobby to row me o'er the ferry. Cheaper transit. By easy stages. Houseboats. Camping out. Also hearses. To heaven by water. Perhaps I will without writing. Come as a surprise, Leixlip, Clonsilla. Dropping down, lock by lock to Dublin. With turf from the midland bogs. Salute. He lifted his brown straw hat, saluting Paddy Dignam.

They drove on. past Brian Boroimhe house. Near it now.

— I wonder how is our friend Fogarty getting on, Mr Power said.

— Better ask Tom Kernan, Mr Dedalus said.

— How is that? Martin Cunningham said. Left him weeping I suppose.

— Though lost to sight, Mr Dedalus said, to memory dear.

The carriage steered left for Finglas road.

The stonecutter's yard on the right. Last lap. Crowded on the spit of land silent shapes appeared, white, sorrowful, holding out calm hands, knelt in grief, pointing. Fragments of shapes, hewn. In white silence : appealing. The best obtainable. Thos. H. Dennany, monumental builder and sculptor.

Passed.

On the curbstone before Jimmy Geary the sexton's, an old tramp sat, grumbling, emptying the dirt and stones out of his huge dustbrown yawning boot. After life's journey.

Gloomy gardens then went by, one by one : gloomy houses.

Mr Power pointed.

— That is where Childs was murdered, he said. The last house.

— So it is, Mr Dedalus said. A gruesome case. Seymour Bushe got him off. Murdered his brother. Or so they said.

— The crown had no evidence, Mr Power said.

— Only circumstantial, Martin Cunningham said. That's the maxim ot the law. Better for ninetynine guilty to escape than for one innocent person to be wrongfully condemned.

They looked. Murderer's ground. It passed darkly. Shuttered, tenantless, unweeded garden. Whole place gone to hell. Wrongfully condemned. Murder. The murderer's image in the eye of the murdered. They love reading about it. Man's head found in a garden. Her clothing consisted of. How she met her death. Recent outrage. The weapon used. Murderer is still at large. Clues. A shoelace. The body to be exhumed. Murder will out.

Cramped in this carriage. She mightn't like me to come that way without letting her know. Must be careful about women. Catch them once with their pants down. Never forgive you after. Fifteen.

The high railings of Prospect rippled past their gaze. Dark poplars, rare white forms. Forms more frequent, white shapes thronged amid the trees, white forms and fragments streaming by mutely, sustaining vain gestures on the air.

The felly harshed against the curbstone : stopped. Martin Cunningham put out his arm and, wrenching back the handle, shoved the door open with his knee. He stepped out. Mr Power and Mr Dedalus followed.

Change that soap now. Mr Bloom's hand unbuttoned his hip pocket swiftly and transferred the paperstuck soap to his inner handkerchief pocket. He stepped out of the carriage, replacing the newspaper his other hand still held.

Paltry funeral : coach and three carriages. It's all the same, Pallbearers gold reins, requiem mass, firing a volley. Pomp of death. Beyond the hind carriage a hawker stood by his barrow of cakes and fruit. Simnel cakes those are, stuck together : cakes for the dead. Dogbiscuits. Who ate them? Mourners coming out.

He followed his companions. Mr Kernan and Ned Lambert followed, Hynes walking after them. Corny Kelleher stood by the opened hearse and took out the two wreaths. He handed one to the boy.

Where is that child's funeral disappeared to ?

A team of horses passed from Finglas with toiling plodding tread, dragging through the funereal silence a creaking waggon on which lay a granite block. The waggoner marching at their head saluted.

Coffin now. Got here before us, dead as he is. Horse looking round at it with his plume skeowways. Dull eye : collar tight on his neck, pressing on a bloodvessel or something. Do they know what they cart out here every day. Must be twenty or thirty funerals every day. Then Mount Jerome for the protestants. Funerals all over the world everywhere every minute. Shovelling them under by the cartload doublequick. Thousands every hour. Too many in the world.

Mourners came out through the gates : woman and a girl. Leanjawed harpy, hard woman at a bargain, her bonnet awry. Girl's face stained with dirt and tears, holding the woman's arm looking up at her for a sign to cry. Fish's face, bloodless and livid.

The mutes shouldered the coffin and bore it in through the gates. So much dead weight. Felt heavier myself steping out of that bath. First the stiff: then the friends of the stiff. Corny Kelleher and the boy followed with their wreaths. Who is that beside them? Ah, the brother-in-law.

All walked after.

Martin Cunningham whispered:

— I was in mortal agony with you talking of suicide before Bloom.

— What? Mr Power whispered. How so?

— His father poisoned himself, Martin Cunningham whispered. Had the Queen's hotel in Ennis. You heard him say he was going to Clare. Anniversary.

— O God! Mr Power whispered. First I heard of it. Poisoned himself!

He glanced behind him to where a face with dark thinking eyes followed towards the cardinal's mausoleum. Speaking.

— Was he insured? Mr Bloom asked.

— I believe so, Mr Kernan answered, but the policy was heavily mortgaged. Martin is trying to get the youngster into Artane.

— How many children did he leave?

— Five. Ned Lambert says he'll try to get one of the girls into Todd's.

— A sad case, Mr Bloom said gently. Five young children.

— A great blow to the poor wife, Mr Kernan added.

— Indeed yes, Mr Bloom agreed.

Has the laugh at him now.

He looked down at the boots he had blacked and polished. She had outlived him, lost her husband. More dead for her than for me. One must outlive the other. Wise men say. There are more women than men in the world. Condole with her. Your terrible loss. I hope you'll soon follow him. For Hindu widows only. She would marry another. Him? No. Yet who knows after? Widowhood not the thing since the old queen died. Drawn on a guncarriage. Victoria and Albert. Frogmore memorial mourning. But in the end she put a few violets in her bonnet. Vain in her heart of hearts. All for a shadow. Consort not even a king. Her son was the substance. Something new to hope for not like the past she wanted back, waiting. It never comes. One must go first: alone, under the ground: and lie no more in her warm bed.

— How are you, Simon? Ned Lambert said softly, clasping hands. Haven't seen you for a month of Sundays.

— Never better. How are all in Cork's own town?

— I was down there for the, Cork park races on Easter Monday, Ned Lambert said. Same old six and eightpence. Stopped with Dick Tivy.

— And how is Dick, the solid man?

— Nothing between himself and heaven, Ned Lambert answered.

— By the holy Paul! Mr Dedalus said in subdued wonder. Dick Tivy bald?

— Martin is going to get up a whip for the youngsters, Ned Lambert said, pointing ahead. A few bob a skull. Just to keep them going till the insurance is cleared up.

— Yes, yes, Mr Dedalus said dubiously. Is that the eldest boy in front?

— Yes, Ned Lambert said, with the wife's brother. John Henry Menton is behind. He put down his name for a quid.

— I'll engage he did, Mr Dedalus said. I often told poor Paddy he ought to mind that job. John Henry is not the worst in the world.

— How did he lose it? Ned Lambert asked. Liquor, what?

— Many a good man's fault, Mr Dedalus said with a sigh.

They halted about the door of the mortuary chapel. Mr Bloom stood behind the boy with the wreath, looking down at his sleek combed hair and the slender furrowed neck inside his brandnew collar. Poor boy! Was he there when the father? Both unconscious. Lighten up at the last moment and recognise for the last time. All he might have done. I owe three shillings to O'Grady. Would he understand? The mutes bore the coffin into the chapel. Which end is his head?

After a moment he followed the others in, blinking in the screened light. The coffin lay on its bier before the chancel four tall yellow candles at its corners. Always in front of us. Corny Kelleher, laying a wreath at each fore corner, beckoned to the boy to kneel. The mourners knelt here and there in praying desks. Mr Bloom stood behind near the font and, when all had knelt dropped carefully his unfolded newspaper from his pocket and knelt his right knee upon it. He fitted his black hat gently on his left knee and, holding its brim, bent over piously.

A server, bearing a brass bucket with something in it, came out through a door. The whitesmocked priest came after him tidying his stole with one hand, balancing with the other a little book against his toad's belly. Who'll read the book? I, said the rook.

They halted by the bier and the priest began to read out of his book with a fluent croak.

Father Coffey. I knew his name was like a coffin. *Dominenamine.* Bully about the muzzle he looks. Bosses the show. Muscular christian. Woe betide anyone that looks crooked at him : priest. Thou art Peter. Burst sideways like a sheep in clover Dedalus says he will. With a belly on him like a poisoned pup. Most amusing expressions that man finds. Hhhn : burst sideways.

— *Non intres in judicium cum servo tuo, Domine.*

Makes them feel more important to be prayed over in Latin. Requiem mass. Crape weepers. Black edged notepaper. Your name on the altarlist. Chilly place this. Want to feed well, sitting in there all the morning in the gloom kicking his heels waiting for the next please. Eyes of a toad too. What swells him up that way? Molly gets swelled after cabbage. Air of the place maybe. Looks full of up bad gas. Must be an infernal lot of bad gas round the place. Butchers for instance : they get like raw beefsteaks. Who was telling me? Mervyn Brown. Down in the vaults of saint Werburgh's lovely old organ hundred and fifty they have to bore a hole in the coffins sometimes to let out the bad gas and burn it. Out it rushes : blue. One whiff of that and you're a goner.

My kneecap is hurting me. Ow. That's better.

The priest took a stick with a knob at the end of it out of the boy's bucket and shook it over the coffin. Then he walked to the other end and shook it again. Then he came back and put it back in the bucket. As you were before you rested. It's all written down : he has to do it.

— *Et ne nos inducas in tentationem.*

The server piped the answers in the treble. I often thought it would be better to have boy servants. Up to fifteen or so. After that of course...

Holy water that was, I expect. Shaking sleep out of it. He must be fed up with that job, shaking that thing over all the corpses they trot up. What harm if he could see what he was shaking it over. Every mortal day a fresh batch : middleaged men, old women, children, women dead in childbirth, men with beards, baldheaded business men, consumptive girls with little sparrows' breasts. All the year round he prayed the same thing over them all and shook water on top of them : sleep. On Dignam now.

— *In paradisum.*

Said he was going to paradise or is in paradise. Says that over everybody. Tiresome kind of a job. But he has to say something.

The priest closed his book and went off, followed by the server. Corny

Kelleher opened the sidedoors and the gravediggers came in, hoisted the coffin again, carried it out and shoved it on their cart. Corny Kelleher gave one wreath to the boy and one to the brother-in-law. All followed them out of the sidedoors into the mild grey air. Mr Bloom came last, folding his paper again into his pocket. He gazed gravely at the ground till the coffin-cart wheeled off to the left. The metal wheels ground the gravel with a sharp grating cry and the pack of blunt boots followed the barrow along a lane of sepulchres.

The ree the ra the ree the ra the roo. Lord, I mustn't lilt here.

— The O'Connell circle, Mr Dedalus said about him.

Mr Power's soft eyes went up to the apex of the lofty cone.

— He's at rest, he said, in the middle of his people, old Dan O'. But his heart is buried in Rome. How many broken hearts are buried here, Simon!

— Her grave is over there, Jack, Mr Dedalus said. I'll soon be stretched beside her. Let Him take me whenever He likes.

Breaking down, he began to weep to himself quietly, stumbling a little in his walk. Mr Power took his arm.

— She's better where she is, he said kindly.

— I suppose so, Mr Dedalus said with a weak gasp. I suppose she is in heaven if there is a heaven.

Corny Kelleher stepped aside from his rank and allowed the mourners to plod by.

— Sad occasions, Mr Kernan began politely.

Mr Bloom closed his eyes and sadly twice bowed his head.

— The others are putting on their hats, Mr Kernan said. I suppose we can do so too. We are the last. This cemetery is a treacherous place.

They covered their heads.

— The reverend gentleman read the service too quickly, don't you think? Mr Kernan said with reproof.

Mr Bloom nodded gravely, looking in the quick bloodshot eyes. Secret eyes, secret searching eyes. Mason, I think: not sure. Beside him again. We are the last. In the same boat. Hope he'll say something else.

Mr Kernan added:

— The service of the Irish church, used in Mount Jerome, is simpler, more impressive, I must say.

Mr Bloom gave prudent assent. The language of course was another thing.

Mr Kernan said with solemnity:

— *I am the resurrection and the life.* That touches a man's inmost heart.

— It does, Mr Bloom said.

Your heart perhaps but what price the fellow in the six feet by two with his toes to the daisies ? No touching that. Seat of the affections. Broken heart. A pump after all, pumping thousands of gallons of blood every day. One fine day it gets bunged up and there you are. Lots of them lying around here : lungs, hearts, livers. Old rusty pumps : damn the thing else. The resurrection and the life. Once you are dead you are dead. That last day idea. Knocking them all up out of their graves. Come forth, Lazarus ! And he came fifth and lost the job. Get up ! Last day ! Then every fellow mousing around for his liver and his lights and the rest of his traps. Find damn all of himself that morning. Pennyweight of powder in a skull. Twelve grammes one pennyweight. Troy measure.

Corny Kelleher fell into step at their side.

— Everything went off A I, he said. What?

He looked on them from his drawling eye. Policeman's shoulders. With your tooraloom tooraloom.

— As it should be, Mr Kernan said.

— What ? Eh ? Corny Kelleher said.

Mr Kernan assured him.

— Who is that chap behind with Tom Kernan ? John Henry Menton asked. I know his face.

Ned Lambert glanced back.

— Bloom, he said Madam Marion Tweedy that was, is, I mean, the soprano. She's his wife.

— O, to be sure, John Henry Menton said. I haven't seen her for some time. She was a finelooking woman. I danced with her, wait, fifteen seventeen golden years ago, at Mat Dillon's. in Roundtown. And a good armful she was.

He looked behind through the others.

— What is he ? he asked. What does he do ? Wasn't he in the stationery line ? I fell foul of him one evening, I remember, at bowls.

Ned Lambert smiled.

— Yes, he was, he said, in Wisdom Hely's. A traveller for blottingpaper.

— In God's name, John Henry Menton said, what did she marry a coon like that for ? She had plenty of game in her then.

— Has still, Ned Lambert said. He does some canvassing ror ads.

John Henry Menton's large eyes stared ahead.

The barrow turned into a side lane. A portly man, ambushed among the grasses, raised his hat in homage. The gravediggers touched their caps.

— John O'Connell, Mr Power said, pleased. He never forgets a friend.

Mr O'Connell shook all their hands in silence. Mr Dedalus said :

— I am come to pay you another visit.

— My dear Simon, the caretaker answered in a low voice. I don't want your custom at all.

Saluting Ned Lambert and John Henry Menton he walked on at Martin Cunningham's side, puzzling two keys at his back.

— Did you hear that one, he asked them, about Mulcahy from the Coombe ?

— I did not, Martin Cunningham said.

They bent their silk hats in concert and Hynes inclined his ear. The caretaker hung his thumbs in the loops of his gold watch chain and spoke in a discreet tone to their vacant smiles.

— They tell the story, he said, that two drunks came out here one foggy evening to look for the grave of a friend of theirs. They asked for Mulcahy from the Coombe and were told where he was buried. After traipsing about in the fog they found the grave, sure enough. One of the drunks spelt out the name : Terence Mulcahy. The other drunk was blinking up at a statue of our Saviour the widow had got put up.

The caretaker blinked up at one of the sepulchres they passed. He resumed :

— And, after blinking up at the sacred figure, *Not a bloody bit like the man,* says he. *That's not Mulcahy,* says he, *whoever done it.*

Rewarded by smiles he fell back and spoke with Corny Kelleher, accepting the dockets given him, turning them over and scanning them as he walked.

— That's all done with a purpose, Martin Cunningham explained to Hynes.

— I know, Hynes said, I know that.

— To cheer a fellow up, Martin Cunningham said. It's pure goodheartedness : damn the thing else.

Mr Bloom admired the caretaker's prosperous bulk. All want to be on good terms with him. Decent fellow, John O'Connell, real good sort. Keys : like Keyes's ad : no fear of anyone getting out, no passout checks. *Habeat corpus.* I must see about that ad after the funeral. Did I write Ballsbridge on the envelope I took to cover when she disturbed me writing to Martha ? Hope it's not chucked in the dead letter office. Be the better of a shave. Grey sprouting beard. That's the first sign when the hairs come out grey and temper getting cross. Silver threads among the grey. Fancy being his wife. Wonder how he had the gumption to propose to any girl. Come out and live in the graveyard. Dangle that before her. It might thrill her first. Courting death.. Shades of night hovering here with all the dead stretched about. The shadows of the tombs when churchyards yawn and Daniel O' Connell must be a descendant I suppose who is this used to say he was a queer breedy man great catholic all the same like a big giant in the dark. Will o' the wisp. Gas of graves. Want to keep her mind off it to conceive at all. Women especially are so touchy. Tell her a ghost story in bed to make her sleep. Have you ever seen a ghost? Well, I have. It was a pitchdark night. The clock was on the stroke of twelve. Still they 'd kiss all right if properly keyed up. Whores in Turkish graveyards. Learn anything if taken young. You might pick up a young widow here. Men like that. Love among the tombstones. Romeo. Spice of pleasure. In the midst of death we are in life. Both ends meet. Tantalising for the poor dead. Smell of grilled beefsteaks to the starving gnawing their vitals. Desire to grig people. Molly wanting to do it at the window. Eight children he has anyway.

He has seen a fair share go under in his time, lying around him field after field. Holy fields. More room if they buried them standing. Sitting or kneeling you couldn't. Standing? His head might come up some day above ground in a landslip with his hand pointing. All honeycombed the ground must be : oblong cells. And very neat he keeps it too, trim grass and edgings. His garden Major Gamble calls Mount Jerome. Well so it is. Ought to be flowers of sleep. Chinese cemeteries with giant poppies growing produce the best opium Mastiansky told me. The Botanic Gardens are just over there. It's the blood sinking in the earth gives new life. Same idea those jews they said killed the christian boy. Every man his price. Well preserved fat corpse gentleman, epicure, invaluable for fruit garden. A bargain. By carcase of William Wilkinson, auditor and accountant, lately deceased, three pounds thirteen and six. With thanks.

I daresay the soil would be quite fat with corpse manure, bones, flesh, nails, charnelhouses. Dreadful. Turning green and pink, decomposing. Rot quick in damp earth lean. The lean old ones tougher. Then a kind of a tallowy kind of a cheesy. Then begin to get black, treacle oozing out of them. Then dried up. Deathmoths. Of course the cells or whatever they are go on living. Changing about. Live for ever practically. Nothing to feed on feed on themselves.

But they must breed a devil of a lot of maggots. Soil must be simply swirling with them. Your head it simply swurls. Those pretty little seaside gurls. He looks cheerful enough over it. Gives him a sense of power seeing all the others go under first. Wonder how he looks at life. Cracking his jokes too : warms the cockles of his heart. The one about the bulletin. Spurgeon went to heaven 4 a. m. this morning. 11 p. m. (closing time). Not arrived yet. Peter. The dead themselves the men anyhow would like to hear an odd joke or the women to know what's in fashion. A juicy pear or ladies' punch, hot, strong and sweet. Keep out the damp. You must laugh sometimes so better do it that way. Gravediggers in *Hamlet*. Shows the profound knowledge of the human heart. Daren't joke about the dead for two years at least. *De mortuis nil nisi prius*. Go out of mourning first. Hard to imagine his funeral. Seems a sort of a joke. Read your own obituary notice they say you live longer. Gives you second wind. New lease of life.

— How many have you for tomorrow ? the caretaker asked.

— Two, Corny Kelleher said. Half ten and eleven.

The caretaker put the papers in his pocket. The barrow had ceased to trundle. The mourners split and moved to each side of the hole, stepping with care round the graves. The gravediggers bore the coffin and set its nose on the brink, looping the bands round it.

Burying him. We come to bury Cæsar. His ides of March or June. He doesn't know who is here nor care.

Now who is that lankylooking galoot over there in the macintosh? Now who is he I'd like to know? Now, I'd give a trifle to know who he is. Always someone turns up you never dreamt of. A fellow could live on his lonesome all his life. Yes, he could. Still he'd have to get someone to sod him after he died though he could dig his own grave. We all do. Only man buries. No ants too. First thing strikes anybody. Bury the dead. Say Robinson Crusoe was true to life. Well then Friday buried him. Every Friday buries a Thursday if you come to look at it.

O, poor Robinson Crusoe,
How could you possibly do so?

Poor Dignam! His last lie on the earth in his box. When you think of them all it does seem a waste of wood. All gnawed through. They could invent a handsome bier with a kind of panel sliding let it down that way. Ay but they might object to be buried out of another fellow's. They're so particular. Lay me in my native earth. Bit of clay from the holy land. Only a mother and deadborn child ever buried in the one coffin. I see what it means. I see. To protect him as long as possible even in the earth. The Irishman's house is his coffin. Embalming in catacombs, mummies, the same idea.

Mr Bloom stood far back, his hat in his hand, counting the bared heads. Twelve. I'm thirteen. No. The chap in the macintosh is thirteen. Death's number. Where the deuce did he pop out of? He wasn't in the chapel, that I'll swear. Silly superstition that about thirteen.

Nice soft tweed Ned Lambert has in that suit. Tinge of purple. I had one like that when we lived in Lombard street west. Dressy fellow he was once. Used to change three suits in the day. Must get that grey suit of mine turned by Mesias. Hello. It's dyed. His wife I forgot he's not married or his landlady ought to have picked out those threads for him.

The coffin dived out of sight, eased down by the men straddled on the gravetrestles. They struggled up and out : and all uncovered. Twenty.

Pause.

If we were all suddenly somebody else.

Far away a donkey brayed. Rain. No such ass. Never see a dead one, they say. Shame of death. They hide. Also poor papa went away.

Gentle sweet air blew round the bared heads in a whisper. Whisper. The boy by the gravehead held his wreath with both hands staring quietly in the black open space. Mr Bloom moved behind the portly kindly caretaker. Well cut frockcoat. Weighing them up perhaps to see which will go next. Well it is a long rest. Feel no more. It's the moment you feel. Must be damned unpleasant. Can't believe it at first. Mistake must be : someone else. Try the house opposite. Wait, I wanted to. I haven't yet. Then darkened deathchamber. Light they want. Whispering around you. Would you like to see a priest? Then rambling and wandering. Delirium all you hid all your life. The death struggle. His sleep is not natural. Press his lower eyelid. Watching is his nose pointed is his jaw sinking are the soles of his feet yellow. Pull the pillow away and finish it off on the floor since he's doomed. Devil in that picture of sinner's death showing him a woman. Dying to embrace her in his shirt. Last act of *Lucia. Shall I nevermore behold thee?* Bam! expires. Gone at last. People talk about you a bit : forget you. Don't forget to pray for him. Remember him in your prayers. Even Parnell. Ivy day dying out. Then they follow : dropping into a hole one after the other.

We are praying now for the repose of his soul. Hoping you're well and not in hell. Nice change of air. Out of the fryingpan of life into the fire of purgatory.

Does he ever think of the hole waiting for himself? They say you do when you shiver in the sun. Someone walking over it. Callboy's warning. Near you. Mine over there towards Finglas, the plot I bought. Mamma, poor mamma, and little Rudy.

The gravediggers took up their spades and flung heavy clods of clay in on the coffin. Mr Bloom turned his face. And if he was alive all the time? Whew! By Jingo, that would be awful! No, no: he is dead, of course. Of course he is dead. Monday he died. They ought to have some law to pierce the heart and make sure or an electric clock or a telephone in the coffin and some kind of a canvas airhole. Flag of distress. Three days. Rather long to keep them in summer. Just as well to get shut of them as soon as you are sure there'sns.

The clay fell softer. Begin to be forgotten. Out of sight, out of mind.

The caretaker moved away a few paces and put on his hat. Had enough of it. The mourners took heart of grace, one by one, covering themselves without show. Mr Bloom put on his hat and saw the portly figure make its way deftly through the maze of graves. Quietly, sure of his ground, he traversed the dismal fields.

Hynes jotting down something in his notebook. Ah, the names. But he knows them all. No: coming to me.

— I am just taking the names, Hynes said below his breath. What is your christian name? I'm not sure.

— L, Mr Bloom said. Leopold. And you might put down M'Coy's name too. He asked me to.

— Charley, Hynes said writing. I know. He was on the *Freeman* once.

So he was before he got the job in the morgue under Louis Byrne. Good idea a postmortem for doctors. Find out what they imagine they know. He died of a Tuesday. Got the run. Levanted with the cash of a few ads. Charley, you're my darling. That was why he asked me to. O well, does no harm. I saw to that, M'Coy. Thanks, old chap: much obliged. Leave him under an obligation: costs nothing.

— And tell us, Hynes said, do you know that fellow in the, fellow was over there in the...

He looked around.

— Macintosh. Yes I saw him, Mr Bloom said. Where is he now?

— M'Intosh, Hynes said, scribbling. I don't know who he is. Is that his name?

He moved away, looking about him.

— No, Mr Bloom began, turning and stopping. I say, Hynes!

Didn't hear. What? Where has he disappeared to? Not a sign. Well of all the. Has anybody here seen? Kay ee double ell. Become invisible. Good Lord, what became of him?

A seventh gravedigger came beside Mr Bloom to take up an idle spade.

— O, excuse me!

He stepped aside nimbly.

Clay, brown, damp, began to be seen in the hole. It rose. Nearly over. A mound of damp clods rose more, rose, and the gravediggers rested their spades. All uncovered again for a few instants. The boy propped his wreath against a corner: the brother-in-law his on a lump. The gravediggers put on their caps and carried their earthy spades towards the barrow. Then knocked the blades lightly on the turf: clean. One bent to pluck from the haft a long tuft of grass. One, leaving his mates, walked slowly on with shouldered weapon, its blade blueglancing. Silently at the gravehead another coiled the coffinband. His navelcord. The brother-in-law, turning away, placed something in his free hand. Thanks in silence. Sorry, sir: trouble. Headshake. I know that. For yourselves just.

The mourners moved away slowly, without aim, by devious paths, staying awhile to read a name on a tomb.

— Let us go round by the chief's grave, Hynes said. We have time.

— Let us, Mr Power said.

They turned to the right, following their slow thoughts. With awe Mr Power's blank voice spoke:

— Some say he is not in that grave at all. That the coffin was filled with stones. That one day he will come again.

Hynes shook his head.

— Parnell will never come again, he said. He's there, all that was mortal of him. Peace to his ashes.

Mr Bloom walked unheeded along his grove by saddened angels, crosses, broken pillars family vaults, stone hopes praying with upcast eyes, old Ireland's hearts and hands. More sensible to spend the money on some charity for the living. Pray for the repose of the soul of. Does anybody really? Plant him and have done with him. Like down a coalshoot. Then lump them together to save time. All souls' day. Twentyseventh I'll be at his grave. Ten shillings for the gardener. He keeps it free of weeds. Old man himself. Bent down double with his shears clipping. Near death's door. Who passed away. Who departed this life. As if they did it of their own accord. Got the shove, all of them. Who kicked the bucket. More interesting if they told you what they were. So and so, wheelwright. I travelled for cork lino. I paid five shillings in the pound. Or a woman's with her saucepan. I cooked good Irish stew. Eulogy in a country churchyard it ought to be that poem of whose is it Wordsworth or Thomas Campbell. Entered into rest the protestants put it. Old Dr Murren's. The great physician called him home. Well it's God's acre for them. Nice country residence. Newly plastered and painted. Ideal spot to have a quiet smoke and read the *Church Times*. Marriage ads they never try to beautify. Rusty wreaths hung on knobs, garlands of bronzefoil. Better value that for the money. Still, the flowers are more poetical. The other gets rather tiresome, never withering. Expresses nothing. Immortelles.

A bird sat tamely perched on a poplar branch. Like stuffed. Like the wedding present alderman Hooper gave us. Hu ! Not a budge out of him. Knows there are no catapults to let fly at him. Dead animal even sadder. Silly-Milly burying the little dead bird in the kitchen matchbox, a daisychain and bits of broken chainies on the grave.

The Sacred Heart that is : showing it. Heart on his sleeve. Ought to be sideways and red it should be painted like a real heart. Ireland was dedicated to it or whatever that. Seems anything but pleased. Why this infliction ? Would birds come then and peck like the boy with the basket of fruit but he said no because they ought to have been afraid of the boy. Apollo that was.

How many! All these here once walked round Dublin. Faithful departed. As you are now so once were we.

Besides how could you remember everybody ? Eyes, walk, voice. Well, the voice, yes : gramophone. Have a gramophone in every grave or keep it in the house. After dinner on a Sunday. Put on poor old greatgrandfather Kraahraark ! Hellohellohello amawfullyglad kraark awfullygladaseeragain hellohello amarawf kopthsth. Remind you of the voice like the photograph reminds you of the face. Otherwise you couldn't remember the face after fifteen years, say. For instance who ? For instance some fellow that died when I was in Wisdom Hely's.

Rtststr ! A rattle of pebbles. Wait. Stop.

He looked down intently into a stone crypt. Some animal. Wait. There he goes.

An obese grey rat toddled along the side of the crypt, moving the pebbles. An old stager : greatgrandfather : he knows the ropes. The grey alive crushed itself in under the plinth, wriggled itself in under it. Good hidingplace for treasure.

Who lives there ? Are laid the remains of Robert Emery. Robert Emmet was buried here by torchlight, wasn't he ? Making his rounds.

Tail gone now.

One of those chaps would make short work ot a fellow. Pick the bones clean no matter who it was. Ordinary meat for them. A corpse is meat gone bad. Well and what's cheese ? Corpse of milk. I read in that *Voyages in China* that the Chinese say a white man smells like a corpse. Cremation better. Priests dead against it. Devilling for the other firm. Wholesale burners and Dutch oven dealers. Time of the plague. Quicklime fever pits to eat them. Lethal chamber. Ashes to ashes. Or bury at sea. Where is that Parsee tower of silence ? Eaten by birds. Earth, fire, water. Drowning they say is the pleasantest. See your whole life in a flash. But being brought back to life no. Can't bury in the air however. Out of a flying machine. Wonder does the news go about whenever a fresh one is let down. Underground communication. We learned that from them. Wouldn't be surprised. Regular square feed for them. Flies come before he's well dead. Got wind of Dignam. They wouldn't care about the smell of it. Saltwhite crumbling mush of corpse : smell, taste like raw white turnips.

The gates glimmered in front : still open. Back to the world again. Enough of this place. Brings you a bit nearer every time. Last time I was here was Mrs Sinico's funeral. Poor papa too. The love that kills. And even scraping up the earth at night with a lantern like that case I read of to get at fresh buried females or even putrefied with running gravesores. Give you the creeps after a bit. I will appear to you after death. You will see my ghost after death. My ghost will haunt you after death. There is another world after death named hell. I do not like that other world she wrote. No more do I. Plenty to see and hear and feel yet. Feel live warm beings near you. Let them sleep in their maggoty beds. They are not going to get me this innings. Warm beds : warm fullblooded life.

Martin Cunningham emerged from a sidepath, talking gravely.

Solicitor, I think. I know his face. Menton. John Henry, solicitor, commissioner for oaths and affidavits. Dignam used to be in his office. Mat Dillon's long ago. Jolly Mat convivial evenings. Cold fowl, cigars, the Tantalus glasses. Heart of gold really. Yes, Menton. Got his rag out that evening on the bowling green because I sailed inside him. Pure fluke of mine: the bias. Why he took such a rooted dislike to me. Hate at first sight. Molly and Floey Dillon linked under the lilactree, laughing. Fellow always like that mortified if women are by.

Got a dinge in the side of his hat. Carriage probably.

— Excuse me, sir, Mr Bloom said beside them.

They stopped.

— Your hat is a little crushed, Mr Bloom said, pointing.

John Henry Menton stared at him for an instant without moving.

— There, Martin Cunningham helped, pointing also.

John Henry Menton took off his hat, bulged out the dinge and smoothed the nap with care on his coatsleeve. He clapped the hat on his head again.

— It's all right now, Martin Cunningham said.

John Henry Menton jerked his head down in acknowledgment.

— Thank you, he said shortly.

They walked on towards the gates. Mr Bloom, chapfallen, drew behind a few paces so as not to overhear. Martin laying down the law. Martin could wind a sappyhead like that round his little finger without his seeing it.

Oyster eyes. Never mind. Be sorry after perhaps when it dawns on him. Get the pull over him that way.

Thank you. How grand we are this morning!

7 - Aeolus

IN THE HEART OF THE HIBERNIAN METROPOLIS

Before Nelson's pillar trams slowed, shunted, changed trolley started for Blackrock, Kingstown and Dalkey, Clonskea, Rathgar and Terenure, Palmerston park and upper Rathmines, Sandymount, Green Rathmines, Ringsend, and Sandymount Tower, Harold's Cross. The hoarse Dublin United Tramway Company's timekeeper bawled them off :

— Rathgar and Terenure !

— Come on, Sandymount Green !

Right and left parallel clanging ringing a doubledecker and a singledeck moved from their railheads, swerved to the down line, glided parallel.

— Start, Palmerston park !

THE WEARER OF THE CROWN

Under the porch of the general post office shoeblacks called and polished. Parked in North Prince's street His Majesty's vermilion mailcars, bearing on their sides the royal initials, E. R., received loudly flung sacks of letters, postcards, lettecards, parcels, insured and paid, for local, provincial, British and overseas delivery.

GENTLEMEN OF THE PRESS

Grossbooted draymen rolled barrels dullthudding out of Prince's stores and bumped them up on the brewery float. On the brewery float bumped dullthudding barrels rolled by grossbooted draymen out of Prince's stores.

— There it is, Red Murray said. Alexander Keyes.

— Just cut it out, will you? Mr Bloom said, and I'll take it round to the *Telegraph* office.

The door of Ruttledge's office creaked again. Davy Stephens, minute in a large capecoat, a small felt hat crowning his ringlets, passed out with a roll of papers under his cape, a king's courier.

Red Murray's long shears sliced out the advertisement from the newspaper in four clean strokes. Scissors and paste.

— I'll go through the printing works, Mr Bloom said, taking the cut square.

— Of course, if he wants a par, Red Murray said earnestly, a pen behind his ear, we can do him one.

— Right, Mr Bloom said with a nod. I'll rub that in.

We.

WILLIAM BRAYDEN, ESQUIRE, OF OAKLANDS, SANDYMOUNT

Red Murray touched Mr Bloom's arm with the shears and whispered:

— Brayden.

Mr Bloom turned and saw the liveried porter raise his lettered cap as a stately figure entered between the newsboards of the *Weekly Freeman and National Press* and the *Freeman's Journal and National Press*. Dullthudding Guinness's barrels. It passed stately up the staircase steered by an umbrella, a solemn beardframed face. The broadcloth back ascended each step: back. All his brains are in the nape of his neck, Simon Dedalus says. Welts of flesh behind on him. Fat folds of neck, fat, neck, fat, neck.

— Don't you think his face is like Our Saviour? Red Murray whispered.

The door of Ruttledge's office whispered: ee: cree. They always build one door opposite another for the wind to. Way in. Way out.

Our Saviour: beardframed oval face: talking in the dusk Mary, Martha. Steered by an umbrella sword to the footlights: Mario the tenor.

— Or like Mario, Mr Bloom said.

— Yes, Red Murray agreed. But Mario was said to be the picture of Our Saviour.

Jesus Mario with rougy cheeks, doublet and spindle legs. Hand on his heart. In *Martha*.

Co-ome thou lost one,
Co-ome thou dear one

THE CROZIER AND THE PEN

— His grace phoned down twice this morning, Red Murray said gravely.

They watched the knees, legs, boots vanish. Neck.

A telegram boy stepped in nimbly, threw an envelope on the counter and stepped off posthaste with a word.

— *Freeman!*

Mr Bloom said slowly:

— Well, he is one of our saviours also.

A meek smile accompanied him as he lifted the counterflap, as he passed in through the sidedoor and along the warm dark stairs and passage, along the now reverberating boards. But will he save the circulation? Thumping, thumping.

He pushed in the glass swingdoor and entered, stepping over strewn packing paper. Through a lane of clanking drums he made his way towards Nannetti's reading closet.

WITH UNFEIGNED REGRET IT IS WE ANNOUNCE THE DISSOLUTION OF A MOST RESPECTED DUBLIN BURGESS

Hynes here too: account of the funeral probably. Thumping thump. This morning the remains of the late Mr Patrick Dignam. Machines. Smash a man to atoms if they got him caught. Rule the world today. His machineries are pegging away too. Like these, got out of hand: fermenting. Working away, tearing away. And that old grey rat tearing to get in.

HOW A GREAT DAILY ORGAN IS TURNED OUT

Mr Bloom halted behind the foreman's spare body, admiring a glossy crown.

Strange he never saw his real country. Ireland my country. Member for Collegegreen. He boomed that workaday worker tack for all it was worth. It's the ads and side features sell a weekly not the stale news in the official gazette. Queen Anne is dead. Published by authority in the year one thousand and. Demesne situate in the townland of Rosenallis, barony of Tinnachinch. To all whom it may concern schedule pursuant to statute showing return of number of mules and jennets exported from Ballina. Nature notes. Cartoons. Phil Blake's weekly Pat and Bull story. Uncle Toby's page for tiny tots. Country bumpkin's queries. Dear Mr Editor, what is a good cure for flatulence? I'd like that part. Learn a lot teaching others. The personal note M. A. P. Mainly all pictures. Shapely bathers on golden strand. World's biggest balloon. Double marriage of sisters celebrated. Two bridegrooms laughing heartily at each other. Cuprani too, printer. More Irish than the Irish.

The machines clanked in threefour time. Thump, thump, thump. Now if he got paralysed there and no one knew how to stop them they'd clank on and on the same, print it over and over and up and back. Monkeydoodle the whole thing. Want a cool head.

— Well, get it into the evening edition, councillor, Hynes said.

Soon be calling him my lord mayor. Long John is backing him they say.

The foreman, without answering, scribbled press on a corner of the sheet and made a sign to a typesetter. He handed the sheet silently over the dirty glass screen.

— Right: thanks, Hynes said moving off.

Mr Bloom stood in his way.

— If you want to draw the cashier is just going to lunch, he said, pointing backward with his thumb.

— Did you? Hynes asked.

— Mm, Mr Bloom said. Look sharp and you'll catch him.

— Thanks, old man, Hynes said. I'll tap him too.

He hurried on eagerly towards the *Freeman's Journal*.

Three bob I lent him in Meagher's. Three weeks. Third hint.

WE SEE THE CANVASSER AT WORK

Mr Bloom laid his cutting on Mr Nannetti's desk.

— Excuse me, councillor, he said. This ad, you see. Keyes, you remember.

Mr Nannetti considered the cutting a while and nodded.

— He wants it in for July, Mr Bloom said.

He doesn't hear it. Nannan. Iron nerves.

The foreman moved his pencil towards it.

— But wait, Mr Bloom said. He wants it changed. Keyes, you see. He wants two keys at the top.

Hell of a racket they make. Maybe he understands what I.

The foreman turned round to hear patiently and, lifting an elbow, began to scratch slowly in the armpit of his alpaca jacket.

— Like that, Mr Bloom said, crossing his forefingers at the top.

Let him take that in first.

Mr Bloom, glancing sideways up from the cross he had made, saw the foreman's sallow face, think he has a touch of jaundice, and beyond the obedient reels feeding in huge webs of paper. Clank it. Clank it. Miles of it unreeled. What becomes of it after? O, wrap up meat, parcels: various uses, thousand and one things.

Slipping his words deftly into the pauses of the clanking he drew swiftly on the scarred woodwork.

HOUSE OF KEY(E)S

— Like that, see. Two crossed keys here. A circle. Then here the name Alexander Keyes, tea, wine and spirit merchant. So on.

Better not teach him his own business.

— You know yourself, councillor, just what he wants. Then round the top in leaded: the house of keys. You see? Do you think that's a good idea?

The foreman moved his scratching hand to his lower ribs and scratched there quietly.

— The idea, Mr Bloom said, is the house of keys. You know, councillor, the Manx parliament. Innuendo of home rule. Tourists, you know, from the isle of Man. Catches the eye, you see. Can you do that?

I could ask him perhaps about how to pronounce that *voglio*. But then if he didn't know only make it awkward for him. Better not.

— We can do that, the foreman said. Have you the design?

— I can get it, Mr Bloom said. It was in a Kilkenny paper. He has a house there too. I'll just run out and ask him. Well, you can do that and just a little par calling attention. You know the usual. High class licensed premises. Longfelt want. So on.

The foreman thought for an instant.

— We can do that, he said. Let him give us a three months' renewal.

A typesetter brought him a limp galleypage. He began to check it silently. Mr Bloom stood by, hearing the loud throbs of cranks, watching the silent typesetters at their cases.

ORTHOGRAPHICAL

Want to be sure of his spelling. Proof fever. Martin Cunningham forgot to give us his spellingbee conundrum this morning. It is amusing to view the unpar one ar alleled embarra two ars is it ? double ess ment of a harassed pedlar while gauging au the symmetry of a peeled pear under a cemetery wall. Silly, isn't it ? Cemetery put in of course on account of the symmetry.

I could have said when he clapped on his topper. Thank you. I ought to have said something about an old hat or something. No, I could have said. Looks as good as new now. See his phiz then.

Sllt. The nethermost deck of the first machine jogged forward its flyboard with sllt the first batch of quirefolded papers. Sllt. Almost human the way it sllt to call attention. Doing its level best to speak. That door too sllt creaking, asking to be shut. Everything speaks in its own way. Sllt.

NOTED CHURCHMAN AN OCCASIONAL CONTRIBUTOR

The foreman handed back the galleypage suddenly, saying :

— Wait. Where's the archbishop's letter ? It's to be repeated in the *Telegraph*. Where's what's his name ?

He looked about him round his loud unanswering machines.

— Monks, sir ? a voice asked from the castingbox.

— Ay. Where's Monks ?

— Monks !

Mr Bloom took up his cutting. Time to get out.

— Then I'll get the design, Mr Nannetti, he said, and you'll give it a good place I know.

— Monks !

— Yes, sir.

Three months' renewal. Want to get some wind off my chest first. Try it anyhow. Rub in August : good idea : horseshow month. Ballsbridge. Tourists over for the show.

A DAYFATHER

He walked on through the caseroom, passing an old man, bowed, spectacled, aproned. Old Monks, the dayfather. Queer lot of stuff he must have put through his hands in his time : obituary notices, pubs' ads, speeches, divorce suits, found drowned. Nearing the end of his tether now. Sober serious man with a bit in the savingsbank I'd say. Wife a good cook and washer. Daughter working the machine in the parlour. Plain Jane, no damn nonsense.

AND IT WAS THE FEAST OF THE PASSOVER

He stayed in his walk to watch a typesetter neatly distributing type. Reads it backwards first. Quickly he does it. Must require some practice that. mangiD. kcirtaP. Poor papa with his hagadah book, reading backwards with his finger to me. Pessach. Next year in Jerusalem. Dear, O dear ! All that long business about that brought us out of the land of Egypt and into the house of bondage *alleluia. Shema Israel Adonai Elohenu.* No, that's the other. Then the twelve brothers, Jacob's sons. And then the lamb and the cat and the dog and the stick and the water and the butcher and then the angel of death kills the butcher and he kills the ox and the dog kills the cat. Sounds a bit silly till you come to look into it well. Justice it means but it's everybody eating everyone else. That's what life is after all. How quickly he does that job. Practice makes perfect. Seems to see with his fingers.

Mr Bloom passed on out of the clanking noises through the gallery on to the landing. Now am I going to tram it out all the way and then catch him out perhaps. Better phone him up first. Number ? Same as Citron's house. Twentyeight. Twentyeight double four.

ONLY ONCE MORE THAT SOAP

He went down the house staircase. Who the deuce scrawled all over these walls with matches ? Looks as if they did it for a bet. Heavy greasy smell there always is in those works. Lukewarm glue in Thom's next door when I was there.

He took out his handkerchief to dab his nose. Citronlemon ? Ah, the soap I put there. Lose it out of that pocket. Putting back his handkerchief he took out the soap and stowed it away, buttoned, into the hip pocket of his trousers.

What perfume does your wife use? I could go home still: tram: something I forgot. Just to see before dressing. No. Here. No.

A sudden screech of laughter came from the *Evening Telegraph* office. Know who that is. What's up? Pop in a minute to phone. Ned Lambert it is.

He entered softly.

ERIN, GREEN GEM OF THE SILVER SEA

— The ghost walks, professor MacHugh murmured softly, biscuitfully to the dusty windowpane.

Mr Dedalus, staring from the empty fireplace at Ned Lambert's quizzing face, asked of it sourly:

— Agonising Christ, wouldn't it give you a heartburn on your arse?

Ned Lambert, seated on the table, read on:

— *Or again, note the meanderings of some purling rill as it babbles on its way, fanned by gentlest zephyrs tho' quarelling with the stony obstacles, to the tumbling waters of Neptune's blue domain, mid mossy banks, played on by the glorious sunlight or 'neath the shadows cast o'er its pensive bosom by the overarching leafage of the giants of the forest.* What about that, Simon? he asked over the fringe of his newspaper. How's that for high?

— Changing his drink, Mr Dedalus said.

Ned Lambert, laughing, struck the newspaper on his knees, repeating:

— *The pensive bosom and the overarsing leafage.* O boys! O, boys!

— And Xenophon looked upon Marathon, Mr Dedalus said, looking again on the fireplace and to the window, and Marathon looked on the sea.

— That will do, professor MacHugh cried from the window. I don't want to hear any more of the stuff.

He ate off the crescent of water biscuit he had been nibbling and, hungered, made ready to nibble the biscuit in his other hand.

High falutin stuff. Bladderbags. Ned Lambert is taking a day off I see. Rather upsets a man's day a funeral does. He has influence they say. Old Chatterton, the vice-chancellor is his granduncle or his greatgranduncle. Close on ninety they say. Subleader for his death written this long time perhaps. Living to spite them. Might go first himself. Johnny, make room for your uncle. The right honourable Hedges Eyre Chatterton. Daresay he writes him an odd shaky cheque or two on gale days. Windfall when he kicks out. Alleluia.

— Just another spasm, Ned Lambert said.

— What is it? Mr Bloom asked.

— A recently discovered fragment of Cicero's, professor Mac Hugh answered with pomp of tone. *Our lovely land.*

SHORT BUT TO THE POINT

— Whose land? Mr Bloom said simply.

— Most pertinent question, the professor said between his chews. With an accent on the whose.

— Dan Dawson's land, Mr Dedalus said.

— Is it his speech last night? Mr Bloom asked.

Ned Lambert nodded.

— But listen to this, he said.

The doorknob hit Mr Bloom in the small of the back as the door was pushed in.

— Excuse me, J. J. O'Molloy said, entering.

Mr Bloom moved nimbly aside.

— I beg yours, he said.

— Good day, Jack.

— Come in. Come in.

— Good day.

— How are you, Dedalus?

— Well. And yourself?

J. J. O'Molloy shook his head.

SAD

Cleverest fellow at the junior bar he used to be. Decline poor chap. That hectic flush spells finis for a man. Touch and go with him. What's in the wind, I wonder. Money worry.

— *Or again if we but climb the serried mountain peaks.*

— You're looking extra.

— Is the editor to be seen? J. J. O'Molloy asked, looking towards the inner door.

— Very much so, professor MacHugh said. To be seen and heard. He's in his sanctum with Lenehan.

J. J. O'Molloy strolled to the sloping desk and began to turn back the pink pages of the file.

Practice dwindling. A mighthavebeen. Losing heart. Gambling. Debts of honour. Reaping the whirlwind. Used to get good retainers from D. and T. Fitzgerald. Their wigs to show their grey matter. Brains on their sleeve like the statue in Glasnevin. Believe he does some literary work for the *Express* with Gabriel Conroy. Wellread fellow. Myles Crawford began on the *Independent.* Funny the way those newspaper men veer about when they get wind of a new opening. Weathercocks. Hot and cold in the same breath. Wouldn't know which to believe. One story good till you hear the next. Go for one another baldheaded in the papers and then all blows over. Hailfellow well met the next moment.

— Ah, listen to this for God' sake, Ned Lambert pleaded. *Or again if we but climb the serried mountain peaks...*

— Bombast! the professor broke in testily. Enough of the inflated windbag!

— *Peaks,* Ned Lambert went on, *towering high on high, to bathe our souls, as it were...*

— Bathe his lips, Mr Dedalus said. Blessed and eternal God! Yes? Is he taking anything for it.

— *As 'twere, in the peerless panorama of Ireland's portfolio, unmatched, despite their wellpraised prototypes in other vaunted prize regions for very beauty, of bosky grove and undulating plain and luscious pastureland of vernal green, steeped in the transcendent translucent glow of our mild mysterious Irish twilight...*

HIS NATIVE DORIC

— The moon, professor MacHugh said. He forgot Hamlet.

— *That mantles the vista far and wide and wait till the glowing orb of the moon shines forth to irradiate her silver effulgence.*

— O! Mr Dedalus cried, giving vent to to a hopeless groan, shite and onions! That'll do, Ned. Life is too short.

He took off his silk hat and, blowing out impatiently his bushy moustache, welshcombed his hair with raking fingers.

Ned Lambert tossed the newspaper aside, chuckling with delight. An instant after a hoarse bark of laughter burst over professor MacHugh's unshaven blackspectacled face.

— Doughy Daw! he cried.

WHAT WETHERUP SAID

All very fine to jeer at it now in cold print but it goes down like hot cake that stuff. He was in the bakery line too wasn't he? Why they call him Doughy Daw. Feathered his nest well anyhow. Daughter engaged to that chap in the inland revenue office with the motor. Hooked that nicely. Entertainments open house. Big blow out. Wetherup always said that. Get a grip of them by the stomach.

The inner door was opened violently and a scarlet beaked face, crested by a comb of feathery hair, thrust itself in. The bold blue eyes stared about them and the harsh voice asked :

— What is it ?

— And here comes the sham squire himself, professor MacHugh said grandly.

— Getououthat, you bloody old pedagogue ! the editor said in recognition.

— Come, Ned. Mr Dedalus said, putting on his hat. I must get a drink after that.

— Drink ! the editor cried. No drinks served before mass.

— Quite right too, Mr Dedalus said, going out. Come on, Ned.

Ned Lambert sidled down from the table. The editor's blue eyes roved towards Mr Bloom's face, shadowed by a smile.

— Will you join us, Myles ? Ned Lambert asked.

MEMORABLE BATTLES RECALLED

— North Cork militia ! the editor cried, striding to the mantelpiece. We won every time ! North Cork and Spanish officers !

— Where was that, Myles ? Ned Lambert asked with a reflective glance at his toecaps.

— In Ohio ! the editor shouted.

— So it was, begad, Ned Lambert agreed.

Passing out, he whispered to J. J. O'Molloy :

— Incipient jigs. Sad case.

— Ohio ! the editor crowed in high treble from his uplifted scarlet face. My Ohio !

— A perfect cretic ! the professor said. Long, short and long.

O, HARP EOLIAN!

He took a reel of dental floss from his waistcoat pocket and, breaking off a piece, twanged it smartly between two and two of his resonant unwashed teeth.

— Bingbang, bangbang.

Mr Bloom, seeing the coast clear, made for the inner door.

— Just a moment, Mr Crawford, he said. I just want to phone about an ad.

He went in.

— What about that leader this evening? professor MacHugh asked, coming to the editor and laying a firm hand on his shoulder.

— That'll be all right, Myles Crawford said more calmly. Never you fret. Hello, Jack. That's all right.

— Good day, Myles, J. J. O'Molloy said, letting the pages he held slip limply back on the file. Is that Canada swindle case on today?

The telephone whirred inside.

— Twenty eight... No, twenty... Double four... Yes.

SPOT THE WINNER

Lenehan came out of the inner office with *Sport's* tissues.

— Who wants a dead cert for the Gold cup? he asked. Sceptre with O. Madden up.

He tossed the tissues on to the table.

Screams of newsboys barefoot in the hall rushed near and the door was flung open.

— Hush, Lenehan said. I hear feetstoops.

Professor Mac Hugh strode across the room and seized the cringing urchin by the collar as the others scampered out of the hall and down the steps. The tissues rustled up in the draught, floated softly in the air blue scrawls and under the table came to earth.

— It wasn't me, sir. It was the big fellow shoved me, sir.

— Throw him out and shut the door, the editor said. There's a hurricane blowing.

Lenehan began to paw the tissues up from the floor, grunting as he stooped twice.

— Waiting for the racing special, sir, the newsboy said. It was Pat Farrell shoved me, sir.

He pointed to two faces peering in round the doorframe.

— Him, sir.

— Out of this with you, professor Mac Hugh said gruffly.

He hustled the boy out and banged the door to.

J. J. O'Molloy turned the files crackingly over, murmuring, seeking :

— Continued on page six, column four.

— Yes... *Evening Telegraph* here, Mr Bloom phoned from the inner office. Is the boss... ? Yes, *Telegraph*... To where ?... Aha ! Which auction rooms ?... Aha ! I see... Right. I'll catch him.

A COLLISION ENSUES

The bell whirred again as he rang off. He came in quickly and bumped against Lenehan who was struggling up with the second tissue.

— *Pardon, monsieur,* Lenehan said, clutching him for an instant and making a grimace.

— My fault, Mr Bloom said, suffering his grip. Are you hurt ? I'm in a hurry.

— Knee, Lenehan said.

He made a comic face and whined, rubbing his knee :

— The accumulation of the *anno Domini.*

— Sorry, Mr Bloom said.

He went to the door and, holding it ajar, paused. J. J. O'Molloy slapped the heavy pages over. The noise of two shrill voices, a mouthorgan, echoed in the bare hallway from the newsboys squatted on the doorsteps :

We are the boys of Wexford
Who fought with heart and hand.

EXIT BLOOM

— I'm just running round to Bachelor's walk, Mr Bloom said, about this ad of Keyes's. Want to fix it up. They tell me he's round there in Dillon's.

He looked indecisively for a moment at their faces. The editor who, leaning against the mantelshelf, had propped his head on his hand suddenly stretched forth an arm amply.

— Begone! he said. The world is before you.

— Back in no time, Mr Bloom said, hurrying out.

J. J. O'Molloy took the tissues from Lenehan's hand and read them, blowing them apart gently, without comment.

— He'll get that advertisement, the professor said, staring through his blackrimmed spectacles over the crossblind. Look at the young scamps after him.

— Show. Where? Lenehan cried, running to the window.

A STREET CORTEGE

Both smiled over the crossblind at the file of capering newsboys in Mr Bloom's wake, the last zigzagging white on the breeze a mocking kite, a tail of white bowknots.

— Look at the young guttersnipe behind him hue and cry, Lenehan said, and you'll kick. O, my rib risible! Taking off his flat spaugs and the walk. Small nines. Steal upon larks.

He began to mazurka in swift caricature cross the floor on sliding feet past the fireplace to J. J. O'Molloy who placed the tissues in his receiving hands.

— What's that? Myles Crawford said with a start. Where are the other two gone?

— Who? the professor said, turning. They're gone round to the Oval for a drink. Paddy Hooper is there with Jack Hall. Came over last night.

— Come on then, Myles Crawford said. Where's my hat?

He walked jerkily into the office behind, parting the vent of his jacket, jingling his keys in his back pocket. They jingled then in the air and against the wood as he locked his desk drawer.

— He's pretty well on, professor MacHugh said in a low voice.

— Seems to be, J. J. O'Molloy said, taking out a cigarette case in murmuring meditation, but it is not always as it seems. Who has the most matches?

THE CALUMET OF PEACE

He offered a cigarette to the professor and took one himself. Lenehan promptly struck a match for them and lit their cigarettes in turn. J. J. O'Molloy opened his case again and offered it.

— *Thanky vous,* Lenehan said, helping himself.

The editor came from the inner office, a straw hat awry on his brow. He declaimed in song, pointing sternly at professor MacHugh :

'Twas rank and fame that tempted thee,
'Twas empire charmed thy heart.

The professor grinned, locking his long lips.

— Eh ? You bloody old Roman empire ? Myles Crawford said.

He took a cigarette from the open case. Lenehan, lighting it for him with quick grace, said :

— Silence for my brandnew riddle !

— *Imperium romanum,* J. J. O'Molloy said gently. It sounds nobler than British or Brixton. The word reminds one somehow of fat in the fire.

Myles Crawford blew his first puff violently towards the ceiling.

— That's it, he said. We are the fat. You and I are the fat in the fire. We haven't got the chance of a snowball in hell.

THE GRANDEUR THAT WAS ROME

— Wait a moment, professor MacHugh said, raising two quiet claws. We mustn't be led away by words, by sounds of words. We think of Rome, imperial, imperious, imperative.

He extended elocutionary arms from frayed stained shirtcuffs, pausing :

— What was their civilisation ? Vast, I allow : but vile. Cloacae : sewers. The Jews in the wilderness and on the mountaintop said : *It is meet to be here. Let us build an altar to Jehovah.* The Roman, like the Englishman who follows in his footsteps, brought to every new shore on which he set his foot (on our shore he never set it) only his cloacal obsession. He gazed about him in his toga and he said : *Is it meet to be here. Let us construct a watercloset.*

— Which they accordingly did do, Lenehan said, Our old ancient ancestors, as we read in the first chapter of Guinness's, were partial to the running stream.

— They were nature's gentlemen, J. J. O'Molloy murmured. But we have also Roman law.

— And Pontius Pilate is its prophet, professor MacHugh responded.

— Do you know that story about chief baron Palles? J. J. O'Molloy asked. It was at the royal university dinner. Everything was going swimmingly...

— First my riddle, Lenehan said. Are you ready?

Mr O'Madden Burke, tall in copious grey of Donegal tweed, came in from the hallway. Stephen Dedalus, behind him, uncovered as he entered.

— *Entrez, mes enfants!* Lenehan cried.

— I escort a suppliant, M. O'Madden Burke said melodiously. Youth led by Experience visits Notoriety.

— How do you do? the editor said, holding out a hand. Come in. Your governor is just gone.

???

Lenehan said to all :

— Silence! What opera resembles a railway line? Reflect, ponder, excogitate, reply.

Stephen handed over the typed sheets, pointing to the title and signature.

— Who? the editor asked.

Bit torn off.

— Mr Garrett Deasy, Stephen said.

— That old pelters, the editor said. Who tore it? Was he short taken?

On swift sail flaming
From storm and south
He comes, pale vampire,
Mouth to my mouth.

— Good day, Stephen, the professor said, coming to peer over their shoulders. Foot and mouth.? Are you turned...?

Bullockbefriending bard.

SHINDY IN WELLKNOWN RESTAURANT

— Good day, sir, Stephen answered, blushing. The letter is not mine. Mr Garrett Deasy asked me to...

— O, I know him, Myles Crawford said, and knew his wife too. The bloodiest old tartar God ever made. By Jesus, she had the foot and mouth disease and no mistake! The night she threw the soup in the waiter's face in the Star and Garter. Oho!

A woman brought sin into the world. For Helen, the runaway wife of Menelaus, ten years the Greeks. O'Rourke, prince of Breffni.

— Is he a widower? Stephen asked.

— Ay, a grass one, Myles Crawford said, his eye running down the typescript. Emperor's horses. Habsburg. An Irishman saved his life on the ramparts of Vienna. Don't you forget! Maximilian Karl O'Donnell, graf von Tirconnel in Ireland. Sent his heir over to make the king an Austrian fieldmarshal now. Going to be trouble there one day. Wild geese. O yes, every time. Don't you forget that!

— The moot point is did he forget it, J. J. O'Molloy said quietly, turning a horseshoe paperweight. Saving princes is a thank you job.

Professor MacHugh turned on him.

— And if not? he said.

— I'll tell you how it was, Myles Crawford began. A Hungarian it was one day...

LOST CAUSES
NOBLE MARQUESS MENTIONED

— We were always loyal to lost causes, the professor said. Success for us is the death of the intellect and of the imagination. We were never loyal to the successful. We serve them. I teach the blatant Latin language. I speak the tongue of a race the acme of whose mentality is the maxim: time is money. Material domination. *Dominus!* Lord! Where is the spirituality? Lord Jesus! Lord Salisbury. A sofa in a westend club. But the Greek!

KYRIE ELEISON!

A smile of light brightened his darkrimmed eyes, lengthened his long lips.

— The Greek! he said again. *Kyrios!* Shining word! The vowels the Semite and the Saxon know not. *Kyrie!* The radiance of the intellect. I ought to profess Greek, the language of the mind. *Kyrie eleison!* The closetmaker and the cloacamaker will never be lords of our spirit. We are liege subjects of the catholic chivalry of Europe that foundered at Trafalgar and of the empire of the spirit, not an *imperium*, that went under with the Athenian fleets at Ægospotami. Yes, yes. They went under. Pyrrhus, misled by an oracle, made a last attempt to retrieve the fortunes of Greece. Loyal to a lost cause.

He strode away from them towards the window.

— They went forth to battle, Mr O'Madden Burke said greyly, but they always fell.

— Boohoo! Lenehan wept with a little noise. Owing to a brick received in the latter half of the *matinée*. Poor, poor, poor Pyrrhus!

He whispered then near Stephen's ear:

LENEHAN'S LIMERICK

— *There's a ponderous pundit MacHugh*
Who wears goggles of ebony hue.
As he mostly sees double
To wear them why trouble?
I can't see the Joe Miller. Can you?

In mourning for Sallust, Mulligan says. Whose mother is beastly dead.

Myles Crawford crammed the sheets into a sidepocket.

— That'll be all right, he said. I'll read the rest after. That'll be all right.

Lenehan extended his hands in protest.

— But my riddle! he said. What opera is like a railway line?

— Opera? Mr O'Madden Burke's sphinx face reriddled.

Lenehan announced gladly:

— *The Rose of Castiile*. See the wheeze? Rows of cast steel. Gee!

He poked Mr O'Madden Burke mildly in the spleen. Mr O'Madden Burke fell back with grace on his umbrella, feigning a gasp.

— Help! he sighed. I feel a strong weakness.

Lenehan, rising to tiptoe, fanned his face rapidly with the rustling tissues.

The professor, returning by way of the files, swept his hand across Stephen's and Mr O'Madden Burke's loose ties.

— Paris, past and present, he said. You look like communards.

— Like fellows who had blown up the Bastille, J. J. O'Molloy said in quiet mockery. Or was it you shot the lord lieutenant of Finland between you? You look as though you had done the deed. General Bobrikoff.

OMNIUM GATHERUM

— We were only thinking about it, Stephen said.

— All the talents, Myles Crawford said Law, the classics...

— The turf, Lenehan put in.

— Literature, the press.

— If Bloom were here, the professor said. The gentle art of advertisement.

— And Madam Bloom, Mr O'Madden Burke added. The vocal muse. Dublin's prime favourite.

Lenehan gave a loud cough.

— Ahem! he said very softly. O, for a fresh of breath air! I caught a co ldin the park. The gate was open.

« YOU CAN DO IT! »

The editor laid a nervous hand on Stephen's shoulder.

— I want you to write something for me, he said. Something with a bite in it. You can do it. I see it in your face. *In the lexicon of youth...*

See it in your face. See it in your eye. Lazy idle little schemer.

— Foot and mouth disease! the editor cried in scornful invective. Great nationalist meeting in Borris-in-Ossory. All balls! Bulldosing the public! Give them something with a bite in it. Put us all into it, damn its soul. Father, Son and Holy Ghost and Jakes M' Carthy.

— We can all supply metanl pabulum, Mr O'Madden Burke said.

Stephen raised his eyes to the bold unheeding stare.

— He wants you for the pressgang, J. J. O'Molloy said.

THE GREAT GALLAHER

— You can do it, Myles Crawford repeated, clenching his hand in emphasis. Wait a minute. We'll paralyse Europe as Ignatius Gallaher used to say when he was on the shaughraun, doing billiardmarking in the Clarence. Gallaher, that was a pressman for you. That was a pen. You know how he made his mark? I'll tell you. That was the smartest piece of journalism ever known. That was in eightyone, sixth of May, time of the invincibles, murder in the Phœnix park, before you were born, I suppose. I'll show you.

He pushed past them to the files.

— Look at here, he said, turning. The *New York World* cabled for a special. Remember that time?

Professor MacHugh nodded.

— *New York World,* the editor said, excitedly pushing back his straw hat, Where it took place. Tim Kelly, or Kavanagh I mean, Joe Brady and the rest of them. Where Skin-the-goat drove the car. Whole route, see?

— Skin-the-goat, Mr O'Madden Burke said. Fitzharris. He has that cabman's shelter, they say, down there at Butt bridge. Holohan told me. You know Holehan?

— Hop and carry one, is it? Myles Crawford said.

— And poor Gumley is down there too, so he told me, minding stones for the corporation. A night watchman.

Stephen turned in surprise.

— Gumley? he said. You don't say so? A friend of my father's, is he?

— Never mind Gumley, Myles Crawford cried angrily. Let Gumley mind the stones, see they don't run away. Look at here. What did Ignatius Gallaher do? I'll tell you. Inspiration of genius. Cabled right away. Have you *Weekly Freeman* of 17 March? Right. Have you got that?

He flung back pages of the files and stuck his finger on a point.

— Take page four, advertisement for Bransome's coffee let us say. Have you got that? Right.

The telephone whirred.

A DISTANT VOICE

— I'll answer it, the professor said going.

— B is parkgate. Good.

His finger leaped and struck point after point, vibrating.

— T is viceregal lodge. C is where murder took place. K is Knockmaroon gate.

The loose flesh of his neck shook like a cock's wattles. An illstarched dicky jutted up and with a rude gesture he thrust it back into his waistcoat.

— Hello? *Evening Telegraph* here... Hello?... Who's there?... Yes... Yes... Yes...

— F to P is the route Skin-the-goat drove the car for an alibi. Inchicore, Roundtown, Windy Arbour, Palmerston Park, Ranelagh. F. A. B. P. Got that? X is Davy's publichouse in upper Leeson street.

The professor came to the inner door.

— Bloom is at the telephone, he said.

— Tell him go to hell, the editor said promptly. X is Burke's public house, see ?

CLEVER, VERY

— Clever, Lenehan said. Very.

— Gave it to them on a hot plate, Myles Crawford said, the whole bloody history.

Nightmare from which you will never awake.

— I saw it, the editor said proudly. I was present, Dick Adams, the besthearted bloody Corkman the Lord ever put the breath of life in, and myself.

Lenehan bowed to a shape of air, announcing :

— Madam, I'm Adam. And Able was I ere I saw Elba.

— History ! Myles Crawford cried. The Old Woman of Prince's street was there first. Thee was weeping and gnashing of teeth over that. Out of an advertisement. Gregor Grey made the design for it. That gave him the leg up. Then Paddy Hooper worked Tay Pay who took him on to the *Star*. Now he's got in with Blumenfeld. That's press. That's talent. Pyatt ! He was all their daddies.

— The father of scare journalism, Lenehan confirmed, and the brother-in-law of Chris Callinan.

— Hello ?... Are you there ?... Yes, he's here still. Come across yourself.

— Where do you find a pressman like that now, eh ? the editor cried.

He flung the pages down.

— Clamn dever, Lenehan said to Mr O'Madden Burke.

— Very smart, Mr O'Madden Burke said.

Professor MacHugh came from the inner office.

— Talking about the invincibles, he said, did you see that some hawkers were up before the recorder...

— O yes, J. J. O'Molloy said eagerly. Lady Dudley was walking home through the park to see all the trees that were blown down by that cyclone last year and thought she'd buy a view of Dublin. And it turned out to be a commemoration postcard of Joe Brady or Number One or Skin-the-goat. Right outside the viceregal lodge, imagine !

— They're only in the hook and eye department, Myles Crawford said.

Psha ! Press and the bar! Where have you a man now at the bar like those fellows, like Whiteside, like Isaac Butt, like silvertongued O'Hagan ? Eh ? Ah, bloody nonsense ! Only in the halfpenny place !

His mouth continued to twitch unspeaking in nervous curls of disdain.

Would anyone wish that mouth for her kiss ? How do you know ? Why did you write it then ?

RHYMES AND REASONS

Mouth, south. Is the mouth south someway ? Or the south a mouth ? Must be some. South, pout, out, shout, drouth. Rhymes: two men dressed the same, looking the same, two by two.

. . . . *la tua pace*
. . . . *che parlar ti piace*
. . . . *mentreche il vento, come fa, si tace.*

He saw them three by three, approaching girls, in green, in rose, in russet, entwining, *per l'aer perso* in mauve, in purple, *quella pacifica oriafiamma,* in gold of oriflamme, *di rimirar fè più ardenti.* But I old men, penitent, leadenfooted, underdarkneath the night : mouth south : tomb womb.

— Speak up for yourself, Mr O'Madden Burke said.

SUFFICIENT FOR THE DAY...

J. J. O'Molloy, smiling palely, took up the gage.

— My dear Myles, he said, flinging his cigarette aside, you put a false construction on my words. I hold no brief, as at present advised, for the third profession *qua* profession but your Cork legs are running away with you. Why not bring in Henry Grattan and Flood and Demosthenes and Edmund Burke ? Ignatius Gallaher we all know and his Chapelizod boss, Harmsworth of the farthing press, and his American cousin of the Bowery gutter sheet not to mention *Paddy Kelly's Budget*, *Pue's Occurrences* and our watchful friend *The Skibereen Eagle.* Why bring in a master of forensic eloquence like Whiteside ? Sufficient for the day is the newspaper thereof.

LINKS WITH BYGONE DAYS OF YORE

— Grattan and Flood wrote for this very paper, the editor cried in his face. Irish volunteers. Where are you now? Established 1763. Dr Lucas. Who have you now like John Philpot Curran? Psha!

— Well, J. J. O'Molloy said, Bushe K. C., for example.

— Bushe? the editor said. Well, yes. Bushe, yes. He has a strain of it in his blood. Kendal Bushe or I mean Seymour Bushe.

— He would have been on the bench long ago, the professor said, only for... But no matter.

J. J. O'Molloy turned to Stephen and said quietly and slowly:

— One of the most polished periods I think I ever listened to in my life fell from the lips of Seymour Bushe. It was in that case of fratricide, the Childs murder case. Bushe defended him.

And in the porches of mine ear did pour.

By the way how did he find that out? He died in his sleep. Or the other story, beast with two backs?

— What was that? the professor asked.

ITALIA, MAGISTRA ARTIUM

— He spoke on the law of evidence, J. J. O'Molloy said, of Roman justice as contrasted with the earlier Mosaic code, the *lex talionis*. And he cited the Moses of Michelangelo in the Vatican.

— Ha.

— A few wellchosen words, Lenehan prefaced. Silence!

Pause. J. J. O'Mollooy too kout his cigarette case.

False lull. Something quite ordinary.

Messenger took out his match box thoughtfully and lit his cigar.

I have often thought since on looking back over that strange time that it was that small act, trivial in itself, that striking of that match, that determined the whole aftercourse of both our lives.

A POLISHED PERIOD

J. J. O'Molloy resumed, moulding his words:

— He said of it: *that stony effigy in frozen music, horned and terrible, of the human form divine, that eternal symbol of wisdom and prophecy which, if aught that the imagination or the hand of sculptor has wrought in marble of soultransfigured and of soultransfiguring deserves to live, deserves to live.*

His slim hand with a wave graced echo and fall.

— Fine! Myles Crawford said at once.

— The divine afflatus, Mr O'Madden Burke said.

— You like it? J. J. O'Molloy asked Stephen.

Stephen, his blood wooed by grace of language and gesture, blushed. He took a cigarette from the case. J. J. O'Molloy offered his case to Myles Crawford. Lenehan lit their cigarettes as before and took his trophy, saying:

— Muchibus thankibus.

A MAN OF HIGH MORALE

— Professor Magennis was speaking to me about you, J. J. O'Molloy said to Stephen. What do you think really of that hermetic crowd, the opal hush poets: A. E. the master mystic? That Blavatsky woman started it. She was a nice old bag of tricks. A. E. has been telling some yankee interviewer that you came to him in the small hours of the morning to ask him about planes of consciousness. Magennis thinks you must have been pulling A. E.'s leg. He is a man of the very highest morale, Magennis.

Speaking about me. What did he say? What did he say? What did he say about me? Don't ask.

— No, thanks, professor MacHugh said, waving the cigarette case aside. Wait a moment. Let me say one thing. The finest display of oratory I ever heard was a speech made by John F. Taylor at the college historical society. Mr Justice Fitzgibbon, the present lord justice of appeal, had spoken and the paper under debate was an essay (new for those days), advocating the revival of the Irish tongue.

He turned towards Myles Crawford and said:

— You know Gerald Fitzgibbon. Then you can imagine the style of his discourse.

— He is sitting withim T Healy, J. J. O'Molloy said, rumour has it, on the Trinity college estates commission.

— He is sitting with a sweet thing in a child's frock, Myles Crawford said. Go on. Well?

— It was the speech, mark you, the professor said, of a finished orator, full of courteous haughtiness and pouring in chastened diction, I will not say the vials of his wrath but pouring the proud man's contumely upon the new movement. It was then a new movement. We were weak, therefore worthless.

He closed his long thin lips an instant but, eager to be on, raised an outspanned hand to his spectacles and, with trembling thumb and ringfinger touching lightly the black rims, steadied them to a new focus.

IMPROMPTU

In ferial tone he addressed J. J. O'Molloy :

— Taylor had come there, you must know, from a sick bed. That he had prepared his speech I do not believe for there was not even one shorthandwriter in the hall. His dark lean face had a growth of shaggy beard round it. He wore a loose neckcloth and altogether he looked (though he was not) a dying man.

His gaze turned at once but slowly from J. J. O'Molloy's towards Stephen's face and then bent at once to the ground, seeking. His unglazed linen collar appeared behind his bent head, soiled by his withering hair. Still seeking, he said :

— When Fitzgibbon's speech had ended John F. Taylor rose to reply. Briefly, as well as I can bring them to mind, his words were these.

He raised his head firmly. His eyes bethought themselves once more. Witless shellfish swam in the gross lenses to and fro, seeking outlet.

He began :

— *Mr chairman, ladies and gentlemen : Great was my admiration in listening to the remarks addressed to the youth of Ireland a moment since by my learned friend. It senned to me that I had been transported into a country far away from this country, into an age remote from this age, that I stood in ancient Egypt and that I was listening to the speech of some highpriest of that land addressed to the youthful Moses.*

His listeners held their cigarettes poised to hear, their smokes ascending in frail stalks that flowered with his speech. *And let our crooked smokes.* Noble words coming. Look out. Could you try your hand at it yourself?

— *And it seemed to me that I heard the voice of that Egyptian highpriest raised in a tone of like haughtiness and like pride. I heard his words and their meaning was revealed to me.*

FROM THE FATHERS

It was revealed to me that those things are good which yet are corrupted which neither if they were supremely good nor unless they were good, could be corrupted. Ah, curse you! That's saint Augustine.

— *Why will you jews not accept our culture, our religion and our language? You are a tribe of nomad herdsmen; we are a mighty people. You have no cities nor no wealth: our cities are hives of humanity and our galleys, trireme and quadrireme, laden with all manner merchandise furrow the waters of the known globe. You have but emerged from primitive conditions: we have a literature, a priesthood, an agelong history and a polity.*

Nile.

Child, man, effigy.

By the Nilebank the babemaries kneel, cradle of bulrushes: a man supple in combat: stonehorned, stonebearded, heart of stone.

— *You pray to a local and obscure idol: our temples, majestic and mysterious, are the abodes of Isis and Osiris, of Horus and Ammon Ra. Yours serfdom, awe and humbleness: ours thunder and the seas. Israel is weak and few are her children: Egypt is an host and terrible are her arms. Vagrants aud daylabourers are you called: the world trembles at our name.*

A dumb belch of hunger cleft his speech. He lifted his voice above it boldly:

— *But, ladies and gentlemen, had the youthful Moses listened to and accepted that view of life, had he bowed his head and bowed his will and bowed his spirit before that arrogant admonition he would never have brought the chosen people out of their house of bondage nor followed the pillar of the cloud by day. He would never have spoken with the Eternal amid lightnings on Sinai's mountaintop nor ever have come down with the light of inspiration shining in his countenance and bearing in his arms the tables of the law, graven in the language of the outlaw.*

He ceased and looked at them, enjoying silence.

OMINOUS — FOR HIM!

J. J. O'Molloy said not without regret:

— And yet he died without having entered the land of promise.

— A-sudden-at-the-moment-though-from-lingering-illness-often-previously-expectorated-demise, Lenehan said. And with a great future behind him.

The troop of bare feet was heard rushing along the hallway and pattering up the staircase.

— That is oratory, the professor said, uncontradicted.

Gone with the wind. Hosts at Mullaghmast and Tara of the kings.

Miles of ears of porches. The tribune's words howled and scattered to the four winds. A people sheltered within his voice. Dead noise. Akasic records of all that ever anywhere wherever was. Love and laud him : me no more.

I have money.

— Gentlemen, Stephen said. As the next motion on the agenda paper may I suggest that the house do now adjourn ?

— You take my breath away. It is not perchance a French compliment? Mr O'Madden Burke asked. 'Tis the hour, methinks, when the winejug, metaphorically speaking, is most grateful in Ye ancient hostelry.

— That it be and hereby is resolutely resolved. All who are in favour say ay, Lenehan announced. The contrary no. I declare it carried. To which particular boosing shed...? My casting vote is : Mooney's!

He led the way, admonishing :

— We will sternly refuse to partake of strong waters, will we not? Yes, we will not. By no manner of means.

Mr O'Madden Burke, following close, said with an ally's lunge of his umbrella :

— Lay on, Macduff!

— Chip of the old block! the editor cried, slapping Stephen on the shoulder. Let us go. Where are those blasted keys?

He fumbled in his pocket, pulling out the crushed typesheets.

— Foot and mouth. I know. That'll be all right. That'll go in. Where are they? That's all night.

He thrust the sheets back and went into the inner office.

LET US HOPE

J. J. O'Molloy, about to follow him in, said quietly to Stephen :

— I hope you will live to see it published. Myles, one moment.

He went into the inner office, closing the door behind him.

— Come along, Stephen, the professor said. That is fine, isn't it? It has the prophetic vision. *Fuit Ilium!* The sack of windy Troy. Kingdoms of this world. The masters of the Mediterranean are fellaheen today.

The first newsboy came pattering down the stairs at their heels and rushed out into the street, yelling :

— Racing special!

Dublin. I have much, much to learn.

They turned to the left along Abbey street.

— I have a vision too, Stephen said.

— Yes, the professor said, skipping to get into step. Crawford will follow.

Another newsboy shot past them, yelling as he ran :

— Racing special!

DEAR DIRTY DUBLIN

Dubliners.

— Two Dublin vestals, Stephen said, elderly and pious, have lived fifty and fiftythree years in Fumbally's lane.

— Where is that? the professor asked.

— Off Blackpitts.

Damp night reeking of hungry dough. Against the wall. Face glistening tallow under her fustian shawl. Frantic hearts. Akasic records. Quicker, darlint!

On now. Dare it. Let there be life.

— They want to see the views of Dublin from the top of Nelson's pillar. They save up three and in tenpence a red tin letterbox moneybox. They shake out the threepenny bits and a sixpence and coax out the pennies with the blade of a knife. Two and three in silver and one and seven in coppers. They put on their bonnets and best clothes and take their umbrellas for fear it may come on to rain.

— Wise virgins, professor Mac Hugh said.

LIFE ON THE RAW

— They buy one and fourpenceworth of brawn and four slices of panloaf at the north city dining rooms in Marlborough street from Miss Kate Collins, proprietress... They purchase four and twenty ripe plums from a girl at the foot of Nelson's pillar to take off the thirst of the brawn. They give two threepenny bits to the gentleman at the turnstile and begin to waddle slowly up the winding staircase, grunting, encouraging each other, afraid of the dark, panting, one asking the other have you the brawn, praising God and the Blessed Virgin, threatening to come down, peeping at the airslits. Glory be to God. They had no idea it was that high.

Their names are Anne Kearns and Florence Mac Cabe. Anne Kearns has the lumbago for which she rubs on Lourdes water given her by a lady who got a bottleful from a passionist father. Florence MacCabe takes a crubeen and a bottle of double X for supper every Saturday.

— Antithesis, the professor said, nodding twice. Vestal virgins. I can see them. What's keeping our friend ?

He turned.

A bevy of scampering newsboys rushed down the steps, scampering in all directions, yelling, their white papers fluttering. Hard after them Myles Crawford appeared on the steps, his hat aureoling his scarlet face, talking with J. J. O'Molloy.

— Come along, the professor cried, waving his arm.

He set off again to walk by Stephen's side.

RETURN OF BLOOM

— Yes, he said. I see them.

Mr Bloom, breathless, caught in a whirl of wild newsboys near the offices of the *Irish Catholic* and *Dublin Penny Journal,* called :

— Mr Crawford ! A moment !

— *Telegraph* ! Racing spécial !

— What is it ? Myles Crawford said, falling back a pace.

A newsboy cried in Mr Bloom's face :

— Terrible tragedy in Rathmines ! A child bit by a bellows !

INTERVIEW WITH THE EDITOR

— Just this ad, Mr Bloom said, pushing through towards the steps, puffing, and taking the cutting from his pocket. I spoke with Mr Keyes just now. He'll give a renewal for two months, he says. After he'll see. But he wants a par to call attention in the *Telegraph* too, the Saturday pink. And he wants it if it's not too late I told councillor Nannetti from the *Kilkenny People.* I can have access to it in the national library. House of keys, don't you see ? His name is Keyes. It's a play on the name. But he practically promised he'd give the renewal. But he wants just a little puff. What will I tell him, Mr Crawford ?

K. M. A.

— Will you tell him he can kiss my arse ? Myles Crawford said, throwing out his arm for emphasis. Tell him that straight from the stable.

A bit nervy. Look out for squalls. All off for a drink. Arm in arm. Lenehan's yachting cap on the cadge beyond. Usual blarney. Wonder is that young Dedalus the moving spirit. Has a good pair of boots on him today. Last time I saw him he had his heels on view. Been walking in muck somewhere. Careless chap. What was he doing in Irishtown?

— Well, Mr Bloom said, his eyes returning, if I can get the design I suppose it's worth a short par. He'd give the ad I think. I'll tell him...

K. M. R. I. A.

— He can kiss my royal Irish arse, Myles Crawford cried loudly over his shoulder. Any time he likes, tell him.

While Mr Bloom stood weighing the point and about to smile he strode on jerkily.

RAISING THE WIND

— *Nulla bona,* Jack, he said, raising his hand to his chin. I'm up to here. I've been through the hoop myself. I was looking for a fellow to back a bill for me no later than last week. You must take the will for the deed. Sorry, Jack. With a heart and a half if I could raise the wind anyhow.

J. J. O'Molloy pulled a long face and walked on silently. They caught up on the others and walked abreast.

— When they have eaten the brawn and the bread and wiped their twenty fingers in the paper the bread was wrapped in, they go nearer to the railings.

— Something for you, the professor explained to Myles Crawford. Two old Dublin women on the top of Nelson's pillar.

SOME COLUMN! — THAT'S WHAT WADDLER ONE SAID

— That's new, Myles Crawford said. That's copy. Out for the waxies' Dargle. Two old trickies, what?

— But they are afraid the pillar will fall, Stephen went on. They see the roofs and argue about where the different churches are: Rathmines'blue dome, Adam and Eve's, saint Laurence O'Toole's. But it makes them giddy to look so they pull up their skirts...

THOSE SLIGHTLY RAMBUNCTIOUS FEMALES

— Easy all, Myles Crawford said, no poetic licence. We're in the archdiocese here.

— And settle down on their striped petticoats, peering up at the statue of the onehandled adulterer.

— Onehandled adulterer! the professor cried. I like that. I see the idea. I see what you mean.

DAMES DONATE DUBLIN'S CITS SPEEDPILLS VELOCITOUS AEROLITHS, BELIEF

— It gives them a crick in their necks, Stephen said, and they are too tired to look up or down or to speak. They put the bag of plums between them and eat the plums out of it, one after another, wiping off with their handkerchiefs the plumjuice that dribbles out of their mouths and spitting the plumstones slowly out between the railings.

He gave a sudden loud young laugh as a close. Lenehan and Mr O'Madden Burke, hearing, turned, beckoned and led on across towards Mooney's.

— Finished? Myles Crawford said. So long as they do no worse.

SOPHIST WALLOPS HAUGHTY HELEN SQUARE ON PROBOSCIS. SPARTANS GNASH MOLARS. ITHACANS VOW PEN IS CHAMP.

— You remind me of Antisthenes, the professor said, a disciple of Gorgias, the sophist. It is said of him that none could tell if he were bitterer against others or against himself. He was the son of a noble and a bondwoman. And he wrote a book in which he took away the palm of beauty from Argive Helen and handed it to poor Penelope.

Poor Penelope. Penelope Rich.

They made ready to cross O'Connell street.

HELLO THERE, CENTRAL!

At various points along the eight lines tramcars with motionless trolleys stood in their tracks, bound for or from Rathmines, Rathfarnham, Kingstown,

Blackrock and Dalkey, Sandymount Green, Ringsend and Sandymount tower Donnybrook, Palmerston Park and Upper Rathmines, all still, becalmed in short circuit. Hackney cars, cabs, delivery waggons, mailvans, private broughams, aerated mineral water floats with rattling crates of bottles, rattled, rolled, horsedrawn, rapidly.

WHAT? — AND LIKEWISE — WHERE?

— But what do you call it? Myles Crawford asked. Where did they get the plums?

VIRGILIAN, SAYS PEDAGOGUE. SOPHOMORE PLUMPS FOR OLD MAN MOSES

— Call it, wait, the professor said, opening his long lips wide to reflect. Call it, let me see. Call it: *deus nobis hæc otia fecit.*

— No, Stephen said, I call it *A Pisgah Sight of Palestine or The Parable of The Plums.*

— I see, the professor said.

He laughed richly.

— I see, he said again with new pleasure. Moses and the promised land. We gave him that idea, he added to J. J. O'Molloy.

HORATIO IS CYNOSURE THIS FAIR JUNE DAY

J. J. O'Molloy sent a weary sidelong glance towards the statue and held his peace.

— I see, the professor said.

He halted on sir John Gray's pavement island and peered aloft at Nelson through the meshes of his wry smile.

DIMINISHED DIGITS PROVE TOO TITILLATING FOR FRISKY FRUMPS. ANNE WIMBLES, FLO WANGLES — YET CAN YOU BLAME THEM?

— Onehandled adulterer, he said grimly. That tickles me I must say.

— Tickled the old ones too, Myles Crawford said, if the God Almighty's truth was known.

8- Lestrygonians

Pineapple rock, lemon platt, butter scotch. A sugarsticky girl shovelling scoopfuls of creams for a christian brother. Some school treat. Bad for their tummies. Lozenge and comfit manufacturer to His Majesty the King. God. Save. Our. Sitting on his throne, sucking red jujubes white.

A sombre Y. M. C. A. young man, watchful among the warm sweet fumes of Graham Lemon's, placed a throwaway in a hand of Mr Bloom.

Heart to heart talks.

Bloo... Me? No.

Blood of the Lamb.

His slow feet walked him riverward, reading. Are you saved? All are washed in the blood of the lamb. God wants blood victim. Birth, hymen, martyr, war, foundation of a building, sacrifice, kidney burntoffering, druids' altars. Elijah is coming. Dr John Alexander Dowie, restorer of the church in Zion, is coming.

Is coming! Is coming!! Is coming!!!
All heartily welcome.

Paying game. Torry and Alexander last year. Polygamy. His wife will put the stopper on that. Where was that ad some Birmingham firm the luminous crucifix? Our Saviour. Wake up in the dead of night and see him on the wall, hanging. Pepper's ghost idea. Iron nails ran in.

Phosphorous it must be done with. If you leave a bit of codfish for instance. I could see the bluey silver over it. Night I went down to the pantry in the kitchen. Don't like all the smells in it waiting to rush out. What was it she wanted? The Malaga raisins. Thinking of Spain. Before Rudy was born. The phosphorescence, that bluey greeny. Very good for the brain.

From Butler's monument house corner he glanced along Bachelor's walk.

Dedalus' daughter there still outside Dillon's auctionrooms. Must be selling off some old furniture. Knew her eyes at once from the father. Lobbing about waiting for him. Home always breaks up when the mother goes. Fifteen children he had. Birth every year almost. That's in their theology or the priest won't give the poor woman the confession, the absolution. Increase and multiply. Did you ever hear such an idea? Eat you out of house and home. No families themselves to feed. Living on the fat of the land. Their butteries and larders. I'd like to see them do the black fast Yom Kippur. Crossbuns. One meal and a collation for fear he'd collapse on the altar. A housekeeper of one of those fellows if you could pick it out of her. Never pick it out of her. Like getting L. s. d. out of him. Does himself well. No guests. All for number one. Watching his water. Bring your own bread and butter. His reverence mum's the word.

Good Lord, that poor child's dress is in flitters. Underfed she looks too. Potatoes and marge, marge and potatoes. It's after they feel it. Proof of the pudding. Undermines the constitution.

As he set foot on O'Connell bridge a puffball of smoke plumed up from the parapet. Brewery barge with export stout. England. Sea air sours it, I heard. Be interesting some day get a pass through Hancock to see the brewery. Regular world in itself. Vats of porter, wonderful. Rats get in too. Drink themselves bloated as big as a collie floating. Dead drunk on the porter. Drink till they puke again like christians. Imagine drinking that! Rats : vats. Well of course if we knew all the things.

Looking down he saw flapping strongly, wheeling between the gaunt quay walls, gulls. Rough weather outside. If I threw myself down? Reuben J's son must have swallowed a good bellyful of that sewage. One and eightpence too much. Hhhhm'. It's the droll way he comes out with the things. Knows how to tell a story too.

They wheeled lower. Looking for grub. Wait.

He threw down among them a crumpled paper ball. Elijah thirtytwo feet per sec is com. Not a bit. The ball bobbed unheeded on the wake of swells, floated under by the bridge piers. Not such damn fools. Also the day I threw that stale cake out of the Erin's King picked it up in the wake fifty yards astern. Live by their wits. They wheeled, flapping.

The hungry famished gull.
Flaps o'er the waters dull.

That is how poets write, the similar sounds. But then Shakespeare has no rhymes: blank verse. The flow of the language it is. The thoughts. Solemn.

Hamlet, I am thy father's spirit
Doomed for a certain time to walk the earth.

— Two apples a penny! Two for a penny!

His gaze passed over the glazed apples serried on her stand. Australians they must be this time of year. Shiny peels: polishes them up with a rag or a handkerchief.

Wait. Those poor birds.

He halted again and bought from the old applewoman two Banbury cakes for a penny and broke the brittle paste and threw its fragments down into the Liffey. See that? The gulls swooped silently two, then all, from their heights, pouncing on prey. Gone. Every morsel.

Aware of their greed and cunning he shook the powdery crumb from his hands. They never expected that. Manna. Live on fishy flesh they have to, all sea birds, gulls, seagoose. Swans from Anna Liffey swim down here sometimes to preen themselves. No accounting for tastes. Wonder what kind is swanmeat. Robinson Crusoe had to live on them.

They wheeled, flapping weakly. I'm not going to throw any more. Penny quite enough. Lot of thanks I get. Not even a caw. They spread foot and mouth disease too. If you cram a turkey, say, on chestnut meal it tastes like that. Eat pig like pig. But then why is it that saltwater fish are not salty? How is that?

His eyes sought answer from the river and saw a rowboat rock at anchor on the treacly swells lazily its plastered board.

Kino's.

11/—.

Trousers.

Good idea that. Wonder if he pays rent to the corporation. How can you own water really? It's always flowing in a stream, never the same, which in the stream of life we trace. Because life is a stream. All kinds of places are good for ads. That quack doctor for the clap used to be stuck up in all the greenhouses. Never see it now. Strictly confidential. Dr Hy Franks. Didn't cost him a red like Maginni the dancing master self advertisement. Got fellows to stick them up or stick them up himself for that matter on the q. t. running in to loosen a button. Fly by night. Just the place too. POST NO BILLS. POST 110 PILLS. Some chap with a dose burning him.

If he...

O!

Eh?

No... No.

No, no. I don't believe it. He wouldn't surely?

No, no.

Mr Bloom moved forward raising his troubled eyes. Think no more about that. After one. Time ball on the ballast office is down. Dunsink time. Fascinating little book that is of Sir Robert Ball's. Parallax. I never exactly understood. There's a priest. Could ask him. Par it's Greek: parallel, parallax. Met him pikehoses she called it till I told her about the transmigration. O rocks!

Mr Bloom smiled O rocks at two windows of the ballast office. She's right after all. Only big words for ordinary things on account of the sound. She's not exactly witty. Can be rude too. Blurt out what I was thinking, Still I don't know. She used to say Ben Dollard had a base barreltone voice. He has legs like barrels and you'd think he was singing into a barrel. Now, isn't that wit? They used to call him big Ben. Not half as witty as calling him base barreltone. Appetite like an albatross. Get outside of a baron of beef. Powerful man he was at storing away number one Bass. Barrel of Bass. See? It all works out.

A procession of whitesmocked men marched slowly towards him along the gutter, scarlet sashes across their boards. Bargains. Like that priest they are this morning: we have sinned: we have suffered. He read the scarlet letters on their five tall white hats: H. E. L. Y. S. Wisdom Hely's. Y lagging behind drew a chunk of bread from under his foreboard, crammed it into his mouth and munched as he walked. Our staple food. Three bob a day, walking along the gutters, street after street. Just keep skin and bone together, bread and skilly. They are not Boyl: no: M'Glade's men. Doesn't bring in any business either. I suggested to him about a transparent show cart with two smart girls sitting inside writing letters, copybooks, envelopes, blotting paper. I bet that would have caught on. Smart girls writing something catch the eye at once. Everyone dying to know what she's writing. Get twenty of them round you if you stare at nothing. Have a finger in the pie. Women too. Curiosity. Pillar of salt. Wouldn't have it of course because he didn't think of it himself first. Or the inkbottle I suggested with a false stain of black celluloid. His ideas for ads like Plumtree's potted under the obituaries, cold meat department. You can't lick 'em. What? Our envelopes. Hello! Jones, where are you going? Can't stop, Robinson, I am hastening to purchase the only reliable inkeraser

Kansell, sold by Hely's Ltd, 85 Dame Street. Well out of that ruck I am. Devil of a job it was collecting accounts of those convents. Tranquilla convent. That was a nice nun there, really sweet face. Wimple suited her small head. Sister? Sister? I am sure she was crossed in love by her eyes. Very hard to bargain with that sort of woman. I disturbed her at her devotions that morning. But glad to communicate with the outside world. Our great day, she said. Feast of Our Lady of Mount Carmel. Sweet name too: caramel. She knew, I think she knew by the way she. If she had married she would have changed. I suppose they really were short of money. Fried everything in the best butter all the same. No lard for them. My heart's broke eating dripping. They like buttering themselves in and out. Molly tasting it, her veil up. Sister? Pat Claffey, the pawnbroker's daughter. It was a nun they say invented barbed wire.

He crossed Westmoreland street when apostrophe S had plodded by. Rover cycleshop. Those races are on today. How long ago is that? Year Phil Gilligan died. We were in Lombard street west. Wait, was in Thom's. Got the job in Wisdom Hely's year we married. Six years. Ten years ago: ninetyfour he died, yes that's right, the big fire at Arnott's. Val Dillon was lord mayor. The Glencree dinner. Alterman Robert O' Reilly emptying the port into his soup before the flag fell, Bobbob lapping it for the inner alderman. Couldn't hear what the band played. For what we have already received may the Lord make us. Milly was a kiddy then. Molly had that elephantgrey dress with the braided frogs. Mantailored with selcovered buttons. She didn't like it because I sprained my ankle first day she wore choir picnic at the Sugarloaf. As if that. Old Goodwin's tall hat done up with some sticky stuff. Flies' picnic too. Never put a dress on her back like it. Fitted her like a glove, shoulder and hips. Just beginning to plump it out well. Rabbit pie we had that day. People looking after her.

Happy. Happier then. Snug little room that was with the red wallpaper, Dockrell's, one and ninepence a dozen. Milly's tubbing night. American soap I bought: elderflower. Cosy smell of her bathwater. Funny she looked soaped all over. Shapely too. Now photography. Poor papa's daguerrotype atelier he told me of. Hereditary taste.

He walked along the curbstone.

Stream of life. What was the name of that priestylooking chap was always squinting in when he passed? Weak eyes, woman. Stopped in Citron's saint Kevin's parade. Pen something. Pendennis? My memory is getting. Pen...? of course it's years ago. Noise of the trams probably. Well, if he couldn't remember the dayfather's name that he sees every day.

Bartell d'Arcy was the tenor, just coming out then. Seeing her home after practice. Conceited fellow with his waxedup moustache. Gave her that song *Winds that blow from the south.*

Windy night that was I went to fetch her there was that lodge meeting on about those lottery tickets after Goodwin's concert in the supper room or oakroom of the mansion house. He and I behind. Sheet of her music blew out of my hand against the high school railings. Lucky it didn't. Thing like that spoils the effect of a night for her. Professor Goodwin linking her in front. Shaky on his pins. poor old sot. His farewell concerts. Positively last appearance on any stage. May be for months an ' may be for never. Remember her laughing at the wind, her blizzard collar up. Corner of Harcourt road remember that gust? Brrfoo! Blew up all her skirts and her boa nearly smothered old Goodwin. She did get flushed in the wind. Remember when we got home raking up the fire and frying up those pieces of lap of mutton for her supper with the Chutney sauce she liked. And the mulled rum. Could see her in the bedroom from the hearth unclamping the busk of her stays. White.

Swish and soft flop her stays made on the bed. Always warm from her. Always liked to let herself out. Sitting there after till near two, taking out her hairpins. Milly tucked up in beddyhouse. Happy. Happy. That was the night...

— O, Mr Bloom, how do you do?

— O, how do you do, Mrs Breen?

— No use complaining. How is Molly those times? Haven't seen her for ages.

— In the pink, Mr Bloom said gaily, Milly has a position down in Mullingar, you know.

— Go away! Isn't that grand for her?

— Yes, in a photographer's there. Getting on like a house on fire. How are all your charges?

— All on the baker's list, Mrs Breen said.

How many has she? No other in sight.

— You're in black I see. You have no...

— No, Mr Bloom said. I have just come from a funeral.

Going to crop up all day, I foresee. Who's dead, when and what did he die of? Turn up like a bad penny.

— O dear me, Mrs Breen said, I hope it wasn't any near relation.

May as well get her sympathy.

— Dignam, Mr Bloom said. An old friend of mine. He died quite suddenly, poor fellow. Heart trouble, I believe. Funeral was this morning.

Your funeral's tomorrow
While you're coming through the rye.
Diddlediddle dumdum
Diddlediddle...

– Sad to lose the old friends, Mrs Breen's womaneyes said melancholily.

Now that's quite enough about that. Just quietly : husband.

— And your lord and master ?

Mrs Breen turned up her two large eyes. Hasn't lost them anyhow.

— O, don't be talking, she said. He's a caution to rattlesnakes. He's in there now with his lawbooks finding out the law of libel. He has me heartscalded. Wait till I show you.

Hot mockturtle vapour and steam of newbaked jampuffs rolypoly poured out from Harrison's. The heavy noonreek tickled the top of Mr Bloom's gullet. Want to make good pastry, butter, best flour, Demerara sugar, or they'd taste it with the hot tea. Or is it from her ? A barefoot arab stood over the grating, breathing in the fumes. Deaden the gnaw of hunger that way. Pleasure or pain is it? Penny dinner. Knife and fork chained to the table.

Opening her handbag, chipped leather hatpin : ought to have a guard on those things. Stick it in a chap's eye in the tram. Rummaging. Open. Money. Please take one. Devils if they lose sixpence. Raise Cain. Husband barging. Where's the ten shillings I gave you on Monday ? Ave you feeding your little brother's family? Soiled handkerchief : medicinebottle. Pastille that was fell. What is she ?...

— There must be a new moon out, she said. He's always bad then. Do you know what he did last night ?

Her hand ceased to rummage. Her eyes fixed themselves on him, wide in alarm, yet smiling.

— What ? Mr Bloom asked.

Let her speak. Look straight in her eyes. I believe you. Trust me.

— Woke me up in the night, she said. Dream he had, a nightmare.

Indiges.

— Said the ace of spades was walking up the stairs

— The ace of spades ! Mr Bloom said.

She took a folded postcard from her handbag.

— Read that, she said. He got it this morning.

— What is it ? Mr Bloom asked, taking the card. U. P. ?

— U. P. : up, she said. Someone taking a rise out of him. It's a great shame for them whoever he is.

— Indeed it is, Mr Bloom said.

She took back the card, sighing.

— And now he's going round to Mr Menton's office. He's going to take an action for ten thousand pounds, he says.

She folded the card into her untidy bag and snapped the catch.

Same blue serge dress she had two years ago, the nap bleaching. Seen its best days. Wispish hair over her ears. And that dowdy toque, three old grapes to take the harm out of it. Shabby genteel. She used to be a tasty dresser. Lines round her mouth. Only a year or so older than Molly.

See the eye that woman gave her, passing. Cruel. The unfair sex.

He looked still at her, holding back behind his look his discontent. Pungent mockturtle oxtail mulligatawny. I'm hungry too. Flakes of pastry on the gusset of her dress : daub of sugary flour stuck to her cheek. Rhubarb tart with liberal fillings, rich fruit interior. Josie Powell that was. In Luke Doyle's long' ago, Dolphin's Barn, the charades. U. P. : up.

Change the subject.

— Do you ever see anything of Mrs Beaufoy, Mr Bloom asked.

— Mina Purefoy ? she said.

Philip Beaufoy I was thinking. Playgoers' club. Matcham often thinks of the masterstroke. Did I pull the chain ? Yes. The last act.

— Yes.

— I just called to ask on the way in is she over it. She's in the lying-in hospital in Holles street. Dr Horne got her in. She's three days bad now.

— O, Mr Bloom said. I'm sorry to hear that.

— Yes, Mrs Breen said. And a houseful of kids at home. It's a very stiff birth, the nurse told me.

— O, Mr Bloom said.

His heavy pitying gaze absorbed her news. His tongue clacked in compassion. Dth ! Dth !

— I'm sorry to hear that, he said. Poor thing ! Three days ! That's terrible for her.

Mrs Breen nodded.

— She was taken bad on the Tuesday.....

Mr Bloom touched her funnybone gently, warning her.

— Mind ! Let this man pass.

A bony form strode along the curbstone from the river, staring with a rapt gaze into the sunlight through a heavy stringed glass. Tight as a skullpiece a tiny hat gripped his head. From his arm a folded dustcoat, a stick and an umbrella dangled to his stride.

— Watch him, Mr Bloom said. He always walks outside the lampposts. Watch!

— Who is he if it's a fair question. Mrs Breen asked. Is he dotty?

— His name is Cashel Boyle O'Connor Fitzmaurice Tisdall Farrell, Mr Bloom said, smiling. Watch!

— He has enough of them, she said. Denis will be like that one of these days.

She broke off suddenly.

— There he is, she said. I must go after him. Good bye. Remember me to Molly, won't you?

— I will, Mr Bloom said.

He watched her dodge through passers towards the shopfronts. Denis Breen in skimpy frockcoat and blue canvas shoes shuffled out of Harrison's, hugging two heavy tomes to his ribs. Blown in from the bay. Like old times He suffered her to overtake him without surprise and thrust his dull grey beard towards her, his loose jaw wagging as he spoke earnestly.

Meshuggah. Off his chump.

Mr Bloom walked on again easily, seeing ahead of him in sunlight the tight skullpiece, the dangling stick, umbrella, dustcoat. Going the two days. Watch him! Out he goes again. One way of getting on in the world. And that other old mosey lunatic in those duds. Hard time she must have with him.

U. P: up. I'll take my oath that's Alf Bergan or Richie Goulding. Wrote it for a lark in the Scotch house, I bet anything. Round to Menton's office. His oyster eyes staring at the postcard. Be a feast for the gods.

He passed the *Irish Times*. There might be other answers lying there. Like to answer them all. Good system for criminals. Code. At their lunch now. Clerk with the glasses there doesn't know me. O, leave them there to simmer. Enough bother wading through fortyfour of them. Wanted smart lady typist to aid gentleman in literary work. I called you naughty darling because I do not like that other world. Please tell me what is the meaning. Please tell me what perfume does your wife. Tell me who made the world. The way they spring those questions on you. And the other one Lizzie Twigg. My literary efforts have had the good fortune to meet with the approval of the eminent poet A. E. (Mr Geo Russell). No time to do her hair drinking sloppy tea with a book of poetry.

Best paper by long chalks for a small ad. Got the provinces now. Cook and general, exc cuisine, housemaid kept. Wanted live man for spirit counter. Resp. girl (R. C.) wishes to hear of post in fruit or pork shop. James Carlisle made that. Six and a half per cent dividend. Made a big deal on Coates's shares. Ca' canny. Cunning old Scotch hunks. All the toady news. Our gracious and popular vicereine. Bought the *Irish Field* now. Lady Mountcashel has quite recovered after her confinement and rode out with the Ward Union staghounds at the enlargement yesterday at Rathoath. Uneatable fox. Pothunters too. Fear injects juices make it tender enough for them. Riding astride. Sit her horse like a man, Weightcarrying huntress. No sidesaddle or pillion for her, not for Joe. First to the meet and in at the death. Strong as a brood mare some of those horsey women. Swagger around livery stables. Toss off a glass of brandy neat while you'd say knife. That one at the Grosvenor this morning. Up with her on the car : wishswish. Stonewall or fivebarred gate put her mount to it. Think that pugnosed driver did it out of spite. Who is this she was like? O yes! Mrs Miriam Dandrade that sold me her old wraps and black underclothes in the Shelbourne hotel. Divorced Spanish American. Didn't take a feather out of her my handling them. As if I was her clotheshorse. Saw her in the viceregal party when Stubbs the park ranger got me in with Whelan of the *Express*. Scavening what the quality left. High tea. Mayonnaise I poured on the plums thinking it was custard. Her ears ought to have tingled for a few weeks after. Want to be a bull for her. Born courtesan. No nursery work for her, thanks.

Poor Mrs Purefoy! Methodist husband. Method in his madness. Saffron bun and milk and soda lunch in the educational dairy. Eating with a stopwatch, thirtytwo chews to the minute. Still his muttonchop whiskers grew. Supposed to be well connected. Theodore's cousin in Dublin Castle. One tony relative in every family. Hardy annuals he presents her with. Saw him out at the Three Jolly Topers marching along bareheaded and his eldest boy carrying one in a marketnet. The squallers Poor thing! Then having to give the breast year after year all hours of the night. Selfish those t.t's are. Dog in the manger. Only one lump of sugar in my tea, if you please.

He stood at Fleet street crossing. Luncheon interval a sixpenny at Rowe's? Must look up that ad in the national library. An eightpenny in the Burton. Better. On my way.

He walked on past Bolton's Westmoreland house. Tea. Tea. Tea. I forgot to tap Tom Kernan.

Sss. Dth, dth, dth! Three days imagine groaning on a bed with a vinegared handkerchief round her forehead, her belly swollen out! Phew! Dreadful simply! Child's head too big : forceps. Doubled up inside her trying to butt its way out blindly, groping for the way out. Kill me that would. Lucky Molly got over hers lightly. They ought to invent something to stop that. Life with hard labour. Twilightsleep idea : queen Victoria was given that. Nine she had. A good layer. Old woman that lived in a shoe she had so many children. Suppose he was consumptive. Time someone thought about it instead of gassing about the what was it the pensive bosom of the silver effulgence. Flapdoodle to feed fools on. They could easily have big establishments. Whole thing quite painless out of all the taxes give every child born five quid at compound interest up to twentyone, five per cent is a hundred shillings and five tiresome pounds, multiply by twenty decimal system, encourage people to put by money save hundred and ten and a bit twentyone years want to work it out on paper come to a tidy sum, more than you think.

Not stillborn of course. They are not even registered. Trouble for nothing.

Funny sight two of them together, their bellies out. Molly and Mrs Moisel. Mothers' meeting. Phthisis retires for the time being, then returns. How flat they look after all of a sudden! Peaceful eyes. Weight off their minds. Old Mrs Thornton was a jolly old soul. All my babies, she said. The spoon of pap in her mouth before she fed them. O, that's nyumyum. Got her hand crushed by old Tom Wall's son. His first bow to the public. Head like a prize pumpkin. Snuffy Dr Murren. People knocking them up at all hours. For God'sake, doctor. Wife in her throes. Then keep them waiting months for their fee. To attendance on your wife. No gratitude in people. Humane doctors, most of them.

Before the huge high door of the Irish house of parliament a flock of pigeons flew. Their little frolic after meals. Who will we do it on? I pick the fellow in black. Here goes Here's good luck. Must be thrilling from the air. Apjohn, myself and Owen Goldberg up in the trees near Goose green playing the monkeys. Mackerel they called me.

A squad of constables debouched from College street, marching in Indian file. Goose step. Foodheated faces, sweating helmets, patting their truncheons. After their feed with a good load of fat soup under their belts. Policeman's lot is oft a happy one. They split up into groups and scattered, saluting towards their beats. Let out to graze. Best moment to attack one in pudding time. A punch in his dinner. A squad of others, marching irregularly, rounded Trinity railings, making for the station. Bound for their troughs. Prepare to receive cavalry. Prepare to receive soup.

He crossed under Tommy Moore's roguish finger. They did right to put him up over a urinal: meeting of the waters. Ought to be places for women. Running into cakeshops. Settle my hat straight. *There is not in this wide world a vallee.* Great song of Julia Morkan's. Kept her voice up to the very last. Pupil of Michael Balfe's, wasn't she?

He gazed after the last broad tunic. Nasty customers to tackle. Jack Power could a tale unfold : father a G man. If a fellow gave them trouble being lagged they let him have it hot and heavy in the bridewell. Can't blame them after all with the job they have especially the young hornies. That horse policeman the day Joe Chamberlain was given his degree in Trinity he got a run for his money. My word he did! His horse's hoofs clattering after us down Abbey street. Luck I had the presenee of mind to dive into Manning's or I was souped. He did come a wallop, by George. Must have cracked his skull on the cobblestones. I oughtn't to have got myself swept along with those medicals. And the Trinity jibs in their mortarboards. Looking for trouble. Still I got to know that young Dixon who dressed that sting for me in the Mater and now he's in Holles street where Mrs Purefoy. Wheels within wheels. Police whistle in my ears still. All skedaddled. Why he fixed on me. Give me in charge. Right here it began.

— Up the Boers!

— Three cheers for De Wet!

— We'll hang Joe Chamberlain on a sourapple tree.

Silly billies : mob of young cubs yelling their guts out. Vinegar hill. The Butter exchange band. Few years time half of them magistrates and civil servants. War comes on : into the army helterskelter : same fellows used to whether on the scaffold high.

Never know who you're talking to. Corny Kelleher he has Harvey Duff in his eye. Like that Peter or Denis or James Carey that blew the gaff on the invincibles. Member of the corporation too. Egging raw youths on to get in the know. All the time drawing secret service pay from the castle. Drop him like a hot potato. Why those plain clothes men are always courting slaveys. Fasily twig a man used to uniform. Squarepushing up against a backdoor. Maul her a bit. Then the next thing on the menu. And who is the gentleman does be visiting there? Was the young master saying anything? Peeping Tom through the keyhole. Decoy duck. Hotblooded young student fooling round her fat arms ironing.

— Are those yours, Mary?

— I don't wear such things... Stop or I'll tell the missus on you. Out half the night.

— There are great times coming, Mary. Wait till you see.

— Ah, get along with your great times coming.

Barmaids too. Tobacco shopgirls.

James Stephens' idea was the best. He knew them. Circles of ten so that a fellow couldn't round on more than his own ring. Sinn Fein. Back out you get the knife. Hidden hand. Stay in. The firing squad. Turkney's daughter got him out of Richmond, off from Lusk. Putting up in the Buckingham Palace hotel under their very noses. Garibaldi.

You must have a certain fascination : Parnell. Arthur Griffith is a squareheaded fellow but he has no go in him for the mob. Want to gas about our lovely land. Gammon and spinach. Dublin Bakery Company's tearoom. Debating societies. That republicanism is the best form of government. That the language question should take precedence of the economic question. Have your daughters inveigling them to your house. Stuff them up with meat and drink. Michaelmas goose. Here's a good lump of thyme seasoning under the apron for you. Have another quart of goosegrease before it gets too cold. Halffed enthusiasts. Penny roll and a walk with the band. No grace for the carver. The thought that the other chap pays best sauce in the world. Make themselves thoroughly at home. Show us over those apricots, meaning peaches. The not far distant day. Home Rule sun rising up in the northwest.

His smile faded as he walked, a heavy cloud hiding the sun slowly, shadowing Trinity's surly front. Trams passed one another, ingoing, outgoing, clanging. Useless words. Things go on same ; day after day : squads of police marching out, back : trams in, out. Those two loonies mooching about. Dignam carted off. Mina Purefoy swollen belly on a bed groaning to have a child tugged out of her. One born every second somewhere. Other dying every second. Since I fed the birds five minutes. Three hundred kicked the bucket. Other three hundred born, washing the blood off, all are washed in the blood of the lamb, bawling maaaaaa.

Cityful passing away, other cityful coming, passing away too : other coming on, passing on. Houses, lines of houses, streets, miles of pavements, piledup bricks, stones. Changing hands. This owner, that. Landlord never dies they say. Other steps into his shoes when he gets his notice to quit. They buy the place up with gold and still they have all the gold. Swindle in it somewhere. Piled up in cities, worn away age after age. Pyramids in sand. Built on bread and onions. Slaves Chinese wall. Babylon. Big stones left. Round towers. Rest rubble, sprawling suburbs, jerrybuilt, Kerwan's mushroom houses, built of breeze. Shelter for the night.

No one is anything.

This is the very worst hour of the day. Vitality. Dull, gloomy : hate this hour. Feel as if I had been eaten and spewed.

Provost's house. The reverend Dr Salmon : tinned salmon. Well tinned in there. Wouldn't live in it if they paid me. Hope they have liver and bacon today. Nature abhors a vacuum.

The sun freed itself slowly and lit glints of light among the silver ware in Walter Sexton's window opposite by which John Howard Parnell passed,unseeing.

There he is : the brother. Image of him. Haunting face. Now that's a coincidence. Course hundreds of times you think of a person and don't meet him. Like a man walking in his sleep. No-one knows him. Must be a corporation meeting today.They say he never put on the city marshal's uniform since he got the job. Charley Boulger used to come out on his high horse, cocked hat, puffed, powdered and shaved. Look at the woebegone walk of him. Eaten a bad egg. Poached eyes on ghost. I have a pain. Great man's brother : his brother's brother. He'd look nice on the city charger. Drop into the D. B. C. probably for his coffee, play chess there. His brother used men as pawns. Let them all go to pot. Afraid to pass a remark on him. Freeze them up with that eye of his. That's the fascination : the name. All a bit touched. Mad Fanny and his other sister Mrs Dickinson driving about with scarlet harness. Bolt upright like surgeon M'Ardle. Still David Sheehy beat him for south Meath. Apply for the Chiltern Hundreds and retire into public life. The patriot's banquet. Eating orangepeels in the park. Simon Dedalus said when they put him in parliament that Parnell would come back from the grave and lead him out of the House of Commons by the arm.

— Of the twoheaded octopus, one of whose heads is the head upon which the ends of the world have forgotten to come while the other speaks with a Scotch accent. The tentacles...

They passed from behind Mr Bloom along the curbstone. Beard and bicycle. Young woman.

And there he is too. Now that's really a coincidence : secondtime. Coming events cast their shadows before. With the approval of the eminent poet Mr Geo. Russell. That might be Lizzie Twigg with him. A. E. : What does that mean? Initials perhaps. Albert Edward, Arthur Edmund, Alphonsus Eb Ed El Esquire. What was he saying? The ends of the world with a Scotch accent. Tentacles : octopus. Something occult : symbolism. Holding forth. She's taking it all in. Not saying a word. To aid gentleman in literary work.

His eyes followed the high figure in homespun, beard and bicycle, a listening woman at his side. Coming from the vegetarian. Only weggebobbles and fruit. Don't eat a beefsteak. If you do the eyes of that cow will pursue you through all eternity. They say it's healthier. Wind and watery though. Tried it. Keep you on the run all day. Bad as a bloater. Dreams all night. Why do they call that thing they gave me nutsteak? Nutarians. Fruitarians. To give you the idea you are eating rumpsteak. Absurd. Salty too. They cook in soda. Keep you sitting by the tap all night.

Her stockings are loose over her ankles. I detest that : so tasteless. Those literary etherial people they are all. Dreamy, cloudy, symbolistic. Esthetes they are. I wouldn't be surpised if it was that kind of food you see produces the like waves of the brain the poetical. For example one of those policemen sweating Irish stew into their shirts; you couldn't squeeze a line of poetry out of him. Don't know what poetry is even. Must be in a certain mood.

The dreamy cloudy gull
Waves o'er the waters dull.

He crossed at Nassau street corner and stood before the window of Yeates and Son, pricing the field glasses. Or will I drop into old Harris's and have a chat with young Sinclair ? Wellmannered fellow. Probably at his lunch. Must get those old glasses of mine set right. Gœrz lenses, six guineas. Germans making their way everywhere. Sell on easy terms to capture trade. Undercutting. Might chance on a pair in the railway lost property office. Astonishing the things people leave behind them in trains and cloak rooms. What do they be thinking about? Women too. Incredible. Last year travelling to Ennis had to pick up that farmer's daughter's bag and hand it to her at Limerick junction. Unclaimed money too. There's a little watch up there on the roof of the bank to test those glasses by.

His lids came down on the lower rims of his irides. Can't see it. If you imagine it's there you can almost see it. Can't see it.

He faced about and, standing between the awnings, held out his right hand at arm's length towards the sun. Wanted to try that often. Yes: completely. The tip of his little finger blotted out the sun's disk. Must be the focus where the rays cross. If I had black glasses. Interesting. There was a lot of talk about those sunspots when we were in Lombard street west. Terrific explosions they are. There will be a total eclipse this year: autumn some time.

Now that I come to think of it, that ball falls at Greenwich time. It's the clock is worked by an electric wire from Dunsink. Must go out there some first Saturday of the month. If I could get an introduction to professor Joly or learn up something about his family. That would do to: man always feels complimented. Flattery where least expected. Nobleman proud to be descended from some king's mistress. His foremother. Lay it on with a trowel. Cap in hand goes through the land. Not go in and blurt out what you know you're not to: what's parallax? Show this gentleman the door.

Ah.

His hand fell again to his side.

Never know anything about it. Waste of time. Gasballs spinning about, crossing each other, passing. Same old dingdong always. Gas, then solid, then world, then cold, then dead shell drifting around, frozen rock like that pineapple rock. The moon. Must be a new moon out, she said. I believe there is.

He went on by la Maison Claire.

Wait. The full moon was the night we were Sunday fortnight exactly there is a new moon. Walking down by the Tolka. Not bad for a Fairview moon. She was humming: The young May moon she's beaming, love. He other side of her. Elbow, arm. He. Glowworm's la-amp is gleaming, love. Touch. Fingers. Asking. Answer. Yes.

Stop. Stop. If it was it was. Must.

Mr Bloom, quick breathing, slowlier walking, passed Adam court.

With a keep quiet relief, his eyes took note: this is street here middle of the day Bob Doran's bottle shoulders. On his annual bend, M'Coy said. They drink in order to say or do something or *cherchez la femme*. Up in the Coombe with chummies and streetwalkers and then the rest of the year as sober as a judge.

Yes. Thought so. Sloping into the Empire. Gone. Plain soda would do him good. Where Pat Kinsella had, his Harp theatre before Whitbred ran the Queen's. Broth of a boy. Dion Boucicault business with his harvestmoon face in a poky bonnet. Three Purty Maids from School. How time flies eh? Showing long red pantaloons under his skirts. Drinkers, drinking, laughed spluttering, their drink against their breath. More power, Pat. Coarse red: fun for drunkards: guffaw and smoke. Take off that white hat. His parboiled eyes. Where is he now? Beggar somewhere. The harp that once did starve us all.

I was happier then. Or was that I? Or am I now I? Twentyeight I was. She twentythree when we left Lombard street west something changed. Could never like it again after Rudy. Can't bring back time. Like holding water in your hand. Would you go back to then? Just beginning then. Would you? Are you not happy in your home, you poor little naughty boy? Wants to sew on buttons for me. I must answer. Write it in the library.

Grafton street gay with housed awnings lured his senses. Muslin prints, silk, dames and dowagers, jingle of harnesses, hoofthuds lowringing in the baking causeway. Thick feet that woman has in the white stockings. Hope the rain mucks them up on her. Country bred chawbacon. All the beef to the heels were in. Always gives a woman clumsy feet. Molly looks out of plumb.

He passed, dallying the windows of Brown Thomas, silk mercers.* Cascades of ribbons. Flimsy China silks. A tilted urn poured from its mouth a flood of bloodhued poplin: lustrous blood. The huguenots brought that here. *La causa è santa!* Tara tara. Great chorus that. Tara. Must be washed in rainwater. Meyerbeer. Tara: bom bom bom.

Pincushions. I'm a long time threatening to buy one. Stick them all over the place. Needles in window curtains.

He bared slightly his left forearm. Scrape: nearly gone. Not today anyhow. Must go back for that lotion. For her birthday perhaps. Junejuly augseptember eighth. Nearly three months off. Then she mightn't like it. Women won't pick up pins. Say it cuts lo.

Gleaming silks, petticoats on slim brass rails, rays of flat silk stockings.

Useless to go back. Had to be. Tell me all.

High voices. Sunwarm silk. Jingling harnesses. All for a woman, home and houses, silk webs, silver, rich fruits, spicy from Jaffa. Agendath Netaim. Wealth of the world.

A warm human plumpness settled down on his brain. His brain yielded. Perfume of embraces all him assailed. With hungered flesh obscurely, he mutely craved to adore.

Duke street. Here we are. Must eat. The Burton. Feel better then.

He turned Combridge's corner, still pursued. Jingling hoofthuds. Perfumed bodies, warm, full. All kissed, yielded : in deep summer fields, tangled pressed grass, in trickling hallways of tenements, along sofas, creaking beds.

— Jack, love!

— Darling!

— Kiss me, Reggy!

— My boy!

— Love!

His heart astir he pushed in the door of the Burton restaurant. Stink gripped his trembling breath : pungent meatjuice, slop of greens. See the animals feed.

Men, men, men.

Perched on high stools by the bar, hats shoved back, at the tables calling for more bread no charge, swilling, wolfing gobfuls of sloppy food, their eyes bulging, wiping wetted moustaches. A pallid suetfaced young man polished his tumbler knife fork and spoon with his napkin. New set of microbes. A man with an infant's saucestained napkin tucked round him shovelled gurgling soup down his gullet. A man spitting back on his plate : halfmasticated gristle : no teeth to chewchewchew it. Chump chop from the grill. Bolting to get it over. Sad booser's eyes. Bitten off more than he can chew. Am I like that? See ourselves as others see us. Hungry man is an angry man. Working tooth and jaw. Don't! O! A bone! That last pagan king of Ireland Cormac in the schoolpoem choked himself at Sletty southward of the Boyne. Wonder what he was eating. Something galoptious. Saint Patrick converted him to Christianity. Couldn't swallow it all however.

— Roast beef and cabbage.

— One stew.

Smells of men. His gorge rose. Spaton sawdust, sweetish warmish cigarette smoke, reek of plug, spilt beer, men's beery piss, the stale of ferment.

Couldn't eat a morsel here. Fellow sharpening knife and fork, to eat all before him, old chap picking his tootles. Slight spasm, full, chewing the cud. Before and after. Grace after meals. Look on this picture then on that. Scoffing up stewgravy with sopping sippets of bread. Lick it off the plate, man! Get out of this.

He gazed round the stooled and tabled eaters, tightening the wings of his nose.

— Two stouts here.

— One corned and cabbage.

That fellow ramming a knifeful of cabbage down as if his life depended on it. Good stroke. Give me the fidgets to look. Safer to eat from his three hands. Tear it limb from limb. Second nature to him. Born with a silver knife in his mouth. That's witty, I think. Or no. Silver means born rich. Born with a knife. But then the allusion is lost.

An illgirt server gathered sticky clattering plates. Rock, the bailiff, standing at the bar blew the foamy crown from his tankard. Well up : it splashed yellow near his boot. A diner, knife and fork upright, elbows on table, ready for a second helping stared towards the foodlift across his stained square of news-paper. Other chap telling him something with his mouth full. Sympathetic listener. Table talk. I munched hum un thu Unchster Bunck un Munchday. Ha? Did you, faith?

Mr Bloom raised two fingers doubtfully to his lips. His eyes said :

— Not here. Don't see him.

Out. I hate dirty eaters.

He backed towards the door. Get a light snack in Davy Byrne's. Stopgap. Keep me going. Had a good breakfast.

— Roast and mashed here.

— Pint of stout.

Every fellow for his own, tooth and nail. Gulp. Grub. Gulp. Gobstuff.

He came out into clearer air and turned back towards Grafton street. Eat or be eaten. Kill! Kill!

Suppose that communal kitchen years to come perhaps. All trotting down with porringers and tommycans to be filled. Devour contents in the street. John Howard Parnell example the provost of Trinity every mother's son don't talk of your provosts and provost of Trinity women and children, cabmen, priests, parsons, fieldmarshals, archbishops. From Ailesbury road, Clyde road, artisans' dwellings, north Dublin union, lord mayor in his gingerbread coach, old queen in a bathchair. My plate's empty. After you with our incorporated drinkingcup. Like sir Philip Crampton's fountain. Rub off the microbes with your handkerchief. Next chap rubs on a new batch with his. Father O'Flynn would make hares of them all. Have rows all the same. All for number one. Children fighting for the scrapings of the pot. Want a soup pot as big as the Phœnix Park. Harpooning flitches and hindquarters out of it. Hate people all round you. City Arms hotel *table d'hôte* she called it. Soup, joint and sweet. Never know whose thoughts you're chewing. Then who'd wash up all the plates and forks? Might be all feeding on tabloids that time. Teeth getting worse and worse.

After all there's a lot in that vegetarian fine flavour of things from the earth garlic, of course, it stinks Italian organgrinders crisp of onions, mushrooms truffles. Pain to the animal too. Pluck and draw fowl. Wretched brutes there at the cattlemarket waiting for the poleaxe to split their skulls open. Moo. Poor trembling calves. Meh. Staggering bob. Bubble and squeak. Butchers' buckets wobble lights. Give us that brisket off the hook. Plup. Rawhead and bloody bones. Flayed glasseyed sheep hung from their haunches, sheepsnouts bloodypapered snivelling nosejam on sawdust. Top and lashers going out. Don't maul them pieces, young one.

Hot fresh blood they prescribe for decline. Blood always needed. Insidious. Lick it up, smoking hot, thick sugary. Famished ghosts.

Ah, I'm hungry.

He entered Davy Byrne's. Moral pub. He doesn't chat. Stands a drink now and then. But in leapyear once in four. Cashed a cheque for me once.

What will I take now? He drew his watch. Let me see now. Shandygaff?

— Hello, Bloom! Nosey Flynn said from his nook.

— Hello, Flynn.

— How's things?

— Tiptop... Let me see. I'll take a glass of burgundy and... let me see.

Sardines on the shelves. Almost taste them by looking. Sandwich? Ham and his descendants musterred and bred there. Potted meats. What is home without Plumtree's potted meat? Incomplete. What a stupid ad! Under the obituary notices they stuck it. All up a plumtree. Dignam's potted meat. Cannibals would with lemon and rice. White missionary too salty. Like pickled pork. Expect the chief consumes the parts of honour. Ought to be tough from exercise. His wives in a row to watch the effect. *There was a right royal old nigger. Who ate or something the somethings of the reverend Mr Mac Trigger.* With it an abode of bliss. Lord knows what concoction. Cauls mouldy tripes windpipes faked and minced up. Puzzle find the meat. Kosher. No meat and milk together. Hygiene that was what they call now. Yom kippur fast spring cleaning of inside. Peace and war depend on some fellow's digestion. Religions. Christmas turkeys and geese. Slaughter of innocents. Eat, drink and be merry. Then casual wards full after. Heads bandaged. Cheese digests all but itself. Mighty cheese.

— Have you a cheese sandwich?

— Yes, sir.

Like a few olives too if they had them. Italian I prefer. Good glass or burgundy; take away that. Lubricate. A nice salad, cool as a cucumber. Tom Kernan can dress. Puts gusto into it. Pure olive oil. Milly served me that cutlet with a sprig of parsley. Take one Spanish onion. God made food, the devil the cooks. Devilled crab.

— Wife well?

— Quite well, thanks... A cheese sandwich, then. Gorgonzola, have you?

— Yes, sir.

Nosey Flynn sipped his grog.

— Doing any singing those times?

Look at his mouth Could whistle in his own ear. Flap ears to match. Music. Knows as much about it as my coachman. Still better tell him. Does no harm. Free ad.

— She's engaged for a big tour end of this month. You may have heard perhaps.

— No. O, that's the style. Who's getting it up?

The curate served.

— How much is that?

— Seven d., sir... Thank you, sir.

Mr Bloom cut his sandwich into slender strips. *Mr MacTrigger*. Easier than the dreamy creamy stuff. *His five hundred wives. Had the time of their lives.*

— Mustard, sir?

— Thank you.

He studded under each lifted strip yellow blobs. *Their lives*. I have it. *It grew bigger and bigger and bigger*.

— Getting it up? he said. Well, it's like a company idea, you see. Part shares and part profits.

— Ay, now I remember, Nosey Flynn said, putting his hand in his pocket to scratch his groin. Who is this was telling me? Isn't Blazes Boylan mixed up in it?

A warm shock of air heat of mustard hauched on Mr Bloom's heart. He raised his eyes and met the stare of a bilious clock. Two. Pub clock five minutes fast. Time going on. Hands moving. Two. Not yet.

His midriff yearned then upward, sank within him, yearned more longly, longingly.

Wine.

He smellsipped the cordial juice and, bidding his throat strongly to speed it, set his wineglass delicately down.

— Yes, he said. He's the organiser in point of fact.

No fear. No brains.

Nosey Flynn snuffled and scratched. Flea having a good square meal.

— He had a good slice of luck, Jack Mooney was telling me, over that boxing match Myler Keogh won again that soldier in the Portobello barracks. By God, he had the little kipper down in the county Carlow he was telling me...

Hope that dewdrop doesn't come down into his glass. No, snuffled it up.

— For near a month, man, before it came off. Sucking duck eggs by God till further orders. Keep him off the boose, see? O, by God, Blazes is a hairy chap.

Davy Byrne came forward from the hindbar in tuckstitched shirt sleeves, cleaning his lips with two wipes of his napkin. Herring's blush. Whose smile upon each feature plays with such and such replete. Too much fat on the parsnips.

— And here's himself and pepper on him, Nosey Flynn said. Can you give us a good one for the Gold cup?

— I'm off that, Mr Flynn, Davy Byrne answered. I never put anything on a horse.

— You're right there, Nosey Flynn said.

Mr Bloom ate his strips of sandwich, fresh clean bread, with relish of disgust, pungent mustard, the feety savour of green cheese. Sips of his wine soothed his palate. Not logwood that. Tastes fuller this weather with the chill off.

Nice quiet bar. Nice piece of wood in that counter. Nicely planed. Like the way it curves there.

— I wouldn't do anything at all in that line, Davy Byrne said. It ruined many a man the same horses.

Vintners' sweepstake. Licensed for the sale of beer, wine and spirits for consumption on the premises. Heads I win tails you lose.

— True for you, Nosey Flynn said. Unless you're in the know. There's no straight sport going now. Lenehan gets some good ones. He's giving Sceptre today. Zinfandel's the favourite, lord Howard de Walden's, won at Epsom. Morny Cannon is riding him. I could have got seven to one against Saint Amant a fortnight before.

— That so? Davy Byrne said...

He went towards the window and, taking up the petty cash book, scanned its pages.

— I could, faith, Nosey Flynn said snuffling. That was a rare bit ot horseflesh. Saint Frusquin was her sire. She won in a thunderstorm, Rothschild's filly, with wadding in her ears. Blue jacket and yellow cap. Bad luck to big Ben Dollard and his John O'Gaunt. He put me off it. Ay.

He drank resignedly from his tumbler, running his fingers down the flutes.

— Ay, he said, sighing.

Mr Bloom, champing, standing, looked upon his sigh. Nosey numskull. Will I tell him that horse Lenehan? He knows already. Better let him forget. Go and lose more. Fool and his money. Dewdrop coming down again. Cold nose he'd have kissing a woman. Still they might like. Prickly beards they like. Dogs' cold noses. Old Mrs Riordan with the rumbling stomach's Skye terrier in the City Arms hotel. Molly fondling him in her lap. O the big doggybowwowsywowsy!

Wine soaked and softened rolled pith of bread mustard a moment mawkish cheese. Nice wine it is. Taste it better because I'm not thirsty. Bath of course does that. Just a bite or two. Then about six o'clock I can. Six, six. Time will be gone then. She...

Mild fire of wine kindled his veins. I wanted that badly. Felt so off colour. His eyes unhungrily saw shelves of tins, sardines, gaudy lobsters' claws. All the odd things people pick up for food. Out of shells, periwinkles with a pin, off trees, snails out of the ground the French eat, out of the sea with bait on a hook. Silly fish learn nothing in a thousand years. If you didn't know risky putting anything into your mouth. Poisonous berries. Johnny Magories. Roundness you think good. Gaudy colour warns you off. One fellow told another and so on. Try it on the dog first. Led on by the smell or the look. Tempting fruit. Ice cones. Cream. Instinct. Orangegroves for instance. Need artificial irrigation. Bleibtreustrasse. Yes but what about oysters. Unsightly like a clot of phlegm. Filthy shells. Devil to open them too. Who found them out? Garbage, sewage they feed on. Fizz and Red bank oysters. Effect on the sexual. Aphrodis. He was in the Red bank this morning. Was he oyster old fish at table. Perhaps he young flesh in bed No. June has no ar no oysters. But there are people like tainted game. Jugged hare. First catch your hare. Chinese eating eggs fifty years old, blue and green again. Dinner of thirty courses. Each dish harmless might mix inside. Idea for a poison mystery. That archduke Leopold was it. No. Yes, or was it Otto one of those Habsburgs?

Or who was it used to eat the scruff off his own head? Cheapest lunch in town. Of course, aristocrats. Then the others copy to be in the fashion. Milly too rock oil and flour. Raw pastry I like myself. Half the catch of oysters they throw back in the sea to keep up the price. Cheap. No one would buy. Caviare. Do the grand. Hock in green glasses. Swell blowout. Lady this. Powdered bosom pearls. The *élite*. *Crème de la crème*. They want special dishes to pretend they' re. Hermit with a platter of pulse keep down the stings of the flesh. Know me come eat with me. Royal sturgeon. High sheriff, Coffey, the butcher, right to venisons of the forest from his ex. Send him back the half of a cow. Spread I saw down in the Master of the Rolls' kitchen area. Whitehatted *chef* like a rabbi. Combustible duck. Curly cabbage *à la duchesse de Parme*. Just as well to write it on the bill of fare so you can know what you've eaten too many drugs spoil the broth. I know it myself. Dosing it with Edwards' desiccated soup. Geese stuffed silly for them. Lobsters boiled alive. Do ptake some ptarmigan. Wouldn't mind being a waiter in a swell hotel. Tips, evening dress, halfnaked ladies. May I tempt you to a little more filleted lemon sole, miss Dubedat? Yes, do bedad. And she did bedad. Huguenot name I expect that. A miss Dubedat lived in Killiney I remember. *Du, de, la,* French. Still it's the same fish, perhaps old Micky Hanlon of Moore street ripped the guts out of making money, hand over first, finger in fishes' gills, can't write his name on a cheque, think he was painting the landscape with his mouth twisted. Moooikill A Aitcha Ha. Ignorant as a kish of brogues, worth fifty thousand pounds.

Stuck on the pane two flies buzzed, stuck.

Glowing wine on his palate lingered swallowed. Crushing in the winepress grapes of Burgundy. Sun's heat it is. Seems to a secret touch telling me memory. Touched his sense moistened remembered. Hidden under wild ferns on Howth. Below us bay sleeping sky. No sound. The sky. The bay purple by the Lion's head. Green by Drumleck. Yellowgreen towards Sutton. Fields of undersea, the lines faint brown in grass, buried cities, Pillowed on my coat she had her hair, earwigs in the heather scrub my hand under her nape, you'll toss me all. O wonder! Coolsoft with ointments her hand touched me, caressed: her eyes upon me did not turn away. Ravished over her I lay, full lips full open, kissed her mouth. Yum. Softly she gave me in my mouth the seedcake warm and chewed. Mawkish pulp her mouth had mumbled sweet and sour with spittle. Joy: I ate it: joy. Young life, her lips that gave me pouting. Soft, warm, sticky gumjelly lips. Flowers her eyes were, take me, willing eyes.

Pebbles fell. She lay still. A goat. No-one. High on Ben Howth rhododendrons a nannygoat walking surefooted, dropping currants. Screened under ferns she laughed warmfolded. Wildly I lay on her, kissed her ; eyes, her lips, her stretched neck, beating, woman's breasts full in her blouse of nun's veiling, fat nipples upright. Hot I tongued her. She kissed me. I was kissed. All yielding she tossed my hair. Kissed, she kissed me.

Me. And me now.

Stuck, the flies buzzed.

His downcast eyes followed the silent veining of the oaken slab. Beauty: it curves : curves are beauty. Shapely goddesses, Venus, Juno : curves the world admires. Can seen them library museum standing in the round hall, naked goddesses. Aids to digestion. They don't care what man looks. All to see. Never speaking. I mean to say to fellows like Flynn. Suppose she did Pygmalion and Galatea what would she say first? Mortal! Put you in your proper place. Quaffing nectar at mess with gods, golden dishes, all ambrosial. Not like a tanner lunch we have, boiled mutton, carrots and turnips, bottle of Allsop. Nectar, imagine it drinking electricity : gods' food. Lovely forms of woman sculped Junonian. Immortal lovely. And we stuffing food in one hole and out behind : food, chyle, blood, dung, earth, food : have to feed it like stoking au engine. They have no. Never looked. I'll look today. Keeper won't see. Bend down let something fall see if she.

Dribbling a quiet message from his bladder came to go to do not to do there to do. A man and ready he drained his glass to the lees and walked, to men too they gave themselves, manly conscious, lay with men lovers, a youth enjoyed her, to the yard.

When the sound of his boots had ceased Davy Byrne said from his book :

— What is this he is? Isn't he in the insurance line?

— He's out of that long ago, Nosey Flynn said. He does canvassing for the *Freeman*.

— I know him well to see, Davy Byrne said. Is he in trouble?

— Trouble? Nosey Flynn said. Not that I heard of. Why?

— I noticed he was in mourning.

— Was he? Nosey Flynn said. So he was, faith. I asked him how was all at home. You're right, by God. So he was.

— I never broach the subject, Davy Byrne said humanely, if I see a gentleman is in trouble that way. It only brings it up fresh in their minds.

— It's not the wife anyhow, Nosey Flynn said. I met him the day before yesterday and he coming out of that Irish farm dairy John Wyse Nolan's wife has in Henry street with a jar of cream in his hand taking it home to his better half. She's well nourished, I tell you. Plovers on toast.

— And is he doing for the *Freeman*? Davy Byrne said.

Nosey Flynn pursed his lips.

— He doesn't buy cream on the ads he picks up. You can make bacon of that.

— How so? Davy Byrne asked, coming from his book.

Nosey Flynn made swift passes in the air with juggling fingers. He winked.

— He's in the craft, he said.

— Do you tell me so? Davy Byrne said.

— Very much so, Nosey Flynn said. Ancient free and accepted order. Light, life and love, by God. They give him a leg up. I was told that by a, well, I won't say who.

— Is that a fact?

— O, it's a fine order, Nosey Flynn said. They stick to you when you're down. I know a fellow was trying to get into it, but they're as close as damn it. By God they did right to keep the women out of it.

Davy Byrne smiledyawnednodded all in one:

— Iiiiichaaaaaaach!

— There was one woman, Nosey Flynn said, hid herself in a clock to find out what they do be doing. But be damned but they smelt her out and swore her in on the spot a master mason. That was one of the Saint Legers of Doneraile.

Davy Byrne, sated after his yawn, said with tearwashed eyes:

— And is that a fact? Decent quiet man he is. I often saw him in here and I never once saw him, you know, over the line.

— God Almighty couldn't make him drunk, Nosey Flynn said firmly. Slips off when the fun gets too hot. Didn't you see him look at his watch? Ah, you weren't there. If you ask him to have a drink first thing he does he outs with the watch to see what he ought to imbibe. Declare to God he does.

— There are some like that, Davy Byrne said. He's a safe man, I'd say.

— He's not too bad, Nosey Flynn said, snuffling it up. He has been known to put his hand down too to help a fellow. Give the devil his due. O, Bloom has his good points. But there's one thing he'll never do.

His hand scrawled a dry pen signature beside his grog.

— I know, Davy Byrne said.

— Nothing in black and white, Nosey Flynn said.

Paddy Leonard and Bantam Lyons came in. Tom Rochford followed, a plaining hand on his claret waistcoat.

— Day, Mr Byrne.

— Day, gentlemen.

They paused at the counter.

— Who's standing? Paddy Leonard asked.

— I'm sitting anyhow, Nosey Flynn answered.

— Well, what'll it be? Paddy Leonard asked.

— I'll take a stone ginger, Bantam Lyons said.

— How much? Paddy Leonard cried Since when, for God' sake? What's yours, Tom?

— How is the main drainage? Nosey Flynn asked, sipping.

For answer Tom Rochford pressed his hand to his breastbone and hiccupped.

— Would I trouble you for a glass of fresh water, Mr Byrne? he said.

— Certainly, sir.

Paddy Leonard eyed his alemates.

— Lord love a duck, he said, look at what I'm standing drinks to! Cold water and gingerpop! Two fellows that would suck whisky off a sore leg. He has some bloody horse up his sleeve for the Gold cup. A dead snip.

— Zinfandel is it? Nosey Flynn asked.

Tom Rochford spilt powder from a twisted paper into the water set before him.

— That cursed dyspepsia, he said before drinking.

— Breadsoda is very good, Davy Byrne said.

Tom Rochford nodded and drank.

— Is it Zinfandel?

— Say nothing, Bantam Lyons winked. I'm going to plunge five bob on my own.

— Tell us if you' re worth your salt and be damned to you, Paddy Leonard said. Who gave it to you?

Mr Bloom on his way out raised three fingers in greeting.

— So long, Nosey Flynn said.

The others turned.

— That's the man now that gave it to me, Bantam Lyons whispered.

— Prrwht! Paddy Leonard said with scorn. Mr Byrne, sir, we'll take two of your small Jamesons after that and a...

— Stone ginger, Davy Byrne added civilly.

— Ay, Paddy Leonard said. A suckingbottle for the baby.

Mr Bloom walked towards Dawson street, his tongue brushing his teeth smooth. Something green it would have to be : spinach say. Then with those Röntgen rays searchlight you could.

At Duke lane a ravenous terrier choked up a sick knuckly cud on the cobble stones and lapped it with new zest. Surfeit. Returned with thanks having fully digested the contents. First sweet then savoury. Mr Bloom coasted warily. Ruminants. His second course. Their upper jaw they move. Wonder if Tom Rochford will do anything with that invention of his. Wasting time explaining it to Flynn's mouth. Lean people long mouths. Ought to be a hall or a place where inventors could go in and invent free. Course then you'd have all the cranks pestering.

He hummed, prolonging in solemn echo, the closes of the bars :

Don Giovanni, a cenar teco
M'invitasti.

Feel better. Burgundy. Good pick me up. Who distilled first? Some chap in the blues. Dutch courage. That *Kilkenny People* in the national library now I must.

Bare clean closestools, waiting, in the window of William Miller, plumber, turned back his thoughts. They could : and watch it all the way down, swallow a pin sometimes come out of the ribs years after, tour round the body, changing biliary duct, spleen squirting liver, gastric juice coils of intestines like pipes. But the poor buffer would have to stand all the time with his insides entrails on show. Science.

— *A cenar teco.*

What does that *teco* mean? Tonight perhaps.

Don Giovanni, thou hast me invited
To come to supper tonight,
The rum the rumdum.

Doesn't go properly.

Keyes : two months if I get Nannetti to. That'll be two pounds ten, about two pounds eight. Three Hynes owes me. Two eleven. Presscott's ad. Two fifteen. Five guineas about. On the pig's back.

Could buy one of those silk petticoats for Molly, colour of her new garters.

Today. Today. Not think.

Tour the south then. What about English watering places? Brighton, Margate. Piers by moonlight. Her voice floating out. Those lovely seaside girls. Against John Long's a drowsing loafer lounged in heavy thought, gnawing a crusted kunckle. Handy man wants job. Small wages. Will eat anything.

Mr Bloom turned at Gray's confectioner's window of unbought tarts and passed the reverend Thomas Connellan's bookstore. *Why I left the church of Rome? Bird's Nest.* Women run him. They say they used to give pauper children soup to change to protestants in the time of the potato blight. Society over the way papa went to for the conversion of poor jews. Same bait. Why we left the church of Rome?

A blind stripling stood tapping the curbstone with his slender cane. No tram in sight. Wants to cross.

— Do you want to cross? Mr Bloom asked.

The blind stripling did not answer. His wall face frowned weakly. He moved his head uncertainly.

— You're in Dawson street, Mr Bloom said. Molesworth street is opposite. Do you want to cross? There's nothing in the way.

The cane moved out trembling to the left. Mr Bloom's eye followed its line and saw again the dyeworks' van drawn up before Drago's. Where I saw his brillantined hair just when I was. Horse drooping. Driver in John Long's. Slaking his drouth.

— There's a van there, Mr Bloom said, but it's not moving. I'll see you across. Do you want to go to Molesworth street?

— Yes, the stripling answered. South Frederick street.

— Come, Mr Bloom said.

He touched the thin elbow gently: then took the limp seeing hand to guide it forward.

Say something to him. Better not do the condescending. They mistrust what you tell them. Pass a common remark.

— The rain kept off.

No answer.

Stains on his coat. Slobbers his food I suppose. Tastes all different for him. Have to be spoonfed first. Like a child's hand his hand. Like Milly's was. Sensitive. Sizing me up I daresay from my hand. Wonder if he has a name. Van. Keep his cane clear of the horse's legs tired drudge get his doze. That's right. Clear. Behind a bull : in front of a horse.

— Thanks, sir.

Knows I'm a man. Voice.

— Right now? First turn to the left.

The blind stripling tapped the curbstone and went on his way, drawing his cane back, feeling again.

Mr Bloom walked behind the eyeless feet, a flatcut suit of herringbone tweed. Poor young fellow! How on earth did he know that van was there? Must have felt it. See things in their foreheads perhaps. Kind of sense of volume. Weight would he feel it if something was removed. Feel a gap. Queer idea of Dublin he must have, tapping his way round by the stones. Could he walk in a beeline if he hadn't that cane? Bloodless pious face like a fellow going in to be a priest.

Penrose! That was that chap's name.

Look at all the things they can learn to do. Read with their fingers. Tune pianos. Or we are surprised they have any brains. Why we think a deformed person or a hunchback clever if he says something we might say. Of course the other senses are more. Embroider. Plait baskets. People ought to help. Work basket I could buy Molly's birthday. Hates sewing. Might take an objection. Dark men they call them.

Sense of smell must be stronger too. Smells on all sides bunched together. Each person too. Then the spring, the summer : smells. Tastes. They say you can't taste wines with your eyes shut or a cold in the head. Also smoke in the dark they say get no pleasure.

And with a woman, for instance. More shameless not seeing. That girl passing the Stewart institution, head in the air. Look at me. I have them all on. Must be strange not to see her. Kind of a form in his mind's eye. The voice, temperature when he touches her with his fingers must almost see the lines, the curves. His hands on her hair, for instance. Say it was black for instance. Good. We call it black. Then passing over her white skin. Different feel perhaps. Feeling of white.

Postoffice. Must answer. Fag today. Send her a postal order two shillings, half a crown. Accept my little present. Stationer's just here too. Wait. Think over it.

With a gentle finger he felt ever so slowly the hair combed back above his ears. Again. Fibres of fine fine straw. Then gently his finger felt the skin of his right cheek. Downy hair there too. Not smooth enough. The belly is the smoothest. No-one about. There he goes into Frederick street. Perhaps to Levenston's dancing academy piano. Might be settling my braces.

Walking by Doran's public house he slid his hand between waistcoat and trousers and, pulling aside his shirt gently, felt a slack fold of his belly. But I know it's whiteyellow. Want to try in the dark to see.

He withdrew his hand and pulled his dress to.

Poor fellow! Quite a boy. Terrible. Really terrible. What dreams would he have, not seeing. Life a dream for him. Where is the justice being born that way. All those women and children excursion beanfeast burned and drowned in New York. Holocaust. Karma they call that transmigration for sins you did in a past life the reincarnation met him pikehoses. Dear, dear, dear. Pity of course : but somehow you can't cotton on to them someway.

Sir Frederick Falkiner going into the freemasons' hall. Solemn as Troy. After his good lunch in Earlsfort terrace. Old legal cronies cracking a magnum. Tales of the bench and assizes and annals of the bluecoat school. I sentenced him to ten years. I suppose he'd turn up his nose at that stuff I drank. Vintage wine for them, the year marked on a dusty bottle. Has his own ideas of justice in the recorder's court. Wellmeaning old man. Police chargesheets crammed with cases get their percentage manufacturing crime. Sends them to the rightabout. The devil on moneylenders. Gave Reuben J a great strawcalling. Now he's really what they call a dirty jew. Power those judges have. Crusty old topers in wigs. Bear with a sore paw. And may the Lord have mercy on your soul.

Hello, placard. Mirus bazaar. His excellency the lord lieutenant. Sixteenth today it is. In aid of funds for Mercer's hospital. *The Messiah* was first given for that. Yes. Handel. What about going out there. Ballsbridge. Drop in on Keyes. No use sticking to him like a leech. Wear out my welcome. Sure to know someone on the gate.

Mr Bloom came to Kildare street. First I must. Library.

Straw hat in sunlight. Tan shoes. Turnedup trousers. It is. It is.

His heart quopped softly. To the right. Museum. Goddesses. He swerved to the right.

Is it? Almost certain. Won't look. Wine in my face. Why did I? Too heady. Yes, it is. The walk. Not see. Not see. Get on.

Making for the museum gate with long windy strides he lifted his eyes. Handsome building. Sir Thomas Deane designed. Not following me?

Didn't see me perhaps. Light in his eyes.

The flutter of his breath came forth in short sighs. Quick. Cold statues : quiet there. Safe in a minute.

No, didn't see me. After two. Just at the gate.

My heart!

His eyes beating looked steadfastly at cream curves of stone. Sir Thomas Deane was the Greek architecture.

Look for something I.

His hasty hand went quick into a pocket, took out, read unfolded Agendath Netaim. Where did I?

Busy looking for.

He thrust back quickly Agendath.

Afternoon she said.

I am looking for that. Yes, that. Try all pockets. Handker. *Freeman.* Where did I? Ah, yes. Trousers. Purse. Potato. Where did I?

Hurry. Walk quietly. Moment more. My heart.

His hand looking for the where did I put found in his hip pocket soap lotion have to call tepid paper stuck. Ah, soap there! Yes. Gate.

Safe!

Urbane, to comfort them, the quaker librarian purred :

— And we have, have we not, those priceless pages of *Wilhelm Meister ?* A great poet on a great brother poet. A hesitating soul taking arms against a sea of troubles, torn by conflicting doubts, as one sees in real life.

He came a step a sinkapace forward on neatsleather creaking and a step backward a sinkapace on the solemn floor.

A noiseless attendant, setting open the door but slightly, made him a noiseless beck.

— Directly, said he, creaking to go, albeit lingering. The beautiful ineffectual dreamer who comes to grief against hard facts. One always feels that Goethe's judgments are so true. True in the larger analysis.

Twicreakingly analysis he corantoed off. Bald, most zealous by the door he gave his large ear all to the attendant's words : heard them : and was gone.

Two left.

— Monsieur de la Palice, Stephen sneered, was alive fifteen minutes before his death.

— Have you found those six brave medicals, John Eglinton asked with elder's gall, to write *Paradise Lost* at your dictation ? *The Sorrows of Satan* he calls it.

Smile. Smile Cranly's smile.

First he tickled her
Then he patted her
Then he passed the female catheter
For he was a medical
Jolly old medi...

— I feel you would need one more for *Hamlet*. Seven is dear to the mystic mind. The shining seven W. B. calls them.

Glittereyed, his rufous skull close to his greencapped desklamp sought the face, bearded amid darkgreener shadow, an ollav, holyeyed He laughed low : a sizar's laugh of Trinity : unanswered.

Orchestral Satan, weeping many a rood
Tears such as angels weep.
Ed egli avea del cul fatto trombetta.

He holds my follies hostage.

Cranly's eleven true Wicklowmen to free their sireland. Gaptoothed Kathleen, her four beautiful green fields, the stranger in her house. And one more to hail him : *ave, rabbi.* The Tinahely twelve. In the shadow of the glen he cooees for them. My soul's youth I gave him, night by night. Godspeed. Good hunting.

Mulligan has my telegram.

Folly. Persist.

— Our young Irish bards, John Eglinton censured, have yet to create a figure which the world will set beside Saxon Shakespeare's Hamlet though I admire him, as old Ben did, on this side idolatry.

— All these questions are purely academic, Russell oracled out of his shadow. I mean, whether Hamlet is Shakespeare or James I or Essex. Clergymen's discussions of the historicity of Jesus. Art has to reveal to us ideas, formless spiritual essences. The supreme question about a work of art is out of how deep a life does it spring. The painting of Gustave Moreau is the painting of ideas. The deepest poetry of Shelley, the words of Hamlet bring our mind into contact with the eternal wisdom, Plato's world of ideas. All the rest is the speculation of schoolboys for schoolboys.

A. E. has been telling some yankee interviewer. Wall, tarnation strike me!

— The schoolmen were schoolboys first, Stephen said superpolitely. Aristotle was once Plato's schoolboy.

— And has remained so, one should hope, John Eglinton sedately said. One can see him, a model schoolboy with his diploma under his arm.

He laughed again at the now smiling bearded face.

Formless spiritual. Father, Word and Holy Breath. Allfather, the heavenly man. Hiesos Kristos, magician of the beautiful, the Logos who suffers in us at every moment. This verily is that. I am the fire upon the altar. I am the sacrificial butter.

Dunlop, Judge, the noblest Roman of them all, A. E., Arval, the Name Ineffable, in heaven hight, K. H., their master, whose identity is no secret to adepts. Brothers of the great white lodge always watching to see if they can help. The Christ with the bridesister, moisture of light, born of en ensouled virgin, repentant sophia, departed to the plane of buddhi. The life esoteric is not for ordinary person. O. P. must work off bad karma first. Mrs Cooper Oakley once glimpsed our very illustrious sister H. P. B's elemental.

O, fie! Out on't! *Pfuiteufel!* You naughtn't to look, missus, so you naughtn't when a lady's ashowing of her elemental.

Mr Best entered, tall, young, mild, light. He bore in his hand with grace a notebook, new, large, clean, bright.

— That model schoolboy, Stephen said, would find Hamlet's musings about the afterlife of his princely soul, the improbable, insignificant and undramatic monologue, as shallow as Plato's.

John Eglinton, frowning, said, waxing wroth:

— Upon my word it makes my blood boil to hear anyone compare Aristotle with Plato.

— Which of the two, Stephen asked, would have banished me from his commonwealth?

Unsheathe your dagger definitions. Horseness is the whatness of allhorse. Streams of tendency and eons they worship. God: noise in the street: very peripatetic. Space: what you damn well have to see. Through spaces smaller than red globules of man's blood they creepycrawl after Blake's buttocks into eternity of which this vegetable world is but a shadow. Hold to the now, the here, through which all future plunges to the past.

Mr Best came forward, amiable, towards his colleague.

— Haines is gone, he said.

— Is he?

— I was showing him Jubainville's book. He's quite enthusiastic, don't you know, about Hyde's *Lovesongs of Connacht*. I couldn't bring him in to hear the discussion. He's gone to Gill's to buy it.

Bound thee forth, my booklet, quick
To greet the callous public.
Writ, I ween, 'twas not my wish
In lean unlovely English.

— The peatsmoke is going to his head, John Eglinton opined.

We feel in England. Penitent thief. Gone. I smoked his baccy. Green twinkling stone. An emerald set in the ring of the sea.

— People do not know how dangerous lovesongs can be, the auric egg of Russell warned occultly. The movements which work revolutions in the world are born out of the dreams and visions in a peasant's heart on the hillside. For them the earth is not an exploitable ground but the living mother. The rarefied air of the academy and the arena produce the sixshilling novel, the music-hall song, France produces the finest flower of corruption in Mallarmé but the desirable life is revealed only to the poor of heart, the life of Homer's Phæacians.

From these words Mr Best turned an unoffending face to Stephen.

— Mallarmé, don't you know, he said, has written those wonderful prose poems Stephen MacKenna used to read to me in Paris. The one about *Hamlet*. He says : *il se promène, lisant au livre de lui-même,* don't you know, *reading the book of himself*. He describes *Hamlet* given in a French town, don't you know, a provincial town. They advertised it.

His free hand graciously wrote tiny signs in air.

Hamlet
ou
Le Distrait
Pièce de Shakespeare

He repeated to John Eglinton's newgathered frown :

— *Pièce de Shakespeare,* don't you know. It's so French, the French point of view. *Hamlet ou...*

— The absentminded beggar, Stephen ended.

John Eglinton laughed.

— Yes, I suppose it would be, he said. Excellent people, no doubt, but distressingly shortsighted in some matters.

Sumptuous and stagnant exaggeration of murder.

— A deathsman of the soul Robert Greene called him, Stephen said. Not for nothing was he a butcher's son wielding the sledded poleaxe and spitting in his palm. Nine lives are taken off for his father's one, Our Father who art in purgatory. Khaki Hamlets don't hesitate to shoot. The bloodboltered shambles in act five is a forecast of the concentration camp sung by Mr Swinburne.

Cranly, I his mute orderly, following battles from afar.

Whelps and dams of murderous foes whom none
But we had spared...

Between the Saxon smile and yankee yawp. The devil and the deep sea.

— He will have it that *Hamlet* is a ghoststory, John Eglinton said for Mr Best's behoof. Like the fat boy in Pickwick he wants to make our flesh creep.

List ! List ! O list !

My flesh hears him : creeping, hears.

If thou didst ever...

— What is a ghost ? Stephen said with tingling energy. One who has faded into impalpability through death, through absence, through change of manners. Elizabethan London lay as far from Stratford as corrupt Paris lies from virgin Dublin. Who is the ghost from *limbo patrum,* returning to the world that has forgotten him ? Who is king Hamlet ?

John Eglinton shifted his spare body, leaning back to judge.

Lifted.

— It is this hour of a day in mid June, Stephen said, begging with a swift glance their hearing. The flag is up on the playhouse by the bankside. The bear Sackerson growls in the pit near it, Paris garden. Canvasclimbers who sailed with Drake chew their sausages among the groundlings.

Local colour. Work in all you know. Make them accomplices.

— Shakespeare has left the huguenot's house in Silver street and walks by the swanmews along the riverbank. But he does not stay to feed the pen chivying her game of cygnets towards the rushes. The swan of Avon has other thoughts.

Composition of place. Ignatius Loyola, make haste to help me !

— The play begins. A player comes on under the shadow, made up in the castoff mail of a court buck, a wellset man with a bass voice. It is the ghost, the king, a king and no king, and the player is Shakespeare who has studied *Hamlet* all the years of his life which were not vanity in order to play the part of the spectre. He speaks the words to Burbage, the young player who stands before him beyond the rack of cerecloth, calling him by a name :

Hamlet, I am thy father's spirit

bidding him list. To a son he speaks, the son of his soul, the prince, young Hamlet and to the son of his body, Hamnet Shakespeare, who has died in Stratford that his namesake may live for ever.

Is it possible that that player Shakespeare, a ghost by absence, and in the vesture of buried Denmark, a ghost by death, speaking his own words to his own son's name (had Hamnet Shakespeare lived he would have been prince Hamlet's twin) is it possible, I want to know, or probable that he did not draw or foresee the logical conclusion of those premises : you are the dispossesed son : I am the murdered father : your mother is the guilty queen, Ann Shakespeare, born Hathaway?

— But this prying into the family life of a great man, Russell began impatiently.

Art thou there, truepenny?

— Interesting only to the parish clerk. I mean, we have the plays. I mean when we read the poetry of *King Lear* what is it to us how the poet lived? As for living, our servants can do that for us, Villiers de l'Isle has said. Peeping and prying into greenroom gossip of the day, the poet's drinking, the poet's debts. We have *King Lear :* and it is immortal.

Mr Best's face appealed to, agreed.

Flow over them with your waves and with your waters, Mananaan,
Mananaan MacLir.....

How now, sirrah, that pound he lent you when you were hungry?

Marry, I wanted it.

Take thou this noble.

Go to! You spent most of it in Georgina Johnson's bed, clergyman's daughter. Agenbite of inwit.

Do you intend to pay it back?

O, yes.

When? Now?

Well... no.

When, then?

I paid my way. I paid my way.

Steady on. He's from beyant Boyne water. The northeast corner. You owe it.

Wait. Five months. Molecules all change. I am other I now. Other I got pound.

Buzz. Buzz.

But I, entelechy, form of forms, am I by memory because under everchanging forms.

I that sinned and prayed and fasted.

A child Conmee saved from pandies.

I, I and I. I.

A. E. I. O. U.

— Do you mean to fly in the face of the tradition of three centuries? John Eglinton's carping voice asked. Her ghost at least has been laid for ever. She died, for literature at least, before she was born.

— She died, Stephen retorted, sixtyseven years after she was born. She saw him into and out of the world. She took his first embraces. She bore his children and she laid pennies on his eyes to keep his eyelids closed when he lay on his deathbed.

Mother's deathbed. Candle. The sheeted mirror. Who brought me into this world lies there, bronzelidded, under few cheap flowers. *Liliata rutilantium.*

I wept alone.

John Eglinton looked in the tangled glowworm of his lamp.

— The world believes that Shakespeare made a mistake, he said, and got out of it as quickly and as best he could.

— Bosh! Stephen said rudely. A man of genius makes no mistakes. His errors are volitional and are the portals of discovery.

Portals of discovery opened to let in the quaker librarian, softcreakfooted, bald, eared and assiduous.

— A shrew, John Eglinton said shrewdly, is not a useful portal of discovery, one should imagine. What useful discovery did Socrates learn from Xanthippe?

— Dialectic, Stephen answered : and from his mother how to bring thoughts into the world. What he learnt from his other wife Myrto *(absit nomen!)* Socratididion's Epipsychidion, no man, not a woman, will ever know. But neither the midwife's lore nor the caudlelectures saved him from the archons of Sinn Fein and their naggin of hemlock.

— But Ann Hathaway? Mr Best's quiet voice said forgetfully. Yes, we seem to be forgetting her as Shakespeare himself forgot her.

His look went from brooder's beard to carper's skull, to remind, to chide them not unkindly, then to the baldpink lollard costard, guitless though maligned.

— He had a good groatsworth of wit, Stephen said, and no truant memory. He carried a memory in his wallet as he trudged to Romeville whistling *The girl I left behind me*. If the earthquake did not time it we should know where to place poor Wat, sitting in his form, the cry of hounds, the studded bridle and her blue windows. That memory, *Venus and Adonis,* lay in the bechamber of every light-of-love in London. Is Katharine the shrew illfavoured? Hortensio calls her young and beautiful. Do you think the writer of *Antony and Cleopatra,* a passionate pilgrim, had his eyes in the back of his head that he chose the ugliest doxy in all Warwickshire to lie withal. Good: he left her and gained the world of men. But his boywomen are the women of a boy. Their life, thought, speech are lent them by males. He chose badly? He was chosen, it seems to me. If others have their will Ann hath a way. By cock, she was to blame. She put the comether on him, sweet and twentysix. The greyeyed goddess who bends over the boy Adonis, stooping to conquer, as prologue to the swelling act, is a boldfaced Stratford wench who tumbles in a cornfield a lover younger than herself.

And my turn? When?

Come!

— Ryefield, Mr Best said brightly, gladly, raising his new book, gladly, brightly.

He murmured then with blond delight for all:

Between the acres of the rye
These pretty countryfolk would lie.

Paris: the wellpleased pleaser.

A tall figure in bearded homespun rose from shadow and unveiled its cooperative watch.

— I am afraid I am due at the *Homestead.*

Whither away? Exploitable ground.

— Are you going, John Eglinton's active eyebrows asked. Shall we see you at Moore's tonight? Piper is coming.

— Piper! Mr Best piped. Is Piper back?

Peter Piper pecked a peck of pick of peck of pickled pepper.

— I don't know if I can. Thursday. We have our meeting. If I can get away in time.

Yogibogeybox in Dawson chambers. *Isis Unveiled.* Their Pali book we tried to pawn. Crosslegged under an umbrel umbershoot he thrones an Aztec logos, functioning on astral levels, their oversoul, mahamahatma. The faithful hermetists await the light, ripe for chelaship, ringroundabout him. Louis H. Victory. T. Caulfield Irwin. Lotus ladies tend them i'the eyes, their pineal glands aglow. Filled with his god he thrones, Buddh under plantain. Gulfer of souls, engulfer. Hesouls, shesouls, shoals of souls. Engulfed with wailing creecries, whirled, whirling, they bewail.

In quintessential triviality
For years in this fleshcase a shesoul dwelt.

— They say we are to have a literary surprise, the quaker librarian said, friendly and earnest. Mr Russell, rumour has it, is gathering together a sheaf of our younger poets' verses. We are all looking forward anxiously.

Anxiously he glanced in the cone of lamplight where three faces, lighted, shone.

See this. Remember.

Stephen looked down on a wide headless caubeen, hung on his ashplant-handle over his knee. My casque and sword. Touch lightly with two index fingers. Aristotle's experiment. One or two? Necessity is that in virtue of which it is impossible that one can be otherwise. Argal, one hat is one hat.

Listen.

Young Colum and Starkey. George Roberts is doing the commercial part. Longworth will give it a good puff in the *Express.* O, will he? I liked Colum's *Drover.* Yes, I think he has that queer thing, genius. Do you think he has genius really? Yeats admired his line: *As in wild earth a Grecian vase.* Did he?

I hope you'll be able to come tonight. Malachi Mulligan is coming too. Moore asked him to bring Haines. Did you hear Miss Mitchell's joke about Moore and Martyn ? That Moore is Martyn's wild oats ? Awfully clever, isn't it ? They remind one of don Quixote and Sancho Panza. Our national epic has yet to be written, Dr Sigerson says. Moore is the man for it. A knight of the rueful countenance here in Dublin. With a saffron kilt ? O'Neill Russell ? O, yes, he must speak the grand old tongue. And his Dulcinea ? James Stephens is doing some clever sketches. We are becoming important, it seems.

Cordelia. *Cordoglio.* Lir's loneliest daughter.

Nookshotten. Now your best French polish.

— Thank you very much, Mr Russell, Stephen said, rising. If you will be so kind as to give the letter to Mr Norman.....

— O, yes. If he considers it important it will go in. We have so much correspondence.

— I understand, Stephen said. Thanks.

God ild you. The pigs' paper. Bullockbefriending.

Synge has promised me an article for *Dana* too. Are we going to be read ? I feel we are. The Gaelic league wants something in Irish. I hope you will come round tonight. Bring Starkey.

Stephen sat down.

The quaker librarian came from the leavetakers. Blushing his mask said :

— Mr Dedalus, your views are most illuminating.

He creaked to and fro, tiptoing up nearer heaven by the altitude of a chopine, and, covered by the noise of outgoing, said low :

— Is it your view, then, that she was not faithful to the poet ?

Alarmed face asks me. Why did he come ? Courtesy or an inward light ?

— Where there is a reconciliation, Stephen said, there must have been first a sundering.

— Yes.

Christfox in leather trews, hiding, a runaway in blighted treeforks from hue and cry. Knowing no vixen, walking lonely in the chase. Women he won to him, tender people, a whore of Babylon, ladies of justices, bully tapsters' wives. Fox and geese. And in New place a slack dishonoured body that once was comely, once as sweet, as fresh as cinnamon, now her leaves falling, all, bare, frighted of the narrow grave and unforgiven.

— Yes. So you think...

The door closed behind the outgoer.

Rest suddenly possessed the discreet vaulted cell, rest of warm and brooding air.

A vestal's lamp.

Here he ponders things that were not: what Cæsar would havé lived to do had he believed the soothsayer: what might have been: possibilities of the possible as possible: things not known: what name Achilles bore when he lived among women.

Coffined thoughts around me, in mummycases, embalmed in spice of words. Thoth, god of libraries, a birdgod, moonycrowned. And I heard the voice of that Egyptian highpriest. *In painted chambers loaded with tilebooks.*

They are still. Once quick in the brains of men. Still: but an itch of death is in them, to tell me in my ear a maudlin tale, urge me to wreak their will.

— Certainly, John Eglinton mused, of all great men he is the most enigmatic. We know nothing but that he lived and suffered. Not even so much. Others abide our question. A shadow hangs over all the rest.

— But *Hamlet* is so personal, isn't it? Mr Best pleaded. I mean, a kind of private paper, don't you know, of his private life. I mean I don't care a button, don't you know, who is killed or who is guilty...

He rested an innocent book on the edge of the desk, smiling his defiance. His private papers in the original. *Ta an bad ar an tir. Taim imo shagart.* Put beurla on it, littlejohn.

Quoth littlejohn Eglinton:

— I was prepared for paradoxes from what Malachi Mulligan told us but I may as well warn you that if you want to shake my belief that Shakespeare is Hamlet you have a stern task before you.

Bear with me.

Stephen withstood the bane of miscreant eyes, glinting stern under wrinkled brows. A basilisk. *E quando vede l'uomo l'attosca.* Messer Brunetto, I thank thee for the word.

— As we, or mother Dana, weave and unweave our bodies, Stephen said, from day to day, their molecules shuttled to and fro, so does the artist weave and unweave his image. And as the mole on my right breast is where it was when I was born, though all my body has been woven of new stuff time after time, so through the ghost of the unquiet father the image of the unliving son looks forth. In the intense instant of imagination, when the mind, Shelley says, is a fading coal that which I was is that which I am and that which in possibility I may come to be. So in the future, the sister of the past, I may see myselr as I sit here now but by reflection from that which then I shall be.

Drummond of Hawthornden helped you at that stile.

— Yes, Mr Best said youngly, I feel Hamlet quite young. The bitterness might be from the father but the passages with Ophelia are surely from the son.

Has the wrong sow by the lug. He is in my father. I am in his son.

— That mole is the last to go, Stephen said, laughing.

John Eglinton made a nothing pleasing mow.

— If that were the birthmark of genius, he said, genius would be a drug in the market. The plays of Shakespeare's later years which Renan admired so much breathe another spirit.

— The spirit of reconciliation, the quaker librarian breathed.

— There can be no reconciliation, Stephen said, if there has not been a sundering.

Said that.

— If you want to know what are the events which cast their shadow over the hell of time of *King Lear, Othello, Hamlet, Troilus and Cressida*, look to see when and how the shadow lifts. What softens the heart of a man, shipwrecked in storms dire, Tried, like another Ulysses, Pericles, prince of Tyre?

Head, redconecapped, buffeted, brineblinded.

— A child, a girl placed in his arms, Marina.

— The leaning of sophists towards the bypaths of apocrypha is a constant quantity, John Eglinton detected. The highroads are dreary but they lead to the town.

Good Bacon: gone musty. Shakespeare Bacon's wild oats. Cypherjugglers going the highroads. Seekers on the great quest. What town, good masters? Mummed in names: A. E, eon: Magee, John Eglinton. East of the sun, west of the moon: *Tir na n-og*. Booted the twain and staved.

How many miles to Dublin?
Three score and ten, sir.
Will we be there by candlelight?

— Mr Brandes accepts it, Stephen said, as the first play of the closing period.

— Does he? What does Mr Sidney Lee, or Mr Simon Lazarus, as some aver his name is, say of it?

— Marina, Stephen said, a child of storm, Miranda, a wonder, Perdita, that which was lost. What was lost is given back to him: his daughter's child.

My dearest wife, Pericles says, *was like this maid*. Will any man love the daughter if he has not loved the mother?

— The art of being a grandfather, Mr Best gan murmur. *L'art d'être grand...*

— His own image to a man with that queer thing genius is the standard of all experience, material and moral. Such an appeal will touch him. The images of other males of his blood will repel him. He will see in them grotesque attempts of nature to foretell or repeat himself.

The benign forehead of the quaker librarian enkindled rosily with hope.

— I hope Mr Dedalus will work out his theory for the enlightenment of the public. And we ought to mention another Irish commentator, Mr George Bernard Shaw. Nor should we forget Mr Frank Harris. His articles on Shakespeare in the *Saturday Review* were surely brilliant. Oddly enough he too draws for us an unhappy relation with the dark lady of the sonnets. The favoured rival is William Herbert, earl of Pembroke. I own that if the poet must be rejected, such a rejection would seem more in harmony with — what shall I say? — our notions of what ought not to have been.

Felicitously he ceased and held a meek head among them, auk's egg, prize of their fray.

He thous and thees her with grave husbandwords. Dost love, Miriam? Dost love thy man?

— That may be too, Stephen said. There is a saying of Goethe's which Mr Magee likes to quote. Beware of what you wish for in youth because you will get it in middle life. Why does he send to one who is a *buonaroba*, a bay where all men ride, a maid of honour with a scandalous girlhood, a lordling to woo for him? He was himself a lord of language and had made himself a coistrel gentleman and had written *Romeo and Juliet*. Why? Belief in himself has been untimely killed. He was overborne in a cornfield first (ryefield, I should say) and he will never be a victor in his own eyes after nor play victoriously the game of laugh and lie down. Assumed dongiovannism will not save him. No later undoing will undo the first undoing. The tusk of the boar has wounded him there where love lies ableeding. If the shrew is worsted yet there remains to her woman's invisible weapon. There is, I feel in the words, some goad of the flesh driving him into a new passion, a darker shadow of the first, darkening even his own understanding of himself. A like fate awaits him and the two rages commingle in a whirlpool.

They list. And in the porches of their ears I pour.

— The soul has been before stricken mortally, a poison poured in the porch of a sleeping ear. But those who are done to death in sleep cannot know the manner of their quell unless their Creator endow their souls with that knowledge in the life to come. The poisoning and the beast with two backs that urged it king Hamlet's ghost could not know of were he not endowed with knowledge by his creator. That is why the speech (his lean unlovely English) is always turned elsewhere, backward. Ravisher and ravished, what he would but would not, go with him from Lucrece's bluecircled ivory globes to Imogen's breast, bare, with its mole cinquespotted. He goes back, weary of the creation he has piled up to hide him from himself, an old dog licking an old sore. But, because loss is his gain, he passes on towards eternity in undiminished personality, untaught by the wisdom he has written or by the laws he has revealed. His beaver is up. He is a ghost, a shadow now, the wind by Elsinore's rocks or what you will, the sea's voice, a voice heard only in the heart of him who is the substance of his shadow, the son consubstantial with the father.

— Amen ! responded from the doorway.

Hast thou found me, O mine enemy ?

Entr'acte.

A ribald face, sullen as a dean's, Buck Mulligan came forward, then blithe in motley, towards the greeting of their smiles. My telegram.

— You were speaking of the gaseous vertebrate, if I mistake not ? he asked of Stephen.

Primrosevested he greeted gaily with his doffed Panama as with a bauble.

They make him welcome. *Was Du verlachst wirst Du noch dienen.*

Brood of mockers : Photius, pseudomalachi, Johann Most.

He Who Himself begot, middler the Holy Ghost, and Himself sent Himself, Agenbuyer, between Himself and others, Who, put upon by His fiends, stripped and whipped, was nailed like bat to barndoor, starved on crosstree, Who let Him bury, stood up, harrowed hell, fared into heaven and there these nineteen hundred years sitteth on the right hand of His Own Self but yet shall come in the latter day to doom the quick and dead when all the quick shall be dead already.

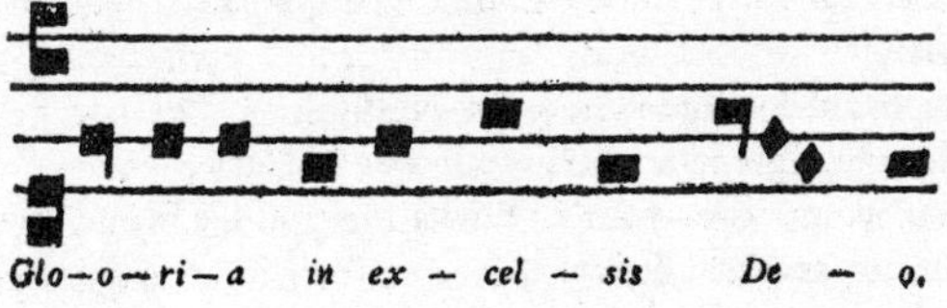

He lifts his hands. Veils fall. O, flowers! Bells with bells with bells aquiring.

— Yes, indeed, the quaker librarian said. A most instructive discussion. Mr Mulligan, I'll be bound, has his theory too of the play and of Shakespeare. All sides of life should be represented.

He smiled on all sides equally.

Buck Mulligan thought, puzzled:

— Shakespeare? he said. I seem to know the name.

A flying sunny smile rayed in his loose features.

— To be sure, he said, remembering brightly. The chap that writes like Synge.

Mr Best turned to him:

— Haines missed you, he said. Did you meet him? He'll see you after at the D. B. C. He's gone to Gill's to buy Hyde's *Lovesongs of Connacht*.

— I came through the museum, Buck Mulligan said. Was he here?

— The bard's fellowcountrymen, John Eglinton answered, are rather tired perhaps of our brilliancies of theorising. I hear that an actress played Hamlet for the fourhundredandeighth time last night in Dublin. Vining held that the prince was a woman. Has no-one made him out to be an Irishman? Judge Barton, I believe, is searching for some clues. He swears (His Highness not His Lordship) by saint Patrick.

— The most brilliant of all is that story of Wilde's, Mr Best said, lifting his brilliant notebook. That *Portrait of Mr W. H.* where he proves that the sonnets were written by a Willie Hughes, a man all hues.

— For Willie Hughes, is it not? the quaker librarian asked.

Or Hughie Wills. Mr William Himself. W. H: who am I?

— I mean, for Willie Hughes, Mr Best said, amending his gloss easily. Of course it's all paradox, don't you know, Hughes and hews and hues the colour, but it's so typical the way he works it out. It's the very essence of Wilde, don't you know. The light touch.

His glance touched their faces lightly as he smiled, a blond ephebe. Tame essence of Wilde.

You're darned witty. Three drams of usquebaugh you drank with Dan Deasy's ducats.

How much did I spend? O, a few shillings.

For a plump of pressmen. Humour wet and dry.

Wit. You would give your five wits for youth's proud livery he pranks in. Lineaments of gratified desire.

There be many mo. Take her for me. In pairing time. Jove, a cool ruttime send them. Yea, turtledove her.

Eve. Naked wheatbellied sin. A shake coils her, fang in's kiss.

— Do you think it is only a paradox, the quaker librarian was asking. The mocker is never taken seriously when he is most serious.

They talked seriously of mocker's seriousness.

Buck Mulligan's again heavy face eyed Stephen awhile. Then, his head wagging, he came near, drew a folded telegram from his pocket. His mobile lips read, smiling with new delight.

— Telegram ! He said. Wonderful inspiration ! Telegram ! A papal bull !

He sat on a corner of the unlit desk, reading aloud joyfully :

— *The sentimentalist is he who would enjoy without incurring the immense debtorship for a thing done.* Signed : Dedalus. Where did you launch it from ? The kips ? No. College Green. Have you drunk the four quid ? The aunt is going to call on your unsubstantial father. Telegram ! Malachi Mulligan, the Ship, lower Abbey street. O, you peerless mummer ! O, you priestified kinchite !

Joyfully he thrust message and envelope into a pocket but keened in querulous brogue :

— It's what I'm telling you, mister honey, it's queer and sick we were, Haines and myself, the time himself brought it in. 'Twas murmur we did for a gallus potion would rouse a friar, I'm thinking, and he limp with leching. And we one hour and two hours and three hours in Connery's sitting civil waiting for pints apiece.

He wailed :

— And we to be there, mavrone, and you to be unbeknownst sending us your conglomerations the way we to have our tongues out a yard long like the drouthy clerics do be fainting for a pussful.

Stephen laughed.

Quickly, warningfully Buck Mulligan bent down :

— The tramper Synge is looking for you, he said, to murder you. He heard you pissed on his halldoor in Glasthule. He's out in pampooties to murder you.

— Me ! Stephen exclaimed. That was your contribution to literature.

Buck Mulligan gleefully bent back, laughing to the dark eavesdropping ceiling.

— Murder you ! he laughed.

Harsh gargoyle face that warred against me over our mess of hash of lights in rue Saint-André-des-Arts. In words of words for words, palabras. Oisin with Patrick. Faunman he met in Clamart woods, brandishing a winebottle. *C'est vendredi saint!* Murthering Irish. His image, wandering, he met. I mine. I met a fool i' the forest.

— Mr Lyster, an attendant said from the door ajar.

—... in which everyone can find his own. So Mr Justice Madden in his *Diary of Master Silence* has found the hunting terms... Yes? What is it?

— There's a gentleman here, sir, the attendant said, coming forward and offering a card. From the *Freeman*. He wants to see the files of the *Kilkenny People* for last year.

— Certainly, certainly, certainly. Is the gentleman?...

He took the eager card, glanced, not saw, laid down, unglanced, looked, asked, creaked, asked:

— Is he?... O, there!

Brisk in a galliard he was off and out. In the daylit corridor he talked with voluble pains of zeal, in duty bound, most fair, most kind, most honest broadbrim.

— This gentleman? *Freeman's Journal? Kilkenny People?* To be sure. Good day, sir. *Kilkenny*... We have certainly...

A patient silhouette waited, listening.

— All the leading provincial... *Northern Whig, Cork Examiner, Enniscorthy Guardian,* 1903... Will you please?... Evans, conduct this gentleman... If you just follow the atten... Or please allow me... This way... Please, sir...

Voluble, dutiful, he led the way to all the provincial papers, a bowing dark figure following his hasty heels.

The door closed.

— The sheeny! Buck Mulligan cried,

He jumped up and snatched the card.

— What's his name? Ikey Moses? Bloom.

He rattled on.

— Jehovah, collector of prepuces, is no more. I found him over in the museum when I went to hail the foamborn Aphrodite. The Greek mouth that has never been twisted in prayer. Every day we must do homage to her. *Life of life, thy lips enkindle.*

Suddenly he turned to Stephen:

— He knows you. He knows your old fellow. O, I fear me, he is Greeker than the Greeks. His pale Galilean eyes were upon her mesial groove. Venus

Kallipyge. O, the thunder of those loins! *The god pursuing the maiden hid.*

— We want to hear more, John Eglinton decided with Mr Best's approval. We begin to be interested in Mrs S. Till now we had thought of her, if at all, as a patient Griselda, a Penelope stayathome.

— Antisthenes, pupil of Gorgias, Stephen said, took the palm of beauty from Kyrios Menelaus' brooddam, Argive Helen, the wooden mare of Troy in whom a score of heroes slept, and handed it to poor Penelope. Twenty years he lived in London and, during part of that time, he drew a salary equal to that of the lord chancellor of Ireland. His life was rich. His art, more than the art of feudalism, as Walt Whitman called it, is the art of surfeit. Hot herringpies, green mugs of sack, honeysauces, sugar of roses, marchpane, gooseberried pigeons, ringocandies. Sir Walter Raleigh, when they arrested him, had half a million francs on his back including a pair of fancy stays. The gombeenwoman Eliza Tudor had underlinen enough to vie with her of Sheba. Twenty years he dallied there between conjugial love and its chaste delights and scortatory love and its foul pleasures. You know Manningham's story of the burgher's wife who bade Dick Burbage to her bed after she had seen him in *Richard III* and how Shakespeare, overhearing, without more ado about nothing, took the cow by the horns and, when Burbage came knocking at the gate, answered from the capon's blankets : *William the conqueror came before Richard III*. And the gay lakin, mistress Fitton, mount and cry O, and his dainty birdsnies, lady Penelope Rich, a clean quality woman is suited for a player, and the punks of the bankside, a penny a time.

Cours-la-Reine. *Encore vingt sous. Nous ferons de petites cochonneries. Minette? Tu veux?*

— The height of fine society. And sir William Davenant of Oxford's mother with her cup of canary for every cockcanary.

Buck Mulligan, his pious eyes upturned, prayed :

— Blessed Margaret Mary Anycock!

— And Harry of six wives' daughter and other lady friends from neighbour seats, as Lawn Tennyson, gentleman poet, sings. But all those twenty years what do you suppose poor Penelope in Stratford was doing behind the diamond panes?

Do and do. Thing done. In a rosery of Fetter Lane of Gerard, herbalist, he walks, greyedauburn. An azured harebell like her veins. Lids of Juno's eyes, violets. He walks. One life is all. One body. Do. But do. Afar, in a reek of lust and squalor, hands are laid on whiteness.

Buck Mulligan rapped John Eglinton's desk sharply.

— Whom do you suspect? he challenged.

— Say that he is the spurned lover in the sonnets. Once spurned twice spurned. But the court wanton spurned him for a lord, his dearmylove.

Love that dare not speak its name.

— As an Englishman, you mean, John sturdy Eglinton put in, he loved a lord.

Old wall where sudden lizards flash. At Charenton I watched them.

— It seems so, Stephen said, when he wants to do for him, and for all other and singular uneared wombs, the holy office an ostler does for the stallion. Maybe, like Socrates, he had a midwife to mother as he had a shrew to wife. But she, the giglot wanton, did not break a bedvow. Two deeds are rank in that ghost's mind : a broken vow and the dullbrained yokel on whom her favour has declined, deceased husband's brother. Sweet Ann I take it, was hot in the blood. Once a wooer twice a wooer.

Stephen turned boldly in his chair.

— The burden of proof is with you not with me, he said, frowning. If you deny that in the fifth scene of *Hamlet* he has branded her with infamy, tell me why there is no mention of her during the thirtyfour years between the day she married him and the day she buried him. All those women saw their men down and under : Mary, her goodman John, Ann, her poor dear Willun, when he went and died on her, raging that he was the first to go, Joan, her four brothers, Judith, her husband and all her sons, Susan, her husband too while Susan's daughter, Elizabeth, to use granddaddy's words, wed her second, having killed her first.

O yes, mention there is. In the years when he was living richly in royal London to pay a debt she had to borrow forty shillings from her father's shepherd. Explain you then. Explain the swansong too wherein he has commended her to posterity.

He faced their silence.

To whom thus Eglinton :

You mean the will.
That has been explained, I believe, by jurists.
She was entitled to her widow's dower
At common law. His legal knowledge was great
Our judges tell us.

Him Satan fleers,

Mocker :

And therefore he left out her name
From the first draft but he did not leave out
The presents for his granddaughter, for his daughters,
For his sister, for his old cronies in Stratford
And in London. And therefore when he was urged,
As I believe, to name her
He left her his
Secondbest
Bed.

Punkt

Leftherhis
Secondbest
Leftherhis
Bestabed
Secabest
Leftabed.

Woa!

— Pretty countryfolk had few chattels then, John Eglinton observed, as they have still if our peasant plays are true to type.

— He was a rich countrygentleman, Stephen said, with a coat of arms and landed estate at Stratford and a house in Ireland yard, a capitalist shareholder, a bill promoter, a tithefarmer. Why did he not leave her his best bed if he wished her to snore away the rest of her nights in peace?

— It is clear that there were two beds, a best and a secondbest, Mr Secondbest Best said finely.

— *Separatio a mensa et a thalamo,* bettered Buck Mulligan and was smiled on.

— Antiquity mentions famous beds, Second Eglinton puckered, bedsmiling, Let me think.

— Antiquity mentions that Stagyrite schoolurchin and bald heathen sage, Stephen said, who when dying in exile frees and endows his slaves, pays tribute to his elders, wills to be laid in earth near the bones of his dead wife and bids his friends be kind to an old mistress (don't forget Nell Gwynn Herpyllis) and let her live in his villa.

— Do you mean he died so? Mr Best asked with slight concern. I mean...

— He died dead drunk, Buck Mulligan capped. A quart of ale is a dish for a king. O, I must tell you what Dowden said!

— What? asked Besteglinton.

William Shakespeare and company, limited. The people's William. For terms apply : E. Dowden, Highfield house.....

— Lovely! Buck Mulligan suspired amorously. I asked him what he thought of the charge of pederasty brought against the bard. He lifted his hands and said : *All we can say is that life ran very high in those days*. Lovely!

Catamite.

— The sense of beauty leads us astray, said beautifulinsadness Best to ugling Eglinton.

Steadfast John replied severe :

— The doctor can tell us what those words mean. You cannot eat your cake and have it.

Sayest thou so? Will they wrest from us, from me the palm of beauty?

— And the sense of property, Stephen said. He drew Shylock out of his own long pocket. The son of a maltjobber and moneylender he was himself a cornjobber and moneylender with ten tods of corn hoarded in the famine riots. His borrowers are no doubt those divers of worship mentioned by Chettle Falstaff who reported his uprightness of dealing. He sued a fellowplayer for the price of a few bags of malt and exacted his pound of flesh in interest for every money lent. How else could Aubrey's ostler and callboy get rich quick? All events brought grist to his mill. Shylock chimes with the jewbaiting that followed the hanging and quartering of the queen's leech Lopez, his jew's heart being plucked forth while the sheeny was yet alive : *Hamlet* and *Macbeth* with the coming to the throne of a Scotch philosophaster with a turn for witchroasting. The lost armada is his jeer in *Love's Labour Lost*. His pageants, the histories, sail fullbellied on a tide of Mafeking enthusiasm. Warwickshire jesuits are tried and we have a porter's theory of equivocation. The *Sea Venture* comes home from Bermudas and the play Renan admired is written with Patsy Caliban, our American cousin. The sugared sonnets follow Sydney's. As for fay Elizabeth, otherwise carrotty Bess, the gross virgin who inspired *The Merry Wives of Windsor* let some meinherr from Almany grope his life long for deephid meanings in the depths of the buckbasket.

I think you're getting on very nicely. Just mix up a mixture of theolologicophilolological. *Mingo, minxi, mictum, mingere*.

— Prove that he was a jew, John Eglinton dared, expectantly. Your dean of studies holds he was a holy Roman.

Sufflaminandus sum.

— He was made in Germany, Stephen replied, as the champion French polisher of Italian scandals.

— A myriadminded man, Mr Best reminded. Coleridge called him myriadminded.

Amplius. In societate humana hoc est maxime necessarium ut sit amicitia inter multos.

— Saint Thomas, Stephen began...

— *Ora pro nobis,* Monk Mulligan groaned, sinking to a chair.

There he keened a wailing rune.

— *Pogue mahone! Acushla machree!* It's destroyed we are from this day! It's destroyed we are surely!

All smiled their smiles.

— Saint Thomas, Stephen, smiling, said, whose gorbellied works I enjoy reading in the original, writing of incest from a standpoint different from that of the new Viennese school Mr Magee spoke of, likens it in his wise and curious way to an avarice of the emotions. He means that the love so given to one near in blood is covetously withheld from some stranger who, it may be, hungers for it. Jews, whom christians tax with avarice, are of all races the most given to intermarriage. Accusations are made in anger. The christian laws which built up the hoards of the jews (for whom, as for the lollards, storm was shelter) bound their affections too with hoops of steel. Whether these be sins or virtues old Nobodaddy will tell us at doomsday leet. But a man who holds so tightly to what he calls his rights over what he calls his debts will hold tightly also to what he calls his rights over her whom he calls his wife. No sir smile neighbour shall covet his ox or his wife or his manservant or his maidservant or his jackass.

— Or his jennyass, Buck Mulligan antiphoned.

— Gentle will is being roughly handled, gentle Mr Best said gently.

— Which will! gagged sweetly Buck Mulligan. We are getting mixed.

— The will to live, John Eglinton philosophised, for poor Ann, Will's widow, is the will to die.

— *Requiescat!* Stephen prayed.

What of all the will to do?
It has vanished long ago...

— She lies laid out in stark stiffness in that secondbest bed, the mobled queen, even though you prove that a bed in those days was as rare as a motorcar is now and that its carvings were the wonder of seven parishes. In old age she takes up with gospellers (one stayed at New Place and drank a quart of sack the town paid for but in which bed he slept it skills not to ask) and heard she had a soul. She read or had read to her his chapbooks preferring them to the *Merry Wives* and, loosing her nightly waters on the jordan, she thought over *Hooks and Eyes for Believers' Breeches* and *The Most Spiritual Snuffbox to Make the Most Devout Souls Sneeze*. Venus has twisted her lips in prayer. Agenbite of inwit : remorse of conscience. It is an age of exhausted whoredom groping for its god.

— History shows that to be true, *inquit Eglintonus Chronolologos*. The ages succeed one another. But we have it on high authority that a man's worst enemies shall be those of his own house and family. I feel that Russell is right. What do we care for his wife and father? I should say that only family poets have family lives Falstaff was not a family man. I feel that the fat knight is his supreme creation.

Lean, he lay back. Shy, deny thy kindred, the unco guid. Shy supping with the godless, he sneaks the cup. A sire in Ultonian Antrim bade it him. Visits him here on quarter days. Mr Magee, sir, there's a gentleman to see you. Me? Says he's your father, sir. Give me my Wordsworth. Enter Magee Mor Matthew, a rugged rough rugheaded kern, in strossers with a buttoned codpiece, his nether stocks bemired with clauber of ten forests, a wand of wilding in his hand.

Your own? He knows your old fellow. The widower.

Hurrying to her squalid deathlair from gay Paris on the quayside I touched his hand. The voice, new warmth, speaking. Dr Bob Kenny is attending her. The eyes that wish me well. But do not know me.

— A father, Stephen said, battling against hopelessness, is a necessary evil. He wrote the play in the months that followed his father's death. If you hold that he, a greying man with two marriageable daughters, with thirtyfive years of life, *nel mezzo del cammin di nostra vita,* with fifty of experience is the beardless undergraduate from Wittemberg then you must hold that his seventyyear old mother is the lustful queen. No. The corpse of John Shakespeare does not walk the night. From hour to hour it rots and rots. He rests, disarmed of fatherhood, having devised that mystical estate upon his son. Boccaccio's Calandrino was the first and last man who felt himself with child. Fatherhood, in the sense of conscious begetting, is unknown to man. It is a mystical estate, an apostolic succession, from only begetter to only begotten On that mystery and not on the madonna which the cunning Italian intellect flung to the mob of Europe the church is founded and founded irremovably because founded, like the world, macro and microcosm, upon the void. Upon incertitude, upon unlikelihood, *Amor matris*, subjective and objective genitive, may be the only true thing in life. Paternity may be a legal fiction. Who is the father of any son that any son should love him or he any son?

What the hell are you driving at?

I know. Shut up. Blast you! I have reasons.

Amplius. Adhuc. Iterum. Postea.

Are you condemned to do this?

— They are sundered by a bodily shame so steadfast that the criminal annals of the world, stained with all other incests and bestialities hardly record its breach. Sons with mothers, sires with daughters, lesbic sisters, loves that dare not speak their name, nephews with grandmothers, jailbirds with keyholes, queens with prize bulls. The son unborn mars beauty : born, he brings pain, divides affection, increases care. He is a male : his growth is his father's decline, his youth his father's envy, his friend his father's enemy.

In rue Monsieur-le-Prince I thought it.

— What links them in nature? An instant of blind rut.

Am I a father? If I were?

Shrunken uncertain hand.

— Sabellius, the African, subtlest heresiarch of all the beasts of the field, held that the Father was Himself His Own Son. The bulldog of Aquin, with whom no word shall be impossible, refutes him. Well : if the father who has not a son be not a father can the son who has not a father be a son? When Rutlandbaconsouthamptonshakespeare or another poet of the same name in the comedy of errors wrote *Hamlet* he was not the father of his own son merely but, being no more a son, he was and felt himself the father of all his race, the father of his own grandfather, the father of his unborn grandson who, by the same token, never was born for nature, as Mr Magee understands her, abhors perfection.

Eglintoneyes, quick with pleasure, looked up shybrightly. Gladly glancing, a merry puritan, through the twisted eglantine.

Flatter. Rarely. But flatter.

— Himself his own father, Sonmulligan told himself. Wait. I am big with child. I have an unborn child in my brain. Pallas Athena ! A play ! The play's the thing ! Let me parturiate !

He clasped his paunchbrow with both birthaiding hands.

— As for his family, Stephen said, his mother's name lives in the forest of Arden. Her death brought from him the scene with Volumnia in *Coriolanus.* His boyson's death is the deathscene of young Arthur in *King John.* Hamlet the black prince, is Hamnet Shakespeare. Who the girls in *The Tempest,* in *Pericles,* in *Winter's Tale* are we know. Who Cleopatra, fleshpot of Egypt, and Cressid and Venus are we may guess. But there is another member of his family who is recorded.

— The plot thickens, John Eglinton said.

The quaker librarian, quaking, tiptoed in, quake, his mask, quake, with haste, quake, quack.

Door closed. Cell. Day.

They list. Three. They.

I you he they.

Come, mess.

STEPHEN

He had three brothers, Gilbert, Edmund, Richard. Gilbert in his old age told some cavaliers he got a pass for nowt from Maister Gatherer one time mass he did and he seen his brud Maister Wull the playwriter up in Lunnon in a wrastling play wud a man on's back. The playhouse sausage filled Gilbert's soul. He is nowhere : but an Edmund and a Richard are recorded in the works of sweet William.

MAGEEGLINJOHN

Names ! What's in a name ?

BEST

That is my name, Richard, don't you know. I hope you are going to say a good word for Richard, don't you know, for my sake.

(Laughter.)

BUCK MULLIGAN

(Piano, diminuendo.)

Then outspoke medical Dick
To his comrade medical Davy...

STEPHEN

In his trinity of black Wills, the villain shakebags, Iago, Richard Crookback, Edmund in *King Lear*, two bear the wicked uncles' names. Nay, that last play was written or being written while his brother Edmund lay dying in Southwark.

BEST

I hope Edmund is going to catch it. I don't want Richard, my name...

(Laughter.)

QUAKERLYSTER

(A tempo.) But he that filches from me my good name...

STEPHEN

(Stringendo.) He has hidden his own name, a fair name, William, in the plays, a super here, a clown there, as a painter of old Italy set his face in a dark corner of his canvas. He has revealed it in the sonnets where there is Will in overplus. Like John O' Gaunt his name is dear to him, as dear as the coat of arms he toadied for, on a bend sable a spear or steeled argent, honorificabilitudinitatibus, dearer than his glory of greatest shakescene in the country. What's in a name? That is what we ask ourselves in childhood when we write the name that we are told is ours. A star, a daystar, a firedrake rose at his birth. It shone by day in the heavens alone, brighter than Venus in the night, and by night it shone over delta in Cassiopeia, the recumbent constellation which is the signature of his initial among the stars. His eyes watched it, lowlying on the horizon, eastward of the bear, as he walked by the slumberous summer fields at midnight, returning from Shottery and from her arms.

Both satisfied. I too.

Don't tell them he was nine years old when it was quenched.

And from her arms.

Wait to be wooed and won. Ay, meacock. Who will woo you?

Read the skies. *Autontimerumenos. Bous Stephanoumenos*. Where's your configuration? Stephen, Stephen, cut the bread even. S. D: sua donna. *Già: di lui. Gelindo risolve di non amar S. D.*

— What is that, Mr Dedalus? the quaker librarian asked. Was it a celestial phenomenon?

— A star by night, Stephen said, a pillar of the cloud by day.

What more's to speak?

Stephen looked on his hat, his stick, his boots.

Stephanos, my crown. My sword. His boots are spoiling the shape of my feet. Buy a pair. Holes in my socks. Handkerchief too.

— You make good use of the name, John Eglinton allowed. Your own name is strange enough. I suppose it explains your fantastical humour.

Me, Magee and Mulligan.

Fabulous artificer, the hawklike man. You flew. Whereto? Newhaven-Dieppe, steerage passenger. Paris and back. Lapwing. Icarus. *Pater, ait.* Seabedabbled, fallen, weltering. Lapwing you are. Lapwing be.

Mr Best eagerquietly lifted his book to say:

— That's very interesting because that brother motive, don't you know, we find also in the old Irish myths. Just what you say. The three brothers Shakespeare. In Grimm too, don't you know, the fairytales. The third brother that marries the sleeping beauty and wins the best prize.

Best of Best brothers. Good, better, best.

The quaker librarian springhalted near.

— I should like to know, he said, which brother you... I understand you to suggest there was misconduct with one of the brothers... But perhaps I am anticipating?

He caught himself in the act: looked at all: refrained.

An attendant from the doorway called:

— Mr Lyster! Father Dineen wants...

— O! Father Dineen! Directly.

Swiftly rectly creaking rectly rectly he was rectly gone.

John Eglinton touched the foil.

— Come, he said Let us hear what you have to say of Richard and Edmund. You kept them for the last, didn't you?

— In asking you to remember those two noble kinsmen nuncle Richie and nuncle Edmund, Stephen answered, I feel I am asking too much perhaps. A brother is as easily forgotten as an umbrella.

Lapwing.

Where is your brother? Apothecaries' hall. My whetstone. Him, then Cranly, Mulligan : now these. Speech, speech. But act. Act speech. They mock to try you. Act. Be acted on.

Lapwing.

I am tired of my voice, the voice of Esau My kingdom for a drink.

On.

— You will say those names were already in the chronicles from which he took the stuff of his plays. Why did he take them rather than others? Richard, a whoreson crookback, misbegotten, makes love to a widowed Ann (what's in a name?), woos and wins her, a whoreson merry widow. Richard the conqueror, third brother, came after William the conquered. The other four acts of that play hang limply from that first. Of all his kings Richard is the only king unshielded by Shakespeare's reverence, the angel of the world. Why is the underplot of *King Lear* in which Edmund figures lifted out of Sidney's *Arcadia* and spatchcocked on to a Celtic legend older than history?

— That was Will's way, John Eglinton defended. We should not now combine a Norse saga with an excerpt from a novel by George Meredith. *Que voulez-vous?* Moore would say. He puts Bohemia on the seacoast and makes Ulysses quote Aristotle.

— Why? Stephen answered himself. Because the theme of the false or the usurping or the adulterous brother or all three in one is to Shakespeare, what the poor is not, always with him. The note of banishment, banishment from the heart, banishment from home, sounds uninterruptedly from *The Two Gentleman of Verona* onward till Prospero breaks his staff, buries it certain fathoms in the earth and drowns his book. It doubles itself in the middle of his life, reflects itself in another, repeats itself, protasis, epitasis, catastasis, catastrophe. It repeats itself again when he is near the grave, when his married daughter Susan, chip of the old block, is accused of adultery. But it was the original sin that darkened his understanding, weakened his will and left in him a strong inclination to evil. The words are those of my lords bishops of Maynooth-an original sin and, like original sin, committed by another in whose sin he too has sinned. It is between the lines of his last written words, it is petrified on his tombstone under which her four bones are not to be laid. Age has not withered it. Beauty and peace have not done it away. It is in infinite variety everywhere in the world he has created, in *Much Ado about Nothing*, twice in *As you like It*, in *The Tempest*, in *Hamlet*, in *Measure for Measure*, and in all the other plays which I have not read.

He laughed to free his mind from his mind's bondage.

Judge Eglinton summed up.

— The truth is midway, he affirmed. He is the ghost and the prince. He is all in all.

— He is, Stephen said. The boy of act one is the mature man of act five. All in all. In *Cymbeline*, in *Othello* he is bawd and cuckold. He acts and is acted on. Lover of an ideal or a perversion, like José he kills the real Carmen. His unremitting intellect is the hornmad Iago ceaselessly willing that the moor in him shall suffer.

— Cuckoo ! Cuckoo ! Cuck Mulligan clucked lewdly. O word of fear !

Dark dome received, reverbed.

— And what a character is Iago ! undaunted John Eglinton exclaimed. When all is said Dumas fils (or is it Dumas père ?) is right. After God Shakespeare has created most.

— Man delights him not nor woman neither, Stephen said. He returns after a life of absence to that spot of earth where he was born, where he has always been, man and boy, a silent witness and there, his journey of life ended, he plants his mulberrytree in the earth. Then dies. The motion is ended. Gravediggers bury Hamlet *père* and Hamlet *fils*. A king and a prince at last in death, with incidental music. And, what though murdered and betrayed, bewept by all frail tender hearts for, Dane or Dubliner, sorrow for the dead is the only husband from whom they refuse to be divorced. If you like the epilogue look long on it : prosperous Prospero, the good man rewarded, Lizzie, grandpa's lump of love, and nuncle Richie, the bad man taken off by poetic justice to the place where the bad niggers go. Strong curtain. He found in the world without as actual what was in his world within as possible. Maeterlinck says : *If Socrates leave his house today he will find the sage seated on his doorstep, If Judas go forth tonight it is to Judas his steps will tend*. Every life is many days, day after day. We walk through ourselves, meeting robbers, ghosts, giants, old men, young men, wives, widows, brothers-in-love. But always meeting ourselves. The playwright who wrote the folio of this world and wrote it badly (He gave us light first and the sun two days later), the lord of things as they are whom the most Roman of catholics call *dio boia*, hangman god, is doubtless all in all in all of us, ostler and butcher, and would be bawd and cuckold too but that in the economy of heaven, foretold by Hamlet, there are no more marriages, glorified man, an androgynous angel, being a wife unto himself.

— *Eureka!*, Buck Mulligan cried. *Eureka!*

Suddenly happied he jumped up and reached in a stride John Eglinton's desk.

— May I? he said. The Lord has spoken to Malachi.

He began to scribble on a slip of paper.

Take some slips from the counter going out.

— Those who are married, Mr Best, douce, herald, said, all save one, shall live. The rest shall keep as they are.

He laughed, unmarried, at Eglinton Johannes, of arts a bachelor.

Unwed, unfancied, ware of wiles, they fingerponder nightly each his variorum edition of *The Taming of the Shrew*.

— You are a delusion, said roundly John Eglinton to Stephen. You have brought us all this way to show us a French triangle. Do you believe your own theory?

— No, Stephen said promptly.

— Are you going to write it? Mr Best asked. You ought to make it a dialogue, don't you know, like the Platonic dialogues Wilde wrote.

John Eclection doubly smiled.

— Well, in that case, he said, I don't see why you should expect payment for it since you don't believe it yourself. Dowden believes there is some mystery in *Hamlet* but will say no more. Herr Bleibtreu, the man Piper met in Berlin, who is working up that Rutland theory, believes that the secret is hidden in the Stratford monument. He is going to visit the present duke, Piper says, and prove to him that his ancestor wrote the plays. It will come as a surprise to his grace. But he believes his theory.

I believe, O Lord, help my unbelief. That is, help me to believe or help me to unbelieve? Who helps to believe? *Egomen*. Who to unbelieve? Other chap.

— You are the only contributor to *Dana* who asks for pieces of silver. Then I don't know about the next number. Fred Ryan wants space for an article on economics.

Fraidrine. Two pieces of silver he lent me. Tide you over. Economics.

— For a guinea, Stephen said, you can publish this interview.

Buck Mulligan stood up from his laughing scribbling, laughing: and then gravely said, honeying malice:

— I called upon the bard Kinch at his summer residence in upper Mecklenburgh street and found him deep in the study of the *Summa contra Gentiles* in the company of two gonorrheal ladies, Fresh Nelly and Rosalie, the coalquay whore.

He broke away.

— Come, Kinch. Come, wandering Ængus of the birds.

Come, Kinch, you have eaten all we left. Ay. I will serve you your orts and offals.

Stephen rose.

Life is many days. This will end.

— We shall see you tonight, John Eglinton said. *Notre ami* Moore says Malachi Mulligan must be there.

Buck Mulligan flaunted his slip and panama.

— Monsieur Moore, he said, lecturer on French letters to the youth of Ireland. I'll be there. Come, Kinch, the bards must drink. Can you walk straight?

Laughing he...

Swill till eleven. Irish nights entertainment.

Lubber...

Stephen followed a lubber...

One day in the national library we had a discussion. Shakes. After his lub back I followed. I gall his kibe.

Stephen, greeting, then all amort, followed a lubber jester, a wellkempt head, newbarbered, out of the vaulted cell into a shattering daylight of no thoughts.

What have I learned? Of them? Of me?

Walk like Haines now.

The constant readers' room. In the readers' book Cashel Boyle O'Connor Fitzmaurice Tisdall Farrell parafes his polysyllables. Item : was Hamlet mad? The quaker's pate godlily with a priesteen in booktalk.

— O please do, sir... I shall be most pleased...

Amused Buck Mulligan mused in pleasant murmur with himself, selfnodding :

— A pleased bottom.

The turnstile.

Is that?... Blueribboned hat... Idly writing... What? Looked?...

The curving balustrade; smoothsliding Mincius.

Puck Mulligan, panamahelmeted, went step by step, iambing, trolling :

John Eglinton, my jo, John.
Why won't you wed a wife?

He spluttered to the air :

— O, the chinless Chinaman! Chin Chon Eg Lin Ton. We went over to their playbox, Haines and I, the plumbers' hall. Our players are creating a new art for Europe like the Greeks or M. Maeterlinck. Abbey theatre! I smell the public sweat of monks.

He spat blank.

Forgot : any more than he forgot the whipping lousy Lucy gave him. And left the *femme de trente ans*. And why no other children born? And his first child a girl?

Afterwit. Go back.

The dour recluse still there (he has his cake) and the douce youngling, minion of pleasure, Phedo's toyable fair hair.

Eh... I just eh... wanted... I forgot... he...

— Longworth and M'Curdy Atkinson were there...

Puck Mulligan footed featly, trilling :

I hardly hear the purlieu cry
Or a Tommy talk as I pass one by
Before my thoughts begin to run
On F. M'Curdy Atkinson,
The same that had the wooden leg
And that filibustering filibeg
That never dared to slake his drouth,
Magee that had the chinless mouth.
Being afraid to marry on earth
They masturbated for all they were worth.

Jest on. Know thyself.

Halted below me, a quizzer looks at me. I halt.

— Mournful mummer, Buck Mulligan moaned. Synge has left off wearing black to be like nature. Only crows, priests and English coal are black.

A laugh tripped over his lips.

— Longworth is awfully sick, he said, after what you wrote about that old hake Gregory. O you inquisitional drunken jew jesuit! She gets you a job on the paper and then you go and slate her drivel to Jaysus. Couldn't you do the Yeats' touch?

He went on and down, mopping, chanting with waving graceful arms:

— The most beautiful book that has come out of our country in my time. One thinks of Homer.

He stopped at the stairfoot.

— I have conceived a play for the mummers, he said solemnly.

The pillared Moorish hall, shadows entwined. Gone the nine men's morrice with caps of indices.

In sweetly varying voices Buck Mulligan read his tablet:

Everyman His Own Wife
or
A Honeymoon in the Hand
(a national immorality in three orgasms)
by
Ballocky Mulligan

He turned a happy patch's smirk to Stephen, saying:

— The disguise, I fear, is thin. But listen.

He read, *marcato:*

— Characters:

TOBY TOSTOFF (a ruined Pole).
CRAB (a bushranger).
MEDICAL DICK and MEDICAL DAVY (two birds with one stone).
MOTHER GROGAN (a watercarrier).
FRESH NELLY
and
ROSALIE (the coalquay whore).

He laughed, lolling a to and fro head, walking on, followed by Stephen: and mirthfully he told the shadows, souls of men:

— O, the night in the Camden hall when the daughters of Erin had to lift their skirts to step over you as you lay in your mulberrycoloured, multicoloured, multitudinous vomit!

— The most innocent son of Erin, Stephen said, for whom they ever lifted them.

About to pass through the doorway, feeling one behind, he stood aside.

Part. The moment is now. Where then? If Socrates leave his house today, if Judas go forth tonight. Why? That lies in space which I in time must come to, ineluctably.

My will: his will that fronts me. Seas between.

A man passed out between them, bowing, greeting.

— Good day again, Buck Mulligan said.

The portico.

Here I watched the birds for augury. Ængus of the birds. They go, they come. Last night I flew. Easily flew. Men wondered. Street of harlots after. A creamfruit melon he held to me. In. You will see.

— The wandering jew, Buck Mulligan whispered with clown's awe. Did you see his eye? He looked upon you to lust after you. I fear thee, ancient mariner. O, Kinch, thou art in peril. Get thee a breechpad.

Manner of Oxenford.

Day. Wheelbarrow sun over arch of bridge.

A dark back went before them. Step of a pard, down, out by the gateway, under portcullis barbs.

They followed.

Offend me still. Speak on.

Kind air defined the coigns of houses in Kildare street. No birds. Frail from the housetops two plumes of smoke ascended, pluming, and in a flaw of softness softly were blown.

Cease to strive. Peace of the druid priests of Cymbeline, hierophantic: from wide earth an altar.

Laud we the gods
And let our crooked smokes climb to their nostrils
From our bless'd altars.

The superior, the very reverend John Conmee S. J. reset his smooth watch in his interior pocket as he came down the presbytery steps. Five to three. Just nice time to walk to Artane. What was that that boy's name again? Dignam, yes. *Vere dignum et iustum est.* Brother Swan was the person to see. Mr Cunningham's letter. Yes. Oblige him, if possible. Good practical catholic: useful at mission time.

A onlegged sailor, swinging himself onward by lazy jerks of his crutches, growled some notes. He jerked short before the convent of the sisters of charity and held out a peaked cap for alms towards the very reverend John Conmee S. J. Father Conmee blessed him in the sun for his purse held, he knew, one silver crown.

Father Conmee crossed to Mountjoy square. He thought, but not for long, of soldiers and sailors, whose legs had been shot off by cannonballs, ending their days in some pauper ward, and of cardinal Wolsey's words: *If I had served my God as I had served my king He would not have abandoned me in my old days.* He walked by the treeshade of sunnywinking leaves and towards him come the wife of Mr David Sheehy. M. P.

— Very well, indeed, father. And you, father?

Father Conmee was wonderfully well indeed. He would go to Buxton probably for the waters. And her boys, were they getting on well at Belvedere? Was that so? Father Conmee was very glad indeed to hear that. And Mr Sheehy himself? Still in London. The house was still sitting, to be sure it was. Beautiful weather it was, delightful indeed. Yes, it was very probable that Father Bernard Vaughan would come again to preach. O, yes: a very great success. A wonderful man really.

Father Conmee was very glad to see the wife of Mr David Sheehy M. P. looking so well and he begged to be remembered to Mr David Sheedy M.P. Yes, he would certainly call.

— Good afternoon, Mrs Sheehy.

Father Conmee doffed his silk hat, as he took leave, at the jet beads of her mantilla inkshining in the sun. And smiled yet again in going. He had cleaned his teeth, he knew, with arecanut paste.

Father Conmee walked and, walking, smiled for he thought on Father Bernard Vaughan's droll eyes and cockney voice.

— Pilate! Wy don't you old back that owlin mob?

A zealous man, however. Really he was. And really did great good in his way. Beyond a doubt. He loved Ireland, he said, and he loved the Irish. Of good family too would one think it? Welsh, were they not?

O, lest he forget. That letter to father provincial.

Father Conmee stropped three little schoolboys at the corner of Mountjoy square. Yes: they were from Belvedere. The little house: Aha. And were they good boys at school? O. That was very good now. And what was his name? Jack Sohan. And his name? Ger. Gallaher. And the other little man? His name was Brunny Lynam. O, that was a very nice name to have.

Father Conmee gave a letter from his breast to master Brunny Lynam and pointed to the red pillarbox at the corner of Fitzgibbon street.

— But mind you don't post yourself into the box, little man, he said.

The boys sixeyed Father Conmee and laughed.

— O, sir.

— Well, let me see if you can post a letter, Father Conmee said.

Master Brunny Lynam ran across the road and put Father Conmee's letter to father provincial into the mouth of the bright red letterbox, Father Conmee smiled and nodded and smiled and walked along Mountjoy square east.

Mr Denis J. Maginni, professor of dancing, &c. in silk hat, slate frock coat with silk facings, white kerchief tie, tight lavender trousers, canary gloves and pointed patent boots, walking with grave deportment most respectfully took the curbstone as he passed lady Maxwell at the corner of Dignam's court.

Was that not Mrs M'Guinness?

Mrs M'Guinness, stately, silverhaired, bowed to Father Conmee from the farther footpath along which she sailed. And Father Conmee smiled and saluted. How did she do?

A fine carriage she had. Like Mary, queen of Scots, something. And to think that she was a pawnbroker. Well, now! Such a... what should he say?... such a queenly mien.

Father Conmee walked down Great Charles Street and glanced at the shutup free church on his left. The reverend T. R Greene B. A. will (D. V.) speak. The incumbent they called him. He felt it incumbent on him to say a few words. But one should be charitable. Invincible ignorance. They acted according to their lights.

Father Conmee turned the corner and walked along the North Circular road. It was a wonder that there was not a tramline in such an important thoroughfare. Surely, there ought to be.

A band of satchelled schoolboys crossed from Richmond street. All raised untidy caps. Father Conmee greeted them more than once benignly. Christian brother boys.

Father Conmee smelled incense on his right hand as he walked. Saint Joseph's church, Portland row. For aged and virtuous females. Father Conmee raised his hat to the Blessed Sacrament. Virtuous : but occasionally they were also badtempered.

Near Aldborough house Father Conmee thought of that spendthrift nobleman. And now it was an office or something.

Father Conmee began to walk along the North Strand road and was saluted by Mr William Gallagher who stood in the doorway of his shop. Father Conmee saluted Mr William Gallagher and perceived the odours that came from baconflitches and ample cools of butter. He passed Grogan's the tobacconist against which newsboards leaned and told of a dreadful catastrophe in New York. In America those things were continually happening. Unfortunate people to die like that, unprepared. Still, an act of perfect contrition.

Father Conmee went by Daniel Bergin's publichouse against the window of which two unlabouring men lounged. They saluted him and were saluted.

Father Conmee passed H. J. O'Neill's funeral establishment where Corny Kelleher totted figures in the daybook while he chewed a blade of hay. A constable on his beat saluted Father Conmee and Father Conmee saluted the constable. In Youkstetter's, the porkbutcher's, Father Conmee observed pig's puddings, white and black and red, lying neatly curled in tubes.

Moored under the trees of Charleville Mall Father Conmee saw a turfbarge, a towhorse with pendent head, a bargeman with a hat of dirty straw seated amidships, smoking and staring at a branch of poplar above him. It was idyllic : and Father Conmee reflected on the providence of the Creator who had made turf to be in bogs where men might dig it out and bring it to town and hamlet to make fires in the houses of poor people.

On Newcomen bridge the very reverend John Conmee S. J. of saint Francis Xavier's church, upper Gardiner street, stepped on to an outward bound tram.

Off an inward bound tram stepped the reverend Nicholas Dudley C. C. of saint Agatha's church, north William street, on to Newcomen bridge.

At Newcomen bridge Father Conmee stepped into an outward bound tram for he disliked to traverse on foot the dingy way past Mud Island.

Father Conmee sat in a corner of the tramcar, a blue ticket tucked with care in the eye of one plump kid glove, while four shillings, a sixpence and five pennies chuted from his other plump glovepalm into his purse. Passing the ivy church he reflected that the ticket inspector usually made his visit when one had carelessly thrown away the ticket. The solemnity of the occupants of the car seemed to Father Conmee excessive for a journey so short and cheap. Father Conmee liked cheerful decorum.

It was a peaceful day. The gentleman with the glasses opposite Father Conmee had finished explaining and looked down. His wife, Father Conmee supposed. A tiny yawn opened the mouth of the wife of the gentleman with the glasses. She raised her small gloved fist, yawned ever so gently, tiptapping her small gloved fist on her opening mouth and smiled tinily, sweetly.

Father Conmee perceived her perfume in the car. He perceived also that the awkward man at the other side of her was sitting on the edge of the seat.

Father Conmee at the altarrails placed the host with difficulty in the mouth of the awkward old man who had the shaky head.

At Annesley bridge the tram halted and, when it was about to go, an old woman rose suddenly from her place to alight. The conductor pulled the bellstrap to stay the car for her. She passed out with her basket and a marketnet: and Father Conmee saw the conductor help her and net and basket down: and Father Conmee thought that, as she had nearly passed the end of the penny fare, she was one of those good souls who had always to be told twice bless you, my child, that they have been absolved, pray for me. But they had so many worries in life, so many cares, poor creatures.

From the hoardings Mr Eugene Stratton grinned with thick niggerlips at Father Conmee.

Father Conmee thought of the souls of black and brown and yellow men and of his sermon of saint Peter Claver S. J. and the African mission and of the propagation of the faith and of the millions of black and brown and yellow souls that had not received the baptism of water when their last hour came like a thief in the night. That book by the Belgian jesuit, *Le Nombre des Élus,* seemed to Father Conmee a reasonable plea. Those were millions of human souls created by God in His Own likeness to whom the faith had not (D. V.) been brought. But they were God's souls created by God. It seemed to Father Conmee a pity that they should all be lost, a waste, if one might say.

At the Howth road stop Father Conmee alighted, was saluted by the conductor and saluted in his turn.

The Malahide road was quiet. It pleased Father Conmee, road and name. The joybells were ringing in gay Malahide. Lord Talbot de Malahide, immediate hereditary lord admiral of Malahide and the seas adjoining. Then came the call to arms and she was maid, wife and widow in one day. Those were old worldish days, loyal times in joyous townlands, old times in the barony.

Father Conmee, walking, thought of his little book *Old Times in the Barony* and of the book that might be written about jesuit houses and of Mary Rochfort, daughter of lord Molesworth, first countess of Belvedere.

A listless lady, no more young, walked alone the shore of lough Ennel, Mary, first countess of Belvedere, listlessly walking in the evening, not startled when an otter plunged. Who could know the truth? Not the jealous lord Belvedere and not her confessor if she had not committed adultery fully, *eiaculatio seminis inter vas naturale mulieris,* with her husband's brother? She would half confess if she had not all sinned as women did. Only God knew and she and he, her husband's brother.

Father Conmee thought of that tyrannous incontinence, needed however for men's race on earth, and of the ways of God which were not our ways.

Don John Conmee walked and moved in times of yore. He was humane and honoured there. He bore in mind secrets confessed and he smiled at smiling noble faces in a beeswaxed drawingroom, ceiled with full fruit clusters. And the hands of a bride and of a bridegroom, noble to noble, were impalmed by don John Conmee.

It was a charming day.

The lychgate of a field showed Father Conmee breadths of cabbages, curtseying to him with ample underleaves. The sky showed him a flock of small white clouds going slowly down the wind. *Moutonner*, the French said. A homely and just word.

Father Conmee, reading his office, watched a flock ot muttoning clouds over Rathcoffey. His thinsocked ankles were tickled by the stubble of Clongowes field He walked there, reading in the evening and heard the cries of the boys' lines at their play, young cries in the quiet evening. He was their rector : his reign was mild.

Father Conmee drew off his gloves and took his rededged breviary out. An ivory bookmark told him the page.

Nones. He should have read that before lunch. But lady Maxwell had come.

Father Conmee read in secret *Pater* and *Ave* and crossed his breast. *Deus in adiutorium.*

He walked calmly and read mutely the nones, walking and reading till he came to *Res* in *Beati immaculati : Principium verborum tuorum veritas : in eternum omnia iudicia iustitiæ tuæ.*

A flushed young man came from a gap of a hedge and after him came a young woman with wild nodding daisies in her hand. The young man raised his hat abruptly : the young woman abruptly bent and with slow care detached from her light skirt a clinging twig.

Father Conmee blessed both gravely and turned a thin page of his breviary. *Sin : Principes persecuti sunt me gratis : et a verbis tuis formidavit cor meum.*

Corny Kelleher closed his long daybook and glanced with his drooping eye at a pine coffinlid sentried in a corner. He pulled himself erect, went to it and, spinning it on its axle, viewed its shape and brass furnishings. Chewing his blade of hay he laid the coffinlid by and came to the doorway. There he tilted his hatbrim to give shade to his eyes and leaned against the doorcase, looking idly out.

Father John Conmee stepped into the Dollymount tram on Newcomen bridge.

Corny Kelleher locked his largefooted boots and gazed, his hat downtilted, chewing his blade of hay.

Constable 57 C, on his beat, stood to pass the time of day.

— That's a fine day, Mr Kelleher.

— Ay, Corny Kelleher said.

— It's very close, the constable said.

Corny Kelleher sped a silent jet of hayjuice arching from his mouth while a generous white arm from a window in Eccles street flung forth a coin.

— What's the best news? he asked.

— I seen that particular party last evening, the constable said with bated breath.

⁂

A onelegged sailor crutched himself round MacConnell's corner, skirting Rabaiotti's icecream car, and jerked himself up Eccles street. Towards Larry O'Rourke, in shirtsleeves in his doorway, he growled unamiably.

— *For England...*

He swung himself violently forward past Katey and Boody Dedalus, halted and growled :

— *home and beauty.*

J. J. O'Molloy's white careworn face was told that Mr Lambert was in the warehouse with a visitor.

A stout lady stopped, took a copper coin from her purse and dropped it into the cap held out to her. The sailor grumbled thanks and glanced sourly at the unheeding windows, sank his head and swung himself forward four strides.

He halted and growled angrily :

— *For England...*

Two barefoot urchins, sucking long liquorice laces, halted near him, gaping at his stump with their yellowslobbered mouths.

He swung himself forward in vigorous jerks, halted, lifted his head towards a window and bayed deeply.

— *home and beauty.*

The gay sweet chirping whistling within went on a bar or two, ceased. The blind of the window was drawn aside. A card *Unfurnished Apartments* slipped from the sash and fell. A plump bare generous arm shone, was seen, held forth from a white petticoatbodice and taut shiftstraps. A woman's hand flung forth a coin over the area railings. It fell on the path.

One of the urchins ran to it, picked it up and dropped it into the minstrel's cap, saying :

— There, sir.

***

Katey and Boody Dedalus shoved in the door of the close steaming kitchen.

— Did you put in the books? Boody asked.

Maggy at the range rammed down a greyish mass beneath bubbling suds twice with her potstick and wiped her brow.

— They wouldn't give anything on them, she said.

Father Conmee walked through Clongowes fields, his thinsocked ankles tickled by stubble.

— Where did you try? Boody asked.

— M'Guinness's.

Boody stamped her foot and threw her satchel on the table.

— Bad cess to her big face! she cried.

Katey went to the range and peered with squinting eyes.

— What's in the pot? she asked.

— Shirts, Maggy said.

Boody cried angrily:

— Crickey, is there nothing for us to eat?

Katey, lifting the kettlelid in a pad of her stained skirt, asked:

— And what's in this?

A heavy fume gushed in answer.

— Peasoup, Maggy said.

— Where did you get it? Katey asked.

— Sister Mary Patrick, Maggy said.

The lacquey rang his bell.

— Barang!

Boody sat down at the table and said hungrily:

— Give us it here!

Maggy poured yellow thick soup from the kettle into a bowl Katey, sitting opposite Boody, said quietly, as her fingertip lifted to her mouth random crumbs.

— A good job we have that much. Where's Dilly?

— Gone to meet father, Maggy said.

Boody, breaking big chunks of bread into the yellow soup, added:

— Our father who art not in heaven.

Maggy, pouring yellow soup in Katey's bowl, exclaimed:

— Boody! For shame!

A skiff, a crumpled throwaway, Elijah is coming, rode lightly down the Liffey, under Loopline bridge, shooting the rapids where water chafed around the bridgepiers, sailing eastward past hulls and anchorchains, between the Customhouse old dock and George's quay.

⁂

The blond girl in Thornton's bedded the wicker basket with rustling fibre. Blazes Boylan handed her the bottle swathed in pink tissue paper and a small jar.

— Put these in first, will you? he said.

— Yes, sir, the blond girl said, and the fruit on top.

— That'll do, game ball, Blazes Boylan said.

She bestowed fat pears neatly, head by tail, and among them ripe shamefaced peaches.

Blazes Boylan walked here and there in new tan shoes about the fruitsmelling shop, lifting fruits, young juicy crinkled and plump red tomatoes, sniffing smells.

H. E. L. Y' S. filed before him, tallwhitehatted, past Tangier lane, plodding towards their goal.

He turned suddenly from a chip of strawberries, drew a gold watch from his fob and held it at its chain's length.

— Can you send them by tram? Now?

A darkbacked figure under Merchant's arch scanned books on the hawker's car.

— Certainly, sir. Is it in the city?

— O, yes, Blazes Boylan said. Ten minutes.

The blond girl handed him a docket and pencil.

— Will you write the address, sir?

Blazes Boylan at the counter wrote and pushed the docket to her.

— Send it at once, will you? he said. It's for an invalid.

— Yes, sir. I will, sir.

Blazes Boylan rattled merry money in his trousers' pocket.

— What's the damage? he asked.

The blond girl's slim fingers reckoned the fruits.

Blazes Boylan looked into the cut of her blouse. A young pullet. He took a red carnation from the tall stemglass.

— This for me? he asked gallantly.

The blond girl glanced sideways at him, got up regardless, with his tie a bit crooked, blushing.

— Yes, sir, she said.

Bending archly she reckoned again fat pears and blushing peaches.

Blazes Boylan looked in her blouse with more favour, the stalk of the red flower between his smiling teeth.

— May I say a word to your telephone, missy? he asked roguishly.

***

— *Ma!* Almidano Artifoni said.

He gazed over Stephen's shoulder at Goldsmith's knobby poll.

Two carfuls of tourists passed slowly, their women sitting fore, gripping frankly the handrests. Pale faces. Men's arms frankly round their stunted forms. They looked from Trinity to the blind columned porch of the bank of Ireland where pigeons roocoocooed.

— *Anch'io ho avuto di queste idee,* Almidano Artifoni said *quand' ero giovine come Lei. Eppoi mi sono convinto che il mondo è una bestia. E peccato. Perchè la sua voce... sarebbe un cespite di rendita, via. Invece, Lei si sacrifica.*

— *Sacrifizio incruento,* Stephen said smiling, swaying his ashplant in slow swingswong from its midpoint, lightly.

— *Speriamo,* the round mustachioed face said pleasantly. *Ma, dia retta a me. Ci rifletta.*

By the stern stone hand of Grattan, bidding halt, an Inchicore tram unloaded straggling Highland soldiers of a band.

— *Ci rifletterò,* Stephen said, glancing down the solid trouserleg.

— *Ma, sul serio, eh?* Almidano Artifoni said.

His heavy hand took Stephen's firmly. Human eyes. They gazed curiously an instant and turned quickly towards a Dalkey tram.

— *Eccolo,* Almidano Artifoni said in friendly haste. *Venga a trovarmi e ci pensi. Addio, caro.*

— *Arrivederla, maestro,* Stephen said, raising his hat when his hand was freed. *E grazie.*

— *Di che?* Almidano Artifano said. *Scusi, eh? Tante belle cose!*

Almidano Artifoni, holding up a baton of rolled music as a signal, trotted on stout trousers after the Dalkey tram. In vain he trotted, signalling in vain among the rout of barekneed gillies smuggling implements of music through Trinity gates.

⁂

Miss Dunne hid the Capel street library copy of *The Woman in White* far back in her drawer and rolled a sheet of gaudy notepaper into her typewriter.

Too much mystery business in it? Is he in love with that one, Marion? Change it and get another by Mary Cecil Haye.

The disk shot down the groove, wobbled a while, ceased and ogled them : six.

Miss Dunne clicked on the keyboard :

— 16 June 1904.

Five tallwhitehatted sandwichmen between Monypeny's corner and the slab where Wolfe Tone's statue was not, eeled themselves turning H. E. L. Y'S. and plodded back as they had come.

Then she stared at the large poster of Marie Kendall, charming soubrette, and listlessy lolling, scribbled on the jotter sixteens and capital esses. Mustard hair and dauby cheeks. She's not nicelooking, is she? The way she is holding up her bit of a skirt. Wonder will that fellow be at the band tonight. If I could get that dressmaker to make a concertina skirt like Susy Nagle's. They kick out grand. Shannon and all the boatclub swells never took his eyes off her. Hope to goodness he won't keep me here till seven.

The telephone rang rudely by her ear.

— Hello. Yes, sir. No, sir. Yes, sir. I'll ring them up after five. Only those two, sir, for Belfast and Liverpool. All right, sir. Then I can go after six if you're not back. A quarter after. Yes, sir. Twentyseven and six. I'll tell him. Yes : one, seven, six.

She scribbled three figures on an envelope.

— Mr Boylan! Hello! That gentleman from *Sport* was in looking for you. Mr Lenehan, yes. He said he'll be in the Ormond at four. No, sir. Yes, sir. I'll ring them up after five.

***

Two pink faces turned in the flare of the tiny torch.

— Who's that? Ned Lambert asked. Is that Crotty?

— Ringabella and Crosshaven, a voice replied, groping for foothold.

— Hello, Jack, is that yourself? Ned Lambert said, raising in salute his pliant lath among the flickering arches. Come on. Mind your steps there.

The vesta in the clergyman's uplifted hand consumed itself in a long soft flame and was let fall. At their feet its red speck died : and mouldy air closed round them.

— How interesting! a refined accent said in the gloom.

— Yes, sir, Ned Lambert said heartily. We are standing in the historic council chamber of saint Mary's abbey where silken Thomas proclaimed himself a rebel in 1534. This is the most historic spot in all Dublin. O 'Madden Burke is going to write something about it one of these days. The old bank of Ireland was over the way till the time of the union and the original jews' temple was here too before they built their synagogue over in Adelaide road. You were never here before, Jack, were you?

— No, Ned.

— He rode down through Dame walk, the refined accent said, if my memory serves me. The mansion of the Kildares was in Thomas court.

— That's right, Ned Lambert said. That's quite right, sir.

— If you will be so kind then, the clergyman said, the next time to allow me perhaps...

— Certainly, Ned Lambert said.Bring the camera whenever you like. I'll get those bags cleared away from the windows. You can take it from here or from here.

In the still faint light he moved about, tapping with his lath the piled seedbags and points of vantage on the floor.

From a long face a beard and gaze hung on a chessboard.

— I'm deeply obliged, Mr Lambert, the clergyman said. I won't trespass on your valuable time...

— You're welcome, sir, Ned Lambert said. Drop in whenever you like. Next week, say. Can you see?

— Yes, yes. Good afternoon, Mr Lambert. Very pleased to have met you.

— Pleasure is mine, sir, Ned Lambert answered.

His followed his guest to the outlet and then whirled his lath away among the pillars. With J. J. O'Molloy he came forth slowly into Mary's abbey where draymen were loading floats with sacks of carob and palm nut meal, O'Connor, Wexford.

He stood to read the card in his hand.

— The reverend Hugh C. Love, Rathcoffey. Present address : Saint Michael's, Sallins. Nice young chap he is. He's writing a book about the Fitzgeralds he told me. He's well up in history, faith.

The young woman with slow care detached from her light skirt a clinging twig.

— I thought you were at a new gunpowder plot, J. J. O'Molloy said.

Ned Lambert cracked his fingers in the air.

— God! he cried. I forgot to tell him that one about the earl of Kildare atter he set fire to Cashel cathedral. You know that one? *I'm bloody sorry I didit*, says he, *but I declare to God I thought the archbishop was inside*. He mightn't like it, though. What? God, I'll tell him anyhow. That was the great earl, the Fitzgerald Mor. Hot members they were all of them, the Geraldines.

The horses he passed started nervously under their slack harness. He slapped a piebald haunch quivering near him and cried :

— Woa, sonny!

He turned to J. J. O'Molloy and asked :

— Well, Jack. What is it? What's the trouble? Wait a while. Hold hard.

With gaping mouth and head far back he stood still and, after an instant, sneezed loudly.

— Chow! he said. Blast you!

— The dust from those sacks, J. J. O'Molloy said politely.

— No, Ned Lambert gasped, I caught a... cold night before... blast your soul... night before last... and there was a hell of a lot of draught...

He held his handkerchief ready for the coming...

— I was... this morning... poor little... what do you call him... Chow!... Mother of Moses!

Tom Rochford took the top disk from the pile he clasped against his claret waistcoat.

— See? he said. Say it's turn six. In here, see. Turn Now On.

He slid it into the left slot for them. It shot down the groove, wobbled a while, ceased, ogling them : six.

Lawyers of the past, haughty, pleading, beheld pass from the consolidated taxing office to Nisi Prius court Richie Goulding carrying the costbag of Goulding, Collis and Ward and heard rustling from the admiralty division of king's bench to the court of appeal an elderly female with false teeth smiling incredulously and a black silk skirt of great amplitude.

— See ? he said. See now the last one I put in is over here : Turns Over. The impact. Leverage, see ?

He showed them the rising column of disks on the right.

— Smart idea, Nosey Flynn said, snuffling. So a fellow coming in late can see what turn is on and what turns are over.

— See ? Tom Rochford said.

He slid in a disk for himself : and watched it shoot, wobble, ogle, stop : four. Turn Now On.

— I'll see him now in the Ormond, Lenehan said, and sound him. One good turn deserves another.

— Do, Tom Rochford said. Tell him I'm Boylan with impatience.

— Goodnight, M'Coy said abruptly, when you two begin...

Nosey Flynn stooped towards the lever, snuffling at it.

— But how does it work here, Tommy ? he asked.

— Tooraloo, Lenehan said, see you later.

He followed M'Coy out across the tiny square of Crampton court.

— He's a hero, he said simply.

— I know, M'Coy said. The drain, you mean.

— Drain ? Lenehan said. It was down a manhole.

They passed Dan Lowry's musichall where Marie Kendall, charming soubrette, smiled on them from a poster a dauby smile.

Going down the path of Sycamore street beside the Empire musichall Lenehan showed M'Coy how the whole thing was. One of those manholes like a bloody gaspipe and there was the poor devil stuck down in it half choked with sewer gas. Down went Tom Rochford anyhow, booky's vest and all, with the rope round him. And be damned but he got the rope round the poor devil and the two were hauled up.

— The act of a hero, he said.

At the Dolphin they halted to allow the ambulance car to gallop past them for Jervis street.

— This way, he said, walking to the right. I want to pop into Lynam's to see Sceptre's starting price. What's the time by your gold watch and chain ?

M'Coy peered into Marcus Tertius Moses' sombre office, then at O'Neill's clock.

— After three, he said. Who's riding her ?

— O. Madden, Lenehan said. And a game filly she is.

While he waited in Temple bar M'Coy dodged a banana peel with gentle pushes of his toe from the path to the gutter. Fellow might damn easy get a nasty fall there coming along tight in the dark.

The gates of the drive opened wide to give egress to the viceregal cavalcade.

— Even money, Lenehan said returning. I knocked against Bantam Lyons in there going to back a bloody horse someone gave him that hasn't an earthly. Through here.

They went up the steps and under Merchants' arch. A darkbacked figure scanned books on the hawker's cart.

— There he is, Lenehan said.

— Wonder what he is buying, M'Coy said, glancing behind.

— *Leopoldo or the Bloom is on the Rye,* Lenehan said.

— He's dead nuts on sales, M'Coy said. I was with him one day and he bought a book from an old one in Liffey street for two bob. There were fine plates in it worth double the money, the stars and the moon and comets with long tails. Astronomy it was about.

Lenehan laughed.

— I'll tell you a damn good one about comet's tails, he said. Come over in the sun.

They crossed to the metal bridge and went along Wellington quay by the river wall.

Master Patrick Aloysius Dignam came out of Mangan's, late Fehrenbach's, carrying a pound and a half of porksteaks.

— There was a big spread out at Glencree reformatory, Lenehan said eagerly. The annual dinner you know. Boiled shirt affair. The lord mayor was there, Val Dillon it was, and Sir Charles Cameron and Dan Dawson spoke and there was music. Bartell D'Arcy sang and Benjamin Dollard...

— I know, M'Coy broke in. My missus sang there once.

— Did she ? Lenehan said.

A card *Unfurnished Apartments* reappeared on the windowsash of number 7 Eccles street.

He checked his tale a moment but broke out in a wheezy laugh.

— But wait till I tell you, he said, Delahunt of Camden street had the catering and yours truly was chief bottlewasher. Bloom and the wife were there. Lashings of stuff we put up : port wine and sherry and curacoa to which we did ample justice. Fast and furious it was. After liquids came solids. Cold joints galore and mince pies...

— I know, M'Coy said. The year the missus was there...

Lenehan linked his arm warmly.

— But wait till I tell you, he said. We had a midnight lunch too after all the jollification and when we sallied forth it was blue o'clock the morning after the night before. Coming home it was a gorgeous winter's night on the Featherbed Mountain. Bloom and Chris Callinan were on one side of the car and I was with the wife on the other. We started singing glees and duets : *Lo, the early beam of morning*. She was well primed with a good load of Delahunt's port under her bellyband. Every jolt the bloody car gave I had her bumping up against me. Hell's delights! She has a fine pair, God bless her. Like that.

He held his caved hands a cubit from him, frowning:

— I was tucking the rug under her and settling her boa all the time. Know what I mean ?

His hands moulded ample curves of air. He shut his eyes tight in delight, his body shrinking, and blew a sweet chirp from his lips.

— The lad stood to attention anyhow, he said with a sigh. She's a gamey mare and no mistake. Bloom was pointing out all the stars and the comets in the heavens to Chris Callinan and the jarvey : the great bear and Hercules and the dragon and the whole jingbang lot. But, by God, I was lost, so to speak, in the milky way. He knows them all, faith. At last she spotted a weeny weeshy one miles away. *And what star is that, Poldy?* says she. By God, she had Bloom cornered. *That one, is it?* says Chris Callinan, *sure that's only what you might call a pinprick.* By God, he wasn't far wide of the mark.

Lenehan stopped and leaned on the riverwall, panting with soft laughter.

— I'm weak, he gasped.

M'Coy's white face smiled about it at instants and grew grave. Lenehan walked on again. He lifted his yachtingcap and scratched his hindhead rapidly. He glanced sideways in the sunlight at M'Coy.

— He's a cultured allroundman, Bloom is, he said seriously. He's not one of your common or garden... you know... There's a touch of the artist about old Bloom.

⁂

Mr Bloom turned over idly pages of *The Awful Disclosures of Maria Monk,* then of Aristotle's *Masterpiece*. Crooked botched print. Plates : infants cuddled in a ball in bloodred wombs like livers of slaughtered cows. Lots of them like that at this moment all over the world. All butting with their skulls to get out of it. Child born every minute somewhere. Mrs Purefoy.

He laid both books aside and glanced at the third : *Tales of the Ghetto* by Leopold von Sacher Masoch.

— That I had, he said, pushing it by.

The shopman let two volumes fall on the counter.

— Them are two good ones, he said.

Onions of his breath came across the counter out of his ruined mouth. He bent to make a bundle of the other books, hugged them against his unbuttoned waistcoat and bore them off behind the dingy curtain.

On O 'Connell bridge many persons observed the grave deportment and gay apparel of Mr Denis J. Maginni, professor of dancing &c.

Mr Bloom, alone, looked at the titles. *Fair Tyrants* by James Lovebirch. Know the kind that is. Had it? Yes.

He opened it. Thought so.

A woman's voice behind the dingy curtain. Listen : The man.

No : she wouldn't like that much. Got her it once.

He read the other title : *Sweets of Sin*. More in her line. Let us see.

He read where his finger opened.

— *All the dollarbills her husband gave her were spent in the stores on wondrous gowns and costliest frillies. For him! For Raoul!*

Yes. This. Here. Try.

— *Her mouth glued on his in a luscious voluptuous kiss while his hands felt for the opulent curves inside her deshabillé.*

Yes. Take this. The end.

— *You are late, he spoke hoarsely, eying her with a suspicious glare.*

The beautiful woman threw off her sabletrimmed wrap, displaying her queenly shoulders and heaving embonpoint. An imperceptible smile played round her perfect lips as she turned to him calmly.

Mr Bloom read again : *The beautiful woman.*

Warmth showered gently over him, cowing his flesh. Flesh yielded amid rumpled clothes. Whites of eyes swooning up. His nostrils arched themselves for prey. Melting breast ointments *(for him! For Raoul!)* Armpits' oniony sweat. Fishgluey slime *(her heaving embonpoint!)*. Feel! Press! Crished! Sulphur dung of lions!

Young! Young!

An elderly female, no more young, left the building of the courts of chancery, king's bench, exchequer and common pleas having heard in the lord chancellor's court the case in lunacy of Potterton, in the admiralty division the summons, exparte motion, of the owners of the Lady Cairns versus the owners of the barque Mona, in the court of appeal reservation of judgment in the case of Harvey versus the Ocean Accident and Guarantee Corporation.

Phlegmy coughs shook the air of the bookshop, bulging out the dingy curtains. The shopman's uncombed grey head came out and his unshaven reddened face, coughing. He raked his throat rudely, spat phlegm on the floor. He put his boot on what he had spat, wiping his sole along it and bent, showing a rawskinned crown, scantily haired.

Mr Bloom beheld it.

Mastering his troubled breath, he said:

— I'll take this one.

The shopman lifted eyes bleared with old rheum.

— *Sweets of Sin*, he said, tapping on it. That's a good one.

***

The lacquey by the door of Dillon's auctionrooms shook his handbell twice again and viewed himself in the chalked mirror of the cabinet.

Dilly Dedalus, listening by the curbstone, heard the beats of the bell, the cries of the auctioneer within. Four and nine. Those lovely curtains. Five shillings. Cosy curtains. Selling new at two guineas. Any advance on five shillings? Going for five shillings.

The lacquey lifted his handbell and shook it:

— Barang!

Bang of the lastlap bell spurred the halfmile wheelmen to their sprint. J. A. Jackson, W. E. Wylie, A. Munro and H. T. Gahan, their stretched necks wagging, negotiated the curve by the College Library.

Mr Dedalus, tugging a long moustache, came round from Williams's row. He halted near his daughter.

— It's time for you, she said.

— Stand up straight for the love of the Lord Jesus, Mr Dedalus said. Are you trying to imitate your uncle John the cornetplayer, head upon shoulders? Melancholy God!

Dilly shrugged her shoulders. Mr Dedalus placed his hands on them and held them back.

— Stand up straight, girl, he said. You'll get curvature of the spine. Do you know what you look like?

He let his head sink suddenly down and forward, hunching his shoulders and dropping his underjaw.

— Give it up, father, Dilly said. All the people are looking at you.

Mr Dedalus drew himself upright and tugged again at his moustache.

— Did you get any money? Dilly asked.

— Where would I get money? Mr Dedalus said. There is no-one in Dublin would lend me fourpence.

— You got some, Dilly said, looking in his eyes.

— How do you know that? Mr Dedalus asked, his tongue in his cheek.

Mr Kernan, pleased with the order he had booked, walked boldly along James's street.

— I know you did, Dilly answered. Were you in the Scotch house now?

— I was not then, Mr Dedalus said, smiling. Was it the little nuns taught you to be so saucy? Here.

He handed her a shilling.

— See if you can do anything with that, he said.

— I suppose you got five. Dilly said. Give me more than that.

— Wait awhile, Mr Dedalus said threateningly. You're like the rest of them, are you? An insolent pack of little bitches since your poor mother died. But wait awhile. You'll all get a short shrift and a long day from me. Low blackguardism! I'm going to get rid of you. Wouldn't care if I was stretched out stiff. He's dead. The man upstairs is dead.

He left her and walked on. Dilly followed quickly and pulled his coat.

— Well, what is it? he said, stopping.

The lacquey rang his bell behind their backs.

— Barang!

— Curse your bloody blatant soul, Mr Dedalus cried, turning on him.

The lacquey, aware of comment, shook the lolling clapper of his bell : but feebly :

— Bang!

Mr Dedalus stared at him.

— Watch him ,he said. It's instructive. I wonder will he allow us to talk.

— You got more than that, father, Dilly said.

— I'm going to show you a little trick, Mr Dedalus said. I'll leave you all where Jesus left the jews. Look, that's all I have. I got two shillings from Jack Power and I spent twopence for a shave for the funeral.

He drew forth a handful of copper coins nervously.

— Can't you look for some money somewhere? Dilly said.

Mr Dedalus thought and nodded.

— I will, he said gravely, I looked all along the gutter in O'Connell street. I'll try this one now.

— You're very funny, Dilly said, grinning.

— Here, Mr Dedalus said, handing her two pennies. Get a glass of milk for yourself and a bun or a something. I'll be home shortly.

He put the other coins in his pocket and started to walk on.

The viceregal cavalcade passed, greeted by obsequious policemen, out of Parkgate.

— I'm sure you have another shilling, Dilly said.

The lacquey banged loudly.

Mr Dedalus amid the din walked off, murmuring to himself with a pursing mincing mouth :

— The little nuns! Nice little things! O, sure they wouldn't do anything! O, sure they wouldn't really! Is it little sister Monica!

From the sundial towards James's Gate walked Mr Kernan pleased with the order he had booked for Pulbrook Robertson, boldly along James's street, past Shackleton's offices. Got round him all right. How do you do, Mr Crimmins? First rate, sir. I was afraid you might be up in your other establishment in Pimlico. How are things going? Just keeping alive. Lovely weather we are having. Yes, indeed. Good for the country. Those farmers are always grumbling. I'll just take a thimbleful of your best gin, Mr Crimmins. A small gin, sir. Yes, sir. Terrible affair that General Slocum explosion. Terrible,

terrible! A thousand casualties. And heartrending scenes. Men trampling down women and children. Most brutal thing. What do they say was the cause? Spontaneous combustion: most scandalous revelation. Not a single lifeboat would float and the firehose all burst. What I can't understand is how the inspectors ever allowed a boat like that... Now you are talking straight, Mr Crimmins. You know why? Palmoil. Is that a fact? Without a doubt. Well now, look at that. And America they say is the land of the free. I thought we were bad here.

I smiled at him. *America,* I said, quietly, just like that. *What is it? The sweepings of every country including our own. Isn't that true?* That's a fact.

Graft, my dear sir. Well, of course, where there's money going there's always someone to pick it up.

Saw him looking at my frockcoat. Dress does it. Nothing like a dressy appearance. Bowls them over.

— Hello, Simon, Father Cowley said. How are things?

— Hello, Bob, old man, Mr Dedalus answered, stopping.

Mr Kernan halted and preened himself before the sloping mirror of Peter Kennedy, hairdresser. Stylish coat, beyond a doubt. Scott of Dawson street. Well worth the half sovereign I gave Neary for it. Never built under three guineas. Fits me down to the ground. Some Kildare street club toff had it probably. John Mulligan, the manager of the Hibernian bank, gave me a very sharp eye yesterday on Carlisle bridge as if he remembered me.

Aham! Must dress the character for those fellows. Knight of the road. Gentleman. And now, Mr Crimmins, may we have the honour of your custom again, sir. The cup that cheers but not inebriates, as the old saying has it.

North wall and sir John Rogerson's quay, with hulls and anchorchains, sailing westward, sailed by a skiff, a crumpled throwaway, rocked on the ferrywash, Elijah is coming.

Mr Kernan glanced in farewell at his image. High colour, of course. Grizzled moustache. Returned Indian officier. Bravely he bore his stumpy body forward on spatted feet, squaring his shoulders. Is that Lambert's brother over the way, Sam? What? Yes. He's as like it as damn it. No, The windscreen of that motorcar in the sun there. Just a flash like that. Damn like him.

Aham! Hot spirit of juniper juice warmed his vitals and his breath. Good drop of gin, that was. His frocktails winked in bright sunshine to his fat strut.

Down there Emmet was hanged, drawn and quartered. Greasy black rope.

Dogs licking the blood off the street when the lord lieutenant's wife drove by in her noddy.

Let me see. Is he buried in saint Michan's? Or no, there was a midnight burial in Glasnevin. Corpse brought in through a secret door in the wall. Dignam is there now. Went out in a puff. Well, well. Better turn down here. Make a detour.

Mr Kernan turned and walked down the slope of Watling street by the corner of Guinness's visitors' waitingroom. Outside the Dublin Distillers Company's stores an outside car without fare or jarvey stood, the reins knotted to the wheel. Damn dangerous thing. Some Tipperary bosthoon endangering the lives of the citizens. Runaway horse.

Denis Breen with his tomes, weary of having waited an hour in John Henry Menton's office, led his wife over O'Connell bridge, bound for the office of Messrs Collis and Ward.

Mr Kernan approached Island street.

Times of the troubles. Must ask Ned Lambert to lend me those reminiscences of sir Jonah Barrington. When you look back on it all now in a kind of retrospective arrangement. Gaming at Daly's. No cardsharping then. One of those fellows got his hand nailed to the table by a dagger. Somewhere here Lord Edward Fitzgerald escaped from major Sirr. Stables behind Moira house.

Damn good gin that was.

Fine dashing young nobleman. Good stock, of course. That ruffian, that sham squire, with his violet gloves, gave him away. Course they were on the wrong side. They rose in dark and evil days. Fine poem that is: Ingram. They were gentlemen. Ben Dollard does sing that ballad touchingly. Masterly rendition.

At the siege of Ross did my father fall.

A cavalcade in easy trot along Pembroke quay passed, outriders leaping, leaping in their, in their saddles. Frockcoats. Cream sunshades.

Mr Kernan hurried forward, blowing pursily.

His Excellency! Too bad! Just missed that by a hair. Damn it! What a pity!

*
* *

Stephen Dedalus watched through the webbed window the lapidary's fingers prove a timedulled chain. Dust webbed the window and the showtrays. Dust darkened the toiling fingers with their vulture nails. Dust slept on dull coils of bronze and silver, lozenges of cinnabar, on rubies, leprous and winedark stones.

Born all in the dark wormy earth, cold specks of fire, evil lights shining in the darkness. Where fallen archangels flung the stars of their brows. Muddy swinesnouts, hands, root and root, gripe and wrest them.

She dances in a foul gloom where gum burns with garlic. A sailorman, rustbearded, sips from a beaker rum and eyes her. A long and seafed silent rut. She dances, capers, wagging her sowish haunches and her hips, on her gross belly flapping a ruby egg.

Old Russell with a smeared shammy rag burnished again his gem, turned it and held it at the point of his Moses' beard. Grandfather ape gloating on a stolen hoard.

And you who wrest old images from the burial earth! The brainsick words of sophists: Antisthenes. A lore of drugs. Orient and immortal wheat standing from everlasting to everlasting.

Two old women fresh from their whiff of the briny trudged through Irishtown along London bridge road, one with a sanded umbrella, one with a midwife's bag in which eleven cockles rolled.

The whirr of flapping leathern bands and hum of dynamos from the powerhouse urged Stephen to be on. Beingless beings. Stop! Throb always without you and the throb always within. Your heart you sing of. I between them. Where? Between two roaring worlds where they swirl, I. Shatter them, one and both. But stun myself too in the blow. Shatter me you who can. Bawd and butcher, were the words. I say! Not yet awhile. A look around.

Yes, quite true. Very large and wonderful and keeps famous time. You say right, sir. A Monday morning, 'twas so, indeed.

Stephen went down Bedford row, the handle of the ash clacking against his shoulderblade. In Clohissey's window a faded 1860 print of Heenan boxing Sayers held his eye. Staring backers with square hats stood round the roped prizering. The heavyweights in light loincloths proposed gently each to other his bulbous fists. And they are throbbing: heroes' hearts.

He turned and halted by the slanted bookcart.

— Twopence each, the huckster said. Four for sixpence.

Tattered pages. *The Irish Beekeeper. Life and Miracles of the Curé of Ars. Pocket Guide to Killarney.*

I might find here one of my pawned schoolprizes. *Stephano Dedalo, alumno optimo, palmam ferenti.*

Father Conmee, having read his little hours, walked through the hamlet of Donnycarney, murmuring vespers.

Binding too good probably, what is this? Eighth and ninth book of Moses. Secret of all secrets. Seal of King David. Thumbed pages : read and read. Who has passed here before me ? How to soften chapped hands. Recipe for white wine vinegar. How to win a woman's love. For me this. Say the following talisman three times with hands folded :

— *Se el yilo nebrakada femininum ! Amor me solo ! Sanktus ! Amen.*

Who wrote this ? Charms and invocations of the most blessed abbot Peter Salanka to all true believers divulged. As good as any other abbot's charms, as mumbling Joachim's. Down, baldynoddle, or we'll wool your wool.

— What are you doing here, Stephen ?

Dilly's high shoulders and shabby dress.

Shut the book quick. Don't let see.

— What are you doing ? Stephen said.

A Stuart face of nonesuch Charles, lank locks falling at its sides. It glowed as she crouched feeding the fire with broken boots. I told her of Paris. Late lieabed under a quilt of old overcoats, fingering a pinchbeck bracelet, Dan Kelly's token. *Nebrakada femininum.*

— What have you there ? Stephen asked.

— I bought it from the other cart for a penny, Dilly said, laughing nervously. Is it any good ?

My eyes they say she has. Do others see me so ? Quick, far and daring. Shadow of my mind.

He took the coverless book from her hand. Chardenal's French primer.

— What did you buy that for ? he asked. To learn French ?

She nodded, reddening and closing tight her lips.

Show no surprise. Quite natural.

— Here, Stephen said. It's all right. Mind Maggy doesn't pawn it on you. I suppose all my books are gone.

— Some, Dilly said. We had to.

She is drowning. Agenbite. Save her. Agenbite. All against us. She will drown me with her, eyes and hair. Lank coils of seaweed hair around me, my heart, my soul. Salt green death.

We.

Agenbite of inwit. Inwit's agenbite.

Misery ! Misery !

⁂

— Hello, Simon, Father Cowley said. How are things?

— Hello, Bob, old man, Mr Dedalus answered, stopping.

They clasped hands loudly outside Reddy and Daughter's. Father Cowley brushed his moustache often downward with a scooping hand.

— What's the best news? Mr Dedalus said.

— Why then not much, Father Cowley said. I'm barricaded up, Simon, with two men prowling around the house trying to effect an entrance.

— Jolly, Mr Dedalus sald. Who is it?

— O, Father Cowley said. A certain gombeen man of our acquaintance.

— With a broken back, is it? Mr Dedalus asked.

— The same, Simon, Father Cowley answered. Reuben of that ilk. I'm just waiting for Ben Dollard. He's going to say a word to Long John to get him to take those two men off. All I want is a little time.

He looked with vague hope up and down the quay, a big apple bulging in his neck.

— I know, Mr Dedalus said, nodding. Poor old bockedy Ben! He's always doing a good turn for someone. Hold hard!

He put on his glasses and gazed towards the metal bridge an instant.

— There he is, by God, he said, arse and pockets.

Ben Dollard's loose blue cutaway and square hat above large slops crossed the quay in full gait from the metal bridge. He came towards them at an amble, scratching actively behind his coattails.

As he came near Mr Dedalus greeted:

— Hold that fellow with the bad trousers.

— Hold him now, Ben Dollard said.

Mr Dedalus eyed with cold wandering scorn various points of Ben Dollard's figure. Then, turning to Fathes Cowley with a nod, he muttered sneeringly:

— That's a pretty garment, isn't it, for a summer's day?

— Why, God eternally curse your soul, Ben Dollard growled furiously, I threw out more clothes in my time than you ever saw.

He stood beside them beaming on them first and on his roomy clothes from points of which Mr Dedalus flicked fluff, saying:

— They were made for a man in his health, Ben, anyhow.

— Bad luck to the jewman that made them, Ben Dollard said. Thanks be to God he's not paid yet.

— And how is that *basso profondo*, Benjamin, Father Cowley asked.

Cashel Boyle O'Connor Fitmaurice Tisdall Farrell, murmuring, glassyeyed, strode past the Kildare street club.

Ben Dollard frowned and, making suddenly a chanter's mouth, gave forth a deep note.

— Aw! he said.

— That's the style, Mr Dedalus said, nodding to its drone.

— What about that? Ben Dollard said. Not too dusty? What?

He turned to both.

— That'll do, Father Cowley said, nodding also.

The reverend Hugh C. Love walked from the old Chapterhouse of saint Mary's abbey past James and Charles Kennedy's, rectifiers, attended by Geraldines tall and personable, towards the Tholsel beyond the Ford of Hurdles.

Ben Dollard with a heavy list towards the shopfronts led them forward, his joyful fingers in the air.

— Come along with me to the subsheriff's office, he said. I want to show you the new beauty Rock has for a bailiff. He's a cross between Lobengula and Lynchehaun. He's well worth seeing, mind you. Come along. I saw John Henry Menton casually in the Bodega just now and it will cost me a fall if I don't... wait awhile... We're on the right lay, Bob, believe you me.

— For a few days tell him, Father Cowley said anxiously.

Ben Dollard halted and stared, his loud orifice open, a dangling button of his coat wagging brightbacked from its thread as he wiped away the heavy shraums that clogged his eyes to hear aright.

— What few days? he boomed. Hasn't your landlord distrained for rent?

— He has, Father Cowley said.

— Then our friend's writ is not worth the paper it's printed on, Ben Dollard said. The landlord has the prior claim. I gave him all the particulars. 29 Windsor avenue. Love is the name?

— That's right, Father Cowley said. The reverend Mr Love. He's a minister in the country somewhere. But are you sure of that?

— You can tell Barabbas from me, Ben Dollard said, that he can put that writ where Jacko put the nuts.

He led Father Cowley boldly forward linked to his bulk.

— Filberts I believe they were, Mr Dedalus said, as he dropped his glasses on his coatfront, following them.

***

— The youngster will be all right, Martin Cunningham said, as they passed out of the Castleyard gate.

The policeman touched his forehead.

— God bless you, Martin Cunningham said, cheerily.

He signed to the waiting jarvey who chucked at the reins and set on towards Lord Edward street.

Bronze by gold, Miss Kennedy's head by Miss Douce's head, appeared above the crossblind of the Ormond hotel.

— Yes, Martin Cunningham said, fingering his beard. I wrote to Father Conmee and laid the whole case before him.

— You could try our friend, Mr Power suggested backward.

— Boyd ? Martin Cunningham said shortly. Touch me not.

John Wyse Nolan, lagging behind, reading the list, came after them quickly down Cork hill.

On the steps of the City hall Councillor Nannetti, descending, hailed Alderman Cowley and Councillor Abraham Lyon ascending.

The castle car wheeled empty into upper Exchange street.

— Look here Martin, John Wyse Nolan said, overtaking them at the *Mail* office. I see Bloom put his name down for five shillings.

— Quite right, Martin Cunningham said, taking the list. And put down the five shillings too.

— Without a second word either, Mr Power said.

— Strange but true, Martin Cunningham added.

John Wyse Nolan opened wide eyes.

— I'll say there is much kindness in the jew, he quoted elegantly.

They went down Parliament street.

— There's Jimmy Henry, Mr Power said, just heading for Kavanagh's.

— Righto, Martin Cunningham said. Here goes.

Outside *la Maison Claire* Blazes Boylan waylaid Jack Mooney's brother-in-law, humpy, tight, making for the liberties.

John Wyse Nolan fell back with Mr Power, while Martin Cunningham took the elbow of a dapper little man in a shower of hail suit who walked uncertainly with hasty steps past Micky Anderson's watches.

— The assistant town clerk's corns are giving him some trouble, John Wyse Nolan told Mr Power.

They followed round the corner towards James Kavanagh's winerooms. The empty castle car fronted them at rest in Essex gate. Martin Cunningham, speaking always, showed often the list at which Jimmy Henry did not glance.

— And long John Fanning is here too, John Wyse Nolan said, as large as life.

The tall form of long John Fanning filled the doorway where he stood.

— Good day, Mr Subsheriff, Martin Cunningham said, as all halted and greeted.

Long John Fanning made no way for them. He removed his large Henry Clay decisively and his large fierce eyes scowled intelligently over all their faces.

— Are the conscript fathers pursuing their peaceful deliberations? he said, with rich acrid utterance to the assistant town clerk.

Hell open to christians they were having, Jimmy Henry said pettishly, about their damned Irish language. Where was the marshal, he wanted to know, to keep order in the council chamber. And old Barlow the macebearer laid up with asthma, no mace on the table, nothing in order, no quorum even and Hutchinson, the lord mayor, in Llandudno and little Lorcan Sherlock doing *locum tenens* for him. Damned Irish language, language of our forefathers.

Long John Fanning blew a plume of smoke from his lips.

Martin Cunningham spoke by turns, twirling the peak of his beard, to the assistant town clerk and the subsheriff, while John Wise Nolan held his peace.

— What Dignam was that? Long John Fanning asked.

Jimmy Henry made a grimace and lifted his left foot.

— O, my corns! he said plaintively. Come upstairs for goodness' sake till I sit down somewhere. Uff! Ooo! Mind!

Testily he made room for himself beside Long John Fanning's flank and passed in and up the stairs.

— Come on up, Martin Cunningham said to the subsheriff. I don't think you knew him or perhaps you did, though.

With John Wyse Nolan Mr Power followed them in.

— Decent little soul he was, Mr Power said to the stalwart back of Long John Fanning ascending towards Long John Fanning in the mirror.

— Rather lowsized, Dignam of Menton's office that was, Martin Cunningham said.

Long John Fanning could not remember him.

Clatter of horsehoofs sounded from the air.

— What's that ? Martin Cunningham said.

All turned where they stood ; John Wyse Nolan came down again. From the cool shadow of the doorway he saw the horses pass Parliament street, harness and glossy pasterns in sunlight shimmering. Gaily they went past before his cool unfriendly eyes, not quickly. In saddles of the leaders, leaping leaders, rode outriders.

— What was it ? Martin Cunningham asked, as they went on up the staircase.

— The lord lieutenant general and general governor of Ireland, John Wyse Nolan answered from the stairfoot.

***

As they trod across the thick carpet Buck Mulligan whispered behind his Panama to Haines,

— Parnell's brother. There in the corner.

They chose a small table near the window opposite a longfaced man whose beard and gaze hung intently down on a chessboard.

— Is that he ? Haines asked, twisting round in his seat.

— Yes, Mulligan said. That's John Howard, his brother, our city marshal.

John Howard Parnell translated a white bishop quietly and his grey claw went up again to his forehead whereat it rested.

An instant after, under its screen, his eyes looked quickly, ghostbright, at his foe and fell once more upon a working corner.

— I'll take a *mélange,* Haines said to the waitress.

— Two *mélanges,* Buck Mulligan said. And bring us some scones and butter and some cakes as well.

When she had gone he said, laughing :

— We call it D. B. C. because they have damn bad cakes. O, but you missed Dedalus on *Hamlet.*

Haines opened his newbought book.

— I'm sorry, he said. Shakespeare is the happy hunting ground of all minds that have lost their balance.

The onelegged sailor growled at the area of 14 Nelson street :

— *England expects*...

Buck Mulligan's primrose waistcoat shook gaily to his laughter.

— You should see him, he said, when his body loses its balance. Wandering Ængus I call him.

— I am sure he has an *idée fixe,* Haines said, pinching his chin thoughtfully with thumb and forefinger. How I am speculating what it would be likely to be. Such persons always have.

Buck Mulligan bent across the table gravely.

— They drove his wits astray, he said, by visions of hell. He will never capture the Attic note. The note of Swinburne, of all poets, the white death and the ruddy birth. That is his tragedy. He can never be a poet. The joy of creation...

— Eternal punishment, Haines said, nodding curtly. I see. I tackled him this morning on beliet. There was something on his mind, I saw. It's rather interesting because Professor Pokorny of Vienna makes an interesting point out of that.

Buck Mulligan's watchful eyes saw the waitress come. He helped her to unload her tray.

— He can find no trace of hell in ancient Irish myth, Haines said, amid the cheerful cups. The moral idea seems lacking, the sense of destiny, of retribution. Rather strange he should have just that fixed idea. Does he write anything for your movement ?

He sank two lumps of sugar deftly longwise through the whipped cream. Buck Mulligan slit a steaming scone in two and plastered butter over its smoking pith. He bit off a soft piece hungrily.

— Ten years, he said, chewing and laughing. He is going to write something in ten years.

— Seems a long way off, Haines said, thoughtfully lifting his spoon. Still, I shouldn't wonder if he did after all.

He tasted a spoonful from the creamy cone of his cup.

— This is real Irish cream I take it, he said with forbearance. I don't want to be imposed on.

Elijah, skiff, light crumpled throwaway, sailed eastward by flanks of ships and trawlers, amid an archipelago of corks, beyond new Wapping street past

Benson's ferry, and by the threemasted schooner *Rosevean* from Bridgewater with bricks.

⁂

Almidano Artifoni walked past Holles street, past Sewell's yard. Behind him Cashel Boyle O'Connor Fiztmaurice Tisdall Farrell with stickumbrelladustcoat dangling, shunned the lamp before Mr Law Smith's house and, crossing, walked along Merrion square. Distantly behind him a blind stripling tapped his way by the wall of College Park.

Cashel Boyle O'Connor Fitzmaurice Tisdall Farrell walked as far as Mr Lewis Werner's cheerful windows, then turned and strode back along Merrion square, his stickumbrelladustcoat dangling.

At the corner of Wilde's he halted, frowned at Elijah's name announced on the Metropolitan Hall, frowned at the distant pleasance of duke's lawn. His eyeglass flashed frowning in the sun. With ratsteeth bared he muttered :

— *Coactus volui.*

He strode on for Clare street, grinding his fierce word.

As he strode past Mr Bloom's dental windows the sway of his dustcoat brushed rudely from its angle a slender tapping cane and swept onwards, having buffeted a thewless body. The blind stripling turned his sickly face after the striding form.

— God's curse on you, he said sourly, whoever you are! You're blinder nor I am, you bitch's bastard!

Opposite Ruggy O'Donohoe's Master Patrick Aloysius Dignam, pawing the pound and a half of Mangan's, late Fehrenbach's, porksteaks he had been sent for, went along warm Wicklow street dawdling. It was too blooming dull sitting in the parlour with Mrs Stoer and Mrs Quigley and Mrs Mac Dowell and the blind down and they all at their sniffles and sipping sups of the superior tawny sherry uncle Barney brought from Tunney's. And they eating crumbs of the cottage fruit cake jawing the whole blooming time and sighing.

After Wicklow lane the window of Madame Doyle, court dress milliner, stopped him He stood looking in at the two puckers stripped to their pelts and putting up their props. From the sidemirrors two mourning Masters Dignam gaped silently. Myler Keogh, Dublin's pet lamb, will meet sergeant major Bennett, the Portobello bruiser, for a purse of fifty sovereigns. Gob, that'd be a good pucking match to see. Myler Keogh, that's the chap sparring out to him with the green sash. Two bar entrance, soldiers half price. I could easy do a bunk on ma. Master Dignam on his left turned as he turned. That's me in mourning. When is it? May the twentysecond. Sure, the blooming thing is all over. He turned to the right and on his right Master Dignam turned, his cap awry, his collar sticking up. Buttoning it down, his chin lifted, he saw the image of Marie Kendall, charming soubrette, beside the two puckers. One ot them mots that do be in the packets of fags Stoer smokes that his old fellow welted hell out of him for one time he found out.

Master Dignam got his collar down and dawdled on. The best pucker going for strength was Fitzsimons. One puck in the wind from that fellow would knock you into the middle of next week, man. But the best pucker for science was Jem Corbet before Fitzsimons knocked the stuffings out of him, dodging and all.

In Grafton street Master Dignam saw a red flower in a toff's mouth and a swell pair of kicks on him and he listening to what the drunk was telling him and grinning all the time.

No Sandymount tram.

Master Dignam walked along Nassau street, shifted the porksteaks to his other hand. His collar sprang up again and he tugged it down. The blooming stud was too small for the buttonhole of the shirt, blooming end to it. He met schoolboys with satchels. I'm not going tomorrow either, stay away till Monday. He met other schoolboys. Do they notice I'm in mourning? Uncle Barney said he'd get it into the paper tonight. Then they'll all see it in the paper and read my name printed and pa's name.

His face got all grey instead of being red like it was and there was a fly walking over it up to his eye. The scrunch that was when they were screwing the screws into the coffin: and the bumps when they were bringing it downstairs.

Pa was inside it and ma crying in the parlour and uncle Barney telling the men how to get it round the bend. A big coffin it was, and high and heavylooking. How was that? The last night pa was boosed he was standing on the landing there bawling out for his boots to go out to Tunney's for to boose more and he looked butty and short in his shirt. Never see him again. Death, that is. Pa is dead. My father is dead. He told me to be a good son to ma. I couldn't hear the other things he said but I saw his tongue and his teeth trying to say it better. Poor pa. That was Mr Dignam, my father. I hope he is in purgatory now because he went to confession to father Conroy on Saturday night.

***

William Humble, earl of Dudley, and Lady Dudley, accompanied by lieutenantcolonel Hesseltine, drove out after luncheon from the viceregal lodge. In the following carriage were the honourable Mrs Paget, Miss de Courcy and the honourable Gerald Ward A. D. C. in attendance.

The cavalcade passed out by the lower gate of Phœnix Park saluted by obsequious policemen and proceeded past Kingsbridge along the northern quays. The viceroy was most cordially greated on his way through the metropolis. At Bloody bridge Mr Thomas Kernan beyond the river greeted him vainly from afar. Between Queen's and Whitworth bridges Lord Dudley's viceregal carriages passed and were unsaluted by Mr Dudley White, B. L., M. A., who stood on Arran Quay outside Mrs M. E. White's, the pawnbroker's, at the corner of Arran street west stroking his nose with his forefinger, undecided whether he should arrive at Phibsborough more quickly by a triple change of tram or by hailing a car or on foot through Smithfield, Constitution hill and Broadstone terminus. In the porch of Four Courts Richie Goulding with the costsbag of Goulding, Collis and Ward saw him with surprise. Past Richmond bridge at the doorstep of the office of Reuben J. Dodd, solicitor, agent for the Patriotic Insurance Company, an elderly female about to enter changed her plan and retracing her steps by King's windows smiled credulously on the representative of His Majesty. From its sluice in Wood quay wall under Tom Devan's office Poddle river hung out in fealty a tongue of liquid sewage. Above the crossblind of the Ormond Hotel, gold by bronze, Miss Kennedy's head by Miss Douce's head watched and admired. On Ormond quay Mr Simon Dedalus, steering his way from the greenhouse for the subsheriff's office, stood still in midstreet and brought his hat low. His Excellency graciously returned Mr Dedalus' greeting. From Cahill's corner the reverend Hugh C. Love, M. A., made obeisance unperceived, mindful of lords deputies whose hands benignant had held of yore rich advowsons. On Grattan bridge Lenehan and M'Coy, taking leave of each other, watched the carriages go by. Passing by Roger Greene's office and Dollard's big red printinghouse Gerty Mac Dowell, carrying the Catesby's cork lino letters for her father who was laid up, knew by the style it was the lord and lady lieutenant but she couldn't see what Her Excellency had on because the tram and Spring's big yellow furniture van had to stop in front of her on account of its being the lord lieutenant. Beyond Lundy Foot's from the shaded door of Kavanagh's winerooms John Wyse Nolan smiled with unseen coldness towards the lord lieutenantgeneral and general governor of Ireland. The Right Honourable William Humble, earl of Dudley, G. C. V. O., passed Micky Anderson's all times ticking watches and Henry and James's wax smartsuited freshcheeked models, the gentleman Henry, *dernier cri* James. Over against Dame gate Tom Rochford and Nosey Flynn watched the approach of the cavalcade. Tom Rochford, seeing the eyes of lady Dudley fixed on him, took his thumbs quickly out of the pockets of his claret waistcoat and doffed his cap to her. A charming *soubrette,* great Marie Kendall, with dauby cheeks and lifted skirt, smiled daubily from her poster upon William Humble, earl of Dudley, and upon lieutenantcolonel H. G. Hesseltine and also upon the honourable Gerald Ward A. D. C. From the window of the D. B. C. Buck Mulligan gaily, and Haines gravely, gazed down on the viceregal equipage over the shoulders of eager guests, whose mass of forms darkened the chessboard whereon John Howard Parnell looked intently. In Fownes's street, Dilly Dedalus, straining her sight upward from Chardenal's first French primer, saw sunshades spanned and wheelspokes spinning in the glare. John Henry Menton, filling the doorway of Commercial Buildings, stared from winebig oyster eyes, holding a fat gold hunter watch not looked at in his fat left hand not feeling it. Where the foreleg of King Billy's horse pawed the air Mrs Breen plucked her hastening husband back from under the hoofs of the outriders. She shouted in his ear the tidings. Understanding, he shifted his tomes to his left breast and saluted the second carriage. The honourable Gerald Ward A. D. C., agreeably surprised, made haste to reply. At Ponsonby's corner a jaded white flagon H. halted and four tallhatted white flagons halted behind him, E. L. Y'. S., while outriders pranced past and carriages. Opposite Pigott's music warerooms Mr Denis J Maginni, professor of dancing &c, gaily apparelled, gravely walked, outpassed by a viceroy and unobserved. By the provost's wall came jauntily Blazes Boylan, stepping in tanned shoes and socks with skyblue clocks to the refrain of *My girl's a Yorkshire girl.*

Blazes Boylan presented to the leaders' skyblue frontlets and high action a skyblue tie, a widebrimmed straw hat at a rakish angle and a suit of indigo serge. His hands in his jacket pockets forgot to salute but he offered to the three ladies the bold admiration of his eyes and the red flower between his lips. As they drove along Nassau street His Excellency drew the attention of his bowing consort to the programme of music which was being discoursed in College park. Unseen brazen highland laddies blared and drumthumped after the *cortège* :

But though she's a factory lass
And wears no fancy clothes.
Baraabum.
Yet I've a sort of a
Yorkshire relish for
My little Yorkshire rose
Baraabum.

Thither of the wall the quartermile flat handicappers, M. C. Green, H. Thrift, T. M. Patey, C. Scaife, J. B. Jeffs, G. N. Morphy, F. Stevenson, C. Adderly, and W. C. Huggard started in pursuit. Striding past Finn's hotel, Cashel Boyle O'Connor Fitzmaurice Tisdall Farrell stared through a fierce eyeglass across the carriages at the head of Mr M. E. Solomons in the window of the Austro-Hungarian viceconsulate. Deep in Leinster street, by Trinity's postern, a loyal king's man, Hornblower, touched his tallyho cap. As the glossy horses pranced by Merrion square Master Patrick Aloysius Dignam, waiting, saw salutes being given to the gent with the topper and raised also his new black cap with fingers greased by porksteak paper. His collar too sprang up. The viceroy, on his way to inaugurate the Mirus bazaar in aid of funds for Mercer's hospital, drove with his following towards Lower Mount street. He passed a blind stripling opposite Broadbent's. In Lower Mount street a pedestrian in a brown macintosh, eating dry bread, passed swiftly and unscathed across the viceroy's path. At the Royal Canal bridge, from his hoarding, Mr Eugene Stratton, his blub lips agrin, bade all comers welcome to Pembroke township. At Haddington road corner two sanded women halted themselves, an umbrella and a bag in which eleven cockles rolled to view with wonder the lord mayor and lady mayoress without his golden chain. On Northumberland and Landsdowne roads His Excellency acknowledged punctually salutes from rare male walkers, the salute of two small schoolboys at the garden gate of the house said to have been admired by the late queen when visiting the Irish capital with her husband, the prince consort, in 1849 and the salute of Almidano Artifoni's sturdy trousers swallowed by a closing door.

Bronze by gold heard the hoofirons, steelyringing.

Imperthnthn thnthnthn.

Chips, picking chips off rocky thumbnail, chips.

Horrid! And gold flushed more.

A husky fifenote blew.

Blew. Blue bloom is on the

Gold pinnacled hair.

A jumping rose on satiny breasts of satin, rose of Castile.

Trilling, trilling: Idolores.

Peep! Who's in the... peepofgold?

Tink cried to bronze in pity.

And a call, pure, long and throbbing. Longindying call.

Decoy. Soft word. But look! The bright stars fade. O rose! Notes chirruping answer. Castile. The morn is breaking.

Jingle jingle jaunted jingling.

Coin rang. Clock clacked.

Avowal. *Sonnez*. I could. Rebound of garter. Not leave thee. Smack. *La cloche!* Thigh smack. Avowal. Warm. Sweetheart, goodbye!

Jingle. Bloo

Boomed crashing chords. When love absorbs. War! War! The tympanum.

A sail! A veil awave upon the waves.

Lost. Throstle fluted. All is lost now.

Horn. Hawhorn.

When first he saw. Alas!

Full tup. Full throb.

Warbling. Ah, lure! Alluring.

Martha! Come!

Clapclop. Clipclap. Clappyclap.

Goodgod henev erheard inall
Deaf bald Pat brought pad knife took up.
A moonlit nightcall : far : far.
I feel so sad. P. S. So lonely blooming.
Listen!
The spiked and winding cold seahorn. Have you the ? Each and for other plash and silent roar.
Pearls : when she. Liszt's rhapsodies. Hissss.
You don't ?
Did not : no, no : believe : Lidlyd. With a cock with a carra.
Black.
Deepsounding. Do, Ben, do.
Wait while you wait. Hee hee. Wait while you hee.
But wait!
Low in dark middle earth. Embedded ore.
Naminedamine. All gone. All fallen.
Tiny, her tremulous fernfoils of maidenhair.
Amen! He gnashed in fury.
Fro. To, fro. A baton cool protruding.
Bronzelydia by Minagold.
By bronze, by gold, in oceangreen of shadow. Bloom. Old Bloom.
One rapped, one tapped with a carra, with a cock.
Pray for him! Pray, good people!
His gouty fingers nakkering.
Big Benaben. Big Benben.
Last rose Castile of summer left bloom I feel so sad alone.
Pwee! Little wind piped wee.
True men. Lid Ker Cow De and Doll. Ay, ay, Like you men. Will lift your tschink with tschunk.
Fff! Oo!
Where bronze from anear? Where gold from afar? Where hoofs?
Rrrpr. Kraa. Kraandl.
Then, not till then. My eppripfftaph. Be pfrwritt.
Done.
Begin!

Bronze by gold, Miss Douce's head by Miss Kennedy's head, over the crossblind of the Ormond bar heard the viceregal hoofs go by, ringing steel.

— Is that her? asked Miss Kennedy.

Miss Douce said yes, sitting with his ex, pearl grey and *eau de Nil.*

— Exquisite contrast, Miss Kennedy said.

When all agog Miss Douce said eagerly:

— Look at the fellow in the tall silk.

— Who? Where? gold asked more eagerly.

— In the second carriage, Miss Douce's wet lips said, laughing in the sun. He's looking. Mind till I see.

She darted, bronze, to the backmost corner, flattening her face against the pane in a halo of hurried breath.

Her wet lips tittered:

— He's killed looking back.

She laughed:

— O wept! Aren't men frightful idiots?

With sadness.

Miss Kennedy sauntered sadly from bright light, twining a loose hair behind an ear. Sauntering sadly, gold no more, she twisted twined a hair. Sadly she twined in sauntering gold hair behind a curving ear.

— It's them has the fine times, sadly then she said.

A man.

Bloowho went by by Moulang's pipes, bearing in his breast the sweets of sin, by Wine's antiques in memory bearing sweet sinful words, by Carroll's dusky battered plate, for Raoul.

The boots to them, them in the bar, them barmaids came. For them unheeding him he banged on the counter his tray of chattering china. And

— There's your teas, he said.

Miss Kennedy with manners transposed the teatray down to an upturned lithia crate, safe from eyes, low.

— What is it? loud boots unmannerly asked.

— Find out, Miss Douce retorted, leaving her spyingpoint.

— Your *beau,* is it?

A haughty bronze replied:

— I'll complain to Mrs de Massey on you if I hear any more of your impertinent insolence.

— Imperthnthn thnthnthn, bootsnout sniffed rudely, as he retreated as she threatened as he had come.

Bloom.

On her flower frowning Miss Douce said :

— Most aggravating that young brat is. If he doesn't conduct himself I'll wring his ear tor him a yard long.

Ladylike in exquisite contrast.

— Take no notice, Miss Kennedy rejoined.

She poured in a teacup tea, then back in the teapot tea. They cowered under their reef of counter, waiting on footstools, crates upturned, waiting for their teas to draw. They pawed their blouses, both of black satin, two and nine a yard, waiting for their teas to draw, and two and seven.

Yes, bronze from anear, by gold from afar, heard steel from anear, hoofs ring from afar, and heard steelhoofs ringhoof ringsteel.

— Am I awfully sunburnt ?

Miss bronze unbloused her neck.

— No, said Miss Kennedy. It gets brown after. Did you try the borax with the cherry laurel water ?

Miss Douce halfstood to see her skin askance in the barmirror gildedlettered where hock and claret glasses shimmered and in their midst a shell.

— And leave it to my hands, she said.

— Try it with the glycerine, Miss Kennedy advised.

Bidding her neck and hands adieu Miss Douce

— Those things only bring out a rash, replied, reseated. I asked that old fogey in Boyd's for something for my skin.

Miss Kennedy, pouring now fulldrawn tea, grimaced and prayed :

— O, don't remind me of him for mercy'sake !

— But wait till I tell you, Miss Douce entreated.

Sweet tea Miss Kennedy having poured with milk plugged both two ears with little fingers.

— No, don't, she cried.

— I won't listen, she cried.

But Bloom ?

Miss Douce grunted in snuffy fogey's tone :

— For your what ? says he.

Miss Kennedy unplugged her ears to hear, to speak : but said, but prayed again :

— Don't let me think of him or I'll expire. The hideous old wretch ! That night in the Antient Concert Rooms.

She sipped distastefully her brew, hot tea, a sip, sipped sweet tea.

— Here he was, Miss Douce said, cocking her bronze head three quarters, ruffling her nosewings. Hufa! Hufa!

Shrill shriek of laughter sprang from Miss Kennedy's throat. Miss Douce huffed and snorted down her nostrils that quivered imperthnthn like a shout in quest.

— O! shrieking, Miss Kennedy cried. Will you ever forget his goggle eye?

Miss Douce chimed in in deep bronze laughter, shouting:

— And your other eye!

Bloowhose dark eye read Aaron Figatner's name. Why do I always think Figather? Gathering figs I think. And Prosper Loré's huguenot name. By Bassi's blessed virgins Bloom's dark eyes went by. Bluerobed, white under, come to me. God they believe she is: or goddess. Those today. I could not see. That fellow spoke. A student. After with Dedalus'son. He might be Mulligan. All comely virgins. That brings those rakes of fellows in: her white.

By went his eyes. The sweets of sin. Sweet are the sweets.

Of sin.

In a giggling peal young goldbronze voices blended, Douce with Kennedy your other eye. They threw young heads back, bronze gigglegold, to let freefly their laughter, screaming, your other, signals to each other, high piercing notes.

Ah, panting, sighing. Sighing, ah, fordone their mirth died down.

Miss Kennedy lipped her cup again, raised, drank a sip and gigglegiggled. Miss Douce, bending again over the teatray, ruffled again her nose and rolled droll fattened eyes. Again Kennygiggles, stooping her fair pinnacles of hair, stooping, her tortoise napecomb showed, spluttered out of her mouth her tea, choking in tea and laughter, coughing with choking, crying:

— O greasy eyes! Imagine being married to a man like that, she cried. With his bit of beard!

Douce gave full vent to a splendid yell, a full yell of full woman, delight, joy, indignation.

— Married to the greasy nose! she yelled.

Shrill, with deep laughter, after bronze in gold, they urged each each to peal after peal, ringing in changes, bronzegold goldbronze, shrilldeep, to laughter after laughter. And then laughed more. Greasy I knows. Exhausted, breathless their shaken heads they laid, braided and pinnacled by glossycombed, against the counterledge. All flushed (O!), panting, sweating (O!), all breathless.

Married to Bloom, to greaseaseabloom.

— O saints above! Miss Douce said, sighed above her jumping rose. I wished I hadn't laughed so much. I feel all wet.

— O, Miss Douce! Miss Kennedy protested. You horrid thing!

And flushed yet more (you horrid!), more goldenly.

By Cantwell's offices roved Greaseabloom, by Ceppi's virgins, bright of their oils. Nannetti's father hawked those things about, wheedling at doors as I. Religion pays. Must see him about Keyes's par. Eat first. I want. Not yet. At four, she said. Time ever passing. Clockhands turning. On. Where eat? The Clarence, Dolphin. On. For Raoul. Eat. If I net five guineas with those ads. The violet silk petticoats. Not yet. The sweets of sin.

Flushed less, still less, goldenly paled.

Into their bar strolled Mr Dedalus. Chips, picking chips off one of his rocky thumbnails. Chips. He strolled.

— O welcome back, Miss Douce.

He held her hand. Enjoyed her holidays?

— Tiptop.

He hoped she had nice weather in Rostrevor.

— Gorgeous, she said. Look at the holy show I am. Lying out on the strand all day.

Bronze whiteness.

— That was exceedingly naughty of you, Mr Dedalus told her and pressed her hand indulgently. Tempting poor simple males.

Miss Douce of satin douced her arm away.

— O go away, she said. You're very simple, I don't think.

He was.

— Well now, I am, he mused. I looked so simple in the cradle they christened me simple Simon.

— You must have been a doaty, Miss Douce made answer. And what did the doctor order today?

— Well now, he mused, whatever you say yourself. I think I'll trouble you for some fresh water and a half glass of whisky.

Jingle.

— With the greatest alacrity, Miss Douce agreed.

With grace of alacrity towards the mirror gilt Cantrell and Cochrane's she turned herself. With grace she tapped a measure of gold whisky from her crystal keg. Forth from the skirt of his coat Mr Dedalus brought pouch and pipe. Alacrity she served. He blew through the flue two husky fifenotes.

— By Jove, he mused. I often wanted to see the Mourne moutains. Must be a great tonic in the air down there. But a long threatening comes at last, they say. Yes, yes.

Yes. He fingered shreds of hair, her maidenhair, her mermaid's, into the bowl. Chips Shreds. Musing. Mute.

None not said nothing. Yes.

Gaily Miss Douce polished a tumbler, trilling :

— *O, Idolores, queen of the eastern seas!*

— Was Mr Lidwell in today?

In came Lenehan. Round him peered Lenehan. Mr Bloom reached Essex bridge. Yes, Mr Bloom crossed bridge of Yessex. To Martha I must write. Buy paper. Daly's. Girl there civil. Bloom. Old Bloom. Blue Bloom is on the rye.

— He was in at lunchtime, Miss Douce said.

Lenehan came forward.

— Was Mr Boylan looking for me?

He asked. She answered :

— Miss Kennedy, was Mr Boylan in while I was upstairs?

She asked. Miss voice of Kennedy answered, a second teacup poised, her gaze upon a page.

— No. He was not.

Miss gaze of Kennedy, heard not seen, read on. Lenehan round the sandwichbell wound his round body round.

— Peep! Who's in the corner?

No glance of Kennedy rewarding him he yet made overtures. To mind her stops. To read only the black ones : round o and crooked ess.

Jingle jaunty jingle.

Girlgold she read and did not glance. Take no notice. She took no notice while he read by rote a solfa fable for her, plappering flatly :

— Ah fox met ah stork. Said thee fox too thee stork : Will you put your bill down inn my troath and pull upp ah bone?

He droned in vain. Miss Douce turned to her tea aside.

He sighed, aside :

— Ah me! O my!

He greeted Mr Dedalus and got a nod.

— Greetings from the famous son of a famous father.

— Who may he be? Mr Dedalus asked.

Lenehan opened most genial arms. Who?

— Who may he be? he asked. Can you ask? Stephen, the youthful bard. Dry.

Mr Dedalus, famous father, laid by his dry filled pipe.

— I see, he said. I didn't recognise him for the moment. I hear he is keeping very select company. Have you seen him lately?

He had.

— I quaffed the nectarbowl with him this very day, said Lenehan. In Mooney's *en ville* and in Mooney's *sur mer*. He had received the rhino for the labour of his muse.

He smiled at bronze's teabathed lips, at listening lips and eyes.

— The *élite* of Erin hung upon his lips. The ponderous pundit. Hugh MacHugh, Dublin's most brilliant scribe and editor and that minstrel boy of the wild wet west who is known by the euphonious appellation of the O'Madden Burke.

After an interval Mr Dedalus raised his grog and

— That must have been highly diverting, said he. I see.

He see. He drank. With faraway mourning mountain eye. Set down his glass.

He looked towards the saloon door.

— I see you have moved the piano.

— The tuner was in today, Miss Douce replied, tuning it for the smoking concert and I never heard such an exquisite player.

— Is that a fact?

— Didn't he, Miss Kennedy? The real classical, you know. And blind too, poor fellow. Not twenty I'm sure he was.

— Is that a fact? Mr Dedalus said.

He drank and strayed away.

— So sad to look at his face, Miss Douce condoled.

God's curse on bitch's bastard.

Tink to her pity cried a diner's bell. To the door of the diningroom came bald Pat, came bothered Pat, came Pat, waiter of Ormond. Lager for diner. Lager without alacrity she served.

With patience Lenehan waited for Boylan with impatience, for jingle jaunty blazes boy.

Upholding the lid he (who?) gazed in the coffin (coffin?) at the oblique triple (piano!) wires. He pressed (the same who pressed indulgently her hand), soft pedalling a triple of keys to sees the thicknesses of felt advancing, to hear the muffled hammerfall in action.

Two sheets cream vellum paper one reserve two envelopes when I was in Wisdom Hely's wise Bloom in Daly's Henry Flower bought. Are you not happy in your home? Flower to console me and a pin cuts lo. Means something, language of flow. Was it a daisy? Innocence that is. Respectable girl meet after mass. Tanks awfully muchly. Wise Bloom eyed on the door a poster, a swaying mermaid smoking mid nice waves. Smoke mermaids, coolest whiff of all. Hair streaming : lovelorn. For some man. For Raoul. He eyed and saw afar on Essex bridge a gay hat riding on a jauntingcar. It is. Third time. Coincidence.

Jingling on supple rubbers it jaunted from the bridge to Ormond quay. Follow. Risk it. Go quick. At four. Near now. Out.

— Twopence, sir, the shopgirl dared to say.

— Aha... I was forgetting... Excuse...

— And four.

At four she. Winsomely she on Bloohimwhom smiled. Bloo smi qui go. Ternoon. Think you're the only pebble on the beach? Does that to all. For men.

In drowsy silence gold bent on her page.

From the saloon a call came, long in dying. That was a tuningfork the tuner had that he forgot that he now struck. A call again. That he now poised that it now throbbed. You hear? It throbbed, pure, purer, softly and softlier, its buzzing prongs. Longer in dying call.

Pat paid for diner's popcorked bottle : and over tumbler tray and popcorked bottle ere he went he whispered, bald and bothered, with Miss Douce.

— *The bright stars fade...*

A voiceless song sang from within, singing :

— ... *the morn is breaking.*

A duodene of birdnotes chirruped bright treble answer under sensitive hands. Brightly the keys, all twinkling, linked, all harpsichording, called to a voice to sing the strain of dewy morn, of youth, of love's leavetaking, life's, love's morn.

— *The dewdrops pearl...*

Lenehan's lips over the counter lisped a low whistle of decoy.

— But look this way, he said, rose of Castile.

Jingle jaunted by the curb and stopped.

She rose and closed her reading, rose of Castile. Fretted forlorn, dreamily rose.

— Did she fall or was she pushed? he asked her.

She answered, slighting :

— Ask no questions and you'll hear no lies.

Like lady, ladylike.

Blazes Boylan's smart tan shoes creaked on the barfloor where he strode. Yes, gold from anear by bronze from afar. Lenehan heard and knew and hailed him :

— See the conquering hero comes.

Between the car and window, warily walking, went Bloom, unconquered hero. See me he might. The seat he sat on : warm. Black wary hecat walked towards Richie Goulding's legal bag, lifted aloft saluting.

— *And I from thee...*

— I heard you were round, said Blazes Boylan.

He touched to fair Miss Kennedy a rim of his slanted straw. She smiled on him. But sister bronze outsmiled her, preening for him her richer hair, a bosom and a rose.

Boylan bespoke potions.

— What's your cry? Glass of bitter? Glass of bitter, please, and a sloegin for me. Wire in yet?

Not yet. At four he. All said four.

Cowley's red lugs and Adam's apple in the door of the sheriff's office. Avoid. Goulding a chance. What is he doing in the Ormond? Car waiting. Wait.

Hello. Where off to? Something to eat? I too was just. In here. What, Ormond? Best value in Dublin. Is that so? Diningroom. Sit tight there. See, not be seen. I think I'll join you. Come on. Richie led on. Bloom followed bag. Dinner fit for a prince.

Miss Douce reached high to take a flagon, stretching her satin arm, her bust, that all but burst, so high.

— O! O! jerked Lenehan, gasping at each stretch. O!

But easily she seized her prey and led it low in triumph.

— Why don't you grow? asked Blazes Boylan.

Shebronze, dealing from her jar thick syrupy liquor for his lips, looked as it flowed (flower in his coat : who gave him?), and syrupped with her voice :

— Fine goods in small parcels.

That is to say she. Neatly she poured slowsyrupy sloe.

— Here's fortune, Blazes said.

He pitched a broad coin down. Coin rang.

— Hold on, said Lenehan, till I...

— Fortune, he wished, lifting his bubbled ale.

— Sceptre will win in a canter, he said.

— I plunged a bit, said Boylan winking aud drinking. Not on my own, you know. Fancy of a friend of mine.

Lenehan still drank and grinned at his tilted ale and at Miss Douce's lips that all but hummed, not shut, the oceansong her lips had trilled. Idolores. The eastern seas.

Clock whirred. Miss Kennnedy passed their way (flower, wonder who gave), bearing away teatray. Clock clacked.

Miss Douce took Boylan's coin, struck boldly the cashregister. It clanged. Clock clacked. Fair one of Egypt teased and sorted in the till and hummed and handed coins in change. Look to the west. A clack. For me.

— What time is that? asked Blazes Boylan. Four?

O'clock.

Lenehan, small eyes ahunger on her humming, bust ahumming, tugged Blazes Boylan's elbowsleeve.

— Let's hear the time, he said.

The bag of Goulding, Colles, Ward led Bloom by ryebloom flowered tables. Aimless he chose with agitated aim, bald Pat attending, a table near the door. Be near. At four. Has he forgotten? Perhaps a trick. Not come : whet appetite. I couldn't do. Wait, wait. Pat, waiter, waited.

Sparkling bronze azure eyed Blazure's skyblue bow and eyes.

— Go on, pressed Lenehan. There's no-one. He never heard.

— *...to Flora's lips did hie.*

High, a high note, pealed in the treble, clear.

Bronzedouce, communing with her rose that sank and rose sought Blazes Boylan's flower and eyes.

— Please, please.

He pleaded over returning phrases of avowal.

— *I could not leave thee...*

— Afterwits, Miss Douce promised coyly.

— No, now, urged Lenehan. *Sonnez la cloche!* O do! There's no-one.

She looked. Quick. Miss Kenn out of earshot. Sudden bent. Two kindling faces watched her bend.

Quavering the chords strayed from the air, found it again, lost chord, and lost and found it faltering.

— Go on! Do! *Sonnez!*

Bending, she nipped a peak of skirt above her knee. Delayed. Taunted them still, bending, suspending, with wilful eyes.

— *Sonnez!*

Smack. She let free sudden in rebound her nipped elastic garter smackwarm against her smackable a woman's warmhosed thigh.

— *La cloche!* cried gleeful Lenehan. Trained by owner. No sawdust there.

She smilesmirked supercilious (wept! aren't men?), but, lightward gliding, mild she smiled on Boylan.

— You're the essence of vulgarity, she in gliding said.

Boylan, eyed, eyed. Tossed to fat lips his chalice, drankoff his tiny, chalice, sucking the last fat violet syrupy drops. His spellbound eyes went after her gliding head as it went down the bar by mirrors, gilded arch for ginger ale, hock and claret glasses shimmering, a spiky shell, where it concerted, mirrored, bronze with sunnier bronze.

Yes, bronze from anearby.

— ...*Sweetheart, goodbye!*

— I'm off, said Boylan with impatience.

He slid his chalice brisk away, grasped his change.

— Wait a shake, begged Lenehan, drinking quickly. I wanted to tell you. Tom Rochford...

— Come on to blazes, said Blazes Boylan, going.

Lenehan gulped to go.

— Got the horn or what? he said. Wait. I'm coming.

He followed the hasty creaking shoes but stood by nimbly by the threshold, saluting forms, a bulky with a slender.

— How do you do, Mr Dollard?

— Eh? How do? How do? Ben Dollard's vague bass answered, turning an instant from Father Cowley's woe. He won't give you any trouble, Bob. Alf Bergan will speak to the long fellow. We'll put a barleystraw in that Judas Iscariot's ear this time.

Sighing, Mr Dedalus came through the saloon, a finger soothing an eyelid.

— Hoho, we will, Ben Dollard yodled jollily. Come on, Simon, give us a ditty. We heard the piano.

Bald Pat, bothered waiter, waited for drink orders, Power for Richie. And Bloom? Let me see. Not make him walk twice. His corns. Four now. How warm this black is. Course nerves a bit. Refracts (is it?) heat. Let me see. Cider. Yes, bottle of cider.

— What's that? Mr Dedalus said. I was only vamping, man.

— Come on, come on, Ben Dollard called. Begone, dull care. Come, Bob.

He ambled Dollard, bulky slops, before them (hold that fellow with the: hold him now) into the saloon. He plumped him Dollard on the stool. His gouty paws plumped chords. Plumped stopped abrupt.

Bald Pat in the doorway met tealess gold returning. Bothered he wanted Power and cider. Bronze by the window watched, bronze from afar.

Jingle a tinkle jaunted.

Bloom heard a jing, a little sound. He's off. Light sob of breath Bloom sighed on the silent bluehued flowers. Jingling. He's gone. Jingle. Hear.

— Love and war, Ben, Mr Dedalus said. God be with old times.

Miss Douce's brave eyes, unregarded, turned from the crossblind, smitten by sunlight. Gone. Pensive (who knows?), smitten (the smiting light), she lowered the dropblind with a sliding cord. She drew down pensive (why did he go so quick when I?) about her bronze, over the bar where bald stood by sister gold, inexquisite contrast, contrast inexquisite nonexquisite, slow cool dim seagreen sliding depth of shadow, *eau de Nil*.

— Poor old Goodwin was the pianist that night, Father Cowley reminded them. There was a slight difference of opinion between himself and the Collard grand.

There was.

— A symposium all his own, Mr Dedalus said. The devil wouldn't stop him. He was a crotchety old fellow in the primary stage of drink.

— God, do you remember? Ben bulky Dollard said, turning from the punished keyboard. And by Japers I had no wedding garment.

They laughed all three. He had no wed. All trio laughed. No wedding garment.

— Our friend Bloom turned in handy that night, Mr Dedalus said. Where's my pipe by the way?

He wandered back to the bar to the lost chord pipe. Bald Pat carried two diners' drinks, Richie and Poldy. And Father Cowley laughed again.

— I saved the situation, Ben, I think.

— You did, averred Ben Dollard. I remember those tight trousers too. That was a brilliant idea, Bob.

Father Cowley blushed to his brilliant purply lobes. He saved the situa. Tight trou. Brilliant ide.

— I knew he was on the rocks, he said. The wife was playing the piano in the coffee palace on Saturdays for a yery trifling consideration and who was it gave me the wheeze she was doing the other business? Do you remember? We had to search all Holles street to find them till the chap in Keogh's gave us the number. Remember?

Ben remembered, his broad visage wondering.

— By God she had some luxurious operacloaks and things there.

Mr Dedalus wandered back, pipe in hand.

— Merrion square style. Balldresses, by God, and court dresses. He wouldn't take any money either. What? Any God's quantity of cocked hats and boleros and trunkhose. What?

— Ay, ay, Mr Dedalus nodded. Mrs Marion Bloom has left off clothes of all descriptions.

Jingle jaunted down the quays. Blazes sprawled on bounding tyres.

Liver and bacon. Steak and kidney pie. Right, sir. Right, Pat.

Mrs Marrion met him pike hoses. Smell of burn of Paul de Kock. Nice name he.

— What's this her name was? A buxom lassy. Marion...

— Tweedy.

— Yes. Is she alive?

— And kicking.

— She was a daughter of...

— Daughter of the regiment.

— Yes, begad. I remember the old drummajor.

Mr Dedalus struck, whizzed, lit, puffed savoury puff after

— Irish? I don't know, faith. Is she, Simon?

Puff after stiff, a puff, strong, savoury, crackling.

— Buccinator muscle is... What?... Bit rusty... O, she is... My Irish Molly, O.

He puffed a pungent plumy blast.

— From the rock of Gibraltar... all the way.

They pined in depth of ocean shadow, gold by the beerpull, bronze by maraschino, thoughtful all two, Mina Kennedy, 4 Lismore terrace, Drumcondra with Idolores, a queen, Dolores, silent.

Pat served uncovered dishes. Leopold cut liverslices. As said before he ate with relish the inner organs, nutty gizzards, fried cods'roes while Richie Goulding, Collis, Ward ate steak and kidney, steak then kidney, bite by bite of pie he ate Bloom ate they ate.

Bloom with Goulding, married in silence, ate. Dinners fit for princes.

By Bachelor's walk jogjaunty jingled Blazes Boylan, bachelor, in sun, in heat, mare's glossy rump atrot, with flick of whip, on bounding tyres : sprawled, warmseated, Boylan impatience, ardentbold. Horn. Have you the? Horn. Have you the? Haw haw horn.

Over their voices Dollard bassooned attack, booming over bombarding chords :

— *When love absorbs my ardent soul...*

Roll of Bensoulbenjamin rolled to the quivery loveshivery roofpanes.

— War! War! cried Father Cowley. You're the warrior.

— So I am, Ben Warrior laughed. I was thinking of your landlord. Love or money.

He stopped. He wagged huge beard, huge face over his blunder huge.

— Sure, you'd burst the tympanum of her ear, man, Mr Dedalus said through smoke aroma, with an organ like yours.

In bearded abundant laughter Dollard shook upon the keyboard. He would.

— Not to mention another membrane, Father Cowley added. Half time, Ben. *Amoroso ma non troppo*. Let me there.

Miss Kennedy served two gentlemen with tankards of cool stout. She passed a remark. It was indeed, first gentleman said, beautiful weather. They drank cool stout. Did she know where the lord lieutenant was going? And heard steelhoofs ringhoof ring. No, she couldn't say. But it would be in the paper. O, she needn't trouble. No trouble. She waved about her outspread *Independent*, searching, the lord lieutenant, her pinnacles of hair slowmoving, lord lieuten. Too much trouble, first gentleman said. O, not in the least. Way he looked that. Lord lieutenant. Gold by bronze heard iron steel.

— . . . . *my ardent soul*
I care not foror the morrow.

In liver gravy Bloom mashed mashed potatoes. Love and war someone is. Ben Dollard's famous. Night he ran round to us to borrow a dress suit for that concert. Trousers tight as a drum on him. Musical porkers. Molly did laugh when he went out. Threw herself back across the bed, screaming, kicking. With all his belongings on show. O, saints above, I'm drenched! O, the women in the front row! O, I never laughed so many! Well, of course, that's what gives him the base barreltone. For instance eunuchs. Wonder who's playing. Nice touch. Must be Cowley. Musical. Knows whatever note you play. Bad breath he has, poor chap. Stopped.

Miss Douce, engaging, Lydia Douce, bowed to suave solicitor, George Lidwell, gentleman, entering. Good afternoom. She gave her moist, a lady's, hand to his firm clasp. Afternoon. Yes, she was back. To the old dingdong again.

— Your friends are inside, Mr Lidwell.

George Lidwell, suave, solicited, held a lydiahand.

Bloom ate liv as said before. Clean here at least. That chap in the Burton, gummy with gristle. No-one here: Goulding and I. Clean tables, flowers, mitres of napkins. Pat to and fro, bald Pat. Nothing to do. Best value in Dub.

Piano again. Cowley it is. Way he sits in to it, like one together, mutual understanding. Tiresome shapers scraping fiddles, eye on the bowend, sawing the 'cello, remind you of toothache. Her high long snore. Night we were in the box. Trombone under blowing like a grampus, between the acts, other brass chap unscrewing, emptying spittle. Conductor's legs too, bagstrousers, jiggedy jiggedy. Do right to hide them.

Jiggedy jingle jaunty jaunty.

Only the harp. Lovely gold glowering light. Girl touched it. Poop of a lovely. Gravy's rather good fit for a. Golden ship. Erin. The harp that once or twice. Cool hands. Ben Howth, the rhododendrons. We are their harps. I. He. Old. Young.

— Ah, I couldn't, man, Mr Dedalus said, shy, listless.

Strongly.

— Go on, blast you, Ben Dollard growled. Get it out in bits.

— *M'appari,* Simon, Father Cowley said.

Down stage he strode some paces, grave, tall in affliction, his long arms outheld. Hoarsely the apple of his throat hoarsed softly. Softly he sang to a dusty seascape there: *A Last Farewell.* A headland, a ship, a sail upon the billows. Farewell. A lovely girl, her veil awave upon the wind upon the headland wind around her.

Cowley sang:

— *M'appari tutt'amor:*
Il mio sguardo l'incontr...

She waved, unhearing Cowley, her veil to one departing, dear one, to wind, love, speeding sail, return.

— Go on, Simon.

— Ah, sure my dancing days are done, Ben... Well...

Mr Dedalus laid his pipe to rest beside the tuningfork and, sitting, touched the obedient keys.

— No, Simon, Father Cowley turned. Play it in the original. One flat.

The keys, obedient, rose higher, told, faltered, confessed, confused.

Up stage strode Father Cowley.

— Here, Simon. I'll accompany you, he said. Get up.

By Graham Lemon's pineapple rock, by Elvery's elephant jingle jogged.

Steak, kidney, liver, mashed at meat fit for princes sat princes Bloom and Goulding. Princes at meat they raised and drank Power and cider.

Most beautiful tenor air ever written, Richie said : *Sonambula*. He heard Joe Maas sing that one night. Ah, what M'Guckin ! Yes. In his way. Choirboy style. Maas was the boy. Massboy. A lyrical tenor if you like. Never forget it. Never.

Tenderly Bloom over liverless bacon saw the tightened features strain. Backache he. Bright's bright eye. Next item on the programme. Paying the piper. Pills, pounded bread, worth a guinea a box. Stave it off awhile. Sings too : *Down among the dead men*. Appropriate. Kidney pie. Sweets to the. Not making much hand of it. Best value in. Characteristic of him. Power. Particular about his drink. Flaw in the glass, fresh Vartry water. Fecking matches from counters to save. Then squander a sovereign in dribs and drabs. And when he's wanted not a farthing. Screwed refusing to pay his fare. Curious types.

Never would Richie forget that night. As long as he lived, never. In the gods of the old Royal with little Peake. And when the first note.

Speech paused on Richie's lips.

Coming out with a whopper now. Rhapsodies about damn all. Believes his own lies. Does really. Wonderful liar. But want a good memory.

— Which air is that ? asked Leopold Bloom.

— *All is lost now.*

Richie cocked his lips apout. A low incipient note sweet banshee murmured : all. A thrush. A throstle. His breath, birdsweet, good teeth he's proud of, fluted with plaintive woe. Is lost. Rich sound. Two notes in one there. Blackbird I heard in the hawthorn valley. Taking my motives he twined and turned them. All most too new call is lost in all. Echo. How sweet the answer. How is that done ? All lost now. Mournful he whistled. Fall, surrender, lost.

Bloom bent leopold ear, turning a fringe of doyley down under the vase. Order. Yes, I remember. Lovely air. In sleep she went to him. Innocence in the moon. Still hold her back. Brave, don't know their danger. Call name.

Touch water. Jingle jaunty. Too late. She longed to go. That's why. Woman. As easy stop the sea. Yes : all is lost.

— A beautiful air, said Bloom lost Leopold. I know it well.

Never in all his life had Richie Goulding.

He knows it well too. Or he feels. Still harping on his daughter. Wise child that knows her father, Dedalus said. Me?

Bloom askance over liverless saw. Face of the all is lost. Rollicking Richie once. Jokes old stale now. Wagging his ear. Napkinring in his eye. Now begging letters he sends his son with. Crosseyed Walter sir I did sir. Wouldn't trouble only I was expecting some money. Apologise.

Piano again. Sounds better than last time I heard. Tuned probably. Stopped again.

Dollard and Cowley still urged the lingering singer out with it.

— With it, Simon.

— It, Simon.

— Ladies and gentlemen, I am most deeply obliged by your kind solicitations.

— It, Simon.

— I have no money but if you will lend me your attention I shall endeavour to sing to you of a heart bowed down.

By the sandwichbell in screening shadow, Lydia her bronze and rose, a lady's grace, gave and withheld : as in cool glaucous *eau de Nil* Mina to tankards two her pinnacles of gold.

The harping chords of prelude closed. A chord longdrawn, expectant drew a voice away.

— *When first I saw that form endearing.*

Richie turned.

— Si Dedalus' voice, he said.

Braintipped, cheek touched with flame, they listened feeling that flow endearing flow over skin limbs human heart soul spine. Bloom signed to Pat, bald Pat is a waiter hard of hearing, to set ajar the door of the bar. The door of the bar. So. That will do. Pat, waiter, waited, waiting to hear, for he was hard of hear by the door.

— *Sorrow from me seemed to depart.*

Through the hush of air a voice sang to them, low, not rain, not leaves in murmur, like no voice of strings of reeds or whatdoyoucallthem dulcimers, touching their still ears with words, still hearts of their each his remembered lives. Good, good to hear : sorrow from them each seemed to from both depart when first they heard. When first they saw, lost Richie, Poldy, mercy of beauty, heard from a person wouldn't expect it in the least, her first merciful lovesoft oftloved word.

Love that is singing : love's old sweet song. Bloom unwound slowly the elastic band of his packet. Love's old sweet *sonnez la* gold. Bloom wound a skein round four forkfingers stretched it, relaxed, and wound it round his troubled double, fourfold, in octave, gyved them fast.

— *Full of hope and all delighted...*

Tenors get women by the score. Increase their flow. Throw flower at his feet when will we meet? My head it simply. Jingle all delighted. He can't sing for tall hats. Your head it simply swurls. Perfumed for him. What perfume does your wife? I want to know. Jing. Stop. Knock. Last look at mirror always before she answers the door. The hall. There? How do you? I do well. There? What? Or? Phial of cachous, kissing comfits, in her satchel. Yes? Hands felt for the opulent.

Alas! The voice rose, sighing, changed : loud, full, shining, proud.

— *But alas, 'twas idle dreaming...*

Glorious tone he has still. Cork air softer also their brogue. Silly man! Could have made oceans of money. Singing wrong words. Wore out his wife : now sings. But hard to tell. Only the two themselves. If he doesn't break down. Keep a trot for the avenue. His hands and feet sing too. Drink. Nerves overstrung. Must be abstemious to sing. Jenny Lind soup : stock, sage, raw eggs, half pint of cream. For creamy dreamy.

Tenderness it welled : slow, swelling, Full it throbbed. That's the chat. Ha, give! Take! Throb, a throb, a pulsing proud erect.

Words? Music? No : it's what's behind.

Bloom looped, unlooped, noded, disnoded.

Bloom. Flood of warm jimjam lickitup secretness flowed to flow in music out, in desire, dark to lick flow, invading. Tipping her tepping her tapping her topping her. Tup. Pores to dilate dilating. Tup. The joy the feel the warm the. Tup. To pour o'er sluices pouring gushes. Flood, gush, flow, joygush, tupthrop. Now! Language of love.

— *... ray of hope...*

Beaming. Lydia for Lidwell squeak scarcely hear so ladylike the muse unsqueaked a ray of hopk.

Martha it is. Coincidence. Just going to write. Lionel's song. Lovely name you have. Can't write. Accept my little pres. Play on her heartstrings pursestrings too. She's a. I called you naughty boy. Still the name : Martha. How strange! Today.

The voice of Lionel returned, weaker but unwearied. It sang again to Richie Poldy Lydia Lidwell also sang to Pat open mouth ear waiting to wait. How first he saw that form endearing, how sorrow seemed to part, how look, form, word charmed him Gould Lidwell, won Pat Bloom's heart.

Wish I could see his face, though. Explain better. Why the barber in Drago's alway's looked my face when I spoke his face in the glass. Still hear it better here than in the bar though farther.

— *Each graceful look...*

First night when first I saw her at Mat Dillon's in Terenure. Yellow, black lace she wore. Musical chairs. We two the last. Fate. After her. Fate. Round and round slow. Quick round. We two. All looked. Halt. Down she sat. All ousted looked. Lips laughing. Yellow knees.

— *Charmed my eye...*

Singing. *Waiting* she sang. I turned her music. Full voice of perfume of what perfume does your lilactrees. Bosom I saw, both full, throat warbling. First I saw. She thanked me. Why did she me? Fate. Spanishy eyes. Under a peartree alone patio this hour in old Madrid one side in shadow Dolores shedolores. At me. Luring. Ah, alluring.

— *Martha! Ah, Martha!*

Quitting all langour Lionel cried in grief, in cry of passion dominant to love to return with deepening yet with rising chords of harmony. In cry or lionel loneliness that she should know, must Martha feel. For only her he waited. Where? Here there try there here all try where. Somewhere.

— *Co-me, thou lost one!*
Co-me thou dear one!

Alone. One love. One hope. One comfort me. Martha, chestnote, return.

— *Come!*

It soared, a bird, it held its flight, a swift pure cry, soar silver orb it leaped serene, speeding, sustained, to come, don't spin it out too long long breath he breath long life, soaring high, high resplendent, aflame, crowned, high in the effulgence symbolistic, high, of the etherial bosom, high, of the high vast irradiation everywhere all soaring all around about the all, the endlessnessnessness...

— *To me!*

Siopold!

Consumed.

Come. Well sung. All clapped. She ought to. Come. To me, to him, to her, you too, me, us.

— Bravo! Clapclap. Goodman, Simon. Clappyclapclap. Encore! Clapclipclap. Sound as a bell. Bravo, Simon! Clapclopclap. Encore, enclap, said, cried, clapped all, Ben Dollard, Lydia Douce, George Lidwell, Pat, Mina, two gentlemen with two tankards, Cowley, first gent with tank and bronze Miss Douce and gold Miss Mina.

Blazes Boylan's smart tan shoes creaked on the barfloor, said before. Jingle by monuments of sir John Gray, Horatio onehandled Nelson, reverend father Theobald Matthew, jaunted as said before just now. Atrot, in heat, heatseated. *Cloche. Sonnez la. Cloche. Sonnez la.* Slower the mare went up the hill by the Rotunda, Rutland square. Too slow for Boylan, blazes Boylan, impatience Boylan, joggled tbe mare.

An afterclang of Cowley's chords closed, died on the air made richer.

And Richie Goulding drank his Power and Leopold Bloom his cider drank, Lidwell his Guinness, second gentleman said they would partake of two more tankards if she did not mind. Miss Kennedy smirked, disserving, coral lips, at first, at second. She did not mind.

— Seven days in jail, Ben Dollard said, on bread and water. Then you'd sing, Simon, like a garden thrush.

Lionel Simon, singer, laughed. Father Bob Cowley played. Mina Kennedy served. Second gentleman paid. Tom Kernan strutted in Lydia, admired, admired. But Bloom sang dumb.

Admiring.

Richie, admiring, descanted on that man's glorious voice. He remembered one night long ago. Never forget that night. Si sang *'Twas rank and fame*: in Ned Lambert's 'twas. Good God he never heard in all his life a note like that he never did *then false one we had better part* so clear so God he never heard *since love lives not* a clinking voice ask Lambert he can tell you too.

Goulding, a flush struggling in his pale, told Mr Bloom, face of the night, Si in Ned Lambert's, Dedalus house, sang *'Twas rank and fame.*

He, Mr Bloom, listened while he, Richie Goulding, told him, Mr Bloom, of the night he, Richie, heard him, Si Dedalus, sing *'Twas rank and fame* in his, Ned Lambert's house.

Brothers-in-law : relations. We never speak as we pass by. Rift in the lute I think. Treats him with scorn. See. He admires him all the more. The night Si sang. The human voice, two tiny silky cords. Wonderful, more than all the others.

That voice was a lamentation. Calmer now. It's in the silence you feel you hear. Vibrations. Now silent air.

Bloom ungyved his crisscrossed hands and with slack fingers plucked the slender catgut thong. He drew and plucked. It buzz, it twanged. While Goulding talked of Barraclough's voice production, while Tom Kernan, harking back in a retrospective sort of arrangement, talked to listening Father Cowley who played a voluntary, who nodded as he played. While big Ben Dollard talked with Simon Dedalus lighting, who nodded as he smoked, who smoked.

Thou lost one. All songs on that theme. Yet more Bloom stretched his string. Cruel it seems. Let people get fond of each other : lure them on. Then tear asunder. Death. Explos. Knock on the head. Outtohelloutofthat. Human life. Dignam. Ugh, that rat's tail wriggling ! Five bob I gave. *Corpus paradisum.* Corncrake croaker : belly like a poisoned pup. Gone. They sing. Forgotten. I too. And one day she with. Leave her : get tired. Suffer then. Snivel. Big Spanishy eyes goggling at nothing. Her wavyavyeavyheavyeavyevyevy hair un comb : 'd.

Yet too much happy bores. He stretched more, more. Are you not happy in your ? Twang. It snapped.

Jingle into Dorset street.

Miss Douce withdrew her satiny arm, reproachful, pleased.

— Don't make half so free, said she, till we are better acquainted.

George Lidwell told her really and truly : but she did not believe.

First gentleman told Mina that was so. She asked him was that so. And second tankard told her so. That that was so.

Miss Douce, Miss Lydia, did not believe : Miss Kennedy, Mina, did not believe : George Lidwell, no : Miss Dou did not : the first, the first : gent with the tank : believe, no, no : did not, Miss Kenn : Lidlydiawell : the tank.

Better write it here. Quills in the postoffice chewed and twisted.

Bald Pat at a sign drew nigh. A pen and ink. He went. A pad. He went. A pad to blot. He heard, deaf Pat.

— Yes, Mr Bloom, said, teasing the curling catgut line. It certainly is.

Few lines will do. My present. All that Italian florid music is. Who is this wrote? Know the name you know better. Take out sheet notepaper, envelope: unconcerned. It's so characteristic.

— Grandest number in the whole opera. Goulding said.

— It is, Bloom said.

Numbers it is. All music when you come to think. Two multiplied by two divided by half is twice one. Vibrations: chords those are. One plus two plus six is seven. Do anything you like with figures juggling. Always find out this equal to that, symmetry under a cemetery wall. He doesn't see my mourning. Callous: all for his own gut. Musemathematics. And you think you're listening to the etherial. But suppose you said it like: Martha, seven times nine minus x is thirtyfive thousand. Fall quite flat. It's on account of the sounds it is.

Instance he's playing now. Improvising. Might be what you like till you hear the words. Want to listen sharp. Hard. Begin all right: then hear chords a bit off: feel lost a bit. In and out of sacks over barrels, through wirefences, obstacle race. Time makes the tune. Question of mood you're in. Still always nice to hear. Except scales up and down, girls learning. Two together nextdoor neighbours. Ought to invent dummy pianos for that. *Blumenlied* I bought for her. The name. Playing it slow, a girl, night I came home, the girl. Door of the stables near Cecilia street. Milly no taste. Queer because we both I mean.

Bald deaf Pat brought quite flat pad ink Pat set with ink pen quite flat pad. Pat took plate dish knife fork. Pat went.

It was the only language Mr Dedalus said to Ben. He heard them as a boy in Ringabella, Crosshaven, Ringabella, singing their barcaroles. Queenstown harbour full of Italian ships. Walking, you know, Ben, in the moonlight with those earthquake hats. Blending their voices. God, such music, Ben. Heard as a boy. Cross Ringabella haven mooncarole.

Sour pipe removed he held a shield of hand beside his lips that cooed a moonlight nightcall, clear from anear, a call from afar, replying.

Down the edge of his *Freeman* baton ranged Bloom's your other eye, scanning for where did I see that. Callan, Coleman, Dignam Patrick. Heigho! Heigho! Fawcett. Aha! Just I was looking ..

Hope he's not looking, cute as a rat. He held unfurled his *Freeman*. Can't see now. Remember write Greek ees. Bloom dipped, Bloo mur: dear sir. Dear Henry wrote: dear Mady. Got your lett and flow. Hell did I put? Some pock or oth. It is utterl imposs. Underline *imposs*. To write today.

Bore this. Bored Bloom tambourined gently with I am just reflecting fingers on flat pad Pat brought.

On. Know what I mean. No, change that ee. Accept my poor little pres enclos. Ask her no answ. Hold on. Five Dig. Two about here. Penny the gulls. Elijah is com. Seven Davy Byrne's. Is eight about. Say half a crown. My poor little pres : p. o. two and six.. Write me a long. Do you despise ? Jingle, have you the ? So excited. Why do you call me naught ? You naughty too ? O, Mairy lost the pin of her. Bye for today. Yes, yes, will tell you. Want to. To keep it up. Call me that other. Other world she wrote. My patience are exhaust. To keep it up. You must believe. Believe. The tank. It. Is. True.

Folly am I writing ? Husbands don't. That's marriage does, their wives. Because I'm away from. Suppose. But how ? She must. Keep young. If she found out. Card in my high grade ha. No, not tell all. Useless pain. If they don't see. Woman. Sauce for the gander.

A hackney car, number three hundred and twentyfour, driver Barton James of number one Harmony avenue, Donnybrook, on which sat a fare, a young gentleman, stylishly dressed in an indigoblue serge suit made by George Robert Mesias, tailor and cutter, of number five Eden quay, and wearing a straw hat very dressy, bought of John Plasto of number one Great Brunswick street, hatter. Eh ? This is the jingle that joggled and jingled. By Dlugacz' porkshop bright tubes of Agendath trotted a gallantbuttocked mare.

— Answering an ad ? keen Richie's eyes asked Bloom.

— Yes, Mr Bloom said. Town traveller. Nothing doing, I expect.

Bloom mur : best references. But Henry wrote : it will excite me. You know now. In haste. Henry. Greek ee. Better add postcript. What is he playing now ? Improvising intermezzo. P. S. The rum tum tum. How will you pun ? You punish me ? Crooked skirt swinging, whack by. Tell me I want to. Know. O. Course if I didn't I wouldn't ask. La la la ree. Trails off there sad in minor. Why minor sad ? Sign H. They like sad tail at end. P. P. S. La la la ree. I feel so sad today. La ree. So lonely. Dee.

He blotted quick on pad of Pat. Envel. Address. Just copy out of paper. Murmured : Messrs Callan, Coleman and Co, limited. Henry wrote :

Miss Martha Clifford
c/o P. O.
Dolphin's barn lane
Dublin.

Blot over the other so he can't read. Right. Idea prize titbit. Something detective read off blottingpad. Payment at the rate of guinea per col. Matcham often thinks the laughing witch. Poor Mrs Purefoy. U. p. : up.

Too poetical that about the sad. Music did that. Music hath charms Shakespeare said. Quotations every day in the year. To be or not to be. Wisdom while you wait.

In Gerard's rosery of Fetter lane he walks, greyedauburn. One life is all. One body. Do. But do.

Done anyhow. Postal order stamp. Postoffice lower down. Walk now. Enough. Barney Kiernan's I promised to meet them. Dislike that job. House of mourning. Walk. Pat! Doesn't hear. Deaf beetle he is.

Car near there now. Talk. Talk. Pat! Doesn't. Settling those napkins. Lot of ground he must cover in the day. Paint face behind on him then he'd be two. Wish they'd sing more. Keep my mind off.

Bald Pat who is bothered mitred the napkins. Pat is a waiter hard of his hearing. Pat is a waiter who waits while you wait. Hee hee hee hee. He waits while you wait. Hee hee. A waiter is he. Hee hee hee hee. He waits while you wait. While you wait if you wait he will wait while you wait. Hee hee hee hee. Hoh. Wait while you wait.

Douce now. Douce Lydia. Bronze and rose.

She had a gorgeous, simply gorgeous, time. And look at the lovely shell she brought.

To the end of the bar to him she bore lightly the spiked and winding seahorn that he, George Lidwell, solicitor, might hear.

— Listen! she bade him.

Under Tom Kernan's ginhot words the accompanist wove music slow. Authentic fact. How Walter Bapty lost his voice. Well, sir, the husband took him by the throat. *Scoundrel*, said he. *You'll sing no more lovesongs*. He did, sir Tom. Bob Cowley wove. Tenors get wom. Cowley lay back.

Ah, now he heard, she holding it to his ear. Hear! He heard. Wonderful. She held it to her own and through the sifted light pale gold in contrast glided. To hear.

Tap.

Bloom through the bardoor saw a shell held at their ears. He heard more faintly that that they heard, each for herself alone, then each for other, hearing the plash of waves, loudly, a silent roar.

Bronze by a weary gold, anear, afar, they listened.

Her ear too is a shell, the peeping lobe there. Been to the seaside. Lovely seaside girls. Skin tanned raw. Should have put on coldcream first make it brown. Buttered toast. O and that lotion mustn't forget. Fever near her mouth. Your head it simply. Hair braided over : shell with seaweed. Why do they hide their ears with seaweed hair? And Turks their mouth, why? Her eyes over the sheet, a yashmak. Find the way in. A cave. No admittance except on business.

The sea they think they hear. Singing. A roar. The blood it is. Souse in the ear sometimes. Well, it's a sea. Corpuscule islands.

Wonderful really. So distinct. Again. George Lidwell held its murmur, hearing : then laid it by, gently.

— What are the wild waves saying? he asked her, smiled.

Charming, seasmiling and unanswering Lydia on Lidwell smiled.

Tap.

By Larry O'Rourke's, by Larry, bold Larry O', Böylan swayed and Boylan turned.

From the forsaken shell Miss Mina glided to her tankard waiting. No, she was not so lonely archly Miss Douce's head let Mr Lidwell know. Walks in the moonlight by the sea. No, not alone. With whom? She nobly answered : with a gentleman friend.

Bob Cowley's twinkling fingers in the treble played again. The landlord has the prior. A little time. Long John. Big Ben. Lightly he played a light bright tinkling measure for tripping ladies, arch and smiling, and for their gallants, gentlemen friends. One : one, one, one : two, one, three, four.

Sea, wind, leaves, thunder, waters, cows lowing, the cattle market, cocks, hens don't crow, snakes hissss. There's music everywhere. Ruttledge's door : ee creaking. No, that's noise. Minuet of *Don Giovanni* he's playing now. Court dresses of all descriptions in castle chambers dancing. Misery. Peasants outside. Green starving faces eating dockleaves. Nice that is. Look: look, look, look, look, look: you look at us.

That's joyful I can feel. Never have written it. Why? My joy is other joy. But both are joys. Yes, joy it must be. Mere fact of music shows you are. Often thought she was in the dumps till she began to lilt. Then know.

M'Coy valise. My wife and your wife Squealing cat. Like tearing silk. When she talks like the clapper of a bellows. They can't manage men's intervals. Gap in their voices too. Fill me. I'm warm, dark, open. Molly in *quis est homo :* Mercadante. My ear against the wall to hear. Want a woman who can deliver the goods.

Jog jig jogged stopped. Dandy tan shoe of dandy Boylan socks skyblue clocks came light to earth.

O, look we are so! Chamber music. Could make a kind of pun on that. It is a kind of music I often thought when she. Acoustics that is. Tinkling. Empty vessels make most noise. Because the acoustics, the resonance changes according as the weight of the water is equal to the law of falling water. Like those rhapsodies of Liszt's, Hungarian, gipsyeyed. Pearls. Drops. Rain. Diddle iddle addle addle oodle oodle. Hiss. Now. Maybe now. Before.

One rapped on a door, one tapped with a knock, did he knock Paul de Kock, with a loud proud knocker, with a cock carracarracarra cock. Cockcock.

Tap.

— *Qui sdegno,* Ben, said Father Cowley.

— No, Ben, Tom Kernan interfered, *The Croppy Boy*. Our native Doric.

— Ay do, Ben, Mr Dedalus said. Good men and true.

— Do, do, they begged in one.

I'll go. Here, Pat, return. Come. He came, he came, he did not stay. To me. How much?

— What key? Six sharps?

— F sharp major, Ben Dollard said.

Bob Cowley's outstretched talons griped the black deepsounding chords.

Must go prince Bloom told Richie prince. No, Richie said. Yes, must. Got money somewhere. He's on for a razzle backache spree. Much? He seehears lipspeech. One and nine. Penny for yourself. Here. Give him twopence tip. Deaf, bothered But perhaps he has wife and family waiting, waiting Patty come home. Hee hee hee hee. Deaf wait while they wait.

But wait. But hear. Chords dark. Lugugugubrious. Low. In a cave of the dark middle earth. Embedded ore. Lumpmusic.

The voice of dark age, of unlove, earth's fatigue made grave approach, and painful, come from afar, from hoary mountains, called on good men and true. The priest he sought, with him would he speak a word.

Tap.

Ben Dollard's voice base barreltone. Doing his level best to say it. Croak of vast manless moonless womoonless marsh. Other comedown. Big ships' chandler's business he did once. Remember: rosiny ropes, ships' lanterns. Failed to the tune of ten thousand pounds. Now in the Iveagh home. Cubicle number so and so. Number one Bass did that for him.

The priest's at home. A false priest's servant bade him welcome. Step in. The holy father. Curlycues of chords.

Ruin them. Wreck their lives. Then build them cubicles to end their days in. Hushaby. Lullaby. Die, dog. Little dog, die.

The voice of warning, solemn warning, told them the youth had entered a lonely hall, told them how solemn fell his footstep there, told them the gloomy chamber, the vested priest sitting to shrive.

Decent soul. Bit addled now. Thinks he'll win in *Answers* poets' picture puzzle. We hand you crisp five pound note. Bird sitting hatching in a nest. Lay of the last minstrel he thought it was. See blank tee what domestic animal ? Tee dash ar most courageous mariner. Good voice he has still. No eunuch yet with all his belongings.

Listen. Bloom listened. Richie Goulding listened. And by the door deaf Pat, bald Pat, tipped Pat, listened.

The chords harped slower.

The voice of penance and of grief came slow, embellished tremulous. Ben's contrite beard confessed : *in nomine Domini,* in God's name. He knelt. He beat his hand upon his breast, confessing : *mea culpa.*

Latin again. That holds them like birdlime. Priest with the communion corpus for those women. Chap in the mortuary, coffin or coffey, *corpusnomine.* Wonder where that rat is by now. Scrape.

Tap.

They listened : tankards and Miss Kennedy, George Lidwell eyelid well expressive, fullbusted satin. Kernan, Si.

The sighing voice of sorrow sang. His sins. Since easter he had cursed three times. You bitch's bast. And once at masstime he had gone to play. Once by the churchyard he had passed and for his mother's rest he had not prayed. A boy. A croppy boy.

Bronze, listening by the beerpull, gazed far away. Soulfully. Doesn't half know I'm. Molly great dab at seeing anyone looking.

Bronze gazed far sideways. Mirror there. Is that best side of her face ? They always know. Knock at the door. Last tip to titivate.

Cockcarracarra.

What do they think when they hear music. Way to catch rattlesnakes. Night Michael Gunn gave us the box. Tuning up. Shah of Persia liked that best. Remind him of home sweet home. Wiped his nose in curtain too. Custom his country perhaps. That's music too. Not as bad as it sounds. Tootling.

Brasses braying asses through uptrunks. Doublebasses, helpless, gashes in their sides. Woodwinds mooing cows. Semigrand open crocodile music hath jaws. Woodwind like Goodwin's name.

She looked fine. Her crocus dress she wore, lowcut, belongings on show. Clove her breath was always in theatre when she bent to ask a question. Told her what Spinoza says in that book of poor papa's. Hypnotised, listening. Eyes like that. She bent. Chap in dresscircle, staring down into her with his operaglass for all he was worth. Beauty of music you must hear twice. Nature woman half a look. God made the country man the tune. Met him pike hoses. Philosophy. O rocks!

All gone. All fallen. At the siege of Ross his father, at Gorey all his brothers fell To Wexford, we are the boys of Wexford, he would. Last of his name and race.

I too, last of my race. Milly young student. Well, my fault perhaps. No son. Rudy. Too late now. Or if not? If not? If still?

He bore no hate.

Hate. Love. Those are names. Rudy. Soon I am old.

Big Ben his voice unfolded. Great voice Richie Goulding said, a flush struggling in his pale, to Bloom, soon old but when was young.

Ireland comes now. My country above the king. She listens. Who fears to speak of nineteen four? Time to be shoving. Looked enough.

— *Bless me, father,* Dollard the croppy cried. *Bless me and let me go.*

Tap.

Bloom looked, unblessed to go. Got up to kill: on eighteen bob a week. Fellows shell out the dibs. Want to keep your weathereye open. Those girls, those lovely. By the sad sea waves. Chorusgirl's romance. Letters read out for breach of promise. From Chickabiddy's own Mumpsypum. Laughter in court. Henry. I never signed it. The lovely name you.

Low sank the music, air and words. Then hastened. The false priest rustling soldier from his cassock. A yeoman captain. They know it all by heart. The thrill they itch for. Yeoman cap.

Tap. Tap.

Thrilled, she listened, bending in sympathy to hear.

Blank face. Virgin should say: or fingered only. Write something on it: page. If not what becomes of them? Decline, despair. Keeps them young. Even admire themselves. See. Play on her. Lip blow. Body of white woman, a flute alive. Blow gentle. Loud. Three holes all women. Goddess I didn't see.

They want it : not too much polite. That's why he gets them. Gold in your pocket, brass in your face. With look to look : songs without words. Molly that hurdygurdy boy. She knew he meant the monkey was sick. Or because so like the Spanish. Understand animals too that way. Solomon did. Gift of nature.

Ventriloquise. My lips closed. Think in my stom. What?

Will? You? I. Want. You. To.

With hoarse rude fury the yeoman cursed. Swelling in apoplectic bitch's bastard. A good thought, boy, to come. One hour's your time to live, your last.

Tap. Tap.

Thrill now. Pity they feel. To wipe away a tear for martyrs. For all things dying, want to, dying to, die. For that all things born. Poor Mrs Purefoy. Hope she's over. Because their wombs.

A liquid of womb of woman eyeball gazed under a fence of lashes, calmly, hearing. See real beauty of the eye when she not speaks. On yonder river. At each slow satiny heaving bosom's wave (her heaving embon) red rose rose slowly, sank red rose. Heartbeats her breath : breath that is life. And all the tiny tiny fernfoils trembled of maidenhair.

But look. The bright stars fade. O rose! Castile. The morn. Ha. Lidwell. For him then not for. Infatuated. I like that? See her from here though. Popped corks, splashes of beerfroth, stacks of empties.

On the smooth jutting beerpull laid Lydia hand lightly, plumply, leave it to my hands. All lost in pity for croppy. Fro, to : to, fro : over the polished knob (she knows his eyes, my eyes, her eyes) her thumb and finger passed in pity : passed, repassed and, gently touching, then slid so smoothly, slowly down, a cool firm white enamel baton protruding through their sliding ring.

With a cock with a carra.

Tap. Tap. Tap.

I hold this house. Amen. He gnashed in fury. Traitors swing.

The chords consented. Very sad thing. But had to be.

Get out before the end. Thanks, that was heavenly. Where's my hat. Pass by her. Can leave that *Freeman*. Letter I have. Suppose she were the? No. Walk, walk, walk. Like Cashel Boylo Connoro Coylo Tisdall Maurice Tisntdall Farrell. Waaaaaaalk.

Well, I must be. Are you off? Yrfmstbyes. Blmstup. O'er ryehigh blue. Bloom stood up. Ow. Soap feeling rather sticky behind. Must have sweated : music. That lotion, remember. Well, so long. High grade. Card inside, yes.

By deaf Pat in the doorway, straining ear, Bloom passed.

At Geneva barrack that young man died. At Passage was his body laid. Dolor! O, he dolores! The voice of the mournful chanter called to dolorous prayer.

By rose, by satiny bosom, by the fondling hand, by slops, by empties, by popped corks, greeting in going, past eyes and maidenhair, bronze and faint gold in deepseashadow, went Bloom, soft Bloom, I feel so lonely Bloom.

Tap. Tap. Tap.

Pray for him, prayed the bass of Dollard. You who hear in peace. Breathe a prayer, drop a tear, good men, good people. He was the croppy boy.

Scaring eavesdropping boots croppy bootsboy Bloom in the Ormond hallway heard growls and roars of bravo, fat blackslapping, their boots all treading, boots not the boots the boy. General chorus off for a swill to wash it down. Glad I avoided.

— Come on, Ben, Simon Dedalus said. By God, you're as good as ever you were.

— Better, said Tomgin Kernan. Most trenchant rendition of that ballad, upon my soul and honour it is.

— Lablache, said Father Cowley.

Ben Dollard bulkily cachuchad towards the bar, mightily praisefed and all big roseate, on heavyfooted feet, his gouty fingers nakkering castagnettes in the air.

Big Benaben Dollard. Big Benben. Big Benben.

Rrr.

And deepmoved all, Simon trumping compassion from foghorn nose, all laughing, they brought him forth, Ben Dollard, in right good cheer.

— You're looking rubicund, George Lidwell said.

Miss Douce composed her rose to wait.

— Ben machree, said Mr Dedalus, clapping Ben's fat back shoulderblade. Fit as a fiddle only he has a lot of adipose tissue concealed about his person.

Rrrrrsss.

— Fat of death, Simon, Ben Dollard growled.

Richie rift in the lute alone sat : Goulding, Collis, Ward. Uncertainly he waited. Unpaid Pat too.

Tap. Tap. Tap. Tap.

Miss Mina Kennedy brought near her lips to ear of tankard one.

— Mr Dollard, they murmured low.

— Dollard, murmured tankard.

Tank one believed : Miss Kenn when she : that doll he was : she doll : the tank.

He murmured that he knew the name. The name was familiar to him, that is to say. That was to say he had heard the name of Dollard, was it? Dollard, yes.

Yes, her lips said more loudly, Mr Dollard. He sang that song lovely, murmured Mina. And *The last rose of summer* was a lovely song. Mina loved that song. Tankard loved the song that Mina.

'Tis the last rose of summer dollard left Bloom felt wind wound round inside.

Gassy thing that cider : binding too. Wait. Postoffice near Reuben J's one and eightpence too. Get shut of it. Dodge round by Greek street. Wish I hadn't promised to meet. Freer in air. Music. Gets on your nerves. Beerpull. Her hand that rocks the cradle rules the. Ben Howth. That rules the world.

Far. Far. Far. Far.

Tap. Tap. Tap. Tap.

Up the quay went Lionelleopold, naughty Henry with letter for Mady, with sweets of sin with frillies for Raoul with met him pike hoses went Poldy on.

Tap blind walked tapping by the tap the curbstone tapping, tap by tap.

Cowley, he stuns himself with it : kind of drunkenness. Better give way only half way the way of a man with a maid. Instance enthusiasts. All ears. Not lose a demisemiquaver. Eyes shut. Head nodding in time. Dotty. You daren't budge. Thinking strictly prohibited. Always talking shop. Fiddlefaddle about notes

All a kind of attempt to talk. Unpleasant when it stops because you never know exac. Organ in Gardiner street. Old Glynn fifty quid a year. Queer up there in the cockloft alone with stops and locks and keys. Seated all day at the organ. Maunder on for hours, talking to himself or the other fellow blowing the bellows. Growl angry, then shriek cursing (want to have wadding or something in his no don't she cried), then all of a soft sudden wee little wee little pipy wind.

Pwee! A wee little wind piped eeee In Bloom's little wee.

— Was he? Mr Dedalus said, returning, with fetched pipe. I was with him this morning at poor little Paddy Dignam's...

— Ay, the Lord have mercy on him

— By the bye there's a tuningfork in there on the...

Tap. Tap. Tap. Tap.

— The wife has a fine voice. Or had. What? Lidwell asked.

— O, that must be the tuner, Lydia said to Simonlionel first I saw, forgot it when he was here.

Blind he was she told George Lidwell second I saw. And played so exquisitely, treat to hear. Exquisite contrast : bronzelid minagold.

— Shout! Ben Dollard shouted, pouring Sing out!

— 'lldo! cried Father Cowley.

Rrrrrr.

I feel I want...

Tap. Tap. Tap. Tap. Tap.

— Very, Mr Dedalus said, staring hard at a headless sardine.

Under the sandwichbell lay on a bier of bread one last, one lonely, last sardine of summer. Bloom alone.

— Very, he stared. The lower register, for choice.

Tap. Tap. Tap. Tap. Tap. Tap. Tap. Tap.

Bloom went by Barry's. Wish I could. Wait. That wonderworker if I had. Twentyfour solicitors in that one house. Litigation. Love one another. Piles of parchment. Messrs Pick and Pocket have power of attorney. Goulding, Collis, Ward.

But for example the chap that wallops the big drum. His vocation : Micky Rooney's band. Wonder how it first struck him. Sitting at home after pig's cheek and cabbage nursing it in the armchair. Rehearsing his band part. Pom. Pompedy. Jolly for the wife. Asses' skins. Welt them through life, then wallop after death. Pom. Wallop. Seems to be what you call yashmak or I mean kismet. Fate.

Tap. Tap. A stripling, blind, with a tapping cane, came taptaptapping by Daly's window where a mermaid, hair all streaming (but he couldn't see), blew whiffs of a mermaid (blind couldn't), mermaid coolest whiff of all.

Instruments. A blade of grass, shell of her hands, then blow. Even comb and tissuepaper you can knock a tune out of. Molly in her shift in Lombard street west, hair down. I suppose each kind of trade made its own, don't you see? Hunter with a horn. Haw. Have you the? *Cloche. Sonnez la!* Shepherd his pipe. Policeman a whistle. Locks and keys! Sweep! Four o'clock's all's well! Sleep! All is lost now. Drum? Pompedy. Wait, I know. Towncrier, bumbailiff. Long John. Waken the dead. Pom. Dignam. Poor little *nominedomine*. Pom.

It is music, I mean of course it's all pom pom pom very much what they call *da capo*. Still you can hear. As we march, we march along, march along. Pom.

I must really. Fff. Now if I did that at a banquet. Just a question of custom shah of Persia. Breathe a prayer, drop a tear. All the same he must have been a bit of a natural not to see it was a yeoman cap. Muffled up. Wonder who was that chap at the grave in the brown macin. O, the whore of the lane!

A frowsy whore with black straw sailor hat askew came glazily in the day along the quay towards Mr Bloom. When first he saw that form endearing. Yes, it is. I feel so lonely. Wet night in the lane. Horn. Who had the? Heehaw. Shesaw. Off her beat here. What is she? Hope she. Psst! Any chance of your wash. Knew Molly. Had me decked. Stout lady does be with you in the brown costume. Put you off your stroke. That appointment we made. Knowing we'd never, well hardly ever. Too dear too near to home sweet home. Sees me, does she? Looks a fright in the day. Face like dip. Damn her! O, well, she has to live like the rest. Look in here.

In Lionel Marks's antique saleshop window haughty Henry Lionel Leopold dear Henry Flower earnestly Mr Leopold Bloom envisaged candlestick melodeon oozing maggoty blowbags. Bargain: six bob. Might learn to play. Cheap. Let her pass. Course everything is dear if you don't want it. That's what good salesman is. Make you buy what he wants to sell. Chap sold me the Swedish razor he shaved me with. Wanted to charge me for the edge he gave it. She's passing now. Six bob.

Must be the cider or perhaps the burgund.

Near bronze from anear near gold from afar they chinked their clinking glasses all, brighteyed and gallant, before bronze Lydia's tempting last rose of summer, rose of Castile. First Lid, De, Cow, Ker, Doll, a fifth: Lidwell, Si Dedalus, Bob Cowley, Kernan and Big Ben Dollard.

Tap. A youth entered a lonely Ormond hall.

Bloom viewed a gallant pictured hero in Lionel Marks's window. Robert Emmet's last words. Seven last words. Of Meyerbeer that is.

— True men like you men.

— Ay, ay, Ben.

— Will lift your glass with us.

They lifted.

Tschink. Tschunk.

Tip. An unseeing stripling stood in the door. He saw not bronze. He saw not gold. Nor Ben nor Bob nor Tom nor Si nor George nor tanks nor Richie nor Pat. Hee hee hee hee. He did not see.

Seabloom, greaseabloom viewed last words. Softly. *When my country takes her place among.*

Prrprr.

Must be the bur.

Fff. Oo. Rrpr.

Nations of the earth. No-one behind. She's passed. *Then and not till then.* Tram. Kran, kran, kran. Good oppor. Coming. Krandlkrankran. I'm sure it's the burgund. Yes. One, two. *Let my epitaph be.* Kraaaaaaa. *Written. I have.*

Pprrpffrrppfff.

Done.

Cyclops

I was just passing the time of day with old Troy of the D. M. P. at the corner of Arbour hill there and be damned but a bloody sweep came along and he near drove his gear into my eye. I turned around to let him have the weight of my tongue when who should I see dodging along Stony Batter only Joe Hynes.

— Lo, Joe, says I. How are you blowing? Did you see that bloody chimneysweep near shove my eye out with his brush?

— Soot's luck, says Joe. Who's the old ballocks you were taking to?

— Old Troy, says I, was in the force. I'm on two minds not to give that fellow in charge for obstructing the thoroughfare with his brooms and ladders.

— What are you doing round those parts? says Joe.

— Devil a much, says I. There is a bloody big foxy thief beyond by the garrison church at the corner of Chicken Lane — old Troy was just giving me a wrinkle about him — lifted any God's quantity of tea and sugar to pay three bob a week said he had a farm in the county Down off a hop of my thumb by the name of Moses Herzog over there near Heytesbury street.

— Circumcised! says Joe.

— Ay, says I. A bit off the top. An old plumber named Geraghty. I'm hanging on to his taw now for the past fortnight and I can't get a penny out of him.

— That the lay you're on now? says Joe.

— Ay, says I. How are the mighty fallen! Collector of bad and doubtful debts. But that's the most notorious bloody robber you'd meet in a day's walk and the face on him all pockmarks would hold a shower of rain. *Tell him,* says he, *I dare him,* says he *and I doubledare him to send you round here again or if he does,* says he, *I'll have him summonsed up before the court, so I will, for trading without a licence.* And he after stuffing himself till he's fit to burst! Jesus, I had to laugh at the little jewy getting his shirt out. *He drink me my teas. He eat me my sugars. Because he no pay me my moneys?*

For nonperishable goods bought of Moses Herzog, of 13 Saint Kevin's parade, Wood quay ward, merchant, hereinafter called the vendor, and sold and delivered to Michael E. Geraghty, Esquire, of 29 Arbour Hill in the city of Dublin, Arran quay ward, gentleman, hereinafter called the purchaser, videlicet, five pounds avoirdupois of first choice tea at three shillings per pound avoirdupois and three stone avoirdupois of sugar, crushed crystal, at three pence per pound avoirdupois, the said purchaser debtor to the said vendor of one pound five shillings and six pence sterling for value received which amount shall be paid by said purchaser to said vendor in weekly instalments every seven calendar days of three shillings and no pence sterling: and the said nonperishable goods shall not be pawned or pledged or sold or otherwise alienated by the said purchaser but shall be and remain and be held to be the sole and exclusive property of the said vendor to be disposed of at his good will and pleasure until the said amount shall have been duly paid by the said purchaser to the said vendor in the manner herein set forth as this day hereby agreed between the said vendor his heirs, successors, trustees and assigns of the one part and the said purchaser, his heirs, successors, trustees and assigns of the other part.

— Are you a strict t. t.? says Joe.

— Not taking anything between drinks, says I.

— What about paying our respects to our friend? says Joe.

— Who? says I. Sure, he's in John of God's off his head, poor man.

— Drinking his own stuff? says Joe.

— Ay, says I. Whisky and water on the brain.

— Come around to Barney Kiernan's, says Joe. I want to see the citizen.

— Barney mavourneen's be it, says I. Anything strange or wonderful, Joe?

— Not a word, says Joe. I was up at that meeting in the City Arms.

— What was that, Joe? says I.

— Cattle traders, says Joe, about the foot and mouth disease. I want to give the citizen the hard word about it.

So we went around by the Linenhall barracks and the back of the courthouse talking of one thing or another. Decent fellow Joe when he has it but sure like that he never has it. Jesus, I couldn't get over that bloody foxy Geraghty, the daylight robber. For trading without a licence, says he.

In Inisfail the fair there lies a land, the land of holy Michan. There rises a watchtower beheld of men afar. There sleep the mighty dead as in life they slept, warriors and princes of high renown. A pleasant land it is in sooth of murmuring waters, fishful streams where sport the gunnard, the plaice, the roach, the halibut, the gibbed haddock, the grilse, the dab, the brill, the flounder, the mixed coarse fish generally and other denizens of the aqueous kingdom too numerous to be enumerated. In the mild breezes of the west and of the east the lofty trees wave in different directions their first class foliage, the wafty sycamore, the Lebanonian cedar, the exalted planetree, the eugenic eucalyptus and other ornaments of the arboreal world with which that region is thoroughly well supplied. Lovely maidens sit in close proximity to the roots of the lovely trees singing the most lovely songs while they play with all kinds of lovely objects as for example golden ingots, silvery fishes, crans of herrings, drafts of eels, codlings, creels of fingerlings, purple seagems and playful insects. And heroes voyage from afar to woo them, from Eblana to Slievemargy, the peerless princes of unfettered Munster and of Connacht the just and of smooth sleek Leinster and of Cruachan's land and of Armagh the splendid and of the noble district of Boyle, princes, the sons of kings.

And there rises a shining palace whose crystal glittering roof is seen by mariners who traverse the extensive sea in barks built expressly for that purpose and thither come all herds and fatlings and first fruits of that land for O'Connell Fitzsimon takes toll of them, a chieftain descended from chieftains. Thither the extremely large wains bring foison of the fields, flaskets of cauliflowers, floats of spinach, pineapple chunks, Rangoon beans, strikes of tomatoes, drums of figs, drills of Swedes, spherical potatoes and tallies of irridescent kale, York and Savoy, and trays of onions, pearls of the earth, and pumets of mushrooms and custard marrows and fat vetches and bere and rape and red green yellow brown russet sweet big bitter ripe pomellated apples and chips of strawberries and sieves of gooseberries, pulpy and pelurious, and strawberries fit for princes and raspberries from their canes.

I dare him, says he, and I doubledare him. Come out here, Geraghty, you notarious bloody hill and dale robber!

And by that way wend the herds innumerable of bellwethers and flushed ewes and shearling rams and lambs and stubble geese and medium steers and roaring mares and polled calves and longwools and storesheep and Cuffe's prime springers and culls and sowpigs and baconhogs and the various different varieties of highly distinguished swine and Angus heifers and polly bullocks of immaculate pedigree together with prime premiated milchcows and beeves : and there is ever heard a trampling, cackling, roaring, lowing, bleating, bellowing, rumbling, grunting, champing, chewing, of sheep and pigs and heavyhooved kine from pasturelands of Lush and Rush and Carrickmines and from the streamy vales of Thomond, from M'Gillicuddy's reeks the inaccessible and lordly Shannon the unfathomable, and from the gentle declivities of the place of the race of Kiar, their udders distended with superabundance of milk and butts of butter and rennets of cheese and farmer's firkins and targets of lamb and crannocks of corn and oblong eggs, in great hundreds, various in size, the agate with the dun.

So we turned into Barney Kiernan's and there sure enough was the citizen up in the corner having a great confab with himself and that bloody mangy mongrel, Garryowen, and he waiting for what the sky would drop in the way of drink.

— There he is, says I, in his gloryhole, with his cruiskeen lawn and his load of papers, working for the cause.

The bloody mongrel let a grouse out of him would give you the creeps. Be a corporal work of mercy if someone would take the life of that bloody dog. I'm told for a fact he ate a good part of the breeches off a constabulary man in Santry that came round one time with a blue paper about a licence.

— Stand and deliver, says he.

— That's all right, citizen, says Joe. Friends here.

— Pass, friends, says he.

Then he rubs his hand in his eye and says he :

— What's your opinion of the times ?

Doing the rapparee and Rory of the hill. But, begob, Joe was equal to the occasion.

— I think the markets are on a rise, say he, sliding his hand down his fork.

So begob the citizen claps his paw on his knee and he says :

— Foreign wars is the cause of it.

And says Joe, sticking his thumb in his pocket :

— It's the Russians wish to tyrannise.

— Arrah, give over your bloody codding Joe, says I, I've a thirst on me I wouldn't sell for half a crown.

— Give it a name, citizen, says Joe.

— Wine of the country, says he.

— What's yours ? says Joe.

— Ditto Mac Anaspey, says I.

— Three pints, Terry, says Joe. And how's the old heart, citizen ? says he.

— Never better, *a chara,* says he. What Garry ? Are we going to win ? Eh ?

And with that he took the bloody old towser by the scruff of the neck and, by Jesus, he near throttled him.

The figure seated on a large boulder at the foot of a round tower was that of a broadshouldered deepchested stronglimbed frankeyed redhaired freely freckled shaggybearded widemouthed largenosed longheaded deepvoiced barekneed brawnyhanded hairylegged ruddyfaced, sinewyarmed hero. From shoulder to shoulder he measured several ells and his rocklike mountainous knees were covered, as was likewise the rest of his body wherever visible, with a strong growth of tawny prickly hair in hue and toughness similar to the mountain gorse *(Ulex Europeus)*. The widewinged nostrils, from which bristles of the same tawny hue projected, were of such capaciousness that within their cavernous obscurity the fieldlark might easily have lodged her nest. The eyes in which a tear and a smile strove ever for the mastery were of the dimensions of a goodsized cauliflower. A powerful current of warm breath issued at regular intervals from the profound cavity of his mouth while in rhythmic resonance the loud strong hale reverberations of his formidable heart thundered rumblingly causing the ground, the summit of the lofty tower and the still loftier walls of the cave to vibrate and tremble.

He wore a long unsleeved garment of recently flayed oxhide reaching to the knees in a loose kilt and this was bound about his middle by a girdle of plaited straw and rushes. Beneath this he wore trews of deerskin, roughly stitched with gut. His nether extremities were encased in high Balbriggan buskins dyed in lichen purple, the feet being shod with brogues of salted cowhide laced with the windpipe of the same beast. From his girdle hung a row of seastones which dangled at every movement of his portentous frame and on these were graven with rude yet striking art the tribal images of many Irish heroes and heroines of antiquity, Cuchulin, Conn of hundred battles, Niall of nine hostages, Brian of Kincora, the Ardri Malachi, Art Mac Murragh, Shane O'Neill, Father John Murphy, Owen Roe, Patrick Sarsfield, Red Hugh O'Donnell, Red Jim MacDermott, Soggarth Eoghan O'Growney, Michael Dwyer, Francy Higgins, Henry Joy M' Cracken, Goliath, Horace Wheatley, Thomas Conneff, Peg Woffington, the Village Blacksmith, Captain Moonlight, Captain Boycott, Dante Alighieri, Christopher Columbus, S. Fursa, S. Brendan, Marshal Mac Mahon, Charlemagne, Theobald Wolfe Tone, the Mother of the Maccabees, the Last of the Mohicans, the Rose of Castile, the Man for Galway, The Man that Broke the Bank at Monte Carlo, The Man in the Gap, The Woman Who Didn't, Benjamin Franklin, Napoleon Bonaparte, John L. Sullivan, Cleopatra, Savourneen Deelish, Julius Caesar, Paracelsus, sir Thomas Lipton, William Tell, Michelangelo, Hayes, Muhammad, the Bride of Lammermoor, Peter the Hermit, Peter the Packer, Dark Rosaleen, Patrick W. Shakespeare, Brian Confucius, Murtagh Gutenberg, Patricio Velasquez, Captain Nemo, Tristan and Isolde, the first Prince of Wales, Thomas Cook and Son, the Bold Soldier Boy, Arrah na Pogue, Dick Turpin, Ludwig Beethoven, the Colleen Bawn, Waddler Healy, Angus the Culdee, Dolly Mount, Sidney Parade, Ben Howth, Valentine Greatrakes, Adam and Eve, Arthur Wellesley, Boss Croker, Herodotus, Jack the Giantkiller, Gautama Buddha, Lady Godiva, The Lily of Killarney, Balor of the Evil Eye, the Queen of Sheba, Acky Nagle, Joe Nagle, Alessandro Volta, Jeremiah O'Donovan Rossa, Don Philip O'Sullivan Beare. A couched spear of acuminated granite rested by him while at his feet reposed a savage animal of the canine tribe whose stertorous gasps announced that he was sunk in uneasy slumber, a supposition confirmed by hoarse growls and spasmodic movements which his master repressed from time to time by tranquilising blows of a mighty cudgel rudely fashioned out of paleolithic stone.

So anyhow Terry brought the three pints Joe was standing and begob the sight nearly left my eyes when I saw him land out a quid. O, as true as I'm telling you. A goodlooking sovereign.

— And there's more where that came from, says he.

— Were you robbing the poorbox, Joe? say I?

— Sweat of my brow, says Joe. 'Twas the prudent member gave me the wheeze.

— I saw him before I met you, says I, sloping around by Pill lane and Greek street with his cod's eye counting up all the guts of the fish.

Who comes through Michan's land, bedight in sable armour? O'Bloom, the son of Rory: it is he. Impervious to fear is Rory's son: he of the prudent soul.

— For the old woman of Prince's street, says the citizen, the subsidised organ. The pledgebound party on the floor of the house. And look at this blasted rag, says he. Look at this, says he. *The Irish Independent*, if you please, founded by Parnell to be the workingman's friend. Listen to the births and deaths in the *Irish all for Ireland Independent* and I'll thank you and the marriages.

And he starts reading them out:

— Gordon, Barnfield Crescent, Exeter; Redmayne of Iffley, Saint Anne's on Sea, the wife of William T. Redmayne, of a son. How's that, eh? Wright and Flint, Vincent and Gillett to Rotha Marion daughter of Rosa and the late George Alfred Gillett 179 Clapham Road, Stockwell, Playwood and Ridsdale at Saint Jude's Kensington by the very reverend Dr Forrest, Dean of Worçester, eh? Deaths. Bristow, at Whitehall lane, London: Carr, Stoke Newington of gastritis and heart disease: Cockburn, at the Moat house, Chepstow...

— I know that fellow, says Joe, from bitter experience.

— Cockburn. Dimsey, wife of David Dimsey, late of the admiralty: Miller, Tottenham, aged eightyfive: Welsh, June 12, at 35 Canning Street, Liverpool, Isabella Helen. How's that for a national press, eh, my brown son! How's that for Martin Murphy, the Bantry jobber?

— Ah, well, says Joe, handing round the boose. Thanks be to God they had the start of us. Drink that, citizen.

— I will, says he, honourable person.

— Health, Joe, says I. And all down the form.

Ah! Ow! Don't be talking! I was blue mouldy for the want of that pint. Declare to God I could hear it hit the pit of my stomach with a click.

And lo, as they quaffed their cup of joy, a godlike messenger came swiftly in, radiant as the eye of heaven, a comely youth and behind him there passed an elder of noble gait and countenance, bearing the sacred scrolls of law and with him his lady wife, a dame of peerless lineage, fairest of her race.

Little Alf Bergan popped in round the door aud hid behind Barney's snug, squeezed up with the laughing, and who was sitting up there in the corner that I hadn't seen snoring drunk, blind to the world, only Bob Doran. I didn't know what was up and Alf kept making signs out of the door. And begob what was it only that bloody old pantaloon Denis Breen in his bath slippers with two bloody big books tucked under his oxter and the wife hotfoot after him, unfortunate wretched woman trotting like a poodle. I thought Alf would split.

— Look at him, says he. Breen. He's traipsing all round Dublin with a postcard someone sent him with u. p.: up on it to take a li...

And he doubled up.

— Take a what? says I.

— Libel action, says he, for ten thousand pounds.

— O hell! says I.

The bloody mongrel began to growl that'd put the fear of God in you seeing something was up but the citizen gave him a kick in the ribs.

— *Bi i dho husht,* says he.

— Who? says Joe.

— Breen, says Alf. He was in John Henry Menton's and then he went round to Collis and Ward's and then Tom Rochford met him and sent him round to the subsheriff's for a lark. O God, I've a pain laughing. U. p : up. The long fellow gave him an eye as good as a process and now the bloody old lunatic is gone round to Green Street to look for a G. man.

— When is long John going to hang that fellow in Mountjoy? says Joe.

— Bergan, says Bob Doran, waking up. Is that Alf Bergan?

— Yes, says Alf. Hanging? Wait till I show you. Here, Terry, give us a pony. That bloody old fool! Ten thousand pounds. You should have seen long John's eye. U. p...

And he started laughing.

— Who are you laughing at? says Bob Doran? Is that Bergan?

— Hurry up, Terry boy, says Alf.

Terence O'Ryan heard him and straightway brought him a crystal cup full of the foaming ebon ale which the noble twin brothers Bungiveagh and Bungardilaun brew ever in their divine alevats, cunning as the sons of deathless Leda. For they garner the succulent berries of the hop and mass and sift and bruise and brew them and they mix therewith sour juices and bring the must to the sacred fire and cease not night or day from their toil, those cunning brothers, lords of the vat.

Then did you, chivalrous Terence, hand forth, as to the manner born, that nectarous beverage and you offered the crystal cup to him that thirsted, the soul of chivalry, in beauty akin to the immortals.

But he, the young chief of the O'Bergan's, could ill brook to be outdone in generous deeds but gave therefor with gracious gesture a testoon of costliest bronze. Thereon embossed in excellent smithwork was seen the image of a queen of regal port, scion of the house of Brunswick, Victoria her name, Her Most Excellent Majesty, by grace of God of the United Kingdom of Great Britain and Ireland and of the British dominions beyond the sea, queen, defender of the faith, Empress of India, even she, who bore rule, a victress over many peoples, the wellbeloved, for they knew and loved her from the rising of the sun to the going down thereof, the pale, the dark, the ruddy and the ethiop.

— What's that bloody freemason doing, says the citizen, prowling up and down outside ?

— What's that ? says Joe.

— Here you are, says Alf, chucking out the rhino. Talking about hanging. I'll show you something you never saw. Hangmens' letters. Look at here.

So he took a bundle of wisps of letters and envelopes out of his pocket.

— Are you codding ? say I.

— Honest injun, says Alf. Read them.

So Joe took up the letters.

— Who are you laughing at ? says Bob Doran.

So I saw there was going to be a bit of a dust Bob's a queer chap when the porter's up in him so says I just to make talk :

— How's Willy Murray those times, Alf?

— I don't know, says Alf. I saw him just now in Capel Street with Paddy Dignam. Only I was running after that...

— You what ? says Joe, throwing down the letters. With who ?

— With Dignam, says Alf.

— Is it Paddy ? says Joe.

— Yes, says Alf. Why ?

— Don't you know he's dead ? says Joe.

— Paddy Dignam dead ? says Alf.

— Ay, says Joe.

— Sure I'm after seeing him not five minutes ago, says Alf, as plain as a pikestaff.

— Who's dead ? says Bob Doran.

— You saw his ghost then, says Joe, God between us and harm.

— What ? says Alf. Good Christ, only five... What ?... and Willy Murray with him, the two of them there near whatdoyoucallhim's... What ? Dignam dead ?

— What about Dignam ? says Bob Doran. Who's talking about... ?

— Dead ! says Alf. He is no more dead than you are.

— Maybe so, says Joe. They took the liberty of burying him this morning anyhow.

— Paddy ? says Alf.

— Ay, says Joe. He paid the debt of nature, God be merciful to him.

— Good Christ ! says Alf.

Begob he was what you might call flabbergasted.

In the darkness spirit hands were felt to flutter and when prayer by tantras had been directed to the proper quarter a faint but increasing luminosity of ruby light became gradually visible, the apparition of the etheric double being particularly lifelike owing to the discharge of jivic rays from the crown of the head and face. Communication was effected through the pituitary body and also by means of the orangefiery and scarlet rays emanating from the sacral region and solar plexus. Questioned by his earthname as to his whereabouts in the heavenworld he stated that he was now on the path of pralaya or return but was still submitted to trial at the hands of certain bloodthirsty entities on the lower astral levels. In reply to a question as to his first sensations in the great divide beyond he stated that previously he had seen as in a glass darkly but that those who had passed over had summit possibilities of atmic development opened up to them. Interrogated as to whether life there resembled our experience in the flesh he stated that he had heard from more favoured beings now in the spirit that their abodes were equipped with every modern home comfort such as talafana, alavatar, hatakalda, wataklasat and that the highest adepts were steeped in waves of volupcy of the very purest nature. Having requested a quart of buttermilk this was brought and evidently afforded relief. Asked if he had any message for the living he exhorted all who were still at the wrong side of Maya to acknowledge the true path for it was reported in devanic circles that Mars and Jupiter were out for mischief on the eastern angle where the ram has power. It was then queried whether there were any special desires on the part of the defunct and the reply was: *We greet you, friends of earth, who are still in the body. Mind C. K. doesn't pile it on*. It was ascertained that the reference was to Mr Cornelius Kelleher, manager of Messrs H. J. O'Neill's popular funeral establishment, a personal friend of the defunct, who had been responsible for the carrying out of the interment arrangements. Before departing he requested that it should be told to his dear son Patsy that the other boot which he had been looking for was at present under the commode in the return room and that the pair should be sent to Cullen's to be soled only as the heels were still good. He stated that this had greatly perturbed his peace of mind in the other region and earnestly requested that his desire should be made known.

Assurances were given that the matter would be attended to and it was intimated that this had given satisfaction.

He is gone from mortal haunts: O'Dignam, sun of our morning. Fleet was his foot on the bracken: Patrick of the beamy brow. Wail, Banba, with your wind: and wail, O ocean, with your whirlwind.

— There he is again, says the citizen, staring out.

— Who? says I.

— Bloom, says he. He's on point duty up and down there for the last ten minutes.

And, begob, I saw his physog do a peep in and then slidder off again.

Little Alf was knocked bawways. Faith, he was.

— Good Christ! says he. I could have sworn it was him.

And says Bob Doran, with the hat on the back of his poll, lowest blackguard in Dublin when he's under the influence.

— Who said Christ is good?

— I beg your parsnips, says Alf.

— Is that a good Christ, says Bob Doran, to take away poor little Willy Dignam?

— Ah, well, says Alf, trying to pass it off. He's over all his troubles.

But Bob Doran shouts out of him.

— He's a bloody ruffian, I say, to take away poor little Willy Dignam.

Terry came down and tipped him the wink to keep quiet, that they didn't want that kind of talk in a respectable licensed premises. And Bob Doran starts doing the weeps about Paddy Dignam, true as you're there.

— The finest man, says he, snivelling, the finest purest character.

The tear is bloody near your eye. Talking through his bloody hat. Fitter for him to go home to the little sleepwalking bitch he married, Mooney, the bumbailiff's daughter, Mother kept a kip in Hardwicke street that used to be stravaging about the landings Bantam Lyons told me that was stopping there at two in the morning without a stitch on her, exposing her person, open to all comers, fair field and no favour.

— The noblest, the truest, says he. And he's gone, poor little Willy, poor little Paddy Dignam.

And mournful and with a heavy heart he bewept the extinction of that beam of heaven.

Old Garryowen started growling again at Bloom that was skeezing round the door.

— Come in, come on, he won't eat you, says the citizen

So Bloom slopes in with his cod's eye on the dog and he asks Terry was Martin Cunningham there.

— O, Christ M'Keown, says Joe, reading one of the letters Listen to this, will you?

And he starts reading out one.

7, Hunter. Street,
Liverpool.

To the High Sheriff of Dublin,
Dublin.

Honoured sir i beg to offer my services in the abovementioned painful case i hanged Joe Gann in Bootle jail on the 12 of Febuary 1900 and i hanged...

— Show us, Joe, says I.

— ... *private Arthur Chace for fowl murder of Jessie Tilsit in Pentonville prison and i was assistant when...*

— Jesus, says I.

— ... *Billington executed the awful murderer Toad Smith...*

The citizen made a grab at the letter.

— Hold hard, says Joe, *i have a special nack of putting the noose once in he can't get out hoping to be favoured i remain, honoured sir, my terms is five ginnees.*

H. Rumbold,
Master Barber.

— And a barbarous bloody barbarian he is too, says the citizen.

— And the dirty scrawl of the wretch, says Joe. Here, says he, take them to hell out of my sight, Alf. Hello, Bloom, says he, what will you have?

So they started arguing about the point, Bloom saying he wouldn't and couldn't and excuse him no offence and all to that and then he said well he'd just take a cigar. Gob, he's a prudent member and no mistake.

— Give us one of your prime stinkers, Terry, says Joe.

And Alf was telling us there was one chap sent in a mourning card with a black border round it.

— There all barbers, says he, from the black country that would hang their own fathers for five quid down and travelling expenses.

And he was telling us there's two fellows waiting below to pull his heels down when he gets the drop and choke him properly and then they chop up the rope after and sell the bits for a few bob a skull.

In the dark land they bide, the vengeful knights of the razor. Their deadly coil they grasp : yea, and therein they lead to Erebus whatsoever wight hath done a deed of blood for I will on nowise suffer it even so saith the Lord.

So they started talking about capital punishment and of course Bloom comes out with the why and the wherefore and all the codology of the business and the old dog smelling him all the time I'm told those Jewies does have a sort of a queer odour coming off them for dogs about I don't know what all deterrent effect and so forth and so on.

— There's one thing it hasn't a deterrent effect on, says Alf.

— What's that? says Joe.

— The poor bugger's tool that's being hanged, says Alf.

— That so? says Joe.

— God's truth, says Alf. I heard that from the head warder that was in Kilmainham when they hanged Joe Brady, the invincible. He told me when they cut him down after the drop it was standing up in their faces like a poker.

— Ruling passion strong in death, says Joe, as someone said.

— That can be explained by science, says Bloom. It's only a natural phenomenon, don't you see, because on account of the...

And then he starts with his jawbreakers about phenomenon and science and this phenomenon and the other phenomenon.

The distinguished scientist Herr Professor Luitpold Blumenduft tendered medical evidence to the effect that the instantaneous fracture of the cervical vertebrae and consequent scission of the spinal cord would, according to the best approved traditions of medical science, be calculated to inevitably produce in the human subject a violent ganglionic stimulus of the nerve centres, causing the pores of the *corpora cavernosa* to rapidly dilate in such a way as to instantaneously facilitate the flow of blood to that part of the human anatomy known as the penis or male organ resulting in the phenomenon which has been denominated by the faculty a morbid upwards and outwards philoprogenetive erection *in articulo mortis per diminutionem capitis.*

So of course the citizen was only waiting for the wink of the word and he starts gassing out of him about the invincibles and the old guard and the men of sixtyseven and who fears to speak of ninetyeight and Joe with him about all the fellows that were hanged, drawn and transported for the cause by drumhead courtmartial and a new Ireland and new this, that and the other. Talking about new Ireland he ought to go and get a new dog sc he ought. Mangy ravenous brute sniffling and sneezing all round the place and scratching his scabs and round be goes to Bob Doran that was standing Alf a half one sucking up for what he could get. So of course Bob Doran starts doing the bloody fool with him :

— Give us the paw! Give the paw, doggy! Good old doggy. Give us the paw here! Give us the paw!

Arrah! bloody end to the paw he'd paw and Alf trying to keep him from tumbling off the bloody stool atop of the bloody old dog and he talking all kinds of drivel about training by kindness and thoroughbred dog and intelligent dog: give you the bloody pip. Then he starts scraping a few bits of old biscuit out of the bottom of a Jacob's tin he told Terry to bring. Gob, he golloped it down like old boots and his tongue hanging out of him a yard long for more. Near ate the tin and all, hungry bloody mongrel.

And the citizen and Bloom having an argument about the point, the brothers Sheares and Wolfe Tone beyond on Arbour Hill and Robert Emmet and die for your country, the Tommy Moore touch about Sara Curran and she's far from the land. And Bloom, of course, with his knockmedown cigar putting on swank with his lardy face. Phenomenon! The fat heap he married is a nice old phenomenon with a back on her like a ballalley. Time they were stopping up in the *City Arms* Pisser Burke told me there was an old one there with a cracked loodheramaun of a nephew and Bloom trying to get the soft side of her doing the mollycoddle playing bézique to come in for a bit of the wampum in her will and not eating meat of a Friday because the old one was always thumping her craw and taking the lout out for a walk. And one time he led him the rounds of Dublin and, by the holy farmer, he never cried crack till he brought him home as drunk as a boiled owl and he said he did it to teach him the evils of alcohol and by herrings if the three women didn't near roast him it's a queer story, the old one, Bloom's wife and Mrs O'Dowd that kept the hotel. Jesus, I had to laugh at Pisser Burke taking them off chewing the fat and Bloom with his *but don't you see?* and *but on the other hand*. And sure, more be token, the lout I'm told was in Power's after, the blender's, round in Cope street going home footless in a cab five times in the week after drinking his way through all the samples in the bloody establishment. Phenomenon!

— The memory of the dead, says the citizen taking up his pintglass and glaring at Bloom.

— Ay, ay, says Joe.

— You don't grasp my point, says Bloom. What I mean is...

— *Sinn Fein!* says the citizen. *Sinn fein amhain!* The friends we love are by our side and the foes we hate before us.

The last farewell was affecting in the extreme. From the belfries far and near the funereal deathbell tolled unceasingly while all around the gloomy precincts rolled the ominous warning of a hundred muffled drums punctuated by the hollow booming of pieces of ordnance. The deafening claps of thunder and the dazzling flashes of lightning which lit up the ghastly scene testified that the artillery of heaven had lent its supernatural pomp to the already gruesome spectacle. A torrential rain poured down from the floodgates of the angry heavens upon the bared heads of the assembled multitude which numbered at the lowest computation five hundred thousand persons. A posse of Dublin Metropolitan police superintended by the Chief Commissioner in person maintained order in the vast throng for whom the York Street brass and reed band whiled away the intervening time by admirably rendering on their blackdraped instruments the matchless melody endeared to us from the cradle by Speranza's plaintive muse. Special quick excursion trains and upholstered charabancs had been provided for the comfort of our country cousins of whom there were large contingents. Considerable amusement was caused by the favourite Dublin streetsingers L-n-h-n and M-ll-g-n who sang *The Night before Larry was stretched* in their usual mirthprovoking fashion. Our two inimitable drolls did a roaring trade with their broadsheets among lovers of the comedy element and nobody who has a corner in his heart for real Irish fun without vulgarity will grudge them their hardearned pennies. The children of the Male and Female Foundling Hospital who thronged the windows overlooking the scene were delighted with this unexpected addition to the day's entertainment and a word of praise is due to the Little Sisters of the Poor for their excellent idea of affording the poor fatherless and motherless children a genuinely instructive treat. The viceregal houseparty which included many wellknown ladies was chaperoned by Their Excellencies to the most favourable positions on the grand stand while the picturesque foreign delegation known as the Friends of the Emerald Isle was accommodated on a tribune directly opposite. The delegation, present in full force, consisted of Commendatore Bacibaci Beninobenone (the semiparalysed *doyen* of the party who had to be assisted to his seat by the aid of a powerful steam crane), Monsieur Pierrepaul Petitépatant, the Grandjoker Vladinmire Pokethankertscheff, the Archjoker Leopold Rudolph von Schwanzenbad-Hodenthaler, Countess Marha Virága Kisászony Putrápesthi, Hiram. Y. Bomboost, Count Athanatos Karamelopulos, Ali Baba Backsheesh Rahat Lokum Effendi, Señor Hidalgo Caballero Don Pecadillo y Palabras y Paternoster de la Malora de la Malaria, Hokopoko Harakiri, Hi Hung Chang, Olaf Kobberkeddelsen, Mynheer Trik van Trumps, Pan Poleaxe Paddyrisky, Goosepond Prhklstr Kratchinabritchisitch,

Herr Hurhausdirektorpresident Hans Chuechli-Steuerli, Nationalgymnasiummuseumsanatoriumandsuspensoriumsordinaryprivatdocentgeneralhistoryspecialprofessordoctor Kriegfried Ueberallgemein. All the delegates without exception expressed themselves in the strongest possible heterogeneous terms concerning the nameless barbarity which they had been called upon to witness. An animated altercation (in which all took part) ensued among the F. O. T. E. I. as to whether the eighth or the ninth of March was the correct date of the birth of Ireland's patron saint. In the course of the argument cannonballs, scimitars, boomerangs, blunderbusses, stinkpots, meatchoppers, umbrellas, catapults, knuckledusters, sandbags, lumps of pig iron were resorted to and blows were freely exchanged. The baby policeman, Constable Mac Fadden, summoned by special courier from Booterstown, quickly restored order and with lightning promptitude proposed the seventeenth of the month as a solution equally honourable for both contending parties. The readywitted ninefooter's suggestion at once appealed to all and was unanimously accepted. Constable Mac Fadden was heartily congratulated by all the F. O. T. E. I., several of whom were bleeding profusely. Commendatore Beninobenone having been extricated from underneath the presidential armchair, it was explained by his legal adviser Avvocato Pagamimi that the various articles secreted in his thirtytwo pockets had been abstracted by him during the affray from the pockets of his junior colleagues in the hope of bringing them to their senses. The objects (which included several hundred ladies' and gentlemen's gold and silver watches) were promptly restored to their rightful owners and general harmony reigned supreme.

Quietly, unassumingly Rumbold stepped on to the scaffold in faultless morning dress and wearing his favourite flower the *Gladiolus Cruentus*. He announced his presence by that gentle Rumboldian cough which so many have tried (unsuccessfully) to imitate — short, painstaking yet withal so characteristic of the man. The arrival of the worldrenowned headsman was greeted by a roar of acclamation from the huge concourse, the viceregal ladies waving their handkerchiefs in their excitement while the even more excitable foreign delegates cheered vociferously in a medley of cries, *hoch, banzai, eljen, zivio, chinchin, polla kronia, hiphip, vive, Allah,* amid which the ringing *evviva* of the delegate of the land of song (a high double F recalling those piercingly lovely notes with which the eunuch Catalani beglamoured our greatgreatgrandmothers) was easily distinguishable. It was exactly seventeen o'clock. The signal for prayer was then promptly given by megaphone and in an instant all heads were bared, the commendatore's patriarchal sombrero, which has been in the possession of his family since the revolution of Rienzi, being removed by his medical adviser in attendance, Dr Pippi. The learned prelate who administered the last comforts of holy religion to the hero martyr when about to pay the death penalty knelt in a most christian spirit in a pool of rainwater, his cassock above his hoary head, and offered up to the throne of grace fervent prayers of supplication. Hard by the block stood the grim figure of the executioner, his visage being concealed in a tengallon pot with two circular perforated apertures through which his eyes glowered furiously. As he awaited the fatal signal he tested the edge of his horrible weapon by honing it upon his brawny forearm or decapitated in rapid succession a flock of sheep which had been provided by the admirers of his fell but necessary office. On a handsome mahogany table near him were neatly arranged the quartering knife, the various finely tempered disembowelling appliances (specially supplied by the worldfamous firm of cutlers, Messrs John Round and Sons, Sheffield) a terracotta saucepan for the reception of the duodenum, colon, blind intestine and appendix etc when successfully extracted and two commodious milkjugs destined to receive the most precious blood of the most precious victim. The housesteward of the amalgamated cats' and dogs' home was in attendance to convey these vessels when replenished to that beneficent institution. Quite an excellent repast consisting of rashers and eggs, fried steak and onions, done to a nicety, delicious hot breakfast rolls and invigorating tea had been considerately provided by the authorities for the consumption of the central figure of the tragedy who was in capital spirits when prepared for death and evinced the keenest interest in the proceedings from beginning to end but he, with an abnegation rare in these our times, rose nobly to the occasion and expressed the dying wish (immediately acceded to) that the meal should be divided in aliquot parts among the members of the sick and indigent roomkeepers' association as a token of his regard and esteem. The *nec* and *non plus ultra* of emotion were reached when the blushing bride elect burst her way through the serried ranks of the bystanders and flung herself upon the muscular bosom of him who was about to be launched into eternity for her sake. The hero folded her willowy form in a loving embrace murmuring fondly *Sheila, my own*. Encouraged by this use of her christian name she kissed passionately all the various suitable areas of his person which the decencies of prison garb permitted her ardour to reach. She swore to him as they mingled the salt streams of their tears that she would cherish his memory, that she would never forget her hero boy who went to his death with a song on his lips as if he were but going to a hurling match in Clonturk park. She brought back to his recollection the happy days of blissful childhood together on the banks of Anna Liffey when they had indulged in the innocent pastimes of the young and, oblivious of the dreadful present, they both laughed heartily, all the spectators, including the venerable pastor, joining in the general merriment. That monster audience simply rocked with delight. But anon they were overcome with grief and clasped their hands for the last time. A fresh torrent of tears burst from their lachrymal ducts and the vast concourse of people, touched to the inmost core, broke into heartrending sobs, not the least affected being the aged prebendary himself. Big strong men, officers of the peace and genial giants of the royal Irish constabulary, were making frank use of their handkerchiefs and it is safe to say that there was not a dry eye in that record assemblage. A most romantic incident occurred when a handsome young Oxford graduate, noted for his chivalry towards the fair sex, stepped forward and, presenting his visiting card, bankbook and genealogical tree solicited the hand of the hapless young lady, requesting her to name the day, and was accepted on the spot. Every lady in the audience was presented with a tasteful souvenir of the occasion in the shape of skull and crossbones brooch, a timely and generous act which evoked a fresh outburst of emotion : and when the gallant young Oxonian (the bearer, by the way, of one of the most timehonoured names in Albion's history) placed on the finger of his blushing *fiancée* an expensive engagement ring with emeralds set in the form of a fourleaved shamrock excitement knew no bounds. Nay, even the stern provostmarshal, lieutenantcolonel Tomkin-Maxwell ffrenchmullan Tomlinson, who presided on the sad occasion, he who had blown a considerable number of sepoys from the cannonmouth without flinching, could not now restrain his natural emotion. With his mailed gauntlet he brushed away a furtive tear and was overheard by those privileged burghers who happened to be in his immediate *entourage* to murmur to himself in a faltering undertone :

— God blimey if she aint a clinker, that there bleeding tart. Blimey it makes me kind of bleeding cry, straight, it does, when I sees her cause I thinks of my old mashtub what's waiting for me down Limehouse way.

So then the citizen begins talking about the Irish language and the corporation meeting and all to that and the shoneens that can't speak their own language and Joe chipping in because he stuck someone for a quid and Bloom putting in his old goo with his twopenny stump that he cadged off of Joe and talking about the Gaelic league and the antitreating league and drink, the curse of Ireland. Antitreating is about the size of it. Gob, he'd let you pour all manner of drink down his throat till the Lord would call him before you'd ever see the froth of his pint. And one night I went in with a fellow into one of their musical evenings, song and dance about she could get up on a truss of hay she could my Maureen Lay and there was a fellow with a Ballyhooly blue ribbon badge spiffing out of him in Irish and a lot of colleen bawns going about with temperance beverages and selling medals and oranges and lemonade and a few old dry buns, gob, flahoolagh entertainment, don't be talking. Ireland sober is Ireland free. And then an old fellow starts blowing into his bagpipes and all the gougers shuffling their feet to the tune the old cow died of. And one or two sky pilots having an eye around that there was no goings on with the females, hitting below the belt.

So howandever, as I was saying, the old dog seeing the tin was empty starts mousing around by Joe and me. I'd train him by kindness, so I would, if he was my dog. Give him a rousing fine kick now and again where it wouldn't blind him.

— Afraid he'll bite you? says the citizen, sneering.

— No, says I. But he might take my leg for a lamppost.

So he calls the old dog over.

— What's on you, Garry? says he.

Then he starts hauling and mauling and talking to him in Irish and the old towser growling, letting on to answer, like a duet in the opera. Such growling you never heard as they let off between them. Someone that has nothing better to do ought to write a letter *pro bono publico* to the papers about the muzzling order for a dog the like of that. Growling and grousing and his eye all bloodshot from the drouth is in it and the hydrophobia dropping out of his jaws.

All those who are interested in the spread of human culture among the lower animals (and their name is legion) should make a point of not missing the really marvellous exhibition of cynanthropy given by the famous old Irish red wolfdog setter formerly known by the *sobriquet* of Garryowen and recently rechristened by his large circle of friends and acquaintances Owen Garry. The exhibition which is the result of years of training by kindness and a carefully thoughtout dietary system, comprises, among other achievements, the recitation of verse. Our greatest living phonetic expert (wild horses shall not drag it from us!) has left no stone unturned in his efforts to delucidate and compare the verse recited and has found it bears a *striking* resemblance (the italics are ours) to the ranns of ancient Celtic bards. We are not speaking so much of those delightful lovesongs with which the writer who conceals his identity under the graceful pseudonym of the Little Sweet Branch has familiarised the bookloving world but rather (as a contributor D. O. C. points out in an interesting communication published by an evening contemporary) of the harsher and more personal note which is found in the satirical effusions of the famous Raftery and of Donald Mac Considine to say nothing of a more modern lyrist at present very much in the public eye. We subjoin a specimen which has been rendered into English by an eminent scholar whose name for the moment we are not at liberty to disclose though we believe that our readers will find the topical allusion rather more than an indication. The metrical system of the canine original, which recalls the intricate alliterative and isosyllabic rules of the Welsh englyn, is infinitely more complicated but we believe our readers will agree that the spirit has been well caught. Perhaps it should be added that the effect is greatly increased if Owen's verse be spoken somewhat slowly and indistinctly in a tone suggestive of suppressed rancour.

The curse of my curses
Seven days every day
And seven dry Thursdays
On you, Barney Kiernan,
Has no sup of water
To cool my courage,
And my guts red roaring
After Lowry's lights.

So he told Terry to bring some water for the dog and, gob, you could hear him lapping it up a mile off. And Joe asked him would he have another.

— I will, says he, *a chara,* to show there's no ill feeling.

Gob, he's not as green as he's cabbagelooking. Arsing around from one pub to another, leaving it to your own honour, with old Giltrap's dog and getting fed up by the ratepayers and corporators. Entertainment for man and beast. And says Joe :

— Could you make a hole in another pint ?

— Could a swim duck ? says I.

— Same again, Terry, says Joe. Are you sure you won't have anything in the way of liquid refreshment? says he.

— Thank you, no, says Bloom. As a matter of fact I just wanted to meet Martin Cunningham, don't you see, about this insurance of poor Dignam's. Martin asked me to go to the house. You see, he, Dignam, I mean, didn't serve any notice of the assignment on the company at the time and nominally under the act the mortgagee can't recover on the policy.

— Holy Wars, says Joe laughing, that's a good one if old Shylock is landed. So the wife comes out top dog, what?

— Well, that's a point, says Bloom, for the wife's admirers.

— Whose admirers ? says Joe.

— The wife's advisers, I mean, says Bloom.

Then he starts all confused mucking it up about the mortgagor under the act like the lord chancellor giving it out on the bench and for the benefit of the wife and that a trust is created but on the other hand that Dignam owed Bridgeman the money and if now the wife or the widow contested the mortgagee's right till he near had the head of me addled with his mortgagor under the act. He was bloody safe he wasn't run in himself under the act that time as a rogue and vagabond only he had a friend in court. Selling bazaar tickets or what do you call it royal Hungarian privileged lottery. True as you're there. O, commend me to an israelite ! Royal and privileged Hungarian robbery.

So Bob Doran comes lurching around asking Bloom to tell Mrs Dignam he was sorry for her trouble and he was very sorry about the funeral and to tell her that he said and everyone who knew him said that there was never a truer, a finer than poor little Willy that's dead to tell her. Choking with bloody foolery. And shaking Bloom's hand doing the tragic to tell her that. Shake hands, brother. You're a rogue and I'm another.

— Let me, said he, so far presume upon our acquaintance which, however slight it may appear if judged by the standard of mere time, is founded, as I hope and believe, on a sentiment of mutual esteem, as to request of you this favour. But, should I have overstepped the limits of reserve let the sincerity of my feelings be the excuse for my boldness.

— No, rejoined the other, I appreciate to the full the motives which actuate your conduct and I shall discharge the office you entrust to me consoled by the reflection that, though the errand be one of sorrow, this proof of your confidence sweetens in some measure the bitterness of the cup.

— Then suffer me to take your hand, said he. The goodness of your heart, I feel sure, will dictate to you better than my inadequate words the expressions which are most suitable to convey an emotion whose poignancy, were I to give vent to my feelings, would deprive me even of speech.

And off with him and out trying to walk straight. Boosed at five o'clock. Night he was near being lagged only Paddy Leonard knew the bobby L, 14 A. Blind to the world up in a shebeen in Bride street after closing time, fornicating with two shawls and a bully on guard, drinking porter out of teacups. And calling himself a Frenchy for the shawls, Joseph Manuo, and talking against the catholic religion and he serving mass in Adam and Eve's when he was young with his eyes shut who wrote the new testament and the old testament and hugging and smugging. And the two shawls killed with the laughing, picking his pockets the bloody fool and he spilling the porter all over the bed and the two shawls screeching laughing at one another. *How is your testament? Have you got an old testament?* Only Paddy was passing there, I tell you what. Then see him of a Sunday with his little concubine of a wife, and she wagging her tail up the aisle of the chapel, with her patent boots on her, no less, and her violets, nice as pie, doing the little lady. Jack Mooney's sister. And the old prostitute of a mother procuring rooms to street couples. Gob, Jack made him toe the line. Told him if he didn't patch up the pot, Jesus, he'd kick the shite out of him.

So Terry brought the three pints.

— Here, says Joe, doing the honours. Here, citizen.

— *Slan leat,* says he.

— Fortune, Joe, says I. Good health, citizen.

Gob, he had his mouth half way down the tumbler already. Want a small fortune to keep him in drinks.

— Who is the long fellow running for the mayoralty, Alf? says Joe.

— Friend of yours, says Alf.

— Nannan? says Joe. The mimber?

— I won't mention any names, says Alf.

— I thought so, says Joe. I saw him up at that meeting now with William Field, M. P., the cattle traders.

— Hairy Iopas, says the citizen, that exploded volcano, the darling of all countries and the idol of his own.

So Joe starts telling the citizen about the foot and mouth disease and the cattle traders and taking action in the matter and the citizen sending them all to the rightabout and Bloom coming out with his sheepdip for the scab and a hoose drench for coughing calves and the guaranteed remedy for timber tongue. Because he was up one time in a knacker's yard. Walking about with his book and pencil here's my head and my heels are coming till Joe Cuffe gave him the order of the boot for giving lip to a grazier. Mister Knowall. Teach your grandmother how to milk ducks. Pisser Burke was telling me in the hotel the wife used to be in rivers of tears sometimes with Mrs O'Dowd crying her eyes out with her eight inches of fat all over her. Couldn't loosen her farting strings but old cod's eye was waltzing around her showing her how to do it. What's your programme today? Ay. Humane methods. Because the poor animals suffer and experts say and the best known remedy that doesn't cause pain to the animal and on the sore spot administer gently. Gob, he'd have a soft hand under a hen.

Ga Ga Gara. Klook Klook Klook. Black Liz is our hen. She lays eggs for us. When she lays her egg she is so glad. Gara. Klook Klook Klook. Then comes good uncle Leo. He puts his hand under black Liz and takes her fresh egg, Ga ga ga ga Gara. Klook Klook Klook.

— Anyhow, says Joe. Field and Nannetti are going over tonight to London to ask about it on the floor of the House of Commons.

— Are you sure, says Bloom, the councillor is going. I wanted to see him, as it happens.

— Well, he's going off by the mailboat, says Joe, tonight.

— That's too bad, says Bloom. I wanted particularly. Perhaps only Mr Field is going. I couldn't phone. No You're sure?

— Nannan's going too, says Joe. The league told him to ask a question tomorrow about the commissioner of police forbidding Irish games in the park. What do you think of that, citizen? *The Sluagh na h-Eireann.*

Mr Cowe Conacre (Multifarnham. Nat.): Arising out of the question of my honourable friend, the member for Shillelagh, may I ask the right honourable gentleman whether the Government has issued orders that these animals shall be slaughtered though no medical evidence is forthcoming as to their pathological condition?

Mr Allfours (Tamoshant. Con.): Honourable members are already in possession of the evidence produced before a committee of the whole house. I feel I cannot usefully add anything to that. The answer to the honourable member's question is in the affirmative.

Mr Orelli O'Reilly (Montenotte. Nat.): Have similar orders been issued for the slaughter of human animals who dare to play Irish games in the Phoenix park?

Mr Allfours : The answer is in the negative.

Mr Cowe Conacre : Has the right honourable gentleman's famous Mitchelstown telegram inspired the policy of gentlemen on the treasury bench? (O! O!)

Mr Allfours : I must have notice of that question.

Mr Staylewit (Buncombe. Ind.) : Don't hesitate to shoot.

(Ironical opposition cheers.)

The speaker : Order! Order!

(The house rises. Cheers.)

— There's the man, says Joe, that made the Gaelic sports revival. There he is sitting there. The man that got away James Stephens. The champion of all Ireland at putting the sixteen pound shot. What was your best throw, citizen?

— *Na bacleis,* says the citizen, letting on to be modest. There was a time I was as good as the next fellow anyhow.

— Put it there, citizen, says Joe. You were and a bloody sight better.

— Is that really a fact? says Alf.

— Yes, says Bloom. That's well known. Do you not know that?

So off they started about Irish sport and shoneen games the like of the lawn tennis and about hurley and putting the stone and racy of the soil and building up a nation once again and all to that. And of course Bloom had to have his say too about if a fellow had a rower's heart violent exercise was bad. I declare to my antimacassar if you took up a straw from the bloody floor and if you said to Bloom : *Look at, Bloom. Do you see that straw? That's a straw.* Declare to my aunt he'd talk about it for an hour so he would and talk steady.

A most interesting discussion took place in the ancient hall of *Brian O'Ciarnain's* in *Sraid na Bretaine Bheag*, under the auspices of *Sluagh na h-Eireann,* on the revival of ancient Gaelic sports and the importance of physical culture, as understood in ancient Greece and ancient Rome and ancient Ireland, for the development of the race. The venerable president of this noble order was in the chair and the attendance was of large dimensions. After an instructive discourse by the chairman, a magnificent oration eloquently and forcibly expressed, a most interesting and instructive discussion of the usual high standard of excellence ensued as to the desirability of the revivability of the ancient games and sports of our ancient panceltic forefathers.

The wellknown and highly respected worker in the cause of our old tongue, Mr Joseph M'Carthy Hynes, made an eloquent appeal for the resuscitation of the ancient Gaelic sports and pastimes, practised morning and evening by Finn Mac Cool, as calculated to revive the best traditions of manly strength and powers handed down to us from ancient ages. L. Bloom, who met with a mixed reception of applause and hisses, having espoused the negative the vocalist chairman brought the discussion to a close, in response to repeated requests and hearty plaudits from all parts of a bumper house house, by a remarkably noteworthy rendering of the immortal Thomas Osborne Davis' evergreen verses (happily too familiar to need recalling here) *A nation once again* in the execution of which the veteran patriot champion may be said without fear of contradiction to have fairly excelled himself. The Irish Caruso-Garibaldi was in superlative form and his stentorian notes were heard to the greatest advantage in the timehonoured anthem sung as only our citizen can sing it. His superb highclass vocalism, which by its superquality greatly enhanced his already international reputation, was vociferously applauded by the large audience amongst which were to be noticed many prominent members of the clergy as well as representatives of the press and the bar and the other learned professions. The proceedings then terminated.

Amongst the clergy present were the very rev. William Delany, S. J., L. L. D.; the rt rev. Gerald Molloy, D. D.; the rev. P. J. Kavanagh, C. S. Sp.; the rev. T. Waters, C. C.; the rev. John M. Ivers, P. P.; the rev. P. J. Cleary, O. S. F.; the rev. L. J. Hickey, O. P.; the very rev. Fr. Nicholas, O. S. F. C.; the very rev. B. Gorman, O. D. C.; the rev. T. Maher. S. J.; the very rev. James Murphy, S. J.; the rev. John Lavery, V. F.; the very rev. William Doherty, D. D.; the rev. Peter Fagan, O. M.; the rev. T. Brangan, O. S. A.; the rev. J. Flavin, C. C.; the rev. M. A. Hackett, C. C.; the rev. W. Hurley, C. C., the rt rev. Mgr M'Manus, V. G.; the rev. B. R. Slattery, O. M. I.; the very rev. M. D. Scally, P. P.; the rev. F. T. Purcell, O. P.; the very rev. Timothy canon Gorman, P. P.; the rev. J. Flanagan, C. C.; The laity included P. Fay, T. Quirke, etc., etc.

— Talking about violent exercise, says Alf, were you at that Keogh-Bennett match?

— No, says Joe.

— I heard So and So made a cool hundred quid over it, says Alf.

— Who? Blazes? says Joe.

And says Bloom:

— What I meant about tennis, for example, is the agility and training of the eye.

— Ay, Blazes, says Alf. He let out that Myler was on the beer to run up the odds and he swatting all the time.

— We know him, says the citizen. The traitor's son. We know what put English gold in his pocket.

— True for you, says Joe.

And Bloom cuts in again about lawn tennis and the circulation of the blood, asking Alf:

— Now don't you think, Bergan?

— Myler dusted the floor with him, says Alf. Heenan and Sayers was only a bloody fool to it. Handed him the father and mother of a beating. See the little kipper not up to his navel and the big fellow swiping. God, he gave him one last puck in the wind. Queensberry rules and all, made him puke what he never ate.

It was a historic and a hefty battle when Myler and Percy were scheduled to don the gloves for the purse of fifty sovereigns. Handicapped as he was by lack of poundage, Dublin's pet lamb made up for it by superlative skill in ringcraft. The final bout of fireworks was a gruelling for both champions. The welterweight sergeantmajor had tapped some lively claret in the previous mixup during which Keogh had been receivergeneral of rights and lefts, the artilleryman putting in some neat work on the pet's nose, and Myler came on looking groggy. The soldier got to business leading off with a powerful left jab to which the Irish gladiator retaliated by shooting out a stiff one flush to the point of Bennett's jaw. The redcoat ducked but the Dubliner lifted him with a left hook, the body punch being a fine one. The men came to handigrips. Myler quickly became busy and got his man under, the bout ending with the bulkier man on the ropes, Myler punishing him. The Englishman, whose right eye was nearly closed, took his corner where he was liberally drenched with water and when the bell went, came on gamey and brimful of pluck, confident of knocking out the fistic Eblanite in jigtime. It was a fight to a finish and the best man for it. The two fought like tigers and excitement ran fever high. The referee twice cautioned Pucking Percy for holding but the pet was tricky and his footwork a treat to watch. After a brisk exchange of courtesies during which a smart upper cut of the military man brought blood freely from his opponent's mouth the lamb suddenly waded in all over his man and landed a terrific left to Battling Bennett's stomach, flooring him flat. It was a knockout clean and clever. Amid tense expectation the Portobello bruiser was being counted out when Bennett's second Ole Pfotts Wettstein threw in the towel and the Santry boy was declared victor to the frenzied cheers of the public who broke through the ringropes and fairly mobbed him with delight.

— He knows which side his bread is buttered, says Alf. I hear he's running a concert tour now up in the north.

— He is, says Joe. Isn't he?

— Who? says Bloom. Ah, yes. That's quite true. Yes, a kind of summer tour, you see. Just a holiday.

— Mrs B. is the bright particular star, isn't she? says Joe.

— My wife? say Bloom. She's singing, yes. I think it will be a success too. He's an excellent man to organise. Excellent.

Hoho begob, says I to myself, says I. That explains the milk in the cocoanut and absence of hair on the animal's chest. Blazes doing the tootle on the flute. Concert tour. Dirty Dan the dodgers's son off Island bridge that sold the same horses twice over to the government to fight the Boers. Old Whatwhat. I called about the poor and water rate, Mr Boylan. You what? The water rate, Mr Boylan. You whatwhat? That's the bucko that'll organise her, take my tip. 'Twixt me and you Caddereesh.

Pride of Calpe's rocky mount, the ravenhaired daughter of Tweedy. There grew she to peerless beauty where loquat and almond scent the air. The gardens of Alameda knew her step: the garths of olives knew and bowed. The chaste spouse of Leopold is she: Marion of the bountiful bosoms.

And lo, there entered one of the clan of the O'Molloy's, a comely hero of white face yet withal somewhat ruddy, his majesty's counsel learned in the law, and with him the prince and heir of the noble line of Lambert.

— Hello, Ned.

— Hello, Alf.

— Hello, Jack.

— Hello, Joe.

— God save you, says the citizen.

— Save you kindly, says J. J. What'll it be, Ned?

— Half one, says Ned.

So J. J. ordered the drinks.

— Were you round at the court? says Joe.

— Yes, says J. J. He'll square that, Ned, says he.

— Hope so, says Ned.

Now what were those two at? J. J. getting him off the grand jury list and the other give him a leg over the stile. With his name in Stubbs's. Playing cards, hobnobbing with flash toffs with a swank glass in their eye, drinking fizz and he half smothered in writs and garnishee orders. Pawning his gold watch in Cummins of Francis street where no-one would know him in the private office when I was there with Pisser releasing his boots out of the pop. What's your name, sir? Dunne, says he. Ay, and done says I. Gob, he'll come home by weeping cross one of these days, I'm thinking.

— Did you see that bloody lunatic Breen round there, says Alf. U. p. up.

— Yes, says J. J. Looking for a private detective.

— Ay, says Ned, and he wanted right go wrong to address the court only Corny Kelleher got round him telling him to get the handwriting examined first.

— Ten thousand pounds, says Alf, laughing. God I'd give anything to hear him before a judge and jury.

— Was it you did it, Alf? says Joe. The truth, the whole truth and nothing but the truth, so help you Jimmy Johnson.

— Me? says Alf. Don't cast your nasturtiums on my character.

— Whatever statement you make, says Joe, will be taken down in evidence against you.

— Of course an action would lie, says J. J. It implies that he is not *compos mentis*. U. p. up.

— *Compos* your eye? says Alf, laughing. Do you know that he's balmy? Look at his head. Do you know that some mornings he has to get his hat on with a shoehorn.

— Yes, says J. J., but the truth of a libel is no defence to an indictment for publishing it in the eyes of the law.

— Ha, ha, Alf, says Joe.

— Still, says Bloom, on account of the poor woman, I mean his wife.

— Pity about her, says the citizen. Or any other woman marries a half and half.

— How half and half? says Bloom. Do you mean he...

— Half and half I mean, says the citizen. A fellow that's neither fish nor flesh.

— Nor good red herring, says Joe.

— That what's I mean, says the citizen. A pishogue, if you know what that is.

Begob I saw there was trouble coming. And Bloom explained he meant on account of it being cruel for the wife having to go round after the old stuttering fool. Cruelty to animals so it is to let that bloody povertystricken Breen out on grass with his beard out tripping him, bringing down the rain. And she with her nose cockahoop after she married him because a cousin of his old fellow's was pew opener to the pope. Picture of him on the wall with his smashall sweeney's moustaches. The signor Brini from Summerhill, the eyetallyano, papal zouave to the Holy Father, has left the quay and gone to Moss street. And who was he, tell us? A nobody, two pair back and passages, at seven shillings a week, and he covered with al kinds of breastplates bidding defiance to the world.

— And moreover, says J. J., a postcard is publication. It was held to be sufficient evidence of malice in the testcase Sadgrove v. Hole. In my opinion an action might lie.

Six and eightpence, please. Who wants your opinion? Let us drink our pints in peace. Gob, we won't be let even do that much itself.

— Well, good health, Jack, says Ned.

— Good health, Ned, says J. J.

— There he is again, says Joe.

— Where? says Alf.

And begob there he was passing the door with his books under his oxter and the wife beside him and Corny Kelleher with his wall eye looking in as they went passed, talking to him like a father, trying to sell him a secondhand coffin.

— How did that Canada swindle case go off? says Joe.

— Remanded, says J. J.

One of the bottlenosed fraternity it was went by the name of James Wought alias Saphiro alias Spark and Spiro, put an ad in the papers saying he'd give a passage to Canada for twenty bob. What? Do you see any green in the white of my eye? Course it was a bloody barney. What? Swindled them all, skivvies and badhachs from the county Meath, ay, and his own kidney too. J. J. was telling us there was an ancient Hebrew Zaretsky or something weeping in the witnessbox with his hat on him, swearing by the holy Moses he was stuck for two quid.

— Who tried the case? says Joe.

— Recorder, says Ned.

— Poor old sir Frederick, says Alf, you can cod him up to the two eyes.

— Heart as big as a lion, says Ned. Tell him a tale of woe about arrears of rent and a sick wife and a squad of kids and, faith, he'll dissolve in tears on the bench.

— Ay, says Alf. Reuben J. was bloody lucky he didn't clap him in the dock the other day for suing poor little Gumley that's minding stones for the corporation there near Butt bridge.

And he starts taking off the old recorder letting on to cry :

— A most scandalous thing ! This poor hardworking man ! How many children ? Ten, did you say ?

— Yes, your worship. And my wife has the typhoid !

— And a wife with typhoid fever ! Scandalous ! Leave the court immediately, sir. No, sir, I'll make no order for payment. How dare you, sir, come up before me and ask me to make an order ! A poor hardworking industrious man ! I dismiss the case.

And whereas on the sixteenth day of the month of the oxeyed goddess and in the third week after the feastday of the Holy and Undivided Trinity the daughter of the skies, the virgin moon being then in her first quarter, it came to pass that those learned judges repaired them to the halls of law. There master Courtenay, sitting in his own chamber, gave his rede and master Justice Andrews sitting without a jury in the probate court, weighed well and pondered the claims of the first chargeant upon the property in the matter of the will propounded and final testamentary disposition *in re* the real and personal estate of the late lamented Jacob Halliday, vintner, deceased, versus Livingstone, an infant, of unsound mind, and another. And to the solemn court of Green street there came sir Frederick the Falconer. And he sat him there about the hour of five o'clock to administer the law of the brehons at the commission for all that and those parts to be holden in and for the county of the city of Dublin. And there sat with him the high sinhedrim of the twelve tribes of Iar, for every tribe one man, of the tribe of Patrick and of the tribe of Hugh and of the tribe of Owen and of the tribe of Conn and of the tribe of Oscar and of the tribe of Fergus and of the tribe of Finn and of the tribe of Dermot and of the tribe of Cormac and of the tribe of Kevin and of the tribe of Caolte and of the tribe of Ossian, there being in all twelve good men and true. And he conjured them by Him who died on rood that they should well and truly try and true deliverance make in the issue joined between their sovereign lord the king and the prisoner at the bar and true verdict give according to the evidence so help them God and kiss the book. And they rose in their seats, those twelve of Iar, and they swore by the name of Him who is from everlasting that they would do His rightwiseness. And straightway the minions of the law led forth from their donjon keep one whom the sleuthhounds of justice had apprehended in consequence of information received. And they shackled him hand and foot and would take of him ne bail ne mainprise but preferred a charge against him for he was a malefactor.

— Those are nice things, says the citizen, coming over here to Ireland filling the country with bugs.

So Bloom lets on he heard nothing and he starts talking with Joe, telling him he needn't trouble about that little matter till the first but if he would just say a word to Mr Crawford. And so Joe swore high and holy by this and by that he'd do the devil and all.

— Because you see, says Bloom, for an advertisement you must have repetition. That's the whole secret.

— Rely on me, says Joe.

— Swindling the peasants, says the citizen, and the poor of Ireland. We want no more strangers in our house.

— O I'm sure that will be all right, Hynes, says Bloom. It's just that Keyes, you see.

— Consider that done, says Joe.

— Very kind of you, says Bloom.

— The strangers, says the citizen. Our own fault. We let them come in. We brought them. The adulteress and her paramour brought the Saxon robbers here.

— Decree *nisi*, says J. J.

And Bloom letting on to be awfully deeply interested in nothing, a spider's web in the corner behind the barrel, and the citizen scowling after him and the old dog at his feet looking up to know who to bite and when.

— A dishonoured wife, says the citizen, that's what the cause of all our misfortunes.

— And here she is, says Alf, that was giggling over the *Police Gazette* with Terry on the counter, in all her warpaint.

— Give us a squint at her, says I.

And what was it only one of the smutty yankee pictures Terry borrows off of Corny Kelleher. Secrets for enlarging your private parts. Misconduct of society belle. Norman W. Tupper, wealthy Chicago contractor, finds pretty but faithless wife in lap of officer Taylor. Belle in her bloomers misconducting herself and her fancy man feeling for her tickles and Norman W. Tupper bouncing in with his peashooter just in time to be late after she doing the trick of the loop with officer Taylor.

— O jakers, Jenny, says Joe, how short your shirt is!

— There's hair, Joe, says I. Get a queer old tailend of corned beef off of that one, what?

So anyhow in came John Wyse Nolan and Lenehan with him with a face on him as long as a late breakfast.

— Well, says the citizen, what's the latest from the scene of action? What did those tinkers in the cityhall at their caucus meeting decide about the Irish language?

O'Nolan, clad in shining armour, low bending made obeisance to the puissant and high and mighty chief of all Erin and did him to wit of that which had befallen, how that the grave elders of the most obedient city, second of the realm, had met them in the tholsel, and there, after due prayers to the gods who dwell in ether supernal, had taken solemn counsel whereby they might, if so be it might be, bring once more into honour among mortal men the winged speech of the seadivided Gael.

— It's on the march, says the citizen.To hell with the bloody brutal Sassenachs and their *patois*.

So J. J. puts in a word doing the toff about one story was good till you heard another and blinking facts and the Nelson policy putting your blind eye to the telescope and drawing un a bill of attainder to impeach a nation and Bloom trying to back him up moderation and botheration and their colonies and their civilisation.

— Their syphilisation, you mean, says the citizen. To hell with them! The curse of a goodfornothing God light sideways on the bloody thicklugged sons of whores' gets! No music and no art and no literature worthy of the name. Any civilisation they have they stole from us. Tonguetied sons of bastards' ghosts.

— The European family, says J. J...

— There're not European, says the citizen. I was in Europe with Kevin Egan of Paris. You wouldn't see a trace of them or their language anywhere in Europe except in a *cabinet d'aisance*.

And says John Wyse:

— Full many a flower is born to blush unseen.

And says Lenehan that knows a bit of the lingo:

— *Conspuez les Anglais! Perfide Albion!*

He said and then lifted he in his rude great brawny strengthy hands the medher of dark strong foamy ale and, uttering his tribal slogan *Lamh Dearg Abu,* he drank to the undoing of his foes, a race of mighty valorous heroes, rulers of the waves, who sit on thrones of alabaster silent as the deathless gods.

— What's up with you, says I to Lenehan. You look like a fellow that had lost a bob and found a tanner.

— Gold cup, says he.

— Who won, Mr Lenehan? says Terry.

— *Throwaway*, says he, at twenty to one. A rank outsider. And the rest nowhere.

— And Bass's mare? says Terry.

— Still running, says he. We 're all in a cart. Boylan plunged two quid on my tip *Sceptre* for himself and a lady friend.

— I had half a crown myself, says Terry, on *Zinfandel* that Mr Flynn gave me. Lord Howard de Walden's.

— Twenty to one, says Lenehan. Such is life in an outhouse. *Throwaway*, says he. Takes the biscuit and talking about bunions. Frailty, thy name is *Sceptre.*

So he went over to the biscuit tin Bob Doran left to see if there was anything he could lift on the nod, the old cur after him backing his luck with his mangy snout up. Old mother Hubbard went to the cupboard.

— Not there, my child, says he.

— Keep your pecker up, says Joe. She'd have won the money only for the other dog.

And J. J. and the citizen arguing about law and history with Bloom sticking in an odd word.

— Some people, says Bloom, can see the mote in others' eyes but they can't see the beam in their own.

— *Raimeis*, says the citizen. There's no-one as blind as the fellow that won't see, if you know what that means. Where are our missing twenty millions of Irish should be here today instead of four, our lost tribes? And our potteries and textiles, the finest in the whole world! And our wool that was sold in Rome in the time of Juvenal and our flax and our damask from the looms of Antrim and our Limerick lace, our tanneries and our white flint glass down there by Ballybough and our Huguenot poplin that we have since Jacquard de Lyon and our woven silk and our Foxford tweeds and ivory raised point from the Carmelite convent in New Ross, nothing like it in the whole wide world. Where are the Greek merchants that came through the pillars of Hercules, the Gibraltar now grabbed by the foe of mankind, with gold and Tyrian purple to sell in Wexford at the fair of Carmen ? Read Tacitus and Ptolemy, even Giraldus Cambrensis, Wine, peltries, Connemara marble, silver from Tipperary, second to none, our farfamed horses even today, the Irish hobbies, with king Philip of Spain offering to pay customs duties for the right to fish in our waters. What do the yellowjohns of Anglia owe us for our ruined trade and our ruined hearths? And the beds of the Barrow and Shannon they won't deepen with millions of acres of marsh and bog to make us all die of consumption.

— As treeless as Portugal we'll be soon, says John Wyse, or Heligoland with its one tree if something is not to reafforest the land. Larches, firs, all the trees of the conifer family are going fast. I was reading a report of lord Castletown's...

— Save them, says the citizen,the giant ash of Galway and the chieftain elm of Kildare with a fortyfoot bole and an acre of foliage. Save the trees of Ireland for the future men of Ireland on the fair hills of Eire, O.

— Europe has its eyes on you, says Lenehan.

The fashionable international world attended *en masse* this afternoon at the wedding of the chevalier Jean Wyse de Neaulan, grand high chief ranger of the Irish National Foresters, with Miss Fir Conifer of Pine Valley. Lady Sylvester Elmshade, Mrs Barbara Lovebirch, Mrs Poll Ash, Mrs Holly Hazeleyes, Miss Daphne Bays, Miss Dorothy Canebrake, Mrs Clyde Twelvetrees, Mrs Rowan Greene, Mrs Helen Vinegadding, Miss Virginia Creeper, Miss Gladys Beech, Miss Olive Garth, Miss Blanche Maple, Mrs Maud Mahogany, Miss Myra Myrtle, Miss Priscilla Elderflower, Miss Bee Honeysuckle, Miss Grace Poplar, Miss O Mimosa San, Miss Rachel Cedarfrond, the Misses Lilian and Viola Lilac, Miss Timidity Aspenall, Mrs Kitty Dewey-Mosse, Miss May Hawthorne, Mrs Gloriana Palme, Mrs Liana Forrest, Mrs Arabella Blackwood and Mrs Norma Holyoake of Oakholme Regis graced the ceremony by their presence. The bride who was given away by her father, the M'Conifer of the Glands, looked exquisitely charming in a creation carried out in green mercerised silk, moulded on an underslip of gloaming grey, sashed with a yoke of broad emerald and finished with a triple flounce of darkerhued fringe, the scheme being relieved by bretelles and hip insertions of acorn bronze. The maids of honour, Miss Larch Conifer and Miss Spruce Conifer, sisters of the bride, wore very becoming costumes in the same tone, a dainty *motif* of plume rose being worked into the pleats in a pinstripe and repeated capriciously in the jadegreen toques in the form of heron feathers of paletinted coral. Senhor Enrique Flor presided at the organ with his wellknown ability and, in addition to the prescribed numbers of the nuptial mass, played a new and striking arrangement of *Woodman, spare that tree* at the conclusion of the service. On leaving the church of Saint Fiacre *in Horto* after the papal blessing the happy pair were subjected to a playful crossfire of hazelnuts, beechmast, bayleaves, catkins of willow, ivytod, hollyberries, mistletoe sprigs and quicken shoots. Mr and Mrs Wyse Conifer Neaulan will spend a quiet honeymoon in the Black Forest.

— And our eyes are on Europe, says the citizen. We had our trade with Spain and the French and with the Flemings before those mongrels were pupped, Spanish ale in Galway, the winebark on the winedark waterway.

— And will again, says Joe.

— And with the help of the holy mother of God we will again, says the citizen, clapping his thigh. Our harbours that are empty will be full again, Queenstown, Kinsale, Galway, Blacksod Bay, Ventry in the kingdom of Kerry, Killybegs, the third largest harbour in the wide world with a fleet of masts oi the Galway Lynches and the Cavan O'Reillys and the O'Kennedys of Dublin when the earl of Desmond could make a treaty with the emperor Charles the Fifth himself. And will again, says he, when the first Irish battleship is seen breasting the waves with our own flag to the fore, none of your Henry Tudor's harps, no, the oldest flag afloat, the flag of the province of Desmond and Thomond, three crowns on a blue field, the three sons of Milesius.

And he took the last swig out of the pint, Moya. All wind and piss like a tanyard cat. Cows in Connacht have long horns. As much as his bloody life is worth to go down and address his tall talk to the assembled multitude in Shanagolden where he daren't show his nose with the Molly Maguires looking for him to let daylight through him for grabbing the holding of an evicted tenant.

— Hear, hear to that, says John Wyse. What will you have?

— An imperial yeomanry, says Lenehan, to celebrate the occasion.

— Half one, Terry, says John Wyse, and a hands up. Terry! Are you asleep?

— Yes, sir, says Terry. Small whisky and bottle of Allsop. Right, sir.

Hanging over the bloody paper with Alf looking for spicy bits instead of attending to the general public Picture of a butting match, trying to crack their bloody skulls, one chap going for the other with his head down like a bull at a gate. And another one : *Black Beast Burned in Omaha. Ga.* A lot of Deadwood Dicks in slouch hats and they firing at a sambo strung up on a tree with his tongue out and a bonfire under him. Gob, they ought to drown him in the sea after and electrocute and crucify him to make sure of their job.

— But what about the fighting navy, says Ned, that keeps our foes at bay ?

— I'll tell you what about it, says the citizen. Hell upon earth it is. Read the revelations that's going on in the papers about flogging on the training ships at Portsmouth. A fellow writes that calls himself *Disgusted One.*

So he starts telling us about corporal punishment and about the crew of tars and officers and rearadmirals drawn up in cocked hats and the parson with his protestant bible to witness punishment and a young lad brought out, howling tor his ma, and they tie him down on the buttend of a gun.

— A rump and dozen, says the citizen, was what that old ruffian sir John Beresford called if but the modern God's Englishman calls it caning on the breech.

And says John Wyse :

— 'Tis a custom more honoured in the breach than in the observance.

Then he was telling us the master at arms comes along with a long cane and he draws out and he flogs the bloody backside off of the poor lad till he yells meila murder.

— That's your glorious British navy, says the citizen, that bosses the earth· The fellows that never will be slaves, with the only hereditary chamber on the face of God's earth and their land in the hands of a dozen gamehogs and cottonball barons. That's the great empire they boast about of drudges and whipped serfs.

— On which the sun never rises, says Joe.

— And the tragedy of it is, says the citizen, they believe it. The unfortunate yahoos believe it.

They believe in rod, the scourger almighty, creator of hell upon earth and in Jacky Tar, the son of a gun, who was conceived of unholy boast, born ot the fighting navy, suffered under rump and dozen, was scarified, flayed and curried, yelled like bloody hell, the third day he arose again from the bed, steered into haven, sitteth on his beamend till further orders whence he shall come to drudge for a living and be paid.

— But, says Bloom, isn't discipline the same everywhere. I mean wouldn't it be the same here if you put force against force ?

Didn't I tell you? As true as I'm drinking this porter if he was at his last gasp he'd try to downface you that dying was living.

— We'll put force against force, says the citizen. We have our greater Ireland beyond the sea. They were driven out of house and home in the black 47. Their mudcabins and their shielings by the roadside were laid low by the batteringram and the *Times* rubbed its hands and told the whitelivered Saxons there would soon be as few Irish in Ireland as redskins in America. Even the Grand Turk sent us his piastres. But the Sassenach tried to starve the nation at home while the land was full of crops that the British hyenas bought and sold in Rio de Janeiro. Ay, they drove out the peasants in hordes. Twenty thousand of them died in the coffinships. But those that came to the land of the free remember the land of bondage. And they will come again and with a vengeance, no cravens, the sons of Granuaile, the champions of Kathleen ni Houlihan.

— Perfectly true, says Bloom. But my point was...

— We are a long time waiting for that day, citizen, says Ned. Since the poor old woman told us that the French were on the sea and landed at Killala.

— Ay, says John Wyse. We fought for the royal Stuarts that reneged us against the Williamites and they betrayed us. Remember Limerick and the broken treatystone. We gave our best blood to France and Spain, the wild geese. Fontenoy, eh? And Sarsfield and O'Donnell, duke of Tetuan in Spain, and Ulysses Browne of Camus that was fieldmarshal to Maria Teresa. But what did we ever get for it?

— The French! says the citizen. Set of dancing masters? Do you know what it is? They were never worth a roasted fart to Ireland. Aren't they trying to make an *Entente cordiale* now at Tay Pay's dinnerparty with perfidious Albion? Firebrands of Europe and they always were.

— *Conspuez les Français,* says Lenehan, nobbling his beer.

— And as for the Prooshians and the Hanoverians, says Joe, haven't we had enough of those sausageeating bastards on the throne from George the elector down to the German lad and the flatulent old bitch that's dead?

Jesus, I had to laugh at the way he came out with that about the old one with the winkers on her blind drunk in her royal palace every night of God, old Vic, with her jorum of mountain dew and her coachman carting her up body and bones to roll into bed and she pulling him by the whiskers and singing him old bits of songs about *Ehren on the Rhine* and come where the boose is cheaper.

— Well! says J. J. We have Edward the peacemaker now.

— Tell that to a fool, says the citizen. There's a bloody sight more pox than pax about that boyo. Edward Guelph-Wettin!

— And what do you think, says Joe, of the holy boys, the priests and bishops of Ireland doing up his room in Maynooth in his Satanic Majesty's racing colours and sticking up pictures of all the horses his jockeys rode. The earl of Dublin, no less.

— They ought to have stuck up all the women he rode himself, says little Alf.

And says J. J.:

— Considerations of space influenced their lordships' decision.

— Will you try another, citizen? says Joe.

— Yes, sir, says he, I will.

— You? says Joe.

— Beholden to you, Joe, says I. May your shadow never grow less.

— Repeat that dose, says Joe.

Bloom was talking and talking with John Wyse and he quite excited with his dunducketymudcoloured mug on him and his old plumeyes rolling about.

— Persecution, says he, all the history of the world is full of it. Perpetuating national hatred among nations.

— But do you know what a nation means? says John Wyse.

— Yes, says Bloom.

— What is it? says John Wyse.

— A nation? says Bloom. A nation is the same people living in the same place.

— By God, then, says Ned, laughing, if that's so I'm a nation for I'm living in the same place for the past five years.

So of course everyone had a laugh at Bloom and says he, trying to muck out of it:

— Or also living in different places.

— That covers my case, says Joe.

— What is your nation if I may ask, says the citizen.

— Ireland, says Bloom. I was born here. Ireland.

The citizen said nothing only cleared the spit out of his gullet and, gob, he spat a Red bank oyster out of him right in the corner.

— After you with the push, Joe, says he, taking out his handkerchief to swab himself dry.

— Here you are, citizen, says Joe. Take that in your right hand and repeat after me the following words.

The muchtreasured and intricately embroidered ancient Irish facecloth attributed to Solomon of Droma and Manus Tomaltach og Mac Donogh, authors of the Book of Ballymote, was then carefully produced and called forth prolonged admiration. No need to dwell on the legendary beauty of the cornerpieces, the acme of art, wherein one can distinctly discern each of the four evangelists in turn presenting to each of the four masters his evangelical symbol a bogoak sceptre, a North American puma (a far nobler king of beasts than the British article, be it said in passing), a Kerry calf and a golden eagle from Carrantuohill. The scenes depicted on the emunctory field, showing our ancient duns and raths and cromlechs and grianauns and seats of learning and maledictive stones, are as wonderfully beautiful and the pigments as delicate as when the Sligo illuminators gave free rein to their artistic fantasy long long ago in the time of the Barmecides. Glendalough, the lovely lakes of Killarney, the ruins of Clonmacnois, Cong Abbey, Glen Inagh and the Twelve Pins, Ireland's Eye, the Green Hills of Tallaght, Croagh Patrick, the brewery of Messrs Arthur Guinness, Son and Company (Limited), Lough Neagh's banks, the vale of Ovoca, Isolde's tower, the Mapas obelisk, Sir Patrick Dun's hospital, Cape Clear, the glen of Aherlow, Lynch's castle, the Scotch house, Rathdown Union Workhouse at Loughlinstown, Tullamore jail, Castleconnel rapids, Kilballymacshonakill, the cross at Monasterboice, Jury's Hotel, S. Patrick's Purgatory, the Salmon Leap, Maynooth college refectory, Curley's hole, the three birthplaces of the first duke of Wellington, the rock of Cashel, the bog of Allen, the Henry Street Warehouse, Fingal's Cave, — all these moving scenes are still there for us today rendered more beautiful still by the waters of sorrow which have passed over them and by the rich incrustations of time.

— Show us over the drink? says I. Which is which?

— That's mine, says Joe, as the devil said to the dead policeman.

— And I belong to a race too, says Bloom, that is hated and persecuted. Also now. This very moment. This very instant.

Gob, he near burnt his fingers with the butt of his old cigar.

— Robbed, says he. Plundered. Insulted. Persecuted. Taking what belongs to us by right. At this very moment, says he, putting up his fist, sold by auction off in Morocco like slaves or cattle.

— Are you talking about the new Jerusalem? says the citizen.

— I'm talking about injustice, says Bloom.

— Right, says John Wyse. Stand up to it then with force like men.

That's an almanac picture for you. Mark for a softnosed bullet. Old lardyface standing up to the business end of a gun. Gob, he'd adorn a sweepingbrush, so he would, if he only had a nurse's apron on him. And then he collapses all of a sudden, twisting around all the opposite, as limp as a wet rag.

— But it's no use, says he. Force, hatred, history, all that. That's not life for men and women, insult and hatred. And everybody knows that it's the very opposite of that that is really life.

— What? says Alf.

— Love, says Bloom. I mean the opposite of hatred. I must go now, says he to John Wyse. Just round to the court a moment to see if Martin is there. If he comes just say I'll be back in a second. Just a moment.

Who's hindering you? And off he pops like greased lightning.

— A new apostle to the gentiles, says the citizen. Universal love.

— Well, says John Wyse. Isn't that what we're told. Love your neighbours.

— That chap? says the citizen. Beggar my neighbour is his motto. Love, Moya! He's a nice pattern of a Romeo and Juliet.

Love loves to love love. Nurse loves the new chemist. Constable 14 A loves Mary Kelly. Gerty Mac Dowell loves the boy that has the bicycle. M. B. loves a fair gentleman. Li Chi Han lovey up kissy Cha Pu Chow. Jumbo, the elephant, loves Alice, the elephant. Old Mr Verschoyle with the ear trumpet loves old Mrs Verschoyle with the turnedin eye. The man in the brown macintosh loves a lady who is dead. His Majesty the King loves Her Majesty the Queen. Mrs Norman W. Tupper loves officer Taylor. You love a certain person. And this person loves that other person because everybody loves somebody but God loves everybody.

— Well, Joe, says I, your very good health and song. More power, citizen.

— Hurrah, there, says Joe.

— The blessing of God and Mary and Patrick on you, says the citizen.

And he ups with his pint to wet his whistle.

— We know those canters, says he, preaching and picking your pocket What about sanctimonious Cromwell and his ironsides that put the women and children of Drogheda to the sword with the bible text *God is love* pasted round the mouth of his cannon? The bible! Did you read that skit in the *United Irishman* today about that Zulu chief that's visiting England?

— What's that? says Joe.

So the citizen takes up one of his paraphernalia papers and he starts reading out:

— A delegation of the chief cotton magnates of Manchester was presented yesterday to His Majesty the Alaki of Abeakuta by Gold Stick in Waiting, Lord Walkup of Walkup on Eggs, to tender to His Majesty the heartfelt thanks of British traders for the facilities afforded them in his dominions. The delegation partook of luncheon at the conclusion of which the dusky potentate, in the course of a happy speech, freely translated by the British chaplain, the reverend Ananias Praisegod Barebones, tendered his best thanks to Massa Walkup and emphasized the cordial relations existing between Abeakuta and the British Empire, stating that he treasured as one of his dearest possessions an illuminated bible, the volume of the word of God and the secret of England's greatness, graciously presented to him by the white chief woman, the great squaw Victoria, with a personal dedication from the august hand of the Royal Donor. The Alaki then drank a lovingcup of firstshot usquebaugh to the toast *Black and White* from the skull of his immediate predecessor in the dynasty Kakachakachak, surnamed Forty Warts, after which he visited the chief factory of Cottonopolis and signed his mark in the visitors' book, subsequently executing an old Abeakutic wardance, in the course of which he swallowed several knives and forks, amid hilarious applause from the girl hands.

— Widow woman, says Ned, I wouldn't doubt her. Wonder did he put that bible to the same use as I would.

— Same only more so, says Lenehan. And thereafter in that fruitful land the broadleaved mango flourished exceedingly.

— Is that by Griffith? says John Wyse.

— No, says the citizen. It's not signed Shanganagh. It's only initialled: P.

— And a very good initial too, says Joe.

— That's how it's worked, says the citizen. Trade follows the flag.

— Well, says J. J., if they're any worse than those Belgians in the Congo Free State they must be bad. Did you read that report by a man what's this his name is?

— Casement, says the citizen. He's an Irishman.

— Yes, that's the man, says J. J. Raping the women and girls and flogging the natives on the belly to squeeze all the red rubber they can out of them.

— I know where he's gone, says Lenehan, cracking his fingers.

— Who? says I.

— Bloom, says he, the courthouse is a blind. He had a few bob on *Throwaway* and he's gone to gather in the shekels.

— Is it that whiteeyed kaffir? says the citizen, that never backed a horse in anger in his life.

— That's where he's gone, says Lenehan. I met Bantam Lyons going to back that horse only I put him off it and he told me Bloom gave him the tip. Bet you what you like he has a hundred shillings to five on. He's the only man in Dublin has it. A dark horse.

— He's a bloody dark horse himself, says Joe.

— Mind, Joe, says I. Show us the entrance out.

— There you are, says Terry.

Goodbye Ireland I'm going to Gort. So I just went round to the back of the yard to pumpship and begob (hundred shillings to five) while I was letting off my (*Throwaway* twenty to) letting off my load gob says I to myself I knew he was uneasy in his (two pints off of Joe and one in Slattery's off) in his mind to get off the mark to (hundred shillings is five quid) and when they were in the (dark horse) Pisser Burke was telling me card party and letting on the child was sick (gob, must have done about a gallon) flabbyarse of a wife speaking down the tube *she's better* or *she's* (ow!) all a plan so he could vamoose with the pool if he won or (Jesus, full up I was) trading without a licence (ow!) Ireland my nation says he (hoik! phthook!) never be up to those bloody (there's the last of it) Jerusalem (ah!) cuckoos.

So anyhow when I got back they were at it dingdong, John Wyse saying it was Bloom gave the idea for Sinn Fein to Griffith to put in his paper all kinds of jerrymandering, packed juries and swindling the taxes off of the Government and appointing consuls all over the world to walk about selling Irish industries. Robbing Peter to pay Paul. Gob, that puts the bloody kybosh on it if old sloppy eyes is mucking up the show. Give us a bloody chance. God save Ireland from the likes of that bloody mouseabout. Mr Bloom with his argol bargol. And his old fellow before him perpetrating frauds, old Methusalem Bloom, the robbing bagman, that poisoned himself with the prussic acid after he swamping the country with his baubles and his penny diamonds. Loans by post on easy terms. Any amount of money advanced on note of hand. Distance no object. No security. Gob he's like Lanty Mac Hale's goat that'd go a piece of the road with every one.

— Well, it's a fact, says John Wyse. And there's the man now that'll tell you all about it, Martin Cunningham.

Sure enough the castle car drove up with Martin on it and Jack Power with him and a fellow named Crofter or Crofton, pensioner out of the collector general's, an orangeman Blackburn does have on the registration and he drawing his pay or Crawford gallivanting around the country at the king's expense.

Our travellers reached the rustic hostelry and alighted from their palfreys.

— Ho, varlet! cried he, who by his mien seemed the leader of the party. Saucy knave! To us!

So saying he knocked loudly with his swordhilt upon the open lattice.

Mine host came forth at the summons girding him with his tabard.

— Give you good den, my masters, said he with an obsequious bow.

— Bestir thyself, sirrah! cried he who had knocked. Look to our steeds. And for ourselves give us of your best for ifaith we need it.

— Lackaday, good masters, said the host, my poor house has but a bare larder I know not what to offer your lordships.

— How now, fellow? cried the second of the party, a man of pleasant countenance, so servest thou the king's messengers, Master Taptun?

An instantaneous change overspread the landlord's visage.

— Cry you mercy, gentlemen, he said humbly. An you be the king's messengers (Gold shield His Majesty!) you shall not want for aught. The king's friends (God bless His Majesty!) shall not go afasting in my house I warrant me.

— Then about! cried the traveller who had not spoken, a lusty trencherman by his aspect. Hast aught to give us?

Mine host bowed again as he made answer:

— What say you, good masters, to a squab pigeon pasty, some collops of venison, a saddle of veal, widgeon with crisp hog's bacon, a boar's head with pistachios, a bason of jolly custard, a medlar tansy and a flagon of old Rhenish?

— Gadzooks! cried the last speaker. That likes me well. Pistachios!

— Aha! cried he of the pleasant countenance. A poor house and a bare larder, quotha! 'Tis a merry rogue.

So in comes Martin asking where was Bloom.

— Where is he? says Lenehan. Defrauding widows and orphans.

— Isn't that a fact, says John Wyse, what I was telling the citizen about Bloom and the Sinn Fein?

— That's so, says Martin. Or so they allege.

— Who made those allegations? says Alf.

— I, says Joe. I'm the alligator.

— And after all, says John Wyse, why can't a jew love his country like the next fellow?

— Why not? says J. J., when he's quite sure which country it is.

— Is he a jew or a gentile or a holy Roman or a swaddler or what the hell is he? says Ned. Or who is he? No offence, Crofton.

— We don't want him, says Crofter the Orangeman or presbyterian.

— Who is Junius? says J. J.

— He's a perverted jew, says Martin, from a place in Hungary and it was he drew up all the plans according to the Hungarian system. We know that in the castle.

— Isn't he a cousin of Bloom the dentist? says Jack Power.

— Not at all, says Martin. Only namesakes. His name was Virag. The father's name that poisoned himself. He changed it by deedpoll, the father did.

— That's the new Messiah for Ireland! says the citizen. Island of saints and sages!

— Well, they're still waiting for their redeemer, says Martin. For that matter so are we.

— Yes, says J. J., and every male that's born they think it may be their Messiah. And every jew is in a tall state of excitement, I believe, till he knows if he's a father or a mother.

— Expecting every moment will be his next, says Lenehan.

— O, by God, says Ned, you should have seen Bloom before that son or his that died was born. I met him one day in the south city markets buying a tin of Neave's food six weeks before the wife was delivered.

— *En ventre sa mère,* says J. J.

— Do you call that a man? says the citizen.

— I wonder did he ever put it out of sight, says Joe.

— Well, there were two children born anyhow, says Jack Power.

— And who does he suspect? says the citizen.

Gob, there's many a true word spoken in jest. One of those mixed middlings he is. Lying up in the hotel Pisser was telling me once a month with headache like a totty with her courses. Do you know what I'm telling you? It'd be an act of God to take a hold of a fellow the like of that and throw him in the bloody sea. Justifiable homicide, so it would. Then sloping off with his five quid without putting up a pint of stuff like a man. Give us your blessing. Not as much as would blind your eye.

— Charity to the neighbour, says Martin. But where is he? We can't wait.

— A wolf in sheep's clothing, says the citizen. That's what he is. Virag from Hungary! Ahasuerus I call him. Cursed by God.

— Have you time for a brief libation, Martin? says Ned.

— Only one, says Martin. We must be quick. J. J. and S.

— You, Jack? Crofton? Three half ones, Terry.

— Saint Patrick would want to land again at Ballykinlar and convert us, says the citizen, after allowing things like that to contaminate our shores.

— Well, says Martin, rapping for his glass. God bless all here is my prayer.

— Amen, says the citizen.

— And I'm sure he will, says Joe.

And at the sound of the sacring bell, headed by a crucifer with acolytes, thurifers, boatbearers, readers, ostiarii, deacons and subdeacons, the blessed company drew nigh of mitred abbots and priors and guardians and monks and friars : the monks of Benedict of Spoleto, Carthusians and Camaldolesi, Cistercians and Olivetans, Oratorians and Vallombrosans, and the friars of Augustine, Brigittines, Premonstratesians, Servi, Trinitarians, and the children of Peter Nolasco : and therewith from Carmel mount the children of Elijah prophet led by Albert bishop and by Teresa of Avila, calced and other : and friars brown and grey, sons of poor Francis, capuchins, cordeliers, minimes and observants and the daughters of Clara : and the sons of Dominic, the friars preachers, and the sons of Vincent : and the monks of S. Wolstan : and Ignatius his children : and the confraternity of the christian brothers led by the reverend brother Edmund Ignatius Rice. And after came all saints and martyrs, virgins and confessors: S. Cyr and S. Isidore Arator and S. James the Less and S. Phocas of Sinope and S. Julian Hospitator and S. Felix de Cantalice and S. Simon Stylites and S. Stephen Protomartyr and S. John of God and S. Ferreol and S. Leugarde and S. Theodotus and S. Vulmar and S. Richard and S. Vincent de Paul and S. Martin of Todi and S. Martin of Tours and S. Alfred and S. Joseph and S. Denis and S. Cornelius and S. Leopold and S. Bernard and S. Terence and S. Edward and S. Owen Caniculus and S. Anonymous and S. Eponymous and S. Pseudonymous and S. Homonymous and S. Paronymous and S. Synonymous and S. Laurence O' Toole and S. James of Dingle and Compostella and S. Columcille and S. Columba and S. Celestine and S. Colman and S. Kevin and S. Brendan and S. Frigidian and S. Senan and S. Fachtna and S. Columbanus and S. Gall and S. Fursey and

S. Fintan and S. Fiacre and S. John Nepomuc and S. Thomas Aquinas and S. Ives of Brittany and S. Michan and S. Herman-Joseph and the three patrons of holy youth S. Aloysius Gonzaga and S. Stanislaus Kostka and S. John Berchmans and the saints Gervasius, Servasius and Bonifacius and S. Bride and S. Kieran and S. Canice of Kilkenny and S. Jarlath of Tuam and S. Finbarr and S. Pappin of Ballymun and Brother Aloysius Pacificus and Brother Louis Bellicosus and the saints Rose of Lima and of Viterbo and S. Martha of Bethany and S. Mary of Egypt and S. Lucy and S. Brigid and S. Attracta and S. Dympna and S. Ita and S. Marion Calpensis and the Blessed Sister Teresa of the Child Jesus and S. Barbara and S. Scholastica and S. Ursula with eleven thousand virgins. And all came with nimbi and aureoles and gloriae, bearing palms and harps and swords and olive crowns, in robes whereon were woven the blessed symbols of their efficacies, inkhorns, arrows, loaves, cruses, fetters, axes, trees, bridges, babes in a bathtub, shells, wallets, shears, keys, dragons, lilies, buckshot, beards, hogs, lamps, bellows, beehives, soupladles, stars, snakes, anvils, boxes of vaseline, bells, crutches, forceps, stags' horns, watertight boots, hawks, millstones, eyes on a dish, wax candles, aspergills, unicorns. And as they wended their way by Nelson's Pillar, Henry Street, Mary Street, Capel Street, Little Britain Street, chanting the introit in *Epiphania Domini* which beginneth *Surge, illuminare* and thereafter most sweetly the gradual *Omnes* which saith *de Saba venient* they did divers wonders such as casting out devils, raising the dead to life, multiplying fishes, healing the halt and the blind, discovering various articles which had beed mislaid, interpreting and fulfilling the scriptures, blessing and prophesying. And last, beneath a canopy of cloth of gold came the reverend Father O'Flynn attended by Malachi and Patrick. And when the good fathers had reached the appointed place, the house of Bernard Kiernan and Co, limited, 8, 9 and 10 little Britain street, wholesale grocers, wine and brandy shippers, licensed for the sale of beer, wine and spirits for consumption on the premises, the celebrant blessed the house and censed the mullioned windows and the groynes and the vaults and the arrises and the capitals and the pediments and the cornices and the engrailed arches and the spires and the cupolas and sprinkled the lintels thereof with blessed water and prayed that God might bless that house as he had blessed the house of Abraham and Isaac and Jacob and make the angels of His light to inhabit therein. And entering he blessed the viands and the beverages and the company of all the blessed answered his prayers.

— *Adiutorium nostrum in nomine Domini.*

— *Qui fecit cœlum et terram.*

— *Dominus vobiscum.*

— *Et cum spiritu tuo.*

And he laid his hands upon that he blessed and gave thanks and he prayed and they all with him prayed :

— *Deus, cuius verbo sanctificantur omnia, benedictionem tuam effunde super creaturas istas : et praesta ut quisquis eis secundum legem et voluntatem Tuam cum gratiarum actione usus fuerit per invocationem sanctissimi nominis Tui corporis sanitatem et animæ tutelam Te auctore percipiat per Christum Dominum nostrum.*

— And so say all of us, says Jack.

— Thousand a year, Lambert, says Crofton or Crawford.

— Right, says Ned, taking up his John Jameson. And butter for fish.

I was just looking round to see who the happy thought would strike when be damned but in he comes again letting on to be in a hell of a hurry.

— I was just round at the courthouse. says he, looking for you. I hope I'm not...

— No, says Martin, we're ready.

Courthouse my eye and your pockets hanging down with gold and silver. Mean bloody scut. Stand us a drink itself. Devil a sweet fear! There's a jew for you! All for number one. Cute as a shithouse rat. Hundred to five.

— Don't tell anyone, says the citizen.

— Beg your pardon, says he.

— Come on boys, says Martin, seeing it was looking blue. Come along now.

— Don't tell anyone, says the citizen, letting a bawl out of him. It's a secret.

And the bloody dog woke up and let a growl.

— Bye bye all, says Martin.

And he got them out as quick as he could, Jack Power and Crofton or whatever you call him and him in the middle of them letting on to be all at sea and up with them on the bloody jaunting car.

— Off with you, says Martin to the jarvey.

The milkwhite dolphin tossed his mane and, rising in the golden poop, the helmsman spread the bellying sail upon the wind and stood off forward with all sail set, the spinnaker to larboard. A many comely nymphs drew nigh to starboard and to larboard and, clinging to the sides of the noble bark, they linked their shining forms as doth the cunning wheelwright when he fashions about the heart of his wheel the equidistant rays whereof each one is sister to another and he binds them all with an outer ring and giveth speed to the feet of men whenas they ride to a hosting or contend for the smile of ladies fair. Even so did they come and set them, those willing nymphs, the undying sisters. And they laughed, sporting in a circle of their foam: and the bark clave the waves.

But begob I was just lowering the heel of the pint when I saw the citizen getting up to waddle to the door, puffing and blowing with the dropsy, and he cursing the curse of Cromwell on him, bell, book and candle in Irish, spitting and spatting out of him and Joe and little Alf round him like a leprechaun trying to peacify him.

— Let me alone, says he.

And begob he got as far as the door and they holding him and be bawls out of him:

— Three cheers for Israel!

Arrah, sit down on the parliamentary side of your arse for Christ' sake and don't be making a public exhibition of yourself. Jesus, there's always some bloody clown or other kicking up a bloody murder about bloody nothing. Gob, it'd turn the porter sour in your guts, so it would.

And all the ragamuffins and sluts of the nation round the door and Martin telling the jarvey to drive ahead and the citizen bawling and Alf and Joe at him to whisht and he on his high horse about the jews and the loafers calling for a speech and Jack Power trying to get him to sit down on the car and hold his bloody jaw and a loafer with a patch over his eye starts singing *If the man in the moon was a jew, jew, jew* and a slut shouts out of her:

— Eh, mister! Your fly is open, mister!

And says he:

— Mendelssohn was a jew and Karl Marx and Mercadante and Spinoza. And the Saviour was a jew and his father was a jew. Your God.

— He had no father, says Martin. That'll do now. Drive ahead.

— Whose God! says the citizen.

— Well, his uncle was a jew, says he. Your God was a jew. Christ was a jew like me.

Gob, the citizen made a plunge back into the shop.

— By Jesus, says he, I'll brain that bloody jewman for using the holy name. By Jesus, I'll crucify him so I will. Give us that biscuitbox here.

— Stop! stop! says Joe.

A large and appreciative gathering of friends and acquaintances from the metropolis and greater Dublin assembled in their thousands to bid farewell to

Nagyaságos uram Lipóti Virag, late of Messrs Alexander Thom's, printers to His Majesty, on the occasion of his departure for the distant clime of Százharminczbrojúgulyás-Dugulás (Meadow of Murmuring Waters). The ceremony which went off with great *éclat* was characterised by the most affecting cordiality. An illuminated scroll of ancient Irish vellum, the work of Irish artists, was presented to the distinguished phenomenologist on behalf on a large section of the community and was accompanied by the gift of a silver casket, tastefully executed in the style of ancient Celtic ornament, a work which reflects every credit on the makers, Messrs Jacob *agus* Jacob. The departing guest was the recipient of a hearty ovation, many of those who were present being visibly moved when the select orchestra of Irish pipes struck up the wellknown strains of *Come Back to Erin,* followed immediately by *Rakóczsy's March.* Tarbarrels and bonfires were lighted along the coastline of the four seas on the summits of the Hill of Howth, Three Rock Mountain, Sugarloaf, Bray Head, the mountains of Mourne, the Galtees, the Ox and Donegal and Sperrin peaks, the Nagles and the Bograghs, the Connemara hills, the reeks of M' Gillicuddy, Slieve Aughty, Slieve Bernagh and Slieve Bloom. Amid cheers that rent the welkin, responded to by answering cheers from a big muster of henchmen on the distant Cambrian and Caledonian hills, the mastodontic pleasureship slowly moved away saluted by a final floral tribute from the representatives of the fair sex who were present in large numbers while, as it proceeded down the river, escorted by a flotilla of barges, the flags of the Ballast office and Custom House were dipped in salute as were also those of the electrical power station at the Pigeonhouse. *Visszontlátásra, kedvés barátom! Visszontlátásra!* Gone but not forgotten.

Gob, the devil wouldn't stop him till he got hold of the bloody tin anyhow and out with him and little Alf hanging on to his elbow and he shouting like a stuck pig, as good as any bloody play, in the Queen's royal theatre.

— Where is he till I murder him?

And Ned and J. G. paralysed with the laughing.

— Bloody wars, says I, I'll be in for the last gospel.

But as luck would have it the jarvey got the nag's head round the other way and off with him.

— Hold on, citizen, says Joe. Stop!

Begob he drew his hand and made a swipe and let fly. Mercy of God the sun was in his eyes or he'd have left him for dead. Gob, he near sent it into the county Longford. The bloody nag took fright and the old mongrel after the car like bloody hell and all the populace shouting and laughing and the old tinbox clattering along the street.

The catastrophe was terrific and instantaneous in its effect. The observatory of Dunsink registered in all eleven shocks, all of the fifth grade of Mercalli's scale, and there is no record extant of a similar seismic disturbance in our island since the earthquake of 1534, the year of the rebellion of Silken Thomas. The epicentre appears to have been that part of the metropolis which constitutes the Inn's Quay ward and parish of Saint Michan covering a surface of fortyone acres, two roods and one square pole or perch. All the lordly residences in the vicinity of the palace of justice were demolished and that noble edifice itself, in which at the time of the catastrophe important legal debates were in progress, is literally a mass of ruins beneath which it is to be feared all the occupants have been buried alive. From the reports of eyewitnesses it transpires that the seismic waves were accompanied by a violent atmospheric perturbation of cyclonic character. An article of headgear since ascertained to belong to the much respected clerk of the crown and peace Mr George Fottrell and a silk umbrella with gold handle with the engraved initials, coat of arms and house number of the erudite and worshipful chairman of quarter sessions sir Frederick Falkiner, recorder of Dublin, have been discovered by search parties in remote parts of the island respectively, the former on the third basaltic ridge of the giant's causeway, the latter embedded to the extent of one foot three inches in the sandy beach of Holeopen bay near the old head of Kinsale. Other eyewitnesses depose that they observed an incandescent object of enormous proportions hurtling through the atmosphere at a terrifying velocity in a trajectory directed southwest by west. Messages of condolence and sympathy are being hourly received from all parts of the different continents and the sovereign pontiff has been graciously pleased to decree that a special *missa pro defunctis* shall be celebrated simultaneously by the ordinaries of each and every cathedral church of all the episcopal dioceses subject to the spiritual authority of the Holy See in suffrage of the souls of those faithful departed who have been so unexpectedly called away from our midst. The work of salvage, removal of *débris,* human remains etc has been entrusted to Messrs Michael Meade and Son 159, Great Brunswick Street, and Messrs T. & C. Martin 77, 78, 79 and 80, North Wall, assisted by the men and officers of the Duke of Cornwall's light infantry under the general supervision of H. R. H., rear admiral, the right honourable sir Hercules Hannibal Habeas Corpus Anderson K. G., K. P., K. T., P. C., K. C. B.,

M. P., J. P., M. B., D. S. O., S. O. D., M. F. H., M. R. I. A., B. L., Mus. Doc., P. L. G., F. T. C. D., F. R. U. I., F. R. C. P. I., and F. R. C. S. I.

You never saw the like of it in all your born puff. Gob, if he got that lottery ticket on the side of his poll he'd remember the gold cup, he would so, but begob the citizen would have been lagged for assault and battery and Joe for aiding and abetting. The jarvey saved his life by furious driving as sure as God made Moses. What? O, Jesus, he did. And he let a volley of oaths after him.

— Did I kill him, says he, or what?

And he shouting to the bloody dog:

— After him, Garry! After him, boy!

And the last we saw was the bloody car rounding the corner and old sheepsface on it gesticulating and the bloody mongrel after it with his lugs back for all he was bloody well worth to tear him limb from limb. Hundred to five! Jesus, he took the value of it out of him, I promise you.

When, lo, there came about them all a great brightness and they beheld the chariot wherein He stood ascend to heaven. And they beheld Him in the chariot, clothed upon in the glory of the brightness, having raiment as of the sun, fair as the moon and terrible that for awe they durst not look upon Him. And there came a voice out of heaven, calling: *Elijah! Elijah!* And He answered with a main cry: *Abba! Adonai!* And they beheld Him even Him, ben Bloom Elijah, amid clouds of angels ascend to the glory of the brightness at an angle of fortyfive degrees over Donohoe's in Little Green Street like a shot off a shovel.

The summer evening had begun to fold the world in its mysterious embrace. Far away in the west the sun was setting and the last glow of all too fleeting day lingered lovingly on sea and strand, on the proud promontory of dear old Howth guarding as ever the waters of the bay, on the weedgrown rocks along Sandymount shore and, last but not least, on the quiet church whence there streamed forth at times upon the stillness the voice of prayer to her who is in her pure radiance a beacon ever to the stormtossed heart of man, Mary, star of the sea.

The three girl friends were seated on the rocks, enjoying the evening scene and the air which was fresh but not too chilly. Many a time and oft were they wont to come there to that favourite nook to have a cosy chat beside the sparkling waves and discuss matters feminine, Cissy Caffrey and Edy Boardman with the baby in the pushcar and Tommy and Jacky Caffrey, two little curlyheaded boys, dressed in sailor suits with caps to match and the name H. M. S. Belleisle printed on both. For Tommy and Jacky Caffrey were twins, scarce four years old and very noisy and spoiled twins sometimes but for all that darling little fellows with bright merry faces and endearing ways about them. They were dabbling in the sand with their spades and buckets, building castles as children do, or playing with their big coloured ball, happy as the day was long. And Edy Boardman was rocking the chubby baby to and fro in the pushcar while that young gentleman fairly chuckled with delight. He was but eleven months and nine days old and, though still a tiny toddler, was just beginning to lisp his first babyish words. Cissy Caffrey bent over him to tease his fat little plucks and the dainty dimple in his chin.

— Now, baby, Cissy Caffrey said. Say out big, big. I want a drink of water.

And baby prattled after her :

— A jink a jink a jawbo.

Cissy Caffrey cuddled the wee chap for she was awfully fond of children, so patient with little sufferers and Tommy Caffrey could never be got to take his castor oil unless it was Cissy Caffrey that held his nose and promised him the scatty heel of the loaf or brown bread with golden syrup on. What a persuasive power that girl had ! But to be sure baby was as good as gold, a perfect little dote in his new fancy bib. None of your spoilt beauties, Flora Mac Flimsy sort, was Cissy Caffrey. A truerhearted lass never drew the breath of life, always with a laugh in her gipsylike eyes and a frolicsome word on her cherryripe red lips, a girl lovable in the extreme. And Edy Boardman laughed too at the quaint language of little brother.

But just then there was a slight altercation between Master Tommy and Master Jacky. Boys will be boys and our two twins were no exception to this golden rule. The apple of discord was a certain castle of sand which Master Jacky had built and Master Tommy would have it right go wrong that it was to be architecturally improved by a frontdoor like the Martello tower had. But if Master Tommy was headstrong Master Jacky was selfwilled too and, true to the maxim that every little Irishman's house is his castle, he fell upon his hated rival and to such purpose that the wouldbe assailant came to grief and (alas to relate !) the coveted castle too. Needless to say the cries of discomfited Master Tommy drew the attention of the girl friends.

— Come here, Tommy, his sister called imperatively, at once ! And you, Jacky, for shame to throw poor Tommy in the dirty sand. Wait till I catch you for that.

His eyes misty with unshed tears Master Tommy came at her call for their big sister's word was law with the twins. And in a sad plight he was after his misadventure. His little man-o'-war top and unmentionables were full of sand but Cissy was a past mistress in the art of smoothing over life's tiny troubles and and very quickly not one speck of sand was to be seen on his smart little suit. Still the blue eyes were glistening with hot tears that would well up so she kissed away the hurtness and shook her hand at Master Jacky the culprit and said if she was near him she wouldn't be far from him, her eyes dancing in admonition.

— Nasty bold Jacky ! she cried.

She put an arm round the little mariner and coaxed winningly :

— What's your name ? Butter and cream ?

— Tell us who is your sweetheart, spoke Edy Boardman. Is Cissy your sweetheart?

— Nao, tearful Tommy said.

— Is Edy Boardman your sweetheart? Cissy queried.

— Nao, Tommy said.

— I know, Edy Boardman said none too amiably with an arch glance from her shortsighted eyes. I know who is Tommy's sweetheart, Gerty is Tommy's sweetheart.

— Nao, Tommy said on the verge of tears.

Cissy's quick motherwit guessed what was amiss and she whispered to Edy Boardman to take him there behind the pushcar where the gentlemen couldn't see and to mind he didn't wet his new tan shoes.

But who was Gerty?

Gerty MacDowell who was seated near her companions, lost in thought, gazing far away into the distance was in very truth as fair a specimen of winsome Irish girlhood as one could wish to see. She was pronounced beautiful by all who knew her though, as folks often said, she was more a Giltrap than a MacDowell. Her figure was slight and graceful, inclining even to fragility but those iron jelloids she had been taking of late had done her a world of good much better than the Widow Welch's female pills and she was much better of those discharges she used to get and that tired feeling. The waxen pallor of her face was almost spiritual in its ivorylike purity though her rosebud mouth was a genuine Cupid's bow, Greekly perfect. Her hands were of finely veined alabaster with tapering fingers and as white as lemon juice and queen of ointments could make them though it was not true that she used to wear kid gloves in bed or take a milk footbath either. Bertha Supple told that once to Edy Boardman, a deliberate lie, when she was black out at daggers drawn with Gerty (the girl chums had of course their little tiffs from time to time like the rest of mortals) and she told her not let on whatever she did that it was her that told her or she'd never speak to her again. No. Honour where honour is due. There wasan innate refinement, a languid queenly *hauteur* about Gerty which was unmistakably evidenced in her delicate hands and higharched instep. Had kind fate but willed her to be born a gentlewoman of high degree in her own right and had she only received the benefit of a good education Gerty MacDowell might easily have held her own beside any lady in the land and have seen herself exquisitely gowned with jewels on her brow and patrician suitors at her feet vying with one another to pay their devoirs to her. Mayhap it was this, the love that might have been, that lent to her softlyfeatured face at whiles a look, tense with suppressed meaning, that imparted a strange yearning tendency to the beautiful eyes, a charm few could resist. Why have women such eyes of witchery? Gerty's were of the bluest Irish blue, set off by lustrous lashes and dark expressive brows. Time was when those brows were not so silkilyseductive. It was Madame Vera Verity, directress of the Woman Beautiful page of the Princess novelette, who had first advised her to try eyebrowleine which gave that haunting expression to the eyes, so becoming in leaders of fashion, and she had never regretted it. Then there was blushing scientifically cured and how to be tall increase your height and you have a beautiful face but your nose? That would suit Mrs Dignam because she had a button one. But Gerty's crowning glory was her wealth of wonderful hair. It was dark brown with a natural wave in it. She had cut it that very morning on account of the new moon and it nestled about her pretty head in a profusion of luxuriant clusters and pared her nails too, Thursday for wealth. And just now at Edy's words as a telltale flush, delicate as the faintest rosebloom, crept into her cheeks she looked so lovely in her sweet girlish shyness that of a surety God's fair land of Ireland did not hold her equal.

For an instant she was silent with rather sad downcast eyes. She was about to retort but something checked the words on her tongue. Inclination prompted her to speak out: dignity told her to be silent. The pretty lips pouted a while but then she glanced up and broke out into a joyous little laugh which had in it all the freshness of a young May morning. She knew right well, no-one better, what made squinty Edy say that because of him cooling in his attentions when it was simply a lover's quarrel. As per usual somebody's nose was out of joint about the boy that had the bicycle always riding up and down in front of her window. Only now his father kept him in the evenings studying hard to get an exhibition in the intermediate that was on and he was going to Trinity college to study for a doctor when he left the high school like his brother W. E. Wylie who was racing in the bicycle races in Trinity college university. Little recked he perhaps for what she felt, that dull aching void in her heart sometimes, piercing to the core. Yet he was young and perchance he might learn to love her in time. They were protestants in his family and of course Gerty knew Who came first and after Him the blessed Virgin and then Saint Joseph. But he was undeniably handsome with an exquisite nose and he was what he looked, every inch a gentleman, the shape of his head too at the back without his cap on that she would know anywhere something off the common and the way he turned the bicycle at the lamp with his hands off the bars and also the nice perfume of those good cigarettes and besides they were both of a size and that was why Edy Boardman thought she was so frightfully clever because he didn't go and ride up and down in front of her bit of a garden.

Gerty was dressed simply but with the instinctive taste of a votary of Dame Fashion for she felt that there was just a might that he might be out. A neat blouse of electric blue, selftinted by dolly dyes (because it was expected in the *Lady's Pictorial* that electric blue would be worn), with a smart vee opening down to the division and kerchief pocket (in which she always kept a piece of cottonwool scented with her favourite perfume because the handkerchief spoiled the sit) and a navy threequarter skirt cut to the strideshowed off her slim graceful figure to perfection. She wore a coquettish little love of a hat of wideleaved nigger straw contrast trimmed with an underbrim of eggblue chenille and at the side a butterfly bow to tone. All Tuesday week afternoon she was hunting to match that chenille but at last she found what she wanted at Clery's summer sales, the very it, slightly shopsoiled but you would never notice, seven fingers two and a penny. She did it up all by herself and what joy was hers when she tried it on then, smiling at the lovely reflection which the mirror gave back to her! And when she put it on the waterjug to keep the shape she knew that that would take the shine out of some people she knew. Her shoes were the newest thing in footwear (Edy Boardman prided herself that she was very *petite* but she never had a foot like Gerty MacDowell, a five, and never would ash, oak or elm) with patent toecaps and just one smart buckle at her higharched instep. Her wellturned ankle displayed its perfect proportions beneath her skirt and just the proper amount and no more of her shapely limbs encased in finespun hose with highspliced heels and wide garter tops. As for undies they were Gerty's chief care and who that knows the fluttering hopes and fears of sweet seventeen (though Gerty would never see seventeen again) can find it in his heart to blame her? She had four dinky sets, with awfully pretty stitchery, three garments and nighties extra, and each set slotted with different coloured ribbons, rosepink, pale blue, mauve and peagreen and she aired them herself and blued them when they came home from the wash and ironed them and she had a brickbat to keep the iron on because she wouldn't trust those washerwomen as far as she'd see them scorching the things. She was wearing the blue for luck, hoping against hope, her own colour and the lucky colour too for a bride to have a bit of blue somewhere on her because the green she wore that day week brought grief because his father brought him in to study for the intermediate exhibition and because she thought perhaps he might be out because when she was dressing that morning she nearly slipped up the old pair on her inside out and that was for luck and lovers' meetings if you put those things on inside out so long as it wasn't of a Friday.

And yet and yet! That strained look on her face! A gnawing sorrow is there all the time. Her very soul is in her eyes and she would give worlds to be in the privacy of her own familiar chamber where, giving way to tears, she could have a good cry and relieve her pentup feelings. Though not too much because she knew how to cry nicely before the mirror. You are lovely, Gerty, it said. The paly light of evening falls upon a face infinitely sad and wistful. Gerty MacDowell yearns in vain. Yes, she had known from the first that her daydream of a marriage has been arranged and the weddingbells ringing for Mrs Reggy Wylie T. C. D. (because the one who married the elder brother would be Mrs Wylie) and in the fashionable intelligence Mrs Gertrude Wylie was wearing a sumptuous confection of grey trimmed with expensive blue fox was not to be. He was too young to understand. He would not believe in love, a woman's birthright. The night of the party long ago in Stoers' (he was still in short trousers) when they were alone and he stole an arm round her waist she went white to the very lips. He called her little one in a strangely husky voice and snatched a half kiss (the first!) but it was only the end of her nose and then he hastened from the room with a remark about refreshments. Impetuous fellow! Strength of character had never been Reggy Wylie's strong point and he who would woo and win Gerty MacDowell must be a man among men. But waiting, always waiting to be asked and it was leap year too and would soon be over. No prince charming is her beau ideal to lay a rare and wondrous love at her feet but rather a manly man with a strong quiet face who had not found his ideal, perhaps his hair slightly flecked with grey, and who would understand, take her in his sheltering arms, strain her to him in all the strength of his deep passionate nature and comfort her with a long long kiss. It would be like heaven. For such a one she yearns this balmy summer eve. With all the heart of her she longs to be his only, his affianced bride for riches for poor, in sickness in health, till death us two part, from this to this day forward.

And while Edy Boardman was with little Tommy behind the pushcar she was just thinking would the day ever come when she could call herself his little wife to be. Then they could talk about her till they went blue in the face, Bertha Supple too, and Edy, the spitfire, because she would be twentytwo in November. She would care for him with creature comforts too for Gerty was womanly wise and knew that a mere man liked that feeling of hominess. Her griddlecakes done to a goldenbrown hue and queen Ann's pudding of delightful creaminess had won golden opinions from all because she had a lucky hand also for lighting a fire, dredge in the fine selfraising flour and always stir in the same direction then cream the milk and sugar and whisk well the white of eggs though she didn't like the eating part when there were any people that made her shy and often she wondered why you couldn't eat something poetical like violets or roses and they would have a beautifully appointed drawingroom with pictures and engravings and the photograph of grandpapa Giltrap's lovely dog Garryowen that almost talked, it was so human, and chintz covers for the chairs and that silver toastrack in Clery's summer jumble sales like they have in rich houses. He would be tall with broad shoulders (she had always admired tall men for a husband) with glistening white teeth under his carefully trimmed sweeping moustache and they would go on the continent for their honeymoon (three wonderful weeks!) and then, when they settled down in a nice snug and cosy little homely house, every morning they would both have brekky, simple but perfectly served, for their own two selves and before he went out to business he would give his dear little wifey a good hearty hug and gaze for a moment deep down into her eyes.

Edy Boardman asked Tommy Caffrey was he done and he said yes, so then she buttoned up his little knickerbockers for him and told him to run off and play with Jacky and to be good now and not to fight. But Tommy said he wanted the ball and Edy told him no that baby was playing with the ball and if he took it there'd be wigs on the green but Tommy said it was his ball and he wanted his ball and he pranced on the ground, if you please. The temper of him! O, he was a man already was little Tommy Caffrey since he was out of pinnies. Edy told him no, no and to be off now with him and she told Cissy Caffrey not to give in to him.

— You're not my sister, naughty Tommy said. It's my ball.

But Cissy Caffrey told baby Boardman to look up, look up high at her finger and she snatched the ball quickly and threw it along the sand and Tommy after it in full career, having won the day.

— Anything for a quiet life, laughed Ciss.

And she tickled tiny tot's two cheeks to make him forget and played here's the lord mayor, here's his two horses, here's his gingerbread carriage and here he walks in, chinchopper, chinchopper, chinchopper chin. But Edy got as cross as two sticks about hin getting him own way like that from everyone always petting him.

— I'd like to give him something, she said, so I would, where I won't say.

— On the beeoteetom, laughed Cissy merrily.

Gerty Mac Dowell bent down her head and crimsoned at the idea of Cissy saying an unladylike thing like that out loud she'd be ashamed of her life to say, flushing a deep rosy red, and Edy Boardman said she was sure the gentleman opposite heard what she said. But not a pin cared Ciss.

— Let him! she said with a pert toss of her head and a piquant tilt of her nose. Give it to him too on the same place as quick as I'd look at him.

Madcap Ciss with her golliwog curls. You had to laugh at her sometimes. For instance when she asked you would you have some more Chinese tea and jaspberry ram and when she drew the jugs too and the men's faces on her nails with red ink make you split your sides or when she wanted to go where you know she said she wanted to run and pay a visit to the Miss White. That was just like Cissycums. O, and will you ever forget the evening she dressed up in her father's suit and hat and the burned cork moustache and walked down Tritonville road, smoking a cigarette. There was none to come up to her for fun. But she was sincerity itself, one of the bravest and truest hearts heaven ever made, not one of your twofaced things, too sweet to be wholesome.

And then there came out upon the air the sound of voices and the pealing anthem of the organ. It was the men's temperance retreat conducted by the missioner, the reverend John Hughes S. J. rosary, sermon and benediction of the Most Blessed Sacrament. They were there gathered together without distinction of social class (and a most edifying spectacle it was to see) in that simple fane beside the waves, after the storms of this weary world, kneeling before the feet of the immaculate, reciting the litany of Our Lady of Loreto, beseeching her to intercede for them, the old familiar words, holy Mary, holy virgin of virgins. How sad to poor Gerty's ears! Had her father only avoided the clutches of the demon drink, by taking the pledge or those powders the drink habit cured in Pearson's Weekly, she might now be rolling in her carriage, second to none Over and over had she told herself that as she mused by the dying embers in a brown study without the lamp because she hated two lights or oftentimes gazing out of the window dreamily by the hour at the rain falling on the rusty bucket, thinking. But that vile decoction which has ruined so many hearths and homes had cast its shadow over her childhood days. Nay, she had even witnessed in the home circle deeds of violence caused by intemperance and had seen her own father, a prey to the fumes of intoxication, forget himself completely for if there was one thing of all things that Gerty knew it was the man who lifts his hand to a woman save in the way of kindness deserves to be branded as the lowest of the low.

And still the voices sang in supplication to the Virgin most powerful, Virgin most merciful. And Gerty, wrapt in thought, scarce saw or heard her companions or the twins at their boyish gambols or the gentleman off Sandymount green that Cissy Caffrey called the man that was so like himself passing along the strand taking a short walk. You never saw him anyway screwed but still and for all that she would not like him for a father because he was too old or something or on account of his face (it was a palpable case of doctor Fell) or his carbuncly nose with the pimples on it and his sandy moustache a bit white under his nose. Poor father! With all his faults she loved him still when he sang *Tell me, Mary, how to woo thee* or *My love and cottage near Rochelle* and they had stewed cockles and lettuce with Lazenby's salad dressing for supper and when he sang *The moon hath raised* with Mr Dignam that died suddenly and was buried, God have mercy on him, from a stroke. Her mother's birthday that was and Charley was home on his holidays and Tom and Mr Dignam and Mrs and Patsy and Freddy Dignam and they were to have had a group taken. No-one would have thought the end was so hear. Now he was laid to rest. And her mother said to him to let that be a warning to him for the rest of his days and he couldn't even go to the funeral on account of the gout and she had to go into town to bring him the letters and samples from his office about Catesby's cork lino, artistic standard designs, fit for a palace, gives tiptop wear and always bright and cheery in the home.

A sterling good daughter was Gerty just like a second mother in the house, a ministering angel too with a little heart worth its weight in gold. And when her mother had those raging splitting headaches who was it rubbed on the menthol cone on her forehead but Gerty though she didn't like her mother taking pinches of snuff and that was the only single thing they ever had words about, taking snuff. Everyone thought the world of her for her gentle ways. It was Gerty who turned off the gas at the main every night and it was Gerty who tacked up on the wall of that place where she never forgot every fortnight the chlorate of lime Mr Tunney the grocer's christmas almanac the picture of halcyon days where a young gentleman in the costume they used to wear then with a threecornered hat was offering a bunch of flowers to his ladylove with oldtime chivalry through her lattice window. You could see there was a story behind it. The colours were done something lovely. She was in a soft clinging white in a studied attitude and the gentleman was in chocolate and he looked a thorough aristocrat. She often looked at them dreamily when she went there for a certain purpose and felt her own arms that were white and soft just like hers with the sleeves back and thought about those times because she had found out in Walker's pronouncing dictionary that belonged to grandpapa Giltrap about the halcyon days what they meant.

The twins were now playing in the most approved brotherly fashion, till at last Master Jacky who was really as bold as brass there was no getting behind that deliberately kicked the ball as hard as ever he could down towards the seaweedy rocks. Needless to say poor Tommy was not slow to voice his dismay but luckily the gentleman in black who was sitting there by himself came gallantly to the rescue and intercepted the ball. Our two champions claimed their plaything with lusty cries and to avoid trouble Cissy Caffrey called to the gentleman to throw it to her please. The gentleman aimed the ball once or twice and then threw it up the strand towards Cissy Caffrey but it rolled down the slope and stopped right under Gerty's skirt near the little pool by the rock. The twins clamoured again for it and Cissy told her to kick it away and let them fight for it so Gerty drew back her foot but she wished their stupid ball hadn't come rolling down to her and she gave a kick but she missed and Edy and Cissy laughed.

— If you fail try again, Edy Boardman said.

Gerty smiled assent and bit her lip. A delicate pink crept into her pretty cheek but she was determined to let them see so she just lifted her skirt a little but just enough and took good aim and gave the ball a jolly good kick and it went ever so far and the two twins after it down towards the shingle. Pure jealousy of course it was nothing else to draw attention on account of the gentleman opposite looking. She felt the warm flush, a danger signal always with Gerty MacDowell, surging and flaming into her cheeks. Till then they had only exchanged glances of the most casual but now under the brim of her new hat she ventured a look at him and the face that met her gaze there in the twilight, wan and strangely drawn, seemed to her the saddest she had ever seen.

Through the open window of the church the fragrant incense was wafted and with it the fragrant names of her who was conceived without stain of original sin, spiritual vessel, pray for us, honourable vessel, pray for us, vessel of singular devotion, pray for us, mystical rose. And careworn hearts were there and toilers for their daily bread and many who had erred and wandered, their eyes wet with contrition but for all that bright with hope for the reverend father Hughes had told them what the great saint Bernard said in his famous prayer of Mary, the most pious Virgin's intercessory power that it was not recorded in any age that those who implored her powerful protection were ever abandoned by her.

The twins were now playing again right merrily for the troubles of childhood are but as fleeting summer showers. Cissy played with baby Boardman till he crowed with glee, clapping baby hands in air. Peep she cried behind the hood of the pushcar and Edy asked where was Cissy gone and then Cissy popped up her head and cried ah! and, my word, didn't the little chap enjoy that! And then she told him to say papa.

— Say papa, baby. Say pa pa pa pa pa pa pa.

And baby did his level best to say it for he was very intelligent for eleven months everyone said and big for his age and the picture of health, a perfect little bunch of love, and he would certainly turn out to be something great, they said.

— Haja ja ja haja.

Cissy wiped his little mouth with the dribbling bib and wanted him to sit up properly and say pa pa pa but when she undid the strap she cried out, holy saint Denis, that he was possing wet and to double the half blanket the other way under him. Of course his infant majesty was most obstreperous at such toilet formalities and he let everyone know it :

— Habaa baaaahabaaa baaaa.

And two great big lovely big tears coursing down his cheeks. It was all no use soothering him with no, nono, baby, no and telling him about the geegee and where was the puffpuff but Ciss, always, readywitted, gave him in his mouth the teat of the suckingbottle and the young heathen was quickly appeased.

Gerty wished to goodness they would take their squalling baby home out of that and not get on her nerves no hour to be out and the little brats of twins. She gazed out towards the distant sea. It was like the paintings that man used to do on the pavement with all the coloured chalks and such a pity too leaving them there to be all blotted out, the evening and the clouds coming out and the Bailey light on Howth and to hear the music like that and the perfume of those incense they burned in the church like a kind of waft. And while she gazed her heart went pitapat. Yes, it was her he was looking at and there was meaning in his look. His eyes burned into her as though they would search her through and through, read her very soul. Wonderful eyes they were, superbly expressive, but could you trust them? People were so queer. She could see at once by his dark eyes and his pale intellectual face that he was a foreigner the image of the photo she had of Martin Harvey, the matinée idol, only for the moustache which she preferred because she wasn't stagestruck like Winny Rippingham that wanted they two to always dress the same on account of a play but she could not see whether he had an aquiline nose or a slightly *retroussé* from where he was sitting. He was in deep mourning, she could see that, and the story of a haunting sorrow was written on his face. She would have given worlds to know what it was. He was looking up so intently, so still and he saw her kick the ball and perhaps he could see the bright steel buckles of her shoes if she swung them like that thoughtfully with the toes down. She was glad that something told her to put on the transparent stockings thinking Reggy Wylie might be out but that was far away. Here was that of which she had so often dreamed. It was he who mattered and there was joy on her face because she wanted him because she felt instinctively that he was like no-one else. The very heart of the girlwoman went out to him, her dreamhusband. because she knew on the instant it was him. If he had suffered, more sinned against than sinning, or even, even, if he had been himself a sinner, a wicked man, she cared not. Even if he was a protestant or methodist she could convert him easily if he truly loved her. There were wounds that wanted healing with heartbalm. She was a womanly woman not like other flighty girls, unfeminine, he had known, those cyclists showing off what they hadn't got and she just yearned to know all, to forgive all if she could make him fall in love with her, make him forget the memory of the past. Then mayhap he would embrace her gently, like a real man, crushing her soft body to him, and love her, his ownest girlie, for herself alone.

Refuge of sinners. Comfortress of the afflicted. *Ora pro nobis*. Well has it been said that whosoever prays to her with faith and constancy can never be lost or cast away: and fitly is she too a haven of refuge for the afflicted because of the seven dolours which transpierced her own heart. Gerty could picture the whole scene in the church, the stained glass windows lighted up, the candles, the flowers and the blue banners of the blessed Virgin's sodality and Father

Conroy was helping Canon O'Hanlon at the altar, carrying things in and out with his eyes cast down. He looked almost a saint and his confessionbox was so quiet and clean and dark and his hands were just like white wax and if ever she became a Dominican nun in their white habit perhaps he might come to the convent for the novena of Saint Dominic. He told her that time when she told him about that in confession crimsoning up to the roots of her hair for fear he could see, not to be troubled because that was only the voice of nature and we were all subject to nature's laws, he said, in this life and that that was no sin because that came from the nature of woman instituted by God, he said, and that Our Blessed Lady herself said to the archangel Gabriel be it done unto me according to Thy Word. He was so kind and holy and often and often she thought and thought could she work a ruched teacosy with embroidered floral design for him as a present or a clock but they had a clock she noticed on the mantelpiece white and gold with a canary bird that came out of a little house to tell the time the day she went there about the flowers for the forty hours' adoration because it was hard to know what sort of a present to give or perhaps an album of illuminated views of Dublin or some place.

The exasperating little brats of twins began to quarrel again and Jacky threw the ball out towards the sea and they both ran after it. Little monkeys common as ditchwater. Someone ought to take them and give them a good hiding for themselves to keep them in their places, the both of them. And Cissy and Edy shouted after them to come back because they were afraid the tide might come in on them and be drowned.

— Jacky! Tommy!

Not they! What a great notion they had! So Cissy said it was the very last time she'd ever bring them out. She jumped up and called them and she ran down the slope past him, tossing her hair behind her which had a good enough colour if there had been more of it but with all the thingamerry she was always rubbing into it she couldn't get it to grow long because it wasn't natural so she could just go and throw her hat at it. She ran with long gandery strides it was a wonder she didn't rip up her skirt at the side that was too tight on her because there was a lot of the tomboy about Cissy Caffrey and she was a forward piece whenever she thought she had a good opportunity to show off and just because she was a good runner she ran like that so that he could see all the end of her petticoat running and her skinny shanks up as far as possible. It would have served her just right if she had tripped up over something accidentally on purpose with her high crooked French heels on her to make her look tall and got a fine tumble. *Tableau!* That would have been a very charming exposé for a gentleman like that to witness.

Queen of angels, queen of patriarchs, queen of prophets, of all saints, they prayed, queen of the most holy rosary and then Father Conroy handed the thurible to Canon O' Hanlon and he put in the incense and censed the Blessed Sacrament and Cissy Caffrey caught the two twins and she was itching to give them a ringing good clip on the ear but she didn't because she thought he might be watching but she never made a bigger mistake in all her life because Gerty could see without looking that he never took his eyes off of her and then Canon O'Hanlon handed the thurible back to Father Conroy and knelt down looking up at the Blessed Sacrament and the choir began to sing *Tantum ergo* and she just swung her foot in and out in time as the music rose and fell to the *Tantumer gosa cramen tum*. Three and eleven she paid for those stockings in Sparrow's of Ceorge's street on the Tuesday, no the Monday before Easter and there wasn't a brack on them and that was what he was looking at, transparent, and not at her insignificant ones that had neither shape nor form (the cheek of her!) because he had eyes in his head to see the difference for himself.

Cissy came up along the strand with the two twins and their ball with her hat anyhow on her to one side after her run and she did look a streel tugging the two kids along with the flimsy blouse she bought only a fortnight before like a rag on her back and a bit of her petticoat hanging like a caricature. Gerty just took off her hat for a moment to settle her hair and a prettier, a daintier head of nutbrown tresses was never seen on a girl's shoulders, a radiant little vision, in sooth, almost maddening in its sweetness. You would have to travel many a long mile before you found a head of hair the like of that. She could almost see the swift answering flush of admiration in his eyes that set her tingling in every nerve. She put on her hat so that she could see from underneath the brim and swung her buckled shoe faster for her breath caught as she caught the expression in his eyes. He was eying her as a snake eyes its prey. Her woman's instinct told her that she had raised the devil in him and at the thought a burning scarlet swept from throat to brow till the lovely colour of her face became a glorious rose.

Edy Boardman was noticing it too because she was squinting at Gerty, half smiling, with her specs, like an old maid, pretending to nurse the baby. Irritable little gnat she was and always would be and that was why no-one could get on with her, poking her nose into what was no concern of hers. And she said to Gerty :

— A penny for your thoughts.

— What? replied Gerty with a smile reinforced by the whitest of teeth. I was only wondering was it late.

Because she wished to goodness they'd take the snottynosed twins and their baby home to the mischief out of that so that was why she just gave a gentle hint about its being late. And when Cissy came up Edy asked her the time and Miss Cissy, as glib as you like, said it was half past kissing time, time to kiss again. But Edy wanted to know because they were told to be in early.

— Wait, said Cissy, I'll ask my uncle Peter over there what's the time by his conundrum.

So over she went and when he saw her coming she could see him take his hand out of his pocket, getting nervous, and beginning to play with his watchchain, looking at the church. Passionate nature though he was Gerty could see that he had enormous control over himself. One moment he had been there, fascinated by a loveliness that made him gaze and the next moment it was the quiet gravefaced gentleman, selfcontrol expressed in every line of his distinguishedlooking figure.

Cissy said to excuse her would he mind telling her what was the right time and Gerty could see him taking out his watch, listening to it and looking up and clearing his throat and he said he was very sorry his watch was stopped but he thought it must be after eight because the sun was set. His voice had a cultured ring in it and though he spoke in measured accents there was a suspicion of a quiver in the mellow tones. Cissy said thanks and came back with her tongue out and said uncle said his waterworks were out of order.

Then they sang the second verse of the *Tantum ergo* and Canon O'Hanlon got up again and censed the Blessed Sacrament and knelt down and he told Father Conroy that one of the candles was just going to set fire to the flowers and Father Conroy got up and settled it all right and she could see the gentleman winding his watch and listening to the works and she swung her leg more in and out in time. It was getting darker but he could see and he was looking all the time that he was winding the watch or whatever he was doing to it and then he put it back and put his hands back into his pockets. She felt a kind of a sensation rushing all over her and she knew by the feel of her scalp and that irritation against her stays that that thing must be coming on because the last time too was when she clipped her hair on account of the moon. His dark eyes fixed themselves on her again drinking in her every contour, literally worshipping at her shrine. If ever there was undisguised admiration in a man's passionate gaze it was there plain to be seen on that man's face. It is for you, Gertrude Mac Dowell, and you know it.

Edy began to get ready to go and it was high time for her and Gerty noticed that that little hint she gave had the desired effect because it was a long way along the strand to where there was the place to push up the pushcar and Cissy took off the twins' caps and tidied their hair to make herself attractive of course and Canon O'Hanlon stood up with his cope poking up at his neck and Father Conroy handed him the card to read off and he read out *Panem de coelo praestitisti eis* and Edy and Cissy were talking about the time all the time and asking her but Gerty could pay them back in their own coin and she just answered with scathing politeness when Edy asked her was she heartbroken about her best boy throwing her over. Gerty winced sharply. A brief cold blaze shone from her eyes that spoke volumes of scorn immeasurable. It hurt. O yes, it cut deep because Edy had her own quiet way of saying things like that she knew would wound like the confounded little cat she was. Gerty's lips parted swiftly to frame the word but she fought back the sob that rose to her throat, so slim, so flawless, so beautifully moulded it seemed one an artist might have dreamed of. She had loved him better than he knew. Lighthearted deceiver and fickle like all his sex he would never understand what he had meant to her and for an instant there was in the blue eyes a quick stinging of tears. Their eyes were probing her mercilessly but with a brave effort she sparkled back in sympathy as she glanced at her new conquest for them to see.

— O, responded Gerty, quick as lightning, laughing, and the proud head flashed up. I can throw my cap at who I like because it's leap year.

Her words rang out crystalclear, more musical than the cooing of the ringdove but they cut the silence icily. There was that in her young voice that told that she was not a one to be lightly trifled with. As for Mr Reggy with his swank and his bit of money she could just chuck him aside as if he was so much filth and never again would she cast as much as a second thought on him and tear his silly postcard into a dozen pieces. And if ever after he dared to presume she could give him one look of measured scorn that would make him shrivel up on the spot. Miss puny little Edy's countenance fell to no slight extent and Gerty could see by her looking as black as thunder that she was simply in a towering rage though she hid it, the little kinnatt, because that shaft had struck home for her petty jealousy and they both knew that she was something aloof, apart in another sphere, that she was not of them and there was somebody else too that knew it and saw it so they could put that in their pipe and smoke it.

Edy straightened up baby Boardman to get ready to go and Cissy tucked in the ball and the spades and buckets and it was high time too because the sandman was on his way for Master Boardman junior and Cissy told him too that Billy Winks was coming and that baby was to go deedaw and baby looked just too ducky, laughing up out of his gleeful eyes, and Cissy poked him like that out of fun in his wee fat tummy and baby, without as much as by your leave, sent up his compliments on to his brandnew dribbling bib.

— O my ! Puddeny pie ! protested Ciss. He has his bib destroyed.

The slight *contretemps* claimed her attention but in two twos she set that little matter to rights.

Gerty stifled a smothered exclamation and gave a nervous cough and Edy asked what and she was just going to tell her to catch it while it was flying but she was ever ladylike in her deportment so she simply passed it off with consummate tact by saying that that was the benediction because just then the bell rang out from the steeple over the quiet seashore because Canon O'Hanlon was up on the altar with the veil that Father Conroy put round him round his shoulders giving the benediction with the Blessed Sacrament in his hands.

How moving the scene there in the gathering twilight, the last glimpse of Erin, the touching chime of those evening bells and at the same time a bat flew forth from the ivied belfry through the dusk, hither, thither, with a tiny lost cry. And she could see far away the lights of the lighthouses so picturesque she would have loved to do with a box of paints because it was easier than to make a man and soon the lamplighter would be going his rounds past the presbyterian church grounds and along by shady Tritonville avenue where the couples walked and lighting the lamp near her window where Reggy Wylie used to turn his freewheel like she read in that book *The Lamplighter* by Miss Cummins, author of *Mabel Vaughan* and other tales. For Gerty had her dreams that no-one knew of. She loved to read poetry and when she got a keepsake from Bertha Supple of that lovely confession album with the coralpink cover to write her thoughts in she laid it in the drawer of her toilettable which, though it did not err on the side of luxury, was scrupulously neat and clean. It was there she kept her girlish treasures trove, the tortoiseshell combs, her child of Mary badge, the whiterose scent, the eyebrowleine, her alabaster pouncetbox and the ribbons to change when her things came home from the wash and there were some beautiful thoughts written in it in violet ink that she bought in Hely's of Dame Street for she felt that she too could write poetry if she could only express herself like that poem that appealed to her so deeply that she had copied out of the newspaper she found one evening round the potherbs. *Art thou real, my ideal?* it was called by Louis J. Walsh, Magherafelt, and after there was something about *twilight, wilt thou ever?* and ofttimes the beauty of poetry, so sad in its transient loveliness, had misted her eyes with silent tears that the years were slipping by for her, one by one, and but for that one shortcoming she knew she need fear no competition and that was an accident coming down Dalkey hill and she always tried to conceal it. But it must end she felt. If she saw that magic lure in his eyes there would be no holding back for her. Love laughs at locksmiths. She would make the great sacrifice. Her every effort would be to share his thoughts. Dearer than the whole world would she be to him and gild his days with happiness. There was the allimportant question and she was dying to know was he a married man or a widower who had lost his wife or some tragedy like the nobleman with the foreign name from the land of song had to have her put into a madhouse, cruel only to be kind. But even if — what then? Would it make a very great difference? From everything in the least indelicate her finebred nature instinctively recoiled. She loathed that sort of person, the fallen women off the accommodation walk beside the Dodder that went with the soldiers and coarse men, with no respect for a girl's honour, degrading the sex and being taken up to the police station. No, no: not that. They would be just good friends like a big brother and sister without all that other in spite of the conventions of Society with a big ess. Perhaps it was an old flame he was in mourning for from the days beyond recall. She thought she understood. She would try to understand him because men were so different. The old love was waiting, waiting with little white hands stretched out, with blue appealing eyes. Heart of mine! She would follow her dream of love, the dictates of her heart that told her he was her all in all, the only man in all the world for her for love was the master guide. Nothing else mattered. Come what might she would be wild, untrammelled, free.

Canon O'Hanlon put the Blessed Sacrament back into the tabernacle and the choir sang *Laudate Dominum omnes gentes* and then he locked the tabernacle door because the benediction was over and Father Conroy handed him his hat to put on and crosscat Edy asked wasn't she coming but Jacky Caffrey called out:

— O, look, Cissy!

And they all looked was it sheet lightning but Tommy saw it too over the trees beside the church, blue and then green and purple.

— It's fireworks, Cissy Caffrey said.

And they all ran down the strand to see over the houses and the church, helterskelter, Edy with the pushcar with baby Boardman in it and Cissy holding Tommy and Jacky by the hand so they wouldn't fall running.

— Come on, Gerty, Cissy called. It's the bazaar fireworks.

But Gerty was adamant. She had no intention of being at their beck and call. If they could run like rossies she could sit so she said she could see from where she was. The eyes that were fastened upon her set her pulses tingling. She looked at him a moment, meeting his glance, and a light broke in upon her. Whitehot passion was in that face, passion silent as the grave and it had made her his. At last they were left alone without the others to pry and pass remarks and she knew he could be trusted to the death, steadfast, a sterling man, a man of inflexible honour to his fingertips. His hands and face were working and a tremour went over her. She leaned back far to look up where the fireworks were and she caught her knee in her hands so as not to fall back looking up and there was no-one to see only him and her when she revealed all her graceful beautifully shaped legs like that, supply soft and delicately rounded, and she seemed to hear the panting of his heart, his hoarse breathing, because she knew about the passion of men like that, hotblooded, because Bertha Supple told her once in dead secret and made her swear she'd never about the gentleman lodger that was staying with them out of the Congested Districts Board that had pictures cut out of papers of those skirtdancers and highkickers and she said he used to do something not very nice that you could imagine sometimes in the bed. But this was altogether different from a thing like that because there was all the difference because she could almost feel him draw her face to his and the first quick hot touch of his handsome lips. Besides there was absolution so long as you didn't do the other thing before being married and there ought to be women priests that would understand without your telling out and Cissy Caffrey too sometimes had that dreamy kind of dreamy look in her eyes so that she too, my dear, and Winny Rippingham so mad about actors' photographs and besides it was on account of that other thing coming on the way it did.

And Jacky Caffrey shouted to look, there was another and she leaned back and the garters were blue to match on account of the transparent and they all saw it and shouted to look, look there it was and she leaned back ever so far to see the fireworks and something queer was flying about through the air, a soft thing to and fro, dark. And she saw a long Roman candle going up over the trees up, up, and, in the tense hush, they were all breathless with excitement as it went higher and higher and she had to lean back more and more to look up after it, high, high, almost out of sight, and her face was suffused with a divine, an entrancing blush from straining back and he could see her other things too, nainsook knickers, the fabric that caresses the skin, better than those other pettiwidth, the green, four and eleven, on account of being white and she let him and she saw that he saw and then it went so high it went out of sight a moment and she was trembling in every limb from being bent so far back that he had a full view high up above her knee where no-one ever not even on the swing or wading and she wasn't ashamed and he wasn't either to look in that immodest way like that because he couldn't resist the sight of the wondrous revealment half offered like those skirtdancers behaving so immodest before gentlemen looking and he kept on looking, looking. She would fain have cried to him chokingly, held out her snowy slender arms to him to come, to feel his lips laid on her white brow, the cry of a young girl's love, a little strangled cry, wrung from her, that cry that has rung through the ages. And then a rocket sprang and bang shot blind blank and O! then the Roman candle burst and it was like a sigh of O! and everyone cried O! O! in raptures and it gushed out of it a stream of rain gold hair threads and they shed and ah! they were all greeny dewy stars falling with golden, O so lovely! O so soft, sweet, soft!

Then all melted away dewily in the grey air: all was silent. Ah! She glanced at him as she bent forward quickly, a pathetic little glance of piteous protest, of shy reproach under which he coloured like a girl. He was leaning back against the rock behind. Leopold Bloom (for it is he) stands silent, with bowed head before those young guileless eyes. What a brute he had been! At it again? A fair unsullied soul had called to him and, wretch that he was, how had he answered? An utter cad he had been. He of all men! But there was an infinite store of mercy in those eyes, for him too a word of pardon even though he had erred and sinned and wandered. Should a girl tell? No, a thousand times no. That was their secret, only theirs, alone in the hiding twilight and there was none to know or tell save the little bat that flew so softly through the evening to and fro and little bats don't tell.

Cissy Caffrey whistled, imitating the boys in the football field to show what a great person she was: and then she cried:

— Gerty! Gerty! We're going. Come on. We can see from farther up.

Gerty had an idea, one of love's little ruses. She slipped a hand into her kerchief pocket and took out the wadding and waved in reply of course without letting him and then slipped it back. Wonder if he's too far to. She rose. Was it goodbye? No. She had to go but they would meet again, there, and she would dream of that till then, tomorrow, of her dream of yester eve. She drew herself up to her full height. Their souls met in a last lingering glance and the eyes that reached her heart, full of a strange shining, hung enraptured on her sweet flowerlike face. She half smiled at him wanly, a sweet forgiving smile, a smile that verged on tears, and then they parted.

Slowly without looking back she went down the uneven strand to Cissy, to Edy, to Jacky and Tommy Caffrey, to little baby Boardman. It was darker now and there were stones and bits of wood on the strand and slippy seaweed. She walked with a certain quiet dignity characteristic of her but with care and very slowly because, because Gerty MacDowell was.....

Tight boots? No. She's lame! O!

Mr Bloom watched her as she limped away. Poor girl! That's why she's left on the shelf and the others did a sprint. Thought something was wrong by the cut of her jib. Jilted beauty. A defect is ten times worse in a woman. But makes them polite. Glad I didn't know it when she was on show. Hot little devil all the same. Wouldn't mind. Curiosity like a nun or a negress or a girl with glasses. That squinty one is delicate. Near her monthlies, I expect, makes them feel ticklish. I have such a bad headache today. Where did I put the letter? Yes, all right. All kinds of crazy longings. Licking pennies. Girl in Tranquilla convent that nun told me liked to smell rock oil. Virgins go mad in the end I suppose. Sister? How many women in Dublin have it today? Martha, she. Something in the air. That's the moon. But then why don't all women menstruate at the same time with same moon, I mean? Depends on the time they were born, I suppose. Or all start scratch then get out of step. Sometimes Molly and Milly together. Anyhow I got the best of that. Damned glad I didn't do it in the bath this morning over her silly I will punish you letter. Made up for that tramdriver this morning. That gouger M'Coy stopping me to say nothing. And his wife engagement in the country valise, voice like a pickaxe. Thankful for small mercies. Cheap too. Yours for the asking. Because they want it themselves. Their natural craving. Shoals of them every evening poured out of offices. Reserve better. Don't want it they throw it at you. Catch em alive, O. Pity they can't see themselves. A dream of wellfilled hose. Where was that? Ah, yes. Mutoscope pictures in Capel street: for men only. Peeping Tom. Willy's hat and what the girls did with it. Do they snapshot those girls or is it all a fake. *Lingerie* does it. Felt for the curves inside her *deshabillé*. Excites them also when they're. I'm all clean come and dirty me. And they like dressing one another for the sacrifice. Milly delighted with Molly's new blouse. At first. Put them all on to take them all off. Molly. Why I bought her the violet garters. Us too : the tie he wore, his lovely socks and turnedup trousers. He wore a pair of gaiters the night that first we met. His lovely shirt was shining beneath his what? of jet. Say a woman loses a charm with every pin she takes out. Pinned together. O Mairy lost the pin of her. Dressed up to the nines for somebody. Fashion part of their charm. Just changes when you're on the track of the secret. Except the east : Mary, Martha : now as then. No reasonable offer refused. She wasn't in a hurry either. Always off to a fellow when they are. They never forget an appointment. Out on spec probably. They believe in chance because like themselves. And the others inclined to give her an odd dig. Girl friends at school, arms round each other's necks or with ten fingers locked, kissing and whispering secrets about nothing in the convent garden. Nuns with whitewashed faces, cool coif and their rosaries going up and down, vindictive too for what they can't get. Barbed wire. Be sure now and write to me. And I'll write to you. Now won't you? Molly and Josie Powell. Till Mr Right comes, along then meet once in a blue moon. *Tableau!* O, look who it is for the love of God! How are you at all? What have you been doing with yourself? Kiss and delighted to, kiss, to see you. Picking holes in each other's appearance. You're looking splendid. Sister souls showing their teeth at one another. How many have you left? Wouldn't lend each other a pinch ot salt.

Ah!

Devils they are when that's coming on them. Dark devilish appearance. Molly often told me feel things a ton weight. Scratch the sole of my foot. O that way! O, that's exquisite! Feel it myself too. Good to rest once in a way. Wonder if it's bad to go with them then. Safe in one way. Turns milk, makes fiddlestrings snap. Something about withering plants I read in a garden. Besides they say if the flower withers she wears she's a flirt. All are. Daresay she felt I. When you feel like that you often meet what you feel. Liked me or what? Dress they look at. Always know a fellow courting : collars and cuffs. Well cocks and lions do the same and stags. Same time might prefer a tie undone or something. Trousers? Suppose I when I was? No. Gently does it. Dislike rough and tumble. Kiss in the dark and never tell. Saw something in me. Wonder what. Sooner have me as I am than some poet chap with bearsgrease plastery hair, lovelock over his dexter optic. To aid gentleman in literary. Ought to attend to my appearance my age. Didn't let her see me in profile. Still, you never know. Pretty girls and ugly men marrying. Beauty and the beast. Besides I can't be so if Molly. Took off her hat to show her hair. Wide brim bought to hide her face, meeting someone might know her, bend down or carry a bunch of flowers to smell. Hair strong in rut. Ten bob I got for Molly's combings when we were on the rocks in Holles street. Why not? Suppose he gave her money. Why not? All a prejudice. She's worth ten, fifteen, more a pound. What? I think so. All that for nothing. Bold hand. Mrs Marion. Did I forget to write address on that letter like the postcard I sent to Flynn. And the day I went to Drimmie's without a necktie. Wrangle with Molly it was put me off. No, I remember. Richie Goulding. He's another. Weighs on his mind. Funny my watch stopped at half past four. Dust. Shark liver oil they use to clean could do it myself. Save. Was that just when he, she?

O, he did. Into her. She did. Done.

Ah!

Mr Bloom with careful hand recomposed his wet shirt. O Lord, that little limping devil. Begins to feel cold and clammy. After effect not pleasant. Still you have to get rid of it someway. They don't care. Complimented perhaps. Go home to nicey bread and milky and say night prayers with the kiddies. Well, aren't they. See her as she is spoil all. Must have the stage setting, the rouge, costume, position, music. The name too. *Amours* of actresses. Nell Gwynn, Mrs Bracegirdle, Maud Branscombe. Curtain up. Moonlight silver effulgence. Maiden discovered with pensive bosom. Little sweetheart come and kiss me. Still I feel. The strength it gives a man. That's the secret of it. Good job I let off there behind coming out of Dignam's. Cider that was. Otherwise I couldn't have. Makes you want to sing after. *Lacaus esant taratara.* Suppose I spoke to her. What about? Bad plan however of you don't know how to end the conversation. Ask them a question they ask you another. Good idea if you're in a cart. Wonderful of course if you say: good evening, and you see she's on for it: good evening. O but the dark evening in the Appian way I nearly spoke to Mrs Clinch O thinking she was. Whew! Girl in Meath street that night. All the dirty things I made her say all wrong of course. My arks she called it. It's so hard to find one who. Aho! If you don't answer when they solicit must be horrible for them till they harden. And kissed my hand when I gave her the extra two shillings. Parrots. Press the button and the bird will squeak. Wish she hadn't called me sir. O, her mouth in the dark! And you a married man with a single girl! That's what they enjoy. Taking a man from another woman. Or even hear of it. Different with me. Glad to get away from other chap's wife. Eating off his cold plate. Chap in the Burton today spitting back gumchewed gristle. French letter still in my pocketbook. Cause of half the trouble. But might happen sometime, I don't think. Come in. All is prepared. I dreamt. What? Worst is beginning. How they change the venue when it's not what they like. Ask you do you like mushrooms because she once knew a gentleman who. Or ask you what someone was going to say when he changed his mind and stopped. Yet if I went the whole hog, say: I want to, something like that. Because I did. She too. Offend her. Then make it up. Pretend to want something awfully, then cry off for her sake. Flatters them. She must have been thinking of someone else all the time. What harm? Must since she came to the use of reason, he, he and he. First kiss does the trick. The propitious moment. Something inside them goes pop. Mushy like, tell by their eye, on the sly. First thoughts are best. Remember that till their dying day. Molly, lieutenant Mulvey that kissed her under the Moorish wall beside the gardens. Fifteen she told me. But her breasts were developed. Fell asleep then. After Glencree dinner that was when we drove home the featherbed mountain. Gnashing her teeth in sleep. Lord mayor had his eye on her too. Val Dillon. Apoplectic.

There she is with them down there for the fireworks. My fireworks. Up like a rocket, down like a stick. And the children, twins they must be, waiting for something to happen. Want to be grownups. Dressing in mother's clothes. Time enough, understand all the ways of the world. And the dark one with the mop head and the nigger mouth. I knew she could whistle. Mouth made for that. Like Molly. Why that high class whore in Jammet's wore her veil only to her nose. Would you mind, please, telling me the right time? I'll tell you the right time up a dark lane. Say prunes and prisms forty times every morning, cure for fat lips. Caressing the little boy too. Onlookers see most of the game. Of course they understand birds, animals, babies. In their line.

Didn't look back when she was going down the strand. Wouldn't give that satisfaction. Those girls, those girls, those lovely seaside girls. Fine eyes she had, clear. It's the white of the eye brings that out not so much the pupil. Did she know what I? Course. Like a cat sitting beyond a dog's jump. Women never meet one like that Wilkins in the high school drawing a picture of Venus with all his belongings on show. Call that innocence? Poor idiot! His wife has her work cut out for her. Never see them sit on a bench marked *Wet Paint*. Eyes all over them. Look under the bed for what's not there. Longing to get the fright of their lives. Sharp as needles they are. When I said to Molly the man at the corner of Cuffe street was goodlooking, thought she might like, twigged at once he had a false arm. Had too. Where do they get that? Typist going up Roger Greene's stairs two at a time to show her understandings. Handed down from father to mother to daughter, I mean. Bred in the bone. Milly for example drying her handkerchief on the mirror to save the ironing. Best place for an ad to catch a woman's eye on a mirror. And when I sent her for Molly's Paisley shawl to Presscott's, by the way that ad I must, carrying home the change in her stocking. Clever little minx! I never told her. Neat way she carries parcels too. Attract men, small thing like that. Holding up her hand, shaking it, to let the blood flow back when it was red. Who did you learn that from? Nobody. Something the nurse taught me. O, don't they know? Three years old she was in front of Molly's dressingtable just before we left Lombard street west. Me have a nice pace. Mullingar. Who knows? Ways of the world. Young student. Straight on her pins anyway not like the other. Still she was game. Lord, I am wet. Devil you are. Swell of her calf. Transparent stockings, stretched to breaking point. Not like that frump today. A. E. Rumpled stockings. Or the one in Grafton street. White. Wow! Beef to the heel.

A monkey puzzle rocket burst, spluttering in darting crackles. Zrads and zrads, zrads, zrads. And Cissy and Tommy ran out to see and Edy after with the pushcar and then Gerty beyond the curve of the rocks. Will she? Watch! Watch! See! Looked round. She smelt an onion. Darling, I saw your. I saw all.

Lord!

Did me good all the same. Off colour after Kiernan's, Dignam's. For this relief much thanks. In *Hamlet*, that is. Lord! It was all things combined. Excitement. When she leaned back felt an ache at the butt of my tongue. Your head it simply swirls. He's right. Might have made a worse fool of myself however. Instead of talking about nothing. Then I will tell you all. Still it was a kind of language between us. It couldn't be? No, Gerty they called her. Might be false name however like my and the address Dolphin's barn a blind.

Her maiden name was Jemima Brown
And she lived with her mother in Irishtown.

Place made me think of that I suppose. All tarred with the same brush. Wiping pens in their stockings. But the ball rolled down to her as if it understood. Every bullet has its billet. Course I never could throw anything straight at school. Crooked as a ram's horn. Sad however because it lasts only a few years till they settle down to potwalloping and papa's pants will soon fit Willy and fullers' earth for the baby when they hold him out to do ah ah. No soft job. Saves them. Keeps them out of harm's way. Nature. Washing child, washing corpse. Dignam. Children's hands always round them. Cocoanut skulls, monkeys, not even closed at first, sour milk in their swaddles and tainted curds. Oughtn't to have given that child an empty teat to suck. Fill it up with wind. Mrs Beaufoy, Purefoy. Must call to the hospital. Wonder is nurse Callan there still. She used to look over some nights when Molly was in the Coffee Palace. That young doctor O'Hare I noticed her brushing his coat. And Mrs Breen and Mrs Dignam once like that too, marriageable. Worst of all at night Mrs Duggan told me in the City Arms. Husband rolling in drunk, stink of pub off him like a polecat. Have that in your nose in the dark, whiff of stale boose. Then ask in the morning : was I drunk last night? Bad policy however to fault the husband. Chickens come home to roost. They stick by one another like glue. Maybe the women's fault also. That's where Molly can knock spots off them. It is the blood of the south. Moorish. Also the form, the figure. Hands felt for the opulent. Just compare for instance those others. Wife locked up at home, skeleton in the cupboard. Allow me to introduce my. Then they trot you out some kind of a nondescript, wouldn't know what to call her. Always see a fellow's weak point in his wife. Still there's destiny in it, falling in love. Have their own secrets between them. Chaps that would go to the dogs if some woman didn't take them in hand. Then little chits of girls, height of a shilling in coppers, with little hubbies. As God made them He matched them. Sometimes children turn out well enough. Twice nought makes one. Or old rich chap of seventy and blushing bride. Marry in May and repent in December. This wet is very unpleasant. Stuck. Well the foreskin is not back. Better detach.

Ow!

Other hand a sixfooter with a wifey up to his watchpocket. Long and the short of it. Big he and little she. Very strange about my watch. Wristwatches are always going wrong. Wonder is there any magnetic influence between the person because that was about the time he. Yes, I suppose at once. Cat's away the mice will play. I remember looking in Pill lane. Also that now is magnetism.

Back of everything magnetism. Earth for instance pulling this and being pulled. That causes movement. And time ? Well that's the time the movement takes. Then if one thing stopped the whole ghesabo would stop bit by bit. Because it's all arranged. Magnetic needle tells you what's going on in the sun, the stars. Little piece of steel iron. When you hold out the fork. Come. Come. Tip. Woman and man that is. Fork and steel. Molly, he. Dress up and look and suggest and let you see and see more and defy you if you're a man to see that and, like a sneeze coming, legs, look, look and if you have any guts in you. Tip. Have to let fly.

Wonder how is she feeling in that region. Shame all put on before third person. More put out about a hole in her stocking. Molly, her underjaw stuck out, head back, about the farmer in the ridingboots and spurs at the horse show. And when the painters were in Lombard street west. Fine voice that fellow had. How Giuglini began. Smell that I did, like flowers. It was too. Violets. Came from the turpentine probably in the paint. Make their own use of everything. Same time doing it scraped her slipper on the floor so they wouldn't hear. But lots of them can't kick the beam, I think. Keep that thing up for hours. Kind of a general all round over me and half down my back.

Wait. Hm. Hm. Yes. That's her perfume. Why she waved her hand. I leave you this to think of me when I'm far away on the pillow. What is it ? Heliotrope ? No, Hyacinth ? Hm. Roses, I think. She'd like scent of that kind. Sweet and cheap : soon sour. Why Molly likes opoponax. Suits her with a little jessamine mixed. Her high notes and her low notes. At the dance night she met him, dance of the hours. Heat brought it out. She was wearing her black and it had the perfume of the time before. Good conductor, is it ? Or bad ? Light too. Suppose there's some connection. For instance if you go into a cellar where it's dark. Mysterious thing too. Why did I smell it only now ? Took its time in coming like herself, slow but sure. Suppose it's ever so many millions of tiny grains blown across. Yes, it is. Because those spice islands, Cinghalese this morning, smell them leagues off. Tell you what it is. It's like a fine fine veil or web they have all over the skin, fine like what do you call it gossamer and they're always spinning it out of them, fine as anything, rainbow colours without knowing it. Clings to everything she takes off. Vamp of her stockings. Warm shoe. Stays. Drawers : little kick, taking them off. Byby till next time. Also the cat likes to sniff in her shift on the bed. Know her smell in a thousand. Bathwater too. Reminds me of strawberries and cream. Wonder where it is really. There or the armpits or under the neck. Because you get it out of all holes and corners. Hyacinth perfume made of oil or ether or something. Muskrat. Bag under their tails one grain pour off odour for years. Dogs at each other behind. Good evening. Evening. How do you sniff? Hm. Hm. Very well, thank you. Animals go by that. Yes now, look at it that way. We're the same. Some women for instance warn you off when they have their period. Come near. Then get a hogo you could hang your hat on. Like what? Potted herrings gone stale or. Boof! Please keep off the grass.

Perhaps they get a man smell off us. What though? Cigary gloves Long John had on his desk the other. Breath? What you eat and drink gives that. No. Mansmell, I mean. Must be connected with that because priests that are supposed to be are different. Women buzz round it like flies round treacle. Railed off the altar get on to it at any cost. The tree of forbidden priest. O father, will you? Let me be the first to. That diffuses itself all through the body, permeates. Source of life and it's extremely curious the smell. Celery sauce. Let me.

Mr Bloom inserted his nose. Hm. Into the. Hm. Opening of his waistcoat. Almonds or. No. Lemons it is. Ah no, that's the soap.

O by the by that lotion. I knew there was something on my mind. Never went back and the soap not paid. Dislike carrying bottles like that hag this morning. Hynes might have paid me that three shillings. I could mention Meagher's just to remind him. Still if he works that paragraph. Two and nine. Bad opinion of me he'll have. Call tomorrow. How much do I owe you? Three and nine? Two and nine, sir. Ah. Might stop him giving credit another time. Lose your customers that way. Pubs do. Fellows run up a bill on the slate and then slinking around the back streets into somewhere else.

Here's this nobleman passed before. Blown in from the bay. Just went as far as turn back. Always at home at dinnertime. Looks mangled out: had a good tuck in. Enjoying nature now. Grace after meals. After supper walk a mile. Sure he has a small bank balance somewhere, government sit. Walk after him now make him awkward like those newsboys me today. Still you learn something. See ourselves as others see us. So long as women don't mock what matter? That's the way to find out. Ask yourself who is he now. *The Mystery Man on the Beach,* prize titbit story by Mr Leopold Bloom. Payment at the rate of one guinea per column. And that fellow today at the graveside in the brown macintosh. Corns on his kismet however. Healthy perhaps absorb all the. Whistle brings rain they say. Must be some somewhere. Salt in the

Ormond damp. The body feels the atmosphere. Old Betty's joints are on the rack. Mother Shipton's prophecy that is about ships around they fly in the twinkling. No. Signs of rain it is. The royal reader. And distant hills seem coming nigh.

Howth. Bailey light. Two, four, six, eight, nine. See. Has to change or they might think it a house. Wreckers. Grace darling. People afraid of the dark. Also glowworms, cyclists : lightingup time. Jewels diamonds flash better. Light is a kind of reassuring. Not going to hurt you. Better now of course than long ago. Country roads. Run you through the small guts for nothing. Still two types there are you bob against. Scowl or smile. Pardon ! Not at all. Best time to spray plants too in the shade after the sun. Some light still. Red rays are longest. Roygbiv Vance taught us : red, orange, yellow, green, blue, indigo, violet. A star I see. Venus ? Can't tell yet. Two, when three it's night. Were those nightclouds there all the time ? Looks like a phantom ship. No. Wait. Trees are they ? An optical illusion. Mirage. Land of the setting sun this. Homerule sun setting in the southeast. My native land, goodnight.

Dew falling. Bad for you, dear, to sit on that stone. Brings on white fluxions. Never have little baby then less he was big strong fight his way up through. Might get piles myself. Sticks too like a summer cold, sore on the mouth. Cut with grass or paper worst, Friction of the position. Like to be that rock she sat on. O sweet little, you don't know how nice you looked. I begin to like them at that age. Green apples. Grab at all that offer. Suppose it's the only time we cross legs, seated. Also the library today : those girl graduates. Happy chairs under them. But it's the evening influence. They feel all that. Open like flowers, know their hours, sunflowers, Jerusalem artichokes, in ballrooms, chandeliers, avenues under the lamps. Nightstock in Mat Dillon's garden where I kissed her shoulder. Wish I had a full length oilpainting of her then. June that was too I wooed. The year returns. History repeats itself. Ye crags and peaks I'm with you once again. Life, love, voyage round your own little world. And now ? Sad about her lame of course but must be on your guard not to feel too much pity. They take advantage.

All quiet on Howth now. The distant hills seem. Where we. The rhododendrons. I am a fool perhaps. He gets the plums and I the plumstones. Where I come in. All that old hill has seen. Names change : that's all. Lovers : yum yum.

Tired I feel now. Will I get up ? O wait. Drained all the manhood out of me, little wretch. She kissed me. My youth. Never again. Only once it comes.

Or hers. Take the train there tomorrow. No. Returning not the same. Like kids your second visit to a house. The new I want. Nothing new under the sun. Care of P. O. Dolphin's barn. Are you not happy in your? Naughty darling. At Dolphin's barn charades in Luke Doyle's house. Mat Dillon and his bevy of daughters: Tiny, Atty, Floey, Maimy, Louy, Hetty. Molly too. Eightyseven that was. Year before we. And the old major partial to his drop of spirits. Curious she an only child, I an only child. So it returns. Think you're escaping and run into yourself. Longest way round is the shortest way home. And just when he and she. Circus horse walking in a ring. Rip van Winkle we played. Rip: tear in Henny Doyle's overcoat. Van: breadvan delivering. Winkle: cockles and periwinkles. Then I did Rip van Winkle coming back. She leaned on the sideboard watching. Moorish eyes. Twenty years asleep in Sleepy Hollow. All changed. Forgotten. The young are old. His gun rusty from the drew.

Ba. What is that flying about? Swallow? Bat probably. Thinks I'm a tree, so blind. Have birds no smell? Metempsychosis. They believed you could be changed into a tree from grief. Weeping willow. Ba. There he goes. Funny little beggar. Wonder where he lives. Belfry up there. Very likely. Hanging by his heels in the odour of sanctity. Bell scared him out, I suppose. Mass seems to be over. Could hear them all at it. Pray for us. And pray for us. And pray for us. Good idea the repetition. Same thing with ads. Buy from us. And buy from us. Yes, there's the light in the priest's house. Their frugal meal. Remember about the mistake in the valuation when I was in Thom's. Twentyeight it is. Two houses they have. Gabriel Conroy's brother is curate. Ba. Again. Wonder why they come out at night like mice. They're a mixed breed. Birds are like hopping mice. What frightens them, light or noise? Better sit still. All instinct like the bird in drouth got water out of the end of a jar by throwing in pebbles. Like a little man in a cloak he is with tiny hands. Weeny bones. Almost see them shimmering, kind of a bluey white. Colours depend on the light you see. Stare the sun for example like the eagle then look at a shoe see a blotch blob yellowish. Wants to stamp his trademark on everything. Instance, that cat this morning on the staircase. Colour of brown turf. Say you never see them with three colours. Not true. That half tabbywhite tortoiseshell in the *City Arms* with the letter em on her forehead. Body fifty different colours. Howth a while ago amethyst. Glass flashing. That's how that wise man what's his name with the burning glass. Then the heather goes on fire. It can't be tourists' matches. What? Perhaps the sticks dry rub together in the wind and light. Or broken bottles in the furze act as a burning glass in the sun. Archimedes. I have it! My memory's not so bad.

Ba. Who knows what they're always flying for. Insects? That bee last week got into the room playing with his shadow on the ceiling. Might be the one bit me, come back to see. Birds too never find out what they say. Like our small talk. And says she and says he. Nerve they have to fly over the ocean and back. Lots must be killed in storms, telegraph wires. Dreadful life sailors have too. Big brutes of oceangoing steamers floundering along in the dark, lowing out like seacows. *Faugh a ballagh.* Out of that, bloody curse to you. Others in vessels, bit of a handkerchief sail, pitched about like snuff at a wake when the stormy winds do blow. Married too. Sometimes away for years at the ends of the earth somewhere. No ends really because it's round. Wife in every port they say. She has a good job if she minds it till Johnny comes marching home again. If ever he does. Smelling the tail end of ports. How can they like the sea? Yet they do. The anchor's weighed. Off he sails with a scapular or a medal on him for luck. Well? And the tephilim no what's this they call it poor papa's father had on his door to touch. That brought us out of the land of Egypt and into the house of bondage. Something in all those superstitions because when you go out never know what dangers. Hanging on to a plank or astride of a beam for grim life, lifebelt round round him, gulping salt water, and that's the last of his nibs till the sharks catch hold of him. Do fish ever get seasick?

Then you have a beautiful calm without a cloud, smooth sea, placid, crew and cargo in smithereens, Davy Jones' locker. Moon looking down. Not my fault, old cockalorum.

A lost long candle wandered up the sky from Mirus bazaar in search of funds for Mercer's hospital and broke, drooping, and shed a cluster of violet but one white stars. They floated, fell : they faded. The shepherd's hour : the hour of folding : hour of tryst. From house to house, giving his everwelcome double knock, went the nine o'clock postman, the glowworm's lamp at his belt gleaming here and there through the laurel hedges. And among the five young trees a hoisted lintstock lit the lamp at Leahy's terrace. By screens of lighted windows, by equal gardens a shrill voice went crying, wailing : *Evening Telegraph, stop press edition! Result of the Gold Cup races!* and from the door of Dignam's house a boy ran out and called. Twittering the bat flew here, flew there. Far out over the sands the coming surf crept, grey. Howth settled for slumber tired of long days, of yumyum rhododendrons (he was old) and felt gladly the night breeze lift, ruffle his fell of ferns. He lay but opened a red eye unsleeping, deep and slowly breathing, slumberous but awake. And far on Kish bank the anchored lightship twinkled, winked at Mr Bloom.

Life those chaps out there must have, stuck in the same spot. Irish Lights board. Penance for their sins. Coastguards too. Rocket and breeches buoy and lifeboat. Day we went out for the pleasure cruise in the Erin's King, throwing them the sack of old papers. Bears in the zoo. Filthy trip. Drunkards out to shake up their livers. Puking overboard to feed the herrings. Nausea. And the women, fear of God in their faces. Milly, no sign of funk. Her blue scarf loose, laughing. Don't know what death is at that age. And then their stomachs clean. But being lost they fear. When we hid behind the tree at Crumlin. I didn't want to. Mamma! Mamma! Babes in the wood. Frightening them with masks too. Throwing them up in the air to catch them. I'll murder you. Is it only half fun? Or children playing battle. Whole earnest. How can people aim guns at each other. Sometimes they go off. Poor kids. Only troubles wildfire and nettlerash. Calomel purge I got her for that. After getting better asleep with Molly. Very same teeth she has. What do they love? Another themselves? But the morning she chased her with the umbrella. Perhaps so as not to hurt. I felt her pulse. Ticking. Little hand it was: now big. Dearest Papli. All that the hand says when you touch. Loved to count my waistcoat buttons. Her first stays I remember. Made me laugh to see. Little paps to begin with. Left one is more sensitive, I think. Mine too. Nearer the heart. Padding themselves out if fat is in fashion. Her growing pains at night, calling, wakening me. Frightened she was when her nature came on her first. Poor child! Strange moment for the mother too. Brings back her girlhood. Gibraltar. Looking from Buena Vista. O'Hara's tower. The seabirds screaming. Old Barbary ape that gobbled all his family. Sundown, gunfire for the men to cross the lines. Looking out over the sea she told me. Evening like this, but clear, no clouds. I always thought I'd marry a lord or a gentleman with a private yacht. *Buenas noches, señorita. El hombre ama la muchaha hermosa.* Why me? Because you were so foreign from the others.

Better not stick here all night like a limpet. This weather makes you dull. Must be getting on for nine by the light. Go home. Too late for *Leah*, *Lily of Killarney*. No. Might be still up. Call to the hospital to see. Hope she's over. Long day I've had. Martha, the bath, funeral, house of keys, museum with those goddesses, Dedalus' song. Then that bawler in Barney Kiernan's. Got my own back there. Drunken ranters. What I said about his God made him wince.

Mistake to hit back. Or? No. Ought to go home and laugh at themselves. Always want to be swilling in company. Afraid to be alone like a child of two. Suppose he hit me. Look at it other way round. Not so bad then. Perhaps not to hurt he meant. Three cheers for Israel. Three cheers for the sister-in-law he hawked about, three fangs in her mouth. Same style of beauty. Particularly nice old party for a cup of tea. The sister of the wife of the wild man of Borneo has just come to town. Imagine that in the early morning at close range. Everyone to his taste as Morris said when he kissed the cow. But Dignam's put the boots on it. Houses of mourning so depressing because you never know. Anyhow she wants the money. Must call to those Scottish widows as I promised. Strange name. Takes it for granted we're going to pop off first. That widow on Monday was is outside Cramer's that looked at me. Buried the poor husband but progressing favourably on the premium. Her widow's mite. Well? What do you expect her to do? Must wheedle her way along. Widower I hate to see. Looks so forlorn. Poor man O'Connor wife and five children poisoned by mussels here. The sewage. Hopeless. Some good matronly woman in a porkpie hat to mother him. Take him in tow, platter face and a large apron. Ladies' grey flanelette bloomers, three shillings a pair, astonishing bargain. Plain and loved, loved for ever, they say. Ugly: no woman thinks she is. Love, lie and be handsome for tomorrow we die. See him sometimes walking about trying to find out who played the trick. U. p: up. Fate that is. He, not me. Also a shop often noticed. Curse seems to dog it. Dreamt last night? Wait. Something confused. She had red slippers on. Turkish. Wore the breeches. Suppose she does. Would I like her in pyjamas? Damned hard to answer. Nannetti's gone. Mailboat. Near Holyhead by now. Must nail that ad of Keyes's. Work Hynes and Crawford. Petticoats for Molly. She has something to put in them. What's that? Might be money.

Mr Bloom stooped and turned over a piece of paper on the strand. He brought it near his eyes and peered. Letter? No. Can't read. Better go. Better. I'm tired to move. Page of an old copybook. All those holes and pebbles. Who could count them? Never know what you find. Bottle with story of a treasure in it thrown from a wreck. Parcels post. Children always want to throw things in the sea. Trust? Bread cast on the waters. What's this? Bit of stick.

O! Exhausted that female has me. Not so young now. Will she come here tomorrow? Wait for her somewhere for ever. Must come back. Murderers do. Will I?

Mr Bloom with his stick gently vexed the thick sand at his foot. Write a message for her. Might remain. What?

I.

Some flatfoot tramp on it in the morning. Useless. Washed away. Tide comes here a pool near her foot. Bend, see my face there, dark mirror, breathe on it, stirs. All these rocks with lines and scars and letters. O, those transparent! Besides they don't know. What is the meaning of that other world. I called you naughty boy because I do not like.

AM. A.

No room. Let it go.

Mr Bloom effaced the letters with his slow boot. Hopeless thing sand. Nothing grows in it. All fades. No fear of big vessels coming up here. Except Guinness's barges. Round the Kish in eighty days. Done half by design.

He flung his wooden pen away. The stick fell in silted sand, stuck. Now if you were trying to do that for a week on end you couldn't. Chance. We'll never meet again. But it was lovely. Goodbye, dear. Thanks. Made me feel so young.

Short snooze now if I had. Must be near nine. Liverpool boat long gone. Not even the smoke. And she can do the other. Did too. And Belfast. I won't go. Race there, race back to Ennis. Let him. Just close my eyes a moment. Won't sleep though. Half dream. It never comes the same. Bat again. No harm in him. Just a few.

O sweety all your little girlwhite up I saw dirty bracegirdle made me do love sticky we two naughty Grace darling she him half past the bed met him pike hoses frillies for Raoul to perfume your wife black hair heave under embon *señorita* young eyes Mulvey plump years dreams return tail end Agendath swoony lovey showed me her next year in drawers return next in her next her next.

A bat flew. Here. There. Here. Far in the grey a bell chimed. Mr Bloom with open mouth, his left boot sanded sideways, leaned, breathed. Just for a few

Cuckoo.
Cuckoo.
Cuckoo.

The clock on the mantelpiece in the priest's house cooed where Canon O'Hanlon and Father Conroy and the reverend John Hughes S. J. were taking tea and sodabread and butter and fried mutton chops with catsup and talking about

Cuckoo.
Cuckoo.
Cuckoo.

Because it was a little canarybird bird that came out of its little house to tell the time that Gerty Mac Dowell noticed the time she was there because she was as quick as anything about a thing like that, was Gerty Mac Dowell, and she noticed at once that that foreign gentleman that was sitting on the rocks looking was

Cuckoo.
Cuckoo.
Cuckoo.

Deshil Holles Eamus. Deshil Holles Eamus. Deshil Holles Eamus.

Send us, bright one, light one, Horhorn, quickening and wombfruit. Send us, bright one, light one, Horhorn, quickening and wombfruit. Send us bright one, light one, Horhorn, quickening and wombfruit.

Hoopsa, boyaboy, hoopsa! Hoopsa, boyaboy, hoopsa! Hoopsa, boyaboy hoopsa.

Universally that person's acumen is esteemed very little perceptive concerning whatsoever matters are being held as most profitably by mortals with sapience endowed to be studied who is ignorant of that which the most in doctrine erudite and certainly by reason of that in them high mind's ornament deserving of veneration constantly maintain when by general consent they affirm that other circumstances being equal by no exterior splendour is the prosperity of a nation more efficaciously asserted than by the measure of how far forward may have progressed the tribute of its solicitude for that proliferent continuance which of evils the original if it be absent when fortunately present constitutes the certain sign of omnipollent nature's incorrupted benefaction. For who is there who anything of some significance has apprehended but is conscious that that exterior splendour may be the surface of a downwardtending lutulent reality or on the contrary anyone so is there inilluminated as not to perceive that as no nature's boon can contend against the bounty of increase so it behoves every most just citizen to become the exhortator and admonisher of his semblables and to tremble lest what had in the past been by the nation excellently commenced might be in the future not with similar excellence accomplished if an inverecund habit shall have gradually traduced the honourable by ancestors transmitted customs to that thither of profundity that that one was audacious excessively who would have the hardihood to rise affirming that no more odious offence can for anyone be than to oblivious neglect to consign that evangel simultaneously command and promise which on all mortals with prophecy of abundance or with diminution's menace that exalted of reiteratedly procreating function ever irrevocably enjoined?

It is not why therefore we shall wonder if, as the best historians relate, among the Celts, who nothing that was not in its nature admirable admired, the art of medicine shall have been highly honoured. Not to speak of hostels, leperyards, sweating chambers, plaguegraves, their greatest doctors, the O'Shiels, the O'Hickeys, the O'Lees, have sedulously set down the divers methods by which the sick and the relapsed found again health whether the malady had been the trembling withering or loose boyconnell flux. Certainly in every public work which in it anything of gravity contains preparation should be with importance commensurate and therefore a plan was by them adopted (whether by having preconsidered or as the maturation of experience it is difficult in being said which the discrepant opinions of subsequent inquirers are not up to the present congrued to render manifest) whereby maternity was so far from all accident possibility removed that whatever care the patient in that allhardest of woman hour chiefly required and not solely for the copiously opulent but also for her who not being sufficiently moneyed scarcely and often not even scarcely could subsist valiantly and for an inconsiderable emolument was provided.

To her nothing already then and thenceforward was anyway able to be molestful for this chiefly felt all citizens except with proliferent mothers prosperity at all not to can be and as they had received eternity gods mortals generation to befit them her beholding, when the case was so having itself, parturient in vehicle thereward carrying desire immense among all one another was impelling on of her to be received into that domicile. O thing of prudent nation not merely in being seen but also even in being related worthy of being praised that they her by anticipation went seeing mother, that she by them suddenly to be about to be cherished had been begun she felt!

Before born babe bliss had. Within womb won he worship. Whatever in that one case done commodiously done was. A couch by midwives attended with wholesome food reposeful cleanest swaddles as though forthbringing were now done and by wise foresight set: but to this no less of what drugs there is need and surgical implements which are pertaining to her case not omitting aspect of all very distracting spectacles in various latitudes by our terrestrial orb offered together with images, divine and human, the cogitation of which by sejunct females is to tumescence conducive or eases issue in the high sunbright wellbuilt fair home of mothers when, ostensibly far gone and reproductitive, it is come by her thereto to lie in, her term up.

Some man that wayfaring was stood by housedoor at night's oncoming. Of Israel's folk was that man that on earth wandering far had fared. Stark ruth of man his errand that him lone led till that house.

Of that house A. Horne is lord. Seventy beds keeps he there teeming mothers are wont that they lie for to thole and bring forth bairns hale so God's angel to Mary quoth. Watchers twey there walk, white sisters in ward sleepless. Smarts they still sickness soothing : in twelve moons thrice an hundred. Truest bedthanes they twain are, for Horne holding wariest ward.

In ward wary the watcher hearing come that man mildhearted eft rising with swire ywimpled to him her gate wide undid. Lo, levin leaping lightens in eyeblink Ireland's westward welkin ! Full she dread that God the Wreaker all mankind would fordo with water for his evil sins. Christ's rood made she on breastbone and him drew that he would rathe infare under her thatch. That man her will wotting worthful went in Horne's house.

Loth to irk in Horne's hall hat holding the seeker stood. On her stow he ere was living with dear wife and lovesome daughter that then over land and seafloor nine years had long outwandered. Once her in townhithe meeting he to her bow had not doffed. Her to forgive now he craved with good ground of her allowed that that of him swiftseen face, hers, so young then had looked. Light swift her eyes kindled, bloom of blushes his word winning.

As her eyes then ongot his weeds swart therefor sorrow she feared. Glad after she was that ere adread was Her he asked if O'Hare Doctor tidings sent from far coast and she with grameful sigh him answered that O'Hare Doctor in heaven was. Sad was the man that word to hear that him so heavied in bowels ruthful. All she there told him, ruing death for friend so young, algate sore unwilling God's rightwiseness to withsay. She said that he had a fair sweet death through God His goodness with masspriest to be shriven, holy housel and sick men's oil to his limbs. The man then right earnest asked the nun of which death the dead man was died and the nun answered him and said that he was died in Mona island through bellycrab three year agone come Childermas and she prayed to God the Allruthful to have his dear soul in his undeathliness. He heard her sad words, in held hat sad staring. So stood they there both awhile in wanhope, sorrowing one with other.

Therefore, everyman, look to that last end that is thy death and the dust that gripeth on every man that is born of woman for as he came naked forth from his mother's womb so naked shall he wend him at the last for to go as he came.

The man that was come into the house then spoke to the nursingwoman and he asked her how it fared with the woman that lay there in childbed. The nursingwoman answered him and said that that woman was in throes now full three days and that it would be a hard birth unneth to bear but that now in a little it would be. She said thereto that she had seen many births of women but never was none so hard as was that woman's birth. Then she set it forth all to him that time was had lived nigh that house. The man hearkened to her words for he felt with wonder women's woe in the travail that they have of motherhood and he wondered to look on her face that was a young face for any man to see but yet was she left after long years a handmaid. Nine twelve bloodflows chiding her childless.

And whiles they spake the door of the castle was opened and there nighed them a mickle noise as of many that sat there at meat. And there came against the place as they stood a young learning knight yclept Dixon. And the traveller Leopold was couth to him sithen it had happed that they had had ado each with other in the house of misericord where this learning knight lay by cause the traveller Leopold came there to be healed for he was sore wounded in his breast by a spear wherewith a horrible and dreadful dragon was smitten him for which he did do make a salve of volatile salt and chrism as much as he might suffice. And he said now that he should go into that castle for to make merry with them that were there. And the traveller Leopold said that he should go otherwhither for he was a man of cautels and a subtle. Also the lady was of his avis and reproved the learning knight though she trowed well that the traveller had said thing that was false for his subtility. But the learning knight would not hear say nay nor do her mandement ne have him in aught contrarious to his list and he said how it was a marvellous castle. And the traveller Leopold went into the castle for to rest him for a space being sore of limb after many marches environing in divers lands and sometimes venery.

And in the castle was set a board that was of the birchwood of Finlandy and it was upheld by four dwarfmen of that country but they durst not move more for enchantment. And on this board were frightful swords and knives that are made in a great cavern by swinking demons out of white flames that they fix in the horns of buffalos and stags that there abound marvellously. And there were vessels that are wrought by magic of Mahound out of seasand and the air by a warlock with his breath that he blares into them like to bubbles. And full fair cheer and rich was on the board that no wight could devise a fuller ne richer. And there was a vat ot silver that was moved by craft to open in the which lay strange fishes withouten heads though misbelieving men nie that this be possible thing without they see it natheless they are so. And these fishes lie in an oily water brought there from Portugal land because of the fatness that therein is like to the juices of the olive press. And also it was a marvel to see in that castle how by magic they make a compost out of fecund wheat kidneys out of Chaldee that by aid of certain angry spirits that they do into it swells up wondrously like to a vast moutain. And they teach the serpents there to entwine themselves up on long sticks out of the ground and of the scales of these serpents they brew out a brewage like to mead.

And the learning knight let pour for childe Leopold a draught and halp thereto the while all they that were there drank every each. And childe Leopold did up his beaver for to pleasure him and took apertly somewhat in amity for he never drank no manner of mead which he then put by and anon full privily he voided the more part in his neighbour glass and his neighbour nist not of his wile. And he sat down in that castle with them for to rest him there awhile. Thanked be Almighty God.

This meanwhile this good sister stood by the door and begged them at the reverence of Jesu our alther liege lord to leave their wassailing for there was above one quick with child a gentle dame, whose time hied fast. Sir Leopold heard on the upfloor cry on high and he wondered what cry that it was whether of child or woman and I marvel, said he, that it be not come or now. Meseems it dureth overlong. And he was ware and saw a franklin that hight Lenehan on that side the table that was older than any of the tother and for that they both were knights virtuous in the one emprise and eke by cause that he was elder he spoke to him full gently. But, said he, or it be long too she will bring forth by God His bounty and have joy of her childing for she hath waited marvellous long. And the franklin that had drunken said, Expecting each moment to be her next. Also he took the cup that stood tofore him for him needed never none asking nor desiring of him to drink and, Now drink, said he, fully delectably, and he quaffed as far as he might to their both's health for he was a passing good man of his lustiness. And sir Leopold that was the goodliest guest that ever sat in scholars' hall and that was the meekest man and the kindest that ever laid husbandly hand under hen and that was the very truest knight of the world one that ever did minion service to lady gentle pledged him courtly in the cup. Woman's woe with wonder pondering.

Now let us speak of that fellowship that was there to the intent to be drunken an they might. There was a sort of scholars along either side the board, that is to wit, Dixon yclept junior of saint Mary Merciable's with other his fellows Lynch and Madden, scholars of medicine, and the franklin that hight Lenehan and one from Alba Longa, one Crotthers, and young Stephen that had mien of a frere that was at head of the board and Costello that men clepen Punch Costello all long of a mastery of him erewhile gested (and of all them, reserved young Stephen, he was the most drunken that demanded still of more mead) and beside the meek sir Leopold. But on young Malachi they waited for that he promised to have come and such as intended to no goodness said how he had broke his avow. And sir Leopold sat with them for he bore fast friendship to sir Simon and to this his son young Stephen and for that his langour becalmed him there after longest wanderings insomuch as they feasted him for that time in the honourablest manner. Ruth red him, love led on with will to wander, loth to leave.

For they were right witty scholars. And he heard their aresouns each gen other as touching birth and righteousness, young Madden maintaining that put such case it were hard the wife to die (for so it had fallen out a matter of some year agone with a woman of Eblana in Horne's house that now was trespassed out of this world and the self night next before her death all leeches and pothecaries had taken counsel of her case). And they said farther she should live because in the beginning they said the woman should bring forth in pain and wherefore they that were of this imagination affirmed how young Madden had said truth for he had conscience to let her die. And not few and of these was young Lynch were in doubt that the world was now right evil governed as it was never other howbeit the mean people believed it otherwise but the law nor his judges did provide no remedy. A redress God grant. This was scant said but all cried with one acclaim nay, by our Virgin Mother, the wife should live and the babe to die. In colour whereof they waxed hot upon that head what with argument and what for their drinking but the franklin Lenehan was prompt each when to pour them ale so that at the least way mirth might not lack. Then young Madden showed all the whole affair and when he said how that she was dead and how for holy religion sake by rede of palmer and bedesman and for a vow he had made to Saint Ultan of Arbraccan her goodman husband would not let her death whereby they were all wondrous grieved. To whom young Stephen had these words following, Murmur, sirs, is eke oft among lay folk. Both babe and parent now glorify their Maker, the one in limbo gloom, the other in purge fire. But, gramercy, what of those Godpossibled souls that we nightly impossibilise, which is the sin against the Holy Ghost, Very God, Lord and Giver of Life? For, sirs, he said, our lust is brief. We are means to those small creatures within us and nature has other ends than we. Then said Dixon junior to Punch Costello wist he what ends. But he had overmuch drunken and the best word he could have of him was that he would ever dishonest a woman whoso she were or wife or maid or leman if it so fortuned him to be delivered of his spleen of lustihead. Whereat Crotthers of Alba Longa sang young Malachi's praise of that beast the unicorn how once in the millennium he cometh by his horn the other all this while pricked forward with their jibes wherewith they did malice him, witnessing all and several by saint Foutinus his engines that he was able to do any manner of thing that lay in man to do. Thereat laughed they all right jocundly only young Stephen and sir Leopold which never durst laugh too open by reason of a strange humour which he would not bewray and also for that he rued for her that bare whoso she might be or wheresoever. Then spoke young Stephen orgulous of mother Church that would cast him out of her bosom, of law of canons, of Lilith, patron of abortions, of bigness wrought by wind of seeds of brightness or by potency of vampires mouth to mouth or, as Virgillius saith, by the influence of the occident or by the reek of moonflower or an she lie with a woman which her man has but lain with, *effectu secuto,* or peradventure in her bath according to the opinions of Averroes and Moses Maimonides. He said also how at the end of the second month a human soul was infused and how in all our holy mother foldeth ever souls for God's greater glory whereas that earthly mother which was but a dam to bring forth beastly should die by canon for so saith he that holdeth the fisherman's seal, even that blessed Peter on which rock was holy church for all ages founded. All they bachelors then asked of sir Leopold would he in like case so jeopard her person as risk life to save life. A wariness of mind he would answer as fitted all and, laying hand to jaw, he said dissembling, as his wont was, that as it was informed him, who had ever loved the art of physic as might a layman, and agreeing also with his experience of so seldom seen an accident it was good for that Mother Church belike at one blow had birth and death pence and in such sort deliverly he scaped their questions. That is truth, pardy, said Dixon, and, or I err, a pregnant word. Which hearing young Stephen was a marvellous glad man and he averred that he who stealeth from the poor lendeth to the Lord for he was of a wild manner when he was drunken and that he was now in that taking it appeared eftsoons.

But sir Leopold was passing grave maugre his word by cause he still had pity of the terrorcausing shrieking of shrill women in their labour and as he was minded of his good lady Marion that had borne him an only manchild which on his eleventh day on live had died and no man of art could save so dark is destiny. And she was wondrous stricken of heart for that evil hap and for his burial did him on a fair corselet of lamb's wool, the flower of the flock, lest he might perish utterly and lie akeled (for it was then about the midst of the winter) and now sir Leopold that had of his body no manchild for an heir looked upon him his friend's son and was shut up in sorrow for his forepassed happiness and as sad as he was that him failed a son of such gentle courage (for all accounted him of real parts) so grieved he also in no less measure for young Stephen for that he lived riotously with those wastrels and murdered his goods with whores.

About that present time young Stephen filled all cups that stood empty so as there remained but little mo if the prudenter had not shadowed their approach from him that still plied it very busily who, praying for the intentions of the sovereign pontiff, he gave them for a pledge the vicar of Christ which also as he said is vicar of Bray. Now drink we, quod he, of this mazer and quaff ye this mead which is not indeed parcel of my body but my soul's bodiment. Leave ye fraction of bread to them that live by bread alone. Be not afeard neither for any want for this will comfort more than the other will dismay. See ye here. And he showed them glistering coins of the tribute and goldsmiths' notes the worth of two pound nineteen shilling that he had, he said, for a song which he writ. They all admired to see the foresaid riches in such dearth of money as was herebefore. His words were then these as followeth: Know all men, he said, time's ruins build eternity's mansions. What means this? Desire's wind blasts the thorntree but after it becomes from a bramblebush to be a rose upon the rood of time. Mark me now. In woman's womb word is made flesh but in the spirit of the maker all flesh that passes becomes the word that shall not pass away. This is the postcreation. *Omnis caro ad te veniet.* No question but her name is puissant who aventried the dear corse of our Agenbuyer, Healer and Herd, our mighty mother and mother most venerable and Bernardus saith aptly that she hath an *omnipotentiam deiparae supplicem,* that is to wit, an almightiness of petition because she is the second Eve and she won us, saith Augustine too, whereas that other, our grandam, which we are linked up with by successive anastomosis of navelcords sold us all, seed, breed and generation, for a penny pippin. But here is the matter now. Or she knew him, that second I say, and was but creature of her creature, *vergine madre figlia di tuo figlio* or she knew him not and then stands she in the one denial or ignorancy with Peter Piscator who lives in the house that Jack built and with Joseph the Joiner patron of the happy demise of all unhappy marriages *parce que M. Leo Taxil nous a dit que qui l'avait mise dans cette fichue position c'était le sacré pigeon, ventre de Dieu! Entweder* transsubstantiality *oder* consubstantiality but in no case subsubstantiality. And all cried out upon it for a very scurvy word. A pregnancy without joy, he said, a birth without pangs, a body without blemish, a belly without bigness. Let the lewd with faith and fervour worship. With will will we withstand, withsay.

Hereupon Punch Costello dinged with his fist upon the board and would sing a bawdy catch *Staboo Stabella* about a wench that was put in pod of a jolly swashbuckler in Almany which he did now attack : *The first three months she was not well, Staboo,* when here nurse Quigley from the door angerly bid them hist ye should shame you nor was it not meet as she remembered them being her mind was to have all orderly against lord Andrew came for because she was jealous that no gasteful turmoil might shorten the honour of her guard. It was an ancient and a sad matron of a sedate look and christian walking, in habit dun beseeming her megrims and wrinkled visage, nor did her hortative want of it effect for incontinently Punch Costello was of them all embraided and they reclaimed the churl with civil rudeness some and with menace of blandishments others whiles all chode with him, a murrain seize the dolt, what a devil he would be at, thou chuff, thou puny, thou got in the peasestraw thou losel, thou chitterling, thou spawn of a rebel, thou dykedropt, thou abortion thou, to shut up his drunken drool out of that like a curse of God ape, the good sir Leopold that had for his cognisance the flower of quiet, margerain gentle, advising also the time's occasion as most sacred and most worthy to be most sacred. In Horne's house rest should reign.

To be short this passage was scarce by when Master Dixon of Mary in Eccles, goodly grinning, asked young Stephen what was the reason why he had not cided to take friar's vows and he answered him obedience in the womb, chastity in the tomb but involuntary poverty all his days. Master Lenehan at this made return that he had heard of those nefarious deeds and how, as he heard hereof counted, he had besmirched the lily virtue of a confiding female which was corruption of minors and they all intershowed it too, waxing merry and toasting to his fathership. But he said very entirely it was clean contrary to their suppose for he was the eternal son and ever virgin. Thereat mirth grew in them the more and they rehearsed to him his curious rite of wedlock for the disrobing and deflowering of spouses, as the priests use in Madagascar island, she to be in guise of white and saffron, her groom in white and grain, with burning of nard and tapers, on a bridebed while clerks sung kyries and the anthem *Ut novetur sexus omnis corporis mysterium* till she was there unmaided. He gave them then a much admirable hymen minim by those delicate poets Master John Fletcher and Master Francis Beaumont that is in their *Maid's Tragedy* that was writ for a like twining of lovers : *To bed, to bed,* was the burden of it to be played with accompanable concent upon the virginals. An exquisite dulcet epithalame of most mollificative suadency for juveniles amatory whom the odoriferous flambeaus of the paranymphs have escorted to the quadrupedal proscenium of connubial communion. Well met they were, said Master Dixon, joyed, but, harkee, young sir, better were they named Beau Mount and Lecher for, by my troth, of such a mingling much might come. Young Stephen said indeed to his best remembrance they had but the one doxy between them and she of the stews to make shift with in delights amorous for life ran very high in those days and the custom of the country approved with it. Greater love than this, he said, no man hath that a man lay down his wife for his friend. Go thou and do likewise. Thus, or words to that effect, saith Zarathustra, sometime regius professor of French letters to the university of Oxtail nor breathed there ever that man to whom mankind was more beholden. Bring a stranger within thy tower it will go hard but thou wilt have the secondbest bed. *Orate, fratres, pro memetipso.* And all the people shall say, Amen. Remember, Erin, thy generations and thy days of old, how thou settedst little by me and by my word and broughtest in a stranger to my gates to commit fornication in my sight and to wax fat and kick like Jeshurum. Therefore hast thou sinned against the light and hast made me, thy lord to be the slave of servants. Return, return, Clan Milly : forget me not, O Milesian. Why hast thou done this abomination before me that thou didst spurn me for a merchant of jalaps and didst deny me to the Roman and the Indian of dark speech with whom thy daughters did lie luxuriously? Look forth now, my people, upon the land of behest, even from Horeb and from Nebo and from Pisgah and from the Horns of Hatten unto a land flowing with milk and money. But thou hast suckled me with a bitter milk : my moon and my sun thou hast quenched for ever. And thou hast left me alone for ever in the dark ways of my bitterness : and with a kiss of ashes hast thou kissed my mouth. This tenebrosity of the interior, he proceeded to say, hath not been illumined by the wit of the septuagint nor so much as mentioned for the Orient from on high which brake hell's gates visited a darkness that was foraneous. Assuefaction minorates atrocities (as Tully saith of his darling Stoics) and Hamlet his father showeth the prince no blister of combustion. The adiaphane in the noon of life is an Egypt's plague which in the nights of prenativity and postmortemity is their most proper *ubi* and *quomodo*. And as the ends and ultimates of all things accords in some mean and measure with their inceptions and originals, that same multiplicit concordance which leads forth growth from birth accomplishing by a retrogressive metamorphosis that minishing and ablation towards the final which is agreeable unto nature so is it with our subsolar being. The aged sisters draw us into life : we wail, batten, sport, clip, clasp, sunder, dwindle, die : over us dead they bend. First saved from water of old Nile, among bulrushes, a bed of fasciated wattles : at last the cavity of a mountain, an occulted sepulchre amid the conclamation of the hillcat and the ossifrage. And as no man knows the ubicity of his tumulus nor to what processes we shall thereby be ushered nor whether to Tophet or to Edenville in the like way is all hidden when we would backward see from what region of remoteness the whatness of our whoness hath fetched his whenceness.

Thereto Punch Costello roared out mainly *Etienne chanson* but he loudly bid them lo, wisdom hath built herself a house, this vast majestic longstablished vault, the crystal palace of the Creator all in applepie order, a penny for him who finds the pea.

Behold the mansion reared by dedal Jack,
See the malt stored in many a refluent sack,
In the proud cirque of Jackjohn's bivouac.

A black crack of noise in the street here, alack, bawled, back. Loud on left Thor thundered : in anger awful the hammerhurler. Came now the storm that hist his heart. And Master Lynch bade him have a care to flout and witwanton as the god self was angered for his hellprate and paganry. And he that had erst challenged to be so doughty waxed pale as they might all mark and shrank together and his pitch that was before so haught uplift was now of a sudden quite plucked down and his heart shook within the cage of his breast as he tasted the rumour of that storm. Then did some mock and some jeer and Punch Costello fell hard again to his yale which Master

Lenehan vowed he would do after and he was indeed but a word and a blow on any the least colour. But the braggart boaster cried that an old Nobodaddy was in his cups it was muchwhat indifferent and he would not lag behind his lead. But this was only to dye his desperation as cowed he crouched in Horne's hall. He drank indeed at one draught to pluck up a heart of any grace for it thundered long rumblingly over all the heavens so that Master Madden, being godly certain whiles, knocked him on his ribs upon that crack of doom and Master Bloom, at the braggart' side spoke to him calming words to slumber his great fear, advertising how it was no other thing but a hubbub noise that he heard, the discharge of fluid from the thunderhead, look you, having taken place, and all of the order of a natural phenomenon.

But was young Boasthard's fear vanquished by Calmer's words? No, for he had in his bosom a spike named Bitterness which could not by words be done away. And was he then neither calm like the one nor godly like the other? He was neither as much as he would have liked to be either. But could he not have endeavoured to have found again as in his youth the bottle Holiness that then he lived withal? Indeed not for Grace was not there to find that bottle. Heard he then in that clap the voice of the god Bringforth or, what Calmer said, a hubbub of Phenomenon? Heard? Why, he could not but hear unless he had plugged up the tube Understanding (which he had not done). For through that tube he saw that he was in the land of Phenomenon where he must for a certain one day die as he was like the rest too a passing show. And would he not accept to die like the rest and pass away? By no means would he and make more shows according as men do with wives which Phenomenon has commanded them to do by the book Law. Then wotted he nought of that other land which is called Believe-on-Me, that is the land of promise which behoves to the king Delightful and shall be for ever where there is no death and no birth neither wiving nor mothering at which all shall come as many as believe on it? Yes, Pious had told him of that land and Chaste had pointed him to the way but the reason was that in the way he fell in with a certain whore of an eyepleasing exterior whose name, she said, is Bird-in-the-Hand and she beguiled him wrongways from the true path by her flatteries that she said to him as, Ho, you pretty man, turn aside hither and I will show you a brave place, and she lay at him so flatteringly that she had him in her grot which is named Two-in-the-Bush or, by some learned, Carnal Concupiscence.

This was it what all that company that sat there at commons in Manse of Mothers the most lusted after and if they met with this whore Bird-in-the-Hand (which was within all foul plagues, monsters and a wicked devil) they would strain the last but they would make at her and know her. For regarding Believe-on-Me they said it was nought else but notion and they could conceive no thought of it for, first, Two-in-the-Bush whither she ticed them was the very goodliest grot and in it were four pillows on which were four tickets with these word printed on them, Pickaback and Topsyturvy and Shameface and Cheek by Jowl and, second, for that foul plague Allpox and the monsters they cared not for them for Preservative had given them a stout shield of oxengut and, third, that they might take no hurt neither from Offspring that was that wicked devil by virtue of this same shield which was named Killchild. So were they all in their blind fancy, Mr Cavil and Mr Sometimes Godly, Mr Ape Swillale, Mr False Franklin, Mr Dainty Dixon, Young Boasthard and Mr Cautious Calmer. Wherein, O wretched company were ye all deceived for that was the voice of the god that was in a very grievous rage that he would presently lift his arm and spill their souls for their abuses and their spillings done by them contrariwise to his word which forth to bring brenningly biddeth.

So Thursday sixteenth June Patk. Dignam laid in clay of an apoplexy and after hard drought, please God, rained, a bargeman coming in by water a fifty mile or thereabout with turf saying the seed won't sprout, fields athirst, very sadcoloured and stunk mightily, the quags and tofts too. Hard to breathe and all the young quicks clean consumed without sprinkle this long while back as no man remembered to be without. The rosy buds all gone brown and spread out blobs and on the hills nought but dry flag and faggots that would catch at first fire All the world saying, for aught they knew, the big wind of last February a year that did havoc the land so pitifully a small thing beside this barrenness. But by and by, as said, this evening after sundown, the wind sitting in the west, biggish swollen clouds to be seen as the night increased and the weatherwise poring up at them and some sheet lightnings at first and after, past ten of the clock, one great stroke with a long thunder and in a brace of shakes all scamper pellmell within door for the smoking shower, the men making shelter for their straws with a clout or kerchief, womenfolk skipping off with kirtles catched up soon as the pour came. In Ely place, Baggot street, Duke's lawn, thence through Merrion green up to Holles street a swash of water running that was before bonedry and not one chair or coach or fiacre seen about but no more crack after that first. Over against the Rt. Hon. Mr Justice Fitzgibbon's door (that is to sit with Mr Healy the lawyer upon the college lands) Mal. Mulligan a gentleman's gentleman that had but come from

Mr Moore's the writer's (that was a papish but is now, folk say, a good Williamite) chanced against Alec. Bannon in a cut bob (which are now in with dance cloaks of Kendal green) that was new got to town from Mullingar with the stage where his coz and Mal M's brother will stay a month yet till Saint Swithin and asks what in the earth he does there, he bound home and he to Andrew Horne's being stayed for to crush a cup of wine, so he said, but would tell him of a skittish heifer, big of her age and beef to the heel and all this while poured with rain and so both together on to Horne's. There Leop. Bloom of Crawford's journal sitting snug with a covey of wags, likely brangling fellows, Dixon jun., scholar of my lady of Mercy, Vin. Lynch, a Scots fellow, Will. Madden, T. Lenehan, very sad for a racinghorse he fancied and Stephen D. Leop. Bloom there for a langour he had but was now better, he having dreamed tonight a strange fancy of his dame Mrs Moll with red slippers on in a pair of Turkey trunks which is thought by those in ken to be for a change and Mistress Purefoy there, that got in through pleading her belly, and now on the stools, poor body, two days past her term, the midwives sore put to it and can't deliver, she queasy for a bowl of riceslop that is a shrewd drier up of the insides and her breath very heavy more than good and should be a bullyboy from the knocks they say, but God give her soon issue. 'Tis her ninth chick to live, I hear, and Lady day bit off her last chick's nails that was then a twelvemonth and with other three all breastfed that died written out in a fair hand in the king's bible. Her hub fifty odd and a methodist but takes the Sacrament and is to be seen any fair sabbath with a pair of his boys off Bullock harbour dapping on the sound with a heavybraked reel or in a punt he has trailing for flounder and pollock and catches a fine bag, I hear. In sum an infinite great fall of rain and all refreshed and will much increase the harvest yet those in ken say after wind and water fire shall come for a prognostication of Malachi's almanac (and I hear that Mr Russell has done a prophetical charm of the same gist out of the Hindustanish for his farmer's gazette) to have three things in all but this a mere fetch without bottom of reason for old crones and bairns yet sometimes they are found in the right guess with their queerities no telling how.

With this came up Lenehan to the feet of the table to say how the letter was in that night's gazette and he made a show to find it about him (for he swore with an oath that he had been at pains about it) but on Stephen's persuasion he gave over to search and was bidden to sit near by which he did mighty brisk. He was a kind or sport gentleman that went for a merryandrew or honest pickle and what belonged of women, horseflesh or hot scandal he had it pat. To tell the truth he was mean in fortunes and for the most part hankered about the coffeehouses and low taverns with crimps, ostlers, bookies, Paul's men, runners, flatcaps, waistcoateers, ladies of the bagnio and other rogues of the game or with a chanceable catchpole or a tipstaff often at nights till broad day of whom he picked up between his sackpossets much loose gossip. He took his ordinary at a boilingcook's and if he had but gotten into him a mess of broken victuals or a platter of tripes with a bare tester in his purse he could always bring himself off with his tongue, some randy quip he had from a punk or whatnot that every mother's son of them would burst their sides. The other, Costello, that is, hearing this talk asked was it poetry or a tale. Faith, no, he says, Frank (that was his name) 'tis all about Kerry cows that are to be butchered along of the plague. But they can go hang, says he with a wink, for me with their bully beef, a pox on it. There's as good fish in this tin as ever came out of it and very friendly he offered to take of some salty sprats that stood by which he had eyed wishly in the meantime and found the place which was indeed the chief design of his embassy as he was sharpset. *Mort aux vaches*, says Frank then in the French language that had been indentured to a brandy shipper that has a winelodge in Bordeaux and he spoke French like a gentleman too. From a child this Frank had been a donought that his father, a headborough, who could ill keep him to school to learn his letters and the use of the globes, matriculated at the university to study the mechanics but he took the bit between his teeth like a raw colt and was more familiar with the justiciary and the parish beadle than with his volumes. One time he would be a playactor, then a sutler or a welsher, then nought would keep him from the bearpit and the cocking main, then he was for the ocean sea or to foot it on the roads with the Romany folk, kidnapping a squire's heir by favour of moonlight or fecking maids' linen or choking chickens behind a hedge. He had been off as many times as a cat has lives and back again with naked pockets as many more to his father the headborough who shed a pint of tears as often as he saw him. What, says Mr Leopold with his hands across, that was earnest to know the drift of it, will they slaughter all? I protest I saw them but this day morning going to the Liverpool boats, says he. I can scarce believe 'tis so bad, says he. And he had experience of the like brood beasts and of springers, greasy hoggets and wether wools having been some years before actuary for Mr Joseph Cuffe, a worthy salesmaster that drove his trade for live stock and meadow auctions hard by Mr Gavin Low's yard in Prussia street. I question with you there, says he. More like 'tis the hoose or the timber tongue. Mr Stephen, a little moved but very handsomely, told him no such matter and that he had dispatches from the emperor's chief tailtickler thanking him for the hospitality, that was sending over Doctor Rinderpest, the bestquoted cowcatcher in all Muscovy with a bolus or two of physic to take the bull by the horns. Come, come, says Mr Vincent, plain dealing. He'll find himself on the horns of a dilemma if he meddles with a bull that's Irish, says he. Irish by name and irish by nature, says Mr Stephen, and he sent the ale purling about. An Irish bull in an English chinashop. I conceive you, says Mr Dixon. It is that same bull that was sent to our island by farmer Nicholas, the bravest cattle breeder of them all with an emerald ring in his nose. True for you, says Mr Vincent cross the table, and a bullseye into the bargain, says he, and a plumper and a portlier bull, says he, never shit on shamrock. He had horns galore, a coat of gold and a sweet smoky breath coming out of his nostrils so that the women of our island, leaving doughballs and rollingpins, followed after him hanging his bulliness in daisychains. What for that, says Mr Dixon, but before he came over farmer Nicholas that was a eunuch had him properly gelded by a college of doctors who were no better off than himself. So be off now, says he, and do all my cousin german the Lord Harry tells you and take a farmer's blessing, and with that he slapped his posteriors very soundly. But the slap and the blessing stood him friend, says Mr Vincent, for to make up he taught him a trick worth two of the other so that maid, wife, abbess and widow to this day affirm that they would rather any time of the month whisper in his ear in the dark of a cowhouse or get a lick on the nape from his long holy tongue than lie with the finest strapping young ravisher in the four fields of all Ireland. Another then put in his word : And they dressed him, says he in a point shift and petticoat with a tippet and girdle and ruffles on his wrists and clipped his forelock and rubbed him all over with spermacetic oil and built stables for him at every turn of the road with a gold manger in each full of the best hay in the market so that he could doss and dung to his heart's content. By this time the father of the faithful (for so they called him) was grown so heavy that he could scarce walk to pasture. To remedy which our cozening dames and damsels brought him his fodder in their apronlaps and as soon as his belly was full he would rear up on his hind quarters to show their ladyships a mystery and roar and bellow out of him in bulls' language and they all after him. Ay, says another, and so pampered was he that he would suffer nought to grow in all the land but green grass for himself (for that was the only colour to his mind) and there was a board put up on a hillock in the middle of the island with a printed notice, saying : By the lord Harry green is the grass that grows on the ground. And, says Mr Dixon, if ever he got scent of a cattleraider in Roscommon or the wilds of Connemara or a husbandman in Sligo that was sowing as much as a handful of mustard or a bag of rapeseed out he run amok over half the countryside rooting up with his horns whatever was planted and all by lord Harry's orders. There was bad blood between them at first says Mr Vincent, and the lord Harry called farmer Nicholas all the old Nicks in the world and an old whoremaster that kept seven trulls in his house and I'll meddle in his matters, says he. I'll make that animal smell hell, says he, with the help of that good pizzle my father left me. But one evening, says Mr Dixon, when the lord Harry was cleaning his royal pelt to go to dinner after winning a boatrace (he had spade oars for himself but the first rule of the course was that the others were to row with pitchforks) he discovered in himself a wonderful likeness to a bull and on picking up a blackthumbed chapbook that he kept in the pantry he found sure enough that he was a lefthanded descendant of the famous champion bull of the Romans, *Bos Bovum*, which is good bog Latin for boss of the show. After that, says Mr Vincent, the lord Harry put his head into a cow's drinkingtrough in the presence of all his courtiers and pulling it it out again told them all his new name. Then, with the water running off him, he got into an old smock and skirt that had belonged to his grandmother and bought a grammar of the bulls' language to study but he could never learn a a word of it except the first personal pronoun which he copied out big and got off by heart and if ever he went out for a walk he filled his pockets with chalk to write it up on what took his fancy, the side of rock or a teahouse table or a bale of cotton or a corkfloat. In short he and the bull of Ireland were soon as fast friends as an arse and a shirt. They were, says Mr Stephen, and the end was that the men of the island, seeing no help was toward as the ungrate women were all of one mind, made a wherry raft, loaded themselves and their bundles of chattels on shipboard, set all masts erect, manned the yards, sprang their luff, heaved to, spread three sheets in the wind, put her head between wind and water, weighed anchor, ported her helm, ran up the jolly Roger, gave three times three, let the bullgine run, pushed off in their bumboat and put to sea to recover the main of America. Which was the occasion, says Mr Vincent, of the composing by a boatswain of that rollicking chanty :

— *Pope Peter's but a pissabed.*
A man's a man for a' that.

Our worthy acquaintance, Mr Malachi Mulligan, now appeared in the doorway as the students were finishing their apologue accompanied with a friend whom he had just rencountered, a young gentleman, his name Alec Bannon, who had late come to town, it being his intention to buy a colour or a cornetcy in the fencibles and list for the wars. Mr Mulligan was civil enough to express some relish of it all the more as it jumped with a project of his own for the cure of the very evil that had been touched on. Whereat he handed round to the company a set of pasteboard cards which he had had printed that day at Mr Quinnell's bearing a legend printed in fair italics : *Mr Malachi Mulligan, Fertiliser and Incubator, Lambay Island.* His project, as he went on to expound, was to withdraw from the round of idle pleasures such as form the chief business of sir Fopling Popinjay and sir Milksop Quidnunc in town and to devote himself to the noblest task for which our bodily organism has been framed. Well, let us hear of it, good my friend, said Mr Dixon. I make no doubt it smacks of wenching. Come, be seated, both. 'Tis as cheap sitting as standing. Mr Mulligan accepted of the invitation and, expatiating on his design, told his hearers that he had been led into this thought by a consideration of the causes of sterility, both the inhibitory and the prohibitory, whether the inhibition in its turn were due to conjugal vexations or to a parsimony of the balance as well as whether the prohibition proceeded from defects congenital or from proclivites acquired. It grieved him plaguily, he said, to see the nuptial couch defrauded of its dearest pledges : and to reflect upon so many agreeable females with rich jointures, a prey for the vilest bonzes, who hide their flambeau under a bushel in a uncongenial cloister or lose their womanly bloom in the embraces of some unaccountable muskin when they might multiply the inlets of happiness, sacrificing the inestimable jewel of their sex when a hundred pretty fellows were at hand to caress, this, he assured them, made his heart weep. To curb this inconvenient (which he concluded due to a suppression of latent heat) having advised with certain counsellors of worth and inspected into this matter, he had resolved to purchase in fee simple for ever the freehold of Lambay island from its holder, lord Talbot de Malahide, a Tory gentleman of note much in favour with our ascendancy party. He proposed to set up there a national fertilising farm to be named *Omphalos* with an obelisk hewn and erected after the fashion of Egypt and to offer his dutiful yeoman services for the fecundation of any female of what grade of life soever who should there direct to him with the desire of fulfilling the functions of her natural. Money was no object, he said, nor would he take a penny for his pains. The poorest kitchenwench no less than the opulent lady of fashion, if so be their constructions and their tempers were warm persuaders for their petitions, would find in him their man. For his nutriment he shewed how he would feed himself exclusively upon a diet of savoury tubercles and fish and coneys there, the flesh of these latter prolific rodents being highly recommended for his purpose, both broiled and stewed with a blade of mace and a pod or two of capsicum chillies. After this homily which he delivered with much warmth of asseveration Mr Mulligan in a trice put off from his hat a kerchief with which he had shielded it. They both, it seems, had been overtaken by the rain and for all their mending their pace had taken water, as might be observed by Mr Mulligan's smallclothes of a hodden grey which was now somewhat piebald. His project meanwhile was very favourably entertained by his auditors and won hearty eulogies from all though Mr Dixon of Mary's excepted to it, asking with a finicking air did he purpose also to carry coals to Newcastle. Mr Mulligan however made court to the scholarly by an apt quotation from the classics which, as it dwelt upon his memory seemed to him a sound and tasteful support of his contention: *Talis ac tanta depravatio hujus seculi, O quirites, ut matres familiarum nostrae lascivas cujuslibet semiviri libici titillationes testibus ponderosis atque excelsis erectionibus centurionum Romanorum magnopere anteponunt* while for those of ruder wit he drove home his point by analogies of the animal kingdom more suitable to their stomach, the buck and doe of the forest glade, the farmyard drake and duck.

Valuing himself not a little upon his elegance, being indeed a proper man of his person, this talkative now applied himself to his dress with animadversions of some heat upon the sudden whimsy of the atmospherics while the company lavished their encomiums upon the project he had advanced. The young gentleman, his friend, overjoyed as he was at a passage that had befallen him, could not forbear to tell it his nearest neighbour. Mr Mulligan, now perceiving the table, asked for whom were those loaves and fishes and, seeing the stranger, he made him a civil bow and said, Pray, sir, was you in need of any professional assistance we could give? Who, upon his offer, thanked him very heartily, though preserving his proper distance, and replied that he was come there about a lady, now an inmate of Horne's house, that was in an interesting condition, poor lady, from woman's woe (and here he fetched a deep sigh) to know if her happiness had yet taken place. Mr Dixon, to turn the table, took on to ask of Mr Mulligan himself whether his incipient ventripotence, upon which he rallied him, betokened an ovoblastic gestation in the prostatic utricle or male womb or was due as with the noted physician, Mr Austin Meldon, to a wolf in the stomach. For answer Mr Mulligan, in a gale of laughter at his smalls, smote himself bravely below the diaphragm, exclaiming with an admirable droll mimic of Mother Grogan (the most excellent creature of her sex though 'tis pity she's a trollop) : There's a belly that never bore a bastard. This was so happy a conceit that it renewed the storms of mirth and threw the whole room into the most violent agitations of delight. The spry rattle had run on in the same vein of mimicry but for some larum in the antechamber.

Here the listener who was none other than the Scotch student, a little fume of a fellow, blond as tow, congratulated in the liveliest fashion with the young gentleman and, interrupting the narrative at a salient point, having desired his visavis with a polite beck to have the obligingness to pass him a flagon of cordial waters at the same time by a questioning poise of the head (a whole century of polite breading had not achieved so nice a gesture) to which was united an equivalent but contrary balance of the head asked the narrator as plainly as was ever done in words if he might treat him with a cup of it. *Mais bien sûr*, noble stranger, said he cheerily, *et mille compliments*. That you may and very opportunely. There wanted nothing but this cup to crown my felicity. But, gracious heaven, was I left with but a crust in my wallet and a cupful of water from the well, my God, I would accept of them and find it in my heart to kneel down upon the ground and give thanks to the powers above for the happiness vouchsafed me by the Giver of good things. With these words he approached the goblet to his lips, took a complacent draught of the cordial, slicked his hair and, opening his bosom, out popped a locket that hung from a silk riband that very picture which he had cherished ever since her hand had wrote therein. Gazing upon those features with a world of tenderness, Ah, Monsieur, he said, had you but beheld her as I did with these eyes at that affecting instant with her dainty tucker and her new coquette cap (a gift for her feast day as she told me) in such an artless disorder, of so melting a tenderness, 'pon my conscience, even you, Monsieur, had been impelled by generous nature to deliver yourself wholly into the hands of such an enemy or to quit the field for ever. I declare, I was never so touched in all my life. God I thank thee as the Author of my days! Thrice happy will he be whom so amiable a creature will bless with her favours. A sigh of affection gave eloquence to these words and, having replaced the locket in his bosom, he wiped his eye and sighed again. Beneficent Disseminator of blessings to all Thy creatures, how greatand universal must be that sweetest of Thy tyrannies which can hold in thrall the free and the bond, the simple swain and the polished coxcomb, the lover in the heyday of reckless passion and the husband of maturer years. But indeed, sir, I wander from the point. How mingled and imperfect are all our sublunary joys. Maledicity! Would to God that foresight had remembered me to take my cloak along! I could weep to think of it. Then, though it had poured seven showers we were neither of us a penny the worse. But beshrew me, he cried, clapping hand to his forehead, tomorrow will be a new day and, thousand thunders, I know of a *marchand de capotes,* Monsieur Poyntz, from whom I can have for a *livre* as snug a cloak of the French fashion as ever kept a lady from wetting. Tut, tut! cries Le Fécondateur, tripping in, my friend Monsieur Moore, that most accomplished traveller (I have just cracked a half bottle *avec lui* in a circle of the best wits of the town) is my authority that in Cape Horn, *ventre biche,* they have a rain that will wet through any, even the stoutest cloak. A drenching of that violence, he tells me, *sans blague,* has sent more than one luckless fellow in good earnest posthaste to another world. Pooh! A *livre!* cries Monsieur Lynch. The clumsy things are dear at a sou. One umbrella, were it no bigger than a fairy mushroom, is worth ten such stopgaps. No woman of any wit would wear one. My dear Kitty told me today that she would dance in a deluge before ever she would starve in such an ark of salvation for, as she reminded me (blushing piquantly and whispering in my ear though there was none to snap her words but giddy butterflies) dame Nature, by the divine blessing, has implanted it in our heart and it has become a household word that *il y a deux choses* for which the innocence of our original garb, in other circumstances a breach of the proprieties, is the fittest, nay the only garment. The first, said she (and here my pretty philosopher, as I handed her to her tilbury, to fix my attention, gently tipped with her tongue the outer chamber of my ear) the first is a bath... but at this point a bell tinkling in the hall cut short a discourse which promised so bravely for the enrichment of our store of knowledge.

Amid the general vacant hilarity of the assembly a bell rang and while all were conjecturing what might be the cause Miss Callan entered and, having spoken a few words in a low tone to young Mr Dixon, retired with a profound bow to the company. The presence even for a moment among a party of debauchees of a woman endued with every quality of modesty and not less severe than beautiful refrained the humourous sallies even of the most licentious but her departure was the signal for an outbreak of ribaldry. Strike me silly, said Costello, a low fellow who was fuddled. A monstrous fine bit of cowflesh! I'll be sworn she has rendezvoused you. What, you dog? Have you a way with them? Gad's bud. Immensely so, said Mr Lynch. The bedside manner it is that they use in the Mater hospice. Demme, does not Doctor O'Gargle chuck the nuns there under the chin. As I look to be saved I had it from my Kitty who has been wardmaid there any time these seven months. Lawksamercy, doctor, cried the young blood in the primrose vest, feigning a womanish simper and immodest squirmings of his body, how you do tease a body! Drat the man! Bless me, I'm all of a wibblywobbly. Why, you're as bad as dear little Father Cantekissem that you are! May this pot of four half choke me, cried Costello, if she ain't in the family way. I knows a lady what's got a white swelling quick as I claps eyes on her. The young surgeon, however, rose and begged the company to excuse his retreat as the nurse had just then informed him that he was needed in the ward. Merciful providence had been pleased to put a period to the sufferings of the lady who was *enceinte* which she had borne with a laudable fortitude and she had given birth to a bouncing boy. I want patience, said he, with those who without wit to enliven or learning to instruct, revile an ennobling profession which, saving the reverence due to the Deity, is the greatest power for happiness upon the earth. I am positive when I say that if need were I could produce a cloud of witnesses to the excellence of her noble exercitations which, so far from being a byword, should be a glorious incentive in the human breast. I cannot away with them. What? Malign such an one, the amiable Miss Callan, who is the lustre of her own sex and the astonishment of ours and at an instant the most momentous that can befall a puny child ot clay? Perish the thought! I shudder to think of the future of a race where the seeds of such malice have been sown and where no right reverence is rendered to mother and maid in house of Horne. Having delivered himself of this rebuke he saluted those present on the by and repaired to the door. A murmur of approval arose from all and some were for ejecting the low soaker without more ado, a design which would have been effected nor would he have received more than his bare deserts had he not abridged his transgression by affirming with a horrid imprecation (for he swore a round hand) that he was as good a son of the true fold as ever drew breath. Stap my vitals, said he, them was always the sentiments of honest Frank Costello which I was bred up most particular to honour thy father and thy mother that had the best hand to a rolypoly or a hasty pudding as you ever see what I always looks back on with a loving heart.

To revert to Mr Bloom who, after his first entry had been conscious of some impudent mocks which he, however, had born with being the fruits of that age upon which it is commonly charged that it knows not pity. The young sparks, it is true, were as full of extravagancies as overgrown children : the words of their tumultuary discussions were difficultly understood and not often nice : their testiness and outrageous *mots* were such that his intellects resiled from : nor were they scrupuluosly sensible of the proprieties though their fund of strong animal spirits spoke in their behalf. But the word of Mr Costello was an unwelcome language for him for he nauseated the wretch that seemed to him a cropeared creature of a misshapen gibbosity born out of wedlock and thrust like a crookback teethed and feet first into the world, which the dint of the surgeon's pliers in his skill lent indeed a colour to, so as it put him in thought of that missing link of creation's chain desiderated by the late ingenious Mr Darwin. It was now for more than the middle span of our allotted years that he had passed through the thousand vicissitudes of existence and, being of a wary ascendancy and self a man of a rare forecast, he had enjoined his heart to repress all motions of a rising choler and, by intercepting them with the readiest precaution, foster within his breast that plenitude of sufferance which base minds jeer at, rash judgers scorn and all find tolerable and but tolerable. To those who create themselves wits at the cost of feminine delicacy (a habit of mind which be never did hold with) to them he would concede neither to bear the name nor to herit the tradition of a proper breeding : while for such that, having lost all forbearance can lose no more, there remained the sharp antidote of experience to cause their insolency to beat a precipitate and inglorious retreat. Not but what he could feel with mettlesome youth which, caring nought for the mows of dotards or the gruntlings of the severe, is ever (as the chaste fancy of the Holy Writer expresses it) for eating of the tree forbid it yet not so far forth as to pretermit humanity upon any condition soever towards a gentlewoman when she was about her lawful occasions. To conclude, while from the sister's words he had reckoned upon a speedy delivery he was, however, it must be owned, not a little alleviated by the intelligence that the issue so ausspicated after an ordeal of such duress now testified once more to the mercy as well as to the bounty of the Supreme Being.

Accordingly he broke his mind to his neighbour, saying that, to express his notion of the thing, his opinion (who ought not perchance to express one) was that one must have a cold constitution and a frigid genius not to be rejoiced by this freshest news of the fruition of her confinement since she had been in such pain through no fault of hers. The dressy young blade said it was her husband's that put her in that expectation or at least it ought to be unless she were another Ephesian matron. I must acquaint you, said Mr Crotthers, clapping on the table so as to evoke a resonant comment of emphasis, old Glory Allelujerum was round again today, an elderly man with dundrearies, preferring through his nose a request to have word of Wilhelmina, my life, as he calls her. I bade him hold himself in readiness for that the event would burst anon. 'Slife, I'll be round with you. I cannot but extol the virile potency of the old bucko that could still knock another child out of her. All fell to praising of it, each after his own fashion, though the same young blade held with his former view that another than her conjugial had been the man in the gap, a clerk in orders, a linkboy (virtuous) or an itinerant vendor of articles needed in every household. Singular, communed the guest with himself, the wonderfully unequal faculty of metempsychosis possessed by them, that the puerperal dormitory and the dissecting theatre should be the seminaries of such frivolity, that the mere acquisition of academic titles should suffice to transform in a pinch of time these votaries of levity into exemplary practitioners of an art which most men anywise eminent have esteemed the noblest. But, he further added, it is mayhap to relieve the pentup feelings that in common oppress them for I have more than once observed that birds of a feather laugh together.

But with what fitness, let it be asked, of the noble lord, his patron, has this alien, whom the concession of a gracious prince has admitted to civil rights, constituted himself the lord paramount of our internal polity? Where is now that gratitude which loyalty should have counselled? During the recent war whenever the enemy had a temporary advantage with his granados did this traitor to his kind not seize that moment to discharge his piece against the empire of which he is a tenant at will while he trembled for the security of his four per cents? Has he forgotten this as he forgets all benefits received? Or is it that from being a deluder of others he has become at last his own dupe as he is, if report belie him not, his own and his only enjoyer? Far be it from candour to violate the bedchamber of a respectable lady, the daughter of a gallant major, or to cast the most distant reflections upon her virtue but if he challenges attention there (as it was indeed highly his interest not to have done) then be it so. Unhappy woman she has been too long and too persistently denied her legitimate prerogative to listen to his objurgations with any other feeling than the derision of the desperate. He says this, a censor of morals, a very pelican in his piety, who did not scruple, oblivious of the ties of nature, to attempt illicit intercourse with a female domestic drawn from the lowest strata of society! Nay, had the hussy's scouringbrush not been her tutelary angel it had gone with her as hard as with

Hagar, the Egyptian! In the question of the grazing lands his peevish asperity is notorious and in Mr Cuffe's hearing brought upon him from an indignant rancher a scathing retort couched in terms as straightforward as they were bucolic. It ill becomes him to preach that gospel. Has he not nearer home a seedfield that lies fallow for the want of a ploughshare? A habit reprehensible at puberty is second nature and an opprobium in middle life. If he must dispense his balm of Gilead in nostrums and apothegms of dubious taste to restore to health a generation of unfledged profligates let his practice consist better with the doctrines that now engross him. His marital breast is the repository of secrets which decorum is reluctant to adduce. The lewd suggestions of some faded beauty may console him for a consort neglected and debauched but this new exponent of morals and healer of ills is at his best an exotic tree which, when rooted in its native orient, throve and flourished and was abundant in balm but, transplanted to a clime more temperate, its roots have lost their quondam vigour while the stuff that comes away from it is stagnant, acid and inoperative.

The news was imparted with a circumspection recalling the ceremonial usages of the Sublime Porte by the second female infirmarian to the junior medical officer in residence, who in his turn announced to the delegation that an heir had been born. When he had betaken himself to the women's apartment to assist at the prescribed ceremony of the afterbirth in the presence of the secretary of state for domestic affairs and the members of the privy council, silent in unanimous exhaustion and approbation the delegates, chafing under the length and solemnity of their vigil and hoping that the joyful occurrence would palliate a licence which the simultaneous absence of abigail and officer rendered the easier broke out at once into a strife of tongues. In vain the voice of Mr Canvasser Bloom was heard endeavouring to urge, to mollify, to restrain. The moment was too propitious for the display of that discursiveness which seemed the only band of union among tempers so divergent. Every phase of the situation was successively eviscerated: the prenatal repugnance of uterine brothers, the Caesarean section, posthumity with respect to the father and, that rarer form, with respect to the mother, the fratricidal case known as the Childs murder and rendered memorable by the impassioned plea of Mr Advocate Bushe which secured the acquittal of the wrongfully accused, the rights of primogeniture and king's bounty touching twins and triplets, miscarriages and infanticides, simulated and dissimulated, acardiac *foetus in foetu,* aprosopia due to a congestion, the agnatia of certain chinless Chinamen (cited by Mr Candidate Mulligan) in consequence of defective reunion of the maxillary knobs along the medial line so that (as he said) one ear could hear what the other spoke, the benefits of anesthesia or twilight sleep, the prolungation of labour pains in advanced gravidancy by reason of pressure on the vein, the premature relentment of the amniotic fluid (as exemplified in the actual case) with consequent peril of sepsis to the matrix, artificial insemination by means of syringes, involution of the womb consequent upon the menopause, the problem of the perpetration of the species in the case of females impregnated by delinquent rape, that distressing manner of delivery called by the Brandenburghers *Sturzgeburt,* the recorded instances of multigeminal, twikindled and monstruous births conceived during the catamenic period or of consanguineous parents — in a word all the cases of human nativity which Aristotle has classified in his masterpiece with chromolithographic illustrations. The gravest problems of obstetrics and forensic medicine were examined with as much animation as the most popular beliefs on the state of pregnancy such as the forbidding to a gravid woman to step over a country stile lest, by her movement, the navelcord should strangle her creature and the injunction upon her in the event of a yearning, ardently and ineffectually entertained, to place her hand against that part of her person which long usage has consecrated as the seat of castigation. The abnormalities of harelip, breastmole, supernumerary digits, negro's inkle, strawberry mark and portwine stain were alleged by one as a *primafacie* and natural hypothetical explanation of swineheaded (the case of Madame Grissel Steevens was not forgotten) or doghaired infants occasionally born. The hypothesis of a plasmic memory, advanced by the Caledonian envoy and worthy of the metaphysical traditions of the land he stood for, envisaged in such cases an arrest of embryonic development at some stage antecedent to the human. An outlandish delegate sustained against both these views with such heat as almost carried conviction the theory of copulation between women and the males of brutes, his authority being his own avouchment in support of fables such as that of the Minotaur which the genius of the elegant Latin poet has handed down to us in the pages of his Metamorphoses. The impression made by his words was immediate but shortlived. It was effaced as easily as it had been evoked by an allocution from Mr Candidate Mulligan in that vein of pleasantry which none better than he knew how to affect, postulating as the supremest object of desire a nice clean old man. Contemporaneously, a heated argument having arisen between Mr Delegate Madden and Mr Candidate Lynch regarding the juridical and theological dilemma in the event of one Siamese twin predeceasing the other, the difficulty by mutual consent was referred to Mr Canvasser Bloom for instant submittal to Mr Coadjutor Deacon Dedalus. Hitherto silent, whether the better to show by preternatural gravity that curious dignity of the garb with which he was invested or in obedience to an inward voice, he delivered briefly, and as some thought perfunctorily, the ecclesiastical ordinance forbidding man to put asunder what God has joined.

But Malachias' tale began to freeze them with horror. He conjured up the scene before them. The secret panel beside the chimney slid back and in the recess appeared... Haines! Which of us did not feel his flesh creep! He had a portfolio full of Celtic literature in one hand, in the other a phial marked *Poison*. Surprise, horror, loathing were depicted on all faces while he eyed them with a ghastly grin. I anticipated some such reception, he began with an eldritch laugh, for which, it seems, history is to blame. Yes, it is true. I am the murderer of Samuel Childs. And how I am punished! The inferno has no terrors for me. This is the appearance is on me. Tare and ages, what way would I be resting at all, he muttered thickly, and I tramping Dublin this while back with my share of songs and himself after me the like of a soulth or a bullawurrus? My hell, and Ireland's, is in this life. It is what I tried to obliterate my crime. Distractions, rookshooting, the Erse language (he recited some), laudanum (he raised the phial to his lips), camping out. In vain! His spectre stalks me. Dope is my only hope... Ah! Destruction! The black panther! With a cry he suddenly vanished and the panel slid back. An instant later his head appeared in the door opposite and said: Meet me at Westland row station at ten past eleven. He was gone! Tears gushed from the eyes of the dissipated host. The seer raised his hand to heaven, murmuring: The vendetta of Mannanaun! The sage repeated *Lex talionis*. The sentimentalist is he who would enjoy without incurring the immense debtorship for a thing done. Malachias, overcome by emotion, ceased. The mystery was unveiled. Haines was the third brother. His real name was Childs. The black panther was himself the ghost of his own father. He drank drugs to obliterate. For this relief much thanks. The lonely house by the graveyard is uninhabited. No soul will live there. The spider pitches her web in the solitude. The nocturnal rat peers from his hole. A curse is on it. It is haunted. Murderer's ground.

What is the age of the soul of man? As she hath the virtue of the chameleon to change her hue at every new approach, to be gay with the merry and mournful with the downcast, so too is her age changeable as her mood. No longer is Leopold, as he sits there, ruminating, chewing the cud of reminiscence, that staid agent of publicity and holder of a modest substance in the funds. He is young Leopold, as in a retrospective arrangement, a mirror within a mirror (hey, presto !), he beholdeth himself. That young figure of then is seen, precociously manly, walking on a nipping morning from the old house in Clambrassil street to the high school, his booksatchel on him bandolierwise, and in it a goodly hunk of wheaten loaf, a mother's thought. Or it is the same figure, a year or so gone over, in his first hard hat (ah, that was a day!), already on the road, a fullfledged traveller for the family firm, equipped with an orderbook, a scented handkerchief (not for show only), his case of bright trinketware (alas, a thing now of the past!), and a quiverful of compliant smiles for this or that halfwon housewife reckoning it out upon her fingertips or for a budding virgin shyly acknowledging (but the heart ? tell me !) his studied baisemoins. The scent, the smile but more than these, the dark eyes and oleaginous address brought home at duskfall many a commission to the head of the firm seated with Jacob's pipe after like labours in the paternal ingle (a meal of noodles, you may be sure, is aheating), reading through round horned spectacles some paper from the Europe of a month before. But hey, presto, the mirror is breathed on and the young knighterrant recedes, shrivels, to a tiny speck within the mist. Now he is himself paternal and these about him might be his sons. Who can say? The wise father knows his own child. He thinks of a drizzling night in Hatch street, hard by the bonded stores there, the first. Together (she is a poor waif, a child of shame, yours and mine and of all for a bare shilling and her luckpenny) together they hear the heavy tread of the watch as two raincaped shadows pass the new royal university. Bridie! Bridie Kelly! He will never forget the name, ever remember the night, first night, the bridenight. They are entwined in nethermost darkness, the willer with the willed, and in an instant (*fiat !*) light shall flood the world. Did heart leap to heart ? Nay, fair reader. In a breath 'twas done but — hold! Back! It must not be! In terror the poor girl flees away through the murk. She is the bride of darkness, a daughter of night. She dare not bear the sunnygolden babe of day. No, Leopold! Name and memory solace thee not. That youthful illusion of thy strength was taken from thee and in vain. No son of thy loins is by thee. There is none now to be for Leopold, what Leopold was for Rudolph.

The voices blend and fuse in clouded silence : silence that is the infinite of space : and swiftly, silently the soul is wafted over regions of cycles of generations that have lived. A region where grey twilight ever descends, never falls on wide sagegreen pasturefields, shedding her dusk, scattering a perennial dew of stars. She follows her mother with ungainly steps, a mare leading her fillyfoal. Twilight phantoms are they yet moulded in prophetic grace of structure, slim shapely haunches, a supple tendonous neck, the meek apprehensive skull. They fade, sad phantoms : all is gone. Agendath is a waste land, a home of screechowls and the sandblind upupa. Netaim, the golden, is no more. And on the highway of the clouds they come, muttering thunder of rebellion, the ghosts of beasts. Huuh ! Hark ! Huuh ! Parallax stalks behind and goads them, the lancinating lightnings of whose brow are scorpions. Elk and yak, the bulls of Bashan and of Babylon, mammoth and mastodon, they come trooping to the sunken sea, *Lacus Mortis*. Ominous, revengeful zodiacal host ! They moan, passing upon the clouds, horned and capricorned, the trumpeted with the tusked, the lionmaned, the giantantlered, snouter and crawler, rodent, ruminant and pachyderm, all their moving moaning multitude, murderers of the sun.

Onward to the dead sea they tramp to drink, unslaked and with horrible gulpings, the salt somnolent inexhaustible flood. And the equine portent grows again, magnified in the deserted heavens, nay to heaven's own magnitude till it looms, vast, over the house of Virgo. And, lo, wonder of metempsychosis, it is she, the everlasting bride, harbinger of the daystar, the bride, ever virgin. It is she, Martha, thou lost one, Millicent, the young, the dear, the radiant. How serene does she now arise, a queen among the Pleiades, in the penultimate antelucan hour, shod in sandals of bright gold, coifed with a veil of what do you call it gossamer ! It floats, it flows about her starborn flesh and loose it streams emerald, sapphire, mauve and heliotrope, sustained on currents of cold interstellar wind, winding, coiling, simply swirling, writhing in the skies a mysterious writing till after a myriad metamorphoses of symbol, it blazes, Alpha, a ruby and triangled sign upon the forehead of Taurus.

Francis was reminding Stephen of years before when they had been at school together in Conmee's time. He asked about Glaucon, Alcibiades, Pisistratus. Where were they now ? Neither knew. You have spoken of the past and its phantoms, Stephen said. Why think of them ? If I call them into life across the waters of Lethe will not the poor ghosts troop to my call ? Who supposes it ? I, Bous Stephanoumenos, bullockbefriending bard, am lord and giver of their life. He encircled his gadding hair with a coronal of vineleaves, smiling at Vincent. That answer and those leaves, Vincent said to him, will adorn you more fitly when something more, and greatly more, than a capful of light odes can call your genius father. All who wish you well hope this for you. All desire to see you bring forth the work you meditate. I heartily wish you may not fail them. O no, Vincent, Lenehan said, laying a hand on the shoulder near him, have no fear. He could not leave his mother an orphan. The young man's face grew dark. All could see how hard it was for him to be reminded of his promise and of his recent loss. He would have withdrawn from the feast had not the noise of voices allayed the smart. Madden had lost five drachmas on Sceptre for a whim of the rider's name : Lenehan as much more. He told them of the race. The flag fell and, huuh, off, scamper, the mare ran out freshly with O. Madden up. She was leading the field : all hearts were beating. Even Phyllis could not contain herself. She waved her scarf and cried : Huzzah ! Sceptre wins ! But in the straight on the run home when all were in close order the dark horse Throwaway drew level, reached, outstripped her. All was lost now. Phyllis was silent : her eyes were sad anemones. Juno, she cried, I am undone. But her lover consoled her and brought her a bright casket of gold in which lay some oval sugarplums which she partook. A tear fell : one only. A whacking fine whip, said Lenehan, is W. Lane. Four winners yesterday and three today. What rider is like him ? Mount him on the camel or the boisterous buffalo the victory in a hack canter is still his. But let us bear it as was the ancient wont. Mercy on the luckless ! Poor Sceptre ! he said with a light sigh. She is not the filly that she was. Never, by this hand, shall we behold such another. By gad, sir, a queen of them. Do you remember her, Vincent? I wish you could have seen my queen today, Vincent said, how young she was and radiant (Lalage were scarce fair beside her) in her yellow shoes and frock of muslin, I do not know the right name of it. The chestnuts that shaded us were in bloom : the air drooped with their persuasive odour and with pollen floating by us. In the sunny patches one might easily have cooked on a stone a batch of those buns with Corinth fruit in them that Periplepomenos sells in his booth near the bridge. But she had nought for her teeth but the arm with which I held her and in that she nibbled mischievously when I pressed too close. A week ago she lay ill, four days on the couch, but today she was free, blithe, mocked at peril. She is more taking then. Her posies too ! Mad romp that it is, she had pulled her fill as we reclined together. And in your ear, my friend, you will not think who met us as we left the field. Conmee himself ! He was walking by the hedge, reading, I think a brevier book with, I doubt not, a witty letter in it from Glycera or Chloe to keep the page. The sweet creature turned all colours in her confusion, feigning to reprove a slight disorder in her dress : a slip of underwood clung there for the very trees adore her. When Conmee had passed she glanced at her lovely echo in the little mirror she carries. But he had been kind. In going by he had blessed us. The gods too are ever kind, Lenehan said. If I had poor luck with Bass's mare perhaps this draught of his may serve me more propensely. He was laying his hand upon a winejar : Malachi saw it and withheld his act, pointing to the stranger and to the scarlet label. Warily, Malachi whispered, preserve a druid silence. His soul is far away. It is as painful perhaps to be awakened from a vision as to be born. Any object, intensely regarded, may be a gate of access to the incorruptible eon of the gods. Do you not think it, Stephen? Theosophos told me so, Stephen answered, whom in a previous existence Egyptian priests initiated into the mysteries of karmic law. The lords of the moon, Theosophos told me, an orangefiery shipload from planet Alpha of the lunar chain would not assume the etheric doubles and these were therefore incarnated by the rubycoloured egos from the second constellation.

However, as a matter of fact though, the preposterous surmise about him being in some description of a doldrums or other or mesmerised which was entirely due to a misconception of the shallowest character, was not the case at all. The individual whose visual organs while the above was going on, were at this juncture commencing to exibit symptoms of animation, was as astute if not astuter than any man living and anybody that conjectured the contrary would have found themselves pretty speedily in the wrong shop. During the past four minutes or thereabouts he had been staring hard at a certain amount of number one Bass bottled by Messrs Bass and Co at Burton-on-Trent which happened to be situated amongst a lot of others right opposite to where he was and which was certainly calculated to attract anyone's remark on account of its scarlet appearance. He was simply and solely, as it subsequently transpired for reasons best known to himself, which put quite an altogether different complexion on the proceedings, after the moment before's observations about boyhood days and the turf, recollecting two or three private transactions of his own which the other two were as mutually innocent of as the babe unborn. Eventually, however, both their eyes met and, as soon as it began to dawn on him that the other was endeavouring to help himself to the thing, he involontarily determined to help him himself and so he accordingly took hold of the mediumsized glass recipient which contained the fluid sought after and made a capacious hole in it by pouring a lot of it out with, also at the same time however, however, a considerable degree of attentiveness in order not to upset any of the beer that was in it about the place.

The debate which ensued was in its scope and progress an epitome of the course of life. Neither place nor council was lacking in dignity. The debaters were the keenest in the land, the theme they were engaged on the loftiest and most vital. The high hall of Horne's house had never beheld an assembly so representative and so varied nor had the old rafters of that establishment ever listened to a language so encyclopaedic. A gallant scene in truth it made. Crotthers was there at the foot of the table in his striking Highland garb, his face glowing from the briny airs of the Mull of Galloway. There too, opposite to him was Lynch whose countenance bore already the stigmata of early depravity and premature wisdom. Next the Scotchman was the place assigned to Costello, the eccentric, while at his side was seated in stolid repose the squat form of Madden. The chair of the resident indeed stood vacant before the hearth but on either flank of it the figure of Bannon in explorer's kit of tweed shorts and salted cowhide brogues contrasted sharply with the primrose elegance and and townbred manners of Malachi Roland St John Mulligan. Lastly at the head of the board was the young poet who found a refuge from his labours of pedagogy and metaphysical inquisition in the convivial atmosphere of Socratic discussion, while to right and left of him were accomodated the flippant prognosticator, fresh from the hippodrome, and that vigilant wanderer, soiled by the dust of travel and combat and stained by the mire of an indelible dishonour, but from whose steadfast and constant heart no lure or peril or threat or degradation could ever efface the image of that voluptuous loveliness which the inspired pencil of Lafayette has limned for ages yet to come.

It had better be stated here and now at the outset that the perverted transcendentalism to which Mr S. Dedalus' (Div. Scep.) contentions would appear to prove him pretty badly addicted runs directly counter to accepted scientific methods. Science, it cannot be too often repeated, deals with tangible phenomena. The man of science like the man in the street has to face hardheaded facts that cannot be blinked and explain them as best he can. There may be, it is true, some questons which science cannot answer — at present — such as the first problem submitted by Mr L. Bloom (Pubb. Canv.) regarding the future determination of sex. Must we accept the view of Empedocles of Trinacria that the right ovary (the postmenstrual period, assert others) is responsible for the birth of males or are the too long neglected spermatozoa or nemasperms the differentiating factors or is it, as most embryologists incline to opine, such as Culpepper, Spallanzani, Blumenbach, Lusk, Hertwig, Leopold and Valenti, a mixture of both. This would be tantamount to a cooperation (one of nature's favourite devices) between the *nisus formativus* of the nemasperm on the one hand and on the other a happily chosen position, *succubitus felix*, of the passive element. The other problem raised by the same inquirer is scarcely less vital : infant mortality. It is interesting because, as he pertinently remarks, we are all born in the same way but we all die in different ways. Mr M. Mulligan (Hyg. et Eug. Doc.) blames the sanitary conditions in which our greylunged citizens contract adenoids, pulmonary complaints etc. by inhaling the bacteria which lurk in dust. These factors, he alleges, and the revolting spectacles offered by our streets, hideous publicity posters, religious ministers of all denominations, mutilated soldiers and sailors, exposed scorbutic cardrivers, the suspened carcases of dead animals, paranoic bachelors and unfructified duennas — these, he said, were accountable for any and every fallingoff in the calibre of the race. Kalipedia, he prophesied, would soon be generally adopted and all the graces of life, genuinely good music, agreeable literature, light philosophy, instructive pictures, plastercast reproductions of the classical statues such as Venus and Apollo, artistic coloured photographs of prize babies, all these little attentions would enable ladies who were in a particular condition to pass the intervening months in a most enjoyable manner. Mr J. Crotthers (Disc. Bacc.) attributes some of these demises to abdominal trauma in the case of women workers subjected to heavy labours in the workshop and to marital discipline in the home but by far the vast majority to neglect, private or official, culminating in the exposure of newborn infants, the practice of criminal abortion or in the atrocious crime of infanticide. Although the former (we are thinking of neglect) is undoubtedly only too true the case he cites of nurses forgetting to count the sponges in the peritoneal cavity is too rare to be normative. In fact when one comes to look into it the wonder is that so many pregnancies and deliveries go off so well as they do, all things considered and in spite of our human shortcomings which often balk nature in her intentions. An ingenious suggestion is that thrown out by Mr V. Lynch (Bacc. Arith.) that both natality and mortality, as well as all other phenomena of evolution, tidal movements, lunar phases, blood temperatures, diseases in general, everything, in fine, in nature's vast workshop from the extinction of some remote sun to the blossoming of one of the countless flowers which beautify our public parks is subject to a law of numeration as yet unascertained. Still the plain straightforward question why a child of normally healthy parents and seemingly a healthy child and properly looked after succumbs unaccountably in early childhood (though other children of the same marriage do not) must certainly in the poet's words, give us pause. Nature, we may rest assured, has her own good and cogent reasons for whatever she does and in all probability such deaths are due to some law of anticipation by which organisms in which morbous germs have taken up their residence (modern science has conclusively shown that only the plasmic substance can be said to be immortal) tend to disappear at an increasingly earlier stage of development, an arrangement, which, though productive of pain to some of our feelings (notably the maternal) is nevertheless, some of us think, in the long run beneficial to the race in general in securing thereby the survival of the fittest. Mr S. Dedalus' (Div. Scep.) remark (or should it be called an interruption?) that an omnivorous being which can masticate, deglute, digest and apparently pass through the ordinary channel with pluterperfect imperturbability such multifarious aliments as cancrenous femoules emaciated by parturition, corpulent professional gentlemen, not to speak of jaundiced politicians and chlorotic nuns might possibly find gastric relief in an innocent collation of staggering bob, reveals as nought else could and in a very unsavoury light the tendency above alluded to. For the enlightenment of those who are not so intimately acquainted with the minutiae of the municipal abattoir as this morbidminded esthete and embryo philosopher who for all his overweening bumptiousness in things scientific can scarcely distinguish an acid from an alkali prides himself on being, it should perhaps be stated that staggering bob in the vile parlance of our lower class licensed victuallers signifies the cookable and eatable flesh of a calf newly dropped from its mother. In a recent public controversy with Mr L. Bloom (Pubb. Canv.) which took place in the commons' hall of the National Maternity Hospital, 29, 30 and 31 Holles street, of which, as is well known, Dr A. Horne (Lic. in Midw., F. K. Q. C. P. I.) is the able and popular master, he is reported by eyewitnesses as having stated that once a woman has let the cat into the bag (an esthetic allusion, presumably, to one of the most complicated and marvellous of all nature's processes, the act of sexual congress) she must let it out again or give it life, as he phrased it, to save her own. At the risk of her own was the telling rejoinder of his interlocutor none the less effective for the moderate and measured tone in which it was delivered.

Meanwhile the skill and patience of the physician had brought about a happy *accouchement*. It had been a weary weary while both for patient and doctor. All that surgical skill could do was done and the brave woman had manfully helped. She had. She had fought the good fight and now she was very very happy. Those who have passed on, who have gone before, are happy too as they gaze down and smile upon the touching scene. Reverently look at her as she reclines there with the motherlight in her eyes, that longing hunger for baby fingers (a pretty sight it is to see), in the first bloom of her new motherhood, breathing a silent prayer of thanksgiving to One above, the Universal Husband. And as her loving eyes behold her babe she wishes only one blessing more, to have her dear Doady there with her to share her joy, to lay in his arms that mite of God's clay, the fruit of their lawful embraces. He is older now (you and I may whisper it) and a trifle stooped in the shoulders yet in the whirligig of years a grave dignity has come to the conscientious second accountant of the Ulster bank, College Green branch. O Doady, loved one of old, faithful lifemate now, it may never be again, that faroff time of the roses! With the old shake of her pretty head she recalls those days. God, how beautiful now across the mist of years! But their children are grouped in her imagination about the bedside, hers and his, Charley, Mary Alice, Frederick Albert (if he had lived), Mamy, Budgy (Victoria Frances), Tom, Violet Constance Louisa, darling little Bobsy (called after our famous hero of the South African war, lord Bobs of Waterford and Candahar) and now this last pledge of their union, a Purefoy if ever there was one, with the true Purefoy nose. Young hopeful will be christened Mortimer Edward after the influential third cousin of Mr Purefoy in the Treasury Remembrancer's office, Dublin Castle. And so time wags on : but father Cronion has dealt lightly here. No, let no sigh break from that bosom, dear gentle Mina. And Doady, knock the ashes from your pipe, the seasoned briar you still fancy when the curfew rings for you (may it be the distant day!) and dout the light whereby you read in the Sacred Book for the oil too has run low and so with a tranquil heart to bed, to rest. He knows and will call in His own good time. You too have fought the good fight and played loyally your man's part. Sir, to you my hand. Well done, thou good and faithful servant!

There are sins or (let us call them as the world calls them) evil memories which are hidden away by man in the darkest places of the heart but they abide there and wait. He may suffer their memory to grow dim, let them be as though they had not been and all but persuade himself that they were not or at least were otherwise. Yet a chance word will call them forth suddenly and they will rise up to confront him in the most various circumstances, a vision or a dream, or while timbrel and harp soothe his senses or amid the cool silver tranquillity of the evening or at the feast at midnight when he is now filled with wine. Not to insult over him will the vision come as over one that lies under her wrath, not for vengeance to cut him off from the living but shrouded in the piteous vesture of the past, silent, remote, reproachful.

The stranger still regarded on the face before him a slow recession of that false calm there, imposed, as it seemed, by habit or some studied trick, upon words so embittered as to accuse in their speaker an unhealthiness, a *flair,* for the cruder things of life. A scene disengages itself in the observer's memory, evoked, it would seem, by a word of so natural a homeliness as if those days were really present there (as some thought) with their immediate pleasures. A shaven space of lawn one soft May evening, the wellremembered grove of lilacs at Roundtown, purple and white, fragrant slender spectators of the game but with much real interest in the pellets as they run slowly forward over the sward or collide and stop, one by its fellow, with a brief alert shock. And yonder about that grey urn where the water moves at times in thoughtful irrigation you saw another as fragrant sisterhood, Floey, Atty, Tiny and their darker friend with I know not what of arresting in her pose then, Our Lady of the Cherries, a comely brace of them pendent from an ear, bringing out the foreign warmth of the skin so daintily against the cool ardent fruit. A lad of four or five in linseywoolsey (blossomtime but there will be cheer in the kindly hearth when ere long the bowls are gathered and hutched) is standing on the urn secured by that circle of girlish fond hands. He frowns a little just as this young man does now with a perhaps too conscious enjoyment of danger but must needs glance at whiles towards where his mother watches from the *piazzetta* giving upon the flowerclose with a faint shadow of remoteness or of reproach *(alles vergängliche)* in her glad look.

Mark this farther and remember. The end comes suddenly. Enter that antechamber of birth where the studious are assembled and note their faces. Nothing, as it seems, there of rash or violent. Quietude of custody rather, befitting their station in that house, the vigilant watch of shepherds and of angels about a crib in Bethlehem of Juda long ago. But as before the lightning the serried stormclouds, heavy with preponderant excess of moisture, in swollen masses turgidly distended, compass earth and sky in one vast slumber, impending above parched field and drowsy oxen and blighted growth of shrub and verdure till in an instant a flash rives their centres and with the reverberation of the thunder the cloudburst pours its torrent, so and not otherwise was the transformation, violent and instantaneous, upon the utterance of the Word.

Burke's! Outflings my lord Stephen, giving the cry, and a tag and bobtail of all them after, cockerel, jackanapes, welsher, pilldoctor, punctual Bloom at heels with a universal grabbing at headgear, ashplants, bilbos, Panama hats and scabbards, Zermatt alpenstocks and what not. A dedale of lusty youth, noble every student there. Nurse Callan taken aback in the hallway cannot stay them nor smiling surgeon coming downstairs with news of placentation ended, a full pound if a milligramme. They hark him on. The door! It is open? Ha! They are out tumultuously, off for a minute's race, all bravely legging it, Burke's of Denzille and Holles their ulterior goal. Dixon follows, giving them sharp language but raps out an oath, he too, and on. Bloom stays with nurse a thought to send a kind word to happy mother and nurseling up there. Doctor Diet and Doctor Quiet. Looks she too not other now? Ward of watching in Horne's house has told its tale in that washedout pallor. Then all being gone, a glance of motherwit helping, he whispers close in going: Madam, when come the storkbird for thee?

The air without is impregnated with raindew moisture, life essence celestial, glistering on Dublin stone there under starshiny *coelum*. God's air, the Allfather's air, scintillant circumambient cessile air. Breathe it deep into thee. By heaven, Theodore Purefoy, thou hast done a doughty deed and no botch! Thou art, I vow, the remarkablest progenitor barring none in this chaffering allincluding most farraginous chronicle. Astounding! In her lay a Godframed Godgiven preformed possibility which thou hast fructified with thy modicum of man's work. Cleave to her! Serve! Toil on, labour like a very bandog and let scholarment and all Malthusiasts go hang. Thou art all their daddies, Theodore. Art drooping under thy load, bemoiled with butcher's bills at home and ingots (not thine!) in the countinghouse? Head up! For every newbegotten thou shalt gather thy homer of ripe wheat. See, thy fleece is drenched. Dost envy Darby Dullman there with his Joan? A canting jay and a rheumeyed curdog is all their progeny. Pshaw, I tell thee! He is a mule, a dead gasteropod, without vim or stamina, not worth a cracked kreutzer. Copulation without population! No, say I! Herod's slaughter of the innocents were the truer name. Vegetables, forsooth, and sterile cohabitation! Give her beefsteaks, red, raw, bleeding! She is a hoary pandemonium of ills, enlarged glands, mumps, quinsy, bunions, hayfever, bedsores, ringworm, floating kidney, Derbyshire neck, warts, bilious attacks, gallstones, cold feet, varicose veins. A truce to threnes and trentals and jeremies and all such congenital defunctive music. Twenty years of it, regret them not. With thee it was not as with many that will and would and wait and never do. Thou sawest thy America, thy lifetask, and didst charge to cover like the transpontine bison. How saith Zarathusthra? *Deine Kuh Truebsal melkest Du. Nun trinkst Du die suesse Milch des Euters.* See! It displodes for thee in abundance. Drink, man, an udderful! Mother's milk, Purefoy, the milk of human kin, milk too of those burgeoning stars overhead, rutilant in thin rainvapour, punch milk, such as those rioters will quaff in their guzzlingden, milk of madness, the honeymilk of Canaan's land. Thy cow's dug was tough, what? Ay, but her milk is hot and sweet and fattening. No dollop this but thick rich bonnyclaber. To her, old patriarch! Pap! *Per deam Partulam et Pertundam nunc est bibendum!*

All off for a buster, armstrong, hollering down the street. Bonafides. Where you slep las nigh? Timothy of the battered naggin. Like ole Billyo. Any brollies or gumboots in the fambly? Where the Henry Nevil's sawbones and ole clo? Sorra one o me knows. Hurrah there, Dix! Forward the ribbon counter. Where's Punch? All serene. Jay, look at the drunken minister coming out of the maternity hospal? *Benedicat vos omnipotens Deus, Pater et Filius.* A make, mister. The Denzille lane boys. Hell, blast ye! Scoot. Righto, Isaacs, shove em out of the bleeding limelight. Yous join uz, dear sir? No hentrusion in life. Lou heap good man. Allee samee this bunch. *En avant, mes enfants!* Fire away number one on the gun. Burke's! Thence they advanced five parasangs. Slattery's mounted foot where's that bleeding awfur? Parson Steve, apostates' creed! No, no. Mulligan! Abaft there! Shove ahead. Keep a watch on the clock. Chuckingout time. Mullee! What's on you? *Ma mère m'a mariée.* British Beatitudes! *Retamplan Digidi Boum Boum.* Ayes have it. To be printed and bound at the Druiddrum press by two designing females. Calf covers of pissedon green. Last word in art shades. Most beautiful book come out of Ireland my time. *Silentium!* Get a spurt on. Tention. Proceed to nearest canteen and there annex liquor stores. March! Tramp, tramp, tramp the boys are (atitudes!) parching. Beer, beef, business, bibles, bulldogs, battleships, buggery and bishops. Whether on the scaffold high. Beerbeef trample the bibles. When for Irelandear. Trample the trampellers. Thunderation! Keep the durned millingtary step. We fall. Bishops boosebox. Halt! Heave to. Rugger. Scrum in. No touch kicking. Wow, my tootsies! You hurt? Most amazingly sorry!

Query. Who's astanding this here do? Proud possessor of damnall. Declare misery. Bet to the ropes. Me nantee saltee. Not a red at me this week gone. Yours? Mead of our fathers for the *Uebermensch.* Dittoh. Five number ones. You, sir? Ginger cordial. Chase me, the cabby's caudle. Stimulate the caloric. Winding of his ticker. Stopped short never to go again when the old. Absinthe for me, savvy? *Caramba!* Have an eggnog or a prairie oyster. Enemy? Avuncular's got my timepiece. Ten to. Obligated awful. Don't mention it. Got a pectoral trauma, eh, Dix? Pos fact. Got bet be a boomblebee whenever he wus settin sleepin in hes bit garten. Digs up near the Mater. Buckled he is. Know his dona? Yup, sartin, I do. Full of a dure. See her in her dishybilly. Peels off a credit. Lovey lovekin. None of your lean kine, not much. Pull down the blind, love. Two Ardilauns. Same here. Look slippery. If you fall don't wait to get up. Five, seven, nine. Fine! Got a prime pair of mincepies, no kid. And her take me to rests and her anker of rum. Must be seen to be believed. Your starving eyes and allbeplastered neck you stole my heart, O gluepot. Sir? Spud again the rheumatiz? All poppycock, you'll scuse me saying. For the hoi polloi. I vear thee beest a gert wool. Well, doc? Back fro Lapland? Your corporosity sagaciating O K? How's the squaws and papooses? Womanbody after going on the straw? Stand and deliver. Password. There's hair. Ours the white death and the ruddy birth. Hi! Spit in your own eye, boss. Mummer's wire. Cribbed out of Meredith. Jesified orchidised polycimical jesuit! Aunty mine's writing Pa Kinch. Baddybad Stephen lead astray goodygood Malachi.

Hurroo! Collar the leather, youngun. Roun wi the nappy. Here, Jock braw Hielentman's your barleybree. Lang may your lum reek and your kailpot boil! My tipple. *Merci*. Here's to us. How's that? Leg before wicket. Don't stain my brandnew sitinems. Give's a shake of pepper, you there. Catch aholt. Caraway seed to carry away. Twig? Shrieks of silence. Every cove to his gentry mort. Venus Pandemos. *Les petites femmes*. Bold bad girl from the town of Mullingar. Tell her I was axing at her. Hauding Sara by the wame. On the road to Malahide. Me? If she who seduced me had left but the name. What do you want for ninepence. Machree, Macruiskeen. Smutty Moll for a mattress jig. And a pull alltogether. *Ex!*

Waiting, guvnor? Most deciduously. Bet your boots on. Stunned like seeing as how no shiners is acoming, Underconstumble? He've got the chink *ad lib*. Seed near free poun on un a spell ago a said war hisn. Us come right in on your invite, see? Up to you, matey. Out with the oof. Two bar and a wing. You larn that go off of they there Frenchy bilks? Won't wash here for nuts nohow. Lil chile velly solly. Ise de cutest colour coon down our side. Gawds teruth, Chawley. We are nae fou. We're nae the fou. Au reservoir, Mossoo. Tanks you.

'Tis, sure. What say? In the speakeasy. Tight. I shee you, shir. Bantam, two days teetee. Bowsing nowt but claretwine. Garn! Have a glint, do. Gum, I'm jiggered. And been to barber he have. Too full for words. With a railway bloke. How come you so? Opera he'd like? Rose of Castile. Rows of cast. Police! Some H_2O for a gent fainted. Look at Bantam's flowers. Gemini, he's going to holler. The colleen bawn, my colleen bawn. O, cheese it! Shut his blurry Dutch oven with a firm hand. Had the winner today till I tipped him a dead cert. The ruffin cly the nab of Stephen Hand as give me the jady coppaleen. He strike a telegramboy paddock wire big bug Bass to the depot. Shove him a joey and grahamise. Mare on form hot order. Guinea to a goosegog. Tell a cram, that. Gospeltrue. Criminal diversion? I think that yes. Sure thing. Land him in chokeechokee if the harman beck copped the game. Madden back Madden's a maddening back. O, lust, our refuge and our strength. Decamping. Must you go? Off to mammy. Stand by. Hide my blushes someone. All in if he spots me. Comeahome, our Bantam. Horryvar, mong vioo. Dinna forget the cowslips for hersel. Cornfide. Wha gev ye thon colt? Pal to pal. Jannock. Of John Thomas, her spouse. No fake, old man Leo. S'elp me, honest injun. Shiver my timbers if I had. There's a great big holy friar. Vyfor you no me tell? Vel, I ses, if that aint a sheeny nachez, vel, I vil get misha mishinnah. Through yerd our lord, Amen.

You move a motion? Steve boy, you're going it some. More bluggy drunkables? Will immensely splendiferous stander permit one stooder of most extreme poverty and one largesize grandacious thirst to terminate one expensive inaugurated libation? Give's a breather. Landlord, landlord, have you good wine, staboo? Hoots, mon, wee drap to pree. Cut and come again. Right Boniface! Absinthe the lot. *Nos omnes biberimus viridum toxicum diabolus capiat posterioria nostria*. Closingtime, gents. Eh? Rome boose for the Bloom toff. I hear you say onions? Bloo? Cadges ads? Photo's papli, by all that's gorgeous. Play low, pardner. Slide. *Bonsoir la compagnie*. And snares of the poxfiend. Where's the buck and Namby Amby? Skunked? Leg bail. Aweel, ye maun e'en gang yer gates. Checkmate. King to tower. Kind Kristyann will yu help, yung man hoose frend tuk bungalo kee to find plais whear to lay crown off his hed 2 night. Crickey, I'm about sprung. Tarnally dog gone my shins if this beent the bestest puttiest longbreak yet. Item, curate, couple of cookies for this child. Cot's plood and prandypalls, none! Not a pite of sheeses? Thrust syphilis down to hell and with him those other licensed spirits. Time. Who wander through the world. Health all. *A la vôtre!*

Golly, whatten tunket's you guy in the mackintosh? Dusty Rhodes. Peep at his wearables. By mighty! What's he got? Jubilee mutton. Bovril, by James. Wants it real bad. D'ye ken bare socks? Seedy cuss in the Richmond? Rawthere! Thought he had a deposit of lead in his penis. Trumpery insanity. Bartle the Bread we calls him. That, sir, was once a prosperous cit. Man all tattered and torn that married a maiden all forlorn. Slung her hook, she did. Here see lost love. Walking Mackintosh of lonely canyon. Tuck and turn in. Schedule time. Nix for the hornies. Pardon? See him today at a runefal? Chum o yourn passed in his checks? Ludamassy! Pore piccanninies! Thou'll no be telling me thot, Pold veg! Did ums blubble bigsplash crytears cos frien Padney was took off in black bag? Of all de darkies Massa Pat was verra best. I never see the like since I was born. *Tiens, tiens,* but it is well sad, that, my faith, yes. O get, rev on a gradient one in nine. Live axle drives are souped. Lay you two to one Jenatzy licks him ruddy well hollow. Jappies? High angle fire, inyah! Sunk by war specials. Be worse for him, says he, nor any Rooshian. Time all. There's eleven of them. Get ye gone. Forward, woozy wobblers! Night. Night. May Allah, the Excellent One, your soul this night ever tremendously conserve.

Your attention! We're nae the fou. The Leith police dismisseth us. The least tholice. Ware hawks tor the chap puking. Unwell in his abominable regions. Yooka. Night. Mona, my thrue love. Yook. Mona, my own love. Ook.

Hark! Shut your obstropolos. Pflaap! Pflaap! Blase on. There she goes. Brigade! Bout ship. Mount street way. Cut up. Pflaap! Tally ho. You not come? Run, skelter, race. Pflaaaap!

Lynch! Hey? Sign on long o me. Denzille lane this way. Change here for Bawdyhouse. We two, she said, will seek the kips where shady Mary is. Righto, any old time. *Laetabuntur in cubilibus suis.* You coming long? Whisper, who the sooty hell's the johnny in the black duds? Hush! Sinned against the light and even now that day is at hand when he shall come to judge the world by fire. Pflaap! *Ut implerentur scripturae.* Strike up a ballad. Then outspake medical Dick to his comrade medical Davy. Christicle, who's this excrement yellow gospeller on the Merrion hall? Elijah is coming. Washed in the Blood of the Lamb. Come on, you winefizzling ginsizzling booseguzzling existences! Come on, you dog-gone, bullnecked, beetlebrowed, hogjowled, peanutbrained, weaseleyed fourflushers, false alarms and excess baggage! Come on, you triple extract of infamy! Alexander J. Christ Dowie, that's yanked to glory most half this planet from 'Frisco Beach to Vladivostok. The Deity aint no nickel dime bumshow. I put it to you that he's on the square and a corking fine business propostion. He's the grandest thing yet and don't you forget it. Shout salvation in King Jesus. You'll need to rise precious early, you sinner there, it you want to diddle the Almighty God. Pflaaaap! Not half. He's got a coughmixture with a punch in it for you, my friend, in his backpocket. Just you try it on.

(*The Mabbot street entrance of nighttown, before which stretches an uncobbled tramsiding set with skeleton tracks, red and green will-o'-the wisps and danger signals. Rows of flimsy houses with gaping doors. Rare lamps with faint rainbow fans. Round Rabaiotti's halted ice gondola stunted men and women squabble. They grab wafers between which are wedged lumps of coal and copper snow. Sucking, they scatter slowly. Children. The swancomb of the gondola, highreared, forges on through the murk, white and blue under a lighthouse. Whistles call and answer.*)

THE CALLS

Wait, my love, and I'll be with you.

THE ANSWERS

Round behind the stable.

(*A deafmute idiot with goggle eyes, his shapeless mouth dribbling, jerks past, shaken in Saint Vitus' dance. A chain of children's hands imprisons him.*)

THE CHILDREN

Kithogue! Salute!

THE IDIOT

(*Lifts a palsied left arm and gurgles.*) Grhahute!

THE CHILDREN

Where's the great light?

THE IDIOT

(*Gobbling.*) Ghaghahest.

(*They release him. He jerks on. A pigmy woman swings on a rope slung between the railings, counting. A form sprawled against a dustbin and muffled by its arm and hat moves, groans, grinding growling teeth, and snores again. On a step a gnome totting among a rubbishtip crouches to shoulder a sack of rags and bones. A crone standing by with a smoky oil lamp rams the last bottle in the maw of his sack. He heaves his booty, tugs askew his peaked cap and hobbles off mutely. The crone makes back for her lair swaying her lamp. A bandy child, asquat on the doorstep with a papershuttlecock, crawls sidling after her in spurts, clutches her skirt, scrambles up. A drunken navvy grips with both hands the railings of an area, lurching heavily. At a corner two night watch in shoulder capes, their hands upon their staffholsters, loom tall. A plate crashes ; a woman screams ; a child wails. Oaths of a man roar, mutter, cease. Figures wander, lurk, peer from warrens. In a room lit by a candle stuck in a bottleneck a slut combs out the tatts from the hair of a scrufulous child. Cissy Caffrey's voice, still young, sings shrill from a lane.*)

CISSY CAFFREY

I gave it to Molly
Because she was jolly,
The leg of the duck
The leg of the duck.

(*Private Carr and Private Compton, swaggersticks tight in their oxters, as they march unsteadily rightaboutface and burst together from their mouths a volleyed fart. Laughter of men from the lane. A hoarse virago retorts.*)

THE VIRAGO

Signs on you, hairy arse. More power the Cavan girl.

CISSY CAFFREY

More luck to me. Cavan, Cootehill and Belturbet. (*She sings.*)

I gave it to Nelly
To stick in her belly
The leg of the duck
The leg of the duck.

(*Private Carr and Private Compton turn and counterretort, their tunics bloodbright in a lampglow, black sockets of caps on their blond cropped polls. Stephen Dedalus and Lynch pass through the crowd close to the redcoats.*)

PRIVATE COMPTON

(*Jerks his finger.*) Way for the parson.

PRIVATE CARR

(*Turns and calls.*) What ho, parson !

CISSY CAFFREY

(*Her voice soaring higher.*)

She has it, she got it,
Wherever she put it
The leg of the duck.

(*Stephen flourishing the ashplant in his left hand, chants with joy the* introit *for paschal time. Lynch, his jockey cap low on his brow, attends him, a sneer of discontent wrinkling his face.*)

STEPHEN

Vidi aquam egredientem de templo a latere dextro. Alleluia.
(*The famished snaggletusks of an elderly bawd protude from a doorway.*)

THE BAWD

(*Her voice whispering huskily.*) Sst ! Come, here till I tell you. Maidenhead inside. Sst.

STEPHEN

(*Altius aliquantulum.*) *Et omnes ad quos pervenit aqua ista.*

THE BAWD

(*Spits in their trail her jet of venom.*) Trinity medicals. Fallopian tube. All prick and no pence.

(*Edy Boardman, sniffling, crouched with Bertha Supple, draws her shawl across her nostrils.*)

EDY BOARDMAN

(*Bickering.*) And says the one : I seen you up Faithful place with your squarepusher, the greaser off the railway, in his cometobed hat. Did you, says I. That's not for you to say, says I. You never seen me in the mantrap with a married highlander, says I. The likes of her ! Stag that one is. Stubborn as a mule ! And her walking with two fellows the one time, Kildbride the enginedriver, and lancecorporal Oliphant.

STEPHEN

(*Triumphaliter.*) *Salvi facti i sunt.*

(*He flourishes his ashplant shivering the lamp image, shattering light over the world. A liver and white spaniel on the prowl slinks after him, growling. Lynch scares it with a kick.*)

LYNCH

So that ?

STEPHEN

(*Looks behind.*) So that gesture, not music not odours, would be a universal language, the gift of tongues rendering visible not the lay sense but the first entelechy, the structural rhythm.

LYNCH

Pornosophical philotheology. Metaphysics in Mecklenburg street !

STEPHEN

We have shrewridden Shakespeare and henpecked Socrates. Even the allwisest stagyrite was bitted, bridled and mounted by a light of love.

LYNCH

Ba!

STEPHEN

Anyway, who wants two gestures to illustrate a loaf and a jug! This movement illustrates the loaf and jug of bread and wine in Omar. Hold my stick.

LYNCH

Damn your yellow stick. Where are we going?

STEPHEN

Lecherous lynx, to *la belle dame sans merci*, Georgina Johnson, *ad deam qui laetificat juventutem meam*.

(*Stephen thrusts the ashplant on him and slowly holds out his hands, his head going back till both hands are a span from his breast, down turned in planes intersecting, the fingers about to part, the left being higher.*)

LYNCH

Which is the jug of bread? It skills not. That or the customhouse. Illustrate thou. Here take your crutch and walk.

(*They pass. Tommy Caffrey scrambles to a gaslamp and, clasping, climbs in spasms. From the top spur he slides down. Jacky Caffrey clasps to climb. The navvy lurches against the lamp. The twins scuttle off in the dark. The navvy, swaying, presses a forefinger against a wing of his nose and ejects from the farther nostril a long liquid jet of snot. Shouldering the lamp he staggers away through the crowd with his flaring cresset.*

Snakes of river fog creep slowly. From drains, clefts, cesspools, middens arise on all sides stagnant fumes. A glow leaps in the south beyond the seaward reaches of the river. The navvy staggering forward cleaves the crowd and lurches towards the tramsiding. On the farther side under the railway bridge Bloom appears flushed, panting, cramming bread and chocolate into a side pocket. From Gillen's hairdresser's window a composite portrait shows him gallant Nelson's image. A concave mirror at the side presents to him lovelorn longlost lugubru Booloohoom. Grave Gladstone sees him level, Bloom for Bloom. He passes, struck by the stare of truculent Wellington but in the convex mirror grin unstruck the bonham eyes and fatchuck cheekchops of Jollypoldy the rixdix doldy.

At Antonio Rabaiotti's door Bloom halts, sweated under the bright arclamps. He disappears. In a moment he reappears and hurries on.)

BLOOM

Fish and taters. N. g. Ah!

(*He disappears into Olhousen's, the pork butcher's, under the downcoming rollshutter. A few moments later he emerges from under the shutter, puffing Poldy, blowing Bloohoom. In each hand he holds a parcel, one containing a lukewarm pig's crubeen, the other a cold sheep's trotter, sprinkled with wholepepper. He gasps, standing upright. Then bending to one side he presses a parcel against his rib and groans.*)

BLOOM

Stitch in my side. Why did I run?

(*He takes breath with care and goes forward slowly towards the lampset siding. The glow leaps again.*)

BLOOM

What is that? A flasher? Searchlight.

(*He stands at Cormack's corner, watching.*)

BLOOM

Aurora borealis or a steel foundry? Ah, the brigade, of course. South side anyhow. Big blaze. Might be his house. Beggar's bush. We're safe. (*He hums cheerfully.*) London's burning, London's burning! On fire, on fire! (*He catches sight of the navvy lurching through the crowd at the farther side of Talbot street.*) I'll miss him. Run. Quick. Better cross here.

(*He darts to cross the road. Urchins shout.*)

THE URCHINS

Mind out, mister!

(Two cyclists, with lighted paper lanterns aswing, swim by him, grazing him, their bells rattling.)

THE BELLS

Haltyaltyaltyall.

BLOOM

(Halts erect stung by a spasm.) Ow.

(He looks round, darts forward suddenly. Through rising fog a dragon sandstrewer, travelling at caution, slews heavily down upon him, its huge red headlight winking, its trolley hissing on the wire. The motorman bangs his footgong.)

THE GONG

Bang Bang Bla Bak Blud Bugg Bloo.

(The brake cracks violently. Bloom, raising a policeman's whitegloved hand, blunders stifflegged, out of the track. The motorman thrown forward, pugnosed, on the guidewheel, yells as he slides past over chains and keys.)

THE MOTORMAN

Hey, shitbreeches, are you doing the hattrick?

BLOOM

(Bloom trickleaps to the curbstone and halts again. He brushes a mudflake from his cheek with a parcelled hand.)

No thoroughfare. Close shave that but cured the stitch. Must take up Sandow's exerciser again. On the hands down. Insure against street accident too. The Providential. *(He feels his trouser pocket.)* Poor mamma's panacea. Heel easily catch in tracks or bootlace in a cog. Day, the wheel of the black Maria, peeled off my shoe at Leonard's corner. Third time is the charm. Shoe trick. Insolent driver. I ought to report him. Tension makes them nervous. Might be the fellow balked me this morning with that horsey woman. Same style of beauty. Quick of him all he same. The stiff walk. True word spoken in jest. That awful cramp in Lad lane. Something poisonous I ate. Emblem of luck. Why? Probably lost cattle. Mark of the beast. (*He closes his eyes an instant.*) Bit light in the head. Monthly or effect of the other. Brainfogfag. That tired feeling. Too much for me now. Ow!

(*A sinister figure leans on plaited legs against O'Beirne's wall, a visage unknown, injected with dark mercury. From under a wideleaved sombrero the figure regards him with evil eye.*)

BLOOM

Bueñas noches, señorita Blanca, que calle es esta?

THE FIGURE

(*Impassive, raises a signal arm.*) Password. *Sraid Mabbot.*

BLOOM

Haha. *Merci.* Esperanto. *Slan leath.* (*He mutters.*) Gaelic league spy, sent by that fireeater.

(*He steps forward. A sackshouldered ragman bars his path. He steps left, ragsackman left.*)

BLOOM

I beg.

(*He swerves, sidles, stepaside, slips past and on.*)

BLOOM

Keep to the right, right, right. If there is a fingerpost planted by the Touring Club at Stepaside who procured that public boon? I who lost my way and contributed to the columns of the *Irish Cyclist* the letter headed, *In darkset Stepaside.* Keep, keep, keep to the right. Rags and bones, at midnight. A fence more likely. First place murderer makes for. Wash off his sins of the world.

(*Jacky Caffrey, hunted by Tommy Caffrey, runs full tilt against Bloom.*)

BLOOM

O.

(*Shocked, on weak hams, he halts. Tommy and Jacky vanish there, there. Bloom pats with parcelled hands watch, fobpocket, bookpocket, pursepoke, sweets of sin, potato soap.*)

BLOOM

Beware of pickpockets. Old thieves dodge. Collide. Then snatch your purse.

(*The retriever approches sniffling, nose to the ground. A sprawled form sneezes. A stooped bearded figure appears garbed in the long caftan of an elder in Zion and a smoking cap with magenta tassels. Horned spectacles hang down at the wings of the nose. Yellow poison streaks are on the drawn face.*)

RUDOLPH

Second halfcrown waste money today. I told you not go with drunken goy ever. So. You catch no money.

BLOOM

(*Hides the crubeen and trotter behind his back and, crestfallen, feels warm and cold feetmeat.*) *Ja, ich weiss, papachi.*

RUDOLPH

What you making down this place? Have you no soul? (*With feeble vulture talons he feels the silent face of Bloom.*) Are you not my son Leopold, the grand son of Leopold? Are you not my dear son Leopold who left the house of his father and left the god of his fathers Abraham and Jacob?

BLOOM

(*With precaution.*) I suppose so, father. Mosenthal. All that's left of him.

RUDOLPH

(*Severely.*) One night they bring you home drunk as dog after spend your good money. What you call them running chaps?

BLOOM

(*In youth's smart blue Oxford suit with white vestslips, narrowshouldered, in brown Alpine hat, wearing gent's sterling silver waterbury keyless watch and double curb Albert with seal attached, one side of him coated with stiffening mud.*) Harriers, father. Only that once.

RUDOLPH

Once! Mud head to foot. Cut your hand open. Lockjaw. They make you kaput, Leopoldleben. You watch them chaps.

BLOOM

(*Weakly.*) They challenged me to a sprint. It was muddy. I slipped.

RUDOLPH

(*With contempt.*) *Goim nachez* Nice spectacles for your poor mother!

BLOOM

Mamma!

ELLEN BLOOM

(*In pantomime dame's stringed mobcap, crinoline and bustle, widow Twankey's blouse with muttonleg sleeves buttoned behind, grey mittens and cameo brooch, her hair plaited in a crispine net, appears over the staircase banisters, a slanted candlestick in her hand and cries out in shrill alarm.*) O blessed Redeemer, what have they done to him! My smelling salts! (*She hauls up a reef of skirt and ransacks the pouch of her striped blay petticoat. A phial, an Agnus Dei, a shrivelled potato and a celluloid doll fall out.*) Sacred Heart of Mary, where were you at all, at all?

(*Bloom, mumbling, his eyes downcast begins to bestow his parcels in his filled pockets but desists, muttering.*)

A VOICE

(*Sharply.*) Poldy!

BLOOM

Who? (*He ducks and wards off a blow clumsily.*) At your service.

(*He looks up. Beside her mirage of datepalms a handsome woman in Turkish costume stands before him. Opulent curves fill out her scarlet *trousers and jacket slashed with gold. A wide yellow cummerbund girdles her. A white yashmak violet in the night, covers her face, leaving free only her large dark eyes and raven hair.*)

BLOOM

Molly!

MARION

Welly? Mrs Marion from this out, my dear man, when you speak to me. (*Satirically.*) Has poor little hubby cold feet waiting so long?

BLOOM

(*Shifts from foot to foot.*) No, no. Not the least little bit.

(*He breathes in deep agitation, swallowing gulps of air, questions, hopes, crubeens for her supper, things to tell her, excuses, desire, spellbound. A coin gleams on her forehead. On her feet are jewelled toerings. Her ankles are linked by a slender fetterchain. Beside her a camel, hooded with a turreting turban, waits. A silk ladder of innumerable rungs climbs to his bobbing howdah. He ambles near with disgruntled hindquarters. Fiercely she slaps his haunch, her goldcurb wristbangles angriling, scolding him in Moorish.*)

MARION

Nebrakada! Feminimum!

(*The camel, lifting a foreleg, plucks from a tree a large mango fruit, offers it to his mistress, blinking, in his cloven hoof then droops his head and, grunting, with uplifted neck, fumbles to kneel. Bloom stoops his back for leapfrog.*)

BLOOM

I can give you... I mean as your business menagerer... Mrs Marion... if you...

MARION

So you notice some change? (*Her hands passing slowly over her trinketed stomacher. A slow friendly mockery in her eyes.*) O Poldy, Poldy, you are a poor old stick in the mud! Go and see life. See the wide world.

BLOOM

I was just going back for that lotion whitewax, orangeflower water. Shop closes early on Thursday. But the first thing in the morning. (*He pats divers pockets.*) This moving kidney. Ah!

(*He points to the south, then to the east. A cake of new clean lemon soap arises, diffusing light and perfume.*)

THE SOAP

We're a capital couple are Bloom and I
He brightens the earth, I polish the sky.

(*The freckled face of Sweny, the druggist, appears in the disc of the soapsun.*)

SWENY

Three and a penny, please.

BLOOM

Yes. For my wife, Mrs Marion. Special recipe.

MARION

(*Softly.*) Poldy!

BLOOM

Yes, ma'am?

MARION

Ti trema un poco il cuore?

(*In disdain she saunters away, plump as a pampered pouter pigeon, humming the duet from* Don Giovanni.)

BLOOM

Are you sure about that *Voglio*? I mean the pronunciati...

(*He follows, followed by the sniffing terrier. The elderly bawd seizes his sleeve, the bristles of her chinmole glittering.*)

THE BAWD

Ten shillings a maidenhead. Fresh thing was never touched. Fifteen. There's no-one in it only her old father that's dead drunk.

(*She points. In the gap of her dark den furtive, rainbedraggled, Bridie Kelly stands.*)

BRIDIE

Hatch street. Any good in your mind?

(*With a squeak she flaps her bat shawl and runs. A burly rough pursues with booted strides. He stumbles on the steps, recovers, plunges into gloom. Weak squeaks of laughter are heard, weaker.*)

THE BAWD

(*Her wolfeyes shining.*) He's getting his pleasure. You won't get a virgin in the flash houses. Ten shillings. Don't be all night before the polis in plain clothes sees us. Sixtyseven is a bitch.

(*Leering, Gerty Mac Dowell limps forward. She draws from behind, ogling, and shows coyly her bloodied clout.*)

GERTY

With all my worldly goods I thee and thou. (*She murmurs.*) You did that. I hate you.

BLOOM

I? When? You're dreaming. I never saw you.

THE BAWD

Leave the gentleman alone, you cheat. Writing the gentleman false letters. Streetwalking and soliciting. Better for your mother take the strap to you at the bedpost, hussy like you.

GERTY

(*To Bloom.*) When you saw all the secrets of my bottom drawer. (*She paws his sleeve, slobbering.*) Dirty married man! I love you for doing that to me.

(*She slides away crookedly. Mrs Breen in man's frieze overcoat with loose *bellows pockets, stands in the causeway, her roguish eyes wideopen, smiling in all her herbivorous buckteeth.*)

MRS BREEN

Mr...

BLOOM

(*Coughs gravely.*) Madam, when we last had this pleasure by letter dated the sixteenth instant...

MRS BREEN

Mr Bloom! You down here in the haunts of sin! I caught you nicely! Scamp!

BLOOM

(*Hurriedly.*) Not so loud my name. Whatever do you think me? Don't give me away. Walls have hears. How do you do? It's ages since I. You're looking splendid. Absolutely it. Seasonable weather we are having this time of year. Black refracts heat. Short cut home here. Interesting quarter. Rescue of fallen women Magdalen asylum. I am the secretary...

MRS BREEN

(*Holds up a finger.*) Now don't tell a big fib! I know somebody won't like that. O just wait till I see Molly! (*Slily.*) Account for yourself this very sminute or woe betide you!

BLOOM

(*Looks behind.*) She often said she'd like to visit. Slumming. The exotic, you see. Negro servants too in livery if she had money. Othello black brute. Eugene Stratton. Even the bones and cornerman at the Livermore christies. Bohee brothers. Sweep for that matter.

(*Tom and Sam Bohee, coloured coons in white duck suits, scarlet socks, upstarched Sambo chokers and large scarlet asters in their buttonholes leap out. Each has his banjo slung. Their paler smaller negroid hands jingle the twingtwang wires. Flashing white Kaffir eyes and tusks they rattle through a breakdown in clumsy clogs, twinging, singing, back to back, toe heel, heel toe, with smackfatclacking nigger lips.*)

TOM AND SAM

There's someone in the house with Dina
There's someone in the house, I know,
There's someone in the house with Dina
Playing on the old banjo.

(*They whisk black masks from raw babby faces : then, chuckling, chortling, trumming, twanging they diddle diddle cakewalk dance away.*)

BLOOM

(*With a sour tenderish smile.*) A little frivol, shall we, if you are so inclined? Would you like me perhaps to embrace you just for a fraction of a second?

MRS BREEN

(*Screams gaily.*) O, you ruck! You ought to see yourself!

BLOOM

For old sake' sake. I only meant a square party, a mixed marriage mingling of our different little conjugials. You know I had a soft corner for you. (*Gloomily.*) 'Twas I sent you that valentine of the dear gazelle.

MRS BREEN

Glory Alice, you do look a holy show! Killing simply. (*She puts out her hand inquisitively.*) What are you hiding behind your back? Tell us, there's a dear.

BLOOM

(*Seizes her wrist with his free hand.*) Josie Powell that was, prettiest deb in Dublin. How time flies by! Do you remember, harking back in a retrospective arrangement, Old Christmas night Georgina Simpson's housewarming while they were playing the Irving Bishop game, finding the pin blindfold and thoughtreading! Subject, what is in this snuffbox!

MRS BREEN

You were the lion of the night with your seriocomic recitation and you looked the part. You were always a favourite with the ladies.

BLOOM

(*Squire of dames, in dinner jacket with watered silkfacings, blue masonic badge in his buttonhole, black bow and mother-of-pear studs, a prismatic champagne glass tilted in his hand.*) Ladies and gentlemen, I give you Ireland, home and beauty.

MRS BREEN

The dear dead days beyond recall. Love's old sweet song.

BLOOM

(*Meaningfully dropping his voice.*) I confess I'm teapot with curiosity to find out whether some person's something is a little teapot at present.

MRS BREEN

(*Gushingly.*) Tremendously teapot! London's teapot and I'm simply teapot all over me. (*She rubs sides with him.*) After the parlour mystery games and the crackers from the tree we sat on the staircase ottoman. Under the mistletoe. Two is company.

BLOOM

(*Wearing a purple Napoleon hat with an amber halfmoon, his fingers and thumb passing slowly down to her soft moist meaty palm which she surrenders gently.*) The witching hour of night. I took the splinter out of this hand, carefully, slowly. (*Tenderly, as he slips on her finger a ruby ring.*) *Là ci darem la mano.*

MRS BREEN

(*In a onepiece evening frock executed in moonlight blue, a tinsel sylph's diadem on her brow with her dancecard fallen beside her moonblue satin slipper, curves her palm softly, breathing quickly.*) *Voglio e non.* You're hot! You're scalding! The left hand nearest the heart.

BLOOM

When you made your present choice they said it was beauty and the beast. I can never forgive you for that. (*His clenched fist at his brow.*) Think what it means. All you meant to me then. (*Hoarsely.*) Woman, it's breaking me!

(*Denis Breen, whitetallhatted, with Wisdom Hely's sandwichboard, shuffles past them in carpet slippers, his dull beard thrust out, muttering to *right and left. Little Alf Bergan, cloaked in the pall of the ace of spades dogs him to left and right, doubled in laughter.)*

ALF BERGAN

(*Points jeering at the sandwich boards.*) U. p : Up.

MRS BREEN

(*To Bloom.*) High jinks below stairs. (*She gives him the glad eye.*) Why didn't you kiss the spot to make it well ! You wanted to.

BLOOM

(*Shocked.*) Molly's best friend ! Could you ?

MRS BREEN

(*Her pulpy tongue between her lips, offers a pigeon kiss.*) Hnhn. The answer is a lemon. Have you a little present for me there ?

BLOOM

(*Offhandedly.*) Kosher. A snack for supper. The home without potted meat is incomplete. I was at *Leah*, Mrs Bandman Palmer. Trenchant exponent of Shakespeare. Unfortunately threw away the programme. Rattling good place round there for pig's feet. Feel.

(*Richie Goulding, three ladies' hats pinned on his head, appears weighted to one side by the black legal bag of Collis and Ward on which a skull and crossbones are painted in white limewash. He opens it and shows it full of polonies, kippered herrings, Findon haddies and tightpacked pills.*)

RICHIE

Best value in Dub.

(*Bald Pat, bothered beetle, stands on the curbstone, folding his napkin, waiting to wait.*)

PAT

(*Advances with a tilted dish of spillspilling gravy.*) Steak and kidney. Bottle of lager. Hee hee hee. Wait till I wait.

RICHIE

Goodgod. Inev erate inall...

(*With hanging head he marches doggedly forward. The navvy, lurching by, gores him with his flaming pronghorn.*)

RICHIE

(*With a cry of pain, his hand to his back.*) Ah! Bright's! Lights!

BLOOM

(*Points to the navvy.*) A spy. Don't attract attention. I hate stupid crowds. I am not on pleasure bent. I am in a grave predicament.

MRS BREEN

Humbugging and deluthering as per usual with your cock and bull story.

BLOOM

I want to tell you a little secret about how I came to be here. But you must never tell. Not even Molly. I have a most particular reason.

MRS BREEN

(*All agog.*) O, not for worlds.

BLOOM

Let's walk on. Shall us?

MRS BREEN

Let's.

(*The bawd makes an unheeded sign. Bloom walks on with Mrs Breen. The terrier follows, whining piteously, wagging his tail.*)

THE BAWD

Jewman's melt!

BLOOM

(*In an oatmeal sporting suit, a sprig of woodbine in the lapel, tony buff shirt, shepherd's plaid Saint Andrew's cross scarftie, white spats, fawn dustcoat on his *arm, tawny red brogues, fieldglasses in bandolier and a grey billycock hat.*) Do you remember a long long time, years and years ago, just after Milly, Marionette we called her, was weaned when we all went together to Fairyhouse races, was it?

MRS BREEN

(*In smart Saxe tailormade, white velours hat and spider veil.*) Leopardstown.

BLOOM

I mean, Leopardstown. And Molly won seven shillings on a three year old named Nevertell and coming home along by Foxrock in that old fiveseater shanderadan of a waggonette you were in your heyday then and you had on that new hat of white velours with a surround of molefur that Mrs Hayes advised you to buy because it was marked down to nineteen and eleven, a bit of wire and an old rag of velveteen, and I'll lay you what you like she did it on purpose...

MRS BREEN

She did, of course, the cat! Don't tell me! Nice adviser!

BLOOM

Because it didn't suit you one quarter as well as the other ducky little tammy toque with the bird of paradise wing in it that I admired on you and you honestly looked just too fetching in it though it was a pity to kill it, you cruel creature, little mite of a thing with a heart the size of a fullstop.

MRS BREEN

(*Squeezes his arm, simpers.*) Naughty cruel I was.

BLOOM

(*Low, secretly, ever more rapidly.*) And Molly was eating a sandwich ot spiced beef out of Mrs Joe Gallaher's lunch basket. Frankly, though she had her advisers or admirers, I never cared much for her style. She was...

MRS BREEN

Too...

BLOOM

Yes. And Molly was laughing because Rogers and Maggot O'Reilly were mimicking a cock as we passed a farmhouse and Marcus Tertius Moses, the tea merchant, drove past us in a gig with his daughter, Dancer Moses was her name, and the poodle in her lap bridled up and you asked me if I ever heard or read or knew or came across...

MRS BREEN

(*Eagerly.*) Yes, yes, yes, yes, yes, yes, yes.

(*She fades from his side. Followed by the whining dog he walks on towards hellsgates. In an archway a standing woman, bent forward, her feet apart, pisses cowily. Outside a shuttered pub a bunch of loiterers listen to a tale which their broken snouted gaffer rasps out with raucous humour. An armless pair of them flop wrestling, growling, in maimed sodden playfight.*)

THE GAFFER

(*Crouches, his voice twisted in his snout.*) And when Cairns came down from the scaffolding in Beaver Street what was he after doing it into only into the bucket of porter that was there waiting on the shavings for Derwan's plasterers.

THE LOITERERS

(*Guffaw with cleft palates.*) O jays!

(*Their paintspeckled hats wag. Spattered with size and lime of their lodges they frisk limblessly about him.*)

BLOOM

Coincidence too. They think it funny. Anything but that. Broad daylight. Trying to walk. Lucky no woman.

THE LOITERERS

Jays, that's a good one. Glauber salts. O jays, into the men's porter.

(*Bloom passes. Cheap whores, singly, coupled, shawled, dishevelled, call from lanes, doors, corners.*)

THE WHORES

Are you going far, queer fellow?
How's your middle leg?
Got a match on you?
Eh, come her till I stiffen it for you.

(*He plodges through their sump towards the lighted street beyond. From a bulge of window curtains a gramophone rears a battered brazen trunk. In the shadow a shebeenkeeper haggles with the navvy and the two redcoats.*)

THE NAVVY

(*Belching.*) Where's the bloody house?

THE SHEBEENKEEPER

Purdon street. Shilling a bottle of stout. Respectable woman.

THE NAVVY

(*Gripping the two redcoats, staggers forward with them.*) Come on, you British army!

PRIVATE CARR

(*Behind his back.*) He aint half balmy.

PRIVATE COMPTON

(*Laughs.*) What ho!

PRIVATE CARR

(*To the navvy.*) Portobello barracks canteen. You ask for Carr. Just Carr.

THE NAVVY

(*Shouts.*)

We are the boys. Of Wexford.

PRIVATE COMPTON

Say! What price the sergeantmajor?

PRIVATE CARR

Bennett? He's my pal. I love old Bennett.

THE NAVVY

(*Shouts.*)

The galling chain.
And free our native land.

(*He staggers forward, dragging them with him. Bloom stops, at fault. The dog approches, his tongue outlolling, panting.*)

BLOOM

Wildgoose chase this. Disorderly houses. Lord knows where they are gone. Drunks cover distance double quick. Nice mixup. Scene at Westland row. Then jump in first class with third ticket. Then too far. Train with engine behind. Might have taken me to Malahide or a siding for the night or collision. Second drink does it. Once is a dose. What am I following him for? Still, he's the best of that lot. If I hadn't heard about Mrs Beaufoy Purefoy I wouldn't have gone and wouldn't have met. Kismet. He'll lose that cash. Relieving office here. Good biz for cheapjacks, organs. What do ye lack? Soon got, soon gone. Might have lost my life too with that mangongwheeltracktrolleyglarejuggernaut only for presence of mind. Can't always save you, though. If I had passed Truelock's window that day two minutes later would have been shot. Absence of body. Still if bullet only went through my coat get damages for shock, five hundred pounds. What was he? Kildare street club toff. God help his gamekeeper.

(*He gazes ahead reading on the wall a scrawled chalk legend* Wet Dream *and a phallic design.*)

Odd! Molly drawing on the frosted carriagepane at Kingstown. What's that like? (*Gaudy dollwomen loll in the lighted doorways, in window embrasures, smoking birdseye cigarettes. The odour of the sicksewet weed floats towards him in slow round ovalling wreaths.*)

THE WREATHS

Sweet are the sweets. Sweets of sin.

BLOOM

My spine's a bit limp. Go or turn? And this food? Eat it and get all pigsticky. Absurd I am. Waste of money. One and eight pence too much. (*The retriever drives a cold snivelling muzzle against his hand, wagging his tail.*) Strange how they take to me. Even that brute today. Better speak to him first. Like women they like *rencontres*. Stinks like a polecat. *Chacun son goût*. He might be mad. Fido. Uncertain in his movements. Good fellow ! Garryowen ! (*The wolfdog sprawls on his back, wriggling obscenely with begging paws, his long black tongue lolling out.*) Influence of his surroundings. Give and have done with it. Provided nobody. (*Calling encouraging words he shambles back with a furtive poacher's tread, dogged by the setter into a dark stalestunk corner. He unrolls one parcel and goes to dump the crubeen softly but holds back and feels the trotter.*) Sizeable for threepence. But then I have it in my left hand. Calls for more effort. Why ? Smaller from want of use. O, let it slide. Two and six.

(*With regret he lets unrolled crubeen and trotter slide. The mastiff mauls the bundle clumsily and gluts himself with growling greed, crunching the bones. Two raincaped watch approach, silent, vigilant. They murmur together.*)

THE WATCH

Bloom. Of Bloom. For Bloom. Bloom.

(*Each lays hand on Bloom's shoulder.*)

FIRST WATCH

Caught in the act. Commit no nuisance.

BLOOM

(*Stammers.*) I am doing good to others.

(*A covey of gulls, storm petrels, rises hungrily from Liffey slime with Banbury cakes in their beaks.*)

THE GULLS

Kaw kave kankury kake.

BLOOM

The friend of man. Trained by kindness.

(*He points. Bob Doran, toppling from a high barstool, sways over the munching spaniel.*)

BOB DORAN

Towser. Give us the paw. Give the paw.

(*The bulldog growls, his scruff standing, a gobbet of pig's knuckle between his molars through which rabid scumspittle dribbles. Bob Doran falls silently into an area.*)

SECOND WATCH

Prevention of cruelty to animals.

BLOOM

(*Enthusiastically.*) A noble work! I scolded that tramdriver on Harold's cross bridge for illusing the poor horse with his harness scab. Bad French I got for my pains. Of course it was frosty and the last tram. All tales of circus life are highly demoralising.

(*Signor Maffei, passion pale, in liontamer's costume with diamonds studs in his shirtfront steps forward, holding a circus paper hoop, a curling carriagewhip and a revolver with which he covers the gorging boarhound.*

SIGNOR MAFFEI

(*With a sinister smile.*) Ladies and gentlemen, my educated greyhound. It was I broke in the bucking broncho Ajax with my patent spiked saddle for carnivores. Lash under the belly with a knotted thong. Block tackle and a strangling pully will bring your lion to heel, no matter how fractious, even *Leo ferox* there, the Libyan maneater. A redhot crowbar and some liniment rubbing on the burning part produced Fritz of Amsterdam, the thinking hyena. (*He glares.*) I possess the Indian sign. The glint of my eye does it with these breastsparklers. (*With a bewitching smile.*) I now introduce Mademoiselle Ruby, the pride of the ring.

FIRST WATCH

Come. Name and address.

BLOOM

I have forgotten for the moment. Ah, yes! (*He takes off his high grade hat, saluting.*) Dr Bloom, Leopold, dental surgeon. You have heard of von Bloom Pasha. Umpteen millions. *Donnerwetter!* Owns half Austria. Egypt. Cousin.

FIRST WATCH

Proof.

(*A card falls from inside the leather headband of Bloom's hat.*)

BLOOM

(*In red fez, cadi's dress coat with broad green sash, wearing a false badge of the Legion of Honour, picks up the card hastily and offers it.*) Allow me. My club is the Junior Army and Navy. Solicitors : Messrs John Henry Menton, 27 Bachelor's Walk.

FIRST WATCH

(*Reads.*) Henry Flower. No fixed abode. Unlawfully watching and besetting.

SECOND WATCH

An alibi. You are cautioned.

BLOOM

(*Produces from his heartpocket a crumpled yellow flower.*) This is the flower in question. It was given me by a man I don't know his name. (*Plausibly.*) You know that old joke, rose of Castile. Bloom. The change of name. Virag. (*He murmurs privately and confidentially.*) We are engaged you see, sergeant. Lady in the case. Love entanglement. (*He shoulders the second watch gently.*) Dash it all. It's a way we gallants have in the navy. Uniform that does it. (*He turns gravely to the first watch.*) Still, of course, you do get your Waterloo sometimes. Drop in some evening and have a glass of old Burgundy. (*To the second watch gaily.*) I'll introduce you, inspector. She's game. Do it in the shake of a lamb's tail.

(*A dark mercurialised face appears, leading a veiled figure.*)

THE DARK MERCURY

The Castle is looking for him. He was drummed out of the army.

MARTHA

(*Thickveiled, a crimson halter round her neck, a copy of the* Irish Times *in her hand, in tone of reproach, pointing.*) Henry ! Leopold ! Leopold ! Lionel, thou lost one ! Clear my name.

FIRST WATCH

(*Sternly.*) Come to the station.

BLOOM

(*Scared, hats himself, steps back then, plucking at his heart and lifting his right forearm on the square, he gives the sign and dueguard of fellowcraft.*) No, no, worshipful master, light of love. Mistaken identity. The Lyons mail. Lesurques and Dubosc. You remember the Childs fratricide case. We medical men. By striking him dead with a hatchet, I am wrongfully accused. Better one guilty escape than ninetynine wrongfully condemned.

MARTHA

(*Sobbing behind her veil.*) Breach of promise. My real name is Peggy Griffin. He wrote to me that he was miserable. I'll tell my brother, the Bective rugger fullback, on you, heartless flirt.

BLOOM

(*Behind his hand.*) She's drunk. The woman is inebriated. (*He murmurs vaguely the past of Ephraim.*) Shitbroleeth.

SECOND WATCH

(*Tears in his eyes, to Bloom.*) You ought to be thoroughly well ashamed of yourself.

BLOOM

Gentlemen of the jury, let me explain. A pure mare's nest. I am a man misunderstood. I am being made a scapegoat of I am a respectable married man, without a stain on my character. I live in Eccles street. My wife, I am the daughter of a most distinguished commander, a gallant upstanding gentleman, what do you call him, Majorgeneral Brian Tweedy, one of Britain's fighting men who helped to win our battles. Got his majority for the heroic defence of Rorke's Drift.

FIRST WATCH

Regiment.

BLOOM

(*Turns to the gallery.*) The royal Dublins, boys, the salt of the earth, known the world over. I think I see some old comrades in arms up there among you. The R. D. F. With our own Metropolitan police, guardians of our homes, the pluckiest lads and the finest body of men, as physique, in the service of our sovereign.

A VOICE

Turncoat ! Up the Boers ! Who booed Joe Chamberlain ?

BLOOM

(His hand on the shoulder of the first watch.) My old dad too was a J. P. I'm as staunch a Britisher as you are, sir. I fought with the colours for king and country in the absentminded war under general Gough in the park and was disabled at Spion Kop and Bloemfontein, was mentioned in dispatches. I did all a white man could. *(With quiet feeling.)* Jim Bludso. Hold her nozzle again the bank.

FIRST WATCH

Profession or trade.

BLOOM

Well, I follow a literary occupation. Author-journalist. In fact we are just bringing out a collection of prize stories of which I am the inventor, something that is an entirely new departure. I am connected with the British and Irish press. If you ring up...

(Myles Crawford strides out jerkily, a quill between his teeth. His scarlet beak blazes within the aureole of his straw hat. He dangles a hank of Spanish onions in one hand and holds with the other hand a telephone receiver nozzle to his ear.)

MYLES CRAWFORD

(His cock's wattles wagging.) Hello, seventyseven eightfour. Hello. *Freeman's Urinal* and *Weekly Arsewiper* here. Paralyse Europe. You which ? Bluebags ? Who writes ? Is it Bloom ?

(Mr Philip Beaufoy, palefaced, stands in the witnessbox, in accurate morning dress, outbreast pocket with peak of handkerchief showing, creased lavender trousers and patent boots. He carries a large portfolio labelled Matcham's Masterstrokes.*)*

BEAUFOY

(*Drawls.*) No, you aren't, not by a long shot if I know it. I don't see it, that's all. No born gentleman, no one with the most rudimentary promptings of a gentleman would stoop to such particularly loathsome conduct. One of those, my lord. A plagiarist. A soapy sneak masquerading as a literateur. It's perfectly obvious that with the most inherent baseness he has cribbed some of my bestselling books, really gorgeous stuff, a perfect gem, the love passages in which are beneath suspicion. The Beaufoy books of love and great possessions with which your lordship is doubtless familiar, are a household word throughout the kingdom.

BLOOM

(*Murmurs with hangdog meekness.*) That bit about the laughing witch hand in hand I take exception to, if I may...

BEAUFOY

(*His lip upcurled, smiles superciliously on the court.*) You funny ass, you ! You're too beastly awfully weird for words ! I don't think you need over excessively disincommodate yourself in that regard. My literary agent Mr J. B. Pinker is in attendance. I presume, my lord, we shall receive the usual witnesses' fees, shan't we ! We are considerably out of pocket over this bally pressman johnny, this jackdaw of Rheims, who has not even been to a university.

BLOOM

(*Indistinctly.*) University of life. Bad art.

BEAUFOY

(*Shouts.*) It's a damnably foul lie showing the moral rottenness of the man ! (*He extends his portfolio.*) We have here damning evidence the *corpus delicti,* my lord, a specimen of my maturer work disfigured by the hallmark of the beast.

A VOICE FROM THE GALLERY

Moses, Moses, king of the jews,
Wiped his arse in the *Daily News.*

BLOOM

(*Bravely*). Overdrawn.

BEAUFOY

You low cad ! You ought to be ducked in the horsepond, you rotter ! (*To the court.*) Why look at the man's private life ! Leading a quadruple existence ! Street angel and house devil. Not fit to be mentioned in mixed society. The arch conspirator of the age.

BLOOM

(*To the court.*) And he, a bachelor, how...

FIRST WATCH

The King versus Bloom. Call the woman Driscoll.

THE CRIER

Mary Driscoll, scullerymaid !

(*Mary Driscoll, a slipshod servant girl approaches. She has a bucket on the crook of her arm and a scouringbrush in her hand.*)

SECOND WATCH

Another ! Are you of the unfortunate class ?

MARY DRISCOLL

(*Indignantly.*) I'm not a bad one. I bear a respectable character and was four months in my last place. I was in a situation, six pounds a year and my chances with Fridays out and I had to leave owing to his carryings on.

FIRST WATCH

What do you tax him with ?

MARY DRISCOLL

He made a certain suggestion but I thought more of myself as poor as I am.

BLOOM

(*In housejacket of ripplecloth flannel trousers, heelless slippers, unshaven, his hair rumpled softly.*) I treated you white. I gave you mementos, smart emerald garters far above your station. Incautiously I took your part when you were accused of pilfering. There's a medium in all things. Play cricket.

MARY DRISCOLL

(*Excitedly.*) As God is looking down on me this night it ever I laid a hand to them oylsters!

FIRST WATCH

The offence complained ot? Did something happen?

MARY DRISCOLL

He surprised me in the rere of the premises, your honour, when the missus was out shopping one morning with a request for a safety pin. He held me and I was discoloured in four places as a result. And he interfered twict with my clothing.

BLOOM

She counterassaulted.

MARY DRISCOLL

(*Scornfully.*) I had more respect for the scouringbrush, so I had. I remonstrated with him, your lord, and he remarked: Keep it quiet!

(*General laughter.*)

GEORGES FOTTRELL

(*Clerk of the crown and peace, resonantly.*) Order in court! The accused will now make a bogus statement.

(*Bloom, pleading not guilty and holding a fullblown waterlily, begins a long unintelligible speech. They would hear what counsel had to say in his stirring address to the grandjury. He was down and out but, through branded as a black sheep, if he might say so, he meant to reform, to retrieve the memory of the past in a purely sisterly way and return to nature as a purely domestic animal. A seven months child he had been carefully brought up and nurtured by an aged bedridden parent. There might have been lapses of an erring father but he wanted to turn over a new leaf and now, when at long last in sight of the whipping post, to lead a homely life in the evening of his days, permeated by the affectionate surroundings of the heaving bosom of the family. An acclimatised Britisher, he had seen that summer eve from the footplate of an engine cab of the Loop line railway company while the rain refrained from falling glimpses, as it were, through the windows of loveful households in Dublin city and urban district of scenes truly rural of happiness of the better land with Dockrell's wallpaper at one and ninepence a dozen, innocent Britishborn bairns lisping prayers to the Sacred Infant, youthful scholars grappling with their pensums, model young ladies playing on the pianoforte or anon all with fervour reciting the family rosary round the crackling Yulelog while in the boreens and green lanes the colleens with their swains strolled what times the strains of the organtoned melodeon Brittania metalbound with four acting stops and twelvefold bellows, a sacrifice, greatest bargain ever...)*

(Renewed laughter. He mumbles incoherently. Reporters complain that they cannot hear.)

LONGHAND AND SHORTHAND

(Without looking up from their notebooks.) Loosen his boots.

PROFESSOR MACHUGH

(From the presstable, coughs and calls.)

Cough it up, man. Get it out in bits.

(The crossexamination proceeds re *Bloom and the bucket. A large bucket. Bloom himself. Bowel trouble. In Beaver street. Gripe, yes. Quite bad. A plasterer's bucket. By walking stifflegged. Suffered untold misery. Deadly agony. About noon. Love or burgundy. Yes, some spinach. Crucial moment. He did not look in the bucket. Nobody. Rather a mess. Not completely. A* Titbits *back number.)*

(Uproar and cat calls. Bloom in a torn frockcoat stained with whitewash, dinged silk hat sideways on his head, a strip of stickingplaster across his nose, talks inaudibly.)

J. J. O'MOLLOY

(In barrister's grey wig and stuffgown, speaking with a voice of pained protest.) This is no place for indecent levity at the expense of an erring mortal disguised in liquor. We are not in a beargarden nor at an Oxford rag nor is this

a travesty of justice. My client is an infant, a poor foreign immigrant who started scratch as a stowaway and is now trying to turn an honest penny. The trumped up misdemeanour was due to a momentary aberration of heredity, brought on by hallucination, such familiarities as the alleged guilty occurrence being quite permitted in my client's native place, the land of the Pharaoh. *Prima facie,* I put it to you that there was no attempt at carnally knowing. Intimacy did not occur and the offence complained of by Driscoll, that her virtue was solicited, was not repeated. I would deal in especial with atavism. There have been cases of shipwreck and somnambulism in my client's family. If the accused could speak he could a tale unfold one of the strangest that have ever been narrated between the covers of a book. He himself, my lord, is a physical wreck from cobbler's weak chest. His submission is that he is of Mongolian extraction and irresponsible for his actions. Not all there, in fact.

BLOOM

(*Barefoot, pigeonbreasted, in lascar's vest and trousers, apologetic toes turned in, opens his tiny mole's eyes and looks about him dazedly, passing a slow hand across his forehead. Then he hitches his belt sailor fashion and with a shrug of oriental obeisance salutes the court, pointing one thumb heavenward.*) Him makee velly muchee fine night. (*He begins to lilt simply.*)

Li li poo lil chile.
Blingee pigfoot evly night.
Payee two shilly...

(*He is howled down.*)

J. J. O'MOLLOY

(*Hotly to the populace.*) This is a lonehand fight. By Hades, I will not have any client of mine gagged and badgered in this fashion by a pack of curs and laughing hyenas. The Mosaic code has superseded the law of the jungle. I say it and I say it emphatically without wishing for one moment to defeat the ends of justice, accused, was not accessory before the act and prosecutrix has not been tampered with. The young person was treated by defendant as if she were his very own daughter. (*Bloom takes J. J. O'Molloy's hand and raises it to his lips.*) I shall call rebutting evidence to prove up to the hilt that the hidden hand is again at its old game. When in doubt persecute Bloom. My client, an innately bashful man, would be the last man in the world to do anything ungentlemanly which injured modesty could object to or cast a stone at a girl who took the wrong turning when some dastard, responsible for her condition, had worked his own sweet will on her. He wants to go straight. I regard him as the whitest man I know. He is down on his luck at present owing to the mortgaging of his extensive property at Agendath Netaim in faraway Asia Minor, slides of which will now be shown. (*To Bloom.*) I suggest that you will do the handsome thing.

BLOOM

A penny in the pound.

(*The mirage of the lake of Kinnereth with blurred cattle cropping in silver haze is projected on the wall. Moses Dlugacz, ferreteyed albino, in blue dungarees, stands up in the gallery, holding in each hand an orange citron and a pork kidney.*)

DLUGACZ

(*Hoarsely.*) Bleibtreustrasse, Berlin, W, 13.

(*J. J. O'Molloy steps on to a low plinth and holds the lapel of his coat with solemnity. His face lengthens, grows pale and bearded, with sunken eyes, the blotches of phthisis and hectic cheekbones of John F. Taylor. He applies his handkerchief to his mouth and scrutinises the galloping tide of rosepink blood.*)

J. J. O'MOLLOY

(*Almost voicelessly.*) Excuse me, I am suffering from a severe chill, have recently come from a sickbed. A few wellchosen words. (*He assumes the avine head, foxy moustache and proboscidal eloquence of Seymour Bushe.*) When the angel's book comes to be opened if aught that the pensive bosom has inaugurated of soultransfigured and of soultransfiguring deserves to live I say accord the prisoner at the bar the sacred benefit of the doubt. (*A paper with something written on it is handed into court.*)

BLOOM

(*In court dress.*) Can give best references. Messrs Callan, Coleman. Mr Wisdom Hely J. P. My old chief Joe Cuffe. Mr. V. B. Dillon, ex-lord mayor of Dublin. I have moved in the charmed circle of the highest... Queens of Dublin Society. (*Carelessly.*) I was just chatting this afternoon at the viceregal lodge to my old pals, sir Robert and lady Ball, astronomer royal, at the levee. Sir Bob, I said...

MRS YELVERTON BARRY

(*In lowcorsaged opal balldress and elbowlength ivory gloves, wearing a sabletrimmed brick quilted dolman, a comb of brilliants and panache of osprey in her hair.*) Arrest him, constable. He wrote me an anonymous letter in prentice backhand when my husband was in the North Riding of Tipperary on the Munster circuit, signed James Lovebirch. He said that he had seen from the gods my peerless globes as I sat in a box of the *Theatre Royal* at a command performance of *La Cigale*. I deeply inflamed him, he said. He made improper overtures to me to misconduct myself at half past four p. m. on the following Thursday, Dunsink time. He offered to send me through the post a work of fiction by Monsieur Paul de Kock, entitled *The Girl with the Three Pairs of Stays*.

MRS BELLINGHAM

(*In cap and seal coney mantle, wrapped up to the nose, steps out of her brougham and scans through tortoiseshell quizzing-glasses which she takes from inside her huge opossum muff.*) Also to me. Yes, I believe it is the same objectionable person. Because he closed my carriage door outside sir Thornley Stoker's one sleety day during the cold snap of February ninetythree when even the grid of the wastepipe and ballstop in my bath cistern were frozen. Subsequently he enclosed a bloom of edelweiss culled on the heights, as he said, in my honour. I had it examined by a botanical expert and elicited the information that it was a blossom of the homegrown potato plant purloined from a forcingcase of the model farm.

MRS YELVERTON BARRY

Shame on him!

(*A crowd of sluts and ragamuffins surges forward.*)

THE SLUTS AND RAGAMUFFINS

(*Screaming.*) Stop thief! Hurrah there, Bluebeard! Three cheers for Ikey Mo!

SECOND WATCH

(*Produces handcuffs.*) Here are the darbies.

MRS BELLINGHAM

He addressed me in several handwritings with fulsome compliments as a

Venus in furs and alleged profound pity for my frostbound coachman Palmer while in the same breath he expressed himself as envious of his earflaps and fleecy sheepskins and of his fortunate proximity to my person, when standing behind my chair wearing my livery and the armorial bearings of the Bellingham escutcheon garnished sable, a buck's head couped or. He lauded almost extravagantly my nether extremities, my swelling calves in silk hose drawn up to the limit and eulogised glowingly my other hidden treasures in priceless lace which, he said, he could conjure up. He urged me, stating that he felt it his mission in life to urge me, to defile the marriage bed, to commit adultery at the earliest possible opportunity.

THE HONOURABLE MRS MERVYN TALBOYS

(*In amazon costume, hard hat, jackboots cockspurred, vermilion waistcoat, fawn musketeer gauntlets with braided drums, long train held up and hunting crop with which she strikes her welt constantly.*) Also me. Because he saw me on the polo ground of the Phœnix park at the match All Ireland versus the Rest of Ireland. My eyes, I know, shone divinely as I watched Captain Slogger Dennehy of the Inniskillings win the final chukkar on his darling cob *Centaur*. This plebeian Don Juan observed me from behind a hackney car and sent me in double envelopes an obscene photograph, such as are sold after dark on Paris boulevards, insulting to any lady. I have it still. It represents a partially nude señorita, frail and lovely (his wife as he solemnly assured me, taken by him from nature) practising illicit intercourse with a muscular torero, evidently a blackguard. He urged me to do likewise, to misbehave, to sin with officers of the garrison. He implored me to soil his letter in an unspeakable manner, to chastise him as he richly deserves, to bestride and ride him, to give him a most vicious horsewhipping.

MRS BELLINGHAM

Me too.

MRS YELVERTON BARRY

Me too.

(*Several highly respectable Dublin ladies hold up improper letters received from Bloom.*)

THE HONOURABLE MRS MERVYN TALBOYS

(*Stamps her jingling spurs in a sudden paroxysm of sudden fury.*) I will, by the God above me. I'll scourge the pigeonlivered cur as long as I can stand over him. I'll flay him alive.

BLOOM

(*His eyes closing, quails expectantly.*) Here? (*He squirms.*) Again! (*He pants cringing.*) I love the danger.

THE HONOURABLE MRS MERVYN TALBOYS

Very much so! I'll make it hot for you. I'll make you dance Jack Latten for that.

MRS BELLINGHAM

Tan his breech well, the upstart! Write the stars and stripes on it!

MRS YELUERTON BARRY

Disgraceful! There's no excuse for him! A married man!

BLOOM

All these people. I meant only the spanking idea. A warm tingling glow without effusion. Refined birching to stimulate the circulation.

THE HONOURABLE MRS MERVYN TALBOYS

(*Laughs derisively.*) O, did you, my fine fellow? Well, by the living God, you'll get the surprise of your life now, believe me, the most unmerciful hiding a man ever bargained for. You have lashed the dormant tigress in my nature into fury.

MRS BELLINGHAM

(*Shakes her muff and quizzing-glasses vindictively.*) Make him smart, Hanna dear. Give him ginger. Thrash the mongrel within an inch of his life. The cat-o'-nine tails. Geld him. Vivisect him.

BLOOM

(*Shuldering, shrinking, joins his hands with hangdog mien.*) O cold! O shivery! It was your ambrosial beauty. Forget, forgive. Kismet. Let me off this once. (*He offers the other cheek.*)

MRS YELVERTON BARRY

(*Severely.*) Don't do so on any account, Mrs Talboys! He should be soundly trounced!

THE HONOURABLE MRS MERVYN TALBOYS

(*Unbuttoning her gauntlet violently.*) I'll do no such thing. Pig dog and always was ever since he was pupped! To dare address me! I'll flog him black and blue in the public streets. I'll dig my spurs in him up to the rowel. He is a wellknown cuckold. (*She swishes her huntingcrop savagely in the air.*) Take down his trousers without loss of time. Come here, sir! Quick! Ready?

BLOOM

(*Trembling, beginning to obey.*) The weather has been so warm.

(*Davy Stephens, ringletted, passes with a bevy of barefoot newsboys.*)

DAVY STEPHENS

Messenger of the Sacred Heart and *Evening Telegraph* with Saint Patrick's Day Supplement. Containing the new addresses of all the cuckolds in Dublin.

(*The very reverend Canon O'Hanlon in cloth of gold cope elevates and exposes a marble timepiece. Before him Father Conroy and the reverend John Hughes S. J. bend low.*)

THE TIMEPIECE

(*Unportalling.*)

Cuckoo.
Cuckoo.
Cuckoo.

(*The brass quoits of a bed are heard to jingle.*)

THE QUOITS

Jigjag, Jigajiga. Jigjag.

(*A panel of fog rolls back rapidly, revealing rapidly in the jurybox the faces of Martin Cunningham, foreman, silkhatted, Jack Power, Simon Dedalus, Tom Kernan, Ned Lambert, John Henry Menton, Myles Crawford, Lenehan, Paddy Leonard, Nosey Flynn, M'Coy and the featureless face of a Nameless One.*)

THE NAMELESS ONE

Bareback riding. Weight for age. Gob, he organised her.

THE JURORS

(*All their heads turned to his voice.*) Really?

THE NAMELESS ONE

(*Snarls.*) Arse over tip. Hundred shillings to five.

THE JURORS

(*All their heads lowered in assent.*) Most of us thought as much.

FIRST WATCH

He is a marked man. Another girl's plait cut. Wanted: Jack the Ripper. A thousand pounds reward.

SECOND WATCH

(*Awed, whispers.*) And in black. A mormon. Anarchist.

THE CRIER

(*Loudly.*) Whereas Leopold Bloom of no fixed abode is a wellknown dynamitard, forger, bigamist, bawd and cuckold and a public nuisance to the citizens of Dublin and whereas at this commission of assizes the most honourable...

(*His Honour, sir Frederick Falkiner, recorder of Dublin, in judicial garb of grey stone rises from the bench, stonebearded. He bears in his arms an umbrella sceptre. From his forehead arise starkly the Mosaic ramshorns.*)

THE RECORDER

I will put an end to this white slave traffic and rid Dublin of this odious pest. Scandalous! (*He dons the black cap.*) Let him be taken, Mr Subsheriff, from the dock where he now stands and detained in custody in Mountjoy prison during His Majesty's pleasure and there be hanged by the neck until he is dead and therein fail not at your peril or may the Lord have mercy on your soul. Remove him. (*A black skullcap descends upon his head.*)

(*The subsheriff Long John Fanning appears, smoking a pungent Henry Clay.*)

LONG JOHN FANNING

Scowls and calls with rich rolling utterance.) Who'll hang Judas Iscariot?

(*H. Rumbold, master barber, in a bloodcoloured jerkin and tanner's apron, a rope coiled over his shoulder, mounts the block. A life preserver and a nailstudded bludgeon are stuck in his belt. He rubs grimly his grappling hands, knobbed with knuckledusters.*)

RUMBOLD

(*To the recorder with sinister familiarity.*) Hanging Harry, your Majesty, the Mersey terror. Five guineas a jugular. Neck or nothing.

(*The bells of George's church toll slowly, loud dark iron.*)

THE BELLS

Heigho! Heigho!

BLOOM

(*Desperately.*) Wait. Stop. Gulls. Good heart. I saw. Innocence. Girl in the monkeyhouse. Zoo. Lewd chimpanzees. (*Breathlessly.*) Pelvic basin. Her artless blush unmanned me. (*Overcome with emotion.*) I left the precincts. (*He turns to a figure in the crowd, appealing.*) Hynes, may I speak to you? You know me. That three shillings you can keep. If you want a little more...

HYNES

(*Coldly.*) You are a perfect stranger.

SECOND WATCH

(*Points to the corner.*) The bomb is here.

FIRST WATCH

Infernal machine with a time fuse.

BLOOM

No, no. Pig's feet. I was at a funeral.

FIRST WATCH

(*Draws his truncheon.*) Liar!

(*The beagle lift his snout, showing the grey scorbutic face of Paddy Dignam. He has gnawed all. He exhales a putrid carcasefed breath. He grows to human size and shape. His dachshund coat becomes a brown mortuary habit. His green eye flashes bloodshot. Half of one ear, all the nose and both thumbs are ghouleaten.*)

PADDY DIGNAM

(*In a hollow voice.*) It is true. it was my funeral. Doctor Finucane pronounced life extinct when I succumbed to the disease from natural causes.

(*He lifts his mutilated ashen face moonwards and bays lugubriously.*)

BLOOM

(*In triumph.*) You hear?

PADDY DIGNAM

Bloom, I am Paddy Dignam's spirit. List, list, O list!

BLOOM

The voice is the voice of Esau.

SECOND WATCH

(*Blesses himself.*) How is that possible?

FIRST WATCH

It is not in the penny catechism.

PADDY DIGNAM

By metempsychosis. Spooks.

A VOICE

O rocks.

PADDY DIGNAM

(*Earnestly.*) Once I was in the employ of Mr J. H. Menton solicitor, commissioner for oaths and affidavits, of 27 Bachelor's Walk. Now I am defunct, the wall of the heart hypertrophied. Hard lines. The poor wife was awfully cut up. How is she bearing it? Keep her off that bottle of sherry. (*He looks round him.*) A lamp. I must satisfy an animal need. That buttermilk didn't agree with me.

(*The portly figure of John O'Connell, caretaker, stands forth, holding a bunch of keys tied with crape. Beside him stands Father Coffey, chaplain, toadbellied, wrynecked, in a surplice and bandanna nightcap, holding sleepily a staff of twisted poppies.*)

FATHER COFFEY

(*Yawns, then chants with a hoarse croak.*) Namine. Jacobs Vobiscuits. Amen.

JOHN O'CONNELL

(*Foghorns stormily through his megaphone.*) Dignam, Patrick T, deceased.

PADDY DIGNAM

(*With pricked up ears, winces.*) Overtones. (*He wriggles forward, places an ear to the ground.*) My master's voice!

JOHN O'CONNELL

Burial docket letter number U. P. Eightyfive thousand. Field seventeen. House of Keys, Plot, one hundred and one.

(*Paddy Dignam listens with visible effort, thinking, his tail stiffpointed, his ears cocked.*)

PADDY DIGNAM

Pray for the repose of his soul.

(*He worms down through a coalhole, his brown habit trailing its tether over rattling pebbles. After him toddles an obese grandfather rat on fungus turtle paws under a grey carapace. Dignam's voice, muffled, is heard baying under ground:* Dignam's dead and gone below. *Tom Rochford, robinredbreasted, in cap and breeches, jumps from his twocolumned machine.*)

TOM ROCHFORD

(*A hand to his breastbone, bows.*) Reuben J. A florin I find him. (*He fixes the manhole with a resolute stare.*) My turn now on. Follow me up to Carlow.

(*He executes a daredevil salmon leap in the air and is engulfed in the coalhole. Two discs on the columns wobble eyes of nought. All recedes. Bloom plodges forward again. He stands before a lighted house, listening. The kisses, winging from their bowers fly about him, twittering, warbling, cooing.*)

THE KISSES

(*Warbling.*) Leo! (*Twittering.*) Icky licky micky sticky for Leo! (*Cooing.*) Coo coocoo! Yummyumm Womwom! (*Warbling.*) Big comebig! Pirouette! Leopopold! (*Twittering.*) Leeolee! (*Warbling.*) O Leo!

(*They rustle, flutter upon his garments, alight, bright giddy flecks, silvery sequins.*)

BLOOM

A man's touch. Sad music. Church music. Perhaps here.

(*Zoe Higgins, a young whore in a sapphire slip, closed with three bronze buckles, a slim black velvet fillet round her throat, nods, trips down the steps and accosts him.*)

ZOE

Are you looking for someone? He's inside with his friend.

BLOOM

Is this Mrs Mack's?

ZOE

No, eightyone. Mrs Cohen's. You might go farther and fare worse. Mother Slipperslapper. (*Familiarly.*) She's on the job herself tonight with the vet, her tipster, that gives her all the winners and pays for her son in Oxford. Working overtime but her luck's turned today. (*Suspiciously.*) You're not his father, are you?

BLOOM

Not I!

ZOE

You both in black. Has little mousey any tickles tonight?

(*His skin, alert, feels her fingertips approach. A hand slides over his left thigh.*)

ZOE

How's the nuts?

BLOOM

Off side. Curiously they are on the right. Heavier I suppose. One in a million my tailor, Mesias, says.

ZOE

(*In sudden alarm.*) You've a hard chancre.

BLOOM

Not likely.

ZOE

I feel it.

(*Her hand slides into his left trouser pocket and brings out a hard black shrivelled potato. She regards it and Bloom with dumb moist lips*)

BLOOM

A talisman. Heirloom.

ZOE

For Zoe? For keeps? For being so nice, eh?

(*She puts the potato greedily into a pocket, then links his arm, cuddling him with supple warmth. He smiles uneasily. Slowly, note by note, oriental music is played. He gazes in the tawny crystal of her eyes, ringed with kohol. His smile softens.*)

ZOE

You'll know me the next time.

BLOOM

(*Forlornly.*) I never loved a dear gazelle but it was sure to...

(*Gazelles are leaping, feeding on the mountains. Near are lakes. Round their shores file shadows black of cedargroves. Aroma rises, a strong hairgrowth of resin. It burns, the orient, a sky of sapphire, cleft by the bronze flight of eagles. Under it lies the womancity, nude, white, still, cool, in luxury. A fountain murmurs among damask roses. Mammoth roses murmur of scarlet winegrapes. A wine of shame, lust, blood exudes, strangely murmuring.*)

ZOE

(*Murmuring singsong with the music, her odalisk lips lusciously smeared with salve of swinefat and rosewater.*)

Schorach ani wenowach, benoith Hierushaloim.

BLOOM

(*Fascinated.*) I thought you were of good stock by your accent.

ZOE

And you know what thought did ?

(*She bites his ear gently with little goldstopped teeth sending on him a cloying breath of stale garlic. The roses draw apart, disclose a sepulchre of the gold of kings and their mouldering bones.*)

BLOOM

(*Draws back, mechanically caressing her right bub with a flat awkward hand.*) Are you a Dublin girl ?

ZOE

(*Catches a stray hair deftly and twists it to her coil.*) No bloody fear. I'm English. Have you a swaggerroot ?

BLOOM

(*As before.*) Rarely smoke, dear. Cigar now and then. Childish device. (*Lewdly.*) The mouth can be better engaged than with a cylinder of rank weed.

ZOE

Go on. Make a stump speech out of it.

BLOOM

(*In workman's corduroy overalls, black gansy with red floating tie and apache cap.*) Mankind is incorrigible. Sir Walter Raleigh brought from the new world that potato and that weed, the one a killer of pestilence by absorption, the other a poisoner of the ear, eye, heart, memory, will, understanding, all. That is to say, he brought the poison a hundred years before another person whose name I forget brought the food. Suicide. Lies. All our habits. Why, look at our public life!

(*Midnight chimes from distant steeples.*)

THE CHIMES

Turn again, Leopold! Lord mayor of Dublin!

BLOOM

(*In alderman's gown and chain.*) Electors of Arran Quay, Inns Quay, Rotunda, Mountjoy and North Dock better run a tramline, I say, from the cattlemarket to the river. That's the music of the future. That's my programme. *Cui bono?* But our bucaneering Vanderdeckens in their phantom ship of finance...

AN ELECTOR

Three times three for our future chief magistrate!

(*The aurora borealis of the torchlight procession leaps.*)

THE TORCHBEARERS

Hooray!

(*Several wellknown burgesses, city magnates and freemen of the city shake hands with Bloom and congratulate him. Timothy Harrington, late thrice Lord Mayor of Dublin, imposing in mayoral scarlet, gold chain and white silk tie, confers with councillor Lorcan Sherlock, locum tenens. They nod vigorously in agreement.*)

LATE LORD MAYOR HARRINGTON

(*In scarlet robe with mace, gold mayoral chain and large white silk scarf.*) That alderman, sir Leo Bloom's speech be printed at the expense of the ratepayers. That the house in which he was born be ornamented with a commemorative tablet and that the thoroughfare hitherto known as Cow Parlour off Cork street be henceforth designated Boulevard Bloom.

COUNCILLOR LORCAN SHERLOCK

Carried unanimously.

BLOOM

(*Impassionedly.*) These flying Dutchmen or lying Dutchmen as they recline in their upholstered poop, casting dice, what reck they? Machines is their cry, their chimera, their panacea. Laboursaving apparatuses, supplanters, bugbears, manufactured monsters for mutual murder, hideous hobgoblins produced by a horde of capitalistic lusts upon our prostituted labour. The poor man starves while they are grassing their royal mountain stags or shooting peasants and phartridges in their purblind pomp of pelf and power. But their reign is rover for rever and ever and ev...

(*Prolonged applause. Venetian masts, maypoles and festal arches spring up. A streamer bearing the legends* Cead Mile Failte *and* Mah Ttob Melek Israel *spans the street. All the windows are thronged with sightseers, chiefly ladies. Along the route the regiments of the royal Dublin fusiliers, the King's own Scottish borderers, the Cameron Highlanders and the Welsh Fusiliers, standing to attention keep back the crowd. Boys from High school are perched on the lampposts, telegraph poles, windowsills, cornices, gutters, chimneypots, railings, rainspouts, whistling and cheering. The pillar of the cloud appears. A fife and drum band is heard in the distance playing the Kol Nidre. The beaters approach with imperial eagles hoisted, trailing banners and waving oriental palms. The chryselephantine papal standard rises high, surrounded by pennons of the civic flag. The van of the procession appears headed by John Howard Parnell, city marshal, in a chessboard tabard, the Athlone Poursuivant and Ulster King of Arms. They are followed by the Right Honourable Joseph Hutchinson, lord mayor of Dublin, the lord mayor of Cork, their worships the mayors of Limerick, Galway,*

Sligo and Waterford, twentyeight Irish representative peers, sirdars, grandees and maharajahs bearing the cloth of estate, the Dublin Metropolitan Fire Brigade, the chapter of the saints of finance in their plutocratic order of precedence, the bishop of Down and Connor, His Eminence Michael cardinal Logue archbishop of Armagh, primate of all Ireland, His Grace, the most reverend Dr William Alexander, archbishop of Armagh, primate of all Ireland, the chief rabbi, the presbyterian moderator, the heads of the baptist, anabaptist, methodist and Moravian chapels and the honorary secretary of the society of friends. After them march the guilds and trades and trainbands with flying colours : coopers, bird fanciers, millwrights, newspaper canvassers, law scriveners, masseurs, vintners, trussmakers, chimney sweeps, lard refiners, tabinet and poplin weavers, farriers, Italian warehousemen, church decorators, bootjack manufacturers, understakers, silk mercers, lapidaries, salesmasters, corkcutters, assessors of fire losses, dyers and cleaners, export bottlers, fellmongers, ticketwriters, heraldic seal engravers, horse repository hands, bullion brokers, cricket and archery outfitters, riddlemakers, egg and potato factors, hosiers and glovers, plumbing contractors. After them march gentlemen of the bedchamber, Black Rod, Deputy Garter, Gold Stick, the master of horse, the lord great chamberlain, the earl marshal, the high constable carrying the sword of state, saint Stephen's iron crown, the chalice and bible. Four buglers on foot blow a sennet. Beefeaters reply, winding clarions of welcome. Under an arch of triumph Bloom appears bareheaded, in a crimson velvet mantletrimmed with ermine, bearing Saint Edward's staff, the orb and sceptre with the dove, the curtana. He is seated on a milkwhite horse with long flowing crimson tail, richly caparisoned, with golden headstall. Wild excitement. The ladies from their balconies throw down rosepetals. The air is perfumed with essences. The men cheer. Bloom's boys run amid the bystanders with branches of hawthorn and wrenbushes.)

BLOOM'S BOYS

The wren, the wren,
The king of all birds,
Saint Stephen's his day
Was caught in the furze.

A BLACKSMITH

(*Murmurs*) For the honour of God! And is that Bloom? He scarcely looks thirtyone.

A PAVIOR and FLAGGER

That's the famous Bloom now, the world's greatest reformer. Hats off!

(*All uncover their heads. Women whisper eagerly.*)

A MILLIONAIRESS

(*Richly.*) Isn't he simply wonderful?

A NOBLEWOMAN

(*Nobly.*) All that man has seen!

A FEMINIST

(*Masculinely.*) And done!

A BELLHANGER

A classic face! He has the forehead of a thinker.

(*Bloom's weather. A sunburst appears in the northwest.*)

THE BISHOP OF DOWN AND CONNOR

I here present your undoubted emperor president and king chairman, the most serene and potent and very puissant ruler of this realm. God save Leopold the First!

ALL

God save Leopold the First!

BLOOM

(*In dalmatic and purple mantle, to the bishop of Down and Connor, with dignity.*) Thanks, somewhat eminent sir.

WILLIAM, ARCHBISHOP OF ARMAGH

(*In purple stock and shovel hat.*) Will you to your power cause law and mercy to be executed in all your judgments in Ireland and territories thereunto belonging?

BLOOM

(*Placing his right hand on his testicles, swears.*) So may the Creator deal with me. All this I promise to do.

MICHAEL, ARCHBISHOP OF ARMAGH

(*Pours a cruse of hairoil over Bloom's head.*) *Gaudium magnum annuntio vobis. Habemus carneficem.* Leopold, Patrick, Andrew, David, George, be thou anointed!

(*Bloom assumes a mantle of cloth of gold and puts on a ruby ring. He ascends and stands on the stone of destiny. The representative peers put on at the same time their twentyeight crowns. Joybells ring in Christ church, Saint Patrick's, George's and gay Malahide. Mirus bazaar fireworks go up from all sides with symbolical phallopyrotechnic designs. The peers do homage, one by one, approaching and genuflecting.*)

THE PEERS

I do become your liege man of life and limb to earthly worship.

(*Bloom holds up his right hand on which sparkles the Koh-i-Noor diamond. His palfrey neighs. Immediate silence. Wireless intercontinental and interplanetary transmitters are set for reception of message.*)

BLOOM

My subjects! We hereby nominate our faithful charger Copula Felix hereditary Grand Vizier and announce that we have this day repudiated our former spouse and have bestowed our royal hand upon the princess Selene, the splendour of night.

(*The former morganatic spouse of Bloom is hastily removed in the Black Maria. The princess Selene, in moonblue robes, a silver crescent on her head, descends from a Sedan chair, borne by two giants. An outburst of cheering.*)

JOHN HOWARD PARNELL

(*Raises the royal standard.*) Illustrious Bloom! Successor to my famous brother!

BLOOM

(*Embraces John Howard Parnell.*) We thank you from our heart, John, for this right royal welcome to green Erin, the promised land of our common ancestors.

(*The freedom of the city is presented to him embodied in a charter. The keys of Dublin, crossed on a crimson cushion, are given to him. He shows all that he is wearing green socks.*)

TOM KERNAN

You deserve it, your honour.

BLOOM

On this day twenty years ago we overcame the hereditary enemy at Ladysmith. Our howitzers and camel swivel guns played on his lines with telling effect. Half a league onward! They charge! All is lost now! Do we yield? No! We drive them headlong! Lo! We charge! Deploying to the left our light horse swept across the heights of Plevna and, uttering thier warcry, *Bonafide Sabaoth*, sabred the Saracen gunners to a man.

THE CHAPEL OF FREEMAN TYPESETTERS

Hear! Hear!

JOHN WYSE NOLAN

There's the man that got away James Stephens.

A BLUECOAT SCHOOLBOY

Bravo!

AN OLD RESIDENT

You're a credit to your country, sir, that's what you are.

AN APPLEWOMAN

He's a man like Ireland wants.

BLOOM

My beloved subjects, a new era is about to dawn. I, Bloom, tell you verily it is even now at hand. Yea, on the word of a Bloom, ye shall ere long enter into the golden city which is to be, the new Bloomusalem in the Nova Hibernia of the future.

(*Thirty two workmen wearing rosettes, from all the counties of Ireland, under the guidance of Derwan the builder, construct the new Bloomusalem. It is a colossal edifice, with crystal roof, built in the shape of a huge pork kidney, containing forty thousand rooms. In the course of its extension several buildings and monuments are demolished. Government offices are temporarily transferred to railway sheds. Numerous houses are razed to the ground. The inhabitants are lodged in barrels and boxes, all marked in red with the letters : L. B. Several paupers fall from a ladder. A part of the walls of Dublin crowded with loyal sightseers, collapses.*)

THE SIGHTSEERS

(*Dying.*) *Morituri te salutant.* (*They die.*)

(*A man in a brown macintosh springs up through a trapdoor. He points an elongated figure at Bloom.*)

THE MAN IN THE MACINTOSH

Don't you believe a word he says. That man is Leopold M'Intosh, the notorious fireraiser. His real name is Higgins.

BLOOM

Shoot him! Dog of a christian! So much for M'Intosh!

(*A cannonshot. The man in the macintosh disppears. Bloom with his sceptre strikes down poppies. The instantaneous deaths of many powerful enemies, graziers, members of parliament, members of standing committees, are reported. Bloom's bodyguard distribute Maundy money, commemoration medals, loaves and fishes, temperance badges, expensive Henry Clay cigars, free cowbones for soup, rubber preservatives, in sealed envelopes tied with gold thread, butter scotch, pineapple rock,* billets doux *in the form of cocked hats, readymade suits, porringers of toad in the hole, bottles of Jeyes' Fluid, purchase stamps, 40 days' indulgences, spurious coins, dairyfed pork sausages, theatre passes, season tickets available for all tram lines, coupons of the royal and prvileged Hungarian lottery, penny dinner counters, cheap reprints of the World's Twelve Worst Books : Froggy and Fritz (politic), Care of the Baby (infantilic), 50 Meals for 7/6 (culinic), Was Jesus a Sun Myth? (historic), Expel that Pain (medic), Infant's Compendium of the*

Universe (cosmic), Let's All Chortle (hilaric), Canvasser's Vade Mecum (journalic), Loveletters of Mother Assistant (erotic), Who's Who in Space (astric), Songs that Reached 'Our Heart (melodic), Pennywise's Way to Wealth (parsimonic). A general rush and scramble. Women press forward to touch the hem of Bloom's robe. The lady Gwendolen Dubedat bursts through the throng, leaps on his horse and kisses him on both cheeks amid great acclamation. A magnesium flashlight photograph is taken. Babes and sucklings are held up.)

THE WOMEN

Little father! Little father

THE BABES and SUCKLINGS

Clap clap hands till Poldy comes home,
Cakes in his pocket for Leo alone.

(*Bloom, bending down, pokes Baby Boardman gently in the stomach.*)

BABY BOARDMAN

(*Hiccups, curdled milk flowing from his mouth.*) Hajajaja.

BLOOM

(*Shaking hands with a blind stripling.*) My more than Brother! (*Placing his arms round the shoulders of an old couple.*) Dear old friends! (*He playes pussy fourcorners with ragged boys and girls.*) Peep! Bopeep! (*He wheels twins in a perambulator.*) Ticktacktwo wouldyousetashoe? (*He performs juggler's tricks, draws red, orange, yellow, green, blue, indigo and violet silk haudherchiefs from his mouth.*) Roygbiv. 32 feet per second. (*He consoles a widow.*) Absence makes the heart grow younger. (*He dances the Highland fling with grotesque antics.*) Leg it, ye devils! (*He kisses the bedsores of a palsied veteran.*) Honourable wounds! (*He trips up a fat policeman.*) U. p : up. U. p : up. (*He whispers in the ear of a blushing waitress and laughs kindly.*) Ah, naughty, naughty! (*He eats a raw turnip offered him by Maurice Butterly, farmer.*) Fine! Splendid! (*He refuses to accept three shillings offered him by Joseph Hynes, journalist.*) My dear fellow, not at all! (*He gives his coat to a beggar.*) Please accept. (*He takes part in a stomach race with elderly male and female cripples.*) Come on, boys! Wriggle it, girls!

THE CITIZEN

(*Choked with emotion, brushes aside a tear in his emerald muffler.*) May the good God bless him!

(*The ram's horns sound for silence. The standard of Zion is hoisted.*)

BLOOM

(*Uncloaks impressively, revealing obesity, unrolls a paper and reads solemnly.*) Aleph Beth Ghimel Daleth Hagadah Tephilim Kosher Yom Kippur Hanukah Roschaschana Beni Brith Bar Mitzvah Mazzoth Askenazim Meshuggah Talith.

(*An official translation is read by Jimmy Henry, assistant town clerk.*)

JIMMY HENRY

The Court of Conscience is now open. His Most Catholic Majesty will now administer open air justice. Free medical and legal advice, solution of doubles and other problems. All cordially invited. Given at this our loyal city of Dublin in the year I of the Paradisiacal Era.

PADDY LEONARD

What am I to do about my rates and taxes?

BLOOM

Pay them, my friend.

PADDY LEONARD

Thank you.

NOSEY FLYNN

Can I raise a mortgage on my fire insurance?

BLOOM

(*Obdurately.*) Sirs, take notice that by the law of torts you are bound over in your own recognisances for six months in the sum of five pounds.

J. J. O'MOLLOY

A Daniel did I say? Nay! A Peter O'Brien!

NOSEY FLYNN

Where do I draw the five pounds?

PISSER BURKE

For bladder trouble?

BLOOM

Acid. nit. hydrochlor dil, 20 minims
Tinct. mix. vom, 5 minims
Extr. taraxel. lig. 30 minims.
Aq. dis. ter in die.

CHRIS CALLINAN

What is the parallax of the subsolar ecliptic of Aldebaran?

BLOOM

Pleased to hear from you, Chris. K. 11.

JOE HYNES

Why aren't you in uniform?

BLOOM

When my progenitor of sainted memory wore the uniform of the Austrian despot in a dank prison where was yours?

BEN DOLLARD

Pansies?

BLOOM

Embellish (beautify) suburban gardens.

BEN DOLLARD

When twins arrive?

BLOOM

Father (pater, dad) starts thinking.

LARRY O' ROURKE

An eight day licence for my new premises. You remember me, sir Leo, when you were in number seven. I'm sending around a dozen of stout for the missus.

BLOOM

(*Coldly.*) You have the advantage of me. Lady Bloom accepts no presents.

CROFTON

This is indeed a festivity.

BLOOM

(*Solemnly.*) You call it a festivity. I call it a sacrament.

ALEXANDER KEYES

When will we have our own house of keys?

BLOOM

I stand for the reform of municipal morals and the plain ten commandments. New worlds for old. Union of all, jew, moslem and gentile. Three acres and a cow for all children of nature. Saloon motor hearses. Compulsory manual labour for all. All parks open to the public day and night. Electric dishscrubbers. Tuberculosis, lunacy, war and mendicancy must now cease. General amnesty, weekly carnival, with masked licence, bonuses for all, esperanto the universal brotherhood. No more patriotism of barspongers and dropsical impostors. Free money, free love and a free lay church in a free lay state.

O'MADDEN BURKE

Free fox in a free henroost.

DAVY BYRNE

(*Yawning.*) Iiiiiiiiiaaaaaaach!

BLOOM

Mixed races and mixed marriage.

LENEHAN

What about mixed bathing?

(*Bloom explains to those near him his schemes for social regeneration. All agree with him. The keeper of the Kildare Street museum appears, dragging a lorry on which are the shaking statues of several naked goddesses, Venus Callipyge, Venus Pandemos, Venus Metempsychosis, and plaster figures, also naked, representing the new nine muses, Commerce, Operatic Music, Amor, Publicity, Manufacture, Liberty of Speech, Plural Voting, Gastronomy, Private Hygiene, Seaside Concert Entertainments, Painless Obstetrics and Astronomy for the People.*)

FATHER FARLEY

He is an episcopalian, an agnostic, an anythingarian seeking to overthrow our holy faith.

MRS RIORDAN

(*Tears up her will.*) I'm disappointed in you! You bad man!

MOTHER GROGAN

(*Removes her boot to throw it at Bloom.*) You beast! You abominable person!

NOSEY FLYNN

Give us a tune, Bloom. One of the old sweet songs.

BLOOM

(*With rollicking humour.*)

I vowed that I never would leave her,
She turned out a cruel deceiver.
With my tooraloom tooraloom tooraloom tooraloom.

HOPPY HOLOHAN

Good old Bloom! There's nobody like him after all.

PADDY LEONARD

Stage Irishman!

BLOOM

What railway opera is like a tramline in Gibraltar? The Rows of Casteele (*Laughter.*)

LENEHAN

Plagiarist! Down with Bloom!

THE VEILED SIBYL

(*Enthusiastically.*) I'm a Bloomite and I glory in it. I believe in him in spite of all. I'd give my life for him, the funniest man on earth.

BLOOM

(*Winks at the bystanders.*) I bet she's a bonny lassie.

THEODORE PUREFOY

(*In fishingcap and oilskin jacket.*) He employs a mechanical device to frustrate the sacred ends of nature.

THE VEILED SIBYL

(*Stabs herself.*) My hero god! (*She dies.*)

(*Many most attractive and enthusiastic women also commit suicide by stabbing, drowning, drinking prussic acid, aconite, arsenic, opening their veins, refusing food, casting themselves under steamrollers, from the top of Nelson's Pillar, into the great vat of Guinness's brewery, asphyxiating themselves by placing their heads in gas ovens, hanging themselves in stylish garters, leaping from windows of different storeys.*)

ALEXANDER J. DOWIE

(*Violently.*) Fellowchristians and antiBloomites, the man called Bloom is from the roots of hell, a disgrace to christian men. A fiendish libertine from his earliest years this stinking goat of Mendes gave precocious signs of infantile debauchery recalling the cities of the plain, with a dissolute granddam. This vile hypocrite, bronzed with infamy, is the white bull mentioned in the Apocalypse. A worshipper of the Scarlet Woman, intrigue is the very breath of his nostrils. The stake faggots and the caldron of boiling oil are for him. Caliban!

THE MOB

Lynch him! Roast him! He's as bad as Parnell was. Mr. Fox!

(*Mother Grogan throws her boot at Bloom. Several shopkeepers from upper and lower Dorset street throw objects of little or no commercial value, hambones, condensed milk tins, unsaleable cabbage, stale bread, sheeps' tails, odd pieces of fat.*)

BLOOM

(*Excitedly.*) This is midsummer madness, some ghastly joke again. By heaven, I am guiltless as the unsunned snow! It was my brother Henry. He is my double. He lives in number 2 Dolphin's Barn. Slander, the viper, has wrongfully accused me. Fellowcountrymen, *sgenl inn ban bata coisde gan capall.* I call on my old friend, Dr Malachi Mulligan, sex specialist, to give medical testimony on my behalf.

DR MULLIGAN

(*In motor jerkin, green motorgoggles on his brow.*) Dr Bloom is bisexually abnormal. He has recently escaped from Dr Eustace's private asylum for demented gentlemen. Born out of bedlock hereditary epilepsy is present, the consequence of unbridled lust. Traces of elephantiasis have been discovered among his ascendants. There are marked symptoms of chronic exhibitionism. Ambidexterity is also latent. He is prematurely bald from selfabuse, perversely idealistic in consequence, a reformed rake, and has metal teeth. In consequence of a family complex he has temporarily lost his memory and I believe him to be more sinned against than sinning. I have made a pervaginal examination and, after application of the acid test to 5427 anal, axillary, pectoral and pubic hairs, I declare him to be *virgo intacta*.

(*Bloom holds his high grade hat over his genital organs.*)

DR MADDEN

Hypsospadia is also marked. In the interest of coming generations I suggest that the parts affected should be preserved in spirits of wine in the national teratological museum.

DR CROTTHERS

I have examined the patient's urine. It is albuminoid. Salivation is insufficient, the patellar reflex intermittent.

DR PUNCH COSTELLO

The *fetor judaicus* is most perceptible.

DR DIXON

(*Reads a bill of health.*) Professor Bloom is a finished example of the new womanly man. His moral nature is simple and lovable. Many have found him a dear man, a dear person. He is a rather quaint fellow on the whole, coy though not feebleminded in the medical sense. He has written a really beautiful letter, a poem in itself, to the court missionary of the Reformed Priests Protection Society which clears up everything. He is practically a total abstainer and I can affirm that he sleeps on a straw litter and eats the most Spartan food, cold dried grocer's peas. He wears a hairshirt winter and summer and scourges himself every Saturday. He was, I understand, at one time a firstclass misdemeanant in Glencree reformatory. Another report states that he was a very posthumous child. I appeal for clemency in the name of the most sacred word our vocal organs have ever been called upon to speak. He is about to have a baby.

(*General commotion and compassion. Women faint. A wealthy American makes a street collection for Bloom. Gold and silver coins, blank cheques, banknotes, jewels, treasury bonds, maturing bills of exchange, I. O. U's, wedding rings, watchchains, lockets, necklaces and bracelets are rapidly collected.*)

BLOOM

O, I so want to be a mother.

MRS THORNTON

(*In nursetender's gown.*) Embrace me tight, dear. You'll be soon over it. Tight, dear.

(*Bloom embraces her tightly and bears eight male yellow and white children. They appear on a redcarpeted staircase adorned with expensive plants. All are handsome, with valuable metallic faces, wellmade, respectably dressed and wellconducted, speaking five modern languages fluently and interested in various arts and sciences. Each has his name printed in legible letters on his shirtfront : Nasodoro, Goldfinger, Chrysostomos, Maindorée, Silversmile, Silberselber, Vifargent, Panargyros. They are immediately appointed to positions of high public trust in several different countries as managing directors of banks, traffic managers of railways, chairmen of limited liability companies, vice chairmen of hotel syndicates.*)

A VOICE

Bloom, are you the Messiah ben Joseph or ben David?

BLOOM

(*Darkly.*) You have said it.

BROTHER BUZZ

Then perform a miracle.

BANTAM LYONS

Prophesy who will win the Saint Leger

(*Bloom walks on a net, covers his left eye with his left ear, passes through several walls, climbs Nelson's Pillar, hangs from the top ledge by his eyelids, eats twelve dozen oysters (shells included), heals several sufferers from king's evil, contracts his face so as to resemble many historical personages, Lord Beaconsfield, Lord Byron, Wat Tyler, Moses of Egypt, Moses Maimonides, Moses Mendelssohn, Henry Irving, Rip van Winkle, Kossuth, Jean Jacques Rousseau, Baron Leopold Rothschild, Robinson Crusoe, Sherlock Holmes, Pasteur, turns each foot simultaneously in different directions, bids the tide turn back, eclipses the sun by extending his little finger.*)

BRINI, PAPAL NUNCIO

(*In papal zouave's uniform, steel cuirasses as breastplate, armplates, thighplates, legplates, large profane moustaches and brown paper mitre.*)

Leopoldi autem generatio. Moses begat Noah and Noah begat Eunuch and Eunuch begat O'Halloran and O'Halloran begat Guggenheim and Guggenheim begat Agendath and Agendath begat Netaim and Netaim begat Le Hirsch and Le Hirsch begat Jesurum and Jesurum begat MacKay and MacKay begat Ostrolopsky and Ostrolopsky begat Smerdoz and Smerdoz begat Weiss and Weiss begat Schwarz and Schwarz begat Adrianopoli and Adrianopoli begat Aranjuez and Aranjuez begat Lewy Lawson and Lewy Lawson begat Ichabudonosor and Ichabudonosor begat O'Donnell Magnus and O'Donnell Magnus begat Christbaum and Christbaum begat ben Maimun and ben Maimun begat Dusty Rhodes and Dusty Rhodes begat Benamor and Benamor begat Jones-Smith and Jones-Smith begat Savorgnanovich and Savorgnanovich begat Jasperstone and Jasperstone begat Vingtetunieme and Vingtetunieme begat Szombathely and Szombathely begat Virag and Virag begat Bloom *et vocabitur nomen eius Emmanuel.*

A DEADHAND

(*Writes on the wall.*) Bloom is a cod.

CRAB

(*In bushranger's kit.*) What did you do in the cattlecreep behind Kilbarrack?

A FEMALE INFANT

(*Shakes a rattle.*) And under Ballybough bridge?

A HOLLYBUSH

And in the devil's glen?

BLOOM

(*Blushes furiously all over from frons to nates, three tears falling from his left eye.*) Spare my past.

THE IRISH EVICTED TENANTS

(*In bodycoats, kneebreeches, with Donnybrook fair shillelaghs.*) Sjambok him!

(*Bloom with asses' ears seats himself in the pillory with crossed arms, his feet protruding. He whistles* Don Giovanni, a cenar teco. *Artane orphans, joining hands, caper round him. Girls of the Prison Gat Mission, joining hands, caper round in the opposite direction.*)

THE ARTANE ORPHANS

You hig, you hog, you dirty dog!
You think the ladies love you!

THE PRISON GATE GIRLS

If you see kay
Tell him he may
See you in tea
Tell him from me.

HORNBLOWER

(*In ephod and huntingcap, announces.*) And he shall carry the sins of the people to Azazel, the spirit which is in the wilderness, and to Lilith, the nighthag. And they shall stone him and defile him, yea, all from Agendath Netaim and from Mizraim, the land of Ham.

(*All the people cast soft pantomime stones at Bloom. Many bonafide travellers and ownerless dogs come near him and defile him. Mastiansky and Citron approach in gaberdines, wearing long earlocks, They wag their beards at Bloom.*)

MASTIANSKY AND CITRON

Belial! Laemlein of Istria! the false Messiah! Abulafia!

(*George S. Mesias, Bloom's tailor, appears, a tailor's goose under his arm, presenting a bill.*)

MESIAS

To alteration one pair trousers eleven shillings.

BLOOM

(*Rubs his hands cheerfully.*) Just like old times. Poor Bloom!

(*Reuben J. Dodd, blackbearded Iscariot, bad shepherd, bearing on his shoulders the drowned corpse of his son, approaches the pillory.*)

REUBEN J.

(*Whispers hoarsely.*) The squeak is out. A split is gone for the flatties. Nip the first rattler.

THE FIRE BRIGADE

Pflaap!

BROTHER BUZZ

(*Invests Bloom in a yellow habit with embroidery of painted flames and high pointed hat. He places a bag of gunpowder round his neck and hands him over to the civil power, sayping.*) Forgive him his trespasses.

(*Lieutenant Myers of the Dublin Fire Brigade by general request sets fire to Bloom. Lamentations.*)

THE CITIZEN

Thank heaven!

BLOOM

(*In a seamless garment marked I. H. S. stands upright amid phoenix flames.*) Weep not for me, O daughters of Erin.

(*He exhibits to Dublin reporters traces of burning. The daughters of Erin, in black garments with large prayerbooks and long lighted candles in their hands, kneel down and pray.*)

THE DAUGHTERS OF ERIN

Kidney of Bloom, pray for us.
Flower of the Bath, pray for us.
Mentor of Menton, pray for us.
Canvasser for the Freeman, pray for us.
Charitable Mason, pray for us.
Wandering Soap, pray for us.
Sweets of Sin, pray for us.
Music without Words, pray for us.
Reprover of the Citizen, pray for us.
Friend of all Frillies, pray for us.
Midwife Most Merciful, pray for us.
Potato Preservative against Plague and Pestilence, pray for us.

(*A choir of six hundred voices, conducted by Mr Vincent O'Brien, sings the Alleluia chorus, accompanied on the organ by Joseph Glynn. Bloom becomes mute, shrunken, carbonised.*)

ZOE

Talk away till you're black in the face.

BLOOM

(*In caubeen with clay pipe stuck in the band, dsuty brogues, an emigrant's red handkerchief bundle in his hand leading a black bogoak pig by a sugaun, with a smile in his eye.*) Let me be going now, woman of the house, for by all the goats in Connemara I'm after having the father and mother of a bating. (*With a tear in his eye.*) All insanity. Patriotism, sorrow for the dead, music, future of the race. To be or not to be. Life's dream is o'er. End it peacefully. They can live on. (*He gazes far away mournfully.*) I am ruined. A few pastilles of aconite. The blinds drawn. A letter. Then lie back to rest. (*He breathes softly.*) No more. I have lived. Fare. Farewell.

ZOE

(*Stiffly, her finger in her neckfillet.*) Honest? Till the next time. (*She sneers.*) Suppose you got up the wrong side of the bed or came too quick with your best girl. O, I can read your thoughts.

BLOOM

(*Bitterly.*) Man and woman, love, what is it? A cork and bottle.

ZOE

(*In sudden sulks.*) I hate a rotter that's insincere. Give a bleeding whore a chance.

BLOOM

(*Repentantly.*) I am very disagreable. You are a necessary evil. Where are you from? London?

ZOE

(*Glibly.*) Hog's Norton where the pigs plays the organs. I'm Yorkshire born (*She holds his hand which is feeling for her nipple.*) I say, Tommy Tittlemouse. Stop that and begin worse. Have you cash for a short time? Ten shillings?

BLOOM

(*Smiles, nods slowly.*) More, houri, more.

ZOE

And more's mother? (*She pats him offhandedly with velvet paws.*) Are you coming into the musicroom to see our new pianola? Come and I'll peel off.

BLOOM

(*Feeling his occiput dubiously with the unparalleled embarrassment of a harassed pedlar gauging the symmetry of her peeled pears.*) Somebody would be dreadfully jealous if she knew. The greeneyed monster (*Earnestly.*) You know how difficult it is. I needn't tell you.

ZOE

(*Flattered.*) What the eye can't see the heart can't grieve for (*She pats him.*) Come.

BLOOM

Laughing witch! The hand that rocks the cradle.

ZOE

Babby!

BLOOM

(*In babylinen and pelisse, bigheaded, with a caul of dark hair, fixes big eyes on her fluid slip and counts its bronze buckles with a chubby finger, his moist tongue lolling and lisping.*) One two tlee : tlee tlwo tlone.

THE BUCKLES

Love me. Love me not. Love me.

ZOE

Silent means consent. (*With little parted talons she captures his hand, her forefinger giving to his palm the passtouch of secret monitor, luring him to doom.*) Hot hands cold gizzard.

(*He hesitates amid scents, music, temptations. She leads him towards the steps, drawing him by the odour of her armpits, the vice of her painted eyes, the rustle of her slip in whose sinuous folds lurks the lion reek of all the male brutes that have possessed her.*)

THE MALE BRUTES

(*Exhaling sulphur of rut and dung and ramping in their loosebox, faintly roaring, their drugged heads swaying to and fro.*) Good!

(*Zoe and Bloom reach the doorway where two sister whores are seated. They examine him curiously from under their pencilled brows and smile to his hasty bow. He trips awkwardly.*)

ZOE

(*Her lucky hand instantly saving him.*) Hoopsa! Don't fall upstairs.

BLOOM

The just man falls seven times (*He stands aside at the threshold.*) After you is good manners.

ZOE

Ladies first, gentlemen after.

(*She crosses the threshold. He hesitates. She turns and, holding out her hands, draws him over. He hops. On the antlered rack of the hall hang a man's hat and waterproof, Bloom uncovers himself but, seeing them, frowns then smiles, preoccupied. A door on the return landing is thrown open. A man in purple shirt and grey trousers brownsocked, passes with an ape's gait, his bald head and goatee beard upheld, hugging a full waterjugjar, his twotailed black braces dangling at heels. Averting his face quickly Bloom bends to examine on the halltable the spaniel eyes of a running fox : then, his lifted head sniffing, follows Zoe into the musicroom. A shade of mauve tissuepaper dims the light of the chandelier. Round and round a moth flies, colliding, escaping. The floor is covered with an oilcloth mosaic of jade and azure and cinnabar rhomboids. Footmarks are stamped over it in all senses, heel to heel, heel to hollow, toe to toe, feet locked, a morris of shuffling feet without body phantoms, all in a scrimmage higgledypiggledy. The walls are tapestried with a paper of yewfronds and clear glades. In the grate is spread a screen of peacock feathers. Lynch squats crosslegged on the hearthrug of matted hair, his cap back to the front. With a wand he beats time slowly. Kitty Ricketts, a bony pallid whore in navy costume, doeskin gloves rolled back from a coral wristlet, a chain purse in her hand, sits perched on the edge of the table swinging her leg and glancing at herself in the gilt mirror over the mantlepiece. A tag of her corset lace hangs slightly below her jacket. Lynch indicates mockingly the couple at the piano.*)

KITTY

(*Coughs behind her hand.*) She's a bit imbecillic. (*She signs with a waggling forefinger.*) Blemblem. (*Lynch lifts up her skirt and white petticoat with the wand. She settles them down quickly.*) Respect yourself. (*She hiccups, then bends quickly her sailor hat under which her hair glows, red with henna.*) O, excuse!

ZOE

More limelight, Charley. (*She goes to the chandelier and turns the gas full cock.*)

KITTY

(*Peers at the gasjet.*) What ails it tonight?

LYNCH

(*Deeply.*) Enter a ghost and hobgoblins.

ZOE

Clap on the back for Zoe.

(*The wand in Lynch's hand flashes : a brass poker. Stephen stands at the pianola on which sprawl his hat and ashplant. With two fingers he repeats once more the series of empty fifths. Florry Talbot, a blond feeble goosefat whore in a tatterdemalion gown of mildewed strawberry lolls spreadeagle in the sofa corner, her limp forearm pendent over the bolster, listening. A heavy stye droops over her sleepy eyelid.*)

KITTY

(*Hiccups again with a kick of her horsed foot.*) O, excuse !

ZOE

(*Promptly.*) Your boy's thinking of you. Tie a knot on your shift.

(*Kitty Ricketts bends her head. Her boa uncoils, slides, glides over her shoulder, back, arm, chair to the ground. Lynch lifts the curled catterpillar on his wand. She snakes her neck, nestling. Stephen glances behind at the squatted figure with its cap back to the front.*)

STEPHEN

As a matter of fact it is of no importance whether Benedetto Marcello found it or made it. The rite is the poet's rest. It may be an old hymn to Demeter or also illustrate *Cœla enarrant gloriam Domini*. It is susceptible of nodes or modes as far apart as hyperphrygian and mixolydian and of texts so divergent as priests haihooping round David's that is Circe's or what am I saying Ceres' altar and David's tip from the stable to his chief bassoonist about the alrightiness of his almightiness. *Mais, nom de nom,* that is another pair of trousers. *Jetez la gourme. Faut que jeunesse se passe.* (*He stops, points at Lynch's cap, smiles, laughs.*) Which side is your knowledge bump ?

THE CAP

(*With saturnine spleen.*) Bah ! It is because it is. Woman's reason. Jewgreek is greekjew. Extremes meet. Death is the highest form of life. Bah !

STEPHEN

You remember fairly accurately all my errors, boasts, mistakes. How long shall I continue to close my eyes to disloyalty ? Whetstone !

THE CAP

Bah !

STEPHEN

Here's another for you. (*He frowns.*) The reason is because the fundamental and the dominant are separated by the greatest possible interval which...

THE CAP

Which ? Finish. You can't.

STEPHEN

(*With an effort.*) Interval which. Is the greatest possible elipse. Consistent with. The ultimate return. The octave. Which.

THE CAP

Which ?

(*Outside the gramophone begins to blare* The Holy City.)

STEPHEN

(*Abruptly.*) What went forth to the ends of the world to traverse not itself, God, the sun, Shakespeare, a commercial traveller, having itself traversed in reality itself becomes that self. Wait a moment. Wait a second. Damn that fellow's noise in the street. Self which it itself was ineluctably preconditioned to become. *Ecco !*

LYNCH

(*With a mocking whinny of laughter grins at Bloom and Zoe Higgins.*) What a learned speech, eh ?

ZOE

(*Briskly.*) God help your head, he knows more than you have forgotten.

(*With obese stupidity Florry Talbot regards Stephen.*)

FLORRY

They say the last day is coming this summer.

KITTY

No!

ZOE

(*Explodes in laughter.*) Great unjust God!

FLORRY

(*Offended.*) Well, it was in the papers about Antichrist. O, my foot's tickling.

(*Ragged barefoot newsboys jogging a wagtail kite, patter past, yelling.*)

THE NEWSBOYS

Stop press edition. Result of the rockinghorse races. Sea serpent in the royal canal. Safe arrival of Antichrist.

(*Stephen turns and sees Bloom.*)

STEPHEN

A time, times and half a time.

(*Reuben J. Antichrist, wandering jew, a clutching hand open on his spine, stumps forward. Across his loins is slung a pilgrim's wallet from which protrude promissory notes and dishonoured bills. Aloft over his shoulder he bears a long boatpole from the hook of which the sodden huddled mass of his only son, saved from Liffey waters hangs from the slack of its breeches. A hobgoblin in the image of Punch Costello, hipshot, crookbacked, hydrocephalic, prognatic with receding forehead and Ally Sloper nose tumbles in somersaults through the gathering darkness.*)

ALL

What?

THE HOBGOBLIN

(*His jaws chattering, capers to and fro, goggling his eyes, squeaking, kangaroohopping, with outstretched clutching arms then all at once thrusts his lipless face through the fork of his thighs.*) *Il vient! C'est moi! L'homme qui rit!*

L'homme primigène! (He whirls round and round with dervish howls.) Sieurs et dames, faites vos jeux! (He crouches juggling. Tiny roulette planets fly from his hands.) Les jeux sont faits! (The planets rush together, uttering crepitant cracks.) Rien n'va plus. (The planets, buoyant balloons, sail swollen up and away. He springs off into vacuum.)

FLORRY

(*Sinking into torpor, crosses herself secretly.*) The end of the world!

(*A female tepid effluvium leaks out from her. Nebulous obscurity occupies space. Through the drifting fog without the gramophone blares over coughs and feetshuffling.*)

THE GRAMOPHONE

Jerusalem!
Open your gates and sing
Hosanna...

(*A rocket rushes up the sky and bursts. A white star falls from it, proclaiming the consummation of all things and second coming of Elijah. Along an infinite invisible tightrope taut from zenith to nadir the End of the World, a twoheaded octopus in gillie's kilts, busby and tartan filibegs whirls through the murk, head over heels, in the form of the Three Legs of Man.*)

THE END OF THE WORLD

(*With a Scotch accent.*) Wha'll dance the keel row, the keel row, the keel row?

(*Over the passing drift and choking breathcoughs, Elijah's voice, harsh as a corncrake's, jars on high. Perspiring in a loose lawn surplice with funnel sleeves he is seen, vergerfaced, above a rostrum about which the banner of old glory is draped. He thumps the parapet.*)

ELIJAH

No yapping, if you please, in this booth. Jake Crane, Creole Sue, Dave Campbell, Abe Kirschner, do your coughing with your mouths shut. Say, I am operating all this trunk line. Boys, do it now. God's time is 12.25. Tell mother you'll be there. Rush your order and you play a slick ace. Join on right here!

Book through to eternity junction, the nonstop run. Just one word more. Are you a god or a doggone clod? If the second advent came to Coney Island are we ready? Florry Christ, Stephen Christ, Zoe Christ, Bloom Christ, Kitty Christ, Lynch Christ, it's up to you to sense that cosmic force. Have we cold feet about the cosmos? No. Be on the side of the angels. Be a prism. You have that something within, the higher self. You can rub shoulders with a Jesus, a Gautama, an Ingersoll. Are you all in this vibration? I say you are. You once nobble that, congregation, and a buck joyride to heaven becomes a back number. You got me? It's a lifebrightener, sure. The hottest stuff ever was. It's the whole pie with jam in. It's just the cutest snappiest line out. It is immense, supersumptuous. It restores. It vibrates. I know and I am some vibrator. Joking apart and getting down to bedrock, A. J. Christ Dowie and the harmonial philosophy have you got that? O. K. Seventyseven west sixtyninth street. Got me? That's it. You call me up by sunphone any old time. Bumboosers, save your stamps. (*He shouts.*) Now then our glory song. All join heartily in the singing. Encore! (*He sings.*) Jeru...

THE GRAMOPHONE

(*Drowning his voice.*)

Whorusalaminyourhighhohhhh... (*The disc rasps gratingly against the needle.*)

THE THREE WHORES

(*Covering their ears, squawk.*) Ahhkkk!

ELIJAH

(*In rolledup shirtsleeves, black in the face, shouts at the top of his voice, his arms uplifted.*) Big Brother up there, Mr President, you hear what I done just been saying to you. Certainly, I sort of believe strong in you, Mr President. I certainly am thinking now Miss Higgins and Miss Ricketts got religion way inside them. Certainly seems to me I don't never see no wusser scared female than the way you been, Miss Florry, just now as I done seed you. Mr President, you come long and help me save our sisters dear. (*He winks at his audience.*) Our Mr President, he twig the whole lot and he ain't saying nothing.

KITTY-KATE

I forgot myself. In a weak moment I erred and did what I did on

Constitution hill. I was confirmed by the bishop. My mother's sister married a Montmorency. It was a working plumber was my ruination when I was pure.

ZOE-FANNY

I let him larrup it into me for the fun of it.

FLORRY-TERESA

It was in consequence of a portwine beverage on top of Hennessy's three stars. I was guilty with Whelan when he slipped into the bed.

STEPHEN

In the beginning was the word, in the enc. the world without end. Blessed be the eight beatitudes.

(The beatitudes, Dixon, Madden, Crotthers, Costello, Lenehan, Bannon, Mulligan and Lynch in white surgical students' gowns, four abreast, goosestepping, tramp fast past in noisy marching.)

THE BEATITUDES

(Incoherently.) Beer beef battledog buybull businum barnum buggerum bishop.

LYSTER

(In quakergrey kneebreeches and broadbrimmed hat, says discreetly.) He is our friend. I need not mention names. Seek thou the light.

(He corantos by. Best enters in hairdresser attire, shinily laundered, his locks in curlpapers. He leads John Eglinton who wears a mandarin's kimono of Nankeen yellow, lizardlettered, and a high pagoda hat.)

BEST

(Smiling, lifts the hat and displays a shaven poll from the crown of which bristles a pigtail toupee tied with an orange topknot.) I was just beautifying him, don't you know. A thing of beauty, don't you know. Yeats says, or I mean, Keats says.

JOHN EGLINTON

(Produces a greencapped dark lantern and flashes it towards a corner; with carping accent.) Esthetics and cosmetics are for the boudoir. I am out for truth.

Plain truth for a plain man. Tanderagee wants the facts and means to get them.

(*In the cone of the searchlight behind the coalscuttle, ollave, holyeyed, the bearded figure of Mananann Mac Lir broods, chin on knees. He rises slowly. A cold seawind blows from his druid mantle. About his head writhe eels and elvers. He is encrusted with weeds and shells. His right hand holds a bicycle pump. His left hand grasps a huge crayfish by its two talons.*)

MHANANANN MAC LIR

(*With a voice of waves.*) Aum! Hek! Wal! Ak! Lub! Mor! Ma! White yoghin of the Gods. Occult pimander of Hermes Trismegistos. (*With a voice of whistling seawind.*) Punarjanam patsypunjaub! I won't have my leg pulled. It has been said by one: beware the left, the cult of Shakti. (*With a cry of stormbirds.*) Shakti, Shiva! Dark hidden Father! (*He smites with his bicycle pump the crayfish in his left hand. On its cooperative dial glow the twelve signs of the zodiac. He wails with the vehemence of the ocean.*) Aum! Baum! Pyjaum! I am the light of the homestead, I am the dreamery creamery butter.

(*A skeleton judashand strangles the light. The green light wanes to mauve. The gasjet wails whistling.*)

THE GASJET

Pooah! Pfuiiiiii!

(*Zoe runs to the chandelier and, crooking her leg, adjusts the mantle.*)

ZOE

Who has a fag as I'm here?

LYNCH

(*Tossing a cigarette on to the table.*) Here.

ZOE

(*Her head perched aside in mock pride.*) Is that the way to hand the *pot* to a lady? (*She stretches up to light the cigarette over the flame, twirling it slowly, showing the brown tufts of her armpits. Lynch with his poker lifts boldly a side of her slip. Bare from her garters up her flesh appears under the sapphire a nixie's green. She puffs calmly at her cigarette.*) Can you see the beauty spot of my behind?

LYNCH

I'm not looking.

ZOE

(*Makes sheep's eyes.*) No? You wouldn't do a less thing. Would you suck a lemon?

(*Squinting in mock shame she glances with sidelong meaning at Bloom then twists round towards him, pulling her slip free of the poker. Blue fluid again flows over her flesh. Bloom stands, smiling desirously, twirling his thumbs. Kitty Ricketts licks her middle finger with her spittle and gazing in the mirror, smooths both eyebrows. Lipoti Virag, basilicogrammate, chutes rapidly down through the chimneyflue and struts two steps to the left on gawky pink stilts. He is sausaged into several overcoats and wears a brown macintosh under which he holds a roll of parchment. In his left eye flashes the monocle of Cashel Boyle O'Connor Fitzmaurice Tisdall Farrell. On his head is perched an Egyptian pshent. Two quills project over his ears.*)

VIRAG

(*Heels together, bows.*) My name is Virag Lipoti, of Szombathely. (*He coughs thoughtfully, drily.*) Promiscuous nakedness is much in evidence hereabouts, eh? Inadvertently her backview revealed the fact that she is not wearing those rather intimate garments of which you are a particular devotee. The injection mark on the thigh I hope you perceived? Good.

BLOOM

Granpapachi. But...

VIRAG

Number two on the other hand, she of the cherry rouge and coiffeuse white, whose hair owes not a little to our tribal elixir of gopherwood is in walking costume and tightly staysed by her sit, I should opine. Backbone in front, so to say. Correct me but I always understood that the act so performed by skittish humans with glimpses of lingerie appealed to you in virtue of its exhibitionististicicity. In a word. Hippogriff. Am I right?

BLOOM

She is rather lean.

VIRAG

(*Not unpleasantly.*) Absolutely! Well observed and those pannier pockets of the skirt and slightly pegtop effect are devised to suggest bunchiness of hip. A new purchase at some monster sale for which a gull has been mulcted. Meretricious finery to deceive the eye. Observe the attention to details of dustspecks. Never put on you tomorrow what you can wear today Parallax! (*With a nervous twitch of his head.*) Did you hear my brain go snap? Pollysyllabax!

BLOOM

(*An elbow resting in a hand, a forefinger against his cheek.*) She seems sad.

VIRAG

(*Cynically, his weasel teeth bared yellow, draws down his left eye wilh a finger and barks hoarsely.*) Hoax! Beware of the flapper and bogus mournful. Lily of the alley. All possess bachelor's button discovered by Rualdus Columbus. Tumble her. Columble her. Chameleon. (*More genially.*) Well then, permit me to draw your attention to item number three. There is plenty of her visible to the naked eye. Observe the mass of oxygenated vegetable matter on her skull. What ho, she bumps! The ugly duckling of the party, longcasted and deep in keel.

BLOOM

(*Regretfully.*) When you come out without your gun.

VIRAG

We can do you all brands mlld, medium and strong. Pay your money, take your choice. How happy caould you be with either...

BLOOM

With?...

VIRAG

(*His tongue upcurling.*) Lyum! Look. Her beam is broad. Sbe is coated with quite a considerable layer of fat. Obviously mammal in weight of bosom you remark that she has in front well to the fore two protuberances of very respectable dimensions, inclined to fall in the noonday soupplate, while on her rere lower down are two additional protuberances, suggestive of potent rectum and tumescent for palpation which leave nothing to be desired save compactness.

Such fleshy parts are the product of careful nurture. When coopfattened their livers reach an elephantine size. Pellets of new bread with fennygreek and gumbenjamin swamped down by potions of green tea endow them during their brief existence with natural pincushions of quite colossal blubber. That suits your book, eh? Fleshhotpots of Egypt to hanker after. Wallow in it. Lycopodium. (*His throat twitches.*) Slapbang! There he goes again.

BLOOM

The stye I dislike.

VIRAG

(*Arches his eyebrows.*) Contact with a goldring, they say. *Argumentum ad feminam*, as we said in old Rome and ancient Greece in the consulship of Diplodocus and Ichthyosaurus. For the rest Eve's sovereign remedy. Not for sale. Hire only. Huguenot. (*He twitches.*) It is a funny sound. (*He coughs encouragingly.*) But possibly it is only a wart. I presume you shall have remembered what I will have taught you on that head? Wheatenmeal with honey and nutmeg.

BLOOM

(*Reflecting.*) Wheatenmeal with lycopodium and syllabax. This searching ordeal. It has been an unusually fatiguing day, a chapter of accidents. Wait. I mean, wartsblood spreads warts, you said...

VIRAG

(*Severely, his nose hardhumped, his side eye winking.*) Stop twirling your thumbs and have a good old thunk. See, you have forgotten. Exercise your mnemotechnic. *La causa è santa*. Tara. Tara. (*Aside.*) He will surely remember.

BLOOM

Rosemary also did I understand you to say or willpower over parasitic tissues. Then nay no I have an inkling. The touch of a deadhand cures. Mnemo?

VIRAG

(*Excitedly.*) I say so. I say so. E'en so. Technic. (*He taps his parchment roll energetically.*) This book tells you how to act with all descriptive particulars. Consult index for agitated fear of aconite, melancholy of muriatic, priapic pulsatilla. Virag is going to talk about amputation. Our old friend caustic.

They must be starved. Snip off with horsehair under the denned neck. But, to change the venue to the Bulgar and the Basque. have you made up your mind whether you like or dislike women in male habiliments. (*With a dry snigger.*) You intended to devote an entire year to the study of the religious problem and the summer months of 1882 to square the circle and win that million. Pomegranate! From the sublime to the ridiculous is but a step. Pyjamas, let us say? Or stockingette gussetted knickers, closed? Or, put we the case, those complicated combinations, camiknickers? (*He crows derisively*) Keekeereekee!

(*Bloom surveys incertainly the three whores then gazes at the veiled mauve light, hearing the everflying moth.*)

BLOOM

I wanted then to have now concluded. Nightdress was never. Hence this. But tomorrow is a new day will be. Past was is today. What now is will then tomorrow as now was be past yester.

VIRAG

(*Prompts into his ear in a pig's whisper.*) Insects of the day spend their brief existence in reiterated coition, lured by the smell of the inferiorly pulchritudinous fumale possessing extendified pudendal verve in dorsal region. Pretty Poll! (*His yellow parrotbeak gabbles nasally.*) They had a proverb in the Carpathians in or about the year five thousand five hundred and fifty of our era. One tablespoonful of honey will attract friend Bruin more than half a dozen barrels of first choice malt vinegar. Bear's buzz bothers bees. But of this apart. At another time we may resume. We were very pleased, we others. (*He coughs and, bending his brow, rubs his nose thoughtfully with a scooping hand.*) You shall find that these night insects follow the light. An illusion for remember their complex unadjustable eye. For all these knotty points see the seventeenth book of my Fundamentals of Sexology or the Love Passion which Doctor L. B. says is the book sensation of the year. Some, to example, there are again whose movements are automatic. Perceive. That is his appropriate sun. Nightbird nightsun nighttown. Chase me, Charley! Buzz!

BLOOM

Bee or bluebottle too other day butting shadow on wall dazed self then me wandered dazed down shirt good job I...

VIRAG

(*His face impassive, laughs in a rich feminine key.*) Splendid! Spanish fly in his fly or mustard plaster on his dibble. (*He gabbles gluttonously with turkey wattles.*) Bubbly jock! Bubbly jock! Where are we? Open Sesame! Cometh forth! (*He unrolls his parchment rapidly and reads, his glowworm's nose running backwards over the letters which he claws.*) Stay, good friend. I bring thee thy answer. Redbank oysters will shortly be upon us. I'm the best o'cook. Those succulent bivalves may help us and the truffles of Perigord, tubers dislodged through mister omnivorous porker, were unsurpassed in cases of nervous debility or viragitis. Though they stink yet they sting. (*He wags his head with cackling raillery.*) Jocular. With my eyeglass in my ocular.

BLOOM

(*Absently*) Ocularly woman's bivalve case is worse. Always open sesame. The cloven sex. Why they fear vermin, creeping things. Yet Eve and the serpent contradict. Not a historical fact. Obvious analogy to my idea. Serpents too are gluttons for woman's milk. Wind their way through miles of omnivorous forest to sucksucculent her breast dry. Like those bubblyjocular Roman matrons one reads of in Elephantuliasis.

VIRAG

(*His mouth projected in hard wrinkles, eyes stonily forlornly closed, psalms in outlandish monotone.*) That the cows with their those distended udders that they have been the known...

BLOOM

I am going to scream. I beg your pardon. Ah? So. (*He repeats.*) Spontaneously to seek out the saurian's lair in order to entrust their teats to his avid suction. Ant milks aphis. (*Profoundly.*) Instinct rules the world. In life. In death.

VIRAG

(*Head askew, arches his back and hunched wingshoulders, peers at the moth out of blear bulged eyes, points a horning claw and cries.*) Who's Ger Ger? Who's dear Gerald? O, I much fear he shall be most badly burned. Will some pleashe pershon not now impediment so catastrophics mit agitation of firstclass tablenumpkin? (*He mews.*) Luss puss puss puss! (*He sighs, draws back and stares sideways down with dropping underjaw.*) Well, well. He doth rest anon.

THE MOTH

I'm a tiny tiny thing
Ever flying in the spring
Round and round a ringaring.
Long ago I was a king,
Now I do this kind of thing
On the wing, on the wing!
Bing!

(*He rushes against the mauve shade flapping noisily*). Pretty pretty pretty pretty pretty pretty petticoats.

(*From left upper entrance with two sliding steps Henry Flower comes forward to left front centre. He wears a dark mantle and drooping plumed sombrero. He carries a silverstringed inlaid dulcimer and a longstemmed bamboo Jacob's pipe, its clay bowl fashioned as a female head. He wears dark velvet hose and silverbuckled pumps. He has the romantic Saviour's face with flowing locks, thin beard and moustache. His spindlelegs and sparrow feet are those of the tenor Mario, prince of Candia. He settles down his goffered ruffs and moistens his lips with a passage of his amorous tongue.*)

HENRY

(*In a low dulcet voice, touching the strings of his guitar.*) There is a flower that bloometh.

(*Virag truculent, his jowl set, stares at the lamp. Grave Bloom regards Zoe's neck. Henry gallant turns with pendant dewlap to the piano.*)

STEPHEN

(*To himself.*) Play with your eyes shut. Imitate pa. Filling my belly with husks of swine. Too much of this. I will arise and go to my. Expect this is the. Steve, thou art in a parlous way. Must visit old Deasy or telegraph. Our interview of this morning has left on me a deep impression. Though our ages. Will write fully tomorrow. I'm partially drunk, by the way. (*He touches the keys again.*) Minor chord comes now. Yes. Not much however.

(*Almidano Artifoni holds out a batonroll of music with vigorous moustachework.*)

ARTIFONI

Ci rifletta. Lei rovina tutto.

FLORRY

Sing us something. Love's old sweet song.

STEPHEN

No voice. I am a most finished artist. Lynch, did I show you the letter about the lute?

FLORRY

(*Smirking.*) The bird that can sing and won't sing.

(*The Siamese twins, Philip Drunk and Philip Sober, two Oxford dons with lawnmowers, appear in the window embrasure. Both are masked with Matthew Arnold's face.*)

PHILIP SOBER

Take a fool's advice. All is not well. Work it out with the buttend of a pencil, like a good young idiot. Three pounds twelve you got, two notes, one sovereign, two crowns, if youth but knew. Mooney's en ville, Mooney's sur mer, the Moira, Larchet's, Holles street hospital, Burke's. Eh? I am watching you.

PHILIP DRUNK

(*Impatiently.*) Ah, bosh, man. Go to hell! I paid my way. If I could only find out about octaves. Reduplication of personality. Who was it told me his name? (*His lawnmower begins to purr.*) Aha, yes. *Zoe mou sas agapo.* Have a notion I was here before. When was it not Atkinson his card I have somewhere. Mac somebody. Unmack I have it. He told me about, hold on, Swinburne, was it, no?

FLORRY

And the song?

STEPHEN

Spirit is willing but the flesh is weak.

FLORRY

Are you out of Maynooth? You're like someone I knew once.

STEPHEN

Out of it now (*To himself.*) Clever.

PHILIP DRUNK AND PHILIP SOBER

(*Their lawnmowers purring with a rigadoon of grasshalms*). Clever ever. Out of it. Out of it. By the bye have you the book, the thing, the ashplant? Yes, there it, yes. Cleverever outofitnow. Keep in condition. Do like us.

ZOE

There was a priest down here two nights ago to do his bit of business with his coat buttoned up. You needn't try to hide, I says to him. I know you've a Roman collar.

VIRAG

Perfectly logical from his standpoint. Fall of man. (*Harshly, his pupils waxing.*) To hell with the pope! Nothing new under the sun. I am the Virag who disclosed the sex secrets of monks and maidens. Why I left the Church of Rome. Read the Priest, the Woman and the Confessional. Penrose. Flipperty Jippert. (*He wriggles.*) Woman, undoing with sweet pudor her belt of rushrope, offers her allmoist yoni to man's lingam. Short time after man presents woman with pieces of jungle meat. Woman shows joy and covers herself with featherskins. Man loves her yoni fiercely with big lingam, the stiff one. (*He cries.*) *Coactus volui*. Then giddy woman will run about. Strong man grapses woman's wrist. Woman squeals, bites, spucks. Man, now fierce angry, strikes woman's fat yadgana. (*He chases his tail.*) Piffpaff! Popo! (*He stops, sneezes.*) Pchp! (*He worries his butt.*) Prrrrrht!

LYNCH

I hope you gave the good father a penance. Nine glorias for shooting a bishop.

ZOE

(*Spouts walrus smoke through her nostrils.*) He couldn't get a connection. Only, you know, sensation. A dry rush.

BLOOM

Poor man!

ZOE

(*Lightly.*) Only for what happened him.

BLOOM

How?

VIRAG

(*A diabolic rictus of black luminosity contracting his visage, cranes his scraggy neck forward. He lifts a mooncalf nozzle and howls.*) *Verfluchte Goim!* He had a father, forty fathers. He never existed. Pig God! He had two left feet. He was Judas Iacchias, a Lybian eunuch, the pope's bastard. (*He leans out on tortured forepaws, elbows bent rigid, his eye agonising in his flat skullneck and yelps over the mute world.*) A son of a whore. Apocalypse.

KITTY

And Mary Shortall that was in the lock with the pox she got from Jimmy Pidgeon in the blue caps had a child off him that couldn't swallow and was smothered with the convulsions in the mattress and we all suscribed for the funeral.

PHILIP DRUNK

(*Gravely.*) *Qui vous a mis dans cette fichue position, Philippe?*

PHILIP SOBER

(*Gaily.*) *C'était le sacré pigeon, Philippe.*

(*Kitty unpins her hat and sets it down calmly, patting her henna hair. And a prettier, a daintier head of winsome curls was never seen on a whore's shoulders. Lynch puts on her hat. She whips it off.*)

LYNCH

(*Laughs.*) And to such delights has Metchnikoff inoculated anthropoid apes.

FLORRY

(*Nods.*) Locomotor ataxy.

ZOE

(*Gaily.*) O, my dictionary.

LYNCH

Three wise virgins.

VIRAG

(*Agueschaken, profuse yellow spawn foaming over his bony epileptic lips.*) She sold lovephiltres, whitewax, orange flower. Panther, the Roman centurion, polluted her with his genitories. (*He sticks out a flickering phosphorescent scorpion tongue, his hand on his fork.*) Messiah! He burst her tympanum. (*With gibbering baboon's cries he jerks his hips in the cynical spasm.*) Hik! Hek! Hak! Hok! Huk! Kok! Kuk!

(*Ben Jumbo Dollard, rubicund, musclebound, hairynostrilled, hugebearded, cabbageeared, shaggychested, shockmaned, fatpapped, stands forth, his loins and genitals tightened into a pair of black bathing bagslops.*)

BEN DOLLARD

(*Nakkering castanet bones in his huge padded paws, yodels jovially in base barreltone.*) When love absorbs my ardent soul.

(*The virgins, Nurse Callan and Nurse Quigley burst through the ringkeepers and the ropes and mob him with open arms.*)

THE VIRGINS

(*Gushingly.*) Big Ben! Ben Mac Chree!

A VOICE

Hold that fellow with the bad breeches.

BEN DOLLARD

(*Smites his thigh in abundant laughter.*) Hold him now.

HENRY

(*Caressing on his breast a severed female head, murmurs.*) Thine heart, mine love. (*He pluks his lutestrings.*) When first I saw...

VIRAG

(*Sloughing his skins, his multitudinous plumage moulting.*) Rats! (*He yawns, showing a coalblack throat and closes his jaws by an upward push of his parchment roll.*) After having said which I took my departure. Farewell. Fare thee well. *Dreck!*

(*Henry Flower combs his moustache and beard rapidly with a pocketcomb and gives a cow's lick to his hair. Steered by his rapier, he glides to the door, his wild harp slung behind him. Virag reaches the door in two ungainly stilthops, his tail cocked, and deftly claps sideways on the wall a pusyellow flybill, butting it with his head.*)

THE FLYBILL

K. 11. post no bills. Strictly confidential. Dr Hy Franks.

HENRY

All is lost now.

(*Virag unscrews his head in a trice and holds it under his arm.*)

VIRAG'S HEAD

Quack!

(*Exeunt severally.*)

STEPHEN

(*Over his shoulder to Zoe.*) You would have preferred the fighting parson who founded the protestant error. But beware Antisthenes, the dog sage, and the last end of Arius Heresiarchus. The agony in the closet.

LYNCH

All one and the same God to her.

STEPHEN

(*Devoutly.*) And Sovereign Lord of all things.

FLORRY

(*To Stephen.*) I'm sure you are a spoiled priest. Or a monk.

LYNCH

He is. A cardinal's son.

STEPHEN

Cardinal sin. Monks of the screw.

(*His Eminence, Simon Stephen Cardinal Dedalus, Primate of all Ireland, appears in the doorway, dressed in red soutane, sandals and socks. Seven dwarf simian acolytes, also in red, cardinal sins, uphold his train, peeping under it. He wears a battered silk hat sideways on his head. His thumbs are stuck in his armpits and his palms outspread. Round his neck hangs a rosary of corks ending on his breast in a corkscrew cross. Releasing his thumbs, he invokes grace from on high with large wave gestures and proclaims with bloated pomp.*)

THE CARDINAL

Conservio lies captured
He lies in the lowest dungeon
With manacles and chains around his limbs
Weighing upwards of three tons.

(*He looks at all for a moment, his right eye closed tight, his left cheek puffed out. Then, unable to repress his merriment, he rocks to and fro, arms akimbo, and sings with broad rollicking humour.*)

O, the poor little fellow
Hi-hi-hi-his legs they were yellow
He was plump, fat and heavy and brisk as a snake
But some bloody savage
To graize his white cabbage
He murdered Nell Flaherty's duckloving drake.

(*A multitude of midges swarms over his robe. He scratches himself with crossed arms at his ribs, grimacing, and exclaims.*)

I'm suffering the agony of the damned. By the hoky fiddle, thanks be to Jesus those funny little chaps are not unanimous. If they were they'd walk me off the face of the bloody globe.

(*His head aslant, he blesses curtly with fore and middle fingers, imparts the Easter kiss and doubleshuffles off comically, swaying his hat from side to side, shrinking quickly to the size of his trainbearers. The dwarf acolytes, giggling, peeping, nudging, ogling, Easter-*

kissing, zigzag behind him. His voice is heard mellow from afar, merciful, male, melodious.)

Shall carry my heart to thee,
Shall carry my heart to thee,
And the breath of the balmy night
Shall carry my heart to thee.

(*The trick doorhandle turns.*)

THE DOORHANDLE

Theeee.

ZOE

The devil is in that door.

(*A male form passes down the creaking staircase and is heard taking the waterproof and hat from the rack. Bloom starts forward involuntarily and, half closing the door as he passes, takes the chocolate from his pocket and offers it nervously to Zoe.*)

ZOE

(*Sniffs his hair briskly.*) Hum. Thank your mother for the rabbits. I'm very fond of what I like.

BLOOM

(*Hearing a male voice in talk with the whores on the doorstep, pricks his ears.*) If it were he? After? Or because not? Or the double event?

ZOE

(*Tears open the silverfoil.*) Fingers was made before forks. (*She breaks off and nibbles a piece, gives a piece to Kitty Ricketts and then turns kittenishly to Lynch.*) No objection to French lozenges? (*He nods. She taunts him.*) Have it now or wait till you get it? (*He opens his mouth, his head cocked. She whirls the prize in left circle. His head follows. She whirls it back in right circle. He eyes her.*) Catch.

(*She tosses a piece. With an adroit snap he catches it and bites it through with a crack.*)

KITTY

(*Chewing.*) The engineer I was with at the bazaar does have lovely ones. Full of the best liqueurs. And the viceroy was there with his lady. The gas we had on the Toft's hobbyhorses. I'm giddy still.

BLOOM

(*In Svengali's fur overcoat, with folded arms and Napoleonic forelock, frowns in ventriloquial exorcism with piercing eagle glance towards the door. Then, rigid, with left foot advanced, he makes a swift pass with impelling fingers and gives the sign of past master drawing his right arm downwards from his left shoulder.*) Go, go, go, I conjure you, whoever you are.

(*A male cough and tread are heard passing through the mist outside. Bloom's features relax. He places a hand in his waistcoat, posing calmly. Zoe offers him chocolate.*)

BLOOM

(*Solemnly.*) Thanks.

ZOE

Do as you're bid. Here.

(*A firm heelclacking is heard on the stairs.*)

BLOOM

(*Takes the chocolate.*) Aphrodisiac? But I bought it. Vanilla calms or? Mnemo. Confused light confuses memory. Red influences lupus. Colours affect women's characters, any they have. This black makes me sad. Eat and be merry for tomorrow. (*He eats.*) Influence taste too, mauve. But it is so long since I. Seems new. Aphro. That priest. Must come. Better late than never. Try truffles at Andrews.

(*The door opens. Bella Cohen, a massive whoremistress enters. She is dressed in a threequarter ivory gown, fringed round the hem with tasselled selvedge and cools herself, flirting a black horn fan like Minnie Hauck in* Carmen. *On her left hand are wedding and keeper rings. Her eyes are deeply carboned. She has a sprouting moustache. Her olive face is heavy, slightly sweated and fullnosed, with orangetainted nostrils. She has large pendant beryl eardrops.*)

BELLA

My word! I'm all of a mucksweat.

(*She glances around her at the couples. Then her eyes rest on Bloom with hard insistence. Her large fan winnows wind towards her heated face, neck and embonpoint. Her falcon eyes glitter.*)

THE FAN

(*Flirting quickly, then slowly.*) Married, I see.

BLOOM

Yes... Partly, I have mislaid...

THE FAN

(*Half opening, then closing.*) And the missus is master. Petticoat government.

BLOOM

(*Looks down with a sheepish grin.*) That is so.

THE FAN

(*Folding together, rests against her eardrop.*) Have you forgotten me?

BLOOM

Nes. Yo.

THE FAN

(*Folded akimbo against her waist.*) Is me her was you dreamed before? Was then she him you us since knew? Am all them and the same now we?

(*Bella approaches, gently tapping with the fan.*)

BLOOM

(*Wincing.*) Powerful being. In my eyes read that slumber which women love.

THE FAN

(*Tapping.*) We have met. You are mine. It is fate.

BLOOM

(*Cowed.*) Exuberant female. Enormously I desiderate your domination. I am exhausted, abandoned, no more young. I stand, so to speak, with an unposted letter bearing the extra regulation fee before the too late box of the general postoffice of human life. The door and window open at a right angle cause a draught of thirtytwo feet per second according to the law of falling bodies. I have felt this instant a twinge of sciatica in my left glutear muscle. It runs in our family. Poor dear papa, a widower, was a regular barometer from it. He believed in animal heat. A skin of tabby lined his winter waistcoat. Near the end, remembering king David and the Sunamite, he shared his bed with Athos, faithful after death. A dog's spittle, as you probably... (*He winces.*) Ah!

RICHIE GOULDING

(*Bagweighted, passes the door.*) Mocking is catch. Best value in Dub. Fit for a prince's liver and kidney.

THE FAN

(*Tapping.*) All things end. Be mine. Now.

BLOOM

(*Undecided.*) All now? I should not have parted with my talisman. Rain, exposure at dewfall on the sea rocks, a peccadillo at my time of life. Every phenomenon has a natural cause.

THE FAN

(*Points downwards slowly.*) You may.

BLOOM

(*Looks downwards and perceives her unfastened bootlace.*) We are observed.

THE FAN

(*Points downwards quickly.*) You must.

BLOOM

(*With desire, with reluctance.*) I can make a true black knot. Learned when

I served my time and worked the mail order line for Kellett's. Experienced hand. Every knot says a lot. Let me. In courtesy. I knelt once before today. Ah!

(*Bella raises her gown slightly and, steadying her pose, lifts to the edge of a chair a plump buskined hoof and a full pastern, silksocked. Bloom, stifflegged, aging, bends over her hoof and with gentle fingers draws out and in her laces.*)

BLOOM

(*Murmurs lovingly.*) To be a shoefitter in Mansfield's was my love's young dream, the darling joys of sweet buttonhooking, to lace up crisscrossed to kneelength the dressy kid footwear satinlined, so incredibly small, of Clyde Road ladies. Even their wax model Raymonde I visited daily to admire her cobweb hose and stick of rhubarb toe, as worn in Paris.

THE HOOF

Smell my hot goathide. Feel my royal weight.

BLOOM

(*Crosslacing.*) Too tight?

THE HOOF

If you bungle, Handy Andy, I'll kick your football for you.

BLOOM

Not to lace the wrong eyelet as I did the night of the bazaar dance. Bad luck. Nook in wrong tache of her... person you mentioned. That night she met... Now!

(*He knots the lace. Bella places her foot on the floor. Bloom raises his head. Her heavy face, her eyes strike him in midbrow. His eyes grow dull, darker and pouched, his nose thickens.*)

BLOOM

(*Mumbles.*) Awaiting your further orders, we remain, gentlemen...

BELLO

(*With a hard basilisk stare, in a baritone voice.*) Hound of dishonour!

BLOOM

(*Infatuated.*) Empress!

BELLO

(*His heavy cheekchops sagging.*) Adorer of the adulterous rump!

BLOOM

(*Plaintively.*) Hugeness!

BELLO

Dungdevourer!

BLOOM

(*With sinews semiflexed.*) Magnificence!

BELLO

Down! (*He taps her on the shoulder with his fan.*) Incline feet forward! Slide left foot one pace back. You will fall. You are falling. On the hands down!

BLOOM

(*Her eyes upturned in the sign of admiration, closing.*) Truffles!

(*With a piercing epileptic cry she sinks on all fours, grunting, snuffling, rooting at his feet, then lies, shamming dead with eyes shut tight, trembling eyelids, bowed upon the ground in the attitude of most excellent master.*)

BELLO

(*With bobbed hair, purple gills, fat moustache rings ronnd his shaven mouth, in mountaineer's puttees, green silverbuttoned coat, sport skirt and alpine hat with moorcock's feather, his hands stuck deep in his breeches pockets, places his heel on her neck and grinds it in.*) Feel my entire weight. Bow, bondslave, before the throne of your despot's glorious heels, so glistening in their proud erectness.

BLOOM

(*Enthralled, bleats.*) I promise never to disobey.

BELLO

(*Laughs loudly.*) Holy smoke! You little know what's in store for you. I'm the tartar to settle your little lot and break you in! I'll bet Kentucky cocktails all round I shame it out of you, old son. Cheek me, I dare you. If you do tremble in anticipation of heel discipline to be inflicted in gym costume.

(*Bloom creeps under the sofa and peers out through the fringe.*)

ZOE

(*Widening her slip to screen her.*) She's not here.

BLOOM

(*Closing her eyes.*) She's not here.

FLORRY

(*Hiding her with her gown.*) She didn't mean it, Mr Bello. She'll be good, sir.

KITTY

Don't be too hard on her, Mr Bello. Sure you won't, ma'amsir.

BELLO

(*Coaxingly.*) Come, ducky dear. I want a word with you, darling, just to administer correction. Just a little heart to heart talk, sweety. (*Bloom puts out her timid head.*) There's a good girly now. (*Bello grabs her hair violently and drags her forward.*) I only want to correct you for your own good on a soft safe spot. How's that tender behind? O, ever so gently, pet. Begin to get ready.

BLOOM

(*Fainting.*) Don't tear my...

BELLO

(*Savagely.*) The nosering, the pliers, the bastinado, the hanging hook, the knout I'll make you kiss while the flutes play like the Nubian slave of old. You're in for it this time. I'll make you remember me for the balance of your natural life. (*His forehead veins swollen, his face congested.*) I shall sit on your ottomansaddleback every morning after my thumping good breakfast of Matterson's fat ham rashers and a bottle of Guinness's porter. (*He belches.*) And suck my thumping good Stock Exchange cigar while I read the *Licensed Victualler's Gazette*. Very possibly I shall have you slaughtered and skewered in my stables and enjoy a slice of you with crisp crackling from the baking tin basted and baked like sucking pig with rice and lemon or currant sauce. It will hurt you.

(*He twists her arm. Bloom squeaks, turning turtle.*)

BLOOM

Don't be cruel, nurse! Don't!

BELLO

(*Twisting.*) Another!

BLOOM

(*Screams.*) O, it's hell itself! Every nerve in my body aches like mad!

BELLO

(*Shouts.*) Good, by the rumping jumping general! That's the best bit of news I heard these six weeks. Here, don't keep me waiting, damn you. (*He slaps her face.*)

BLOOM

(*Whimpers.*) You're after hitting me. I'll tell...

BELLO

Hold him down, girls, till I squat on him.

ZOE

Yes. Walk on him! I will.

FLORRY

I will. Don't be greedy.

KITTY

No, me. Lend him to me.

(*The brothel cook, Mrs Keogh, wrinkled, greybearded, in a greasy bib, men's grey and green socks and brogues, floursmeared, a rollingpin stuck with raw pastry in her bare red arm and hand, appears at the door.*)

MRS KEOGH

(*Ferociously.*) Can I help? (*They hold and pinion Bloom.*)

BELLO

(*Squats, with a grunt on Bloom's upturned face, puffing cigarsmoke, nursing a fat leg.*) I see Keating Clay is elected chairman of the Richmond Asylum and bytheby Guinness's preference shares are at sixteen three quarters. Curse me for a fool that I didn't buy that lot Craig and Gardner told me about. Just my infernal luck, curse it. And that Goddamned outsider *Throwaway* at twenty to one. (*He quenches his cigar angrily on Bloom's ear.*) Where's that Goddamned cursed ashtray?

BLOOM

(*Goaded, buttocksmothered.*) O! O! Monsters! Cruel one!

BELLO

Ask for that every ten minutes. Beg, pray for it as you never prayed before. (*He thrusts out a figged fist and foul cigar.*) Here, kiss that. Both. Kiss. (*He throws a leg astride and, pressing with horseman's knees, calls in a hard voice.*) Gee up! A cockhorse to Banbury cross. I'll ride him for the Eclipse stakes. (*He bends sideways and squeezes his mount's testicles roughly, shouting.*) Ho! off we pop! I'll nurse you in proper fashion. (*He horserides cockhorse, leaping in the, in the saddle.*) The lady goes a pace a pace and the coachman goes a trot a trot and the gentleman goes a gallop a gallop a gallop a gallop.

FLORRY

(*Pulls at Bello.*) Let me on him now. You had enough. I asked before you.

ZOE

(*Pulling at Florry.*) Me Me. Are you not finished with him yet, suckeress?

BLOOM

(*Stifling.*) Can't.

BELLO

Well, I'm not. Wait. (*He holds in his breath.*) Curse it. Here. This bung's about burst. (*He uncorks himself behind: then, contorting his features, farts loudly.*) Take that! (*He recorks himself.*) Yes, by Jingo, sixteen three quarters.

BLOOM

(*A sweat breaking out over him.*) Not man. (*He sniffs.*) Woman.

BELLO

(*Stands up.*) No more blow hot and cold. What you longed for has come to pass. Henceforth you are unmanned and mine in earnest, a thing under the yoke. Now for your punishment frock. You will shed your male garments, you understand, Ruby Cohen? and don the shot silk luxuriously rustling over head and shoulders and quickly too.

BLOOM

(*Shrinks.*) Silk, mistress said! O crinkly! scrapy! Must I tiptouch it with my nails?

BELLO

(*Points to his whores.*) As they are now, so will you be, wigged, singed, perfumesprayed, ricepowdered, with smoothshaven armpits. Tape measurements will be taken next your skin. You will be laced with cruel force into vicelike corsets of soft dove coutille, with whalebone busk, to the diamond trimmed pelvis, the absolute outside edge, while your figure, plumper than when at large, will be restrained in nettight frocks, pretty two ounce petticoats and fringes and things stamped, of course, with my houseflag, creations of lovely lingerie for Alice and nice scent for Alice. Alice will feel the pullpull. Martha and Mary will be a little chilly at first in such delicate thighcasing but the frilly flimsiness of lace round your bare knees will remind you...

BLOOM

(*A charming soubrette with dauby cheeks, mustard hair and large male hands and nose, leering mouth.*) I tried her things on only once, a small prank, in Holles street. When we were hardup I washed them to save the laundry bill. My own shirts I turned. It was the purest thrift.

BELLO

(*Jeers.*) Little jobs that make mother pleased, eh! and showed off coquettishly in your domino at the mirror behind closedrawn blinds your unskirted thighs and hegoat's udders, in various poses of surrender, eh? Ho! Ho! I have to laugh! That secondhand black operatop shift and short trunk leg naughties all split up the stitches at her last rape that Mrs Miriam Dandrade sold you from the Shelbourne Hotel, eh?

BLOOM

Miriam. Black. Demimondaine.

BELLO

(*Guffaws.*) Christ Almighty, it's too tickling, this! You were a nicelooking Miriam when you clipped off your backgate hairs and lay swooning in the thing across the bed as Mrs Dandrade, about to be violated by Lieutenant

Smythe-Smythe, Mr Philip Augustus Blockwell, M. P., Signor Laci Daremo, the robust tenor, blueeyed Bert, the liftboy, Henry Fleury of Gordon Bennett fame, Sheridan, the quadroon Crœsus, the varsity wetbob eight from old Trinity, Ponto, her splendid Newfoundland and Bobs, dowager duchess of Manorhamilton. (*He guffaws again.*) Christ, wouldn't it make a Siamese cat laugh?

BLOOM

(*Her hands and features working.*) It was Gerald converted me to be a true corsetlover when I was female impersonator in the High School play *Vice Versa*. It was dear Gerald. He got that kink, fascinated by sister's stays. Now dearest Gerald uses pinky greasepaint and gilds his eyelids. Cult of the beautiful.

BELLO

(*With wicked glee.*) Beautiful! Give us a breather! When you took your seat with womanish care, lifting your billowy flounces, on the smoothworn throne.

BLOOM

Science. To compare the various joys we each enjoy. (*Earnestly.*) and really it's better the position... because often I used to wet...

BELLO

(*Sternly.*) No insubordination. The sawdust is there in the corner for you. I gave you strict instructions, didn't I? Do it standing, sir! I'll teach you to behave like a jinkleman! If I catch a trace on your swaddles. Aha! By the ass of the Dorans' you'll find I'm a martinet. The sins of your past are rising against you. Many. Hundreds.

THE SINS OF THE PAST

(*In a medley of voices.*) He went through a form of clandestine marriage with at least one woman in the shadow of the Black Church. Unspeakable messages he telephoned mentally to Miss Dunn at an address in d'Olier Street while he presented himself indecently to the instrument in the callbox. By word and deed he encouraged a nocturnal strumpet to deposit fecal and other matter in an unsanitary outhouse attached to empty premises. In five public conveniences he wrote pencilled messages offering his nuptial partner to all strongmembered males. And by the offensively smelling vitriol works did he not pass night after night by loving courting couples to see if and what and how much he could see? Did he not lie in bed, the gross boar, gloating over a nauseous fragment of wellused toilet paper presented to him by a nasty harlot, stimulated by gingerbread and a postal order?

BELLO

(*Whistles loudly.*) Say! What was the most revolting piece of obscenity in all your career of crime? Go the whole hog. Puke it out. Be candid for once.

(*Mute inhuman faces throng forward, leering, vanishing, gibbering, Booloohoom. Poldy Kock, Bootlaces a penny. Cassidy's hag, blind stripling, Larry Rhinoceros, the girl, the woman, the whore, the other, the...*)

BLOOM

Don't ask me: Our mutual faith. Pleasants street. I only thought the half of the... I swear on my sacred oath...

BELLO

(*Peremptorily.*) Answer. Repugnant wretch! I insist on knowing. Tell me something to amuse me, smut or a bloody good ghoststory or a line of poetry, quick, quick, quick! Where? How? What time? With how many? I give you just three seconds. One! Two! Thr...!

BLOOM

(*Docile, gurgles.*) I rererepugnosed in rerererepugnant...

BELLO

(*Imperiously.*) O get out, you skunk! Hold your tongue! Speak when you're spoken to.

BLOOM

(*Bows.*) Master! Mistress! Mantamer!

(*He lifts his arms. His bangle bracelets fall.*)

BELLO

(*Satirically.*) By day you will souse and bat our smelling underclothes, also when we ladies are unwell, and swab out our latrines with dress pinned up and a dishclout tied to your tail, Won't that be nice? (*He places a ruby ring on her finger.*) And there now! With this ring I thee own. Say, thank you, mistress.

BLOOM

Thank you, mistress.

BELLO

You will make the beds, get my tub ready, empty the pisspots in the different rooms, including old Mrs Keogh's the cook's, a sandy one. Ay, and rinse the seven of them well, mind, or lap it up like champagne. Drink me piping hot. Hop! you will dance attendance or I'll lecture you on your misdeeds, Miss Ruby, and spank your bare bot right well, miss, with the hairbrush. You'll be taught the error of your ways. At night your wellcreamed braceletted hands will wear fortythreebutton gloves newpowdered with talc and having delicately scented fingertips. For such favours knights of old laid down their lives (*He chuckles.*) My boys will be no end charmed to see you so ladylike, the colonel, above all. When they come here the night before the wedding to fondle my new attraction in gilded heels. First, I'll have a go at you myself. A man I know on the turf named Charles Alberta Marsh (I was in bed with him just now and another gentleman out of the Hanaper and Petty Bag office) is on the lookout for a maid of all work at a short knock. Swell the bust. Smile. Droop shoulders. What offers? (*He points.*) For that lot trained by owner to fetch and carry, basket in mouth. (*He bares his arm and plunges it elbowdeep in Bloom's vulva.*) There's fine depth for you! What, boys? That give you a hardon? (*He shoves his arm in a bidder's face.*) Here wet the deck and wipe it round!

A BIDDER

A florin.

(*Dillon's lacquey rings his handbell.*)

A VOICE

One and eightpence too much.

THE LACQUEY

Barang!

CHARLES ALBERTA MARSH.

Must be virgin. Good breath. Clean.

BELLO

(*Gives a rap with his gavel.*) Two bar. Rockbottom figure and cheap at the price. Fourteen hands high. Touch and examine shis points. Handle hrim. This downy skin, these soft muscles, this tender flesh. If I had only my gold piercer here! And quite easy to milk. Three newlaid gallons a day. A pure stockgetter, due to lay within the hour. His sire's milk record was a thousand gallons of whole milk in forty weeks. Whoa, my jewel! Beg up! Whoa! (*He brands his initial C on Bloom's croup.*) So! Warranted Cohen! What advance on two bob, gentlemen?

A DARKVISAGED MAN

(*In disguised accent.*) Hoondert punt sterlink.

VOICES

(*Subdued.*) For the Caliph Haroun Al Raschid.

BELLO

(*Gaily.*) Right. Let them all come. The scanty, daringly short skirt, riding up at the knee to show a peep of white pantelette, is a potent weapon and transparent stockings, emeraldgartered, with the long straight seam trailing up beyond the knee, appeal to the better instincts of the *blasé* man about town. Learn the smooth mincing walk on four inch Louis XV heels, the Grecian bend with provoking croup, the thighs fluescent, knees modestly kissing. Bring all your power of fascination to bear on them. Pander to their Gomorrahan vices.

BLOOM

(*Bends his blushing face into his armpit and simpers with forefinger in mouth.*) O, I know what you're hinting at now.

BELLO

What else are you good for, an impotent thing like you? (*He stoops and, peering, pokes with his fan rudely under the fat suet folds of Bloom's haunches.*) Up! Up! Manx cat! What have we here? Where's your curly teapot gone to or who docked it on you, cockyolly? Sing, birdy, sing. It's as limp a boy of six's doing his pooly behind a cart. Buy a bucket or sell your pump. (*Loudly.*) Can you do a man's job?

BLOOM

Eccles Street...

BELLO

(*Sarcastically.*) I wouldn't hurt your feelings for the world but there's a man of brawn in possession there. The tables are turned, my gay young fellow! He is something like a fullgrown outdoor man. Well for you, you muff, if you had that weapon with knobs and lumps and warts all over it. He shot his bolt, I can tell you! Foot to foot, knee to knee, belly to belly, bubs to breast! He's no eunuch. A shock of red hair he has sticking out of him behind like a furzebush! Wait for nine months, my lad! Holy ginger, it's kicking and coughing up and down in her guts already! That makes you wild, don't it? Touches the spot? (*He spits in contempt.*) Spittoon!

BLOOM

I was indecently treated, I... inform the police. Hundred pounds. Unmentionable. I...

BELLO

Would if you could, lame duck. A downpour we want not your drizzle.

BLOOM

To drive me mad! Moll! I forgot! Forgive! Moll!... We... Still...

BELLO

(*Ruthlessly.*) No, Leopold Bloom, all is changed by woman's will since you slept horizontal in Sleepy Hollow your night of twenty years. Return and see.

(*Old Sleepy Hollow calls over the wold.*)

SLEEPY HOLLOW

Rip Van Winkle! Rip Van Winkle!

BLOOM

(*In tattered mocassins with a rusty fowlingpiece, tiptoing, fingertipping, his haggard bony bearded face peering through the diamond panes, cries out.*) I see her! It's she! The first night at Mat Dillon's! But that dress, the green! And her hair is dyed gold and he...

BELLA

(*Laughs mockingly.*) That's your daughter, you owl, with a Mullingar student.

(*Milly Bloom, fairhaired, greenvested, slimsandalled, her blue scarf in the seawind simply swirling, breaks from the arms of her lover and calls, her young eyes wonderwide.*)

MILLY

My! It's Papli! But, O Papli, how old you've grown!

BELLO

Changed, eh? Our whatnot, our writing table where we never wrote, Aunt Hegarty's armchair, our classic reprints of old masters. A man and his menfriends are living there in clover. The *Cuckoos' Rest!* Why not? How many women had you, say? Following them up dark streets,, flatfoot, exciting them by your smothered grunts. What, you male prostitute? Blameless dames with parcels of groceries. Turn about. Sauce for the goose, my gander, O.

BLOOM

They... I...

BELLO

(*Cuttingly.*) Their heelmarks will stamp the Brusselette carpet you bought at Wren's auction. In their horseplay with Moll the romp to find the buck flea in her breeches they will deface the little statue you carried home in the rain for art for art' sake. They will violate the secrets of your bottom drawer. Pages will be torn from your handbook of astronomy to make them pipespills. And they will spit in your ten shilling brass fender from Hampton Leedom's.

BLOOM

Ten and six. The act of low scoundrels. Let me go. I will return. I will prove...

A VOICE

Swear!

(*Bloom clenches his fists and crawls forward, a bowie knife between his teeth.*)

BELLO

As a paying guest or a kept man? Too late. You have made your secondbest bed and others must lie in it. Your epitaph is written. You are down and out and don't you forget it, old bean.

BLOOM

Justice! All Ireland versus one! Has nobody...?

(*He bites his thumb.*)

BELLO

Die and be damned to you if you have any sense of decency or grace about you. I can give you a rare old wine that'll send you skipping to hell and back. Sign a will and leave us any coin you have. If you have none see you damn well get it, steal it, rob it! We'll bury you in our shrubbery jakes where you'll be dead and dirty with old Cuck Cohen, my stepnephew I married, the bloody old gouty procurator and sodomite with a crick in his neck, and my other ten or eleven husbands, whatever the buggers' names were, suffocated in the one cesspool. (*He explodes in a loud phlegmy laugh.*) We'll manure you, Mr Flower! (*He pipes scoffingly.*) Byby, Poldy! Byby. Papli!

BLOOM

(*Clasps his head.*) My will power! Memory! I have sinned! I have suff...

(*He weeps tearlessly.*)

BELLO

(*Sneers.*) Crybaby! Crocodile tears!

(*Bloom, broken, closely veiled for the sacrifice, sobs, his face to the earth. The passing bell is heard. Darkshawled figures of the circumcised, in sackcloth and ashes, stand by the wailing wall. M. Shulomowitz, Joseph Goldwater, Moses Herzog, Harris Rosenberg, M. Moisel, J. Citron, Minnie Watchman, O. Mastiansky, the Reverend Leopold Abramovitz, Chazen. With swaying arms they wail in pneuma over the recreant Bloom.*)

THE CIRCUMCISED

(*In a dark guttural chant as they cast dead sea fruit upon him, no flowers.*) *Shema Israel Adonai Elohenu Adonai Echad.*

VOICES

(*Sighing.*) So he's gone. Ah yes. Yes, indeed. Bloom? Never heard of him. No? Queer kind of chap. There's the widow. That so? Ah, yes.

(*From the suttee pyre the flame of gum camphire ascends. The pall of incense smoke screens and disperses. Out of her oak frame a nymph with hair unbound, lightly clad in teabrown art colours, descends from her grotto and passing under interlacing yews, stands over Bloom.*)

THE YEWS

(*Their leaves whispering.*) Sister. Our sister. Ssh.

THE NYMPH

(*Softly.*) Mortal! (*Kindly.*) Nay, dost not weepest!

BLOOM

(*Crawls jellily forward under the bought, streaked by sunlight, with dignity.*) This position. I felt it was expected of me. Force of habit.

THE NYMPH

Mortal! You found me in evil company, highkickers, coster picnic makers, pugilists, popular generals, immoral panto boys in flesh tights and the nifty shimmy dancers, La Aurora and Karini, musical act, the hit of the century. I was hidden in cheap pink paper that smelt of rock oil. I was surrounded by the stale smut of clubmen, stories to disturb callow youth, adsf or transparencies, truedup dice and bustpads, proprietary articles and why wear a truss with testimonial from ruptured gentleman. Useful hints to the married.

BLOOM

(*Lifts a turtle head towards her lap.*) We have met before. On another star.

THE NYMPH

(*Sadly.*) Rubber goods. Neverrip. Brand as supplied to the aristocracy. Corsets for men. I cure fits or money refunded. Unsolicited testimonials for Professor Waldmann's wonderful chest exuber. My bust developed four inches in three weeks, reports Mrs Gus Rublin with photo.

BLOOM

You mean *Photo Bits*?

THE NYMPH

I do. You bore me away, framed me in oak and tinsel, set me above your marriage couch. Unseen, one summer eve, you kissed me in four places. And with loving pencil you shaded my eyes, my bosom and my shame.

BLOOM

(*Humbly kisses her long hair.*) Your classic curves, beautiful immortal. I was glad to look on you, to praise you, a thing of beauty, almost to pray.

THE NYMPH

During dark nights I heard your praise.

BLOOM

(*Quickly.*) Yes, yes. You mean that I... Sleep reveals the worst side of everyone, children perhaps excepted. I know I fell out of my bed or rather was pushed Steel wine is said to cure snoring. For the rest there is that English invention, pamphlet of which I received some days ago, incorrectly addressed. It claims to afford a noiseless inoffensive vent. (*He sighs.*) 'Twas ever thus. Frailty, thy name is marriage.

THE NYMPH

(*Her fingers in her ears.*) And words. They are not in my dictionary.

BLOOM

You understood them ?

THE YEWS

Ssh.

THE NYMPH

(*Covers her face with her hand.*) What have I not seen in that chamber ? What must my eyes look down on ?

BLOOM

(*Apologetically.*) I know. Soiled personal linen, wrong side up with care. The quoits are loose. From Gibraltar by long sea, long ago.

THE NYMPH

(*Bends her head.*) Worse ! Worse !

BLOOM

(*Reflects precautiously.*) That antiquated commode. It wasn't her weight. She scaled just eleven stone nine. She put on nine pounds after weaning. It was a crack and want of glue. Eh ? And that absurd orangekeyed utensil which has only one handle.

(*The sound of a waterfall is heard in bright cascade.*)

THE WATERFALL

Poulaphouca Poulaphouca
Poulaphouca Poulaphouca.

THE YEWS

(*Mingling their boughs.*) Listen. Whisper. She is right, our sister. We grew by Poulaphouca waterfall. We gave shade on languorous summer days.

JOHN WYSE NOLAN

(*In the background, in Irish National Forester's uniform, doffs his plumed hat.*) Prosper! Give shade on languorous days, trees of Ireland!

THE YEWS

(*Murmuring.*) Who came to Poulaphouca with the high school excursion? Who left his nutquesting classmates to seek our shade?

BLOOM

(*Pigeonbreasted, bottleshouldered, padded, in nondescript juvenile grey and black striped suit, too small for him, white tennis shoes, bordered stockings with turnover tops, and a red school cap with badge.*) I was in my tens, a growing boy. A little then sufficed, a jolting car, the mingling odours of the ladies' cloakroom and lavatory, the throng penned tight on the old Royal stairs for they love crushes, instinct of the herd, and the dark sexsmelling theatre unbridles vice. Even a pricelist of their hosiery. And then the heat. There were sunspots that summer. End of school. And tipsycake. Halcyon days.

(*Halcyon Days, high school boys in blue and white football jerseys and shorts, Master Donald Turnbull, Master Abraham Chatterton, Master Owen Goldberg, Master Jack Meredith, Master Percy Apjohn, stand in a clearing of the trees and shout to Master Leopold Bloom.*)

THE HALCYON DAYS

Mackerel! Live us again. Hurray! (*They cheer.*)

BLOOM

(*Hobbledehoy, warmgloved, mammamufflered, stunned with spent snowballs, struggles to rise.*) Again! I feel sixteen! What a lark! Let's ring all the bells in Montague Street (*He cheers feebly.*) Hurray for the High School!

THE ECHO

Fool!

THE YEWS

(*Rustling.*) She is right, our sister. Whisper. (*Whispered kisses are heard in all the wood. Faces of hamadryads peep out from the boles and among the leaves and break blossoming into bloom.*) Who profaned our silent shade?

THE NYMPH

(*Coyly through parting fingers.*) There! In the open air?

THE YEWS

(*Sweeping downward.*) Sister, yes. And on our virgin sward.

THE WATERFALL

Poulaphouca Poulaphouca
Phoucaphouca Phoucaphouca

THE NYMPH

(*With wide fingers.*) O! Infamy!

BLOOM

I was precocious. Youth. The fauns. I sacrificed to the god of the forest. The flowers that bloom in the spring. It was pairing time. Capillary attraction is a natural phenomenon. Lotty Clarke, flaxenhaired, I saw at her night toilette trough illclosed curtains, with poor papa's operaglasses. The wanton ate grass wildly. She rolled downhill at Rialto Bridge to tempt me with her flow of animal spirits. She climbed their crooked tree and I... A saint couldn't resist it. The demon possessed me. Besides, who saw?

(*Staggering Bob, a white polled calf, thrusts a ruminating head with humid nostrils through the foliage.*)

STAGGERING BOB

Me. Me see.

BLOOM

Simply satisfying a need. (*With pathos.*) No girl would when I went girling. Too ugly. They wouldn't play...

(*High on Ben Howth through rhododendrons a nannygoat passes, plumpuddered, buttytailed, dropping currants.*)

THE NANNYGOAT

(*Bleats.*) Megegaggegg! Nannannanny!

BLOOM

(*Hatless, flushed, covered with burrs of thistledown and gorsepine.*) Regularly engaged. Circumstances alter cases. (*He gazes intently downwards on the water.*) Thirtytwo head over heels per second. Press nightmare. Giddy Elijah. Fall from cliff. Sad end of government printer's clerk. (*Through silversilent summer air the dummy of Bloom, rolled in a mummy, rolls roteatingly from the Lion's Head cliff into the purple waiting waters.*)

THE DUMMYMUMMY

Bbbbblllllbbbbblblobschbg!

(*Far out in the bay between Bailey and Kish lights the* Erin's King *sails, sending a broadening plume of coalsmoke from her funnel towards the land.*)

COUNCILLOR NANNETTI

(*Alone on deck, in dark alpaca, yellow kitefaced, his hand in his waistcoat, opening, declaims.*) When my country takes her place among the nations of the earth, then, and not till then, let my epitaph be written. I have...

BLOOM

Done. Prff!

THE NYMPH

(*Loftily.*) We immortals, as you saw today have not such a place and no hair there either. We are stonecold and pure. We eat electric light. (*She arches her body in lascivious crispation, placing her forefinger in her mouth.*) Spoke to me. Heard from behind. How then could you...?

BLOOM

(*Pacing the heather abjectly.*) O, I have been a perfect pig. Enemas too, I have administered. One third of a pint of quassia to which add a tablespoonful of rocksalt. Up the fundament. With Hamilton Long's syringe, the ladies' friend.

THE NYMPH

In my presence. The powderpuff. (*She blushes and makes a knee.*) And the rest.

BLOOM

(*Dejected.*) Yes. *Peccavi!* I have paid homage on that living altar where the back changes name. (*With sudden fervour.*) For why should the dainty scented jewelled hand, the hand that rules...?

(*Figures wind serpenting in slow woodland pattern around the treestems, cooeeing.*)

THE VOICE OF KITTY

(*In the thicket.*) Show us one of them cushions.

THE VOICE OF FLORRY

Here.

(*A grouse wings clumsily through the underwood.*)

THE VOICE OF LYNCH

(*In the thicket.*) Whew! Piping hot!

THE VOICE OF ZOE

(*From the thicket.*) Came from a hot place.

THE VOICE OF VIRAG

(*A birdchief, bluestreaked and feathered in war panoply with his assegai, striding through a crackling canebrake over beechmast and acorns.*) Hot! Hot! Ware Sitting Bull!

BLOOM

It overpowers me. The warm impress of her warm form. Even to sit where a woman has sat, especially with divaricated thighs, as though to grant the last favours, most especially with previously well uplifted white sateen coatpans. So womanly full. It fills me full.

THE WATERFALL

Phillaphulla Poulaphouca
Poulaphouca Poulaphouca

THE YEWS

Ssh! Sister, speak!

THE NYMPH

(*Eyeless, in nun's white habit, coif and huge winged wimple, softly, with remote *eyes.*) Tranquilla convent. Sister Agatha. Mount Carmel, the apparitions of Knock and Lourdes. No more desire. (*She reclines her head, sighing.*) Only the ethereal. Where dreamy creamy gull waves o'er the waters dull.

(*Bloom half rises. His back trousers' button snaps.*)

THE BUTTON

Bip!

(*Two sluts of the Coombe dance rainily by, shawled, yelling flatly.*)

THE SLUTS

O Leopold lost the pin of his drawers
He didn't know what to do,
To keep it up,
To keep it up.

BLOOM

(*Coldly.*) You have broken the spell. The last straw. If there were only ethereal where would you all be, postulants and novices? Shy but willing like an ass pissing.

THE YEWS

(*Their silverfoil of leaves precipitating, their skinny arms aging and swaying.*) Deciduously!

THE NYMPH

Sacrilege! To attempt my virtue! (*A large moist stain appears on her robe.*) Sully my innocence! You are not fit to touch the garment of a pure woman. (*She clutches in her robe.*) Wait, Satan. You'll sing no more lovesongs. Amen. Amen. Amen. Amen. (*She draws a poniard and, clad in the sheathmail of an elected knight of nine, strikes at his loins.*) Nekum!

BLOOM

(*Starts up, seizes her hand.*) Hoy! Nebrakada! Cat of nine lives! Fair play, madam. No pruning knife. The fox and the grapes, is it? What do we lack with your barbed wire? Crucifix not thick enough? (*He clutches her veil.*) A holy abbot you want or Brophy, the lame gardener, or the spoutless statue of the watercarrier or good Mother Alphonsus, eh Reynard?

THE NYMPH

(*With a cry, flees from him unveiled, her plaster cast cracking, a cloud of stench escaping from the cracks.*) Poli...!

BLOOM

(*Calls after her.*) As if you didn't get it on the double yourselves. No jerks and multiple mucosities all over you. I tried it. Your strength our weakness. What's our studfee ? What will you pay on the nail ? You fee men dancers on the Riviera, I read. (*The fleeing nymph raises a keen.*) Eh ? I have sixteen years of black slave labour behind me. And would a jury give me five shillings alimony to morrow, eh ? Fool someone else, not me. (*He sniffs.*) But, Onions. Stale. Sulphur. Grease.

(*The figure of Bella Cohen stands before him.*)

BELLA

You'll know me the next time.

BLOOM

(*Composed, regards her.*) *Passée.* Mutton dressed as lamb. Long in the tooth and superflous hair. A raw onion the last thing at night would benefit your complexion. And take some double chin drill. Your eyes are as vapid as the glass eyes of your stuffed fox. They have the dimensions of your other features, that's all. I'm not a triple screw propeller.

BELLA

(*Contemptuously.*) You're not game, in fact. (*Her sowcunt barks*). Fohracht!

BLOOM

(*Contemptuously.*) Clean your nailless middle finger first, the cold spunk o your bully is dripping from your cockscomb. Take a handful of hay and wipe yourself.

BELLA

I know you, canvasser! Dead cod!

BLOOM

I saw him, kipkeeper! Pox and gleet vendor!

BELLA

(*Turns to the piano.*) Which of you was playing the dead march from *Saul*?

ZOE

Me. Mind your cornflowers. (*She darts to the piano and bangs chords on it with crossed arms.*) The cat's ramble through the slag. (*She glances back.*) Eh? Who's making love to my sweeties? (*She darts back to the table.*) What's yours is mine and what's mine is my own.

(*Kitty disconcerted coats her teeth with the silver paper. Bloom approaches Zoe.*)

BLOOM

(*Gently.*) Give me back that potato, will you?

ZOE

Forfeits, a fine thing and a superfine thing.

BLOOM

(*With feeling.*) It is nothing but still a relic of poor mamma.

ZOE

Give a thing and take it back
God'll ask you where is that
You'll say you don't know
God'll send you down below.

BLOOM

There is a memory attached to it. I should like to have it.

STEPHEN

To have or not to have, that is the question.

ZOE

Here. (*She hauls up a reef of her slip, revealing her bare thigh and unrolls the potato from the top of her stocking.*) Those that hides knows where to find.

BELLA

(*Frowns.*) Here. This isn't a musical peepshow. And don't you smash that piano. Who's paying here ?

(*She goes to the pianola. Stephen fumbles in his pocket and, taking out a banknote by its corner, hands it to her.*)

STEPHEN

(*With exagerated politeness.*) This silken purse I made out of the sow's ear of the public. Madam, excuse me. If you allow me. (*He indicates vaguely Lynch and Bloom.*) We are all in the same sweepstake, Kinch and Lynch. *Dans ce bordel où tenons nostre état.*

LYNCH

(*Calls from the hearth.*) Dedalus ! Give her your blessing for me.

STEPHEN

(*Hands Bella a coin.*) Gold. She has it.

BELLA

(*Looks at the money, then at Zoe, Florrie and Kitty.*) Do you want three girls? It's ten shillings here.

STEPHEN

(*Delightedly.*) A hundred thousand apologies. (*He fumbles again and takes out and hands her two crowns.*) Permit, *brevi manu*, my sight is somewhat troubled.

(*Bella goes to the table to count the money while Stephen talks to himself in monosyllabbes. Zoe bounds over to the table. Kitty leans over Zoe's neck, Lynch gets up, rights his cap and clasping Kitty's waist, adds his head to the group.*)

FLORRY

(*Strives heavily to rise.*) Ow ! My foot's asleep. (*She limps over to the table. Bloom approaches.*)

BELLA, ZOE, KITTY, LYNCH, BLOOM

(*Chattering and squabbling.*) The gentleman... ten shillings... paying for the three... allow me a moment... this gentleman pays separate... who's touching it ?... ow ... mind who you're pinching... are you staying the night or a short time?... who did?... you're a liar, excuse me... the gentleman paid down like a gentleman... drink... it's long after eleven.

STEPHEN

(*At the pianola, making a gesture of abhorrence.*) No bottles! What, eleven? A riddle.

ZOE

(*Lifting up her pettigown and folding a half sovereign into the top of her stocking.*) Hard earned on the flat of my back.

LYNCH

(*Lifting Kitty from the table.*) Come!

KITTY

Wait. (*She clutches the two crowns.*)

FLORRY

And me?

LYNCH

Hoopla!

(*He lifts her, carries her and bumps her down on the sofa.*)

STEPHEN

The fox crew, the cocks flew,
The bells in heaven
Were striking eleven.
'Tis time for her poor soul
To get out of heaven.

BLOOM

(*Quietly lays a half sovereign on the table between Bella and Florry.*) So. Allow me. (*He takes up the poundnote.*) Three times ten. We're square.

BELLA

(*Admiringly.*) You're such a slyboots, old cocky. I could kiss you.

ZOE

(*Points.*) Hum? Deep as a drawwell. (*Lynch bends Kitty back over the sofa and kisses her. Bloom goes with the poundnote to Stephen.*)

BLOOM

This is yours.

STEPHEN

How is that? *Le distrait* or absentminded beggar. (*He fumbles again in his pocket and draws out a handful of coins. An object falls.*) That fell.

BLOOM

(*Stooping, picks up and hands a box of matches.*) This.

STEPHEN

Lucifer. Thanks.

BLOOM

(*Quietly.*) You had better hand over that cash to me to take care of. Why pay more?

STEPHEN

(*Hands him all his coins.*) Be just before you are generous.

BLOOM

I will but is it wise? (*He counts.*) One, seven, eleven, and five. Six. Eleven. I don't answer for what you may have lost.

STEPHEN

Why striking eleven? Proparoxyton. Moment before the next Lessing says. Thirsty fox. (*He laughs loudly.*) Burying his grandmother. Probably he killed her.

BLOOM

That is one pound six and eleven. One pound seven, say.

STEPHEN

Doesn't matter a rambling damn.

BLOOM

No, but...

STEPHEN

(*Comes to the table.*) Cigarette, please. (*Lynch tosses a cigarette from the sofa to the table.*) And so Georgina Johnson is dead and married. (*A cigarette appears on the table Stephen looks at it.*) Wonder. Parlour magic. Married. Hm. (*He strikes a match and proceeds to light the cigarette with enigmatic melancholy.*)

LYNCH

(*Watching him.*) You would have a better chance of lighting it if you held the match nearer.

STEPHEN

(*Brings the match nearer his eye.*) Lynx eye. Must get glasses. Broke them yesterday. Sixteen years ago. Distance. The eye sees all flat. (*He draws the match away. It goes out.*) Brain thinks. Near : far. Ineluctable modality of the visible. (*He frowns mysteriously.*) Hm. Sphinx. The beast that has two backs at midnight. Married.

ZOE

It was a commercial traveller married her and took her away with him.

FLORRY

(*Nods.*) Mr Lambe from London.

STEPHEN

Lamb of London, who takest away the sins of our world.

LYNCH

(*Embracing Kitty on the sofa, chants deeply.*) *Dona nobis pacem.*

(*The cigarette slips from Stephen's fingers. Bloom picks it up and throws it into the gate.*)

BLOOM

Don't smoke. You ought to eat. Cursed dog I met. (*To Zoe.*) You have nothing?

ZOE

Is he hungry?

STEPHEN

(*Extends his hand to her smiling and chants to the air of the bloodoath in the* Dusk of the Gods.)

Hangende Hunger,
Fragende Frau,
Macht uns alle kaput.

ZOE

(*Tragically.*) Hamlet, I am thy father's gimlet! (*She takes his hand.*) Blue eyes beauty I'll read your hand. (*She points to his forehead.*) No wit, no wrinkles (*She counts.*) Two, three, Mars, that's courage. (*Stephen shakes his head.*) No kid.

LYNCH

Sheet lightning courage. The youth who could not shiver and shake. (*To Zoe.*) Who taught you palmistry?

ZOE

(*Turns.*) Ask my ballocks that I haven't got. (*To Stephen.*) I see it in your face. The eye, like that. (*She frowns with lowered head.*)

LYNCH

(*Laughing, slaps Kitty behind twice.*) Like that. Pandy bat.

(*Twice loudly a pandybat cracks, the coffin of the pianola flies open, the bald tittle round jack-in-the-box head of Father Dolan springs up.*)

FATHER DOLAN

Any boy want flogging? Broke his glasses? Lazy idle little schemer. See it in your eye.

(*Mild, benign, rectorial, reproving, the head of Don John Connee rises from the pianola coffin.*)

DON JOHN CONNEE

Now, Father Dolan! Now. I'm sure that Stephen is a very good little boy.

ZOE

(*Examining Stephen's palm.*) Woman's hand.

STEPHEN

(*Murmurs.*) Continue. Lie. Hold me. Caress. I never could read His handwriting except His criminal thumbprint on the haddock.

ZOE

What day were you born?

STEPHEN

Thursday. Today.

ZOE

Thursday's child has far to go. (*She traces lines on his hand.*) Line of fate. Influential friends.

FLORRY

(*Pointing.*) Imagination.

ZOE

Mount of the moon. You'll meet with a... (*She peers at his hands abruptly.*) I won't tell you what's not good for you. Or do you want to know?

BLOOM

(*Detaches her fingers and offers his palm.*) More harm than good. Here. Read mine.

BELLA

Show. (*She turns up Bloom's hand.*) I thought so. Knobby knuckles, for the women.

ZOE

(*Peering at Bloom's palm.*) Gridiron. Travels beyond the sea and marry money.

BLOOM

Wrong.

ZOE

(*Quickly.*) O, I see. Short little finger. Henpecked husband. That wrong?

(*Black Liz, a huge rooster hatching in a chalked circle, rises, stretches her wings and clucks.*)

BLACK LIZ

Gara. Klook. Klook. Klook.

(*She sidles from her newlaid egg and waddles off.*)

BLOOM

(*Points to his hand.*) That weal there is an accident. Fell and cut it twenty two years age. I was sixteen.

ZOE

I see, says the blind man. Tell us news.

STEPHEN

See? Moves to one great goal. I am twentytwo too. Sixteen years ago I twentytwo tumbled, twentytwo years ago he sixteen fell off his hobbyhorse (*He winces.*) Hurt my hand somewhere. Must see a dentist. Money?

(*Zoe whispers to Florry. They giggle. Bloom releases his hand and writes idly on the table in backhand, pencilling slow curves.*)

FLORRY

What?

(*A hackneycar, number three hundred and twentyfour, with a gallant buttocked mare, driven by James Barton, Harmony Avenue, Donnybrook, trots past. Blazes Boylan and Lenehan sprawl swaying on the sideseats. The Ormond boots crouches behind on the axle. Sadly over the crossblind Lydia Douce and Mina Kennedy gaze.*)

THE BOOTS

(*Jogging, mocks them with thumb and wriggling wormfingers.*) Haw, haw, have you the horn?

(*Bronze by gold they whisper.*).

ZOE

(*To Florry.*) Whisper.

(*They whisper again.*)

(*Over the well of the car Blazes Boylan leans, his boater straw, set sideways, a red flower in his mouth. Lenehan, in a yachtsman's cap and *white shoes, officiously detaches a long hair from Blazes Boylan's shoulder.*)

LENEHAN

Ho ! What do I here behold ? Were you brushing the cobwebs off a few quims ?

BOYLAN

(*Sated, smiles.*) Plucking a turkey.

LENEHAN

A good night's work.

BOYLAN

(*Holding up four thick bluntungulated fingers, winks.*) Blazes Kate ! Up to sample or your money back. (*He holds out a forefinger.*) Smell that.

LENEHAN

(*Smells gleefully.*) Ah ! Lobster and mayonnaise. Ah !

ZOE and FLORRY

(*Laugh together.*) Ha ha ha ha.

BOYLAN

(*Jumps surely from the car and calls loudly for all to hear.*) Hello, Bloom ! Mrs Bloom up yet ?

BLOOM

(*In a flunkey's plum plush coat and kneebreeches, buff stockings and powdered wig.*) I'm afraid not, sir, the last articles.....

BOYLAN

(*Tosses him sixpence.*) Here, to buy yourself a gin and splash. (*He hangs his hat smartly on a peg of Bloom's antlered head.*) Show me in. I have a little private business with your wife. You understand ?

BLOOM

Thank you, sir. Yes, sir, Madam Tweedy is in her bath, sir.

MARION

He ought to feel himself highly honoured. (*She plops splashing out of the water.*) Raoul, darling, come and dry me. I'm in my pelt. Only my new hat and a carriage sponge.

BOYLAN

(*A merry twinkle in his eye.*) Topping!

BELLA

What? What is it?

(*Zoe whispers to her.*)

MARION

Let him look, the pishogue! Pimp! And scourge himself! I'll write to a powerful prostitute or Bartholomona, the bearded woman, to raise weals out on him an inch thick and make him bring me back a signed and stamped receipt.

BELLA

(*Laughing.*) Ho ho ho ho.

BOYLAN

(*To Bloom, over his shoulder.*) You can apply your eye to the keyhole and play with yourself while I just go through her a few times.

BLOOM

Thank you, sir. I will, sir. May I bring two men chums to witness the deed and take a snapshot? (*He holds an ointment jar.*) Vaseline, sir? Orangeflower?... Lukewarm water?...

KITTY

(*From the sofa.*) Tell us, Florry. Tell us. What...

(*Florry whispers to her. Whispering lovewords murmur liplapping loudly, poppysmic plopslop.*)

MINA KENNEDY

(*Her eyes upturned.*) O, it must be like the scent of geraniums and lovely peaches! O, he simply idolises every bit of her! Stuck together! Covered with kisses!

LYDIA DOUCE

(*Her mouth opening.*) Yumyum. O, he's carrying her round the room doing it! Ride a cock horse. You could hear them in Paris and New York. Like mouthfuls of strawberries and cream.

KITTY

(*Laughing.*) Hee hee hee.

BOYLAN'S VOICE

(*Sweetly, hoarsely, in the pit of his stomach.*) Ah ! Gooblazeqruk brukarchkrasht !

MARION'S VOICE

(*Hoarsely, sweetly rising to her throat.*) O ! Weeshwashtkissimapooisthnapoohuck !

BLOOM

(*His eyes wildy dilated, clasps himself.*) Show ! Hide ! Show ! Plough her ! More ! Shoot !

BELLA, ZOE, FLORRY, KITTY

Ho ho ! Ha ha ! Hee hee !

LYNCH

(*Points.*) The mirror up to nature. (*He laughs.*) Hu hu hu hu hu.

(*Stephen and Bloom gaze in the mirror. The face of William Shakespeare, beardless, appears there, rigid in facial paralysis, crowned by the reflection of the reindeer antlered hatrack in the hall.*)

SHAKESPEARE

(*In dignified ventriloquy.*) 'Tis the loud laugh bespeaks the vacant mind. (*To Bloom.*) Thou thoughtest as how thou wastest invisible. Gaze. (*He crows with a black capon's laugh.*) Iagogo ! How my Oldfellow chokit his Thursdaymomun. Iagogogo !

BLOOM

(*Smiles yellowly at the whores.*) When will I hear the joke ?

ZOE

Before you're twice married and once a widower.

BLOOM

Lapses are condoned. Even the great Napoleon, when measurements were taken near the skin after his death...

(*Mrs Dignam, widow woman, her snubnose and cheeks flushed with deathtalk, fears and Tunny's tawny sherry, hurries by in her weeds, her bonnet awry, rouging and powdering her cheeks, lips and nose a pen chivvying her brood of cygnets. Beneath her skirt appear her late husband's everyday trousers and turnedup boots, large eights. She holds a Scottish widow's insurance policy and large marqueeumbrella under which her brood runs with her, Patsy, hopping on one short foot, his collar loose, a hank of porksteaks dangling, Freddy, whimpering, Susy with a crying cods' mouth, Alice, struggling with the baby. She cuffs them on, her streamers flaunting aloft.*)

FREDDY

Ah, ma, you're dragging me along!

SUSY

Mamma, the beeftea is fizzing over!

SHAKESPEARE

(*With paralytic rage.*) Weda seca whokilla farst.

(*The face of Martin Cunningham, bearded, refeatures Shakespeare's beardless face. The marqueeumbrella sways drunkenly, the children run aside. Under the umbrella appears Mrs Cunningham in Merry Widow hat and kimono gown. She glides sidling and bowing, twisting japanesily.*)

MRS CUNNINGHAM

(*Sings.*)

And they call me the jewel of Asia.

MARTIN CUNNINGHAM

(*Gazes on her impassive.*) Immense! Most bloody awful demirep!

STEPHEN

Et exaltabuntur cornua iusti. Queens lay with prize bulls. Remember Pasiphae for whose lust my grandoldgrossfather made the first confessionbox. Forget not Madam Grissel Steevens nor the suine scions of the house of Lambert. And Noah was drunk with wine. And his ark was open.

BELLA

None of that here. Come to the wrong shop.

LYNCH

Let him alone. He's back from Paris.

ZOE

(*Runs to Stephen and links him.*) O go on! Give us some parleyvoo.

(*Stephen claps hat on head and leaps over to the fireplace, where he stands with shrugged shoulders, finny hands outspread, a painted smile on his face.*)

LYNCH

(*Pommelling on the sofa.*) Rmm Rmm Rmm Rrrrrrmmmmm.

STEPHEN

(*Gabbles, with marionette jerks.*) Thousand places of entertainment to expenses your evenings with lovely ladies saling gloves and other things perhaps her heart beerchops perfect fashionable house very eccentric where lots cocottes beautiful dressed much about princesses like are dancing cancan and walking there parisian clowneries extra foolish for bachelors foreigns the same if talking a poor english how much smart they are on things love and sensations voluptuous. Misters very selects for is pleasure must to visit heaven and hell show with mortuary candles and they tears silver which occur every night. Perfectly shocking terrific of religion's things mockery seen in universal world. All chic womans which arrive full of modesty then disrobe and squeal loud to see vampire man debauch nun very fresh young with *dessous troublants* (*He clacks his tongue loudly.*) *Ho, la la! Ce pif qu'il a!*

LYNCH

Vive le vampire!

THE WHORES

Bravo! Parleyvoo!

STEPHEN

(*Grimacing with head back, laughs loudly, clapping himself.*) Great success of laughing. Angels much prostitutes like and holy apostles big damn ruffians. *Demimondaines* nicely handsome sparkling of diamonds very amiable costumed. Or do you are fond better what belongs they moderns pleasure turpitude of old mans? (*He points about him with grotesque gestures which Lynch and the whores reply to.*) Caoutchouc statue woman reversible or lifesize tompeeptoms virgins nudities very lesbic the kiss five ten times. Enter gentlemen to see in mirrors every positions trapezes all that machine there besides also if desire act awfully bestial butcher's boy pollutes in warm veal liver or omlette on the belly *pièce de Shakespeare.*

BELLA

(*Clapping her belly sinks back on the sofa with a shout of laughter.*) An omelette on the... Ho! ho! ho! ho!... Omelette on the...

STEPHEN

(*Mincingly.*) I love you, Sir darling. Speak you englishman tongue for *double entente cordiale.* O yes, *mon loup.* How much cost? Waterloo. Watercloset. (*He ceases suddenly and holds up a forefinger.*)

BELLA

(*Laughing.*) Omelette...

THE WHORES

(*Laughing.*) Encore! Encore!

STEPHEN

Mark me. I dreamt of a watermelon.

ZOE

Go abroad and love a foreign lady.

LYNCH

Across the world for a wife.

FLORRY

Dreams go by contraries.

STEPHEN

(*Extending his arms.*) It was here. Street of harlots. In Serpentine Avenue Beelzebub showed me her, a fubsy widow. Where's the red carpet spread?

BLOOM

(*Approaching Stephen.*) Look...

STEPHEN

No, I flew My foes beneath me. And ever shall be. World without end. (*He cries.*) *Pater!* Free!

BLOOM

I say, look...

STEPHEN

Break my spirit, will he? *O merde alors!* (*He cries, his vulture talons sharpened.*) Hola! Hillyho!

(*Simon Dedalus' voice hilloes in answer, somewhat sleepy but ready.*)

SIMON

That's all right. (*He swoops uncertainly through the air, wheeling, uttering cries of hearkening, on strong ponderous buzzard wings.*) Ho, boy! Are you going to win? Hoop! Pschatt! Stable with those halfcastes. Wouldn't let them within the bawl of an ass. Head up! Keep our flag flying! An eagle gules volant in a field argent displayed. Ulster king at arms! hai hoop! (*He makes the beagle's call giving tongue.*) Bulbul! Burblblbrurblbl! Hai, boy!

(*The fronds and spaces of the wall paper file rapidly across country. A stout fox drawn from covert, brush pointed, having buried his grandmother, runs swift, for the open brighteyed, seeking badger earth, under the leaves. The pack of staghounds follows, nose to the ground, sniffing their quarry, beaglebaying, burblbrbling to be blooded. Ward Union huntsmen and huntswomen live with them, hot for a kill. From Six Mile Point, Flathouse, Nine Mile Stone follow the footpeople with knotty sticks, salmongaffs, lassos, flockmasters with stockwhips, bearbaiters with tomtoms, toreadors with bullswords, grey negroes waving torches. The crowd bawls of dicers, crown and anchor players, thimbleriggers, broadsmen. Crows and touts, hoarse bookies in high wizard hats clamour deafeningly.)*

THE CROWD

Card of the races. Racing card !
Ten to one the field !
Tommy on the clay here ! Tommy on the clay !
Ten to on. bar one. Ten to one bar one.
Try your luck on spinning Jenny !
Ten to one bar one !
Sell the monkey, boys ! Sell the monkey !
I'll give ten to one !
Ten to one bar one !

(A dark horse riderless, bolts like a phantom past the winningpost, his mane moonfoaming, his eyeballs stars. The field follows, a bunch of bucking mounts. Skeleton horses : Sceptre, Maximum the Second, Zinfandel, the Duke of Westminster's Shotover, Repulse, The Duke of Beaufort's Ceylon, prix de Paris. Dwarfs ride them, rusty armoured, leaping, leaping in their, in their saddles. Last in a drizzle of rain, on a broken-winded isabelle nag. Cock of the North, the favourite, honey cap, green jacket, orange sleeves, Garrett Deasy up, gripping the reins, a hockey stick at the ready. His nag, stumbling on whitegaitered feet, jogs along the rocky road.)

THE ORANGE LODGES

(Jeering.) Get down and push, mister. Last lap ! You'll be home the night !

GANETT DEARY

(Bolt upright, his nailscraped face plastered with postage stamps, brandishes his hockeystick, his blue eyes flashing in the prism of the chandelier as his mount lopes by at schooling gallop.)

Per vias rectas !

(A yoke of buckets leopards all over him and his rearing nag, a torrent of mutton broth with dancing coins of carrots, barley, onions, turnips, potatoes.)

THE GREEN LODGES

Soft day, sir John! Soft day, your honour!

(*Private Carr, Private Compton and Cissy Caffrey pass beneath the windows, singing in discord.*)

STEPHEN

Hark! Our friend, noise in the street!

ZOE

(*Holds up her hand.*) Stop!

PRIVATE CARR, PRIVATE COMPTON and CISSY CAFFREY

Yet I've a sort a
Yorkshire relish for ...

ZOE

That's me. (*She claps her hands.*) Dance! Dance! (*She runs to the pianola.*) Who has twopence?

BLOOM

Who'll?...

LYNCH

(*Handing her coins.*) Here.

STEPHEN

(*Cracking his fingers impatiently.*) Quick! Quick! Where's my augur's rod? (*He runs to the piano and takes his ashplant, beating his foot in tripudium.*)

ZOE

(*Turns the drumhandle.*) There.

(*She drops two pennies in the slot. Gold pink and violet lights start forth. The drum turns purring in low hesitation waltz. Professor Goodwin, in a bowknotted periwig, in court dress, wearing a stained inverness cape, bent in two from incredible age, totters across the room, his hands fluttering. He sits tinily on the piano stool and lifts and beats handless sticks of arms on the keyboard, nodding with damsel's grace, his bowknot bobbing.*)

ZOE

(*Twirls around herself, heeltapping.*) Dance. Anybody here for there? Who'll dance?

(*The pianola, with changing lights plays in waltz time the prelude of* My Girl's a Yorkshire Girl. *Stephen throws his ashplant on the table and seizes Zoe around the waist. Florry and Bella push the table towards the fireplace. Stephen, arming Zoe with exaggerated grace, begins to waltz her around the room. Her sleeve, falling from gracing arms, reveals a white fleshflower of vaccination. Bloom stands aside. Between the curtains, Professor Maginni inserts a leg on the toepoint of which spins a silk hat. With a deft kick, he sends it spinning to his crown and jauntyhatted skates in. He wears a slate frockcoat with claret silk lapels, a gorget of cream tulle, a green lowcut waistcoat, stock collar with white kerchief, tight lavender trousers, patent pumps and canary gloves. In his buttonhole is a dahlia. He twirls in reversed directions a clouded cane, then wedges it tight in his oxter. He places a hand limply on his breastbone, bows and fondles his flower and buttons.*)

MAGINNI

The poetry of motion, art of calisthenics. No connection with Madam Legget Byrne's or Levinstone's. Fancy dress balls arranged. Deportment. The Katty Lanner steps. So. Watch me! My terpsichorean abilities. (*He minuets forward three paces on tripping bee's feet.*) *Tout le monde en avant! Reverence! Tout le monde en place!*

(*The prelude ceases. Professor Goodwin, beating vague arms, shrivels, shrinks, his live cape falling about the stool. The air, in firmer waltz time, pounds. Stephen and Zoe circle freely. The lights change, glow, fade, gold, rose, violet.*)

THE PIANOLA

Two young fellows were talking about their girls, girls, girls,
Sweethearts they'd left behind...

(*From a corner the morning hours run out, goldhaired, slim, in girlish blue, waspwaisted, with innocent hands. Nimbly they dance, twirling their skipping ropes. The hours of noon follow in amber gold. Laughing linked, high haircombs flashing, they catch the sun in mocking mirrors, lifting their arms.)*

MAGINNI

(*Clipclaps glovesilent hands.*) *Carré! Avant deux!* Breathe evenly! *Balance!*

(*The morning and noon hours waltz in their places, turning, advancing to each other, shaping their curves, bowing vis a vis. Cavaliers behind them arch and suspend their arms, with hands descending to, touching, rising from their shoulders.*)

HOURS

You may touch my...

CAVALIERS

May I touch your?

HOURS

O, but lightly!

CAVALIERS

O, so lightly!

THE PIANOLA

My little shy little lass has a waist.

(*Zoe and Stephen turn boldly with looser swing. The twilight hours advance, from long landshadows, dispersed, lagging, languideyed, their cheeks delicate with cipria and false faint bloom. They are in grey gauze with dark bat sleeves that flutter in the land breeze.*)

MAGINNI

Avant huit! Traversé! Salut! Cours de mains! Croisé!

(*The night hours steal to the last place. Morning, noon and twilight hours retreat before them. They are masked, with daggered hair and bracelets of dull bells. Weary, they curchycurchy under veils.*)

THE BRACELETS

Heigho! Heigho!

ZOE

(*Twisting, her hand to her brow.*) O!

MAGINNI

Les tiroirs! Chaîne de dames! La corbeille! Dos à dos!

(*Arabesquing wearily, they weave a pattern on the floor, weaving, unweaving, curtseying, twisting, simply swirling.*)

ZOE

I'm giddy.

(*She frees herself, droops on a chair, Stephen seizes Florry and turns with her.*)

MAGINNI

Boulangère! Les ronds! Les ponts! Chevaux de bois! Escargots!

(*Twining, receding, with interchanging hands, the night hours link, each with arching arms, in a mosaic of movements, Stephen and Florry turn cumbrously.*)

MAGINNI

Dansez avec vos dames! Changez de dames! Donnez le petit bouquet à votre dame! Remerciez!

THE PIANOLA

Best, best of all,
Baraabum!

KITTY

(*Jumps up.*) O, they played that on the hobbyhorses at the *Mirus* bazaar!

(*She runs to Stephen. He leaves Florry brusquely and seizes Kitty. A screaming bittern's harsh high whistle shrieks. Groangrousegurgling Toft's cumbersome whirligig turns slowly the room right roundabout the room.*)

THE PIANOLA

My girl's a Yorkshire girl.

ZOE

Yorkshire through and through.

Come on all!

(*She seizes Florry and waltzes her.*)

STEPHEN

Pas seul!

(*He wheels Kitty into Lynch's arms, snatches up his ashplant from the table and takes the floor. All wheel, whirl, waltz, twirl. Bloombella, Kittylynch, Florryzoe, jujuby women. Stephen with hat ashplant frogsplits in middle highkicks with skykicking mouth shut hand clasp part under thigh, with clang tinkle boomhammer tallyho hornblower blue green yellow flashes Toft's cumbersome turns with hobbyhorse riders from gilded snakes dangled, bowels fandango leaping spurn soil foot and fall again.*)

THE PIANOLA

Though she's a factory lass
And wears no fancy clothes.

(*Closeclutched swift swifter with glareblareflare scudding they scotlootshoot lumbering by. Baraabum!*)

TUTTI

Encore! Bis! Bravo! Encore!

SIMON

Think of your mother's people!

STEPHEN

Dance of death.

(*Bang fresh barang bang of lacquey's bell, horse, nag, steer, piglings. Conmee on Christass lame crutch and leg sailor in cockboat armfolded ropepulling hitching stamp hornpipe through and through, Baraabum! On nags, hogs, bellhorses, Gadarene swine, Corny in coffin. Steel shark stone onehandled Nelson, two trickies Frauenzimmer plumstained from pram falling bawling. Gum, he's a champion. Fuseblue peer from barrel rev. evensong Love on hackney jaunt Blazes blind coddoubled bicyclers Dilly with snowcake no fancy clothes. Then in last wiswitchback lumbering up and down bump mashtub sort of viceroy and reine relish for tublumber bumpshire rose.. Baraabum!)*

(The couples fall aside. Stephen whirls giddily. Room whirls back. Eyes closed, he totters. Red rails fly spacewards. Stars all around suns turn roundabout. Bright midges dance on wall. He stops dead.)

STEPHEN

Ho!

(Stephen's mother, emaciated, rises stark through the floor in leper grey with a wreath of faded orange blossoms and a torn bridal veil, her face worn and noseless, green with grave mould. Her hair is scant and lank. She fixes her bluecircled hollow eyesockets on Stephen and opens her toothless mouth uttering a silent word. A choir of virgins and confessors sing voicelessly.)

THE CHOIR

Liliata rutilantium te confessorum...
Jubilantium te virginum...

(From the top of a tower Buck Mulligan, in particoloured jester's dress of puce and yellow and clown's cap with curling bell, stands gaping at her, a smoking buttered split scone in his hand.)

BUCK MULLIGAN

She's beastly dead. The pity of it! Mulligan meets the afflicted mother. *(He upturns his eyes.)* Mercurial Malachi.

THE MOTHER

(With the subtle smile of death's madness.) I was once the beautiful May Goulding. I am dead.

STEPHEN

(Horrorstruck.) Lemur, who are you? What bogeyman's trick is this?

BUCK MULLIGAN

(Shakes his curling capbell.) The mockery of it! Kinch killed her dogsbody

bitchbody. She kicked the bucket. (*Tears of molten butter fall from his eyes into the scone.*) Our great sweet mother! *Epi oinopa ponton.*

THE MOTHER

(*Comes nearer, breathing upon him softly her breath of wetted ashes.*) All must go through it, Stephen. More women than men in the world. You too. Time will come.

STEPHEN

(*Choking with fright, remorse and horror.*) They said I killed you, mother. He offended your memory. Cancer did it, not I. Destiny.

THE MOTHER

(*A green rill of bile trickling from a side of her mouth.*) You sang that song to me. *Love's bitter mystery.*

STEPHEN

(*Eagerly.*) Tell me the word, mother, if you know now. The word known to all men.

THE MOTHER

Who saved you the night you jumped into the train at Dalkey with Paddy Lee? Who had pity for you when you were sad among the strangers? Prayer is all powerful. Prayer for the suffering souls in the Ursuline manual, and forty days indulgence. Repent, Stephen.

STEPHEN

The ghoul! Hyena!

THE MOTHER

I pray for you in my other world. Get Dilly to make you that boiled rice every night after your brain work. Years and years I loved you, O my son, my firstborn, when you lay in my womb.

ZOE

(*Fanning herself with the grate fan.*) I'm melting!

FLORRY

(*Points to Stephen.*) Look! He's white.

BLOOM

(*Goes to the window to open it more.*) Giddy.

THE MOTHER

(*With smouldering eyes.*) Repent! O, the fire of hell!

STEPHEN

(*Panting.*) The corpsechewer! Raw head and bloody bones!

THE MOTHER

(*Her face drawing near and nearer, sending out an ashen breath.*) Beware! (*She raises her blackened, withered right arm slowly towards Stephen's breast with outstretched fingers.*) Beware! God's hand! (*A green crab with malignant red eyes sticks deep its grinning claws in Stephen's heart.*)

STEPHEN

(*Strangled with rage.*) Shite! (*His features grow drawn and grey and old.*)

BLOOM

(*At the window.*) What?

STEPHEN

Ah non, par exemple! The intellectual imagination! With me all or not at all. *Non serviam!*

FLORRY

Give him some cold water. Wait. (*She rushes out.*)

THE MOTHER

(*Wrings her hands slowly, moaning desperately.*) O Sacred Heart of Jesus, have mercy on him! Save him from hell, O divine Sacred Heart!

STEPHEN

No! No! No! Break my spirit all of you if you can! I'll bring you all to heel!

THE MOTHER

(*In the agony of her deathrattle.*) Have mercy on Stephen, Lord, for my sake! Inexpressible was my anguish when expiring with love, grief and agony on Mount Calvary.

STEPHEN

Nothung!

(*He lifts his ashplant high with both hands and smashes the chandelier. Time's livid final flame leaps and, in the following darkness, ruin of all space, shattered glass and toppling masonry.*)

THE GASJET

Pwfungg!

BLOOM

Stop!

LYNCH

(*Rushes forward and seizes Stephen's hand.*) Here! Hold on! Don't run amok!

BELLA

Police!

(*Stephen, abandoning his ashplant, his head and arms thrown back stark, beats the ground and flees from the room past the whores at the door.*)

BELLA

(*Screams.*) After him!

(*The two whores rush to the halldoors. Lynch and Kitty and Zoe stampede from the room. They talk excitedly. Bloom follows, returns.*)

THE WHORES

(*Jammed in the doorway, pointing.*) Down there.

ZOE

(*Pointing.*) There. There's something up.

BELLA

Who pays for the lamp? (*She seizes Bloom's coattail.*) There. You were with him. The lamp's broken.

BLOOM

(*Rushes to the hall, rushes back.*) What lamp, woman ?

A WHORE

He tore his coat.

BELLA

(*Her eyes hard with anger and cupidity, points.*) Who's to pay for that ? Ten shillings. You're a witness.

BLOOM

(*Snatches up Stephen's ashplant.*) Me ? Ten shillings ? Haven't you lifted enough off him ? Didn't he... !

BELLA

(*Loudly.*) Here, none of your tall talk. This isn't a brothel. A ten shilling house.

BLOOM

(*His hand under the lamp, pulls the chain. Pulling, the gasjet lights up a crushed mauve purple shade. He raises the ashplant.*) Only the chimney's broken. Here is all he...

BELLA

(*Shrinks back and screams.*) Jesus ! Don't !

BLOOM

(*Warding off a blow*). To show you how he hit the paper. There's not a sixpenceworth of damage done. Ten shillings !

FLORRY

(*With a glass of water, enters.*) Where is he ?

BELLA

Do you want me to call the police ?

BLOOM

O, I know. Bulldog on the premises. But he's a Trinity student. Patrons of your establishment. Gentlemen that pay the rent. (*He makes a masonic sign.*) Know what I mean ? Nephew of the vicechancellor. You don't want a scandal.

BELLA

(*Angrily.*) Trinity. Coming down here ragging after the boat races and paying nothing. Are you my commander here ? Where is he ? I'll charge him. Disgrace him, I will. (*She shouts.*) Zoe ! Zoe !

BLOOM

(*Urgently.*) And if it were your own son in Oxford ! (*Warningly.*) I know.

BELLA

(*Almost speechless.*) Who are you incog ?

ZOE

(*In the doorway.*) There's a row on.

BLOOM

What ? Where ? (*He throws a shilling on the table and shouts.*) That's for the chimney. Where ? I need mountain air.

(*He hurries out through the hall. The whores point. Florry follows, spilling water from her tilted tumbler. On the doorstep all the whores clustered talk volubly, pointing to the right where the fog has cleared off. From the left arrives a jingling hackney car. It slows to in front of the house. Bloom at the halldoor perceives Corny Kelleher who is about to dismount from the car with two silent lechers. He averts his face. Bella from within the hall urges on her whores. They blow ickylickysticky yumyum kisses. Corny Kelleher replies with a ghostly lewd smile. The silent lechers turn to pay the jarvey. Zoe and Kitty still point right. Bloom, parting them swiftly, draws his caliph's hood and poncho and hurries down the steps with sideways face. Incog Haroun al Raschid, he flits behind the silent lechers and hastens on by the railings with fleet step of a pard strewing the drag behind him, torn envelopes drenched in aniseed. The ashplant marks his stride. A pack of bloodhounds led by Hornblower of Trinity brandishing a dogwhip in tallyho cap, and an old pair of grey trousers, follows from far, picking up the scent, nearer, baying, panting, at fault, breaking away, throwing their tongues, biting his heels, leaping at his tail. He walks, runs, zigzags, gallops, lugs laid back. He is pelted with gravel, cabbagestumps, biscuitboxes, eggs, potatoes, dead codfish, woman's slipperslappers. After him, freshfound, the hue and cry zigzag gallops in hot pursuit of follow my leader: 65 C 66 C night watch, John Henry Menton, Wisdom Hely, V. B. Dillon, Councillor Nannetti, Alexander Keyes, Larry O'Rourke, Joe Cuffe, Mrs O'Dowd, Pisser Burke, The Nameless One, Mrs Riordan, The Citizen, Garryowen, Whatdoyoucallhim, Strangeface, Fellowthatslike, Sawhimbefore, Chapwith, Chris Callinan, sir Charles Cameron, Benjamin Dollard, Lenehan, Bartell d'Arcy, Joe Hynes, red Murray, editor Brayden, T. M. Healy, Mr Justice Fitzgibbon, John Howard Parnell, the reverend Tinned Salmon, Professor Joly, Mrs Breen, Denis Breen, Theodore Purefoy, Mina Purefoy, the Westland Row postmistress, C. P. McCoy, friend of Lyons, Hoppy Holohan, man in the street, other man in the street, Footballboots, pugnosed driver, rich protestant lady, Davy Byrne, Mrs Ellen Mc Guinness, Mrs Joe Gallaher, George Lidwell, Jimmy Henry on corns, Superintendent Laracy, Father Cowley, Crofton out of the Collector General's, Dan Dawson, dental surgeon Bloom with tweezers, Mrs Bob Doran, Mrs Kennefick, Mrs Wyse Nolan, John Wyse Nolan, handsomemarriedwomanrubbedagainstwidebehindin-Clonskea tram, the bookseller of* Sweets of Sin, *Miss Dubedatandshedidbedad, Mesdames Gerald and Stanislaus Moran of Roebuck, the managing clerk of Drimmie's, colonel Hayes, Mastiansky, Citron, Penrose, Aaron Figatner, Moses Herzog, Michael E. Geraghty, Inspector Troy, Mrs Galbraith, the constable off Eccles Street corner, old doctor Brady with stethoscope, the mystery man on the beach, a retriever, Mrs Miriam Dandrade and all her lovers.)*

THE HUE AND CRY

(*Helterskelterpelterwelter.*) He's Bloom! Stop Bloom! Stopabloom! Stopperrobber! Hi! Hi! Stop him on the corner!

(*At the corner of Beaver Street beneath the scaffolding Bloom panting stops on the fringe of the noisy quarelling knot, a lot not knowing a jot what hi! hi! row and wrangle round the whowhat brawlaltogether.*)

STEPHEN

(*With elaborate gestures, breathing deeply and slowly.*) You are my guests.

The uninvited. By virtue of the fifth of George and seventh of Edward. History to blame. Fabled by mothers of memory.

PRIVATE CARR

(*To Cissy Caffrey.*) Was he insulting you?

STEPHEN

Addressed her in vocative feminine. Probably neuter. Ungenitive.

VOICES

No, he didn't. The girl's telling lies. He was in Mrs Cohen's. What's up? Soldiers and civilians.

CISSY CAFFREY

I was in company with the soldiers and they left me to do — you know and the young man ran up behind me. But I'm faithful to the man that's treating me though I'm only a shilling whore.

STEPHEN

(*Catches sight of Kitty's and Lynch's heads.*) Hail, Sisyphus. (*He points to himself and the others.*) Poetic. Neopoetic.

VOICES

She's faithfultheman.

CISSY CAFFREY

Yes, to go with him. And me with a soldier friend.

PRIVATE COMPTON

He doesn't half want a thick ear, the blighter. Biff him one, Harry.

PRIVATE CARR

(*To Cissy.*) Was he insulting you while me and him was having a piss?

LORD TENNYSON

(*In Union Jack blazer and cricket flannels, bareheaded, flowingbearded.*) Their's not to reason why.

PRIVATE COMPTON

Biff him, Harry.

STEPHEN

(*To Private Compton.*) I don't know your name but you are quite right. Doctor Swift says one man in armour will beat ten men in their shirts. Shirt is synechdoche. Part for the whole.

CISSY CAFFREY

(*To the crowd.*) No, I was with the private.

STEPHEN

(*Amiably.*) Why not? The bold soldier boy. In my opinion every lady for example...

PRIVATE CARR

(*His cap awry, advancing to Stephen.*) Say, how would it be, governor, if I was to bash in your jaw?

STEPHEN

(*Looks up in the sky.*) How? Very unpleasant. Noble art of selfpretence. Personally, I detest action. (*He waves his hand.*) Hand hurts me slightly. *Enfin, ce sont vos oignons.* (*To Cissy Caffrey.*) Some trouble is on here. What is it, precisely?

DOLLY GRAY

(*From her balcony waves her handkerchief, giving the sign of the heroine of Jericho.*) Rahab. Cook's son, goodbye. Safe home to Dolly. Dream of the girl you left behind and she will dream of you.

(*The soldiers turn their swimming eyes.*)

BLOOM

(*Elbowing through the crowd, plucks Stephen's sleeve vigorously.*) Come now, professor, that carman is waiting.

STEPHEN

(*Turns.*) Eh? (*He disengages himself.*) Why should I not speak to him or to any human being who walks upright upon this oblate orange? (*He points his finger.*) I'm not afraid of what I can talk to if I see his eye. Retaining the perpendicular.

(*He staggers a pace back.*)

BLOOM

(*Propping him.*) Retain your own.

STEPHEN

(*Laughs emptily.*) My centre of gravity is displaced. I have forgotten the trick. Let us sit down somewhere and discuss. Struggle for life is the law of existence but modern philirenists, notably the tsar and the king of England, have invented arbitration. (*He taps his brow.*) But in here it is I must kill the priest and the king.

BIDDY THE CLAP

Did you hear what the professor said? He's a professor out of the college

CUNTY KATE

I did. I heard that.

BIDDY THE CLAP

He expresses himself with much marked refinement of phraseology.

CUNTY KATE

Indeed, yes. And at the same time with such apposite trenchancy.

PRIVATE CARR

(*Pulls himself free and comes forward.*) What's that you're saying about my king?

(*Edward the Seventh appears in an archway. He wears a white jersey on which an image of the Sacred Heart is stitched, with the insignia of Garter and Thistle, Golden Fleece, Elephant of Denmark, Skinner's and Probyn's horse, Lincoln's Inns' bencher and ancient and honourable artillery company of Massachussets. He sucks a red jujube. He is robed as a grand elect perfect and sublime mason with trowel and apron, marked* made in Germany. *In his left hand he holds a plasterer's bucket on which is printed :* Défense d'uriner. *A roar of welcome greets him.*)

EDWARD THE SEVENTH

(*Slowly, solemnly but indistinctly.*) Peace, perfect peace. For identification bucket in my hand. Cheerio, boys. (*He turns to his subjects.*) We have come here to witness a clean straight fight and we heartily wish both men the best of good luck. Mahak makar a back.

(*He shakes hands with Private Carr, Private Compton, Stephen, Bloom and Lynch. General applause. Edward the Seventh lifts the bucket graciously in acknowledgement.*)

PRIVATE CARR

(*To Stephen.*) Say it again.

STEPHEN

(*Nervous, friendly, pulls himself up.*) I understand your point of view though I have no king myself for the moment. This is the age of patent medicine. A discussion is difficult down here. But this is the point. You die for your country, suppose. (*He places his arm on Private Carr's sleeve.*) Not that I wish it for you. But I say : Let my country die for me. Up to the present it has done so. I don't want it to die. Damn death. Long live life!

EDWARD THE SEVENTH

(*Levitates over heaps of slain in the garb and with the halo of Joking Jesus, a white jujube in his phosphorescent face.*)

My methods are new and are causing surprise.
To make the blind see I throw dust in their eyes.

STEPHEN

Kings and unicorns! (*He falls back a pace.*) Come somewhere and we'll... What was that girl saying?...

PRIVATE COMPTON

Eh, Harry, give him a kick in the knackers. Stick one into Jerry.

BLOOM

(*To the privates, softly.*) He doesn't know what he's saying. Taking a little more than is good for him. Absinthe, the greeneyed monster. I know him. He's a gentleman, a poet. It's all right.

STEPHEN

(*Nods, smiling and laughing.*) Gentleman, patriot, scholar and judge of impostors.

PRIVATE CARR

I don't give a bugger who he is.

PRIVATE COMPTON

We don't give a bugger who he is.

STEPHEN

I seem to annoy them. Green rag to a bull.

(*Kevin Egan of Paris in black Spanish tasselled shirt and peep-o'-day boy's hat signs to Stephen.*)

KEVIN EGAN

H'lo! *Bonjour!* The *vieille ogresse* with the *dents jaunes.*

(*Patrice Egan peeps from behind, his rabbit face nibbling a quince leaf.*)

PATRICE

Socialiste!

DON EMILE PATRIZIO FRANZ RUPERT POPE HENNESSY

(*In medieval hauberk, two wild geese valant on his helm, with noble indignation points a mailed hand against the privates.*) Werf those eykes to footboden, big grand porcos of johnyellows todos covered of gravy!

BLOOM

(*To Stephen.*) Come home. You'll get into trouble.

STEPHEN

(*Swaying.*) I don't avoid it. He provokes my intelligence.

BIDDY THE CLAP

One immediately observes that he is of patrician lineage.

THE VIRAGO

Green above the red, says he. Wolfe Tone.

THE BAWD

The red's as good as the green, and better. Up the soldiers! Up King Edward!

A ROUGH

(*Laughs.*) Ay! Hands up to De Wet.

THE CITIZEN

(*With a huge emerald muffler and shillelagh, calls.*)

May the God above
Send down a dove
With teeth as sharp as razors
To slit the throat
Of the English dogs
That hanged our Irish leaders.

THE CROPPY BOY

(*The rope noose round his neck, gripes in his issuing bowels with both hands.*)

I bear no hate to a living thing,
But I love my country beyond the king.

RUMBOLD, DEMON BARBER

(*Accompanied by two blackmasked assistants, advances with a gladstone bag which he opens.*) Ladies and gents, cleaver purchased by Mrs Pearcy to slay Mogg. Knife with which Voisin dismembered the wife of a compatriot and hid remains in a sheet in the cellar, the unfortunate female's throat being cut from ear to ear. Phial containing arsenic retrieved from the body of Miss Barron which sent Seddon to the gallows.

(*He jerks the rope, the assistants leap at the victim's legs and drag him downward, grunting: the croppy boy's tongue protrudes violently.*)

THE CROPPY BOY

Horhot ho hray ho rhother's hest

(*He gives up the ghost. A violent erection of the hanged sends gouts of sperm spouting through his death clothes on to the cobblestones. Mrs Bellingham, Mrs Yelverton Barry and the Honourable Mrs Mervy Talboys rush forward with their handkerchiefs to sop it up.*)

RUMBOLD

I'm near it myself. (*He undoes the noose.*) Rope which hanged the awful rebel. Ten shillings a time as applied to His Royal Highness. (*He plunges his head into the gaping belly of the hanged and draws out his head again clotted with coiled and smoking entrails.*) My painful duty has now been done. God save the king!

EDWARD THE SEVENTH

(*Dances slowly, solemnly, rattling his bucket and sings with soft contentment.*)

On coronation day, on coronation day,
O, won't we have a merry time,
Drinking whisky, beer and wine!

PRIVATE CARR

Here. What are you saying about my king?

STEPHEN

(*Throws up his hands.*) O, this is too monotonous! Nothing. He wants my money and my life, though want must be his master, for some brutish empire of his. Money I haven't. (*He searches his pockets vaguely.*) Gave it to someone.

PRIVATE CARR

Who wants your bleeding money?

STEPHEN

(*Tries to move off.*) Will some one tell me where I am least likely to meet these necessary evils? *Ça se voit aussi à Paris.* Not that I... But by Saint Patrick!...

(*The women's heads coalesce. Old Gummy Granny in sugarloaf hat appears seated on a toadstool, the deathflower of the potato blight on her breast.*)

STEPHEN

Aha! I know you, gammer! Hamlet, revenge! The old sow that eats her farrow!

OLD GUMMY GRANNY

(*Rocking to and fro.*) Ireland's sweetheart, the king of Spain's daughter, alanna. Strangers im my house, bad manners to them! (*She keens with banshee *woe.*) Ochone! Ochone! Silk of the kine! (*She wails.*) You met with poor old Ireland and how does she stand?

STEPHEN

How do I stand you? The hat trick! Where's the third person of the Blessed Trinity? Soggarth Aroon? The reverend Carrion Crow.

CISSY CAFFREY

(*Shrill.*) Stop them from fighting!

A ROUGH

Our men retreated.

PRIVATE CARR

(*Tugging at his belt.*) I'll wring the neck of any bugger says a word against my fucking king.

BLOOM

(*Terrified.*) He said nothing. Not a word. A pure misunderstanding.

THE CITIZEN

Erin go bragh!

(*Major Tweedy and the Citizen exhibit to each other medals, decorations, trophies of war, wounds. Both salute with fierce hostility.*)

PRIVATE COMPTON

Go it, Harry. Do him one in the eye. He's a proboer.

STEPHEN

Did I? When?

BLOOM

(*To the redcoats*) We fought for you in South Africa, Irish missile troops. Isn't that history? Royal Dublin Fusiliers. Honoured by our monarch.

THE NAVVY

(*Staggering past.*) O, yes. O, God, yes! O, make the kwawr a krowawr! O! Bo!

(*Casqued halberdiers in armour thrust forward a pentice of gutted spear points. Major Tweedy, moustached like Turko the terrible, in bearskin *cap with hackle plume and accoutrements, with epaulette, gilt chevrons and sabretache, his breast bright with medals, toes the line. He gives the pilgrim warrior's sign of the knights templars.)*

MAJOR TWEEDY

(*Growls gruffly.*) Rorke's Drift! Up, guards, and at them! Mahal shalal hashbaz.

PRIVATE CARR

I'll do him in.

PRIVATE COMPTON

(*Waves the crowd back.*) Fair play, here. Make a bleeding butcher's shop o. the bugger.

(*Massed bands blare* Garryowen *and* God save the king.)

CISSY CAFFREY

They're going to fight. For me!

CUNTY KATE

The brave and the fair.

BIDDY THE CLAP

Methinks yon sable knight will joust it with the best.

CUNTY KATE

(*Blushing deeply.*) Nay, Madam. The gules doublet and merry Saint George for me!

STEPHEN

The harlot's cry from street to street
Shall weave old Ireland's windingsheet.

PRIVATE CARR

(*Loosening his belt, shouts.*) I'll wring the neck of any fucking bastard says a word against my bleeding fucking king.

BLOOM

(*Shakes Cissy Caffrey's shoulders.*) Speak, you! Are you struck dumb? You are the link between nations and generations. Speak, woman, sacred life giver!

CISSY CAFFREY

(*Alarmed, seizes Private Carr's sleeve.*) Amn't I with you? Amn't I your girl? Cissy's your girl. (*She cries.*) Police!

STEPHEN

(*Ecstatically, to Cissy Caffrey.*)

White thy fambles, red thy gan
And thy quarrons dainty is.

VOICES

Police!

DISTANT VOICES

Dublin's burning! Dublin's burning! On fire, on fire!

(*Brimstone fires spring up. Dense clouds roll past. Heavy Gatling guns boom. Pandemonium. Troops deploy. Gallop of hoofs. Artillery. Hoarse commands. Bells clang. Backers shout. Drunkards bawl Whores screech. Foghorns hoot. Cries of valour. Shrieks of dying. Pikes clash on cuirasses. Thieves rob the slain. Birds of prey, winging from the sea, rising from marshlands, swooping from eyries, hover screaming, gannets, cormorants, vultures, goshawks, climbing woodcocks, peregrines, merlins, blackgrouse, sea eagles, gulls, albatrosses, barnacle geese. The midnight sun is darkened. The earth trembles. The dead of Dublin from Prospect and Mount Jerome in white sheepskin overcoats and black goatfell cloaks arise and appear to many. A chasm opens with a noisless yawn. Tom Rochford, winner in athlete's singlet and breeches, arrives at the head of the national hurdle handicap and leaps into the void. He is followed by a race of runners and leapers. In wild attitudes they spring from the brink. Their bodies plunge. Factory lasses with fancy clothes toss redhot Yorkshire baraabombs. Society ladies lift their skirts above their heads to protect themselves. Laughing witches in red cutty sarks ride through the air on broomsticks. Quakerlyster plasters blisters. It rains dragon's teeth. Armed heroes spring up from furrows. They exchange in amity the pass of knights of the red cross and fight duels with cavalry sabres: Wolfe Tome against Henry Grattan, Smith O'Brien against Daniel O'Connell, Michael Davitt against Isaac Butt, Justin M'Carthy against Parnell, Arthur Griffith against John Redmond, John O'Leary against Lear O'Johnny, Lord Edward Fitzgerald against Lord Gerald Fitzedward, The O'Donoghue of the Glens against The Glens of The Donoghue. On an eminence, the centre of the earth, rises the field altar of Saint Barbara. Black candles rise from its gospel and epistle horns. From the high barbacans of the tower two shafts of light fall on the smokepalled altarstone. On the altarstone Mrs Mina Purefoy, goddess of unreason, lies, naked, fettered, a chalice resting on her swollen belly. Father Malachi O'Flynn in a long petticoat and reversed chasuble, his two left feet back to the front, celebrates camp mass. The Reverend Mr Hugh C Haines Love M. A. in a plain cassock and mortar board, his head and collar back to the front, holds over the celebrant's head an open umbrella.*)

FATHER MALACHI O'FLYNN

Introibo ad altare diaboli.

THE REVEREND MR HAINES LOVE

To the devil which hath made glad my young days.

FATHER MALACHI O'FLYNN

(*Takes from the chalice and elevates a blooddripping host.*) Corpus Meum.

THE REVEREND MR HAINES LOVE

(*Raises high behind the celebrant's petticoats, revealing his grey bare hairy buttocks between which a carrot is stuck.*) My body.

THE VOICE OF ALL THE DAMNED

Htengier Lnetopinmo Dog Drol eht rof, Aiulella!

(*From on high the voice of Adonai calls.*)

ADONAI

Dooooooooooog!

THE VOICE OF ALL THE BLESSED

Alleluia, for the Lord God Omnipotent reigneth!

(*From on high the voice of Adonai calls.*)

ADONAI

Goooooooooood!

(*In strident discord peasants and townsmen of Orange and Green factions sing* Kick the Pope *and* Daily, daily sing to Mary.)

PRIVATE CARR

(*With ferocious articulation.*) I'll do him in, so help me fucking Christ! I'll wring the bastard fucker's bleeding blasted fucking windpipe!

OLD GUMMY GRANNY

(*Thrusts a dagger towards Stephen's hand.*) Remove him, acushla. At 8.35 a.m. you will be in heaven and Ireland will be free. (*She prays.*) O good God, take him!

BLOOM

(*Runs to Lynch.*) Can't you get him away?

LYNCH

He likes dialectic, the universal language. Kitty! (*To Bloom.*) Get him away, you. He won't listen to me.

(*He drags Kitty away.*)

STEPHEN

(*Points.*) *Exit Judas. Et laqueo se suspendit.*

BLOOM

(*Runs to Stephen.*) Come along with me now before worse happens. Here's your stick.

STEPHEN

Stick, no. Reason. This feast of pure reason.

CISSY CAFFREY

(*Pulling Private Carr.*) Come on, you're boosed. He insulted me but I forgive him. (*Shouting in his ear.*) I forgive him for insulting me.

BLOOM

(*Over Stephen's shoulder.*) Yes, go. You see he's incapable.

PRIVATE CARR

(*Breaks loose.*) I'll insult him.

(*He rushes towards Stephen, fists outstretched, and strikes him in the face. Stephen totters, collapses, falls stunned. He lies prone, his face to the sky, his hat rolling to the wall. Bloom follows and picks it up.*)

MAJOR TWEEDY

(*Loudly.*) Carbine in bucket! Cease fire! Salute!

THE RETRIEVER

(*Barking furiously.*) Ute ute ute ute ute ute ute ute.

THE CROWD

Let him up! Don't strike him when he's down! Air! Who? The soldier hit him. He's a professor. Is he hurted? Don't manhandle him! he's fainted!

(*The retriever, nosing on the fringe of the crowd, barks noisily.*)

A HAG

What call had the redcoat to strike the gentleman and he under the influence. Let them go and fight the Boers!

THE BAWD

Listen to who's talking! Hasn't the soldier a right to go with his girl? He gave him the coward's blow.

(*They grab at each other's hair, claw at each other and spit.*)

THE RETRIEVER

(*Barking.*) Wow wow wow.

BLOOM

(*Shoves them back, loudly.*) Get back, stand back!

PRIVATE COMPTON

(*Tugging his comrade.*) Here bugger off, Harry. There's the cops! (*Two raincaped watch, tall, stand in the group.*)

FIRST WATCH

What's wrong here?

PRIVATE COMPTON

We were with this lady and he insulted us and assaulted my chum. (*The retriever barks.*) Who owns the bleeding tyke?

CISSY CAFFREY

(*With expectation.*) Is he bleeding?

A MAN

(*Rising from his knees.*) No. Gone off. He'll come to all right.

BLOOM

(*Glances sharply at the man.*) Leave him to me. I can easily...

SECOND WATCH

Who are you? Do you know him?

PRIVATE CARR

(*Lurches towards the watch.*) He insulted my lady friend.

BLOOM

(*Angrily.*) You hit him without provocation. I'm a witness. Constable, take his regimental number.

SECOND WATCH

I don't want your instructions in the discharge of my duty.

PRIVATE COMPTON

(*Pulling his comrade.*) Here, bugger off, Harry. Or Bennett'll have you in the lockup.

PRIVATE CARR

(*Staggering as he is pulled away.*) God fuck old Bennett! He's a whitearsed bugger. I don't give a shit for him.

FIRST WATCH

(*Taking out his notebook.*) What's his name?

BLOOM

(*Peering over the crowd.*) I just see a car there. If you give me a hand a second, sergeant...

FIRST WATCH

Name and address.

(*Corny Kelleher, weepers round his hat, a death wreath in his hand, appears among the bystanders.*)

BLOOM

(*Quickly.*) O, the very man! (*He whispers.*) Simon Dedalus' son. A bit sprung. Get those policemen to move those loafers back.

SECOND WATCH

Night, Mr Kelleher.

CORNY KELLEHER

(*To the watch, with drawling eye.*) That's all right. I know him. Won a bit on the races. Gold cup. Throwaway. (*He laughs.*) Twenty to one. Do you follow me?

FIRST WATCH

(*Turns to the crowd.*) Here, what are you all gaping at? Move on out of that.

(*The crowd disperses slowly, muttering, down the lane.*)

CORNY KELLEHER

Leave it to me, sergeant. That 'll be all right. (*He laughs, shaking his head.*) We were often as bad ourselves, ay or worse. What? Eh, what?

FIRST WATCH

(*Laughs.*) I suppose so.

CORNY KELLEHER

(*Nudges the second watch.*) Come and wipe your name off the slate. (*He lilts, wagging his head.*) With my tooraloom tooraloom tooraloom tooraloom. What, eh, do you follow me?

SECOND WATCH

(*Genially.*) Ah, sure we were too.

CORNY KELLEHER

(*Winking.*) Boys will be boys. I've a car round there.

SECOND WATCH

All right, Mr Kelleher. Good night.

CORNY KELLEHER

I'll see to that.

BLOOM

(*Shakes hands with both of the watch in turn.*) Thank you very much, gentlemen, thank you. (*He mumbles confidentially.*) We don't want any scandal, you understand. Father is a well known, highly respected citizen. Just a little wild oats, you understand.

FIRST WATCH

O, I understand, sir.

SECOND WATCH

That's all right, sir.

FIRST WATCH

It was only in case of corporal injuries I'd have to report it at the station.

BLOOM

(*Nods rapidly.*) Naturally. Quite right. Only your bounden duty.

SECOND WATCH

It's our duty.

CORNY KELLEHER

Good night, men.

THE WATCH

(*Saluting together.*) Night, gentlemen. (*They move off with slow heavy tread.*)

BLOOM

(*Blows.*) Providential you came on the scene. You have a car?...

CORNY KELLEHER

(*Laughs, pointing his thumb over his right shoulder to the car brought up against the scaffolding.*) Two commercials that were standing fizz in Jammet's. Like princes, faith. One of them lost two quid on the race. Drowning his grief and were on for a go with the jolly girls. So I landed them up on Behan's car and down to nighttown.

BLOOM

I was just going home by Gardiner street when I happened to...

CORNY KELLEHER

(*Laughs.*) Sure they wanted me to join in with the mots. No, by God, says I. Not for old stagers like myself and yourself. (*He laughs again and leers with lacklustre eye.*) Thanks be to God we have it in the house what, eh, do you follow me? Hah! hah! hah!

BLOOM

(*Tries to laugh.*) He, he, he! Yes. Matter of fact I was just visiting an old friend of mine there, Virag, you don't know him (poor fellow he's laid up for the past week) and we had a liquor together and I was just making my way home...

(*The horse neighs.*)

THE HORSE

Hohohohohohoh! Hohohohome!

CORNY KELLEHER

Sure it was Behan, our jarvey there, that told me after we left the two commercials in Mrs Cohen's and I told him to pull up and got off to see. (*He laughs.*) Sober hearsedrivers a specialty. Will I give him a lift home? Where does he hang out? Somewhere in Cabra, what?

BLOOM

No, in Sandycove, I believe, from what he let drop.

(*Stephen, prone, breathes to the stars. Corny Kelleher, asquint, drawls at the horse. Bloom in gloom, looms down.*)

CORNY KELLEHER

(*Scratches his nape.*) Sandycove! (*He bends down and calls to Stephen.*) Eh! (*He calls again.*) Eh! He's covered with shavings anyhow. Take care they didn't lift anything off him.

BLOOM

No, no, no. I have his money and his hat here and stick.

CORNY KELLEHER

Ah, well he'll get over it. No bones broken. Well, I'll shove along. (*He laughs.*) I've a rendezvous in the morning. Burying the dead. Safe home!

THE HORSE

(*Neighs.*) Hohohohohome.

BLOOM

Good night. I'll just wait and take him along in a few...

(*Corny Kelleher returns to the outside car and mounts it. The horse harness jingles.*)

CORNY KELLEHER

(*From the car, standing.*) Night.

BLOOM

Night.

(*The jarvey chucks the reins and raises his whip encouragingly. The car and horse back slowly, awkwardly and turn. Corny Kelleher on the sideseat sways his head to and fro in sign of mirth at Bloom's plight. The jarvey joins in the mute pantomimic merriment nodding from the farther seat. Bloom shakes his head in mute mirthful reply. With thumb and palm Corny Kelleher reassures that the two bobbies will allow the sleep to continue for what else is to be done. With a slow nod Bloom conveys his gratitude as that is exactly what Stephen needs. The car jingles tooraloom round the corner of the tooraloom lane. Corny Kelleher again reassuralooms with his hand. Bloom with his hand assuralooms Corny Kelleher that he is reassuraloomtay. The tinkling hoofs and jingling harness grow fainter with their tooralooloo looloo lay. Bloom, holding in his hand Stephen's hat festooned with shavings and ashplant, stands irresolute. Then he bends to him and shakes him by the shoulder.*)

BLOOM

Eh! Ho! (*There is no answer; he bends again.*) Mr Dedalus! (*There is no answer.*) The name if you call. Somnambulist. (*He bends again and, hesitating, brings his mouth near the face of the prostrate form.*) Stephen! (*There is no answer. He calls again.*) Stephen!

STEPHEN

(*Groans.*) Who? Black panther vampire. (*He sighs and stretches himself, then murmurs thickly with prolonged vowels.*)

Who... drive... Fergus now.
And pierce... wood's woven shade?...

(*He turns on his left side, sighing, doubling himself together.*)

BLOOM

Poetry. Well educated. Pity. (*He bends again and undoes the buttons of Stephen's waistcoat.*) To breathe. (*He brushes the woodshavings from Stephen's clothes with light hands and fingers.*) One pound seven. Not hurt anyhow. (*He listens.*) What!

STEPHEN

(*Murmurs.*)

...shadows... the woods.
...white breast... dim...

(*He stretches out his arms, sighs again and curls his body. Bloom holding his hat and ashplant stands erect. A dog barks in the distance. Bloom tightens and loosens his grip on the ashplant. He looks down on Stephen's face and form.*)

BLOOM

(*Communes with the night.*) Face reminds me of his poor mother. In the shady wood. The deep white breast. Ferguson, I think I caught. A girl. Some girl. Best thing could happen him... (*He murmurs.*)... swear that I will always hail, ever conceal, never reveal, any part or parts, art or arts... (*He murmurs.*)... in the rough sands of the sea... a cabletow's length from the shore... where the tide ebbs... and flows...

(*Silent, thoughtful, alert, he stands on guard, his fingers at his lips in the attitude of secret master. Against the dark wall a figure appears slowly, a fairy boy of eleven, a changeling, kidnapped, dressed in an Eton suit with glass shoes and a little bronze helmet, holding a book in his hand. He reads from right to left inaudibly, smiling, kissing the page.*)

BLOOM

(*Wonderstruck, calls inaudibly.*) Rudy!

RUDY

(*Gazes unseeing into Bloom's eyes and goes on reading, kissing, smiling. He has a delicate mauve face. On his suit he has diamond and ruby buttons. In his free left hand he holds a slim ivory cane with a violet bowknot. A white lambskin peeps out of his waistcoat pocket.*)

Preparatory to anything else Mr Bloom brushed off the greater bulk of the shavings and handed Stephen the hat and ashplant and bucked him up generally in orthodox Samaritan fashion, which he very badly needed. His (Stephen's) mind was not exactly what you would call wandering but a bit unsteady and on his expressed desire for some beverage to drink Mr Bloom, in view of the hour it was and there being no pumps of Vartry water available for their ablutions, let alone drinking purposes, hit upon an expedient by suggesting, off the reel, the propriety of the cabman's shelter, as it was called, hardly a stonesthrow away near Butt Bridge where they might hit upon some drinkables in the shape of a milk and soda or a mineral. But how to get there was the rub. For the nonce he was rather nonplussed but inasmuch as the duty plainly devolved upon him to take some measures on the subject he pondered suitable ways and means during which Stephen repeatedly yawned. So far as he could see he was rather pale in the face so that it occurred to him as highly advisable to get a conveyance of some description which would answer in their then condition, both of them being e. d. ed, particularly Stephen, always assuming that there was such a thing to be found. Accordingly, after a few such preliminaries, as, in spite of his having forgotten to take up his rather soapsuddy handkerchief after it had done yeoman service in the shaving line, brushing they both walked together along Beaver Street, or, more properly, lane, as far as the farrier's and the distinctly fetid atmosphere of the livery stables at the corner of Montgomery street where they made tracks to the left from thence debouching into Amiens Street round by the corner of Dan Bergin's. But, as he confidently anticipated, there was not a sign of a Jehu plying for hire anywhere to be seen except a fourwheeler, probably engaged by some fellows inside on the spree, outside the North Star Hotel and there was no symptom of its budging a quarter of an inch when Mr Bloom, who was anything but a professional whistler, endeavoured to hail it by emitting a kind of a whistle, holding his arms arched over his head, twice.

This was a quandary but, bringing commonsense to bear on it, evidently there was nothing for it but put a good face on the matter and foot it which they accordingly did. So, bevelling around by Mullet's and the Signal House, which they shortly reached, they proceeded perforce in the direction of Amiens Street railway terminus, Mr Bloom being handicapped by the circumstance that one of the back buttons of his trousers had, to vary the timehonoured adage, gone the way of all buttons, though, entering thoroughly into the spirit of the thing, he heroically made light of the mischance. So as neither of them were particularly pressed for time, as it happened, and the temperature refreshing since it cleared up after the recent visitation of Jupiter Pluvius, they dandered along past by where the empty vehicle was waiting without a fare or a jarvey. As it so happened a Dublin United Tramways Company's sandstrewer happening to be returning and the elder man recounted to his companion *à propos* of the incident his own truly miraculous escape of some little while back. They passed the main entrance of the Great Northern railway station, the starting point for Belfast, where of course all traffic was suspended at that late hour, and passing the back door of the morgue (a not very enticing locality, not to say gruesome to a degree, more especially at night), ultimately gained the Dock Tavern and in due course turned into Store Street, famous for its C division police station. Between this point and the high, at present unlit, warehouses of Beresford Place Stephen thought to think of Ibsen, associated with Baird's, the stonecutter's in his mind somehow in Talbot Place, first turning on the right, while the other, who was acting as his *fidus Achates* inhaled with internal satisfaction the smell of James Rourke's city bakery, situated quite close to where they were, the very palatable odour indeed of our daily bread, of all commodities of the public the primary and most indispensable. Bread, the staff of life, earn your bread, O tell me where is fancy bread? At Rourke's the baker's, it is said.

En route, to his taciturn, and, not to put too fine a point on it, not yet perfectly sober companion, Mr Bloom, who at all events, was in complete possession of his faculties, never more so, in fact disgustingly sober, spoke a word of caution *re* the dangers of nighttown, women of ill fame and swell mobsmen, which, barely permissible once in a while, though not as a habitual practice, was of the nature of a regular deathtrap for young fellows of his age particularly if they had acquired drinking habits under the influence of liquor unless you knew a little juijitsu for every contingency as even a fellow on the broad of his back could administer a nasty kick if you didn't look out. Highly providential was the appearance on the scene of Corny Kelleher when Stephen was blissfully unconscious that, but for that man in the gap turning up at the eleventh hour, the finis might have been that he might have been a candidate for the accident ward, or, failing that, the bridewell and an appearance in the court next day before Mr Tobias, or, he being the solicitor, rather old Wall, he meant to say, or Malony which simply spelt ruin for a chap when it got bruited about. The reason he mentioned the fact was that a lot of those policemen, whom he cordially disliked, were admittedly unscrupulous in the service of the Crown and, as Mr Bloom put it, recalling a case or two in the A Division in Clanbrassil Street, prepared to swear a hole through a ten gallon pot. Never on the spot when wanted but in quiet parts of the city, Pembroke Road, for example, the guardians of the law were well in evidence, the obvious reason being they were paid to protect the upper classes. Another thing he commented on was equipping soldiers with firearms or sidearms of any description, liable to go off at any time which was tantamount to inciting them against civilians should by any chance they fall out over anything. You frittered away your time, he very sensibly maintained, and health and also character besides which the squandermania of the thing, fast women of the *demimonde* ran away with a lot of £. s. d. into the bargain and the greatest danger of all was who you got drunk with though, touching the much vexed question of stimulants he relished a glass of choice old wine in season as both nourishing and bloodmaking and possessing aperient virtues (notably a good burgundy which he was a staunch believer in) still never beyond a certain point where he invariably drew the line as it simply led to trouble all round to say nothing of your being at the tender mercy of others pratically. Most of all he commented adversely on the desertion of Stephen by all his pubhunting *confrères* but one, a most glaring piece of ratting on the part of his brother medicos under all the circs.

— And that one was Judas, said Stephen, who up to then had said nothing whatsoever of any kind.

Discussing these and kindred topics they made a beeline across the back of the Customhouse and passed under the Loop Line bridge when a brazier of coke burning in front of a sentrybox, or something like one, attracted their rather lagging footsteps. Stephen of his own accord stopped for no special reason to look at the heap of barren cobblestones and by the light emanating from the brazier he could just make out the darker figure of the corporation watchman inside the gloom of the sentrybox. He began to remember that this had happened, or had been mentioned as having happened, before but it cost him no small effort before he remembered that he recognised in the sentry a quondam friend of his father's, Gumley. To avoid a meeting he drew nearer to the pillars of the railway bridge.

— Someone saluted you, Mr Bloom said.

A figure of middle height on the prowl, evidently, under the arches saluted again, calling : *Night!* Stephen, of course, started rather dizzily and stopped to return the compliment. Mr Bloom, actuated by motives of inherent delicacy, inamsuch as he always believed in minding his own business, moved off but nevertheless remained on the *qui vive* with just a shade of anxiety though not funkyish in the least. Although unusual in the Dublin area, he knew that it was not by any means unknown for desperadoes who had next to nothing to live on to be about waylaying and generally terrorising peaceable pedestrians by placing a pistol at their head in some secluded spot outside the city proper, famished loiterers of the Thames embankment category they might be hanging about there or simply marauders ready to decamp with whatever boodle they could in one fell swoop at a moment's notice, your money or your life, leaving you there to point a moral, gagged and garrotted.

Stephen, that is when the accosting figure came to close quarters, though he was not in any over sober state himself, recognised Corley's breath redolent of rotten cornjuice. Lord John Corley, some called him, and his genealogy came about in this wise. He was the eldest son of Inspector Corley of the G Division, lately deceased, who had married a certain Katherine Brophy, the daughter of a Louth farmer. His grandfather, Patrick Michael Corley, of New Ross, had married the widow of a publican there whose maiden name had been Katherine (also) Talbot. Rumour had it, though not proved, that she descended from the house of the Lords Talbot de Malahide, in whose mansion, really an unquestionably fine residence of its kind and well worth seeing, her mother or aunt or some relative had enjoyed the distinction of being in service in the washkitchen. This, therefore, was the reason why the still comparatively young though dissolute man who now addressed Stephen was spoken of by some with facetious proclivities as Lord John Corley.

Taking Stephen on one side he had the customary doleful ditty to tell. Not as much as a farthing to purchase a night's lodgings. His friends had all deserted him. Furthermore, he had a row with Leneban and called him to Stephen a mean bloody swab with a sprinkling of other uncalledfor expressions. He was out of a job and implored of Stephen to tell him where on God's earth he could get something, anything at all to do. No, it was the daughter of the mother in the washkitchen that was fostersister to the heir of the house or else they were connected through the mother in some way, both occurrences happening at the same time if the whole thing wasn't a complete fabrication from start to finish. Anyhow, he was all in.

— I wouldn't ask you, only, pursued he, on my solemn oath and God knows I'm on the rocks.

— There'll be a job to morrow or the next day, Stephen told him, in a boys' school at Dalkey for a gentleman usher. Mr Garrett Deasy. Try it. You may mention my name.

— Ah, God, Corley replied, sure I couldn't teach in a school, man. I was never one of your bright ones, he added with a half laugh, Got stuck twice in the junior at the Christian Brothers.

— I have no place to sleep myself, Stephen informed him.

Corley, at the first go-off, was inclined to suspect it was something to do with Stephen being fired out of his digs for bringing in a bloody tart off the street. There was a dosshouse in Marlborough Street, Mrs Maloney's, but it was only a tanner touch and full of undesirables but M'Conachie told him you got a decent enough do in the Brazen Head over in Winetavern Street (which was distantly suggestive to the person addressed of friar Bacon) for a bob. He was starving too though he hadn't said a word about it.

Though this sort of thing went on every other night or very near it still Stephen's feelings got the better of him in a sense though he knew that Corley's brandnew rigmarole, on a par with the others, was hardly deserving of much credence. However, *haud ignarus malorum miseris succurrere disco,* etcetera, as the Latin poet remarks, especially as luck would have it he got paid his screw after every middle of the month on the sixteenth which was the date of the month as a matter of fact though a good bit of the wherewithal was demolished. But the cream of the joke was nothing would get it out of Corley's head that he was living in affluence and hadn't a thing to do but hand out the needful — whereas. He put his hand in a pocket anyhow, not with the idea of finding any food there, but thinking he might lend him anything up to a bob or so in lieu so that he might endeavour at all events and get sufficient to eat. But the result was in the negative for, to his chagrin, he found his cash missing. A few broken biscuits were all the result of his invetiongstia. He tried his hardest to recollect for the moment whether he had lost, as well he might have, or left, because in that contingency it was not a pleasant lookout, very much the reverse, in fact. He was altogether too fagged out to institute a thorough search though he tried to recollect about biscuits he dimly remembered. Who now exactly gave them, or where was, or did he buy? However, in another pocket he came across what he surmised in the dark were pennies, erroneously, however, as it turned out.

— Those are halfcrowns, man, Corley corrected him.

And so in point of fact they turned out to be. Stephen lent him one of them.

— Thanks, Corley answered. You're a gentleman. I'll pay you back some time. Who's that with you ? I saw him a few times in the Bleeding Horse in Camden street with Boylan the billsticker. You might put in a good word for us to get me taken on there. I'd carry a sandwichboard only the girl in the office told me they're full up for the next three weeks, man. God, you've to book ahead, man, you'd think it was for the Carl Rosa. I don't give a shite anyway so long as I get a job even as a crossing sweeper.

Subsequently, being not quite so down in the mouth after the two-and-six he got, he informed Stephen about a fellow by the name of Bags Comisky that he said Stephen knew well out of Fullam's, the shipchandler's, bookkeeper there, that used to be often round in Nagle's back with O'Mara and a little chap with a stutter the name of Tighe. Anyhow, he was lagged the night before last and fined ten bob for a drunk and disorderly and refusing to go with the constable.

Mr Bloom in the meanwhile kept dodging about in the vicinity of the cobblestones near the brazier of coke in front of the corporation watchman's sentrybox, who, evidently a glutton for work, it struck him, was having a quiet forty winks for all intents and purposes on his own private account while Dublin slept. He threw an odd eye at the same time now and then at Stephen's anything but immaculately attired interlocutor as if he had seen that nobleman somewhere or other though where he was not in a position to truthfully state nor had he the remotest idea when. Being a levelheaded individual who could give points to not a few in point of shrewd observation, he also remarked on his very dilapidated hat and slouchy wearing apparel generally, testifying to a chronic impecuniosity. Probably he was one of his hangerson but for the matter of that it was merely a question of one preying on his nextdoor neighbour all round, in every deep, so to put it, a deeper depth and for the matter of that if the man in the street chanced to be in the dock himself penal servitude, with or without the option of a fine, would be a very *rara avis* altogether. In any case he had a consummate amount of cool assurance intercepting people at that hour of the night or morning. Pretty thick that was certainly.

The pair parted company and Stephen rejoined Mr Bloom, who with his practised eye, was not without perceiving that he had succumbed to the blandiloquence of the other parasite. Alluding to the encounter he said, laughingly, Stephen, that is:

— He's down on his luck. He asked me to ask you to ask somebody named Boylan, a billsticker, to give him a job as a sandwichman.

At this intelligence, in which he seemingly evinced little interest, Mr Bloom gazed abstractedly for the space of a half a second or so in the direction of a bucket dredger, rejoicing in the farfamed name of Eblana, moored alongside Customhouse Quay and quite possibly out of repair, whereupon he observed evasively:

— Everybody gets their own ration of luck, they say. Now you mention it his face was familiar to me. But leaving that for the moment, how much did you part with, he queried, if I am not too inquisitive?

— Half-a-crown, Stephen responded. I daresay he needs it to sleep somewhere.

— Needs, Mr Bloom ejaculated, professing not the least surprise at the intelligence, I can quite credit the assertion and I guarantee he invariably does. Everyone according to his needs and everyone according to his deeds. But talking about things in general, where, added he with a smile, will you sleep yourself? Walking to Sandycove is out of the question and, even supposing you did, you won't get in after what occurred at Westland Row station. Simply fag out there for nothing. I don't mean to presume to dictate to you in the slightest degree but why did you leave your father's house?

— To seek misfortune, was Stephen's answer.

— I met your respected father on a recent occasion, Mr Bloom diplomatically returned, Today, in fact, or, to be strictly accurate, on yesterday. Where does he live at present? I gathered in the course of conversation that he had moved.

— I believe he is in Dublin somewhere, Stephen answered unconcernedly. Why?

— A gifted man, Mr Bloom said of Mr Dedalus senior, in more respects than one and a born *raconteur* if ever there was one. He takes great pride, quite legitimately, out of you. You could go back, perhaps, he hazarded, still thinking of the very unpleasant scene at Westland Row terminus when it was perfectly evident that the other two, Mulligan, that is, and that English tourist friend of his, who eventually euchred their third companion, were patently trying,as if the whole bally stationbelonged to them, to give Stephen the slip in the confusion.

There was no response forthcoming to the suggestion, however, such as it was, Stephen's mind's eye being too busily engaged in repicturing his family hearth the last time he saw it, with his sister Dilly sitting by the ingle, her hair hanging down, waiting for some weak Trinidad shell cocoa that was in the sootcoated kettle to be done so that she and he could drink it with the oatmeal water for milk after the Friday herrings they had eaten at two a penny, with an egg apiece for Maggy, Boody and Katey, the cat meanwhile under the mangle devouring a mess of eggshells and charred fish heads and bones on a square of brown paper in accordance with the third precept of the church to fast and abstain on the days commanded, it being quarter tense or, if not, ember days or something like that.

— No, Mr Bloom repeated again, I wouldn't personally repose much trust in that boon companion of yours who contributes the humorous element, Dr Mulligan, as a guide, philosopher, and friend, if I were in your shoes. He knows which side his bread is buttered on through in all probability he never realised what it is to be without regular meals. Of course you didn't notice as much as I did but it wouldn't occasion me the least surprise to learn that a pinch of tobacco or some narcotic was put in your drink for some ulterior object.

He understood, however, from all he heard, that Dr Mulligan was a versatile allround man, by no means confined to medicine only, who was rapidly coming to the fore in his line and, if the report was verified, bade fair to enjoy a flourishing practice in the not too distant future as a tony medical practitioner drawing a handsome fee for his services in addition to which professional status his rescue of that man from certain drowning by artificial respiration and what they call first aid at Skerries, or Malahide was it? was, he was bound to admit, an exceedingly plucky deed which he could not too highly praise, so that frankly he was utterly at a loss to fathom what earthly reason could be at the back of it except he put it down to sheer cussedness or jealousy, pure and simple.

— Except it simply amounts to one thing and he is what they call picking your brains, he ventured to throw out.

The guarded glance of half solicitude, half curiosity, augmented by friendliness which he gave at Stephen's at present morose expression of features did not throw a flood of light, none at all in fact, on the problem as to whether he had let himself be badly bamboozled, to judge by two or three lowspirited remarks he let drop, or, the other way about, saw through the affair, and, for some reason or other best known to himself, allowed matters to more or less... Grinding poverty did have that effect and he more than conjectured that, high educational abilities though he possessed, he experienced no little difficulty in making both ends meet.

Adjacent to the men's public urinal he perceived an icecream car round which a group of presumably Italians in heated altercation were getting rid of voluble expressions in their vivacious language in a particularly animated way, there being some little differences between the parties.

— *Putanna madonna, che ci dia i quattrini! Ho ragione? Culo rotto!*

— *Intendiamoci. Mezzo sovrano più...*

— *Dice lui, però.*

— *Farabutto! Mortacci sui!*

Mr Bloom and Stephen entered the cabman's shelter, an unpretentious wooden structure, where, prior to then, he had rarely, it ever, been before; the former having previously whispered to the latter a few hints anent the keeper of it, said to be the once famous Skin-the-Goat, Fitzharris, the invincible, though he wouldn't vouch for the actual facts, which quite possibly there was not one vestige of truth in. A few moments later saw our two noctambules safely seated in a discreet corner, only to be greeted by stares from the decidedly miscellaneous collection of waifs and strays and other nondescript specimens of the genus *homo,* already there engaged in eating and drinking, diversified by conversation, for whom they seemingly formed an object of marked curiosity.

— Now touching a cup of coffee, Mr Bloom ventured to plausibly suggest to break the ice, it occurs to me you ought to sample something in the shape of solid food, say a roll of some description.

Accordingly his first act was with characteristic *sangfroid* to order these commodities quietly. The *hoi polloi* of jarvies or stevedores, or whatever they were, after a cursory examinatiou, turned their eyes, apparently dissatisfied, away, though one redbearded bibulous individual, portion of whose hair was greyish, a sailor, probably, still stared for some appreciable time before transferring his rapt attention to the floor.

Mr Bloom, availing himself of the right of free speech, he having just a bowing acquaintance with the language in dispute though, to be sure, rather in a quandary over *voglio*, remarked to his *protégé* in an audible tone of voice, *apropos* of the battle royal in the street which was still raging fast and furious :

— A beautiful language. I mean for singing purposes. Why do you not write your poetry in that language? *Bella Poetria!* it is so melodious and full. *Belladonna voglio.*

Stephen, who was trying his dead best to yawn, if he could, suffering from dead lassitude generally, replied :

— To fill the ear of a cow elephant. They were haggling over money.

— Is that so? Mr Bloom asked. Of course, he subjoined pensively, at the inward reflection of there being more languages to start with than were absolutely necessary, it may be only the southern glamour that surrounds it.

The keeper of the shelter in the middle of this *tête-à-tête* put a boiling swimming cup of a choice concoction labelled coffee on the table and a rather antediluvian specimen of a bun, or so it seemed, after which he beat a retreat to his counter. Mr Bloom determining to have a good square look at him later on so as not to appear to... for which reason he encouraged Stephen to proceed with his eyes while he did the honours by surreptitiously pushing the cup of what was temporarily supposed to be called coffee gradually nearer him.

— Sounds are impostures, Stephens aid after a pause of some little time. Like names, Cicero, Podmore, Napoleon, Mr Goodbody, Jesus, Mr Doyle, Shakespeares were as common as Murphies. What's in a name?

— Yes, to be sure, Mr Bloom unaffectedly concurred. Of course. Our name was changed too, he added, pushing the socalled roll across.

The redbearded sailor, who had his weather eye on the newcomers, boarded Stephen, whom he had singled out for attention in particular, squarely by asking :

— And what might your name be?

Just in the nick of time Mr Bloom touched his companion's boot but Stephen, apparently disregarding the warm pressure, from an unexpected quarter, answered :

— Dedalus.

The sailor stared at him heavily from a pair of drowsy baggy eyes, rather bunged up from excessive use of boose, preferably good old Hollands and water.

— You know Simon Dedalus? he asked at length.

— I've heard of him, Stephen said.

Mr Bloom was all at sea for a moment, seeing the others evidently eavesdropping too.

— He's Irish, the seaman bold affirmed, staring still in much the same way and nodding. All Irish.

— All too Irish, Stephen rejoined.

As for Mr Bloom he could neither make head or tail of the whole business and he was just asking himself what possible connection when the sailor, of his own accord, turned to the other occupants of the shelter with the remark :

— I seen him shoot two eggs off two bottles at fifty yards over his shoulder. The left hand dead shot.

Though he was slightly hampered by an occasional stammer and his gestures being also clumsy as it was still he did his best to explain.

— Bottle out there, say. Fifty yards measured. Eggs on the bottles. Cocks his gun over his shoulder. Aims.

He turned his body half round, shut up his right eye completely, then he screwed his features up some way sideways and glared out into the night with an unprepossessing cast of countenance.

— Pom, he then shouted once.

The entire audience waited, anticipating an additional detonation, there being still a further egg.

— Pom, he shouted twice.

— Egg two evidently demolished, he nodded and winked, adding bloodthirstily :

— Buffalo Bill shoots to kill,
Never missed nor he never will.

A silence ensued till Mr Bloom for agreeableness' sake just felt like asking him whether it was for a marksmanship competition like the Bisley.

— Beg pardon, the sailor said.

— Long ago ? Mr Bloom pursued without flinching a hairsbreadth.

— Why, the sailor replied, relaxing to a certain extent under the magic influence of diamond cut diamond, it might be a matter of ten years. He toured the wide world with Hengler's Royal Circus. I seen him do that in Stockholm.

— Curious coincidence, Mr Bloom confided to Stephen unobtrusively.

— Murphy's my name, the sailor continued, W. B. Murphy, of Carrigaloe. Know where that is ?

— Queenstown Harbour, Stephen replied.

— That's right, the sailor said. Fort Camden and Fort Carlisle. That's where I hails from. My little woman's down there. She's waiting for me, I know. *For England, home and beauty*. She's my own true wife I haven't seen for seven years now, sailing about.

Mr Bloom could easily picture his advent on this scene — the homecoming to the mariner's roadside shieling after having diddled Davy Jones — a rainy night with a blind moon. Across the world for a wife. Quite a number of stories there were on that particular Alice Ben Bolt topic, Enoch Arden and Rip van Winkle and does anybody hereabouts remember Caoc O'Leary, a favourite and most trying declamation piece, by the way, of poor John Casey and a bit of perfect poetry in its own small way. Never about the runaway wife coming back, however much devoted to the absentee. The face at the window! Judge of his astonishment when he finelly did breast the tape and the awful truth dawned upon him anent his better half, wrecked in his affections. You little expected me but I've come to stay and make a fresh start. There she sits, a grass widow, at the selfsame fireside. Believes me dead. Rocked in the cradle of the deep. And there sits uncle Chubb or Tomkin, as the case might be, the publican of the Crown and Anchor, in shirtsleeves, eating rumpsteak and onions. No chair for father. Boo! The wind! Her brandnew arrival is on her knee, *post mortem* child. With a high ro! and a randy ro and my galloping tearing tandy O! Bow to the inevitable. Grin and bear it. I remain with much love your brokenhearted husband, W. B. Murphy.

The sailor, who scarcely seemed to be a Dublin resident, turned to one of the jarvies with the request:

— You don't happen to have such a thing as a spare chaw about you, do you?

The jarvey addressed, as it happened, had not but the keeper took a die of plug from his good jacket hanging on a nail and the desired object was passed from hand to hand.

— Thank you, the sailor said.

He deposited the quid in his gob and, chewing, and with some slow stammers, proceeded:

— We come up this morning eleven o'clock. The threemaster *Rosevean* from Bridgwater with bricks. I shipped to get over. Paid off this afternoon. There's my discharge. See? W. B. Murphy, A. B. S.

In confirmation of which statement he extricated from an inside pocket and handed to his neighbours a not very cleanlooking folded document.

— You must have seen a fair share of the world, the keeper remarked, leaning on the counter.

— Why, the sailor answered, upon reflection upon it, I've circumnavigated a bit since I first joined on. I was in the Red Sea. I was in China and North America and South America. I seen icebergs plenty, growlers. I was in Stockholm and the Black Sea, the Dardanelles, under Captain Dalton, the best bloody man that ever scuttled a ship. I seen Russia. *Gospodi pomilooy*. That's how the Russians prays.

— You seen queer sights, don't be talking, put in a jarvey.

— Why, the sailor said, shifting his partially chewed plug, I seen queer things too, ups and downs. I seen a crocodile bite the fluke of an anchor same as I chew that quid.

He took out of his mouth the pulpy quid and, lodging it between his teeth, bit ferociously.

— Khaan! Like that. And I seen maneaters in Peru that eats corpses and the livers of horses. Look here. Here they are. A friend of mine sent me.

He fumbled out a picture postcard from his inside pocket, which seemed to be in its way a species of repository, and pushed it along the table. The printed matter on it stated : *Choza de Indios. Beni, Bolivia.*

All focussed their attention on the scene exhibited, at a group of savage women in striped loincloths, squatted, blinking, suckling, frowning, sleeping, amid a swarm of infants (there must have been quite a score of them) outside some primitive shanties of osier.

— Chews coca all day long, the communicative tarpaulin added. Stomachs like breadgraters. Cuts off their diddies when they can't bear no more children. See them there stark ballocknaked eating a dead horse's liver raw.

His postcard proved a centre of attraction for Messrs the greenhorns for several minutes, if not more.

— Know how to keep them off ? he inquired genially.

Nobody volunteering a statement, he winked, saying :

— Glass. That boggles 'em. Glass.

Mr Bloom, without evincing surprise, unostentatiously turned over the card to peruse the partially obliterated address and postmark. It ran as follows: *Tarjeta Postal. Señor A. Boudin, Galeria Becche, Santiago, Chile.* There was no message evidently, as he took particular notice. Though not an implicit believer in the lurid story narrated (or the eggsniping transaction for that matter despite William Tell and the Lazarillo - Don Cesar de Bazan incident depicted in *Maritana* on which occasion the former's ball passed through the latter's hat) having detected a discrepancy between his name (assuming he was the person he represented himself to be and not sailing under false colours after having boxed the compass on the strict q. t. somewhere), and the fictitious addressee of the missive which made him nourish some suspicions of our friend's *bona fides* nevertheless it reminded him in a way of a longcherished plan he meant to one day realise some Wednesday or Saturday of travelling to London *via* long sea not to say that he had ever travelled extensively to any great extent but he was at heart a born adventurer though by a trick of fate he had consistently remained a landlubber except you call going to Holyhead which was his longest. Martin Cunningham frequently said he would work a pass through Egan but some deuced hitch or other eternally cropped up with the net result that the scheme fell through. But even suppose it did come to planking down the needful and breaking Boyd's heart it was not so dear, purse permitting, a few guineas at the ouside, considering the fare to Mullingar where he figured on going was five and six there and back. The trip would benefit health on account of the bracing ozone and be in every way thoroughly pleasurable, especially for a chap whose liver was out of order, seeing the different places along the route, Plymouth, Falmouth, Southampton and so on, culminating in an instructive tour of the sights of the great metropolis, the spectacle of our modern Babylon where doubtless he would see the greatest improvement tower, abbey, wealth of Park Lane to renew acquaintance with. Another thing just struck him as a by no means bad notion was he might have a gaze around on the spot to see about trying to make arrangements about a concert tour of summer music embracing the most prominent pleasure resorts, Margate with mixed bathing and firstrate hydros and spas, Eastbourne, Scarborough, Margate and so on, beautiful Bournemouth, the Channel islands and similar bijou spots, which might prove highly remunerative. Not, of course, with a hole and corner scratch company or local ladies on the job, witness Mrs C. P. M'Coy type — lend me your valise and I'll post you the ticket. No, something top notch, an all star Irish caste, the Tweedy-Flower grand opera company with his own legal consort as leading lady as a sort of counterblast to the Elster Grimes and Moody-Manners, perfectly simple matter and he was quite sanguine of success, providing puffs in the local papers could be managed by some fellow with a bit of bounce who could pull the indispensable wires and thus combine business with pleasure. But who? That was the rub.

Also, without being actually positive, it struck him a great field was to be opened up in the line of opening up new routes to keep pace with the times *apropos* of the Fishguard-Rosslare route which, it was mooted, was once more on the *tapis* in the circumlocution departments with the usual quantity of red tape and dillydallying of effete fogeydom and dunderheads generally. A great opportunity there certainly was for push and enterprise to meet the travelling needs of the public at large, the average man, i. e. Brown, Robinson and Co.

It was a subject of regret and absurd as well on the face of it and no small blame to our vaunted society that the man in the street, when the system really needed toning up, for a matter of a couple of paltry pounds, was debarred from seeing more of the world they lived in instead of being always cooped up since my old stick-in-the-mud took me for a wife. After all, hang it, they had their eleven and more humdrum months of it and merited a radical change of *venue* after the grind of city life in the summertime, for choice, when Dame Nature is at her spectacular best, constituting nothing short of a new lease of life. There were equally excellent opportunities for vacationists in the home island, delightful sylvan spots for rejuvenation, offering a plethora of attractions as well as a bracing tonic for the system in and around Dublin and its picturesque environs, even, Poulaphouca, to which there was a steam tram, but also farther away from the madding crowd, in Wicklow, rightly termed the garden of Ireland, an ideal neighbourhood for elderly wheelmen, so long as it didn't come down, and in the wilds of Donegal where, if report spoke true, the *coup d'œil* was exceedingly grand, though the lastnamed locality was not easily getatable so that the influx of visitors was not as yet all that it might be considering the signal benefits to be derived from it, while Howth with its historic associations and otherwise, Silken Thomas, Grace O'Malley, George IV, rhododendrons several hundred feet above sealevel was a favourite haunt with all sorts and conditions of men, especially in the spring when young men's fancy, though it had its own toll of deaths by falling off the cliffs by design or accidentally, usually, by the way, on their left leg, it being only about three quarters of an hour's run from the pillar. Because of course uptodate tourist travelling was as yet merely in its infancy, so to speak, and the accommodation left much to be desired. Interesting to fathom, it seemed to him, from a motive of curiosity pure and simple, was whether it was the traffic that created the route or viceversa or the two sides in fact. He turned back the other side of the card picture and passed it along to Stephen.

— I seen a Chinese one time, related the doughty narrator, that had little pills like putty and he put them in the water and they opened, and every pill was something different. One was a ship, another was a house, another was a flower. Cooks rats in your soup, he appetisingly added, the Chinese does.

Possibly perceiving an expression of dubiosity on their faces, the globetrotter went on adhering to his adventures.

— And I seen a man killed in Trieste by an Italian chap. Knife in his back. Knife like that.

Whilst speaking he produced a dangerous looking claspknife, quite in keeping with his character, and held it in the striking position.

— In a knockingshop it was count of a tryon between two smugglers. Fellow hid behind a door, come up behind him. Like that. *Prepare to meet your God,* says he. Chuk! It went into his back up to the butt.

His heavy glance, drowsily roaming about, kind of defied their further questions even should they by any chance want to. That's a good bit of steel, repeated he, examining his formidable *stiletto.*

After which harrowing *dénouement* sufficient to appal the stoutest he snapped the blade to and stowed the weapon in question away as before in his chamber of horrors, otherwise pocket.

— They're great for the cold steel, somebody who was evidently quite in the dark said for the benefit of them all. That was why they thought the park murders of the invincibles was done by foreigners on account of them using knives.

At this remark, passed obviously in the spirit of *where ignorance is bliss,* Mr Bloom and Stephen, each in his own particular way, both instinctively exchanged meaning glances, in a religious silence of the strictly *entre nous* variety however, towards where Skin-the-Goat, *alias* the keeper, was drawing spurts of liquid from his boiler affair. His inscrutable face, which was really a work of art, a perfect study in itself, beggaring description, conveyed the impression that he didn't understand one jot of what was going on. Funny, very.

There ensued a somewhat lengthy pause. One man was reading by fits and starts a stained by coffee evening journal; another, the card with the natives *choza de*; another, the seaman's discharge. Mr Bloom, so far as he was personally concerned, was just pondering in pensive mood. He vividly recollected when the occurrence alluded to took place as well as yesterday, some score of years previously, in the days of the land troubles when it took the civilised world by storm, figuratively speaking, early in the eighties, eightyone to be correct, when he was just turned fifteen.

— Ay, boss, the sailor broke in. Give us back them papers.

The request being complied with, he clawed them up with a scrape.

— Have you seen the Rock of Gibraltar? Mr Bloom inquired.

The sailor grimaced, chewing, in a way that might be read as yes, ay, or no.

— Ah, you've touched there too, Mr Bloom said, Europa point, thinking he had, in the hope that the rover might possibly by some reminiscences but he failed to do so, simply letting spurt a jet of spew into the sawdust, and shook his head with a sort of lazy scorn.

— What year would that be about? Mr Bloom interpolated. Can you recall the boats?

Our *soi-disant* sailor munched heavily awhile, hungrily, before answering.

— I'm tired of all them rocks in the sea, he said, and boats and ships. Salt junk all the time.

Tired, seemingly, he ceased. His questioner, perceiving that he was not likely to get a great deal of change out of such a wily old customer, fell to woolgathering on the enormous dimensions of the water about the globe. Suffice it to say that, as a casual glance at the map revealed, it covered fully three fourths of it and he fully realised accordingly what it meant, to rule the waves. On more than one occasion — a dozen at the lowest — near the North Bull at Dollymount he had remarked a superannuated old salt, evidently derelict, seated habitually near the not particularly redolent sea on the wall, staring quite obviously at it and it at him, dreaming of fresh woods and pastures new as someone somewhere sings. And it left him wondering why. Possibly he had tried to find out the secret for himself, floundering up and down the antipodes and all that sort of thing and over and under — well, not exactly under — tempting the fates. And the odds were twenty to nil there was really no secret about it at all. Nevertheless, without going into the *minutiae* of the business, the eloquent fact remained that the sea was there in all its glory and in the natural course of things somebody or other had to sail on it and fly in the face of providence though it merely went to show how people usually contrived to load that sortof onus on to the other fellow like the hell idea and the lottery and insurance, which were run on identically the same lines so that for that very reason, if no other, lifeboat Sunday was a very laudable institution to which the public at large, no matter where living, inland or seaside, as the case might be, having it brought home to them like that, should extend its gratitude also to the harbourmasters and coastguard service who had to man the rigging and push off and out amid the elements, whatever the season, when duty called *Ireland expects that every man* and so on, and sometimes had a terrible time ot it in the wintertime not forgetting the Irish lights, Kish and others, liable to capsize at any moment rounding which he once with his daughter had experienced some remarkably choppy, not to say stormy, weather.

— There was a fellow sailed with me in the *Rover*, the old seadog, himself a rover, proceeded. Went ashore and took up a soft job as gentleman's valet at six quid a month. Them are his trousers I've on me and he gave me an oilskin and that jackknife. I'm game for that job, shaving and brushup. I hate roaming about. There's my son now, Danny, run off to sea and his mother got him took in a draper's in Cork where he could be drawing easy money.

— What age is he? queried one hearer who, by the way, seen from the side, bore a distant resemblance to Henry Campbell, the townclerk, away from the carking cares of office, unwashed, of course, and in a seedy getup and a a strong suspicion of nosepaint about the nasal appendage.

— Why, the sailor answered with a slow puzzled utterance. My son Danny? He'd be about eighteen now, way I figure it.

The Skibereen father hereupon tore open his grey or unclean anyhow shirt with his two hands and scratched away at his chest on which was to be seen an image tattooed in blue Chinese ink, intended to represent an anchor.

— There was lice in that bunk in Bridgwater, he remarked. Sure as nuts. I must get a wash tomorrow or next day. It's them black lads I objects to. I hate those buggers. Sucks your blood dry, they does.

Seeing they were all looking at his chest, he accomodatingly dragged his shirt more open so that, on top of the timehonoured symbol of the mariner's hope and rest, they had a full view of the figure 16 and a young man's sideface looking frowningly rather.

— Tattoo, the exhibitor explained. That was done when we were lying becalmed off Odessa in the Black Sea under Captain Dalton. Fellow the name of Antonio done that. There he is himself, a Greek.

— Did it hurt much doing it? one asked the sailor.

That worthy, however, was busily engaged in collecting round the someway in his. Squeezing or...

— See here, he said, showing Antonio. There he is, cursing the mate. And there he is now, he added. The same fellow, pulling the skin with his fingers, some special knack evidently, and he laughing at a yarn.

And in point of fact the young man named Antonio's livid face did actually look like forced smiling and the curious effect excited the unreserved admiration of everybody, including Skin-the-Goat who this time stretched over.

— Ay, ay, sighed the sailor, looking down on his manly chest. He's gone too. Ate by sharks after. Ay, ay.

He let go of the skin so that the profile resumed the normal expression of before.

— Neat bit of work, longshoreman one said.

— And what's the number for? loafer number two queried.

— Eaten alive? a third asked the sailor.

— Ay, ay, sighed again the latter personage, more cheerily this time, with some sort of a half smile, for a brief duration only, in the direction of the questioner about the number. A Greek he was.

And then he added, with rather gallowsbird humour, considering his alleged end:

— *As bad as old Antonio,*
For he left me on my ownio.

The face of a streetwalker, glazed and haggard under a black straw hat, peered askew round the door of the shelter, palpably reconnoitring on her own with the object of bringing more grist to her mill. Mr Bloom, scarcely knowing which way to look, turned away on the moment, flusterfied but outwardly calm, and picking up from the table the pink sheet of the Abbey street organ which the jarvey, if such he was, had laid aside, he picked it up and looked at the pink of the paper though why pink? His reason for so doing was he recognised on the moment round the door the same face he had caught a fleeting glimpse of that afternoon on Ormond Quay, the partially idiotic female, namely, of the lane, who knew the lady in the brown costume does be with you (Mrs B.), and begged the chance of his washing. Also why washing, which seemed rather vague than not?

Your washing. Still, candour compelled him to admit that he had washed his wife's undergarments when soiled in Holles Street and women would and did too a man's similar garments initialled with Bewley and Draper's marking ink (hers were, that is) if they really loved him, that is to say. Love me, love my dirty shirt. Still, just then, being on tenterhooks, he desired the female's room more than her company so it came as a genuine relief when the keeper made her a rude sign to take herself off. Round the side of the

Evening Telegraph he just caught a fleeting glimpse of her face round the side of the door with a kind of demented glassy grin showing that she was not exactly all there, viewing with evident amusement the group of gazers round Skipper Murphy's nautical chest and then there was no more of her.

— The gunboat, the keeper said.

— It beats me, Mr Bloom confided to Stephen, medically I am speaking, how a wretched creature like that from the Lock Hospital, reeking with disease, can be barefaced enough to solicit or how any man in his sober senses, if he values his health in the least. Unfortunate creature! Of course, I suppose some man is ultimately responsible for her condition. Still no matter what the cause is from...

Stephen had not noticed her and shrugged his shoulders, merely remarking:

— In this country people sell much more than she ever had and do a roaring trade. Fear not them that sell the body but have not power to buy the soul. She is a bad merchant. She buys dear and sells cheap.

The elder man, though not by any manner of means an old maid or a prude, said that it was nothing short of a crying scandal that ought to be put a stop to *instanter* to say that women of that stamp (quite apart from any oldmaidish squeamishness on the subject), a necessary evil, were not licensed and medically inspected by the proper authorities, a thing he could truthfully state he, as a *paterfamilias,* was a stalwart advocate of from the very first start. Whoever embarked on a policy of the sort, he said, and ventilated the matter thoroughly would confer a lasting boon on everybody concerned.

— You, as a good catholic, he observed, talking of body and soul, believe in the soul. Or do you mean the intelligence, the brainpower as such, as distinct from any outside object, the table, let us say, that cup? I believe in that myself because it has been explained by competent men as the convolutions of the grey matter. Otherwise we would never have such inventions as X rays, for instance. Do you?

Thus cornered, Stephen had to make a superhuman effort of memory to try and concentrate and remember before he could say.

— They tell me on the best authority it is a simple substance and therefore incorruptible. It would be immortal, I understand, but for the possibility of its annihilation by its First Cause, Who, from all I can hear, is quite capable of adding that to the number of His other practical jokes, *corruptio per se* and *corruptio per accidens* both being excluded by court etiquette.

Mr Bloom thoroughly acquiesced in the general gist of this though the mystical finesse involved was a bit out of his sublunary depth still he felt bound to enter a demurrer on the head of simple, promptly rejoining :

— Simple? I shouldn't think that is the proper word. Of course, I grant you, to concede a point, you do knock across a simple soul once in a blue moon. But what I am anxious to arrive at is it is one thing for instance to invent those rays Röngten did, or the telescope like Edison, though I believe it was before his time, Galileo was the man I mean. The same applies to the laws, for example, of a farreaching natural phenomenon such as electricity but it's a horse of quite another colour to say you believe in the existence of a supernatural God.

— O that, Stephen expostulated, has been proved conclusively by several of the best known passages in Holy Writ, apart from circumstantial evidence.

On this knotty point, however, the views of the pair, poles apart as they were, both in schooling and everything else, with the marked difference in their respective ages, clashed.

— Has been ? the more experienced of the two objected, sticking to his original point. I'm not so sure about that. That's a matter of every man's opinion and, without dragging in the sectarian side of the business, I beg to differ with you *in toto* there. My belief is, to tell you the candid truth, that those bits were genuine forgeries all of them put in by monks most probably or it's the big question of our national poet over again, who precisely wrote them, like *Hamlet* and Bacon, as you who know your Shakespeare infinitely better than I, of course I needn't tell you. Can't you drink that coffee, by the way ? Let me stir it and take a piece of that bun. It's like one of our skipper's bricks disguised. Still, no one can give what he hasn't got. Try a bit.

— Couldn't, Stephen contrived to get out, his mentlal organs for the moment refusing to dictate further.

Faultfinding being a proverbially bad hat, Mr Bloom thought well to stir, or try to, the clotted sugar from the bottom and reflected with something approaching acrimony on the Coffee Palace and its temperance (and lucrative) work. To be sure it was a legitimate object and beyond yea or nay did a world of good. Shelters such as the present one they were in run on teetotal lines for vagrants at night, concerts, dramatic evenings, and useful lectures (admittance free) by qualified men for the lower orders. On the other hand, he had a distinct and painful recollection they paid his wife, Madam Marion Tweedy who had been prominently associated with it at one time, a very modest remuneration indeed for her pianoplaying. The idea he was strongly inclined to believe, was to do good and net a profit, there being no competition to speak of. Sulphate of copper poison, S O_4 or something in some dried peas he remembered reading of in a cheap eatinghouse somewhere but he couldn't remember when it was or where. Anyhow, inspection, medical inspection, of all eatables, seemed to him more than ever necessary which possibly accounted for the vogue of Dr Tibble's Vi-Cocoa on account of the medical analysis involved.

— Have a shot at it now, he ventured to say of the coffee after being stirred.

Thus prevailed on to at any rate taste it, Stephen lifted the heavy mug from the brown puddle — it clopped out of it when taken up — by the handle and took a sip of the offending beverage.

— Still, it's solid food, his good genius urged, I'm a stickler for solid food, his one and only reason being not gormandising in the least but regular meals as the *sine qua non* for any kind of proper work, mental or manual. You ought to eat more solid food. You would feel a different man.

— Liquids I can eat, Stephen said. But oblige me by taking away that knife. I can't look at the point of it. It reminds me of Roman history.

Mr Bloom promptly did as suggested and removed the incriminated article, a blunt hornhandled ordinary knife with nothing particularly Roman or antique about it to the lay eye, observing that the point was the least conspicuous point about it.

— Our mutual friend's stories are like himself, Mr Bloom, *apropos* of knives, remarked to his *confidante sotto voce*. Do you think they are genuine? He could spin those yarns for hours on end all night long and lie like old boots. Look at him.

Yet still, though his eyes were thick with sleep and sea air, life was full of a host of things and coincidences of a terrible nature and it was quite within the bounds of possibility that it was not an entire fabrication though at first blush there was not much inherent probability in all the spoof he got off his chest being strictly accurate gospel.

He had been meantime taking stock of the individual in front of him and Sherlockholmesing him up, ever since he clapped eyes on him. Though a wellpreserved man of no little stamina, if a trifle prone to baldness, there was something spurious in the cut of his jib that suggested a jail delivery and it required no violent stretch of imagination to associate such a weirdlooking specimen with the oakum and treadmill fraternity.

He might even have done for his man, supposing it was his own case he told, as people often did about others, namely, that he killed him himself and had served his four or five goodlooking years in durance vile to say nothing of the Antonio personage (no relation to the dramatic personage of identical name who sprang from the pen of our national poet) who expiated his crimes in the melodramatic manner above described. On the other hand he might be only bluffing, a pardonable weakness, because meeting unmistakable mugs, Dublin residents, like those jarvies waiting news from abroad, would tempt any ancient mariner who sailed the ocean seas to draw the long bow about the schooner *Hesperus* and etcetera. And when all was said and done, the lies a fellow told about himself couldn't probably hold a proverbial candle to the wholesale whoppers other fellows coined about him.

— Mind you, I'm not saying that it's all a pure invention, he resumed. Analogous scenes are occasionally, if not often, met with. Giants, though, that is rather a far cry you see once in a way. Marcella, the midget queen. In those waxworks in Henry street I myself saw some Aztecs, as they are called, sitting bowlegged. They couldn't straighten their legs if you paid them because the muscles here, you see, he proceeded, indicating on his companion the brief outline, the sinews, or whatever you like to call them, behind the right knee, were utterly powerless from sitting that way so long cramped up, being adored as gods. There's an example again of simple souls.

However, reverting to friend Sinbad and his horrifying adventures (who reminded him a bit of Ludwig, *alias* Ledwidge, when he occupied the boards of the Gaiety when Michael Gunn was identified with the management in the *Flying Dutchman*, a stupendous success, and his host of admirers came in large numbers, everyone simply flocking to hear him though ships of any sort, phantom or the reverse, on the stage usually fell a bit flat as also did trains), there was nothing intrinsically incompatible about it, he conceded. On the contrary, that stab in the back touch was quite in keeping with those Italianos, though candidly he was none the less free to admit those ice creamers and friers in the fish way, not to mention the chip potato variety and so forth, over in little Italy there, near the Coombe, were sober thrifty hardworking fellows except perhaps a bit too given to pothunting the harmless necessary animal of the feline persuasion of others at night so as to have a good old succulent tuckink with garlic *de rigueur* off him or her next day on the quiet and, he added, on the cheap.

— Spaniards, for instance, he continued, passionate temperaments like that, impetuous as Old Nick, are given to taking the law into their own hands and give you your quietus double quick with those poignards they carry in the abdomen. It comes from the great heat, climate generally. My wife is, so to speak, Spanish, half, that is. Point of fact she could actually claim Spanish nationality if she wanted, having been born in (technically) Spain, i. e. Gibraltar. She has the Spanish type. Quite dark, regular brunette, black. I, for one, certainly believe climate accounts for character. That's why I asked you if you wrote your poetry in Italian.

— The temperaments at the door, Stephen interposed with, were very passionate about ten shillings. *Roberto ruba roba sua.*

— Quite so, Mr Bloom dittoed.

— Then, Stephen said, staring and rambling on to himself or some unknown listener somewhere, we have the impetuosity of Dante and the isosceles triangle, Miss Portinari, he fell in love with and Leonardo and san Tommaso Mastino.

— It's in the blood, Mr Bloom acceded at once. All are washed in the blood of the sun. Coincidence, I just happened to be in the Kildare Street Museum today, shortly prior to our meeting, if I can so call it, and I was just looking at those antique statues there. The splendid proportions of hips, bosom. You simply don't knock against those kind of women here. An exception here and there. Handsome, yes, pretty in a way you find, but what I'm talking about is the female form. Besides, they have so little taste in dress, most of them, which greatly enhances a woman's natural beauty, no matter what you say. Rumpled stockings — it may be, possibly is, a foible of mine, but still it's a thing I simply hate to see.

Interest, however, was starting to flag somewhat all round and the others got on to talking about accidents at sea, ships lost in a fog, collisions with icebergs, all that sort of thing. Shipahoy, of course, had his own say to say. He had doubled the Cape a few odd times and weathered a monsoon, a kind of wind, in the China seas and through all those perils of the deep there was one thing, he declared, stood to him, or words to that effect, a pious medal he had that saved him.

So then after that they drifted on to the wreck of Daunt's rock, wreck of that illfated Norwegian barque — nobody could think of her name for the moment till the jarvey who had really quite a look of Henry Campbell remembered it, *Palme*, on Booterstown Strand, that was the talk of the town that year (Albert William Quill wrote a fine piece of original verse of distinctive merit on the topic for the Irish *Times*) breakers running over her and crowds and crowds on the shore in commotion petrified with horror. Then someone said something about the case of the s. s. *Lady Cairns* of Swansea, run into by the *Mona*, which was on an opposite tack, in rather muggyish weather and lost with all hands on deck. No aid was given. Her master, the *Mona*'s, said he was afraid his collision bulkhead would give way. She had no water, it appears, in her hold.

At this stage an incident happened. It having become necessary for him to unfurl a reef, the sailor vacated his seat.

— Let me cross your bows, mate, he said to his neighbour, who was just gently dropping off into a peaceful doze.

He made tracks heavily, slowly, with a dumpy sort of a gait to the door, stepped heavily down the one step there was out of the shelter and bore due left. While he was in the act of getting his bearings, Mr Bloom, who noticed when he stood up that he had two flasks of presumably ship's rum sticking one out of each pocket for the private consumption of his burning interior, saw him produce a bottle and uncork it, or unscrew, and, applying its nozzle to his lips, take a good old delectable swig out of it with a gurgling noise. The irrepressible Bloom, who also had a shrewd suspicion that the old stager went out on a manœuvre after the counterattraction in the shape of a female, who, however, had disappeared to all intents and purposes, could, by straining, just perceive him, when duly refreshed, by his rum puncheon exploit, gazing up at the piers and girders of the Loop Line, rather out of his depth, as of course it was all radically altered since his last visit and greatly improved. Some person or persons invisible directed him to the male urinal erected by the cleansing committee all over the place for the purpose but, after a brief space of time during which silence reigned supreme, the sailor, evidently giving it a wide berth, eased himself close at hand, the noise of his bilgewater some little time subsequently splashing on the ground where it apparently woke a horse of the cabrank.

A hoof scooped anyway for new foothold after sleep and harness jingled. Slightly disturbed in his sentrybox by the brazier of live coke, the watcher of the corporation, who, though now broken down and fast breaking up, was none other in stern reality than the Gumley aforesaid, now practically on the parish rates, given the temporary job by Pat Tobin in all human probability, from dictates of humanity, knowing him before — shifted about and shuffled in his box before composing his limbs again in the arms of Morpheus. A truly amazing piece of hard times in its most virulent form on a fellow most respectably connected and familiarised with decent home comforts all his life who came in for a cool £ 100 a year at one time which of course the doublebarrelled ass proceeded to make general ducks and drakes of. And there he was at the end of his tether after having often painted the town tolerably pink, without a beggarly stiver. He drank, needless to be told, and it pointed only once more a moral when he might quite easily be in a large way of business if — a big if, however — he had contrived to cure himself of his particular partiality.

All, meantime, were loudly lamenting the falling off in Irish shipping, coastwise and foreign as well, which was all part and parcel of the same thing. A Palgrave Murphy boat was put off the ways at Alexandra Basin, the only launch that year. Right enough the harbours were there only no ships ever called.

There were wrecks and wrecks, the keeper said, who was evidently *au fait*.

What he wanted to ascertain was why that ship ran bang against the only rock in Galway Bay when the Galway Harbour scheme was mooted by a Mr Worthington or some name like that, eh? Ask her captain, he advised them, how much palmoil the British Government gave him for that day's work. Captain John Lever of the Lever line.

— Am I right, skipper? he queried of the sailor now returning after his private potation and the rest of his exertions.

That worthy, picking up the scent of the fagend of the song or words, growled in wouldbe music, but with great vim, some kind of chanty or other in seconds or thirds. Mr Bloom's sharp ears heard him then expectorate the plug probably (which it was), so that he must have lodged it for the time being in his fist while he did the drinking and making water jobs and found it a bit sour after the liquid fire in question. Anyhow in he rolled after his successful libation — *cum* — potation, introducing an atmosphere of drink into the *soirée*, boisterously trolling, like a veritable son of a seacook:

— *The biscuits was as hard as brass,*
And the beef as salt as Lot's wife's arse.
O Johnny Lever!
Johnny Lever, O!

After which effusion the redoutable specimen duly arrived on the scene and, regaining his seat, he sank rather than sat heavily on the form provided.

Skin-the-Goat, assuming he was he, evidently with an axe to grind, was airing his grievances in a forcible-feeble philippic anent the natural resources of Ireland, or something of that sort, which he described in his lengthy dissertation as the richest country bar none on the face of God's earth, far and away superior to England, with coal in large quantities, six million pounds' worth of pork exported every year, ten millions between butter and eggs, and all the riches drained out of it by England levying taxes on the poor people that paid through the nose always, and gobbling up the best meat in the market, and a lot more surplus steam in the same vein. Their conversation accordingly became general and all agreed that that was a fact. You could grow any mortal thing in Irish soil, he stated, and there was Colonel Everard down there in Cavan growing tobacco. Where would you find anywhere the like of Irish bacon? But a day of reckoning, he stated *crescendo* with no uncertain voice — thoroughly monopolising all the conversation — was in store for mighty England, despite her power of pelf on account of her crimes. There would be a fall and the greatest fall in history. The Germans and the Japs were going to have their little lookin, he affirmed. The Boers were the beginning of the end. Brummagem England was toppling already and her downfall would be Ireland, her Achilles heel, which he explained to them about the vulnerable point ot Achilles, the Greek hero — a point his auditors at once seized as he completely gripped their attention by showing the tendon referred to on his boot. His advice to every Irishman was: stay in the land of your birth and work for Ireland and live for Ireland. Ireland, Parnell said, could not spare a single one of her sons.

Silence all round marked the termination of his *finale*. The impervious navigator heard these lurid tidings undismayed.

— Take a bit of doing, boss, retaliated that rough diamond palpably a bit peeved in response to the foregoing truism.

To which cold douche, referring to downfall and so on, the keeper concurred but nevertheless held to his main view.

— Who's the best troops in the army? the grizzled old veteran irately interrogated. And the best jumpers and racers? And the best admirals and generals we've got? Tell me that.

— The Irish for choice, retorted the cabby like Campbell, facial blemishes apart.

— That's right, the old tarpaulin corroborated. The Irish catholic peasant. He's the backbone of our empire. You know Jem Mullins ?

While allowing him his individual opinions, as every man, the keeper added he cared nothing for any empire, ours or his, and considered no Irishman worthy of his salt that served it. Then they began to have a few irascible words, when it waxed hotter, both, needless to say, appealing to the listeners who followed the passage of arms with interest so long as they didn't indulge in recriminations and come to blows.

From inside information extending over a series of years Mr Bloom was rather inclined to poohpooh the suggestion as egregious balderdash for, pending that consummation devoutly to be or not to be wished for, he was fully cognisant of the fact that their neighbours across the channel, unless they were much bigger fools than he took them for, rather concealed their strength than the opposite. It was quite on a par with the quixotic idea in certain quarters that in a hundred million years the coal seam of the sister island would be played out and if, as time went on, that turned out to be how the cat jumped all he could personally say on the matter was that as a host of contingencies, equally relevant to the isssue, might occur ere then it was highly advisable in the interim to try to make the most of both countries, even though poles apart. Another littleinteresting point, the amours of whores and chummies, to put it in common parlance, reminded him Irish soldiers had as often fought for England as against her, more so, in fact. And now, why ? So the scene between the pair of them, the licensee of the place, rumoured to be or have been Fitzharris, the famous invincible, and the other, obviously bogus, reminded him forcibly as being on all fours with the confidence trick, supposing, that is, it was prearranged, as the lookeron, a student of the human soul, if anything, the others seeing least of the game. And as for the lessee or keeper, who probably wasn't the other person at all, he (Bloom) couldn't help feeling, and most properly, it was better to give people like that the goby unless you were a blithering idiot altogether and refuse to have anything to do with them as a golden rule in private life and their felonsetting, there always being the offchance of a Dannyman coning forward and turning queen's evidence — or king's, now — like Denis or Peter Carey, an idea he utterly repudiated. Quite apart from that, he disliked those careers of wrongdoing and crime on principle. Yet, though such criminal propensities had never been an inmate of his bosom in any shape or form, he certainly did feel, and no denying it (while inwardly remaining what he was), a certain kind of admiration for a man who had actually brandished a knife, cold steel, with the courage of his political convictions though, personally, he would never be a party to any such thing, off the same bat as those love vendettas of the south — have her or swing for her — when the husband frequently, after some words passed between the two concerning her relations with the other lucky mortal (he man having had the pair watched) inflicted fatal injuries on his adored one as a result of an alternative postnuptial *liaison* by plunging his knife into her until it just struck him that Fitz, nicknamed Skin-the-Goat, merely drove the car for the actual perpetrators of the outrage and so was not, if he was reliabl-- informed, actually party to the ambush which, in point of fact, was the plea some legal luminary saved his skin on. In any case that was very ancient history by now and as for our friend, the pseudo Skin-the-etcetera, he had transparently outlived his welcome. He ought to have either died naturally or on the scaffold high. Like actresses, always farewell — positively last performance — then come up smiling again. Generous to a fault, of course, temperamental, no economising or any idea of the sort, always snapping at the bone for the shadow. So similarly he had a very shrewd suspicion that Mr Johnny Lever got rid of some £. s. d. in the course of his perambulations round the docks in the congenial atmosphere of the *Old Ireland* tavern, come back to Erin and so on. Then as for the others, he had heard not so long before the same identical lingo, as he told Stephen how he simply but effectually silenced the offender.

— He took umbrage at something or other, that muchinjured but on the whole eventempored person declared, I let slip. He called me a jew, and in a heated fashion, offensively. So I, without deviating from plain facts in the least, told him his God, I mean Christ, was a jew too, and all his family, like me, though in reality I'm not. That was one for him. A soft answer turns away wrath. He hadn't a word to say for himself as everyone saw. Am I not right?

He turned a long you are wrong gaze on Stephen of timorous dark pride at the soft impeachment, with a glance also of entreaty for he seemed to glean in a kind of a way that it wasn't all exactly...

— *Ex quibus*, Stephen mumbled in a noncommital accent, their two or four eyes conversing. *Christus* or Bloom his name is, or, after all, any other, *secundum carnem.*

— Of course, Mr Bloom proceeded to stipulate, you must look at both sides of the question. It is hard to lay down any hard and fast rules as to right and wrong but room for improvement all round there certainly is though every country, they say, our own distressful included, has the government it deserves. But with a little goodwill all round. It's all very fine to boast of mutual superiority but what about mutual equality ? I resent violence or intolerance in any shape or form. It never reaches anything or stops anything. A revolution must come on the due instalments plan. It's a patent absurdity on the face of it to hate people because they live round the corner and speak another vernacular, so to speak.

— Memorable bloody bridge battle and seven minutes' war, Stephen assented, between Skinner's alley and Ormond market.

— Yes, Mr Bloom thoroughly agreed, entirely endorsing the remark, that was overwhelmingly right and the whole world was overwhelmingly full of that sort of thing.

— You just took the words out of my mouth, he said. A hocuspocus of conflicting evidence that candidly you couldn't remotely...

All those wretched quarrels, in his humble opinion, stirring up bad blood — bump of combativeness or gland of some kind, erroneously supposed to be about a punctilio of honour and a flag, — were very largely a question of the money question which was at the back of everything, greed and jealousy, people never knowing when to stop.

— They accuse — remarked he audibly. He turned away from the others, who probably... and spoke nearer to, so as the others... in case they...

— Jews, he softly imparted in an aside in Stephen's ear, are accused of ruining. Not a vestige of truth in it, I can safely say. History, — would you be surprised to learn ? — proves up to the hilt Spain decayed when the Inquisition hounded the jews out and England prospered when Cromwell, an uncommonly able ruffian, who, in other respects has much to answer for, imported them. Why ? Because they are practical and are proved to be so. I don't want to indulge in any... because you know the standard works on the subject, and then, orthodox as you are... But in the economic, not touching religion, domain, the priest spells poverty. Spain again, you saw in the war, compared with goahead America. Turks, it's in the dogma. Because if they didn't believe they'd go straight to heaven when they die they'd try to live better — at least, so I think. That's the juggle on which the p. p.'s raise the wind on false pretences. I'm, he resumed, with dramatic force, as good an Irishman as that rude person I told you about at the outset and I want to see everyone, concluded he, all creeds and classes *pro rata* having a comfortable tidysized income, in no niggard fashion either, something in the neighbourhood of £ 300 per annum. That's the vital issue at stake and it's feasible and would be provocative of friendlier intercourse between man and man. At least that's my idea for what it's worth. I call that patriotism. *Ubi patria,* as we learned a small smattering of in our classical day in *Alma Mater, vita beni.* Where you can live well, the sense is, if you work.

Over his untasteable apology for a cup of coffee, listening to this synopsis of things in general, Stephen stared at nothing in particular. He could hear, of course, all kinds of words changing colour like those crabs about Ringsend in the morning, burrowing quickly into all colours of different sorts of the same sand where they had a home somewhere beneath or seemed to. Then he looked up and saw the eyes that said or didn't say the words the voice he heard said — if you work.

— Count me out, he managed to remark, meaning to work.

The eyes were surprised at this observation, because as he, the person who owned them pro. tem. observed, or rather, his voice speaking did: All must work, have to, together.

— I mean, of course, the other hastened to affirm, work in the widest possible sense. Also literary labour, not merely for the kudos of the thing. Writing for the newspapers which is the readiest channel nowadays. That's work too. Important work. After all, from the little I know of you, after all the money expended on your education, you are entitled to recoup yourself and command your price. You have every bit as much right to live by your pen in pursuit of your philosophy as the peasant has. What? You both belong to Ireland, the brain and the brawn. Each is equally important.

— You suspect, Stephen retorted with a sort of a half laugh, that I may be important because I belong to the *faubourg Saint-Patrice* called Ireland for short.

— I would go a step farther, Mr Bloom insinuated.

— But I suspect, Stephen interrupted, that Ireland must be important because it belongs to me.

— What belongs? queried Mr Bloom, bending, fancying he was perhaps under some misapprehension. Excuse me. Unfortunately I didn't catch the latter portion. What was it you?...

Stephen, patently crosstempered, repeated and shoved aside his mug of coffee, or whatever you like to call it, none too politely, adding:

— We can't change the country. Let us change the subject.

At this pertinent suggestion, Mr Bloom, to change the subject, looked down, but in a quandary, as he couldn't tell exactly what construction to put on belongs to which sounded rather a far cry. The rebuke of some kind was clearer than the other part. Needless to say, the fumes of his recent orgy spoke then which some asperity in a curious bitter way, foreign to his sober state. Probably the home life, to which Mr Bloom attached the utmost importance, had not been all that was needful or he hadn't been familiarised with the the right sort of people. With a touch of fear for the young man beside him, whom he furtively scrutinised with an air of some consternation, remembering he had just come back from Paris, the eyes more especially reminding him forcibly of father and sister, failing to throw much light on the subject, however, he brought to mind instances of cultured fellows that promised so brilliantly, nipped in the bud of premature decay. and nobody to blame but themselves. For instance, there was the case of O'Callaghan, for one, the half crazy faddist, respectably connected, though of inadequate means, with his mad vagaries, among whose other gay doings when rotto and making himself a nuisance to everybody all round he was in the habit of ostentatiously sporting in public a suit of brown paper (a fact). And then the usual *dénouement* after the fun had gone on fast and furious he got landed into hot water and had to be spirited away by a few friends, after a strong hint to a blind horse from John Mallon of Lower Castle Yard, so as not to be made amenable under section two of the Criminal Law Amendment Act, certain names of those subpœnaed being handed in but not divulged, for reasons which will occur to anyone with a pick of brains. Briefly, putting two and two together, six sixteen, which he pointedly turned a deaf ear to, Antonio and so forth, jockeys and esthetesand the tattoo which was all the go in the seventies or thereabouts, even in the House of Lords, because early in life the occupant of the throne, then heir apparent, the other members of the upper ten and other high personages simply following in the footsteps of the head of the state, he reflected about the errors of notorieties and crowned heads running counter to morality such as the Cornwall case a number of years before under their veneer in a way scarcely intended by nature, a thing good Mrs Grundy as the law stands, was terribly down on, though not for the reason they thought they were probably, whatever it was, except women chiefly, who were always fiddling more or less at one another, it being largely a matter of dress and all the rest of it. Ladies who like distinctive underclothing should, and every welltailored man must, trying to make the gap wider between them by innuendo and give more of a genuine filip to acts of impropriety between the two, she unbuttoned his and then he untied her, mind the pin, whereas savages in the cannibal islands, say, at ninety degrees in the shade not caring a continental. However, reverting to the original, there were on the other hand others who had forced their way to the top from the lowest rung by the aid of their bootstraps. Sheer force of natural genius, that. With brains, sir.

For which and further reasons he felt it was interest and duty even to wait on and profit by the unlookedfor occasion, though why, he could not exactly tell, being, as it was, already several shillings to the bad, having, in fact, let himself in for it. Still, to cultivate the acquaintance of someone of no uncommon calibre who could provide food for reflection would amply repay any small... Intellectual stimulation as such was, he felt, from time to time a firstrate tonic for the mind. Added to which was the coincidence of meeting, discussion, dance, row, old salt, of the here today and gone tomorrow type, night loafers, the whole galaxy of events, all went to make up a miniature cameo of the world we live in, especially as the lives of the submerged tenth, viz., coalminers, divers, scavengers etc., were very much under the microscope lately. To improve the shining hour he wondered whether he might meet with anything approaching the same luck as Mr Philip Beaufoy if taken down in writing. Suppose he were to pen something out of the common groove (as he fully intended doing) at the rate of one guinea per column, *My Experiences,* let us say, *in a Cabman's Shelter*.

The pink edition, extra sporting, of the *Telegraph,* tell a graphic lie, lay, as luck would have it, beside his elbow and as he was just puzzling again, far from satisfied, over a country belonging to him and the preceding rebus the vessel came from Bridgwater and the postcard was addressed to A. Boudin, find the captain's age, his eyes went aimlessly over the respective captions which came under his special province, the allembracing give us this day our daily press. First he got a bit of a start but it turned out to be only something about somebody named H. du Boyes, agent for typewriters or something like that. Great battle Tokio. Lovemaking in Irish £ 200 damages. Gordon Bennett. Emigration swindle. Letter from His Grace William ✠. Ascot *Throwaway* recalls Derby of '92 when Captain Marshall's dark horse, *Sir Hugo,* captured the blue ribband at long odds. New-York disaster, thousand lives lost. Foot and Mouth. Funeral of the late Mr Patrick Dignam.

So to change the subject he read about Dignam, R. I. P., which, he reflected, was anything but a gay sendoff.

— *This morning* (Hynes put in, of course), *the remains of the late Mr Patrick Dignam were removed from his residence, n° 9 Newbridge Avenue, Sandymount, for interment in Glasnevin. The deceased gentleman was a most popular and genial personality in city life and his demise, after a brief illness, came as great shock to citizens of all classes by whom he is deeply regretted. The obsequies, at which many friends of the deceased were present, were carried out* (certainly Hynes wrote it with a nudge from Corny) *by Messrs. H. J. O'Neill & Son, 164 North Strand road. The mourners included : Patk. Dignam (son), Bernard Corrigan (brother-in-law), John Henry Menton, solr., Martin Cunningham, John Power eatondph 1/8 ador dorador douradora* (must be where he called Monks the dayfather about Keyes's ad.) *Thomas Kernan, Simon Dedalus, B. A., Edward J. Lambert, Cornelius Kelleher, Joseph M'C. Hynes, L. Bloom, C. P. M'Coy — M'Intosh, and several others.*

Nettled not a little by *L. Boom* (as it incorrectly stated) and the line of bitched type, but tickled to death simultaneously by C. P. M'Coy and Stephen Dedalus, B. A., who were conspicuous, needless to say, by their total absence (to say nothing of M'Intosh), L. Boom pointed it out to his companion B. A., engaged in stifling another yawn, half nervousness, not forgetting the usual crop of nonsensical howlers of misprints.

— Is that first epistle to the Hebrews, he asked, as soon as his bottom jaw would let him, in ? Text : open thy mouth and put thy foot in it.

— It is, really, Mr Bloom said (though first he fancied he alluded to the archbishop till he added about foot and mouth with which there could be no possible connection) overjoyed to set his mind at rest and a bit flabbergasted at Myles Crawford's after all managing the thing, there.

While the other was reading it on page two Boom (to give him for the nonce his new misnomer) whiled away a few odd leisure moments in fits and starts with the account of the third event at Ascot on page three, his side-value 1,000 sovs., with 3,000 sovs. in specie added for entire colts and fillies. Mr F. Alexander's *Throwaway*, b. h. by *Rightaway*, 5 yrs, 9 st 4 lbs, Thrale (W. Lane) 1. Lord Howard de Walden's *Zinfandel* (M. Cannon) 2. Mr W. Bass's *Sceptre*, 3. Bettings 5 to 4 on *Zinfandel*, 20 to 1 *Throwaway* (off). *Throwaway* and *Zinfandel* stood close order. It was anybody's race then the rank outsider drew to the fore got long lead, beating lord Howard de Walden's chestnut colt and Mr W. Bass's bay filly Sceptre on a 2 1/2 mile course. Winner trained by Braine so that Lenehan's version of the business was all pure buncombe. Secured the verdict cleverly by a length. 1,000 sovs. with 300 in specie. Also ran J. de Bremond's (French horse Bantam Lyons was anxiously inquiring after not in yet but expected any minute) *Maximum II*. Different ways of bringing off a coup. Lovemaking damages. Though that halfbaked Lyons ran off at a tangent in his impetuosity to get left. Of course, gambling eminently lent itself to that sort of thing though, as the event turned out, the poor fool hadn't much reason to congratulate himself on his pick, the forlorn hope. Guesswork it reduced itself to eventually.

— There was every indication they would arrive at that, Mr Bloom said.

— Who? the other, whose hand by the way was hurt, said.

— One morning you would open the paper, the cabman affirmed, and read, *Return of Parnell*. He bet them what they liked. A Dublin fusilier was in that shelter one night and said he saw him in South Africa. Pride it was killed him. He ought to have done away with himself or lain low for a time after Committee Room nº 15 until he was his old self again with no-one to point a fiinger at him. Then they would all to a man have gone down on their marrowbones to him to come back when he had recovered his senses. Dead he wasn't. Simply absconded somewhere. The coffin they brought over was full of stones. He changed his name to De Wet, the Boer general. He made a mistake to fight the priests. And so forth and so on.

All the same Bloom (properly so dubbed) was rather surprised at their memories for in nine cases out of ten it was a case of tarbarrels, and not singly but in their thousands, and then complete oblivion because it was twenty odd years. Highly unlikely, of course, there was even a shadow of truth in the stones and, even supposing, he thought a return highly inadvisable, all things considered. Something evidently riled them in his death. Either he petered out too tamely of acute pneumonia just when his various different political arrangements were nearing completion or whether it transpired he owed his death to his having neglected to change his boots and clothes after a wetting when a cold resulted and failing to consult a specialist he being confined to his room till he eventually died of it amid widespread regret before a fortinght was at an end or quite possibly they were distressed to find the job was taken out of their hands. Of course nobody being acquainted with his movements even before, there was absolutely no clue as to his whereabouts which were decidedly of the *Alice, where art thou* order even prior to his starting to go under several aliases such as Fox and Stewart, so the remark which emanated from friend cabby might be within the bounds of possibility. Naturally then, it would prey on his mind as a born leader of men, which undoubtedly he was, and a commanding figure, a sixfooter or at any rate five feet ten or eleven in his stockinged feet, whereas Messrs. So-and-So who, though they weren't even a patch on the former man, ruled the roost after their redeeming features were very few and far between. It certainly pointed a moral, the idol with feet of clay. And then seventytwo of his trusty henchmen rounding on him with mutual mudslinging. And the identical same with murderers. You had to come back — that haunting sense kind of drew you — to show the understudy in the title *rôle* how to. He saw him once on the auspicious occasion when they broke up the type in the *Insuppressible* or was it *United Ireland*, a privilege he keenly appreciated, and, in point of fact, handed him his silk hat when it was knocked off and he said *Thank you,* excited as he undoubtedly was under his frigid expression notwithstanding the little misadventure mentioned between the cup and the lip, — what's bred in the bone. Still, as regards return, you were a lucky dog if they didn't set the terrier at you directly you got back. Then a lot of shillyshally usually followed. Tom for and Dick and Harry against. And then, number one, you came up against the man in possession and had to produce your credentials, like the claimant in the Tichborne case, Roger Charles Tichborne, *Bella* was the boat's name to the best of his recollection he, the heir, went down in, as the evidence went to show, and there was a tattoo mark too in Indian ink, Lord Bellew, was it? As he might very easily have picked up the details from some pal on board ship and then, when got up to tally with the description given, introduce himself with, *Excuse me, my name is So-and-So* or some such commonplace remark. A more prudent course, Mr Bloom said to the not over effusive, in fact like the distinguished personage under discussion beside him, would have been to sound the lie of the land first.

— That bitch, that English whore, did for him, the shebeen proprietor commented. She put the first nail in his coffin.

— Fine lump of a woman, all the same, the *soi-disant* townclerk, Henry Campbell remarked, and plenty of her. I seen her picture in a barber's. Her husband was a captain or an officer.

— Ay, Skin-the-Goat amusingly added. He was, and a cottonball one.

This gratuitous contribution of a humorous character occasioned a fair amount of laughter among his *entourage*. As regards Bloom, he, without the faintest suspicion of a smile, merely gazed in the direction of the door and reflected upon the historic story which had aroused extraordinary interest at the time when the facts, to make matters worse, were made public with the usual affectionate letters that passed between them, full of sweet nothings. First, it was strictly platonic till nature intervened and an attachment sprang up between them, till it bit by bit matters came to a climax and the matter became the talk of the town till the staggering blow came as a welcome intelligence to not a few evildisposed however, who were resolved upon encouraging his downfal though the thing was public property all along though not to anything like the sensational extent that it subsequently blossomed into. Since their names were coupled, though, since he was her declared favorite, where was the particular necessity to proclaim it to the rank and file from the housetops, the fact namely, that he had shared her bedroom, which came out in the witnessbox on oath when a thrill went through the packed court literally electrifying everybody in the shape of witnesses swearing to having witnessed him on such and such a particular date in the act of scrambling out of an upstairs apartment with the assistance of a ladder in night apparel, having gained admittance in the same fashion, a fact that the weeklies, addicted to the lubric a little, simply coined shoals of money out of. Whereas the simple fact of the case was it was simply a case of the husband not being up to the scratch with nothing in common between them beyond the name and then a real man arriving on the scene, strong to the verge of weakness, falling a victim to her siren charms and forgetting home ties. The usual sequel, to bask in the loved one's smiles. The eternal question of the life connubial, needless to say, cropped up. Can real love, supposing there happens to be another chap in the case, exist between married folk? Though it was no concern of theirs absolutely if he regarded her with affection carried away by a wave of folly. A magnificent specimen of manhood he was truly, augmented obviously by gifts of a high order as compared with the other military supernumerary, that is (who was just the usual everyday *farewell, my gallant captain* kind of an individual in the light dragoons, the 18th hussars to be accurate), and inflammable doubtless (the fallen leader, that is not the other) in his own peculiar way which she of course, woman, quickly perceived as highly likely to carve his way to fame, which he almost bid fair to do till the priests and ministers of the gospel as a whole, his erstwhile staunch adherents and his beloved evicted tenants for whom he had done yeoman service in the rural parts of the country by taking up the cudgels on their behalf in a way that exceeded their most sanguine expectations, very effectually cooked his matrimonial goose, thereby heaping coals of fire on his head-much in the same way as the fabled ass's kick. Looking back now in a retrospective kind of arrangement, all seemed a kind of dream. And the coming back was the worst thing you ever did because it went without saying you would feel out of place as things always moved with the times. Why, as he reflected, Irishtown Strand, a locality he had not been in for quite a number of years, looked different somehow since, as it happened, he went to reside on the north side. North or south however, it was just the wellknown case of hot passion, pure and simple, upsetting the applecart with a vengeance and just bore out the very thing he was saying, as she also was Spanish or half so, types that wouldn't do things by halves, passionate abandon of the south, casting every shred of decency to the winds.

— Just bears out what I was saying, he, with glowing bosom said to Stephen. And, if I don't greatly mistake, she was Spanish too.

— The king of Spain's daughter, Stephen answered, adding something or other rather muddled about farewell and adieu to you Spanish onions and the first land called the Deadman and from Ramhead to Scilly was so and so many...

— Was she? Bloom ejaculated surprised, though not astonished by any means. I never heard that rumour before. Possible, especially there it was, as she lived there. So, Spain.

Carefully avoiding a book in his pocket *Sweets of,* which reminded him by the by of that Capel street library book out of date, he took out his pocketbook and, turning over the various contents rapidly, finally he...

— Do you consider, by the by, he said, thoughtfully selecting a faded photo which he laid on the table, that a Spanish type?

Stephen, obviously addressed, looked down on the photo showing a large sized lady, with her fleshy charms on evidence in an open fashion, as she was in the full bloom of womanhood, in evening dress cut ostentatiously low for the occasion to give a liberal display of bosom, with more than vision of breasts, her full lips parted, and some perfect teeth, standing near, ostensibly with gravity, a piano, on the rest of which was *In old Madrid*, a ballad, pretty in its way, which was then all the vogue. Her (the lady's) eyes, dark, large, looked at Stephen, about to smile about something to be admired, Lafayette of Westmoreland street, Dublin's premier photographic artist, being responsible for the esthetic execution.

— Mrs Bloom, my wife the *prima donna*, Madam Marion Tweedy, Bloom indicated. Taken a few years since. In or about '96. Very like her then.

Beside the young man he looked also at the photo of the lady now his legal wife who, he intimated, was the accomplished daughter of Major Brian Tweedy and displayed at an early age remarkable proficiency as a singer having even made her bow to the public when her years numbered barely sweet sixteen. As for the face, it was a speaking likeness in expression but it did not do justice to her figure, which came in for a lot of notice usually and which did not come out to the best advantage in that getup. She could without difficulty, he said, have posed for the ensemble, not to dwell on certain opulent curves of the... He dwelt, being a bit of an artist in his spare time, on the female form in general developmentally because, as it so happened, no later than that afternoon, he had seen those Grecian statues, perfectly develop d as works of art, in the National Museum. Marble could give the original, shoulders, back, all the symmetry. All the rest, yes, Puritanism. It does though, St Joseph's sovereign... whereas no photo could, because it simply wasn't art, in a word.

The spirit moving him, he would much have liked to follow Jack Tar's good example and leave the likeness there for a very few minutes to speak for itself on the plea he... so that the other could drink in the beauty for himself, her stage presence being, frankly, a treat in itself which the camera could not at all do justice to. But it was scarcely professional etiquette so, though it was a warm pleasant sort of a night now yet wonderfully cool for the season considering, for sunshine after storm... And he did feel a kind of need there and then to follow suit like a kind of inward voice and satisfy a possible need by moving a motion. Nevertheless, he sat tight, just viewing the slightly soiled photo creased by opulent curves, none the worse for wear, however, and looked away thoughfully with the intention of not further increasing the other's possible embarrassement while gauging her symmetry of heaving *embonpoint*. In fact, the slight soiling was only an added charm, like the case of linen slightly soiled, good as new, much better, in fact, with the starch out. Suppose she was gone when he ?... I looked for the lamp which she told me came into his mind but merely as a passing fancy of his because he then recollected the morning littered bed etcetera and the book about Ruby with met him pike hoses (*sic*) in it which must have fell down sufficiently appropriately beside the domestic chamberpot with apologies to Lindley Murray.

The vicinity of the young man he certainly relished, educated, *distingué*, and impulsive into the bargain, far and away the pick of the bunch, though you wouldn't think he had it in him... yet you would. Besides he said the picture was handsome which, say what you like, it was, though at the moment she was distinctly stouter. And why not? An awful lot of makebelieve went on about that sort of thing involving a lifelong slur with the usual splash page of letterpress about the same old matrimonial tangle alleging misconduct with professional golfer or the newest stage favourite instead of being honest and aboveboard about the whole business. How they were fated to meet and an attachment sprang up between the two so that their names were coupled in the public eye was told in court with letters containing the habitual mushy and compromising expressions, leaving no loophole, to show that they openly cohabited two or three times a week at some wellknown seaside hotel and relations, when the thing ran its normal course, became in due course intimate. Then the decree *nisi* and the King's Proctor to show cause why and, he failing to quash it, *nisi* was made absolute. But as for that, the two misdemeanants, wrapped up as they largely were in one another, could safely afford to ignore it as they very largely did till the matter was put in the hands of a solicitor, who filed a petition for the party wronged in due course. He, Bloom, enjoyed the distinction of being close to Erin's uncrowned king in the flesh when the thing occurred on the historic *fracas* when the fallen leader's — who notoriously stuck to his guns to the last drop even when clothed in the mantle of adultery — (leader's) trusty henchmen to the number of ten or a dozen or possibly even more than that penetrated into the prinitng worsk of the *Insuppressible* or no it was *United Ireland* (a by no means, by the by appropriate appellative) and broke up the typecases with hammers or something like that all on account of some scurrilous effusions from the facile pens of the O'Brienite scribes at the usual mudslinging occuaption, reflecting on the erstwhile tribune's private morals. Though palpably a radically altered man, he was still a commanding figure, though carelessly garbed as usual, with that look of settled purpose which went a long way with the shillyshallyers till they discovered to their vast discomfiture that their idol had feet of clay, after placing him upon a pedestal, which she, however, was the first to perceive. As those were particularly hot times in the general hullaballoo Bloom sustained a minor injury from a nasty prod of some chap's elbow in the crowd that of course congregated lodging some place about the pit of the stomach, fortunately not of a grave character. His hat (Parnell's), was inadvertently knocked off and, as a matter of strict history, Bloom was the man who picked it up in the crush after witnesssing the occurrence meaning to return it to him (and return it to him he did with the utmost celerity) who, panting and hatless and whose thoughts were miles away from his hat at the time, being a gentleman born with a stake in the country, he, as a matter of fact, having gone into it more for the kudos of the thing than anything else, what's bred in the bone, instilled into him in infancy at his mother's knee in the shape of knowing what good form was came out at once because he turned round to the donor and thanked him with perfect *aplomb*, saying: *Thank you, sir* though in a very different tone of voice from the ornament of the legal profession whose headgear Bloom also set to rights earlier in the course of the day, history repeating itself with a difference, after the burial of a mutual friend when they had left him alone in his glory after the grim task of having committed his remains to the grave.

On the other hand what incensed him more inwardly was the blatant jokes of the cabmen and so on, who passed it all off as a jest, laughing immoderately, pretending to understand everything, the why and the wherefore, and in reality not knowing their own minds, it being a case for the two parties themselves unless it ensued that the legitimate husband happened to be a party to it owing to some anonymous letter from the usual boy Jones, who happened to come across them at the crucial moment in a loving position locked in one another's arms drawing attention to their illicit proceedings and leading up to a domestic rumpus and the erring fair one begging forgiveness of her lord and master upon her knees and promising to sever the connection and not receive his visits any more if only the aggrieved husband would overlook the matter and let bygones be bygones, with tears in her eyes, though possibly with her tongue in her fair cheek at the same time, as quite possibly there were several others. He personally, being of a sceptical bias, believed, and didn't make the smallest bones about saying so either, that man, or men in the plural, were always hanging around on the waiting list about a lady, even supposing she was the best wife in the world and they got on fairly well together for the sake of argument, when, neglecting her duties, she chose to be tired of wedded life, and was on for a little flutter in polite debauchery to press their attentions on her with improper intent, the upshot being that her affections centred on another, the cause of many *liaisons* between still attractive married women getting on for fair and forty and younger men, no doubt as several famous cases of feminine infatuation proved up to the hilt.

It was a thousand pities a young fellow blessed with an allowance of brains, as his neighbour obviously was, should waste his valuable time with profligate women, who might present him with a nice dose to last him his lifetime. In the nature of single blessedness he would one day take unto himself a wife when when Miss Right came on the scene but in the interim ladies' society was a *conditio sine qua non* though he had the gravest possible doubts, not that he wanted in the smallest to pump Stephen about Miss Ferguson (who was very possibly the particular lodestar who brought him down to Irishtown so early in the morning), as to whether he would find much satisfaction basking in the boy and girl courtship idea and the company of smirking misses without a penny to their names bi-or tri-weekly with the orthodox preliminary canter of complimentpaying and walking out leading up to fond lovers' ways and flowers and chocs. To think of him house and homeless, rooked by some landlady worse than any stepmother, was really too bad at his age. The queer suddenly things he popped out with attracted the elder man who was several years the other's senior or like his father. But something substantial he certainly ought to eat, were it only an eggflip made on unadulterated maternal nutriment or, failing that, the homely Humpty Dumpty boiled.

— At what o'clock did you dine ? he questioned of the slim form and tired though unwrinkled face.

— Some time yesterday, Stephen said.

— Yesterday, exclaimed Bloom till he remembered it was already tomorrow, Friday. Ah, you mean it's after twelve!

— The day before yesterday, Stephen said, improving on himself.

Literally astounded at this piece of intelligence Bloom, reflected. Though they didn't see eye to eye in everything, a certain analogy there somehow was, as if both their minds were travelling, so to speak, in the one train of thought. At his age when dabbling in politics roughly some score of years previously when he had been a *quasi* aspirant to parliamentary honours in the Buckshot Foster days he too recollected in retrospect (which was a source of keen satisfaction in itself) he had a sneaking regard for those same ultra ideas. For instance, when the evicted tenants question, then at its first inception, bulked largely in people's mind though, it goes without saying, not contributing a copper or pinning his faith absolutely to its dictums, some of which wouldn't exactly hold water, he at the outset in principle, at all events, was in thorough sympathy with peasant possession, as voicing the trend of modern opinion, a partiality, however, which, realising his mistake, he was subsequently partially cured of, and even was twitted with going a step further than Michael Davitt in the striking views he at one time inculcated as a backtothelander, which was one reason he strongly resented the innuendo put upon him in so barefaced a fashion at the gathering of the clans in Barney Kiernan's so that he, though often considerably misunderstood and the least pugnacious of mortals, be it repeated, departed from his customary habit to give him (metaphorically) one in the gizzard though so far as politics themselves were concerned, he was only too conscious of the casualties invariably resulting from propaganda and displays of mutual animosity and the misery and suffering it entailed as a foregone conclusion on fine young fellows, chiefly, destruction of the fittest, in a word.

Anyhow, upon weighing the pros and cons, getting on for one as it was, it was high time to be retiring for the night. The crux was it was a bit risky to bring him home as eventualities might possibly ensue (somebody having a temper of her own sometimes) and spoil the hash altogether as on the night he misguidedly brought home a dog (breed unknown) with a lame paw, not that the cases were either identical or the reverse, though he had hurt his hand too, to Ontario Terrace, as he very distinctly remembered, having been there, so to speak. On the other hand it was altogether far and away too late for the Sandymount or Sandycove suggestion so that he was in some perplexity as to which of the two alternatives... Everything pointed to the fact that it behoved him to avail himself to the full of the opportunity, all things considered. His initial impression was that he was a bit standoffish or not over effusive but it grew on him someway. For one thing he mightn't what you call jump at the idea, if approached, and what mostly worried him was he didn't know how to lead up to it or word it exactly, supposing he did entertain the proposal, as it would afford him very great personal pleasure if he would allow him to help to pu coin in his way or some wardrobe, if found suitable. At all events he wound up by concluding, eschewing for the nonce hidebound precedent, a cup of Epps's cocoa and a shakedown for the night plus the use of a rug or two and overcoat doubled into a pillow. At least he would be in safe hands and as warm as a toast on a trivet. He failed top erceive any very vast amount of harm in that always with the proviso no rumpus of any sort was kicked up. A move had to be made because that merry old soul, the grasswidower in question who appeared to be glued to the spot, didn't appear in any particular hurry to wend his way home to his dearly beloved Queenstown and it was highly likely some sponger's bawdyhouse of retired beauties off Sheriff street lower would be the best clue to that equivocal character's whereabouts for a few days to come, alternately racking their feelings (the mermaids') with sixchamber revolver anecdotes verging on the tropical calculated to freeze the marrow of anybody's bones and mauling their largesized charms between whiles with rough and tumble gusto to the accompaniment of large potations of pottheen and the usual blarney about himself for as to who he in reality was let XX equal my right name and address, as Mr Algebra remarks *passim*. At the same time he inwardly chuckled over his repartee to the blood and ouns champion about his God being a jew. People could put up with being bitten by a wolf but what properly riled them was a bite from a sheep. The most vulnerable point too of tender Achilles, your God was a jew, because mostly they appeared to imagine he came from Carrick-on-Shannon or somewhere abouts in the county Sligo.

— I propose, our hero eventually suggested, after mature reflection, while prudently pocketing her photo, as it's rather stuffy here, you just come home with me and talk things over. My diggings are quite close in the vicinity. You can't drink that stuff. Wait, I'll just pay this lot.

The best plan clearly being to clear out, the remainder being plain sailing, he beckoned, while prudently pocketing the photo, to the keeper, of the shanty, who didn't seem to...

— Yes, that's the best, he assured Stephen, to whom for the matter of that Brazen Head or him or anywhere else was all more or less...

All kinds of Utopian plans were flashing through his (Bloom's) busy brain. Education (the genuine article), literature, journalism, prize titbits, up to date billing, hydros and concert tours in English watering resorts packed with theatres, turning money away, duets in Italian with the accent perfectly true to nature and a quantity of other things, no necessity of course to tell the world and his wife from the housetops about it and a slice of luck. An opening was all was wanted. Because he more than suspected he had his father's voice to bank his hopes on which it was quite on the cards he had so it would be just as well, by the way no harm, to trail the conversation in the direction of that particular red herring just to...

The cabby read out of the paper he had got hold of that the former viceroy, Earl Cadogan, had presided at the cabdrivers' association dinner in London somewhere. Silence with a yawn or two accompanied this thrilling announcement. Then the old specimen in the corner who appeared to have some spark of vitality left read out that Sir Anthony MacDonnell had left Euston for the chief secretary's lodge or words to that effect. To which absorbing piece of intelligence echo answered why.

— Give us a squint at that literature, grandfather, the ancient mariner put in, manifesting some natural impatience.

— And welcome, answered the elderly party thus addressed.

The sailor lugged out from a case he had a pair of greenish goggles which he very slowly hooked over his nose and both ears.

— Are you bad in the eyes? the sympathetic personage like the town clerk queried.

— Why, answered the seafarer with the tartan beard, who seemingly was a bit of a literary cove in his own small way, staring out of seagreen portholes as you might well describe them as, I uses goggles reading. Sand in the Red Sea done that. One time I could read a book in the dark, manner of speaking, *The Arabian Nights Entertainment* was my favourite and *Red as a Rose is She*.

Thereupon he pawed the journal open and pored upon Lord only knows what, found drowned or the exploits of King Willow, Iremonger having made a hundred and something second wicket not out for Notts, during which time (completely regardless of Ire) the keeper was intensely occupied loosening an apparently new or secondhand boot which manifestly pinched him, as he muttered against whoever it was sold it, all of them who were sufficiently awake enough to be picked out by their facial expressions, that is to say, either simply looking on glumly or passing a trivial remark.

To cut a long story short Bloom, grasping the situation, was the first to rise from his feet so as not to outstay their welcome having first and foremost, being as good as his word that he would foot the bill for the occasion, taken the wise precaution to unobtrusively motion to mine host as a parting shot a scarcely perceptible sign when the others were not looking to the effect that the amount due was forthcoming, making a grand total of fourpence (the amount he deposited unobtrusively in four coppers, literally the last of the Mohicans) he having previously spotted on the printed pricelist for all who ran to read opposite to him in unmistakable figures, coffee 2d., confectionery d°, and honestly well worth twice the money once in a way, as Wetherup used to remark.

— Come, he counselled, to close the *séance*.

Seeing that the ruse worked and the coast was clear, they left the shelter or shanty together and the *élite* society of oilskin and company whom nothing short of an earthquake would move out of their *dolce far niente*. Stephen, who confessed to still feeling poorly and fagged out, paused at the, for a moment... the door to...

— One thing I never understood, he said, to be original on the spur ot the moment, why they put tables upside down at night, I mean chairs upside down on the tables in cafés.

To which impromptu the neverfailing Bloom replied without a moment's hesitation, saying straight off:

— To sweep the floor in the morning.

So saying he skipped around nimbly, considering frankly, at the same time apologetic, to get on his companion's right, a habit of his, by the bye the right side being, in classical idiom, his tender Achilles. The night air was certainly now a treat to breathe though Stephen was a bit weak on his pins.

— It will (the air) do you good, Bloom said, meaning also the walk, in a moment. The only thing is to walk then you'll feel a different man. It's not far. Lean on me.

Accordingly he passed his left arm in Stephen's right and led him on accordingly.

— Yes, Stephen said uncertainly, because he thought he felt a strange kind of flesh of a different man approach him, sinewless and wobbly and all that.

Anyhow, they passed the sentrybox with stones, brazier, etc. where the municipal supernumerary, ex-Gumley, was still to all intents and purposes wrapped in the arms of Murphy, as the adage has it, dreaming of fresh fields and pastures new. And *apropos* of coffin of stones, the analogy was not at all bad, as it was in fact a stoning to death on the part of seventytwo out of eighty odd constituencies that ratted at the time of the split and chiefly the belauded peasant class, probably the selfsame evicted tenants he had put in their holdings.

So they passed on to chatting about music, a form of art for which Bloom, as a pure amateur, possessed the greatest love, as they made tracks arm-in-arm across Beresford Place. Wagnerian music, though confessedly grand in its way, was a bit too heavy for Bloom and hard to follow at the first go off but the music of Mercadante's *Huguenots*, Meyerbeer's *Seven Last Words on the Cross,* and Mozart's *Twelfth Mass,* he simply revelled in, the *Gloria* in that being to his mind the acme of first class music as such, literally knocking everything else into a cocked hat. He infinitely preferred the sacred music of the catholic church to anything the opposite shop could offer in that line such as those Moody and Sankey hymns or *Bid me to live and I will live thy protestant to be.* He also yielded to none in his admiration of Rossini's *Stabat Mater,* a work simply abounding in immortal numbers, in which his wife, Madam Marion Tweedy, made a hit, a veritable sensation, he might safely say greatly adding to her other laurels and putting the others totally in the shade in the jesuit fathers' church in Upper Gardiner Street, the sacred edifice being thronged to the doors to hear her with virtuosos, or *virtuosi* rather. There was the unanimous opinion that there was none to come up to her and, suffice it to say in a place of worship for music of a sacred character, there was a generally voiced desire for an encore. On the whole, though favouring preferably light opera of the *Don Giovanni* description, and *Martha,* a gem in its line, he had a *penchant,* though with only a surface knowledge, for the severe classical school such as Mendelssohn. And talking of that, taking it for granted he knew all about the old favourites, he mentioned *par excellence* Lionel's air in *Martha, M'appari,* which, curiously enough, he heard, or overheard, to be more accurate, on yesterday, a privilege he keenly appreciated, from the lips of Stephen's respected father, sung to perfection, a study of the number, in fact, which made all the others take a back seat. Stephen, in reply to a politely put query, said he didn't but launched out into praises of Shakespeare's songs, at least of in or about that period, the lutenist Dowland who lived in Fetter Lane near Gerard the herbalist, who *anno ludendo hausi, Doulandus,* an instrument he was contemplating purchasing from Mr Arnold Dolmetsch, whom Bloom did not quite recall, though the name certainly sounded familiar, for sixtyfive guineas and Farnaby and son with their *dux* and *comes* conceits and Byrd (William), who played the virginals, he said, in the Queen's Chapel or anywhere else he found them and one Tomkins who made toys or airs and John Bull.

On the roadway which they were approaching whilst still speaking beyond the swing chain, a horse, dragging a sweeper, paced on the paven ground, brushing a long swathe of mire up so that with the noise Bloom was not perfectly certain whether he had caught aright the allusion to sixtyfive guineas and John Bull. He inquired if it was John Bull the political celebrity of that ilk, as it struck him, the two identical names, as a striking coincidence.

By the chains, the horse slowly swerved to turn, which perceiving, Bloom, who was keeping a sharp lookout as usual plucked the other's sleeve gently, jocosely remarking:

— Our lives are in peril to night. Beware of the steamroller.

They thereupon stopped. Bloom looked at the head of a horse not worth anything like sixtyfive guineas, suddenly in evidence in the dark quite near, so that it seemed new, a different grouping of bones and even flesh, because palpably it was a fourwalker, a hipshaker, a blackbuttocker, a taildangler, a headhanger, putting his hind foot foremost the while the lord of his creation sat on the perch, busy with his thoughts. But such a good poor brute, he was sorry he hadn't a lump of sugar but, as he wisely reflected, you could scarcely be prepared for every emergency that might crop up. He was just a big foolish nervous noodly kind of a horse, without a second care in the world. But even a dog, he reflected, take that mongrel in Barney Kiernan's, of the same size, would be a holy horror to face. But it was no animal's fault in particular if he was built that way like the camel, ship of the desert, distilling grapes into potheen in his hump. Nine tenths of them all could be caged or trained, nothing beyond the art of man barring the bees; whale with a harpoon hairpin, alligator, tickle the small of his back and he sees the joke; chalk a circle for a rooster; tiger, my eagle eye. These timely reflections anent the brutes of the field occupied his mind, somewhat distracted from Stephen's words, while the ship of the street was manœuvring and Stephen went on about the highly interesting old...

— What's this I was saying? Ah, yes! My wife, he intimated, plunging *in medias res,* would have the greatest of pleasure in making your acquaintance as she is passionately attached to music of any kind.

He looked sideways in a friendly fashion at the sideface of Stephen, image of his mother, which was not quite the same as the usual blackguard type they unquestionably had an indubitable hankering after as he was perhaps not that way built.

Still, supposing he had his father's gift, as he more than suspected, it opened up new vistas in his mind, such as Lady Fingall's Irish industries concert on the preceding Monday, and aristocracy in general.

Exquisite variations he was now describing on a air *Youth here has End* by Jans Pieter Sweelinck, a Dutchman of Amsterdam where the frows come from. Even more he liked an old German song of *Johannes Jeep* about the clear sea and the voices of sirens, sweet murderers of men, which boggled Bloom a bit:

Von der Sirenen Listigkeit
Tun die Poeten dichten.

These opening bars he sang and translated *extempore*. Bloom, nodding, said he perfectly understood and begged him to go on by all means, which he did.

A phenomenally beautiful tenor voice like that, the rarest of boons, which Bloom appreciated at the very first note he got out, could easily, if properly handled by some recognised authority on voice production such as Barraclough and being able to read music into the bargain, command its own price where baritones were ten a penny and procure for its fortunate possessor in the near future an *entrée* into fashionable houses in the best residential quarters of financial magnates in a large way of business and titled people where, with his university degree of B. A. (a huge ad in its way) and gentlemanly bearing to all the more influence the good impression he would infallibly score a distinct success, being blessed with brains which also could be utilised for the purpose and other requisites, if his clothes were properly attended to, so as to the better worm his way into their good graces as he, a youthful tyro in society's sartorial niceties, hardly understood how a little thing like that could militate against you. It was in fact only a matter of months and he could easily foresee him participating in their musical and artistic *conversaziones* during the festivities of the Christmas season, for choice, causing a slight flutter in the dovecotes of the fair sex and being made a lot of by ladies out for sensation, cases of which, as he happened to know, were on record, in fact, without giving the show away, he himself once upon a time, if he cared to, could easily have... Added to which of course, would be the pecuniar y emolument by no means to be sneezed at, going hand in hand with his tuition fees. Not, he parenthesised, that for the sake of filthy lucre he need necessarily embrace the lyric platform as a walk in life for any lengthy space of time but a step in the required direction it was, beyond yea or nay, and both monetarily and mentally it contained no reflection on his dignity in the smallest and it often turned in uncommonly handy to be handed a cheque at a muchneeded moment when every little helped. Besides, though taste latterly had deteriorated to a degree, original music like that, different from the conventional rut, would rapidly have a great vogue, as it would be a decided novelty for Dublin's musical world after the usual hackneyed run of catchy tenor solos foisted on a confiding public by Ivan St Austell and Hilton St Just and their *genus omne*. Yes, beyond a shadow of a doubt, he could, with all the cards in his hand and he had a capital opening to make a name for himself and win a high place in the city's esteem where he could command a stiff figure and, booking ahead, give a grand concert for the patrons of the King Street house, given a backer-up, if one were forthcoming to kick him upstairs, so to speak, — a big *if*, however — with some impetus of the goahead sort to obviate the inevitable procrastination which often tripped up a too much fêted prince of good fellows and it need not detract from the other by one iota as, being his own master, he would have heaps of time to practise literature in his spare moments when desirous of so doing without its clashing with his vocal career or containing anything derogatory what soever as it was a matter for himself alone. In fact, he had the ball at his feet and that was the very reason why the other, possessed of a remarkably sharp nose for smelling a rat of any sort, hung on to him at all.

The horse was just then... and later on, at a propitious opportunity he purposed (Bloom did), without anyway prying into his private affairs on the *fools step in where angels* principle advising him to sever his connection with a certain budding practitioner, who, he noticed, was prone to disparage, and even, to a slight extent, with some hilarious pretext, when not present, deprecate him, or whatever you like to call it, which, in Bloom's humble opinion, threw a nasty sidelight on that side of a person's character — no pun intended.

The horse, having reached the end of his tether, so to speak, halted, and, rearing high a proud feathering tail, added his quota by letting fall on the floor, which the brush would soon brush up and polish, three smoking globes of turds. Slowly, three times, one after another, from a full crupper, he mired. And humanely his driver waited till he (or she) had ended, patient in his scythed car.

Side by side Bloom, profiting by the *contretemps,* with Stephen passed through the gap of the chains, divided by the upright, and, stepping over a strand of mire, went across towards Gardiner Street lower, Stephen singing more boldly, but not loudly, the end of the ballad :

Und alle Schiffe brücken.

The driver never said a word, good, bad or indifferent. He merely watched the two figures, as he sat on his lowbacked car, both black — one full, one lean — walk towards the railway bridge, *to be married by Father Maher*. As they walked, they at times stopped and walked again, continuing their *tête à tête* (which of course he was utterly out of). about sirens, enemies of man's reason, mingled with a number of other topics of the same category, usurpers, historical cases of the kind while the man in the sweeper car or you might as well call it in the sleeper car who in any case couldn't possibly hear because they were too far simply sat in his sest near the end of lower Gardiner street *and looked after their lowbacked car*.

What parallel courses did Bloom and Stephen follow returning ?

Starting united both at normal walking pace from Beresford Place they followed in the order named Lower and Middle Gardiner streets and Mountjoy square, west : then, at reduced pace, each bearing left, Gardiner's place by an inadvertence as far as the farther corner of Temple street, north : then, at reduced pace with interruptions of halt, bearing right, Temple street, north, as far as Hardwicke place. Approaching, disparate, at relaxed walking pace they crossed both the circus before George's church diametrically, the chord in any circle being less than the arc which it subtends.

Of what did the duumvirate deliberate during their itinerary ?

Music, literature, Ireland, Dublin, Paris, friendship, woman, prostitution, diet, the influence of gaslight or the light of arc and glowlamps on the growth of adjoining paraheliotropic trees, exposed corporation emergency dustbuckets, the Roman catholic church, ecclesiastical celibacy, the Irish nation, jesuit education, careers, the study of medicine, the past day, the maleficent influence ot the presabbath, Stephen's collapse.

Did Bloom discover common factors of similarity between their respective like and unlike reactions to experience ?

Both were sensitive to artistic impressions musical in preference to plastic or pictorial. Both preferred a continental to an insular manner of life, a cisatlantic to a transatlantic place of residence. Both indurated by early domestic training and an inherited tenacity of heterodox resistance professed their disbelief in many orthodox religions, national, social and ethical doctrines. Both admitted the alternately stimulating and obtunding influence of heterosexual magnetism.

Were their views on some points divergent ?

Stephen dissented openly from Bloom's views on the importance of dietary and civic selfhelp while Bloom dissented tacitly from Stephen's views on the eternal affirmation of the spirit of man in literature. Bloom assently covertly to Stephen's rectification of the anachronism involved in assigning the date of the conversion of the Irish nation to christianity from druidism by Patrick son of Calpornus, son of Potitus, son of Odyssus, sent by pope Celestine I in the year 432 in the reign of Leary to the year 260 or thereabouts in the reign of Cormac Mac Art († 266 A. D.) suffocated by imperfect deglutition of aliment at Sletty and interred at Rossnaree. The collapse which Bloom ascribed to gastric inanition and certain chemical compounds of varying degrees of adulteration and alcoholic strength, accelerated by mental exertion and the velocity of rapid circular motion in a relaxing atmosphere, Stephen attributed to the reapparition of a matutinal cloud (perceived by both from two different points of observation, Sandycove and Dublin), at first no bigger than a woman's hand.

Was there one point on which their views were equal and negative ?

The influence of gaslight or electric light on the growth of adjoining paraheliotropic trees.

Had Bloom discussed similar subjects during nocturnal perambulations in the past ?

In 1884 with Owen Goldberg and Cecil Turnbull at night on public thoroughfares between Longwood avenue and Leonard's corner and Leonard's corner and Synge street and Synge street and Bloomfield Avenue. In 1885 with Percy Apjohn in the evenings, reclined against the wall between Gibraltar villa and Bloomfield house in Crumlin, barony of Uppercross. In 1886 occusionally with casual acquaintances and prospective purchasers on doorsteps, in front parlours, in third class railway carriages of suburban lines. In 1888 frequently with major Brian Tweedy and his daughter Miss Marion Tweedy, together and separately on the lounge in Matthew Dillon's house in Roundtown. Once in 1892 and once in 1893 with Julius Mastiansky, on both occasions in the parlour of his (Bloom's) house in Lombard street, west.

What reflection concerning the irregular sequence of dates 1884, 1885, 1886, 1888, 1892, 1893, 1904 did Bloom make before their arrival at their destination ?

He reflected that the progressive extension of the field of individual development and experience was regressively accompanied by a restriction of the converse domain of interindividual relations.

As in what ways?

From inexistence to existence he came to many and was as one received: existence with existence he was with any as any with any: from existence to nonexistence gone he would be by all as none perceived.

What did Bloom make on their arrival at their destination?

At the housesteps of the 4th of the equidifferent uneven numbers, number 7 Eccles street, he inserted his hand mechanically into the back pocket of his trousers to obtain his latchkey.

Was it there?

It was in the corresponding pocket of the trousers which he had worn on the day but one preceding.

Why was he doubly irritated?

Because he had forgotten and because he remembered that he had reminded himself twice not to forget.

What were then the alternatives before the, premeditatedly (respectively) and inadvertently, keyless couple?

To enter or not to enter. To knock or not to knock.

Bloom's decision?

A stratagem. Resting his feet on the dwarf wall, he climbed over the area railings, compressed his hat on his head, grasped two points at the lower union of rails and stiles, lowered his body gradually by its length of five feet nine inches and a half to within two feet ten inches of the area pavement, and allowed his body to move freely in space by separating himself from the railings and crouching in preparation for the impact of the fall.

Did he fall?

By his body's known weight of eleven stone and four pounds in avoirdupois measure, as certified by the graduated machine for periodical selfweighing in the premises of Francis Frœdman, pharmaceutical chemist of 19 Frederick street, north, on the last feast of the Ascension, to wit, the twelfth day of May of the bissextile year one thousand nine hundred and four of the christian era, (jewish era five thousand six hundred and sixtyfour, mohammadan era one thousand three hundred and twentytwo), golden number 5, epact 13, solar cycle 9, dominical letters C B, Roman indication 2, Julian period 6617, MXMIV.

Did he rise uninjured by concussion ?

Regaining new stable equilibrium he rose uninjured though concussed by the impact, raised the latch of the area door by the exertion of force at its freely moving flange and by leverage of the first kind applied at its fulcrum gained retarded access to the kitchen through the subadjacent scullery, ignited a lucifer match by friction, set free inflammable coal gas by turning on the ventcock, lit a high flame which, by regulating, he reduced to quiescent candescence and lit finally a portable candle.

What discrete succession of images did Stephen meanwhile perceive ?

Reclined against the area railings he perceived through the transparent kitchen panes a man regulating a gasflame of 14 C P, a man lighting a candle, a man removing in turn each of his two boots, a man leaving the kitchen holding a candle of 1 C P.

Did the man reappear elsewhere ?

After a lapse of four minutes the glimmer of his candle was discernible through the semitransparent semicircular glass fanlight over the halldoor. The halldoor turned gradually on its hinges. In the open space of the doorway the man reappeared without his hat, with his candle.

Did Stephen obey his sign ?

Yes, entering softly, he helped to close and chain the door and followed softly along the hallway the man's back and listed feet and lighted candle past a lighted crevice of doorway on the left and carefully down a turning staircase of more than five steps into the kitchen of Bloom's house.

What did Bloom do ?

He extinguished the candle by a sharp expiration of breath upon its flame, drew two spoonseat deal chairs to the hearthstone, one for Stephen with its back to the area window, the other for himself when necessary, knelt on one knee, composed in the grate a pyre of crosslaid resintipped sticks and various coloured papers and irregular polygons of best Abram coal at twentyone shillings a ton from the yard of Messrs Flower and M'Donald of 14 D'Olier street, kindled it at three projecting points of paper with one ignited lucifer match, thereby releasing the potential energy contained in the fuel by allowing its carbon and hydrogen elements to enter into free union with the oxygen of the air.

Of what similar apparitions did Stephen think ?

Of others elsewhere in other times who, kneeling on one knee or on two, had kindled fires for him, of Brother Michael in the infirmary of the college of the Society of Jesus at Clongowes Wood, Sallins, in the county of Kildare : of his father, Simon Dedalus, in an unfurnished room of his first residence in Dublin, number thirteen Fitzgibbon street : of his godmother Miss Kate Morkan in the house of her dying sister Miss Julia Morkan at 15 Usher's Island : of his mother Mary, wife of Simon Dedalus, in the kitchen of number twelve North Richmond street on the morning of the feast of Saint Francis-Xavier 1898 : of the dean of studies, Father Butt, in the physics' theatre of university College, 16 Stephen's Green, north : of his sister Dilly (Delia) in his father's house in Cabra.

What did Stephen see on raising his gaze to the height of a yard from the fire towards the opposite wall ?

Under a row of five coiled spring housebells a curvilinear rope, stretched between two holdfasts athwart across the recess beside the chimney pier, from which hung four smallsized square handkerchiefs folded unattached consecutively in adjacent rectangles and one pair of ladies' grey hose with Lisle suspender tops and feet in their habitual position clamped by three erect wooden pegs two at their outer extremities and the third at their point of junction.

What did Bloom see on the range ?

On the right (smaller) hob a blue enamelled saucepan : on the left (larger) hob a black iron kettle.

What did Bloom do at the range ?

He removed the saucepan to the left hob, rose and carried the iron kettle to the sink in order to tap the current by turning the faucet to let it flow.

Did it flow ?

Yes. From Roundwood reservoir in county Wicklow of a cubic capacity of 2.400 million gallons, percolating through a subterranean aqueduct of filtre mains of single and double pipeage constructed at an initial plant cost of £ 5 per linear yard by way of the Dargle, Rathdown, Glen of the Downs and Callowhill to the 26 acre reservoir at Stillorgan, a distance of 22 statute miles, and thence, through a system of relieving tanks, by a gradient of 250 feet to the city boundary at Eustace bridge, upper Leeson street, though from prolonged summer drouth and daily supply of 12 1/2 million gallons the water had fallen below the sill of the overflow weir for which reason the borough surveyor and waterworks engineer, Mr Spencer Harty, C. E., on the instructions of the waterworks committee had prohibited the use of municipal water for purposes other than those of consumption (envisaging the possibility of recourse being had to the impotable water of the Grand and Royal canals as in 1893) particulary as the South Dublin Guardians, notwithstanding their ration of 15 gallons per day per pauper supplied through a 6 inch meter had been convicted of a wastage of 20.000 gallons per night by a reading of their meter on the affirmation of the law agent of the corporation, Mr Ignatius Rice, solicitor, thereby acting to the detriment of another section of the public, selfsupporting taxpayers, solvent, sound.

What in water did Bloom, waterlover, drawer of water, watercarrier, returning to the range, admire?

Its universality : its democratic equality and constancy to its nature in seeking its own level : its vastness in the ocean of Mercator's projection : its umplumbed profundity in the Sundam trench of the Pacific exceeding 8.000 fathoms : the restlessness of its waves and surface particles visiting in turn all points of its seaboard : the independence of its units : the variability of states of sea : its hydrostatic quiescence in calm : its hydrokinetic turgidity in neap and spring tides : its subsidence after devastation : its sterility in the circumpolar icecaps, arctic and antarctic : its climatic and commercial significance : its preponderance of 3 to 1 over the dry land of the globe : its indisputable hegemony extending in square leagues over all the region below the subequatorial tropic of Capricorn : the multisecular stability of its primeval basin : its luteosfulvous bed : its capacity to dissolve and hold in solution all soluble substances including millions of tons of the most precious metals : its slow erosions of peninsulas and downwardtending promontories : its alluvial deposits : its weight and volume and density : its imperturbability in lagoons and highland tarns : its gradation of colours in the torrid and temperate and frigid zones : its vehicular ramifications in continental lakecontained streams and confluent oceanflowing rivers with their tributaries and transoceanic currents : gulfstream, north and south equatorial courses : its violence in seaquakes, waterspouts, Artesian wells, eruptions, torrents, eddies, freshets, spates, groundswells, watersheds, waterpartings, geysers, cataracts, whirlpools, maelstroms, inundations, deluges, cloudbursts : its vast circumterrestrial ahorizontal curve : its secrecy in springs, and latent humidity, revealed by rhabdomantic or hygrometric instruments and exemplified by the hole in the wall at Ashtown gate, saturation of air; distillation of dew : the simplicity of its composition, two constituent parts of hydrogen with one constituent part of oxygen : its healing virtues : its buoyancy in the waters of the Dead Sea : its persevering penetrativeness in runnels, gullies, inadequate dams, leaks on shipboard : its properties for cleansing, quenching thirst and fire, nourishing vegetation : its infaillibility as paradigm and paragon : its metamorphoses as vapour, mist, cloud, rain, sleet, snow, hail : its strength in rigid hydrants : its variety of forms in loughs and bays and gulfs and bights and guts and lagoons and atolls and archipelagos and sounds and fjords and minches and tidal estuaries and arms of sea : its solidity in glaciers, icebergs, icefloes : its docility in working hydraulic millwheels, turbines, dynamos, electric power stations, bleachworks, tanneries, scutchmills : its utility in canals, rivers, ifnavigable, floating and graving docks : its potentiality derivable from harnessed tides or watercourses falling from level to level : its submarine fauna and flora (anacoustic, photophobe) numerically, if not literally, the inhabitants of the globe : its ubiquity as constituting 90 % of the human body : the noxiousness of its effluvia in lacustrine marshes, pestilential fens, faded flowerwater, stagnant pools in the waning moon.

Having set the halffilled kettle on the now burning coals, why did he return to the stillflowing tap ?

To wash his soiled hands with a partially consumed tablet of Barrington's lemonflavoured soap, to which paper still adhered (bought thirteen hours previously for fourpence and still unpaid for), in fresh cold neverchanging everchanging water and dry them, face and hands, in a long redbordered holland cloth passed over a wooden revolving roller.

What reason did Stephen give for declining Bloom's offer ?

That he was hydrophobe, hating partial contact by immersion or total by submersion in cold water (his last bath having taken place in the month of

October of the preceding year), disliking the aqueous substances of glass and crystal, distrusting aquacities of thought and language.

What impeded Bloom from giving Stephen counsels of hygiene and prophylactic to which should be added suggestions concerning a preliminary wetting of the head and contraction of the muscles with rapid splashing of the face and neck and thoracic and epigastric region in case of sea or river bathing, the parts of the human anatomy most sensitive to cold being the nape, stomach and thenar or sole of foot?

The incompatibility of aquacity with the erratic originality of genius.

What additional didactic counsels did he similarly repress?

Dietary: concerning the respective percentage of protein and caloric energy in bacon, salt ling and butter, the absence of the former in the lastnamed and the abundance of the latter in the firstnamed.

Which seemed to the host to be the predominant qualities of his guest?

Confidence in himself, an equal and opposite power of abandonment and recuperation.

What concomitant phenomenon took place in the vessel of liquid by the agency of fire?

The phenomenon of ebullition. Fanned by a constant updraught of ventilation between the kitchen and the chimneyflue, ignition was communicated from the faggots of precombustible fuel to polyhedral masses of bituminous coal, containing in compressed mineral form the foliated fossilised decidua of primeval forests which had in turn derived their vegetative existence from the sun, primal source of heat (radiant), transmitted through omnipresent luminiferous diathermanous ether. Heat (convected), a mode of motion developed by such combustion, was constantly and increasingly conveyed from the course of calorification to the liquid contained in the vessel, being radiated through the uneven unpolished dark surface of the metal iron, in part reflected, in part absorbed, in part transmitted, gradually raising the temperature of the water from normal to boiling point, a rise in temperature expressible as the result of an expenditure of 72 thermal units needed to raise 1 pound of water from 50° to 212° Fahrenheit.

What announced the accomplishment of this rise in temperature?

A double falciform ejection of water vapour from under the kettlelid at both sides simultaneously.

For what personal purpose could Bloom have applied the water so boiled?

To shave himself.

What advantages attended shaving by night?

A softer beard : a softer brush if intentionally allowed to remain from shave to shave in its agglutinated lather : a softer skin if unexpectedly encountering female acquaintances in remote places at incustomary hours : quiet reflections upon the course of the day : a cleaner sensation when awaking after a fresher sleep since matutinal noises, premonitions and perturbations, a clattered milkcan, a postman's double knock, a paper read, reread while lathering, relathering the same spot, a shock, a shoot, with thought of aught he sought though fraught with nought might cause a faster rate of shaving and a nick on which incision plaster with precision cut and humected and applied adhered which was to be done.

Why did absence of light disturb him less than presence of noise?

Because of the surety of the sense of touch in his firm full masculine feminine passive active hand.

What quality did it (his hand) possess but with what counteracting influence?

The operative surgical quality but that he was reluctant to shed human blood even when the end justified the means, preferring, in their natural order, heliotherapy, psychophysicotherapeutics, osteopathic surgery.

What lay under exposure on the lower middle and upper shelves of the kitchen dresser opened by Bloom?

On the lower shelf five vertical breakfast plates, six horizontal breakfast saucers on which rested inverted breakfast cups, a moustachecup, uninverted, and saucer of Crown Derby, four white goldrimmed eggcups, an open shammy purse dispaying coins, mostly copper, and a phial of aromatic violet comfits. On the middle shelf a chipped eggcup containing pepper, a drum of table salt, four conglomerated black olivesin oleaginous paper, an empty pot of

Plumtree's potted meat, an oval wicker basket bedded with fibre and containing one Jersey pear, a halfempty bottle of William Gilbey and Co's white invalid port, half disrobed of its swathe of coralpink tissue paper, a packet of Epps's soluble cocoa, five ounces of Anne Lynch's choice tea at 2/- per lb. in a crinkled leadpaper bag, a cylindrical canister containing the best crystallised lump sugar, two onions, one the larger, Spanish, entire, the other, smaller, Irish, bisected with augmented surface and more redolent, a jar of Irish Model Dairy's cream, a jug of brown crockery containing a naggin and a quarter of soured adulterated milk, converted by heat into water, acidulous serum and semisolidified curds, which added to the quantity subtracted for Mr Bloom's and Mrs Fleming's breakfasts made one imperial pint, the total quantity originally delivered, two cloves, a halfpenny and a small dish containing a slice of fresh ribsteak. On the upper shelf a battery of jamjars of various sizes and proveniences.

What attracted his attention lying on the apron of the dresser?

Four polygonal fragments of two lacerated scarlet betting tickets, numbered 8 87, 8 86.

What reminiscences temporarily corrugated his brow?

Reminiscences of coincidences, truth stranger than fiction, preindicative of the result of the Gold Cup flat handicap, the official and definitive result of which he had read in the *Evening Telegraph*, late pink edition, in the cabman's shelter, at Butt bridge.

Where had previous intimations of the result, effected or projected, been received by him?

In Bernard Kiernan's licensed premises 8, 9 and 10 Little Britain street: in David Byrne's licensed premises, 14 Duke street: in O'Connell street lower, outside Graham Lemon's when a dark man had placed in his hand a throwaway (subsequently thrown away), advertising Elijah, restorer of the church in Zion: in Lincoln place outside the premises of F. W Sweny and Co (Limited), dispensing chemists, when, when Frederick M. (Bantam) Lyons had rapidly and successively requested, perused and restituted the copy of the current issue of the *Freeman's Journal* and *National Press* which he had been about to throw away (subsequently thrown away), he had proceeded towards the oriental edifice of the Turkish and Warm Baths, 11 Leinster street, with the light of inspiration shining in his countenance and bearing in his arms the secret of the race, graven in the language of prediction.

What qualifying considerations allayed his perturbations?

The difficulties of interpretation since the significance of any event followed its occurrence as variably as the acoustic report followed the electrical discharge and of counterestimating against an actual loss by failure to interpret the total sum of possible losses proceeding originally from a successful interpretation.

His mood?

He had not risked, he did not expect, he had not been disappointed, he was satisfied.

What satisfied him?

To have sustained no positive loss. To have brought a positive gain to others. Light to the gentiles.

How did Bloom prepare a collation for a gentile?

He poured into two teacups two level spoonfuls, four in all, of Epps's soluble cocoa and proceeded according to the directions for use printed on the label, to each adding after sufficient time for infusion the prescribed ingredients for diffusion in the manner and in the quantity prescribed.

What supererogatory marks of special hospitality did the host show his guest?

Relinquishing his symposiarchal right to the moustache cup of imitation Crown Derby presented to him by his only daughter, Millicent (Milly), he substituted a cup identical with that of his guest and served extraordinarily to his guest and, in reduced measure, to himself, the viscous cream ordinarily reserved for the breakfast of his wife Marion (Molly).

Was the guest conscious of and did he acknowledge these marks of hospitality?

His attention was directed to them by his host jocosely and he accepted them seriously as they drank in jocoserious silence Epps's massproduct, the creature cocoa.

Were there marks of hospitality which he contemplated but suppressed, reserving them for another and for himself on future occasions to complete the act begun ?

The reparation of a fissure of the length of 1 1/2 inches in the right side of his guest's jacket. A gift to his guest of one of the four lady's handkerchiefs, if and when ascertained to be in a presentable condition.

Who drank more quickly ?

Bloom, having the advantage of ten seconds at the initiation and taking, from the concave surface of a spoon along the handle of which a steady flow of heat was conducted, three sips to his opponent's one, six to two, nine to three.

What cerebration accompanied his frequentative act ?

Concluding by inspection but erroneously that his silent companion was engaged in mental composition he reflected on the pleasures derived from literature of instruction rather than of amusement as he himself had applied to the works of William Shakespeare more than once for the solution of difficult problems in imaginary or real life.

Had he found their solution ?

In spite of careful and repeated reading of certain classical passages, aided by a glossary, he had derived imperfect conviction from the text, the answers not bearing in all points.

What lines concluded his first piece of original verse written by him, potential poet, at the age of 11 in 1877 on the occasion of the offering of three prizes of 10/-, 5/- and 2/6 respectively by the *Shamrock,* a weekly newspaper ?

An ambition to squint
At my verses in print
Makes me hope that for these you'll find room
If you so condescend
Then please place at the end
The name of yours truly, L. Bloom.

Did he find four separating forces between his temporary guest and him ?

Name, age, race, creed.

What anagrams had he made on his name in youth ?

Leopold Bloom
Ellpodbomool
Molldopeloob
Bollopedoom
Old Ollebo, M. P.

What acrostic upon the abbreviation of his first name had he (kinetic poet) sent to Miss Marion Tweedy on the 14 February 1888 ?

Poets oft have sung in rhyme
Of music sweet their praise divine.
Let them hymn it nine times nine.
Dearer far than song or wine.
You are mine. The world is mine.

What had prevented him from completing a topical song (music by R. G. Johnston) on the events of the past, or fixtures for the actual, years, entitled *If Brian Boru could but come back and see old Dublin now,* commissioned by Michael Gunn, lessee of the Gaiety Theatre, 46, 47, 48, 49 South King street, and to be introduced into the sixth scene, the valley of diamonds, ot the second edition (30 January 1893) of the grand annual Christmas pantomime *Sinbad the Sailor* (written by Greenleaf Whittier, scenery by George A. Jackson and Cecil Hicks. costumes by Mrs and Miss Whelan produced by R. Shelton 26 December 1892 under the personal supervision of Mrs Michael Gunn, ballets by Jessie Noir, harlequinade by Thomas Otto) and sung by Nelly Bouverist, principal girl ?

Firstly, oscillation between events of imperial and of local interest, the anticipatep diamond jubilee of Queen Victoria (born 1820, acceded 1837) and the posticipated opening of the new municipal fish market : secondly, apprehension of opposition from extreme circles on the questions of the respective visits of Their Royal Highnesses, the duke and duchess of York (real), and of His Majesty King Brian Boru (imaginary) : thirdly, a conflict between professional etiquette and professional emulation concerning the recent erections of the Grand Lyric Hall on Burgh Quay and the Theatre Royal in Hawkins Street : fourthly, distraction resultant from compassion for Nelly Bouverist's non-intellectual, non-political, non-topical expression of countenance and concupiscence caused by Nelly

Bouverist's revelations of white articles of non-intellectual, non-political, non-topical underclothing while she (Nelly Bouverist) was in the articles : fifthly, the difficulties of the selection of appropriate music and humorous allusions from *Everybody's Book of Jokes* (1000 pages and a laugh in every one) : sixthly, the rhymes homophonous and cacophonous, associated with the names of the new lord mayor, Daniel Tallon, the new high sheriff, Thomas Pile and the new sollicitorgeneral, Dunbar Plunket Barton.

What relation existed between their ages ?

16 years before in 1888 when Bloom was of Stephen's present age Stephen was 6. 16 years after in 1920 when Stephen would be of Bloom's present age Bloom would be 54. In 1936 when Bloom would be 70 and Stephen 54 their ages initially in the ratio of 16 to 0 would be as 17 1/2 to 13 1/2, the proportion increasing and the disparity diminishing according arbitrary as future years were added for if the proportion existing in 1883 had continued immutable, conceiving that to be possible, till then 1904 when Stephen was 22 Bloom would be 374 and in 1920 when Stephen would be 38, as Bloom then was, Bloom would be 646 while in 1952 when Stephen would have attained the maximum postdiluvian age of 70 Bloom, being 1190 years alive having been born in the year 714, would have surpassed by 221 years the maximum antediluvian age, that of Methusalah, 969 years, while, if Stephen would continue to live until he would attain that age in the year 3072 A. D., Bloom would have been obliged to have been alive 83,300 years, having been obliged to have been born in the year 81,396 B. C.

What events might nullify these calculations ?

The cessation of existence of both or either, the inauguration of a new era or calendar, the annihilation of the world and consequent extermination of the human species, inevitable but impredictable.

How many previous encounters proved their preexisting acquaintance ?

Two. The first in the lilacgarden of Matthew Dillon's house. Medina Villa, Kimmage road, Roundtown, in 1887, in the company of Stephen's mother, Stephen being then of the age of 5 and reluctant to give his hand in salutation. The second in the cofferoom of Breslin's hotel on a rainy Sunday in the January of 1892, in the company of Stephen's father and Stephen's granduncle, Stephen being then 5 years older.

Did Bloom accept the invitation to dinner given then by the son and afterwards seconded by the father?

Very gratefully, with grateful appreciation, with sincere appreciative gratitude, in appreciatively grateful sincerity of regret, he declined.

Did their conversation on the subject of these reminiscences reveal a third connecting link between them ?

Mrs Riordan, a widow of independent means, had resided in the house of Stephen's parents from 1 September 1888 to 29 December 1891 and had also resided during the years 1892, 1893 and 1894 in the City Arms Hotel owned by Elizabeth O'Dowd of 54 Prussia street where during parts of the years 1893 and 1894 she had been a constant informant of Bloom who resided also in the same hotel, being at that time a clerk in the employment of Joseph Cuffe of 5 Smithfield for the superintendence of sales in the adjacent Dublin Cattle market on the North Circular road.

Had he performed any special corporal work of mercy for her ?

He had sometimes propelled her on warm summer evenings, an infirm widow of independent, if limited means, in her convalescent bathchair with slow revolutions of its wheels as far as the corner of the North Circular road opposite Mr Gavin Low's place of business where she had remained for a certain time scanning through his onelensed binocular fieldglasses unrecognisable citizens on tramcars, roadster bicycles. equipped with inflated pneumatic tyres, hackney carriages, tandems, private and hired landaus, dogcarts, ponytraps and brakes passing from the city to the Phœnix Park and *vice versa*.

Why could he then support that his vigil with the greater equanimity ?

Because in middle youth he had often sat observing through a rondel of bossed glass of a multicoloured pane the spectacle offered with continual changes of the thoroughfare without, pedestrians, quadrupeds, velocipedes, vehicles, passing slowly, quickly, evenly, round and round and round the rim of a round precipitous globe.

What distinct different memories had each of her now eight years deceased ?

The older, her bezique cards and counters, her Skye terrier, her suppositious wealth, her lapses of responsiveness and incipient catarrhal deafness : the younger, her lamp of colza oil before the statue of the Immaculate Conception, her green and maroon brushes for Charles Stewart Parnell and for Michael Davitt, her tissue papers.

Were there no means still remaining to him to achieve the rejuvenation which these reminiscences divulged to a younger companion rendered the more desirable?

The indoor exercices, formerly intermittently practised, subsequently abandoned, prescribed in Eugen Sandow's *Physical Strength and How To Obtain It* which, designed particularly for commercial men engaged in sedentary occupations, were to be made with mental concentration in front of a mirror so as to bring into play the various families of muscles and produce successively a pleasant relaxation and the most pleasant repristination of juvenile agility.

Had any special agility been his in earlier youth?

Though ringweight lifting had been beyond his strength and the full circle gyration beyond his courage yet as a High School scholar he had excelled in his stable and protracted execution of the half lever movement on the parallel bars in consequence of his abnormally developed abdominal muscles.

Did either openly allude to their racial difference?

Neither.

What, reduced to their simplest reciprocal form, were Bloom's thoughts about Stephen's thoughts about Bloom about Stephen's thoughts about Bloom's thoughts about Stephen?

He thought that he thought that he was a jew whereas he knew that he knew that he knew that he was not.

What, the enclosures of reticence removed, were their respective parentages?

Bloom, only born male transubstantial heir of Rudolf Virag (subsequently Rudolf Bloom) of Szombathely, Vienna, Budapest. Milan, London and Dublin and of Ellen Higgins, second daughter of Julius Higgins (born Karoly) and Fanny Higgins (born Hegarty). Stephen, eldest surviving male consubstantial heir of Simon Dedalus of Cork and Dublin and of Mary, daughter of Richard and Christina Goulding (born Grier).

Had Bloom and Stephen been baptised, and where and by whom, cleric or layman?

Bloom (three times) by the reverend Mr Gilmer Johnston M. A. alone in the protestant church of Saint Nicolas Without, Coombe, by James O'Connor, Philip Gilligan and James Fitzpatrick, together, under a pump in the village of Swords, and by the reverend Charles Malone C. C., in the church of the Three Patrons, Rathgar. Stephen (once) by the reverend Charles Malone, C. C. alone, in the church of the Three Patrons, Rathgar.

Did they find their educational careers similar?

Substituting Stephen for Bloom Stoom would have passed successively through a dame's school and the high school. Substituting Bloom for Stephen Blephen would have passed successively through the preparatory, junior, middle and senior grades of the intermediate and through the matriculation, first arts second arts and arts degree courses of the royal university.

Why did Bloom refrain from stating that he had frequented the university of life?

Because of his fluctuating incertitude as to whether this observation had or had not been already made by him to Stephen or by Stephen to him.

What two temperaments did they individually represent?

The scientific. The artistic.

What proofs did Bloom adduce to prove that his tendency was towards applied, rather than towards pure, science?

Certain possible inventions of which he had cogitated when reclining in a state of supine repletion to aid digestion, stimulated by his appreciation of the importance of inventions now common but once revolutionary, for example, the aeronautic parachute, the reflecting telescope, the spiral corkscrew, the safety pin, the mineral water siphon, the canal lock with winch and sluice, the suction pump.

Were these inventions principally intended for an improved scheme of kindergarten?

Yes, rendering obsolete popguns, elastic airbladders, games of hazard, catapults. They comprised astronomical kaleidoscopes exhibiting the twelve constellations of the zodiac from Aries to Pisces, miniature mechanical orreries, arithmetical gelatine lozenges, geometrical to correspond with zoological biscuits, globemap playing balls, historically costumed dolls.

What also stimulated him in his cogitations?

The financial success achieved by Ephraim Marks and Charles A. James, the former by his 1d. bazaar at 42 George's Street, South, the latter at his 6 1/2 d. shop and world's fancy fair and waxwork exhibition at 30 Henry Street, admission 2d., children 1d.; and the infinite possibilities hitherto unexploited of the modern art of advertisement if condensed in triliteral monoideal symbols, vertically of maximum visibility (divined), horizontally of maximum legibility (deciphered) and of magnetising efficacy to arrest involuntary attention, to interest, to convince, to decide.

Such as?

K. 11. Kino's 11/- Trousers.

House of Keys. Alexander J. Keyes.

Such as not?

Look at this long candle. Calculate when it burns out and you receive gratis 1 pair of our special non-compo boots, guaranteed 1 candle power. Address: Barclay and Cook, 18 Talbot Street.

Bacilikil (Insect Powder).

Veribest (Boot Blacking).

Uwantit (Combined pocket twoblade penknife with corkscrew, nailfile and pipecleaner).

Such as never?

What is home without Plumtree's Potted Meat?

Incomplete.

With it an abode of bliss.

Manufactured by George Plumtree, 23 Merchant's quay, Dublin, put up in 4 oz.. pots, and inserted by Councillor Joseph P. Nannetti, M. P., Rotunda Ward, 19 Hardwicke Street, under the obituary notices and anniversaries of deceases. The name on the label is Plumtree. A plumtree in a meatpot, registered trade mark. Beware of imitations. Peatmot. Trumplee. Montpat. Plamtroo.

Which example did he adduce to induce Stephen to deduce that originality, though producing its own reward, does not invariably conduce to success?

His own ideated and rejected project of an illuminated showcart, drawn by a beast of burden, in which two smartly dressed girls were to be seated engaged in writing.

What suggested scene was then constructed by Stephen?

Solitary hotel in mountain pass. Autumn. Twilight. Fire lit. In dark corner young man seated. Young woman enters. Restless. Solitary. She sits. She goes to window. She stands. She sits. Twilight. She thinks. On solitary hotel paper she writes. She thinks. She writes. She sighs. Wheels and hoofs. She hurries out. He comes from his dark corner. He seizes solitary paper. He holds it towards fire. Twilight. He reads. Solitary.

What?

In sloping, upright and backhands: Queen's hotel, Queen's hotel Queen's Ho...

What suggested scene was then reconstructed by Bloom?

The Queen's Hotel, Ennis, County Clare where Rudolph Bloom (Rudolf Virag) died on the evening of the 27 June 1886, at some hour unstated, in consequence of an overdose of monkshood (aconite) selfadministered in the form of a neuralgic liniment, composed of 2 parts of aconite liniment to 1 of chloroform liniment (purchased by him at 10. 20 a. m. on the morning of 27 June 1886 at the medical hall of Francis Dennehy, 17 Church street, Ennis) after having, though not in consequence of having, purchased at 3. 15 p. m. on the afternoon of 27 June 1886 a new boater straw hat, extra smart (after having, though not in consequence of having, purchased at the hour and in the place aforesaid), the toxin aforesaid, at the general drapery store of James Cullen, 4 Main street, Ennis.

Did he attribute this homonymity to information or coincidence or intuition?

Coincidence.

Did he depict the scene verbally for his guest to see?

He preferred himself to see another's face and listen to another's words by which potential narration was realised and kinetic temperament relieved.

Did he see only a second coincidence in the second scene narrated to him, described by the narrator as *A Pisgah Sight of Palestine* or *The Parable of the Plums?*

It, with the preceding scene and with others unnarrated but existent by implication, to which add essays on various subjects or moral apothegms (e. g. *My Favourite Hero* or *Procrastination is the Thief of Time*) composed during schoolyears, seemed to him to contain in itself and in conjunction with the personal equation certain possibilities of financial, social, personal and sexual success, whether specially collected and selected as model pedagogie themes (of cent per cent merit) for the use of preparatory and junior grade students or contributed in printed form, following the precedent of Philip Beaufoy or Doctor Dick or Heblon's *Studies in Blue*, to a publication of certified circulation and solvency or employed verbally as intellectual stimulation for sympathetic auditors, tacitly appreciative of successful narrative and confidently augurative of successful achievement, during the increasingly longer nights gradually following the summer solstice on the day but three following, videlicet, Tuesday, 21 June (S. Aloysius Gonzaga), sunrise, 3.33 a. m., sunset 8.29 p. m.

Which domestic problem as much as, if not more than, any other frequently engaged his mind?

What to do with our wives.

What had been his hypothetical singular solutions?

Parlour games (dominos, halma, tiddledywinks, spilikins, cup and ball, nap, spoil five, bezique, twentyfive, beggar my neighbour, draughts, chess or backgammon) : embroidery, darning or knitting for the policeaided clothing society : musical duets, mandoline and guitar, piano and flute, guitar and piano : legal scrivenery or envelope addressing : biweekly visits to variety entertainments : commercial activity as pleasantly commanding and pleasingly obeyed mistress proprietress in a cool dairy shop or warm cigar divan : the clandestine satisfaction of erotic irritation in masculine brothels, state inspected and medically controlled : social visits, at regular infrequent prevented intervals and with regular frequent preventive superintendence, to and from female acquaintances of recognised respectability in the vicinity : courses of evening instruction specially designed to render liberal instruction agreeable.

What instances of deficient mental development in his wife inclined him in favour of the lastmentioned (ninth) solution?

In disoccupied moments she had more than once covered a sheet of paper with signs and hieroglyphics which she stated were Greek and Irish and Hebrew characters. She had interrogated constantly at varying intervals as to the correct method of writing the capital initial of the name of a city in Canada, Quebec. She understood little of political complications, internal, or balance of power, external. In calculating the addenda of bills she frequently had recourse to digital aid. After completion of laconic epistolary compositions she abandoned the implement of calligraphy in the encaustic pigment exposed to the corrosive action of copperas, green vitriol and nutgall. Unusual polysyllables of foreign origin she interpreted phonetically or by false analogy or by both: metempsychosis (met him pike hoses), *alias* (a mendacious person mentioned in sacred Scripture).

What compensated in the false balance of her intelligence for these and such deficiencies of judgment regarding persons, places and things?

The false apparent parallelism of all perpendicular arms of all balances, proved true by construction. The counterbalance of her proficiency of judgment regarding one person, proved true by experiment.

How had he attemped to remedy this state of comparative ignorance?

Variously. By leaving in a conspicuous place a certain book open at a certain page: by assuming in her, when alluding explanatorily, latent knowledge: by open ridicule in her presence of some absent other's ignorant lapse.

With what success had he attempted direct instruction?

She followed not all, a part of the whole, gave attention with interest, comprehended with surprise, with care repeated, with greater difficulty remembered, forgot with ease, with misgiving reremembered, rerepeated with error.

What system had proved more effective?

Indirect suggestion implicating self-interest.

Example?

She disliked umbrella with rain, he liked woman with umbrella, she disliked new hat with rain, he liked woman with new hat, he bought new hat with rain, she carried umbrella with new hat.

Accepting the analogy implied in his guest's parable which examples of postexilic eminence did he adduce?

Three seekers of the pure truth, Moses of Egypt, Moses Maimonides, author of *More Nebukim* (Guide of the Perplexed) and Moses Mendelssohn of such eminence that from Moses (of Egypt) to Moses (Mendelssohn) there arose none like Moses (Maimonides).

What statement was made, under correction, by Bloom concerning a fourth seeker of pure truth, by name Aristotle, mentioned, with permission, by Stephen?

That the seeker mentioned had been a pupil of a rabbinical philosopher, name uncertain.

Were other anapocryphal illustrious sons of the law and children of a selected or rejected race mentioned?

Felix Bartholdy Mendelssohn (composer), Baruch Spinoza (philosopher), Mendoza (pugilist), Ferdinand Lassalle (reformer, duellist).

What fragment of verse from the ancient Hebrew and ancient Irish languages were cited with modulations of voice and translation of texts by guest to host and by host to guest?

By Stephen: *suil, suil, suil arun, suil go siocair agus suil go cuin* (walk, walk, walk your way, walk in safety, walk with care).

By Bloom: *Kifeloch, harimon rakatejch m'baad l'zamatejch* (thy temple amid thy hair is as a slice of pomegranate).

How was a glyphic comparison of the phonic symbols of both languages made in substantiation of the oral comparison?

On the penultimate blank page of a book entituled of inferior literary style, *Sweets of Sin* (produced by Bloom and so manipulated that its front cover came in contact with the surface of the table) with a pencil (supplied by Stephen) Stephen wrote the Irish characters for gee, eh, dee, em, simple and modified, and Bloom in turn wrote the Hebrew characters ghimel, aleph, daleth and (in the absence of mem) a substituted goph, explaining their arithmetical values as ordinal and cardinal numbers, videlicet 3, 1, 4 and 100.

Was the knowledge possessed by both of each of these languages, the extinct and the revived, theoretical or practical?

Theoretical, being confined to certain grammatical rules of accidence and syntax and practically excluding vocabulary.

What points of contact existed between these languages and between the peoples who spoke them?

The presence of guttural sounds, diacritic aspirations, epenthetic and servile letters in both languages: their antiquity, both having taught on the plain of Shinar 242 years after the deluge in the seminary instituted by Fenius Farsaigh, descendant of Noah, progenitor of Israel, and ascendant of Heber and Heremon, progenitors of Ireland: their archeological, genealogical, hagiographical, exegetical, homilectic, toponomastic, historical and religious literatures comprising the works of rabbis and culdees, Torah, Talmud (Mischna and Ghemara) Massor, Pentateuch, Book of the Dun Cow, Book of Ballymote, Garland of Howth, Book of Kells: their dispersal, persecution, survival and revival: the isolation of their synagogical and ecclesiastical rites in ghetto (S. Mary's Abbey) and masshouse (Adam and Eve's tavern): the proscription of their national costumes in penal laws and jewish dress acts: the restoration in Chanan David of Zion and the possibility of Irish political autonomy or devolution.

What anthem did Bloom chant partially in anticipation of that multiple, ethnically irreducible consummation?

Kolod balejwaw pnimah
Nefesch, jehudi, homijah.

Why was the chant arrested at the conclusion of this first distich?

In consequence of defective mnemotechnic.

How did the chanter compensate for this deficiency?

By a periphrastic version of the general text.

In what common study did their mutual reflections merge?

The increasing simplification traceable from the Egyptian epigraphic hieroglyphs to the Greek and Roman alphabets and the anticipation of modern stenography and telegraphic code in the cuneiform inscriptions (Semitic) and the virgular quinquecostate ogham writing (Celtic).

Did the guest comply with his host's request?

Doubly, by appending his signature in Irish and Roman characters.

What was Stephen's auditive sensation?

He heard in a profound ancient male unfamiliar melody the accumulation of the past.

What was Bloom's visual sensation?

He saw in a quick young male familiar form the predestination of a future.

What were Stephen's and Bloom's quasisimultaneous volitional quasisensations of concealed identities?

Visually, Stephen's : The traditional figure of hypostasis, depicted by Johannes Damascenus, Lentulus Romanus and Epiphanius Monachus as leucodermic, sesquipedalian with winedark hair.

Auditively, Bloom's : The Traditionnal accent af the ecstasy of catastrophe.

What future careers had been possible for Bloom in the past and with what exemplars?

In the church, Roman, Anglican, or Nonconformist : exemplars, the very reverend John Conmee S.J., the reverend T. Salmon, D.D., provost of Trinity college, Dr Alexander J. Dowie. At the bar, English or Irish : exemplars, Seymour Bushe, K. C., Rufus Isaacs, K. C. On the stage, modern or Shakespearean : examplars Charles Wyndham, high comedian, Osmond Tearle († 1901), exponent of Shakespeare.

Did the host encourage his guest to chant in a modulated voice a strange legend on an allied theme?

Reassuringly, their place where none could hear them talk being secluded, reassured, the decocted beverages, allowing for subsolid residual sediment of a mechianacal mixture, water plus sugar plus cream plus cocoa, having been consumed.

Recite the first (major) part of this chanted legend ?

Little Harry Hughes and his schoolfellows all
Went out for to play ball.
And the very first ball little Harry Hughes played
He drove it o'w'er the je's garden wall.
And the very second ball little Harry Hughes played
He broke the jew's windows all.

How did the son of Rudolph receive this first part ?

With unmixed feeling. Smiling, a jew, he heard with pleasure and saw the unbroken kitchen window.

Recite the second part (minor) of the legend.

Then out came the jew's daughter
And she all dressed in green.
« Come back, come back, you pretty little boy,
And play your ball again. »

« I can't come back and I won't come back
Without my schoolfellows all.
For if my master he did hear
He'd make it a sorry ball. »

She took him by the lilywhite hand
And led him along the hall
Until she led him to a room
Where none could hear him call.

She took a penknife out of her pocket
And cut off his little head
And now he'll play his ball no more
For he lies among the dead.

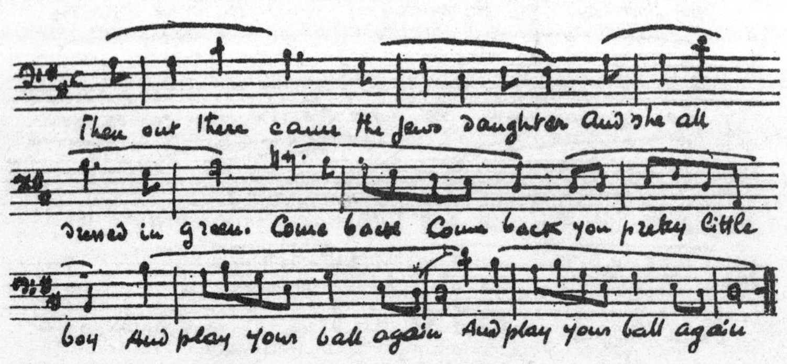

How did the father of Millicent receive this second part?

With mixed ſeelings. Unsmiling, he heard and saw with wonder a jew's daughter, all dressed in green.

Condense Stephen's commentary.

One of all, the least of all, is the victim predestined. Once by inadvertence, twice by design he challenges his destiny. It comes when he is abandoned and challenges him reluctant and, as an apparition of hope and youth, holds him unresisting. It leads him to a strange habitation, to a secret infidel apartment, and there, implacable, immolates him, consenting.

Why was the host (victim predestined) sad?

He wished that a tale of a deed should be told of a deed not by him should by him not be told.

Why was the host (reluctant, unresisting) still?

In accordance with the law of the conservation of energy.

Why was the host (secret infidel) silent?

He weighed the possible evidences for and against ritual murder: the incitation of the hierarchy, the superstition of the populace, the propagation of rumour in continued fraction of veridicity, the envy of opulence, the influence of retaliation, the sporadic reappearance of atavistic delinquency, the mitigating circumstances of fanaticism, hypnotic suggestion and somnambulism.

From which (if any) of these mental or physical disorders was he not totally immune?

From hypnotic suggestion: once, waking, he had not recognised his sleeping apartment: more than once, waking, he had been for an indefinite time incapable of moving or uttering sounds. From somnambulism: once, sleeping, his body had risen, crouched and crawled in the direction of a heatless fire and, having attained its destination, there, curled, unheated, in night attire had lain, sleeping.

Had this latter or any cognate phenomenon declared itself in any member of his family?

Twice, in Holles street and in Ontario terrace, his daughter Millicent (Milly) at the ages of 6 and 8 years had uttered in sleep an exclamation of terror and had replied to the interrogations of two figures in night attire with a vacant mute expression.

What other infantile memories had he of her ?

15 June 1889. A querulous newborn female infant crying to cause and lessen congestion. A child renamed Padney Socks she shook with shocks her moneybox : counted his three free moneypenny buttons one, tloo, tlee : a doll, a boy, a sailor she cast away : blond, born of two dark, she had blond ancestry, remote, a violation, Herr Hauptmann Hainau, Austrian army, proximate, ahallucination, lieutenant Mulvey, British navy.

What endemic characteristics were present ?

Conversely the nasal and frontal formation was derived in a direct line of lineage which, though interrupted, would continue at distant intervals to its most distant intervals.

What memories had he of her adolescence ?

She relegated her hoop and skippingrope to a recess. On the duke's lawn entreated by an English visitor, she declined to permit him to make and take away her photographic image (objection not stated). On the South Circular road in the company of Elsa Potter, followed by an individual of sinister aspect, she went half way down Stamer street and turned abruptly back (reason of change not stated). On the vigil of the 15th anniversary of her birth she wrote a letter from Mullingar, county Westmeath, making a brief allusion to a local student (faculty and year not stated).

Did that first division, portending a second division, afflict him ?

Less than he had imagined, more than he had hoped.

What second departure was contemporaneously perceived by him similarly if differently ?

A temporary departure of his cat.

Why similarly, why differently ?

Similarly, because actuated by a secret purpose the quest of a new male (Mullingar student) or of a healing herb (valerian). Differently, because of different possible returns to the inhabitants or to the habitation.

In other respects were their differences similar ?

In passivity, in economy, in the instinct of tradition, in unexpectedness.

As ?

Inasmuch as leaning she sustained her blond hair for him to ribbon it for her (cf. neckarching cat). Moreover, on the free surface of the lake in Stephen's green amid inverted reflections of trees her uncommented spit, describing concentric circles of waterrings, indicated by the constancy of its permanence the locus of a somnolent prostrate fish (cf. mousewatching cat). Again, in order to remember the date, combatants, issue and consequences of a famous military engagement she pulled a plait of her hair (cf. earwashing cat). Furthermore, silly Milly, she dreamed of having had an unspoken unremembered conversation with a horse whose name had been Joseph to whom (which) she had offered a tumblerful of lemonade which it (he) had appeared to have accepted (cf. hearthdreaming cat). Hence, in passivity, in economy, in the instinct of tradition, in unexpectedness, were differences were similar.

In what way had he utilised gifts 1) an owl, 2) a clock), given as matrimonial auguries, to interest and to instruct her ?

As object lessons to explain : 1) the nature and habits of oviparous animals, the possibility of aerial flight, certain abnormalities of vision, the secular process of imbalsamation : 2) the principle of the pendulum, exemplified in bob, wheelgear and regulator, the translation in terms of human or social regulation of the various positions clockwise of moveable indicators on an unmoving dial, the exactitude of the recurrence per hour of an instant in each hour, when the longer and the shorter indicator were at the same angle of inclination, *videlicet*, 5 5/11 minutes past each hour per hour in arithmetical progression.

In what manners did she reciprocate ?

She remembered : on the 27th anniversary of his birth she presented to him a breakfast moustachecup of imitation crown Derby porcelain ware. She provided : at quarter day or thereabouts if or when purchases had been made by him not for her she showed herself attentive to his necessities, anticipating his desires. She admired : a natural phenomenon having been explained by him not for her she expressed the immediate desire to possess without gradual acquisition a fraction of his science, the moiety, the quarter, a thousandth part.

What proposal did Bloom, diambulist, father of Milly, somnambulist, make to Stephen, noctambulist?

To pass in repose the hours intervening between Thursday (proper) and Friday (normal) on an extemporised cubicle in the apartment immediately above the kitchen and immediateiy adjacent to the sleeping apartment of his host and hostess.

What various advantages would or might have resulted from a prolungation of such extemporisation?

For the guest: security of domicile and seclusion of study. For the host: rejuvenation of intelligence, vicarious satisfaction. For the hostess: disintegration of obsession, acquisition of correct Italian pronunciation.

Why might these several provisional contingencies between a guest and a hostess not necessarily preclude or be precluded by a permanent eventuality of reconciliatory union between a schoolfellow and a jew's daughter?

Because the way to daughter led through mother, the way to mother through daughter.

To what inconsequent polysyllabic question of his host did the guest return a monosyllabic negative answer?

If he had known the late Mrs Emily Sinico, accidentally killed at Sydney Parade railway station, 14 October 1903.

What inchoate corollary statement was consequently suppressed by the host?

A statement explanatory of his absence on the occasion of the interment of Mrs Mary Goulding, 26 June 1903, vigil of the anniversary of the decease of Rudolph Bloom (born Virag).

Was the proposal of asylum accepted?

Promptly, inexplicably, with amicability, gratefully it was declined.

What exchange of money took place between host and guest?

The former returned to the latter, without interest, a sum of money (£ 1-7-0), one pound seven shilling, advanced by the latter to the former.

What counterproposals were alternately advanced, accepted, modified, declined, restated in other terms, reaccepted, ratified, reconfirmed?

To inaugurate a prearranged course of Italian instruction, place the residence of the instructed. To inaugurate a course of vocal instruction, place the residence of the instructress. To inaugurate a series of static, semistatic and peripatetic intellectual dialogues, places the residence of both speakers (if both speakers were resident in the same place) the *Ship* hotel and tavern, 6 Lower Abbey street (W. and E. Connery, proprietors), the National Library of Ireland, 10 Kildare street, the National Maternity Hospital, 29, 30 and 31 Holles street, a public garden, the vicinity of a place of worship, a conjunction of two or more public thoroughfares, the point of bisection of a right line drawn between their residences (if both speakers were resident in different places).

What rendered problematic for Bloom the realisation of these mutually selfexcluding propositions?

The irreparability of the past: once at a performance of Albert Hengler's circus in the Rotunda, Rutland Square, Dublin, anintuitive particoloured clown in quest of paternity had penetrated from the ring to a place in the auditorium where Bloom, solitary, was seated and had publicly declared to an exhilarated audience that he (Bloom) was his (the clown's) papa. The imprevidibility of the future: once in the summer of 1898 he (Bloom) had marked a florin (2/-) with three notches on the milled edge and tendered it in payment of an account due to and received by J. and T. Davy family grocers, 1 Charlemont Mall, Grand Canal, for circulation on the waters of civic finance, for possible, circuitous or direct, return.

Was the clown Bloom's son?

No.

Had Bloom's coin returned?

Never.

Why would a recurrent frustration the more depress him?

Because at the critical turningpoint of human existence he desired to amend many social conditions, the product of inequality and avarice and international animosity.

He believed then that human life was infinitely perfectible, eliminating these conditions?

There remained the generic conditions imposed by natural, as distinct from human law, as integral parts of the human whole; the necessity of destruction to procure alimentary sustenance; the painful character of the ultimate functions of separate existence, the agonies of birth and death: the monotonous menstruation, of simian and (particularly) human females extending from the age of puberty to the menopause; inevitable accidents at sea, in mines and factories: certain very painful maladies and their resultant surgical operations, innate lunacy and congenital criminality, decimating epidemics: catastrophic cataclyms which make terror the basis of human mentality: seismic upheavals the epicentres of which are located in densely populated regions: the fact of vital growth, through convulsions of metamorphosis, from infancy through maturity to decay.

Why did he desist from speculation?

Because it was a task for a superior intelligence to substitute other more acceptable phenomena in place of the less acceptable phenomena to be removed.

Did Stephen participate in his dejection?

He affirmed his significance as a conscious rational animal proceeding syllogistically from the known to the unknown and a conscious rational reagent between a micro and a macrocosm ineluctably constructed upon the incertitude of the void.

Was this affimation apprehended by Bloom?

Not verbally. Substantially.

What comforted his misapprehension?

That as a competent keyless citizen he had proceeded energetically from the unknown to the known through the incertitude of the void.

In what order of precedence, with what attendant ceremony was the exodus from the house of bondage to the wilderness of inhabitation effected?

Lighted Candle in Stick borne by
BLOOM
Diaconal Hat on Ashplant borne by
STEPHEN.

With what intonation *secreto* of what commemorative psalm?

The 113 th, *modus peregrinus : In exitu Israël de Egypto : domus Jacob de populo barbaro.*

What did each so at the door of egress?

Bloom set the candlestick on the floor. Stephen put the hat on his head.

For what creature was the door of egress a door of ingress?

For a cat.

What spectacle confronted them when they, first the host, then the guest, emerged silently, doubly dark, from obscurity by a passage from the rere of the house into the penumbra of the garden?

The heaventree of stars hung with humid nightblue fruit.

With what meditations did Bloom accompany his demonstration to his companion of various constellation?

Meditations of evolution increasingly vaster : of the moon invisible in incipient lunation, approaching perigee : of the infinite lattiginous scintillating uncondensed milky way, discernible by daylight by an observer placed at the lower end of a cylindrical vertical shaft 5000 ft deep sunk from the surface towards the centre of the earth : of Sirius (alpha in Canis Maior) 10 lightyears (57, 000, 000, 000, 000, miles) distant and in volume 900 times the dimension of our planet : of Arcturus : of the precession of equinoxes : of Orion with belt and sextuple sun theta and nebula in which 100 of our solar systems could be contained : of moribund and of nascent new stars such as Nova in 1901 : of our system plunging towards the constellation of Hercules : of the parallax or parallactic drift of socalled fixed stars, in reality evermoving from immeasurably remote eons to infinitely remote futures in comparison with which the years, threscore and ten, of allotted human life formed a parenthesis of infinitesimal brevity.

Were there obverse meditations of involution increasingly less vast?

Of the eons of geological periods recorded in the stratifications of the earth : of the myriad minute entomological organic existences concealed in cavities of the earth, beneath removable stones, in hives and mounds, of microbes, germs, bacteria, bacilli, spermatozoa : of the incalculable trillions of billions of millions of imperceptible molecules contained by cohesion of molecular affinity in a single pinhead : of the universe of human serum constellated with red and white bodies, themselves universes of void space constellated with other bodies, each, in continuity, its universe of divisible component bodies of which each was again divisible in divisions of redivisible component bodies, dividends and divisors ever diminishing without actual division till, if the progress were carried far enough, nought nowhere was never reached.

Why did he not elaborate these calculations to a more precise result?

Because some years previously in 1886 when occupied with the problem of the quadrature of the circle he had learned of the existence of a number computed to a relative degree of accuracy to be of such magnitude and of so many places, e. g., the 9th power of the 9th power of 9, that, the result having been obtained, 33 closely printed volumes of 1000 pages each of innumerable quires and reams of India paper would have to be requisitioned in order to contain the complete tale of its printed integers of units, tens, hundreds, thousands, tens of thousands, hundreds of thousands, millions, tens of millions, hundreds ot millions, billions, the nucleus of the nebula of every digit of every series containing succinctly the potentiality of being raised to the utmost kinetic elaboration of any power of any of its powers.

Did he find the problem of the inhabitability of the planets and their satellites by a race, given in species, and of the possible social and moral redemption of said race by a redeemer, easier of solution?

Of a different order of difficulty. Conscious that the human organism, normally capable of sustaining an atmospheric pressure of 19 tons, when elevated to a considerable altitude in the terrestrial atmosphere suffered with arithmetical progression of intensity, according as the line of demarcation between troposphere and statosphere was approximated, from nasal hemorrhage, impeded respiration and vertigo, when proposing this problem for solution, he had conjectured as a working hypothesis which could not be proved impossible that a more adaptable and differently anatomically constructed race of beings might subsist otherwise under Martian, Mercurial, Veneral, Jovian, Saturnian, Neptunian or Uranian sufficient and equivalent conditions, though an apogean humanity of beings created in varying forms wiih finite differences resulting similar to the whole and to one another would probably there as here remain inalterably and inalienably attached to vanities, to vanities of vanities and to all that is vanity.

And the problem of possible redemption?

The minor was proved by the major.

Which various features of the constellations were in turn considered?

The various colours significant of various degrees of vitality (white, yellow, crimson, vermilion, cinnabar): their degrees of brilliancy: their magnitudes revealed up to and including the 7th: their positions: the waggoner's star: Walsingham way: the chariot of David: the annular cinctures of Saturn: the condensation of spiral nebulae into suns: the interdependant gyrations of double suns: the independent synchronous discoveries of Galileo, Simon Marius, Piazzi, Le Verrier, Herschel, Galle: the systematisations attempted by Bode and Kepler of cubes of distances and squares of times of revolution: the almost infinite compressibility of hirsute comets and their vast elliptical egressive and reentrant orbits from perihelion to aphelion: the sidereal origin of meteoric stones: the Libyan floods on Mars about the period of the birth of the younger satroscopist: the annual recurrence of meteoric showers about the period of the feast of S. Lawrence (martyr, 10 August): the monthly recurrence known as the new moon with the old moon in her arms: the posited influence of celestial on human bodies: the appearance of a star (1st magnitude) of exceeding brilliancy dominating by night and day (a new luminous sun generated by the collision and amalgamation in incandescence of two nonluminous exsuns) about the period of the birth of William Shakespeare over delta in the recumbent neversetting constellation of Cassiopeia and of a star (2nd magnitude) of similar origin but lesser brilliancy which had appeared in and dissapeared from the constellation of the Corona Septentrionalis about the period of the birth of Leopold Bloom and of other stars of (presumably) similar origin which had (effectively or presumably) appeared in and disappeared from the constellation of Andromeda about the period of the birth of Stephen Dedalus, and in and from the constellation of Auriga some years after the birth and death of Rudolph Bloom, junior, and in and from other constellations some years before or after the birth or death of other persons, the attendant phenomena of eclipses, solar and lunar, from immersion to emersion, abatement of wind, transit of shadow, taciturnity of winged creatures, emergence of nocturnal or crepuscular animals, persistance of infernal light, obscurity of terrestrial waters, pallor of human beings.

His (Bloom's) logical conclusion, having weighed the matter and allowing for possible error?

That it was not a heaventree, not a heavengrot, not a heavenbeast, not a heavenman. That it was a Utopia, there being no known method from the known to the unknown: an infinity, renderable equally finite by the suppositious probable apposition of one or more bodies equally of the same and of different magnitudes: a mobility of illusory forms immobilised in space, remobilised in air: a past which possibly had ceased to exist as a present before its spectators had entered actual present existence.

Was he more convinced of the esthetic value of the spectacle?

Indubitably in consequence of the reiterated examples of poets in the delirium of the frenzy of attachment or in the abasement of rejection invoking ardent sympathetic constellations or the frigidity of the satellite of their planet.

Did he then accept as an article of belief the theory of astrological influences upon sublunary disasters?

It seemed to him as possible of proof as of confutation and the nomenclature employed in its selenographical charts as attributable to verifiable intuition as to fallacious analogy: the lake of dreams, the sea of rains, the gulf of dews, the ocean of fecundity.

What special affinities appeared to him to exist between the moon and woman?

Her antiquity in preceding and surviving successive tellurian generations: her nocturnal predominance: her satellitic dependence: her luminary reflection: her constancy under all her phases, rising, and setting by her appointed times, waxing and waning: the forced invariability of her aspect: her indeterminate response to inaffirmative interrogation: her potency over effluent and refluent waters: her power to enamour, to mortify, to invest with beauty, to render insane, to incite to and aid delinquency: the tranquil inscrutability of her visage: the terribility of her isolated dominant implacable resplendent propinquity: her omens of tempest and of calm: the stimulation of her light, her motion and her presence: the admonition of her craters, her arid seas, her silence: her splendour, when visible: her attraction, when invisible.

What visible luminous sign attracted Bloom's, who attracted Stephen's gaze?

In the second storey (rere) of his (Bloom's) house the light of a paraffin oil lamp with oblique shade projected on a screen of roller blind supplied by Frank O'Hara, window blind, curtain pole and revolving shutter manufacturer, 16 Aungier street.

How did he elucidate the mystery of an invisible person, his wife Marion (Molly) Bloom, denoted by a visible splendid sign, a lamp?

With indirect and direct verbal allusions or affirmations: with subdued affection and admiration: with description; with impediment; with suggestion.

Both then were silent?

Silent, each contemplating the other in both mirrors of the reciprocal flesh of theirhisnothis fellowfaces.

Were they indefinitely inactive?

At Stephen's suggestion, at Bloom's instigation both, first Stephen, then Bloom, in penumbra urinated, their sides contiguous, their organs of micturition reciprocally rendered invisible by manual circumposition, their gazes, first Bloom's, then Stephen's, elevated to the projected luminous and semiluminous shadow.

Similarly?

The trajectories of their, first sequent, then simultaneous, urinations were dissimilar: Bloom's longer, less irruent, in the incomplete form of the bifurcated penultimate alphabetical letter who in his ultimate year at High School (1880) had been capable of attaining the point of greatest altitude against the whole concurrent strength of the institution, 210 scholars: Stephen's higher, more sibilant, who in the ultimate hours of the previous day had augmented by diuretic consumption an insistent vescical pressure.

What different problems presented themselves to each concerning the invisible audible collateral organ of the other?

To Bloom: the problems of irritability, tumescence, rigidity, reactivity, dimension, sanitariness, pelosity. To Stephen: the problem of the sacerdotal integrity of Jesus circumcised (1st January, holiday of obligation to hear mass and abstain from unnecessary servile work) and the problem as to whether the divine prepuce, the carnal bridal ring of the holy Roman catholic apostolic church, conserved in Calcata, were deserving of simple hyperduly or of the fourth degree of latria accorded to the abscission of such divine excrescences as hair and toenails.

What celestial sign was by both simultaneously observed ?

A star precipitated with great apparent velocity across the firmament from Vega in the Lyre above the zenith beyond the stargroup of the Tress of Berenice towards the zodiacal sign of Leo.

How did the centripetal remainer afford egress to the centrifugal departer ?

By inserting the barrel of an arruginated male key in the hole of an unstable female lock, obtaining a purchase on the bow of the key and turning its wards from right to left, withdrawing a bolt from its staple, pulling inward spasmodically an obsolescent unhinged door and revealing an aperture for free egress and free ingress.

How did they take leave, one of the other, in separation ?

Standing perpendicular at the same door and on different sides of its base, the lines of their valedictory arms, meeting at any point and forming any angle less than the sum of two right angles.

What sound accompanied the union of their tangent, the disunion of their (respectively) centrifugal and centripetal hands ?

The sound of the peal of the hour of the night by the chime of the bells in the church of Saint George.

What echoes of that sound were by both and each heard ?

By Stephen :

Liliata rutilantium. Turma circumdet.
Jubilantium te virginum. Chorus excipiat.

By Bloom :

Heigho, heigho,
Heigho, heigho.

Where were the several members of the company which with Bloom that day at the bidding of that peal had travelled from Sandymount in the south to Glasnevin in the north?

Martin Cunningham (in bed), Jack Power (in bed), Simon Dedalus (in bed), Tom Kernan (in bed), Ned Lambert (in bed), Joe Hynes (in bed), John Henry Menton (in bed), Bernard Corrigan (in bed), Patsy Dignam (in bed), Paddy Dignam (in the grave).

Alone, what did Bloom hear?

The double reverberation of retreating feet on the heavenborn earth, the double vibration of a jew's harp in the resonant lane.

Alone, what did Bloom feel?

The cold of interstellar space, thousands of degrees below freezing point or the absolute zero of Fahrenheit, Centigrade or Réaumur: the incipient intimations of proximate dawn.

Of what did bellchime and handtouch and footstep and lonechill remind him?

Of companions now in various manners in different places defunct: Percy Apjohn (killed in action, Modder River) Philip Gilligan (phthisis, Jervis Street hospital), Matthew F. Kane (accidental drowning, Dublin Bay), Philip Moisel (pyemia, Heytesbury street) Michael Hart (phthisis, Mater Misericordiæ hospital), Patrick Dignam (apoplexy, Sandymount).

What prospect of what phenomena inclined him to remain?

The disparition of three final stars, the diffusion of daybreak, the apparition of a new solar disk.

Had he ever been a spectator of those phenomena?

Once, in 1887 after a protracted performance of charades in the house of Luke Doyle, Kimmage, he had awaited with patience the apparition of the diurnal phenomenon, seated on a wall, his gaze turned in the direction of Mizrach, the east.

He remembered the initial paraphenomena?

More active air, a matutinal distant cock, ecclesiastical clocks at various points, avine music, the isolated tread of an early wayfarer, the visible diffusion of the light of an invisible luminous body, the first golden limb of the resurgent sun perceptible low on the horizon.

Did he remain?

With deep inspiration he returned, retraversing the garden, reentering the passage, reclosing the door. With brief suspiration he reassumed the candle, reascended the stairs, reapproached the door of the front room, hallfloor, and reentered.

What suddenly arrested his ingress?

The right temporal lobe of the hollow sphere of his cranium came into contact with a solid timber angle where, an infinitesimal but sensible fraction of a second later, a painful sensation was located in consequence of anetcedent sensations transmitted and registered.

Describe the alterations effected in the disposition of the articles of furniture?

A sofa upholstered in prune plush had been translocated from opposite the door to the ingleside near the compactly furled Union Jack (an alteration which he had frequently intended to execute): the blue and white checker inlaid majolicatopped table had been placed opposite the door in the place vacated by the prune plush sofa: the walnut sideboard (a projecting angle of which had momentarily arrested his ingress) had been moved from its position beside the door to a more advantageous but more perilous position in front of the door: two chairs had been moved from right and left of the ingleside to the position originally occupied by the blue and white checker inlaid majolicatopped table.

Describe them.

One: a squat stuffed easychair with stout arms extended and back slanted to the rere, which, repelled in recoil, had then upturned an irregular fringe of a rectangular rug and now displayed on its amply upholstered seat a centralised diffusing and diminishing discolouration. The other: a slender splayfoot chair of glossy cane curves, placed directly opposite the former, its frame from top to seat and from seat to base being varnished dark brown, its seat being a bright circle of white plaited rush.

What significances attached to these two chairs?

Significances of similitude, of posture, of symbolism, of circumstantial evidence, of testimonial supermanence.

What occupied the position originally occupied by the sideboard?

A vertical piano (Cadby) with exposed keyboard, its closed coffin supporting a pair of long yellow ladies' gloves and an emerald ashtray containing four consumed matches, a partly consumed cigarette and two discoloured ends of cigarettes, its musicrest supporting the music in the key of G natural for voice and piano of *Love's Old Sweet Song* (words by G. Clifton Bingham, composed by J. L. Molloy, sung by Madam Antoinette Sterling) open at the last page with the final indications *ad libitum, forte,* pedal, *animato,* sustained, pedal, *ritirando,* close.

With what sensations did Bloom contemplate in rotation these objects?

With strain, elevating a candlestick: with pain, feeling on his right temple a contused tumescence: with attention, focussing his gaze on a large dull passive and slender bright active: with solicitation, bending and downturning the upturned rugfringe: with amusement, remembering Dr Malachi Mulligan's scheme of colour containing the gradation of green: with pleasure, repeating the words and antecedent act and perceiving through various channels of internal sensibility the consequent and concomitant tepid pleasant diffusion of gradual discolouration.

His next proceeding?

From an open box on tbe majolicatopped table he extracted a black diminutive cone, one inch in height, placed it on its circular base on a small tin plate, placed his candlestick on the right corner of the mantelpiece, produced from his waistcoat a folded page of prospectus (illustrated) entitled Agendath Netaim, unfolded the same, examined it superficially, rolled it into a thin cylinder, ignited it in the candleflame, applied it when ignited to the apex of the cone till the latter reached the stage of rutilance, placed the cylinder in the basin of the candlestick disposing its unconsumed part in such a manner as to facilitate total combustion.

What followed this operation?

That truncated conical crater summit of the diminutive volcano emitted a vertical and serpentine fume redolent of aromatic oriental incense.

What homothetic objects, other than the candlestick, stood on the mantelpiece?

A timepiece of striated Connemara marble, stopped at the hour of 4.46 a. m. on the 21 March 1896, matrimonial gift of Matthew Dillon : a dwarf tree of glacial arborescence under at ransparent bellshade, matrimonial gift of Luke and Caroline Doyle : an embalmed owl, matrimonial gift of Alderman John Hooper.

What interchanges of looks took place between these three objects and Bloom?

In the mirror of the giltbordered pierglass the undecorated back of the dwarf tree regarded the upright back of the embalmed owl. Before the mirror the matrimonial gift of Alderman John Hooper with a clear melancholy wise bright motionless compassionate gaze regarded Bloom while Bloom with obscure tranquil profound motionless compassionated gaze regarded the matrimonial gift of Luke and Caroline Doyle.

What composite asymmetrical image in the mirror then attracted his attention?

The image of a solitary (ipsorelative) mutable (aliorelative) man.

Why solitary (ipsorelative)?

Brothers and sisters had he none.
Yet that man's father was his grandfather's son.

Why mutable (aliorelative)?

From infancy to maturity he had resembled his maternal procreatrix. From maturity to senility he would increasingly resemble his paternal procreator.

What final visual impression was communicated to him by the mirror?

The optical reflection of several inverted volumes improperly arranged and not in the order of their common letters with scintillating titles on the two bookshelves opposite.

Catalogue these books.

Thom's Dublin Post Office Directory, 1886.

Denis Florence M'Carthy's *Poetical Works* (copper beechleaf bookmark at p. 5).

Shakespeare's *Works* (dark crimson morocco, goldtooled).

The Useful Ready Reckoner (brown cloth).

The Secret History of the Court of Charles II (red cloth, tooled binding).

The Child's Guide (blue cloth).

When We Were Boys by William O'Brien M. P. (green cloth, slightly faded, envelope bookmark at p. 217).

Thoughts from Spinoza (maroon leather).

The Story of the Heavens by Sir Robert Ball (blue cloth).

Ellis's *Three Trips to Madagascar* (brown cloth, title obliterated).

The Stark-Munro Letters by A. Conan Doyle, property of the City of Dublin Public Library, 106 Capel Street, lent 21 May (Whitsun Eve) 1904, due 4 June 1904, 13 days overdue (black cloth binding, bearing white letternumber ticket).

Voyages in China by « Viator » (recovered with brown paper, red ink title).

Philosophy of the Talmud (sewn pamphlet).

Lockart's *Life of Napoleon* (cover wanting, marginal annotations, minimising victories, aggrandising defeats of the protagonist).

Soll und Haben by Gustav Freytag (black boards, Gothic characters, cigarette coupon bookmark at p. 24).

Hozier's *History of the Russo-Turkish War* (bronw cloth, 2 volumes, with gummed label, Garrison Library Governor's Parade, Gibraltar, on verso of cover).

Laurence Bloomfield in Ireland by William Allingham (second edition, green cloth, gilt trefoil design, previous owner's name on recto of flyleaf erased).

A Handbook of Astronomy (cover, brown leather, detached, 5 plates, antique letterpress long primer, author's footnotes nonpareil. marginal clues brevier, captions small pica).

The Hidden Life of Christ (black boards).

In the Track of the Sun (yellow cloth, titlepage missing recurrent title intestation).

Physical Strength and How to Obtain It by Eugen Sandow (red cloth).

Short but yet Plain Elements of Geometry written in French by F. Ignat. Pardies and rendered into Engſlih by John Harris D. D. London, printed for R. Knaplock at the Biſhop's Head MDCCXI, with dedicatory epiſtle to his worthy friend Charles Cox, eſquire, Member of Parliament for the burgh of Southwark and having ink calligraphed statement on the flyleaf certifying that the book was the property of Michael Gallagher, dated this 10th day of May 1822 and requeſting the perſon who should find it, if the book should be loſt or go aſtray, to reſtore it to Michael Gallagher, carpenter, Duſery Gate, Enniſcorthy, county Wicklow, the fineſt place in the world.

What reflections occupied his mind during the process of reversion of the inverted volumes?

The necessity of order, a place for everything and everything in its place: the deficient appreciation of literature possessed by females: the incongruity of an apple incuneated in a tumbler and of an umbrella inclined in a closestool: the insecurity of hiding any secret document behind, beneath or between the pages of a book.

Which volume was the largest in bulk?

Hozier's *History of the Russo-Turkish War*.

What among other data did the second volume of the work in question contain?

The name of a decisive battle (forgotten), frequently remembered by a decisive officer, major Brian Cooper Tweedy (remembered).

Why, firstly and secondly, did he not consult the work in question?

Firstly, in order to exercise mnemotechnic: secondly, because after an interval of amnesia, when seated at the central table, about to consult the work in question, he remembered by mnemotechnic the name of the military engagement, Plevna.

What caused him consolation in his sitting posture?

The candour, nudity, pose, tranquillity, youth, grace, sex, counsel of a statue erect in the centre of the table, an image of Narcissus purchased by auction from P. A. Wren, 9 Bachelor's Walk.

What caused him irritation in his sitting posture?

Inhibitory pressure of collar (size 17) and waistcoat (5 buttons), two articles of clothing superfluous in the costume of mature males and inelastic to alterations of mass by expansion.

How was the irritation allayed?

He removed his collar, with contained black necktie and collapsible stud, from his neck to a position on the left of the table. He unbuttoned successively in reversed direction waistcoat, trousers, shirt and vest along the medial line of irregular incrispated black hairs extending in triangular convergence from the pelvic basin over the circumference of the abdomen and umbilicular fossicle along the medial line of nodes to the intersection of the sixth pectoral vertebrae, thence produced both ways at right angles and terminating in circles described about two equidistant points, right and left, on the summits of the mammary prominences. He unbraced successively each of six minus one braced trouser buttons, arranged in pairs, of which one incomplete.

What involuntary actions followed?

He compressed between 2 fingers the flesh circumjacent to a cicatrice in the left infracostal region below the diaphragm resulting from a sting inflicted 2 weeks and 3 days previously (23 May 1904) by a bee. He scratched imprecisely with his right hand, though insensible of prurition, various points and surfaces of his partly exposed, wholly abluted skin. He inserted his left hand into the left lower pocket of his waistcoat and extracted and replaced a silver coin (1 shilling), placed there (presumably) on the occasion (10 October 1903) of the interment of Mrs Emily Sinico, Sydney Parade.

Compile the budget for 16 June 1904.

Debit	£. s. d.	*Credit*	£. s. d.
1 Pork kidney	0. 0. 3	Cash in hand	0. 4. 9
1 Copy *Freeman's Journal*	0. 0. 1	Commission recd. *Freeman's Journal*	1. 7. 6
1 Bath and gratification	0. 1. 6	Loan (Stephen Dedalus)	1. 7. 0
Tramfare	0. 0. 1		
1 In Memoriam Patrick Dignam	0. 5. 0		
2 Banbury cakes	0. 0. 1		
1 Lunch	0. 0. 7		
1 Renewal fee for book	0. 1. 0		
1 Packet notepaper and envelopes	0. 0. 2		
1 Dinner and gratification	0. 2. 0		
1 Postal order and stamp	0. 2. 8		
Tramfare	0. 0. 1		
1 Pig's Foot	0. 0. 4		
1 Sheep's Trotter	0. 0. 3		
1 Cake Fry's plain chocolate	0. 0. 1		
1 Square soda bread	0. 0. 4		
1 Coffee and bun	0. 0. 4		
Loan (Stephen Dedalus) refunded	1. 7. 0		
BALANCE	0.16. 6		
£.	2.19. 3	£.	2.19. 3

Did the process of divestiture continue?

Sensible of a benignant persistant ache in his footsoles he extended his foot to one side and observed the creases, protuberances and salient points caused by foot pressure in the course of walking repeatedly in several different directions, then, inclined, he disnoded the laceknots, unhooked and loosened the laces, took off each of his two boots for the second time, detached the partially moistened right sock through the fore part of which the nail of his great toe had again effracted, raised his right and, having unhooked a purple elastic sock suspender, took off his right sock, placed his unclothed right foot on the margin of the seat of his chair, picked at and gently lacerated the protruding part of the great toenail, raised the part lacerated to his nostrils and inhaled the odour of the quick, then with satisfaction threw away the lacerated unguial fragment.

Why with satisfaction?

Because the odour inhaled corresponded to other odours inhaled of other unguial fragments, picked and lacerated by Master Bloom, pupil of Mrs Ellis's juvenile school, patiently each night in the act of brief genuflection and nocturnal prayer and ambitious meditation.

In what ultimate ambition had all concurrent and consecutive ambitions now coalesced?

Not to inherit by right of primogeniture, gavelkind or borough English, or possess in perpetuity an extensive demesne of a sufficient number of acres, roods and perches, statute land measure (valuation £ 42), of grazing turbary surrounding a baronial hall with gatelodge and carriage drive nor, on the other hand, a terracehouse or semidetached villa, described as *Rus in Urbe* or *Qui Si Sana*, but to purchase by private treaty in fee simple a thatched bungalowshaped 2 storey dwellinghouse of southerly aspect, surmounted by vane and lightning conductor, connected with the earth, with porch covered by parasitic plants (ivy or Virginia creeper), halldoor, olive green, with smart carriage finish and neat doorbrasses, stucco front with gilt tracery at eaves and gable, rising, if possible, upon a gentle eminence with agreeable prospect from balcony with stone pillar parapet over unoccupied and unoccupyable interjacent pastures and standing in 5 or 6 acres of its own ground, at such a distance from the nearest public thoroughfare as to render its houselights visible at night above and through a quickset hornbeam hedge of topiary cutting, situate at a given point not less than 1 statute mile from the periphery of the metropolis, within a time limit of not more than 5 minutes from tram or train line, (e. g. Dundrum, south, or Sutton, north, both localities equally reported by trial to resemble the terrestrial poles in being favourable climates for phthisical subjects), the premises to be held under feefarmgrant, lease 999 years, the messuage to consist of 1 drawingroom with baywindow (2 lancets), thermometer affixed, 1 sittingroom, 4 bedrooms, 2 servants' rooms, tiled kitchen with close range and scullery, lounge hall fitted with linen wallpresses, fumed oak sectional bookcase containing the Encyclopaedia Brittanica and New Century Dictionary, transverse obsolete medieval and oriental weapons, dinner gong, alabaster lamp, bowl pendant, vulcanite automatic telephone receiver with adjacent directory, handtufted Axminster carpet with cream ground and trellis border, loo table with pillar and claw legs, hearth with massive firebrasses and ormolu mantel chronometer clock, guaranteed timekeeper with cathedral chime, barometer with hygrographic chart, comfortable lounge settees and corner fitments, upholstered in ruby plush with good springing and sunk centre, three banner Japanese screen and cuspidors (club style, rich winecoloured leather, gloss renewable with a minimum of labour by use of linseed oil and vinegar) and pyramidically prismatic central chandelier lustre, bentwood perch with a fingertame parrot (expurgated language), embossed mural paper at 10/- per dozen with transverse swags of carmine floral design and top crown frieze, staircase, three continuous flights at successive right angles, of varnished cleargrained oak, treads and risers, newel, balusters and handrail, with steppedup panel dado, dressed with camphorated wax, bathroom, hot and cold supply, reclining and shower : water closet on mezzanine provided with opaque singlepane oblong window, tipup seat, bracket lamp, brass tierod brace, armrests, footstool and artistic oleograph on inner face of door : ditto, plain : servants' apartments with separate sanitary and hygienic necessaries for cook, general and betweenmaid (salary, rising by biennial unearned increments of £ 2, with comprehensive fidelity insurance, annual bonus (£ 1) and retiring allowance (based on the 65 system) after 30 years' service, pantry, buttery, larder, refrigerator, outoffices, coal and wood cellarage with winebin (still and sparkling vintages) for distinguished guests, if entertained to dinner (evening dress), carbon monoxide gas supply throughout.

What additional attractions might the grounds contain ?

As addenda, a tennis and fives court, a shrubbery, a glass summerhouse with tropical palms, equipped in the best botanical manner, a rockery with waterspray, a beehive arranged on humane principles, oval flowerbeds in rectangular grassplots set with eccentric ellipses of scarlet and chrome tulips blue scillas, crocuses, polyanthus, sweet William, sweet pea, lily of the valley, [bulbs obtainable, from sir James W. Mackey (Limited)] wholesale and retail seed and bulb merchant and nurseryman, agent for chemical manures, 23 Sackville Street, upper), an orchard, kitchen garden and vinery, protected against illegal trespassers by glasstopped mural enclosures, a lumbershed with padlock for various inventoried implements.

As ?

Eeltraps, lobsterpots, fishingrods, hatchet, steelyard, grindstone, clodcrusher, swatheturner, carriagesack, telescope ladder, 10 tooth rake, washing clogs, haytedder, tumbling rake, billhook, paintpot, brush, hoe and so on.

What improvements might be subsquently introduced ?

A rabbitry and fowlrun, a dovecote, a botanical conservatory, 2 hammocks (lady's and gentleman's), a sundial shaded and sheltered by laburnum or lilac trees, an exotically harmonically accorded Japanese tinkle gatebell affixed to left lateral gatepost, a capacious waterbutt, a lawnmower with side delivery and grassbox, a lawnsprinkler with hydraulic hose.

What facilities of transit were desirable ?

When citybound frequent connection by train or tram from their respective intermediate station or terminal. When countrybound velocipedes, a chainless freewheel roadster cycle with side basketcar attached, or draught conveyance, a donkey with wicker trap or smart phaeton with good working solidungular cob (roan gelding, 14h).

What might be the name of this erigible or erected residence ?

Bloom Cottage. Saint Leopold's. Flowerville.

Could Bloom of 7 Eccles Street foresee Bloom of Flowerville ?

In loose allwool garments with Harris tweed cap, price 8/6, and useful garden boots with elastic gussets and wateringcan, planting aligned young firtrees, syringing, pruning, staking, sowing hayseed, trundling a weedladen wheelbarrow without excessive fatigue at sunset amid the scent of newmown hay, ameliorating the soil, multiplying wisdom, achieving longevity.

What syllabus of intellectual pursuits was simultaneously possible ?

Snapshot photography, comparative study of religions, folklore relative to various amatory and superstitious practices, contemplation of the celestial constellations.

What lighter recreations ?

Outdoor : garden and fieldwork, cycling on level macadamised causeways, ascents of moderately high hills, natation in secluded fresh water and unmolested river boating in secure wherry or light curricle with kedge anchor on reaches free from weirs and rapids (period of estivation), vespertinal perambulation or equestrian circumprocession with inspection of sterile landscape and contrastingly agreeable cottagers' fires of smoking peat turves (period of hibernation). Indoor discussion in tepid security of unsolved historical and criminal problems : lecture of unexpurgated exotic erotic masterpieces : house carpentry with toolbox containing hammer, awl, nails, screws, tintacks, gimlet, tweezers, bullnose plane and turnscrew.

Might he become a gentleman farmer of field produce and live stock?

Not impossibly, with 1 or 2 stripper cows, 1 pike of upland hay and requisite farming implements, e. g., an end-to-end churn, a turnip pulper etc.

What would be his civic functions and social status among the county families and landed gentry?

Arranged successively in ascending powers of hierarchical order, that of gardener, groundsman, cultivator, breeder, and at the zenith of his career, resident magistrate or justice of the peace with a family crest and coat of arms and appropriate classical moto (*Semper paratus*), duly recorded in the court directory (Bloom, Leopold P., M. P., P. C., K. P., L. L. D. *honoris causa*, Bloomville, Dundrum) and mentioned in court and fashionable intelligence (Mr and Mrs Leopold Bloom have left Kingstown for England).

What course of action did he outline for himself in such capacity?

A course that lay between undue clemency and excessive rigour: the dispensation in a heterogeneous society of arbitrary classes, incessantly rearranged in terms of greater and lesser social inequality, of unbiassed homogeneous indisputable justice, tempered with mitigants of the widest possible latitude but exactable to the uttermost farthing with confiscation of estate, real and personal, to the crown. Loyal to the highest constituted power in the land, actuated by an innate love of rectitude his aims would be the strict maintenance of public order, the repression of many abuses though not of all simultaneously (every measure of reform or retrenchment being a preliminary solution to be contained by fluxion in the final solution) the upholding of the letter of the law (common, statute and law merchant) against all traversers in covin and trespassers acting in contravention of bylaws and regulations, all resuscitators (by trespass and petty larceny of kindlings) of venville rights, obsolete by desuetude, all orotund instigators of international persecution, all perpetuators of international animosities, all menial molestors of domestic conviviality, all recalcitrant violators of domestic connubiality.

Prove that he had loved rectitude from his earliest youth?

To Master Percy Apjohn at High School in 1880 he had divulged his disbelief in the tenets of the Irish (protestant) church (to which his father Rudolf Virag, later Rudolph Bloom, had been converted from the Israelitic faith and communion in 1865 by the Society for promoting Christianity among the jews) subsequently abjured by him in favour of Roman catholicism at the epoch of and with a view to his matrimony in 1888. To Daniel Magrane and Francis Wade in 1882 during a juvenile friendship (terminated by the premature emigration of the former) he had advocated during nocturnal perambulations the political theory of colonial (e. g. Canadian) expansion and the evolutionary theories of Charles Darwin, expounded in *The Descent of Man* and *The Origin of Species*. In 1885 he had publicly expressed his adherence to the collective and national economic programme advocated by James Fintan Lalor, John Fisher Murray, John Mitchel, J. F. X. O'Brien and others, the agrarian policy of Michael Davitt, the constitutional agitation of Charles Stewart Parnell (M. P. for Cork City), the programme of peace, retrenchment and reform of William Ewart Gladstone (M. P. for Midlothian, N. B.) and, in support of his political convictions, had climbed up into a secure position amid the ramifications of a tree on Northumberland road to see the entrance (2 Febuary 1888) into the capital of a demonstrative torchlight procession of 20.000 torchbearers, divided into 120 trade corporations, bearing 2.000 torches in escort of the marquess of Ripon and John Morley.

How much and how did he propose to pay for this country residence?

As per prospectus of the Industrious Foreign Acclimatised Nationalised Friendly Stateaided Building Society (incorporated 1874), a maximum of £ 60 par annum, being 1/6 of an assured income, derived from giltedged securities, representing at 5 % simple interest on capital of £ 1.200 (estimate of price at 20 years purchase) of which 1/3 to be paid on acquisition and the balance in the form of annual rent, viz. £ 800 plus 2 1/2 % interest on the same, repayable quarterly in equal annual instalments until extinction by amortisation of loan advanced for purchase within a period of 20 years, amounting to an annual rental of £ 64, headrent included, the titledeeds to remain in possession of the lender or lenders with a saving clause envisaging forced sale, foreclosure and mutual compensation in the event of protracted failure to pay the terms assigned, otherwise the messuage to become the absolute property of the tenant occupier upon expiry of the period of years stipulated.

What rapid but insecure means to opulence might facilitate immediate purchase?

A private wireless telegraph which would transmit by dot and dash system the result of a national equine handicap (flat or steeplechase) of 1 or more miles and furlongs won by an outsider at odds of 50 to 1 at 3 hr. 8 m. p. m. at Ascot (Greenwich time) the message being received and available for betting purposes in Dublin at 2.59 p. m. (Dunsink time). The unexpected discovery of an object of great monetary value (precious stone, valuable adhesive or unpressed posrage stamps (7 shilling, mauve, imperforate, Hamburg, 1866: 4 pence, rose, blue paper, perforate, Great Britain, 1855: 1 franc, stone, official, rouletted, diagonal surcharge, Luxemburg, 1878, antique dynastical ring, unique relic) in unusual repositories or by unusual means: from the air (dropped by an eagle in flight), by fire (amid the carbonised remains of an incendiated edifice), in the sea (amid flotsam, jetsam, lagan and derelict), on earth (in the gizzard of a commestible fowl). A Spanish prisoner's donation of a distant treasure of valuables or specie or bullion lodged with a solvent banking corporation 100 years previously at 5 % compound interest of the collective worth of £ 5.000.000 stg (five million pounds sterling). A contract with an inconsiderate contractee for the delivery of 32 consignments of some given commodity in consideration of cash payment on delivery at the initial rate of 1/4 d. to be increased constantly in the geometrical progression of 2 (1/4, 1/2, 1 d., 2 d., 4 d., 8 d., 1 s. 4 d., 2 s. 8 d. to 32 terms). A prepared scheme based on a study of the laws of probability to break the bank at Monte Carlo. A solution of the secular problem of the quadrature of the circle, government premium £ 1.000.000 sterling.

Was vast wealth acquirable through industrial channels?

The reclamation of dunams of waste arenary soil, proposed in the prospectus of Agendath Netaim, Bleibtreustrasse, Berlin, W. 15, by the cultivation of orange plantations and melonfields and reafforestation. The utilisation of waste paper, fells of sewer rodents, human excrement possessing chemical properties, in view of the vast production of the first, vast number of the second and immense quantity of the third, every normal human being of average vitality and appetite producing annually, cancelling byproducts of water, a sum total of 80 lbs. (mixed animal and vegetable diet), to be multiplied by 4.386.035 the total population of Ireland according the census returns of 1901.

Were there schemes of wider scope?

A scheme to be formulated and submitted for approval to the harbour commissioners for the exploitation of white coal (hydraulic power), obtained by hydroelectric plant at peak of tide at Dublin bar or at head of water at Poulaphouca or Powerscourt or catchment basins of main streams for the economic production of 500.000 W. H. P. of electricity. A scheme to enclose the peninsular delta of the North Bull at Dollymount and erect on the space of the foreland, used for golf links and rifle ranges, an asphalted esplanade with casinos, booths, shooting galleries, hotels, boardinghouses, readingrooms, establishments for mixed bathing. A scheme for the use of dogvans and goatvans for the delivery of early morning milk. A scheme for the development of Irish tourist traffic in and around Dublin by means of petrolpropelled riverboats, plying in the fluvial fairway between Island bridge and Ringsend, charabancs, narrow gauge local railways, and pleasure steamers for coastwise navigation [10/- per person per day, guide (trilingual) included]. A scheme for the repristination of passenger and goods traffics over Irish waterways, when freed from weedbeds. A scheme to connect by tramline the Cattle Market (North Circular road and Prussia Street) with the quays (Sheriff street, lower and East Wall), parallel with the Link line railway laid (in conjunction with the Great Southern and Western railway line) between the cattle park, Liffey junction, and terminus of Midland Great Western railway 43 to 45 North Wall, in proximity to the terminal stations or Dublin branches of Great Central Railway, Midland Railway of England, City of Dublin Steam Packet Company, Lancashire Yorkshire Railway Company, Dublin and Glasgow Steam Packet Company, Glasgow Dublin and Londonderry Steam Packet Company (Laird line) British and Irish Steam Packet Company, Dublin and Morecambe Steamers, London and North Western Railway Company, Dublin Port and Docks Board Landing Sheds and transit sheds of Palgrave, Murphy and Company, steamship owners, agents for steamers from Mediterranean, Spain, Portugal, France, Belgium and Holland and for Liverpool Underwriters' Association, the cost of acquired rolling stock for animal transport and of additional mileage operated by the Dublin United Tramways Company, limited, to be covered by graziers' fees.

Positing what protasis would the contraction for such several schemes become a natural and necessary apodosis?

Given a guarantee equal to the sum sought, the support, by deed of gift and transfer vouchers during donor's lifetime or by bequest after donor's painless extinction, of eminent financiers (Blum Pasha, Rothschild, Guggenheim, Hirsch, Montefiore, Morgan, Rockefeller) possessing fortunes in 6 figures, amassed during a successful life, and joining capital with opportunity the thing required was done.

What eventually would render him independent of such wealth?

The independent discovery of a goldseam of inexhaustible ore.

For what reason did he meditate on schemes so difficult of realisation?

It was one of his axioms that similar meditations or the automatic relation to himself of a narrative concerning himself or tranquil recollection of the past when practised habitually before retiring for the night allievated fatigue and produced as a result sound repose and renovated vitality.

His justifications?

As a physicist he had learned that of the 70 years of complete human life at least 2/7, viz., 20 years are passed in sleep. As a philosopher he knew that at the termination of any allotted life only an infinitesimal part of any person's desires has been realised. As a physiologist he believed in the artificial placation of malignant agencies chiefly operative during somnolence.

What did he fear?

The commital of homicide or suicide during sleep by an aberration of the light of reason, the incommensurable categorical intelligence situated in the cerebral convolutions.

What were habitually his final meditations?

Of some one sole unique advertisement to cause passers to stop in wonders a poster novelty, with all extraneous accretions excluded, reduced to its simplest and most efficient terms not exceeding the span of casual vision and congruous with the velocity of modern life.

What did the first drawer unlocked contain?

A Vere Foster's handwriting copybook, property of Milly (Millicent) Bloom, certain pages of which bore diagram drawings marked *Papli*, which showed a large globular head with 5 hairs erect, 2 eyes in profile, the trunk full front with 3 large buttons, 1 triangular foot : 2 fading photographs of queen Alexandra of England and of Maud Branscombe, actress and professional beauty: a Yuletide card, bearing on it a pictorial representation of a parasitic plant, the legend *Mizpah*, the date Xmas 1892, the name of the senders : from Mr and Mrs M. Comerford, the versicle : *May this Yuletide bring to thee, Joy and peace and welcome glee* : a butt of red partly liquefied sealing wax, obtained from the stores department of Messrs Hely's, Ltd., 89, 90 and 91 Dame street : a box containing the remainder of a gross of gilt « J » pennibs, obtained from same department of same firm : an old sandglass which rolled containing sand which rolled : a sealed prophecy (never unsealed) written by Leopold Bloom in 1886 concerning the consequences of the passing into law of William Ewart Gladstone's Home Rule bill of 1886 (never passed into law): a bazaar ticket N° 2004, of S. Kevin's Charity Fair, price 6 d. 100 prizes: an infantile epistle, dated, small em monday, reading: capital pee Papli comma capital aitch How are you note of interrogation capital eye I am very well full stop new paragraph signature with flourishes capital em Milly no stop : a cameo brooch, property of Ellen Bloom (born Higgins), deceased : 3 typewritten letters, addressee, Henry Flower, c/o P. O. Westland Row, addresser, Martha Clifford, c/o P. O. Dolphin's Barn : the transliterated name and address of the addresser of the 3 letters in reversed alphabetic boustrephodontic punctated quadrilinear cryptogram (vowels suppressed) N. IGS./ WI. UU. OX/ W. OKS. MH / Y. IM: a press cutting from an English weekly periodical *Modern Society*, subject corporal chastisement in girls' schools : a pink ribbon which had festooned an Easter egg in the year 1899 : two partly uncoiled rubber preservatives with reserve pockets, purchased by post from Box 32, P. O., Charing Cross, London, W. C. : 1 pack of 1 dozen creamlaid envelopes and feintruled notepaper, watermarked, now reduced by 3 : some assorted Austrian-Hungarian coins : 2 coupons of the Royal and Privileged Hungarian Lottery . a lowpower magnifying glass : 2 erotic photocards showing. a) buccal coition between nude senorita (rere presentation, superior position) and nude torero (fore presentation, inferior position). b) anal violation by male religious (fully clothed, eyes abject) of female religious (partly clothed, eyes direct), purchased by post from Box 32, P. O., Charing Cross, London, W. C. : a press cutting of recipe for renovation of old tan boots: 1d. ad hesive stamp, lavender, of the reign of Queen Victoria: a chart of measurements of Leopold Bloom compiled, before, during and after 2 months of consecutive use of Sandow-Whiteley's pulley exerciser (men's 15/-, athlete's 20/-) viz., chest 28 in and 29 1/2 in, biceps 9 in and 10 in, forearm 8 1/2 and 9 in, thigh 10 in and 12 in, calf, 11 in and 12 in: 1 prospectus of the Wonderworker, the world's greatest remedy for rectal complaints, direct from Wonderworker, Coventry House, South Place, London E. C., addressed to Mrs L. Bloom with brief accompanying note commencing: Dear Madam.

Quote the textual terms in which the prospectus claimed advantages for this thaumaturgic remedy.

It heals and soothes while you sleep, in case of trouble in breaking wind, assists nature in the most formidable way insuring, instant relief in discharge of gases, keeping parts clean and free natural action, an initial outlay of 7/6 making a new man of you and life worth living. Ladies find Wonderworker especially useful, a pleasant surprise when they note delightful result like a cool drink of fresh spring water on a sultry summer's day. Recommend it to your lady and gentlemen friends, lasts a lifetime. Insert long round end. Wonderworker.

Were there testimonials?

Numerous. From clergyman, British naval officer, wellknown author, city man, hospital nurse, lady, mother of five, absentminded beggar.

How did absentminded beggar's concluding testimonial conclude?

What a pity the government did not supply our men with wonderworkers during the South African campaign! What a relief it would have been!

What object did Bloom add to this collection of objects?

A 4th typewritten letter received by Henry Flower (let H. F. be L. B.) from Martha Clifford (find M. C.)

What pleasant reflection accompanied this action?

The reflection that, apart from the letter in question, his magnetic face, form and address had been favourably received during the course of the preceding day by a wife (Mrs Josephine Breen, born Josie Powell); a nurse, Miss Callan (Christian name unknown) a maid, Gertrude (Gerty, family name unkown).

What possibility suggested itself?

The possibility of exercising virile power of fascination in the most immediate future after an expensive repast in a private apartment in the company of an elegant courtesan, of corporal beauty, moderately mercenary, variously instructed, a lady by origin.

What did the 2nd drawer contain?

Documents : the birth certificate of Leopold Paula Bloom : an endowment assurance policy of £ 500 in the Scottish Widow's Assurance Society intestated Millcent (Milly) Bloom, coming into force at 25 years as with profit policy of £ 430, £ 462-10-0 and £ 500 at 60 years or death, 65 years or death and death, respectively, or with profit policy (paidup) of £ 299-10-0 together with cash payment of £ 133-10-0, at option : a bank passbook issued by the Ulster Bank, College Green branch showing statement of a/c for halfyear ending 31 December 1903, balance in depositor's favour : £ 18-14-6 (eighteen pounds, fourteen shillings and sixpence, sterling), net personalty : certificate of possession of £ 900, Canadian 4 % (inscribed) government stock (free of stamp duty) : dockets of the Catholic Cemeteries' (Glasnevin) Committee, relative to a graveplot purchased : a local press cutting concerning change of name by deedpoll.

Quote the textual terms of this notice.

I, Rudolph Virag, now resident at n° 52 Clanbrassil street, Dublin, formerly of Szombathely in the kingdom of Hungary, hereby give notice that I have assumed and intend henceforth upon all occasions and at all times to be known by the name of Rudolph Bloom.

What other objects relative to Rudolph Bloom (born Virag) were in the 2nd drawer?

An indistinct daguerrotype of Rudolph Virag and his father Leopold Virag executed in the year 1852 in the portrait atelier of their (respectively) 1st and 2nd cousin, Stefan Virag of Szesfehervar, Hungary. An ancient hagadah book in which a pair of hornrimmed convex spectacles inserted marked the passage of thanksgiving in the ritual prayers for Pessach (Passover) : a photocard of the Queen's Hotel, Ennis, proprietor, Rudolph Bloom : an envelope addressed: *To My Dear Son Leopold.*

What fractions of phrases did the lecture of those four whole words evoke ?

Tomorrow will be a week that I received... it is no use Leopold to be... wlth your dear mother... that is not more to stand... to her... all for me is out... be kind to Athos, Leopold... my dear son... always... of me... *das Herz... Gott... dein...*

What reminiscences of a human subject suffering from progressive melancholia did these objects evoke in Bloom ?

An old man widower, unkempt hair, in bed, with head covered, sighing : an infirm dog, Athos : aconite, resorted to by increasing doses of grains and scruples as a palliative of recrudescent neuralgia : the face in death of a septuagenarian suicide by poison.

Why did Bloom experience a sentiment of remorse ?

Because in immature impatience he had treated with disrespect certain beliefs and practices.

As ?

The prohibition of the use of fleshmeat and milk at one meal, the hebdomadary symposium of incoordinately abstract, perfervidly concrete mercantile coexreligionist excompatriots : the circumcision of male infants : the supernatural character of Judaic scripture: the ineffability of the tetragrammation : the sanctity of the sabbath.

How did these beliefs and practices now appear to him ?

Not more rational than they had then appeared, not less rational than other beliefs and practices now appeared.

What first reminiscence had he of Rudolph Bloom (deceased) ?

Rudolph Bloom (deceased) narrated to his son Leopold Bloom (aged 6) a retrospective arrangement of migrations and settlements in and between Dublin, London, Florence, Milan, Vienna, Budapest, Szombathely with statements of satisfaction (his grandfather having seen Maria Theresia, empress of Austria, queen of Hungary), with commercial advice (having taken care of pence, the pounds having taken care of themselves). Leopold Bloom (aged 6) had accompanied these narrations by constant consultation of a geographical map of Europe (political) and by suggestions for the establishment of affiliated business premises in the various centres mentioned.

Had time equally but differently obliterated the memory of these migrations in narrator and listener?

In narrator by the access of years and in consequence of the use of narcotic toxin: in listener by the access of years and in consequence of the action of distraction upon vicarious experiences.

What idiosyncracies of the narrator were concomitant products of amnesia?

Occasionally he ate without having previously removed his hat. Occasionally he drank voraciously the juice of gooseberry fool from an inclined plate. Occasionally he removed from his lips the traces of food by means of a lacerated envelope or other accessible fragment of paper.

What two phenomena of senescence were more frequent?

The myopic digital calculation of coins, eructation consequent upon repletion.

What object offered partial consolation for these reminiscences?

The endowment policy, the bank passbook, the certificate of the possession of scrip.

Reduce Bloom by cross multiplication of reverses of fortune, from which these supports protected him, and by elimination of all positive values to a negligible negative irrational unreal quantity.

Successively, in descending helotic order: Poverty: that of the outdoor hawker of imitation jewellery, the dun for the recovery of bad and doubtful debts, the poor rate and deputy cess collector. Mendicancy: that of the fraudulent bankrupt with negligible assets paying 1/4d in the £, sandwichman, distributor of throwaways, nocturnal vagrant, insinuating sycophant, maimed sailor, blind stripling, superannuated bailiff's man, marfeast, lickplate, spoilsport, pickthank, eccentric public laughingstock seated on bench of public park under discarded perforated umbrella. Destitution: the inmate of Old Man's House (Royal Hospital), Kilmainham, the inmate of Simpson's Hospital for reduced but respectable men permanently disabled by gout or want of sight. Nadir of misery : the aged impotent disfranchised ratesupported moribund lunatic pauper.

With which attendant indignities ?

The unsympathetic indifference of previously amiable females, the contempt of muscular males, the acceptance of fragments of bread, the simulated ignorance of casual acquaintances, the latration of illegitimate unlicensed vagabond dogs, the infantile discharge of decomposed vegetable missiles, worth little or nothing, nothing or less than nothing.

By what could such a situation be precluded ?

By decease (change of state), by departure (change of place).

Which preferably ?

The latter, by the line of least resistance.

What considerations rendered it not entirely undesirable ?

Constant cohabitation impeding mutual toleration of personal defects. The habit of independent purchase increasingly cultivated. The necessity to counteract by impermanent sojourn the permanence of arrest.

What considerations rendered it not irrational ?

The parties concerned, uniting, had increased and multiplied, which being done, offspring produced and educed to maturity, the parties, if not disunited were obliged to reunite, for increase and multiplication which was absurd, to form by reunion the original couple of uniting parties, which was impossible.

What considerations rendered it desirable ?

The attractive character of certain localities in Ireland and abroad, as represented in general geographical maps of polychrome design or in special ordnance survey charts by employment of scale numerals and hachures.

In Ireland ?

The cliffs of Moher, the windy wilds of Connemara, lough Neagh with submerged petrified city, the Giant's Causeway, Fort Camden and Fort Carlisle, the Golden Vale of Tiperrary, the islands of Aran, the pastures of royal Meath, Brigid's elm in Kildare, the Queen's Island shipyard in Belfast, the Salmon Leap, the lakes of Killarney.

Abroad?

Ceylon, (with spicegardens supplying tea to Thomas Kernan, agent for Pulbrook, Robertson and Co, 2 Mincing Lane, London, E. C, 5 Dame Street, Dublin). Jerusalem, tbe holy city (with mosque of Omar and gate of Damascus, goal of aspiration), the straits of Gibraltar (the unique birthplace of Marion Tweedy), the Parthenon (containing statues, nude Grecian divinities) the Wall street money market (which controlled international finance), the Plaza de Toros at La Linea, Spain (where O'Hara of the Camerons had slain the bull), Niagara (over which no human being had passed with impunity), the land of the Eskimos (eaters of soap), the forbidden country of Thibet (from which no traveller returns), the bay of Naples (to see which was to die), the Dead Sea.

Under what guidance, following what signs?

At sea, septentrional, by night the polestar, located at the point of intersection of the right line from beta to alpha in Ursa Major produced and divided externally at omega and the hypotenuse of the rightangled triangle formed by the line alpha omega so produced and the line alpha delta of Ursa Major. On land, meridional, a bispherical moon, reveated in imperfect varying phases of lunation through the posterior interstice of the imperfectly occluded skirt of a carnose negligent perambulating female, a pillar of the cloud by day.

What public advertisement would divulge the occultation of the departed?

£ 5 reward, lost, stolen or strayed from his residence 7 Eccles street, missing gent about 40, answering to the name of Bloom Leopold (Poldy), height 5 ft., 9 1/2 inches, full build, olive complexion, may have since grown a beard, when last seen was wearing a black suit. Above sum will be paid for information leading to his discovery.

What universal binomial denominations would be his as entity and nonentity?

Assumed by any or known to none. Everyman or Noman.

What tributes his?

Honour and gifts of strangers, the friends of Everyman A nymph immortal, beauty, the bride of Noman.

Would the departed never nowhere nohow reappear ?

Ever he would wander, selfcompelled, to the extreme limit of his cometary orbit, beyond the fixed stars and variable suns and telescopic planets, astronomical waifs and strays, to the extreme boundary of space, passing from land to land, among peoples, amid events. Somewhere imperceptibly hea would her and somehow reluctantly, suncompelled, obey the summons of recall. Whence, disappearing from the constellation of the Northern Crown he would somehow reappear reborn above delta in the constellation of Cassiopeia and after incalculable eons of peregrination return an estranged avenger, a wreaker of justice on malefactors, a dark crusader, a sleeper awakened, with financial resources (by supposition) surpassing those of Rothschild or the silver king.

What would render such return irrational ?

An unsatisfactory equation between an exodus and return in time through reversible space and an exodus and return in space through irreversible time.

What play of forces, inducing inertia, rendered departure undesirable ?

The lateness of the hour, rendering procrastinatory : the obscurity of the night, rendering invisible the uncertainty of thoroughfares, rendering perilous the necessity for repose, obviating movement : the proximity of an occupied bed, obviating research : the anticipation of warmth (human) tempered with coolness (linen) obviating desire and rendering desirable : the statue of Narcissus, sound without echo, desired desire.

What advantages were possessed by an occupied, as distinct from an unoccupied bed ?

The removal of nocturnal solitude, the superior quality of human (mature female) to inhuman (hotwaterjar) calefaction, the stimulation of matutinal contact, the economy of mangling done on the premises in the case of trousers accurately folded and placed lengthwise between the spring mattress (striped) and the woollen mattress (biscuit section).

What past consecutive causes, before rising preapprehended, of accumulated fatigue did Bloom, before rising, silently recapitulate ?

The preparation of breakfast (burnt offering) : intestinal congestion and premeditative defecation (holy of holies) : the bath (rite of John) : the funeral (rite of Samuel) : the advertisement of Alexander Keyes (Urim and

Thummim) : the unsubstantial lunch (rite of Melchisedek) : the visit to museum and national library (holy place) : the bookhunt along Bedford row, Merchants Arch, Wellington Quay (Simchath Torah) : the music in the Ormond Hotel (Shira Shirim) : the altercation with a truculent troglodyte in Bernard Kiernan's premises (holocaust) : a blank period of time including a cardrive, a visit to a house of mourning, a leavetaking (wilderness) : the eroticism produced by feminine exhibitionism (rite of Onan) : the prolonged delivery of Mrs Mina Purefoy (heave offering) : the visit to the disorderly house of Mrs Bella Cohen, 82 Tyrone street, lower, and subsequent brawl and chance medley in Beaver street (Armageddon) : nocturnal perambulation to and from the cabman's shelter, Butt Bridge (atonement).

What selfimposed enigma did Bloom about to rise in order to go so as to conclude lest he should not conclude involuntarily apprehend?

The cause of a brief sharp unforeseen heard loud lone crack emitted by the insentient material of a strainveined timber table.

What selfinvolved enigma did Bloom risen, going, gathering multicoloured multiform mutitudinous garments, voluntarily apprehending, not comprehend?

Who was M'Intosh?

What selfevident enigma pondered with desultory constancy during 30 years did Bloom now, having effected natural obscurity by the extinction of artificial light, silently suddenly comprehend?

Where was Moses when the candle went out?

What imperfections in a perfect day did Bloom, walking, silently, successively, enumerate?

A provisional failure to obtain renewal of an advertisement, to obtain a certain quantity of tea from Thomas Kernan (agent for Pulbrook, Robertson and C°, 5 Dame Street, Dublin, and 2 Mincing Lane, London E. C.), to certify the presence or absence of posterior rectal orifice in the case of Hellenic female divinities, to obtain admission (gratuitous or paid) to the performance of *Leah* by Mrs Bandmann Palmer at the Gaiety Theatre, 46, 47, 48, 49 South King street.

What impression of an absent face did Bloom, arrested, silently recall?

The face of her father, the late Major Brian Cooper Tweedy, Royal Dublin Fusiliers, of Gibraltar and Rehoboth, Dolphin's Barn.

What recurrent impressions of the same were possible by hypothesis?

Retreating, at the terminus of the Great Northern Railway, Amiens street, with constant uniform acceleration, along parallel lines meeting at infinity, if produced: along parallel lines, reproduced from infinity, with constant uniform retardation, at the terminus of the Great Nothern Railway Amiens street, returning.

What miscellaneous effects of female personal wearing apparel were perceived by him?

A pair of new inodorous halfsilk black ladies' hose, a pair of new violet garters, a pair of outsize ladies' drawers of India mull, cut on generous lines, redolent of opoponax, jessamine and Muratti's Turkish cigarettes and containing a long bright steel safety pin, folded curvilinear, a camisole of batiste with thin lace border, a accordion underskirt of blue silk moirette, all these objects being disposed irregularly on the top of a rectangular trunk, quadruple battened, having capped corners, with multicoloured labels, initialled on its fore side in white lettering B. C. T. (Brian Cooper Tweedy).

What impersonal objects were perceived?

A commode, one leg fractured, totally covered by square cretonne cutting, apple design, on which rested a lady's black straw hat. Orangekeyed ware, bought of Henry Price, basket, fancy goods, chinaware and ironmongery manufacturer, 21, 22, 23 Moore Street, disposed irregularly on the washstand and floor, and consisting of basin, soapdish and brushtray (on the washstand, together), pitcher and night article (on the floor, separate).

Bloom's acts?

He deposited the articles of clothing on a chair, removed his remaining articles of clothing, took from beneath the bolster at the head of the bed a folded long white nightshirt, inserted his head and arms into the proper apertures of the nightshirt, removed a pillow from the head to the foot of the bed, prepared the bedlinen accordingly and entered the bed.

How ?

With circumspection, as invariably when entering an abode (his own or not his own): with solicitude, the snakespiral springs of the mattress being old, the brass quoits and pendent viper radii loose and tremulous under stress and strain : prudently, as entering a lair or ambush of lust or adders : lightly, the less to disturb: reverently, the bed of conception and of birth, of consummation of marriage and of breach of marriage, of sleep and of death.

What did his limbs, when gradually extended, encounter ?

New clean bedlinen, additional odours, the presence of a human form, female, hers, the imprint of a human form, male, not his, some crumbs, some flakes of potted meat, recooked, which he removed.

If he had smiled why would he have smiled ?

To reflect that each one who enters imagines himself to be the first to enter whereas he is always the last term of a preceding series even if the first term of a succeeding one, each imagining himself to be first, last, only and alone whereas, he is neither first nor last nor only nor alone in a series originating in and repeated to infinity.

What preceding series ?

Assuming Mulvey to be the first term of his series, Penrose, Bartell d'Arcy, professor Goodwin, Julius Mastiansky, John Henry Menton, Father Bernard Corrigan, a farmer at the Royal Dublin Society's Horse Show, Maggot O'Reilly, Matthew Dillon, Valentine Blake Dillon (Lord Mayor of Dublin), Christopher Callinan, Lenehan, an Italian organgrinder, an unknown gentleman in the Gaiety Theatre, Benjamin Dollard, Simon Dedalus, Andrew (Pisser) Burke, Joseph Cuffe, Wisdom Hely, Alderman John Hooper, Dr Francis Brady, Father Sebastian of Mount Argus, a bootblack at the General Post Office, Hugh E. (Blazes) Boylan and so each and so on to no last term.

What were his reflections concerning the last member of this series and late occupant of the bed ?

Reflections on his vigour (a bounder), corporal proportion (a billsticker), commercial ability (a bester), impressionability (a boaster).

Why for the observer impressionability in addition to vigour, corporal proportion and commercial ability?

Because he had observed with augmenting frequency in the preceding members of the same series the same concupiscence, inflammably transmitted first with alarm, then with understanding, then with desire, finally with fatigue, with alternating symptoms of epicene comprehension and apprehension.

With what antagonistic sentiments were his subsequent reflections affected?

Envy, jealousy, abnegation, equanimity.

Envy?

Of a bodily and mental male organism specially adapted for the superincumbent posture of energetic human copulation and energetic piston and cylinder movement necessary for the complete satisfaction of a constant but not acute concupiscence resident in a bodily and mental female organism, passive but not obtuse.

Jealousy?

Because a nature full and volatile in its free state, was alternately the agent and reagent of attraction. Because attraction between agents and reagents at all instants varied, with inverse proportion of increase and decrease, with incessant circular extension and radial reentrance. Because the controlled contemplation of the fluctuation of attraction produced, if desired, a fluctuation of pleasure.

Abnegation?

In virtue of a) acquaintance initiated in September 1903 in the establishment of George Mesias, merchant tailor and outfitter, 5 Eden Quay, b) hospitality extended and received in kind, reciprocated and reappropriated in person, c) comparative youth subject to impulses of ambition and magnanimity, colleagual altruism and amorous egoism, d) extraracial attraction, intraracial inhibition, supraracial prerogative, e) an imminent provincial musical tour, common current expenses, net proceeds divided.

Equanimity?

As natural as any and every natural act of a nature expressed or understood executed in natured nature by natural creatures in accordance with his, her and their natured natures, of dissimilar similarity. As not as calamitous as a cataclysmic annihilation of the planet in consequence of a collision with a dark sun. As less reprehensible than theft, highway robbery, cruelty to children and animals, obtaining money under false pretences, forgery, embezzlement, misappropriation of public money, betrayal of public trust, malingering, mayhem, corruption of minors, criminal libel, blackmail, contempt of court, arson, treason, felony, mutiny on the high seas, trespass, burglary, jailbreaking, practice of unnatural vice, desertion from armed forces in the field, perjury, poaching, usury, intelligence with the king's enemies, impersonation, criminal assault, manslaughter, wilful and premeditated murder. As not more abnormal than all other altered processes of adaptation to altered conditions of existence, resulting in a reciprocal equilibrium between the bodily organism and its attendant circumstances, foods, beverages, acquired habits, indulged inclinations, significant disease. As more than inevitable, irreparable.

Why more abnegation than jealousy, less envy than equanimity?

From outrage (matrimony) to outrage (adultery) there arose nought but outrage (copulation) yet the matrimonial violator of the matrimonially violated had not been outraged by the adulterous violator of the adulterously violated.

What retribution, if any?

Assassination, never, as two wrongs did not make one right. Duel by combat, no. Divorce, not now. Exposure by mechanical artifice (automatic bed) or individual testimony (concealed ocular witnesses), not yet. Suit for damages by legal influence or simulation of assault with evidence of injuries sustained (selfinflicted), not impossibly. If any, positively, connivance, introduction of emulation (material, a prosperous rival agency of publicity: moral, a successful rival agent of intimacy), depreciation, alienation, humiliation, separation protecting the one separated from the other, protecting separator from both.

By what reflections did he, a conscious reactor against the void of incertitude, justify to himself his sentiments?

The preordained frangibility of the hymen, the presupposed intangibility of the thing in itself: the incongruity and disproportion between the selfprolonging tension of the thing proposed to be done and the selfabbreviating relaxation of the thing done : the fallaciously inferred debility of the female, the muscularity of the male : the variations of ethical codes : the natural grammatical transition by inversion involving no alteration of sense of an aorist preterite proposition (parsed as masculine subject, monosyllabic onomatopœic transitive verb with direct feminine object) from the active voice into its correlative aorist preterite proposition (parsed as feminine subject, auxiliary verb and quasimonosyllabic onomatopœic past participle with complementary masculine agent) in the passive voice : the continued product of seminators by generation : the continual production of semen by distillation : the futility of triumph or protest or vindication : the inanity of extolled virtue: the lethargy of nescient matter : the apathy of the stars.

In what final satisfaction did these antagonistic sentiments and reflections reduced to their simplest forms, converge ?

Satisfaction at the ubiquity in eastern and western terrestrial hemispheres, in all habitable lands and islands explored or unexplored (the land of the midnight sun, the islands of the blessed, the isles of Greece, the land of promise) of adipose posterior female hemispheres, redolent of milk and honey and of excretory sanguine and seminal warmth, reminiscent of secular families of curves of amplitude, insusceptible of moods of impression or of contrarieties of expression, expressive of mute immutable mature animality.

The visible signs of antesatisfaction ?

An approximate erection : a solicitous adversion : a gradual elevation : a tentative revelation ; a silent contemplation.

Then ?

He kissed the plump mellow yellow smellow melons of her rump, on each plump melonous hemisphere, in their mellow yellow furrow, with obscure prolonged provocative melonsmellonous osculation.

The visible signs of postsatisfaction ?

A silent contemplation : a tentative velation : a gradual abasement : a solicitous aversion : a proximate erection.

What followed this silent action ?

Somnolent invocation, less somnolent recognition, incipient excitation, catechetical interrogation.

With what modifications did the narrator reply to this interrogation?

Negative: he omitted to mention the clandestine correspondence between Martha Clifford and Henry Flower, the public altercation at, in and in the vicinity of the licensed premises of Bernard Kiernan and C°, Limited, 8, 9 and 10 Little Britain street, the erotic provocation and response thereto caused by the exhibitionism of Gertrude (Gerty), surname unknown. Positive: he included mention of a performance by Mrs Bandmann Palmer of *Leah* at the Gaiety Theatre, 46, 47, 48, 49 South King street, an invitation to supper at Wynn's (Murphy's) Hotel 35, 36 and 37 Lower Abbey street, a volume of peccaminous pornographical tendency entituled *Sweets of Sin,* anonymous, author a gentlemen of fashion, a temporary concussion caused by a falsely calculated movement in the course of a postcenal gymnastic display, the victim (since completely recovered) being Stephen Dedalus, professor and author, eldest surviving son of Simon Dedalus, of no fixed occupation, an aeronautical feat executed by him (narrator) in the presence of a witness, the professor and author aforesaid, with promptitude of decision and gymnastic flexibility.

Was the narration otherwise unaltered by modifications?

Absolutely.

Which event or person emerged as the salient point of his narration?

Stephen Dedalus, professor and author.

What limitations of activity and inhibitions of conjugal rights were perceived by listener and narrator concerning themselves during the course of this intermittent and increasingly more laconic narration?

By the listener a limitation of fertility inasmuch as marriage had been celebrated 2 calendar months after the 18th anniversary of her birth (8 September 1870), viz. 8 October, and consummated on the same date with female issue born 15 June 1889, having been anticipatorily consummated on the 10 September of the same year and complete carnal intercourse, with ejaculation of semen within the natural female organ, having last taken place 5 weeks previous, viz. 27 November 1893, to the birth on 29 December 1893 of second (and only male) issue, deceased 9 January 1895, aged 11 days, there remained a period of 10 years, 5 months and 18 days during which carnal intercourse had been incomplete, without ejaculation of semen within the natural female organ. By the narrator a limitation of activity, mental and corporal, inasmuch as complete mental intercourse between himself and the listener had not taken place since the consummation of puberty, indicated by catamenic hemorrhage, of the female issue of narrator and listener, 15 September 1903, there remained a period of 9 months and 1 day during which in consequence of a preestablished natural comprehension in incomprehension between the consummated females (listener and issue), complete corporal liberty of action had been circumscribed.

How?

By various reiterated feminine interrogation concerning the masculine destination whither, the place where, the time at which, the duration for which, the object with which in the case of temporary absences, projected or effected.

What moved visibly above the listener's and the narrator's invisible thoughts?

The upcast reflection of a lamp and shade, an inconstant series of concentric circles of varying gradations of light and shadow.

In what directions did listener and narrator lie?

Listener: S. E. by E.: Narrator N. W. by W.: on the 53rd parallel of latitude, N. and 6th meridian of longitude, W.: at an angle of 45° to the terrestrial equator.

In what state of rest or motion?

At rest relatively to themselves and to each other. In motion being each and both carried westward, forward and rereward respectively, by the proper perpetual motion of the earth through everchanging tracks of neverchanging space.

In what posture?

Listener: reclined semilaterally, left, left hand under head, right leg extended in a straight line and resting on left leg, flexed, in the attitude of Gea-Tellus, fulfilled, recumbent, big with seed. Narrator: reclined laterally, left, with right and left legs flexed, the indexfinger and thumb of the right hand resting on the bridge of the nose, in the attitude depicted on a snapshot photograph made by Percy Apjohn, the childman weary, the manchild in the womb.

Womb? Weary?
He rests. He has travelled.

With?
Sinbad the Sailor and Tinbad the Tailor and Jinbad the Jailer and Whinbad the Whaler and Ninbad the Nailer and Finbad the Failer and Binbad the Bailer and Pinbad the Pailer and Minbad the Mailer and Hinbad the Hailer and Rinbad the Railer and Dinbad the Kailer and Vinbad the Quailer and Linbad the Yailer and Xinbad the Phthailer.

When?
Going to dark bed there was a square round Sinbad the Sailor roc's auk's eggin the night of the bed of all the auks of the rocs of Darkinbad the Brightdayler.

Where?

●

Yes because he never did a thing like that before as ask to get his breakfast in bed with a couple of eggs since the *City Arms* hotel when he used to be pretending to be laid up with a sick voice doing his highness to make himself interesting to that old faggot Mrs Riordan that he thought he had a great leg of and she never left us a farthing all for masses for herself and her soul greatest miser ever was actually afraid to lay out 4d for her methylated spirit telling me all her ailments she had too much old chat in her about politics and earthquakes and the end of the world let us have a bit of fun first God help the world if all the women were her sort down on bathingsuits and lownecks of course nobody wanted her to wear I suppose she was pious because no man would look at her twice I hope Ill never be like her a wonder she didnt want us to cover our faces but she was a welleducated woman certainly and her gabby talk about Mr Riordan here and Mr Riordan there I suppose he was glad to get shut of her and her dog smelling my fur and always edging to get up under my petticoats especially then still I like that in him polite to old women like that and waiters and beggars too hes not proud out of nothing but not always if ever he got anything really serious the matter with him its much better for them to go into a hospital where everything is clean but I suppose Id have to dring it into him for a month yes and then wed have a hospital nurse next thing on the carpet have him staying there till they throw him out or a nun maybe like the smutty photo he has shes as much a nun as Im not yes because theyre so weak and puling when theyre sick they want a woman to get well if his nose bleeds youd think it was O tragic and that dyinglooking one off the south circular when he sprained his foot at the choir party at the sugarloof Mountain the day I wore that dress Miss Stack bringing him flowers the worst old ones she could find at the bottom of the basket anything at all to get into a mans bedroom with her old maids voice trying to imagine he was dying on account of her to never see thy face again though he looked more like a man with his beard a bit grown in the bed father was the same besides I hate bandaging and dosing when he cut his toe with the razor paring his corns afraid hed get blood poisoning but if it was a thing I was sick then wed see what attention only of course the woman hides it not to give all the trouble they do yes he came somewhere Im sure by his appetite anyway love its not or hed be off his feed thinking of her so either it was one of those night women if it was down there he was really and the hotel story he made up a pack of lies to hide it planning it Hynes kept me who did I meet ah yes I met do you remember Menton and who else who let me see that big babbyface I saw him and he not long married flirting with a young girl at Pooles Myriorana and turned my back on him when he slinked out looking quite conscious what harm but he had the impudence to make up to me one time well done to him mouth almighty and his boiled eyes of all the big stupoes I ever met and thats called a solicitor only for I hate having a long wrangle in bed or else if its not that its some little bitch or other he got in with somewhere or picked up on the sly if they only knew him as well as I do yes because the day before yesterday he was scribbling something a letter when I came into the front room for the matches to show him Dignams death in the paper as if something told me and he covered it up with the blottingpaper pretending to be thinking about business so very probably that was it to somebody who thinks she has a softy in him because all men get a bit like that at his age especially getting on to forty he is now so as to wheedle any money she can out of him no fool like an old fool and then the usual kissing my bottom was to hide it not that I care two straws who he does it with or knew before that way though Id like to find out so long as I dont have the two of them under my nose all the time like that slut that Mary we had in Ontario Terrace padding out her false bottom to excite him bad enough to get the smell of those painted women off him once or twice I had a suspicion by getting him to come near me when I found the long hair on his coat without that one when I went into the kitchen pretending he was drinking water 1 woman is not enough for them it was all his fault of course ruining servants then proposing that she could eat at our table on Christmas if you please O no thank you not in my house stealing my potatoes and the oysters 2/6 per doz going out to see her aunt if you please common robbery so it was but I was sure he had something on with that one it takes me to find out a thing like that he said you have no proof it was her proof O yes her aunt was very fond of oysters but I told her what I thought of her suggesting me to go out to be alone with her I wouldnt lower myself to spy on them the garters I found in her room the Friday she was out that was enough for me a little bit too much I saw to that her face swelled up on her with temper when I gave her her weeks notice better do without them altogether do out the rooms myself quicker only for the damn cooking and throwing out the dirt I gave it to him anyhow either she or me leaves the house I couldnt even touch him if I thought he was with a dirty barefaced liar and sloven like that one deuying it up to my face and singing about the place in the W C too because she knew she was too well off yes because he couldnt possibly do without it that long so he must do it somewhere and the last time he came on my bottom when was it the night Boylan gave my hand a great squeeze going along by the Tolka in my hand there steals another I just pressed the back of his like that with my thumb to squeeze back singing the young May Moon shes beaming love because he has an idea about him and me hes not such a fool he said Im dining out and going to the Gaiety though Im not going to give him the satisfaction in any case God knows hes change in a way not to be always and ever wearing the same old hat unless I paid some nicelooking boy to do it since I cant do it myself a young boy would like me Id confuse him a little alone with him if we were Id let him see my garters the new ones and make him turn red looking at him seduce him I know what boys feel with that down on their cheek doing that frigging drawing out the thing by the hour question and answer would you do this that and the other with the coalman yes with a bishop yes I would because I told him about some Dean or Bishop was sitting beside me in the jews Temples gardens when I was knitting that woollen thing a stranger to Dublin what place was it and so on about the monuments and he tired me out with statues encouraging him making him worse than he is who is in your mind now tell me who are you thinking of who is it tell me his name who tell me who the German Emperor is it yes imagine Im him think of him can you feel him trying to make a whore of me what he never will he ought to give it up now at this age of his life simply ruination for any woman and no satisfaction in it pretending to like it till he comes and then finish it off myself anyway and it makes your lips pale anyhow its done now once and for all with all the talk of the world about it people make its only the first time after that its just the ordinary do it and think no more about it why cant you kiss a man without going and marrying him first you sometimes love to wildly when you feel that way so nice all over you you cant help yourself I wish some man or other would take me sometime when hes there and kiss me in his arms theres nothing like a kiss long and hot down to your soul almost paralyses you then I hate that confession when I used to go to Father Corrigan he touched me father and what harm if he did where and I said on the canal bank like a fool but whereabouts on your person my child on the leg behind high up was it yes rather high up was it where you sit down yes O Lord couldnt he say bottom right out and have done with it what has that got to do with it and did you whatever way he put it I forget no father and I always think of the real father what did he want to know for when I already confessed it to God he had a nice fat hand the palm moist always I wouldnt mind feeling it neither would he Id say by the bullneck in his horsecollar I wonder did he know me in the box I could see his face he couldnt see mine of course hed never turn or let on still his eyes were red when his father died theyre lost for a woman of course must be terrible when a man cries let alone them Id like to be embraced by one in his vestments and the smell of incense off him like the pope besides theres no danger with a priest if youre married hes too careful about himself then give something to H H the pope for a penance I wonder was he satisfied with me one thing I didnt like his slapping me behind going away so familiarly in the hall though I laughed Im not a horse or an ass am I I suppose he was thinking of his father I wonder is he awake thinking of me or dreaming am I in it who gave him that flower he said he bought he smelt of some kind of a drink not whisky or stout or perhaps the sweety kind of paste they stick their bills up with some liquor Id like to sip those richlooking green and yellow expensive drinks those stagedoor johnnies drink with the opera hats I tasted once with my finger dipped out of that American that had the squirrel talking stamps with father he had all he could do to keep himself from falling asleep after the last time we took the port and potted meat it had a fine salty taste yes because I felt lovely and tired myself and fell asleep as sound as a top the moment I popped straight into bed till that thunder woke me up as if the world was coming to an end God be merciful to us I thought the heavens were coming down about us to punish when I blessed myself and said a Hail Mary like those awful thunderbolts in Gibraltar and then they come and tell you theres no God what could you do if it was running and rushing about nothing only make an act of contrition the candle I lit that evening in Whitefriars street chapel for the month of May see it brought its luck though hed scoff if he heard because he never goes to church burst though his nose is not so big after I took off all my things with the blinds down after my hours dressing and perfuming and combing it like iron or some kind of a thick crowbar standing all the time he must have eaten oysters I think a few dozen he was in great singing voice no I never in all my life felt anyone had one the size of that to make you feel full up he must have eaten a whole sheep after whats the idea making us like that with a big hole in the middle of us like a Stallion driving it up into you because thats all they want out of you with that determined vicious look in his eye I had to halfshut my eyes still he hasnt such a tremendous amount of spunk in him when I made him pull it out and do it on me considering how big it is so much the better in case any of it wasnt washed out properly the last time I let him finish it in me nice invention they made for women for him to get all the pleasure but if someone gave them a touch of it themselves theyd know what I went through with Milly nobody would believe cutting her teeth too and Mina Purefoys husband give us a swing out of your whiskers filling her up with a child or twins once a year as regular as the clock always with a smell of children off her the one they called budgers or something like a nigger with a shock of hair on it Jesusjack the child is a black the last time I was there a squad of them falling over one another and bawling you couldnt hear your ears supposed to be healthy not satisfied till they have us swollen out like elephants or I dont know what supposing I risked having another not off him though still if he was married Im sure hed have a fine strong child but I dont know Poldy has more spunk in him yes thatd be awfully jolly I suppose it was meeting Josie Powell and the funeral and thinking about me and Boylan set him off well he can think what he likes now if thatll do him any good I know they were spooning a bit when I came on the scene he was dancing and sitting out with her the night of Georgina Simpsons housewarming and then he wanted to ram it down my neck on account of not liking to see her a wallflower that was why we had the standup row over politics he began it not me when he said about Our Lord being a carpenter at last he made me cry of course a woman is so sensitive about every thing I was fuming with myself after forgiving in only for I knew he was gone on me and the first socialist he said He was he annoyed me so much I couldnt put him into a temper still he knows a lot of mixed up things especially about the body and the insides I often wanted to study up that myself what we have inside us in that family physician I could always hear his voice talking when the room was crowded and watch him after that I pretended I had on a coolness with her over him mass or meeting he says your soul you have no soul inside only grey matter because he doesnt know what it is to have one yes when I lit the lamp yes because he must have come 3 or 4 times with that tremendous big red brute of a thing he has I thought the vein or whatever the dickens they call it was going to because he used to be a bit on the jealous side whenever he asked who are you going to and I said over to Floey and he made me the present of lord Byrons poems and the three pairs of gloves so that finished that I could quite easily get him to make it up any time I know how Id even supposing he got in with her again and was going out to see her somewhere Id know if he refused to eat the onions I know plenty of ways ask him to tuck down the collar of my blouse or touch him with my veil and gloves on going out 1 kiss then wouldsend them all spinning however alright well see then let him go to her she of course would only be too delighted to pretend shes mad in love with him that I wouldnt so much mind Id just go to her and ask her do you love him and look her square in the eyes she couldnt fool me but he might imagine he was and make a declaration with his plabbery kind of a manner to her like he did to me though I had the devils own job to get it out of him though I liked him for that it showed he could hold in and wasnt to be got for the asking he was on the pop of asking me too the night in the kitchen I was rolling the potato cake theres something I want to say to you only for I put him off letting on I was in a temper with my hands and arms full of pasty flour in any case I let out too much the night before talking of dreams so I didnt want to let him know more than was good for him she used to be always embracing me Josie whenever he was there meaning him of course glauming me over and when I said I washed up and down as far as possible asking me did you wash possible the women are always egging on to that putting it on thick when hes there they know by his sly eye blinking a bit putting on the indifferent when they come out with something the kind he is what spoils him I dont wonder in the least because he was very handsome at that time trying to look like lord Byron I said I liked though he was too beautiful for a man and he was a little before we got engaged afterwards though she didnt like it so much the day I was in fits of laughing with the giggles I couldnt stop about all my hairpins falling one after another with the mass of hair I had youre always in great humour she said yes because it grigged her because she knew what it meant because I used to tell her a good bit of what went on between us not all but just enough to make her month water but that wasnt my fault she didnt darken the door much after we were married I wonder what shes got like now after living with that dotty husband of hers she had her face beginning to look drawn and run down the last time I saw her she must have been just after a row with him because I saw on the moment she was edging to draw down a conversation about husbands and talk about him to run him down what was it she told me O yes that sometimes he used to go to bed with his muddy boots on when the maggot takes him just imagine having to get into bed with a thing like that that might murder you any moment what a man well its not the one way everyone goes mad Poldy anyway whatever he does always wipes his feet on the mat when he comes in wet or shine and always blacks his own boots too and he always takes off his hat when he comes up in the street like that and now hes going about in his slippers to look for £ 10000 for a postcard up up O Sweetheart May wouldnt a thing like that simply bore you stiff to extinction actually too stupid even to take his boots off now what could you make of a man like that Id rather die 20 times over than marry another of their sex of course hed never find another woman like me to put up with him the way I do know me come sleep with me yes and he knows that too at the bottom of his heart take that Mrs Maybrick that poisoned her husband for what I wonder in love with some other man yes it was found out on her wasnt she the downright villain to go and do a thing like that of course some men can be dreadfully aggravating drive you mad and always the worst word in the world what do they ask us to marry them for if were so bad as all that comes to yes because they cant get on without us white Arsenic she put in his tea of flypaper wasnt it I wonder why they call it that if I asked him hed say its from the Greek leave us as wise as we were before she must have been madly in love with the other fellow to run the chance of being hanged O she didnt care if that was her nature what could she do besides theyre not brutes enough to go and hang a woman surely are they

theyre all so different Boylan talking about the shape of my foot he noticed at once even before he was introduced when I was in the D B C with Poldy laughing and trying to listen I was waggling my foot we both ordered 2 teas and plain bread and butter I saw him looking with his two old maids of sisters when I stood up and asked the girl where it was what do I care with it dropping out of me and that black closed breeches he made me buy takes you half an hour to let them down wetting all myself always with some brandnew fad every other week such a long one I did I forgot my suede gloves on the seat behind that I never got after some robber of a woman and he wanted me to put it in the Irish Times lost in the ladies lavatory D B C Dame street finder return to Mrs Marion Bloom and I saw his eyes on my feet going out through the turning door he was looking when I looked back and I went there for tea 2 days after in the hope but he wasnt now how did that excite him because I was crossing them when we were in the other room first he meant the shoes that are too tight to walk in my hand is nice like that if I only had a ring with the stone for my mouth a nice aquamarine Ill stick him for one and a gold bracelet I dont like my foot so much still I made him spend once with my foot the night after Goodwins botchup of a concert so cold and windy it was well we had that rum in the house to mull and the fire wasnt black out when he asked to take off my stockings lying on the hearthrug in Lombard street well and another time it was my muddy boots hed like me to walk in all the horses dung I could find but of course hes not natural like the rest of the world that I what did he say I could give 9 points in 10 to Katty Lanner and beat her what does that mean I asked him I forget what he said because the stoppress edition just passed and the man with the curly hair in the Lucan dairy thats so polite I think I saw his face before somewhere I noticed him when I was tasting the butter so I took my time Bartell dArcy too that he used to make fun of when he commenced kissing me on the choir stairs after I sang Gounods *Ave Maria* what are we waiting for O my heart kiss me straight on the brow and part which is my brown part he was pretty hot for all his tinny voice too my low notes he was always raving about if you can believe him I liked the way he used his mouth singing then he said wasnt it terrible to do that there in a place like that I dont see anything so terrible about it Ill tell him about that some day not now and surprise him ay and Ill take him there and show him the very place too we did it so now there you are like it or lump it he thinks nothing can happen without him knowing he hadnt an idea about my mother till we were engaged otherwise hed never have got me so cheap as he did he was 10 times worse himself anyhow begging me to give him a tiny bit cut off my drawers that was the evening coming along Kenilworth Square he kissed me in the eye of my glove and I had to take it off asking me questions is it permitted to inquire the shape of my bedroom so I let him keep it as if I forgot it to think of me when I saw him slip it into his pocket of course hes mad on the subject of drawers thats plain to be seen always skeezing at those brazenfaced things on the bicycles with their skirts blowing up to their navels even when Milly and I were out with him at the open air fete that one in the cream muslin standing right against the sun so he could see every atom she had on when he saw me from behind following in the rain I saw him before he saw me however standing at the corner of the Harolds cross road with a new raincoat on him with the muffler in the Zingari colours to show off his complexion and the brown hat looking slyboots as usual what was he doing there where hed no business they can go and get whatever they like from anything at all with a skirt on it and were not to ask any questions but they want to know where were you where are you going I could feel him coming along skulking after me his eyes on my neck he had been keeping away from the house he felt it was getting too warm for him so I halfturned and stopped then he pestered me to say yes till I took off my glove slowly watching him he said my openwork sleeves were too cold for the rain anything for an excuse to put his hand anear me drawers drawers the whole blessed time till I promised to give him the pair off my doll to carry about in his waistcoat pocket *O Maria Santisima* he did look a big fool dreeping in the rain splendid set of teeth he had made me hungry to look at them and beseeched of me to lift the orange petticoat I had on with sunray pleats that there was nobody he said hed kneel down in the wet if I didnt so persevering he would too and ruin his new raincoat you never know what freak theyd take alone with you theyre so savage for it if anyone was passing so I lifted them a bit and touched his trousers outside the way I used to Gardner after with my ring hand to keep him from doing worse where it was too public I was dying to find out was he circumcised he was shaking like a jelly all over they want to do everything too quick take all the pleasure out of it and father waiting all the time for his dinner he told me to say I left my purse in the butchers and had to go back for it what a Deceiver then he wrote me that letter with all those words in it how could he have the face to any woman after his company manners making it so awkward after when we met asking me have I offended you with my eyelids down of course he saw I wasnt he had a few brains not like that other fool Henny Doyle he was always breaking or tearing something in the charades I hate an unlucky man and if I knew what it meant of course I had to say no for form sake dont understand you I said and wasnt it natural so it is of course it used to be written up with a picture of a womans on that wall in Gibraltar with that word I couldnt find anywhere only for children seeing it too young then writing a letter every morning sometimes twice a day I liked the way he made love then he knew the way to take a woman when he sent me the 8 big poppies because mine was the 8th then I wrote the night he kissed my heart at Dolphins barn I couldnt describe it simply it makes you feel like nothing on earth but he never knew how to embrace well like Gardner I hope hell come on Monday as he said at the same time four I hate people who come at all hours answer the door you think its the vegetables then its somebody and you all undressed or the door of the filthy sloppy kitchen blows open the day old frostyface Goodwin called about the concert in Lombard street and I just after dinner all flushed and tossed with boiling old stew dont look at me professor I had to say Im a fright yes but he was a real old gent in his way it was impossible to be more respectful nobody to say youre out you have to peep out through the blind like the messengerboy today I thought it was a putoff first him sending the port and the peaches first and I was just beginning to yawn with nerves thinking he was trying to make a fool of me when I knew his tattarrattat at the door he must have been a bit late because it was 1/4 after 3 when I saw the 2 Dedalus girls coming from school I never know the time even that watch he gave me never seems to go properly Id want to get it looked after when I threw the penny to that lame sailor for England home and beauty when I was whistling there is a charming girl I love and I hadnt even put on my clean shift or powdered myself or a thing then this day week were to go to Belfast just as well he has to go to Ennis his fathers anniversary the 27 th it wouldnt be pleasant if he did suppose our rooms at the hotel were beside each other and any fooling went on in the new bed I couldnt tell him to stop and not bother me with him in the next room or perhaps some protestant clergyman with a cough knocking on the wall then he wouldnt believe next day we didnt do something its all very well a husband but you cant fool a lover after me telling him we never did anything of course he didnt believe me no its better hes going where he is besides something always happens with him the time going to the Mallow Concert at Maryborough ordering boiling soup for the two of us then the bell rang out he walks down the platform with the soup splashing about taking spoonfuls of it hadnt he the nerve and the waiter after him making a holy show of us screeching and confusion for the engine to start but he wouldnt pay till he finished it the two gentlemen in the 3rd class carriage said he was quite right so he was too hes so pigheaded sometimes when he gets a thing into his head a good job he was able to open the carriage door with his knife or theyd have taken us on to Cork I suppose that was done out of revenge on him O I love jaunting in a train or a car with lovely soft cushions I wonder will he take a 1st class for me he might want to do it in the train by tipping the guard well O I suppose there'll be the usual idiots of men gaping at us with their eyes as stupid as ever they can possibly be that was an exceptional man that common workman that left us alone in the carriage that day going to Howth Id like to find out something about him 1 or 2 tunnels perhaps then you have to look out of the window all the nicer then coming back suppose I never came back what would they say eloped with him that gets you on on the stage the last concert I sang at where its over a year ago when was it St Teresas hall Clarendon St little chits of missies they have now singing Kathleen Kearney and her like on account of father being in the army and my singing the absentminded beggar and wearing a brooch for lord Roberts when I had the map of it all and Poldy not Irish enough was it him managed it this time I wouldnt put it past him like he got me on to sing in the *Stabat Mater* by going around saying he was putting Lead Kindly Light to music I put him up to that till the jesuits found out he was a freemason thumping the piano lead Thou me on copied from some old opera yes and he was going about with some of them Sinner Fein lately or whatever they call themselves talking his usual trash and nonsense he says that little man he showed me without the neck is very intelligent the coming man Griffith is he well he doesnt look it thats all I can say still it must have been him he knew there was a boycott I hate the mention of politics after the war that Pretoria and Ladysmith and Bloemfontein where Gardner Lieut Stanley G 8th Bn 2nd East Lancs Rgt of enteric fever he was a lovely fellow in khaki and just the right height over me Im sure he was brave too he said I was lovely the evening we kissed goodbye at the canal lock my Irish beauty he was pale with excitement about going away or wed be seen from the road he couldnt stand properly and I so hot as I never felt they could have made their peace in the beginning or old oom Paul and the rest of the old Krugers go and fight it out between them instead of dragging on for years killing any finelooking men there were with their fever if he was even decently shot it wouldnt have been so bad I love to see a regiment pass in review the first time I saw the Spanish cavalry at La Roque it was lovely after looking across the bay from Algeciras all the lights of the rock like fireflies or those sham battles on the 15 acres the Black Watch with their kilts in time at the march past the 10th hussars the prince of Wales own or the lancers O the lancers theyre grand or the Dublins that won Tugela his father made his money over selling the horses for the cavalry well he could buy me a nice present up in Belfast after what I gave him theyve lovely linen up there or one of those nice kimono things I must buy a mothball like I had before to keep in the drawer with them it would be exciting going around with him shopping buying those things in a new city better leave this ring behind want to keep turning and turning to get it over the knuckle there or they might bell it round the town in their papers or tell the police on me but theyd think were married O let them all go and smother themselves for the fat lot I care he has plenty of money and hes not a marrying man so somebody better get it out of him if I could find out whether he likes me I looked a bit washy of course when I looked close in the handglass powdering a mirror never gives you the expression besides scrooching down on me like that all the time with his big hipbones hes heavy too with his hairy chest for this heat always having to lie down for them better for him put it into me from behind the way Mrs Mastiansky told me her husband made her like the dogs do it and stick out her tongue as far as ever she could and he so quiet and mild with his tingating cither can you ever be up to men the way it takes them lovely stuff in that blue suit he had on and stylish tie and socks with the skyblue silk things on them hes certainly welloff I know by the cut his clothes have and his heavy watch but he was like a perfect devil for a few minutes after he came back with the stop press tearing up the tickets and swearing blazes because he lost 20 quid he said he lost over that outsider that won and half he put on for me on account of Lenehans tip cursing him to the lowest pits that sponger he was making free with me after the Glencree dinner coming back that long joult over the featherbed mountain after the lord Mayor looking at me with his dirty eyes Val Dillon that big heathen I first noticed him at dessert when I was cracking the nuts with my teeth I wished I could have picked every morsel of that chicken out of my fingers it it was so tasty and browned and as tender as anything only for I didnt want to eat everything on my plate those forks and fishslicers were hallmarked silver too I wish I had some I could easily have slipped a couple into my muff when I was playing with them then always hanging out of them for money in a restaurant for the bit you put down your throat we have to be thankful for our mangy cup of tea itself as a great compliment to be noticed the way the world is divided in any case if its going to go on I want at least two other good chemises for one thing and but I dont know what kind of drawers he likes none at all I think didnt he say yes and half the girls in Gibraltar never wore them either naked as God made them that Andalusian singing her Manola she didnt make much secret of what she hadnt yes and the second pair of silkette stockings is laddered after one days wear I could have brought them back to Lewers this morning and kick up a row and made that one change them only not to upset myself and run the risk of walking into him and ruining the whole thing and one of those kidfitting corsets Id want advertised cheap in the Gentlewoman with elastic gores on the hips he saved the one I have but thats no good what did they say they give a delightful figure line 11/6 obviating that unsightly broad appearance across the lower back to reduce flesh my belly is a bit too big Ill have to knock off the stout at dinner or am I getting too fond of it the last they sent from O Rourkes was as flat as a pancake he makes his money easy Larry they call him the old mangy parcel he sent at Xmas a cottage cake and a bottle of hogwash he tried to palm off as claret that he couldnt get anyone to drink God spare his spit for fear hed die of the drouth or I must do a few breathing exercises I wonder is that antifat any good might overdo it thin ones are not so much the fashion now garters that much I have the violet pair I wore today thats all he bought me out of the cheque he got on the first O no there was the face lotion I finished the last of yesterday that made my skin like new I told him over and over again get that made up in the same place and dont forget it God only knows whether he did after all I said to him Ill know by the bottle anyway if not I suppose Ill only have to wash in my piss like beeftea or chickensoup with some of that opoponax and violet I thought it was beginning to look coarse or old a bit the skin underneath is much finer where it peeled off there on my finger after the burn its a pity it isnt all like that and the four paltry handerchiefs about 6/- in all sure you cant get on in this world without style all going in food and rent when I get it Ill lash it around I tell you in fine style I always want to throw a handful of tea into the pot measuring and mincing if I buy a pair of old brogues itself do you like those new shoes yes how much were they Ive no clothes at all the brown costume and the skirt and jacket and the one at the cleaners 3 whats that for any woman cutting up this old hat and patching up the other the men wont look at you and women try to walk on you because they know youve no man then with all the things getting dearer every day for the 4 years more I have of life up to 35 no Im what am I at all Ill be 33 in September will I what O well look at that Mrs Galbraith shes much older than me I saw her when I was out last week her beautys on the wane she was a lovely woman magnificent head of hair on her down to her waist tossing it back like that like Kitty OShea in Grantham street 1st thing I did every morning to look across see her combing it as if she loved it and was full of it pity I only got to know her the day before we left and that Mrs Langtry the Jersey Lily the prince of Wales was in love with I suppose hes like the first man going the roads only for the name of a king theyre all made the one way only a black mans Id like to try a beauty up to what was she 45 there was some funny story about the jealous old husband what was it at all and an oyster knife he went no he made her wear a kind of a tin thing around her and the prince ot Wales yes he had the oyster knife cant be true a thing like that like some of those books he brings me the works of Master Francois somebody supposed to be a priest about a child born out of her ear because her bumgut fell out a nice word for any priest to write and her a — e as if any fool wouldnt know what that meant I hate that pretending of all things with the old blackguards face on him anybody can see its not true and that Ruby and Fair Tyrants he brought me that twice I remember when I came to page 50 the part about where she hangs him up out of a hook with a cord flagellate sure theres nothing for a woman in that all invention made up about he drinking the champagne out of her slipper after the ball was over like the infant Jesus in the crib at Inchicore in the Blessed Virgins arms sure no woman could have a child that big taken out of her and I thought first it came out of her side because how could she go to the chamber when she wanted to and she a rich lady of course she felt honoured H. R. H. he was in Gibraltar the year I was born I bet he found lilies there too where he planted the tree he planted more than that in his time he might have planted me too if hed come a bit sooner then I wouldnt be here as I am he ought to chuck that Freeman with the paltry few shillings he knocks out of it and go into an office or something where hed get regular pay or a bank where they could put him up on a throne to count the money all the day of course he prefers plottering about the house so you cant stir with him any side whats your programme today I wish hed even smoke a pipe like father to get the smell of a man or pretending to be mooching about for advertisements when he could have been in Mr Cuffes still only for what he did then sending me to try and patch it up I could have got him promoted there to be the manager he gave me a great mirada once or twice first he was as stiff as the mischief really and truly Mrs Bloom only I felt rotten simply with the old rubbishy dress that I lost the leads out of the tails with no cut in it but theyre coming into fashion again I bought it simply to please him I knew it was no good by the finish pity I changed my mind of going to Todd and

Burns as I said and not Lees it was just like the shop itself rummage sale a lot of trash I hate those rich shops get on your nerves nothing kills me altogether only he thinks he knows a great lot about a womans dress and cooking mathering everything he can scour off the shelves into it if I went by his advices every blessed hat I put on does that suit me yes take that thats alright the one like a wedding cake standing up miles off my head he said suited me or the dishcover one coming down on my backside on pins and needles about the shop girl in that place in Grafton street I had the misfortune to bring him into and she as insolent as ever she could be with her smirk saying Im afraid were giving you too much trouble whats she there for but I stared it out of her yes he was awfully stiff and no wonder but he changed the second time he looked Poldy pigheaded as usual like the soup but I could see him looking very hard at my chest when he stood up to open the door for me it was nice of him to show me out in any case Im extremely sorry Mrs Bloom believe me without making it too marked the first time after him being insulted and me being supposed to be his wife I just half smiled I know my chest was out that way at the door when he said Im extremely sorry and Im sure you were

yes I think he made them a bit firmer sucking them like that so long he made me thirsty titties he calls them I had to laugh yes this one anyhow stiff the nipple gets for the least thing Ill get him to keep that up and Ill take those eggs beaten up with marsala fatten them out for him what are all those veins and things curious the way its made 2 the same in case of twins theyre supposed to represent beauty placed up there like those statues in the museum one of them pretending to hide it with her hand are they so beautiful of course compared with what a man looks like with his two bags full and his other thing hanging down out of him or sticking up at you like a hatrack no wonder they hide it with a cabbageleaf the woman is beauty of course thats admitted when he said I could pose for a picture naked to some rich fellow in Holles street when he lost the job in Helys and I was selling the clothes and strumming in the coffee palace would I be like that bath of the nymph with my hair down yes only shes younger or Im a little like that dirty bitch in that Spanish photo he has the nymphs used they go about like that I asked him that disgusting Cameron highlander behind the meat market or that other wretch with the red head behind the tree where the statue of the fish used to be when I was passing pretending he was pissing standing out for me to see it with his babyclothes up to one side the Queens own they were a nice lot its well the Surreys relieved them theyre always trying to show it to you every time nearly I passed outside the mens greenhouse near the Harcourt street station just to try some fellow or other trying to catch my eye or if it was 1 of the 7 wonders of the world O and the stink of those rotten places the night coming home with of those rotten places the night coming home with Poldy after the Comerfords party oranges and lemonade to make you feel nice and watery I went into 1 of them it was so biting cold I couldnt keep it when was that 93 the canal was frozen yes it was a few months after a pity a couple of the Camerons werent there to see me squatting in the mens place meadero I tried to draw a picture of it before I tore it up like a sausage or something I wonder theyre not afraid going about of getting a kick or a bang of something there and that word met something with hoses in it and he came out with some jawbreakers about the incarnation he never can explain a thing simply the way a body can understand then he goes and burns the bottom out of the pan all for his Kidney this one not so much theres the mark of his teeth still where he tried to bite the nipple I had to scream out arent they fearful trying to hurt you I had a great breast of milk with Milly enough for two what was the reason of that he said I could have got a pound a week as a wet nurse all swelled out the morning that delicate looking student that stopped in nº 28 with the Citrons Penrose nearly caught me washing through the window only for I snapped up the towel to my face that was his studenting hurt me they used to weaning her till he got doctor Brady to give me the Belladonna prescription I had to get him to suck them they were so hard he said it was sweeter and thicker than cows then he wanted to milk me into the tea well hes beyond everything I declare somebody ought to put him in the budget if I only could remember the one half of the things and write a book out of it the works of Master Poldy yes and its so much smoother the skin much an hour he was at them Im sure by the clock like some kind of a big infant I had at me they want everything in their mouth all the pleasure those men get out of a woman I can feel his mouth O Lord I must stretch myself I wished he was here or somebody to let myself go with and come again like that I feel all fire inside me or if I could dream it when he made me spend the 2nd time tickling me behind with his finger I was coming for about 5 minutes with my legs round him I had to hug him after O Lord I wanted to shout out all sorts of things fuck or shit or anything at all only not to look ugly or those lines ftom the strain who knows the way hed take it you want to feel your way with a man theyre not all like him thank God some of them want you to be so nice about it I noticed the contrast he does it and doesnt talk I gave my eyes that look with my hair a bit loose from the tumbling and my tongue between my lips up to him the savage brute Thursday Friday one Saturday two Sunday three O Lord I cant wait till Monday

frseeeeeeeefronnnng train somewhere whistling the strength those engines have in them like big giants and the water rolling all over and out of them all sides like the end of Loves old sweet sonnnng the poor men that have to be out all the night from their wives and families in those roasting engines stifling it was today Im glad I burned the half of those old Freemans and Photo bits leaving things like that lying around hes getting very careless and threw the rest of them up in the W C Ill get him to cut them tomorrow for me instead of having them there for the next year to get a few pence for them have him asking wheres last Januarys paper and all those old overcoats I bundled out of the hall making the place hotter than it is the rain was lovely just after my beauty sleep I thought it was going to get like Gibraltar my goodness the heat there before the levanter came on black as night and the glare of the rock standing up in it like a big giant compared with their 3 Rock mountain they think is so great with the red sentries here and there the poplars and they all whitehot and the mosquito nets and the smell of the rainwater in those tanks watching the sun all the time weltering down on you faded all that lovely frock fathers friend Mrs Stanhope sent me from the B Marche paris what a shame my dearest Doggerina she wrote on what she was very nice whats this her other name was just a P C to tell you I sent the little present have just had a jolly warm bath and feel a very clean dog now enjoyed it wogger she called him wogger wd give anything to be back in Gib and hear you sing in old Madrid or Waiting Concone is the name of those exercises he bought me one of those new some word I couldnt make out shawls amusing things but tear for the least thing still there lovely I think dont you will always think of the lovely teas we had together scrumptious currant scones and raspberry wafers I adore well now dearest Doggerina be sure and write soon kind she left out regards to your father also Captain Grove with love yes affly x x x x x she didnt look a bit married just like a girl he was years older than her wogger he was awfully fond of me when he held down the wire with his foot for me to step over at the bullfight at La Linea when that matador Gomez was given the bulls ear clothes we have to wear whoever invented them expecting you to walk up Killiney hill then for example at that picnic all staysed up you cant do a blessed thing in them in a crowd run or jump out of the way thats why I was afraid when that other ferocious old Bull began to charge the banderilleros with the sashes and the 2 things in their hats and the brutes of men shouting bravo toro sure the women were as bad in their nice white mantillas ripping all the whole insides out of those poor horses I never heard of such a thing in all my life yes he used to break his heart at me taking off the dog barking in bell lane poor brute and it sick what became of them ever I suppose theyre dead long ago the 2 of them its like all through a mist makes you feel so old I made the scones of course I had everything all to myself then a girl Hester we used to compare our hair mine was thicker than hers she showed me how to settle it at the back when I put it up and whats this else how to make a knot on a thread with the one hand we were like cousins what age was I then the night of the storm I slept in her bed she had her arms round me then we were fighting in the morning with lhe pillow what fun he was watching me whenever he got an opportunity at the band on the Alameda esplanade when I was with father and Captain Grove I looked up at the church first and then at the windows then down and our eyes met I felt something go through me like all needles my eyes were dancing I remember after when I looked at myself in the glass hardly recognized myself the change I had a splendid skin from the sun and the excitement like a rose I didnt get a wink of sleep it wouldnt have been nice on account of her but I could have stopped it in time she gave me the Moonstone to read that was the first I read of Wilkie Collins East Lynne I read and the shadow of Ashlydyat Mrs Henry Wood Henry Dunbar by that other woman I lent him afterwards with Mulveys photo in it so as he see I wasnt without and Lord Lytton Eugene Aram Molly bawn she gave me by Mrs Hungerford on account of the name I dont like books with a Molly in them like that one he brought me about the one from Flanders a whore always shopifting anything she could cloth and stuff and yards of it this blanket is too heavy on me thats better I havent even one decent nightdress this thing gets all rolled up under me besides him and his fooling thats better I used to be weltering then in the heat my shift drenched with the sweat stuck in the cheeks of my bottom on the chair when I stood up they were so fattish and firm when I got up on the sofa cushions to see with my clothes up and the bugs tons of them at night and the mosquito nets I couldnt read a line Lord how long ago it seems centuries of course they never come back and she didnt put her address right on it either she may have noticed her wogger people were always going away and we never I remember that day with the waves and the boats with their high heads rocking and the swell of the ship those Officers uniforms on shore leave made me seasick he didnt say anything he was very serious I had the high buttoned boots on and my skirt was blowing she kissed me six or seven times didnt I cry yes I believe I did or near it my lips were taittering when I said goodbye she had a Gorgeous wrap of some special kind of blue colour on her for the voyage made very peculiarly to one side like and it was extremely pretty it got as dull as the devil after they went I was almost planning to run away mad out of it somewhere were never easy where we are father or aunt or marriage waiting always waiting to guiiiide him toooo me waiting nor speeeed his flying feet their damn guns bursting and booming all over the shop especially the Queens birthday and throwing everything down in all directions of you didnt open the windows when general Ulysses Grant whoever he was or did supposed to be some great fellow landed off the ship and old Sprague the codsul that was there from before the flood dressed up poor man and he in mourning for the son then the same old reveille in the morning and drums rolling and the unfortunate poor devils of soldiers walking about with messtins smelling the place more than the old longbearded jews in their jellibees and levites assembly and sound clear and gunfire for the men to cross the lines and the warden marching with his keys to lock the gates and the bagpipes and only Captain Groves and father talking about Rorkes drift and Plevna and sir Garnet Wolseley and Gordon at Khartoum lighting their pipes for them everytime they went out drunken old devil with his grog on the windowsill catch him leaving any of it picking his nose trying to think of some other dirty story to tell up in a corner but he never forgot himself when I was there sending me out of the room on some blind excuse paying his compliments the Bushmills whisky talking of course but hed do the same to the next woman that came along I supposed he died of galloping drink ages ago the days like years not a letter from a living soul except the odd few I posted to myself with bits of paper in them so bored sometimes I could fight with my nails listening to that old Arab with the one eye and his heass of an instrument singing his heah heah heah aheah all my compriments on your hotchapotch of your heass as bad as now with the hands hanging off me looking out of the window if there was a nice fellow even in the opposite house that medical in Holles street the nurse was after when I put on my gloves and hat at the window to show I was going out not a notion what I meant arent they thick never understand what you say even youd want to print it up on a big poster for them not even if you shake hands twice with the left he didnt recognise me either when I half frowned at him outside Westland row chapel where does their great intelligence come in Id like to know grey matter they have it all in their tail if you ask me those country gougers up in the City Arms intelligence they had a damn sight less than the bulls and cows they were selling the meat and the coalmans bell that noisy bugger trying to swindle me with the wrong bill he took out of his hat what a pair of paws and pots and pans and kettles to mend any broken bottles for a poor man today and no visitors or post ever except his cheques or some advertisement like that wonderworker they sent him addressed dear Madam only his letter and the card from Milly this morning see she wrote a letter to him who did I get the last letter from O Mrs Dwenn now whatever possessed her to write after so many years to know the recipe I had for pisto madrileno Floey Dillon since she wrote to say she was married to a very rich architect if Im to believe all I hear with a villa and eight rooms her father was an awfully nice man he was near seventy always good humour well now Miss Tweedy or Miss Gillespie theres the pyannyer that was a solid silver coffee service he had too on the mahogany sideboard then dying so far away I hate people that have always their poor story to tell everybody has their own troubles that poor Nancy Blake died a month ago of acute pneumonia well I didnt know her so well as all that she was Floeys friend more than mine its a bother having to answer he always tells me the wrong things and no stops to say like making a speech your sad bereavement symphathy I always make that mistake and newphew with 2 double yous in I hope hell write me a longer letter the next time if its a thing he really likes me O thanks be to the great God I got somebody to give me what I badly wanted to put some heart up into me youve no chances at all in this place like you used long ago I wish somebody would write me a loveletter his wasnt much and I told him he could write what he liked yours ever Hugh Boylan in Old Madrid silly women believe love is sighing I am dying still if he wrote it I suppose thered be some truth in it true or no it fills up your whole day and life always something to think about every moment and see it all around you like a new world I could write the answer in bed to let him imagine me short just a few words not those long crossed letters Atty Dillon used to write to the fellow that was something in the four courts that jilted her after out of the ladies letterwriter when I told her to say a few simple words he could twist how he liked not acting with precipit precipitancy with equal candour the greatest earthly happiness answer to a gentlemans proposal affirmatively my goodness theres nothing else its all very fine for them but as for being a woman as soon as youre old they might as well throw you out in the bottom of the ashpit.

Mulveys was the first when I was in bed that morning and Mrs Rubio brought it in with the coffee she stood there standing when I asked her to hand me and I pointing at them I couldnt think of the word a hairpin to open it with ah horquilla disobliging old thing and it staring her in the face with her switch of false hair on her and vain about her appearance ugly as she was near 80 or a 100 her face a mass of wrinkles with all her religion domineering because she never could get over the Atlantic fleet coming in half the ships of the world and the Union Jack flying with all her carabineros because 4 drunken English sailors took all the rock from them and because I didnt run into mass often enough in Santa Maria to please her with her shawl up on her except when there was a marriage on with all her miracles of the saints and her black blessed virgin with the silver dress and the sun dancing 3 times on Easter Sunday morning and when the priest was going by with the bell bringing the vatican to the dying blessing herself for his Majestad an admirer he signed it I near jumped out of my skin I wanted to pick him up when I saw him following me along the Calle Real in the shop window then he tipped me just in passing I never thought hed write making an appointment I had it inside my petticoat bodice all day reading it up in every hole and corner while father was up at the drill instructing to find out by the handwriting or the language of stamps singing I remember shall I wear a white rose and I wanted to put on the old stupid clock to near the time he was the first man kissed me under the Moorish wall my sweetheart when a boy it never entered my head what kissing meant till he put his tongue in my mouth his mouth was sweetlike young I put my knee up to him a few times to learn the way what did I tell him I was engaged for fun to the son of a Spanish nobleman named Don Miguel de la Flora and he believed that I was to be married to him in 3 years time theres many a true word spoken in jest there is a flower that bloometh a few things I told him true about myself just for him to be imagining the Spanish girls he didnt like I suppose one of them wouldnt have him I got him excited he crushed all the flowers on my bosom he brought me he couldnt count the pesetas and the perragordas till I taught him Cappoquin he came from he said on the Blackwater but it was too short then the day before he left may yes it was May when the infant king of Spain was born Im always like that in the spring Id like a new fellow every year up on the tiptop under the rockgun near OHaras tower I told him it was struck by lightning and all about the old

Barbary apes they sent to Clapham without a tail careering all over the show on each others back Mrs Rubio said she was a regular old rock scorpion robbing the chickens out of Inces farm and throw stones at you if you went anear he was looking at me I had that white blouse on open at the front to encourage him as much as I could without too openly they were just beginning to be plump I said I was tired we lay over the firtree cove a wild place I suppose it must be the highest rock in existence the galleries and casemates and those frightful rocks and Saint Michaels cave with the icicles or whatever they call them hanging down and ladders all the mud plotching my boots Im sure thats the way down the monkeys go under the sea to Africa when they die the ships out far like chips that was the Malta boat passing yes the sea and the sky you could do what you liked lie there for ever he caressed them outside they love doing that its the roundness there I was leaning over him with my white ricestraw hat to take the newness out of it the left side of my face the best my blouse open for his last day transparent kind of shirt he had I could see his chest pink he wanted to touch mine with his for a moment but I wouldnt let him he was awfully put out first for fear your never know consumption or leave me with a child embarazada that old servant Ines told me that one drop even if it got into you at all after I tried with the Banana but I was afraid it might break and get lost up in me somewhere yes because they once took something down out of a woman that was up there for years covered with limesalts theyre all mad to get in there where they come out of youd think they could never get far enough up and then theyre done with you in a way till the next time yes because theres a wonderful feeling there all the time so tender how did we finish it off yes O yes I pulled him off into my handkerchief pretending not to be excited but I opened my legs I wouldnt let him touch me inside my petticoat I had a skirt opening up the side I tortured the life out of him first tickling him I loved rousing that dog in the hotel rrrsssst awokwokawok his eyes shut and a bird flying below us he was shy all the same I liked him like that morning I made him blush a little when I got over him that way when I unbuttoned him and took his out and drew back the skin it had a kind of eye in it theyre all Buttons men down the middle on the wrong side of them Molly darling he called me what was his name Jack Joe Harry Mulvey was it yes I think a lieutenant he was rather fair he had a laughing kind of a voice so I went around to the whatyoucallit everything was whatyoucallit moustache had he he said hed come back Lord its just like yesterday to me and if I was married hed do it to me and I promised him yes faithfully Id let him block me now flying perhaps hes dead or killed or a Captain or admiral its nearly 20 years if I said firtree cove he would if he came up behind me and put his hands over my eyes to guess who I might recognize him hes young still about 40 perhaps hes married some girl on the black water and is quite changed they all do they havent half the character a woman has she little knows what I did with her beloved husband before he ever dreamt of her in broad daylight too in the sight of the whole world you might say they could have put an article about it in the Chronicle I was a bit wild after when I blew out the old bag the biscuits were finrom Benady Bros and exploded it Lord what a bang all the woodcocks and pigeons screaming coming back the same way that we went over middle hill round by the old guardhouse and the jews burialplace pretending to read out the Hebrew on them I wanted to fire his pistol he said he hadnt one he didnt know what to make of me with his peaked cap on that he always wore crooked as often as I settled it straight H M S Calypso swinging my hat that old Bishop that spoke off the altar his long preach about womans higher functions about girls now riding the bicycle and wearing peak caps and the new woman bloomers God send him sense and me more money I suppose theyre called after him I never tho ught that would be my name Bloom when I used to write it in print to see how it looked on a visiting card or practising for the butcher and oblige M Bloom youre looking blooming Josie used to say after I married him well its better than Breen or Briggs does brig or those awful names with bottom in them Mrs Ramsbottom or some other kind of a bottom Mulvey I wouldnt go mad about either or suppose I divorced him Mrs Boylan my mother whoever she was might have given me a nicer name the Lord knows after the lovely one she had Lunita Laredo the fun we had running along Willis road to Europe point twisting in and out all round the other side of Jersey they were shaking and dancing about in my blouse like Millys little ones now when she runs up the stairs I loved looking down at them I was jumping up at the pepper trees and the white poplars pulling the leaves off and throwing them at him he went to India he was to write the voyages those men have to make to the ends of the world and back its the least they might get a squeeze or two at a woman while they can going out to be drowned or blown up somewhere I went up windmill hill to the flats that Sunday morning with Captain Rubios that was dead spyglass like the sentry had he said hed have one or two from on board I wore that frock from the B Marche Paris and the coral necklace the straits shining I could see over to Morocco almost the bay of Tangier white and the Atlas mountain with snow on it and the straits like a river so clear Harry Molly Darling I was thinking of him on the sea all the time after at mass when my petticoat began to slip down at the elevation weeks and weeks I kept the handerchief under my pillow for the smell of him there was no decent perfume to be got in that Gibraltar only that cheap peau despagne that faded and left a stink on you more than anything else I wanted to give him a memento he gave me that clumsy Claddagh ring for luck that I gave Gardner going to South Africa where those Boers killed him with their war and fever but they were well beaten all the same as if it brought its bad luck with it like an opal or pearl must have been pure 16 carat gold because it was very heavy I can see his face clean shaven Frseeeeeeeeeeeeeeeeeeeefrong that train again weeping tone once in the dear deaead days beyondre call close my eyes breath my lips forward kiss sad look eyes open piano ere oer the world the mists began I hate that istsbeg comes loves sweet ssooooooong Ill let that out full when I get in front of the footlights again Kathleen Kearney and her lot of squealers Miss This Miss That Miss Theother lot of sparrowfarts skitting around talking about politics they know as much about as my backside anything in the world to make themselves someway interesting Irish homenade beauties soldiers daughter am I ay and whose are you bootmakers and publicasn I beg your pardon coach I thought you were a wheelbarrow theyd die down dead off their feet if ever they got a chance of walking down the Alameda on an officers arm like me on the bandnight my eyes flash my bust that they havent passion God help their poor head I knew more about men and life when I was 15 than theyll all know at 50 they dont know how to sing a song like that Gardner said no man could look at my mouth and teeth smiling like that and not think of it I was afraid he mightnt like my accent first he so English all father left me in spite of his stamps Ive my mothers eyes and figure anyhow he always said theyre so snotty about themselves some of those cads he wasnt a bit like that he was dead gone on my lips let them get a husband first thats fit to be looked at and a daughter like mine or see if they can excite a swell with money that can pick and choose whoever he wants like Boylan to do it 4 or 5 times locked in each others arms or the voice either I could have been a prima donna only I married him comes looooves old deep down chin back not too much make it double My Ladys Bower is too long for an encore about the moated grange at twilight and vaunted rooms yes Ill sing Winds that blow from the south that he gave after the choirstairs performance Ill change that lace on my black dress to show off my bubs and Ill yes by

God Ill get that big fan mended make them burst with envy my hole is itching me always when I think of him I feel I want to I feel some wind in me better go easy not wake him have him at it again slobbering after washing every bit of myself back belly and sides if we had even a bath itself or my own room anyway I wish hed sleep in some bed by himself with his cold feet on me give us room even to let a fart God or do the least thing better yes hold them like that a bit on my sidep iano quietly sweeeee theres that train far away pianissimo eeeeeeee one more song

that was a relief wherever you be let your wind go free who knows if that pork chop I took with my cup of tea after was quite good with the heat I couldnt smell anything off it Im sure that queerlooking man in the porkbutchers is a great rogue I hope that lamp is not smoking fill my nose up with smuts better than having him leaving the gas on all night I couldnt rest easy in my bed in Gibraltar even getting up to see why am I so damned nervous about that though I like it in the winter its more company O Lord it was rotten cold too that winter when I was only about ten was I yes I had the big doll with all the funny clothes dressing her up and undressing that icy wind skeeting across from those mountains the something Nevada sierra nevada standing at the fire with the little bit of a short shift I had up to heat myselr I loved dancing about in it then make a race back into bed Im sure that fellow opposite used to be there the whole time watching with the lights out in the summer and I in my skin hopping around I used to love myself then stripped at the washstand dabbing and creaming only when it came to the chamber performance I put out the light too so then there were 2 of us Goodbye to my sleep for this night anyhow I hope hes not going to get in with those medicals leading him astray to imagine hes young again coming in at 4 in the morning it must be if not more still he had the manners not to wake me what do they find to gabber about all night squandering money and getting drunker and drunker couldnt they drink water then he starts giving us his orders for eggs and tea Findon haddy and hot buttered toast I suppose well have him sitting up like the king of the country pumping the wrong end of the spoon up and down in his egg wherever he learned that from and I love to hear him falling up the stairs of a morning with the cups rattling on the tray and then play with the cat she rubs up against you for her own sake I wonder has she fleas shes as bad as a woman always licking and lecking but I hate their claws I wonder do they see anything that we cant staring like that when she sits at the top of the stairs so long and listening as I wait always what a robber too that lovely fresh place I bought I think Ill get a bit of fish tomorrow or today is it Friday yes I will with some blancmange with black currant jam like long ago not those 2 lb pots of mixed plum and apple from the London and Newcastle Williams and Woods goes twice as far only for the bones I hate those eels cod yes Ill get a nice piece of cod Im always getting enough for 3 forgetting anyway Im sick of that everlasting butchers meat from Buckleys loin chops and leg beef and rib steak and scrag of mutton and calfs pluck the very name is enough or a picnic suppose we all gave 5/ each and or let him pay and invite some other woman for him who Mrs Fleming and drove out to the furry glen or the strawberry beds wed have him examining all the horses toenails first like he does with the letters no not with Boylan there yes with some cold veal and ham mixed sandwiches there are little houses down at the bottom of the banks there on purpose but its as hot as blazes he says not a bank holiday anyhow I hate those ruck of Mary Ann coalboxes out for the day Whit Monday is a cursed day too no wonder that bee bit him better the seaside but Id never again in this life get into a boat with him after him at Bray telling the boatmen he knew how to row if anyone asked could he ride the steeplechase for the gold cup hed say yes then it came on to get rough the old thing crookeding about and the weight all down my side telling me to pull the right reins now pull the left and the tide all swamping in floods in through through the bottom and his oar slipping out of the stirrup its a mercy we werent all drowned he can swim of course me no theres no danger whatsoever keep yourself calm in his flannel trousers Id like to have tattered them down off him before all the people and give him what that one calls flagellate till he was black and blue do him all the good in the world only for that longnosed chap I dont know who he is with that other beauty Burke out of the City Arms hotel was there spying around as usual on the slip always where he wasnt wanted if there was a row on youd vomit a better face there was no love lost between us thats 1 consolation I wonder what kind is that book he brought me Sweets of Sin by a gentleman of fashion some other Mr de Kock I suppose the people gave him that nickname going about with his tube from one woman to another I couldnt even change my new white shoes all ruined with the saltwater and the hat I had with that feather all blowy and tossed on me how annoying and provoking because the smell of the sea excited me of course the sardines and the bream in Catalan bay round the back of the rock they were fine all silver in the fishermens baskets old Luigi near a hundred they said came from Genoa and the tall old chap with the earrings I dont like a man you have to climb up to to get at I suppose theyre all dead and rotten long ago besides I dont like being alone in this big barracks of a place at night I suppose Ill have to put up with it I never brought a bit of salt in even when we moved in the confusion musical academy he was going to make on the first floor drawingroom with a brassplate or Blooms private hotel he suggested go and ruin himself altogether the way his father did down in Ennis like all the things he told father he was going to do and me but I saw through him telling me all the lovely places we could go for the honeymoon Venice by moonlight with the gondolas and the lake of Como he had a picture cut out of some paper of and mandolines and lanterns O how nice I said whatever I liked he was going to do immediately if not sooner will you be my man will you carry my can he ought to get a leather medal with a putty rim for all the plans he invents then leaving us here all day youd never know what old beggar at the door for a crust with his long story might be a tramp and put his foot in the way to prevent me shutting it like that picture of that hardened criminal he was called in Lloyd's Weekly News 20 years in jail then he comes out and murders an old woman for her money imagine his poor wife or mother or whoever she is such a face youd run miles away from I couldnt rest easy till I bolted all the doors and windows to make sure but its worse again being locked up like in a prison or a madhouse they ought to be all shot or the cat of nine tails a big brute like that that would attack a poor old woman to murder her in her bed Id cut them off him so I would not that hed be much use still better than nothing the night I was sure I heard burglars in the kitchen and he went down in his shirt with a candle and a poker as if he was looking for a mouse as white as a sheet frightened out of his wit making as much noise as he possibly could for the burglars benefit there isnt much to steal indeed the Lord knows still its the feeling especially now with Milly away such an idea for him to send the girl down there to learn to take photographs on account of his grandfather instead of sending her to skerrys academy where shed have to learn not like me getting all at school only hed do a thing like that all the same on account of me and Boylan thats why he did it Im certain the way he plots and plans everything out I couldnt turn round with her in the place lately unless I bolted the door first gave me the fidgets coming in without knocking first when I put the chair against the door just as I was washing myself there below with the glove get on your nerves then doing the loglady all day put her in a glasscase with two at a time to look at her it he knew she broke off the hand off that little gimcrack statue with her roughness and carelessness before she left that I got that little Italian boy to mend so that you cant see the join for 2 shillings wouldnt even teem the potatoes for you of course shes right not to ruin her hands I noticed he was always talking to her lately at the table explaining things in the paper and she pretending to understand sly of course that comes from his side of the house and helping her into her coat but if there was anything wrong with her its meshed tell not him he cant say I pretend things can he Im too honest as a matter of fact I suppose he thinks Im finished out and laid on the shelf well Im not no nor anything like it well see well see now shes well on for flirting too with Tom Devans two sons imitating me whistling with those romps of Murray girls calling for her can Milly come out please shes in great demand to pick what they can out of her round in Nelson street riding Harry Devans bicycle at night its as well he sent her where she is she was just getting out of bounds wanting to go on the skatingrink and smoking their cigarettes through their nose I smelt it off her dress when I was biting off the thread of the button I sewed on to the bottom of her jacket she couldnt hide much from me I tell you only I oughtnt to have stitched it and it on her it brings a parting and the last plumpudding too split in 2 halves see it comes out no matter what they say her tongue is a bit too long for my taste your blouse is open too low she says to me the pan calling the kettle blackbottom and I had to tell her not to cock her legs up like that on show on the windowsill before all the people passing they all look at her like me when I was her age of course any old rag looks well on you then a great touchmenot too in her own way at the Only Way in the Theatre royal take your foot away out of that I hate people touching me afraid of her life Id crush her skirt with the pleats a lot of that touching must go in theatres in the crush in the dark theyre always trying to wiggle up to you that fellow in the pit at the pit at the Gaiety for Beerbohm Tree in Trilby the last time Ill ever go there to be squashed like that for any Trilby or her barebum every two minutes tipping me there and looking away hes a bit daft I think I saw him after trying to get near two stylish dressed ladies outside Switzers window at the same little game I recognised him on the moment the face and everything but he didnt remember me and she didnt even want me to kiss her at the Broadstone going away well I hope shell get someone to dance attendance on her the way I did when she was down with the mumps and her glands swollen wheres this and wheres that of course she cant feel anything deep yet I never came properly till I was what 22 or so it went into the wrong place always only the usual girls nonsense and giggling that Conny Connolly writing to her in white ink on black paper sealed with sealingwax though she clapped when the curtain came down because he looked so handsome then we had Martin Harvey for breakfast dinner and supper I thought to myself afterwards it must be real love if a man gives up his life for her that way for nothing I suppose there are few men like that left its hard to believe in it though unless it really happened to me the majority of them with not a particle of love in their natures to find two people like that nowadays full up of each other that would feel the same way as you do theyre usually a bit foolish in the head his father must have been a bit queer to go and poison himself after her still poor old man I suppose he felt lost always making love to my things too the few old rags I have wanting to put her hair up at 15 my powder too only ruin her skin on her shes time enough for that all her life after of course shes restless knowing shes pretty with her lips so red a pity they wont stay that way I was too but theres no use going to the fair with the thing answering me like a fishwoman when I asked to go for a half a stone of potatoes the day we met Mrs Joe Gallaher at the trottingmatches and she pretended not to see us in her trap with Friery the solicitor we werent grand enough till I gave her 2 damn fine cracks across the ear for herself take that now for answering me like that and that for your impudence she had me that exasperated of course contradicting I was badtempered too because how was it there was a weed in the tea or I didnt sleep the night before cheese I ate was it and I told her over and over again not to leave knives crossed like that because she has nobody to command her as she said herself well if he doesnt correct her faith I will that was the last time she turned on the teartap I was just like that myself they darent order me about the place its his fault of course having the two of us slaving here instead of getting in a woman long ago am I ever going to have a proper servant again of course then shed see him coming Id have to let her know or shed revenge it arent they a nuisance that old Mrs Flemming you have to be walking round after her putting the things into her hands sneezing and farting into the pots well of course shes old she cant help it a good job I found that rotten old smelly dishcloth that got lost behind the dresser I knew there was something and opened the window to let out the smell bringing in his friends to entertain them like the night he walked home with a dog if you please that might have been mad especially Simon Dedalus son his father such a criticiser with his glasses up with his tall hat on him at the cricket match and a great big hole in his sock one thing laughing at the other and his son that got all those prizes for whatever he won them in the intermediate imagine climbing over the railings if anybody saw him that knew us wonder he didnt tear a big hole in his grand funeral trousers as if the one nature gave wasnt enough for anybody hawking him down into the dirty old kitchen now is he right in his head I ask pity it wasnt washing day my old pair of drawers might have been hanging up too on the line on exhibition for all hed ever care with the ironmould mark the stupid old bundle burned on them he might think was something else and she never even rendered down the fat I told her and now shes going such as she was on account of her paralysed husband getting worse theres always something wrong with them disease or they have to go under an operation or if its not that its drink and he beats her Ill have to hunt around again for someone every day I get up theres some new thing on sweet God sweet God well when Im stretched out dead in my grave I suppose Ill have some peace I want to get up a minute if Im let wait O Jesus wait yes that thing has come on me yes now wouldnt that afflicty ou of course all the poking and rooting and ploughing he had up in me now what am I to do Friday Saturday Sunday wouldnt that pester the soul out of a body unless he likes it some men do God knows theres always something wrong with us 5 days every 3 or 4 weeks usual monthly auction isnt it simply sickening that night it came on me like that the one and only tim ewe were in a box that Michael Gunn gave him to see Mrs Kendal and her husband at the Gaiety something he did about insurance for him Drimmies I was fit to be tied though I wouldnt give in with that gentleman of fashion staring down at me with his glasses and him the other side of me talking about Spinoza and his soul thats dead I suppose millions of years ago I smiled the best I could all in a swamp leaning forward as if I was interested having to sit it out then to the last tag I wont forget that wife of Scarli in a hurry supposed to be a fast play about adultery that idiot in the gallery hissing the woman adulteress he shouted I suppose he went and had a woman in the next lane running round all the back ways after to make up for it I wish he had what I had then hed boo I bet the cat itself is better off than us have we too much blood up in us or what O patience above its pouring out of me like the sea anyhow he didnt make me pregnant as big as he is I dont want to ruin the clean sheets the clean linen I wore brought it on too damn it damn it and they always want to see a stain on the bed to know youre a virgin for them all thats troubling them theyre such fools too you could be a widow or divorced 40 times over a daub of red ink would do or blackberry juice no thats too purply O Jamesy let me up out of this pooh sweets of sin whoever suggested that business for women what between clothes and cooking and children this damned old bed too jingling like the dickens I suppose they could hear us away over the other side of the park till I suggested to put the quilt on the floor with the pillow under my bottom I wonder is it nicer in the day I think it is easy I think Ill cut all this hair off me there scalding me I might look like a young girl wouldnt he get the great suckin the next time he turned up my clothes on me Id give anything to see his face wheres the chamber gone easy Ive a holy horror of its breaking under me after that old commode I wonder was I too heavy sitting on his knee I made him sit on the easychair purposely when I took off only my blouse and skirt first in the other room he was so busy where he oughtnt to be he never felt me I hope my breath was sweet after those kissing comfits easy God I remember one time I could scout it out straight whistling like a man almost easy O Lord how noisy I hope theyre bubbles on it for a wad of money from some fellow Ill have to perfume it in the morning dont forget I bet he never saw a better pair of thighs than that look how white they are the smoothest place is right there between this bit here how soft like a peach easy God I wouldnt mind being a man and get up on a lovely woman O Lord what a row youre making like the jersey lily easy easy O how the waters come down at Lahore

who knows is there anything the matter with my insides or have I something growing in me getting that thing like that every week when was it last I Whit Monday yes its only about 3 weeks I ought to go to the doctor only it would be like before I married him when I had that white thing coming from me and Floey made me go to that dry old stick Dr Collins for womens diseases on Pembroke road your vagina he called it I suppose thats how he got all the gilt mirrors and carpets getting round those rich ones off Stephens green running up to him for every little fiddlefaddle her vagina and her cochinchina theyve money of course so theyre all right I wouldnt marry him not if he was the last man in the world besides theres something queer about their children always smelling around those filthy bitches all sides asking me if what I did had an offensive odour what did he want me to do but the one thing gold maybe what a question if I smathered it all over his wrinkly old face for him with all my compriment I suppose hed know then and could you pass it easily pass what I thought he was talking about the rock of Gibraltar the way he put it thats a very nice invention too by the way only I like letting myself down after in the hole as far as I can squeeze and pull the chain then to flush it nice cool pins and needles still theres something in it I suppose I always used to know by Millys when she was a child whether she had worms or not still all the same paying him for that how much is that doctor one guinea please and asking me had I frequent omissions where do those old fellows get all the words they have omissions with his shortsighted eyes on me cocked sideways I wouldnt trust him too far to give me chloroform or God knows what else still I liked him when he sat down to write the thing out frowning so severe his nose intelligent like that you be damned you lying strap O anything no matter who except an idiot he was clever enough to spot that of course that was all thinking of him and his mad crazy letters my Precious one everything connected with your glorious Body everything underlined that comes from it is a thing of beauty and of joy for ever something he got out of some nonsensical book that he had me always at myself 4 or 5 times a day sometimes and I said I hadnt are you sure O yes I said I am quite sure in a way that shut him up I knew what was coming next only natural weakness it was he excited me I dont know how the first night ever we met when I was living in Rehoboth terrace we stood staring at one another for about 10 minutes as if we met somewhere I suppose on account of my being jewess looking after my mother he used to amuse me the things he said with the half sloothering smile on him and all the Doyles said he was going to stand for a member of Parliament O wasnt I the born fool to believe all his blather about home rule and the land league sending me that long strool of a song out of the Huguenots to sing in French to be more classy O beau pays de la Touraine that I never even sang once explaining and rigmaroling about religion and persecution he wont let you enjoy anything naturally then might he as a great favour the very 1st opportunity he got a chance in Brighton square running into my bedroom pretending the ink got on his hands to wash it off with the Albion milk and sulphur soap I used to use and the gelatine still round it O I laughed myself sick at him that day I better not make an alnight sitting on this affair they ought to make chambers a natural size so that a woman could sit on it properly he kneels down to do it I suppose there isnt in all creation another man with the habits he has look at the way hes sleeping at the foot of the bed how can he without a hard bolster its well he doesnt kick or he might knock out all my teeth breathing with his hand on his nose like that Indian god he took me to show one wet Sunday in the museum in Kildare street all yellow in a pinafore lying on his side on his hand with his ten toes sticking out that he said was a bigger religion than the jews and Our Lords both put together all over Asia imitating him as hes always imitating everybody I suppose he used to sleep at the foot of the bed too with his big square feet up in his wifes mouth damn this stinking thing anyway wheres this those napkins are ah yes I know I hope the old press doesnt creak ah I knew it would hes sleeping hard had a good time somewhere still she must have given him great value for his money of course he has to pay for it from her O this nuisance of a thing I hope theyll have something better for us in the other world tying ourselves up God help us thats all right for tonight now the lumpy old jingly bed always reminds me of old Cohen I suppose he scratched himself in it often enough and he thinks father bought it form Lord Napier that I used to admire when I was a little girl because I told him easy piano O I like my bed God here we are as bad as ever after 16 years how many houses were we in at all Raymond terrace and Ontario terrace and Lombard street and Holles street and he goes about whistling every time were on the run again his huguenots or the frogs march pretending to help the men with our 4 sticks of furniture and then the City Arms hotel worse and worse says Warden Daly that charming place on the landing always somebody inside praying then leaving all their stinks after them always know who was in there last every time were just getting on right something happens or he puts his big foot in it Thoms and Helys and Mr Cuffes and Drimmies either hes going to be run into prison over his old lottery tickets that was to be all our salvations or he goes and gives impudence well have him coming home with the sack soon out of the Freeman too like the rest on account of those Sinner Fein or the freemasons then well see if the little man he showed me dribbling along in the wet all by himself round by Coadys lane will give him much consolation that he says is so capable and sincerely Irish he is indeed judging by the sincerity of the trousers I saw on him wait theres Georges church bells wait 3 quarters the hour wait 2 oclock well thats a nice hour of the night for him to be coming home at to anybody climbing down into the area if anybody saw him Ill knock him off that little habit tomorrow first Ill look at his shirt to see or Ill see if he has that French letter still in his pocketbook I suppose he thinks I dont know deceitful men all their 20 pockets arent enough for their lies then why should we tell them even if its the truth they dont believe you then tucked up in bed like those babies in the Aristocrats Masterpiece he brought me another time as if we hadnt enough of that in real life without some old Aristocrat or whatever his name is disgusting you more with those rotten pictures children with two heads and no legs thats the kind of villainy theyre always dreaming about with not another thing in their empty heads they ought to get slow poison the half of them then tea and toast for him buttered on both sides and newlaid eggs I suppose Im nothing any more when I wouldnt let him lick me in Holles street one night man man tyrant as ever for the one thing he slept on the floor half the night naked the way the jews used when somebody dies belonged to them and wouldnt eat any breakfast or speak a word wanting to be petted so I thought I stood out enough for one time and let him he does it all wrong too thinking only of his own pleasure his tongue is too flat or I dont know what he forgets that wethen I dont Ill make him do it again if he doesnt mind himself and lock him down to sleep in the coalcellar with the blackbeetles I wonder was it her Josie off her head with my castoffs hes such a born liar too no hed never have the courage with a married woman thats why he wants me and Boylan though as for her Denis as she calls him that forlornlooking spectacle you couldnt call him a husband yes its some little bitch hes got in with even when I was with him with Milly at the College races that Hornblower with the childs bonnet on the top of his nob let us into by the back way he was throwing his sheeps eyes at those two doing skirt duty up and down I tried to wink at him first no use of course and thats the way his money goes this is the fruits of Mr Paddy Dignam yes they were all in great style at the grand funeral in the paper Boylan brought in if they saw a real officers funeral thatd be something reversed arms muffled drums the poor horse walking behind in black L Boom and Tom Kernan that drunken little barrelly man that bit his tongue off falling down the mens W C drunk in some place or other and Martin Cunningham and the two Dedaluses and Fanny M Coys husband white head of cabbage skinny thing with a turn in her eye trying to sing my songs shed want to be born all over again and her old green dress with the lowneck as she cant attract them any other way like dabbling on a rainy day I see it all now plainly and they call that friendship killing and then burying one another and they all with their wives and families at home more especially Jack Power keeping that barmaid he does of course his wife is always sick or going to be sick or just getting better of it and hes a goodlooking man still though hes getting a bit grey over the ears theyre a nice lot all of them well theyre not going to get my husband again into their clutches if I can help it making fun of him then behind his back I know well when he goes on with his idiotics because he has sense enough not to squander every penny piece he earns down their gullets and looks after his wife and family goodfornothings poor Paddy Dignam all the same Im sorry in a way for him what are his wife and 5 children going to do unless he was insured comical little teetotum always stuck up in some pub corner and her or her son waiting Bill

Bailey wont you please come home her widows weeds wont improve her appearance theyre awfully becoming though if youre goodloking what men wasnt he yes he was at the Glencree dinner and Ben Dollard base barreltone the night he borrowed the swallowtail to sing out of in Holles street squeezed and squashed into them and grinning all over his big Dolly face like a wellwhipped childs botty didnt he look a balmy ballocks sure enough that must have been a spectacle on the stage imagine paying 5/- in the preserved seats for that to see him and Simon Dedalus too he was always turning up half screwed singing the second verse first the old love is the new was one of his so sweetly sang the maiden on the hawthorn bough he was always on for flirtyfying too when I sang Maritana with him at Freddy Mayers private opera he had a delicious glorious voice Phoebe dearest goodbye *sweet*heart he always sang it not like Bartell D'Arcy sweet *tart* goodbye of course he had the gift of the voice so there was no art in it all over you like a warm showerbath O Maritana wildwood flower we sang splendidly though it was a bit too high for my register even transposed and he was married at the time to May Goulding but then hed say or do something to knock the good out of it hes a widower now I wonder what sort is his son he says hes an author and going to be a university professor of Italian and Im to take lessons what is he driving at now showing him my photo its not good of me I ought to have got it taken in drapery that never looks out of fashion still I look young in it I wonder he didnt make him a present of it altogether and me too after all why not I saw him driving down to the Kingsbridge station with his father and mother I was in mourning thats 11 years ago now yes hed be 11 though what was the good in going into mourning for what was neither one thing nor the other of course he insisted hed go into mourning for the cat I suppose hes a man now by this time he was an innocent boy then and a darling little fellow in his lord Fauntleroy suit and curly hair like a prince on the stage when I saw him at Mat Dillons he liked me too I remember they all do wait by God yes wait yes hold on he was on the cards this morning when I laid out the deck union with a young stranger neither dark nor fair you met before I thought it meant him but hes no chicken nor a stranger either besides my face was turned the other way what was the 7th card after that the 10 of spades for a Journey by laud then there was a letter on its way and scandals too the 3 queens and the 8 of diamonds for a rise in society yes wait it all came out and 2 red 8s for new garments look at that and didnt I dream something too yes there was something about poetry in it I hope he hasnt long greasy hair hanging into his eyes or standing up like a red Indian what do they go about like that for only getting themselves and their poetry laughed at I always liked poetry when I was a girl first I thought he was a poet like Byron and not an ounce of it in his composition I thought he was quite different I wonder is he too young hes about wait 88 I was married 88 Milly is 15 yesterday 89 what age was he then at Dillons 5 or 6 about 88 I suppose hes 20 or more Im not too old for him if hes 23 or 24 I hope hes not that stuck up university student sort no otherwise he wouldnt go sitting down in the old kitchen with him taking Eppss cocoa and talking of course he pretended to understand it all probably he told him he was out of Trinity college hes very young to be a profes:or I hope hes not a professor like Goodwin was he was a patent professor of John Jameson they all write about some woman in their poetry well I suppose he wont find many like me where softly sighs of love the light guitar where poetry is in the air the blue sea and the moon shining so beautifully coming back on the nightboat from Tarifa the lighthouse at Europa point the guitar that fellow played was so expressive will I ever go back there again all new faces two glancing eyes a lattice hid Ill sing that for him theyre my eyes if hes anything of a poet two eyes as darkly bright as loves own star arent those beautiful words as loves young star itll be a change the Lord knows to have an intelligent person to talk to about yourself not always listening to him and Billy Prescotts ad and Keyess ad and Tom the Devils ad then if anything goes wrong in their business we have to suffer Im sure hes very distinguished Id like to meet a man like that God not those other ruck besides hes young those fine young men I could see down in Margate strand bathing place from the side of the rock standing up in the sun naked like a God or something and then plunging into the sea with them why arent all men like that thered be some consolation for a woman like that lovely little statue he bought I could look at him all day long curly head and his shoulders his finger up for you to listen theres real beauty and poetry for you I often felt I wanted to kiss him all over also his lovely young cock there so simple I wouldnt mind taking him in my mouth if nobody was looking as if it was asking you to suck it so clean and white he looked with his boyish face I would too in 1/2 a minute even if some of it went down what its only like gruel or the dew theres no danger besides hed be so clean compared with those pigs of men I suppose never dream of washing it from 1 years end to the other the most of them only thats what gives the women the moustaches Im sure itll be grand if I can only get in with a handsome young poet at my age Ill throw them the

1st thing in the morning till I see if the wishcard come out or Ill try pairing the lady herself and see if he comes out Ill read and study all I can find or learn a bit off by heart if I knew who he likes so he wont think me stupid if he thinks all women are the same and I can teach him the other part Ill make him feel all over him till he half faints nnder me then hell write about me lover and mistress publicly too with our 2 photographs in all the papers when he becomes famous O but then what am I going to do about him though

no thats no way for him has he no manners nor no refinement nor no nothing in his nature slapping us behind like that on my bottom because I didnt call him Hugh the ignoramus that doesnt know poetry from a cabbage thats what you get for not keeping them in their proper place pulling off his shoes and trousers there on the chair before me so barefaced without even asking permission and standing out that vulgar way in the half of a shirt they wear to be admired like a priest or a butcher or those old hypocrites in the time of Julius Caesar of course hes right enough in his way to pass the time as a joke sure you might as well be in bed with what with a lion God Im sure hed have something better to say for himself an old Lion would O well I suppose its because they were so plump and tempting in my short petticoat he couldnt resist they excite myself sometimes its well for men all the amount of pleasure they get off a womans body were so round and white for them always I wished I was one myself for a change just to try with that thing they have swelling upon you so hard and at the same time so soft when you touch it my uncle John has a thing long I heard those cornerboys saying passing the corner of Marrowbone lane my aunt Mary has a thing hairy because it was dark and they knew a girl was passing it didnt make me blush why should it either its only nature and he puts his thing long into my aunt Marys hairy etcetera and turns out to be you put the handle in a sweepingbrush men again all over they can pick and choose what they please a married woman or a fast widow or a girl for their different tastes like those houses round behind Irish street no but were to be always chained up theyre not going to be chaining me up no damn fear once I start I tell you for stupid husbands jealousy why cant we all remain friends over it instead of quarrelling her husband found it out what they did together well naturally and if he did can he undo it hes coronado anyway whatever he does and then he going to the other mad extreme about the wife in Fair Tyrants of course the man never even casts a 2nd thought on the husband or wife either its the woman he wants and he gets her what else were we given all those desires for Id like to know I cant help it if Im young still can I its a wonder Im not an old shrivelled hag before my time living with him so cold never embracing me except sometimes when hes asleep the wrong end of me not knowing I suppose who he has any man thatd kiss a womans bottom Id throw my hat at him after that hed kiss anything unnatural where we havent 1 atom of any kind of expression in us all of us the same 2 lumps of lard before ever Id do that to a man pfooh the dirty brutes the mere thought is enough I kiss the feet of you senorita theres some sense in that didnt he kiss our halldoor yes he did what a madman nobody understands his cracked ideas but me still of course a woman wants to be embraced 20 times a day almost to make her look young no matter by who so long as to be in love or loved by somebody if the fellow you want isnt there sometimes by the Lord God I was thinking would I go around by the quays there some dark evening where nobodyd know me and pick up a sailor off the sea thatd be hot on for it and not care a pin whose I was only to do it off up in a gate somewhere or one of those wildlooking gipsies in Rathfarnham had their camp pitched near the Bloomfield laundry to try and steal our things if they could I only sent mine there a few times for the name model laundry sending me back over and over some old ones odd stockings that blackguardlooking fellow with the fine eyes peeling a switch attack me in the dark and ride me up against the wall without a word or a murderer anybody what they do themselves the fine gentlemen in their silk hats that K. C. lives up somewhere this way coming out of Hardwicke lane the night he gave us the fish supper on account of winning over the boxing match of course it was for me he gave it I knew him by his gaiters and the walk and when I turned round a minute after just to see there was a woman after coming out of it too some filthy prostitute then he goes home to his wife after that only I suppose the half of those sailors are rotten again with disease O move over your big carcass out of that for the love of Mike listen to him the winds that waft my sighs to thee so well he may sleep and sigh the great Suggester Don Poldo de la Flora if he knew how he came out on the cards this morning hed have something to sigh for a dark man in some perplexity between 2 7s too in prison for Lord knows what he does that I dont know and Im to be slooching around down in the kitchen to get his lordship his breakfast while hes rolled up like a mummy will I indeed did you ever see me running Id just like to see myself at it show them attention and they treat you like dirt I dont care what anybody says itd be much better for the world to be governed by the women in it you wouldnt see women going and killing one another and slaughtering when do you ever see women rolling around drunk like they do or gambling every penny they have and losing it on horses yes because a woman whatever she does she knows where to stop sure they wouldnt be in the world at all only for us they dont know what it is to be a woman and a mother how could they where would they all of them be if they hadnt all a mother to look after them what I never had thats why I suppose hes running wild now out at night away from his books and studies and not living at home on account of the usual rowy house I suppose well its a poor case that those that have a fine son like that theyre not satisfied and I none was he not able to make one it wasnt my fault we came together when I was watching the two dogs up in her behind in the middle of the naked street that disheartened me altogether I suppose I oughtnt to have buried him in that little woolly jacket I knitted crying as I was but give it to some poor child but I knew well Id never have another our 1st death too it was we were never the same since O Im not going to think myself into the glooms about that any more I wonder why he wouldnt stay the night I felt all the time it was somebody strange he brought in instead of roving around the city meeting God knows who nightwalkers and pickpockets his poor mother wouldnt like that if she was alive ruining himself for life perhaps still its a lovely hour so silent I used to love coming home after dances the air of the night they have friends they can talk to weve none either he wants what he wont get or its some woman ready to stick her knife in you I hate that in women no wonder they treat us the way they do we are a dreadful lot of bitches I suppose its all the troubles we have makes us so snappy Im not like that he could easy have slept in there on the sofa in the other room I suppose he was as shy as a boy he being so young hardly 20 of me in the next room hed have heard me on the chamber arrah what harm Dedalus I wonder its like those names in Gibraltar Delapaz Delagracia they had the devils queer names there father Vial plana of Santa Maria that gave me the rosary Rosales y O'Reilly in the Calle las Siete Revueltas and Pisimbo and Mrs Opisso in Governor street O what a name Id go and drown myself in the first river if I had a name like her O my and all the bits of streets Paradise ramp and Bedlam ramp and Rodgers ramp and Crutchetts ramp and the devils gap steps well small blame to me if I am a harumscarum I know I am a bit I declare to God I dont feel a day older than then I wonder could I get my tongue round any of the Spanish como esta usted muy bien gracias y usted see I havent forgotten it all I thought I had only for the grammar a noun is the name of any person place or thing pity I never tried to read that novel cantankerous Mrs Rubio lent me by Valera with the questions in it all upside down the two ways I always knew wed go away in the end I can tell him the Spanish and he tell me the Italian then hell see Im not so ignorant what a pity he didnt stay Im sure the poor fellow was dead tired and wanted a good sleep badly I could have brought him in his breakfast in bed with a bit of toast so long as I didnt do it on the knife for bad luck or if the woman was going her rounds with the watercress and something nice and tasty there are a few olives in the kitchen he might like I never could bear the look of them in Abrines I could do the criada the room looks all right since I changed it the other way you see something was telling me all the time Id have to introduce myself not knowing me from Adam very funny wouldnt it Im his wife or pretend we were in Spain with him half awake without a Gods notion where he is dos huevos estrellados senor Lord the cracked things come into my head sometimes itd be great fun supposing he stayed with us why not theres the room upstairs empty and Millys bed in the back room he could do his writing and studies at the table in there for all the scribbling he does at it and if he wants to read in bed in the morning like me as hes making the breakfast for 1 he can make it for 2 Im sure Im not going to take in lodgers off the street for him if he takes a gesabo of a house like this Id love to have a long talk with an intelligent welleducated person Id have to get a nice pair of red slippers like those Turks with the fez used to sell or yellow and a nice semitransparent morning gown that I badly want or a peachblossom dressing jacket like the one long ago in Walpoles only 8/6 or 18/6 Ill just give him one more chance Ill get up early in the morning Im sick of Cohens old bed in any case I might go over to the markets to see all the vegetables and cabbages and tomatoes and carrots and all kinds of splendid fruits all coming in lovely and fresh who knows whod be the 1st man Id meet theyre out looking for it in the morning Mamy Dillon used to say they are and the night too that was her massgoing Id love a big juicy pear now to melt in your mouth like when I used to be in the in the longing way then Ill throw him up his eggs and tea in thc moustachecup she gave him to make his mouth bigger I suppose hed like my nice cream too I know what Ill do Ill go about rather gay not too much singing a bit now and then mi fa pieta Masetto then Ill start dressing myself to go out presto non son più forte Ill put on my best shift and drawers let him have a good eyeful out of that to make his micky stand for him Ill let him know if thats what he wanted that his wife is fucked yes and damn well fucked too up to my neck nearly not by him 5 or 6 times handrunning theres the mark of his spunk on the clean sheet I wouldnt bother to even iron it out that ought to satisfy him if you dont believe me feel my belly unless I made him stand there and put him into me Ive a mind to tell him every scrap and make him do it in front of me serve him right its all his own fault if I am an adulteress as the thing in the gallery said O much about it if thats all the harm ever we did in this vale of tears God knows its not much doesnt everybody only they hide it I suppose thats what a woman is supposed to be there for or He wouldn't have made us the way He did so attractive to men then if he wants to kiss my bottom Ill drag open my drawers and bulge it right out in his face as large as life he can stick his tongue 7 miles up my hole as hes there my brown part then Ill tell him I want £ 1 or perhaps 30/ Ill tell him I want to buy underclothes then if he gives me that well he wont be too bad I dont want to soak it all out of him like other women do I could often have written out a fine cheque for myself and write his name on it for a couple of pounds a few times he forgot to lock it up besides he wont spend it Ill let him do it off on me behind provided he doesnt smear all my good drawers O I suppose that cant be helped Ill do the indifferent 1 or 2 questions Ill know by the answers when hes like that he cant keep a thing back I know every turn in him Ill tighten my bottom well and let out a few smutty words smellrump or lick my shit or the first mad thing comes into my head then Ill suggest about yes O wait now sonny my turn is coming Ill be quite gay and friendly over it O but I was forgetting this bloody pest of a thing pfooh you wouldnt know which to laugh or cry were such a mixture of plum and apple no Ill have to wear the old things so much the better itll be more pointed hell never know whether he did it or not there thats good enough for you any old thing at all then Ill wipe him off me just like a business his omission then Ill go out Ill have him eying up at the ceiling where is she gone now make him want me thats the only way a quarter after what an unearthly hour I suppose theyre just getting up in China now combing out their pigtails for the day well soon have the nuns ringing the angelus theyve nobody coming in to spoil their sleep except an odd priest or two for his night office the alarmclock next door at cockshout clattering the brains out of itself let me see if I can doze off 1 2 3 4 5 what kind of flowers are those they invented like the stars the wallpaper in Lombard street was much nicer the apron he gave me was like that something only I only wore it twice better lower this lamp and try again so as I can get up early Ill go to Lambes there beside

Findlaters and get them to send us some flowers to put about the place in case he brings him home tomorrow today I mean no no Fridays an unlucky day first I want to do the place up someway the dust grows in it I think while Im asleep then we can have music and cigarettes I can accompany him first I must clean the keys of the piano with milk whatll I wear shall I wear a white rose or those fairy cakes in Liptons I love the smell of a rich big shop at 7 1/2 d a lb or the other ones with the cherries in them and the pinky sugar 11 d a couple of lbs of course a nice plant for the middle of the table Id get that cheaper in wait wheres this I saw them not long ago I love flowers Id love to have the whole place swimming in roses God of heaven theres nothing like nature the wild mountains then the sea and the waves rushing then the beautiful country with fields of oats and wheat and all kinds of things and all the fine cattle going about that would do your heart good to see rivers and lakes and flowers all sorts of shapes and smells and colours springing up even out of the ditches primroses and violets nature it is as for them saying theres no God I wouldnt give a snap of my two fingers for all their learning why dont they go and create something I often asked him atheists or whatever they call themselves go and wash the cobbles off themselves first then they go howling for the priest and they dying and why why because theyre afraid of hell on account of their bad conscience ah yes I know them well who was the first person in the universe before there was anybody that made it all who ah that they dont know neither do I so there you are they might as well try to stop the sun from rising tomorrow the sun shines for you he said the day we were lying among the rhododendrons on Howth head in the grey tweed suit and his straw hat the day I got him to propose to me yes first I gave him the bit of seedcake out of my mouth and it was leapyear like now yes 16 years ago my God after that long kiss I near lost my breath yes he said I was a flower of the mountain yes so we are flowers all a womans body yes that was one true thing he said in his life and the sun shines for you today yes that was why I liked him because I saw he understood or felt what a woman is and I knew I could always get round him and I gave him all the pleasure I could leading him on till he asked me to say yes and I wouldnt answer first only looked out over the sea and the sky I was thinking of so many things he didnt know of Mulvey and Mr Stanhope and Hester and father and old captain Groves and the sailors playing all birds fly and I say stoop and washing up dishes they called it on the pier and the sentry in front of the governors house with the thing round his white helmet poor devil half roasted and the Spanish girls laughing in their shawls and their tall combs and the auctions in the morning the Greeks and the jews and the Arabs and the devil knows who else from all the ends of Europe and Duke street and the fowl market all clucking outside Larby Sharons and the poor donkeys slipping half asleep and the vague fellows in the cloaks asleep in the shade on the steps and the big wheels of the carts of the bulls and the old castle thousands of years old yes and those handsome Moors all in white and turbans like kings asking you to sit down in their little bit of a shop and Ronda with the old windows of the posadas glancing eyes a lattice hid for her lover to kiss the iron and the wineshops half open at night and the castanets and the night we missed the boat at Algeciras the watchman going about serene with his lamp and O that awful deepdown torrent O and the sea the sea crimson sometimes like fire and the glorious sunsets and the figtrees in the Alameda gardens yes and all the queer little streets and pink and blue and yellow houses and the rosegardens and the jessamine and geraniums and cactuses and Gibraltar as a girl where I was a Flower of the mountain yes when I put the rose in my hair like the Andalusian girls used or shall I wear a red yes and how he kissed me under the Moorish wall and I thought well as well him as another and then I asked him with my eyes to ask again yes and then he asked me would I yes to say yes my mountain flower and first I put my arms around him yes and drew him down to me so he could feel my breasts all perfume yes and his heart was going like mad and yes I said yes I will Yes.

Trieste-Zurich-Paris,

1914-1921.

APPENDICES AND EXPLANATORY NOTES

Appendix A

The Gilbert and Linati Schemata
Table of Correspondences

THE GILBERT SCHEMA

Title	Scene	Hour	Organ	Art	Colour	Symbol	Technic	Correspondences
I. TELEMACHIA								
1. Telemachus	The Tower	8 a.m.		Theology	white, gold	Heir	Narrative (young)	Stephen: Telemachus, Hamlet; Buck Mulligan: Antinous; Milkwoman: Mentor.
2. Nestor	The School	10 a.m.		History	brown	Horse	Catechism (personal)	Deasy: Nestor; Sargent: Pisistratus; Helen: Mrs O'Shea.
3. Proteus	The Strand	11 a.m.		Philology	green	Tide	Monologue (male)	Proteus: Primal Matter; Menelaus: Kevin Egan; Megapenthes: The Cocklepicker.
II. ODYSSEY								
4. Calypso	The House	8 a.m.	Kidney	Economics	orange	Nymph	Narrative (mature)	Calypso: The Nymph; The Recall: Dlugascz; Ithaca: Zion.
5. Lotus Eaters	The Bath	10 a.m.	Genitals	Botany, Chemistry		Eucharist	Narcissism	Lotus Eaters: Cabhorses, Communicants, Soldiers, Eunuchs, Bather, Watchers of Cricket.
6. Hades	The Graveyard	11 a.m.	Heart	Religion	white, black	Caretaker	Incubism	The 4 Rivers: Dodder, Grand and Royal Canals, Liffey; Sisyphus: Cunningham; Cerberus: Father Coffey; Hades: Caretaker; Hercules: Daniel O'Connell; Elpenor: Dignam; Agamemnon: Parnell; Ajax: Menton.

7. Aeolus	The Newspaper	12 noon	Lungs	Rhetoric	red	Editor	Enthymemic	Aeolus: Crawford; Incest: Journalism; Floating Island: Press.
8. Lestrygonians	The Lunch	1 p.m.	Esophagus	Architecture		Constables	Peristaltic	Antiphates: Hunger; The Decoy: Food; Lestrygonians: Teeth.
9. Scylla and Charybdis	The Library	2 p.m.	Brain	Literature		Stratford, London	Dialectic	Rock: Aristotle, Dogma, Stratford; Whirlpool: Plato, Mysticism, London; Ulysses: Socrates, Jesus, Shakespeare.
10. Wandering Rocks	The Streets	3 p.m.	Blood	Mechanics		Citizens	Labyrinth	Bosphorus: Liffey; European bank: Viceroy; Asiatic bank: Conmee; Symplegades: Groups of citizens.
11. Sirens	The Concert Room	4 p.m.	Ear	Music		Barmaids	Fuga per canonem	Sirens: Barmaids; Isle: Bar.
12. Cyclops	The Tavern	5 p.m.	Muscle	Politics		Fenian	Gigantism	Noman: I; Stake: cigar; Challenge: apotheosis.
13. Nausicaa	The Rocks	8 p.m.	Eye, Nose	Painting	grey, blue	Virgin	Tumescence, detumescence	Nausicaa: Nymph; Phaecia: Star of the Sea.
14. Oxen of the Sun	The Hospital	10 p.m.	Womb	Medicine	white	Mothers	Embryonic development	Trinacria: Hospital; Lampetie, Phaethusa: Nurses; Helios: Horne; Oxen: Fertility; Crime: Fraud.
15. Circe	The Brothel	12 midnight	Locomotor apparatus	Magic		Whore	Hallucination	Circe: Bella.
				III. NOSTOS				
16. Eumaeus	The Shelter	1 a.m.	Nerves	Navigation		Sailors	Narrative (old)	Eumaeus: Skin-the-Goat; Ulysses Pseudangelos: Sailor; Melanthius: Corley.
17. Ithaca	The House	2 a.m.	Skeleton	Science		Comets	Catechism (impersonal)	Eurymachus: Boylan; Suitors: scruples; Bow: reason.
18. Penelope	The Bed	—	Flesh	—		Earth	Monologue (female)	Penelope: Earth; Web: movement.

THE LINATI SCHEMA

	Title	Hour	Colour	Persons	Technic	Science, Art	Sense (Meaning)	Organ	Symbol
I.					DAWN				
1	Telemachus	8–9	gold, white	Telemachus { Mentor { Pallas Antinous The Suitors Penelope (Mother)	Dialogue for 3 & 4 Narration Soliloquy	Theology	The Dispossessed Son in Contest	—	Hamlet, Ireland, Stephen
2.	Nestor	9–10	brown	Nestor Telemachus Pisistratus Helen	Dialogue for 2 Narration Soliloquy	History	The Wisdom of the Ancients	—	Ulster, Woman, Practical sense
3	Proteus	10–11	blue	Proteus Menelaus Helen Megapenthes Telemachus	Soliloquy	Philology	Primal Matter (*ΠΡΩΤΕΥΣ*)	—	Word, Tide, Moon, Evolution, Metamorphosis
								(Telemachus does not yet suffer the body)	
II.					MORNING				
1 (4)	Calypso	8–9	orange	Calypso (Penelope wife) Ulysses Callidike	Dialogue for 2 Soliloquy	Mythology	The Departing Wayfarer	Kidneys	Vagina, Exile, Kin, Nymph, Israel in captivity
2 (5)	Lotus Eaters	9–10	dark brown	Eurylochus Polites Ulysses Nausicaa (2)	Dialogue Soliloquy Prayer	Chemistry	The Temptation of Faith	Skin	Host, Penis in the bath, Froth, Flower, Drugs, Castration, Oats

3 (6)	Hades	11–12	black-white	Ulysses Elpenor Ajax Agamemnon Hercules Eriphyle Sisyphus Orion Laertes etc. Prometheus Cerberus Tiresias Hades Proserpina Telemachus Antinous	Narration Dialogue		The Descent into Nothingness	Heart	Cemetery, Sacred Heart, The Past, The Unknown Man, The Unconscious, Heart defect, Relics, Heartbreak
					MIDDAY				
4 (7)	Aeolus	12–1	red	Aeolus Sons Telemachus Mentor Ulysses (2)	Simbouleutike[1] Dikanike[1] Epideictic[1] Tropes	Rhetoric	The Derision of Victory	Lungs	Machines, Wind, Fame, Kite, Failed destinies, The press, Mutability
5 (8)	Lestrygonians	1–2	blood red	Antiphates The Seductive Daughter Ulysses	Peristaltic prose	Architecture	Despondency	Esophagus	Bloody sacrifice, Food, Shame
6 (9)	Scylla and Charybdis	2–3	—	Scylla and Charybdis Ulysses Telemachus Antinous	Whirlpools	Literature	The Two-edged Sword[2]	Brain	Hamlet, Shakespeare, Christ, Socrates, London & Stratford, Scholasticism & Mysticism, Plato & Aristotle, Youth & Maturity

Title	Hour	Colour	Persons	Technic	Science, Art	Sense (Meaning)	Organ	Symbol
				DAY Central point—Umbilicus				
7 (10) Wandering Rocks	3–4	rainbow	Objects Places Forces Ulysses	Shifting labyrinth between two shores	Mechanics	The Hostile Milieu	Blood	Christ & Caesar, Errors, Homonyms, Synchronisms, Resemblances
8 (11) Sirens	4–5	coral	Leucothea Parthenope Ulysses Orpheus Menelaus Argonauts	Fuga per canonem	Music	The Sweet Deceit	Ear	Promises, Female, Sounds, Embellishments
9 (12) Cyclops	5–6	green	Prometheus Noman (I) Ulysses Galatea	Alternating asymmetry	Surgery	Egocidal Terror	(1) Muscles (2) Bones	Nation, State, Religion, Dynasty,[3] Idealism, Exaggeration, Fanaticism, Collectivity
10 (13) Nausicaa	8–9	grey	Nausicaa Handmaidens Alcinous Arete Ulysses	Retrogressive progression	Painting	The Projected Mirage	Eye Nose	Onanism, Feminine, Hypocrisy
11 (14) Oxen of the Sun	10–11	white	Lampetie Phaethusa Helios Hyperion Jove Ulysses	Prose Embryo— Foetus— Birth	Physics[4]	The Eternal Herds	Matrix Uterus	Fertilization, Frauds, Parthenogenesis
12 (15) Circe	11–12	violet	Circe The Swine Telemachus Ulysses Hermes	Exploding vision	Dance	The Man-hating Ogress	Locomotor apparatus Skeleton	Zoology, Personification, Pantheism, Magic, Poison, Antidote, Reel

III.

MIDNIGHT
(Fusion of Bloom & Stephen)
(Ulysses & Telemachus)

1 (16) Eumaeus	12–1	—	Eumaeus Ulysses Telemachus The Bad Goat-herd Ulysses Pseudangelos	Relaxed prose	The Ambush on Home Ground	Nerves
2 (17) Ithaca	1–2	— starry milky[5]	Ulysses Telemachus Eurycleia The suitors	Dialogue Pacified style Fusion	Armed Hope	Juices
3 (18) Penelope	∞	starry milky *then* new dawn	Laertes Ulysses Penelope	Monologue Resigned style	The Past Sleeps	Fat

DEEP NIGHT—DAWN

Ulysses (Bloom) Telemachus (Stephen)

---

[1] Simbouleutike, Dikanike, and Epideictic are the three branches of Classical Rhetoric: deliberative, judicial, and public oratory.

[2] Joyce uses the phrase 'Dilemma Bitagliente'; *bitagliente* means a double cutting edge, hence 'two-edged sword'. The only other option for translation is 'double cutting-edged dilemma' which, as well as being tautologous, loses entirely the flavour of the metaphor.

[3] Joyce's handwriting is difficult at this point. Richard Ellmann reads Joyce as having written 'Ginnastica', or Gymnastics, while Claude Jacquet reads him as having written 'Dinastia', or Dynasty. I think the initial letter is an upper-case 'D', which lends credence to the latter. However, there is no question that if Joyce meant 'Dinastia' he misspelled it as 'Dinnastia'. See Richard Ellmann, *Ulysses on the Liffey* (1972; corr. edn., London: Faber & Faber, 1974), Appendix, and Claude Jacquet, 'Les Plans de Joyce pour *Ulysses*', in Louis Bonnerot, ed., *'Ulysses': Cinquante ans après* (Paris: Didier, 1974), 66, 76.

[4] Joyce may have meant Physic or Medicine, but he wrote 'Fisica' which means Physics.

[5] As in the Milky Way.

Appendix B
Ulysses: Serialization and Editions

As with the text of *Ulysses* itself, the book's publishing history is a matter of dispute. The full facts (complete histories of all impressions of each edition) are not known, have not been published, or are contested. Slocum and Cahoon—the standard bibliography—has long been considered in need of correction.[1] Certainly, the traditional list of 'Previous Editions of *Ulysses*' inevitably printed with each successive resetting, reissue, or reimpression is inaccurate on many counts (most notably in its endless repetition of the folktale that 499 of the 500 copies of the *Egoist*'s second impression were seized and burned).[2] The two leading contestants in the latest battle over textual authenticity—Hans Walter Gabler and John Kidd—disagree on the printing history. Or, to be more precise, Kidd disagrees with a number of claims made by Gabler in his list of 'Editions [of *Ulysses*]'.[3] What follows is as full a publication history as it is possible to reconstruct from what has been published and argued so far.

Little Review

Joyce, James. ['Telemachus.'] *Little Review*, 4/11 (Mar. 1918), 3–22 [incorrectly numbered vol. v; pp. 3–23 of this edition].

— ['Nestor.'] *Little Review*, 4/12 (Apr. 1918), 32–45 [incorrectly numbered vol. v; pp. 24–36 of this edition].

— ['Proteus.'] *Little Review*, 5/1 (May 1918), 31–45 [pp. 37–50 of this edition].

— ['Calypso.'] *Little Review*, 5/2 (June 1918), 39–52 [incorrectly numbered vol. iv; pp. 53–67 of this edition].

— ['Lotus Eaters.'] *Little Review*, 5/3 (July 1918), 37–49 [pp. 68–83 of this edition].

— ['Hades.'] *Little Review*, 5/5 (Sept. 1918), 15–37 [pp. 84–111 of this edition].

— ['Aeolus.'] *Little Review*, 5/6 (Oct. 1918), 26–51 [pp. 112–43 of this edition].

— ['Lestrygonians.'] *Little Review*, 5/9 (Jan. 1919), 27–50 [pp. 144–71 of this edition]; and 5/10–11 (Feb.–Mar. 1919), 58–62 [pp. 171–5 of this edition].

— ['Scylla and Charybdis.'] *Little Review*, 5/12 (Apr. 1919), 30–43 [incorrectly

[1] John J. Slocum and Herbert Cahoon, *A Bibliography of James Joyce (1882-1941)* (1953; repr. Westport, Conn.: Greenwood Press, 1971).

[2] More copies survive than the one which this story allows for.

[3] Gabler's list is included in James Joyce, *Ulysses: A Critical and Synoptic Edition*, prepared by Hans Walter Gabler with Wolfhard Steppe and Claus Melchior (New York and London: Garland Publishing, 1984), iii. 1855–6. Kidd's counter-arguments are most succinctly found in his 'An Inquiry into *Ulysses: The Corrected Text*', *Papers of the Bibliographical Society of America*, 82 (Dec. 1988), 509–14, 516–17.

numbered 11; pp. 176–89 of this edition]; and 6/1 (May 1919), 17–35 [pp. 189–209 of this edition].

— ['Wandering Rocks.'] *Little Review*, 6/2 (June 1919), 34–45 [pp. 210–22 of this edition], and 6/3 (July 1919), 28–47 [pp. 222–44 of this edition].

— ['Sirens.'] *Little Review*, 6/4 (Aug. 1919), 41–64 [pp. 245–69 of this edition]; and 6/5 (Sept. 1919), 46–55 [pp. 269–79 of this edition].

— ['Cyclops.'] *Little Review*, 6/7 (Nov. 1919), 38–54 [pp. 280–300 of this edition]; 6/8 (Dec. 1919), 50–60 [pp. 300–13 of this edition]; 6/9 (Jan. 1920), 53–61 [pp. 313–24 of this edition]; and 6/10 (Mar. 1920), 54–60 [pp. 324–30 of this edition].

— ['Nausicaa.'] *Little Review*, 6/11 (Apr. 1920), 43–50 [pp. 331–8 of this edition]; 7/1 (May–June 1920), 61–72 [pp. 338–48 of this edition]; and 7/2 (July–Aug. 1920), 42–58 [pp. 348–65 of this edition].

— ['Oxen of the Sun.'] *Little Review*, 7/3 (Sept.–Dec. 1920), 81–92 [pp. 366–76 of this edition].

Egoist

— ['Nestor.'] *Egoist*, 6/1 (Jan.–Feb. 1919), 11–14 [pp. 24–36 of this edition].

— ['Proteus.'] *Egoist*, 6/2 (Mar.–Apr. 1919), 26–30 [pp. 37–50 of this edition].

— ['Hades.'] *Egoist*, 6/3 (July 1919), 42–6 [pp. 84–97 of this edition]; and 6/4 (Sept. 1919), 56–60 [pp. 97–111 of this edition].

— ['Wandering Rocks.'] *Egoist*, 6/5 (Dec. 1919), 74–8 [pp. 210–20 of this edition].

Ulysses by James Joyce. Paris: Shakespeare and Company, 1922. [First Edition. First impression, 2 February 1922, comprising three issues, numbered: 1–100 (100 copies signed on Dutch handmade paper); 101–250 (150 copies on vergés d'Arches); 251–1000 (750 copies on handmade paper). This text is No. 785, original in the Bodleian Library, Oxford.]

[Second impression, 12 October 1922, issued with imprint 'Published for Egoist Press, London by John Rodker, Paris', 'ERRATA' list laid in. 2,000 numbered copies.]

[Third impression, January 1923, issued with imprint 'Published for Egoist Press, London by John Rodker, Paris', 'ERRATA' list laid in though corrections worked into plates over the course of the print run.[4] 500 numbered copies.]

[Fourth impression, January 1924, 'Ulysses/Additional corrections' (second errata) list printed and bound with impression (pp. [733]–736).]

[4] John Kidd claims that of the two copies of the third impression now at Yale, one 'has the errata changes throughout and the other only in the first two gatherings, the remainder of the book being made up of October 1922 gatherings' ('An Inquiry', 509). Assuming he is correct, this would mean that the changes were worked into the plates over the course of the print run (which was only 500 copies, give or take a copy or two). This accords with the chronology implied (or at least wished for) in Joyce's letter of 17 Oct. 1922 to Harriet Weaver: 'I spoke to Mr Darantière who thinks that the corrections of plates ought to be begun at once so that whenever a third edition is called for the book can appear letter perfect' (*LI* 188).

[Fifth (September 1924), Sixth (August 1925), and Seventh (December 1925) impressions; all contain 'Additional corrections' list.]

Ulysses by James Joyce. Paris: Shakespeare and Company, 1926. [Second edition, set from the first. Type entirely reset with corrections from 'Additional corrections' list (for the most part) worked into the text. Four impressions: May 1926, May 1927, November 1928, May 1930. Labelled the '8th printing', '9th printing', '10th printing', '11th printing', though they were actually the first through fourth of this setting. Extensive plate corrections to the 1927 impression (and lesser corrections to the 1928 impression).[5]]

Ulysses by James Joyce. Paris: Shakespeare and Company, 1927. [Third edition, set from the second impression of the second edition. The imprint is false as this is the infamous Roth pirated edition, printed in New York in 1929.]

Ulysses by James Joyce. Hamburg, Paris, Bologna: The Odyssey Press, 1932. [Fourth edition, set from the second. First impression in one volume on thin paper, December 1932. Second impression in two volumes and two issues: Regular and Special Editions, December 1932. Both first and second impressions include on title-page verso the statement 'The present edition may be regarded as the definitive standard edition, as it has been specially revised, at the author's request, by *Stuart Gilbert*.' Third impression (labelled 'Second Impression'), October 1933; Fourth impression (labelled 'Third Impression') in two issues: a one-volume and a two-volume issue, August 1935; Fifth impression (labelled 'Fourth Impression'), April 1939.[6]]

Ulysses [by] James Joyce. New York: Random House, 1934. [Fifth edition set from the third (perhaps corrected from the fourth for one or more of its subsequent impressions). First authorized American edition. Ten impressions from 25 January 1934 to August 1939. Modern Library Giant sub-edition, fifth edition corrected from the fourth, September 1940; numerous impressions until 1960. Random House edition reissued in new binding, 1949; continued until 1960.]

Ulysses by James Joyce. With an Introduction by Stuart Gilbert and Illustrations by Henri Matisse. New York: Limited Editions Club, 1935. [Sixth edition, (probably) set from fourth.[7]]

Ulysses [by] James Joyce. London: John Lane The Bodley Head, 1936. [Seventh edition, set from the fourth. First English edition published in England. First impression in two issues limited to 1,000 copies, October 1936; second impression, September 1937, printed from reduced plates with authorial corrections, in eight issues: 1937, 1941, 1947, 1949, 1952, 1954, 1955 (with an errata list),[8] 1958.]

[5] According to Kidd, 'An Inquiry', 510.

[6] See James F. Spoerri, 'The Odyssey Press Edition of James Joyce's *Ulysses*', *Papers of the Bibliographical Society of America*, 50 (1956), 195–8, and Kidd, 'An Inquiry', 510–11.

[7] The precise status of this text is uncertain. Apparently the unpublished correspondence between Joyce, George Macy (publisher), Stuart Gilbert, and Paul Léon at the Harry Ransom Research Center, Austin, Texas, demonstrates that Joyce played some part in its correction. See Kidd, 'An Inquiry', 512.

[8] Kidd maintains that for the 1955 impression, 'the uncorrected pages of the 1936 [limited

Ulysses [by] James Joyce. London: The Bodley Head, 1960. [Eighth edition, set from the (?) 1958 impression of the seventh.[9] Ten impressions to 1969; 1967 (seventh) impression 'with corrections'; 1969 (tenth) impression 'revised'. Standard English trade edition in hardback pre-Gabler. First impression (?) offset and reissued by Penguin, 1992.[10]]

Ulysses [by] James Joyce. New York: Random House, 1961. [Ninth edition, set from the eighth. Ten (?) impressions until 1986; reissued in 1990. Modern Library sub-edition resumed, 1961. Vintage imprint, 1965. Standard American trade edition in hardback and paperback pre-Gabler.]

Ulysses [by] James Joyce. Harmondsworth: Penguin, 1968. [Tenth edition, set from the eighth, but corrected from another (unknown) source. Three impressions, 1968–9; corrected for the fourth impression, 1971; corrected again for the 1982 'centenary' impression. Standard English paperback trade edition pre-Gabler.]

Ulysses [by] James Joyce. *A Critical and Synoptic Edition*. 3 vols. Prepared by Hans Walter Gabler with Wolfhard Steppe and Claus Melchior. New York: Garland Publishing, 1984. [Eleventh edition.[11] Reissued in paperback with corrections,

edition] were reproduced, along with an errata list which has different corrections from those made in 1937'. Further, while the text of the 1958 impression has had the corrections listed in the 1955 errata list (plus a few more) worked into the text, it 'still carries many readings found in the 1936 but not in the 1937 to 1954 printings' ('An Inquiry', 517).

[9] A difference of opinion exists as to which impression of the seventh edition the eighth edition was set from. Gabler lists the 'first (limited) impression of the seventh' (G 1856) (an assumption shared by Walter Hettche and Claus Melchior in their 'A Famous Fighter and Mairy's Drawers: Joyce's Corrections for the 1936 John Lane Edition of *Ulysses*', *James Joyce Quarterly*, 21/2 (Winter 1984), 165–9). Kidd, on the other hand, maintains that 'The 1960 resetting was not composed from the 1936 limited edition . . . but from the 1958 reimpression' ('An Inquiry', 512). As Kidd's explanation is the most economical for explaining why, as Gabler says, the eighth edition 'lacks about half the authorial corrections made in the unlimited impression of 1937' (G 1856) but contains the other half, I have accepted his argument in the absence of a published full collation.

[10] The 1992 Penguin reissue states on its cover, 'this edition returns to the standard Random House/Bodley Head text that first appeared in 1960'. The copyright notice reads: 'This edition first published in Great Britain by The Bodley Head 1960 and in the USA by Random House 1961[.] Reset and published in Penguin Books 1968[.] The 1960 Bodley Head text offset and reissued with an introduction 1992.' This appears to mean that the first impression was used (rather than the 1967 ('corrected') or 1969 ('revised') impression). Certainly, those corrections made to the text for the 1968 Penguin which found their way into the 1969 'revised' Bodley Head text are not included in this text.

[11] Gabler's claim that the 1984 edition is the 'Eleventh' is contested by Kidd who maintains that 'Somehow Gabler overlooked seven typesettings of *Ulysses* which came before his own, making his not the eleventh but the eighteenth' ('An Inquiry', 514). Kidd does not justify his claim, though in an article by Jerome P. Frank ('Trade Edition of Corrected *Ulysses* is Due from Random House', *Publisher's Weekly*, 229/24 (13 June 1986), 50–1), Kidd is cited as claiming that Gabler missed *five* further editions: a Literary Guild

1986. Rectos ('Reading Text') extracted and published: New York: Random House, 1986; London: Bodley Head, 1986; Harmondsworth: Penguin, 1986. American and English standard trade editions, paperback and hardback, until the recent controversy.]

Ulysses [by] James Joyce. *A Facsimile of the Manuscript*. With a critical introduction by Harry Levin and a bibliographical preface by Clive Driver. 3 vols. London: Faber; Philadelphia: Rosenbach Foundation, 1975. Vol. iii: *The Manuscript and First Printings Compared*; contains facsimile of first impression of the first edition.

Various book club printings and/or editions as well as various stray reprintings have been published. Among them are:

Ulysses [by] James Joyce. City of Industry, Calif.: Collectors Publications, (*c.* 1965). [No title-page; includes 43 pp. of pornography advertisements at back.]

Ulysses [by] James Joyce. New York: Milestone editions, 1972.

Ulysses [by] James Joyce. Franklin Center, Pa.: Franklin Library, 1976. [Limited edition.]

Ulysses [by] James Joyce. With illustrations by Paul Hogarth. Franklin Center, Pa.: Franklin Library, 1976. [Limited edition. 'The Greatest Books of the Twentieth-Century' series.]

Ulysses [by] James Joyce. Franklin Center, Pa.: Franklin Library, 1979. [Limited edition.]

Ulysses [by] James Joyce. With a new foreword by Anthony Burgess and illustrations by Susan Stillman. New York: Book of the Month Club, 1982.

Ulysses [by] James Joyce. New York: Oxford University Press, 1983. ['Oxford Library of the World's Great Books' series.]

edition from the 1960s, a 1982 Book-of-the-Month-Club edition, a Milestone edition, an OUP World's Great Literature edition, and an International Collector's Library edition. Whether these are actually new 'typesettings' (and hence new 'editions') or merely reprintings remains to be shown.

Ulysses Publishing History Stemma

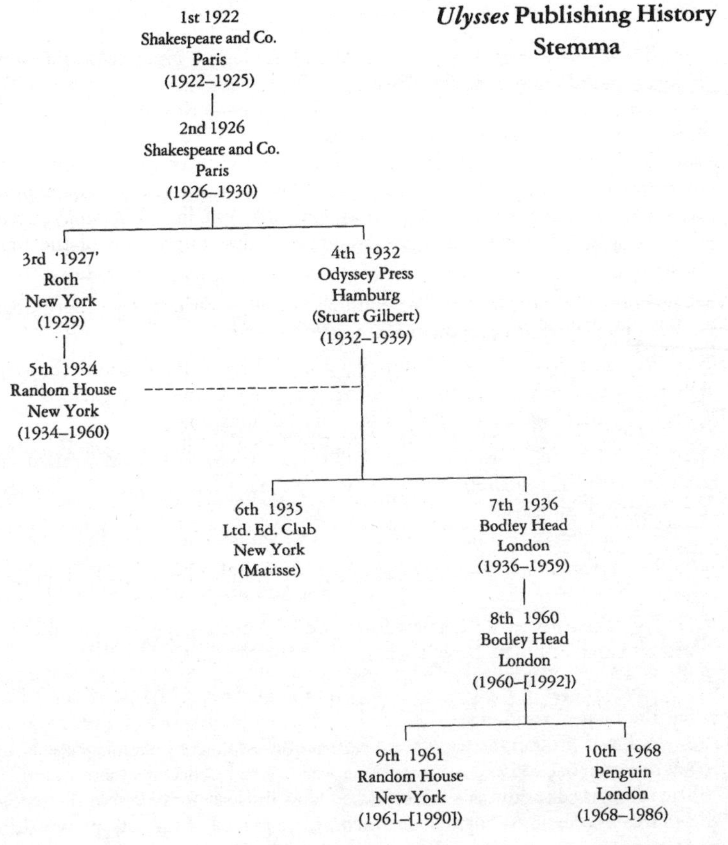

11th 1984
Garland
New York
(Gabler)

1986
Garland paper
w. emendations

1986
Bodley Head, Penguin,
and Random House
Trade editions

APPENDIX C
Errata

Sylvia Beach's caveat in the first edition—'The publisher asks the reader's indulgence for typographical errors unavoidable in the exceptional circumstances'—proved warranted. Almost immediately upon publication on 2 February 1922, Joyce began compiling errata lists. A first list ('ERRATA') was printed and laid in with the second impression of the first edition on 12 October 1922 (issued with the imprint 'Published for Egoist Press, London by John Rodker, Paris', though the original Shakespeare and Company plates were used). These corrections were worked into the plates over the course of the print run of the third impression (issued January 1923, the second 'Egoist Press' imprint). A second list, apparently drawn from a reading of the second impression, was compiled by Joyce and Harriet Weaver. This list ('ULYSSES Additional corrections') was printed and bound in with the fourth impression (January 1924, a return to the 'Shakespeare and Company' imprint).

Already in the second impression, errors which were not present in the first edition cropped up. *Ulysses* had been set by hand in movable type. Unfortunately, the type began to move of its own accord: letters dropped out or lines shifted, causing words to be incorrectly divided. (Some of these new errors become readily apparent in the list below: corrections cited on the 'Additional corrections' list which are not errors in the first edition are most frequently errors which have crept into the plates by the printing of the second impression.) Thus began the now notorious saga of successive attempts to correct the text being hampered by a proliferation of errors: correction moved two steps forward only to fall one step back.

The following list contains the errata cited in the lists appended to the second and fourth impressions. Further, the incomplete record of the lists' composition and transmission contained in British Library Add. MS 57356 has been consulted and variants or transmission histories of interest or significance have been included (either in the list or as footnotes). Every erratum which survives as authorial autograph in this MS is marked. Though Joyce's wording may vary slightly from that reproduced here (which is taken from the printed lists), only significant variations have been noted. (For example, when Joyce has written 'for were?' read were', and the list reads 'change questionmark to comma after *were*' the difference goes unnoted in this list. Unnoted, too, are Joyce's mistaken line numbers. He was a very bad line counter.)

For the sake of the usefulness of this compilation for this printing, the lists have been amalgamated and some slight emendations have been made when, for example, a line or page number in the original is incorrect with reference to the first edition. All such emendations have been noted. Further, page and line references are for the most part presented in a standardized form (e.g. 'Page 3, line 6 from foot' becomes '3.22'). Citations which have been altered in this way are marked with an asterisk (*). (Obsessive readers can check the original wording of such citations and of Joyce's autograph errata by referring to the facsimile lists reproduced in Michael Groden, ed., *The James Joyce Archive*, 63 vols. (New York and London: Garland, 1977–80), xii. 117–80, 182–4, 203–16, 218–21.

The source of each erratum is noted thus:

(*U2*) 'ERRATA'—list printed and laid in with the second impression.

(*U4*) 'ULYSSES Additional corrections'—list printed and bound with the fourth impression.

Further, the following citations are to the original documents contained in British Library Add. MS 57356. All contain holographic additions and/or emendations:

(*A1*) Joyce's autograph errata list (incomplete) made for 'ERRATA' list for second impression (*U2*).

(*A2*) Joyce's autograph errata list made for 'Additional corrections' list for fourth impression (*U4*).

(*A2 W*) Holographic emendations and 'clarifications' of, and additions to, *A2* in pencil in a hand not Joyce's (most likely Harriet Weaver's). These are cited in the following list only when they continue or clarify the transmission record, or are the only surviving source for an erratum on *U4*.

(*A2R*) Citations on *A2* which have been crossed through in red crayon (probably by Harriet Weaver).

(*E1*) Holographically emended copy of printed 'ERRATA' list (*U2*).

(*E2*) Second holographically emended copy of printed 'ERRATA' list (*U2*).

(*T1*) Typescript (carbon) of Joyce's autograph errata for 'Additional corrections' list (*U4*).

(*T2*) One page (original) of typescript of errata.

(*T3*) Complete typescript (carbon) of 'Additional corrections' list (*U4*).

(*T4*) One page (original) of typescript of corrections to 'Eolus' (*sic*).

When the printed texts other than the first edition are referred to, the citations take the form:

(*UP2*) *Ulysses*, second impression of first edition, copy in the Bodleian Library.

(*UP4*) *Ulysses*, fourth impression of first edition, copy in the British Library.

Full bibliographical information and a chronology of the various errata lists are given at the end of this list.

3.7: for *Jesuit* read *jesuit* (*A2*, *U4*)

*3.22: insert comma after *call* (*A2*, *U4*)

*4.36: for *razor blade* read *razorblade* (*A2*, *U4*)

5.12: for *great* read *grey* (*U4*)[1]

[1] This is a mis-correction. The emendation should be made at 5.19, not here. See n. 2.

5.19: for *great* read *grey* (*A2*)[2]
6.23: for *Genera* read *General* (*A2R*, *U2*)
*9.31: for *above* read *alone* (*A2*, *U4*)
10.1: for *tassled* read *tasseled* (*A2*, *U4*)
10.4: for *pantomine* read *pantomime* (*A2*, *U4*)
13, after verse insert: *He crammed his mouth with fry and munched and droned.* (*A2*, *U4*)
*13.30: insert dash at beginning of line to mark conversation (*A2*, *U4*)
14.23: insert comma before *the* (*A2*, *U4*)
17.12: after *suppose* new paragraph (*A2*)[3]
18.3: for *aimiably* read *amiably* (*A2*, *U4*)
21, last line: for *breastbone* read *lips and breastbone* (*A2*, *U4*)
22.7: for *rotten* read *rotto* (*A2*, *U4*)
30.31: delete fullstop after *A poet* (*U2*)
31.4: for *Goood* read *Good* (*A2*, *U4*)
31.10: for *borard* read *board* (*U2*)[4]
34.9: for *bellied* read *belied* (*A2R*, *U2*)
34.22: for *gave a* read *gave* (*A2*, *U4*)
35.10: delete dash at beginning of line (*A2R*, *U2*)
37.8: for *throught* read *through* (*A2R*, *U2*)
37.19: for *Dominic* read *Dominie* (*U2*)
*37.22: for *Acatalectic* read *A catalectic* (*A2*, *U4*)[5]

[2] On *A2* Joyce wrote 'p 5 l 19 for great read grey'; *T1* typist typed 'Page 5, line 9' to which a '1' was added by hand in ink (to read '19'). *T2* and *T3* carry the unemended 'Page 5, line 9'. Most likely someone noted that there was no 'great' at line 9, located the nearest 'great' (unfortunately not at line 19, but at line 12) and changed the line numbering accordingly for *U4*. The text should read 'grey searching eyes' at line 12 and 'great sweet mother' at line 19.

[3] An *A2W* addition to *A2* reads 'can't be done'; the entire entry has then been crossed through in pencil. The change was not included on any printed list.

[4] Correct on *UP2* and *UP4*.

[5] *A2*, Joyce's holograph, reads in his hand (in ink): 'p 37 l 2 from foot a catalectic'. The first 'a' has been subsequently overwritten in pencil and the underscoring extended thus: 'A catalectic'. This is followed by the phrase, again in pencil, '(for A catalectic)'. Joyce's hand clearly separates the 'a' from 'catalectic', though why he should do so since they are already separated on both the first and second printings remains a mystery (let alone why he should make the first letter of the word lower-case). The typist read the emended *A2* text as reading 'for A catalectic read Acatalectic' as this is what s/he has typed on *T1*, though this has been crossed through in pencil and followed by a notation 'See below'. An addition to the bottom of the page in ink reads, 'Page 37, line 2 from foot, divide A/catalectic better'; and above the dividing line 'more space' has been written. *E1* carries a holographic addition in ink: 'divide A//catalectic better: more space'. *T2*, *T3*, and *U4* transmit this as 'for Acatalectic read A catalectic'. Part of this history can be reconstructed from the facsimiles of these documents in *JJA* xii. 177, 189, 192–5, 210, though the facsimile of Joyce's holograph does not

37.22: for *march ing* read *marching* (*U2*, *U4*)
39.28: delete fullstop after *law* (*A2R*, *U2*)
39.31: for *put toit* read *to put it* (*U2*)
40.6: delete comma after *bay* (*A2R*, *U2*)
40.14: for *basliskeyed* read *basiliskeyed* (*U2*)[6]
*40.33: for *what else* read *What else* (*A2*, *U4*)
41.2: for *deeeply* read *deeply* (*A2*, *U4*)
41.16: [see note below][7]
42, last line: for *well pleased* read *wellpleased* (*A2*, *U4*)
43.4, 5:[8] for *Irlandais* read *irlandais* (*A2*, *U4*)
43.19: for messieurs *not* read messieurs. *Not* (*A2*, *U4*)
43.26: insert comma after *veil* (*U2*)
*43.32, 33: divide *Shatte- red* so: *Shatter- ed* (*A2*, *U4*)
*44.30: for *carcase* read *carcass* (*A2*, *U4*)
45.7: for *mong* read *among* (*U2*)[9]
45.7: retain word *mong* (*A2*)[10]
45.7: for *among* read *mong* (*U4*)[11]
47.5: for *A bout* read *About* (*A2R*, *U2*)[12]
55.7: for *off must* read *off. Must* (*A2*, *U4*)
59.23: for *ihe* read *the* (*U2*)
61.9: change questionmark ? to comma after *were* (*A2*, *U4*)
68.15: for whatyoumay call read whatyoumaycall (*A2*)[13]
70.1, 2: divide word *reviewing* so: *review- ing* (*A2*, *U4*)
71.23: change comma to questionmark ? after *him* (*A2*, *U4*)
73.13, 14: divide *difference* so: *differ- ence* (*A2*, *U4*)[14]

make the numerous additions and emendations clearly discernible. Anyone relying on the facsimile alone might conclude that Joyce had written not 'a catalectic' but 'Acatalectic'. (See entry in 'Explanatory Notes' below.)

[6] *U2* actually reads 'for *basliskedeyed* read *basiliskeyed*', though both the first printing and *UP2* have 'basliskeyed'.

[7] *A2* has an entry 'p 41 l 16 for My read my', though there is no 'My' on this line. Unfortunately the reference is so vague as to be unretrievable. *A2 W* addition: 'p 41 l. 16 paging wrong have asked Joyce HW'. The correction never makes it on to *U4*.

[8] Mis-cited as 'lines 5 and 6' on *U4*.

[9] This mis-correction is listed on *U2*. Joyce amends it on *A2*: 'retain word mong', which is then transmitted on *T1* and *T3*, then included on *U4* as 'for *among* read *mong*'.

[10] See previous note.

[11] See n. 6.

[12] *U2* actually reads 'for *A bout* read *about*'. *A2* reads 'for A bout read About'.

[13] *A2* actually reads 'p 61 l 16', which clearly left Harriet Weaver baffled as *A2 W* has 'p. 61 l 16 paging wrong have asked Joyce HW'. Fortunately, this is a unique usage and therefore a recoverable correction.

[14] *U4* actually reads 'divide *differing* so: *differ- ing*' but the word in the text is 'difference' not 'differing'. On *A2* Joyce wrote only 'divide differ-'; *A2 W* mistakenly adds 'ing (not differing)'.

77.6:	insert fullstop after *mission* (*A2, U4*)
77.16:	for *whit* read *with* (*A2R, U2*)
*78.34:	for *show* read *shew* (*A2, U4*)
80.26:	for *rhe* read *the* (*U2, E2, U4*)
82.16:	change fullstop to questionmark ? after *soap* (*A2, U4*)
82.19:	delete ' after *Lyons'* (*A2, U4*)
85.2:	for *ten* read *nine* (*A2, U4*)
85.22:	for *aying* read *saying* (*A2, U4*)
*86.32:	change questionmark ? to comma after *this* (*A2, U4*)
92.27:[15]	for *Matew* read *Mathew* (*U2*)
*92.30:	for *tinycoffin* read *tiny coffin* (*A2, U4*)
95.24:	for *pance* read *pause* (*U2*)
96.9:	delete fullstop after *on* (*U2*)
98.1:	for *steping* read *stepping* (*A2, U4*)
99.1:	delete comma after *the* (*A2, U4*)
100.13:	for *full of up* read *full up of* (*U2*)
*104.29:	for *carcase* read *carcass* (*A2, U4*)
*104.34:	delete first *lean* (*A2, U4*)
107.14:	for *there'sns* read *there's no* (*A2, U4*)
*108.34:	insert comma after *pillars* (*A2, U4*)
112.4:	for *Sandymount, Green Rathmines, Ringsend, and* read *Sandymount Green, Rathmines, Ringsend and* (*A2, U4*)[16]
112.16:	for *lettecards* read *lettercards* (*A2, U4*)
126.27:	change comma to fullstop after *said* (*U2*)
127.7:	for *M. O'Madden* read *Mr O'Madden* (*U2*)
130.11:	for *coldin* read *cold in* (*A2, U4*)
132.15:	for *Thee* read *There* (*U2*)
132.16:	[see note below][17]
134.24:	for *O'Mollooy* read *O'Molloy* (*T3, U4*)
134.24:	for *too kout* read *took out* (*U2*)[18]
134.26:	for *match box* read *matchbox* (*A2, U4*)
136.22:	for *senned* read *seemed* (*U2*)
*136.33:	delete comma after *were good* (*A2, U4*)
138.24:	for *That's all night* read *That's all right* (*U2*)
139.17:	for *and in tenpence* read *and tenpence in* (*A2R, U2*)
142, last line:	for *Kingstown* read *Blackrock* (*A2, U4*)
143.1:	for *Blackrock* read *Kingstown* (*A2, U4*)

[15] Mis-cited as 'line 26' on *U2*.

[16] Joyce does not delete the comma after 'Sandymount'; that is done as *A2 W* clarification.

[17] *A2* has an entry: 'p. 132 l 16 for Grey'. While there is a 'Grey' on this page at this line ('Gregor Grey made the design for it.'), what Joyce's intentions for it were remain unrecoverable. *A2 W* has 'p 132 l 16 for Grey have asked Joyce HW'.

[18] Correct on both *UP2* and *UP4*.

143.1:	insert comma after *tower* (*U4*)[19]
145.12:	insert fullstop after *reverence* (*A2*, *U4*)
145.13:	for *mum's* read *Mum's* (*A2*, *U4*)
147.8:	for *Time ball* read *Timeball* (*A2*, *U4*)[20]
148.22:	for *selcovered* read *selfcovered* (*A2*, *U4*)
148.30:	for *daguerrotype* read *daguerreotype* (*U2*)
150.18:	insert comma after *leather* (*A2*, *U4*)
151.[14]:	[see note below][21]
151.17:	for *long'* read *long* (*U2*)
155.16:	for *presenee* read *presence* (*U2*)
*159.32:	delete comma after *relief* (*A2*, *U4*)
160.1:	delete comma after *had* (*A2R*, *U2*)
162.11:	for *news-paper* read *newspaper* (*A2*, *U4*)
167.30:	change comma to fullstop after *cities* (*U2*)
168.20:	for *au* read *an* (*U2*)
171 ff.:	[see note below][22]
173.1:	for *food suppose* read *food, I suppose* (*A2*, *U4*)[23]
178.9:	for *en* read *an* (*A2R*, *U2*)
183.9:	for *guitless* read *guiltless* (*U2*)
185.17:	insert dash at beginning of line (*U2*)
188.3:	for *grand*... read *grandp*... (*A2*, *U4*)
192.7:	for *Master Silence* read *Master William Silence* (*A2*, *U4*)
197.31:[24]	for *Gentle will* read *Gentle Will* (*U2*, *E2*, *U4*)
202.4:	italics for *sua donna* (*A2*, *U4*)
204.16:	italics for *fils* and for *père* (*A2*, *U4*)

[19] Listed on *T4*; holograph addition on *T3*.

[20] *A2* and *U4* actually read: 'for *time ball* read *timeball*'.

[21] *A2* has an entry: 'p. 151 for mulligatawny' which is then heavily crossed through in pencil. What Joyce intended remains unrecoverable.

[22] *A2* and *A2 W* contain numerous instructions at this point to the printer to reset various occurrences of the letter 'f' which have broken in type, as well as one instruction to insert a full stop. *A2*: 'p 171 l 10 reset fully' and 'p 172 l 13 for Nest read Nest.' (crossed through in red crayon and followed by *A2 W*: 'it has stop in my copy'). *A2 W*: 'p 182 5 from foot softcreakrooted reset f'; 'p 182 3 from foot or reset f'; 'p 183 l 1 rrom (reset from)'; 'p 183 l 6 rorgetfully reset 1st fo'. Clearly Harriet Weaver lost patience with this exercise as it does not continue beyond this locus, although *UP2* is replete with broken 'f's.

[23] The first printing has 'food I suppose.' The 'I' has dropped out on *UP2* (at least in the copy in the Bodleian Library). The one thing that troubles the hypothesis that Joyce was using a copy of the second impression to draw up his list of corrections is the fact that *A2* has 'for I suppose read , I suppose', thereby including an 'I' in the misprint when at least two other copies of *UP2* do not have it (Bodley's and Harriet Weaver's). *A2 W*'s pencilled clarification (undoubtedly drawn by Weaver from a copy of *UP2*) has 'for food suppose read food, I suppose'.

[24] Mis-cited as 'line 32' on both *U2* and *U4*.

204.30:	change comma to fullstop after *doorstep* (*A2R*, *U2*)
205.10:	delete comma after *douce* (*A2*, *U4*)
205.21:	for *Eclection* read *Eclecticon* (*A2*, *U4*)
*207.24:	for *filibeg* read *fillibeg* (*A2*, *U4*)[25]
210.7:	for *onlegged* read *onelegged* (*U2*)
210.17:	for *come* read *came* (*U2*)
211.2:	for *Sheedy* read *Sheehy* (*A2*, *U4*)
211.15:	for *stropped* read *stopped* (*A2R*, *U2*)
*213.32:	italics for *bless you, my child* (*A2*, *U4*)
*213.32:	italics for *pray for me* (*A2*, *U4*)
215.7:	for *Anivory* read *An ivory* (*A2*, *U4*)[26]
215.16:	for *hat* read *cap* (*A2*, *U4*)
216.6:	for *onlegged* read *onelegged* (*A2R*, *U4*)[27]
219.14:	for *Pale faces* read *Palefaces* (*A2*, *U4*)
222.15:	for *didit* read *did it* (*A2R*, *U2*)
226.2:	for *Pates* read *Plates* (*A2*, *U4*)[28]
237.26:	for *Wise* read *Wyse* (*A2*, *U4*)
239.9:	for *How* read *Now* (*A2*, *U4*)
240.1:	for *Bridgewater* read *Bridgwater* (*A2*, *U4*)
*243.32:	for *tanned* read *tan* (*A2*, *U4*)
*245.20:	for *cranshig* read *crashing* (*A2*, *U4*)[29]
*245.20:	for *Whe loven* read *When love* (*A2*, *U4*)[30]
249.5:	for *shout* read *snout* (*A2*, *U4*)
252.11:	change fullstop to comma after *pundit* (*U2*)
256.10:	delete comma after *tiny* (*T1*, *U4*)
258.1:	for *yery* read *very* (*A2R*, *U2*)
258.15:	for *Marrion* read *Marion* (*A2*, *U4*)[31]
261, last line:	insert fullstop after *moon* (*U2*)[32]

[25] *A2* has only 'p 207 filibeg'; it is another hand which adds in pencil: '10 from foot' and 'read fillibeg'.

[26] This is not a misprint in the first printing, though both *UP2* and *UP4* read 'Ani vory'.

[27] This is not a misprint in the first printing, though it is on *UP2* and *UP4* (the 'e' has dropped out). This is the only *A2R* correction which is not an already noted *U2* correction. Clearly Harriet Weaver mistook it initially for a misnumbered repetition of 'Page 210, line 7'. It is not transmitted to *T1*, but is on *T3*.

[28] This is not a misprint in the first printing, though it is on *UP2* and *UP4*.

[29] This is not a misprint in the first printing, though it is on *UP2* and *UP4*.

[30] This is not a misprint in the first printing, though it is on *UP2* and *UP4*.

[31] This is the last correction on *A2*. As Joyce had another eye attack shortly after sending this list to Harriet Weaver (3 Nov. 1922 (*LI* 192)), it is likely that he never continued his corrections of *UP2*. No further (later) autograph corrections survive in British Library Add. MS 57356.

[32] Correct on both *UP2* and *UP4*; the fullstop is present but faint in the first printing.

270.8:	for *Corpuscule* read *Corpuscle* (*U2*)[33]
270.14:	for *Böylan* read *Boylan* (*U2*)
274, last line:	insert fullstop after *music* (*U2*)[34]
280.8:	for *taking* read *talking* (*U2*)
301.6:	for *bobby L* read *bobby* (*U2*)
304.8:	for *house house* read *house* (*U2*)
308.9:	for *al* read *all* (*U2*)
315.15:	for *called if* read *called it* (*U2*)
325.23:	for *beed* read *been* (*U2*, *E2*, *U4*)
326.15:	change fullstop to comma after *courthouse* (*U2*)
327.11:	for *be bawls* read *he bawls* (*U2*)
328.6:	for *on behalf on* read *on behalf of* (*U2*)
328.28:	delete comma after *play* (*U2*)
338.3:	for *about hin getting him own way* read *about him getting his own way* (*U2*)[35]
341.31:	delete comma after *readywitted* (*U2*)[36]
341.31:	delete comma after *always* (*U4*)[37]
341.31:	insert comma after *readywitted* (*U4*)[38]
352.19:	delete comma after *comes* (*U2*)
360.14:	for *drew* read *dew* (*U2*)
363.12:	for *was is* read *was it* (*U2*)
383.19:	for *proclivites* read *proclivities* (*U2*)
388.4:	for *scrupuluosly* read *scrupulously* (*U2*)
391.3:	for *prolungation* read *prolongation* (*U2*)
391.7:	for *perpetration* read *perpetuation* (*U2*)
398.11:	for *suspened* read *suspended* (*U2*)
399.13:	for *femoules* read *females* (*U2*)
409.18:	for *scrufulous* read *scrofulous* (*U2*)
414.3:	for *awsing* read *aswing* (*U2*)
423.2:	for *watered silkfacings* read *wateredsilk facings* (*U2*)
429.27:[39]	for *sicksewet* read *sicksweet* (*U2*)

33 *U2* actually reads '*corpuscule . . . corpuscle*'.

34 This is not a misprint in the first printing, nor on *UP2*; it is on *UP4*.

35 Only half this correction is made on *UP2* ('hin' is corrected to 'him'); the entire correction is made on *UP4*.

36 This is a mis-correction, as is noted on *E2*: pencil holograph addition 'my mistake'. The intended correction seems to have been that noted on *T3*: 'Page 341, line 31, delete comma after always' where the next entry restores the mistakenly deleted comma after *readywitted*: 'Page 341, line 31, insert comma after readywitted.' This re-correction is also on *U4*.

37 See previous note.

38 See n. 36.

39 Mis-cited as 'line 28' on *U2*.

433.9: for *escapethan nin etynine* read *escape than ninetynine* (*T3, U4*)[40]
436.27: insert comma after *ripplecloth* (*U2*)
437.25: for *through* read *though* (*U2*)
439.29:[41] delete comma after *accused* (*U2*)
442.3: for *ffeecy* read *fleecy* (*U2, E2, U4*)
447.5: for *lift* read *lifts* (*U2*)
447.11: for *it was* read *It was* (*U2*)
457.13: for *thier* read *their* (*U2*)
458.29: for *prvileged* read *privileged* (*U2*)
459.20: for *playes* read *plays* (*U2*)
470.26: for *dsuty* read *dusty* (*U2, E2, U4*)
482.22:[42] for *mlld* read *mild* (*U2*)
482.23: for *caould* read *could* (*U4*)[43]
484.5: for 1882 read 1886 (*U4*)[44]
490.4: For *Agueschaken* read *Agueshaken* (*U2*)
490.26: for *pluks* read *plucks* (*U2*)
510.4: for *bought* read *boughs* (*U2*)
510.11: for *adsf or* read *ads for* (*U2*)
513.14: for *trough* read *through* (*U2*)
513.18: for *white polled* read *whitepolled* (*U2*)
514.12: delete comma after *waistcoat* (*U2*)
519.7: for *exagerated* read *exaggerated* (*U2*)
519.23: for *monosyllabbes* read *monosyllables* (*U2*)
523.20: for *tittle* read *little* (*U2, E2, U4*)
526.25: for *autlered* read *antlered* (*U2*)
529.8: insert comma after *nose* (*U2*)
532.26: for *runs swift, for the open brighteyed* read *runs swift for the open, brighteyed,* (*U2*)
537.14:[45] change comma to fullstop after *movements* (*U2*)
552, last line: for *im my house* read *in my house* (*U2*)
576.19: for *through* read *though* (*U2*)
578.20: for *Stephens aid* read *Stephen said* (*U2*)
579.22: delete dash before *Egg two* (*U2*)
580.14: for *finelly* read *finally* (*U2*)
589.27: for *mentlal* read *mental* (*U2*)

[40] This is not a misprint in the first printing, though it is on *UP2* and *UP4*.
[41] Mis-cited as 'Page 429' on *U2*.
[42] Mis-cited as 'line 21' on *U2*.
[43] Mis-cited as 'line 26' on *U4*. The correction is a holographic addition to *E2*: '482 l 23 caould could' where '23' could easily be mistaken for '26' which is what *T3* has.
[44] This is a holograph addition on both *E1* and *E2*, and is present on *T3*.
[45] Mis-cited as 'line 10' on *U2*.

597.6:	for *he man* read *the man* (*U2*)
597.24:	for *eventempored* read *eventempered* (*U2*)
600.5:	for *which some asperity* read *with some asperity* (*U2*)
600.26:	for *esthetesand* read *esthetes and* (*U2*)
602.13:	for *Simon Dedalus, B.A.* read *Simon Dedalus, Stephen Dedalus B.A.* (*U2*)[46]
602.14:	for *L. Bloom* read *L. Boom* (*U2*)
603.17:	for *fiinger* read *finger* (*U2*)
608.21:	for *prinitng worsk* read *printing works* (*E2*)[47]
608.21:	for *worsk* read *works* (*U2, U4*)[48]
608.25:	for *occuaption* read *occupation* (*U2, E2, U4*)
610.2:	delete *when* (*U2*)
610.22:	for *Bloom, reflected* read *Bloom reflected* (*U2*)
611.23:	for *pu* read *put* (*U2*)
611.28:	for *top erceive* read *to perceive* (*U2*)
617.19:	for *pecuniar y* read *pecuniary* (*U2*)[49]
618.34:	for *sest* read *seat* (*U2*)
619.23:	for *religions* read *religious* (*A1, U2*)
620.4:	for *assently* read *assented* (*A1, U2*)
620.26:	for *occusionally* read *occasionally* (*U2*)
621.8:	for *What did Bloom* read *What action did Bloom* (*U2*)
624.12:	for *particulary* read *particularly* (*U2*)
625.13:	for *infaillibility* read *infallibility* (*U2*)
625.20:	for *ifnavigable* read *if navigable* (*U2*)
626.27:	for *the course of calorification* read *the source of calorification* (*U2*)[50]
627, last line:	for *olivesin* read *olives in* (*U2*)
631.21:	insert comma after *Miss Whelan* (*U2*)
631.26:	for *anticipatep* read *anticipated* (*U2*)
632.13:	for *arbitrary as* read *as arbitrary* (*A1, U2*)
632.29:	change fullstop to comma after *Matthew Dillon's house* (*U2*)
632.32:	for *cofferoom* read *coffeeroom* (*U2*)

[46] *U2* actually reads 'for *Simon Dedalus B.A.*' thereby missing out the comma after 'Dedalus'.

[47] *U2* reads 'for *worsk* read *works*'. *E2* has as holograph addition: '608: 21 prinitng worsk = printing works'. *T3* and *U4* fail to transmit the full correction and instead include only the change from 'worsk' to 'works'.

[48] See previous note.

[49] *U2* actually reads '*pecunair y . . . pecuniary*'.

[50] *U2* actually reads 'for *the cource. . .* read *the source. . .*' though the first printing and *UP2* both have 'course' not 'cource'.

634.6:	for *exercices* read *exercises* (*U2*)
634.20:	for *Bloom* read *Bloom and Bloom's thoughts* (*A1*, *U2*)
*637.26–7:	for *in the place aforesaid), the toxin aforesaid,* read *in the place aforesaid, the toxin aforesaid),* (*U2*)[51]
638.9:	for *pedagogie* read *pedagogic* (*A1*, *U2*)
641.8:	for *taught* read *been taught* (*A1*, *U2*)
641.10:	for *Farsaig* read *Farsaigh* (*U4*)[52]
642.14:	for *Traditionnal accent af* read *traditional accent of* (*U2*, *U4*)[53]
642.27:	for *mechianacal* read *mechanical* (*U2*)
643.5:	for *ow'er the je's* read *o'er the jew's* (*U2*)
646.7:	for *ahallucination* read *a hallucination* (*A1*, *U2*)
647.13:	for *were differences* read *their differences* (*U2*)
648.24:	for *Goulding* read *Dedalus (born Goulding)* (*A1*, *U2*)[54]
648, last line:	for *shilling* read *shillings* (*A1*, *U2*)
649.16:	for *anintuitive parti coloured clown* read *an intuitive particoloured clown* (*U2*)
650.7:	delete comma (*A1*, *U2*)
650.11:	for *cataclyms* read *cataclysms* (*U2*)
651.4:	for *so* read *do* (*A1*, *U2*)
651.13:	for *constellation* read *constellations* (*U2*)
651.26:	for *threscore* read *threescore* (*U2*)
652.32:	for *wiih* read *with* (*U2*)
653.8:	for *interdependant* read *interdependent* (*A1*, *U2*)
653.15:	for *satroscopist* read *astroscopist* (*A1*, *U2*)
653.30:	for *persons,* read *persons:* (*A1*, *U2*)
654.9:	for *spectators* read *future spectators* (*A1*, *U2*)
658.11:	for *anetcedent* read *antecedent* (*U2*)
660.3:	for *at ransparent* read *a transparent* (*U2*)

[51] *U2* actually reads 'for *in the place aforesaid), the toxin aforesaid* read *in the place aforesaid, the toxin aforesaid),*'.

[52] This is not a misprint in either the first printing or *UP2*, though it is on *UP4*.

[53] *U2* actually reads: 'for *traditionnal accent of* read *traditional accent of*', thereby missing two of the three misprints in its citation of the first printing: 'Traditionnal accent af', while nevertheless correcting them. *E1* contains an erasure of the printed 'o' of 'of' in the citation to the text; this is overwritten in pencil as 'af'. On *E2*, a holographic correction catches one of them: '642, 14 The Traditionnal: The traditional' but still misses the 'af' misprint. *T3* reproduces, correctly, all three misprints: 'for The Traditionnal accent af read The traditional accent of', though these are not transmitted on to *U4* which reverts to 'for *The Traditionnal accent of* read *The traditional accent of*'.

[54] *U2* cites the correction as 'Dedalus born Goulding'. On *A1* Joyce wrote: 'p. 648 l 24 for Goulding read Dedalus (born Goulding)'. The brackets are not transmitted on to *U2*. *UP4*, corrected from *U2*, has 'Dedalus, born Goulding,'.

661.23:	for *bronw* read *brown* (*U2*)
663.29:	for *10 October* read *17 October* (*A1*, *U2*)
664.24:[55]	for *0.16.6* read *0.17.5* (*A1*, *U2*)
664.33:[56]	for *right* read *right foot* (*A1*, *U2*)
664, last line:	for *unguial* read *unguical* (*U2*)
665.3:	for *unguial* read *unguical* (*U2*)
669.20:	for *Febuary* read *February* (*A1*, *U2*)
669.27:	for *par annum* read *per annum* (*U2*)
670.11:	for *posrage* read *postage* (*U2*)
670.13:	for *1878,* read *1878),* (*A1*, *U2*)
671.2:	for *according the* read *according to the* (*U2*)
672.27:	for *in wonders a poster novelty* read *in wonder, a poster novelty* (*U2*)
674.1:	for *a1d.* read *a 1d.* (*U4*)[57]
674.1:	for *ad hesive* read *adhesive* (*U2*)
674.13:	insert comma after *way,* delete comma after *insuring* (*U2*)
675.27:	for *daguerrotype* read *daguerreotype* (*U2*)
676.1:	for *four* read *five* (*U2*)
676.21:	for *tetragrammation* read *tetragrammaton* (*U2*)[58]
676.21:	for *tetragrammatou* read *tetragrammaton* (*U4*)[59]
677.11:	for *grooseberry* read *gooseberry* (*U2*)
678.20:	delete comma after *reunite,* insert comma after *multiplication* (*U2*, *U4*)[60]
679.15:	for *Major* read *Maior* (*U2*)
679.18:	for *Major* read *Maior* (*U2*)
679.18:	for *reveated* read *revealed* (*U2*)
680.5:	for *hea would her* read *he would hear* (*U2*)
680.11:	for *or* read *or of* (*U2*)

[55] Mis-cited as 'line 23' on both *A1* and *U2*.

[56] Mis-cited as 'line 32' on both *A1* and *U2*.

[57] *U4* actually reads 'for *a1d* read *a 1d.*'.

[58] When the plates were corrected for the third impression, this misprint was mis-corrected. *UP4* reads 'tetragrammatou'. This is picked up and noted as a holograph addition to *E2*: '676 have ended word tou not ton'. *T3* and *U4* both then correct this as: 'for tetragrammatou read tetragrammaton'.

[59] See preceding note.

[60] The plate corrections failed to 'delete comma after *reunite*', though they did 'insert comma after *multiplication*'. *UP4* reads: 'to reunite, for increase and multiplication, which was absurd'. This is picked up in a holograph addition to *E1*: 'have not deleted comma after reunite'. Despite the partial correction having been made, the entire correction is repeated on *T3* and *U4*.

680.17:	insert colon after *invisible*, insert colon after *perilous* (*U2, U4*)[61]
682.16:	for *a accordion* read *an accordion* (*U2*)
687.25:	for *2 calendar months* read *1 calendar month* (*U2*)
689.11:	for *eggin* read *egg in* (*U2*)
692.8:	for *deuying* read *denying* (*U2*)
701.26:	for *it it was* read *it was* (*U2*)
705.5, 6:	delete words repeated: *of those rotten places the night coming home with* (*U2*)
710.34:	for *may* read *May* (*U2*)
712.9:	for *finrom* read *from* (*U2*)
712.18:	for *tho ught* read *thought* (*U2*)
713.18:	for *homenade* read *homemade* (*U4*)[62]
713.19:	for *publicasn* read *publicans* (*U2*)
714.7:	for *sidep iano* read *side piano* (*U2*)
719.14:	for *afflicty ou* read *afflict you* (*U2*)
719.18:	for *tim ewe* read *time we* (*U2*)
722.7:	for *form Lord Napier* read *from Lord Napier* (*U2*)
724.34:	for *laud* read *land* (*U2*)
726.5:	for *nnder* read *under* (*U2*)

UP2 *Ulysses* by James Joyce. Paris: John Rodker, [12 October] 1922. 'ERRATA' list printed and laid in. (This is the second impression of the first (Shakespeare & Company) edition, issued under the imprint of the Egoist Press, printed from the original plates. The title-page reads: 'PUBLISHED FOR THE // EGOIST PRESS, LONDON // BY JOHN RODKER, PARIS // 1922'. (Copy consulted in the Bodleian Library, Oxford.)

UP4 *Ulysses* by James Joyce. Paris: Shakespeare and Company, [January] 1924. 'Additional corrections' list printed and bound with text (as pp. [733]–736). (This is the fourth impression of the first edition. The errata noted in the list for the second impression were worked into the plates for the third impression (January 1923, also issued under the imprint of the Egoist Press). This impression is from those plates. Copy consulted in the British Library, London.)

U2 'ERRATA'. Printed list laid in: *Ulysses* by James Joyce. Paris: John Rodker, [12 October] 1922. (Copies consulted in British Library Add. MS 57356, pp. 28–31, 32–5.)

[61] Only the first correction is repeated on *U4* (as 'insert colon : after *invisible*'), despite the fact that the plate corrections failed to make the correct emendation. *UP4* reads: 'rendering invisible the uncertainty of thoroughfares, rendering perilous; the necessity . . .' when if properly corrected it would read 'rendering invisible: the uncertainty of thoroughfares, rendering perilous: the necessity . . . .'.

[62] Holograph addition to *E2*.

U4 'ULYSSES Additional corrections'. Printed and bound in: *Ulysses* by James Joyce. Paris: Shakespeare and Company, [January] 1924. Pp. [733]–736. (Copy consulted in British Library, London.)

A1 Joyce's autograph errata list (incomplete) made for 'ERRATA' list for second impression (*U2* above); British Library Add. MS 57356, pp. 10–11. These are two sheets (three pages: recto, verso, recto only) originally loose, now fixed to pages in the cahier described in *A2* below. The list comprises 20 corrections in Joyce's hand, all of which are contained on *U2* above. Thus, while they are now included with *A2*, they may well constitute the only surviving portion of Joyce's original list of errata (made from the first printing) drawn up for the list which now forms *U2*. They would therefore chronologically precede both *U2* and *A2* and would have been drawn up some time before 28 September 1922 (*LI* 187).

A2 Joyce's autograph errata list made for 'Additional corrections' list of fourth impression (*U4* above); British Library Add. MS 57356, pp. 7–8[v]. The list is contained on the first four pages (7, 7verso, 8, 8verso) of a 'cahier'—small paper-covered manuscript notebook. Probably drawn up from a reading of the second impression. Sent to Harriet Weaver. *T1* below is a typescript of these corrections. This is undoubtedly the list Joyce refers to in two letters to Harriet Weaver: 17 October 1922: 'I am reading steadily through the book and am preparing the list [of corrections] though it is not amusing work and I cannot do more than 30 pages a day' (*LI* 188). 3 November 1922: 'I send you my list of corrections page 1 to 290 which you can perhaps check and forward' (*LI* 192). (While Joyce says the corrections are complete up to and including p. 290, they end after a correction to p. 258. On *T2*, Harriet Weaver refers to 'Joyce's corrections as far as page 260'.) Beyond Joyce's autograph corrections in ink, the document contains additions and emendations in pencil and red crayon, probably made by Harriet Weaver. The list contains 14 corrections already printed in *U2*, each of which has been crossed through in red crayon (cited as *A2R* in the list above). Also mistakenly crossed through in red is one correction not included on *U2* nor on *T1* (the typescript made from this list), but nevertheless on *T3* and *U4* ('Page 216, line 6') (also cited as *A2R*). Pencil emendations (cited as *A2W* above) usually seem intended to clarify Joyce's instructions for the typist, though occasionally these confuse or may even contradict Joyce's rather vague intentions. All such instances have been noted in the above list. Also included in the cahier is a page of pencil autograph (p. 9 of MS), probably Harriet Weaver's hand, of clarifications of confusing points in Joyce's list (also cited as *A2W* above). Finally, also included at the back of the cahier (pp. 12[v]–14 of the MS) are lists (in Joyce's and another hand) of names of persons to whom advertising leaflets are to be sent (see *LI* 192).

E1 Holographically emended copy of 'ERRATA' list (*U2* above) laid in with second impression (*UP2* above); British Library Add. MS 57356, pp. 32–5. Additions and emendations in ink, pencil, and red crayon. Holographic notation on first page: '200 on this slip. These made and paid for December 6, 1922 frs. 750.95—but see that penciled corrections are made.' Four holographic additions and one erasure and emendation of printed text. Of the four cited corrections, all but one are made to the plates. This list was probably therefore made for the printer for correction of the plates for the third impression.

E2 Second holographically emended copy of 'ERRATA' list (*U2* above) laid in with second impression (*UP2* above); British Library Add. MS 57356, pp. 28–31. Additions in pencil and blue crayon. Holographic notation on first page: 'See a few to add to typed list'—probably Harriet Weaver's instructions to the typist who was compiling the typescript of 'Additional corrections' for *UP4*. Lines marked are those not corrected in the plates for the third impression and which are therefore cited again on *U4*. Also seven holographic additions (either clarifications of marked corrections or newly noted). The list could have been drawn up any time after the third impression and before *U4/UP4*. It pre-dates *T3* (which contains all of the marked passages).

T1 Typescript (carbon) of Joyce's autograph errata for 'Additional corrections' list; British Library Add. MS 57356, pp. 15–17. Holographic additions and emendations in ink, pencil, and blue crayon. A typed copy of *A2* as emended by Harriet Weaver(?). Holographic notation on first page: 'Mr Darantiere had a copy of these corrections—should now work from new list.' One holographic addition in ink (see n. 2 above). Typed list contains one erratum not on *A2*: ('Page 256, line 10') and therefore succeeds it.

T2 One page (original) of typescript of errata; British Library Add. MS 57356, p. 18. Holographic additions in ink: 'Sent to Miss Beach 6.12.23 This list includes Joyce's corrections as far as page 260. Also the few overlooked in errata slip & few others noticed by me HW.' The first page of a different and later typing beyond *T1*. The holographic additions may be much later additions to the sheet.

T3 Complete typescript (carbon) of 'Additional corrections' list; British Library Add. MS 57356, pp. 21–5. Corrections in ink. Blue crayon marks. Also one holographic addition in ink (also typed on *T4* below): 'Page 143, line 1 insert comma after tower.' This is the list for *U4* developed yet further beyond that represented on *A2* and *T1*.

T4 One page (original) of typescript of corrections to 'Eolus' (*sic*); British Library Add. MS 57356, p. 26. Holographic additions and emendations in pencil and ink. Heading reads: 'Please make the following corrections to the text before resetting chapter VII (Eolus episode):—.' Holographic addition in pencil: 'Sent to Miss Beach.' This may have been intended to be sent to Darantière for the plate corrections for the third printing. If so, it either never arrived or was disregarded, as all the listed errata remain errata in *UP4*. One entry carries the list beyond *A2* ('Page 143, line 1 insert comma after tower'). This correction is a holograph addition to *T3*. Probably, therefore, this list chronologically succeeds first stage (typing) of *T3*, and pre-dates its second stage (holographic additions).

Tentative chronological ordering: *A1*, *UP2*, *U2*, *E1*, plate corrections, *A2*, *T1*, *T2*, *E2*, *T3*, *T4*, *UP4*, *U4*. The plate changes were made while Joyce was drawing up *A2*, sometime between September and December 1922 (for the third impression (Dec. 1922)). No corrections from *A2* are made on *UP4*. *UP4* was issued in January 1924, but it carried no corrections beyond those made from *U2* in late 1922. (See letter of 17/10/22 to Weaver (*LI* 188).)

EXPLANATORY NOTES

The very idea of annotating *Ulysses* overwhelms. Both of the questions 'Where does one begin?' and, perhaps more practically, 'Where does one stop?' utterly disconcert. Still, the labour has already been lovingly and admirably performed by two previous publications: Don Gifford with Robert J. Seidman, *'Ulysses' Annotated* (rev. edn. Berkeley, Los Angeles, and London: University of California Press, 1988), and the earlier Weldon Thornton, *Allusions in 'Ulysses': An Annotated List* (Chapel Hill: University of North Carolina Press, 1968). I recommend these books to anyone left bemused when faced with the polyglot, polymath Joyce's 'abstrusiosities'. The aim of these notes is much more modest for two reasons. The first is practical: to provide anything remotely approaching 'full annotation' would require that the book appear in at least two volumes (the second of which would simply repeat much of Gifford and Thornton's work). The second is a more principled decision: understanding the allusions removes one mystifying barrier to understanding, but really only a very small one. Searching out the references does not bestow claritas. Both the difficulties and the joys of the book are more fundamental than superficial knowledge. So, instead of simply providing glosses, I have tried to ask, 'What would help the student coming to the book for the first time?' In attempting to answer this, I have tried to provide here sufficient contextualizing information, episode by episode, to allow students to read the book. That such background is necessary, Joyce was the first to admit. He slowly fed clues to his devoted readership so they could begin to grasp what it was that confronted them. I have strayed very little from Joyce's own hints about how to read his tome. Nor do I subscribe to the school which believes that a predigested *Ulysses* is helpful for students. Nothing can substitute for the intimate first-hand experience of *reading* the book. So, no plot summaries. I have tried to anchor the narrative action in the real Dublin by indicating (with reference by grid number (e.g. E4) to the map at the front of this volume) exactly which part of the city provides the setting for each episode and where the characters move within that setting. A rule of thumb about the topography of Dublin: assume the streets, shops, buildings, institutions referred to are actual places in 1904 Dublin. Joyce anchored this fiction in fact (aided in his task by Thom's Directory and, when that failed, his Aunt Josephine (see 'Introduction', p. xxvi)). Similarly, the impersonal events are almost inevitably actual (such as the Gold Cup horserace—winner: dark outsider Throwaway—which plays such a significant part in the narrative). Joyce consulted various Dublin newspapers for topical information.

The relevant episodes of the *Odyssey* have been outlined (quotations are from Homer, *The Odyssey*, trans. Walter Shewring (Oxford: Oxford University Press, 1980)), though I would recommend that serious students read that classic for themselves. According to Stanislaus, Joyce used Butcher and Lang's translation

(1879) and Samuel Butler's (1900) 'modernisation' of Homer.[1] One might also usefully follow Joyce's advice to his Aunt Josephine: 'You say there is a lot of it you don't understand. I told you to read the *Odyssey* first. . . . Then buy at once the *Adventures of Ulysses* (which is Homer's story told in simple English much abbreviated) by Charles Lamb. . . . Then have a try at *Ulysses* again' (*LI* 193). He also recommended that she read Valéry Larbaud's article 'The *Ulysses* of James Joyce'.[2] Take note. Joyce's two schemata sketching his conceived correspondences have been provided in Appendix A, but are further referred to here.

Joyce's hints, his own comments on and advice about how to read the episodes, so freely provided in letters and conversation, are also supplied. The headnote commentaries are meant to be merely suggestive, to tickle the critical fancy, not to direct a reading.

A final word about the principles of selection underlying the list of annotations. One enormous category of allusion is significantly under-represented below: popular culture. *Ulysses* is saturated with, for example, the music that was in the air in 1904 Dublin. To list every song hummed, strummed, or thought (and its lyrics) and the plots of every pantomime or play recently performed, the actors and actresses who starred in them, and the music hall acts which enjoyed popularity would fill an entire volume. Only the most significant (those repeatedly returned to) are cited below. To delete the rest has been a hard decision and one which runs the risk of falsely representing *Ulysses* as a text of 'high' rather than 'popular' culture. In fact, *Ulysses* combines the two in unequal proportions, the 'popular' being the more pervasive (except, of course, in Stephen's episodes). However, the songs seldom stand between the reader and understanding while the philosophy of Aristotle or the facts of Irish history often do. I recommend that those interested in pursuing the particularities of popular music in the book seek out the following: Matthew J. C. Hodgart and Mabel P. Worthington, *Song in the Work of James Joyce* (New York: Columbia University Press, 1959); Zack Bowen, *Musical Allusions in the Works of James Joyce* (Albany, New York: State University of New York Press, 1974); Ruth Bauerle, *The James Joyce Songbook* (New York and London: Garland, 1982). Gifford and, less so, Thornton provide reasonably full glosses of texts and contexts for songs, plays, acts, and Gifford identifies relevant performers. For a critical analysis of the workings of popular culture in Joyce, I recommend Cheryl Herr's *Joyce's Anatomy of Culture* (Urbana and Chicago: University of Illinois Press, 1986).

For the rest, glosses have been supplied selectively, that is, when particular knowledge is required for an understanding of the narrative. A final caution: for the sake of space, allusions once cited are not repeated. Citations are to page and line number in the form: 376.22 (page 376, line 22). All citations of Shakespeare are

[1] W. B. Stanford, *The Ulysses Theme: A Study in the Adaptability of a Traditional Hero* (1954; 2nd edn. rev. Oxford: Basil Blackwell, 1968) 276 n. 6.

[2] *Criterion*, 1/1 (Oct. 1922), 94–103.

to *The Riverside Shakespeare*, ed. G. Blakemore Evans *et al.* (Boston: Houghton Mifflin, 1974). The following works are repeatedly referred to by the abbreviations listed below, either as source for the gloss, or as indication that readers may find fuller, more detailed information in these works.

Adams	Robert M. Adams, *Surface and Symbol: The Consistency of James Joyce's 'Ulysses'* (New York: Oxford University Press, 1962)
Brewer	*Brewer's Dictionary of Phrase and Fable*, 14th edn., ed. Ivor H. Evans (London: Cassell, 1989)
Budgen	Frank Budgen, *James Joyce and the Making of 'Ulysses'* (1934; repr. Bloomington: Indiana University Press, 1960)
CW	James Joyce, *The Critical Writings of James Joyce*, ed. Ellsworth Mason and Richard Ellmann (New York: Viking Press, 1959)
Dubliners	James Joyce, *Dubliners* (1914), ed. Robert Scholes with Richard Ellmann (New York: Viking, 1967)
G	Don Gifford with Robert J. Seidman, *'Ulysses' Annotated* (1974; 2nd edn. Berkeley: University of California Press, 1988)
Foster	R. F. Foster, *Modern Ireland: 1600-1972* (1988; repr. Harmondsworth: Penguin, 1989) (though Foster is rarely cited below, his work informs the facts of Irish history that are provided)
Gabler	James Joyce, *'Ulysses': The Corrected Text*, ed. Hans Walter Gabler with Wolfhard Steppe and Claus Melchior (New York and London: Garland, 1984)
Gilbert	Stuart Gilbert, *James Joyce's 'Ulysses'* (1930; repr. New York: Vintage, 1955)
Hart & Hayman	Clive Hart and David Hayman, eds., *James Joyce's 'Ulysses': Critical Essays* (Berkeley: University of California Press, 1974)
Janusko	Robert Janusko, *The Sources and Structures of James Joyce's 'Oxen'* (Ann Arbor, Mich.: UMI Research Press, 1983)
JJ	Richard Ellmann, *James Joyce* (1959; rev. edn. New York: Oxford University Press, 1982)
JJA	*The James Joyce Archive*, ed. Michael Groden, et al., (63 vols.; New York and London: Garland, 1977–80); vols. xii–xvii
Kenner	Hugh Kenner, *Ulysses* (1980; rev. edn. Baltimore: Johns Hopkins University Press, 1987)
Odyssey	Homer, *The Odyssey*, trans. Walter Shewring (Oxford: Oxford University Press, 1980)
OED	*The Oxford English Dictionary*
OEED	Joyce M. Hawkins and Robert Allen, *The Oxford Encyclopedic English Dictionary* (Oxford: Clarendon Press, 1991)
O Hehir	Brendan O Hehir, *A Gaelic Lexicon for 'Finnegans Wake' and Glossary for Joyce's Other Works* (Berkeley: University of

	California Press, 1967) (unless otherwise stated, all glosses of Gaelic words come from O Hehir)
Portrait	James Joyce, *A Portrait of the Artist as a Young Man* (1916), ed. Chester G. Anderson (New York: Viking, 1964)
Power	Arthur Power, *Conversations with James Joyce*, ed. Clive Hart (Chicago: University of Chicago Press, 1974)
PSW	James Joyce, *Poems and Shorter Writings*, ed. Richard Ellmann, A. Walton Litz, and John Whittier-Ferguson (London: Faber & Faber, 1991)
P. W. Joyce	P. W. Joyce, *English as We Speak it in Ireland* (1910; repr. Portmarnock: Wolfhound Press, 1979)
RM	*'Ulysses': A Facsimile of the Manuscript* [*'Rosenbach Manuscript'*], ed. Clive Driver (3 vols.; London: Faber & Faber; Philadelphia: Rosenbach Foundation, 1972); vols. i and ii
Stephen Hero	James Joyce, *Stephen Hero*, ed. Theodore Spencer (1944); rev. edn., John J. Slocum and Herbert Cahoon (St Albans: Triad/ Panther, 1977)
T	Weldon Thornton, *Allusions in 'Ulysses': An Annotated List* (Chapel Hill: University of North Carolina Press, 1968)

TELEMACHUS

Location: Martello Tower, Sandycove (on Dublin Bay, 7 miles south-east of central Dublin).

Time: 8 a.m., Thursday, 16 June 1904.

Homer: The *Odyssey* opens (after an invocation to the gods) *in medias res* ('in the midst of things'). The council of gods is meeting to decide the fate of Odysseus, who has been becalmed on Calypso's island in retaliation for his having angered Poseidon by slaying the god's son, Polyphemus, the Cyclops. Pallas Athena, grey-eyed goddess of wisdom and Odysseus's patron, argues his case, and it is decided that it is time he be allowed to return home to Ithaca. Athena, in the guise of Mentes, king of Taphos and Odysseus's friend, travels to Ithaca to find Telemachus, Odysseus's son, and to urge him to seek his father and his own fortune.

She finds Telemachus worrying about his father, wishing he would return to disperse the overbearing suitors who have gathered in an attempt to woo Penelope, Telemachus's mother and Odysseus's wife, and so acquire his lands. When Athena asks Telemachus if he is his father's son, he replies, 'My mother says that I am his son, though I myself have no knowledge of it—what man can be sure of his parentage?' (6) He worries, too, that the suitors are devouring his inheritance. They mock Telemachus, plot his death, and claim they will slay Odysseus should he return home. Loudest of the boasters are Antinous and

Eurymachus. Athena appears again to Telemachus, this time disguised as Mentor, faithful friend to Odysseus and guardian of his property in his absence. As Mentor, Athena again urges Telemachus to seek news of his father and helps him prepare for the journey. He defiantly faces the suitors and leaves. (Books I and II)

Schemata: Linati ('*L*') lists the personae for this episode as Telemachus, Mentor and Pallas [Athena] (bracketed together), Antinous, the suitors and Penelope (Mother), while Gilbert ('*G*') provides three of the correspondences: Stephen is Telemachus (and Hamlet), Buck Mulligan is Antinous, the milkwoman is Mentor. It is tempting to align Haines, the Englishman, with the suitors, but we ought perhaps to cast more widely to include Stephen's own definitions of those who vie for his servitude: 'I am a servant of two masters ... an English and an Italian. ... And a third ... there is who wants me for odd jobs. ... The imperial British state ... and the holy Roman catholic and apostolic church' (20). While he does not name the third, the most obvious candidate is 'Mother Ireland'. 'Penelope (Mother)' is clear enough: Stephen's mother, May Dedalus.

L and *G* agree on the Art (Theology), Organ (none), and Colour (white, gold), but not on Technic (*L*: 'Dialogue for 3 & 4, Narration, Soliloquy'; *G*: 'Narrative (young)') or Symbol (*L*: Hamlet, Ireland, Stephen; *G*: Heir). Further, *L* gives the 'Sense' as 'The Dispossessed Son in Contest'.

'Stately, plump Buck Mulligan came from the stairhead, bearing a bowl of lather on which a mirror and a razor lay crossed.' *Ulysses*'s first 'narrator' provides no scene setting nor, for that matter, any authoritative thematic exposition; no comforting voice intones 'It is a truth universally acknowledged ...' or 'Who cares much to know the history of man ...' (opening words of, respectively, Jane Austen's *Pride and Prejudice* (1813) and George Eliot's *Middlemarch* (1871–2)). We hear only Buck Mulligan intoning '*Introibo ad altare Dei*'. But two words (at least) stand out in that opening sentence as being in excess of what is required for simple description of the physical actions narrated: 'bearing' and 'crossed'. Why '*bearing* a bowl of lather' instead of '*carrying* a bowl of lather'? The former provides a note of ritual solemnity utterly lacking in the latter. When two sentences later Mulligan '[holds] the bowl aloft and intone[s]', the ritual note becomes sacramental chord. Similarly 'crossed'. Try 'crossing' a mirror and a razor on a bowl and 'crossed' may come to seem a verb ill-suited to the action. It is not, however, inappropriate to the 'eucharistic' purpose to which the bowl will soon be put. Here, with miserly economy, the verbs tell two tales at once: the first of Mulligan's mundane preparations for his morning shave, the second of his imposition of a symbolic significance on this routine—mock Mass supplants morning shave.

Mulligan persistently (usually perversely) assigns symbolic significance to actions, objects, people: the sea becomes (after Swinburne) 'a great sweet mother', the Martello Tower on which he stands becomes the Hellenic '*omphalos*', Stephen

Dedalus (soon to enter from the same stairhead) becomes by turns 'an ancient Greek', 'Kinch, the knifeblade', the 'bard', 'a lovely mummer', 'dogsbody'. Stephen's polysemic capacity exceeds even Mulligan's; his figures are finer, his assignments more apt. The cracked lookingglass pinched by Mulligan from the serving girl becomes in Stephen's appellation 'a symbol of Irish art. The cracked lookingglass of a servant.' To Stephen, the milkwoman merges with Mother Ireland, known 'in old times' as 'Silk of the kine and poor old woman'. Haines, the Englishman who speaks better Irish than the natives, is to Stephen simply the 'conqueror'. By the time some pages later that the narrative calmly records 'Haines stopped to take out a smooth silver case in which twinkled a green stone. He sprang it open with his thumb and offered it [to Stephen]', we have begun to read as Stephen would and recognize the silver case with its green stone as a troping of 'Erin, green gem of the silver sea', significantly held in the palm of the 'conqueror' and offered back to the 'bard'. It is as if the physical world (and its readers) have conspired to conform to Stephen's propensity for metaphor. (And while we began with Mulligan, it is only fair to point out that his manner is more mocking: his favourite phrase, his twice-uttered 'the mockery of it': 'To me it's all a mockery', he declaims; 'Idle mockery', Stephen thinks.)

Here, the circumambient world is pregnant with meaning because the 'narrator' verbalizes it—and the characters and their actions—in a language simultaneously precisely denotative and symbolically connotative ('bearing ... crossed'). Paradoxically, in doing so, he takes his lead from his characters; he plays a game that they play, follows the connections they make. Narrative sympathy (or should we say complicity?) with characters has never been greater (except perhaps in *A Portrait of the Artist as a Young Man*). But, as 'thing' and 'symbolic meaning of thing' converge, distinguishing action from its 'significance' becomes more difficult. Is Stephen peering at Dublin bay or at the bowl of bile standing beside his mother's bed (6)? Keeping hold of the narrative thread thus demands wary vigilance.

In *Telemachus*, Stephen and Mulligan perform most of these acts of metaphorical nomination though frequently as internal mental action in their 'interior monologues' (see 'Introduction', pp. xix ff.). Though as these arrive unsignalled to the reader, recognizing them requires 'rapt attention': 'He peered sideways up and gave a long low whistle of call then paused awhile in rapt attention, his even white teeth glistening here and there with gold points. Chrysostomos. Two strong shrill whistles answered through the calm' (3). Here, into the middle of a paragraph previously proceeding in the third person, pops 'Chrysostomos', Greek for 'golden-mouthed' and the name of two ancient orators (one a Church prelate) so named for their 'golden-mouthed orations' (see note). The epithet is doubly appropriate here: literally, Mulligan has gold fillings in his teeth; figuratively, he's playing the part of prelate. The punning is apt; it is also recondite, sufficiently so to identify Stephen immediately as its source. It is undeniably his kind of joke. This abrupt eruption into the narrative of Stephen's (unsignalled) thought disconcerts; recognizing it *as* Stephen's thought clears up some of the confusion (though we can probably only so recognize 'Chrysostomos' as Stephen's once we later realize that other more obviously segregated narrative passages must be emanating from his mind). As the narrative proceeds, it crosses into and out of Stephen's thoughts with increasing frequency until distinguishing them *as* his thoughts poses no problem. Making sense of them does. Stephen's self-conscious erudition sets up one kind of obstacle; the elliptical, fragmentary nature of this internal mode of narration another. The former difficulty—who is Chrysostomos when he's at home?—can usually be resolved fairly easily (through recourse to notes, dictionaries, encyclopaedias, other texts). The latter—itself the direct result of the requirement of psychological verisimilitude: we seldom 'think' coherently—allows only approximate (re)construction. Limiting itself strictly to what a character admits to consciousness, the narrative slyly asserts that what is most 'real' is perhaps also most elusive.

3.5 *Introibo ad altare Dei*: 'I will go unto the altar of God' (Ps. 43: 4). Spoken by the priest at the opening of the former Latin Mass.

3.19–20 *For this . . . blood and ouns*: parody of Jesus's words at the Last Supper: 'Take, eat; this is my body . . . Drink ye all of it; for this is my blood' (Matt. 26: 26–8). 'Blood and ouns': God's blood and wounds; 'Christine': feminization of Christ's name. Mocking Mulligan is performing a pseudo Black Mass.

3.24 *Chrysostomos*: Greek: 'golden-mouthed'; name of two early orators: Dion Chrysostomos (*c.*50–*c.*117), Greek rhetorician, and St John Chrysostomos (*c.*345–407), early Father of the Church.

4.5–6 *an ancient Greek*: the 'Greek' in question is Daedalus, the cunning artificer who fashioned for King Minos the labyrinth to hold fast the Minotaur. Minos, angered at Daedalus's having built a wooden cow for Queen Pasiphaë so she might copulate with a prize bull, placed Daedalus and his son, Icarus, inside the labyrinth. To escape, Daedalus fashioned wings of wax and feathers, and he and his son flew out. Icarus, however, overcome by the ecstasy of flight, flew too near the sun, his wings melted, and he fell into the sea and drowned. (See Ovid, *Metamorphoses*, VIII.) Stephen's forename derives from St Stephen, the first Christian martyr.

4.13 *Malachi*: Hebrew: 'my messenger'; the Old Testament prophet who foretells the coming of Elijah.

5.12–13 *Algy . . . a great sweet mother*: Algernon Charles Swinburne (1837–1909), English poet and author of 'The Triumph of Time' (1866), which includes the line, 'the great sweet mother . . . the sea'.

5.13 *Epi oinopa ponton*: Homeric epithet: 'over the winedark sea'.

5.15 *Thalatta! Thalatta!*: Attic Greek: 'The sea! The sea!' From the Greek historian Xenophon's (*c.*428–*c.*354 BC) *Anabasis*, chronicle of the expedition of the Ten Thousand Greek mercenaries in siege against the Persians. This was the cry of the Ten Thousand on reaching the sea (IV. vii. 24) (*T*).

5.17 *Kingstown*: former English name for Dun Laoghaire, town on the south shore of Dublin Bay.

5.24 *hyperborean*: Friedrich Nietzsche (1844–1900), German philosopher, uses the term to describe those who, like the Übermensch ('Superman' (see 22.16 n.)), were 'above the crowd' (*Der Wille zur Macht* ('The Will to Dominate') (1896), 'The Antichrist', sect. 1).

6.33–4 *Lead him not... temptation*: Lord's Prayer (Matt. 6: 13).

6.34 *Ursula*: perhaps after St Ursula, the early Christian saint, renowned for her chastity, legendary leader of eleven thousand virgins.

6.36 *The rage of Caliban ... mirror*: after Oscar Wilde (1854–1900), Preface to *Dorian Gray* (1891): 'The nineteenth century dislike of Realism is the rage of Caliban seeing his own face in the glass. The nineteenth century dislike of Romanticism is the rage of Caliban not seeing his own face in the glass.'

7.2 *a symbol... of a servant*: see Oscar Wilde, 'The Decay of Lying' (1889), where Cyril says that treating art as a mirror 'would reduce genius to the position of a cracked looking-glass'. The servant here is, literally, the servant girl from whom Mulligan has 'borrowed' the mirror, but obviously, metaphorically, the servant is Ireland.

7.14 *Hellenise it*: in *Culture and Anarchy* (1869), ch. 4, Matthew Arnold (1822–88) suggests that Western culture is driven by two contrary but, ideally, complementary forces, the Hebraic ('energy driving at practice' with an attendant 'obligation of duty, self-control, and work') and the Hellenic ('the indomitable impulse to know', 'to see things as they really are ... in their essence and beauty'). By the end of the nineteenth century, 'to Hellenize' had become synonymous with 'to bring culture to, or to aestheticize'.

7.15 *Cranly's arm. His arm*: Cranly is Stephen's (now estranged) friend from *Portrait*, ch. 5, pp. 226 ff.

7.21–30 *Young shouts... grasshalms*: Stephen imagines an Oxford scene. Oliver St John Gogarty, real-life model for Mulligan, spent a term there in 1904.

7.29 *Matthew Arnold*: see 7.14 n. Joyce saw Arnold as a distasteful 'tidier', a man of 'little opinion' as he says in his 1898/99 essay 'The Study of Languages' (*CW* 26).

7.31 *To ourselves*: English for the Gaelic *Sinn Féin*—'ourselves'; motto for various groups militating for the revival of Irish culture and a return to Gaelic as the principal language of Ireland; adopted by Arthur Griffith (1871–1922) as the name of a political organization pursuing Irish nationalism.

7.31 *omphalos*: Greek: 'navel'; Odysseus's epithet for Calypso's island; a stone used in Greek religious rites, most famously at Delphi, supposed centre of the earth and principal site of prophecy in Ancient Greece.

8.12 *and I went across the landing*: should read 'and went across the landing'.

8.29 *Sir Peter Teazle*: character in Richard Brinsley Sheridan's (1751–1816) play *The School for Scandal* (1777).

8.31 *Lalouette's*: Dublin funeral establishment.

9.12 *Loyola*: St Ignatius of Loyola (1491–1556), founder of the Society of Jesus (Jesuits).

9.13 *Sassenach*: Gaelic: 'the Saxon' or 'Englishman'.

9.21–3 *And no more . . . cars*: W. B. Yeats (1865–1939), 'Who Goes with Fergus' (1892), a song from his play *The Countess Cathleen*, sung to comfort Cathleen who has sold her soul to buy food for her people. The verse continues: 'And rules the shadow of the wood, | And the white breast of the dim sea | And all dishevelled wandering stars.' Quoted further at 9.24, 26–7.

10.4 *Turko the terrible*: pantomime (1873) by Edwin Hamilton (1849–1919) immensely popular in Dublin in its various editions throughout the 1880s and 1890s. In it, the magical Fairy Rose grants invisibility (*T*).

10.21–2 *Liliata . . . excipiat*: Latin: 'May the lilied throng of radiant Confessors encompass thee; may the choir of rejoicing Virgins welcome thee'; prayer offered at the bedside of the dying (*T*).

11.9 *druidy druids*: priests of the ancient, pagan, Celtic religion.

11.12–17 *O, won't we have a merry time . . . On coronation day?*: version of 'De Golden Wedding' (1880), song by African-American songwriter James A. Bland (1854–1911) (*T*).

11.23 *Clongowes*: Clongowes Wood College, Jesuit boys' school attended by both Stephen (in *Portrait*, ch. 1) and Joyce.

11.24 *A server of a servant*: strictly, Stephen as altar boy (server) helping the priest (servant of God); but also figuratively as Irishman attending an Englishman (servant of English colonialism).

12.26 *In nomine . . . Sancti*: Latin: 'In the name of the Father and of the Son and of the Holy Ghost'; blessing of the Holy Trinity.

13.4–5 *Dundrum. Printed . . . weird sisters . . . big wind*: parody of the colophon of Yeats's *In the Seven Woods* (1903), printed at the Dun Emer press in Dundrum by Yeats's two sisters, Elizabeth and Lily, though Mulligan's sarcastic comments are aimed at the contemporary Irish antiquarian impulse in general; 'weird sisters': the witches in *Macbeth* (*T*).

13.9 *Mabinogian*: collection of classical Welsh myths.

13.9 *Upanishads*: mystic ancient Hindu scriptures, much read by Yeats and the Theosophists. (See 135.13–14n.)

13.31 *collector of prepuces*: the Hebrew God, Jehovah, who required circumcision; 'prepuces': foreskins.

14.1 *tilly*: Gaelic: *tuile*: 'extra, addition, little added bit'.

14.6 *Silk of the kine and poor old woman*: two traditional names for Ireland; direct translations from the Gaelic: *Síoda na mbó* and *Sean bhean bhocht*. (See also 17.30–1 n.)

14.8 *cuckquean*: 'female cuckold'.

14.22–3 *woman's unclean loins . . . serpent's prey*: Old Testament descriptions of woman: 'unclean loins': after childbirth (Lev. 12: 2, 5) and during menstruation

(15: 19–28); 'of man's flesh': Eve made from Adam's rib (Gen. 2: 22); and 'serpent's prey': she fell for the serpent's (Satan's) ploy (Gen. 3).

14.30 *[the] west*: the Gaelic-speaking remote western districts of Ireland.

15.6–9 *it's seven mornings . . . a shilling and one and two*: as it stands, this is mathematical nonsense; should read 'it's seven mornings . . . a shilling. That's a shilling and one and two'.

15.18, 24–5 *Ask nothing more . . . give | Heart of my heart . . . feet*: Swinburne, 'The Oblation', *Songs Before Sunrise* (1871), ll. 1–2 and 3–4.

15.28–9 *Ireland expects . . . duty*: parody of Lord Nelson's reported words at the Battle of Trafalgar (21 Oct. 1805): 'England expects . . .'; the words also form part of the song 'The Death of Nelson' by S. J. Arnold and John Braham.

16.6 *Agenbite of inwit*: Middle English: 'remorse of conscience', and title of Dan Michel of Northgate's translation (1340) of French medieval moral treatise (*T*).

16.12 *Hamlet*: obviously, Shakespeare's tragedy; an important repeated motif for Stephen who often throughout the day returns to the role of Hamlet. To paraphrase Kenner, Stephen thinks he's in a book called *Hamlet* and never discovers that it's really called *Ulysses* and that he is a supporting actor, not the lead (Kenner, 28).

16.35 *Mulligan . . . garments*: parody of the tenth Station of the Cross (from Matt. 27: 28; John 19: 23–4): 'Christ is stripped of his garments'.

17.5 *Do I contradict myself? . . . myself*: Walt Whitman (1819–92), *Song of Myself* (1855), sect. 51, ll. 6–7.

17.7 *Latin quarter hat*: Stephen's hat, like the characters of *Ulysses* themselves, changes roles to suit the situation. Here, it invokes Stephen's stay in the Latin Quarter in Paris; later it will become his Hamlet hat (47.20). Similarly, Mulligan wears 'Mercury's hat' (19.14) in keeping with Stephen's characterization of him as 'Mercurial Malachi' (17.6): 'Mercury': the messenger of the gods in Greek mythology; just as, in Hebrew, 'Malachi' means 'my messenger'.

17.30 *Billy Pitt*: William Pitt the Younger (1759–1806), Prime Minister of England at the time that the Martello towers were built (1803–6) as safeguard against the possible invasion of Ireland by the French during the Napoleonic Wars.

17.30–1 *when the French were on the sea*: general allusion to attempts (in 1796 and 1798) by the French to intervene on behalf of the Irish in their rebellion against England's repressive measures. Specific allusion to the Irish ballad, 'The Shan Van Vocht' (Gaelic: *Sean Bhean Bhocht*: The Poor Old Woman, see 14.6 n.): 'O, the French are on the sea, | Says the Shan Van Vocht, | . . . | Yes! Ireland shall be free'.

17.33–4 *Thomas Aquinas*: St Thomas Aquinas (1225–74), Dominican, theologian, Scholastic philosopher. In *Portrait* (ch. 5, p. 209), Stephen describes his aesthetic theory as 'applied Aquinas'.

18.10 *Japhet in search of a father!*: title of 1836 novel by Captain Frederick Marryat (1792–1848); concerns foundling's (eventually successful) search for his father.

Also, of course, sounds the theme of a son in pursuit of a father which resounds throughout *Ulysses*.

18.16–17 *Elsinore. That beetles . . . sea*: Elsinore: the setting of *Hamlet*, the allusion is to *Hamlet*, I. iv. 71.

18.23 *The seas' ruler*: England (or Haines as an Englishman), after James Thomson's (1700–48) ode 'Rule Britannia' (1740), set to music by Thomas Arne (1710–78).

18.33–19.12 *I'm the queerest young fellow . . . goodbye!*: the first of several near-verbatim citations of verses written by Oliver St John Gogarty. The theme, blasphemously stated here, of Jesus's actual physical existence (as opposed to his divinity) will recur.

19.28–9 *silver case . . . a green stone*: the first appearance of a recurrent image for Ireland, the Green Gem of the Silver Sea (another version of the 'Emerald Isle'; see 119.6 n. and 179.7 n.); here, clearly, used as a symbol of colonialism, as the case is held in the palm of the Englishman Haines.

20.19 *servant of two masters*: see headnote.

20.32 *et unam . . . ecclesiam*: Latin: 'And in one holy, catholic, and apostolic church'; from the Nicene Creed (325).

20.34 *Symbol of the apostles . . . pope Marcellus*: 'Symbol of the apostles': the Apostles' Creed in the Mass (*G*); the Italian musician Giovanni Pierluigi da Palestrina (1525–94) wrote a mass for Pope Marcellus II (1501–55), a composition which Joyce described to Budgen as having 'saved music for the Church' (Budgen, 182).

20.36 *vigilant angel . . . militant*: the Archangel Michael; the struggle alluded to is the 16th-c. battle of the Catholic Church against the rising tide of the Protestant heresy. (See 21.7 n.)

20.37 *Photius* : (*c.*815–*c.*897): appointed patriarch of Constantinople (857) against Pope Nicholas I's wishes, refused to accept that the Holy Spirit proceeds from the Father *and* the Son, excommunicated (863), initiated the schism which culminated in the separation of the Eastern Orthodox and Roman Catholic Churches in 1054.

21.1 *Arius*: (*c.*256–336), his heresy was to maintain that the Father and the Son were not of the same, but merely of similar, substance (the Son being the Father's first creation and therefore inferior to Him); the Council of Nicaea (325), convened to address Arius's teachings, produced the Nicene Creed—an explicit refutation of the Arian heresy, through its use of the term 'consubstantial' to emphasize that Father and Son are of the same substance.

21.2 *Valentine*: (d. *c.*166), an Egyptian Gnostic who maintained that Christ neither had a real body nor actually suffered.

21.3 *Sabellius*: 3rd-c. heretic who maintained that the three members of the Trinity were a strict unity, i.e. merely different modes of the same substance.

21.7 *Michael's host*: Michael the Archangel, valiant leader of the host of Angels in the battle against Satan. (See 20.36 n.)

21.10–11 *I don't want to see my country . . . German jews*: Haines gives voice to the anti-Semitic attitudes (prevalent in 1904 Europe) against which *Ulysses* is written. (See *G* 4.)

22.16 *Uebermensch* German: 'Superman'; coined by Nietzsche in his *Thus Spake Zarathustra* (1883) where Zarathustra, a Persian prophet, becomes the mouthpiece of Nietzsche's theories. (See 5.24 n.)

22.36 *He who stealeth . . . poor*: parody of Prov. 19: 17: 'He that hath pity upon the poor lendeth unto the Lord'.

23.4 *Horn of a bull . . . Saxon*: proverbial three things an Irishman should beware.

23.16 *Usurper*: compare Telemachus's indictment of Antinous, who would marry Penelope and usurp Telemachus's inheritance, and Hamlet's of Claudius who in marrying Queen Gertrude has, as Hamlet says, 'Popp'd in between th' election and my hopes' (*Hamlet*, v. ii. 65).

NESTOR

Location: Boys' school, Dalkey (village on Dublin Bay, 1 mile south-east of Martello Tower, Sandycove; 8 miles south-east of central Dublin).

Time: 10 a.m.

Homer: Having arrived in Pylos, Telemachus approaches Nestor, 'master of horsemanship' (23), for news of his father. Telemachus worries about his lack of grace in speech, and Athena assures him that 'some words you will find in your own heart unaided: others a god will prompt you with' (23). On nearing Nestor's house, Telemachus is greeted by Pisistratus, Nestor's youngest son. Unfortunately, Nestor has no news of Odysseus, but relates instead part of the tale of the return of the Greek warriors from the Trojan War. Included here is the tale of Agamemnon's return, his murder, and the avenging of it by his son Orestes. Nestor provides Telemachus with horses and a chariot for his journey, and Telemachus and Pisistratus travel to Menelaus's court where they meet Helen ('of Troy'). Menelaus recounts his travels home from Troy. (Books III and IV)

Schemata: *L* and *G* both list the personae of the episode as Nestor, Pisistratus, Helen (*L* adds Telemachus); *G* provides the correspondences: Deasy is Nestor; Sargent, Pisistratus; Mrs O'Shea (Katherine O'Shea, *de facto* and later actual wife of Charles Stewart Parnell (see 34.37 n. below)), Helen (of Troy). *L* and *G* agree on the Art (History), Organ (none), and Colour (brown), but disagree on Technic (*L*: 'Dialogue for 2, Narration, Soliloquy'; *G*: 'Catechism (personal)') and Symbol (*L*: Ulster, Woman, Practical sense; *G*: Horse). *L* gives as Sense, 'The Wisdom of the Ancients'.

In *Telemachus* Haines, the 'ponderous Saxon' and 'seas' ruler', admits to a guilty conscience over England's treatment of the Irish, then, as if by reflex action, attempts to erase that guilt with his next words: 'We feel in England that we have treated you rather unfairly. It seems history is to blame' (20). As a chronicle of England's colonial occupation of Ireland, history both implicates Haines as Englishman in that narrative and indicts him for it. In a gesture of attempted self-absolution, Haines displaces his guilt by troping history as an infernal agent, much like the schoolboy caught redhanded who seeks to escape imminent punishment by squealing 'I didn't do it. History did.'

An hour-and-a-half later finds Stephen teaching history to other schoolboys and pondering Blake's conception of human history. For Blake, humanity sees only partially: vision is required to transform mundane reality into God's greater Truth. So, Blake's history is a debased narrative, human, fabled, unlike Truth which is divine and visionary. To a degree then, Blake would agree with Mr Deasy who will declare that 'All human history moves towards one great goal, the manifestation of God.' (In this Deasy reveals himself a Hegelian to the extent that in his *Philosophy of History* (1832) Hegel declared human history to be teleologically progressive, moving ever nearer a state of perfection, of completion.)

But Stephen is more Aristotelian than Blakean and so dismisses Blake's assertion of history as fable. Julius Caesar and Pyrrhus 'are not to be thought away'. Theirs was an actual existence. And it is the actuality of Irish history which yokes Stephen to the schoolboys. Milton's 'Lycidas' reminds him that 'over these [the boy's] craven hearts [Christ's] shadow lies and on the scoffer's heart and lips and on mine'. 'For them too history was a tale like any other too often heard, their land a pawnshop.' This accords with Stephen's earlier comment to Haines: 'I am the servant of two masters ... an English and an Italian ... And a third ... who wants me for odd jobs.' History has cast Stephen in the role of factotum, 'jester', 'dogsbody'.

No wonder, then, his remark to Deasy, 'History ... is a nightmare from which I am trying to awake.' Significantly, Stephen's definition of history, unlike Deasy's and Haines's, includes no gesture of attempted self-absolution. A nightmare arises from the dreaming subject as product of that subject's innermost fears. While Stephen the Aristotelian acknowledges the actuality of others and the part they play in history, he accepts his own position of responsibility in the narrative. It is this Stephen who will reject the too-easy answers of xenophobia, racism, and sentimental nationalism which the 'tale ... too often heard' seduces one to adopt.

24.2, 12, 18 *Tarentum; Asculum; Pyrrhus*: Stephen's history lesson concerns Pyrrhus (318–272 BC), King of Epirus, who was sent for (in 281 BC) by the people of Tarentum (Greek city in Italy) to defend them against the Romans. He was successful, but his victories were so costly (especially at Asculum in 279) that the eventual collapse of the Tarentines was inevitable. Thus a 'Pyrrhic victory': a victory obtained at too great a cost.

24.7–9 *Fabled by the daughters of memory ... Blake's wings of excess*: in his commentary 'A Vision of the Last Judgment' (1810), William Blake (1757–1827) contrasts 'Vision' with the 'inferior Poetry' of 'Fable or Allegory': 'Vision or

Imagination is a Representation of what Eternally Exists, Really & Unchangeably. Fable or Allegory is Form'd by the daughters of Memory. Imagination is surrounded by the daughters of Inspiration, who in the aggregate are called Jerusalem' (Blake, *Complete Writings*, ed. Geoffrey Keynes (1957; repr. Oxford: Oxford University Press, 1972), 604). For Blake, then, history—the so-called 'Reality' 'Remember'd' as 'the Vanities of Time & Space' (p. 605)—is Fabled Reality and is debased by comparison with Visionary Reality (what 'Eternally Exists'). Stephen's impatience with Blake's displacement of temporal history with 'Eternal Reality' leads him to suggest that Blake's assertions were themselves born of impatience and of his predilection for 'excess' (cf. Blake, *The Marriage of Heaven and Hell*, 'Proverbs of Hell' (*c.*1790–3): 'The road of excess leads to the palace of wisdom'; 'No bird soars too high, if he soars with his own wings' (ll. 3, 15)).

24.9–10 *ruin of all space . . . flame*: Blake repeatedly asserted (in e.g. *A Vision of the Last Judgment* and *The Marriage of Heaven and Hell*) that the corrupt temporal world ('the Vanities of Time & Space') would be destroyed by apocalyptic fire and thus supplanted by 'Truth and Eternity'. As he wrote to William Hayley on 6 May 1800, 'every Mortal loss is an Immortal Gain. The Ruins of Time build Mansions in Eternity' (Blake, *Complete Writings*, 797) (see 373.28 n. and *T*). Note that Stephen's emphasis is on the destruction of Time and Space, not their replacement with glorified 'Eternal Truth'.

24.14 *Another victory . . . done for*: Pyrrhus's statement after the 'victory' at Asculum, according to Plutarch's *Lives*, 'Pyrrhus'.

24.18 *the end of Pyrrhus*: killed with the help of the mother of an assailant (Zopyrus) whom Pyrrhus was about to kill; she threw a roof-tile at him, stunned him, and Zopyrus then cut his head off.

25.21–2 *Had . . . Julius Caesar not been knifed to death*: Caesar (100–44 BC), Roman general, statesman, and dictator, murdered by the aristocratic conspirators who feared his power. Stephen ponders whether history could have been other than it was; these events, having happened, can not now be 'thought away'.

25.23 *the infinite possibilities*: in the *Metaphysics* (esp. Bk. IX), Aristotle argues the distinction between the 'actual' (what really happened) and the 'possible' (what might have happened). At any moment in time, there are infinite possibilities for what might happen, but only one thing which does or will happen (the 'actual'). Stephen wonders whether these 'possibilities' were really possible since they never happened—is Aristotle's distinction merely nominal? See, too, Aristotle's distinction (in the *Poetics*, IX (1451b1–5) between poetry and history: the poet's distinctive role is to write of what might happen (the 'possible') while the historian's is to write of what has happened (the 'actual'). (See, too, 26.4 n.)

26.1–3, 15 *Weep no more . . . walked the waves*: John Milton (1608–74), 'Lycidas' (1638), ll. 165–7, 173; pastoral elegy on the death, by drowning, of Edward King, Milton's fellow student at Christ's College, Cambridge.

26.4 *movement then, an actuality of the possible as possible*: Aristotle's definition of movement from his *Physics*, III.i (201a10–11), in Joyce's translation from the French translation. While in Paris in 1903–4, Joyce read Aristotle in French, jotting his own translations into English down in a (now lost) notebook. Some survived as copied down by Joyce's first biographer, Herbert Gorman (published in full by Richard F. Peterson, 'More Aristotelian Grist for the Joycean Mill', *JJQ* 17/2 (Winter 1980), 213–16; this quotation is on 215). Jacques Aubert identifies Joyce's sources in the French translations (see Aubert, *The Aesthetics of James Joyce* (1973; trans. Baltimore: Johns Hopkins University Press, 1992), 'Appendix B', 131–7, 136). The allusions to Aristotle throughout *Ulysses* have been elusive precisely because Joyce read Aristotle in French rather than in any standard English translation.

26.11 *Thought is the thought of thought*: again Joyce's translation of the French Aristotle, this time from *Metaphysics*, XII. vii (1072b20) (Peterson, 215; Aubert, 136).

26.11–12 *soul... form of forms*: Joyce from Aristotle, *De Anima*, III. viii (431b21 and 432a2): 'The soul is in a manner all that is'; 'The intellectual soul is the form of forms' (Peterson, 214; Aubert, 134).

26.22–3 *To Caesar what is Caesar's*: Christ, when asked whether tribute should be paid to Caesar (Caesar's image was stamped on Roman coins) (Matt. 22: 21, Mark 12: 17, Luke 20: 25).

26.25–6 *Riddle me ... to sow*: opening of traditional riddle which continues: 'The seed was black and the ground was white ... | Riddle me that and I'll give you a pipe'. Answer: Writing a Letter.

27.5–10 *The cock crew ... To go to heaven*: adaptation of another riddle, cited by P. W. Joyce, 187: 'Riddle me, riddle me right: | What did I see last night? | The wind blew, | The cock crew, | The bells of heaven | Struck eleven. | 'Tis time for my poor *sowl* to go to heaven. Answer: the fox burying his mother under the holly tree.' He also remarks 'the delightful inconsequence of riddle and answer'. Note that Stephen substitutes 'grandmother' for 'mother'.

28.10 *The only true thing in life?*: Stephen means, of course, 'a mother's love' (a theme to which he returns in *Scylla and Charybdis*) and echoes Cranly's statement in *Portrait* (ch. 5, pp. 241–2): 'Whatever else is unsure in this stinking dunghill of a world a mother's love is not'.

28.11 *Columbanus*: St Columbanus (543–615), Irish saint and writer, whom Joyce mentions in his essay, 'Ireland, Island of Saints and Sages' (1907) (*CW* 157–8). Supposedly, in going as a missionary to Europe, he left his mother against her will.

28.24 *imps of... Moors*: the Moors brought algebra to Europe.

28.25 *Averroes and Moses Maimonides*: Averroës (1126–98), Spanish–Arabian philosopher, commentator on Aristotle, attempted to reconcile Aristotelian philosophy with Muslim orthodoxy; similarly, Moses Maimonides (1135–1204), Jewish rabbi and philosopher, attempted to reconcile Aristotelian thought with orthodox Judaism. Both strongly influenced medieval Christian Scholasticism.

28.26 *soul of the world*: a recurrent phrase in (esp. medieval and mystical) philosophy; Stephen probably gets the phrase from Giordano Bruno (1548–1600), Italian philosopher, whose *anima del mondo* was the unifying principle and cause of nature (*G*); Joyce quoted him in 'The Day of the Rabblement' (1901) and devoted an entire essay to him, 'The Bruno Philosophy', in 1903 (*CW* 69–72, 132–4).

28.26–7 *a darkness shining in brightness*: parodic inversion of John 1: 5: 'And the light shineth in darkness; and the darkness comprehended it not'. Stephen is preoccupied (as is Joyce) with the persistence of an incommensurable darkness (or error, or heresy) in the midst of 'light' (of law or Church), a darkness which is more 'true' than the 'truth' of 'light'.

28.32 *Amor matris: subjective and objective genitive*: Latin: 'mother love'; meaning either 'mother's love for [another]' (subjective) or '[another's] love for mother' (objective).

29.29 *As it was in the beginning*: conclusion to the Gloria Patri: 'Glory be to the Father, and to the Son, and to the Holy Ghost; as it was in the beginning, is now and ever shall be, world without end'.

29.29 *Stuart coins*: when the Stuart king, James II of England (1633–1701; r. 1685–8), a Catholic, was deposed by William of Orange (1650–1702; r. 1689–1702), a Protestant, he fled first to France then (1689) came to Ireland which had remained loyal to him. He led the Irish troops to defeat (by the now King William III) at the Battle of the Boyne (1690), a defeat which helped ensure a strongly Protestant northern Ireland. While in Ireland, he minted coin from inferior metals (so debasing the currency). Ironically, the coins became valuable as rarities.

29.37 *table strapping and*: should read 'table.'.

30.27–9 *Put but money in thy purse . . . Iago*: Deasy (favourably and presumably ignorantly) quotes Iago in *Othello*, I. iii. 345–6.

31.7 *brogues*: from the Gaelic: *bróg*: 'shoe'.

31.8, 9 *Fred Ryan; Russell*: Fred Ryan (1876–1913), Irish economist, journalist, and editor of the magazine *Dana* (coedited by W. K. Magee, 'Eglinton' in *Scylla and Charybdis*). Russell: George William Russell (1867–1935), pseudonym 'AE', Theosophist, journalist (with *The Irish Homestead* in which Joyce too published), agrarian reformer, and leading figure in the Irish literary renaissance.

31.18 *fillibegs*: Gaelic: *filleadh beig*: '"little fold", kilt'.

31.18 *Albert Edward, prince of Wales*: (1841–1910), by 1904 King Edward VII of England (r. 1901–10).

31.20 *O'Connell's time*: Daniel O'Connell (1775–1847), Irish political leader ('the Liberator') who successfully militated for Catholic Emancipation (1829). (Catholics had suffered severe restriction of their political and religious rights and freedoms from the time of Henry VIII (r. 1509–47).) He also, unsuccessfully, agitated for repeal of the Act of Union which in 1800 had dissolved the Irish Parliament and brought Ireland entirely under the rule of the British Parliament in Westminster.

31.20 *the famine*: should read 'the famine in '46'; 'The Great Famine' (1845–8) during which the potato crop was destroyed by blight. As the crop was the staple diet of the vast majority of the Irish 'peasantry' (at least half the population by mid-century), and as Ireland had purposely been prevented from developing independent industries which would threaten those of England so that there was no economic industrial base to fall back on, the effects were cataclysmic: a reduction in the population (from either death or emigration) from 8.2 million in 1841 to 6.6 million in 1851. (By 1901, it had fallen still further to 4.5 million.) (Foster, 606–7, 611.)

31.21 *orange lodges*: Protestant (often violently anti-Catholic) societies formed in the 1790s and united by the Orange Society (1795), the stated purpose of which was 'the maintenance of British authority in Ireland'; concentrated in Ulster, the northernmost counties of Ireland.

31.21 *repeal of the union*: 'the union' is the Act of Union of 1800 (see 31.20n.). The orange lodges were initially—and only briefly—anti-union. Deasy presents either an ignorant or a highly selective and distorted version of history.

31.23 *fenians*: after the Fianna army in the medieval Gaelic saga of Fionn Mac Cumhail, the popular name of the Irish Republican Brotherhood, founded by James Stephens (1825–1901) in 1858; political organization committed to bringing about Irish independence through whatever means necessary. Also a general term for an Irish republican.

31.24–7 *Glorious, pious . . . Croppies lie down*: Stephen's condensation of various moments in the history of Protestant–Catholic contestation: 'Glorious . . . memory': Orangeman's toast to memory of William III ('who saved us from popery, slavery, arbitrary power, brass money, and wooden shoes'). 'Lodge . . . papishes': on 21 Sept. 1795, twenty or thirty 'Defenders' (Catholic tenants organized to defend themselves against Protestant 'enforcers' of the anti-Catholic laws) were massacred at Diamond in the northern county of Armagh ('papishes': papists or Catholics); the incident led to the formation of the Orange Society. 'Planters covenant': apparently an allusion to the oath of loyalty to the English monarch (as head of State and Church) exacted in exchange for land (or plantations) in Ireland from the time of Elizabeth I (r. 1558–1603). 'Black north': Protestant northern Ireland. 'True blue': originally a Scottish Presbyterian anti-Royalist, many of the immigrants under the Plantation system were of this ilk. 'Croppies lie down': a 'loyalist' (Orange, Protestant) slogan; 'croppy' a general name for any Irish 'rebel' after the Wexford rebels who fought in the 1798 Rebellion against continuing English domination. (*G*)

31.30 *sir John Blackwood*: (1722–99), an Ulster MP who 'died in the act of putting on his topboots to go to Dublin to vote *against* the Union' (italics added; *SL*

201–2; Joyce quoting Henry N. Blackwood Price (a model for Deasy and descendant of sir John) who wrote to him in 1912 trying to solicit his help in the battle against foot and mouth disease (see 32.36–7 n.)).

31.31 *all Irish, all kings' sons*: Deasy quotes the Irish proverb 'All Irishmen are kings' sons', the 'kings' in question being the ancient kings of Ireland. Stephen's 'Alas' addresses the irony of 'kings' also being English kings, hence all Irishmen are the subjects of English colonialism.

31.33 *Per vias rectas*: Latin: 'by straight roads', sir John's motto; by now it should be clear that Deasy's 'roads' are anything but 'straight'.

31.35–6 *Lal the ral . . . road to Dublin*: 'The Rocky Road to Dublin', anonymous Irish ballad.

32.15 *images of vanished horses . . .*: various English aristocrats and their prize-winning horses; Homer's Nestor was, of course, a 'master of horsemanship' who provided Telemachus with horses and a chariot for his continued travels.

32.24 *slush. Even money Fair rebel: ten*: should read 'slush *Fair Rebel! Fair Rebel!* Even money the favourite: ten'.

32.36–7 *foot and mouth disease*: there was an outbreak of foot and mouth disease (aphthous fever which had no dependable cure) in Ireland, but not until 1912. Joyce transfers the disease to 1904 along with Henry N. Blackwood Price as Deasy (see 31.30 n.).

33.3 *Liverpool ring . . . harbour scheme*: various schemes to transform Galway into a transatlantic port were about in the mid-19th c.; all failed, but through ignorance of shipping rather than a conspiracy of self-serving Liverpool shipping interests.

33.6 *Cassandra*: daughter of Priam and Hecuba whose prophecy of the downfall of Troy was disregarded. Because she refused Apollo's love, he condemned her to utter true prophecies which no one would believe.

33.31–2 *The harlot's cry . . . winding sheet*: Blake, 'Auguries of Innocence' (*c.* 1803), ll. 115–16.

34.19 *History . . . trying to awake*: after Jules Laforgue (1860–87), *Mélanges posthumes* (Paris, 1903), 279: 'L'histoire est un vieux chauchemar bariolé qui ne se doute pas que les meilleures plaisanteries sont les plus courtes' ('History is an old gaudy nightmare who does not suspect that the best jokes are the shortest').

34.23–4 *All history . . . manifestation of God*: should read 'All human history . . .'; generally accepted Victorian sentiment about the divine ends of history, but also the more respectable philosophy of history espoused by, among others, Georg Wilhelm Friedrich Hegel (1770–1831) in his *Philosophy of History* (1832).

34.33–5 *For a woman who . . . Troy*: Helen of Troy, who was awarded to Paris by Aphrodite as prize for his having judged her more beautiful than either Hera or Athena. To reclaim her, her husband Menelaus invaded and brought the downfall of Troy. See, especially, Homer's *Iliad*.

34.35–7 *A faithless wife . . . Breffni*: another Deasy mistake: MacMurrough was

Devorgilla's lover (or 'leman'); O'Rourke, her husband. Dermot MacMurrough, King of Leinster, was deposed in 1167 (by the joined forces of Tiernan O'Rourke, Prince of Breffni, and Roderick O'Connor, High King of Ireland, ostensibly in retaliation for MacMurrough's elopement with O'Rourke's wife fifteen years earlier). He fled to England, whence he launched (in 1169, joined by the forces of Henry II) the first successful Anglo-Norman invasion of Ireland.

34.37 *A woman too brought Parnell low*: Charles Stewart Parnell (1846–91), an Anglo-Irish Protestant landlord, became an MP in 1875 and subsequently head of the Land League and the Irish Parliamentary Party—a parliamentarian militating for Irish Home Rule and the head of an organization dedicated to guaranteeing, through direct action, an equitable solution to the oppresive landlord/tenant system of land ownership and management. Arrested and imprisoned for his Land League involvement, he re-entered Parliament on his release, where he secured the support of Gladstone (the Liberal Prime Minister: see 77.8 n.) for Home Rule. In Dec. 1889 he was cited as co-respondent in the divorce petition of Captain William O'Shea against his wife Katherine ('Kitty'), an Englishwoman with whom Parnell had for years been living in a *de facto*, though (somewhat openly) secret, 'marriage'. Though Parnell fought valiantly to maintain his position as leader of the Irish Party, he was deserted by them and denounced by the Catholic Church (Dec. 1890). He died fourteen weeks after marrying Katherine (in June 1891).

35.3–4 *For Ulster will fight ... right*: Ulster: the northernmost of the ancient provinces of Ireland, now virtually synonymous with Northern Ireland. Coined by Lord Randolph Churchill (1849–94), opponent of Gladstone and Irish Home Rule, in a letter of 7 May 1886; the phrase became a slogan of the pro-Protestant, anti-Home Rule campaigners.

36.13 *she never let them in*: Irish history includes the presence of Jewish residents from the 11th c., though they were expelled from Ireland (as from England) in 1290. Under Cromwell (1650s), they were resettled in both countries. In 1904 there were, according to census, 3,898 Jews in Ireland. (*G*)

PROTEUS

Location: Sandymount Strand (a beach on Dublin Bay, south of the mouth of the River Liffey (Map: I6)). A breakwater, the Pigeon House, extends the south bank of the Liffey out into Dublin Bay.

Time: 11 a.m.

Homer: Telemachus arrives at Menelaus's court during the wedding feast of Menelaus's son, Megapenthes, born to him by a slave girl outside the walls of Troy. Menelaus narrates his return home from the Trojan War. Having neglected the rules of sacrifice, he was punished by the gods by being waylaid on the island of Pharos. Having taken pity on him, Eidothea, daughter of Proteus 'the ancient sea-god', told him her father possessed the gift of prophecy but that he must be held fast before he will speak. If caught, he will both foretell the future and recount what has happened at home in Menelaus's absence. As Proteus can assume 'the shape of every creature that moves on earth, and of water and of portentous fire' (44), catching him is difficult. Eidothea revealed to Menelaus the secrets of how to both find and hold him. Using them, Menelaus captured Proteus who then told him how to break the spell holding him to the island and recounted the deaths of Ajax and Agamemnon. Most relevantly for Telemachus, Proteus told Menelaus that Odysseus was being held on Calypso's island. Meanwhile, back in Ithaca, the suitors have set sail in pursuit of Telemachus with the intention of killing him when they find him. (Book IV)

Schemata: *L* and *G* both list the personae as Proteus, Menelaus, and Megapenthes (to which *L* adds Telemachus and Helen). *G* provides the correspondences: Primal Matter is Proteus; Kevin Egan, Menelaus; the cocklepicker, Megapenthes. The intended correspondent of *L*'s Helen remains unclear.

L and *G* agree only on the Art (Philology) and Organ (none) of the episode. They differ on Colour (*L*: blue; *G*: brown), Technic (*L*: Soliloquy; *G*: Monologue (Male)), Symbol (*L*: Word, Tide, Moon, Evolution, Metamorphosis; *G*: Tide). *L* gives as Sense, 'Primal Matter (πρωτευσ)'.

'Ineluctable'—that from which one cannot escape even by struggling—fittingly opens *Proteus*, the episode named after the endlessly mutating sea god forced into fixed form by the 'ineluctable' Menelaus. Fixity and flux, space and time, actuality and imagination: these are the twin poles between which *Proteus* moves. Stephen, after Aristotle, regards the material world—space—as 'what you damn well have to see' (178). But Aristotle regarded vision as the action of the eyes in concert with the mind, and sight and thought interweave with one another as Stephen transforms the material world around him through mental acts of speculation. Here Stephen plays simultaneously the parts of speculator and spectator (both of which have their roots in the Latin *specere*: 'see, look'). One problem for the reader comes in trying to sort out when he is playing which. For, with only a handful of sentences excepted, the narrative proceeds through Stephen's interior monologue; thus, what we see depends entirely on what he thinks and this in turn is prompted by what he sees.

As he walks, thinks, sits, writes a poem, pisses, and picks his nose, Stephen observes two midwives, the sea, sand, boulders, a man and a woman cocklepicking, a dead dog, a live dog, his shadow, Cock lake, no black clouds, and a ship. His thoughts are more active and carry him back to fourteenth-century Dublin, sixteenth-century Denmark, seventeenth-century London; to the words of heretics, philosophers, Renaissance writers; to memories of visits to his aunt Sara's, of sighting a woman outside Hodges Figgis bookstore, of conversations with the wild goose Kevin Egan, of his own adolescent writerly pretensions, of an early morning dream; to imagined sightings of drowned corpses and imagined enactments of the role of Hamlet and Actaeon (in his stag form). Matter, space, time, all mutate in response to Stephen's thoughts.

While Stephen likes looking and freely transforming the spectacle in his mind, he is himself frequently anxious that he might be seen: 'Who watches me here?'; 'Can't see! who's behind me?' For he is much happier as spectator than as spectacle, and his transformations of matter, derived as they are from his acts of seeing, place him in the position of power as the subject, not the object, of the gaze. In his early experiment ('Shut your eyes and see') Stephen attempts to determine whether space is dependent on his perceiving it. His admission that the world exists 'there all the time without you' ('without': both 'independently of' and 'outside') corresponds to his earlier thoughts (in *Nestor*) that historical figures and events are not to be 'thought away'.

Still, he unhappily inhabits the position of object just as he persistently resents his existence as matter. Note how he identifies himself with his father's voice, his ended shadow, Aristotle's 'soul . . . form of forms'—all insubstantial entities. Just so, the '*lex eterna* . . . wherein Father and Son are consubstantial'. Matter means mortality, a body which can become 'a bag of corpsegas' through whose 'buttoned trouserfly' minnows may flit and grow fat in eating 'a spongy titbit'. However much Stephen accepts the material existence of the world and its cycles of birth and death, he prefers the regeneration more easily accomplished in the artist's imagination. But as Stephen Dogsbody (as Mulligan has named him) speculates, live dog 'moves to one great goal . . . poor dogsbody's body'. That much is ineluctable.

37.1 *Ineluctable modality of the visible . . . my eyes*: in 'plain English', the phrase means 'the inescapable nature of that which can be seen'. The exact phrase has not been located, but it probably comes from Joyce's translation of the French Aristotle (see 26.4n.). In both *De Sensu et Sensibili* and *De Anima* (II–III), Aristotle considers how individuals perceive the material world (through the action of the senses in concert with the intellect). Each sense perceives particularly by means of the sensible qualities of the bodies perceived: hearing through sound; taste through savour; smell through odour; touch through weight, temperature, hardness/softness. Sight (in concert with the mind) perceives through colour which lies at the boundary of determined bodies. So, Stephen is contemplating (through Aristotle) the inescapability of the material world, and, in particular, that aspect of it which is perceptible through the sense of sight.

37.2 *Signatures of all . . . to read*: the phrase derives from Jakob Boehme (1575–1624), *Signatura Rerum* (Latin: 'Signature of all Things'), but, in context, Stephen remarks his role as the perceiver of the characteristic forms of nature. Because perception results from the action of the senses (here the eyes) in concert with the mind (thought), the world becomes real *to Stephen* as he 'reads' (sees/thinks) it—though the emphasis is on his being there to perceive it, not on its being there to be perceived by him. The world exists before him (there must be a text to be read), but comes alive *to him* in the act of 'reading' it.

37.3 *coloured signs*: 'coloured' because, after Aristotle, colour is what allows determined non-transparent bodies to be seen.

37.4 *Limits of the diaphane . . . in bodies*: Joyce from the French Aristotle: 'Colour is the limit of the diaphane in any determined body' (Aristotle, *De Sensu et Sensibilia*, III (439b11); Peterson, 214; Aubert, 134). 'Diaphane': the transparent. (See 37.1–2 n.)

37.5 *By knocking his sconce against them*: if Aristotle knew they were bodies before he formulated a theory of how he perceived them visually, how so? Because he bumped his head against them.

37.6 *Bald he was and a millionaire*: traditional stories about Aristotle.

37.6 *maestro di color che sanno*: Italian: 'master of those that know'; from Dante's description of Aristotle in the *Inferno*, IV. 131.

37.7 *adiaphane*: the non-transparent or opaque.

37.13, 15 *nacheinander, nebeneinander*: German: *nacheinander*: one after another, successively; *nebeneinander*: next to one another, adjacent. Stephen distinguishes the two terms as being, respectively, the distinctive characteristic of time (one thing after another) and of space (things next to one another). He also links the audible with time (and *nacheinander*) and the visible with space (and *nebeneinander*). Fritz Senn suggests that the distinction follows Gotthold Lessing's (1729–81) characterization (in *Laocoön* (1766)) of the difference between the objects appropriate to poetry (those which occur *nacheinander*, in succession, in time) and those appropriate to painting (those which occur *nebeneinander*, in coexistence, in space) (*JJQ* 2 (Winter 1965), 134–6).

37.17 *made by the mallet of Los Demiurgos*: William Blake, 'The Book of Los' (1795); 'Los, the creator' embodies creative imagination. In Blake's *Milton* (1804–8), he writes: 'For every Space larger than a red Globule of Man's blood | Is visionary, and is created by the Hammer of Los' (Bk. I, plate 29, ll. 19–20), a line paraphrased by Joyce in his lecture on Blake (1912) (*CW* 222); hence Stephen puns (silently) on 'visionary' and 'visible': Los created the visible world. 'Demiurgos': the demiurge (from Platonic, Neoplatonic, and Gnostic philosophies), a subordinate god, creator of the physical world (*T*).

37.19 *Dominic Deasy kens them a'*: 'Dominic' should read 'Dominie': Scots: 'teacher'; 'kens': 'knows'; but also a pun on the Latin *Dominus Deus*: 'Lord God'.

37.22 *A catalectic*: see ERRATA for discussion of whether this should be 'A catelectic' or 'Acatalectic'. 'Catalectic': 'poetic metrics—lacking either a syllable in the last foot, or an initial unstressed syllable'; 'Acatalectic': 'not catalectic, so complete in its syllables'. If Stephen is right and these lines are iambic (only the first would be tetrameter), then they would be 'catalectic'—missing the first unstressed syllable. (David Hayman cites an unpublished letter from Joyce to Harriet Weaver of 3 November 1922 with a postscript: 'divide better A catalectic' ('What the Unpublished Letters can Tell Us: or, Is Anyone Watching', *Studies in the Novel*, 22/2 (Summer 1990), 187–8). That ought to settle the matter.)

38.3–4 *and ever shall be, world without end*: see 29.29 n.

38.13–14 *Will you be as gods?*: Satan to Eve (Gen. 3: 5): 'For God doth know that in the day ye eat thereof, then your eyes shall be opened, and ye shall be as gods, knowing good and evil'.

38.15 *Aleph, alpha*: Hebrew and Greek, respectively, for the first letter of the alphabet.

38.16 *Adam Kadmon*: Theosophical name for prelapsarian human: complete, androgynous, and unfallen.

38.16 *Heva, naked Eve*: 'Heva': from the Hebrew *Cheva*: 'Life'; an early name for Eve.

38.20 *made not begotten*: reversal of the Nicene Creed which states that Christ was 'begotten, but not made', a phrase intended to refute the Arian heresy by asserting the consubstantiality of God the Father and Christ; by reversing the phrase, Stephen admits his humanity and mortality.

38.23 *lex eterna*: Latin: 'eternal law'. In the *Summa Theologica*, Aquinas discusses the implications of the fact that God's law is eternal. As God is eternal, all things exist in Him; thus, things which have not yet come about (in human time) nevertheless already exist in God; therefore he knows what will be and it may appear from the human perspective that he ordains or summons future things (Part I(II), question XCI, art. 1, 'Varieties of Law').

38.24–5 *divine substance . . . consubstantial?*: Stephen seems to suggest that Father and Son are consubstantial only in their sharing of an eternal law. See 199.9 n.

38.25 *Arius*: see 21.1 n. According to tradition, Arius did die of 'hemorrhage of the bowels' in a public toilet on the eve of his being reinstated into the Church.

38.31–2 *the steeds of Mananaan*: Mananaan MacLir (Gaelic: *Manannán Mac Lir*) is the Irish god of the sea, the waves the manes of his horses. He shares Proteus's ability to change form.

39.16 *—Morrow, nephew.*: should read '—Morrow, nephew. Sit down and take a walk.'

39.19 *Duces Tecum*: Latin: 'Bring with you'; legal writ demanding that person appear in court with a specified piece of evidence.

39.20 *Wilde's Requiescat*: Latin: 'Let her rest'; Wilde's poem (1881) on the death of his sister.

39.35–6 *All'erta . . . aria di sortita*: Italian: 'On guard!'; opening words of the opening aria (Ferrando's *aria di sortita*: 'entrance aria') in Giuseppe Verdi's (1813–1901) opera *Il Trovatore* (1852).

40.6 *Marsh's library*: St Sepulchre Library, St Patrick's Cathedral, Dublin, founded

(1707) by Narcissus Marsh, Church of Ireland archbishop; oldest public library in Ireland.

40.7 *Joachim Abbas*: Father Joachim of Floris (*c.*1145–1202), Italian mystic theologian, divided history into three ages corresponding to the three members of the Trinity.

40.8–10 *A hater of his kind . . . Houyhnhnm*: Jonathan Swift (1667–1745), dean of St Patrick's Cathedral from 1713; widely believed to hate mankind, he suffered from Ménière's disease, increasing deafness, and finally premature senility. The Houyhnhnms were the utterly rational horses met by the eponymous hero of *Gulliver's Travels* (1726). The 'furious dean' (40.11) is obviously Swift.

40.11 *Foxy Campbell, Lantern jaws*: nicknames for Stephen's teacher, Father Campbell, at Belvedere college (*Portrait*, ch. 4, p. 161).

40.12 *Descende, calve . . . decalveris*: Latin: 'Come down, bald one, lest you be made balder'; allusion to 2 Kgs. 2: 23 (children's taunt to Elisha) by way of Joyce's reading of (spuriously attributed) Joachim Abbas text in Marsh's Library. (See Adams, 125–6.)

40.13 *comminated*: 'threatened'.

40.17 *fat of the kidneys of wheat*: bread, from Deut. 32: 12–14 where Moses celebrates Jacob's blessedness.

40.21–2 *Dan Occam . . . hypostasis tickled his brain*: William of Occam (*c.*1285–1389), philosopher and theologian, who argued that the body of Christ was not present in the host in quality or quantity, but merely in 'faith', thus there is only one body of Christ no matter how many celebrations of the eucharist take place simultaneously. 'Hypostasis': the whole person of Christ combining human and divine natures (*OEED*).

40.26 *Cousin Stephen . . . saint*: after comment on Swift by John Dryden (1631–1700): 'Cousin Swift, you will never be a poet'.

40.26 *Isle of saints*: medieval name for Ireland: *Insula Sanctorum* (Latin).

41.2 *epiphanies*: Stephen defines 'epiphany' in *Stephen Hero* (188): 'a sudden spiritual manifestation' of the essence of a thing; from the Feast of Epiphany (6 Jan.), the celebration of the showing forth to the Magi of the body of God in the form of the infant Jesus. (For Joyce's own epiphanies, see *PSW* 161–200.)

41.3 *Alexandria*: greatest library of the ancient world, first severely damaged (47 BC) then completely destroyed by fire (AD 641).

41.4 *mahamanvantara*: Hindu: 'great year'; large span of time (*c.*4 billion years).

41.4–5 *Pico della Mirandola*: (1463–94), Italian Renaissance humanist, philosopher, scholar who attempted to blend Christian theology with cabbalistic and pre-Christian philosophy.

41.5 *Ay, very like a whale*: Polonius in agreement with Hamlet about the shape of a cloud (*Hamlet*, III. ii. 382).

41.5–6 *When one reads . . . once*: parody of (possibly) Walter Pater (1839–94), particularly his essay 'Pico della Mirandola' in *The Renaissance* (1873).

41.8–9 *that on the unnumbered pebbles beats*: Edgar to Gloucester (to, falsely, convince him of the nearness of the sea) in *King Lear*, IV. vi. 21.

41.9–10 *Unwholesome sandflats . . . sewage breath*: true enough; the River Liffey, which emptied into Dublin Bay (and the sandflats of Sandymount), carried untreated sewage.

41.10 *breath. He*: should read 'breath, a pocket of seaweed smouldered in seafire under a midden of man's ashes. He'.

41.18 *Pigeonhouse*: formerly a fort, now the electricity power station on the breakwater which extends into Dublin Bay.

41.19–20 *Qui vous a mis . . . le pigeon*: French: 'Who has put you in this wretched position?' 'It's the pigeon, Joseph.' From Léo Taxil's *La Vie de Jésus* (1884). Taxil was the pseudonym of Gabriel Jogand-Pages (1854–1907), who wrote several such comically blasphemous volumes. (See 41.25.)

41.21–2 *Patrice . . . Son of the wild goose, Kevin Egan*: 'wild geese': Irish expatriates; initially those who, having supported the losing Stuart cause in the battle against William III, chose exile rather than English rule. The portrait of Kevin Egan resembles that of John Casey, Fenian imprisoned for his part in the (1867) rescue of two Fenians from a police van in Manchester; he was in Clerkenwell Prison when the Fenians used dynamite (killing twelve Londoners) in an attempt to destroy the wall and rescue those inside.

41.25 *Michelet*: Jules Michelet (1798–1874), French historian, and author of *La Femme* (1860), a romantic 'history' of woman.

41.27–30 *C'est . . . oui*: 'It's a scream, you know. Myself, I'm a socialist. I don't believe in the existence of God. Don't tell my father.' 'He believes?' 'My father? yes.'

41.31 *Schluss*: German: 'Enough!'

41.35 *mou en civet*: very cheap stew.

41.35 *fleshpots of Egypt*: in Exod. 16: 2–3, the children of Israel complain of Moses's leading them into the wilderness and long to return to 'Egypt when we sat by the flesh pots, and when we did eat bread to the full'.

42.3 *Lui, c'est moi*: French: 'I am he.'

42.13 *Columbanus. Fiacre and Scotus*: for Columbanus, see 28.11 n. All three were Irish missionaries to the Continent: St Fiacre, a 7th-c. saint; Scotus, John Duns Scotus (1266–1308), a Scholastic.

42.18 *Mother dying*: should read 'Nother dying' (hence 'a curiosity to show').

43.4–5 *Il est Irlandais . . . oui!*: French: 'He is Irish'. 'Dutch?' 'Not cheese. Two Irishmen, we, Ireland, you understand?' 'Oh yes!'

43.8 *slainte!*: Gaelic: *sláinte*: 'health' (a toast).

43.11 *Dalcassians*: from the Gaelic: *Dál gCais*: 'Race of *Cas* ("Twist"); clan of which Brian Boru (see 96.9 n.) was chief; family in the Munster dynasty.

43.11–12 *Arthur Griffith*: (1872–1922), Irish nationalist, founder of Sinn Féin (see 7.31 n.), the Celtic Literary Society, and the *United Irishman* (nationalist newspaper), and first president of the Irish Free State (1922).

43.12 *now. To*: should read 'now, AE, pimander, good shepherd of me. To'.

43.13 *You're your father's son ... voice*: allusion to the oft-remarked similarity between Telemachus's and Odysseus's voices, as well as to Jacob's duping his father Isaac into believing he is his elder brother Esau so that he receives Esau's birthright (Gen. 27). (See 203.8 and n.)

43.14 *M. Drumont*: Edouard Adolphe Drumont (1844–1917), French journalist, editor of *La Libre Parole*, a virulently anti-Semitic newspaper.

43.16 *Vieille ogresse ... dents jaunes*: French: 'Old ogresse ... yellow teeth'.

43.16 *Maud Gonne*: (1866–1953), Irish nationalist, famed beauty, beloved of Yeats, refugee to Paris.

43.16–17 *La Patrie, M. Millevoye*: French newspaper edited by Lucien Millevoye (1850–1918), lover of Maud Gonne and father of her daughter, Iseult.

43.17 *Félix Faure*: (1841–99), president of the French Republic (1895–9), died of a cerebral haemorrhage rumoured to have been brought about by sexual excess.

43.25 *peep of day boy*: Late 18th-c. Ulster Protestants (later joined with the Orangemen) who raided Catholics' homes at 'peep o' day'.

43.25 *How the head centre got away*: James Stephens, the Head Centre of the Irish Republican Brotherhood (see 31.23 n.), was arrested and imprisoned in Richmond Jail (1865), later escaped, remained hidden in Dublin until Apr. 1866 when he fled to America. Rumour had it that he disguised himself in women's clothing to effect his escape.

43.27 *Of lost leaders ...* : Robert Browning (1812–89), 'The Lost Leader' (1845), in which he laments the once radical Wordsworth's increasing conservatism on being made Poet Laureate in 1843.

43.29 *gossoon*: Gaelic: *garsún*: 'boy', 'lad'.

43.31 *colonel Richard Burke*: American Fenian, effected Manchester rescue of two Fenian leaders, one of those (with Casey) meant to be freed by the Clerkenwell attempt (see 41.21–2 n.).

43.31 *tanist of his sept*: 'sept': ancient Irish tribe; 'tanist': Gaelic: *tánaiste*: 'second-in-command, heir presumptive', more generally, 'leader'.

44.5 *saint Canice, Strongbow's castle*: St Canice (or Kenny) (6th c.) gave his name to Kilkenny ('kil': church). Richard de Clare, called 'Strongbow' (d. 1176), MacMurrough's successor as King of Leinster, successful in the Anglo-Norman invasion in 1169. His castle is in Kilkenny.

44.6 *O, O. He takes me ... hand*: from 'The Wearing of the Green', anonymous Irish ballad from the late 18th c. (as adapted by Dion Boucicault: see 160.2 n.), which laments that in Ireland 'They're hanging men and women ... for wearin' of the green'. James Napper Tandy (1740–1803), revolutionary, founder of United Irishmen, supporter of French Revolution.

44.10 *Remembering thee, O Sion*: lament of the dispersed Jews for their homeland.

44.31–2 *Un coche ensablé ... prose*: French: 'A coach stuck in the sand'. French journalist Louis Veuillot's (1813–83) description of Théophile Gautier's (1811–

72) prose style. Veuillot was an ardent supporter of the Church; Gautier a romantic poet, critic, and novelist.

44.34 *Sir Lout's toys*: perhaps Joyce's creation, a prehistoric giant, sexually weak according to Joyce, who had rocks in his mouth instead of teeth (see Budgen, 52).

45.6 *The two maries*: Mary Magdalene and Mary the mother of James and Joses, the two who see Christ risen.

45.9 *Lochlanns*: Gaelic: '"Lake-Place", Scandinavia or Scandinavians'; name for the 8th-c. Norwegian invaders of Ireland.

45.11 *when Malachi wore the collar of gold*: from Thomas Moore's (1779–1852) 'Let Erin Remember the Days of Old'. Malachi II (948–1022), High King of Ireland, who with Brian Boroimhe (see 96.9n.) helped to free Ireland from the Norse invaders; Malachi took the collar as prize from a defeated Dane.

45.12 *school of turlehide whales*: in 1331, during a famine, a school of whales beached themselves on the shores of Dublin Bay; the Dubliners killed and ate them.

45.15 *Famine, plague and slaughters*: 14th-c. Dublin saw all three: the famine mentioned above, the visitation of the Black Plague (1348), and the slaughters of the Bruce invasion (1314–18) (see 45.21–4n.).

45.16 *the frozen Liffey*: in the winter of 1338–9, the Liffey froze so solidly that the people could light fires on it.

45.19 *stood pale, silent, bayed about*: Stephen as Actaeon who, having spied on Diana bathing, was turned into a stag hunted by his own dogs. See too 'A Portrait' (1904) (*PSW* 212) and 'The Holy Office' (1904), ll. 83–8 (*PSW* 99), where Joyce uses the image of the disdainful stag flashing his antlers at the rabble.

45.19 *Terribilia meditans*: Latin: 'meditating on terrible things'.

45.21–4 *The Bruce's brother . . . Paradise of pretenders*: all made attempts to claim either the Irish or the English throne: 'The Bruce's brother': Edward Bruce (d. 1318), brother of Robert Bruce who freed Scotland from the English at Bannockburn in 1314 after which Edward invaded Ireland and attempted to establish himself as king—slain by the Irish; 'Thomas Fitzgerald': Lord Thomas Fitzgerald (1513–37), tenth earl of Kildare ('silken' because his followers wore tokens of silk), raised a rebellion against Henry VIII, defeated and executed at Tyburn; 'Perkin Warbeck': (1474–99), a commoner and Yorkist pretender to the throne by claiming to be Richard, Duke of York, son of Edward IV (and one of the two young princes supposedly murdered by Richard III), supported by the Anglo-Irish lords of Ireland—eventually executed at Tyburn; 'Lambert Simnel': (*c.*1475–1525), son of an Irish baker, trained by Yorkists to impersonate the Earl of Warwick in attempt to overthrow Henry VII, crowned in Dublin (1487) as Edward VI, invaded England, captured and used by Henry as scullion in his kitchens. 'Paradise of pretenders': Ireland's history of oppression made it all too ready to entertain the ambitions of those who would challenge the English monarchy.

45.26–7 *But the courtiers . . . House of . . .* : Guido Cavalcanti (*c.* 1250–1300), Italian poet; this story is told in Boccaccio's (1313–75) *Decameron* (1349–51), Day VI, Tale 9: Guido, while walking among the tombs in a church in Or' San Michele, is mocked by his friends for brooding. He responds by saying they can mock as they will in their house—one friend realizes he means the House of Death (which Stephen too avoids saying).

46.6–7 *On a field tenney . . . unattired*: the dog on the beach becomes a heraldic device; in plain English: a stag without antlers in natural colours, walking, displayed against a tawny background.

46.31–2 *a pard, a panther, got in spousebreach*: 'spousebreach': adultery; according to one bestiary tradition, the leopard (or panther) is born of 'spousebreach' between a lioness and a pard (for 'pard', see 209.21 n.; see also *T*).

46.34 *Haroun al Raschid*: (763–809), caliph of Baghdad, known for the splendour of his court and for his appearance in several of the tales of the *Arabian Nights*; he supposedly disguised himself to walk unnoticed among his people.

47.4 *mort*: 16th–17th-c. cant for 'woman'; first allusion to 17th-c. canting song 'The Rogue's Delight in Praise of his Mort' (printed in Richard Head's *The Canting Academy* (1673); repr. in *G*).

47.6 *bing . . . Romeville*: 16th–17th-c. cant: 'Go away to London' (first line of seventh stanza of 'Rogue's Delight'; see 47.4 n.).

47.8–9 *wap in . . . dell*: 16th–17th-c. cant: 'Make love in rogue's fine talk, for O, my pretty loving wench' ('O . . . dell': second line of seventh stanza of 'Rogue's Delight'; see 47.4 n.).

47.11–14 *White thy fambles . . . kiss*: 16th–17th-c. cant: 'White thy hands, red thy mouth, | and thy body dainty is. | Lie down to sleep with me then, | In the night embrace and kiss' (second stanza of 'Rogue's Delight'; see 47.4 n.).

47.15 *Morose delectation*: Aquinas in *Summa Theologica* (Part I(II), question XXXI, art. 2; question LXXIV, art. 6; and question LXXXIII, art. 5): *Delectatio morosa*, an internal sin, taking pleasure in sinful thoughts (*T*).

47.15 *frate porcospino*: Italian: 'Brother Porcupine', Aquinas, whose thought is prickly.

47.21–2 *Across the sands . . . lands*: perhaps a free allusion to Percy Bysshe Shelley's (1792–1822) *Hellas* (1821), ll. 1023–49 (*G*); an allusion, too, to the flaming sword that God placed outside the Garden of Eden after evicting Adam and Eve (Gen. 3: 24).

47.22 *She trudges . . . trascines her load*: 'She' is Eve (see Gen. 3: 16); the verbs are all synonyms with different linguistic origins.

47.25 *Behold . . . moon*: adaptation of Luke 1: 38: (of Mary) 'Behold the handmaid of the Lord'.

47.26–7: *Omnis caro ad te veniet*: Latin: 'All flesh will come to thee', from Ps. 65: 2: 'O thou that hearest prayer, unto thee shall all flesh come'; part of the Introit of the requiem mass.

47.27–8 *He comes . . . kiss*: Stephen's 'poem' is a freely borrowed, free adaptation of

'My Grief on the Sea', Gaelic poem translated by Douglas Hyde (see 299.3–4 n.) in his *Love Songs of Connacht* (1893); the last stanza: 'And my love came behind me— | He came from the South; | His breast to my bosom, | His mouth to my mouth'.

47.31–2 *her womb. Oomb,*: should read 'her moomb. Oomb,'.

48.5 *delta of Cassiopeia*: a 'delta' is a star of relatively low magnitude: Cassiopeia is the constellation resembling a W turned on its side in the northern skies, the delta being the star at the bottom of the first stroke in the W.

48.5–6 *augur's rod of ash*: in Ancient Roman culture, an augur was a soothsayer or diviner who sought knowledge through the observation of the flight and cries of birds; his sign of office: the *lituus*, the rod or staff with which he marked out the portion of sky where the birds' omens were to be 'read'. (Cf. *Portrait*, ch. 5, p. 224.) Stephen's 'augur's rod' is his ashplant (see 17.15), a walking staff made from an ash sapling.

48.9–10 *Who ever anywhere . . . words?*: answer: see 363.28–9.

48.11 *bishop of Cloyne*: George Berkeley (1685–1753), philosopher, Church of Ireland bishop of Cloyne, idealist philosopher.

48.11–14 *the veil of the temple . . . frozen in stereoscope*: Berkeley argued that reality itself is mental—things do not exist, ideas alone exist—so Berkeley found reality inside his own head. The 'veil of the temple' (see Exod. 26: 31–5) separates the 'holy place' from the 'most holy' place, perhaps an indication that Berkeley goes beyond idealist philosophy to super-idealism in making all reality mental. The rest of the passage follows Berkeley's experiments with vision (in *Essay Towards a New Theory of Vision* (1709)): we can't see without the mind, what we see we see as flat, distance is thought not seen; the veil, like a screen, is like the visible world upon which God projects signs (or ideas) to be read and thought; we think them into 'stereoscope'.

48.28 *What is that word known to all men?*: Stephen returns to the question in *Circe* (540.14). In the *Rosenbach Manuscript* (*RM*) holograph of *Scylla and Charybdis*, Stephen knew the answer: 'Love, yes. Word known to all men' (*RM*, *S&C*, fol. 13). The 1984 *Ulysses* reinstates the phrase there (see 188.3 n.).

48.32–3 *Et vidit . . . bona*: Latin: (from Gen. 1: 31) 'And God saw [every thing that he had made,] and, [behold,] it was very good'.

48.33–7 *Under its leaf . . . Pain is far*: an improvisation on Stéphane Mallarmé's (1842–98) 'L'Après-midi d'un faune' (1876–7). Noon is both Pan's hour (the Greek nature god's most active time) and the hour of Proteus's downfall (the time when, readying himself for sleep, he is caught by Menelaus).

49.4 *tripudium*: Latin: 'a triple beat', but also a dance.

49.6–7 *Wilde's love that dare not speak its name*: the phrase appears in 'Two Loves', a poem by Lord Alfred Douglas (1870–1945), friend of Oscar Wilde: 'I am the Love that dare not speak its name'. In his trial for 'indecency and sodomy', Wilde declared that 'The "Love that dare not speak its name" in this century is such a great affection of an elder for a younger man as there was between David and Jonathan' (qtd. in Richard Ellmann, *Oscar Wilde* (London: Hamish Hamilton, 1987), 435).

49.7 *name. He*: should read 'name. His arm: Cranly's arm. He'; see 7.15 n.

49.20–2 *Saint Ambrose; diebus ac noctibus ... ingemiscit*: St Ambrose (*c.*340–97), bishop of Milan, one of the four Doctors of the Western Church, in his *Commentary on Romans*: Latin: 'Days and nights [the Creation] groans over wrongs' (on Rom. 8: 22).

49.26 *Full fathom five thy father lies*: opening of Ariel's song in *The Tempest*, I. ii. 397.

49.32–3 *God becomes man ... featherbed mountain*: the protean, ever-changing, transformation of matter. 'Featherbed mountain': a mountain south of Dublin. See, too, Hamlet tracing the movement of Alexander's noble dust (*Hamlet*, v. i. 207 ff.).

50.4 *Allbright he falls... occasum*: 'Lucifer' means 'light-bringing' in Latin; in pride of intellect he refused to serve God and so fell; the phrase in Latin: 'The morning star, I say, that [or who] knows no setting'. See *Portrait*, ch. 3, p. 117.

50.5 *My cockle hat... hismy sandal shoon*: Ophelia's song in *Hamlet*, IV. v. 23 ff.: 'How should I your true-love know | From another one? | By his cockle hat and staff, | And his sandal shoon'.

50.9–10 *Of all the glad new year, mother*: from Alfred, Lord Tennyson's (1809–92) 'The May Queen' (1833), l. 3.

50.10 *Lawn Tennyson*: Lord Tennyson, genteel gentleman poet in Stephen's opinion.

CALYPSO

Location: 7 Eccles Street, home of Leopold and Molly Bloom, and close environs, a middle-class neighbourhood in north-east Dublin (Map: E2–3).

Time: 8 a.m.

Homer: At a council of the gods, Athena complains that Odysseus is still being held by Calypso, the nymph, while the suitors are in pursuit of Telemachus. Zeus tells Athena to send word to Telemachus to return home, while he sends Hermes to instruct Calypso to release Odysseus. Hermes finds Calypso weaving at her loom. On hearing Hermes' message, Calypso agrees not only to let Odysseus go, but to give him best advice on how to reach home unscathed. Odysseus, who is found weeping by the shore, admits to having slept with Calypso, but unwillingly: 'she was loving and he unloving' (58). Suspicious of Calypso's decision to release him, Odysseus ('cunning' and 'no innocent') extracts from her an oath that she will do him no more harm. Then he leaves for Phaecia (or 'Scheria'). Poseidon, whose ire was the cause of Odysseus's detention, responds to his release with fury, sending a storm to drown him. Leucothea ('slender ankled' sea-goddess) intercedes to help Odysseus, but he still nearly drowns before Athena strengthens him. He survives to land on Scheria. (Book V)

Schemata: *L* lists as personae Calypso (Penelope Wife), Ulysses, and Callidike, while *G* provides different correspondences: Calypso is the Nymph; Dlugascz, The Recall; Zion, Ithaca. Callidike (not mentioned in the *Odyssey* but rather in a (now lost) post-Homeric epic *The Telegonia*) was the queen of Threspotia who married Odysseus when he left Ithaca for further adventures. As to 'Penelope Wife' (see 'Penelope (Mother)' under *Telemachus*), Joyce clearly thought of Penelope as having human as well as pre- and post-human aspects. The latter are reserved for the final episode, *Penelope*, the former takes various forms as he makes plain in a letter to Harriet Weaver: '[In *Penelope*] I have rejected the usual interpretation of her as a human apparition—that aspect being better represented by Calypso, Nausikaa and Circe' (*LI* 180).

L and *G* agree on the Organ (Kidney) and Colour (orange) but disagree on all else: Art (*L*: Mythology; *G*: Economics), Technic (*L*: 'Dialogue for 2, Soliloquy'; *G*: Narrative (mature)), Symbol (*L*: Vagina, Exile, Kin, Nymph, Israel in Captivity; *G*: Nymph). Further, *L* gives as the Sense, 'The Departing Wayfarer'.

Mr Leopold Bloom opens *Calypso* eating and closes it excreting. His is most obviously a bodied text, a corpus. He is corporeal man to Stephen Dedalus's mental man (note that neither Linati nor Gilbert assign Telemachus bodily organs). Where Stephen *metaphorically* 'devour[s] a urinous offal from all dead' (49), Bloom *literally* ingests 'the inner organs of beasts and fowls' and likes most 'grilled mutton kidneys which gave to his palate a fine tang of faintly scented urine'. Etymologically, 'offal' concerns things that have 'fallen off' (animal bits more usually thrown away) and Bloom's preference for it harmonizes with his habit of tidying rooms (picking up Molly's strewn undergarments, fetching her book from under the bed), his endless attempts to retrieve factual knowledge which has slipped away ('Black conducts, reflects (refracts is it?)'; 'whatdoyoucallhim'), his acceptance, even appreciation, of excrement ('flop and fall of dung', 'manure the whole place over', 'Dirty cleans'). His defecation completes a libidinal rhythm introduced with his earlier ingestion (complementary expulsion to his earlier introjection in somatic rhythm of primary impulses). Not surprisingly, it stimulates (and is prompted by) simultaneous acts of reading and (imagined) writing, for creation for Bloom is never far removed from the body, just as the body (and its correlate the mundane physical world) obtrudes whenever Bloom is around.

In keeping with this somatizing of the text, *Calypso* repeats *Telemachus*—with a difference. We meet again a tower, a feline creature, green gems, a deliverer of milk. There they became in turn *omphalos*, nightmarish panther, Ireland itself, Mother Ireland (a symbol of a symbol). Here they cling tenaciously to banality: Bloom is the height of a *tower* to the *cat* which has eyes like *green gems* and laps milk brought by *Hanlon's milkman.* There Stephen's penchant for metaphor urged narrative transformation of mundane objects into symbols, here Bloom's solid pragmatic presence seems to cause every attempt at metaphor to founder on mundane physicality: 'Mr Leopold Bloom ate with relish' (that 'relish' is as much 'condiment' as 'gusto'). In *Calypso*, 'Kidneys were in his mind' (where 'mind' is as much 'organic brain' as 'thoughts') is perhaps Bloom's most fitting motto.

54.32 *Gibraltar*: another colonial city: on the tip of the Iberian peninsula, gateway to the Mediterranean, captured by the English in 1704; Molly Bloom's birthplace; her father, Major Brian Tweedy, served there with the Royal Dublin Fusiliers.

54.35 *Plevna*: site of famous siege during the Russo-Turkish War (1877–8) which the Turks ultimately lost to the Russians; as the English remained neutral, Tweedy would not, in fact, have been there, though he may have been in fiction.

55.25 *sherbert. Wander along*: should read 'sherbert. Dander along'.

55.32–3 *in the track of the sun*: a book of this title is on Bloom's bookshelf (672.1–2), probably Frederick Diodati Thompson, *In the Track of the Sun* (1893), an account of a round-the-world trip, focusing especially on his travels in the Orient.

55.33–5 *What Arthur Griffith . . . Ireland*: the headpiece of *The Freeman's Journal*, a Dublin moderately pro-Home Rule newspaper, depicts a sunburst behind the Bank of Ireland above the motto 'Ireland a Nation' (given the location of the Bank, the sun would be rising in the north-west); the building which housed the Bank housed the Irish Parliament before the Act of Union.

56.12–13 *the Russians . . . Japanese*: one of the few references to contemporary world events in *Ulysses*: the Russo-Japanese War (Feb. 1904–Sept. 1905) which was currently being waged.

56.22 *country Leitrim*: should read 'county Leitrim'.

56.33 *Inishturk, Inishark, Inishboffin*: Gaelic: *Inis Tuirc* ('Boar's Island'), *Inis Eirc* ('Ox's Island'), *Inis Bó Finn* ('White Cow's Island'): small islands off the west coast of Ireland.

56.34 *Slieve Bloom*: mountain range in central Ireland ('Slieve': Gaelic: *sliabh*: mountain).

56.36 *white. Fifty multiplied*: should read 'white. Fifteen multiplied'.

57.11–12 *model farm at Kinnereth . . . Tiberias*: 'Kinneret': small town on south-west shore of Lake Tiberias (the Sea of Galilee); the 'model farm' actually existed.

57.14 *Moses Montefiore*: Sir Moses Haim Montefiore (1784–1885), an early Zionist and wealthy English philanthropist who used his wealth to secure Jewish emancipation in England.

58.11 *Agendath Netaim*: Hebrew: 'a company of planters'.

58.12 *Turkish government*: Palestine was part of the Turkish empire (from 1516 until after the First World War); the government looked favourably on Jewish settlement by the means Bloom describes.

58.14 *pay eight marks*: should read 'pay eighty marks'.

58.30 *Must be without a flaw*: technically, according to the *Talmud*, correct: the citron brought to the Feast of the Tabernacles should be perfect in every way. Feast of the Tabernacles: Succoth: Jewish autumn thanksgiving in commemoration of the Israelites' sheltering in the Wilderness (*G*).

58.35–6 *On earth as it is in heaven*: part of the Lord's Prayer: Matt. 6: 10: 'Thy will be done in earth, as it is in heaven'.

59.3–4 *Brimstone ... Sodom, Gommorrah, Edom*: all, except Edom, cities of the plain (Gen. 14: 2) upon which God rained down brimstone (Gen. 19: 24–5). 'Edom' is the name God gives to Esau (Gen. 36: 8), father of the Edomites.

59.15 *Sandow's exercises*: another book on Bloom's shelf (662.3) by Eugen Sandow, famous strong man.

60.23 *seaside girls*: a recurrent song, attached throughout to Blazes Boylan, written and composed by Harry B. Norris (1899). (Qtd. in full in *G*.)

61.20 *Là ci darem*: full phrase in Italian: '*Là ci darem la mano*': 'Then we'll go hand in hand'; first of many allusions to a duet in Wolfgang Amadeus Mozart's (1756–91) opera *Don Giovanni* (1787) (I. iii) between Don Giovanni and Zerlina, the innocent peasant girl, as he attempts to seduce her away from her fiancé. He sings: 'This summer house is mine; we shall be alone, | and then, my jewel, we'll be married. | Then we'll go hand in hand. | Then you'll say yes. | Look it isn't far; | Let's be off from here, my darling'.

61.20 *Love's Old Sweet Song*: first of many allusions to this popular song, written by G. Clifton Bingham (1859–1913), words by James Lyman Molloy (1837–1909) (as we are told on 659.6–7). (Qtd. in full in *G*.)

61.33 *Voglio... vorrei*: Italian: 'I want to and I wouldn't like to', a misquotation of Zerlina's response to Don Giovanni (see 61.20n.); she sings 'Vorrei et non vorrei': '*I would like to and I wouldn't like to*; | My heart beats a little faster. | It's true I would be happy, | But he can still make a fool of me'.

62.9 *Metempsychosis*: Greek for, as Bloom says, the transmigration of the soul: the belief in reincarnation, held in ancient Indian thought, Greek Orphic teachings, and late 19th-c. Theosophy (though the latter believed only in human-to-human migration, not human-to-animal as did the others). (*G*)

62.16 *Ruby: the Pride of the Ring*: after an actual novel, *Ruby. A Novel. Founded on the Life of a Circus Girl*, by Amye Reade (1889), a moral, reformist tale of the dangers for young women of circus life (see Mary Power, *JJQ* 18/2 (1981), 115–21).

62.18 *The monster Maffei desisted ... oath*: an illustration, nearly exactly as described, occurs in the book with the inscription: 'The monster desisted and threw his victim from him with an oath'. In the actual novel, the monster is named Mr Henry, not Maffei.

62.27 *Paul de Kock*: Charles Paul de Kock (1794–1871), popular French novelist, not a pornographer.

62.37 *The Bath of the Nymph*: Calypso in one of her guises.

63.1 *Photo Bits*: London pennyweekly magazine (est. 1898), ostensibly photographic, really soft pornography.

65.25 *Titbits: Titbits from all the Most Interesting Books, Periodicals and Newspapers in the World* (est. 1881), London pennyweekly, for which it seems Joyce himself held ambitions (as an adolescent) to write. (See 66.24n.)

66.13 *James Stephens*: see 31.23n. and 43.25n.

66.14 *O'Brien*: if Bloom is thinking that 'O'Brien' helped with the escape of James Stephens from Richmond Jail, he is either mistaken or the man is lost to history. Stephens *was* associated with William Smith O'Brien (1803–64), Protestant landowner, MP, and leader in the Repeal Movement (of whom Bloom clearly thinks in *Hades*, 90.10). During the famine in 1848, Smith O'Brien participated in a raid on a police garrison in Tipperary during which several were killed (Stephens was there and wounded but escaped by feigning death). O'Brien was sentenced to death, his sentence was commuted to transportation for life, and he was later unconditionally pardoned. Only in rumour could he have helped Stephens to escape Richmond.

66.24 *Matcham's Masterstroke*: Stanislaus Joyce maintained that this was Joyce's joke at the expense of his own adolescent story (written with an eye to *Titbits*) which contained a reference to a 'laughing witch' (66.36) (Stanislaus Joyce, *My Brother's Keeper: James Joyce's Early Years*, ed. Richard Ellmann (1958; repr. New York: Viking, 1969), 91–2).

67.7 *Gretta Conroy*: a character from Joyce's *Dubliners* story 'The Dead'. *Ulysses* is populated by characters first seen in *Dubliners*: Gretta and Gabriel Conroy, Bob Doran, M'Coy, Tom Kernan, Martin Cunningham, Jack Power, Long John Fanning, Bantam Lyons, Joe Hynes, Ignatius Gallaher, Hoppy Hollohan, O'Madden Burke, T. Lenehan, John Corley, Bartell d'Arcy, Julia and Kate Morkan, Mrs Sinico, Kathleen Kearney, Fogarty, Crofton, all made their first fictional appearance in the earlier book. Knowledge of their past lives is often helpful to an understanding of their actions and motivations in *Ulysses*.

67.11 *Ponchielli's dance of the hours*: a popular number from Amilcare Ponchielle's (1834–86) opera *La Gioconda* (1876): an elaborate ballet, including costume changes, to illustrate the passing of the hours from dusk to dawn.

LOTUS EATERS

Location: The area around Westland Row station, south of the Liffey (F/G4). Bloom strolls east along Sir John Rogersons Quay (G4), turns right down Lime Street, right again into Hanover Street, then left into Lombard Street (F4), crosses Great Brunswick Street into Westland Row where he visits the Westland Row Post Office (F4). Leaving, he goes back up Westland Row, turns right into Great Brunswick Street, right again into Cumberland Street to All Hallows (St Andrew's) church (F4). He then passes through the church back into Westland Row, turns left down the street to Sweny's (the chemist) in Lincoln Place (F4), then continues on to the Leinster Street baths.

Time: 10 a.m.

Homer: Having landed on Scheria, Odysseus is entertained at the court of King Alcinous, to whom he reveals himself: 'Among all mankind I am known for subtleties' (99). He begins the tale of his encounters prior to landing on Calypso's island. First he tells of having arrived at the land of the Lotus-Eaters, 'whose only fare is that fragrant fruit' (101). Odysseus and his men ate and drank. Those who accepted the offer of lotus lost their desire to leave. Odysseus forced his men back aboard ship and set sail at once. Among Odysseus's companions are 'bold' Eurylochus and Polites ('of all my companions the trustiest and closest to me' (118)). (Book IX)

Schemata: *L* lists the personae as Eurylochus, Polites, Ulysses, and 'Nausicaa (2)' (by which he presumably means another aspect of Nausicaa (see note to *Nausicaa*, below), the beautiful Phaecian princess who fantasizes marriage to Odysseus—Martha Clifford(?)). No correspondents are provided for Eurylochus and Polites. *G* provides instead an entirely different scheme of correspondence, citing various 'inhabitants' of Dublin as manifestations of the drugged Lotus Eaters: cabhorses, communicants, soldiers, eunuchs, bather, watchers of cricket.

L and *G* agree on virtually nothing. The single (half) exception is that *L* lists the Art as Chemistry, while *G* gives Botany and Chemistry. Otherwise they part company: Colour (*L*: dark brown; *G*: none), Organ (*L*: Skin; *G*: Genitals), Technic (*L*: Dialogue, Soliloquy, Prayer; *G*: Narcissism), Symbol (*L*: Host, Penis in the bath, Froth, Flower, Drugs, Castration, Oats; *G*: Eucharist). Further *L* provides as Sense, 'The Temptation of the Faith'.

Homer's Lotus Eaters ate lotus and so achieved narcosis (from the Greek '*ναρκῦν*: to benumb'). As Gilbert tells us, *Ulysses*'s material equivalent is the Eucharist; its verbal counterpart, the Latin of the Mass, helpfully 'stupefies them first'. Numbness and stupefaction, libidinal and mental narcosis, are close correlatives in *Lotus Eaters* where the effects of 'lotus' can be located in the gelded cabhorses, the potions of Sweney the chemist, 'Lovephiltres' or the 'Lourdes cure, waters of oblivion'. Such thematic tropes are easily identified. Beyond this, a linguistic process, marked most obviously in the figurative operations of the metaphoric manœuvres of the central symbol of the Eucharist, is at work in this episode. The Eucharist itself is a material symbol of the Word made Flesh, intended for incorporation by the devout communicant; as Bloom thinks: 'They don't seem to chew it: only swallow it down. Rum idea: eating bits of a corpse why the cannibals cotton on to it.' In Catholic theology, the Eucharist is more than symbol of Jesus's body; transubstantiation transforms the symbol into material entity; the symbol has been occupied by the matter. Bloom blasphemously insists that it be seen as such—as mere matter.

In this episode more generally, 'worlds' have a habit of supplanting 'words' as Martha Clifford's 'I called you naughty boy because I do not like that other world' reveals. Martha's preference for material signs registers, too, in her sending

'Henry Flower' a flower (both name and thing appropriate to such a floral episode). In this materializing of language Martha shows herself Bloom's worthy cohort. Bloom too likes tangible signs: 'Clever idea Saint Patrick the shamrock', he thinks in praise of the saint's use of the trefoil shamrock to demonstrate the theological precept of the Trinity. For Bloom's mind works to substantiate the ephemeral and incorporeal. '*Corpus*: Body' thinks Bloom during the communion, and later he will blasphemously appropriate Jesus's 'This is my body' in deictic citation to his own (imagined) corpus in the bath. Here the sacred becomes profane, transubstantiation in reverse, performed by the man who is ever wary of what he will 'put . . . into [*his*] mouth'.

Lotus Eaters flourishes in the light of such verbal play, its favourite games being the pun and *double entendre*. 'Who's getting it up?' asks M'Coy, and Bloom carefully avoids responding 'Blazes Boylan'—the required answer to both (actual and implied) questions. 'Another gone', he sighs earlier, meaning both Dignam and a chance for a glance at a bit of thigh. In such 'throwaway' lines (see 'Introduction', pp. xxviii–xxix), we see the mutual incorporation of two meanings in one word or phrase, and an exuberant recognition that language is dynamic, not static. We will miss the point if we catch only the nominative punning substitution of 'Henry *Flower*' for 'Leopold *Bloom*', for a 'Flower' is also one who (or that which) 'flows', just as 'bloom' is as much verb as noun. (Recognition of this fact transforms Bloom's 'languid floating flower' through a kinetic pun more suited to an organ of dissemination and micturition.) Blooming Bloom suspects insubstantial symbols and their narcotizing effects, prefers the realized 'here and now', and so addresses material reality, even embraces the incarnate body and urges it into doing rather than being. In this he is a fittingly *Ulyssean* corporeal signifier, one which opens up '*The* Word' to a commodious accommodation of alternative wor(l)ds.

68.10–11 *Bethel . . . Beth*: Hebrew: *Beth*: 'house of'; *El*: 'God'.

68.27 *His right hand . . . over again*: should read 'His right hand . . . over his brow and hair. Then he put on his hat again, relieved: and read again:'.

69.4 *dolce far niente*: Italian: 'sweet doing nothing'.

69.13 *a law*: the law Bloom struggles to enunciate is Archimedes's (*c*.287–212 BC) principle: a body immersed in a fluid is subject to an upward force equal to the weight of fluid it displaces.

69.15 *Thirtytwo feet per second, per second*: the rate at which falling bodies accelerate.

70.6 *Maud Gonne's letter*: in response to the fact that, during the Boer War (1899–1902), British troops in Dublin were not confined to barracks at night and so were creating a nuisance on the streets, *Inghinidhe na hÉireann* ('Daughters of Ireland') militated to get troops off the streets; they circulated a pamphlet ostensibly written by Maud Gonne (see 43.16 n.) urging young Irish women not to consort with the soldiers of the enemy.

70.7 *Griffith's paper*: see 43.11–12 n. and 55.33–5 n.

70.8 *halfseasover*: 'drunk'.

71.3 *Brutus is an honourable man*: ironic comment spoken by Mark Antony over Caesar's body impugning Brutus's motives for slaying Caesar (*Julius Caesar*, III. ii. 87).

71.15 *fostering*: should read 'foostering' (*RM, Lotus Eaters*, fol. 4); from Gaelic: *fuadar*: 'rush'; 'clumsy bustling' (*G*).

71.29–30 *Paradise and the peri*: phrase roughly equivalent to 'So near and yet so far'; second tale in Thomas Moore's *Lalla Rookh* (1817): the peri (one of the beautiful fallen spirits who direct the faithful to heaven) sitting outside the gates of Heaven weeps at not being allowed in; eventually her offering of the Repentant Tear gains her admission.

73.15 *that smallpox up there*: there was an actual outbreak of smallpox in Belfast in May–June 1904.

73.21 *Leah . . . Ristori*: *Leah, the Forsaken* (1862), an adaptation by John Augustin Daly (1838–99) of *Deborah* (1850), a play by the German-Austrian playwright Salomon Hermann Mosenthal (1821–77), the central concern of which is to expose and attack anti-Semitism; the actresses named all played the part of Leah at various points; Millicent Bandmann Palmer (1865–1905) did act the role of Hamlet on 15 June 1904 at Dublin's Gaiety (*G*).

73.26–7 *Mosenthal . . . Rachel*: Bloom, struggling for Mosenthal's original title, mistakenly hits on *Rachel*; in Gen. 29, Rachel is the more beautiful sister of Leah, second and first wives, respectively, of Jacob.

73.27–31 *where the old blind Abraham . . . his father*: a scene apparently from the original German play (*T*), where blind Abraham recognizes the voice of Nathan, the apostate Jew who, disguised as an anti-Semitic Christian, hounds the Jewish Deborah to her death.

73.29 *—Nathan's*: delete dialogue dash.

74.22–3 *Mohammed cut a piece*: a traditional story about the prophet Muhammad.

76.9 *Martha, Mary*: the two sisters of Lazarus (John 11); when Jesus visited them, Martha was burdened with chores, Mary listened at his feet, Martha complained. Jesus said that Mary had chosen the 'good part' (Luke 10: 38–42).

76.24, 26 *Lord Iveagh; lord Ardilaun*: the two Guinness brothers: Edward Cecil Guinness (1847–1927, became Baron Iveagh in 1891) and Arthur Edward Guinness (1840–1915, became Baron Ardilaun in 1880); partners in the Dublin Brewery.

77.6 *saint Peter Claver*: (1581–1654), Spanish Jesuit saint, ministered to the African-American slaves in Cartagena, Colombia; later patron saint of all missionaries who work among African peoples.

77.8 *Prayers for the conversion of Gladstone*: William Ewart Gladstone (1809–98), four times Prime Minister (between 1868 and 1894) and qualified supporter of Irish Home Rule. He was by conviction anti-Catholic, but tolerant in his attitudes. Prayers were to be offered at his death, but not specifically for his conversion.

77.10 *Dr William. J. Walsh D.D.*: (1841–1921), Catholic archbishop of Dublin (1885–1921); the one who urged Irish Catholics to offer prayers for Gladstone at his death; for Joyce's attitude toward him, see his 'Gas from a Burner' (1912), ll. 23–4 (*PSW* 103).

77.12 *Ecce Home. Crown of thorns and cross*: should read 'Ecce Homo', Latin: 'Behold the Man'; Pilate's words (John 19: 5) when Jesus was brought before him wearing the crown of thorns and purple robe. (See Joyce on the painting 'Ecce Homo' by the Hungarian painter Michael Munkacsy (1844–1900) in his essay 'Royal Hibernian Academy "Ecce Homo"' (1899) (*CW* 31–7).)

77.12–13 *Clever idea Saint Patrick the shamrock*: St Patrick (*c.*389–*c.*481), patron saint of Ireland, supposedly taught the Irish king Laoghaire about the Trinity using the three-leafed shamrock.

77.23 *Who is my neighbour?*: the lawyer's question to Jesus when told to love his neighbour, in response to which Jesus tells of the Good Samaritan (Luke 10: 25–37).

78.3–4 *mazzoth ... unleavened shewbread*: 'matzoth', Yiddish: the unleavened bread eaten during the Hebrew Feast of the Passover; not the same as 'shewbread'—the twelve loaves of bread that were displayed in the ancient temple and renewed each sabbath.

78.10 *Lourdes; Knock apparition*: 'Lourdes': town in south-west France where the Virgin Mary reputedly appeared in vision to the peasant girl Bernadette Soubirous (later St Bernadette) in 1858, famous for its miraculous cures; 'Knock': village in County Mayo where the Virgin, St Joseph, and St John reputedly appeared (1879–80), also famous for its miracles.

78.16 *I.N.R.I. ... I.H.S.*: abbreviations: 'I.N.R.I.' for the Latin: *Iesus Nazarenus, Rex Iudaeorum* ('Jesus of Nazareth, King of the Jews'), the inscription on Jesus's cross (John 19: 19); and 'I.H.S.', originally from the first three letters of Jesus's name in Greek (iota: *I*, eta: *H*, sigma: *Σ*), and coming by tradition to be associated with the Latin phrases: *Iesus Hominum Salvator* ('Jesus the Saviour of Man'), *In Hoc Signo (Vinces)* ('In this sign (thou shalt conquer)'), and *In Hac Salus*' ('In this [cross] is salvation'). Needless to say, Molly gets it wrong.

78.22–4 *That fellow that turned ... invincibles ... Denis Carey*: the Invincibles, a militant faction of the Fenians, formed in 1881 with the express intention of assassinating British figures responsible for carrying out repressive British policy in Ireland. On 6 May 1882 in Phoenix Park, they murdered Lord Frederick Cavendish (1836–82), chief secretary of Ireland, and T. H. Burke, an Irish Catholic undersecretary at Dublin Castle who they thought responsible for the coercion policy (repressive measures meant to coerce Irish compliance with English rule). James Carey (1845–83), a Dublin leader of the Invincibles involved in the murders, turned queen's evidence; the tried men were convicted. While trying to emigrate from Dublin in 1883, Carey was recognized and shot by a Patrick O'Donnell (who was subsequently hanged). Carey had a brother named Peter, also involved in the murders, but none named Denis. Bloom's confusion continues at 155.32 and 596.33.

79.4 *Stabat Mater of Rossini*: Latin: 'The Mother was Standing' (as Mary at the Cross), a medieval poem and hymn celebrating Mary's compassion and suffering, with various musical settings. Bloom's is that by Gioacchino Rossini (1792–1868), Italian composer.

79.9 *Quis est homo?*: Latin: 'Who is the man?'; opening words of soprano duet in Rossini's setting of the *Stabat Mater*.

79.10 *Mercadante: seven last words*: Giuseppe Saverio Raffaelo Mercadante (1795–1870), Italian composer. *The Seven Last Words* ('Le sette ultime parole') is an oratorio composed around the seven last words of Christ on the cross (see *T* and *G*).

79.11 *Mozart's twelfth mass: the Gloria*: Bloom is probably thinking of the 'Twelfth Mass' (popularized as *Gloria*) spuriously attributed to Mozart, rather than Mozart's actual 'Twelfth Mass' (K. 262).

79.12 *Palestrina*: see 20.34 n.

79.27 O, *God ... strength*: one of the two prayers (in English) the priest was required to read after celebrating low mass; Bloom overhears further phrases from it at 79.29–30, while he catches the second prayer at 80.12–16.

81.27–8 *One of the old queen's sons ... Leopold*: the 'old queen' is, of course, Queen Victoria (1819–1901; r. 1837–1901), whose youngest son, Prince Leopold, Duke of Albany (1853–84), suffered from haemophilia.

81.30–1 *That orangeflower. Pure curd soap. Water is so fresh. Nice smell these soaps have*: should read 'That orangeflower water is so fresh. Nice smell these soaps have. Pure curd soap.'

82.24 *Ascot. Gold cup.*: an important event for Dubliners in *Ulysses*; the actual Gold Cup, an annual event, was run in 1904 at Ascot (in England) at 3.00 p.m., 16 June.

83.16 *Donnybrook fair*: a fair established during the reign of King John (r. 1199–1216) at the village of Donnybrook, south-east of Dublin, famous for its 'bacchanalian routs' (Brewer). Abolished in 1855, its name became synonymous with riotous goings-on.

83.18–19 *Always passing ... than them all*: a slight misquotation from the ballad 'In Happy Moments Day by Day', Act II of *Maritana*, an opera by W. Vincent Wallace (1814–65) and Edward Fitzball (1792–1873). The ballad ends with the line 'Which [the memory of first seeing the beloved] in the flight of years we trace, | Is dearer than them all'. The song and the opera recur throughout *Ulysses*. For plot, see *G*.

83.21 *This is my body*: spoken in the mass during the Consecration of the Host, taken from Jesus's words at the Last Supper (Matt. 26: 26; Mark 14: 22; Luke 22: 19).

HADES

Location: The funeral cortège travels across Dublin from Paddy Dignam's house (9 Newbridge Avenue in Sandymount (H5)), north along Tritonville Road (I5), west across the River Dodder (H5) and along Ringsend Road to cross the Grand Canal (G4), continues on Great Brunswick Street to cross the River Liffey on O'Connell Bridge (F4), up Sackville Street (F4, F/E3). Continuing along Cavendish Row (E3), Frederick and Blessington Streets, it then turns into Berkeley Street and Road (passing thereby the west end of Eccles Street (E2)), turns left on to the North Circular Road, then right into Phibsborough Road (D/E2), crosses the Royal Canal at Crossguns Bridge (E1), bears left into Finglas Road (D1) to arrive at Prospect Cemetery, Glasnevin (D1).

Time: 11 a.m.

Homer: Odysseus continues his tale, telling how he landed on Circe's island. She advised him that, before continuing his voyage, he consult Tiresias whose shade could be found in the house of 'dread Persephone (Latin: *Proserpina*) and Hades' (125). Crossing the four rivers of Hades (the Styx, Acheron, Cocytus, and Pyriphlegethon), Odysseus arrived in Hades, where he encountered, first, the shade of Elpenor, one of his men ('neither brave in battle nor firm in mind' (127)) who, having drunk too much in Circe's house, climbed on to the roof only to walk off it and break his neck when Odysseus summoned him to leave. Elpenor asked that he not remain unburied. Odysseus found Tiresias, who warned him, first, that Poseidon, 'Earthshaker', would try to prevent his return home and, second, not to slay the sacred Oxen of Helios the sun-god lest his men all be lost and his journey be made more difficult. Still, he promised Odysseus that he would return home safely. Odysseus met, too, the shades of his mother, Anticleia, and of various famous women including 'loathsome Eriphyle, who took a great bribe of gold to lure her own husband to his doom' (135). Agamemnon told him of his own murder and what he knew of the fates of the others present at Troy. Odysseus approached Aias (Latin: *Ajax*) who, nursing his pride at having been bested by Odysseus in the contest for Achilles's armour, refused to speak to him. Further, he met Achilles, 'huge' Orion, Sisyphus heaving his stone, Tityus (a character who, like Prometheus, is condemned to an eternity of having his liver plucked at by vultures), and Heracles (Latin: *Hercules*), not really a shade since he rests among the gods. Heracles sympathized with Odysseus, recounting how he too laboured and suffered; among his tasks was his trip to Hades to fetch Cerberus, the hound of Hades. Odysseus then left Hades, returned to his men, and saw to the burial of Elpenor. (Book XI)

Schemata: In addition to Ulysses, Elpenor, Ajax, Agamemnon, Hercules, Eriphyle, Sisyphus, Orion, Prometheus, Cerberus, Tiresias, Hades, and Proserpina, *L* lists Telemachus, 'Laertes etc.', and Antinous among the personae. None is present in Hades, though Laertes and Telemachus are at least mentioned in this Book. Laertes, Odysseus's father, and Telemachus are still alive, though Anticleia related how both were suffering in Ithaca in Odysseus's absence. Entirely absent from the episode is Antinous, the chief suitor, who, with the others, currently lies in wait for Telemachus on the island of Asteris. *G* provides correspondences: the four rivers of Hades are the Grand and Royal Canals, and the rivers Dodder and Liffey; Cunningham is Sisyphus; Father Coffey, Cerberus; the Caretaker, Hades; Daniel O'Connell (the 'Liberator', see 31.20 n.), Hercules; Dignam, Elpenor; Parnell (see 34.37 n.), Agamemnon; Menton, Ajax.

L and *G* agree on the Organ (Heart) and Colour (white, black), but not on Technic (*L*: Narration, Dialogue; *G*: Incubism), Art (*L*: none; *G*: Religion), Symbol (*L*: Cemetery, Sacred Heart, The Past, The Unknown Man, The Unconscious, Heart defect, Relics, Heartbreak; *G*: Caretaker). *L* gives the Sense as 'The Descent into Nothingness'.

Ghosts haunt *Hades*, an episode the technique of which Joyce defined as 'Incubism'. According to Augustine's *The City of God*, one could not rule out the possible existence of incubi (spirits which took sufficiently fleshly form to accomplish carnal intercourse with unsuspecting women). But incubi have developed etymologically from such specifically seductive, into more run-of-the-mill spectres: nightmares generally, or anything which oppresses like a nightmare. Here they run the gamut from Bloom's imagined 'poor old greatgrandfather' speaking from the grave gramophone ('Kraahraark! Hellohellohello amawfullyglad kraark awfullygladaseeragain hellohello amarawf kopthsth') to his haunting feeling of being out of place (note his frequent embarrassment: at the anti-Semitic jokes, the mention of suicide, the sighting of Boylan, the rebuff from John Henry Menton). More deeply disturbing for Bloom are the ghostly memories of his dead son ('If little Rudy had lived') and father ('Death by misadventure. The letter. For my son Leopold'), and his recognition that it is those who survive who suffer ('More sensible to spend the money [used to buy memorials] on some charity for the living'). The text is haunted too by 'deadly' verbal nuances: 'dead letter office', 'He's dead nuts on that', 'So much dead weight', 'Priests dead against it', 'Martin Cunningham's eyes and beard, gravely shaking', 'He gazed gravely at the ground', even 'the metal wheels ground the gravel'.

But Bloom's recognition that 'Once you are dead you are dead', so much 'corpse manure' (however 'dreadful' and 'cheesy' this might be), and that the concern of the living must be with the living displaces the deadliness, reconfigures the episode around the organ of life and emotions, the heart. It too appears in all its literal and metaphorical permutations, from actual organ ('A pump after all, pumping thousands of gallons of blood every day') to metaphorical location of emotion ('Seat of the affections', 'touches a man's inmost heart', 'How many broken hearts are buried here'), to the Sacred Heart, 'Heart on his sleeve', 'Heart of gold', 'the mourners took heart of grace' and 'Wear the heart out of a stone'. In the end, it is the 'pure goodheartedness' of those such as the caretaker which does most to banish the ghosts.

85.23 *fidus Achates*: Latin: 'the faithful Achates' (Virgil, *Aeneid*, I. 188); Achates was Aeneas's loyal friend.

86.3 *I'll tickle his catastrophe*: Page to the hostess at the attempted arrest of Falstaff in *2 Henry IV*, II. i. 60; 'catastrophe': backside.

86.14–15 *the wall of the cease to do evil*: the motto over the door of the Richmond jail (by 1904 absorbed into the Wellington barracks in the South Circular Road, opposite Raymond Terrace (D6)): 'Cease to do evil—learn to do well'.

88.4 *The Croppy Boy*: ballad by William B. McBurney (*c.*1844–*c.*1892) about a young boy who, about to join the Rebellion of 1798, goes to confession and admits 'I bear no grudge against living thing; | But I love my country above the king.' The 'priest' turns out to be an English captain in disguise and the croppy boy 'swings' as a 'traitor'. Ben Dollard sings the ballad in *Sirens*. (Complete text given in *G* and *T*; for 'croppy', see 31.24–7 n.)

88.10 *Dan Dawson's speech*: Charles (Dan) Dawson, Dublin businessman, MP, Lord Mayor of Dublin and (in 1904) Rates Collector; his 'speech' is scrutinized in *Aeolus.*

88.21 *Month's mind*: properly the requiem mass said for the deceased on the 30th day after burial; here, a memorial, printed in the newspaper, one month after the death of a loved one; the verse which follows is an example.

89.7 *Eugene Stratton*: stage-name of Eugene Augustus Ruhlmann (1861–1918), music-hall star, 'negro impersonator'; he returns in *Circe*.

89.9 *Lily of Killarney*: an opera written by John Oxenford (1812–77) and Dion Boucicault (1822–90), a musical version of Boucicault's play *The Colleen Bawn* (figuratively, 'fair-haired girl'; see 285.9 n.) (*G*).

89.13 *Sir Philip Crampton . . . Who was he?*: answer: a famous Dublin surgeon (1777–1858); the memorial has been removed.

90.7 *J. C. Doyle and John MacCormack*: renowned Irish baritone and tenor, respectively; Joyce, himself a promising tenor, shared the stage with the two on 27 Aug. 1904 (*JJ* 168).

90.10 *Smith O'Brien*: see 66.14 n.

90.22 *voglio . . . vorrei e non*: see 61.33 n.; Bloom here corrects his earlier mistake.

90.23 *Mi trema un poco il*: part of a line from Zerlina's duet with Don Giovanni (see 61.33 n.), which in full reads '*Mi trema un poco il cuore*' (Italian: 'My heart beats a little faster!'); '*cuore*', the missing word in Bloom's citation, means 'heart'.

90.33 *the hugecloaked Liberator's form*: the 'Liberator' is Daniel O'Connell (see 31.20 n.); his statue—a 12-ft. figure on a 28-ft. pedestal—stands in the middle of Sackville Street (now O'Connell Street) at O'Connell Bridge (F4).

90.35 *the tribe of Reuben*: Gen. 29: 32: Reuben was the eldest of Jacob's twelve sons (the twelve being in turn the heads of the 'Twelve Tribes of Israel'); here, Cunningham uses the appellation punningly to identify Reuben J. Dodd, since

Dodd's first name is Reuben and he is Jewish. *G* says that Judas who betrayed Jesus is referred to in Christian tradition as 'of the tribe of Reuben', in which case this becomes one of many anti-Semitic remarks made by Dubliners during the course of the day.

91.5 *Gray's statue*: statue in the middle of Sackville Street (F4) of Sir John Gray (1816–75), Protestant editor and proprietor of the *Freeman's Journal*, advocate of land reform.

91.20 *Drown Barabbas!*: the original Barabbas was the murderer whom the Jewish multitude wished released instead of Jesus (Matt. 27: 16–26; Mark 15: 11–15; Luke 23: 18–25; John 18: 40); his namesake is the eponymous villain in Christopher Marlowe's (1564–93) *The Jew of Malta* (1633) who, after great treachery, falls into the cauldron of boiling water he has prepared for his adversaries and dies cursing Christians and infidels alike (v. 348–76).

92.2 *Nelson's pillar*: another statue in the middle of Sackville Street (F3), this one a 134-ft. monument to the British Admiral Horatio, Viscount Nelson (1758–1805), flamboyant and triumphant admiral of the Napoleonic wars (see 15.28–9 n.).

92.27–8 *Foundation stone for Parnell*: the monument to Parnell had not yet been placed on its base (which had been erected 8 Oct. 1899), though it would be in 1911.

93.2–3 *Rattle his bones. Over . . . owns*: from 'The Pauper's Drive', song by Thomas Noel; supposedly the song was suggested to Noel by his 'seeing a funeral where the body was borne upon a cart at full speed' (*G*); the lines here are an abbreviated form of the refrain.

94.4 *The Gordon Bennett*: annual international road race; in 1904 it was to be held on 17 June outside Homburg, Germany.

94.8 *Dead march from Saul*: from George Frideric Handel's (1685–1759) *Saul* (1738), an oratorio, Act III, a not uncommon funeral march.

94.32 *the corporation*: the Dublin Corporation, the ruling civic body (like a city council).

96.9 *Brian Boroimhe house*: Brian Boroimhe ('Boru') (Gaelic: *Bóroimhe*) (926–1014), king of Ireland, best known for his defeat of the Danes at Clontarf on Good Friday 1014, after which he was slain in his tent. This house is a pub with a painting of Boroimhe in battle over the door.

96.25 *where Childs was murdered*: 76-year-old Thomas Childs was murdered on 2 Sept. 1898 at 5 Bengal Terrace, Glasnevin; his brother Samuel was charged, tried, and acquitted; his council was Seymour Bushe, KC. (*G*)

96.33 *unweeded garden*: Hamlet, in his 'too, too sallied flesh' soliloquy, refers to the world as an 'unweeded garden' (*Hamlet*, I. ii. 135–7).

96.37 *Murder will out*: proverbial, as in Chaucer's 'The Nun's Priest's Tale' where Chauntecleer declares: 'Morder wol out, that se we day by day' (l. 3052).

97.26 *Got here before us, dead as he is*: remember Elpenor.

98.28–9 *Widowhood . . . Victoria and Albert. Frogmore memorial mourning*: Prince

Albert, husband of Queen Victoria, died 14 Dec. 1861, forty years before she did; the queen made a great show of mourning him and widowhood became fashionable as a result; 'Frogmore memorial': the mausoleum, in the grounds of Windsor Castle, commissioned by the queen for herself, Prince Albert, and her mother.

99.34–5 *Who'll read the book? I, said the rook*: after the nursery rhyme 'Who Killed Cock Robin?': 'Who'll be the parson? | I said the Rook | With my little book, | I'll be the parson'.

100.1 *Dominenamine*: echo of words Bloom hears the priest saying; the phrase would be *In nomine Domine*: Latin: 'In the name of the Lord'.

100.3 *Thou art Peter*: Jesus renames Simon as Peter ('rock'—the rock upon which Jesus will build his church) (Matt. 16: 18).

100.7/24/34 *Non intres . . . Domine* | *Et ne nos . . . tentationem* | *In paradisum*: Latin (respectively): 'Enter not into judgement with thy servant, Lord'; 'And lead us not into temptation'; 'Into paradise'; phrases from, again respectively, the prayer of absolution, the Lord's Prayer, and the anthem, which form that portion of the Catholic burial ceremony which follows the mass and precedes the placement of the coffin in the grave.

101.10; 12–13 *The O'Connell circle* | *his heart is buried in Rome*: at the centre of Glasnevin cemetery lies the Daniel O'Connell memorial formed of a replica Irish round tower, at the base of which O'Connell is buried; he died in 1847 in Italy returning from a pilgrimage to Rome; his heart was placed in the church of St Agatha (the Irish College) in Rome and his body returned to Dublin.

101.34 *the Irish church*: i.e. the Church of Ireland, Irish counterpart of the Church of England.

102.1 *I am the resurrection and the life*: Jesus to Martha when she doubts his ability to raise Lazarus from the dead (John 11: 25), the opening of the service of the Burial of the Dead (for the Church of Ireland); the same verse is used in the Catholic funeral service just witnessed, though in Latin.

102.9 *Come forth, Lazarus!*: Jesus's command to the dead Lazarus, who then arises (John 11: 43).

104.7 *when churchyards yawn*: Hamlet, after the play he's staged to trap Claudius: ''Tis now the very witching time of night, | When churchyards yawn and hell itself breathes out | Contagion to this world' (*Hamlet*, III. ii. 388–90).

104.14–15 *Love among the tombstones. Romeo*: mixed allusion to Robert Browning's 'Love Among the Ruins' (1855) and the last act of *Romeo and Juliet*, when the deaths of both lovers are played out in Juliet's tomb (Act V).

104.17 *grig*: Gaelic: *griog*: 'excite desire or envy'.

104.27–8 *those jews they said killed the christian boy*: Bloom thinks of (perhaps a specific case, but certainly) the general, repeated anti-Semitic accusations made by Christians that Jews killed children, drained their blood, and used it in various rituals; the accusations are known collectively as the 'blood libel' and have been repeated since the 12th c. (See the song Stephen sings in *Ithaca*, 643–4.)

105.10 *Gravediggers in Hamlet*: the scene of 'comic relief' as the gravediggers prepare Ophelia's grave (*Hamlet*, v. i).

105.11–12 *De mortuis nil nisi prius*: Bloom's misquotation of the Latin *De mortuis nil nisi bonum*: 'Of the dead speak nothing but good'. The phrase *nisi prius* means 'unless before' (a specific legal term for the local courts which hear civil cases or the writ requiring the summoning of such a court). Bloom's phrase means: 'Of the dead speak nothing unless before' and thus implies the desirability of a period of reverence before the dead can be mocked.

105.21 *We come to bury Caesar. His ides of March or June*: Mark Antony's ironic remark in his funeral oration for Julius Caesar through which he succeeds in stirring the people to fury against the conspirators who have slain him (*Julius Caesar*, III. ii. 74); Caesar was stabbed on the Ides of March, the 15th, after having been warned by a soothsayer 'Beware the ides of March' (I. ii. 18); Dignam died on the Ides of June (the 13th).

105.28–9 *Robinson Crusoe . . . Friday*: Daniel Defoe (1660–1731), *The Life and strange and surprising Adventures of Robinson Crusoe* (1719): the hero, shipwrecked on an island, and his native servant whom he names Friday; though, as Crusoe survives to leave the island, Friday does not bury him.

106.34 *Lucia. Shall I . . . thee*: in Gaetano Donizetti's (1797–1848) opera *Lucia di Lammermoor* (1835), the hero Edgar laments the death of Lucia before he commits suicide. Bloom, thinking of Edgar's declaration 'Yet once more shall I behold thee', conflates it with a line from Stephen Foster's (1826–64) song 'Gentle Annie': 'Shall we never more behold thee?'.

106.36 *Even Parnell. Ivy day dying out*: Ivy Day: 6 Oct., the anniversary of Parnell's death on which his followers wore a sprig of ivy in remembrance. (See 'Ivy Day in the Committee Room', *Dubliners*.)

108.24 *the chief's grave*: Parnell, 'the chief', was buried in a grave opposite the door of the mortuary chapel.

109.1 *All souls' day*: 2 Nov., when prayers are said for the faithful dead yet in purgatory.

109.7–9 *Eulogy in a country . . . Thomas Campbell*: actually, '*Elegy* Written in a Country Churchyard' (1751) by Thomas Gray (1716–71) not by either William Wordsworth (1770–1850) or Thomas Campbell (1777–1844).

109.21 *The Sacred Heart that is*: the Blessed Margaret Mary Alacoque (1647–90) (sanctified 1920) had repeated visions in which Jesus took his heart, held it out for her to see, and then placed it in hers; she established the Litany of the Sacred Heart.

109.24–5 *Would birds come then . . . Apollo*: the name of the Greek painter Bloom is reaching for is Apelles (not Apollo), though the story really concerns another Greek painter Zeuxis (d. *c.*400 BC) who was famed for his realistic pictures. Pliny the Elder (AD 23–79) in his *Natural History* (*c.*77) tells the story of Zeuxis painting so realistically a picture of a child carrying grapes that the birds came to peck at the grapes; Zeuxis was cross because, he said, if he had painted the child as well as he had painted the grapes, the birds would have been frightened away.

110.5–6 *Robert Emmet . . . wasn't he?*: Robert Emmet (1778–1803), leader of the United Irishmen, distinguished orator, discussed Irish independence with Napoleon; leader of a rebellion and march on Dublin Castle (1803) which disintegrated into a brutal and bloody farce; escaped, returned (according to legend) partly to see his sweetheart Sarah Curren; was captured, tried, hanged, and beheaded. His burial place remains a matter of speculation. From the dock he declared, 'When my country takes her place among the nations of the earth then and not till then, let my epitaph be written. I have done.' He became in popular myth the romantics' archetypal tragic Irish hero.

110.10 *Voyages in China*: a book, by 'Viator' (Latin: 'traveller'), on Bloom's bookshelf (661.16).

110.14 *Ashes to ashes: Book of Common Prayer*, 'Burial of the Dead': 'Earth to earth, ashes to ashes, dust to dust, in sure and certain hope of the resurrection to eternal life, through our Lord Jesus Christ'.

AEOLUS

Location: Offices of the *Freeman's Journal* (and *Evening Telegraph*), 4–8 Princes Street North (E4, behind the General Post Office), off Sackville Street and around the corner from Nelson's Pillar (F3).

Time: 12 noon.

Homer: Earlier at Menelaus's court, Odysseus told the tale of landing on the floating island of Aeolia, ruled by Aeolus, 'warden of all the winds' (113), and father of six sons and six daughters, all married to one another. After entertaining Odysseus (who repaid the debt of hospitality by recounting his adventures), Aeolus gave Odysseus a bag in which he had 'penned up every wind that blows' (113), the west wind being intended to carry him safely home. Odysseus set sail and after nine days came within sight of Ithaca, only to collapse with exhaustion. His men, convinced that he was hiding precious gifts in the bag, opened it and released the winds. They were blown back to Aeolus's island where Odysseus again sought his help. Aeolus, recognizing one whom the gods have cursed, banished him. (Book X)

Schemata: *L* lists as personae Aeolus, Sons, Telemachus, Mentor, and Ulysses (2). Neither Telemachus nor Mentor (see *Telemachus* headnote above) are present in the Homeric episode, Telemachus being at Menelaus's court and Mentor in Ithaca. What Joyce meant by 'Ulysses (2)' (Ulysses in another aspect, but what? or whom?) remains unclear. *G* provides correspondences: Crawford, Aeolus; Journalism, Incest; the Press, Floating Island.

L and *G* agree on Colour (red), Art (Rhetoric), Organ (Lungs), but disagree on Technic (*L*: Simbouleutike, Dikanike, Epideictic (respectively deliberative, judicial, and public oratory) and Tropes; *G*: Enthymemic (a syllogism the premisses of which are only probably, rather than demonstrably, true)) and Symbol (*L*: Machines, Wind, Fame, Kite, Failed destinies, The Press, Mutability; *G*: Editor). *L*'s Sense is 'The Derision of Victory'.

In keeping with its Art, 'Rhetoric' (or in less reverent tones, windy bombast, hot air), *Aeolus* is a virtual handbook of rhetorical tropes. Stuart Gilbert, who first catalogued these (with hints from Joyce), lists 95 examples (Gilbert, 194–8). *G* provides an even longer list: multiple examples of 113 separate types of figure (in *G*, 'Appendix: Rhetorical Figures in *Aeolus*', 635–43). Often the two lists disagree. Since one person's metonymy is another's synecdoche, this is hardly surprising, but, rather than compound the confusion, the figures go unlisted below.

The other use of rhetoric—oratorical persuasion—also plays its part in *Aeolus*: famous Irish (and Greek) orators parade past, their speeches alluded to or dissected. Similarly, the modern mode of persuasion—the daily newspaper—provides more than the setting. Newspapers and journalists abound; the institution of the Press is treated with both scepticism and affection (remember that the young Joyce, under the pseudonym Stephen Daedalus, published in *The Irish Homestead*). But more than this, the 'Sllt . . . Sllt . . . Sllt' (117.10, 11, 13) of the presses themselves beat the steady rhythm of mechanical inhalation and exhalation. This is the home of the modern mechanized material production of words, the place where paper and ink come together, the ink having been spread on inverted lead letters already distributed by a typesetter who 'reads it backwards first . . . mangiD. kcirtaP' (118.9–10).

Note, too, that this episode has been fiddled with by the Arranger, that figure distinctly different from the narrator, not least in 'his' awareness of the book as a material object consisting of paper and ink juxtaposed to form words, sentences, and a non-continuous narrative, all of which can be played with, moved about, taken out and reinserted in different places to create surprising effects (see 'Introduction', pp. xxxiii–xxxiv). Here the Arranger becomes Editor, an editor who has taken to the copy with a pair of scissors and a blue pencil, has cut it up and inserted 'Headlines' into the gaps (headlines which often have a flippant disregard for their relevance to what follows; ironic irreverence is this Editor's hallmark).

112.3–5 *Blackrock . . . Harold's Cross*: the tramlines radiating out from Nelson's Pillar; in 1904 Dublin's public transportation system was considered the nonpareil of modern efficiency.

112.15 *the royal initials, E.R.*: for Edward Rex: Edward VII (see 31.18 n.).

113.13 *WILLIAM BRAYDEN*: William Henry Brayden (1865–1933), Irish barrister and editor of the *Freeman's Journal* (1892–1916).

113.28 *Mario the tenor*: Giovanni Matteo, Cavaliere di Candia (1810–83), stage-name 'Mario', Italian tenor.

113.33 *Martha*: *Martha, oder der Markt von Richmond* (1847), a light opera composed by Friedrich von Flotow (1812–83); two songs from the opera—'M'appari' (lines from a free adaptation of which follow at 113.34–5; see, further, 260.23 and 262.26) and Thomas Moore's 'The Last Rose of Summer' (see 276.8 n.)—recur throughout *Ulysses* (*G*).

114.15 *Nannetti*: Joseph Patrick Nannetti (1851–1915), Irish-Italian politician and printer, MP for the College Division of Dublin ('College Green', 114.27–8), member of the Dublin Corporation.

114.16–18 *WITH UNFEIGNED . . . BURGESS*: should be moved to follow (as new lines) 'Thumping. Thump.' (114.19).

114.27 *Ireland my country*: a lot of talk goes on throughout the day about just exactly who is and, perhaps more vehemently, who is not Irish; the debate was topical: Arthur Griffith's *United Irishman* frequently took up the issue; the purist line: only Gaels; the liberal line: anyone born in Ireland. Bloom is clearly a liminal figure, sometimes in, sometimes out.

114.29 *the official gazette*: *Dublin Gazette*, printed by His Majesty's Stationer's Office, included legal notices and 'official' news.

114.30 *Queen Anne is dead*: 'A slighting retort made to a teller of stale news' (Brewer); ostensibly from the fact that Joseph Addison (1672–1719) reported the fact of Queen Anne's death in the pages of *The Spectator* (1711–12, 1714) long after its occurrence.

114.31 *Tinnachinch*: should read 'Tinnahinch'; house presented to Henry Grattan (1746–1820), Irish statesman and orator, by the Irish Parliament in appreciation for his services to the cause of Irish independence; helped organize political movement for Catholic emancipation; retired 1797; re-emerged to fight the Act of Union and to become an MP (1805–20) once the Act was passed.

114.31–115.7 *To all whom . . . heartily at each other*: these are parodies of actual columns in the *Weekly Freeman* (weekly paper also owned and published by Freeman's Journal, Ltd.).

115.5 *M.A.P.*: *M(ainly) A(bout) P(eople)*, 'society' pennyweekly. Bloom's comment is more applicable to the photo supplements that came with the Sunday weeklies.

115.32 *He doesn't hear it. Nanaan. Irons nerves.*: should follow 'racket they make' (116.1).

116.13 *HOUSE OF KEY(E)S*: the orthographical equivalent of Bloom's desired visual pun on 'Keys' and 'Keyes'; the House of Keys: lower house of the Parliament of the Isle of Man; the island was under the British Crown but not subject to acts of the British Parliament, hence, its symbolism of home rule.

116.22 *Innuendo of home rule*: see 116.13 n.

118.1 *DAYFATHER*: a 'dayfather': father of the union chapel for the day staff.

118.8 *AND IT WAS THE FEAST OF THE PASSOVER*: Passover (from Hebrew:

pesach: 'to pass over'): the feast in commemoration of the Lord's 'passing over' the Israelites' homes when He 'smote all the firstborn of Egypt' (Exod. 12: 12; 12: 1–14). The phrase here is an echo of the recurrent 'And the feast of the passover was nigh' in the Gospels (particularly John 2: 13, 6: 4, 11: 55).

118.11 *hagadah book*: 'hagadah': Hebrew: 'tale'; the book, brought out at the first 'seder' (the ritual of the first day of the Feast of the Passover), for the ritual retelling and re-enactment of the story of the exodus of the Children of Israel from Egypt.

118.12 *Pessach*: Passover (see 118.8 n.).

118.12 *Next year in Jerusalem*: traditional conclusion to the seder on the first night of the Passover.

118.13 *that brought us out . . . house of bondage*: Bloom's mistaken version of (or ironic commentary on) the oft-repeated phrase of the Old Testament: 'the Lord brought us out from Egypt, from the house of bondage' (Exod. 13: 14).

118.14 *Shema Israel Adonai Elohenu*: Hebrew: 'Hear, oh Israel, the Lord our God' (Deut. 6: 4); beginning of the best-known Hebrew prayer, the 'Shema'. It is a daily prayer, not part of the Passover.

118.15 *the twelve brothers, Jacob's sons*: the twelve sons (fathers of the 'twelve tribes') of Jacob (known as 'Israel') (Gen. 35: 22–6).

118.15–17 *the lamb . . . butcher . . . cat*: the 'Chad Gadya' (One Kid), an Aramaic song sung at the conclusion of the Passover festival; cumulative chant (like 'The House that Jack Built'); Bloom's interpretation is not far off.

119.6 *ERIN, GREEN GEM OF THE SILVER SEA*: see 19.28–9 n.; also an allusion to John Philpot Curran's (1750–1817) 'Cuisle Mo Chroidhe' (Gaelic: 'pulse of my heart'): 'Dear Erin . . . an emerald set in the ring of the sea'. (See also *G* and *T*).

119.7 *the ghost walks*: theatrical slang for 'salaries are about to be paid' (Brewer); allusion to *Hamlet*, I. i.

119.22 *And Xenophon . . . sea*: from George Gordon, Lord Byron's (1788–1824) 'The Isles of Greece', an interpolated lyric in *Don Juan*, Canto III (1821) (between stanzas 86 and 87), iii. 1–2: 'The mountains look on Marathon, | And Marathon looks on the sea'. For Xenophon, see 5.15 n.

120.2 *Cicero*: (106–43 BC), greatest Roman orator and statesman, renowned for his moderate rhetorical style (*G*).

121.4 *Reaping the whirlwind*: Hos. 8: 7: 'For they have sown the wind, and they shall reap the whirlwind'.

121.6 *the Express*: *Daily Express* (1851–1921), conservative and basically pro-union.

121.7 *Gabriel Conroy*: protagonist of Joyce's 'The Dead' who, in that story, is teased by Miss Ivors over his columns in the *Daily Express*.

121.7 *the Independent*: *Irish Daily Independent*, established by Parnell after his fall (though not published until 18 Dec. 1891—after his death) but taken over by anti-Parnellites.

121.24 *HIS NATIVE DORIC*: should be moved to follow (as new line) 'He forgot Hamlet' (121.25).

121.25 *The moon . . . He forgot Hamlet*: i.e. having done Ireland by moonlight, he forgot to carry the rhetorical flourish forward to Ireland at dawn, as Horatio does in *Hamlet*, I. i. 166–7 (*G*).

122.12 *the sham squire*: Francis Higgins (1746–1802) defrauded a young woman by pretending to be a country squire, married her, was discovered, prosecuted, and imprisoned; later became owner and editor of the *Freeman's Journal*; libelled Grattan; supposedly accepted bribe to reveal the hiding place of Edward Fitzgerald, one of the military leaders in the 1798 Rebellion.

122.23 *North Cork militia!*: the context makes it clear that Lambert at least thinks the editor has his history scrambled. For a partial unscrambling, see *G*.

122.33 *cretic*: poetic metrics: a foot comprising one short syllable between two long.

123.1 *HARP EOLIAN*: Aeolian harp: stringed instrument which makes 'music' when the wind passes through it, named, of course, for Aeolus; the harp, instrument of Celtic poets, is also the national emblem of Ireland. (See too, 'The Eolian Harp' (1795) by Samuel Taylor Coleridge (1772–1834).)

123.14 *Canada swindle case*: case currently before the court of a man (known variously as Saphiro, Sparks, James Wought) charged with swindling people by promising to secure passage to Canada for 20*s*. (usual fare *c*.£2). (*G*)

124.21 *anno Domini*: Latin: 'in the year of our Lord'.

124.26–7 *We are the boys . . . hand*: from the ballad 'The Boys of Wexford' by R. Dwyer Joyce (1830–83) about the Rebellion of 1798; describes the routing of the English by the boys of Wexford, then their subsequent decline into drink.

125.3 *Begone! . . . The world is before you*: an almost proverbial phrase, but see the ending of Milton's *Paradise Lost* (1667), XII. 646, when Adam and Eve leave the Garden of Eden: 'The world was all before them'; and Byron's 'Epistle to Augusta' (1816; 1830), XI.1: 'The world is all before me'.

125.15 *spaugs*: Gaelic: *spág*: 'paw; long flat foot; clubfoot'; but perhaps instead a variant of 'spaught': 'youth, lad, stripling' (*OED*).

125.31 *CALUMET*: Native American peace pipe.

126.4–5 *'Twas rank and fame . . . heart*: from an aria in Act III of the Irish composer Michael William Balfe's (1808–70) opera *The Rose of Castille* (1857), which is repeatedly alluded to in *Ulysses*. (*G* provides a plot outline.)

126.11 *Imperium romanum*: Latin: 'the Roman empire'.

126.16 *THE GRANDEUR THAT WAS ROME*: from Edgar Allan Poe's (1809–49) 'To Helen' (1831), l. 10.

126.25 *(on our shore he never set it)*: a classical issue with Irish historians: what was the extent of Roman dominion over Ireland? Limited, it seems.

126.25 *cloacal obsession*: the phrase used by H. G. Wells (1866–1946) in his review of *Portrait* ('James Joyce', *Nation*, 20 (24 Feb. 1917), 710, 712; repr. in Robert H. Deming (ed.), *A Bibliography of James Joyce Studies* (2nd edn., Boston: Hall, 1977), i. 86–8): 'Like Swift and another living Irish writer, Mr. Joyce has a cloacal obsession. He would bring back into the general picture of life aspects which modern drainage and modern decorum have taken out of ordinary intercourse and conversation' (ibid. 86).

126.32 *Pontius Pilate is its prophet*: after the traditional Muslim statement 'There is no god but God and Muhammad is his prophet'; the Roman law of Pilate, of course, eventually condemned Jesus (John 18: 28–19: 22).

127.20–3 *On swift sail . . . my mouth*: Stephen's poem, written in *Proteus*, a 'free adaptation' of a poem by Douglas Hyde (see 47.27–8 n.).

128.7–9 *An Irishman saved . . . in Ireland*: according to *G*, Maximilian Karl Lamoral Graf O'Donnell von Tirconnell (b. 1812), an Irish expatriate's son, saved the life of Emperor Francis Joseph (18 Feb. 1853) when he was attacked by a Hungarian tailor.

128.24–5 *Lord Jesus! Lord Salisbury*: two very different 'Lords': the second, Robert Arthur Talbot Gascoigne-Cecil, 3rd Marquess of Salisbury (1830–1903), Conservative, anti-Gladstone, anti-Home Rule Prime Minister (1885–6, 1886–92, 1895–1902), supporter of the policies which led to the Boer War (1899–1902).

128.26, 28 *KYRIE ELEISON! . . . Kyrios!*: Greek: 'Lord, have mercy'; litany sung in regular mass. 'Kyrios': Greek: 'Lord'.

128.28–9 *vowels the Semite and the Saxon know not*: the twentieth letter of the Greek alphabet *upsilon* (*Υ*) has no direct equivalent in either the Hebrew or the English alphabet.

128.32 *Trafalgar*: the battle of Trafalgar (21 Oct. 1805), decisive sea battle in the Napoleonic wars; the British fleet, under the command of Admiral Nelson, defeated the combined fleets of France and Spain, and thus hastened the collapse of Napoleon's empire. Nelson was mortally wounded in the battle.

129.2 *Ægospotami*: decisive battle in the Peloponnesian War when the Spartans defeated the Athenians (by destroying their fleet and 3,000 men) at Ægospotami in Thrace (405 BC).

129.2–3 *Pyrrhus . . . Greece*: *G* and *T* give two different accounts of how Pyrrhus was misled by the 'oracle'. For 'Pyrrhus', see 24.2, 12, 18 n.

129.5–6 *They went forth . . . always fell*: original title (1892) of Yeats's poem 'The Rose of Battle', taken from Matthew Arnold's epigraph to his *Study of Celtic Literature* (1867).

129.15 *the Joe Miller*: slang: a joke (Brewer claims 'a stale joke').

129.16 *Sallust*: Gaius Sallustius Crispus (86–35 BC), Roman historian, supporter of Caesar, after retirement a distinguished historian, in public life corrupt.

129.23 *The Rose of Castille*: see 126.4–5 n.

129.30 *communards*: members of the left-wing, communalistic, Commune de Paris who after the Franco-Prussian War (1870–1) briefly (Mar.–May 1871) seized control of the municipal government of Paris.

129.31 *Bastille*: 14th-c. French fortress, used as prison in 17th and 18th c., symbol of despotism, stormed by the people of Paris on 14 July 1789, an event which marked the start of the French Revolution.

129.32–3 *shot the lord lieutenant of Finland... General Bobrikoff*: an actual event of 16 June 1904; the despotic Nikolai Ivanovitch Bobrikoff (1857–1904), governor-general of Finland, was assassinated by Eugen Schaumann at 11.00 a.m. (*G*, *T*).

130.1 *OMNIUM GATHERUM*: dog Latin: 'a motley collection'; this headline should be moved to follow 'Stephen said.' (130.2).

130.15 *In the lexicon of youth* ...: from Edward Bulwer-Lytton's (1803–73) play *Richelieu, or the Conspiracy* (1839), III. i: 'In the lexicon of youth, which fate reserves | For a bright manhood, there is no such word | As "fail"'.

130.16 *See it in your face... schemer*: Stephen recalls his unjust punishment at the hands of Father Dolan, prefect of studies at Clongowes (*Portrait*, ch. 1, pp. 47–59).

130.18 *nationalist meeting in Borris-in-Ossory*: in 1843 O'Connell held one of his 'monster meetings' here to agitate for repeal of the Act of Union; the Nationalists were considering re-staging the meeting in 1904.

130.21 *metanl pabulum*: should read 'mental pabulum'.

130.27 *shaughraun*: Gaelic: *seachrán*: 'wandering' (*G*).

130.30–1 *murder in the Phoenix Park*: see 78.22–4 n.; the date was 1882 (Joyce's year of birth), not 1881.

131.5–6 *Tim Kelly ... drove the car*: all three were Invincibles involved in the Phoenix Park murders: Brady (as principal assassin), Kelly (as second), and Kavanagh (who drove the getaway cab in the route Crawford later describes). 'Skin-the-Goat' (James Fitzharris) drove a decoy cab in a direct route from Phoenix Park to the centre of Dublin (*T*). He returns in *Eumaeus* to a job he did not hold, proprietor of the cabman's shelter. For more on the Invincibles, see 78.22–4 n.

132.14 *The Old Woman of Prince's Street*: nickname for the *Freeman's Journal*.

132.30 *Lady Dudley*: wife of William Ward, 2nd Earl of Dudley (1866–1932), Lord-Lieutenant of Ireland (1902–6).

132.31–2 *that cyclone last year*: on 26–7 Feb. 1903, severe gales caused great damage in Dublin.

133.2 *Whiteside; Isaac Butt; silver tongued O'Hagan*: Irish barristers and orators all, and in varying degrees supporters of Home Rule (*G* and *T*).

133.11–13 *la tua pace ... tace*: Italian: 'thy peace', 'it pleases thee to speak', 'while the wind, as now, is silent for us'; all from the speech of Paolo and Francesca to Dante in the *Inferno*, v. 92, 94, 96; quoted by Stephen as rhymes but the last also appropriately 'windy'. (*G* and *T* quote the lines in context.)

133.14–17 *He saw them ... womb*: all Dantean phrases. Dante's mellifluous words are multicoloured like the rainbow, Stephen's rhymes leadenfooted and dark. The passage echoes Dante's Divine Pageant in *Purgatorio* XXIX. The line phrases, in order cited by Stephen, mean: 'through the black (ruined) air' (*Inferno*, v. 89); 'that peaceful oriflamme' (*Paradiso*, XXXI. 127); 'more ardent to regaze' (*Paradiso*, XXXI. 142). Stephen's penitent 'old men' are like those seen by Dante after the Divine Pageant (*Purgatorio*, XXIX. 142–4) (*G*).

133.24 *Flood*: Henry Flood (1732–91), Irish statesman and orator, somewhat eclipsed by Grattan (see 114.31 n.) in the Irish Parliament of 1782; did accept public office where Grattan refused.

133.24 *Demosthenes*: (*c.* 384–322 BC), Athenian orator, reputedly the greatest; like his Irish descendants, a leader of opposition politics.

133.24–5 *Edmund Burke*: (1729–97), Anglo-Irish MP, barrister, orator, political philosopher; advocated Irish, Catholic, American, and Indian emancipation; opposed the slave trade and (latterly) the 'atheistical' excesses of the French Revolution.

133.25–6 *Harmsworth... gutter sheet*: Alfred C. Harmsworth (1865–1922), English editor and publisher, born in Chapelizod, founder of the London *Daily Mail*; 'his American cousin': American publisher Joseph Pulitzer (1847–1911), friend of Harmsworth, owner of the *New York World*.

133.27–8 *Paddy Kelly's Budget... the Skibereen Eagle*: actual Irish newspapers (*G*).

134.3 *Irish volunteers*: formed as a national defence force in 1778 when English troops were withdrawn from Ireland to fight in America; largely (at first solely) Protestant, in favour of an independent Irish Parliament, but opposed to independence; helped bring about legislative independence in 1782 which was lost eighteen years later with the Act of Union which dissolved the Irish Parliament.

134.3 *Dr Lucas*: Charles Lucas (1713–71), Irish physician and contributor to *Freeman's Journal*, of whom Grattan said, 'He laid the groundwork of Irish liberty'.

134.4 *John Philpot Curran*: (1750–1817), Irish barrister, orator, and MP, supporter of Catholic relief and parliamentary reform, opponent of Union, defended a number of United Irishmen throughout the 1790s.

134.14 *And in the porches... did pour*: the Ghost in *Hamlet* relates the manner of his death: poison in the ear courtesy of Claudius (*Hamlet*, I, v. 63).

134.15 *how did he find that out?*: how could the Ghost know how he died if he was sleeping at the time? How did he discover that Gertrude was committing adultery ('making the beast with two backs' (*Othello*, I. i. 116–17)) before he died?

134.18 *ITALIA, MAGISTRA ARTIUM*: Latin: 'Italy, Mistress of the Arts'.

134.20 *lex talionis*: Latin: 'law of the same'; the law of exacting exact retribution: 'eye for eye, tooth for tooth' (Exod. 21: 24). Bushe did speak on the law of evidence, but seems not to have contrasted Mosaic and Roman law (*G* and *T*).

134.21 *Moses of Michelangelo in the Vatican*: Michelangelo Buonarotti (1475–1564), Italian sculptor, painter, architect, poet, sculpted the *Moses* (1513–16) as part of the tomb for Pope Julius II, not in the Vatican, but in San Pietro in Vincoli in Rome.

134.27–9 *I have often thought... lives*: whose sentence? Certainly in the manner of the Charles Dickens (1812–70) of *David Copperfield* (1849–50) or *Great Expectations* (1860–1).

134.33 *the human form divine*: German philosopher Frederick von Schelling's (1775–1854) description of architecture: 'music in space, as it were a frozen music' (*Philosophy of Art*, trans. 1845).

135.13–14 *that hermetic crowd ... A.E. ... That Blavatsky woman*: the Theosophists were much about in Dublin around the turn of the century. Following Hindu and Buddhist teachings, they believed in 'the transmigration of souls, the brotherhood of man irrespective of race or creed, and complicated systems of psychology and cosmology' and denied a personal god (*OEED*). Helena Petrovna Blavatsky (1831–91), Russian traveller, founded the Theosophical Society in 1875; published *Isis Unveiled* in 1876; was not infrequently investigated for charlatanism. Yeats was her most famous 'follower', though in Ireland, AE (George Russell, see 31.8, 9n.) was perhaps her most ardent.

135.23 *John F. Taylor*: (*c.*1850–1902), Irish barrister, orator, and journalist who did (on 24 Oct. 1901) make a speech on the Irish language.

135.24 *Mr Justice Fitzgibbon*: Gerald Fitzgibbon (1837–1909), Lord Justice of the Appeal (1878), anti-Home Rule, Conservative, and considered, as commissioner of education, to be attempting to Anglicize Ireland.

135.26 *revival of the Irish tongue*: for centuries Irish nationalism was tied to the battle between the conqueror's language (English) and the native tongue (Gaelic). In the late 19th c. the issue was revived, directly linked to the battle for Irish independence by the Gaelic League (founded in 1893 by Douglas Hyde (see 299.3–4n.) and Eoin MacNeill (1867–1945)), dedicated specifically to the re-establishment of the Irish language (and generally to a policy of 'de-Anglicization').

135.30 *sitting withim T Healy*: should read 'sitting with Tim Healy'. Timothy Michael Healy (1855–1931), secretary to Parnell (at first his 'lieutenant', later, on leading the move to oust him, his 'betrayer'), MP, ardent nationalist, first Governor-General of the Irish Free State (1922–8).

136.1 *the proud man's contumely*: from Hamlet's most famous soliloquy (*Hamlet*, III. i. 70).

136.16 *Briefly ... his words were these*: Taylor's speech was not recorded, though see *JJ* 91 for the *Freeman's Journal* version.

136.26 *And let our croked smokes*: '... climb to their nostrils | From our blest altars' (*Cymbeline*, v. v. 477–8). (See 209.30–2.)

136.32–4 *It was revealed to me ... Augustine*: verbatim quotation from St Augustine's (354–430) *Confessions* (397), vii. 12.

137.3 *tireme*: should read 'trireme'.

137.12 *Isis and Osiris, of Horus and Ammon Ra*: Egyptian deities: Isis and Osiris: respectively, the female and male principles (sister and brother, wife and husband); Horus: son of Isis and Osiris, avenged his father's death, god of light; Ammon Ra: sun-god and supreme deity.

137.35 *Gone with the wind*: from Ernest Dowson's (1867–1900) 'Non Sum Qualis

Eram Bonae Sub Regno Cynarae' (1896), stanza 3 (Latin: 'I am no longer the man I was under the kind reign of Cynara' (Horace, *Odes*, IV. i. 3–4)).

137.35–138.2 *Hosts at Mullaghmast . . . within his voice*: the 'hosts' who came to Daniel O'Connell's two most successful 'monster meetings' agitating for repeal of the Act of Union, 13 Aug. 1843 (Tara) and 1 Oct. 1843 (Mullaghmast). O'Connell, of course, died before the establishment of the Irish Free State (see 31.20 n.).

138.2–3 *Akasic records*: Theosophical term: the Akasa is the eternal memory of Nature (Gilbert, 189).

138.31 *Fuit Ilium!*: Latin: 'Troy has been!' (Virgil, *Aeneid*, II. 325).

139.9 *Two Dublin vestals*: the vestals were the virgin priestesses of Vesta, Roman goddess of the hearth.

139.15 *Let there be life*: from 'Let there be light' (Gen. 1: 3).

139.22 *Wise virgins*: from Jesus's parable of the prepared and the unprepared virgins—those who have lamps and oil and those who have lamps but no oil (Matt. 25: 1–13).

140.1 *passionist father*: member of the Catholic order 'Barefooted Clerks of the Holy Cross and Passion of Our Lord', established in 1737 by St Paul of the Cross (1697–1775).

140.1 *crubeen*: Gaelic: *crúibín*: 'pig's trotter'.

140.12 *RETURN OF BLOOM*: should be moved to follow (as new line) 'I see them.' (140.13).

141.13 *RAISING THE WIND*: 'Obtaining necessary money or funds' (Brewer).

141.14 *Nulla bona*: Latin: 'No goods or possessions'; legal phrase: nothing that can be sold for the payment of debts.

141.26–7 *the waxies' Dargle*: 'waxies': cobblers; 'Dargle': picturesque spot near Bray; perhaps an annual picnic.

142.5 *the onehandled adulterer*: Admiral Nelson (see 92.2 n.), who lost an arm in the battle of Santa Cruz (1797), and had a famous affair with Lady Emma Hamilton (*c.*1765–1815), wife of the British minister at Naples.

142.21–5 *Antisthenes . . . Penelope*. Antisthenes (*c.*445–360 BC), Greek cynic philosopher, ascetic; the work alluded to is lost, but his argument was supposedly that Penelope was the more beautiful because the more virtuous of the two women (*G* and *T*). 'Gorgias', Greek Sophist and rhetorician, and Antisthenes's teacher.

142.26 *Penelope Rich*: (*c.*1562–1607), Sir Philip Sidney's (1554–86) beloved 'Stella' of his *Astrophel and Stella* (1591), a sonnet sequence. She was unhappily married to Robert, Lord Rich, but lived openly with Lord Mountjoy whom she married after her divorce from Rich.

143.12 *Deus nobis hæc otia fecit*: Latin: 'god has made this peace for us'; Virgil, *Eclogues*, I. 6.

143.13 *A Pisgah Sight of Palestine*: Mount Pisgah: the mountain from which God showed Moses the Promised Land (though he was not allowed to enter) at the end of the forty years in the wilderness (Deut. 34: 1–5); as usual, Stephen's words are borrowed, this time from the title of Thomas Fuller's (1608–61) *A Pisgah-Sight of Palestine and the Confines Thereof with the History of the Old and New Testament Acted Thereon* (1650), a descriptive geography of the Holy Land.

143.19 *cynosure*: a centre of attraction or admiration.

LESTRYGONIANS

Location: Both sides of the Liffey, not far from Trinity College (F4–5). In search of food, Bloom strolls south down Sackville Street (F4) past the end of Bachelor's Walk (on the north bank of the Liffey), crosses the Liffey on O'Connell Bridge (F4), continues south on Westmoreland Street past the gates of Trinity College, and on down Grafton Street. He then turns left into Duke Street (F4–5) and enters, first, the Burton Hotel (rejected), then Davy Byrne's pub (at 21 Duke Street). After eating, he walks east on Duke Street to Dawson Street, turns right then immediately left into Molesworth Street (F5), starts to turn left into Kildare Street and the National Library when he sees Boylan approaching from the opposite direction so swerves back right and ducks into the National Museum (F5).

Time: 1 p.m.

Homer: Odysseus continues his tale. After leaving Aeolia, he and his men came to Telepylus, the town of the Lestrygonians. Two promontories formed the mouth of the harbour which was itself encircled by high stone cliffs. While the other ships had anchored well inside the harbour, wily Odysseus moored 'outside where the harbour ended' (115), and sent three men to discover who dwelt there. They encountered King Antiphates's daughter ('tall and powerful') who directed them to her father's house. Here they met, first, his wife (who stood 'mountain-high') and, then, the king himself (whose only thought was to kill and eat the men). He caught only one; the other two escaped. In fury, Antiphates sounded an alarm. In response, his subjects ran to the cliffs, threw huge rocks down upon the ships in the harbour, 'speared men like fish' (116), and carried them away to be eaten. Odysseus, whose ship lay safely outside the harbour, quickly severed the mooring line with a sword, and he and his crew escaped. (Book X)

Schemata: *L* lists as personae Antiphates, the Seductive Daughter, and Ulysses, but provides no correspondences. *G* aligns Antiphates with Hunger, The Decoy with Food, and the Lestrygonians with Teeth. *L* and *G* agree on Organ (Esophagus), Art (Architecture), and Technic (*L*: Peristaltic prose; *G*: Peristaltic), but disagree on Colour (*L*: blood red; *G*: none) and Symbol (*L*: Bloody sacrifice, Food, Shame; *G*: Constables). *L*'s Sense is 'Despondency'.

One o'clock is lunchtime and Bloom is preoccupied with thoughts of food. The human body's need for nourishment registers on him as an awareness that everyone is eating, and that he too must eat. Everything is subject to the (at times subliminal, at times conscious if unstated) question, 'Can it be eaten?' His body is played over by the antithetical impulses of desire and disgust, hunger and despondency. 'Feel as if I had been eaten and spewed' (157.10). Also, he unconsciously enacts, in his movement about the streets, the rhythm of peristalsis as he walks past Davy Byrne's then back, into Kildare Street then back. And if Bloom doubles back so does time: contemplating coincidence (of thinking of Parnell's brother then seeing him, of AE then passing him) Bloom theorizes, 'Coming events cast their shadows before' (158.1–2). That's a narrative fact readers would be wise to attend to, one which reaches beyond *Lestrygonians* and reverberates throughout *Ulysses*.

144.6–9 *a throwaway . . . Blood of the Lamb*: one of Bloom's many identifications with the 'throwaway' motif; here he thinks he's the addressee of the casual correspondence, but the word turns out to be 'Blood', a reminder of his corporeality, an identification of Bloom, the dark outsider, with a very different Messiah; 'Blood of the Lamb': see Rev. 7: 14: 'These are they which came out of great tribulation, and have washed their robes, and made them white in the blood of the Lamb'. Also an allusion to the evangelical hymn 'Washed in the Blood of the Lamb' by E. A. Hoffmann (*T*).

144.11 *God wants blood victim*: the connection between the 'blood of the lamb' and 'blood sacrifice' (whether the throwaway's or Bloom's) echoes the rhetoric of Mikhail Bakunin (1814–76), Russian revolutionary and anarchist exiled to London: 'All religions are cruel, all founded on blood; for all rest principally on the idea of sacrifice—that is, on the perpetual immolation of humanity to the insatiable vengeance of divinity' (*God and the State* (1882), as quoted in Dominic Manganiello, *Joyce's Politics* (London: Routledge, 1980), 102).

144.13 *Elijah is coming*: in Jewish tradition, the second coming of Elijah must precede the coming of the Messiah; based on Mal. 4: 5: 'Behold, I will send you Elijah the prophet before the coming of the great and dreadful day of the Lord'.

144.13 *John Alexander Dowie*: (1847–1907), Scottish-born American evangelist, founded his own church (and town, Zion City, Illinois), announced himself Elijah the Restorer, tried to convert New York City, pursued an evangelical Round the World campaign, was finally ousted by his followers for his abuses; he was in London, though not preaching, in the week of 11–18 June 1904, but not in Dublin (*T*).

144.17 *Torry and Alexander*: American revivalists who were in Britain between 1903 and 1905 (*G*).

145.5–6 *Increase and multiply*: the commandment to Adam and Eve in the Garden of Eden (Gen. 1: 28).

145.8 *black fast Yom Kippur*: the Day of Atonement, holiest day of Jewish religious year and in Mosaic law the only fast, a day of penitence (see Lev. 16 and 23: 26–32).

145.19 *the brewery*: Guinness's Brewery (C4).

146.3–4 *Hamlet, I am . . . earth*: the Ghost in *Hamlet*, I. v. 9–10; Bloom substitutes 'time' for the Ghost's 'term', and mistakenly has the Ghost call Hamlet by name (see 181.7).

146.15 *Live on fishy flesh they have to, all*: should read 'Live on fish, fishy flesh they have, all'.

146.16 *Anna Liffey*: the River Liffey, which runs through the centre of Dublin; 'Anna' derives from the Gaelic: *ahba* (pronounced 'avain'): 'river' (though see O Hehir, 354–9, for an alternative etymology); in the *Wake*, she becomes Anna Livia Plurabelle.

146.18 *Robinson Crusoe had to live on them*: if he did, he kept it a secret.

146.31–2 *greenhouses*: public urinals.

147.8 *Time ball . . . Dunsink time*: the Ballast Office (on Aston's Quay (F4)) clock was the Big Ben of Dublin; the 'timeball' (a large ball on a pole) dropped at a specified time each day, 1.00 *Greenwich* time; as Dublin time was 'Dunsink time' (time at the Royal Observatory of Ireland, 25 minutes *earlier* than Greenwich time), the ball would drop every day at 12.35 p.m. Dublin time; thus, all Bloom can tell from seeing that the ball has dropped is that it is some time after 12.35.

147.9 *Sir Robert Ball's*: (1840–1913), Astronomer Royal, director of the Cambridge observatory, author of *The Story of the Heavens* (1885) on Bloom's shelf (661.10).

147.9 *Parallax*: 'the apparent difference in the position or direction of an object caused when the observer's position is changed' (*OEED*); a principle with more than physical repercussions in *Ulysses*.

147.32–3 *Women too. Curiosity. Pillar of salt*: Lot and his family were spared destruction (unlike the others in Sodom) on condition that, on leaving, they did not look back; Lot's wife looked and was turned into a pillar of salt (Gen. 19: 26).

148.12 *a nun . . . invented barbed wire*: not so; three Americans (Smith, Hunt, and Kelly) invented it in 1867–8; Joseph Farwell Glidden invented a machine which made its manufacture commercially viable (1874).

149.4–5 *that lodge meeting . . . lottery tickets*: as *Cyclops* and *Penelope* repeat, Bloom flirted with arrest by attempting to sell tickets for 'The Royal and Privileged Hungarian Lottery' only to be saved by the Masons; there was actually a prosecution in Dublin against a printer who printed the tickets (*G*).

150.17 *Penny dinner*: charitable dinners for the poor, provided at the Christian Union Buildings, Lower Abbey Street (F4).

150.36 *U.P.*: the exact meaning is Joyce's secret, though the French translation (produced by the 'team' of Auguste Morel, Stuart Gilbert, and Valéry Larbaud with Joyce occasionally reviewing and answering queries) reads: 'Fou. Tu.: foutu' (*Ulysse*, i. 227)—a phrase itself beautifully ambiguous, but roughly 'you're mad' or 'done for' or even 'buggered'. Ellmann always maintained it meant 'when erect you urinate rather than ejaculate'.

151.25 *Dr Horne*: Andrew J. Horne, one of the two masters of the National Maternity Hospital.

152.21 *Meshuggah*: Yiddish: 'crazy'.

152.29 *Irish Times*: Dublin daily newspaper, solid, conservative, generally Protestant Anglo-Irish, generally staidly opposed to Home Rule; Henry Flower has placed his ad. which connects him with Martha Clifford here.

153.10 *Uneatable fox*: in Act I of Oscar Wilde's *A Woman of No Importance*, Lord Illingworth remarks: 'The English country gentleman galloping after a fox—the unspeakable in full pursuit of the uneatable'.

153.22 *scavening*: should read 'scavenging'.

153.29 *Dublin Castle*: city residence of the Lord-Lieutenant of Ireland, offices of the chief secretary, law offices of the Crown, the Royal Irish Constabulary, etc.

154.8 *Twilightsleep*: 'A state of partial narcosis, especially to ease the pain of child-birth' (*OEED*); used by Queen Victoria (as induced by chloroform) for the birth of Prince Leopold (Apr. 1853).

154.20 *Phthisis retires . . . returns*: 'Phthisis': any progressive wasting disease but especially pulmonary tuberculosis which can lie dormant and then become active again.

154.29 *the Irish house of parliament*: the building viewed did house the Irish House of Parliament (dissolved under the Act of Union in 1800), but in 1904 was the Bank of Ireland.

155.5–6 *Tommy Moore's roguish finger . . . meeting of the waters*: Thomas Moore (1779–1852), Irish poet, made his home in England, published *Irish Melodies* (a series of volumes of sentimental Irish verse (1807–34)) and *Captain Rock* (1824) which showed that he was aware of the plight of rural Catholics; often referred to as Ireland's 'national poet'; see *G* for a gleeful gloss of 'roguish'; Moore's verse 'The Meeting of the Waters' celebrates the beauties of the vale of Avoca; Bloom recalls a line at 155.7–8.

155.9 *Michael Balfe*: see 126.4–5 n.

155.12 *bridewell*: house of correction or prison, after the Bridewell, Blackfriars, London, a penitentiary until it was demolished in 1863 (Brewer).

155.14 *Joe Chamberlain*: Joseph Chamberlain (1836–1914), industrialist and politician, Liberal MP who left the party (1886) over Gladstone's support of Home Rule, formed the Liberal Unionists, led them into alliance with the Conservatives (1895), served as Colonial Secretary (1895–1903)—an aggressive defender of British imperialist policies: anti-Home Rule, often held in some part responsible for the Boer War. Irish nationalists were pro-Boer (largely on the grounds of a belief in a shared oppression by Britain). When Chamberlain came to Trinity College to receive an honorary degree (18 Dec. 1899), nationalists organized a pro-Boer demonstration in which the police intervened.

155.24 *Up the Boers!*: see previous note; radical nationalists even raised troops to fight on the Boer side.

155.25 *De Wet*: Christian R. DeWet (1854–1922), distinguished Boer commander.

155.26 *We'll hang ... sourapple tree*: adaptation of line from one version of the American civil war song 'John Brown's Body': 'We'll hang Jeff Davis to a sour-apple tree!' (Davis was the president of the southern states Confederacy.)

155.27 *Vinegar hill*: in County Wexford, home of the Wexford rebels and scene of their final defeat (21 June 1798).

156.10 *James Stephens' idea*: James Stephens organized the Irish Republican Brotherhood on the cell principle: no more than ten members in a cell, more than that and the cell divided, each cell had a leader (or 'centre')—the only leader the cell member would know and the only one who would know anyone further up the chain of command—and so on up numerous levels; only the highest leaders really knew what was going on. (See 31.23 n. and 43.25 n.)

156.11 *Sinn Fein*: see 7.31 n. Originally without a secret 'military' wing, Sinn Féin policy was economic and cultural: refusal to support England economically, independent development of Ireland's economy and culture whether or not constitutionally recognized by Britain.

156.12 *Turkney's*: should read 'Turnkey's'.

156.14 *Garibaldi*: Giuseppe Garibaldi (1807–82), Italian patriot and military leader, influential in the establishment of a united kingdom of Italy; he relied heavily on his popular support and, on one occasion, walked into a Naples held by hostile forces with only two companions.

156.16 *no go in him for the mob*: Arthur Griffith's policies (see 156.11 n.) were frankly 'élitist' rather than populist and he contented himself with gaining the support of those who could understand them.

156.18–19 *That the language question ... economic question*: an independent Ireland, so the line went, was best achieved through establishing a strong Irish cultural identity, not through attention to economic independence—a slight parody of Griffith's position.

157.5 *Big stones left. Round towers*: the remains of ancient Ireland: the standing stones and stone circles, and the pre-Norman round towers of 9th–12th-c. monasteries.

157.6 *Kerwan's mushroom houses*: low-cost housing built by Michael Kirwan, Dublin contractor.

157.15 *John Howard Parnell*: (1843–1923), brother of Charles Stewart Parnell, MP (1895–1900), city marshal of Dublin in 1904; (157.28–9: David Sheehy did beat him—by a huge vote—in the 1903 election).

157.27 *Mad Fanny*: Frances (Fanny) Parnell (1845–82), sister of Charles Stewart Parnell, and the most romantically nationalist of the siblings, emigrated to America (1874) where she wrote Irish nationalist pieces for the *Nation* and patriotic verses and established the Ladies' Land League (New York, 1880). 'Mrs. Dickinson' was yet another sister.

157.30 *The patriot's ... orangepeels*: the eating of oranges by nationalists at patriotic assemblies was meant to taunt the Orangemen.

158.1–2 *Coming events cast their shadows before*: from Thomas Campbell's (1777–1844) 'Lochiel's Warning' (1802), l. 56, in which a wizard foretells the fall of Bonnie Prince Charlie (1720–88) at the battle of Culloden (1745) and warns Lochiel not to ride to his death.

158.3–4 *A.E.: What does that mean?*: George Russell's pen-name, AE, did not stand, as one Dublin wit put it, for 'Agricultural Economist', but for the first two letters in the word 'aeon', ostensibly a typesetter's misreading for Russell's attempted use of this word as his pseudonym (*G*).

158.27–8: *Germans making their way*: Germany's policies before the First World War were militaristic, colonialist, and economically expansionist.

159.11 *professor Joly*: Charles Jasper Joly (1864–1906), Astronomer Royal of Ireland, professor of astronomy at Trinity, director of Dunsink observatory.

159.20 *Gas, then solid ... frozen rock*: Pierre Simon, marquis de Laplace (1749–1827), French astronomer, held that the movement of matter was toward a perpetual cooling: from gas, to solid, etc., until the earth would become like the moon, a 'dead shell' (*G*).

160.2 *Dion Boucicault*: (1822–90), Irish-American playwright and actor; contemporary opinion held that he made up in humour whatever other talent he lacked.

160.7 *The harp that once did starve us all*: punning parody of title of Thomas Moore's song 'The Harp that Once Through Tara's Halls' from his *Irish Melodies*.

160.21–3 *La causa è santa! ... Meyerbeer*: Italian: 'The cause is sacred'; allusion to Giacomo Meyerbeer's (1791–1864) opera *Les Huguenots* (1836). See *T* and *G*.

161.22 *See ourselves as others see us*: after Robert Burns's (1759–96) 'To a Louse; on Seeing One on a Lady's Bonnet at Church' (1786), ll. 43–4: 'O wad some Power the giftie gie us | To see oursels as ithers see us!' Note Stephen's thought at 6.30–1.

161.23–6 *That last pagan king ... swallow it all however*: legend and history collide here; Bloom recalls Sir Samuel Ferguson's (1810–86) poem 'The Burial of King Cormac': 'He choked upon the food he ate | At Sletty, southward of the Boyne'; Cormac (r. *c.*254–*c.*277), reputedly the founder of Ireland as a nation (established Tara as 'the ancient seat of Irish kings'), *not* the last pagan king, though legend does have him being converted to Christianity by St Patrick (who didn't arrive in Ireland until *c.*432); Laoghaire was high king when St Patrick arrived and legend has him neither accepting nor interfering with St Patrick's mission.

161.33 *Look on this picture then on that*: Hamlet to Gertrude, urging her to compare the picture of his father with that of Claudius (*Hamlet*, III, iv. 53–4).

162.5–6 *Born with a silver knife in his mouth*: a Bloomism for 'Born with a silver spoon in his mouth': proverbial for 'born wealthy'.

162.27, 33 *don't talk of ... provost of Trinity | Father O'Flynn ... hares of them all*: allusion to Alfred Percival Graves's (1846–1931) ballad 'Father O'Flynn', the second verse of which begins, 'Don't talk of your Provost and Fellows of Trinity | Famous for ever at Greek and Latinity, | Dad and the divels and all at Divinity, | Father O'Flynn'd make hares of them all'; 'to make a hare of': 'to make a fool of'.

162.29 *artisans' dwellings, north Dublin union*: houses of the Dublin poor on the east edge of Phoenix Park (C3); the North Union Workhouse was a poorhouse just east of there (D4).

163.31–2 *Kosher. No meat and milk together*: 'Kosher': of food or premises which handle it, fulfilling the requirements of Jewish law (for its ceremonial preparation and cleanliness); 'no meat . . .': one of the laws.

163.32–3 *Yom Kippur fast spring cleaning*: see 145.8 n.; the fast of Yom Kippur can only metaphorically be a 'spring cleaning' as it occurs in autumn.

163.34 *Slaughter of innocents*: King Herod's command, on hearing a prophecy that the Messiah (Jesus) was about to be born, that all young male children in Bethlehem be slain (Matt. 2: 16).

163.34–5 *Eat, drink and be merry*: now proverbial; similar phrases are littered throughout the Bible (*T*).

163.36 *Mighty cheese*: should read 'Mity cheese'.

164.32 *hauched*: should read 'hanched'.

165.6–7 *that boxing match Myler Keogh . . . soldier*: an event repeatedly alluded to, though Joyce has changed the details: an actual match occurred between Keogh and one Garry of the 6th Dragoons on 29 Apr. 1904; Keogh won in the third round. Joyce makes his opponent one 'sergeantmajor Percy Bennett', an Englishman (see 305.11–306.4), and changes the date to 22 May (241.7).

166.37 *That archduke Leopold . . . Otto one of those Habsburgs*: a confusion of Leopold von Bayern (1821–1912), prince regent of Bavaria (1886–1912), with Otto I (1848–1916), king of Bavaria (1886–1912). The latter went insane in 1872, was kept under strict scrutiny (a secrecy which bred stories of strange goings-on) until he was finally deposed in 1912; he was not a Habsburg (rulers of the Austro-Hungarian empire).

167.20 *over first*: should read 'over fist'.

167.22 *kish*: Gaelic: *cis*: 'wickerwork, hamper'.

168.13–14 *Pygmalion and Galatea*: Greek myth of the King of Cyprus who fell in love with an ivory statue of a woman (which he may or may not have sculpted); he asked Aphrodite to grant him such a woman and returned to find the statue had come to life. Also an 1871 verse play by Sir William Schwenck Gilbert (1836–1911) (of Gilbert and Sullivan fame), a satire in which Galatea, the statue-come-alive, disrupts the lives of Pygmalion, the sculptor, and his jealous wife, Cynisca (played at the Gaiety Theatre in Nov. 1891).

168.19 *food, chyle, blood, dung, earth, food*: this sequence of matter endlessly recycled echoes that described by Giordano Bruno (see 28.26 n.) in his *Cause, Principle, and Unity* (1584) (*G*).

168.23 *A man and ready . . . to the lees*: Homer repeatedly refers to Odysseus's 'readiness'; Tennyson's 'Ulysses' (1842), ll. 6–7: 'I cannot rest from travel; I will drink | Life to the lees'.

169.11, 13–15 *the craft. | Ancient free and... won't say who*: 'The craft': Freemasonry: the 'Free and Accepted Masons', 'an international fraternity for mutual help and fellowship with an elaborate ritual and system of secret signs' (*OEED*); their ostensible goal is the establishment of a better world through individual purity and fraternal harmony; the phrases that follow echo phrases from the Masonic ritual; Bloom has (at least) been a Mason.

169.22–4 *There was one woman ... Doneraile*: traditionally, not the only, but the first woman to invade the Masons, Elizabeth Aldworth (d. 1773), daughter of Arthur St Leger, first Viscount Doneraile, who supposedly saw a Masonic ceremony in her father's house and was sworn in to ensure secrecy, though not as a Master (highest degree) Mason.

171.6–7 *Something green it... searchlight you could*: Bloom imagines following food through the body through the use of Röntgen rays (or 'X-rays'), discovered in 1895 by Wilhelm Konrad von Röntgen (1845–1923).

171.17–18 *Don Giovanni, a cenar teco | M'invitasti*: in *Don Giovanni*, Mozart's opera (see 61.20 n.), Don Giovanni mockingly invites the statue of his enemy to supper; in the final act, the statue appears and (unsuccessfully) solicits Don Giovanni's repentance; on entering he sings the line (in Italian:) 'Don Giovanni, you invited me to sup with you' and continues '*e son venuto*'—'and I have come'. Bloom returns to the lines at 171.28 and 'translates' them at 171.30–2; 'teco' means, not 'tonight' (which Bloom mistakenly adds in his translation), but 'with you [thee]'.

172.2–3 *Presscott's ad*: should read 'Prescott's dyeworks over there. If I got Billy Prescott's ad'.

172.12–13 *Why I left the church of Rome*: pamphlet by Presbyterian minister Charles Pascal Telesphore Chiniquy (1809–99), who was ordained a Catholic priest but left, principally over the concept of the Virgin Mary (*G*).

172.13 *Birds' Nest. Women run him*: should read 'Bird's nest women run him'; 'Bird's nest women': women who ran Protestant missionary societies for poor and orphaned children.

173.14 *Weight would*: should read 'Weight or size of it, something blacker than the dark. Wonder would'.

173.25–6 *bunched together. Each person too.*: should read 'bunched together. Each street different smell. Each person too.'

174.12–13 *All those women ... Holocaust*: an American steamer, the *General Slocum*, hired for a Lutheran Sunday School trip, caught fire and burned killing over 1,000 in Long Island Sound, New York; the story was carried in the 16 June *Freeman's Journal*.

174.16 *Sir Frederick Falkiner*: the Honourable Sir Frederick Richard Falkiner (1831–1908), recorder (chief judicial officer) of Dublin (1876–1905).

174.16 *Solemn as Troy*: not the city of the *Iliad*, but the anti-nationalist Roman

Catholic archbishop of Dublin, the Most Revd John Thomas Troy (1739–1823), who issued a 'solemn condemnation' of the 1798 Rebellion.

174.27 *Mirus bazaar*: bazaar in Ballsbridge (H6) to raise funds for the Mercer's Hospital, opened (on 31 May, not 16 June, 1904) by the Lord-Lieutenant, who did not conduct a viceregal cavalcade through Dublin.

174.28–9 *The Messiah was first given for that*: Handel's *Messiah*, an oratorio, was first performed, in aid of the Mercer's Hospital, 13 Apr. 1742, in the Music Hall, Fishamble Street (E4), Dublin, Handel conducting.

175.2 *Sir Thomas Deane*: actually, the architects for the National Museum and National Library (the same design) were Sir Thomas Newenham Deane (1830–99) and Sir Thomas Manly Deane (1851–1933), son and grandson of Sir Thomas Deane (1792–1871), architect for the Trinity College Museum.

SCYLLA AND CHARYBDIS

Location: National Library, Kildare Street (F5).

Time: 2 p.m.

Homer: Odysseus continues his tale. After escaping the Lestrygonians, Odysseus and his men landed on Circe's island (see *Circe* below). In order to leave, Odysseus had to choose between two routes: to go past either the Wandering Rocks or Scylla and Charybdis. Having chosen the latter, he faced another dilemma: whether to sail close to Scylla (the fearsome, twelve-footed, six-necked, six-headed (each with a 'triple row of crowded and close-set teeth, fraught with black death' (145)) monster who dwelt in a cave half-way up a tremendously high cliff, wailed furiously and fished for whatever large animals swam by) or Charybdis (a dark whirlpool who lived under the opposite cliff and thrice each day sucked in, then belched forth, the sea). He chose Scylla, paid the price of a loss of men, but managed eventually to pass by. (Book XII)

Schemata: As well as Ulysses and Scylla and Charybdis, *L* lists Antinous and Telemachus. Neither is present in the episode. Telemachus remains at Menelaus's court while Antinous still waits on Asteris (with the other suitors) to ambush Telemachus on his return. *G* entirely changes the register of correspondences providing for the Rock (Scylla), Aristotle, Dogma, and Stratford; for the Whirlpool (Charybdis), Plato, Mysticism, and London; for Ulysses (the one who passes between), Socrates, Jesus, and Shakespeare.

L and *G* agree on Colour (none), Art (Literature), and Organ (Brain), but disagree on Technic (*L*: Whirlpools; *G*: Dialectic). *L* lists most of *G*'s correspondences under Symbol: Hamlet, Shakespeare, Christ, Socrates, London and Stratford, Scholasticism and Mysticism, Plato and Aristotle, Youth and Maturity, while in the same category, *G* lists only Stratford and London. *L*'s Sense is 'The Two-edged Sword'.

Scylla or Charybdis, the rocks or the whirlpool; in Bloom lingo, the fryingpan or the fire: it is between such extremes that the wary traveller must steer a careful course. The journey here is Stephen's, most specifically his aesthetic theorizing—not simply what he says but the rhetorical flourish with which he says it. The twin dangers present themselves most glaringly as form versus formlessness, body versus mind, actual history versus pure ideation, or in the terms of Gilbert and Linati, Scholasticism (or Dogma) versus Mysticism, Aristotle versus Plato. Ulysses (the successful traveller) has his correlates in Shakespeare, Socrates, Jesus (inasmuch as he was 'God *incarnate*')—those who successfully steer the course between. Ulysses chose to sail by way of Scylla the Rock. Just so, Stephen prefers Aristotle (whose theories advocate a necessary recognition of 'Space: what you damn well have to see' and 'the now, the here') to Plato (much preferred by AE and Eglinton for he is thought by them to advocate 'ideas, formless spiritual essences'). Hence, his theory of Shakespeare attempts to demonstrate the incorporation into Shakespeare's art of 'the now, the here' of his actual life (however far-fetched the posited 'facts' that Stephen must muster to such a defence).

Still, art for Stephen is the imaginative transformation of life and in this is linked more to what he calls the 'legal fiction' of paternity than to his 'only-true-thing-in-life' materiality of maternity. Stephen distrusts the flesh, preferring even 'impalpable' paternal ghosts through whom 'the image of the unliving son looks forth' to maternal ghosts who remind him of his own corporeality. However close Stephen comes in what follows to acknowledging actuality, materiality, body, he inevitably attempts to protect himself from them through his repeated assertion of the artist's authority to control the unruly material world through the distantiating transformative power of language. Watch carefully, for in *Scylla and Charybdis*, *Ulysses* steers a more successful course than does Stephen.

In this episode, Stephen musters numerous 'facts' about Shakespeare's life to the cause of his argued aesthetic. In relying on Shakespeare biography (however irreverently), Stephen shows himself a child of the late nineteenth century—the age of Shakespeare biography. Very little is actually known about the details of Shakespeare's life, but this has not stopped the proliferation of biographies. Stephen's contribution to this imaginative art relies heavily on 'facts' gleaned by Joyce from the following works: George Brandes, *William Shakespeare* (London, 1898) (cited below as *GB*); Frank Harris, *The Man Shakespeare and his Tragic Life-Story* (New York, 1909) (cited below as *FH*), most of which had appeared in the 1890s in the *Saturday Review* which Harris edited; Sidney Lee, *A Life of William Shakespeare* (London, 1898) (cited below as *Lee*). See *G* for further details.

This being the discussion of 'clever young men' intent as much on demonstrating their capacity for citation as their gift of argument, the episode is heavily interlarded with Shakespearian allusion. Aside from the central consideration of *Hamlet* (a first-hand knowledge of which is indispensable to an understanding of, not only this episode, but *Ulysses* generally, especially Stephen's part in it), particular knowledge of either the play cited or the context of the specific allusion usually adds little insight. These boys wear their learning on their sleeves. Unless contextual knowledge of a particular Shakespeare citation is crucial, it is not provided below; instead, references alone are given. *T* and *G* provide fuller glosses. In all instances, citations are to *The Riverside Shakespeare*, ed. G. Blakemore Evans *et al.* (Boston: Houghton Mifflin, 1974).

176.1 *the quaker librarian*: Thomas William Lyster (1855–1922), librarian of the National Library of Ireland (1895–1920), translator of Dunster's *Life of Goethe* (1883) and editor of the series *English Poems for Young Students* (1893–).

176.2 *Wilhelm Meister*: Johann Wolfgang von Goethe (1749–1832), *Wilhelm Meister's Apprenticeship* (1796; trans. Thomas Carlyle (1795–1881) in 1824); Wilhelm translates, interprets, revises, and performs in his revised version of Shakespeare's *Hamlet* (Bk. IV, ch. 13–Bk. V, ch. 2).

176.3–4 *A hesitating soul . . . doubts*: in *Wilhelm Meister* (Bk. IV, ch. 13), Wilhelm theorizes that Hamlet's character renders him inadequate to the task he faces; the play thus 'represent[s] the effects of a great action laid upon a soul unfit for the performance of it'; of Hamlet himself he remarks: 'a lovely, pure, noble, and most moral nature, without the strength of nerve which forms a hero, sinks beneath a burden it cannot bear and must not cast away'. See too *Hamlet* III. i. 56–9.

176.5 *a sinkapace; neatsleather*: 'sinkapace': five-stepped dance (*Twelfth Night*, I. iii. 130–1); 'neatsleather': oxhide (*Julius Caesar*, I. i. 25; *Tempest*, II. ii. 70).

176.9–10 *The beautiful ineffectual . . . hard facts*: Wilhelm Meister on *Hamlet* (see 176.3–4 n.); but also Goethe's attitude toward Wilhelm himself who is in danger of being lured by the theatre into ineffectuality (*G*); 'beautiful ineffectual dreamer': Matthew Arnold, 'Shelley', *Essays in Criticism: Second Series* (1888): 'And in poetry, no less than in life, he is a beautiful "and ineffectual" angel, beating in the void his luminous wings in vain'.

176.17 *John Eglinton*: pseudonym of William Kirkpatrick Magee (1868–1961), essayist, assistant librarian of National Library (*c.*1904–1922); he resigned in protest at the formation of the Irish Free State and retired to England (*G*).

176.18 *The Sorrows of Satan*: novel (1895) by Marie Corelli (pseudonym of Mary McKay (1855–1924)); a record-breaking bestseller; Satan sorrows because of the failure of his (therefore endless) quest to find someone strong enough to withstand him; variously adapted for the stage.

176.21–5 *First he tickled . . . medi . . .* : part of an unpublished verse by Oliver St John Gogarty.

177.2 *The shining seven W.B. calls them*: in 'A Cradle Song' (1895 version), l. 7, W. B. Yeats refers to the planets (the seven known in 1895) as 'The Shining Seven'.

177.4 *an ollav*: pre-Christian Irish master of arts; here referring to AE (George Russell).

177.5 *a sizar*: scholarship student at Trinity College, Dublin (one whose fees were paid by the College and who worked as servant in exchange); sizars wore red hats to distinguish them from ordinary students.

177.6–8 *Orchestral Satan ... trombetta*: three disparate lines: (1) after Milton's *Paradise Lost*, I. 196 where Satan is described as 'floating many a rood'; (2) *Paradise Lost*, I. 619–20, of Satan, trying to speak to the fallen angels: 'and thrice in spite of scorn, | Tears such as Angels weep, burst forth'; (3) Dante's *Inferno*, XXI. 139: Italian: 'And of his arse he made a trumpet'.

177.10–11 *Gaptoothed Kathleen*: Cathleen ni Houlihan in Yeats's 1902 play of that name; Cathleen is a characterization of the Shan Van Vocht ('the Poor Old Woman', see 14.6 n. and 17.30–1 n.); the 'four beautiful green fields' are the four pre-Norman provinces of Ireland: Ulster, Connacht, Munster, Leinster.

177.11–12 *And one more to hail him: ave, rabbi*: one to play Judas; 'ave, rabbi': Vulgate Latin: 'Hail, Master'; Matt. 26: 49: Judas identifying Jesus: 'and forthwith he came to Jesus, and said, Hail, Master!'

177.12–13 *In the shadow of the glen*: title of 1903 one-act play by John Millington Synge (see 185.17 n.); the play is set in Wicklow, where Tinahely is.

177.19 *I admire him ... idolatry*: from Ben ('Old Ben') Jonson's eulogy for Shakespeare printed in his *Timber, or Discoveries* (1640): 'for I lov'd the man, and doe honour his memory (on this side Idolatry)' (*GB* 20; *T*).

177.21 *whether Hamlet is Shakespeare or James I or Essex*: various answers to the endlessly repeated critical question, 'On whom is Hamlet modelled?'; James I (of England, VI of Scotland) (1566–1625); Robert Devereux (1566–1601), second earl of Essex.

177.23 *formless spiritual essences*: an AE catchphrase; see e.g. AE on Yeats: 'spirituality is the power of apprehending formless spiritual essences, of seeing the eternal in the transitory' ('Religion and Love' (1904), repr. in *Imaginations and Reveries* (Dublin, 1915), 122) (*G*).

177.24 *Gustave Moreau*: (1826–98), French Romantic painter much admired by AE.

177.25 *the deepest poetry of Shelley*: Percy Bysshe Shelley (1792–1822), whose poetry was much admired by the hermetic crowd.

177.26 *Plato's world of ideas*: the transcendentalist view of Plato (*c*.427–347 BC) held him to be the ultimate symbolist: truth was an abstraction, an ideal embodied elsewhere, this world its mere shadow. See, particularly, the parable of the cave in Bk. VII of *Republic*.

177.30 *Aristotle was once Plato's schoolboy*: he was, for twenty years: Plato was head of the Academy in Athens, Aristotle (384–322 BC) was a pupil there 367–347 BC.

178.2–13 *Formless spiritual. Father, Word ... Pfuiteufel!*: this passage is an extended parody of Theosophical beliefs (see 135.13–14 n.); for full background, see Annie Besant, *Esoteric Christianity* (1901), or *The Ancient Wisdom* (1897); Helena Petrovna Blavatsky, *Isis Unveiled: A Master Key to the Mysteries of Ancient and Modern Science and Philosophy* (1876), or Powis Hoult, *A Dictionary of some Theosophical Terms* (1910).

178.2–3 *Allfather, the heavenly man*: 'Allfather': Jesus to Theosophists; 'heavenly man': Adam Kadmon (see 38.16 n.).

178.3 *Hiesos Kristos*: Greek: 'Jesus Christ'.

178.3 *Logos*: Greek: 'the word'; as in John 1: 1: 'In the beginning was the Word, and the Word was with God, and the Word was God'.

178.4–5 *I am the fire . . . butter*: parody of the *Bhagavadgītā*: 'I am the ritual action, I am the sacrifice, I am the ancestral oblation, I am the (medicinal) herb, I am the (sacred) hymn, I am also the melted butter, I am the fire and I am the offering' (trans. S. Radhakrishnan (London, 1948), 245) (*G*).

178.6 *Dunlop*: Daniel Nicol Dunlop, editor of *Irish Theosophist* (*c.* 1896–1915), and permanent chair of the Theosophical Society of Europe (from 1896) (*G*).

178.6 *Judge*: William Q. Judge (1851–96), co-founder with Madame Blavatsky of the Theosophical Society (1875) and head of Aryan Theosophical Society, New York.

178.6 *the noblest Roman of them all*: Mark Antony in praise of the now dead Brutus in *Julius Caesar*, v. v. 68: 'This was the noblest Roman of them all'.

178.6 *Arval*: ruling council of the Theosophical Society.

178.6–7 *The Name Ineffable*: name (not to be spoken, but known by the 'adepts') of one of Blavatsky's two masters 'K.H.' or Koot Hoomi who 'spoke' to her in spiritual messages.

178.8 *Brothers of the great white lodge*: another name for Judge's Aryan Theosophical Society (see 178.6 n.).

178.9–10 *The Christ with . . . plane of buddhi*: synopsis of Jesus's life according to the Theosophists (see *G*).

178.11 *O.P. must work off bad karma first*: 'O.P.': ordinary people; 'karma': 'the sum of a person's actions in previous states of existence, viewed as deciding his or her fate in future existences' (*OEED*); so, to attain the perfected state, a soul had to work through its previous 'bad karma' in successive incarnations.

178.12–13 *Mrs Cooper Oakley*: Isabel Cooper-Oakley (b. 1854), wealthy London businesswoman and close friend of Madame Blavatsky.

178.13 *H.P.B.'s elemental*: Helena Petrovna Blavatsky (see 135.13–14 n.); 'elemental': mortal aspect.

178.14 *O, fie! Out on't!*: after Hamlet's various oaths; see *Hamlet*, I. ii. 135 and II. ii. 587.

178.14 *Pfuiteufel!*: German: *pfui*: 'fie'; *teufel*: 'devil'; an oath.

178.15 *Mr Best*: Richard Irvine Best (1872–1959), assistant director (1904–23) then director (1924–40) of the National Library, founder of School of Irish Learning, translator of Marie Henri d'Arbois de Joubainville's (1827–1910) *Le Cycle mythologique irlandais* (as *The Irish Mythological Cycle and Celtic Mythology* (1903)).

178.17–19 *That model schoolboy . . . Plato's*: the 'model schoolboy': Aristotle; Hamlet's 'musings on the afterlife' occur, of course, in his 'To be or not to be' soliloquy (III. i. 55–87); for Plato's 'musings' see e.g. *Republic*, x. 611: 'the soul which cannot be destroyed by an evil, whether inherent or external, must exist for ever, and if existing for ever, must be immortal' (trans. Jowett).

178.23–4 *Which of the two ... commonwealth*: answer: Plato, *Republic*, x. 607: 'hymns to the gods and praises of famous men are the only poetry which ought to be admitted into our State. For if you go beyond this and allow the honeyed muse to enter, either in epic or lyric verse, not law and the reason of mankind, which by common consent have ever been deemed best, but pleasure and pain will be the rulers in our State' (trans. Jowett).

178.25 *Horseness is the whatness of allhorse*: Aristotle's theory of substance in a nutshell; he held that abstractions (or universals) had no existence outside the particular substances in which they inhered, but could be distinguished by their coexistence in similar substances (see *T*).

178.26 *Streams of tendency and eons they worship*: 'they' being the Theosophists; 'eons' puns on AE, Russell's pseudonym, which derives from the word 'aeon' (see 158.3–4 n.).

178.27 *Space: what you damn well have to see*: Aristotle's view; see *Proteus*, especially 37.1 n.

178.27–9 *Through spaces smaller ... shadow*: after Blake's *Milton* (Bk. I, plate 29, ll. 21–2): 'every Space smaller than a Globule of Man's blood opens | Into Eternity, of which this vegetable Earth is but a shadow' (see 37.17 n. where Stephen alludes to the two preceeding lines); and Dante's *Inferno*, XXXIV, where Dante and Virgil leave Hell by crawling over Satan's buttocks (he being waist-deep in ice) and emerging into Purgatory.

178.29–30 *Hold to the now ... past*: see St Augustine's (353–430) *De Immortalitate Animae*: 'The intention to act is of the present, through which the future flows into the past' (*G*).

178.35 *Jubainville's book*: see 178.16 n.

178.36 *Hyde's Lovesongs of Connacht*: see 47.26–8 n.

179.1–4 *Bound thee forth ... English*: after the first stanza of Douglas Hyde's imitation of a *deibhidh*, a metre used by Celtic bards: 'Bound thee forth my Booklet quick. | To greet the Polished Public. | Writ—I ween't was not my Wish— | In Lean unLovely English' (in *The Story of Early Gaelic Literature* (1895)).

179.7 *An emerald set ... sea*: after John Philpot Curran's 'Cuisle Mo Chroidhe', ll. 1–2 (see 119.6 n.): 'Dear Erin, how sweetly thy green bosom rises | An emerald set in the ring of the sea'. (See too 19.28–9 n.)

179.8 *auric egg*: Theosophical term for the 'Causal Body' (the meditator or 'Thinker') at his most 'in tune' (see *G*).

179.9–13 *The movements which work ... the musichall song*: AE's general opinion of popular culture when weighed against traditional Irish art (see e.g. 'Nationality and Imperialism', in *Ideals in Ireland* (Dublin, 1901)).

179.13 *Mallarmé*: Stéphane Mallarmé (1842–98), French poet, aesthete, symbolist, 'decadent', author of, *inter alia*, *Le Cygne*, *Hérodiade*, *L'Après-midi d'un faune*, and the 'prose poem' to which Best alludes in 179.17, 'Hamlet et Fortinbras' (1896).

179.14–15 *the life of Homer's Phæacians*: see *Odyssey*, Books V–VIII, XIII; the Phaecians lived lives of peace, prosperity, and beauty; their supreme hospitality to Odysseus is punished by Poseidon.

179.18 *Stephen Mac Kenna*: (1872–1954), Irish journalist, linguist, and philosopher.

179.18–19 *The one about Hamlet*: see 179.13 n.

179.19 *il se promène . . . de lui-même*: French: 'he strolls, reading the book of himself' (from 'Hamlet et Fortinbras').

179.23–6 *HAMLET ou LE DISTRAIT . . . Shakespeare*: French: 'Hamlet, or the Distracted One. Play by Shakespeare'; Mallarmé does cite this in 'Hamlet et Fortinbras'.

179.30 *The absentminded beggar*: poem written by Rudyard Kipling (1865–1936), set to music by Arthur Sullivan, written to raise funds for British soldiers in the Boer War.

179.34 *Sumptuous and stagnant exaggeration of murder*: from Mallarmé's 'Hamlet et Fortinbras'.

180.1 *A deathsman . . . called him*: Robert Greene (*c.*1558–92), Elizabethan playwright, in *A Groat's Worth of Wit bought with a Million of Repentance* (1592) (see 183.11), calls 'lust' (not Shakespeare) 'the deathsman of the soul'; he does attack Shakespeare as 'an upstart Crow, beautified with our feathers . . . in his owne conceit, the only Shake-scene in a countrie' (*G*).

180.2 *a butcher's son*: a traditional story about John Shakespeare started by John Aubrey (1629–97), antiquarian.

180.3 *Nine lives*: actually only eight die (to the 'father's one'): Polonius, Ophelia, Rosencrantz, Guildenstern, Gertrude, Laertes, Claudius, Hamlet.

180.3–4 *Our Father who art in purgatory*: parody of the opening of the Lord's Prayer (Matt. 6: 9), though the Ghost in *Hamlet* does state he is 'confined to fast in fires | Till the foul crimes done in my days of nature | Are burnt and purged away' (I. v. 11–13).

180.4 *Khaki Hamlets don't hesitate to shoot*: 'khaki': colour of British troops' uniforms after the 1840s; 'don't hesitate to shoot': the charge of Irish protesters against those who enforced the coercion policy in 19th-c. Ireland; thus, Stephen aligns the slaughter in the last act of *Hamlet* with militaristic readiness to kill.

180.4–5 *The bloodboltered shambles in act five*: i.e. Act V of *Hamlet* in which four characters are slain; 'bloodboltered': *Macbeth*, IV. i. 123.

180.5 *the concentration camp sung by Mr Swinburne*: in Swinburne's sonnet 'On the Death of Colonel Benson' (1901), he laments Benson's death in the Boer War, indicts in jingoistic terms the Boers, and refuses to accept the charges made against English concentration camps (established under Kitchener, they held Boer civilians—including women and children—in reputedly inhumane conditions): 'Nor heed we more than he what liars say | Of mercy's holiest duties left undone | Toward whelps and dams of murderous foes whom none | Save we had spared or feared to starve and slay' (ll. 5–8).

180.6 *Cranly ... battles from afar*: i.e. Stephen finds himself continuing the lines of argument maintained by his friend Cranly in *Portrait*, ch. 5.

180.7–8 *Whelps and dams ... spared*: Swinburne's sonnet, ll. 7–8; see 180.5 n.

180.11 *the fat boy in Pickwick*: Joe, the fat boy, in Dickens's *The Pickwick Papers* (1836–7), ch. 8, who in telling Mrs Wardle of his having seen Mr Tupman kissing her daughter Rachel's hand says, 'I wants to make your flesh creep.'

180.13, 15 *List! List! O list! | If thou didst ever ...* : Ghost to Hamlet: 'List, list, oh, list! | If thou didst ever thy dear father love ...' (*Hamlet*, I. v. 22–3).

180.19 *limbo patrum*: in Shakespeare, slang for 'jail' (*Henry VIII*, v. iii. 64); but in Catholic theology, *Limbus Patrum* was the destination of the virtuous who died before Jesus came to earth and who could not ascend to heaven until after his resurrection.

180.23–5 *It is the hour ... bear Sackerson ... Paris garden*: the 'local colour' comes largely from *GB* (*T*): 'the bear Sackerson': the bear kept chained in the Bear Garden (the 'Paris Garden') on Bankside near the Globe Theatre where Shakespeare's plays were performed.

180.26 *Drake*: Sir Francis Drake (*c.*1540–96), English mariner, explorer, and vice-admiral, circumnavigated the globe (1577–80), raided Spanish settlements in South America, instrumental in England's defeat of the Spanish Armada (1588).

180.28–9 *Shakespeare has left ... the rushes*: anachronism, for this information was not known until 1910, when Charles Wallace published an article establishing Shakespeare's residence in Silver Street (*T*).

180.30 *The swan of Avon*: Ben Jonson's epithet for Shakespeare, from his poem published with the first Folio (see 177.19 n.).

180.31 *Composition of place. Ignatius Loyola*: St Ignatius Loyola uses the term 'composition of place' in his *Spiritual Exercises* (1548), 'The First Exercise', Item 47, 'First Prelude', to designate the act of imagining the physical counterpart of the thing (or person or place) to be meditated upon; cf. *Portrait*, ch. 3, p. 127.

181.3 *a king and no king*: title of Francis Beaumont (*c.*1584–1616) and John Fletcher's (1579–1625) tragicomic play *A King and No King* (1611); (*GB* 599).

181.3 *the player is Shakespeare*: both *GB* and *Lee* refer to Shakespeare having played the part of the Ghost in *Hamlet*; from Nicholas Rowe (1674–1718), poet, dramatist, editor of Shakespeare (1709).

181.5 *Burbage*: Richard Burbage (*c.*1567–1619), actor and manager of the Globe Theatre, acted the title role in *Hamlet* (*Lee* 222).

181.6 *beyond the rack of cerecloth*: 'beyond the grave'; 'rack': 'clouds'; 'cerecloth': 'waxed cloth used in embalming'.

181.7 *Hamlet, I am thy father's spirit*: *Hamlet*, I. v. 9: the Ghost addresses Hamlet: 'I am thy father's spirit', but does not call him by name; Bloom makes the same mistake at 146.3.

181.9 *Hamnet Shakespeare*: Hamnet, Shakespeare's only son, twin brother of Judith, died aged 11 (1585–96); *GB* connects Hamlet and Hamnet (140).

181.11–12 *in the vesture of buried Denmark*: Horatio to the Ghost in *Hamlet*, I. i. 46–9: 'What art thou that usurp'st this time of night, | Together with that fair and warlike form | In which the majesty of buried Denmark | Did sometimes march?'

181.16–17 *Ann Shakespeare, born Hathaway*: (1556–1623), Shakespeare's wife, to whom he famously left his 'second best bed'.

181.20 *Art thou there, truepenny*: Hamlet to the Ghost (*Hamlet*, I. v. 150).

181.23 *As for living... Villiers de l'Isle has said*: Comte Jean Marie Mathais Philippe Auguste de Villiers de l'Isle Adam (1838–89), French poet and dramatist, in his last play Axel (1890); cited by Yeats as epigraph to *The Secret Rose* (1897), which he dedicated to AE (George Russell).

181.27–8 *Flow over them... Mananaan Mac Lir*: from George Russell's verse play *Deirdre* (1902), Act III; Cathvah, the Druid mage, chants a curse which brings about the downfall of Naisi and Deirdre: 'Let thy waves rise, | Mananaun Mac Lir. | Let the earth fail | Beneath their feet, | Let thy waves flow over them, | Mananaun: | Lord of Ocean!' (see 38.31–2 n.).

182.7 *He's from beyant... northeast corner*: Russell was born in County Armagh in Ulster, i.e. (in 1904) northern Ireland, the largely Protestant, pro-British area of Ireland; the Boyne: river between northern and southern Ireland, site of the Battle of the Boyne in which William of Orange defeated James II (see 29.29 n.).

182.12 *entelechy, form of forms*: two different ways of saying 'soul' as Aristotle means the term; Stephen takes the terms from two discussions of the 'soul' in *De Anima* (as translated by Joyce from the French translation (see 26.4 n.)); from *De Anima*, II. i. 412a27: 'The soul is the first entelechy of a naturally organic body' (Peterson 213; Aubert 131) and III. viii. 432a2: 'The intellectual soul is the form of forms' (see 26.11–12 n.); 'entelechy' (or *entelechia*): 'actuality'; for Aristotle, the form-giving cause capable of reproducing itself (*G*).

182.14–15 *I that sinned... pandies*: Stephen recalls his childhood as recounted in *Portrait*; especially ch. 1, pp. 56–9 (see 523.19–28).

182.16 *I, I and I. I.*: in this shorthand, Stephen illustrates the continuity ('I, I') vs. the discontinuity ('I. I.') of his existence; the former because of 'memory', the latter because of the 'everchanging forms' (186.12–13) though 'I, I and I.' can also be read as a Trinity of 'I's (see Hélène Cixous, *The Exile of James Joyce* (1968) trans. Sally A. J. Purcell (New York: David Lewis, 1972), 591.

182.36 *Socrates*: (469–399 BC), Greek philosopher, teacher of Plato in whose dialogues he appears as the great teacher of reason and morality.

182.37 *Xanthippe*: wife of Socrates whose behaviour was, in tradition, ill-tempered, shrewish, argumentative.

183.1–2 *from his mother... into the world*: Socrates's mother, Phaenareté, was a midwife.

183.2 *Myrto*: in some traditions, first wife of Socrates.

183.2–3 *absit nomen!*: Latin: 'let the name be absent'; pun on *absit omen*: 'let there be no ill omen' (Latin equivalent of knocking on wood to avoid the potential bad luck of something just said).

183.3 *Socratididion's Epipsychidion*: 'Socratididion': diminutive of Socrates; 'Epipsychidion': a Greek coinage of P. B. Shelley and the title of a poem by him (1821); from *epi-* (upon) and *psychidion* (diminutive of 'soul', 'little soul'): 'On the Subject of the Soul', though also translated as meaning (as in l. 238) 'this soul of my soul'.

183.4 *caudlelectures*: from Douglas Jerrold (1803–57), *Curtain Lectures* (1846), in which Margaret Caudle nightly harangues her long-suffering husband Job (*G*).

183.4–5 *the archons of Sinn Fein*: 'archons': Athenian rulers who sentenced Socrates to his death for his corruption of the youth of Athens (he drank a cup of hemlock); for Sinn Féin, see 7.31 n.

183.12 *Romeville*: 17th-c. cant: London (see 47.6 n.).

183.13 *The girl I left behind me*: anonymous ballad, chosen by Stephen merely because of the appropriateness of its title to his meaning.

183.13 *If the earthquake did not time it*: in *Venus and Adonis*, ll. 1046–8, Shakespeare describes an earthquake; Stephen implies that scholars have attempted to date the poem by tying its composition to the time of an actual earthquake; they have not.

183.14 *poor Wat, sitting in his form, the cry of the hounds*: 'wat': hare; 'form': hare's lair; *Venus and Adonis*, ll. 697–9: 'By this, poor Wat, far off upon a hill, | Stands on his hinder legs with list'ning ear, | To hearken if his foes pursue him still'.

183.14–15 *the studded bridle and her blue windows*: *Venus and Adonis*, ll. 37–8; 481–3.

183.15–16 *Venus and Adonis . . . light-of-love in London*: cf. *GB* (56): '[*Venus and Adonis*] is an entirely erotic poem, and contemporaries aver that it lay on the table of every light woman in London'; 'Light of Love': 16th-c. popular song, the phrase later came to mean 'an inconstant capricious or loose woman; a harlot' (Brewer).

183.16 *bechamber*: should read 'bedchamber'.

183.16–17 *Is Katharine . . . beautiful*: Hortensio to Petruchio in *Taming of the Shrew*, I. ii. 86, describes Katherina as 'young and beauteous'.

183.18 *a passionate pilgrim*: after *The Passionate Pilgrime. By W. Shakespeare. At London printed . . . 1599*; of the twenty-odd poems contained, only four or five are attributed (and then contentiously) to Shakespeare.

183.20 *his boywomen*: the parts of women were played by boys until 1660 when the first English actress appeared on stage.

183.22 *He was chosen*: according to *GB* (10), Anne Hathaway's family hurried the marriage on because she was pregnant (the first child being born less than six months later).

183.23 *By cock, she was to blame*: note Stephen's alteration of Ophelia's song: 'Young men will do't if they come to't; | By Cock, they are to blame' (*Hamlet*, IV. v. 60–1).

183.23–4 *sweet and twentysix*: after Feste's song in *Twelfth Night*, II. iii. 51–2: 'Then come kiss me sweet and twenty; | Youth's a stuff will not endure'; Anne Hathaway was 26, Shakespeare 18, when they married in 1582.

183.24 *The greyeyed goddess*: epithet for Athena, but also Venus to Adonis: 'Mine eyes are grey' (*Venus and Adonis*, l. 140).

183.24 *the boy Adonis*: Adonis, 'the tender boy' (*Venus and Adonis*, l. 32).

183.24–5 *stooping to conquer*: after Oliver Goldsmith's (1728–74) play *She Stoops to Conquer* (1773).

183.25 *as prologue to the swelling act*: Stephen's crude pun appropriates Macbeth's words on discovering the witches have truly prophesied his becoming Thane of Cawdor (and may therefore be right about his becoming king): 'Two truths are told, | As happy prologues to the swelling act | Of the imperial theme' (*Macbeth*, I. iii. 127–9).

183.25–6 *a boldfaced Stratford ... herself*: from *FH* (368): 'I, too, Shakespeare tells us practically, was wooed by an older woman against my will'.

183.32–3 *Between the acres ... would lie*: Page's song in *As You Like It*, v. iii. 22–4 (second verse): 'Between the acres of the rye, | With a hey, and a ho, and a hey nonino, | These pretty country folks would lie'; but Stephen's use of 'cornfield' (183.26) is supported by the first verse: 'It was a lover and his lass, | ... | That o'er the green corn-field did pass' (ll. 16–18).

183.34 *Paris: the wellpleased pleaser*: after the Greek myth in which Paris was asked who (of Hera, Athena, and Aphrodite) was the most beautiful; he pleased Aphrodite by awarding her the prize; she pleased him by awarding him the love of Helen of Troy. (Result: Trojan war.)

184.3 *Homestead*: see 31.8, 9 n.

184.6 *Moore*: George Moore (1852–1933), Irish novelist, poet, dramatist; lived in Paris, then London, until 1901 when he returned to Dublin and joined the Irish literary revival; friend of Yeats, Synge, Lady Gregory, *et al.*

184.11–18 *Isis Unveiled ... they bewail*: further Stephen parody of Theosophy. *Isis Unveiled*: see 178.2–13 n.

184.11 *Pali book*: Pali, a form of Sanskrit, in which (Blavatsky claimed) the most ancient myths were written (*G*).

184.12 *umbrel umbershoot*: umbrella.

184.12 *Aztec logos*: for Blavatsky, the universal truth ('logos') found in Aztec (as well as Hindu, Egyptian, and Babylonian) myth (*G*).

184.13 *astral levels*: most rarefied (undetectable to ordinary people) substance and/or level of existence (*G*).

184.13 *oversoul*: a bit like god—omnipresent, transcendental being (see Ralph Waldo Emerson (1803–82), 'The Over-Soul' (1841)) (*G*).

184.13 *mahamahatma*: Sanskrit: 'great-great-soul' (*G*).

184.14 *chelaship*: Buddhist term for novitiate (*G*).

184.14–15 *Louis H. Victory*: minor figure in Irish literary circles (late 19th c.), wrote on Shakespeare, author of lines at 184.19–20.

184.15 *T. Caulfield Irwin*: (1823–92), Irish poet, suffered a 'gentle mania' (*G*).

184.15 *Lotus ladies tend them i'the eyes*: 'Lotus ladies': Asparas, Hindu seductive nymphs; 'tend them i'the eyes': *Antony and Cleopatra*, II. ii. 206–8.

184.16 *Buddh under plantain*: Buddha, meditating beneath a bo (not a plantain) tree, reached enlightenment.

184.16–17 *Gulfer of souls, engulger*: the Theosophical God (see *G*).

184.19–20 *In quintessential... shesoul dwelt*: misquotation of opening lines of Louis H. Victory poem 'Soul-Perturbing Mimicry': 'In quintessential triviality | of flesh, for four fleet years, a she-soul dwelt' (*G* and *T*).

184.22–3 *Mr Russell... poets' verses*: the May 1904 issue of *Dana* carried a literary notice by Oliver St John Gogarty for George Russell's *New Songs, a Lyric Selection; Made by AE from Poems by Padraic Colum, Eva Gore-Booth, Thomas Koehler, Alice Milligan, Susan Mitchell, Seamus O'Sullivan, George Roberts, and Ella Young* (1904); note the absence of James Joyce from the list of contributors.

184.27 *caubeen*: Gaelic: *cáibín*: 'old hat'.

184.28–9 *Touch lightly ... Aristotle's experiment*: Aristotle, *Problemata*, XXXV. 10 (965a36 *et seq.*): 'Why is it that an object which is held between two crossed fingers appears to be two? Is it because we touch it with two sense-organs? For when we hold the hand in its natural position we cannot touch an object with the outer sides of the two fingers' (rev. Oxford trans., ed. Jonathan Barnes (Princeton University Press, 1984)).

184.29–30 *Necessity is that... hat is one hat*: Aristotle, *Metaphysics*, v. 5 (1015b2–3): 'necessity is that because of which the thing cannot be otherwise' (rev. Oxford trans.); 'Argal': dog Latin for *ergo*: 'therefore' (used by the gravediggers in *Hamlet*, v. i. 12, 19, 48).

184.32 *Young Colum ... Starkey ... George Roberts*: Padraic Colum (1881–1972), Irish poet, dramatist, and Joyce's friend (see Padraic and Mary Colum, *Our Friend James Joyce* (New York, 1958)), poems in Russell's *New Songs* (184.22–3 n.); James Sullivan Starkey (1879–1958), who changed his name to Seamus O'Sullivan, Irish poet and editor, poems included in *New Songs*; George Roberts (d. 1952), publisher, as managing director of Maunsel & Co. contracted to publish *Dubliners* but failed to do so.

184.33 *Longworth... the Express*: Ernest Victor Longworth (1874–1935), editor of the *Daily Express* (pro-British, conservative 'West Briton' newspaper; see 'The Dead').

184.33–4 *Colum's Drover*: Padraic Colum's 'A Drover', published in *New Songs*.

184.35 *Yeats admired... Grecian vase*: the final line of Padraic Colum's poem 'A Portrait', published in *New Songs*.

185.2–3 *Miss Mitchell's joke about Moore and Martyn*: Susan Mitchell (1866–1926), Irish poet, parodist, associate editor of *Irish Homestead*, author of *Aids to the Immortality of Certain Persons in Ireland, Charitably Administered* (1908) and

George Moore (1916); Edward Martyn (1859–1923), wealthy (fervently) Catholic landlord, supporter of Gaelic League, co-founder of Irish Literary Theatre (1898), president of Sinn Féin (1906–8), co-founder of Irish Theatre (1914); he and Moore were cousins, friends, then mutually bound, oddly affectionate antagonists. See *G* for an account of their relationship and the adroitness of Mitchell's joke.

185.3–4 *They remind one of . . . Sancho Panza*: central characters in Miguel de Cervantes's *Don Quixote* (1605, 1615); Quixote is the gentleman, Panza the pig farmer; Quixote the idealistic eccentric, Panza the earthy, no-nonsense pragmatist.

185.4–5 *Our national epic . . . Dr Sigerson says*: Dr George Sigerson (1838–1925), Irish physician, poet, translator; in the essay 'Ireland's Influence on European Literature' (*Irish Literature*, ed. Justin McCarthy, Maurice Egan, Douglas Hyde (1904)), he argues that Irish influence on the European epic has been tremendous, and that the Irish literary revivalists should set their minds to producing a new national epic. The irony of this challenge being repeated here is, of course, that *Ulysses* is the desired epic, but one which challenges rather than perpetuates the romantic nationalism advocated by Sigerson and the raconteurs in the Library.

185.5–6 *A knight of the rueful countenance*: one of the epithets attached to Quixote.

185.6 *O'Neill Russell*: Thomas O'Neill Russell (1828–1908), Celtic revivalist, linguist, novelist; lived in self-imposed exile in the USA (*G*).

185.7 *Dulcinea*: 'Dulcinea del Toboso': the name Don Quixote gives to the peasant woman Alonza Lorenzo, whom he idealizes as a 'princess and great lady'.

185.7 *James Stephens*: (1882–1950), Irish poet, folklorist, writer of sketches of peasant life, author of memoirs, notably *The Insurrection in Dublin* (1916).

185.9 *Cordelia. Cordoglio*: 'Cordelia': King Lear's youngest (and only faithful) daughter; 'Cordoglio': Italian: 'deep sorrow'.

185.9 *Lir's loneliest daughter*: 'Lir': Gaelic: 'Ocean; ancient Irish sea-god'; after a line in Thomas Moore's 'The Song of Fionnuala': 'Silent, oh Moyle, be the roar of thy water, | Break not, ye breezes, your chain of repose, | While, murmuring mournfully, Lir's lonely daughter | Tells to the night star her tale of woes'; here, Lir is the ancient Danaan sea deity, displaced by his son Mananaan; Lir's daughter, Fionnuala, is transformed into a swan by her stepmother.

185.10 *Nookshotten*: 'running out into corners or angles' (*OED*); *Henry V*, III. v. 14.

185.16 *God ild you*: 'God reward you'; Touchstone in *As You Like It*, III. iii. 74–5; V. iv. 54, and Ophelia to Hamlet in *Hamlet*, IV. v. 42.

185.17 *Synge*: John Millington Synge (1871–1909), Irish poet and dramatist, convert to the Irish literary revival, left Paris to live in and write of the Aran islands, author of *In the Shadow of the Glen* (1903), *Riders to the Sea* (1904), *Playboy of the Western World* (1907), and *Deirdre of the Sorrows* (1910).

185.17 *Dana: A Magazine of Independent Thought*, Dublin magazine (1904–5) edited by John Eglinton and Fred Ryan, named after the ancient goddess Dana (see 186.30 n.); Joyce published 'Song' ('My love is in a light attire', *Chamber Music*, VII) in the Aug. 1904 issue.

185.18 *The Gaelic league*: see 135.26 n.

185.23 *tiptoing up nearer heaven by the altitude of a chopine*: Hamlet to boy actor: 'your ladyship is nearer to heaven than when I saw you last, by the altitude of a chopine' (*Hamlet*, II. ii. 425–7); 'chopine': thick-soled woman's shoe.

185.26 *Courtesy or an inward light?*: an allusion to Lyster's being a Quaker; George Fox (1624–91), founder of the Society of Friends (Quakers), advocated reliance on an 'inward light' for the reception of divine truth; he was also famously courteous.

185.30–3 *Christfox in leather trews ... geese*: in this passage, Stephen links Shakespeare and George Fox (see 185.26 n.), the latter dressed simply (in 'leather trews' or trousers), was persecuted for his beliefs, remained unmarried until he was 45 (when he wed Margaret Fell, widow of Judge Fell), converted many (including prostitutes). See *G* and *FH* for Shakespeare parallels, and 188.19 n.

185.33–5 *And in New place ... unforgiven*: 'New Place': Shakespeare's house in Stratford; according to *GB*, Anne Hathaway was extremely pious (unlike her husband); Stephen describes her in the terms of the Irish song 'Fair Maidens' Beauty Will Soon Fade Away' (second stanza): 'My love is as sweet as the cinnamon tree; | She clings to me as close as the bark to the tree: | But the leaves they will wither and the roots will decay, | And fair maidens' beauty will soon fade away!' (*T*).

186.4–5 *what Caesar would... soothsayer*: Shakespeare depicts Caesar as disregarding the soothsayer's advice ('Beware the ides of March' (*Julius Caesar*, I. ii. 18, 23)) to his own detriment.

186.6–7 *what name Achilles ... women*: Sir Thomas Browne (1605–82), *Hydriotaphia, Urn-Burial* (1658), ch. 5: 'What song the Syrens sang, or what name Achilles assumed, when he hid himself among women, though puzzling questions, are not beyond all conjecture'; post-Homeric elaborations of the legend of Achilles recount that Thetis (Achilles's mother), knowing that her son was prophesied to die at the gates of Troy, disguised him in women's clothing and sent him to live among women in the court of King Lycomedes; Odysseus, seeking to acquire Achilles's help in the Trojan War, discovered through ruse who he was and persuaded him to join the battle, where, of course, he died.

186.9 *Thoth, god of... moonycrowned*: Thoth: Egyptian god of wisdom, learning, magic, inventor of writing, messenger and scribe of the gods; personified as ibis-headed man, often crowned with the moon (or its horns).

186.15 *Others abide our question*: opening line of Matthew Arnold's sonnet 'Shakespeare' (1844): 'Others abide our question. Thou art free. | We ask and ask—Thou smilest and art still, | Out-topping knowledge'.

186.20 *Ta an bad . . . Taim imo shagart*: Gaelic: *Tá an bád ar an tír. Táim i mo shagart*: 'The boat is on the land. I am a priest'; a near-verbatim quotation from Revd Eugene O'Growney's (1863–99) Gaelic primer, *Simple Lessons in Irish* (1897), i. 22; cf. *Stephen Hero*, 55.

186.21 *beurla*: Gaelic: 'English (language)'.

186.28 *A basilisk. E quando . . . Messer Brunetto*: Brunetto Latini (*c.*1210–*c.*1295), Florentine writer admired by Dante, in his compendium of medieval lore, *Li livres dou trésor* (1262–6?), *Histoire Naturelle, Des Basiliques*, discusses the 'basilisk'—a fabulous beast, hatched by a serpent from a cock's egg, with a lethal breath and look (it can kill with a glance); *E quando vede l'uomo l'attosca*: Italian: 'and when it looks at a man, it poisons him' (*T* and *G*).

186.30 *mother Dana*: mother of ancient Irish gods (the tribe of Dana), simultaneously the goddess of fertility, youth, knowledge, and of disintegration and death (*G*).

186.30–2 *weave and unweave our bodies . . . unweave his image*: cf. Walter Pater, *The Renaissance* (1873), 'Conclusion': 'It is with this movement, with the passage and dissolution of impressions, images, sensations, that analysis leaves off—that continual vanishing away, that strange, perpetual, weaving and unweaving of ourselves'.

186.35–6 *the mind . . . a fading coal*: P. B. Shelley in 'A Defence of Poetry' (1821; 1840): 'Poetry is not like reasoning, a power to be exerted according to the determination of the will. A man cannot say, "I will compose poetry." The greatest poet even cannot say it; for the mind in creation is as a fading coal, which some invisible influence, like an inconstant wind, awakens to transitory brightness; this power arises from within, like the colour of a flower which fades and changes as it is developed, and the conscious portions of our natures are unprophetic either of its approach or its departure.'

186.37–187.2 *So in the future . . . Drummond of Hawthornden*: William Drummond of Hawthornden (1585–1649), Scottish poet, passages from whose best-known prose work *A Cypresse Grove* (1623), a meditation on death, Stephen reworks: 'If thou dost complain that there shall be a Time in which thou shalt not be, why dost thou not also grieve that there was a time in which thou was not; and so that thou art not as old as that enlivening Planet of Time? . . . That will be after us, which, long long before we were, was' (*G*).

187.9: *Renan*: Ernest Renan (1823–92), French philologist, historian, essayist, applied the scientific historical method to an account of Christianity; admired Shakespeare's late plays as 'mature philosophical dramas' and wrote a sequel to *The Tempest*, entitled *Caliban, Suite de La Tempête* (1878) (*G* and *T*).

187.17–18 *What softens the heart . . . prince of Tyre*: Stephen argues that the Shakespeare who writes *Pericles* (1606–8) has experienced a change of heart, a point made by all his consulted commentators; see esp. *GB* (585): 'When he consented to rewrite parts of this *Pericles*, it was that he might embody the feeling by which he is now possessed. Pericles is a romantic Ulysses, a far-travelled, sorely tried, much-enduring man, who has, little by little, lost all that was dear to him.'

187.20 *Marina*: in Act III of *Pericles*, Thaisa (Pericles's wife) gives birth to a daughter, Marina, at the height of a storm and then (apparently) dies; the nurse, Lychordia, places Marina in Pericles's arms, saying: 'Take in your arms this piece | Of your dead queen' (III. i. 17–18).

187.21 *apocrypha*: writings not considered genuine, after the books of the Old Testament contained in the Greek, but not the Hebrew, version; Catholicism admits them as authoritative; Protestantism does not; Eglinton considers *Pericles* 'apocrypha' as it was not included in the First Folio, and is (now) generally considered to be (at least) a work of collaboration rather than (wholly) Shakespearian.

187.24 *Good Bacon: gone musty*: *G* persuasively argues that in his thought, Stephen is suggesting that Eglinton has used (badly) Sir Francis Bacon (1561–1626), who in *The Advancement of Learning* (1605) warns against 'vain affectation, vain disputes, and vain imaginations' and suggests that, to avoid the affectation of 'two extremes: antiquity and novelty . . . The advice of the prophet is just . . .: "Stand upon the old ways, and see which is the good way, and walk therein" [Jer. 6: 16].'

187.24 *Shakespeare Bacon's wild oats*: alludes to the theory that Shakespeare's plays were really written by Bacon; both *GB* and *Lee* discuss the arguments, which often depended on the detection of a cipher hidden in the texts of some plays; hence the Baconians were 'Cypherjugglers' (187.24). (See *T*).

187.26–7 *East of the sun . . . Tir na n-og*: Gaelic: *Tír na nÓg*: 'Land of the Young; legendary elysium'; 'East of the Sun, West of the Moon': title story of Peter Christen Asbjörnsen's (1812–85) collection of Norse folktales (1842–5) (*G*).

187.28–30 *How many miles . . . candlelight?*: Stephen's adaptation of the nursery rhyme 'How many miles to Babylon? | Three score and ten. | Can I get there by candlelight? | Yes, and back again, | If your heels are nimble and light, | You may get there by candlelight.'

187.31 *Mr Brandes accepts . . . closing period*: George Morris Cohen Brandes (1842–1927), Danish literary critic, championed scientific criticism of literature and the new realism of such writers as Émile Zola and Henrik Ibsen; in *GB* (see headnote), he does accept *Pericles* as written by Shakespeare (572); he also argues that the late plays are repeatedly concerned with 'girlish and forsaken creatures [who] are lost and found again, suffer grievous wrongs, and are in no case cherished as they deserve; but their charm, purity and nobility of nature triumph over everything' (572).

187.32 *Mr Sidney Lee*: (1859–1926) (originally named Solomon Lazarus Levi), editor of the *Dictionary of National Biography* (after 1891), biographer of Queen Victoria (1902) and Shakespeare (see headnote); in *Lee*, he does not group *Pericles* with the 'last plays' (198–9).

187.34–5 *Marina . . . which was lost*: for Marina, see 187.20 n.; Miranda, Prospero's daughter in *The Tempest*, to whom Ferdinand says: 'My prime request, | Which I do last pronounce, is (O you wonder!) | If you be maid, or no?'; her response: 'No wonder, sir, | But certainly a maid' (I. ii. 426–9); Perdita ('the lost one'), Leontes's daughter in *The Winter's Tale* who is left to die as a baby but survives to return to her father years later. Shakespeare's elder daughter, Susanna, married Dr John Hall and had a daughter, Elizabeth, in 1608 (the date coinciding with *GB*'s dating of Shakespeare's late period).

188.1 *My dearest wife . . . this maid*: in *Pericles*, v. i. 107–8, when Marina and Pericles are reunited, he remarks: 'My dearest wife was like this maid, and such a one | My daughter might have been'.

188.3 *L'art d'être grand . . .* : should read '*L'art d'être grandp . . .*'; French: 'The art of being a grandf[ather]'; in *RM* this passage reads in full: '—The art of being a grandfather, Mr Best murmured. ¶—Will he not see reborn in her, with memory of his own youth added, another image? ¶Do you know what you are talking about? Love, yes. Word known to all men. *Amor vero aliquid alicui bonum vult unde et ea quae concupiscimus* . . . ¶—His own image to a man with that queer thing genius is the standard of all experience, material and moral.' (*RM*, *S&C*, fol. 13.) The typescript (Buffalo V.B.7) adds the French phrase '*L'art d'être grandp* . . .' (and changes 'murmured' to 'gan murmur'). This passage, which was either deleted by Joyce or accidentally dropped by the typist (it is impossible to know which as the relevant documents are missing), was restored in the 1984 edition—perhaps the single most controversial decision of that edition. The Latin comes from St Thomas Aquinas's *Summa Contra Gentiles*, I. 91, 'That in God There is Love', joins (arguably incoherently) two disparate phrases; here Aquinas is contrasting 'love' (which requires an object, an 'other', to which we wish good) with 'desire' (which arises from the self, and concerns only the self and that which we want for it).

188.10–11 *Mr George Bernard Shaw*: (1856–1950), Dublin-born novelist, critic, playwright, whose views about Shakespeare were contained in both his drama criticism and his play *The Dark Lady of the Sonnets* (1910) in the preface of which he suggests that every critic of Shakespeare draws the bard in his (the critic's) own image.

188.12 *Mr Frank Harris*: (born James Thomas) (1856–1931), Galway-born editor (of, *inter alia*, the *Saturday Review*), critic, novelist, short-story writer, and hyperbolic memoirist; wrote *The Man Shakespeare and his Tragic Life-Story* (1909) (see headnote); Shaw in his preface to *The Dark Lady* (see 188.10–11 n.) suggested that Harris's portrait of Shakespeare was (like most of Harris's writing) thinly disguised autobiographical self-projection.

188.12–14 *he too draws . . . earl of Pembroke*: *FH* identifies the 'dark lady' of Shakespeare's sonnets as Mary Fitton, suggests that Shakespeare sent his friend William Herbert, earl of Pembroke, to her so that he could commend Shakespeare to her, that she fell in love with Pembroke and this brought 'the loss of both friend and mistress' (202); Shaw identifies the 'dark lady' as Mary Fitton in his play (see 188.10–11 n.), but refutes it in his preface.

188.19 *He thous and thees*: the Quaker address to persons with whom a relationship of familiarity existed; also a yoking of George Fox with Shakespeare as the American poet and essayist Walt Whitman (1819–92) had done in his 'George Fox (and Shakspere)', the last essay in *November Boughs* (1888), where he says of Fox that he felt 'resistless commands not to be explain'd, but follow'd, to abstain from taking off his hat, to say *Thee* and *Thou*, and not bid others Good morning or Good evening' (repr. Walt Whitman, *Complete Poetry and Collected Prose*, comp. Justin Kaplan (New York: Library of America, 1982), 1246).

188.22–3 *Beware of what ... middle life*: free translation of Goethe's epigraph to Part II of his autobiographical *Wahrheit und Dichtung* (1811–14): 'Was man in der Jugend wünscht, hat man im Alter die Fülle': German: 'What one wishes for in youth, one has in abundance in old age'.

188.23 *buonaroba*: literally, Italian: 'good thing'; in Elizabethan slang, a harlot (as in *2 Henry IV*, III. ii. 23).

188.23–4 *a bay where all men ride*: Sonnet 137, ll. 5–8: 'If eyes, corrupt by overpartial looks, | Be anchor'd in the bay where all men ride, | Why of eyes' falsehood hast thou forged hooks, | Whereto the judgement of my heart is tied?'

188.24 *a maid of honour with a scandalous girlhood*: *FH* (212–13) says that Mary Fitton, who became a maid of honour to Queen Elizabeth in 1595 (aged 17), had already been married (which suggests 'a certain recklessness of character'), and that she later had three illegitimate children (one by Pembroke).

188.25 *a lord of language*: phrase used by both Tennyson (in his poem 'To Virgil', l. 5: 'Landscape-lover, lord of language') and Oscar Wilde (in his *De Profundis* (1905 version): 'Three months [after arriving at Reading Gaol] my mother dies. No one knew how deeply I loved and honoured her. Her death was terrible to me; but I, once a lord of language, have no words in which to express my anguish and my shame.')

188.26 *coistrel*: Shakespearian for 'knave' or 'ruffian'.

188.26 *had written Romeo and Juliet*: *c.*1596; *FH* dates it 1597, after Shakespeare had met Fitton, but before Pembroke stole her away.

188.27 *untimely killed*: *Macbeth*, V. viii. 15–16: 'Macduff was from his mother's womb | Untimely ripp'd'.

188.29 *dongiovannism*: to play the part of Don Giovanni, infamous 'ladykiller'; *FH* argues that Shakespeare loathed Anne and attempted to compensate for his failed marriage by having (inevitably unsuccessful) relations with numerous women.

188.30–1 *The tusk of the boar ... love lies ableeding*: multiple allusions: Odysseus was wounded in the thigh by a boar (which left the scar by which his faithful nurse recognizes him (*Odyssey*, Bk. XIX)); *Venus and Adonis*, in which Adonis dies from a wound in the thigh from a boar: 'nousling in his flank, the loving swine | Sheath'd unaware the tusk in his soft groin' (ll. 1115–16); 'love lies ableeding': after Beaumont and Fletcher's *Philaster: or, Love Lies Ableeding* (1609).

188.34–5 *darkening even his own understanding of himself*: cf. the *Maynooth Catechism* (1882), Lesson 6: 'Q. What other particular effects follow from the sin of our first parents? A. Our whole nature was corrupted by the sin of our first parents—it darkened our understanding, weakened our will, and left in us a strong inclination to evil'; and see 203.32–4.

188.36 *They list. And in the porches... I pour*: Ghost in *Hamlet*, I. v. 63–4: 'And in the porches of my ears did pour | The leprous distillment'.

188.37–189.5 *The soul has been ... by his creator*: as he wondered earlier (at 134.15), Stephen questions how the Ghost could have known the manner of his death if he were sleeping (or that Gertrude was committing adultery with Claudius).

189.7 *Lucrece's bluecircled ivory globes*: of Lucrece in *The Rape of Lucrece*, l. 407: 'Her breasts like ivory globes circled with blue', as Tarquin gazes on Lucrece just prior to raping her.

189.8 *Imogen's breast, bare, with its mole cinquespotted*: in *Cymbeline*, Jachimo dupes Posthumus into believing his virtuous wife Imogen has been unfaithful; having spied on Imogen in her sleep, Jachimo reports the 'corporal' details back to Posthumus in a manner intended to persuade the husband that his 'friend' has more than intellectual 'knowledge' of his wife: 'On her left breast | A mole cinque-spotted, like the crimson drops | I' th' bottom of a cowslip. Here's a voucher, | Stronger than ever law could make; this secret | Will force him think I have pick'd the lock and ta'en | The treasure of her honor' (*Cymbeline*, II. ii. 37–42).

189.16 *Hast thou found me, O mine enemy?*: Ahab to Elijah in 1 Kgs. 21: 20: 'Hast thou found me, O mine enemy?'

189.23 *Was Du verlachst wirst Du noch dienen*: German: 'What you laugh at, you will still serve'.

189.24 *Brood of mockers... Johann Most*: for 'Photius', see 20.37 n.; 'pseudomalachi': false Malachi (the one pretending to be Malachi (Hebrew: 'the messenger of the Lord')), i.e. Mulligan (see 20.37–21.1); 'Johann Most': (1846–1906), German anarchist, bookbinder, pamphleteer, publisher of anarchist newspaper *Die Freiheit* (German: 'Freedom'), who praised the Phoenix Park murderers and, in the spirit of true anarchism, published *Down with the Anarchists!* (1901). See Adams, 138.

189.25–31 *He Who Himself begot... dead already*: parody of the Apostles' Creed after that published by Johann Most in *The Deistic Pestilence* (1902): [The Judaeo-Christian god is] a Godly Charlatan who created himself through the Holy Ghost, and then sent himself as mediator between himself and others, and who held in contempt and derided by his enemies, was nailed to a cross, like a bat on a barndoor; who was buried—arose from the dead—descended to hell—ascended to Heaven, and since then for eighteen hundred years has been sitting at his own right hand to judge the living—and the dead when the living have ceased to exist' (quoted in Manganiello, *Joyce's Politics*, 101–2).

189.32 *Glo–o–ri–a in ex–cel–sis De–o*: Latin: 'Glory be to God on high' (Luke 2: 14), opening of Angelic Hymn sung in Mass.

190.9–10 *The chap that writes like Synge*: joke after Yeats's comment that Synge wrote like Aeschylus (see Oliver St John Gogarty, *As I Was Going Down Sackville Street* (1937; repr. Harmondsworth: Penguin, 1954), 303).

190.17–18 *Vining held . . . a woman*: Edward Payson Vining (1847–1920), *The Mystery of Hamlet; An Attempt to Solve an Old Problem* (1881), did so hold.

190.18–19 *Has no-one made . . . Judge Barton*: Dunbar Plunket Barton (1853–1937), Irish High Court Justice (from 1900), author of *Links Between Ireland and Shakespeare* (Dublin, 1919); though he did not maintain that Hamlet was Irish.

190.19–20 *He swears . . . by saint Patrick*: Hamlet in *Hamlet*, I. v. 136: 'Yes, by Saint Patrick, but there is, Horatio'.

190.22 *Portrait of Mr W.H.*: Oscar Wilde, in *The Portrait of Mr W.H.* (1889 version), proposes (as did Thomas Tyrwhitt in 1766) that the dedicatee of the Sonnets ('The Onlie Begetter Of These Insuing Sonnets Mr. W.H.') was Mr Willie Hughes, a young actor.

190.23–5 *Willie Hughes . . . Mr William Himself*: see previous note; Wilde says the Sonnets were written *for* (not *by*) Willie Hughes; 'a man all hues': 'Sonnet 20', l. 7: 'A man in hue all hues in his controlling'; 'Hughie Wills' and 'Mr William Himself': parodies of names supplied as possible answers to the question 'Who is Mr. W.H.?'

190.32 *usquebaugh*: Gaelic: *uisce beatha*: '"water of life", whiskey'.

190.35 *Humour wet and dry*: see, not only the medieval theory of humours, but Joyce's 'Gas from a Burner', ll. 19–20: ''Twas Irish humour, wet and dry, | Flung quicklime into Parnell's eye' (*CW*, 103).

190.36 *five wits*: 'common sense, imagination, fantasy, estimation and memory' (Brewer); cf. *Romeo and Juliet*, II. iv. 71–3.

190.36–7 *youth's proud livery he pranks in*: see Sonnet 2, ll. 3–4: 'Thy youth's proud livery, so gaz'd on now, | Will be a totter'd weed, of small worth held'; 'pranks': 'adorns'.

190.37 *Lineaments of gratified desire*: William Blake, Poems from the *Notebook*, *c.*1791–2, XXXVI: 'In a wife I would desire | What in whores is always found— | The lineaments of gratified desire'; and LI: 'Several Questions Answered', ll. 11–14: 'What is it men in women do require?— | The lineaments of gratified desire. | What is it women do in men require?— | The lineaments of gratified desire' (*Complete Poems*, ed. W. H. Stevenson, 2nd edn. (London: Longman, 1989) 162, 167).

191.1–2 *Jove, a cool ruttime send them*: Falstaff in *The Merry Wives of Windsor*, v. v. 13–15: 'Send me a cool rut-time, Jove, or who can blame me to piss my tallow?'

191.3 *Eve. Naked wheatbellied . . . kiss*: see 38.16–19; and Gen. 3: 1–6 where the serpent seduces Eve.

191.12–13 *The sentimentalist . . . done*: George Meredith (1828–1909), *The Ordeal of*

Richard Feverel (1859; though Joyce quotes from the 1875 Tauchnitz edition (see *G*)): '"Sentimentalists," says the PILGRIM'S SCRIPT, "are they who seek to enjoy, without incurring the Immense Debtorship for a thing done"'.

191.17 *keened*: Gaelic: *caoin*: 'wail, lament'.

191.18 *brogue*: Gaelic: *barróg*: 'defect in speech'.

191.20 *mavrone*: Gaelic: *mo bhrón*: 'my sorrow'.

191.21 *gallus*: dialect: 'gallows'.

191.31 *pampooties*: Gaelic: *pampútí*: 'primitive shoes'.

191.37–192.1 *Harsh gargoyle face . . . Saint-André-des-Arts*: Stephen recalls meeting Synge, as Joyce recalled meeting him to his first biographer Herbert Gorman (*James Joyce*, 101).

192.1 *palabras*: Spanish: 'words'.

192.1–2 *Oisin with Patrick*: *Oisín* (Gaelic: 'faun'), mythic poet-hero, son of Fionn Mac Cumhail, who in legend met St Patrick, was converted to Christianity by him, and recounted to him the heroic tales of the Fianna; see W. B. Yeats, *The Wanderings of Oisin* (1889); and *JJ* 124–5 for an account of Joyce's meeting Synge in Paris in 1903; Synge did apparently tell of having met a 'faunman' in the woods.

192.3 *C'est vendredi saint!*: French: 'It's Good Friday!'

192.4 *I met a fool i' the forest*: Jacques of Touchstone in *As You Like It* (II. vii. 12–13): 'A fool, a fool! I met a fool i' th' forest, | A motley fool.'

192.6 *Mr Justice Madden*: The Right Honourable Dodgson Hamilton Madden (1840–1928), author of *The Diary of Master William Silence: A Study of Shakespeare and of Elizabethan Sport* (1897), in which he argued that Shakespeare's extensive knowledge of field sport made him an aristocrat and/or that the earl of Rutland (1576–1612) was his ghostwriter (*T* and *G*).

192.29 *Ikey Moses*: a 'comic' depiction of a Jewish 'type' who attempts to insinuate himself into middle-class Gentile society; see *Ally Sloper's Half-Holiday* (a London illustrated weekly); not surprisingly, anti-Semitic.

192.32 *the foamborn Aphrodite*: in one version of Greek myth, Aphrodite, goddess of love, was born of the seafoam into which Uranus's genitals (cut off by his son Chronos) had fallen.

192.33–4 *Life of life, thy lips enkindle*: from P. B. Shelley's *Prometheus Unbound: A Lyrical Drama* (1820; 1839) II. v. 48–51: 'VOICE (*in the air, singing*) | Life of Life! thy lips enkindle | With their love the breath between them | And thy smiles before they dwindle | Make the cold air fire'.

192.36–7 *he is Greeker than the Greeks*: variation on 'More Irish than the Irish', but here implying homosexuality.

192.37 *pale Galilean*: from Swinburne's 'Hymn to Prosperine' (1866), l. 35: 'Thou hast conquered, O pale Galilean; the world has grown grey from thy breath'; after the reputed final words of the Roman emperor Julian the Apostate (d. 363) who, during his lifetime, repudiated Christianity: 'Vicisti, Galilae' (Latin: 'Thou has conquered, Galilean'); the 'Galilean' is, specifically, Jesus.

192.37 *mesial groove*: the 'midline groove of the buttocks'.

192.37–193.1 *Venus Kallipyge*: statue found in the Domus Aureo ('Golden House') of Nero, now in the Museo Nazionale, Naples; 'Kallipyge': Greek: 'beautiful buttocks'.

193.1 *The god pursuing the maiden hid*: from Swinburne's *Atalanta in Calydon* (1865), first chorus, stanza 6: 'The laughing leaves of the trees divide, | And screen from seeing and leave in sight | The god pursuing, the maiden hid'.

193.4 *patient Griselda*: archetypal obedient and long-suffering wife; after character in last tale of Boccaccio's *Decameron*, and 'The Clerk's Tale' in Chaucer's *Canterbury Tales.*

193.5–7 *Antisthenes, pupil of Gorgias . . . poor Penelope*: for Antisthenes, Gorgias, and Penelope (in this context), see 142.21–5 n.; 'Kyrios Menelaus': Lord Menelaus, husband of Helen, who went to Troy (where she had gone with Paris) to retrieve her; 'the wooden mare of Troy': combines Helen (as 'brooddam') with the Trojan horse which contained Greek warriors being smuggled inside the gates of Troy.

193.7–9 *Twenty years he . . . chancellor of Ireland*: *GB*, *FH*, *Lee* date Shakespeare's residence in London as 1592–1613; *Lee* suggests he was earning £600 per year (the equivalent, says *FH*, of £5,000 in 1904, which was the salary of the Chancellor of Ireland) (*G*).

193.9–10 *the art of feudalism, as Whitman called it*: Whitman (see 118.19n.) frequently argued that the 'New World' possessed a freedom and democratic spirit lacking in the 'Old', and that Shakespeare, while 'the loftiest of the singers life has yet given voice to' ('A Backward Glance o'er Travel'd Roads' (1888)), had 'much in him ever offensive to democracy. He is not only the tally of feudalism, but I should say Shakspere is incarnated, uncompromising feudalism, in literature' ('British Literature' (1892)) (both repr. in Whitman, *Complete Poetry and Collected Prose*, 663, 1058).

193.12 *Sir Walter Raleigh* (?1554–1618), explorer and poet, arrested in 1603 for treason (on largely trumped-up charges) when James I took the throne; the source of Stephen's information is *GB* ('he had gems to the value of £4,000 (£20,000 in modern money) on his breast' (417); in 1904, £20,000 was roughly equivalent to half a million francs).

193.13–14 *gombeenwoman Eliza Tudor*: 'gombeen': Gaelic: *gaimbín*: 'usury'; 'Eliza Tudor': Queen Elizabeth I; usurous presumably because the plantation system (the practice of transferring ownership of confiscated Irish lands to English settlers who then used the Irish to work the land) was established in her reign.

193.15 *between conjugial love . . . and scortatory love*: the two contrasting 'types' of love are borrowed from the (English) title of Emanuel Swedenborg's (1688–1772) *Delights of Wisdom Concerning Conjugal Love: After which follow the pleasures of Insanity concerning Scortatory Love* (London, 1794); 'scortatory': illicit; fornicatory. (*G*)

193.16–17 *Manningham's . . . Richard III*: contemporary account (recorded in the diary of John Manningham, of the Middle Temple, under the date 13 Mar. 1601) and cited in full in *GB* (196).

193.19 *knocking at the gate*: the famous scene of light relief in *Macbeth*, II. iii.

193.21 *mount and cry O*: from Posthumus's account (in his remarkable misogynist soliloquy) of what Jachimo might have done with Imogen in *Cymbeline*, II. v: 'Perchance he spoke not, but | Like a full-acorn'd boar, a German [one], | Cried "O!" and mounted' (15–17).

193.21 *Penelope Rich*: see 142.26 n.; arguments proliferated in the 19th c. that Lady Penelope Rich was the 'dark lady' (see *G* and, further, 142.21–5 n.).

193.24–5 *Cours-la-Reine . . . Tu veux?*: French: 'Queen's Parade' (a street on the right bank in Paris); the rest, prostitutes' patter: 'Another twenty sous. We'll do dirty little things. Tart? You want?'

193.26–7 *sir William Davenant of Oxford's mother*: after a spurious story circulated by John Aubrey that Shakespeare, in travelling to and from Stratford, stopped at John D'Avenant's pub in Oxford, where he fell in love with Mrs D'Avenant and sired (her son)Sir William D'Avenant (1606–68), poet and dramatist.

193.29 *Blessed Margaret Mary Anycock*: after Blessed Margaret Mary Alacoque (1647–90) (see 109.21 n.).

193.30 *Harry of six wives' daughter*: i.e. Henry VIII's daughter, Elizabeth I.

193.30–1 *other lady friends . . . Lawn Tennyson*: from Tennyson's *The Princess* (1847), 'Prologue', ll. 96–8: 'And here we lit on Aunt Elizabeth, | And Lilia with the rest, and lady friends | From neighbour seats'.

193.34 *Do and do*: witch's pledge of vengeance in *Macbeth*, I. iii. 10: 'I'll do, I'll do, and I'll do'.

193.34–5 *In a rosery . . . greyedauburn*: John Gerard (1545–1612), gardener, herbalist, and author of *The Herball or Generall Historie of Plantes* (1597), had a rose garden ('rosery') in Fetter Lane; his connection with Shakespeare was postulated by Maurice Clare (May Byron), *A Day with William Shakespeare* (London, 1913) (Ellmann, *The Consciousness of Joyce* (London, 1977), 60–1); *Lee* and *FH* give Shakespeare grey eyes and auburn hair; though Stephen's epithet turns his auburn hair grey.

193.35 *An azured harebell like her veins*: Arviragus to the (mistakenly presumed) dead youth 'Fidele' (Imogen disguised) concerning the adornments he will place on Fidele's grave (in *Cymbeline*, IV. ii. 220–2): 'Thou shalt not lack | The flower that's like thy face, pale primrose, nor | The azur'd harebell, like thy veins'.

193.35 *Lids of Juno's eyes*: Perdita, in *The Winter's Tale*, IV. iv. 113, 120–1: 'I would I had some flow'rs o' th' spring . . . // . . . violets, dim, | But sweeter than the lids of Juno's eyes'.

194.10 *uneared wombs*: 'uneared': 'untilled'; so 'virgin wombs'; from Sonnet 3, ll. 5–6: 'For where is she so fair whose unear'd womb | Disdains the tillage of thy husbandry?'

194.12 *But she, the giglot . . . bedvow*: 'she': Xanthippe (see 182.37 n.); 'giglot wanton': a tautology, since 'giglot' means 'wanton'—a lascivious woman (see *1 Henry VI*, IV. vii. 41); 'break a bedvow': Sonnet 152, l. 3: 'In act thy bed-vow broke and new faith torn'.

194.18 *the fifth scene of Hamlet*: i.e. Act I, scene v: when the Ghost addresses Hamlet.

194.19 *no mention of her*: *Lee* asserts that there is only one contemporary account of Anne Hathaway—her borrowing of some money from her father's former shepherd (187) (see 194. 26–8).

194.21–4 *Mary, her goodman ... Elizabeth*: all Shakespeare's relatives, all accurately accounted for (see *T*).

194.24–5 *granddaddy's words ... killed her first*: *Hamlet*, III. ii. 180: 'None wed the second but who kill'd the first'.

194.28 *the swansong*: Shakespeare's will, to which (having previously failed to make provision for her) he appended a clause leaving his 'secondbest bed' to Anne Hathaway.

194.31–195.11 *thus Eglinton ... Secondbest Bed*: the information in Eglinton's speech comes from the various sources *Lee*, *GB*, *FH*, Madden (see 192.6 n.) and Barton (see 190.18–19 n.).

195.28 *Separatio a mensa et a thalamo*: Latin: 'Separation from board and bedchamber'; variant of decree *Separatio a mensa et a thoro* ('Separation of board and bed') granted at law before divorce was freely allowable (1857).

195.31–5 *Antiquity mentions ... villa*: Aristotle, born in Stageira, exiled himself (fearing for his life after the death of Alexander); Diogenes Laertius's *Lives of Eminent Philosophers* (3rd c. BC) provides the information about his will: that he freed his slaves, asked to be buried near his wife (Phythias), and that his mistress (Herpyllis) be allowed to live in any one of his houses. On his deathbed, Charles II reputedly said, 'Let not poor Nelly [Nell Gwynn, actress and his mistress] starve.'

196.2–3 *A quart of ale is a dish for a king*: from Autolycus's song in *The Winter's Tale*, VI. iii. 5, 7–8: 'The white sheet bleaching on the hedge, | ... | Doth set my pugging tooth an edge, | For a quart of ale is a dish for a king'.

196.3 *Dowden*: Edward Dowden (1843–1913), English professor and orator, Trinity College, Dublin.

196.5 *William Shakespeare and company, limited*: in another era, publishers of *Ulysses*.

196.9 *All we can say ... very high in those days*: typical of Dowden's evasive language when addressing the homosexual implications of the Sonnets, in his *The Sonnets of William Shakespeare* (1881); though, as Kenner points out, the sentence echoes 'the first sentence of a *Shakespeare* Dowden published in 1877 for the use of schoolchildren: "In the closing years of the sixteenth century the life of England ran high"' (Kenner, 113).

196.14 *The doctor can tell us ... mean*: Perhaps Sigmund Freud (1856–1939), in 1904 the new 'father' of psychoanalysis.

196.17–35 *He drew Shylock . . . buckbasket*: in this paragraph, Stephen fleshes his portrait of Shakespeare out with the help of the biographical readings of *GB*, *FH*, *Lee*, John Aubrey's (1626–97) *Brief Lives* (1898) (see *T* and *G* for full references). 'Shylock': the Jewish money lender in *The Merchant of Venice*; there was a corn-famine in 1598, during which period Shakespeare is recorded (according to *GB* and *Lee*) as possessing stores of corn and malt.

196.20–1 *His borrowers are . . . uprightness of dealing*: 'Chettle Falstaff': Henry Chettle (*c.*1560–*c.*1607), printer, playwright, publisher of Robert Greene's *Groat's Worth of Wit* (see 180.1 n.), author of *Kind-Hart's Dream* (1592), in which he apologizes for publishing Greene's attack on Shakespeare: 'Divers of worship have reported his uprightness of dealing, which argues his honesty, and his facetious grace in writing, that approves his Art' (quoted in *GB*, *Lee*, and *FH*); rumoured model for Falstaff.

196.21–3 *He sued a fellowplayer . . . get rich quick?*: he did sue (not a 'fellowplayer', but) Philip Rogers (an apothecary) to recover debts owed (*GB* and *Lee*); 'pound of flesh': what Antonio must forfeit Shylock if he fails to repay his debt in *Merchant of Venice*, I. iii. 146–51; 'Aubrey's ostler and callboy': Aubrey (see 196.17-35 n.) says that Shakespeare was a butcher and a schoolmaster; others that he began in the theatre as the one who held visitors' horses, or as a 'callboy', or prompter's assistant (see *G*).

196.24–6 *Shylock chimes with . . . was yet alive*: Elizabeth I's Jewish physician, Roderigo Lopez, was accused of having accepted a bribe to poison the queen, tried (in Feb. 1594), executed (June 1594) by being hanged, drawn, and quartered (but did not, it seems, have his heart cut out); an outbreak of anti-Semitism followed.

196.26–7 *Hamlet and Macbeth . . . witchroasting*: 'philophaster': a dabbler in philosophy; James I (came to the English throne in 1603) believed in witchcraft, published *Daemonologie* (1597), and as king James VI of Scotland (1567–1625) promoted numerous witch trials (and attendant burnings).

196.28 *The lost armada . . . Love's Labour Lost*: the Spanish Armada was defeated by the English in 1588; Stephen suggests (after *Lee*) that Don Adriano Armado (vain, foolish, 'stage Spaniard') in *Love's Labour's Lost* takes his name from 'Armada' in a bit of 'jolly' jingoistic Spaniard-bashing.

196.28–9 *His pageants, the histories . . . Mafeking enthusiasm*: 'Mafeking': South African town held by the British, and besieged by the Boers for 217 days, in the Boer War; when the relief of Mafeking became known in London (18 May 1900), there were 'uproarious scenes and unrestrained exultation'; any such 'extravagant and boisterous celebration of an event, especially on an occasion of national rejoicing', became known as 'Mafficking' (Brewer); the 'Mafeking enthusiasm' Shakespeare expresses is that of the English at their defeat of the Spanish Armada.

196.29–30 *Warwickshire jesuits . . . theory of equivocation*: in the trials following the Gunpowder Plot (attempt by English Catholics to blow up the Houses of

Parliament (5 Nov. 1605)), Henry Garnett (Warwickshire provincial of the Jesuits) produced his 'theory of equivocation'—that he could lie under oath if he were doing so for 'the Greater Glory of God' (Jesuit motto); in *Macbeth*, II. iii. 8–11, the porter remarks: 'Faith, here's an equivocator, that could swear in both the scales against either scale, who committed treason enough for God's sake, yet could not equivocate to heaven'; *Lee* draws the connection (*G*).

196.30 *The Sea Venture*: or, *Sea Adventure*, ship sailing for Virginia but driven by storm to the Bermudas in 1609; often said to have influenced *The Tempest*.

196.31–2 *the play Renan admired . . . Patsy Caliban our American cousin*: for Renan, see 187.9 n.; he admired *The Tempest*; 'Patsy': stage Irishman; 'Caliban': 'a savage and deformed slave', offspring of Sycorax the witch, half-human possessor of the island in *The Tempest* before Prospero arrives; 'our American cousin': title of play (1858) by Tom Taylor (1817–80), but see 133.25–6 n.

196.32 *sugared sonnets follow Sydney's*: Sir Philip Sidney's (1554–86) sonnet sequence *Astrophel and Stella* (written *c.*1582) is cited by both *Lee* and *GB* as an (only mildly) influential predecessor of Shakespeare's; 'sugared sonnets': phrase used of Shakespeare's sonnets by Francis Meres in *Palladis Tamia: Wits Treasury* (1598).

196.32–5 *fay Elizabeth . . . of the buckbasket*: 'fay': 'fairy', so 'fay Elizabeth': Elizabeth I, after Edmund Spenser's (*c.*1552–99) allegorization of her in his *Faerie Queene* (1590, 1596); 'carroty Bess': because of her red hair; 'gross virgin': because of her reputedly crude sense of humour and her insistence on remaining unmarried; her command that Shakespeare write *The Merry Wives* is traditional; 'meinherr from Almany': gentleman from Germany (a dig at German scholars); 'buckbasket': dirty clothes' basket (from *Merry Wives*, as in III. iii. 2–3).

196.37 *Mingo, minxi, mictum, mingere*: principal parts of the Latin verb *mingere*: 'to urinate'.

197.3 *Sufflaminandus sum*: Latin: 'I ought to be slowed down'; after Ben Jonson's remarks about Shakespeare in his *Timber, or Discoveries* (1640): 'He flow'd with that facility, that sometime it was necessary he should be stop't: *Sufflaminandus erat* [he should have been slowed down]; as Augustus said of Haterius [prolix Roman senator and orator]'.

197.6 *myriadminded man . . . Coleridge*: Samuel Taylor Coleridge (1772–1834), *Biographia Literaria* (1817), ch. xv: 'the greatest genius, that perhaps human nature has yet produced, our *myriad-minded* Shakespeare'.

197.8–9 *Amplius. In societate . . . inter multos*: Latin: 'Furthermore, in human society it is of the utmost necessity that there be friendship among the many'; source unknown.

197.11 *Ora pro nobis*: Latin: 'Pray for us'.

197.13 *Pogue mahone! Acushla machree!*: Gaelic: *Póg mo thón. A chúisle mo chroidhe*: 'Kiss my arse! O pulse of my heart!'

197.13–14 *It's destroyed . . . surely!*: after Cathleen's keening lament (on hearing

Maurya's vision of her son's death) in J. M. Synge's (185.17 n.) *Riders to the Sea*: 'It's destroyed we are from this day. It's destroyed, surely.'

197.16–21 *Saint Thomas, Stephen ... hungers for it*: St Thomas Aquinas (after Augustine (see *G*)) likens 'lust' (which includes incest here) to avarice in *Summa Theologica*, Part I(II), question CLIV, art. 10, and in art. 9 condemns incest because, *inter alia*, it hinders the making of extrafamilial friendships, and is 'contrary to the natural respect we owe persons related to us' (*T* and *G*); 'gorbellied': fat (as Falstaff uses it in *1 Henry IV*, II. ii. 93).

197.18 *the new Viennese school*: the 'school' of psychoanalysis founded by Sigmund Freud (see 196.14 n.).

197.22–4 *The christian laws... hoops of steel*: 'christian laws': those that prohibited Christians lending money at interest; Jews were not so prohibited, and were (at various points in history) valued ('sheltered') precisely because of their practice of money-lending; 'lollards': 14th-c. followers of John Wyclif (*c.* 1330–84), translator of the Bible and religious reformer who held that the Church should lead people to live lives of evangelical poverty in imitation of Christ; he was 'sheltered' by John of Gaunt (1340–99) when under attack for his beliefs; 'affections ... steel': Polonius to Laertes in *Hamlet*, I. iii. 62–3: 'Those friends thou hast ... | Grapple them unto thy soul with hoops of steel'.

197.25 *old Nobodaddy*: Blake's anthropomorphic, wrathful, jealous god, in 'To Nobodaddy' (*c.* 1792), 'When Klopstock England defied' (*c.* 1800), and 'Let the brothels of Paris be opened' (*c.* 1792): 'Then old Nobodaddy aloft | Farted and belched and coughed, | And said, "I love hanging and drawing and quartering | Every bit as well as war and slaughtering"' (ll. 5–8) (Stevenson, ed., 169).

197.25 *at doomsday leet*: 'leet': court held by certain manorial lords; so the Last Judgement.

197.28 *sir smile neighbour*: Leontes, on the inevitability of man's being cuckolded 'by his next neighbour—by | Sir Smile, his neighbour' (*Winter's Tale*, I. ii. 195–6).

197.28–9 *shall covet... his jackass*: tenth commandment (in Exod. 20: 17): 'Thou shalt not covet thy neighbour's house, thou shalt not covet thy neighbour's wife, nor his manservant, nor his maidservant, nor his ox, nor his ass, nor any thing that is thy neighbour's'.

197.31 *Gentle will*: after Ben Jonson's epithet 'Gentle Shakespeare' in his 'To the Reader' and 'To the Memory of Shakespeare', both printed with the First Folio (1623).

197.36 *Requiescat!*: Latin from the prayer for the dead: *Requiescat in pace*: 'May he rest in peace'.

198.1–2 *What of all... ago*: opening lines of AE's (George Russell's) poem 'Sung on a By-Way', first stanza: 'What of all the will to do? | It has banished long ago. | For a dream-shaft pierced it through | From the Unknown Archer's bow'.

198.3–4 *the mobled queen*: one of the players engaged by Hamlet recites (of Hecuba): '"But who, ah woe, had seen the mobled queen"' (*Hamlet*, II. ii. 502); 'mobled': 'muffled'.

198.5–7 *In old age . . . town paid for*: 'gospeller': Puritan; the spending of money for a quart of sack for a preacher is recorded in the municipal records, but whether spent by Anne or her son-in-law is not (*GB*, *Lee*, *FH*).

198.9–11 *Hooks and Eyes . . . Sneeze*: Joyce seems to have found these titles of Puritan tracts from a review article in the 15 June 1904 issue of the *Irish Independent*, which lists *Hooks and Eyes for Believers' Breechers* and *The Spiritual Snuffbox to make the Most Devout Souls Sneeze* (Adams, 127).

198.13 *inquit Eglintonus Chronolologus*: Latin: 'cited Eglinton the Chronologist'.

198.19 *deny thy kindred*: Juliet to Romeo in the balcony scene: 'Deny thy father and refuse thy name' (*Romeo and Juliet*, II. ii. 34).

198.19 *the unco guid*: after Robert Burns's (1759–96) poem 'Address to the Unco Guid, or the Rigidly Righteous' (1786, 1787); 'unco': 'uncouth or uncommon'; 'guid': 'good'.

198.20 *A sire in Ultonian Antrim*: 'Ultonian': Ulster inhabitant; 'Antrim': county in Ulster; Eglinton (pseudonym of W. K. Magee) was actually the Dublin son of a Protestant clergyman (*G*).

198.22 *Give me my Wordsworth*: Eglinton's *Two Essays on the Remnant* (1896) praises Wordsworth (*G* and *T*).

198.22 *Magee Mor*: Gaelic: *Mag Aodha Mór*: 'Great Son of *Aodh* ("Fire"); Magee the Great'; or Magee Senior, Magee's father.

198.23 *a rugged rough rugheaded kern*: 'kern': Gaelic: *ceatharn*: 'mercenary foot soldier'; but also Richard in *Richard II*, II. i. 155–8: 'Now for our Irish wars: | We must supplant those rough rug-headed kerns, | Which live like venom where no venom else | But only they have privilege to live'.

198.23 *strossers*: 'trousers'; the dauphin in *Henry V*, III. vii. 52–4: 'you rode like a kern of Ireland, your French hose off, and in your strait strossers'.

198.24 *clauber of ten forests*: 'clauber': Gaelic: *clábar*: 'filth, dirt, mud'; after Yeats's *The Countess Cathleen* (1895 version), Shemus to his wife: 'the dead leaves and clauber of four forests cling to my footsole' (*T*).

198.24–5 *a wand of wilding in his hand*: after Wordsworth's 'The Two April Mornings': 'Matthew is in his grave, yet now, | Methinks, I see him stand, | As at that moment, with a bough | Of wilding in his hand'; 'wilding': 'wild crab-apple'.

198.31 *He wrote the play . . . his father's death*: John Shakespeare died 8 Sept. 1601; *GB* argues that *Hamlet* was written in 1601 (341).

198.33 *nel mezzo del cammin di nostra vita*: Italian: 'In the middle of the journey of our life'; opening line of Dante's *Inferno*.

198.34 *beardless undergraduate from Wittemberg*: Hamlet, who is a student at the University in 'Wittenberg'.

198.36 *From hour to hour it rots and rots*: Jacques, quoting the 'fool i' the forest' in *As You Like It*, II. vii. 26–8: 'From hour to hour, we ripe and ripe, | And then from hour to hour, we rot and rot; | And thereby hangs a tale'.

199.2 *Boccaccio's Calandrino*: Giovanni Boccaccio's (1313–75) *Decameron*, Day 9, story 3, concerns the duping of Calandrino into believing he's pregnant and his subsequent expensive 'cure'.

199.8 *Amor matris, subjective and objective genitive*: Latin: 'mother love'; ambiguously either 'mother's love for child' (subjective genitive) or 'child's love for mother' (objective genitive). (See also 28.32 n.)

199.9 *the only true thing in life . . . a legal fiction*: See *Portrait*, ch. 5, pp. 241–2 (see 28.10 n.); 'legal fiction': 'an assertion accepted as true (though probably fictitious) to achieve a useful purpose, esp. in legal matters' (*OEED*).

199.13 *Amplius. Adhuc. Iterum. Postea*: Latin rhetorical terms: 'Furthermore. Heretofore. Once again. Hereafter.'

199.19 *queens with prize bulls*: for Queen Pasiphaë's lust for the prize bull, see Ovid's *Metamorphoses*, Bk. VIII, and 4.5–6 n.

199.27–8 *The bulldog of Aquin . . . refutes him*: St Thomas Aquinas, a Dominican (in a medieval Latin pun, *Domini canis*: 'dog of god', hence 'bulldog'), refutes Sabellius (see 21.3 n.) in various places in *Summa Theologica*, but particularly in Part I(I), question XXXI, article 2 (*T*).

199.30 *Rutlandbaconsouthamptonshakespeare*: the 'familiar compound ghost' often asserted to be behind Shakespeare's writings: Roger Manners, fifth earl of Rutland (1576–1612); Francis Bacon (1561–1626); Henry Wriothesley, third earl of Southampton (1573–1624) (the last, dedicatee of *Venus and Adonis*).

199.34–5 *nature, as Mr Magee understands . . . abhors perfection*: from Eglinton's statement in *Pebbles from a Brook* (1901), 'Apostolic Succession', p. 45: 'Nature abhors perfection. Things perfect in their way, whether manners, poetry, painting, scientific methods, philosophical systems, architecture, ritual, are only so by getting into some backwater or shoal out of the eternal currents, where life has ceased to circulate. The course of time is fringed with perfections but bears them not upon its bosom.'

199.37 *through the twisted eglantine*: Milton's 'L'Allegro' (1631/2), of the lark greeting the lyric 'I' of the poem: 'Through the sweet-briar, or the vine, | Or the twisted eglantine' (ll. 47–8).

200.3 *Pallas Athena!*: Odysseus's patron; goddess of wisdom; springs full-grown from the head of Zeus.

200.3–4 *The play's the thing*: Hamlet in *Hamlet*, II. ii. 604–5: 'the play's the thing | Wherein I'll catch the conscience of the King'.

200.6–7 *his mother's name . . . Arden*: Shakespeare's mother was named Mary Arden; Stephen suggests that the Forest of Arden in *As You Like It* takes its name from her; Shakespeare's source for the play, Thomas Lodge's (*c.*1558–1625) *Rosalynde or Euphues' Golden Legacy* (1590), employed a forest of Arden; but see Stephen's answer to this at 203.10–11.

200.7 *Her death brought . . . Coriolanus*: Mary Arden died in 1608, supposed date of composition of *Coriolanus*; both *GB* and *FH* agree with Coriolanus's view of his mother, Volumnia, as 'the most noble mother of the world' (V. iii. 49) (*G*).

200.8 *His boyson's death . . . King John*: Hamnet Shakespeare died Aug. 1596; *GB* and *FH* date *King John* as 1596–7 and link Arthur, King John's nephew, to Hamnet (*G*).

200.8–9 *Hamlet, the black prince*: Hamlet, mourning his father, wears black (*Hamlet*, I. ii); also an allusion to Edward, the Black Prince (1330–76), who never became king because he predeceased his father, Edward III (1312–77).

200.10–11 *Who Cleopatra ... we may guess*: Cleopatra (in *Antony and Cleopatra*), Cressida (in *Troilus and Cressida*), Venus (in *Venus and Adonis*) would all, in Stephen's theory, be cast after Anne Hathaway, the seductress.

200.21 *Gilbert, Edmund, Richard*: Gilbert Shakespeare (b. 1566) seems to have survived his brother; Edmund Shakespeare (1580–1607); Richard Shakespeare (1574–1613).

200.21–5 *Gilbert in his old age ... Gilbert's soul*: these lines, in ostensible Warwickshire accent, embellish *Lee*'s report (44) that Gilbert went to London to see Shakespeare act in his own plays (particularly Adam in *As You Like It*) (Adams, 127).

200.28 *What's in a name?*: Juliet to Romeo: 'What's in a name? That which we call a rose | By any other word would smell as sweet' (*Romeo and Juliet*, II. ii. 43–4).

201.3–4 *Then outspoke ... Davy ...* : more fragments from the unpublished bawdiness of Oliver St John Gogarty.

201.6–7 *In his trinity ... names*: 'black Wills': Iago (in *Othello*), the eponymous Richard III, and Edmund (Gloucester's bastard son in *King Lear*) all admit their 'willful' villainy; Black Will and Shakebag: two roguish villains in the anonymous *Arden of Feversham* (1592) (*G*).

201.7–9 *that last play ... Southwark*: *King Lear* was entered on the Stationer's Register 26 Nov. 1607, as having played at James's court on St Stephen's Day (26 Dec.) 1606; Edmund Shakespeare (as *Lee* records) was buried 31 Dec. 1607.

201.13 *But he that filches ... name*: Iago to Othello: 'Good name in man and woman, dear my lord, | Is the immediate jewel of their souls. | Who steals my purse steals trash ... | But he that filches my good name | Robs me of that which not enriches him, | And makes me poor indeed' (*Othello*, III, iii. 155–7; 159–61).

201.15–16 *He has hidden ... a clown there*: 'super': 'supernumerary', an actor (one up from an 'extra') who appears on stage, but doesn't speak; Shakespeare sprinkles *1* and *2 Henry VI* and *2 Henry IV* with such 'super' Williams; William, a page, appears the object of humour in *Merry Wives of Windsor*, but the most relevant William is Audrey's pursuer in *As You Like It* whose exchange with Touchstone provides the verbal allusion here: 'Touchstone: "Is thy name William?" William: "William, sir". Touchstone: "A fair name"' (V. i. 20–2).

201.18 *Will in overplus*: see Sonnet 135, ll. 1–2: 'Whoever hath her wish, thou hast thy *Will*, | And *Will* to boot, and *Will* in overplus'.

201.18 *Like John O'Gaunt*: on the eve of his death, John of Gaunt puns on his name: 'Old Gaunt indeed, and gaunt in being old. | ... | Gaunt am I for the grave, gaunt as a grave, | Whose hollow womb inherits nought but bones' (*Richard II*, II. i. 74, 82–3).

201.19 *on a bend sable a spear or steeled argent*: Shakespeare's coat of arms; motto: *Non sans droict* ('Not without right').

201.19–20 *honorificabilitudinitatibus*: Dr Johnson records that it was often cited as the longest Latin word: 'the state of being loaded with honours'; Shakespeare uses it in *Love's Labour's Lost*, v. i. 41.

201.20 *his glory as greatest shakescene in the country*: see 180.1 n.

201.22 *A star, a daystar*: On 11 Nov. 1572 (when Shakespeare was 8 years old), Tycho Brahe (1546–1601), Danish astronomer, discovered a new star above the star delta in Cassiopeia (the constellation shaped like a W on its side; see 48.5 n.); it became so bright that it could be seen in the day, then faded (by Mar. 1574, when Will was nearly 10).

202.2 *meacock*: 'timid [man]'; Petruchio to Kate in *Taming of the Shrew*, II. i. 311–13: ''Tis a world to see | How tame, when men and women are alone, | A meacock wretch can make the curstest shrew'.

202.3 *Autontimerumenos*: *Autontimorumenos* or *Heauton-timoroumenos*: Greek: 'self-tormentor'; the latter being a play by Terence (*c.*185–*c.*159 BC); also used (as 'L'heautinouroumenos') by Charles Baudelaire in *Les Fleurs du mal* (1857) (*G* and *T*).

202.3 *Bous Stephanoumenos*: Greek neologism for 'Stephen's ox (or bull) soul'; an epithet of self-sacrifice as invoking the wreathed bull killed in ancient festivals (see *T*); it occurs also in *Portrait*, ch. 4, p. 168.

202.4–5 *S.D.: sua donna . . . non amar S.D.*: should read '*amare*'; Italian: 'S.D.: his woman. Sure: his. Gelindo resolves not to love S.D.'

202.8 *a pillar of cloud by day*: Exod. 13: 21: 'And the Lord went before them [the Israelites in the wilderness] by day in a pillar of a cloud, to lead them the way; and by night in a pillar of fire'; see, too, 137.21.

202.11 *Stephanos*: Greek: 'crown or garland'.

202.16 *Fabulous artificer*: Daedalus, the mythical maker of the labyrinth and the wings to fly out of it (see 4.5–6 n.).

202.17 *Lapwing*: 'Lapwing' carries a dense allusive history. In some English translations of Ovid, Daedalus's nephew, whose cleverness at invention is viewed so jealously by Daedalus that he throws the boy off the Acropolis, is saved by Pallas Athena, who changes him to a lapwing (in other translations, a partridge); he flutters joyfully about the grave when Daedalus buries Icarus. The bird is renowned for its careful seclusion of its nest, its flight away from the nest to distract predators, its jerky, fluttering movements in flight. In the Bible, it is an 'abomination' which 'shall not be eaten' (Lev. 11: 13, 19); in Celtic mythology (according to Robert Graves's *The White Goddess*), it is known as 'Disguise the Secret' and is associated with the stag ('Hide the Secret') and the dog ('Guard the Secret') (*G*). See, too, Blake's 'O lapwing, thou flyest around the heath, | Nor seest the net that is spread beneath. | Why dost thou not fly among the cornfields? | They cannot spread nets where a harvest yields' (Poems from the *Notebook*, XVII (*c.*1791–2)), and *Measure for Measure*, I. iv. 31–3,

Comedy of Errors, IV. ii. 27, *Much Ado About Nothing*, III. i. 24–5, *Hamlet*, V. ii. 185–6 (*T*).

202.17 *Icarus*: son of Daedalus, whose delight at flight got the better of him; he flew too near the sun, his wings melted, and he fell into the sea and drowned (see 4.5–6 n.).

202.17 *Pater, ait*: Latin: 'Father, he cries'; according to Ovid (*Metamorphoses*, Bk. VIII), on falling from the skies, Icarus calls—too late—for Daedalus; see too Luke 23: 46, where Jesus on the cross calls 'Father'.

202.31 *Father Dineen*: Father Patrick S. Dineen (1860–1934), Irish linguist, translator, editor, and philologist, compiler of Gaelic–English dictionary, assisted in the translation of Geoffrey Keating's (*c.*1570–*c.*1644) *History of Ireland* (*G*).

202.37 *two noble kinsmen*: title of play (*c.*1613) by John Fletcher in which, according to tradition, Shakespeare is meant to have collaborated.

203.4 *Where is your brother? Apothecaries' hall*: Stanislaus Joyce was employed (until 30 Jan. 1904) as a clerk at the Apothecaries' Hall, Dublin (*JJ* 144).

203.4–5 *My whetstone. Him, then Cranly, Mulligan*: those against whom Stephen sharpens his wit: his brother ('Maurice' in *Stephen Hero*), Cranly (in *Portrait*), and, of course, Buck Mulligan. (See, too, *T* and *G*.)

203.8 *the voice of Esau. My kingdom for a drink*: Jacob gains his elder brother Esau's blessing from their blind, elderly father, Isaac, by disguising himself as Esau: 'The voice is Jacob's voice, but the hands are the hands of Esau' (Gen. 27: 22); (see, too, 43.13 n. and 73.27–31 n.); Esau has earlier sold his birthright to Jacob for food when he was hungry (Gen. 25). 'My kingdom . . .': *Richard III*, V. iv. 7, 13: 'A horse, a horse! my kingdom for a horse!'; according to Shakespeare, Richard too usurped a birthright by having the two young princes, sons of his brother Edward IV, killed in the Tower.

203.10–11 *the chronicles . . . his plays*: Shakespeare's principal source for the history plays (and parts of *Macbeth*, *King Lear*, and *Cymbeline*) was Raphael Holinshed's (d. *c.*1580) *Chronicles* (1578).

203.12–13 *Richard . . . a whoreson merry widow*: in *Richard III*, I. ii, Richard succeeds in wooing Anne, widow of his brother the deceased king Edward IV (though she was a sincere widow who at the outset loathed Richard as the one responsible for her husband's death); 'whoreson': lit. 'bastard', fig. 'villain'; *The Merry Widow* (English title of *Die lustige Witwe* (1905)), Franz Lehar's (1870–1948) light opera.

203.13–14: *Richard the conqueror . . . William the conquered*: Richard III, conqueror of his eldest brother's throne and widow, was the 'third brother' (after Edward IV and Clarence); Richard Shakespeare, Stephen contends (having erased Gilbert), was the 'third brother' of William and conqueror of his brother's wife.

203.14–15 *The other four acts . . . first*: Stephen's argument: after Richard's villainy in Act I (having eliminated his brother and wooed his widow), the villainy in the rest of the play pales into insignificance.

203.16 *reverence, the angel of the world*: *Cymbeline*, IV. ii. 247–9: 'reverence | (That angel of the world) doth make distinction | Of place 'tween high and low'.

203.17–18 *Why is the underplot . . . history*: Stephen suggests, after *GB*, that the principal *Lear* plot (Lear and his daughters) derives from Celtic legend; the second plot (Gloucester and his sons) is borrowed from Sidney's *Arcadia* (1590), Bk. II, ch. 10, where the Paphlagonian King is estranged from his legitimate son through the devices of his bastard son who then deposes and blinds his father.

203.20 *George Meredith*: (1828–1909), English novelist, poet, and reviewer, whose principal works include the novels *The Ordeal of Richard Feverel* (see 191.12–13 n.), *The Egoist* (1879), and *Diana of the Crossways* (1885), as well as the bleak poem-cycle *Modern Love* (1862).

203.20–1 *Que voulez vous?*: French: 'What do you want [or 'desire']?; Moore was renowned for his French 'tags'.

203.21–2 *He puts Bohemia . . . quote Aristotle*: two Shakespearian errors: the first in *The Winter's Tale*, III. iii; in the second, Stephen compounds Shakespeare's error by making one of his own: in *Troilus and Cressida*, II. ii. 166–7, Hector (not Ulysses) cites Aristotle (who lived centuries *after* the Trojan War).

203.24–5 *what the poor is not, always with him*: see Matt. 26:11: 'ye have the poor always with you'.

203.25–8 *The note of banishment . . . drowns his book*: in *Two Gentlemen of Verona* (an early, Stephen suggests the earliest, play), Valentine is banished by the Duke of Milan; in *The Tempest* (generally considered the last), Prospero, rightful duke of Milan, is banished by his brother Antonio; having worked his magic repeatedly (and to Antonio's detriment) on his island, Prospero vows at last to abjure 'this rough magic', declaring, 'I'll break my staff, | Bury it certain fadoms in the earth, | And deeper than did ever plummet sound | I'll drown my book' (*Tempest*. v. i. 54–7).

203.29–30 *protasis*, *epitasis*, *catastasis*, *catastrophe*: critical terms, the four structural parts into which drama was divided (as articulated by the Hellenistic Alexandrian school, 3rd and 2nd c. BC): *protasis*: introduction or exposition; *epitasis*: the rising action or complication leading to the climax; *catastasis*: the falling action; *catastrophe*: the resolution (glibly, death or marriage).

203.30–1 *married daughter . . . accused of adultery*: *Lee* (266–7) provides the background: 15 July 1613, Susanna Shakespeare brought a charge of slander (with her father's help) against 'one Lane' in ecclesiastical court for his having accused her of having illicit relations with 'Ralph Smith'; Lane did not appear; verdict for Susanna (*G*).

203.32–4 *original . . . bishops of Maynooth*: see 188.34–5 n.

203.34–5 *like original sin . . . in whose sin he too has sinned*: *Maynooth Catechism* (see 188.34–5 n.), Lesson 6: 'We were all made partakers of the sin and punishment of our first parents'.

203.36 *it is petrified . . . to be laid*: Shakespeare's epitaph: 'Good frend for Iesus sake forbeare, | To digg the dust encloased here! | Bleste be y[e] man y[t] spares thes stones, | And curst be he y[t] moves my bones'; *FH* (362) maintains that the inscription was intended to prevent Anne's being buried with him.

203.37 *Age has not withered it*: Enobarbus of Cleopatra in *Antony and Cleopatra*, II. ii. 234–5: 'Age cannot wither her, nor custom stale | Her infinite variety'.

204.1–3 *Much Ado ... Measure for Measure*: Stephen asserts that 'it'—the theme 'banishment' or 'original sin'—resounds throughout these plays, an assertion which is tenable only if one accepts 'it' as broadly metaphorical. See *G* for possible readings of the plays in this light.

204.6–7 *He is all in all*: Hamlet of his father in *Hamlet*, I. ii. 188–9: ''A was a man, take him for all in all, | I shall not look upon his like again'.

204.9 *Cymbeline ... cuckold*: i.e. Shakespeare is both Jachimo/Iago and Posthumus/Othello.

204.10 *José... Carmen*: Don José, hero of George Bizet's (1838–75) opera *Carmen* (1857), falls in love with the beautiful gypsy Carmen and kills her when she prefers Escamillo.

204.11 *hornmad*: 'excessively jealous'.

204.13 *Cuckoo!... O word of fear*: from Spring's song in *Love's Labour's Lost*, V. ii. 900–1, 909–10: '"Cuckoo; | Cuckoo, cuckoo"—O word of fear, | Unpleasing to a married ear'; 'unpleasing' as it implies cuckolding.

204.16 *Dumas fils (or is it Dumas père?)*: of the two Alexandre Dumas, father (1802–70) and son (1824–95), it is the former who wrote, in his *Comment je devins auteur dramatique* ('How I Became a Dramatist') (1836): 'I recognized that [Shakespeare's] works, his alone, included as many types as the works of all [playwrights] put together. I recognized finally that he was the man who had, after God, created the most' (*T*).

204.18 *Man delights him not nor woman neither*: Hamlet in *Hamlet*, II. ii. 309: 'Man delights not me—nor women neither'.

204.21 *he plants his mulberrytree*: both *GB* and *Lee* repeat the traditional story of Shakespeare planting a mulberry tree in the garden of New Place.

204.26 *prosperous Prospero, the good man rewarded*: in keeping with generations of criticism, Stephen reads Prospero as the image of Shakespeare himself, retired to Stratford (*The Tempest* having been his last play); Lizzie (at 204.26): Shakespeare's first grandchild, Elizabeth Hall (b. 1608); 'nuncle Richie': Shakespeare's brother, Richard (but see 39.13).

204.28 *where the bad niggers go*: after the chorus of Stephen Foster's (1826–64) 'Uncle Ned': 'Den lay down de shubble and de hoe, | Hang up de fiddle and de bow, | No more hard work for poor old Ned, | He's gone whar de good niggers go'.

204.29–30 *Maeterlinck says... will tend*: Maurice Maeterlinck (1862–1949), Belgian poet and dramatist, in his *La Sagesse et la destinée* ('Wisdom and Destiny') (1899), sect. 10: 'If Judas go forth to-night, it is towards Judas his steps will tend, nor will chance for betrayal be lacking; but let Socrates open his door, he shall find Socrates asleep on the threshold before him, and there will be occasion for wisdom' (trans. Alfred Smith (New York, 1901)) (*T*).

204.34–5 *The playwright who . . . two days later)*: God, the clumsy creator, in Gen. 1: 1–19, who created light on day one, the sun and moon on day four.

204.36–7 *whom the most Roman . . . in all of us*: *Dio boia*: Italian: 'hangman god'; the vengeful, wrathful god; 'all in all': see 204.6–7 n.

205.1–3 *economy of heaven . . . wife unto himself*: Hamlet to Ophelia in *Hamlet*, III. i. 146–9: 'Go to, I'll no more on't, it hath made me mad. I say we will have no more marriage. Those that are married already (all but one) shall live, the rest shall keep as they are. To a nunn'ry go'; and Jesus to the Sadducees (Matt. 22: 30): 'In the resurrection they neither marry, nor are given in marriage, but are as the angels of God in heaven'.

205.4 *Eureka!*: Greek: 'I have found it!'; by tradition, Archimedes's words on discovering the law of specific gravity (see *T* for a different version).

205.13–14 *they fingerponder . . . Taming of the Shrew*: a sexually suggestive pun behind the indictment of the examiners of minutiae in Shakespeare criticism; see Swinburne's charge in 'The Three Stages of Shakespeare' (1875): 'metre-mongers, scholiasts, finger-counters, pedagogues, and figure-casters' (*G*).

205.20 *the Platonic dialogues Wilde wrote*: Platonic only in their dialogic form are Wilde's two essays 'The Decay of Lying' and 'The Critic as Artist' (1891); his *The Portrait of Mr. W.H.* (1889), while not itself a dialogue, narrates two.

205.23–4 *Dowden believes . . . mystery in Hamlet*: see Dowden's (see 196.3 n.) assertion in *Shakspere: A Critical Study of his Mind and Art* (1875) that 'Shakspere created [*Hamlet*] a mystery, and therefore it is forever suggestive; forever suggestive, and never wholly explicable' (126) (*G*).

205.24–6 *Herr Bleibtreu . . . the Stratford monument*: Karl Bleibtreu (1859–1928), *Die Lösung der Shakespeare-Frage* ('The Solution to the Shakespeare Problem') (Berlin, 1907), identifies Shakespeare's ghostwriter as Roger Manners, earl of Rutland (see 199.30 n.); note the anachronism and see Adams, 8, and *JJ* 411.

205.26 *the present duke*: John James Robert Manners (1818–1906), seventh earl of Rutland, English MP, and poetaster (*G*).

205.29 *I believe, O Lord, help my unbelief*: Mark 9: 24: 'Lord, I believe; help thou mine unbelief'.

205.30 *Egomen*: Greek: 'I on the one hand'.

205.31 *the only contributor to Dana*: see 185.17 n.

205.34 *Fraidrine*: 'Fred Ryan'.

206.2–3 *the Summa contra Gentiles*: short title of St Thomas Aquinas's *Summa de Veritate Catholicae Fidei contra Gentiles* ('Treatise on the Truth of the Catholic Church, against Unbelievers') (1261–4).

206.3–4 *Fresh Nelly and Rosalie, the coalquay whore*: two Oliver St John Gogarty creations (see *T* and *G*).

206.6 *wandering Ængus* of the birds: in Irish myth, Ængus (one of the Tuatha de Danaan) was the god of youth, beauty, love; portrayed (like St Francis) with birds hovering around his head; see Yeats's 'The Song of Wandering Aengus' (1899).

206.11 *Notre ami Moore*: French: 'Our friend Moore'; after Martyn's phrase for him 'Mon ami Moore' (see *G* and *T*).

206.18 *Irish nights entertainment*: after the *Arabian Nights' Entertainment* and Patrick J. McCall's (1861–1919) collection of Ossianic tales *The Fenian Nights' Entertainment* (1897).

206.22 *I gall his kibe*: 'I rub his chilblain'; after Hamlet to Horatio of the grave-digger's wordplay in *Hamlet*, v. i. 139–41: 'the age is grown so pick'd that the toe of the peasant comes so near the heel of the courtier, he galls his kibe'.

206.23 *all amort*: 'dispirited, dejected'; *Taming of the Shrew*, IV. iii. 36 and *1 Henry VI*, III. ii. 124.

206.29 *parafes*: paraphs: 'to place a flourish after a signature'.

206.37 *smoothsliding Mincius*: the river Mincius, Lombardy plain, near Virgil's birthplace (see *Eclogues*, VII. 12); and Milton, *Lycidas*, ll. 85–6: 'thou honor'd flood, | Smooth-sliding Mincius'.

207.1 *Puck*: otherwise known as Robin Goodfellow, the mischievous attendant of Oberon in *A Midsummer Night's Dream*.

207.2–3 *John Eglinton . . . wife*: after Robert Burns's 'John Anderson My Jo' (1789, 1790) which begins 'John Anderson, my jo ['sweetheart'], John'.

207.5 *Chin Chon Eg Lin Ton*: perhaps after 'Chin Chin Chinaman' from *The Geisha*, a light opera by James Philip and Harry Greenbank (another song from the opera is alluded to at 93.24–6) (see *G*).

207.6–7 *Our players are creating . . . for Europe*: comments like this were much in the air during the Irish literary revival (see *G*).

207.8 *public sweat*: should read 'pubic sweat'.

207.10 *the whipping lousy Lucy gave him*: traditional story (first mentioned by Richard Davies (1688–1708) and Nicholas Rowe (1674–1718) and repeated by *GB*, *FH*, and *Lee*) that Shakespeare stole deer from Sir Thomas Lucy who as a result had him whipped and imprisoned.

207.11 *femme de trente ans*: French: 'thirty-year-old woman'; also the title of a novel (1831) by Honoré de Balzac (1799–1850).

207.15 *minion of pleasure*: Sonnet 126, l. 9: of Nature: 'Yet fear her, O thou minion of her pleasure'.

207.15 *Phedo's toyable fair hair*: in Plato's *Phaedo*, 89, Socrates plays with Phaedo's hair while arguing about the immortality of the soul (*T*).

207.17 *Longworth and M'Curdy Atkinson*: for Longworth, see 184.33n.; F. McCurdy Atkinson: also involved in Moore's circle and the Irish National Theatre.

207.18 *Puck Mulligan footed featly*: Ariel's song guiding Ferdinand to Prospero in *The Tempest*, I. ii. 359: 'Foot it featly here and there'.

207.19–28 *I hardly hear . . . were worth*: parody of first stanza of Yeats's 'Baile and Aillinn' (1903 version): 'I hardly hear the curlew cry, | Nor the grey rush when wind is high, | Before my thoughts begin to run | On the heir of Ulad, Buan's son, | Baile, who had the honey mouth; | And that mild woman of the south, | Aillinn, who was King Lugaid's heir, | Their love was never drowned in care | Of this or that thing, nor grew cold | Because their bodies had grown old. | Being forbid to marry on earth, | They blossomed to immortal mirth'; 'purlieu': one's usual neighbourhood or haunts; 'Tommy': British soldier.

208.1–3 *Longworth is awfully sick... Jaysus*: Joyce's 'The Soul of Ireland', a review of Lady Gregory's *Poets and Dreamers* (1903), appeared in Longworth's *Daily Express*, 26 Mar. 1903; she had recommended him to Longworth; typical of Joyce's tone: 'her book, wherever it treats of the "folk", sets forth in the fulness of its senility a class of mind which Mr. Yeats has set forth with such delicate scepticism in his happiest book, "The Celtic Twilight"' (*CW* 102–5, 104); 'hake': a gossip.

208.4 *Yeats' touch*: Yeats, on the other hand, was always careful to praise Lady Gregory, as he did with her *Cuchulain of Muirthemne* (1902): 'I think this book is the best that has come out of Ireland in my time' (in his 'Preface' to her book).

208.10–11 *Gone the nine men's morrice*: after Titania's remark to Oberon in *A Midsummer Night's Dream*, II. i. 98: 'The nine men's morris is fill'd up with mud'.

208.21 *marcato*: Italian: 'marked'; musical direction to play with emphasis.

209.13 *Here I watched... augury*: In *Portrait*, ch. 5, p. 224, Stephen stands outside the Library watching the birds ('For an augury of good or evil?'); see 48.5–6 and n.

209.16 *The wandering jew*: legendary; according to one version, a Jew who mocked Jesus as he carried the cross, and to whom Jesus replied 'thou shalt tarry till I return'; thus, condemned to wander until Judgement Day (see *G*).

209.17 *He looked upon you to lust after you*: after Jesus's comment 'whosoever looketh on a woman to lust after her hath committed adultery with her already in his heart' (Matt. 5: 28).

209.17–18 *I fear thee, ancient mariner*: the Wedding Guest to the Ancient Mariner in Coleridge's *The Rime of the Ancient Mariner* (1798), ll. 224, 228: 'I fear thee, ancient Mariner! | ... | I fear thee and thy glittering eye'.

209.19 *Manner of Oxenford*: in this regard, see Joyce's essay 'Oscar Wilde: The Poet of "Salomé"' (1909): 'But the truth is that Wilde, far from being a perverted monster who sprang in some inexplicable way from the civilization of modern England, is the logical and inescapable product of the Anglo-Saxon college and university system, with its secrecy and restrictions' (*CW* 201–5, 204).

209.21 *Step of a pard*: 'pard': in medieval bestiaries, the most beautiful of all beasts, many-coloured, eats sweet herbs, allegorical of Christ (because it sleeps for three days after feasting), beloved of all animals (except the dragon); see 544.28–9.

209.25 *coigns of houses... No birds*: see *Macbeth*, I. vi. 6–10, where Banquo, watching a martlet, remarks: 'no jutty, frieze, | Buttress, nor coign of vantage, but this bird | Hath made his pendant bed and procreant cradle. | Where they most breed and haunt, I have observ'd | The air is delicate'; 'no birds': no augury to be read.

209.28 *Peace of the druid... hierophantic*: in the final scene of *Cymbeline* (v. v. 458, 466–7), the soothsayer, Philarmonus, interprets a prophecy, saying it 'Promises Britain peace and plenty. ... The fingers of the pow'rs above do tune | The harmony of this peace'.

209.30–2 *Laud we the gods//... altars*: opening lines of Cymbeline's final speech (the final speech of the play) in *Cymbeline*, v. v. 476–7.

WANDERING ROCKS

Location: The streets of Dublin. (See list of scenes and settings below.)
Time: 3 p.m.

Homer: Odysseus continues his tale. Having chosen Scylla and Charybdis, Odysseus avoided the Wandering Rocks. Thus there is no *Wandering Rocks* adventure in the *Odyssey*. Still, Odysseus has heard from Circe what might have happened had he chosen that route. Only Jason, blessed by Hera, has ever managed to sail past these Wanderers, 'overshadowing rocks against which dash the mighty billows of the goddess of blue-glancing seas' (144). Not even birds escape. Odysseus escapes them by choosing not to go that way. (Book XII) (The Rocks have been associated with the Symplegades, the two rocks on either side of the Hellespont which reputedly crashed together until, charmed by the music of Orpheus, they stayed still for Jason's Argo to sail by.)

Schemata: As personae, *L* lists, not characters from the *Odyssey* (except Ulysses)—this episode does not actually occur there—but instead, 'Objects, Places, Forces'. *G*'s correspondences lie with the actual geographic locations ostensibly underlying the myth: so, the Liffey is (oddly) aligned with the Bosphorus (instead of the Hellespont; both divide Europe and Asia, but the Bosphorus is the strait separating the Black Sea from the Sea of Marmara, while the Hellespont (at the mouth of which lie the Symplegades, the 'Wandering Rocks') is the strait separating the Sea of Marmara from the Aegean); the Viceroy with the European bank; Conmee with the Asiatic bank; groups of citizens with the Symplegades.

L and *G* agree on the Art (Mechanics), Organ (Blood), and, largely, Technic (*L*: 'Shifting labyrinth between two shores'; *G*: Labyrinth), but differ on Symbol (*L*: Christ and Caesar, Errors, Homonyms, Synchronisms, Resemblances; *G*: Citizens). *L*'s Sense is 'The Hostile Milieu'.

The episode consists of 18 short scenes and a 'Coda', each with its own setting. Into the scenes, at irregular intervals, various 'interpolations' intrude. An interpolation is defined as a narrative interruption because it could not properly be witnessed by those present in the scene itself. These interpolations occur in simultaneous narrative time but outside the range of vision of the characters proper to the scene itself. Some are events clearly belonging to other scenes in the episode; others have no such narrative 'home'. Further, there are two 'false interpolations'—'false' because they appear to be interpolations because they do not register on the consciousnesses of the characters in a scene but could actually have been witnessed by them if they had happened to have been looking in the right direction at the right moment. The scenes and their settings are given below; the interpolations ('true' and 'false') are cited in their proper place in the annotations list.

1. Father Conmee (210.1–215.20). Father John Conmee walks from St Francis Xavier Church, Upper Gardiner Street (F2), past Mountjoy Square (North, then East), up Great Charles Street to the North Circular Road, then down Portland Row (F3, G3), up North Strand Road to Newcomen Bridge where he mounts the tram. This he takes along North Strand and Fairview Roads to Malahide Road (H1) where he dismounts. He continues his walk up the Malahide Road toward Artane. He also visits Clongowes School in his memory.
2. Corny Kelleher (215.21–216.5). Corny Kelleher stands in the doorway of H J O'Neill's funeral establishment, 164 North Strand Road near Newcomen Bridge (G2).
3. Onelegged sailor; Eccles Street (216.6–32). The onelegged sailor, having earlier been seen on Upper Gardiner Street (F2), crutches his way up Eccles Street (E2), begging.
4. The Dedalus family kitchen (217.1–218.5). Katey, Boody, and Maggy Dedalus are at home in their father Simon Dedalus's house in Cabra (D2). (The Joyce family lived briefly at 7 St Peter's Terrace, Cabra.)
5. Blazes Boylan in Thornton's (218.6–219.10). Blazes Boylan buys fruit for Molly in Thornton's fruiterers, 63 Grafton Street (F4–5), and phones his secretary Miss Dunne.
6. Stephen Dedalus and Almidano Artifoni (219.11–220.5). Stephen Dedalus talks to his Italian tutor, Almidano Artifoni, outside the gates of Trinity College (F4).
7. Miss Dunne, Boylan's secretary (220.6–32). Miss Dunne types a letter and receives a phone call from her employer at his office (probably in D'Olier Street (F4)).
8. Ned Lambert, J J O'Molloy, and the Reverend Hugh C. Love (221.1–222.31). Ned Lambert shows the Reverend Hugh C. Love the 'historic council chamber of St. Mary's abbey', where they are joined by J J O'Molloy. All three emerge into 'Mary's abbey', the street (E4).
9. Lenehan, M'Coy, and Rochford (222.32–225.37). Tom Rochford shows Nosey

Flynn, Lenehan, and M'Coy his machine designed to reveal at a glance which 'turn' is on-stage at the musichall. Lenehan and M'Coy walk out into 'the tiny square of Crampton court', past the Empire Theatre (Dame Street), up Sycamore Street, east along Temple Bar, up the steps to and through Merchants' Arch to Wellington Quay and then back west along the river wall (all in E4).

10. Bloom at a bookstall (226.1–227.22; the central episode of the central episode). Bloom peruses books at a bookstall in Merchants' Arch (leading from Temple Bar to Crampton Quay (E4)).

11. Dilly and Simon Dedalus at Dillon's auctionrooms (227.23–229.26). Dilly Dedalus asks her father Simon for money outside Dillon's auctionrooms (25 Bachelor's Walk on the north bank of the Liffey (E4)).

12. Tom Kernan (229.27–231.31). Tom Kernan admires his attire as he walks east along James Street (C4), turns north into Watling Street and, passing Guinness's Brewery, heads for the Liffey. The viceregal cavalcade passes along Pembroke Quay (on the opposite bank of the river, too far away from Kernan for him to be noticed) (C/D4).

13. Stephen and Dilly Dedalus at a bookcart (231.32–233.37). Stephen Dedalus walks west along Fleet Street (E/F4), turns right into Bedford Row, and stops at a bookcart outside Clohissey's (10–11 Bedford Row) where he meets his sister Dilly.

14. Simon Dedalus, Father Bob Cowley, Ben Dollard (234.1–236.2). Simon Dedalus meets Father Bob Cowley outside Richard Reddy's antique shop, 19 Lower Ormond Quay (on the north bank of the Liffey (E4)), where they are joined by Ben Dollard who has just crossed the Metal Bridge. They then all walk west towards the subsheriff's office on Upper Ormond Quay.

15. Martin Cunningham, John Wyse Nolan, Jack Power with Long John Fanning and Jimmy Henry (236.3–238.14). Martin Cunningham, collecting money for the Dignams and accompanied by Jack Power and John Wyse Nolan, passes out of Castleyard gate (Dublin Castle (E4)), walks down Cork Hill, past the City Hall, continues into Parliament Street (where he approaches Jimmy Henry), and stops at Kavanagh's winerooms (where Long John Fanning stands in the doorway).

16. Buck Mulligan and Haines in the D.B.C. (238.15–240.2). Mulligan and Haines have tea in the Dublin Bread (later Bakery) Company tearooms (33 Dame Street (E4)).

17. Almidano Artifoni and Cashel Boyle O'Connor Fitzmaurice Tisdall Farrell and the blind stripling (240.3–21). Artifoni, having left Trinity College after speaking to Stephen, walks east along the north side of Merrion Square (F5) (which becomes Lower Mount Street (G5)). He is heading for his home in Landsdowne Road (H6). At the same time, CBOFT Farrell follows him east along Merrion Square North to the corner of Holles Street where he turns, retraces his steps, then continues into Clare Street. Simultaneously a blind

stripling taps his way along Leinster Street (F4), then Clare Street (F5) where he is passed and buffeted by CBOFT Farrell.

18. Master Patrick Aloysius Dignam (240.22–242.2). Young Master Dignam emerges from Mangan's butchers on the corner of William Street South and Wicklow Street (E4), proceeds east on Wicklow Street, turns left on to Grafton Street, then right into Nassau Street (F4).
19. Coda: the Viceregal Cavalcade (242.3–244.34). The Viceregal Cavalcade leaves the Viceregal Lodge in Phoenix Park (A2), passes through the lower gate of the park, travels along the quays on the north bank of the Liffey (C/D/E4), crosses the river at Grattan Bridge (E4), turns east into Dame Street, then south into Grafton Street and east into Nassau Street (F4). It continues along this street (through several name changes), across the Grand Canal (mistaken by the Viceroy for the 'Royal Canal') (G5) towards Ballsbridge (H6).

The disorienting effects of the 'Objects, Places, Forces' that comprise this 'Hostile Milieu' register variously on reader and characters. The latter are caught briefly in a narrative frame in the act of doing nothing very special. Paradoxically, it is the mere fact of their inclusion in the narrative that makes these characters appear culpable. ('What sinister motive lies behind such seemingly innocent acts?' we wonder; 'why are we being told *this* story?') In more than one sense, then, the characters are 'framed'. Who sees who doing what when matters a lot here. The problem for the characters seems to be that they cannot count on the narratorial eye not falling on them, cannot rely on only the apparently significant event being recorded, cannot depend on a narratorial logic beyond mere arbitrary selection. The reader's problem situates itself similarly: how to contend with the seeming capriciousness of the narrative. Is there some underlying significance here? Just as a plot-line appears to be gaining momentum, an interpolation intrudes. These interruptions force the fact of narrative simultaneity to the reader's consciousness, but how do we make sense of the juxtaposition? At the thematic level, these synchronous narrations bring home a fact about urban existence: the modern city brings individuals into (chance) relations by the mere fact of their coexistence within the giant mechanistic organism. It is the fact of the city which produces the relation. Similarly, narratively: *Wandering Rocks* teasingly hints that it is the fact of the narrative frame which bestows significance on narrated events, not vice versa (though once they are included, we will probably work overtime finding reasons to justify these erstwhile arbitrary vignettes). If the milieu is hostile here, that is because *it* (whether city or narrative frame) and *not* the characters dictates who meets who where and whether it will be glimpsed or overheard. Not they, then, but *it* produces meaning and determines guilt. Miss Dunne has no idea that a disk from Rochford's machine 'ogled' her as she 'hid the Capel street library copy of *The Woman in White* far back in her drawer'. It does so through narrative interpolation, the arrangement of a frame. No wonder she thinks there is 'Too much mystery business in it'. But as to just *how* much, she hasn't a clue.

210.4 *Vere dignum et iustum est*: Latin: 'It is indeed fitting and right', opening phrase of the Preface (which begins the Eucharist) in the Mass.

210.14–16 *cardinal Wolsey's words . . . in my old days*: Thomas, Cardinal Wolsey (*c.*1474–1530), archbishop of York (1514–30), Lord Chancellor of England (1515–29), powerful statesman favoured by Henry VIII until he failed to secure the papal dispensation necessary for the king's divorce from Catherine of Aragon, charged with treason, died on his way to trial; his final words: 'Had I served God as diligently as I have the king, he would not have given me over in my gray hairs'; (see, too, Shakespeare's version in *Henry VIII*, III. ii. 455–7).

210.23–4 *Father Bernard Vaughan*: (1847–1922), English Jesuit, famous for his sermons; a Cockney, hence the rendition of his words regarding Pilate (the governor of Judea who handed Jesus over to be crucified) at 211.10.

211.29–32 **Interpolation**: Denis Maginni and lady Maxwell.

211.37 *Mary, queen of Scots*: Mary Stuart (1542–87), daughter of James V of Scotland, a Catholic, imprisoned by Elizabeth I, beheaded on charge of conspiracy against the queen; renowned for her beauty, courage, and religious devotion.

212.3–5 *the shutup free church . . . will (D.V.) speak*: Free Church, a dissenting Church of Ireland chapel; 'shutup': not open for prayer; 'D.V.': abbreviation of the Latin: *Deo volente*: 'God willing'.

212.6 *Invincible ignorance*: Catholic theology: ignorance of which a person is not able to rid himself despite 'moral diligence'; Protestants are, according to Catholicism, invincibly ignorant.

212.18–19 *Aldborough house . . . spendthrift nobleman*: Lord Aldborough (d. 1801), already owner of various town and country houses, built this house (1792–98) at the cost of £40,000; his wife then refused to live in it; his name became synonymous with the excesses of the nobility.

214.3–4 *That book by the Belgian jesuit, Le Nombre des Élus*: Father A. Castelein, SJ, *Le Rigorisme, le nombre des élus et la doctrine du salut* (Brussels, 1899) (French: 'Rigorism, the Number of the Elect and the Doctrine of Salvation'), a 'liberal' book which suggested that the great majority of souls would be saved, thus bringing condemnation upon the author by strict Catholics who maintained that only baptized Catholics would be saved.

214.11 *The joybells were ringing in gay Malahide*: opening line of Gerald Griffin's (1803–40) poem 'The Bridal of Malahide' which tells the tale of Maud Plunkett's marriage (see 214.11–13 n.).

214.11–13 *Lord Talbot de Malahide . . . widow in one day*: the Lords Talbot of Malahide were (since 1476) hereditary lords admiral of Malahide (coast above Dublin); however, the story of 'maid, wife and widow' concerns Maud Plunkett: at his wedding to Maud, her 'husband' Hussey was called from the altar to battle where he died; her third husband was Sir Richard Talbot of Malahide (d. 1329), namesake of the first Lord Talbot.

214.16 *Old Times in the Barony*: actual book by actual Father John Conmee, SJ (1847–1910).

214.17–18 *Mary Rochfort*: (1720–*c.*1790), married to the first Earl of Belvedere who, after obtaining a verdict against her and his brother (for adultery), locked her away on his estate until he died (1774); she evidently had nothing to do with Belvedere House, which was actually built by the second earl in 1786.

214.23 *eiaculatio seminis inter vas naturale mulieris*: Latin: 'ejaculation of semen within the natural female organ'; technical definition of sexual intercourse, full completion of which was not necessary to have committed the sin of adultery.

215.3 *Clongowes field*: Father Conmee was rector of Clongowes Wood College (1885–91) during Stephen's (and Joyce's) time there (see *Portrait*, ch. 1).

215.4 *the boys' lines*: the divisions of the boys by age.

215.9–10 *Deus in adiutorium*: Latin: 'O God, to our aid [come]'; opening phrase of Ps. 70, beginning of the Nones (the daily prayer to be read at the 'ninth hour', *c.*3.00 p.m.).

215.12–13 *Res in Beati . . . tuæ*: Ps. 119 (which Conmee now reads) is divided into sections, each headed by a letter of the Hebrew alphabet (and, when the Vulgate version is alluded to, given Latin short titles); sect. 20 (vv. 153–60) is headed by the Hebrew letter *Res* (or *Resh*: ר), its Latin head is *Beati immaculati* ('Blessed are the undefiled'). The rest of the Latin quotation is from v. 160: 'Thy word is true from the beginning; and every one of thy righteous judgments endureth for ever'.

215.19–20 *Sin: Principes . . . meum*: '*Sin*' is the Hebrew letter (*Schin*: ש) which heads sect. 21 (vv. 161–8) of Ps. 119; the Latin quotation is from v. 161: 'Princes have persecuted me without a cause: but my heart standeth in awe of thy word'.

215.27–8 **False interpolation**: Father John Conmee.

216.2 **Interpolation**: 'generous white arm'.

216.9, 12 *For England . . . ; home and beauty*: from the song 'The Death of Nelson', about Nelson's death at the Battle of Trafalgar: 'Vict'ry crown'd the day | But dearly was that conquest bought, | Too well the gallant hero fought, | For England, home, and beauty, | For England, home, and beauty, | He cried, as 'midst the fire he ran, | "England expects that ev'ry man | This day will do his duty"'.

216.13–14 **Interpolation:** J J O'Molloy.

217.6–7 **Interpolation:** Father John Conmee.

217.11 *Bad cess to*: slang: 'In Ireland the word is used as a contraction of success, meaning luck, as, "Bad cess to you!"' (Brewer).

217.23–4 **Interpolation:** Lacquey's bell.

217.33 *Our father who art not in heaven*: literally, Simon Dedalus; adaptation of the Pater Noster: 'Our father which art in heaven' (Matt. 6: 9).

218.2–5 **Interpolation**: Throwaway.
218.22–3 **Interpolation**: Bloom ('darkbacked figure').
219.12 *Goldsmith's knobby poll*: statue of Oliver Goldsmith (?1730–74), Anglo-Irish clergyman, reviewer, essayist, poet, novelist, playwright; the statue, by the Irish sculptor John Henry Foley (1818–74), stands on Trinity College grounds facing College Green (F4).
219.17–220.1 *Anch'io ho avuto ... belle cose!*: Stephen's (S) and Almidano Artifoni's (A) conversation in Italian: (A): 'I too had the same idea when young as you are. At the time I was convinced that the world was a beast. It's too bad. Because your voice ... would be a source of income, come now. But instead, you are sacrificing yourself.' (S): 'Bloodless sacrifice.' (A): 'Let's hope ... But listen to me. Think about it.' (S): 'I'll think about it.' (A): 'Are you serious, eh?' (A): 'Here it is. Come see me and think about it. Goodbye dear man.' (S): 'Goodbye master ... And thank you.' (A): 'For what? Excuse me, eh? All the best!'
220.4 *gillies*: Scots; but also Gaelic: *giolla*: 'lad, servant'.
220.6 *The Woman in White*: novel (1860) by Wilkie Collins (1824–89) with a plot of extreme intricacy (and no little melodrama) involving romance, false identities, inheritance, madness, violent death, and, eventually, virtue rewarded.
220.9 *Mary Cecil Haye*: (*c.*1840–86), popular sentimental novelist.
220.10–11 **Interpolation**: Rochford's machine.
220.14–16 **Interpolation**: H E L Y'S men.
220.15 *slab where Wolfe Tone's statue was not*: Theobald Wolfe Tone (1763–98), Irish patriot and revolutionary, one of the founders of the Society of United Irishmen (1791), regarded republicanism as a necessary part of patriotism, solicited the aid of the French for various uprisings in the 1790s, particularly for the 1798 Rebellion, captured at sea, committed suicide when denied a soldier's death; treated with some ambivalence by both Protestants and Catholics. The foundation stone was laid in 1898 at the north-west corner of St Stephen's Green, but the statue never made it; now a monument sits in the north-east corner of the green (F5).
221.6 *vesta*: a match (named after the Roman goddess of the hearth).
221.10–12 *the historic council chamber ... 1534*: site: the old chapter house of St Mary's abbey (E4), the remains of which were used (by 1904) as storerooms for seed merchants; Silken Thomas (see 45.21–4n.) summoned the Council to the abbey 11 June 1534 and renounced his allegiance to Henry VIII.
221.14–15 *the original jews' temple ... Adelaide road*: the chapter house was used as a Jewish synagogue (1835–92), but it was not the first in Dublin; that was across the Liffey (*c.*1650).
221.18–19 *He rode down through ... Thomas court*: no he didn't; fanciful history involving among other things his crossing bridges that weren't built until the 17th c.; history records him approaching from the west (G).
221.28 **Interpolation**: 'beard'.
222.8 *Fitzgeralds*: one of Ireland's most famous families going back to the 12th c.;

by the 16th c. they comprised two houses, the earls of Kildare and the earls of Desmond; by the 18th c. they were the dukes of Leinster.

222.9–10 **Interpolation**: 'young woman'.

222.11 *gunpowder plot*: conspiracy by small group of extremist Catholics to blow up James I and the Houses of Parliament on 5 Nov. 1605 (now Guy Fawkes Day in memory of the conspirator captured in the vaults of the House attempting to set a mine).

222.13–17 *the earl of Kildare . . . the Fitzgerald Mor*: Gerald Fitzgerald (1456–1513), 8th Earl of Kildare; fiery Anglo-Irish lord caught up in a series of conflicts, including a fight with Archbishop Creagh which resulted in his setting fire to Cashel Cathedral (1495); the accusation (before Henry VII) apparently ended, 'All Ireland cannot rule this Earl', to which Henry is said to have responded: 'Then in good faith shall the Earl rule all Ireland'; Fitzgerald returned to Ireland as Henry's deputy.

222.30 *was . . . this*: should read 'was . . . Glasnevin this'.

222.34 *Turn Now On*: Rochford's machine will indicate at a glance which musichall 'turn' is on-stage (for the benefit of those who come in late).

223.3–7 **Interpolation**: Richie Goulding.

223.3–4 *Lawyers of the past . . . court*: Four Courts, 18th-c. building (D4), the great hall of which is filled with statues of famous Irish men of law; housed numerous courts.

224.10 **Interpolation**: Viceregal Cavalcade.

224.18 *the Bloom is on the Rye*: after refrain in Edward Fitzball and Sir Henry Bishop's song 'When the Bloom is on the Rye': 'meet me, meet me in the ev'ning | While the bloom is on, is on the rye'.

224.28–9 **Interpolation**: Master Dignam.

224.36–7 **Interpolation**: *Unfurnished Apartments.*

225.13–14 *Lo, the early beam of morning*: a quartet (not duet) from Michael Balfe's opera *The Siege of Rochelle* (1835).

226.1–2 *The Awful Disclosures of Maria Monk*: Maria Monk (*c.*1817–50) wrote a book in which she claimed to have escaped from a Montreal nunnery and to be revealing the hideous events within; revealed as a fraud; nevertheless sold a quarter of a million copies; prompted intense anti-Catholic sentiment.

226.2 *Aristotle's Masterpiece*: not actually by Aristotle: a semi-pornographic supposed medical treatise, widely circulated since the 16th c.

226.6 *Tales of the Ghetto by Leopold von Sacher Masoch*: Leopold von Sacher-Masoch (1835–95), Austrian novelist ('masochism' derives from his name), author of *Venus in Furs*; his *Tales of the Ghetto* was in Joyce's Trieste library (Ellmann, *The Consciousness of Joyce* (1977; repr. New York: Oxford University Press, 1981), 126).

226.14–15 **Interpolation**: Denis Maginni.

226.16 *Fair Tyrants by James Lovebirch*: not uncommon pseudonym for authors of flagellation literature, though no work of this name has yet surfaced.

226.21 *Sweets of Sin*: if not Joyce's creation, as yet to be found.

227.6–12 **Interpolation**: 'elderly female'.

227.31–3 **Interpolation**: cycle race.

228.20–1 **Interpolation**: Tom Kernan.

229.19–20 **Interpolation**: Viceregal Cavalcade.

230.15–16 **Interpolation**: Simon Dedalus and Bob Cowley.

230.25 *The cup that ... inebriates*: Bishop Berkeley said this of tar-water (*Siris* (1744), ¶217); William Cowper (1731–1800) of tea (*The Task* (1785), IV. 34).

230.26–8 **Interpolation**: Throwaway.

230.37 *Down there Emmet ... quartered*: see 110.5–6 n. Emmet was hanged and beheaded (though not drawn and quartered) in front of St Catherine's church in Thomas Street (D4).

231.1 *the lord lieutenant's wife*: tradition holds that the witness was merely a woman nearby; the pretentious Kernan increases her status to that of the wife (Elizabeth) of the then Lord-Lieutenant of Ireland, Philip Yorke (1757–1834).

231.2–3 *in her noddy*: should be followed by entirely new paragraph: 'Bad times those were. Well, well. Over and done with. Great topers too. Fourbottle men.'

231.10 *Tipperary bosthoon*: 'bosthoon': Gaelic: *bastún*: 'poltroon, blockhead'; so, a country bumpkin.

231.12–14 **Interpolation**: Denis Breen.

231.16 *Times of the troubles*: the 1798 Rebellion.

231.16–17 *those reminiscences of sir Jonah Barrington*: (1760–1834), self-proclaimed patriot, judge, voted against the Union, but procured others' votes for it (Foster 169, n. x); author of the disingenuous *Personal Sketches* and *Historic Memoirs of Ireland*.

231.20 *Lord Edward Fitzgerald*: (1763–98), leading figure in the United Irishmen, supposed architect of the plans for the 1798 Rebellion; denounced; went into hiding; reward offered for his capture by (the notoriously brutal) Henry Charles Sirr (1764–1841), mayor of Dublin; caught and mortally wounded in house in Thomas Street (D4); his wife hid in Moira House on Usher's Quay (D4).

231.22–3 *that sham squire*: see 122.12 n.

231.23 *Course they were on the wrong side*: which statement puts Kernan on the anti-nationalist, pro-British side.

231.24 *They rose in dark and evil days ... Ingram*: from John Kells Ingram's (1823–1907) poem 'The Memory of the Dead' (1843), l. 33; the poem begins: 'Who fears to speak of Ninety-Eight ... He's a knave or half a slave'; Kernan's line begins stanza 5.

231.27 *At the siege ... father fall*: from 'The Croppy Boy' (see 88.4 n.); Ross was the site of a confrontation between 'croppies' and an English garrison; the latter won.

232.3–5 *Born all in the dark ... wrest them*: Stephen's thoughts echo, somewhat distantly, John 1: 5 and Rev. 12: 4.

232.11–12 *Grandfather ape . . . hoard*: after Yeats's description (in 'The Eaters of Precious Stones' in *The Celtic Twilight* (1893)) of 'the Hell of the artist' in which he sees apes devouring precious green and crimson stones out of their hands (*Mythologies* (London: 1959), 100).

232.14 *Antisthenes*: see 142.21–5 n.

232.16–18 **Interpolation:** 'Two old women'; *cf.* 38.5–12.

232.20–1: *Throb always . . . within*: echoes a line from James Lane Allen's (1849–1925) novel *The Mettle of the Pasture* (1903) which Joyce reviewed for the *Daily Express* (*CW* 117–18); as Joyce quotes the phrase from Mettle: 'without us and within us moves one universe that saves us or ruins us only for its own purposes' (*CW* 117).

232.22 *Between two . . . swirl*: *G* cites Arnold's 'Stanzas from the Grande Chartreuse' and Richard Henry Stoddard's 'The Castle in the Air', neither of which are very convincing.

232.25–6 *You say right . . . indeed*: Hamlet mocking Polonius: 'You say right, sir: a' Monday morning; 'twas then indeed' (*Hamlet*, II. ii. 387–8).

232.28–9 *1860 print . . . Sayers*: an actual fight between the world champion Tom Sayers, an Englishman, and John Heenan, an American, 7 Apr. 1860, which was so brutal that boxing was suppressed in England, only to be allowed again under the Marquess of Queensberry rules.

232.36–7 *Stephano Dedalo . . . ferenti*: Latin: 'To Stephen Dedalus, one of the best alumni, the class prize'.

233.1–2 **Interpolation:** Father Conmee.

233.3–4 *Eighth and ninth . . . secrets*: cabbalistic tradition holds that Moses wrote not only the first five books of the Old Testament (as Moses the Lawgiver), but also another four (or five) books now lost (as Moses the Magician); various 'translations' of these 'lost' books (containing, *inter alia*, esoteric lore and magical charms) circulated in the 19th c. (*G*).

233.4 *Seal of King David*: the six-pointed star formed of two interlaced triangles.

233.8 *Se el yilo . . . Amen*: *G* gives a possible 'translation': 'My little heaven of blessed femininity, love only me. Holy! Amen.'

233.16 *A Stuart face . . . Charles*: 'Nonesuch': most eminent; Charles I (1600–49; r. 1625–49), second Stuart king of England.

234.16 *bockedy*: Gaelic: *bacach*: 'lame, halt, clumsy'.

235.4–5 **Interpolation:** CBOFT Farrell.

235.13–16 **Interpolation:** Hugh C. Love.

235.15–16 *the Tholsel . . . Hurdles*: 'Tholsel': literally, 'toll collector's booth', an early (14th-c.) municipal building in Christchurch Place (D4); 'Ford of Hurdles': a direct translation of the Gaelic: *Áth Cliath*: the ancient name for Dublin, from an ancient wicker bridge crossing the Liffey.

235.20 *Lobengula*: Zulu king of the Matabele (*c.*1833–94), fierce protector of his territory against invasions.

235.21 *Lynchehaun*: should read 'Lynchebaun'; an alias of James Walshe who assaulted and left for dead a woman on Achil island; tried and sentenced to life (1895); escaped and fled to America; recaptured, but the United States refused extradition accepting his story that he was a political prisoner; came into legend as one whom the police couldn't touch (*G*).

235.27 *shraums*: Gaelic: *sream*: 'rheum'.

236.14 *Touch me not*: Jesus's words to Mary Magdalene after the resurrection (John 20: 17).

236.9–10 **Interpolation**: 'Bronze by gold'.

236.27 *there is much kindness in the jew*: Antonio, upon sealing his bond that he'll give a pound of flesh if he can't repay his loan from Shylock: 'I'll seal to such a bond, | And say there is much kindness in the jew' (*The Merchant of Venice*, I. iii. 152–3).

236.17–18 **False interpolation**: Councillor Nannetti.

236.31–2 **Interpolation**: Boylan.

237.13–14 *Henry Clay*: cigar named after American politician Henry Clay (1777–1852).

237.16 *the conscript fathers*: name given to Roman senators.

237.18 *Hell open to christians*: after the tract *Hell Opened to Christians; To Caution Them from Entering into It* (1688) by Giovanni Pietro Pinamonti (1632–1703), the principal source for the sermons on hell in *Portrait*, ch. 3.

237.23 *locum tenens*: Latin: 'holding the place'; a stand-in.

239.3–4 **Interpolation**: onelegged sailor.

239.13 *the Attic note*: aesthetic rather than instructive (Athenian culture in 5th-c. BC).

239.13 *The note of Swinburne*: Mulligan's constant reference to Swinburne marks him as a self-styled aesthete.

239.13–14 *the white death and the ruddy birth*: from Swinburne's 'Genesis', *Songs Before Sunrise* (1871), stanza 9: 'For the great labour of growth, being many, is one; | One thing the white death and the ruddy birth'.

239.18 *Professor Pokorny of Vienna*: Julius P. Pokorny (b. 1887), a Viennese Celticist.

239.22 *no trace of hell in ancient Irish myth*: not quite accurate; *Tír na nÓg*, the Celtic otherworld, has no hell, but an underworld of demons did exist in Celtic myth.

239.23–4 *The moral idea . . . retribution*: the thoughts more of an Englishman towards the Irish than of Pokorny.

239.29–30 *He is going to write something in ten years*: i.e. *Dubliners* (1914).

239.36–240.2 **Interpolation**: Throwaway.

240.11–12 *Elijah's name . . . Metropolitan Hall*: Farrell mistakes Merrion Hall (at which he is looking (F5) and on which Stephen and Lynch later see the poster) for Metropolitan Hall (F4) on the other side of the Liffey.

240.14 *Coactus volui*: Latin: 'Having been forced, I was willing'.

240.16 *Mr Bloom's dental windows*: Marcus J. Bloom, no relation.

241.2–3 *Keogh . . . Bennett*: see 165.6–7 n.
241.11 *mots . . . fags*: 'mots': prostitute; 'fags': cigarettes.
242.3 *William Humble*: William Humble Ward, 2nd Earl of Dudley (1866–1932), a Conservative, Lord-Lieutenant of Ireland (1902–6).
242.10 *Bloody bridge*: name of a former bridge where Barrack Bridge stood in 1904 (Victoria Bridge on the map (D4)); site of a bloody skirmish between military and those whose interests lay with money from the docks (1670), hence Bloody Bridge.
243.23 *King Billy's horse*: equestrian statue of King William III (William of Orange), victor at the Battle of the Boyne, stood opposite Trinity College (E/F4); much-despised, the statue was removed in 1929.
243.33 *My girl's a Yorkshire girl*: song by C. W. Murphy and Dan Lipton, repeatedly alluded to (particularly in *Circe*); *G* reproduces the lyrics.
244.21 *Mirus bazaar*: see 174.27 n.
244.25 *the Royal Canal bridge*: actually, at this point the cavalcade must be crossing not the Royal Canal (which circles around the northern periphery of Dublin), but the Grand Canal.
244.31–3 *the house said . . . 1849*: Queen Victoria and Prince Albert visited Dublin (entering from the south-east via Pembroke Road) 6–10 Aug. 1849, but history does not record the queen admiring a particular house.

SIRENS

Location: The bar of the Ormond Hotel (8 Upper Ormond Quay, north bank of the River Liffey (E4)). While the principal action occurs in the bar, Bloom is seen to have left Merchants' Arch and to be walking along Wellington Quay (E4) toward, then across, Grattan ('Essex') Bridge. He then turns left into Upper Ormond Quay to the Hotel. On leaving, he continues west along the quay on his way to buy a postal order at the post office further along. He will later be seen on the corner of Pill Lane and Greek Street (D4). Blazes Boylan, spied earlier by Bloom, crosses Essex Bridge by car and turns into Upper Ormond Quay, stopping, too, at the Ormond Hotel; he leaves shortly thereafter on his way to 7 Eccles Street. The blind stripling, earlier seen being buffeted on Clare Street, returns across O'Connell Bridge to retrieve his tuningfork from the Hotel.
Time: 4 p.m.

Homer: Before encountering Scylla and Charybdis, Odysseus and his men had first to sail past the Sirens' island. Here the two sirens (one of whom is named Parthenope) sit in a meadow surrounded by the corpses of men they had enraptured. For they sing an enchanting song, 'honey-sweet music' (147) which men find irresistible. Determined to hear the song, Odysseus demanded that his men fill their ears with wax to block the music and bind him to the mast so he could both hear and not be lost. Though Odysseus was enchanted and bid his men untie him, the crew refused and all sailed safely by. Parthenope, outraged at their escape, threw herself into the sea. (Book XII)

Schemata: In addition to Parthenope and Ulysses, *L* lists Leucothea, Menelaus, Orpheus, and the Argonauts. Neither Menelaus nor Telemachus is either present at the adventure, or hears the telling of the tale. In simultaneous narrative time, they are in one another's company at Menelaus's court. Leucothea is the sea-goddess who has earlier helped Odysseus (see n. to *Calypso*, above). Orpheus, not in the *Odyssey* at all, is the renowned poet-musician whose music charmed all nature. The Argonauts solicited his help in their quest for the Golden Fleece. His music charmed the Wandering Rocks and the Colchian dragon, thus allowing the Argo twice to sail past danger. On approaching the Sirens, Orpheus provided music more beautiful than theirs and so prevented the Argonauts from listening to their song. *G* provides only two correspondences: the Barmaids with the Sirens, and the Bar with the Isle.

L and *G* agree on the Art (Music), Organ (Ear), and Technic (*fuga per canonem* ('fugue according to rule', an eight-part fugue (in five sections) following the pattern of (in the first section) (1) a subject, (2) answer, and (3)repetition; (in the second) a (4) statement and (5) answer; (the third) (6) a free exposition; (the fourth) (7) the climax; and (the final section) (8) a Coda)). They differ on Colour (*L*: coral; *G*: none) and Symbol (*L*: Promises, Female, Sounds, Embellishments; *G*: Barmaids), *L*'s Sense is 'The Sweet Deceit'.

Joyce's Hints: In a letter to Harriet Weaver, Joyce refers to the episode as comprising 'all the eight regular parts of a *fuga per canonem*: and I did not know in what other way to describe the seductions of music beyond which Ulysses travels' (*LI* 129; 6/8/19).

'All art constantly aspires towards the condition of music' wrote Walter Pater in *The Renaissance.* If *Sirens* is Joyce's response to this truism, it is a riposte at once serious and parodic (see Lawrence, *The Odyssey of Style in Ulysses*, 91 ff.). *Sirens* takes quite seriously the problem of how words might perform like the tonal sounds of music. Hence the proliferation of onomatopoeic noises ('With a cock with a carra', 'Pwee', 'Hee hee', 'Hissss'), the reduction of words to rhythmically repeated, syllabic units ('Imperthnthn thnthnthn'), the transcription of sequences of words as received sound rather than as conventional or standardized morphemes ('Goodgod henev erheard inall'). The governing rules here are acoustic, not linguistic. More broadly, *Sirens* ostensibly follows the structure of a fugue (see 'Joyce's Hints' above) and the 'prelude' (pp. 245–6) most resembles a quick flick through the score by the conductor before its performance (see 'Introduction', p. xxxiii). But all this suggests that Joyce's episode merely imitates music—its sounds, structural organizations, performative conventions—as secondary parasitic repetition.

Pater's point was more serious than an intended prompting of such flippant mimetic gestures, and Joyce's experiments in *Sirens* are responsively unsettling. Pater's contention was that in music, it is virtually impossible to distinguish the matter from the form, and that the obliteration of this distinction is the aim of all art. In so far as the 'form' of novels is verbal and narrative, *Sirens* performs the most dramatic challenge to that form yet seen in *Ulysses*. The aural logic of the episode—passages spawn other passages through similarities of sound; words arrange themselves into alliterative, mellifluous, cacophonous, rhythmic, assonantal, rhyming patterns; the acoustic voice (as sound) nudges out the graphic mark (as sense)—produces a noisy static profoundly disruptive of narrative coherence. But *Sirens* remains this side of (mere graphic transcription of) insensible sound, whatever its challenges to the matter/form divide. That is, narrative prevails beneath the dissonant hiss (and Bloom even succeeds in writing a letter). If Joyce takes Pater seriously in pushing narrative as far as it might go toward imitating the form/matter dissolution in music, he also parodically pushes Pater into an admission that the sensible words formed into narratives which are novels necessarily refuse the decomposition into pure sound required in music. For Ulysses (and no less *Ulysses*) resists the Sirens' song.

In the following notes, the annotation begins with the 'text proper' (that is, after the 'prelude'). Though the 'prelude' itself is replete with musical allusions, these all recur in the main narrative and are annotated there. Note that the 'prelude' is itself a proleptic synthesis of the motifs sounded in the succeeding narrative; each note heard here can be traced forward to its corresponding chord in the text.

249.12 *Bluerobed*, *white under*: the Virgin Mary's traditional colours.

251.4 *mermaid's*: a brand of tobacco.

251.8 *O, Idolores . . . eastern seas!*: refrain from 'The Shade of the Palm' from the light opera *Floradora* (1899), music by 'Leslie Stuart' (Thomas A. Barrett), book by Owen Hall, lyrics by E. Boyd-Jones and Paul Rubens; the song is a pledge of love sung by the hero (a lord in disguise) who is parting from Dolores ('my Dolores': 'Idolores' to Miss Douce), the heroine: 'Oh, my Dolores, Queen of the Eastern sea, | Fair one of Eden look to the West for me, | My star will be shining, love, | When you're in the moonlight calm, | So be waiting for me by the Eastern sea, | In the shade of the sheltering palm'.

251.28 *solfa*: as in 'do, re, mi, fa, sol, la, ti, do', the syllables sung to the scale.

251.29–30 *Ah fox met ah stork . . . bone*: two of Aesops' fables combined: 'The Wolf and the Crane' (wolf has a bone stuck in his throat which the crane removes, wolf says his payment is not being eaten) and 'The Fox and the Stork' (fox invites stork to dinner, serves him soup in a flat plate so he can't eat'; stork invites fox to dine, serves him mince in a narrow-necked jar so he can't eat).

252.12–13 *minstrel boy of the wild wet west*: the 'west of Ireland', typically regarded as wild because still rural; 'The Minstrel Boy', a song from Thomas Moore's *Irish Melodies*.

252.17 *faraway mourning mountain eye*: echoes Percy French's (1854–1920) song 'The Mountains of Mourne' where the good boy prefers the girl at home in Ireland to all the lights of London.

253.22 *bothered*: from the Gaelic: *bodhar*: 'deaf, used as both a noun and a verb' (P. W. Joyce, 221).

253.23, 25, 30; 254.10 *The bright stars fade . . . | . . . | . . . And I from thee*: from Goodbye, Sweetheart, Goodbye', words by Jane Williams (1806–85), music by John L. Hatton (1809–86), first verse: 'The bright stars fade, that morn is breaking, | The dew drops pearl each bud and leaf, | And I from thee my leave am taking, | With bliss too brief, with bliss too brief, | How sinks my heart with fond alarms, | The tear is hiding in mine eye, | For time doth thrust me from thine arms; | Goodbye, sweetheart, goodbye! Goodbye, sweetheart, goodbye!'

253.32 *rose of Castile*: see 126.4–5 n.

254.6 *See the conquering hero comes*: opening line of a poem by the same name by Thomas Morell (1703–84), used by Handel in two of his oratorios, *Judas Maccabaeus* (1747) and *Joshua* (1748).

255.11–12 *Fair one of Egypt . . . For me* : adaptation of line from 'The Shade of the Palm' (see 251.8 n.) in substituting 'Fair one of Egypt' for 'Fair one of Eden'.

255.24, 30 *To Flora's lips did hie | I could not leave thee . . .* : adaptation of lines in second verse of 'Goodbye, Sweetheart, Goodbye' (see 253.23 n.): 'The sun is up, the lark is soaring, | Loud swells the song of chanticleer, | The levret bounds o'er earth's soft flooring, | Yet I am here, yet I am here. | For since night's gems from heav'n did fade | And morn to floral lips doth hie, | I could not leave thee though I said, | Goodbye, sweetheart, goodbye'.

255.32 *Sonnez la cloche!*: French: 'sound the bell'.

256.29–30 *Judas Iscariot's*: Reuben J. Dodd under the name of Judas, the betrayer of Jesus.

257.2 *Begone, dull care*: anonymous drinking song from at least the 17th c.

257.11 *Love and war*: a duet (known variously as 'Love and War' and 'When [or 'While'] Love Absorbs my Ardent Soul') by T. Cooke, in which a Lover and Soldier echo one another's lines in a musical contest: Lover: 'When love absorbs my ardent soul, I think not of the morrow', Soldier: 'When war absorbs my ardent soul I think not of the morrow', etc.; the battle is resolved by recourse to the marriage of Venus (goddess of love) and Mars (god of war).

257.30 *the lost chord*: song by Adelaide A. Procter (1825–64) and Arthur Sullivan (1842–1900) in which the singer recounts playing idly at the organ and coming across 'one chord of music, | Like the sound of a great Amen', only to lose it: 'I have sought, but I seek it vainly, | That one lost chord divine | Which came from the soul of an organ | And enter'd into mine'.

258.22 *Daughter of the regiment*: title of Gaetano Donizetti's (1797–1848) comic opera *La Fille du régiment* (1840).

258.27–8 *My Irish Molly, O*: anonymous Irish ballad: Scottish youth mourns because his Irish beloved's father has forbidden her to marry a foreigner.

259.8 *When love absorbs my ardent soul* . . .: see 257.11 n.

259.10 —*War! War!* . . . *You're the warrior*: bass Ben Dollard has mistakenly begun to sing the part of the (tenor or soprano) Lover.

259.14 *you'd burst the tympanum*: 'tympanum': eardrum; in medieval tradition (often depicted in painting), the Virgin Mary was thought to have conceived (by hearing the Word of God) through the unbroken membrane of her tympanum.

259.18 *Amoroso ma non troppo*: musical instruction: Italian: 'soft and tender, but not too much'.

260.16–18 *Poop of a lovely* . . . *Cool hands*: echoes Enobarbus's description of Cleopatra in *Antony and Cleopatra*, II. ii. 191–2, 208–11.

260.17–18 *The harp that once or twice*: see 160.7 n.

260.23/30–1: *M'appari* | *M'appari* . . . *l'incontr* . . .: Lionel's aria from Flotow's *Martha* (see 113.33 n.) which begins: '*M'appari, tutt' amor, il mio sguardo l'incontro*': 'All [perfect] love appeared to me, that meeting filled my eyes'.

260.26 *A Last Farewell*: the print on the wall illustrates John Willis's song 'The Last Farewell'.

260.27 *A lovely girl, her veil awave upon the wind*: Leucothea, perhaps.

260.35 *Ah, sure my dancing days are done*: from v. 3 of 'Johnny, I Hardly Knew Ye' an anti-war folk-song in which Peggy laments (through numerous choruses enumerating yet more mutilated body parts) the change which war has brought to Johnny: 'Where are the legs with which you run | When you went to carry a gun? | Indeed your dancing days are done! | Faith, Johnny, I hardly knew ye'.

261.9 *Sonambula*: Vincenzo Bellini's (1801–35) opera *La Sonnambula* ('The Sleepwalker') (1831), from which the aria '*Tutto è sciolto*' ('All is Lost') comes; the innocent sleepwalking heroine gets into a compromising situation and her fiancé, mistakenly believing her unfaithful, sings the aria: 'All is lost now, | By all hope and joy | Am I forsaken. | Nevermore can love awaken | Past enchantment, no, nevermore'.

261.10 *Joe Maas*: (1847–86), famous English tenor.

261.10 *M'Guckin*: Barton M'Guckin (1852–1913), Irish tenor.

261.16 *Down among the dead men*: by (?) John Dyer (fl. 1714) English drinking song: 'he that will this health deny [i.e. he that won't drink] . . . Down among the dead men let him lie!'

261.28 *All is lost now*: see 261.9 n.

261.29 *banshee*: Gaelic: *bean sidhe*: female fairy spirit who wailed at the deaths of loved ones.

261.33 *Echo. How sweet the answer*: opening line of Thomas Moore's song 'Echo' in *Irish Melodies*.

261.36–7 *In sleep she* . . . *in the moon*: the heroine of *La Sonnambula* (see 261.9 n.).

262.5 *Still harping on his daughter*: when Hamlet taunts Polonius with crude innuendoes about Ophelia, the latter says 'How say you by that? Still harping on my daughter' (*Hamlet*, II. ii. 187–8).

262.20 *a heart bowed down*: title of song in Michael Balfe's opera *The Bohemian Girl* (1843).

262.26–265.3 *When first I saw that form endearing* . . . | —*To me!*: the italicized lines on these three pages all come from the popular English version of Lionel's song '*M'appari*' (see 113.33n.) from Flotow's *Martha* (see 260.23/30–1n.): Charles Jeffreys's 'When first I saw that form endearing'.

262.36 *strings of reeds*: should read 'strings or reeds'.

263.5 *love's old sweet song*: see 61.20n.

263.11–12 *My head it simply* . . . *swurls*: 'Those lovely seaside girls'; see 60.23n.

263.16 *Hands felt for the opulent*: from *Sweets of Sin*; see 226.26–7.

263.20 *Singing wrong words*: it's hard to tell from what we're given whether or not Bloom is right.

263.30–2 *Tipping her* . . . *Tup*: all archaic verbs for 'to copulate' (specifically as animals do); 'tipping' also means double-tonguing in the musical sense.

264.17 *Waiting*: song (1867) by Ellen H. Flagg and H. Millard, of a woman awaiting the arrival of her lover.

264.20 *in old Madrid*: song by G. Clifton Bingham and 'Henry Trotere' (Henry Trotter), of which Molly thinks later.

264.27–8 —*Co-me* . . . —*Co-me*: should read '—*Co-ome* . . . —*Co-ome*'.

265.31 *'Twas rank and fame* . . . : aria from Balfe's *The Rose of Castille*; see 126.4–5n.

266.3 *We never speak as we pass by*: title of song (1882) by Frank Egerton.

266.3 *Rift in the lute*: after Tennyson's song 'The Rift in the Lute' in *Idylls of the King*, 'Merlin and Vivien' (1859): 'It is the little rift within the lute, | That by and by will make the music mute, | And ever widening slowly silence all' (ll. 388–90).

266.15 *Thou lost one* . . . *on that theme*: from Jeffreys's English version (see 262.26–265.3n.) of Flotow's '*M'appari*' (see 260.23/30–1n.): 'Come thou lost one | Come thou dear one, | Thou alone can'st comfort me: | Ah! Martha return! | Come to me!'

266.18 *Corpus paradisum*: Latin: 'the body of paradise'; Bloom's combination of two earlier heard liturgical fragments (see 77.31 and 100.34).

267.19 *Blumenleid*: German: 'flower song'. The lines from here through 'Cecilia street' (267.19–21) should be moved to follow 'I mean' (267.21).

269.4–5 *Music hath charms Shakespeare said*: no; William Congreve (1670–1729), *The Mourning Bride* (1697) I. i. 1–2: 'Music hath charms to soothe the savage breast, | To soften rocks, and bend the knotted oak'.

269.5 *To be or not to be*: *Hamlet*, III. i. 55 ff.

269.7–8 *In Gerard's rosery* . . . *Do. But do.*: a narratological conundrum: whose words are these? In *Scylla and Charybdis* (193.34–6), they were Stephen's.

269.27 *How Walter Bapty lost his voice*: Walter Bapty (1850–1915), professor of singing in Dublin and an organizer of the *Feis Ceoil* (1897), the annual Dublin music festival. (See Adams, 73.)

270.11 *What are the wild waves saying?*: title of a duet by Joseph Edwards Carpenter and Stephen Glover, in which 'the voice of the great Creator | Dwells in that mighty tone' of the wild waves.

270.23 *One: one, one . . . four*: a description, not of the music, but of the dancers dancing.

270.26 *Minuet of Don Giovanni*: the minuet (in I. v of *Don Giovanni*) to which Don Giovanni dances with Zerlina.

270.33 *My wife and your wife*: from an American folk-song 'The Grey Goose'.

270.33 *silk. When she talks*: should read 'silk. Tongue when she talks'.

270.35–46 *quis est homo: Mercadante*: combines Rossini's *Stabat Mater* and Mercadante (who did not compose it) as Bloom has thought of them in the same context in *Lotus Eaters* (79.9, 10).

271.3 *Chamber music*: aside from the obvious musical term, the title of Joyce's volume of short lyrics (1907).

271.5–6 *Empty vessels . . . water*: Bloom, popular scientist, combines the acoustical principle that the pitch produced by a vessel changes with the volume of liquid it contains, with Archimedes's law of specific gravity (see 69.13 n.) and the rate of acceleration of falling bodies (see 69.15 n.) to produce nonsense.

271.7 *those rhapsodies of Liszt's, Hungarian*: Franz Liszt (1811–86), Hungarian pianist and composer, 'Hungarian Rhapsodies'.

271.13 *Qui sdegno*: Italian: 'Here indignation'; from the Italian libretto of Mozart's *Die Zauberflöte* (The Magic Flute), opening words of the high priest's aria (to Pamina: in German '*In diesen heiligen Hallen*').

271.14 *The Croppy Boy*: see 88.4 n.; allusions to this song punctuate the remainder of the episode: 271.31, 272:1–2, 5–7, 17–18, 25–8, 273.11–13, 16, 20, 22, 29–30, 274.8–9, 15–16, 29, 275.2, 9–10.

271.27–8 *In a cave of the dark . . . Embedded ore*: the dark chords prompt a thought of Richard Wagner's (1813–83) *Das Rheingold* (the first opera in his tetralogy *Der Ring des Nibelungen* (1853–74)), especially Wotan's descent to Alberich's cavern to retrieve the Rhinegold the dwarf has stolen, the magical properties of which have allowed him to rule the world; through trickery Wotan succeeds.

272.10 *Lay of the last minstrel*: title of a poem by Sir Walter Scott (1771–1832).

272.17 *in nomine Domini*: the actual phrase from 'The Croppy Boy' is 'Nomine Dei' (Latin: 'in God's name') which Bloom switches to the Latin rhyme which translated means 'in the Lord's name'.

272.20 *corpusnomine*: Bloom compound: Latin: 'body-name'.

272.35 *Shah of Persia*: Nasr-al Din (d. 1896), Shah of Persia, made two state visits to England (1873, 1889) where he was hosted by the Prince of Wales; the 1889 visit prompted numerous popular songs and stories (*G*).

272.36 *home sweet home*: song (1823) by John Howard Payne and Henry Rowley Bishop.

273.6 *what Spinoza says*: Baruch Spinoza (1632–77), Dutch-Jewish philosopher, a collection of whose 'thoughts' can be found on Bloom's bookshelf (661.9); see *G* for one guess at what Bloom might be thinking.

273.9 *God made the country man the tune*: adaptation of William Cowper's 'God made the country, and man made the town' (*The Task*, 1. 749).

273.11–13 *All gone ... race*: see 231.27 n.; 'Gorey' recalls another unsuccessful attempt by the 'croppies'; it was from here that they launched their (failed) attack on Arklow.

273.20–1 *Who fears to speak of nineteen four?*: a change to the line 'Who fears to speak of ninety-eight?'; see 231.24 n.

274.2 *songs without words*: Felix Mendelssohn (1809–47) composed forty-eight piano pieces under the title *Lieder ohne Worte* (German: Songs without words) (1834–45).

274.11–12 *martyrs. For all... things born*: should read 'martyrs that want to, dying to, die. For all things dying, for all things born'.

275.19 *Lablache*: Luigi Lablache (1794–1858), most famous European bass of his time; intermittently gave Queen Victoria singing lessons.

276.8 *The last rose of summer*: song by Thomas Moore, ''Tis the Last Rose of Summer' in his *Irish Melodies*, used in Flotow's *Martha* (see 113.33 n.); first verse: ''Tis the last rose of summer | Left blooming alone; | All her lovely companions | Are faded and gone; | No flower of her kindred, | No rosebud is nigh, | To reflect back her blushes, | To give sigh for sigh'.

276.14–15 *Her hand ... world*: echoes William Ross Wallace's (*c.*1819–81) 'What Rules the World', each stanza of which ends with the refrain 'For the hand that rocks the cradle | Is the hand that rules the world'.

276.22–3 *Better give way ... man with a maid*: the line 'the way of a man with a maid' is found in Prov. 30: 18–19 (where it is listed as one of the four things that Solomon doesn't know), in Kipling's poem 'The Long Trail', l. 30 (which alludes to Solomon's list), and, most relevantly for Bloom, as the title of a 19th-c. pornographic novel *The Way of a Man with a Maid* where the innocent heroine, having been ruined by the 'hero', goes more than half-way and joins him in his future seductions (*G*).

276.30 *Maunder*: to talk aimlessly, but also the composer of sentimental church music John Henry Maunder (1858–1920) (*G*).

276.32 *no don't she cried*: *G* points out that this occurs as a refrain throughout *The Way of a Man with a Maid.*

278.2 *da capo*: Italian: 'from the beginning' (musical term).

278.13 *we'd never, well hardly ever*: from Gilbert and Sullivan's *HMS Pinafore: or, The Lass that Loved a Sailor* (1878) where it serves as Captain Corcoran's 'tag': 'I'm never, never sick at sea!' 'What never?' 'Hardly ever' (and so on).

278.23–4 *they chinked their clinking glasses*: echoes Timothy Daniel Sullivan's (1827–1914) drinking song 'The Thirty-Two Counties' (of Ireland, all of which it names), with the chorus: 'Then clink, glasses, clink, 'tis a toast we all must drink, | And let every voice come in at the chorus. | For Ireland is our home, and wherever we may roam | We'll be true to the dear land that bore us'.

278.28–9 *Robert Emmet's last words*: see 110.5–6n. His last words: 'Let no man write my epitaph; for as no man who knows my motives dares now vindicate them, let not prejudice or ignorance asperse them. When my country takes her place among the nations of the earth then and not till then, let my epitaph be written. I have done.'

278.29 *Seven last words. Of Meyerbeer*: another mistaken juxtaposition; Mercadante wrote *The Seven Last Words*, not Meyerbeer (who wrote *Les Huguenots*); see 160.21–3n.

278.30 *True men like you . . . glass with us*: the last two lines of the first stanza of John Kells Ingram's 'The Memory of the Dead' (see 231.24n.): 'But a true man, like you, man, | Will fill your glass with us', while those of the poem are 'And true men, be you, men, | Like those of Ninety-eight.'

CYCLOPS

Location: Barney Kiernan's pub (8–10 Little Britain Street, near the corner with Green Street (E3–4)). 'I' meets Joe Hynes at the corner of Arbour Hill and Stony Batter (D3). They walk down North King Street (passing south of Linenhall Barracks) and turn south into Halston Street (past the back of the courthouse) (D3, E3–4). Bloom, Cunningham, Power, and Crofton leave Kiernan's in a car which will head south towards Dignam's house on Newbridge Avenue (H5).

Time: 5 p.m.

Homer: Earlier in his account of his travails before landing in Phaecia (Book IX), Odysseus told of arriving at the land of the giant Cyclops, 'arrogant lawless beings' (101) who dwell in caves, and never leave (or till) their own land. Leaving most of his men on board his ship, Odysseus chose the twelve bravest to go with him to meet the Cyclops, Polyphemus. Finding his cavern empty, they awaited his return. When he arrived, they begged in the name of Zeus to be treated as guests. The Cyclops, who had blocked the entrance to the cavern with a huge stone, decried Zeus, grabbed two men, tore them apart, and ate them raw. As the stone was too large for Odysseus and his men to move themselves, they could not kill the giant in his sleep or they would be unable to escape. The next morning, Polyphemus again killed and ate two men, left the cavern, and replaced the stone. Realizing he would have to use his wits rather than his strength to best Polyphemus, Odysseus formed a plan, first, to blind the one-eyed giant and then to trick his way out. He found a great cudgel of wood which he cut, sharpened, then hid. When the Cyclops returned that evening, he removed then replaced the stone, and ate two more men. Odysseus offered him wine which he drank. When he asked Odysseus's name, the wily one replied, 'My name is Noman' (108). In a drunken stupor, the Cyclops fell asleep. Odysseus placed the tip of the stake in the fire, heated it until it was glowing, then, with his four best men, drove the stake into the Cyclops's single eye. In fury, the Cyclops shouted for his kinsmen to come help him, but when asked who was threatening him, he replied, 'It is Noman's craft and no violence that is threatening death to me' (109). Thinking him drunk or mad, the kinsmen left.

The now-blind Cyclops then removed the stone blocking the entrance, but placed himself with outstretched arms in the centre of the egress, thus aiming both to allow his flocks (penned for the night in the cavern) to leave and to prevent the men's escape. He carefully felt each sheep as it passed. But wily Odysseus had already taken the rams, tied them together into units each comprising three rams, and bound one man each to the underbelly of the middle ram. Odysseus himself crawled under, and clung to, the shaggy belly of Polyphemus's largest and favourite ram. While the Cyclops felt the back of each ram and sheep, he missed Odysseus and his men who thus escaped. Once outside, they turned and taunted Polyphemus who, enraged, 'wrenched away the top of a towering crag and hurled it' (110) at the ship, nearly driving it on to land. Having saved the ship, Odysseus turned once more to taunt (despite the warning of his men), 'The one who blinded you was Odysseus the city-sacker, son of Laertes and dweller in Ithaca' (111). At his words, Polyphemus realized the fulfilment of a prophecy that he would be blinded by Odysseus, whom he assumed would be 'handsome, visibly clothed with heroic strength', not 'puny and strengthless and despicable' (111). He then begged Odysseus to return so he could fête him and so appease the gods and perhaps regain his sight. Odysseus refused. In fury, Polyphemus prayed to his father, Poseidon, to curse Odysseus and, if not prevent his return to Ithaca, to make it painful. Then he flung another stone, 'much larger than the first' (112); the wave caused drove the ship on to the shore of the island opposite, where Odysseus had left the rest of his men and ships. They feasted on Polyphemus's sheep, departed, and eventually arrived at Aeolia. (Book IX)

Schemata: *L* lists as personae Ulysses and his pseudonym 'Noman' but also two characters absent from the *Odyssey*, Galatea and Prometheus. Galatea, a sea-nymph, was beloved of Polyphemus but loved Acis instead. One day Polyphemus came upon Galatea and Acis lying by the sea and, in a jealous fury, hurled a giant boulder at Acis, killing him. Prometheus, whose name means 'foresight', was the Titan who returned fire to mankind after Zeus, in rage, had deprived them of it. If Bloom is meant to be not only Ulysses and Noman, but also Prometheus, he is less the Prometheus of Greek myth than Shelley's protagonist in his *Prometheus Unbound* who triumphs over the tyranny of his antagonist, Jupiter, by countering it, not with force or power but with 'love':'I wish no living thing to suffer pain' (P. B. Shelley, *Prometheus Unbound* (1820), I. 305).

L and *G* disagree on virtually everything in this episode except, in part, the Organ (*L*: (1) Muscles (2) Bones; *G*: Muscle). On all else they differ: Art (*L*: Surgery; *G*: Politics), Technic (*L*: 'Alternating asymmetry'; *G*: Gigantism),

Colour (*L*: green; *G*: none), Symbol (*L*: Nation, State, Religion, Dynasty, Idealism, Exaggeration, Fanaticism, Collectivity; *G*: Fenian). *L*'s Sense is 'Egocidal Terror'.

Joyce's Hints: 'The chapter of the *Cyclops* is being lovingly moulded in the way you know. The Fenian is accompanied by a wolfhound who speaks (or curses) in Irish. He unburdens his soul about the Saxo-Angles in the best Fenian style and with colossal vituperativeness alluding to their standard industry. The epic proceeds explanatorily "He spoke of the English, a noble race, rulers of the waves, who sit on thrones of alabaster, silent as the deathless gods" . . .' (*LI* 126; 19/6/19).

Polyphemus (Greek: *Πολύφημος*; literally 'many-voiced') would have fared better in his battle against Odysseus had he been 'many-eyed'. At the very least, Odysseus's task would have been twice as hard. Since monocularity allows no depth perception (it takes two eyes sufficiently widely spaced and forward-looking for that), it sits fittingly with bigotry, self-centredness, and rage. No wonder then the attitudes espoused here, by the first-person narrator (known only as 'I'), the xenophobic citizen (spokesman for Ireland right or wrong), and those sucked into the drunken antagonism against Bloom 'the bloody jewman', sole dissenting voice.

But Polyphemus's many-voicedness has its correlates not so much in Bloom's discordant humanitarian exhortations as in the other half of the narration, that portion not assignable to 'I'. 'I' recounts an anecdote (racist, unsurprisingly) about 'a bloody big foxy thief' who successfully swindles Moses Herzog out of goods by threatening to report Herzog for trading without a licence if he continues to pursue him for payment of the debt. Suddenly, into the narrative breaks a legal contract (whether actually or only wishfully drawn up): 'For non-perishable goods bought of Moses Herzog . . . sold and delivered to Michael E. Geraghty . . . five pounds avoirdupois of first choice tea', etc., etc., etc. Here the narrative stops abruptly; this 'document' carries the action not one step further forward. Nor can it even really be considered narration. There is no 'narrative voice' narrating this 'text'; it stands out as announcing its status as a *written* document, and as rejecting any claim to be *telling* a tale. Similarly, the other intrusive eruptions most resemble other texts: newspaper sports columns, society pages, news items, letters, translations of 'Gaelic' verses, court records, descriptions of artefacts, biblical parodies, and lists, lists, lists. In this, *Cyclops* is more intertextual than polyphonic.

'Many-voiced' is only a literal translation of 'Polyphemus'; figuratively (and more suitably) his name means 'much spoken of'. Fame in Homer's oral culture spread from voice to voice; *Cyclops*'s verbal equivalent: the seemingly endless capacity these men have for talk and the spreading of rumour. But *Ulysses* itself is situated at the height of the age of print, just at the beginning of the rise of those modern machines the telephone, radio, and television which will once again promote the voice. *Cyclops* proudly announces its textual supremacy, for even as it depicts a struggle between the 'narrative voice' and the 'text as text' it contains them both. Novel and anti-novel: *Cyclops* accommodates both and so flaunts a binocularity Polyphemus might have yearned for.

280.1–3 *I . . . eye*: typical of the kind of punning *Ulysses* delights in: the Cyclops has only one eye, and visionary puns abound in his episode; one of the most obvious (and most formative) is the nameless narrator's (seemingly endless) reiteration of the first-person pronoun (and the monocular—i.e. bigoted—view he has of the world).

281.4–21 *For nonperishable goods . . . the other part*: **Parody**; in the manner of a legal document in a civil proceeding for collection of debt.

281.5 *parade, Wood*: should read 'parade in the city of Dublin, Wood'.

281.8 *shillings per*: should read 'shillings and no pence per'.

281.29 *mavourneen*: Gaelic: *mo mhúirnín*: 'my darling'.

281.33 *the citizen*: modelled on Michael Cusack (1847–1907) (as Joyce names him in an early draft of this episode), founder of the Gaelic Athletic Association (see *JJ* 61, 61 n. and *JJA* xiii. 137).

282.1–30 *In Inisfail the fair . . . canes*: **Parody**; after James Clarence Mangan's (1803–49) translation of Aldfrid's (7th-c. king of Northumbria) poem 'Aldfrid's Itinerary', which begins 'I found in Innisfail the fair, | In Ireland, while in exile there, | Women of worth, both grave and gay men, | Many clerics and many laymen. // I travelled its fruitful provinces round, | And in every one of the five I found, | Alike in church and in palace hall, | Abundant apparel and food for all'. It continues in much the same vein for another fifty lines, listing the counties of Ireland and their bounty. 'Inisfail': Gaelic: *Inis Fál*: 'Island of Destiny (*Fál* is also the name of the fetish stone at Tara): a poetic name for Ireland.

282.1 *the land of holy Michan*: Kiernan's pub lies in St Michan's parish (a Dublin municipal district).

282.6 *flounder, the mixed*: should read 'flounder, the pollock, the mixed'.

282.15–18 *from Eblana . . . Boyle*: all ancient provinces, towns, districts, sites around Ireland (*G*).

282.19 *a shining palace*: the Dublin Corporation Fruit, Vegetable, and Fish Market, between St Michan's Street and Boot Lane (E4). Quite clearly, what follows is a gigantic list of the bounties of Ireland.

282.26 *pumets*: should read 'punnets'.

282.33–283.10 *And by that way wend . . . the dun*: **Parody**; now we get the livestock which have come from rural Ireland.

283.8 *crannocks*: Gaelic: *crannóg*: 'box, vessel'.

283.15 *cruiskeen lawn*: Gaelic: *crúiscín lán*: 'full little jug'; also the title of an Irish folk-song (*G* provides lyrics).

283.26 *Doing the rapparee*: from the Gaelic: *rapaire*: 'half pike'; commonly 'robbers, outlaws'; initially those Catholic lords who, dispossessed by

Cromwell (1653), took to raiding the estates of the *bodachs* (the Protestant landowners); later the Irish soldiers who, after the Treaty of Limerick (1691), refused expatriation to France and instead took to the hills.

283.26 *Rory of the hill*: the signature of those who, at the urging of the Irish Land League, sent threatening letters to those who took or paid rents or occupied the farms of evicted tenants; also title of a ballad by Fenian poet, essayist, and novelist Charles Joseph Kickham (1828–82): Rory is a peasant farmer who keeps his rake for the day he will need it to fight for Ireland.

283.33 *Arrah*: Gaelic: *ara*: figuratively 'nonsense'.

283.33 *codding*: joking.

284.3 *a chara*: Gaelic: 'my friend'.

284.6–285.19 *The figure seated . . . paleolithic stone*: **Parody**; the description of 'the figure seated' is indebted to Homer's description of the Cyclops; the list of Irish heroes typifies the lists in this episode: from Cuchulin through Henry Joy M'Cracken, the persons listed are genuine Irish 'heroes' (kings, rebels, patriots, founders of nationalist societies), then, quite obviously, things begin to go awry; the list expands (in a colonizing fashion) to include those less heroic, those less (and less and finally not at all) Irish, those more and more fictional. Most of the jokes are obvious. *G* gives glosses for the dramatis personae.

284.16 *a tear and a smile*: from Thomas Moore's poem, 'Erin, the Tear and the Smile in Thine Eyes' (in *Irish Melodies*).

284.31 *Ardri Malachi*: Gaelic: *Árd Rí*: 'High King' Malachi.

284.32 *Patrick Sarsfield*: (*c.*1650–93), earl of Lucan, Irish general, supporter of James II (see 29.29 n.), brilliant leader of troops in battle of Limerick (see 316.19 n.), exiled to France with 11,000 troops as condition of Treaty of Limerick (see 41.21–2 n. and 316.20–1 n.), joined French army and died in battle of Landen.

284.33 *Soggarth*: Gaelic: *sagart*: 'priest'.

285.4 *Savourneen Deelish*: Gaelic: *'s a mhúirnín dílis*: 'and, my precious darling'.

285.9 *Arrah na Pogue*: Gaelic: *ara na bpóg*: 'one given to kissing'.

285.9 *Colleen Bawn*: Gaelic: *cailín bán*: '"white" (pretty) girl'; title of Boucicault play (see 89.9 n.) and a song 'The Colleen Bawn' in *The Lily of Killarney* (see 89.9 n.).

285.29–30 *Who comes through . . . prudent soul*: **Parody**; after reworked Irish legend.

285.31–2 *the old woman of Prince's . . . subsidised organ*: the *Freeman's Journal*, considered to be the official paper of the Irish Nationalists, was sufficiently moderate in its expression of the nationalist cause to be considered the mouthpiece of the Home Rule party with its mildly conservative policies.

285.32 *The pledgebound party . . . house*: the phrase refers to members of a political party who pledge in advance of a vote loyalty to a particular party or issue: here the Irish members of the British Parliament who pledged loyalty to the Liberal party during Parnell's tenure (so that the Irish members could hold the balance of power, in exchange for Liberal assurances on the issue of Home Rule) but who continued loyal to the pledge long after the Liberals had pursued policies favourable to Ireland.

285.33–4 *The Irish Independent . . . founded by Parnell*: it was; but it did not begin publication until after his death and was quickly taken over by anti-Parnellites.

286.1–11 *Gordon, Barnfield Crescent . . . Isabella Helen*: the citizen reads from the actual columns of the *Irish Daily Independent* for 16 June 1904, but skips the Irish names (*G*).

286.12 *Martin Murphy, the Bantry jobber*: William Martin Murphy (1844–1921), owner of the *Irish Daily Independent* born in Bantry and worked as a contractor, MP, joined the anti-Parnellites in the 1890 split; 'jobber': 'one who improperly uses a public office, trust, or service for private gain' (*OED*).

286.19–23 *And lo, as they . . . race*: **Parody**; more parody of 19th-c. recyclings of Irish legend.

287.3 *Bi i dho husht*: Gaelic: *bí i do thost*: 'be quiet'.

287.18–37 *Terence O'Ryan . . . ethiop*: **Parody**; after reworked Irish legend, medieval romance and myth.

287.19–20 *the noble twin brothers . . . Bungardilaun*: the Guinness brothers (not twins) who owned the brewery: Lord Iveagh and Lord Ardilaun (see 76.24, 26 n.); 'Bung' from a cask's stopper, for one who serves grog.

287.20–1 *the sons of deathless Leda*: Castor and Pollux, the twin brothers born of the union of Leda (the Swan) and Zeus; brothers to Helen and Clytemnestra.

289.1–37 *In the darkness . . . whirlwind*: **Parody**; a seance for Paddy Dignam conducted in the terms of the tenets of Theosophy (a neo-Hindu, neo-Buddhist philosophy articulated and espoused by 'Madame' H. P. Blavatsky (see 135.13–14 n.)); ending with a return to mock Irish legend (289.35–7).

289.2 *tantras*: Hindu ceremonial treatise (*G*).

289.3 *etheric double*: the less material of the two bodies every person is believed by Theosophists to have; it slowly disintegrates after death (*G*).

289.4 *jivic rays*: energy rays; *jiva*: life source or energy (*G*).

289.8 *prālāyā*: the period after death and before rebirth (*G*).

289.11 *he had seen as in a glass darkly*: St Paul to the Corinthians (13: 12): 'For now we see through a glass, darkly; but then face to face'.

289.12 *atmic development*: the 'atmic plane' is the plane of pure being at which the soul arrives after completing the cycle of reincarnation (*G*).

289.16 *tālāfānā*, *ālāvātār*, *hātākāldā*, *wātāklāsāt*: the puns are obvious; the spelling in imitation of the Theosophists' predilection for Sanskrit.

289.19 *Māyā*: the deceitful physical, sensuous world (*G*).

289.20 *devanic circles*: '*Deva*': deity; thus, hobnobbing with the gods (*G*).

289.36 *Banba*: in Irish legend, one of the three daughters of Cain, son of Adam and Eve, and with her sisters, Erin and Fotha, the original settlers of Ireland; another legend has it that she was a queen of the *Tuatha de Danaan*, the original Irish heroes; also, hers is a poetic name for Ireland.

291.16 *H. Rumbold*: after Sir Horace Rumbold, the British minister to Switzerland (*JJ* 458).

291.32–4 *In the dark land . . . Lord*: **Parody**; this time of medieval romance.

291.33 *Erebus*: Greek mythology: home of the infernal Shades; the underworld between Hades and earth.

292.11 *Joe Brady, the invincible*: see 131.5–6 n.; Brady was hanged in Kilmainham jail (14 May 1883).

292.13 *Ruling passion strong in death*: Alexander Pope (1688–1744), *Moral Essays*, 'Epistle I. To Richard Temple, Viscount Cobham', ll. 262–5: 'And you! brave COBHAM, to the latest breath | Shall feel your ruling passion strong in death: | Such in those moments as in all the past, | "Oh, save my Country, Heav'n!" shall be your last'.

292.18–27 *The distinguished scientist . . . capitis*: **Parody**; medical journalese describing a medical conference.

292.18 *Luitpold Blumenduft*: German: 'Leopold flowerscent'.

292.22–3 *centres, causing the pores*: should read 'centres of the genital apparatus, thereby causing the elastic pores'.

292.23 *corpora cavernosa*: Latin: 'the cavernous bodies'; medical terminology for erectile tissue.

292.27 *in articulo mortis per diminutionem capitis*: Latin: 'at the moment of death caused by breaking the neck'.

292.29 *the invincibles*: see 78.22–4 n.

292.29–30 *the men of sixtyseven*: failed Fenian rebellion of 1867.

293.7 *a Jacob's tin*: W. and R. Jacobs & Co.: biscuit manufacturers in Dublin.

293.11 *the brothers Sheares*: Henry (1755–98) and John (1766–98) Sheares, United Irishmen, participated in the 1798 Rebellion, executed (in legend, hand-in-hand).

293.11 *Wolfe Tone beyond on Arbour Hill*: reputed site of Tone's suicide (see 220.15 n.).

293.11–12 *Robert Emmet and die for your country*: see 110.5–6 n.

293.12 *the Tommy Moore touch*: Sarah Curren (d. 1808), Robert Emmet's (secret) fiancée, was the subject of Thomas Moore's song 'She is Far From the Land' (in *Irish Melodies*), a sentimental account of her love for the dead hero; it begins: 'She is far from the land where her young hero sleeps, | And lovers are round her, sighing: | But coldly she turns from their gaze, and weeps, | For her heart in his grave is lying'.

293.17 *loodheramaun*: Gaelic: *ludramán*: 'lazy idle fellow, fool'.

293.34 *Sinn Fein! . . . Sinn fein amhain!*: Gaelic: *Sinn féin . . . amhain*: toast: 'Ourselves . . . Ourselves alone!'

293.34–5 *The friends we love . . . before us*: adaptation of Thomas Moore's 'Oh, Where's the Slave?' (in *Irish Melodies*): 'We tread the land that bore us, | Her green flag glitters o'er us, | The friends we've tried | Are by our side, | And the foe we hate before us'.

293.36–297.33 *The last farewell was affecting . . . Limehouse way*: **Parody**; of a front-page story of a major event, in this instance the execution of Robert Emmet.

294.11 *Speranza*: pseudonym of Jane Francesca Elgee, Lady Wilde (1821–96), Oscar Wilde's mother; involved with the literary nationalists, the Young Irelanders (1848); wrote nationalist verse. Perhaps her poem 'The Brothers: Henry and John Sheares' (see 293.11 n.) is behind this parody.

294.28–295.3 *Commendatore Bacibaci Beninobenone . . . Ueberallgemein*: names of the foreign delegation all involve multi-level, often multilingual, puns (see *G*); the languages represented: Italian, French, German, Hungarian, Greek, Arabic, Albanian-Turkish, Chinese, Danish, Polish, Russian, Swiss-German; obviously one of the places in *Ulysses* where one can detect the future writer of the *Wake* busily at work. (The text should read 'Přhklštř' for 'Prhklstr' and the name 'Boris Hupinkoff' should follow 'Kratchinabritchisitch' at 294.37.)

295.6 *F.O.T.E.I.*: Friends of the Emerald Isle.

295.7–8 *whether the eighth . . . patron saint*: an actual uncertainty exists over the date of birth of St Patrick; Joyce's comic account of the arbitrary nature of the resolution is borrowed from Samuel Lover's 'The Birth of St Patrick'.

295.32–3 *hoch . . . evviva*: 'national toasts': all (more or less) meaning 'long life': German; Japanese; Hungarian; Serbo-Croatian; pidgin English; Greek; American; French; Arabic; Italian.

296.29 *nec and non plus ultra*: Latin: *nec* (or *ne*) *plus ultra* and *non plus ultra* both mean 'none higher'.

297.2 *hurling match*: traditional Irish sport.

297.14–17 *handsome young Oxford . . . accepted on the spot*: three years after Emmet's death, Sarah Curren married Captain Henry Sturgeon (*c.*1781–1814), an Englishman, though he was not from Oxford.

297.26 *blown . . . sepoys from the cannonmouth*: actual mode of execution of 'mutinous' Indian troops ('sepoys'), in the time of the Mogul emperors (1526–1857), and continued by the British, especially during the Sepoy Mutiny (1857–8).

297.35 *shoneens*: Gaelic: *Seóinín*: 'little John', i.e. imitator of John Bull; aper of English ways.

298.1 *the Gaelic league*: see 135.26 n.

298.1 *the antitreating league*: St Patrick's Anti-Treating League, a temperance society whose tactics involved trying to stop the practice of buying rounds ('treating').

298.7 *Ballyhooly blue ribbon badge*: worn by temperance workers; also, the song 'The Ballyhooly Blue Ribbon Army' about 'the water drinkin' band'.

298.9 *flahoolagh*: Gaelic: *flaitheamhlach*: 'generous, chieftain-like'.

298.25 *pro bono publico*: Latin: 'for the public good'.

298.28–299.25 *All those who are . . . Lowry's lights*: **Parody**; of a newspaper 'puff' for an upcoming 'event'.

298.29 *(and their name is legion)*: Mark 5: 9: the 'name' of the spirits inhabiting the Gadarene swine.

298.30 *cynanthropy*: species of madness in which a person imagines himself a dog.

298.32–3 *Owen Garry*: legendary king of Leinster in the time of Fionn Mac Cumhail, 3rd c. (see 304.4 n.).

299.1 *ranns*: Gaelic: 'verses, sayings, rhymes, songs'.

299.3–4 *Little Sweet Branch*: from Gaelic: *An Craoibhín Aoibhinn*: 'The Sweet Little Branch'; pseudonym of Douglas Hyde (1860–1947), Irish literary nationalist, poet, scholar, translator (of *Love Songs of Connacht*, see 47.27–8 n.), friend of Yeats with whom he founded the Irish Literary Society (1891), founder of the Gaelic League (see 135.26 n.); president of Ireland (1938–45).

299.7–8 *Raftery*: Anthony Raftery (*c.* 1784–1834), blind Irish bard; his work was rediscovered during the late 19th-c. literary revival.

299.18–25 *The curse of my curses ... lights*: parodic imitation of contemporary attempts to write classical Irish verse; 'Lowry's lights': on the stage of Lowry's musichall.

300.29–301.4 *Let me, said he ... even of speech*: **Parody**; of 19th-c. sentimental fiction.

301.7 *shebeen*: Gaelic: *síbín*: 'illicit tavern'.

301.8 *shawls*: slang for 'prostitutes'.

301.24 *Slan leat*: Gaelic: *slán leat*: 'goodbye'.

301.34 *Hairy Iopas*: 'Long-haired Iopas', a poet in Virgil's *Aeneid* (I. 740–6) who sings in Dido's palace.

302.14–17 *Ga Ga Gara ... Klook*: **Parody**; of a children's primer?

302.27 *The Sluagh na h-Eireann*: Gaelic: *Sluagh na hÉireann*: 'Host (Army) of Ireland', patriotic society that persuaded Nannetti to complain to Parliament (16 June 1904) about the police prohibiting the playing of Irish games in Phoenix Park (*G*).

302.28–303.11 *Mr Cowe Conacre ... Cheers)*: **Parody**; of reports of Parliamentary proceedings.

302.28 *Conacre*: the Conacre System: the system of absentee landlords, managers, and exploited tenants who paid exorbitant rates for the privilege of subsistence farming in the 19th c. (see *G*).

302.33 *Allfours*: suggests the Rt. Hon. Arthur James Balfour, Leader of the House of Commons, Conservative Prime Minister in 1904. While Secretary for Ireland (1887–91), he was committed to the policy of 'coercion' (punitive intervention in the face of nationalist action) and earned the nickname 'Bloody Balfour'.

303.5 *Mitchelstown telegram*: when in Sept. 1887 the Parnellite John Dillon (1851–1927) spoke in Mitchelstown, a riot ensued in which the police shot three men. In responding to hostile questions in the House, Balfour merely quoted the brief police report contained in a telegram (*G*).

303.13 *The man that got away James Stephens*: a rumour that could be laid at the door of virtually any Fenian around at the time of Stephens's escape, and Cusack was probably a Fenian, though most certainly not involved with the Invincibles (see 43.25 n.).

303.15 *Na bacleis*: Gaelic: *Ná bac leis*: 'don't bother with it'.

303.21 *racy of the soil*: nationally characteristic.

303.22 *a nation once again*: title of song by Thomas Osborne Davis (1814–45): 'And then I prayed I yet might see | Our fetters rent in twain, | And Ireland, long a province, be | A nation once again!'; see 304.9–11.

303.28–304.31 *A most interesting discussion ... T. Quirke, etc., etc.*: **Parody**; of minutes of the meeting of a social or political organization written up as a newspaper puff. The clergymen listed are genuine.

303.28–9 *Brian O'Ciarnain's in Sraid na Bretaine Bheag*: Gaelic: 'Barney O'Kiernan's in Little Britain Street'.

304.4 *Finn Mac Cool*: Fionn Mac Cumhail (d. *c.*284), Irish chieftain and poet, leader of the Fianna (an army), central figure of the medieval Ossian or Finn sagas.

305.14 *puck*: Gaelic: *poc*: 'short sharp blow'.

305.16–306.4 *It was historic ... him with delight*: **Parody**; of a sports column.

306.14 *Caddereesh*: Gaelic: *Cad arís*: 'What, again?'

306.20 *Calpe's rocky mount*: Greek mythology: one of the pillars of Hercules, now the Rock of Gibraltar.

307.35 *pishogue*: Gaelic: *piseog*: 'spell or talisman'.

308.7 *papal zouave*: devout young Catholics recruited to the aid of the Pope in the defence of Rome against Italian occupation (1860s).

308.11–12 *Sadgrove v. Hole*: an actual libel action, which did turn on the issue of whether a postcard constituted publication; the trial court held it did; court of appeals reversed, but the ruling was limited (under the facts of this case), thus JJ is right: an action might lie.

308.24 *that Canada swindle case*: see 123.14 n.

308.30 *badhachs*: Gaelic: *bodach*: 'lout'.

309.14–310.5 *And whereas on the sixteenth ... a malefactor*: **Parody**; a trial record in the manner of a classical Irish legend.

309.25 *brehons*: Gaelic: *breitheamhain*: 'judges in ancient Irish legal system'.

309.27–32 *the high sinhedrim of the twelve tribes of Iar ... Ossian*: after the patriarchs of the twelve tribes of Israel and the twelve members of a jury; 'Iar': Gaelic: 'west, remote', i.e. Ireland; the twelve are real 'classical' Irish names, most of them having more than one referent (see *G*).

310.4 *ne bail ne mainprise*: Middle English legal phrase: 'without bail or guardian'.

310.22 *The adulteress and her paramour*: see 34.35–7 n.

310.22 *the Saxon robbers*: not actually Saxons, rather Anglo-Norman overlords.

311.11–17 *O'Nolan, clad in ... seadivided Gael*: **Parody**; in manner of high classical legend and medieval romance.

311.19 *Sassenachs*: Gaelic: Englishmen.

311.21–2 *the Nelson policy . . . telescope*: Admiral Nelson, having lost his right eye in the battle of Corsica (1793) and not wanting to heed the signal to withdraw from the battle of Copenhagen (1801), put the glass to his right eye and proclaimed that he did not see the signal; he went on to a brilliant victory.

311.22 *drawing un a bill of attainder . . . a nation*: 'un' should read 'up'. One of the first policies of Sinn Féin was to do just this to indict England in the eyes of the world.

311.33 *cabinet d'aisance*: French: 'cabinet of assistance'; euphemism for toilet.

311.35 *Full many a flower . . . unseen*: Thomas Gray's 'Elegy Written in a Country Church-Yard' (1751), l. 55.

311.37 *Conspuez les Anglais! Perfide Albion!*: French: 'Scorn the English! Perfidious Albion!'

312.1–4 *He said and then . . . deathless gods*: **Parody**; still in the manner of legend and romance.

312.2 *medher*: Gaelic: *meadar*: 'one piece quadrangular wooden cup'.

312.2–3 *Lamh Dearg Abu*: Gaelic: *Lámh Dearg Abú*: 'Red Hand to Victory'; the Red Hand was the heraldic symbol of Ulster and O'Neill.

312.28 *Raimeis*: Gaelic: *ráiméis*: '"romance", nonsense'.

312.29–30 *our missing twenty millions . . . four*: the citizen's comments, though in general hyperbolic, are true.

312.30 *our lost tribes*: after the Jewish tradition of the lost ten tribes of Israel.

312.30–7 *And our potteries . . . whole wide world*: again, though in the exaggerated language of chauvinism which he speaks, the citizen is basically right about the devastation of Irish industries under English rule, the central policy of which was to keep Ireland rural (and not allow it to become competitive with England); throughout the 18th c. this was done through high taxation.

313.2 *Tacitus*: (*c.*56–*c.*117) Roman historian and orator, mentions Ireland in his *Agricola* (98), 24, largely an account of Agricola's achievements in Britain.

313.2 *Ptolemy*: Claudius Ptolemaeus (*c.*100–178), Greek astronomer, mathematician, geographer; mentions Ireland in his 'Outline of Geography' (which also lists some 8,000 other places).

313.3 *Giraldus Cambrensis*: Girald de Barri (*c.*1146–*c.*1220), Welsh chronicler, whose two books on Ireland, *Topographia Hibernica* and *Expugnatio Hibernica*, are in the long tradition of anti-Irish justifications for others' colonialist aspirations there (in his case, a justification of the Anglo-Norman invasions).

313.6 *yellowjohns*: translation of the Gaelic: *Seón Buidhe*: 'yellow (i.e. "filthy") John (i.e. John Bull)', filthy English.

313.10 *As treeless as Portugal*: English deforestation of Ireland had been proceeding for centuries; one of the issues of the land reform movement was reforestation.

313.12–13 *a report of lord Castletown's*: report issued by a committee (in 1907) drawn up to investigate the status of Ireland's forests; recommendation: immediate action for reforestation.

313.18–314.9 *The fashionable international world . . . Black Forest*: **Parody**; newspaper society column. Behind it may lie Edmund Spenser's (*c.*1552–99) catalogue of trees in his *The Faerie Queene* (1589), I. i, stanzas 8–9. Again the jokes are, for the most part, obvious.

314.2: *Senhor Enrique Flor*: Portuguese: 'Mr Henry Flower'.

314.17–18 *Queenstown . . . Killybegs*: all flourishing harbours in the 16th and 17th cs., gradually becoming less prosperous over the course of the 18th and 19th cs.

314.19–21 *Galway Lynches . . . Charles the Fifth*: the Lynches, O'Reillys, and O'Kennedys were all ancient powerful Irish families; 'the earl of Desmond': James Fitzmaurice Fitzgerald (d. 1529), 10th earl of Desmond, an extremely powerful lord who could refuse royal demands with impunity, on his death was about to enter into an alliance with Charles V (1500–58), Holy Roman Emperor, against England.

314.22–3 *Henry Tudor's harps*: the harp was incorporated into Henry VIII's royal arms as an emblem of his rule of Ireland.

314.23–4 *the oldest flag afloat . . . sons of Milesius*: Milesians were the last legendary invaders of Ireland whose flag was (according to legend) 'three crowns on a blue field'; Ireland's oldest flag.

314.25 *Moya*: Gaelic: *mar bh´eadh*: 'as if it were' (ironic).

314.28 *the Molly Maguires*: by 1904, general term for terrorists; originally, rebel group formed by Cornelius Maguire to fight in the 1641 rebellion; disguised themselves in women's clothing, hence the name 'Molly'; occasionally revived for other direct action groups in the 19th c.

315.2 *Black Beast Burned in Omaha. Ga.*: actual event but on 28 Sept. 1919 in Omaha, Nebraska (not Georgia); the London *Times* (30/9/19) substituted Georgia (see Timothy Weiss, *JJQ*, 19/2 (Winter 1982), 183–6).

315.8–9 *the revelations that's going . . . Disgusted One*: Joyce's joke at George Bernard Shaw's (1856–1950) expense; Shaw engaged in a debate in the London *Times*'s correspondence columns over the issue of the continued use of corporal punishment in the Royal Navy (flogging having been outlawed), the debate having begun because of protests raised in the House of Commons by the Irish Nationalist MP John Gordon Swift MacNeill. Shaw ended his letter: 'I should blush to offer a lady or a gentleman more reasons for my disgust at it. Yours truly, G. Bernard Shaw' (*Times* (14/6/1904)).

315.14–15 *sir John Beresford*: Conflation of two figures: Sir John Poo Beresford (*c.*1768–1844), Irish-born British admiral and English MP, and John Beresford (1738–1805), Ireland's commissioner of revenue, supporter of the English cause during the 1798 Rebellion, his riding school was the site of the infliction of corporal punishment on the rebels.

315.21 *meila murder*: Gaelic: *míle marbhadh*: '"a thousand killings", great commotion'.

315.23 *The fellows that never . . . slaves*: after James Thompson's (1700–48) ode, set to music by Thomas Arne (1710–78), 'Rule Britannia': 'Rule Britannia, Britannia rule the waves, | Britons never, never, never will be slaves'.

315.23–4 *the only hereditary... earth*: not strictly true: the House of Lords was not solely hereditary, nor was it the sole surviving hereditary chamber.

315.29 *yahoos*: from Jonathan Swift's *Gulliver's Travels*, Pt. IV: the yahoos were the degenerate animals in human form who contrast with the noble Houyhnhnms, the reasonable horses.

315.30–5 *They believe in rod... and be paid*: **Parody**; in the form of the Apostles' Creed (statement of Christian belief dating from the 4th c.; ostensibly drafted by the twelve apostles of Jesus).

316.3–4 *greater Ireland beyond the sea*: i.e. the United States, where Irish immigrants continually raised support for the cause of Irish nationalism.

316.4–5 *the black 47*: the great potato famine of 1845–8, worst year 1847.

316.5 *shielings*: small cottages.

316.10–11 *Twenty thousand... coffinships*: deaths of Irish emigrants to America travelling by ship were notorious (though no actual figures exist), especially aboard the opportunistic (and hideously inadequate) ships sailing unlicensed from small harbours; the term 'coffin ships', however, dates from 1833 as a more general nautical term for unseaworthy vessels (*OED*).

316.13 *Granuaile*: Gaelic name (*Gráinne Ní Mháille*) of Grace O'Malley (*c.*1530–*c.*1600), a western Ireland chieftain, sea captain, and rebel.

316.13–14 *Kathleen ni Houlihan*: traditional feminine embodiment of the spirit of Ireland, name of play by Yeats (1902) (see 177.10–11 n.).

316.17 *poor old woman ... landed at Killala*: 'poor old woman': the *Sean Bhean Bhocht* (see 14.6 n. and 17.30–1 n.); Killala, village in west of Ireland at which French forces landed in 1798 too late to be of any use to the Irish in the Rebellion which had already virtually collapsed.

316.18–19 *We fought for the royal... betrayed us*: the Irish supported the Stuart king James II, even after his removal as king, and especially when he landed in Ireland and fought William III to regain his title (see 29.29 n.); on losing, James fled to France, thus deserting Ireland.

316.19 *Remember Limerick*: after losing at the Battle of the Boyne (see 29.29 n.) the Irish (with French assistance) continued to fight, their last battle being at Limerick, under Sarsfield's leadership. (See 284.32 n.) The Treaty of Limerick (3 Oct. 1691) granted some liberties to Catholics in exchange for Sarsfield and some 11,000 troops accepting exile to France. In 1695 the treaty was repudiated by the (Protestant) Irish Parliament.

316.20–1 *We gave... wild geese*: 'wild geese' those exiled after Limerick, most of whom went to France and Spain.

316.26 *Entente cordiale*: French: 'Cordial understanding', policy of friendship with a country; the resolution of France and England's acrimonious relationship (8 Apr. 1904) by agreement to such an understanding.

316.29–31 *the Prooshians... bitch that's dead*: Hanover: North German state and (as of 1866) a province of Prussia; an electorate of the Holy Roman empire; in 1714 the Elector of Hanover succeeded to the British throne as George I; Hanover was the name of the British royal family until Queen Victoria's death. 'The German lad' was Victoria's husband, Albert, prince of Saxe-Coburg-Gotha (and German, as were Victoria's parents).

316.33–7 *blind drunk ... boose is cheaper*: after Prince Albert's death and Queen Victoria's taking to perpetual mourning and reclusion, stories about 'what really went on' abounded; this is typical; the 'coachman' is her faithful attendant Scotsman John Brown (1826–83).

317.1–11 *Edward the peacemaker ... lordships' decision*: King Edward VII, after his attempts to establish peaceful relations with France, Germany, and Austria; notorious ladies' man; 'Guelph-Wettin': a conjunction of 'Guelph', the family name of the House of Hanover, and 'Wettin', Prussian version of Wetter, Prince Albert's family name. The King was also a famous horse fancier, and when he visited Ireland in 1903 he was fêted at the Catholic college in Maynooth, where the decorative theme was Edward's horses; seen as sign of Church's willingness to curry English favour.

318.3–27 *The muchtreasured ... incrustations of time*: **Parody**; 'journalese' description of an ancient artefact. The citizen's handkerchief bears on it representations of traditional Irish symbols, books, ancient monuments, even modern buildings, all genuine.

318.4–5 *Solomon of Droma ... Ballymote*: the *Book of Ballymote* (Gaelic: *Leabhar Baile an Mhota*), an anthology of Irish histories, genealogies, legends of early kings, produced in *c.*1391 in Sligo, was the work of numerous scribes, chief among whom were Solomon O'Droma, Manus O'Duigenan, and Robert mac Sheehy.

318.8–11 *four evangelists ... Carrantuohill*: the four evangelists' symbols: Matthew, a winged man with a lance; Mark, a lion; Luke, an ox; and John, an eagle; from Rev. 4: 7–8, which also describes the 'beasts' as winged. 'Four masters': compilers of *The Annals of the Four Masters* (1632–6), the Franciscans Michael O'Clery, Conaire O'Clery, Cucoigcriche O'Clery, and Fearfeasa O'Mulchonry. 'Carrantuohill' is the highest mountain in Ireland.

318.11 *emunctory*: of or pertaining to nose-blowing.

318.12 *duns, raths, cromlechs, grianauns*: Gaelic: *dún*: 'fort'; *ráth*: 'ring-fort'; *cromleac*: 'stooped flagstone, dolmen'; *grianán*: 'solar, sunroom'.

318.13 *maledictive stones*: pile of stones as monument of disaster.

318.22 *Kilballymacshonakill*: a Gaelic made-up name: *Cill/Coill Baile mhic Seóin á Chill*: Church (or Wood) of the Town of the son of John of the Church.

318.23 *Curley's hole*: dangerous Dollymount bathing pool; see Joyce's satiric poem 'Gas from a Burner' (1912) where the speaker (Maunsel & Co.'s printer—the firm which refused to publish *Dubliners* fearing that if real names were printed libel would ensue) says: 'Do you think I'll print | The name of the Wellington Monument, | Sydney Parade and the Sandymount tram, | Downes's cakeshop and Williams's jam? | I'm damned if I do—I'm damned to blazes! | Talk about *Irish Names of Places*! | It's a wonder to me, upon my soul, | He forgot to mention Curly's [*sic*] Hole' (ll. 55–62) (*PSW* 104).

319.15 *apostle to the gentiles*: after St Paul the missionary, who preached the gospel to everyone (1 Tim. 2: 7).

319.15–16 *Love your neighbours*: Jesus's second commandment: 'Thou shalt love thy neighbour as thyself' (Matt. 22: 39).

319.20–8 *Love loves ... loves everybody*: **Parody**; in the manner of lovers' cooing babytalk.

319.34 *sanctimonious Cromwell ... cannon*: Oliver Cromwell (1599–1658) and his Protestant troops ('Ironsides') began their anti-Stuart campaign in Ireland with an assault on Drogheda (coastal town south of Dublin) in 1649, after the resolution of the Civil War in England; some 3,000 Irish were killed (including women and children); Cromwell justified the action by saying, 'I am persuaded that this is the righteous judgement of God upon these barbarous wretches'.

320.4–21 *A delegation ... girl hands*: though it looks like one, this is not technically a parody as it is announced as a 'skit' from the *United Irishman*; the *Freeman's Journal* carried a similar announcement on 2 June 1904.

320.5 *His Majesty ... Abeakuta*: ruler of a province in western Nigeria; not a Zulu.

320.30–3 *those Belgians in the Congo ... Irishman*: Sir Roger Casement (1864–1916), British Consul to the Congo in 1904, issued a report condemning the treatment, under the Belgian government, of natives in the Congo; resulted in some measure of reform (Casement was executed as a traitor in 1916 for attempting to procure German help for the Irish nationalist cause).

321.22 *Jerusalem (ah!) cuckoos*: 'Jerusalem cuckoos': slang: Zionists.

321.24–7 *Bloom gave the idea for ... industries*: Sinn Féin's strategies were influenced by 19th-c. Hungarian resistance to Austrian domination; Kenner claims Griffith was rumoured to have had a 'Jewish adviser-ghostwriter' (133).

322.5–31 *Our travellers reached ... merry rogue*: **Parody**; of 19th-c. revivals of medieval romance.

323.8 *Who is Junius?*: Junius was an anonymous 18th-c. satirist, author of a series of letters published in the *Public Advertiser* (1769–72), highly critical attacks on George III and his ministers; in 1904 'Junius' was often claimed to have been the Irish-born Sir Philip Francis (1740–1818). (*G*)

323.10 *according to the Hungarian system*: Arthur Griffith wrote (and published serially in the *United Irishman*, Jan.–June 1904) *The Resurrection of Hungary*, an account of Hungary's attempts to win independence from Austria, urging Hungary as a model for Ireland.

323.26 *En ventre sa mère*: French: 'in the belly of his mother'.

324.3 *Ahasuerus I call him. Cursed by God*: traditional name of the Wandering Jew.

324.13–326.9 *And at the sound of ... Dominum nostrum* **Parody**; of account of religious festival, here the blessing of Barney Kiernan's pub; the blessing follows the forms specified in Catholic liturgy for (1) blessing a house, (2) the consecration of a church, and, finally, (3) the consecration of a cathedral. The saints, their symbols, their accoutrements all derive from Catholic history and liturgical lore. *G* provides complete glosses and biographies. Watch for the occasional extra joke and note that the majority of these saints are Irish.

324.30–2 *S. Martin of Tours ... S. Owen Caniculus*: 'patron saints' of Martin Cunningham, Alf Bergan, J J O'Molloy, Denis Breen, Corny Kelleher, Bloom, Barney Kiernan, Terry Ryan, Ned Lambert, and Garryowen ('S. Owen Caniculus': Saint Owen of the Dogs (*Canicula*: Latin: 'small dog, bitch')).

325.19–20 *the introit in Epiphania ... Surge, illuminare*: Latin: *Introit*: 'entrance chant'; *Epiphania Domini*: 'Epiphany of Our Lord' (thus, together, the opening chant for the Mass celebrating the Feast of the Epiphany (6 Jan.), though the chant which follows is from the Epistle for Epiphany, not the Introit); *Surge, illuminare*: 'Arise, shine' (from Isa. 60:1).

325.20–1 *the gradual Omnes which saith de Saba venient*: Latin: *Omnes*: 'All of the people'; *de Saba venient*: 'of Sheba are coming' (the Gradual of the Mass for the Epiphany begins 'Omnes de Saba venient' (from Isa. 60:6)).

325.21–2 *casting out devils ... halt and the blind*: the saints repeat the miracles of Jesus.

325.33 *blessed the house of Abraham and Isaac and Jacob*: an oddly Hebraic ending to a Catholic parade.

325.37–326.3 *Audiutorium nostrum ... cum spiritu tuo*: Latin: 'Our help is in the name of the Lord'; 'who made heaven and earth'; 'the Lord be with you'; 'And with thy spirit'.

326.6–9 *Deus, cuius verbo sanctificantur ... Christum Dominum nostrum*: 'animoe' should read 'animae'; the prescribed 'Blessing for all things': Latin: 'O God, by whose word all things are made holy, pour down your blessing on these which you created. Grant that whoever, giving thanks to you, uses them in accordance with your law and your will, may by calling on your holy name receive through your aid health of body and protection of soul, through Christ our Lord.'

326.31–327.4 *The milkwhite dolphin ... clave the waves*: **Parody**; of 19th-c. translations of medieval romance.

327.7 *bell, book and candle*: to curse by 'bell, book and candle' is to pronounce major excommunication (Brewer).

327.20 *whisht*: Gaelic: *thoist*: 'silence'.

327.22–3 *If the man in the moon ... jew*: after a similarly racist American popular song by Fred Fisher, 'If the Man in the Moon were a Coon' (1905).

327.26 *Mendelssohn ... Spinoza*: an odd list of the 'Jewish faithful'; more a list of the 'doubtfully Jewish': 'Mendelssohn': either Moses Mendelssohn (1729–86), Jewish German philosopher and campaigner for increased tolerance by and toward Jews, or Felix Mendelssohn-Bartholdy (1809–47) German composer, whose father left Judaism (and added the second name); Karl Marx: (1818–83), German political philosopher, born of parents who had abandoned Judaism before he was born, antipathetic to Jews and Judaism; Saverio Mercadante (see 79.10 n.), Italian composer, not Jewish at all; Baruch Spinoza (1632–77), Dutch philosopher, Jewish but so unorthodox in his views as to be excommunicated by the Sephardic Jewish community in 1656.

327.36–328.25 *A large and appreciative ... not forgotten*: **Parody**; of journalist account of the end of a state visit.

328.1 *Nagyaságos uram Lipóti Virag*: Hungarian: 'Your greatness, my lord, Leopold Flower [or Virag of Lipot]' (see *G*).

328.3 *Százharminczbrojúgulyás-Dugulás*: Hungarian: according to *G*: '130-calf-shepherd-sticking-into'.

328.12 *Come Back to Erin*: song by English sentimental balladeer 'Claribel' (Mrs Charlotte Allington Barnard (1830–69)).

328.12–13 *Rakóczsy's March*: Hungarian national march (1809 song by Miklos Scholl, popularized by the army of Francis Rakoczy II of Transylvania), banned by the Austrians.

328.13–17 *the four seas ... Slieve Bloom*: signals are sent from the four seas surrounding Ireland and every significant mountain peak (as well as from the Cambrian (Welsh) and Caledonian (Scottish) hills).

328.24 *Pigeonhouse.*: should read 'Pigeonhouse, and the Poolbeg Light.'

328.24 *Visszontlátásra, kedvés barátom! Visszontlátásra!*: Hungarian: 'See you again, my dear friend! See you again!' (*G*)

328.30 *J.G.*: should read 'J.J.'

329.3–330.3 *The catastrophe was terrific ... F.R.C.S.I.*: **Parody**; of a sensational newspaper account of a disaster. All of the honorifics (except 'S.O.D.'—an obvious joke) refer to real degrees, offices, or societies.

329.28 *missa pro defunctis*: Latin: 'mass for the dead'.

330.17–25 *When, lo, there came ... a shovel*: **Parody**; of biblical event; specifically Bloom departs in the manner of Elijah's ascent to heaven (2 Kgs. 2: 11–12): 'And it came to pass, as they [Elijah and Elisha] still went on, and talked, that, behold, there appeared a chariot of fire, and horses of fire, and parted them both asunder; and Elijah went up by a whirlwind into heaven. And Elisha saw it, and he cried, My father, my father, the chariot of Israel and the horsemen thereof'; *Abba*: Syriac Greek: 'Father/God'; *Adonai*: Hebrew: 'Lord'.

NAUSICAA

Location: Sandymount Strand below Leahy's Terrace (small road leading due east off Tritonville Road just north of Sandymount Road (I5)). (The Star of the Sea Church is not the church marked on the map, but sits between Leahy's Terrace and Sandymount Road.)

Time: 8 p.m.

Homer: When Odysseus left Calypso's island (Book V), he was nearly drowned (see *Calypso* above), but eventually swam to shore at Scheria or Phaecia, home of

King Alcinous (to whom he has related the tale of his travails from the time of his having left Troy to his arrival on and departure from Calypso's island). Athena, guarding his safety, gives him sleep, then goes to Nausicaa, daughter of Alcinous, an 'unwedded girl beyond compare' (69), and tells her in a dream to offer to take and do the family washing at the river's mouth near where Odysseus sleeps. She gathers her handmaidens, they go, do the laundry, then bathe, eat, and play. In a game of catch, the catcher misses the ball which lands in deep water. At this the girls shriek and wake sleeping Odysseus. Covering his naked body with a leaf, he approaches the girls, all of whom except Nausicaa flee. Odysseus praises her beauty: 'I am all wonder and astonishment, and deepest reverence forbids me to touch your knees' (71), tells her briefly of his afflictions and begs her help. She provides him with clothing, oil with which to anoint himself after he has bathed, food and drink, and instructions on how to reach the city. He must not travel with her lest the people see him and think him to be her future husband. He travels to a grove of Athena within the city where he prays for the goddess's help. She shrouds him in mist so that he may walk safely through the city to Alcinous's palace. Once inside the palace, he kneels before Arete (wife of Alcinous), the mist clears, he greets the assembled company, and is welcomed by Alcinous. (Books V, VI, VII)

Schemata: *L* lists as personae Nausicaa, Handmaidens, Alcinous, Arete, and Ulysses, but *G* provides correspondences only for Nausicaa as Nymph, and Phaecia as the Star of the Sea [church].

L and *G* agree on the Organ (Eye, Nose), Art (Painting) and, in part, Colour (*L*: grey; *G*: grey, blue), but differ on the Technic (*L*: Retrogressive progression; *G*: Tumescence, detumescence) and Symbol (*L*: Onanism, Feminine, Hypocrisy; *G*: Virgin). *L*'s Sense is 'The Projected Mirage'.

Joyce's Hints: '*Nausikaa* is written in a namby-pamby jammy marmalady drawersy (alto là!) style with effects of incense, mariolatry, masturbation, stewed cockles, painter's palette, chitchat, circumlocutions, etc. etc.' (*LI* 135; 3/1/20). In response to Arthur Power's question about what actually happened between Gerty and Bloom on the beach, Joyce said, 'Nothing happened between them. It all took place in Bloom's imagination' (Power, 32).

Nausicaa divides neatly between Gerty's narrative and Bloom's, though the two stand in asymmetrical relation to one another. This is no relationship of parity. In Bloom's half of the episode, the narrative returns (after the narrative disruptions of *Wandering Rocks*, *Sirens*, and *Cyclops*) to interior monologue. So, Bloom is thus accorded (whatever his vocabulary) the illusion of an integral subjectivity and narrative control. Not so Miss MacDowell. Gerty has no voice of her own. Her narrative proceeds in the third person as free indirect discourse, the lexicon provided courtesy of Madame Vera Verity, Miss Cummins, the litany of Our Lady of Loreto, the *Lady's Pictorial*, with a passing glance at Walker's pronouncing dictionary. Here popular discourses vie with one another for air time: **romance fiction** ('the picture of halcyon days where a young gentleman . . . was offering a bunch of flowers to his ladylove with oldtime chivalry'), **fashion magazines** ('it was expected in the *Lady's Pictorial* that electric blue would be worn'), **advertising** ('the newest thing in footwear'), **mariolatry** ('the old familiar words, holy Mary, holy virgin of virgins'), **cliché** ('if you fail try again'), **proverb** ('Love laughs at locksmiths'), **folk wisdom** ('when she was dressing that morning she nearly slipped up the old pair on her inside out and that was for luck and lovers' meetings'), **fairy tale** ('she knew how to cry nicely before the mirror. You are lovely, Gerty, it said'), **colloquialism** ('as cross as two sticks'), and **euphemism** ('his waterworks were out of order'). Persuaded as she is of the enhancing capacities of 'eyebrowleine', 'dolly dyes', 'queen of ointments', and 'iron jelloids', Gerty is a real commodity fetishist.

More to the point, she is 'in very truth as fair a specimen of winsome Irish girlhood as one could wish to see'. That is, she is femininity 'to a tee' and she is 'on show'. Her narrative comprises various discourses, all perceived by Irish manhood (Bloom, at least) as constitutive of femininity. Or, put slightly differently, her discourse emerges as a veritable code of femininity—at least as perceived from the standpoint of the masculine observer. For Gerty here is the object of this discourse, not its subject; she is constructed by and through it, not vice versa. Similarly, she is the fantasy, not the fantasist. As fantasy, as object, she is also a cultural commodity, a product of societal notions of what 'woman' is or should be. If as Joyce remarked to Power, 'it all took place in Bloom's imagination', Gerty is *Bloom's* 'Projected Mirage' (Linati); she is *his* fantasy, a product of the masculine desire of what a woman would be *for him*—'as fair a specimen of winsome Irish girlhood *as one could wish to see*'. Or as Gerty says, she is 'more sinned against than sinning'.

331.8 *Mary, star of the sea*: Catholic church of Mary, Star of the Sea, off Leahy's terrace; *Stella maris* (Latin: 'star of the sea') is one of the Virgin Mary's many appellations.

331.24 *plucks*: Gaelic: *pluc*: 'cheek'.

332.8–9 *Flora Mac Flimsy*: heroine of William Allen Butler's (1825–1902) comic poem 'Nothing to Wear' (1857), a real 'fashion victim' who finally collapses 'in utter despair | Because she had nothing whatever to wear' (*G*).

334.6–7 *Madame Vera Verity . . . Princess novelette*: *The Princess's Novelettes* (1886–1904) was a London weekly women's magazine, though no Madame Verity wrote for it.

334.33–4 *They were protestants in his family*: despite what Gerty intimates, a significant obstacle to marriage (since she is Catholic).

335.9 *the Lady's Pictorial*: London weekly illustrated fashion magazine.

336.15 *T.C.D.*: Trinity College, Dublin.

336.33–5 *for riches for poor . . . forward*: misquotation from the wedding ceremony;

the Catholic vows (for both bride and groom) were 'I, —, take you, —, for my lawful wife [husband], to have and to hold, from this day forward, for better, for worse, for richer, for poorer, in sickness and in health, until death do us part'.

338.27–8 *benediction of the Most Blessed Sacrament*: evening service to celebrate the Virgin Mary; it can include the Litany of Our Lady of Loreto (see 338.31–3 n.), the 'Tantum ergo' (see 344.11 n.) and Ps. 117 (see 348.32 n.), as it does here.

338.30 *fane*: poetic: 'temple or church'.

338.31–3 *the litany of Our Lady . . . virgins*: prayer of supplication; begins with appeal to the Trinity, followed by lengthy application to the Virgin through her various names (e.g. Holy Mary, Holy Mother of God, Virgin Most Powerful, Virgin Most Merciful, Tower of Ivory, House of Gold, etc.); portions of the Litany are heard at 341.3–4, 342.2, 344.3–4.

338.34 *taking the pledge*: vowing to abstain from alcohol.

338.35 *Pearson's Weekly*: London pennyweekly which combined 'instructive' sensational tales with advertisements for patent medicines and miracle cures.

339.15–16 *a palpable case of doctor Fell*: Dr John Fell (1625–86), dean of Christ Church, Oxford, threatened the satirist Thomas Browne (1663–1704) with expulsion unless he could produce an impromptu paraphrase of Martial's 32nd epigram; Browne's effort: 'I do not love thee, Doctor Fell, | The reason why I cannot tell; | But this I know, and know full well: | I do not love thee, Doctor Fell'.

341.2–3 *her who was conceived without stain of original sin*: i.e. the Virgin Mary, whose immaculate conception became Church dogma in 1854.

341.7–10 *what the great saint Bernard . . . abandoned by her*: the 'Memorare' (a prayer to the Virgin Mary popularized but not written by St Bernard) which asks confidently for the Virgin's intercession on behalf of the pleader as no one who had ever asked for her help had been 'left forsaken' (*G*).

341.25 *possing*: *poss*: dialect: 'to beat or stamp (clothes, etc.) in water, in the process of washing' (*OED*); so, figuratively, 'dripping wet' (?).

342.8 *Martin Harvey*: Sir John Martin-Harvey (1863–1944), English actor who played to great success in Dublin at the turn of the century.

342.32 *Ora pro nobis*: Latin: 'pray for us'.

342.35 *the seven dolours which transpierced her own heart*: the seven sorrows in the life of the Virgin Mary (*G* lists them); the effigy of 'Our Lady of Sorrows' (one of Mary's names) is depicted with seven swords piercing her heart.

343.5 *the novena of Saint Dominic*: 'novena': in Catholic liturgy, a devotion consisting of specific prayers to be said over nine days; St Dominic: saint known for his devotion to the Virgin, popularizer of the rosary as a devotion.

343.10–11 *Our Blessed Lady . . . Thy Word*: Mary when told by Archangel Gabriel that she will bear the Son of God: 'Behold the handmaid of the Lord; be it unto me according to thy word' (Luke 1: 38).

343.15–16 *the forty hours' adoration*: a devotion celebrated during which the

'Blessed Sacrament' is exposed to 'the faithful' for forty consecutive hours (as forty hours was the time Jesus stayed in the tomb).

344.1 *Tableau!*: parlour game where players strike a pose meant to represent a 'message'; when ready to be 'read', they declare 'Tableau!' Bloom also invokes the command at 352.19.

344.11 *Tantum ergo*: hymn sung during the benediction of the Most Blessed Sacrament, after the Litany and exposure of the Sacrament, comprising the last two verses of St Thomas Aquinas's *Pange, lingua*; *Tantum ergo sacramentum*: Latin: 'So great a sacrament, therefore'.

344.13 *Tantumer gosa cramen tum*: Gerty's metrical version of *Tantum ergo sacramentum*.

344.15 *brack*: Gaelic: *breac*: 'speck'.

344.19 *streel*: Gaelic: *sraoille*: 'loose-hanging garment'; also *sraoilleog*: 'slut'.

345.21 *after eight*: on 16 June 1904 in Dublin, the sun set at 8.27 p.m.

346.10 *Panem de coelo praestitisti eis*: Latin: 'You have given them bread from heaven'; spoken by the celebrant after the *Tantum ergo* in the Benediction.

346.35 *kinnatt*: Hiberno-English: 'impertinent, conceited, impudent little puppy' (P. W. Joyce, 281).

346.37 *them and*: should read 'them and never would be and'.

347.9 *compliments on*: should read 'compliments to all and sundry on'.

347.28–9 *The Lamplighter by Miss Cummins ... Vaughan and other tales*: Maria Cummins (1827–66), *The Lamplighter* (1854), sentimental novel with a heroine named Gerty, who is orphaned, later adopted by the kindly lamplighter Trueman Flint, grows from being sweet but hot-tempered to practising a constant religious self-sacrifice, and is rewarded by marriage to her childhood sweetheart, Willie, who has made good (*G*).

348.3–4 *Art thou real, my ideal... Magherafelt*: verse by Louis J. Walsh (1880–1942), known in his youth as 'the boy orator'; *Stephen Hero* quotes at greater length: 'Art thou real, my ideal? | Wilt thou ever come to me | In the soft and gentle twilight | With your baby on your knee?' (77); Walsh was Joyce's fellow student at University College.

348.19 *the accommodation walk*: prostitutes' soliciting area.

348.32 *Laudate Dominum omnes gentes*: Latin: 'Praise the Lord, all ye people' (Ps. 117: 1); spoken at the conclusion of the Benediction.

349.5 *the bazaar fireworks*: the fireworks of the Mirus bazaar, opened earlier in the day by the Lord-Lieutenant, held approximately one mile south of Gerty and Bloom.

349.7 *rossies*: Gaelic: *rásaidhe*: 'wandering woman'.

349.21–2 *the Congested Districts Board*: governmental board established in 1891 with power to redistribute land in the west of Ireland to alleviate problems of over-population of unproductive land (*G*).

351.36 *Mutoscope pictures*: a 'mutoscope' was a device for animating still photographs, though the movement produced was erratic and jerky.

353.23–4 *Nell Gwynn; Mrs Bracegirdle; Maud Branscombe*: all English actresses and famous beauties; for Nell Gwynn, see 195.31–5 n.; Anne Bracegirdle (1663–1748), apparently more virtuous than was rumoured; Maud Branscombe (?; popular 1875–1910) renowned beauty, seemingly virtuous as well.

353.28 *Lacaus esant taratara*: Bloom's metrical version of *La causa è santa* (see 160.21–3 n.).

353.31 *Good idea if you're in a cart*: should read 'Good idea if you're stuck. Gain time. But then you're in a cart.'

354.29 *Say prunes and prisms*: from Charles Dickens's *Little Dorrit* (1857), Book II, ch. 5, where Mrs General advises Amy to repeat this phrase on entering a room to form 'a demeanour'.

356.3 *Every bullet has its billet*; fatalistic proverb attributed to William III (see 29.29 n.).

357.3 *ghesabo*: *G* claims this is slang for 'gazebo' and means 'the whole show'.

358.6 *hogo*: from the French *haut-goût*: 'high flavour'; slang: 'a high or putrescent flavour; a taint, a stench, a stink' (*OED*).

359.2–3 *Mother Shipton's prophecy . . . twinkling*: Mother Shipton (*c.*1487–*c.*1561), fabled English prophetess (perhaps fictitious) who supposedly predicted, among other things, the deaths of Cardinal Wolsey and others in Henry VIII's court; though 'her' 'prophecies' were not published until 1641; 1862 hoax version included 'prophecies' of the telegraph ('Around the world thoughts shall fly | In the twinkling of an eye'), iron steamships, and submarines (*G*).

359.3 *The royal reader*: 1870s English textbooks (in six volumes) which formed part of the Irish school curriculum.

359.6 *Grace darling*: Grace Darling (1815–42), daughter of a lighthouse keeper who, with her father, saved nine (of the 63) passengers of a foundered steamer; praised by Wordsworth on her death in his poem 'Grace Darling' (1843).

359.12 *Roygbiv Vance*: named after the mnemonic for recalling the colours of the rainbow in order: *r*ed, *o*range, *y*ellow, *g*reen, *b*lue, *i*ndigo, *v*iolet.

359.16 *My native land, goodnight*: from a lyric in Byron's *Childe Harold's Pilgrimage* (1812), Canto 1, after stanza 13; begins 'Adieu, my native shore' and the first and last stanzas end with 'My native Land—Good Night!'.

359.29 *Ye crags and peaks . . . again*: from a monologue spoken by the eponymous hero of *William Tell* (1825), I. ii. 1, a tragedy by the Anglo-Irish dramatist James Sheridan Knowles (1784–1862).

360.9–10 *Rip van Winkle*: after the story 'Rip Van Winkle', *The Sketch Book* (1819–20) by American author Washington Irving (1783–1859); Rip fell asleep for twenty years and woke to find his gun rusted, his wife dead, and his son grown and married.

360.13 *Sleepy Hollow*: not the place where Rip Van Winkle fell asleep, but another story from Irving's *Sketch Book*, 'The Legend of Sleepy Hollow', about schoolmaster Ichabod Crane.

360.14 *drew*: should read 'dew'.

360.16 *Metempsychosis*: see 62.9n., 147.11, and 705.12.

360.35–6 *that wise Man ... burning glass*: an apocryphal story that Archimedes set Roman ships on fire by using mirrors to focus the sun's rays.

361.9 *Faugh a ballagh*: Gaelic: *fág a' bealach*: 'Clear the way'.

361.16–17 *the tephilim no what's ... door to touch*: searching for 'mezuzah' (Hebrew: 'doorpost'; a small case containing the verses from Deut. 6: 4–9 and 11: 13–21 placed next to the door of devout Jewish homes), Bloom finds instead 'tephilim': phylacteries, small leather boxes, containing four parts of the Pentateuch, worn on the arms of religious Jews to remind them of their duties to God (*T*).

362.29–30 *Buenas noches, señorita ... la muchaha hermosa*: should read '*muchacha*'; Spanish: 'Good evening, miss. The man loves the beautiful young girl.'

362.33–4 *Leah, Lily of Killarney*: For *Leah*, see 73.21n.; for *Lily of Killarney*, see 89.9n.

363.10 *Scottish widows*: the Scottish Widows' Fund (Mutual) Life Assurance Society.

364.3, 9 *I | AM. A*: Note the parallel in John 8: 6–8, when Jesus, confronting the woman accused of committing adultery, writes in the sand; note, too, that Bloom does not complete the copula.

364.26 *plump years*: should read 'plump bubs me breadvan Winkle red slippers she rusty sleep wander years'.

364.30–2; 365.3–5, 11–13 *Cuckoo. / Cuckoo. / Cuckoo ... Cuckoo. / Cuckoo. / Cuckoo*: obviously connoting the cuckold (see 204.13n.); but see also the traditional rhyme: 'Cuckoo, cuckoo, | Tell me true, | When shall I be married?'; the number of cuckoo calls then heard foretells the number of years before marriage.

OXEN OF THE SUN

Location: Holles Street Maternity Hospital (29–31 Holles Street, corner of Holles and Lower Mount Streets (G5)).

Time: 10 p.m.

Homer: In narrating his tale to Alcinous, Odysseus tells of having come (after passing Scylla and Charybdis) to Thrinacia, the land where Phaethusa and Lampetie, daughters of Helios Hyperion (god of the sun), tend their father's sacred cattle. Odysseus had twice been warned (once by Tiresias in Hades, once by Circe) not to harm the cattle if he desired to return safely to Ithaca. Hence, he was wary of letting his men go ashore. 'Bold' Eurylochus pleaded the case for the men who, exhausted and hungry, hoped to find food ashore. Odysseus agreed, but made them swear a solemn oath not to slaughter any of Helios's cattle. The men acceded, went ashore, and ate. Odysseus walked inland, prayed to the gods for a safe journey home, and fell asleep. Meanwhile, Eurylochus has persuaded the men that to die of hunger would be a horrible death and that, to ward it off, they should slaughter the cattle, offer a sacrifice, and eat their fill. Though they had no wine for libation and had to substitute water instead, they nevertheless slaughtered, sacrificed, and ate. On waking, Odysseus returned to find the sacrilege. Lampetie, discovering the events, rushed to tell her father, Hyperion, who in rage pleaded with Zeus to take revenge, saying he would descend to Hades and shine there if his wishes were refused. Zeus agreed to destroy Odysseus's ship in mid-ocean. As there was no wind, the ship could not yet leave so the men continued to feast. The gods sent them 'signs and wonders': the slaughtered beasts began to bellow. On the seventh day, the wind rose, and the ship set sail, only to be struck by Zeus's thunderbolt. The men jumped overboard and were lost. Odysseus made a raft for himself from the mast, set off, was nearly drowned, and finally landed on Calypso's island where he would remain for seven years (Book XII)

Schemata: *L* lists as personae Lampetie, Phaethusa, Helios Hyperion, Jove (Jupiter or Zeus), and Ulysses, while *G* provides correspondences as follows: Trinacria (Gr. Thrinacia), Hospital; Lampetie and Phaethusa, Nurses [Callan and Quigley]; Helios, Horne [Andrew J. Horne, one of the two masters of the National Maternity Hospital]; Oxen, Fertility; Crime, Fraud.

L and *G* agree in whole only on the Colour (white) and in part on the Organ (*L*: Matrix, Uterus; *G*: Womb), while they sympathetically differ on Technic (*L*: Prose Embryo-Foetus-Birth; *G*: Embryonic development). For the Art, Joyce wrote '*Fisica*' on *L*, which means 'Physics', but he may have been aiming at the Italian equivalent of the English 'Physic' (which would have been '*Medicina*'). *G* has 'Medicine'. For Symbol, *L* gives Fertilization, Frauds, Parthenogenesis and *G*, Mothers. *L*'s Sense is 'The Eternal Herds'.

Joyce's Hints: In Mar. 1920 Joyce wrote a letter to Budgen which has often been read as a virtual guide to this episode. Use it with care: '*Oxen of the Sun*, the idea being the crime committed against fecundity by sterilizing the act of coition. Scene, lying-in hospital. Technique: a nineparted episode without divisions introduced by a Sallustian-Tacitean prelude (the unfertilized ovum), then by way of earliest English alliterative and monosyllabic and Anglo-Saxon ("Before born the babe had bliss. Within the womb he won worship." [367.31] "Bloom dull dreamy heard: in held hat stony staring" [cf. 368.35]) then by way of Mandeville ("there came forth a scholar of medicine that men clepen etc" [cf. 369.15–17]) then Malory's *Morte d'Arthur* ("but that franklin Lenehan was prompt ever to pour them so that at the least way mirth should not lack" [cf. 371.32–3]), then the Elizabethan chronicle style ("about that present time young Stephen filled all cups" [373.16]), then a passage solemn, as of Milton, Taylor, Hooker, followed by a choppy Latin-gossipy bit, style of Burton-Browne, then a passage Bunyanesque ("the reason was that in the way he fell in with a certain whore whose name she said is Bird in the hand" [cf. 377.30–1]) after a diarystyle bit Pepys-Evelyn ("Bloom sitting snug with a party of wags, among them Dixon jun., Ja. Lynch,

Doc. Madden and Stephen D. for a languor he had before and was now better, he having dreamed tonight a strange fancy and Mistress Purefoy there to be delivered, poor body, two days past her time and the midwives hard put to it, God send her quick issue" [cf. 379.9–20]) and so on through Defoe-Swift and Steele-Addison-Sterne and Landor-Pater-Newman until it ends in a frightful jumble of Pidgin English, nigger English, Cockney, Irish, Bowery slang and broken doggerel. This progression is also linked back at each part subtly with some foregoing episode of the day and, besides this, with the natural stages of development in the embryo and the periods of faunal evolution in general. The double-thudding Anglo-Saxon motive recurs from time to time ("Loth to move from Horne's house" [cf. 368.18, 374.30, 397.4, and 402.11–12]) to give the sense of the hoofs of oxen. Bloom is the spermatozoon, the hospital the womb, the nurse the ovum, Stephen the embryo. How's that for high?' (*LI* 139–40; ?20/3/1920). To Harriet Weaver, he commented that the episode comprised 'nine circles of development (enclosed between the headpiece and tailpiece of opposite chaos)' (*LIII* 16; 16/10/20).

Joyce himself described *Oxen of the Sun* as 'the most difficult episode in an odyssey, I think, both to interpret and to execute' (*SL* 249, 25/2/20). The letter is typically ambiguous. For whom is it difficult 'to interpret and to execute'—the writer who attempts to adapt Homer to *Ulysses* or the reader who tries to understand it? How might one (a writer or a reader) be thought to 'execute' *Oxen* and what would the punishment be for such a slaying?

In *Oxen*, the narrative (an account of the events in the Holles Street Maternity Hospital the night that Mortimer Edward Purefoy is born) proceeds through a series of (historically successive) English prose styles. It is in this dense growth that most first-time readers come to grief in the struggle to distinguish the discursive or stylistic trees from the narrative wood. But taking to the trees with an axe will not help, for the characters and events themselves are produced through the styles (not despite them). So Bloom becomes by turns a wayfarer (Anglo-Saxon), the traveller Leopold (Mandeville's *Travels*), childe Leopold (Malory), Mr Cautious Calmer (Bunyan), Leop. Bloom (Pepys), Mr Bloom (Burke), this alien (Junius), Mr Canvasser Bloom (Gibbon), young Leopold (by 'retrospective arrangement' courtesy of Charles Lamb), Mr L. Bloom (Pubb. Canv.) (Huxley), the stranger (Pater), Bloom (Carlyle), 'the johnny in the black duds' (slang). He becomes the character to suit the style: the enlightened, rational gentleman calmly asserting that 'to those who create themselves wits at the cost of feminine delicacy . . . he would concede neither to bear the name nor to herit the tradition of a proper breeding' when narrated in Edmund Burke's style, for example. The words make the man. One cannot see through them to a character underneath; there is no underneath. Or, to return to the metaphor, one cannot chop down the trees to find the wood; the trees are the wood.

This stylistic development parallels the growth of the foetus in the womb—or so Joyce steadfastly maintained even while he drew the correspondence quite loosely (see his 'embryological charts' drawn to make clear which part of the embryo developed when (*JJA* xii. 23 and xiv. 2a)). We will misread if we assume that the history of styles follows the growth of the foetus in any teleologically progressive way. The episode's end in doggerel and pidgin English belies this much (though Joyce would probably have liked such a reading's placing of *Ulysses* near the apex of English stylistic development). How then is the parallel to be drawn? Comparing the episode's mode (narration through a history of English styles) with its stated theme ('Copulation without population! No, say I! Herod's slaughter of the innocents were the truer name') appears to elicit a contradiction. By so easily using (and discarding?) so many styles, *Oxen* could be read as using up, even killing, these styles.

T. S. Eliot certainly read it that way. Virginia Woolf records him in her diary (entry for 26 Sept. 1922) as remarking that *Ulysses* 'destroyed the whole of the 19th Century.... It showed up the futility of all English styles.' (For Eliot this was high praise.) How can the text be advocating fertility on the one hand and futility on the other? If we follow Eliot's line, *Ulysses* here seems to be hoisting itself by its own petard. Or might it not be Eliot who 'executes' *Oxen*? Joyce was not Eliot nor did he share Eliot's desire to purify language or find an uncorrupted original tongue. Fertility for Joyce came in recirculation and recycling, not purifying and sterilizing. It came in the recognition that to reuse Burke was to renew Burke not kill him (nor was it to reinstall him in a position of prior authority; Burke once used by Joyce is no longer the same Burke—something Eliot knew in 'Tradition and the Individual Talent' but seemed to forget later). The final paradox, of course, is that in its admission that it is not new, in its admission—even flaunting—of its dependence on its precursors, *Oxen* becomes (like Theodore Purefoy) 'the remarkablest progenitor barring none in this chaffering allincluding most farraginous chronicle'. Let us not 'execute' it.

In his 'execution' of *Oxen*, Joyce removed himself even one step further from the originating fathers by using not their texts themselves, but the texts as they had been dismembered and recirculated in two histories of English prose style: George Saintsbury, *A History of English Prose Rhythm* (London: Macmillan, 1912) and William Peacock, *English Prose from Mandeville to Ruskin* (London: Oxford University Press, 1903). The diligent will discover much about Joyce's magpie-like methods of composition in an examination of the two texts.

In what follows, Robert Janusko's division of the episode into 'months of gestation' is used. Janusko convincingly argues that in his drafting of this episode, Joyce divided the manuscript across nine notebooks, each corresponding to one month of foetal gestation (Janusko, 43–4; and see *JJA* xiv. 59–132)).

366.1–6 *Deshil Holles Eamus ... boyaboy hoopsa*: according to Gilbert, 'three incantations, in the manner of the *Fratres Arvales*' (Gilbert, 296); *Fratres Arvales*:

ancient Roman priests who conducted fertility rites, their formalized chant (see *G*) was repeated three times; 'Deshil': Gaelic: *deiseal*: 'turning to the right, sunwise'; 'Holles': Holles Street, the site of the Maternity Hospital; 'Eamus': Latin: 'Let us go'; 'Horhorn': suggests both Andrew J. Horne, master of the hospital, and the 'horn of plenty'; 'Hoopsa boyaboy hoopsa': the chant of celebration at the birth of a boy.

366.7–367.4 *Universally . . . enjoined?*: **Style**: imitation of the Latin prose styles of e.g. the Roman historians Sallust (86–34 BC) and Tacitus (d. AD 120). This section also forms the 'Headpiece' and signifies the coming together of the ovum (Nurse Callan) and the sperm (Bloom).

366.16 *omnipollent* 'all powerful'.

366.19 *lutulent*: 'muddy'.

366.24 *inverecund*: 'immodest'.

367.5–30 *It is not why therefore . . . begun she felt!*: **Style**: after medieval Latin prose chronicles (*G*).

367.11 *trembling withering*: St Vitus's dance, or chorea, a disease characterized by jerky involuntary movements (*OEED*).

367.13 *a plan was by them adopted*: the plan to build maternity hospitals, the first in Britain being that built in Dublin in 1745.

367.31–368.36 *Before born babe bliss had . . . one with other*: **Style**: after Aelfric's (*c.*955–*c.*1010) Anglo-Saxon alliterative rhythmic prose, particularly in his *Homilies*.

368.1 *sejunct*: 'separated'.

368.4 *Some man that wayfaring was*: echoes the Anglo-Saxon elegy *The Wanderer*, from *The Exeter Book* (*c.*940 AD); **Embryo**: beginning of the first month of gestation.

368.9 *God's angel to Mary quoth*: the Archangel Gabriel's announcement to Mary that she will bear the son of God (Luke 1: 26–8).

368.13 *swire ywimpled*: 'swire': Anglo-Saxon: 'throat or neck'; 'ywimpled': Middle English: 'covered with a wimple'.

368.13 *levin*: 'lightning'.

368.16 *rathe*: 'quickly'.

368.26 *grameful*: 'full of grief'.

368.28 *algate*: 'always'.

368.30 *housel* 'the Eucharist'.

368.33 *bellycrab*: 'stomach cancer'.

368.33 *Childermas*: 28 Dec.; Holy Innocents Day (commemorating the Slaughter of the Innocents).

368.36 *wanhope*: 'despair'.

368.37–369.14 *Therefore, everyman, look to that . . . childless*: **Style**: after the late medieval (*c.*1509–19) morality play *Everyman*.

369.1 *every man that is born of woman*: Job 14: 1: 'Man that is born of a woman is of few days, and full of trouble'.

369.1–3 *as he came naked forth . . . he came*: Job 1: 21: 'Naked came I out of my mother's womb, and naked shall I return thither'.

369.7 *unneth*: 'difficult'.

369.13–14 *Nine twelve bloodflows*: nine years of menstruation.

369.15–370.19 *And whiles they spake . . . Almighty God*: **Style**: after the *Travels of Sir John Mandeville* (*c.*1356–7), a late 14th-c. collection of travel tales. **Embryo**: beginning of the second month of gestation.

369.21 *a horrible and dreadful dragon*: a bee.

369.26 *reproved*: should read 'repreved'.

369.26 *avis*: 'advice'.

369.28 *mandement*: 'command'.

369.37 *Mahound*: Middle English name for the prophet Muhammad; the word meant 'heathen god or monster'.

370.15 *apertly*: 'openly'.

370.17 *nist*: 'knew not'.

370.20–373.15 *This meanwhile . . . goods with whores*: **Style**: *G* identifies this entire section as being in the manner of Sir Thomas Malory's (d. 1471) medieval romance *Le Morte d'Arthur* (1485), whereas Janusko argues that the Malory imitation proper ends at 371.2.

371.3–17 *Now let us speak . . . loth to leave*: **Style**: Janusko identifies this as an imitation of John Bourchier, Lord Berners (1467–1533), especially his 'The Insurrection of Wat Tyler' from his translation of the *Chronicles of Froissart* (1523–5).

371.7 *Alba Longa*: the most ancient town in Latium (Latin Italy), but *Alba* is also Gaelic for Scotland.

371.18–373.2 *For they were right . . . appeared eftsoons*: **Style**: Janusko identifies this as an imitation of the styles of Berners (see 371.3–371.17 n.), Sir Thomas More's (?1477–1535) 'The Death of Lord Hastings', *History of Richard III* (1513–18), and Sir Thomas Elyot's (*c.*1490–1546) 'Prince Hal and Judge Gascoigne', *Boke Named the Governour* (1531).

371.24 *the woman should bring forth in pain*: Gen. 3: 16: God to Eve: 'In sorrow thou shalt bring forth children'.

371.30–1 *the wife should live . . . babe to die*: not the view of the Catholic Church, which was that, faced with a necessary choice, the child was to live and the mother die.

372.2–3 *the one in limbo gloom, the other in purge fire*: the unbaptized child (stillborn) would, according to Catholic theology, go to limbo, while the mother would go to purgatory.

372.4 *sin against the Holy Ghost*: or 'blasphemy against the Holy Spirit', the one unforgivable sin, remains ill-defined in Catholic theology, but Stephen here clearly equates it with masturbation (such an equation might itself be blasphemous).

372.13 *saint Foutinus*: St Foutin, 3rd-c. French bishop, seen by locals as a fertility saint (*G*); note the similarity of his name to the French verb *foutre*: coarse slang: 'to fuck'.

372.18 *orgulous*: 'haughty'.

372.19–20 *Lilith, patron of abortions*: Lilith: Hebrew: 'night hag'; in legend, Adam's lustful first wife; in her demonic form, she tormented children and pregnant women (*T*).

372.20–4 *bigness wrought by wind of seeds of brightness . . . Maimonides*: all legends concerning fabulous impregnations.

372.21 *vampires mouth to mouth*: see Stephen's poem, 47.27–8 and n.

372.21 *Virgillius saith*: Virgil, *Georgics*, III. 271–7, where he describes mares being impregnated by (and so seeking out) the west wind.

372.23 *effectu secuto*: Latin: 'one performance following another'.

372.23–4 *in her bath according . . . Moses Maimonides*: not, it seems, the opinion held by Maimonides, but Averroës cites such a case in his *Colliget* (*T* and *G*).

372.24–5 *at the end of the second month a human soul was infused*: Aquinas, after Aristotle, held that the foetus had first a 'vegetative', then a 'sensitive', and finally a 'rational' soul, only the latter being truly a soul; modern Catholic theology maintains the soul is present from the moment of conception (*G*).

372.27–9 *he that holdeth the fisherman's . . . founded*: the holder of 'the fisherman's seal' is the Pope; Peter was the first 'Bishop of Rome' (see Matt. 16: 18).

373.3–373.15 *But sir Leopold . . . goods with whores*: Janusko identifies John Wyclif's (*c.*1330–84) *Sermons*, particularly his sermon on the Prodigal Son, as a source of this passage.

373.9 *akeled*: 'cooled'.

373.16–374.30 *About that present time . . . rest should reign*: **Style**: after Elizabethan prose chronicles; **Embryo**: here begins the third month of gestation.

373.20 *vicar of Bray*: after 'The Vicar of Bray' (on the west coast of Ireland), a song of a churchman whose beliefs conveniently changed with his monarchs.

373.20–2 *Now drink we, quod . . . my soul's bodiment*: parody of Jesus's words at the Last Supper (Matt. 26: 26–8).

373.22 *them that live by bread alone*: Matt. 4: 4: 'Man shall not live by bread alone, but by every word that proceedeth out of the mouth of God'.

373.28 *time's ruins build eternity's mansions*: William Blake in a letter to William Hayley, 6 May 1800: 'Every Mortal loss is an Immortal Gain. The Ruins of Time build Mansions in Eternity' (quoted by Yeats in his 'Preface' to Lady Gregory's *Cuchulain of Muirthemne* (1902)).

373.29–30 *Desire's wind blasts . . . the rood of time*: here Stephen blends together elements of Blake, St Bernard, Dante, and Yeats (see *G* and *T*).

373.30–2 *In woman's womb . . . shall not pass away*: the 'word made flesh': Jesus Christ (John 1: 14); but Stephen contrasts woman's physical creation with the paternal artist's imaginative creation.

373.33–4 *aventried . . . Healer and Herd*: sense: 'took into her womb the body of our Redeemer, Healer and Shepherd'.

373.35 *omnipotentiam deiparae supplicem*: Latin: 'The mother of god's omnipotence in petition' (and see *T*).

373.36–374.2 *second Eve . . . penny pippin*: the idea, expressed by St Augustine among others, that Eve willingly succumbed to Satan and thereby brought death into the world, whereas Mary, full of grace, brought forth Jesus and thereby brought life (the rebirth of resurrection) back into the world (*T* and *G*).

374.2–3 *Or she knew him . . . creature*: Stephen puns on 'to know', as in 'to have sexual knowledge of'; so, 'either she knew him (sexually)' in which case this was a physical creation.

374.3–4 *vergine madre figlia di tuo figlio*: Italian: 'Virgin Mother, daughter of thy son'.

374.4 *or she knew him not*: the other half of the pun (374.2–3 n.): had no knowledge of him, with the possible meanings of 'she was not impregnated by him' or 'she did not know what was happening'.

374.4–5 *the one denial . . . Peter Piscator*: Peter, 'the Fisherman', thrice denied knowing Jesus (after his death) (Matt. 26: 34); 'the house that Jack built': the Catholic church (see 372.27–9 n. and 376.24–6 n.).

374.5–6 *Joseph the Joiner*: Joseph the carpenter, husband of Mary (see 18.33–19.12 and n.).

374.6–8 *parce que M. Leo Taxil . . . de Dieu!*: French: 'because Mr Leo Taxil has told us that the one who put her in this wretched condition was the sacred pigeon, God's bowels!' (the last phrase being a curse). (See 41.19–20 and n.)

374.8–9 *Entweder transsubstantiality . . . subsubstantiality*: 'Entweder/oder': German: 'Either/or'; should read 'transubstantiality': changing from one substance into another (as the Eucharist into the body and blood of Christ); 'consubstantiality': the uniting as one substance (or the existence as one and the same substance); 'subsubstantiality': (Joyce coinage) less than substance or, perhaps, the debasing of substance. All this returns to Stephen's earlier preoccupations with the Arian and Sabellian heresies (see 21.1 n. and 21.3 n.).

374.14–16 *Staboo Stabella . . . Staboo*: another unpublished lewd verse by Oliver St John Gogarty.

374.19 *gasteful*: 'wasteful'.

374.24 *chode*: past tense of 'to chide'.

374.31–377.11 *To be short this passage . . . natural phenomenon*: **Style**: after 16th- and 17th-c. Latinate prose styles, including John Milton and Jeremy Taylor (1613–67) (374.31–375.25), Sir Thomas Browne (1605–82) (375.35–376.19), especially his *Christian Morals* (1650s, pub. 1716) and *Urn Burial* (1650s, pub. 1690); *T* and *G* point out that 375.25–35 recalls the *Improperia* ('The Reproaches') of the Catholic liturgy for Good Friday.

375.2 *the eternal son and ever virgin*: Jesus, who was flesh but free from all sin.

375.7 *Ut novetur sexus omnis corporis mysterium*: Latin: 'That the whole mystery of physical sexuality may be known', not an actual anthem.

375.9–10 *Master John Fletcher . . . to bed*: song from *The Maid's Tragedy* (*c.*1610), a play by Francis Beaumont (*c.*1584–1616) and John Fletcher (1579–1625): 'To bed, to bed! Come, Hymen, lead the bride, | And lay her by her husband's side' (I. ii. 130–1).

375.12 *suadency*: 'persuasiveness'.

375.19 *custom of the country*: title of a play (*c.*1628, pub. 1647) by John Fletcher and Philip Massinger (1583–1640).

375.20–1: *Go thou and do likewise*: Jesus admonishing the lawyer to follow the example of the Good Samaritan (Luke 10: 37).

375.24–5 *Orate, fratres, pro memetipso*: Latin: 'Pray, brothers, for me myself'.

375.25–6 *Remember, Erin, thy generations and thy days of old*: combines Thomas Moore's song 'Let Erin Remember the Days of Old' (from *Irish Melodies*) with Deut. 32: 7: 'Remember the days of old, consider the years of many generations'.

375.28 *Jeshurum*: Hebrew: *Jeshurun*: 'righteous'; poetic name for Israel; Deut. 32: 15: 'But Jeshurun waxed fat, and kicked'.

375.29–30 *Return, return, Clan Milly . . . O Milesian*: echoes S. of S. 6: 13: 'Return, return, O Shulamite; return, return, that we may look upon thee'; 'Clan Milly': Gaelic: *Clann Mílidh*: 'the race of *Míleadh*' '(the legendary ancestor of the Celtic Irish), so the Irish race'.

375.34 *Horeb . . . Nebo . . . Pisgah . . . Horns of Hatten*: mountains associated with Moses's leadership of the Israelites (see *G*).

375.35 *land flowing with milk and money*: the 'promised land' to which Moses leads the children of Israel (see Exod. 33: 3).

376.2 *septuagint*: 3rd-c. BC Greek translation of the Old Testament; includes the Apocrypha.

376.4 *Assuefaction minorates atrocities*: i.e. repeated contact with an 'atrocity' lessens its impact; after Sir Thomas Browne's argument in *Christian Morals*, III. 10.

376.4 *Tully*: Marcus Tullius Cicero (106–43 BC), a Stoic, did urge the contemplation of coming events because 'anticipation . . . of the future mitigates the approach of evils whose coming one has long foreseen' (*Tusculan Disputations* (45 BC), III. xiv).

376.6 *The adiaphane . . . Egypt's plague*: see Dante, *Inferno*, I. 1–3, where he tells of arriving in 'a dark wood' in 'the middle of the journey of our life'; Egypt was stricken with plagues because of the Pharaoh's refusal to free the Israelites (see esp. Exod. 10: 21).

376.7 *ubi and quomodo*: Latin: 'the where and the manner'.

376.13–15 *First saved from water . . . occulted sepulchre*: Moses's birth and death; he was hidden (and found) among the bulrushes (Exod. 2: 5) and died without being allowed to enter the promised land, buried where 'no man knoweth of his sepulchre' (Deut. 34: 6).

376.16 *ossifrage*: 'osprey'.

376.21 *wisdom hath built herself a house*: Prov. 9: 1: 'Wisdom hath builded her house'.

376.24–6 *Behold the mansion ... bivouac*: opening lines of George Shepherd Burleigh's parody of 'The House that Jack Built', 'The Domicile Erected by Jack' (1857) (*G*).

376.28 *Thor thundered*: Thor: the Norse god of thunder and lightning.

377.12–378.16 *But was young Boasthard's ... brenningly biddeth*: **Style**: after John Bunyan (1628–88), especially *Pilgrim's Progress* (1678, 1684) with its characteristic use of personification; **Embryo**: here begins the fourth month of gestation.

377.18 *Bringforth*: see Gen. 3: 16: God to Eve: 'in sorrow shalt thou bring forth children'.

377.23–4 *By no means would he and make*: should read 'By no means would he though he must nor would he make'.

377.26 *Believe-on-Me*: see John 6: 35: Jesus to the multitude: 'He that believeth on me shall never thirst'.

377.27–8 *no death and no birth neither wiving nor mothering*: Jesus to the Sadducees in Mark 12: 25: '[In the resurrection] they neither marry, nor are given in marriage'.

378.16 *brenningly*: 'burningly'.

378.17–379.32 *So Thursday sixteenth ... queerities no telling how*: **Style**: after the diarists Samuel Pepys (1633–1703) and John Evelyn (1620–1706); **Embryo**: here begins the fifth month of gestation.

378.24 *the big wind*: the tremendous gale which hit Dublin on 26–27 Feb. 1903 (*T*).

379.1–2 *(that was a papish ... good Williamite)*: George Moore, whose attitude to religion was reputedly equivocal: having been Catholic, he became Protestant and pro-English (*G*).

379.16 *pleading her belly*: see Daniel Defoe's *Moll Flanders* (1722), where Moll says her mother got a stay of execution by 'pleading her belly'—announcing her pregnancy.

379.27 *after wind and water fire shall come*: biblical in its prophetic tone, though not, apparently, a direct quotation.

379.28–30 *Mr Russell has done ... farmer's gazette*: for George Russell, see 31.8, 9 n.; Russell, 'AE', was eccentrically interested in both agrarian reform and the occult.

379.33–381.8 *With this came up ... ale purling about*: **Style**: after Daniel Defoe (1660–1731), pamphleteer and novelist, especially his *Colonel Jack* (1722); see, too, Joyce on Defoe (*Buffalo Studies*, 1/1 (Dec. 1964), 3–27); **Embryo**: here begins the sixth month of gestation.

380.6 *sackpossets*: drink made of eggs, sugar, and sack.

380.17 *Mort aux vaches*: French: 'death to the cows'.

380.30 *What, says Mr Leopold*: **Style**: Janusko argues that the imitation of Jonathan Swift (1667–1745) begins here (see 381.8–382.36 n.).

381.6–7 *a bull that's Irish*: 'Irish bull': a statement containing a contradiction in terms or implying ludicrous inconsistency; 'Papal bull': an edict from the Pope.

381.8–382.36 *An Irish bull . . . a man for a' that*: **Style**: a parody in the manner of Jonathan Swift's *A Tale of a Tub* (1704), particularly Part IV, in which Swift exposes the history of Catholicism to ridicule by parodying Peter's (Catholicism's) recourse to papal bulls. Joyce provides a different parodic account: Ireland's history of exploitation at the hands of the Catholic Church and the English monarchy from the 12th through the 16th cs.

381.9 *farmer Nicholas*: Nicholas Breakspear, Pope Adrian IV (pope 1154–9), the only English pope; he granted Ireland to the English King Henry II (r. 1154–89) by means of the papal bull 'Laudibiliter' (1155), ostensibly so that Henry might exterminate Ireland's irreligious vices.

381.10 *an emerald ring*: according to John of Salisbury, Adrian IV gave Henry II a gold ring with an inset emerald as token of his overlordship of Ireland (1155).

381.18 *the Lord Harry*: see 381.9n.; Henry II of England; in what follows, 'lords Harry' multiply: Henry II, VII, and VIII all go by this name.

381.24–5 *four fields of all Ireland*: the four 'ancient kingdoms' of Ireland: Munster, Leinster, Ulster, and Connacht.

381.30 *father of the faithful*: the title 'Defender of the Faith' was (ironically, as it turned out) bestowed by the pope on Henry VIII (r. 1509–47) in acknowledgement of his treatise *Assertio Septem Sacramentorum* (1521), a defence of the Church against Luther's attacks.

382.1 *By the lord Harry*: Henry VII (r. 1485–1509), who reasserted the English claim to Ireland and imposed English land-use laws on Ireland.

382.7–8 *the lord Harry called farmer Nicholas . . . seven trulls in his house*: Henry VIII's arguments with the Catholic Church over Pope Clement VII's refusal to grant Henry a divorce from Catherine of Aragon; 'Old Harry' and 'Old Nick' are both names for the devil; the accusation is that, if Henry had six wives, the pope outdid him by having seven mistresses.

382.16 *famous champion bull of the Romans*: St Peter, supposed founder of Catholicism.

382.16 *Bos Bovum*: dog-Latin: 'Bull of Bulls'.

382.19 *his new name*: 'Defender of the Faith' (see 381.30n.).

382.25 *he and the bull of Ireland*: by act of Parliament (May 1536), Henry VIII was proclaimed Head of Church and State and, in 1541, King of Ireland.

382.37–385.6 *Our worthy acquaintance . . . antechamber*: **Style**: after the essayists Joseph Addison (1672–1719) and Richard Steele (1672–1729) in the *Tatler* (1709–11) and the *Spectator* (1711–12); **Embryo**: here begins the seventh month of gestation.

383.22 *who hide their flambeau under a bushel*: Matt. 5: 15: 'Neither do men light a candle, and put it under a bushel'.

383.23–4 *some unaccountable muskin*: William Cowper (1731–1800), English poet, coined the term 'muskin' ('a pretty face'), an endearment when addressed to a woman, an insult when to a man; but see Samuel Johnson (1709–84): 'Those who call a man an unaccountable muskin, should never come into company without an interpreter' (*OED*).

384.14–18 *an apt quotation . . . magnopere anteponunt*: '*matres familiarum*' should read '*matresfamiliarum*'; not a quotation (from Cicero) but an invention (of Mulligan): Latin: 'Of such a kind and so great is the depravity of our generation, O citizens, that our matrons much prefer the lascivious titillations of Gallic half-men to the weighty testicles and extraordinary erections of the Roman centurion'.

384.34 *ventripotence*: 'big belliedness; gluttony'.

384.35 *ovoblastic gestation in the prostatic utricle*: medical description of a 'male pregnancy': gestation of an embryo in the prostate gland.

385.7–386.27 *Here the listener who . . . store of knowledge*: **Style**: after Laurence Sterne (1713–68), Irish-born minister and novelist, especially his *Sentimental Journey through France and Italy* (1768).

385.12 *breading*: should read 'breeding'.

386.6 *marchand de capotes*: French: 'a cloak merchant'; but *capote* is also slang for 'condom'.

386.8 *Le Fécondateur*: French: 'The Impregnator'.

386.14 *umbrella*: slang: a diaphragm.

386.28–387.34 *Amid the general vacant . . . a loving heart*: **Style**: after Oliver Goldsmith (?1730–74), Irish-born essayist, dramatist, poet, novelist.

387.12 *enceinte*: French: 'pregnant'.

387.35–388.30 *To revert to Mr Bloom . . . Supreme Being*: **Style**: after various 18th-c. essayists: Edmund Burke (1729–97), political philosopher; Samuel Johnson, essayist, poet, lexicographer; David Hume (1711–76), Scottish sceptical philosopher; Gilbert White (1720–93), naturalist and essayist; Lord Chesterfield (1694–1773), statesman and political essayist; Sir Joshua Reynolds (1723–92), artist and essayist; **Embryo**: here begins the eighth month of gestation.

388.7–8 *a cropeared creature . . . feet first into the world*: after the descriptions of Richard III in Shakespeare's *3 Henry VI*, v. vi. 71–9, and *Richard III*.

388.9 *his skill lent*: should read 'his skull lent'.

388.10–11 *missing link . . . Mr Darwin*: Charles Darwin's (1809–82) hypothesis in *The Descent of Man* (1871) to account for the great differences between man and apes.

388.31–389.17 *Accordingly he broke his mind . . . feather laugh together*: **Style**: after Dublin-born Richard Brinsley Sheridan (1751–1816), dramatist, MP, and political essayist.

389.10–15 *Singular, communed the guest . . . esteemed the noblest*: **Style**: a much disputed section; Atherton (Hart & Hayman, 327) suggests Samuel Johnson, though the first sentence comes from Sir Walter Scott (1771–1832), *In A Besieged Castle*, as quoted in Peacock (259).

389.18–390.15 *But with what fitness . . . acid and inoperative*: **Style**: after the satirist 'Junius' (see 323.8 n.).

389.19–20 *this alien . . . admitted to civil rights*: 'civil' should read 'civic'; the Jews were expelled from the British Isles in 1290, readmitted under Cromwell and Charles II, but only gradually 'admitted to civic rights', e.g. they were not allowed to become MPs until 1858.

390.1 *Hagar, the Egyptian*: handmaid to Sarah, wife of Abraham, she conceived a child (Ishmael, traditional 'father' of Arabic peoples) with Abraham when Sarah proved (initially) barren (Gen. 16).

390.7 *balm of Gilead*: a highly prized 'balm' made from the resin of the trees of Gilead (Jer. 8: 22).

390.16–392.6 *The news was imparted . . . God has joined*: **Style**: after Edward Gibbon (1737–94), sceptical philosopher and historian.

390.36 *acardiac foetus in foetu*: here follows a series of 'monstrous births': the first, being born without a heart; 'aprosopia': 'lacking a face'; 'agnathia' (not 'agnatia'): 'lacking a jaw'.

391.9 *Sturzgeburt*: German: 'sudden birth'.

391.12 *Aristotle has classified in his masterpiece*: allusion to the apocryphal, quasi-pornographic work *Aristotle's Masterpiece* (see 226.2 n.) upon which, according to Janusko, Joyce is heavily reliant in this episode.

391.29–31 *Minotaur . . . Metamorphoses*: the account in Ovid's *Metamorphoses*, Bk. VIII, of Queen Pasiphaë's copulation with the prize bull, of which union was born the Minotaur (see 4.5–6 n.).

392.5–6 *the ecclesiastical ordinance . . . God has joined*: Matt. 19: 6: 'What therefore God hath joined together [wife and husband], let not man put asunder'.

392.7–33 *But Malachias' tale began . . . Murderer's ground*: **Style**: after the late 18th-c./early 19th-c. genre of the Gothic novel, especially Horace Walpole's (1717–97) *The Castle of Otranto* (1764) and Sheridan Le Fanu's (1814–73) *The House by the Churchyard* (1861).

392.10 *portfolio full of Celtic literature*: Douglas Hyde's *Love Songs of Connacht* (1893), see 47.27–8 and n.; 299.3–4 n.

392.15 *This is the appearance is on me*: a literal translation of the Gaelic: *'Seo é an chuma atá orm*: 'This is the condition I am in'.

392.17 *soulth*: Gaelic: *samhailt*: 'apparition, ghost'.

392.17 *bullawurrus*: disputed meaning; O Hehir: from Gaelic: *boladh a' mharbhadha*: 'smell of murder'; P. W. Joyce (227): 'the spectral bull, with fire blazing from eyes and nose and mouth'.

392.19 *the Erse language*: Gaelic, technically Scots Gaelic, but loosely also Irish Gaelic.

392.24–5 *The seer . . . Mannanaun!*: Mulligan's tale that at the gathering of the literati which he has attended in the afternoon, AE ('the seer', George Russell) recited the Mananaan chant from his play *Deirdre* (see 181.27–8 n. and 38.31–2 n.).

392.26 *Lex talionis*: see 134.20n.

392.34–393.33 *What is the age . . . Leopold was for Rudolph*: **Style**: after Charles Lamb (1775–1834), essayist, dramatist, poet, and author of *The Adventures of Ulysses* (1808).

393.13 *baisemoins*: 'baisemains': archaic French: 'compliments'.

393.20 *The wise father knows his own child*: *The Merchant of Venice*, II. ii. 76–7: the Clown (Launcelot Gobbo) to his father (Old Gobbo) who has failed to recognize his own son: 'it is a wise father that knows his own son'. (Compare 85.27.)

393.27 *in an instant . . . flood the world*: as in God's creation of the world as recorded in Gen. 1: 1–3.

393.34–394.27 *The voices blend and fuse . . . the forehead of Taurus*: **Style**: after Thomas De Quincey (1785–1859), English essayist and memoirist, especially 'The English Mail Coach' (1849), pts. 1 and 3.

394.7 *the ghosts of beasts*: compare the *Odyssey* where the ghosts of the slaughtered oxen of Helios stir and bellow.

394.8 *the lancinating lightenings . . .*: for a gloss of the zodiacal significance of Bloom's vision, see *G*.

394.10 *Lacus Mortis*: Latin: 'Lake of the Dead'; i.e. the Dead Sea.

394.28–396.14 *Francis was reminding . . . second constellation*: **Style**: after Walter Savage Landor (1775–1864), especially his *Imaginary Conversations* (1824–9, 1853), Landor's version of conversations that might have been held between figures from history and classical literature; **Embryo**: here begins the ninth month of gestation.

394.29 *Glaucon*: appears in Plato's *Republic*, often assumed to be Plato's brother.

394.29 *Alcibiades*: (*c*.450–404 BC), Athenian general, pupil of Socrates.

394.30 *Pisistratus*: (*c*.600–527 BC), Athenian tyrant *c*.560 BC, but also, of course, the name of Nestor's son in the *Odyssey*.

394.33 *Bous Stephanoumenos*: see 202.3n. and *Portrait*, ch. 4, p. 168.

394.33 *bullockbefriending bard*: see 36.2.

395.10, 23, 36 *Phyllis/Lalage/Glycera or Chloe*: conventional names for 'beautiful maidens' in pastoral poetry (*G*).

395.28 *Periplepomenos*: as 'Periplipomenes' a Greek neologism: 'itinerant fruit merchant' (*G*).

395.37 *a slight disorder in her dress*: from Robert Herrick's (1591–1674) 'Delight in Disorder' (1648): 'A sweet disorder in the dress | Kindles in clothes a wantonness'.

396.15–397.23 *However, as a matter of fact . . . ages yet to come*: **Style**: after Thomas Babington Macaulay (1800–59), essayist and historian.

397.1 *The debate which ensued*: Janusko maintains that the Macaulay does not begin until this point.

397.24–399.32 *It had better be stated . . . in which it was delivered*: **Style**: after Thomas Henry Huxley (1825–95), natural historian and evolutionist.

397.32–4 *Empedocles ... birth of males*: a version of a theory held by Empedocles of Acragas (*c*.495–*c*.435 BC) (Acragas being a city in Sicily, Trinacria being the ancient name of Sicily): according to Aristotle, Empedocles maintained that the sex of a child was determined by whether the fluid entering the womb were hot or cold (*T*).

397.36–7 *Culpepper ... Valenti*: 17th–20th-c. physicians, biologists, naturalists, embryologists, all of whom wrote embryological treatises (*G* provides glosses).

398.1 *nisus formativus*: Latin: 'formative tendency'.

398.2 *succubitus felix*: Latin: 'the fertile one who lies beneath'.

398.13 *Kalipedia*: Greek: 'the study of beauty'.

399.9 *survival of the fittest*: Herbert Spencer's (1820–1903) phrase, now virtually proverbial, synthesizing Charles Darwin's argument for natural selection as articulated in his *On the Origin of Species* (1859).

399.33–400.28 *Meanwhile the skill ... good and faithful servant!*: **Style**: after Charles Dickens, particularly *David Copperfield* (1849–50), ch. 53.

400.21 *father Cronion*: 'Father Time', from a conflation of the Greek *chronos* ('time') with *Cronus*, the god of harvests.

400.24 *dout*: 'put out'.

400.27–8 *Well done ... servant*: Matt. 25: 23: the master to the servant who used his talents wisely.

400.29–401.2 *There are sins or ... remote, reproachful*: **Style**: after John Henry, Cardinal Newman (1801–90), essayist and Catholic convert.

401.3–24 *The stranger still regarded ... glad look*: **Style**: after Walter Pater (1839–94), essayist and aesthetic philosopher, especially his memoir, 'The Child in the House' (1878).

401.24 *alles vergängliche*: German: 'all that is transitory'; from Goethe's *Faust*, II (1832), v. vii, final stanza of the play: 'All that is transitory | Is only an image; | The insufficient | Here becomes an event; | The indescribable | Here is achieved; | The eternal feminine | Draws us upward'.

401.25–36 *Mark this farther ... utterance of the Word*: **Style**: after John Ruskin (1819–1900), art critic and aesthetic philosopher, especially his description of St Mark's in *The Stones of Venice* (1851–3). **Embryo**: 'the utterance of the Word' undoubtedly marks the birth of the 'child'.

401.37–403.9 *Burke's! ... nunc est bibendum!*: **Style**: after Thomas Carlyle (1795–1881), Scots essayist and historian. **Embryo**: the 'Tailpiece' of the episode (see headnote).

402.16 *coelum*: Latin: 'the vault of heaven'.

402.17 *cessile*: 'yielding'.

402.23 *Malthusiasts*: followers of the philosophies of Thomas Robert Malthus (1766–1834), social philosopher who argued in his *An Essay on the Principle of Population* (1798; 2nd edn. 1803) that population growth (a geometric progression) inevitably outstripped the resources available from agricultural and economic growth (an arithmetic progression), so population control was necessary or disaster (in the form of plagues, famines) was inevitable.

402.35 *threnes and trentals and jeremies*: all lamentations, elegies, or dirges.

403.1 *transpontine bison*: 'transpontine': 'across the bridge', i.e. across the supposed land bridge connecting eastern and western hemispheres; so, the American buffalo.

403.2 *Deine Kuh Truebsal... Milch des Euters*: German: 'You are milking your cow Affliction. Now you are drinking the sweet milk of her udder.'

403.8 *bonnyclabber*: Gaelic: *bainne clabair*: 'sour thick milk'.

403.8–9 *Per deam Partulam... nunc est bibendum!*: Latin: 'By the goddesses Partula and Pertunda now must we drink'; Partula: the Roman goddess of childbirth; Pertunda: the Roman goddess presiding over the loss of virginity; 'Nunc est bibendum' is the opening phrase of Horace's Ode 37.

403.10–407.7 *All off for a buster... Just you try it on*: **Style**: fragments of dialect and slang; *G* glosses them all. **Embryo**: Janusko suggests that this represents the afterbirth.

403.15 *Benedicat vos omnipotens Deus, Pater et Filius*: Latin: 'May Almighty God, the Father and the Son, bless you'; from the Filial Blessing in the Dismissal portion of the Mass (the phrase 'et Spiritus Sanctus' ('and the Holy Spirit') is omitted here).

403.19–20 *Thence they advanced five parasangs*: after distances remarked in Xenophon's *Anabasis* (see 5.15 n.)—a day's march, *c.* 3½ miles.

403.22–3 *Ma mère m'a mariée*: French: 'My mother married me'; opening of bawdy French song 'Ma mère m'a mariée un mari' ('... to a husband').

403.23 *British Beatitudes!*: after Jesus's Beatitudes ('Blessed are the ...') in the Sermon on the Mount (Matt. 5: 2–11); the British version is listed at 403.28–9.

403.23 *Retamplan Digidi Boum Boum*: nonsense choric refrain often added to 'Ma mère m'a mariée (403.22–3 n.).

404.17 *orchidised*: 'with inflammed testicles'.

404.17 *polycimical*: 'full of varied insects'.

404.25 *Venus Pandemos*: Venus 'of all the people'; originally goddess 'of all the people' of Greece; later the goddess of lust.

405.8–10 *The ruffian cly the nab of Stephen Hand... grahamise*: 'The ruffian ... nab': 17th-c. cant: 'The devil take the head'; Stephen Hand, as *G* claims Joyce explained to his German translator, bribed a telegraph boy to hand over a telegram supposedly carrying inside information on a horse race; he steamed open the telegram ('grahamised' it: after Sir Charles Graham (1792–1861), British Home Secretary who steamed open the correspondence of Giuseppe Mazzini, Italian revolutionary, and conveyed the contents to Austrian ministers), bet on the tipped horse, re-sealed the envelope, sent it on its way, and lost his bet (*G* cites JJ letter to Goyert of 6 Mar. 1927, but this explanation is not included in the letter as published in *LIII* 156); 'coppaleen': Gaelic: *capaillín*: 'little horse'.

405.26–7 *Nos omnes biberimus . . . capiat posterioria nostria*: Latin: 'We will all drink green poison, and the devil take the hindmost' (*G*).

406.19 *The Leith police dismisseth us*: traditional test of sobriety: can this line from the nursery rhyme be clearly articulated?

406.28 *Laetabuntur in cubilibus suis*: Latin: 'Let them sing aloud upon their beds' (Ps. 149: 5).

406.31 *Ut implerentur scripturae*: Latin: 'That the scriptures might be fulfilled'.

406.37 *Alexander J. Christ Dowie*: The evangelist whose 'throwaway' announces the Coming of Elijah (see 144.13 n.).

CIRCE

Location: Bella Cohen's brothel (82 Lower Tyrone Street, though number 81 in the text (F3)). We enter 'nighttown' by way of the Mabbot Street entrance (F3). Stephen and Lynch have come by train from Westland Row station (F4) to Amiens Street station (F3), then have walked along Talbot and Mabbot Streets to Tyrone Street. Bloom, too, has come by train, but he missed the Amiens Street station and has been carried to the next stop. He makes his way back (presumably by the next train) and follows (somewhat later) Stephen and Lynch's route.

Time: Midnight. (*L*: 11–12; *G*: 12 midnight.)

Homer: When narrating his tale to King Alcinous, Odysseus tells of landing on Circe's island ('Aeaea') after having escaped the Lestrygonians. On arriving, Odysseus divided his men into two groups, the first led by himself, the second by Eurylochus. The second he sent to scout the island. Coming upon Circe's palace, they found it surrounded by wild beasts (bewitched by Circe) and the goddess herself inside weaving a web. All entered except Eurylochus, and the 'goddess of braided hair' offered them food into which, unbeknownst to them, she 'intermingled pernicious drugs' (118). Once they had eaten, she waved her wand and turned them into swine. Eurylochus returned to tell Odysseus, who set out to rescue them. On the way, he met Hermes (disguised as a youth) who gave him the magic antidote, the herb *moly*, and advice on how to thwart Circe's charms. Arriving at Circe's palace, Odysseus followed Hermes's wisdom: he took the herb and thus was neither affected by Circe's drugs, nor turned to swine. Instead, seizing his sword, he rushed toward her as if to kill her. Astonished, she nevertheless recognized him as Odysseus whose arrival Hermes had prophesied, pleaded for gentleness, and asked him to her bed. Odysseus made her vow she would plot no more mischief toward him before he would sleep with her. Later her handmaids bathed, anointed, clothed, and fed him. Odysseus refused to eat until his men had been freed from the charm. Circe released the men, then provided a feast for them. Here they stayed until the year was out, when the men, restless for home, urged Odysseus to seek Circe's help in returning to Ithaca. Circe bade

Odysseus first travel to Hades to seek counsel from Tiresias, the blind seer. After the trip to Hades (see *Hades* above), Odysseus returned to Circe's island and sought her advice on how to return to Ithaca. She outlined the necessary route: past the Sirens, past either the Wandering Rocks or Scylla and Charybdis. She also warned him of the danger of slaughtering the sacred Oxen of Helios. Armed with her advice, Odysseus and his men set sail. (Books X and XII)

Schemata: *L* lists as personae Circe, The Swine, Telemachus, Ulysses, Hermes, while *G* provides a correspondence only for Circe: Bella. *L* and *G* differ on virtually everything except, in part, the Organ (*L*: Locomotor apparatus, Skeleton; *G*: Locomotor apparatus). In all else they vary: Art (*L*: Dance; *G*: Magic); Colour (*L*: violet; *G*: none), Technic (*L*: Exploding vision (literally, 'vision animated to the bursting point'); *G*: Hallucination), Symbol (*L*: Zoology, Personification, Pantheism, Magic, Poison, Antidote, Reel; *G*: Whore). *L*'s sense is 'The Man-hating Ogress'.

Joyce's Hints: Regarding the prophylactic herb 'moly', Joyce wrote to Budgen: '"moly" ... can be chance, also laughter, the enchantment killer, the knockout blow delivered at end brings all things back to their sordid reality' (*LI* 144; ?9/20). '*Moly* is a nut to crack. My latest is this. Moly is the gift of Hermes, god of public ways, and is the invisible influence (prayer, chance, agility, *presence of mind*, power of recuperation) which saves in case of accident. This would cover immunity from syphilis.... Hermes is the god of signposts: i.e. he is, specially for a traveller like Ulysses, the point at which roads parallel merge and roads contrary also. He is an accident of providence. In this special case his plant may be said to have many leaves, indifference due to masturbation, pessimism congenital, a sense of the ridiculous, sudden fastidiousness in some detail, experience. It is the only occasion on which Ulysses is not helped by Minerva [Athena] but by her male counterpart or inferior.' In this letter, he further remarks: 'I want to make *Circe* a costume episode also. Bloom for instance appears in five or six different suits' (*LI* 147–8; Michaelmas 1920). Of the repeated musical motif, he writes: 'The whirligig movement in *Circe* is on the refrain *My Girl's a Yorkshire* etc, but to unify the action[,] the preceding *pas seul* of S.D. which I intended to balance on the gramophone of the opposite kip should be on the air of that same ditty played on Mrs Cohen's pianola with lights' (*LI* 151; 10/12/20). Finally, he refers to the entire episode as a '*Walpurgisnacht*' (*LI* 157; 4/2/21). ('*Walpurgisnacht*': according to German legend, the witches' Sabbath, on eve of 1 May; in Goethe's *Faust*, 1 (1808) Mephistopheles takes Faust to this fête.)

Ulysses's most extreme departure from narrative norms arrives with *Circe* which looks like a drama but doesn't act like one. Here buttons, caps, yews speak ('Bip!' 'Bah!' 'Deciduously!'), a rooster lays an egg (squawking 'Gara. Klook. Klook. Klook'), night hours dance (and 'curchycurchy under veils'), Edward the Seventh 'levitates'. Beside this, the appearance of the ghost of Stephen's mother ('Save him from hell, O divine Sacred Heart!') and the transformation of Bloom into a woman ('charming soubrette with dauby cheeks') seem comparatively 'normal'. Indeed, the 'normal' and the 'phantasmagoric' become indistinguishable in *Circe*. As Daniel Ferrer points out, nothing in the formal apparatus of the drama allows us objectively to distinguish between the characters and events we might wish to assign to fantasy and those we might seek to call 'real' ('*Circe*, regret and regression', in Attridge and Ferrer, eds., *Post-Structuralist Joyce: Essays from the French*, 132). The stage directions command all performances (whether Bloom's or button's) in the same deadpan, objective way. And what is it that appears on stage? From the characters' perspectives (most specifically, Stephen's and Bloom's), their most closely held secrets. For them, interiority (whether nightmare, fantasy, memory, or anything repressed) is exteriorized, given an objective reality. Whatever they have sought most actively to internalize, to keep private (even from themselves), hauntingly returns as uncannily familiar, externalized 'hallucination'. This is Freud's 'Return of the Repressed' with a vengeance.

But if Stephen and Bloom cannot (seemingly) distinguish 'hallucination' from 'actual event', no more can the reader. And, just as what they see seems both uncannily familiar *and* strange, the text before us seems oddly simultaneously like and unlike the *Ulysses* we have so far read. For just as Stephen and Bloom re-member their pasts into present drama, *Circe* re-members *Ulysses*'s textual past into present dramatic narrative. The text recirculates its prior self, re-presenting elements in new configurations. So *Cyclops*'s Black Liz reappears as an egg-laying rooster; Gerty MacDowell limps forward 'leering . . . ogling'; Rabaiotti's icecream car (first glimpsed in *Wandering Rocks*) now provides 'wafers between which are wedged lumps of coral and copper snow'. There are literally hundreds of such displaced repetitions. The textual titbits we have ignored or passed over or even repressed return with the accusation (overtly voiced by Virag): 'I presume you shall have remembered what I will have taught you on that head?'

To his grandson Bloom, Virag advocates 'mnemotechnic'—the 'science' of using a system (such as key words, or phrases, or initial letters) to aid the memory. In the mnemonically helpful year 1904, the word 'mneme' was coined (from the Greek μνήμθ: 'memory') by a German psychologist to name 'the capacity which a living substance or organism possesses for retaining after-effects of experience or stimulation undergone by itself or its progenitors' (*OED Supplement*, 'Mneme'). Within *Ulysses*, itself such a 'living substance or organism', *Circe* employs textual mnemotechnics to draw our readerly attention to *Ulysses*'s, Stephen's, Bloom's and our own 'mneme'. To paraphrase Virag, 'We will all surely remember'; if not, it will surely return.

Various literary and psychological texts fed Joyce's imagination in his writing of *Circe*. Those with the greatest influence on the episode—those a reading of which would prove most useful—are (with the edition used if the texts are cited in the notes below): Gustave Flaubert (1821–80), *The Temptation of Saint Antony* (1874), trans. Kitty Mrosovsky (1980; repr. Harmondsworth: Penguin, 1983); Johann Wolfgang von Goethe (1749–1832), *Faust*, I and II (1808; 1832); Henrik Ibsen (1828–1906), *Ghosts* (1881); Richard von Krafft-Ebing (1840–1902), *Psychopathia Sexualis* (1886); Leopold von Sacher-Masoch (1836–95), *Venus in Furs* (written 1870, pub. 1904), trans. Uwe Moeller and Laura Lindgren (1928; repr. New York: Blast, 1989); August Strindberg (1849–1912), *Ghost Sonata* (1907).

408.1 *nighttown*: Joyce's name for Dublin's prostitution district, north of the Liffey, west of the Amiens Street railway station (F3).

408.6 *of coal and*: should read '*of coral and*'.

408.17 *Kithogue*: Gaelic: *ciotóg*: 'left-handed person'.

410.18–19 *the introit for paschal time*: the entrance chant of the Mass sung in the period between Easter and Pentecost ('paschal time'), a Mass of celebration.

410.22 *Vidi aquam egredientem . . . Alleluia*: Latin: 'I saw a stream of water welling forth from the right of the temple. Alleluia!'; not the introit for paschal time, but the opening phrase of the antiphon sung with asperges (the sprinkling of the altar with holy water) for paschal. Stephen continues the antiphon at 410.29 and 411.14.

410.29 *(Altius aliquantulum.) . . . aqua ista*: Latin: '(With great profundity.) And all among them came to the water'; see 410.22 n.

411.14 *(Triumphaliter.) Salvi facti i sunt*: should read '*facti sunt*'; Latin: '(Triumphantly.) And they are made whole'; see 410.22 n.

411.22 *the gift of tongues*: the manifestation of the Holy Spirit to the Apostles on the day of Pentecost (Acts 2: 4).

411.22–3 *the first entelechy . . . structural rhythm*: for a discussion of Joyce's theories of 'rhythm', see Jacques Aubert, *Aesthetics of James Joyce*, 69–70, 89–93. For 'entelechy', see 182.12 n. See also *CW* 145.

411.27–8 *Even the allwisest stagyrite . . . by a light of love*: Aristotle (born at Stageira); after a print of Aristotle by Hans Baldung (1476–1545) (*G*); Aristotle, Stephen suggests, was the victim of a woman's love (probably that of his mistress Herpyllis).

412.5 *the loaf . . . in Omar*: after the most famous line of Edward Fitzgerald's (1809–83) translation of *The Rubáiyát of Omar Khayyám* (1859).

412.10 *la belle dame sans merci*: French: 'the beautiful merciless woman'; the title of a poem (1819) by John Keats (1795–1821).

412.10–11 *ad deam qui laetificat juventutem meam*: Latin: 'to the goddess who has gladdened the days of my youth'; by the change of a letter (from 'Deum' to 'deam') Stephen has blasphemed: the response to the Introit in the Mass is 'ad Deum . . .' ('to God . . .').

413.4 *bonham*: dialect: 'young pig'.

414.26 *The Providential*: a London-based insurance firm.

415.4 *Mark of the beast*: see Rev. 13: 1, 16–17; 'the beast' is the beast with seven heads and ten horns.

415.7–8 *a visage unknown, injected with dark mercury*: literally, mercury used to be injected to cure syphilis; metaphorically, Mercury (Gk. Hermes), the messenger from the gods who greets Odysseus as he approaches Circe's palace and gives him the prophylactic herb 'moly'.

415.11 *Bueñas noches, señorita Blanca, que calle es esta?*: Spanish: 'Good evening, Miss White, what street is this?'

415.13 *Sraid Mabbot*: Gaelic: *Sráid*: 'Street'; so Mabbot Street.

415.15 *Slan leath*: Gaelic: *slán leat*: 'safe with you', 'good-bye'.

415.15 *Gaelic league*: see 135.26 n.

415.20 *I beg*: following this, insert (as new line) '(*He leaps right, sackragman right.*)', followed by (as new line) 'BLOOM', followed by (as new line) 'I beg'.

415.23 *fingerpost*: should read 'signpost'.

416.4 *hands watch, fobpocket, bookpocket, pursepoke*: should read '*hands watchfob, pocketbookpocket, pursepoke*'.

416.19 *Ja, ich weiss, papachi*: German: 'Yes, I know, papa'.

417.12 *Goim nachez!*: Yiddish: 'The proud pleasure of the gentiles!' (an indictment).

417.16 *mobcap, crinoline and bottle, widow Twankey's*: should read '*mobcap, Widow Twankey's crinoline and bottle*'.

417.21 *an Agnus Dei*: Latin: 'Lamb of God'; a religious badge bearing the image of a lamb (representing Jesus).

417.30–418.3 *Beside her mirage . . . raven hair*: compare Flaubert's description of the Queen of Sheba in *St Antony*, ch. 2, pp. 83–4.

418.20 *Nebrakada! Feminimum!*: should read 'Femininum!'; see 233.8 and n.

419.20 *Ti trema un poco il cuore?*: after Zerlina's line in her duet with Don Giovanni (see 61.33 n. and 90.23 n.); here, Italian: 'Does your heart tremble a little?'

421.24 *the bones and cornerman at the Livermore christies*: music-hall act of white men in black face performing a 'minstrel show'; 'christies' after the Christy Minstrels (*c.* 1843), the most famous such group.

422.26 *the Irving Bishop game*: a 'mind-reading' game named after Washing Irving Bishop (1847–89), an American magician.

423.8–12 *I confess I'm teapot . . . teapot all over me*: guessing game involving the substitution of one word (here 'teapot') for another to be guessed (here 'burning').

423.19 *Là ci darem la mano*: see 61.20 n.

423.23 *Voglio e non*: see 61.33 n.

425.11 *deluthering*: G and O Hehir (somewhat hesitantly) suggest 'fawning, cringing, making up to' from the Gaelic: *lútáil*; but I suspect it to be Joyce's neologistic anglicization (by means of a simple consonant shift from '*d*' to '*th*') of the Latin *deludere* (root of 'delude'): 'to mock at, banter, deceive' (especially 'to deceive'); the French translation has '*à blaguer et à tromper*' ('joking and deceiving') for 'Humbugging and deluthering' (*Ulysse*, II, 145). (See 389.2 where Bloom is referred to as a 'deluder'.)

427.20 *Spattered with size and lime of their lodges*: the first of many Masonic images in *Circe* in keeping with Bloom's (past?) membership (*G*).

427.26 *Glauber salts*: sodium sulphate, used medicinally as a purgative.

430.4 *Chacun son goût*: French: 'Everyone to his own taste'.

430.18 *Bloom... Bloom*: the declension of the (supposedly 'Latin') noun 'Bloom'; in order: nominative, genitive, dative, (most appropriately) accusative.

431.31–2 *von Bloom Pasha*: should read 'von Blum Pasha'.

431.32 *Donnerwetter!*: German: 'thunderstorm'; also used as curse (as Joyce, a hater of thunderstorms, would be likely to use it).

433.4–5: *plucking at his heart... fellowcraft*: Freemason 'distress signal'; 'fellowcraft': the second degree (of three) in Freemasonry.

433.6 *worshipful master, light of love*: 'master': highest degree in Freemasonry; 'light of love': see 183.15–16n.

433.6–7 *The Lyons mail. Lesurques and Dubosc*: Charles Reade's (1814–84) play *The Lyons Mail* (adapted from a French play), about an actual case of mistaken identity: in 1796, Joseph Lesurques (1763–96) was executed for the crime of holding up the Lyons mail coach; in 1800 Duboscq (who bore a striking resemblance to the now-dead Lesurques) was discovered actually to have committed the crime; he too was executed (*T* and *G*).

433.16 *the past of Ephraim.) Shitbroleeth*: should read 'the pass of Ephraim'; in Judg. 12: 1–6, Jephthah, in need of a password to distinguish the Israelites from the captured Ephraimites, chose the Hebrew word 'shibboleth' which the Ephraimites could not pronounce; the bad pun is obvious.

433.26–7 *Got his majority... Rorke's Drift*: a battle at the beginning of the Zulu War, Jan. 1879 (Britain invaded Zululand), in which *c.*140 British troops successfully defended a communications post against *c.*4,000 Zulu troops.

434.9 *in the absentminded war under general Gough in the park*: 'the absentminded war': the Boer War (1899–1902) (after Kipling's verse 'The Absentminded Beggar', see 179.30n.); 'general Gough in the park': Irish-born General Hugh Gough (1779–1869), veteran of the Peninsular Wars (1808–14) against Napoleon, an equestrian statue of him stood in Phoenix Park; not the same as the Gough who fought in the Boer War (see *G*).

434.10 *Spion Kop ... Bloemfontein*: 'Spion Kop': mountain in Natal, site of important Boer victory (Jan. 1900); 'Bloemfontein': capital of Orange Free State, South Africa, Boer stronghold until it fell to the British in March 1900.

434.11–12 *Jim Bludso. Hold her nozzle again the bank*: should read 'against'; 'Jim Bludso': a ballad by American John Hay (1838–1905), about a Mississippi riverboat captain who died holding the prow of his burning boat against the bank to allow the passengers to escape.

435.17–18 *My literary agent Mr J. B. Pinker*: J. B. Pinker was Joyce's London literary agent (*JJ* 384).

435.20 *jackdaw of Rheims*: verse legend in Richard Harris Barham's (1788–1845) *The Ingoldsby Legends* (1840) in which a jackdaw who steals, then admits to having stolen, a cardinal's ring is canonized as 'Jem Crow'.

435.26–7 *corpus delicti*: Latin: 'body of offence'; the facts constituting a breach of law.

438.8 *pensums*: 'homework or lessons'.

438.10 *boreens*: Gaelic: *bóthairín*: 'little roads'.

439.6 *Prima facie*: Latin: 'first face': at first glance; evidence which appears conclusive on first examination.

441.1 MRS YELVERTON BARRY: after Barry Yelverton, first Viscount Avonmore (1736–1805), Irish self-made man, teacher, KC, member of Irish Parliament, Attorney-General (1782), created an Irish Viscount for his vigorous support of Union (1800).

441.8 *La Cigale*: *La Cigale et la Fourmi* ('The Grasshopper and the Ant'): an opera (1886; English adaptation, 1890) by Henry Chivot, Alfred Duru, and Edmond Audran, based on La Fontaine's famous fable of the hardworking ant and the frivolous grasshopper.

441.10 *Dunsink time*: it was, of course, at half past four on *this* Thursday, 16 June, that Molly and Blazes Boylan 'misconducted' themselves.

441.11–12 *Paul de Kock... Three Pairs of Stays*: actual novel (1878) by Paul de Kock (see 62.27 n).

441.27 *Bluebeard*: legendary murderer of several wives; see Charles Perrault's (1628–1703) version in *Histoires ou Contes du tems passé* (1697).

442.1 *Venus in furs*: *Venus im Pelz* (written 1870, pub. 1904), a novel by Leopold von Sacher-Masoch (1836–94), who gave his name to 'masochism'; the protagonist, Severin, desires to be enslaved and humiliated by his beloved, Wanda, who (reluctantly at first) agrees; she comes to enjoy her role as sadist.

443.9 *I'll make you dance Jack Latten*: legendary Irishman who bet he could dance the more-than-twenty miles home, changing step every furlong; he won (P. W. Joyce, 172–3).

444.31 *the featureless face of a Nameless One*: after 'The Nameless One', a poem by James Clarence Mangan, the protagonist of which 'pawned his soul for the Devil's dismal'; but also, of course, the narrator of *Cyclops*.

445.21–2 *From his forehead ... Mosaic ramshorns*: Sir Frederick Falkiner (see 174.16 n.) appears as Michelangelo's *Moses* (see 134.21 n.); the statue depicts Moses horned because of a mistranslation in the Vulgate Bible of Exod. 34: 29 ('his face shone' has become 'his face was horned').

447.17 *Bloom, I am... list, O list*: after the Ghost in *Hamlet*, I. v. 9, 22.

447.19 *The voice is the voice of Esau*: for 'Esau' see 203.8 n.; but also see 73.27–31 n.

448.11 *a staff of twisted poppies*: Morpheus, god of sleep, carries such a staff.

448.13 *Namine. Jacobs Vobiscuits. Amen*: see 100.1; 'Jacobs Vobiscuits': after Jacob's Biscuits, Bloom-Latin for *Dominus vobiscum*: 'the Lord be with you'.

449.4 *a daredevil salmon leap*: one of the favourite tricks of Cúchulainn, legendary (1st c. AD) 'hound of Ulster' and Celtic hero *par excellence*; see 284.30.

449.6 *Bloom plodges forward again. He stands*: should read '*Bloom plodges forward again through the sump. Kisses chirp amid the rifts of fog. A piano sounds. He stands*'.

451.2 *I never loved a dear gazelle but it was sure to . . .*: after Thomas Moore's *Lalla Rookh* (see 71.29–30n.), sect. 3, ll. 283–6: 'I never nursed a dear gazelle, | To glad me with its soft black eye, | But when it came to know me well, | And love me, it was sure to die!'; though see also Dickens's parody of these lines in *The Old Curiosity Shop*, ch. 56, where Dick Swiveller says 'I never nursed . . . and love me, it was sure to marry a market-gardener'.

451.6 *womancity*: Jerusalem; from, among others, Blake's description in *The Four Zoas* (written and revised 1797–1804), 'Night the Ninth' ll. 220–2: '[T]he Lamb of God creates himself a bride & wife | That we his Children evermore may live in Jerusalem | Which now descendeth out of heaven, a City, yet a Woman' (Keynes ed.); see, too, Rev. 21: 2: 'And I John saw the holy city, new Jerusalem, coming down from God out of heaven, prepared as a bride adorned for her husband'.

451.13 *Schorach ani wenowach . . . Hierushaloim*: bad Hebrew for S. of S. 1: 5: 'I am black, but comely, O ye daughters of Jerusalem'.

451.26 *swaggerroot*: 'cigarette'.

452.13 *Turn again, Leopold . . . Dublin!*: after nursery tale of 'Dick Whittington and his Cat' where the bells of Bow Church say, 'Turn again, Whittington, | Thrice Lord Mayor of London'.

452.18 *Cui bono?*: Latin: 'Whom does it benefit?'

452.18–19 *Vanderdeckens in their phantom ship of finance*: 'Vanderdecken': The Flying Dutchman (in English versions of the legend), condemned to sail forever in a phantom ship; 'of finance': links Vanderdecken to Cornelius Vanderbilt (1794–1877), American financier.

453.16–17 *their reign is rover for rever and ever and ev . . .* : after Rev. 11: 15: 'he [Christ] shall reign for ever and ever'; used by Handel as a refrain in the 'Hallelujah Chorus' in his *Messiah* (see 174.28–9n.).

453.19 *Cead Mile Failte*: Gaelic: *Céad Míle Fáilte*: 'A hundred thousand welcomes'.

453.19–20 *Mah Ttob Melek Israel*: Hebrew: 'How beautiful is thy king, O Israel'.

453.27 *Kol Nidre*: Hebrew: 'All vows'; prayer chanted on the eve of Yom Kippur (see 145.8n.) to annul all previous vows in preparation for the ceremony of cleansing.

453.31 *John Howard Parnell . . .* : most of the city officials and churchmen in the list that follows derive from actual offices (and real officers), though the Chief Rabbinate for Ireland was not created until 1919. (*G* provides full glosses.)

453.33–4 *mayor of Dublin, the lord mayor*: should read '*mayor of Dublin, his lordship the lord mayor*'.

454.10 *guilds and trades and trainbands*: the traditional groups of craftsmen who enjoyed special privileges in London and participated in ceremonial occasions;

Bloom's installation as Lord Mayor becomes a parodic 'coronation', after the manner of the coronation of Edward VII in 1901, and of Arthur Griffith's description of Franz Joseph's coronation in his *The Resurrection of Hungary* (see 323.10 n.); the tokens or symbols of authority are likewise actual (see *G* for full glosses).

454.33–6 *The wren, the wren ... caught in the furze*: traditional chant for St Stephen's Day (26 Dec.), when Irish children 'seek a penny to bury the wren' (the bird of the old year).

456.2 *placing his right hand on his testicles, swears*: ancient form of oath-swearing (or '*testi*fying'); see e.g. Gen. 24: 2–3.

456.5–6 *Gaudium magnum ... carneficem*: Latin: 'A great joy I announce to you. We have an executioner'; after the formula for the announcement of a new pope: *Annuntio vobis gaudium magnum: habemus pontificem* [or *papem*]' (*T*).

456.20–1 *nominate our faithful ... Grand Vizier*: Bloom, like the Roman emperor Caligula (12–41 AD), elevates his horse to public office; 'Copula felix': Latin: 'the fortunate bond' (parodic of *felix culpa*: 'the fortunate fall' (of Adam and Eve)).

456.22 *Selene*: in Greek myth, the goddess of the moon and sister of Helios; an early version of Artemis.

457.10 *Ladysmith*: town in Natal, site of long siege of the British by the Boers (29 Jan. 1899–28 Feb. 1900); the British finally won; Bloom, of course, has his dates wrong, and, from the standpoint of Irish nationalist politics, supports the wrong side (*T* and *G*).

457.11 *Half a league onward!*: from Tennyson's 'Charge of the Light Brigade' (1854) which celebrates the foolhardy heroism of the British at Balaclava (25 Oct. 1854) in the Crimean War (1853–6).

457.14 *Bonafide Sabaoth*: 'Bonafide': Latin: 'good faith', 'genuine'; 'Sabaoth': Greek form of the Hebrew *tsebâôth*: 'armies' (often 'hosts').

458.11 *Morituri te salutant*: Latin: 'They [who are] about to die salute you'; Roman gladiators' statement to Caesar on entering the arena.

458.13 *elongated figure*: should read '*elongated finger*'.

458.30–1 *the World's Twelve Worst Books*: all apparently fictitious.

459.5 *Women press forward ... hem of Bloom's robe*: see Matt. 9: 20, where the diseased woman 'touched the hem of [Christ's] garment', seeking, in so doing, to be made whole.

460.4 *The ram's horns ... standard of Zion*: the Israelites' battle trumpet, the *shofar*, was made from rams' horns; 'the standard of Zion': emblem of the Israelites' status as God's chosen people.

460.7 *Aleph Beth Ghimel Daleth*: first four letters of the Hebrew alphabet: א, ב, ג, ד.

460.7 *Hagadah*: see 118.11 n.

460.7 *Tephilim*: see 361.16–17 n.

460.7 *Yom Kippur*: see 145.8 n.

460.7 *Hanukah*: 'Hannukah': the Feast of Dedication, in commemoration of the rededication of the Temple and altar after the victory of Judah of Maccabee over Antiochus Epiphanes, an eight-day celebration.

460.8 *Roschaschana*: 'Rosh Hashana': the two-day holiday celebrating the Jewish new year.

460.8 *Beni Brith*: 'B'nai B'rith': Hebrew: 'sons of the covenant', Jewish fraternity (from 1843).

460.8 *Bar Mitzvah*: Hebrew: 'son of command'; ceremonial celebration of Jewish male's coming of age (at 13).

460.8 *Mazzoth*: Hebrew: 'unleavened'; the bread eaten during Passover.

460.8 *Askenazim*: the Jews of eastern Europe (as opposed to the Sephardim, the Jews of Spain and Portugal).

460.8 *Meshuggah*: see 152.21 n.

460.8 *Talith*: prayer shawl worn by Jewish men.

460.27 *A Daniel did I say?*: after *The Merchant of Venice*, IV. i. 223, 333, 340: when the disguised Portia wisely intervenes in the legal battle between Antonio and Shylock, she is compared to Daniel, the youth who acts as judge when Susannah is accused by the Elders (in the Apocryphal story of Susannah and the Elders); Portia, like Daniel, succeeds in turning the tables on the accusers.

460.27 *A Peter O'Brien*: (1842–1914), Lord Chief Justice of Ireland, thought to be hostile to nationalists, suspected of packing the juries (hence 'Peter the Packer', 285.6), unpopular, but grudgingly admitted to be a perceptive judge (*G*).

462.12–13 *Three acres and a cow*: the demand (and hence slogan) of those seeking Irish land reform.

462.17 *esperanto the universal brotherhood*: should read 'esperanto the universal language with universal brotherhood'.

463.2 *the new nine muses*: 'new' not only in their function, but also in their number—here, twelve; the originals: Calliope (epic poetry), Clio (history), Polyhymnia (mime), Euterpe (flute), Terpsichore (light verse and dance), Erato (lyric choral poetry, esp. love poetry), Melpomene (tragedy), Talia (comedy), Urania (astronomy).

463.8 *an anythingarian*: see Swift's *Polite Conversation* (1738), first conversation; Lady Smart: 'What Religion is he of?' Lord Sparkish: 'Why; he is an Anythingarian'; many of the proverbial or cliché phrases in *Circe* come from this source; see *T*.

464.20 *this stinking goat of Mendes*: one of the three sacred animals of ancient Egypt, symbolic of generative power.

464.22–3 *white bull . . . Scarlet Woman*: there is no white bull in Revelation (the Christian Apocalypse); the 'Scarlet Woman': the 'Whore of Babylon' (Rev. 17: 4–5).

464.29 *condensed milk tins*: when first produced, tinned condensed milk was routinely stripped of all its nutritional value; the consequent malnutrition among children of the poor led to a scandal and ultimately to legislation controlling the milk's production.

465.3 *guiltless as the unsunned snow*: Posthumus of Imogen in *Cymbeline*, II. v. 12–13: 'I thought her | As chaste as unsunn'd snow'.

465.5 *sgenl inn ban bata coisde gan capall*: should read '*sgeul im barr bata coisde gan capall*'; Gaelic: *sgéal i mbarr bata cóisde gan capall*: 'a pointless tale is a horseless coach'.

465.22 *Hypsospadia*: 'hypospadias': 'malformation consisting in a fissure of the lower wall of the male urethra' (*OED*).

465.29 *fetor judaicus*: Latin: 'Jewish stench'.

465.31–2 *the new womanly man*: according to Ellmann, an idea Joyce borrows from Otto Weininger's (1880–1903) *Sex and Character* (1903), a virulently sexist and anti-Semitic 'study' which suggested that Jews were feminine, non-men (*JJ* 463).

466.6 *hairshirt winter*: should read 'hairshirt of pure Irish manufacture winter'.

466.24 *All are*: should read '*All the octuplets are*'.

466.27–9 *Nasodoro . . . Panargyros*: the offspring are all named for 'precious' metals: *Nasodoro*: Italian: 'golden nose'; *Chrysostomos*: Greek: 'golden mouthed'; *Maindorée*: French: 'golden handed'; *Silberselber*: German: 'silverself'; *Vifargent*: French: 'quicksilver'; *Panargyros*: Greek: 'allsilver'.

466.33 *the Messiah ben Joseph or ben David*: in Jewish apocalyptic legends, the Messiah of the House of Joseph will prepare the way for the true Messiah of the House of David who will bring rebirth to the world.

467.2 *You have said it*: Luke 23: 3: when accused by the elders of claiming to be 'Christ a King', Jesus answers, 'Thou sayest it'.

467.4 *a miracle*: should read 'a miracle like Father Charles'.

467.11 *Lord Beaconsfield*: Benjamin Disraeli (1804–81), novelist, statesman, and Prime Minister (1868, 1874–80), of Italian-Jewish descent.

467.11–12 *Wat Tyler*: (d. 1381), leader of the Peasants' Revolt in 1381, ill-fated uprising against poor economic conditions and repressive legislation under Richard II.

467.12 *Moses Maimonides*: see 28.25 n.

467.12 *Moses Mendelssohn*: see 327.26 n.

467.13 *Henry Irving*: (1838–1905), famous English actor.

467.13 *Rip Van Winkle*: see 360.9–10 n.

467.13 *Kossuth*: Lajos Kossuth (1802–94), Hungarian reformer and a leader of the Hungarian revolution (1848–9).

467.13 *Jean Jacques Rousseau*: (1712–78), French political philosopher.

467.14: *Baron Leopold Rothschild*: (1845–1917), Jewish banker, son of Baron Lionel Nathan de Rothschild (1808–79), first Jewish MP.

467.14 *Sherlock Holmes*: famous detective created by Sir Arthur Conan Doyle (1859–1930) in his 1887 story 'A Study in Scarlet'.

467.15–16 *bids the tide turn back*: after the legend recounted in Holinshed of King Canute (?995–1035), Danish king of England, who in response to fawning courtiers claiming he was all-powerful, set his throne on the seashore and 'bid the tide turn back'; when it didn't, he pointed the lesson of his own human limitations.

467.17 *BRINI, PAPAL NUNCIO*: for Brini, see 308.6; a 'papal nuncio' is an ambassador for the pope.

467.21 *Leopoldi autem generatio*: after Matt. 1: 18 (describing the birth of Jesus): Latin: 'Now the generation of Leopold'; what follows is a mock genealogy modelled on those in the Bible (*cf.* Matt. 1: 1–17). *G* glosses the jokes.

467.33–4 *et vocabitur nomen eius Emmanuel*: Latin: 'and shall call his name Emmanuel'; from Isa. 7: 14: 'Behold, a virgin shall conceive, and bear a son, and shall call his name Immanuel'.

468.1–2 A DEADHAND *(Writes on the wall.)*: 'Deadhand': literal meaning of *mortmain* (legal term for lands held inalienably by ecclesiastical bodies; so symbolic of absolute ecclesiastical authority); at Belshazzar's Feast, 'fingers of a man's hand' write on the wall a message which only Daniel can interpret: that Belshazzar's days are numbered, he has been weighed and 'found wanting', and his kingdom will be divided among the Medes and the Persians (Dan. 5: 5–8, 25–8).

468.13 *Sjambok*: Afrikaans: 'to whip with a heavy rhinoceros-hide whip'.

468.15 *Don Giovanni, a cenar teco*: see 171.17–18 n.

468.22–5 *If you see kay . . . Tell him from me*: a vulgar acrostic: 'F. U. C. K. | Tell him he may | C. U. N. T. | Tell him from me'.

468.27 *ephod*: garment decorated with sacred symbols, worn by the high priests in the Old Testament.

468.27–8 *And he shall carry . . . in the wilderness*: 'Azazel' (Hebrew: 'dismissal'), the symbolic scapegoat used in ceremonies to receive the sins of the people; see Lev. 16: 8, 10, 26.

469.2 *Mizraim, the land of Ham*: 'Mizraim': Old Testament name for Egypt; also (in Ps. 78: 51) called 'the land of Ham' after Noah's son who was cursed for having looked upon his father when he was drunk and naked (Gen. 9: 21–5).

469.8 *Belial*: associated with Satan; 'the sons of Belial': those who would lead the Israelites to idolatry (Deut. 13: 13; Judg. 19: 20).

469.8 *Laemlein of Istria*: Jewish heretic who appeared in Istria (near Venice) and proclaimed himself a herald of the Messiah (1502).

469.8 *Messiah! Abulafia!* : should read 'Messiah! Abulafia! Recant!'; 'Abulafia': Abraham Ben Samuel Abulafia (1240–*c.*1291), Spanish Jew who proclaimed himself the Messiah and attempted to convert Pope Nicholas III.

470.3 *Weep not for me, O daughters of Erin*: after Jesus's statement to the women weeping at his crucifixion: 'Daughters of Jerusalem, weep not for me' (Luke 23: 28).

470.8–19 *Kidney of Bloom . . . Pestilence, pray for us*: parody of a Catholic litany, especially the Litany of the Sacred Heart (e.g. 'Heart of Jesus . . . have mercy on us'); summary of Bloom's episodes so far.

470.14 *Sweets of Sin*: see 226.21 and n.

470.15 *Music without Words*: see 274.2 n.

470.21 *the Alleluia chorus, accompanied*: should read '*the chorus from Handel's Messiah* Alleluia for the Lord God omnipotent reigneth, *accompanied*'.

470.26–8 *In caubeen with clay . . . smile in his eye*: Bloom as the stereotypical 'stage Irishman'.

471.6 *A cork and bottle*: should read 'A cork and bottle. I'm sick of it. Let everything rip.'

471.27 *sugaun*: Gaelic: *súgán*: 'hay or straw rope'.

472.10–11 *her forefinger giving . . . secret monitor*: clearly here a sign of willingness to have sex, but 'the pass touch of secret monitor' is also a Masonic secret signal warning of impending danger.

472.26 *The just man falls seven times*: Prov. 24: 16: 'For a just man falleth seven times, and riseth up again; but the wicked shall fall into mischief'.

474.20–1 *whether Benedetto Marcello found it or made it*: Benedetto Marcello (1686–1739), Italian composer who set paraphrases of the Psalms to music; claimed he tried to find actual ancient Hebrew settings to compose from.

474.21–2 *an old hymn to Demeter*: 'Demeter': goddess of fertility and agriculture; the hymn, a 7th-c. BC 'Homeric Hymn' supposedly celebrating the Eleusinian mysteries (*G* and *T*).

474.22 *Cœla enarrant gloriam Domini*: Latin: 'The heavens declare the glory of the Lord', adaptation of Ps. 19: 1.

474.23 *hyperphrygian and mixolydian*: two 'modes' (or 'keys') of ancient Greek music; each 'mode' was thought expressive of particular emotions; the (properly) 'hypophrygian' was thought frenetic, the 'mixolydian' ordered yet tender (*G*).

474.25 *Ceres*: the Roman counterpart of the Greek Demeter: goddess of the harvest.

474.27 *Jetez la gourme . . . jeunesse se passe*: French: 'Sow wild oats. Youth must pass.'

475.20–3 *having itself traversed . . . preconditioned to become. Ecco!*: Stephen revisits the theory he articulated earlier (see e.g. 204.29–30 and n.); for 'Damn that fellow's noise in the street', compare 34.26, 29, and Prov. 1: 20–2: 'Wisdom crieth without; she uttereth her voice in the streets . . . How long, ye simple ones, will ye love simplicity? and the scorners delight in their scorning, and fools hate knowledge?'; 'Ecco!': Latin: 'Behold!'.

476.15 *A time, times and half a time*: from Rev. 12: 13–14, the length of time for which 'the woman which brought forth the man child' is 'nourished . . . from the face of the serpent'.

476.22 *hydrocephalic, prognatic*: should read '*prognathic*': possessing a projecting jaw; 'hydrocephalic': possessing an enlarged head as the result of excess fluid within the brain.

476.30–477.1 *Il vient!... primigène*: French: 'He comes! It's me! The laughing man! The primordial man!'

477.1–2 *Sieurs et dames, faites vos jeux!*: French: 'Gents and ladies, place your bets!'

477.3 *Les jeux sont faits!*: French: 'The bets are made!'

477.4 *Rien n'va plus*: French: 'Nothing more goes'.

477.12–14 *Jerusalem!... Hosanna*: after the chorus of Frederick Edward Weatherly and Stephen Adams's (1892) song 'The Holy City': 'Jerusalem, Jerusalem, | Lift up your gates and sing, | Hosanna in the highest, | Hosanna to your king'.

477.20 *the Three Legs of Man*: three human legs joined at the thigh; emblem of Mananaan (see 38.31–2 n.) and of the Isle of Man.

477.28 *ELIJAH*: see 144.13 n.

478.5 *Be on the side of the angels*: speaking against Darwin's theories in 1864, Disraeli proclaimed, 'The question is this: is man an ape or an angel? I, my lord, am on the side of the angels' (*T*).

478.7 *Guatama*: Siddharta Gautama, the name of Buddha.

478.7 *Ingersoll*: Robert Ingersoll (1833–99), American politician, orator, passionate agnostic and defender of scientific rationalism (*G*).

478.26–31 *certainly, I sort of believe... ain't saying nothing*: see *T* for an argument that this pastiche of American speech parodies e.g. Gertrude Stein's (1874–1946) *Melanctha* (1909) and Joel Chandler Harris's (1848–1908) Uncle Remus stories.

479.1 *confirmed by the bishop. My*: should read 'confirmed by the bishop and enrolled in the brown scapular. My'.

479.9 *In the beginning was the word... without end*: John 1: 1: 'In the beginning was the Word, and the Word was with God, and the Word was God'; 'world without end': from the Gloria Patri (see 29.29 n.).

479.10–16 *eight beatitudes... buggerum bishop*: see 403.28–9; as with everything met again in *Circe*, the 'British beatitudes' have changed a bit since their earlier appearance; 'buybull': not only Bible, but 'buy [John] Bull', i.e. 'buy English'.

479.26 *A thing of beauty*: the opening of Keats's *Endymion* (1818): 'A thing of beauty is a joy forever'.

479.28 *JOHN EGLINTON*: Eglinton (W. K. Magee (see 176.17 n.)) appears in the guise of Diogenes the Cynic (412–323 BC) who reputedly carried a lantern even during the daytime to aid him in his search for one honest man (*G*).

480.4 *Mananann Mac Lir*: see 38.31–2 n.

480.10 *Aum! Hek! Wal! Ak! Lub! Mor! Ma!*: in AE's theory of the origins of human speech, these sounds appear with their corresponding hypothesized meanings; see *G* for a defence of the argument that Joyce orders the sounds here to suggest the progression of sexual intercourse.

480.10–11 *White yoghin of the Gods*: in this speech, Mananaan utters Theosophical 'nonsense' mainly concerning the differences between the male (right) and female (left) principles; 'white yoghin of the gods': the white stone awarded to a successful initiate into the precepts of Theosophy; 'Punarjanam': *Punarjanman*: both rebirth and the power for creating 'objective' manifestations; 'Shakti': the Hindu female deity, generative energy, left hand; 'Shiva': *Siva*: one of the two principal Hindu male deities, darkness, asceticism, the Destroyer, often paired with Shakti; 'I am the light . . . butter': see 178.4–5 n.; for AE, see 31.8, 9 n. and 379.28–30 n. (*G*).

480.11 *Hermes Trismegistos*: legendary great mage (ostensibly combining the Greek Hermes and the Egyptian Thoth); supposed author of numerous treatises which combine Neoplatonism, cabbalistic theories, Judaism, astrology, and alchemy; 'pimander': *Poimandres*: a Hermetic book, after the higher being who appears to Hermes and reveals occult esoteric truths to him (*T*).

481.16 *an Egyptian pshent*: the double crown of the rulers of Egypt.

481.24 *Grandpapachi*: Yiddish: 'grandfather'; Virag's predilection for home remedies, popular science, garbled half-knowledge has clearly left an impact on the only slightly more sceptical and better-informed Bloom.

481.31 *Hippogrif*: fabulous beast with head of a griffin and body of a horse.

482.13 *bachelor's button discovered by Rualdus Columbus*: the clitoris, which the anatomist Rualdus Columbus (1516–59) claimed to have discovered.

483.6 *Lycopodium*: fine powder from the spores of club moss, used in medicine (and in the making of fireworks).

483.10–11 *Argumentum ad feminam*: Latin: 'argument to the woman'; an *ad hominem* argument is the logical fallacy of attempting to refute an argument by attacking the arguer rather than the argument.

483.24 *mnemotechnic*: the 'science' of memory.

483.32–3 *priapic pulsatilla*: pasqueflower (*Anemone pulsatilla*), the oil of which was believed to be an aphrodisiac.

484.5 *to square the circle and win that million*: a mathematical impossibility (as proved in 1882); see Kenner, 166–7; note that ERRATA changes the date to '1886'.

484.18 *pudendal verve*: should read 'pudendal nerve'.

484.30 *Charley! Buzz!*: should read 'Charley! (*He blows in Bloom's ear.*) Buzz!'

485.9 *virigitis*: supposed masculine characteristics in a woman.

485.11 *my ocular*: should read 'my ocular. (*He sneezes.*) Amen!'.

485.18 *Elephantuliasis*: conflation of elephantiasis (skin disease causing enlargement of limbs) with Elephantis, Greek writer of erotica, supposed to have been a woman.

485.30–1 *Who's Ger Ger? Who's dear Gerald? O, I much fear*: should read 'Who's moth moth? Who's dear Gerald? Dear Ger, that you? O dear, he is Gerald. O, I much fear'.

485.33 *Luss*: should read 'Puss'.

485.34 *rest anon.*: should read 'rest anon. (*He snaps his jaws suddenly in the air.*)'.

486.21–2 *There is a flower that bloometh*: song from Wallace and Fitzball's *Maritana* (see 83.18–19n.).

486.24–5 *Filling my belly with husks of swine . . . I will arise and go to my*: both phrases occur in the parable of the Prodigal Son: Luke 15: 16: 'he would fain have filled his belly with the husks that the swine did eat'; Luke 15: 18: 'I will arise and go to my father, and I will say unto him, Father, I have sinned against heaven and before thee'.

487.2 *Ci rifletta. Lei rovina tutto*: Italian: 'Think it over. You ruin everything.'

487.10 *Philip Drunk and Philip Sober*: 'to appeal from Philip drunk to Philip sober': proverbial: to seek a different judgement once circumstances have changed; after a tale of Philip of Macedon having reversed a judgement made in drunkenness once he sobered up.

487.22 *Zoe mou sas agapo*: Greek: 'My life, I love you'; epigraph to Byron's 'Maid of Athens, Ere We Part' (1810, 1812).

487.31 *Maynooth*: the Royal College of St Patrick founded (1795) to educate Catholic males for the priesthood; the theological centre of Irish Catholicism.

488.16 *pudor*: modesty, chastity (from Latin: *pudicus*: 'chaste').

488.17 *yoni . . . lingam*: Sanskrit for the female and male sexual organs respectively.

488.21 *spucks*: spits (from German: *spucken*: 'to spit').

488.22 *yadgana*: from the Sanskrit for 'rump'.

489.7 *Verfluchte Goim!*: Yiddish: 'Cursed gentiles!'.

489.8 *He had two left feet*: a *Book of Kells* illustration of 'The Virgin and Child' shows the child with two left feet, the virgin with two right (*G*).

489.9 *Judas Iacchias*: after a similar passage in Flaubert's *St Antony* (ch. 4, pp. 116–21) concerned with irreligious explanations of the identity of Jesus; 'Judas': the apostle who betrayed Jesus; 'Iacchia': a name for Bacchus, the Roman god of wine and mystic ecstasy; *G* points to the Cainites, an obscure Gnostic sect (mentioned in Flaubert, ch. 4, p. 115) which inverted the biblical narrative, made Judas the hero, Jesus the villain, and combined the former with Bacchus, hence 'Judas Iacchias'; 'Lybian' should read 'Libyan'.

489.18–20 *Qui vous a mis . . . pigeon, Phillipe*: French: 'Who put you in this wretched position, Philip? It was the sacred pigeon, Philip' (variation of Mulligan's verse in *Proteus* (see 41.19–20n.)).

489.25–6 *Metchnikof inoculated anthropoid apes*: Ilya Metchnikoff (1845–1916), Russian embryologist who succeeded in infecting apes with syphilis through inoculation.

490.4–5 *She sold love philtres . . . genitories*: after Flaubert's *St Antony* (ch. 4, pp. 118–19), where Antony is taunted by a leprotic Jew with tales that Mary was a perfume seller who had sex with Pantherus, a Roman soldier (who was thus the presumed, all-too-mortal father of Jesus); the source of the tale is Celsus (2nd c. AD), a vehement anti-Christian who survives only through Origen's (AD 185–254) refutation of him in his *Contra Celsum*.

490.19 *Mac Chree*: Gaelic: *mo chroidhe*: '[of] my heart'.

491.2 *Dreck!*: Yiddish: 'trash'.

491.11 *Virag unscrews his head . . . under his arm*: as does the 'sower of discord' Bertrand de Born (*c.*1140–1215) giver of evil counsel, whom Dante meets in *Inferno*, XXVIII.

491.17–18 *the fighting parson who founded the protestant error*: Martin Luther (1483–1546), leader of the Protestant Reformation.

491.18 *Antisthenes, the dog sage*: see 142.21–5 n.; Antisthenes, founder of the School of Cynics, who took their name from the Cynosargos Gymnasium where Antisthenes taught, but who were nicknamed *kunikos*: Greek: 'dog-like'.

492.1 *Monks of the screw*: 18th-c. non-religious Irish pleasure-seeking fraternal society, also known as the Order of St Patrick; John Philpot Curran (see 119.6 n., 134.4 n.) was 'prior' of the 'order' (*T* and *G*).

492.12–15 *Conservio lies . . . three tons*: source unknown, but Joyce identified these as 'the verses [his father] quote[d] most' ('Alphabetical Notebook', Cornell MS 25 (*JJA* vii. 109–56)).

492.19–24 *O, the poor little fellow . . . duckloving drake*: adaptation of second stanza of Irish ballad 'Nell Flaherty's Drake' (*G*).

494.6 *Svengali*: mesmerizing schemer in George du Maurier's (1834–96) popular novel *Trilby* (1894) (which Stephen discusses with Wells in *Stephen Hero*, 68).

494.8–9 *the sign of past master*: in Freemasonry, the Past Master is a Master Mason who acts as chairman.

494.20 *Aphrodisiac? But*: should read 'Aphrodisiac? Tansy and pennyroyal. But'.

495.23–4 *Powerful being . . . slumber which women love*: loose allusion to *Venus in Furs* (see 442.1 n.), as, in the scenario which follows, Bloom acts the part of the masochistic Severin, Bella/Bello that of Wanda, the dominatrix; Richard von Krafft-Ebing's (1840–1902) discussion of masochism in his *Psychopathia Sexualis* (1886) also informs the passage.

496.10 *king David and the Sunamite*: the story in 1 Kgs. 1: 1–4 of the provision by his people of a young Shunammite virgin to minister to the infirm King David.

496.19 *I should not have parted with my talisman*: unlike Odysseus who has kept and used Hermes's gift of *moly*.

497.10 *incredibly small*: should read 'incredibly impossibly small'.

498.2 *Adorer of the adulterous rump*: after Krafft-Ebing's description of *oscula ad nates* ('bum kissing'); mild coprophilia, a symptom of masochism (*G*).

498.14–15 *on all fours, grunting, snuffling, rooting*: compare Circe's charm which turns Odysseus's men to swine.

498.16–17 *the attitude of most excellent master*: the postures and oaths of Freemasonry begin to combine with the symptoms of masochism.

498.22 *grinds it in.) Feel*: should read '*grinds it in.*) Footstool! Feel'.

501.7 *a figged fist*: obscene Italian gesture (the thumb stuck between the first two fingers of the clenched fist) meaning 'Fuck you!'.

502.17 *only once*: should read 'only twice'.

502.25 *Mrs Miriam Dandrade*: for Mrs Dandrade, see 153.18; her 'suitors'' names are typical Joyce jokes (see *G*).

503.9 *Vice Versa*: either one of two stage adaptations of Thomas Anstey Guthrie's (1856–1934) novel *Vice Versa: A Lesson to Fathers* (1882); the role reversal involves a father and son, rather than a woman and man; Joyce acted in the play at Belvedere (*JJ* 56).

507.25 BELLA: should read 'BELLO'.

508.13–14 *the little statue . . . art for art' sake*: the statue will reappear (see 663.5 and 725.27–32); 'art for art's sake': the slogan of the Aesthetes.

509.15–16 *the circumcised . . . the wailing wall*: if Minnie Watchman were male, there would be, including Bloom, the requisite ten Jewish males to form a *minyan* (or quorum); 'the wailing wall': the last surviving remnant of Solomon's Temple in Jerusalem, a place of lamentation (though such ritual lamentation was forbidden before 1917).

509.16–19 *M. Shulomowitz . . . Leopold Abramovitz*: were Bloom real, these would have been his neighbours when he lived in Lombard Street West; actual members of the Jewish community there (*G*).

509.23 *Shema Israel . . . Adonai Echad*: see 118.14 n.; '*Adonai Echad*': Hebrew: 'The Lord is One'; the entire phrase is the Hebrew prayer chanted for one dying (Deut. 6: 4).

511.28 *Poulaphouca*: waterfall on the Upper Liffey.

512.6–7 *our shade?*: following this, insert (as new line) 'BLOOM', followed by (as new lines) '(*Scared.*) High school of Poula? Mnemo? Not in full possession of faculties. Concussion. Run over by tram.', followed by (as new line) 'THE ECHO', followed by (as new line) 'Sham!'.

512.23 *stunned*: should read '*starred*'.

513.11 *fauns*: should read 'fauna'.

513.18 *Staggering Bob*: see 163.7; 'bob': a newborn calf.

513.21 *Me. Me see.*: should read '(*Large teardrops rolling from his prominent eyes, snivels.*) Me. Me see.'.

514.23 *Pacing*: should read '*Pawing*'.

514.30 *Peccavi!*: Latin: 'I have sinned!'

516.21 *Sacrilege!*: should read '(*Her features hardening, gropes in the folds of her habit.*) Sacrilege!'.

516.24–5 *an elected knight of nine*: one of the Knights Templar (medieval chivalric order founded in 1188 during the Crusades; suppressed in 1312).

517.10–11 *(He sniffs.) But, Onions.*: should read '(*He sniffs.*). Rut. Onions.'.

518.2–3 *the dead march from Saul*: see 94.8 n.

518.25 *To have or not to have, that is the question*: adaptation of Hamlet's most famous soliloquy (*Hamlet*, III. i. 55 ff.).

519.9–10 *Dans ce bordel . . . nostre état*: French: 'In this brothel where we hold our "court"'; after a line from François Villon's (1431–*c.*1463) *Ballade de la grosse Margot* (*T*).

519.16 *(Looks at the money, then at Zoe*: should read '(*Looks at the money, then at Stephen, then at Zoe*'.

519.20 *brevi manu*: Italian: 'short changed'.

521.2 *Hum?*: should read 'Him?'.

521.12 *Lucifer*: see 50.4 n.; here, a match.

521.22 *Proparoxyton*: Greek metrics: word with an accented antepenultimate syllable.

521.22–3 *Moment before the next Lessing says*: Gotthold Lessing (1729–81), aesthetic philosopher, in his *Laocoön* (1766) distinguishes poetry from painting and sculpture in various ways, one of which is their determination by (and treatment of) different relations to the 'moment': the latter two capture small moments, the former presents continuing moments (see 37.13, 15 n.).

522.22 *Dona nobis pacem*: Latin: 'Give us peace'; final phrase from prayer uttered during the Rites of Communion in the Mass: *Agnus Dei, qui tollis peccata mundi, miserere nobis. [Repeat.] Agnus Dei, qui tollis peccata mundi, dona nobis pacem*' (Latin: 'Lamb of God, who takest away the sins of the world, have mercy on us. Lamb of God ... give us peace' (see 522.20)).

523.2–3 *the bloodoath in the Dusk of the Gods*: 'The Dusk of the Gods': English name of Richard Wagner's opera *Die Götterdämmerung* (1869–74); in Act I, Siegfried and Gunther seal a pact (which eventually results in the end of the gods) with an oath of blood brotherhood.

523.4–6 *Hangende Hunger... Macht uns alle kaputt*: German: 'unfulfilled longing, a questioning wife, ruin us everyone'.

523.19–28 *a pandybat ... very good little boy*: recalls Stephen's misadventure at Clongowes when Father Dolan unjustly punished the 'lazy idle little schemer' with strikes of the pandybat; Stephen had in fact broken his glasses and so appealed the injustice to Father Conmee (*Portrait*, ch. 1, pp. 47–59; and see 130.16).

523.24 *John Connee*: should read '*John Conmee*' (and at 523.36).

524.2–3 *I never could read His handwriting ... thumbprint on the haddock*: after the popular legend that the haddock bears the thumbprint of St Peter on its gills where the saint held it when he removed the 'tribute money' from its mouth (Matt. 17: 24–7) (Adams, 202–3).

525.10 *twentytwo too.*: should read 'twentytwo. Sixteen years ago he was twenty-two too.'

527.13 *stamped receipt.*: following this, insert (as new line) 'BOYLAN', followed by (as new lines) '(*Clasps himself.*) Here, I can't hold this little lot much longer. (*He strides off on stiff cavalry legs.*)'.

528.24 *'Tis the loud laugh bespeaks the vacant mind*: after Oliver Goldsmith's (1728–74) *The Deserted Village* (1770), l. 122: 'And the loud laugh that spoke the vacant mind'.

529.21 *Weda seca whokilla farst*: *Hamlet*, III. ii. 180: 'None wed the second but who kill'd the first!' (see 194.24–5 n.).

530.2 *Et exaltabuntur cornua iusti*: Latin: 'And the horns of the righteous shall be exalted' (Ps. 75: 10).

530.3 *grandoldgrossfather*: Daedalus, the cunning artificer.

530.4 *the suine scions of the house of Lambert*: 'A family of Lamberts who for several generations were born with bristles all over their bodies' (Adams, 204).

530.28 *dessous troublants*: French: 'disordered underwear'.

530.29 *Ce pif qu'il a*: French slang: 'The nose he has'; figuratively 'What a face!'

531.9 *Caoutchouc*: unvulcanized rubber.

532.5 *Beelzebub*: Hebrew: 'Lord of the flies'; (also see 2 Kgs. 1: 2); a name for Satan or (in Milton's *Paradise Lost*) one of his henchmen.

532.9–10 *No, I flew . . . Pater! Free!*: see 202.17 and n.

532.21–2 *An eagle gules . . . argent displayed*: the coat of arms of the Galway Joyces.

533.15 *A dark horse . . . past the winningpost*: Throwaway, of course.

533.28 GANETT DEARY: should read 'GARRETT DEASY'.

534.1 *THE GREEN LODGES*: pre-Home-Rule Irishmen; anti-Orangemen.

535.23 *Tout le monde . . .* : the phrases in French which follow (to 537.18) are Maginni's elaborate dancing instructions (*G* translates the phrases).

535.32 *goldhaired, slim,*: should read '*goldhaired, slimsandalled,*'.

536.25 *hours steal*: should read '*hours, one by one, steal*'.

538.18 *scotlootshoot*: should read '*scootlootshoot*'.

538.29 *Gadarene swine*: the swine into which Jesus cast the devils that had possessed two men; the swine went wild and jumped off a cliff into the sea (Matt. 8: 28–34).

539.27 *Lemur*: Roman ghost of the dead; lemurs appear in the 'Burial' scene in Goethe's *Faust*, Pt. II, Act V (*T*).

539.30–540.1 *Kinch killed her dogsbody bitchbody.*: should read 'Kinch dogsbody killed her bitchbody.'.

540.22 *Hyena!*: see Brunetto Latini's *Il Tesoro*, II. 253: 'The hyena is a beast that at one time is male and at another female. It lives wherever it can near a cemetery of dead men, and it digs out the bodies of the men, and eats them' (*T*).

541.6 *O, the fire of hell!*: should read 'O, the fire of hell! His noncorrosive sublimate!'.

541.10 *A green crab*: cancer, green, like Stephen's mother's green bile.

541.13 *(Strangled with rage.) Shite! (His features grow drawn and grey and old.)*: should read '(*Strangled with rage, his features drawn grey and old.*) Shite!'.

541.18 *Non serviam!*: Latin: 'I will not serve!'; according to the priest at the retreat Stephen attends in *Portrait* (ch. 3, p. 117), Lucifer's 'sinful thought conceived in an instant: *non serviam: I will not serve*'; Stephen echoes Lucifer when he tells Cranly, 'I will not serve that in which I no longer believe whether it call itself my home, my fatherland or my church' (*Portrait*, ch. 5, pp. 246–7).

541.22–3 *O Sacred Heart of Jesus . . . him*: the prayer is more usually spoken by the devout for themselves: 'Most Sacred Heart of Jesus, have mercy on us'.

542.1–2 *Inexpressible was my anguish . . . Calvary*: after Jesus's suffering during the crucifixion (or of Mary's anguish at his death); 'Calvary': site of the crucifixion (Luke 23: 33).

542.4 *Nothung!*: German: 'Needful'; the name of Siegfried's magical sword in Wagner's *Der Ring des Nibelungen* (1853–74), with which (in *Siegfried*) he slays the dragon Fafner and (eventually) brings about the demise of the gods.

544.28–9 *a pard ... drenched in aniseed*: for 'pard', see 209.21 n.; in the chase that follows, Bloom is pursued by those he's thought of—or encountered—in the course of his day.

546.1 *the fifth of George and seventh of Edward*: half-anachronistic reference: King George V did not become so until the death of his father Edward VII in 1910.

546.8 *No, he didn't. The girl's telling lies.*: should read 'No, he didn't. I seen him. The girl there.'.

546.15 *Sisyphus*: Odysseus encountered him in Hades where he had been condemned to roll a stone to the top of a hill, but inevitably, before reaching the summit, it would roll down, and the whole process had to begin again.

546.16 *Neopoetic*: should read 'Uropoetic', which means 'of the production of urine', an aesthetic with which Stephen (and Joyce, especially in *Finnegans Wake*) has sympathy.

546.26–7 *Their's not to reason why*: Tennyson's 'Charge of the Light Brigade' again (see 457.11), this time ll. 11–12: 'Theirs not to reason why | Theirs but to do and die'.

547.3 *Doctor Swift says ... men in their shirts*: from Swift's *Drapier's Letters* (1724), 'Letter IV': 'For, in reason, all government without the consent of the governed is the very definition of slavery: but, in fact, eleven men well armed will certainly subdue one single man in his shirt'.

547.16 *Enfin, ce sont vos oignons*: French: 'After all, those are your onions', e.g. 'It's your fight, not mine'.

547.18 *DOLLY GRAY*: from a popular Boer War song 'Good-bye, Dolly Gray' by Will D. Cobb and Paul Barnes.

547.19–20 *giving the sign of the heroine of Jericho.) Rahab*: 'Rahab': the Jericho harlot who protected Joshua's spies and in return was spared when Joshua destroyed Jericho; her 'sign': a 'line of scarlet thread in the window' (Josh. 2 (esp. 2: 15–16) and 6: 22–5).

548.6 *philirenists*: 'peace lovers'.

548.6 *the tsar*: Tsar Nicholas II of Russia (1868–1918; r. 1894–1917) whose petition for peace in 1898 led to the Hague Conference on international disarmament in 1899; five years later (1904) Russia entered into war with Japan.

548.6 *the king of England*: Edward VII fancied himself an international diplomat for peace (see 317.1–11 n.), but he was suspected of having ulterior (anti-German) motives in e.g. his attempted alliances with Russia and France.

548.7–8 *But in here it is ... priest and the king*: compare William Blake's 'Merlin's Prophecy' (*c.*1793), ll. 3–4: 'The King & the Priest must be tied in a tether | Before two virgins can meet together' (Keynes ed.).

548.22–6 *Garter and Thistle . . . made in Germany*: here, Edward VII wears various real and farcical insignia: the first three are actual orders of knighthood; 'Skinner's' and 'Probyn's Horse': cavalry regiments; 'Lincoln's Inns' bencher': a senior member of Lincoln's Inn (one of the Inns of Court in London); 'ancient . . . Massachusetts': a 17th-c. artillery company; 'made in Germany': slighting reference to the German origins of the British royal family (*T*).

548.27 *Défense d'uriner*: French: 'Urination prohibited'.

550.14 *DON EMILIO PATRIZIO FRANZ RUPERT POPE HENNESSY*: allusive generally of the families of the 'wild geese' (those who left Ireland with Sarsfield after the Battle of the Boyne (see 41.21–2n.)); 'Pope Hennessy': Sir John Pope Hennessy (1834–91), lawyer and MP, won Kilkenny seat in 1890 on anti-Parnellite ticket.

550.15 *valant*: should read '*volant*'.

550.16–17 *Werf those eykes . . . todos covered of gravy!*: garbled polyglossia: German: *Werf . . . footboden*: approximates 'Throw those disgusting ones to the ground at your feet'; '*porcos*': Spanish: *puercos*: 'pigs'; '*todos*': Spanish: 'entirely' (*G*).

550.25 *Green above the red*: song by Thomas Osborne Davis: '[Our fathers] proudly set the Irish Green above the English Red'.

550.25 *Wolfe Tone*: see 220.15 n.

551.17–21 *cleaver purchased by Mrs Pearcy . . . Seddon to the gallows*: Mrs Pearcy, Louis Voisin, and Seddon were all convicted of the murders described (*G* provides glosses).

551.25 *Horhot ho hray ho rhother's hest*: should read 'hor hother's'; the Croppy Boy's ghoulish 'Forgot to pray for mother's rest' (see 88.4 n.).

552.20 *Ça se voit aussi à Paris*: 'This is found too in Paris'.

552.26–7 *The old sow that eats her farrow!*: Stephen's description of Ireland in *Portrait*, ch. 5, p. 203.

552.30–553.16 *alanna/keens/banshees/Ochone!/Soggarth Aroon/Erin go hragh!*: (Last word should read '*bragh*'.) All Gaelic (in order): *a leanbh*: 'child'; *caoin*: 'wail, lament'; *bean sidhe*: 'fairy woman'; *ochón*: 'alas'; *sagart a rún*: 'my beloved priest'; *Éire go brágh*: 'Ireland until Judgement Day!'

553.11 *bugger*: should read 'fucker'.

553.15–18 *THE CITIZEN . . . fierce hostility.*): should be moved to follow (as new lines) 'Mahal shalal hashbaz.' (554.6).

554.5–6 *Mahal shalal hashbaz*: Hebrew ('*maher*' not 'mahal'): 'Hasten to the spoils'; see Isa. 8: 1 and 3, where Isaiah is commanded to write these words on a scroll and to name his son this as a reminder of the constant Assyrian threat.

554.23–4 *The harlot's cry . . . Ireland's windingsheet*: after Blake's 'Auguries of Innocence' (*c.*1803), ll. 115–16: 'The Harlot's cry from Street to Street | Shall weave Old England's winding sheet' (Keynes ed.).

555.14 *Brimstone fires spring up*: the scene invoked is that of Armageddon, the great battle which will precede the Last Judgement (see Rev. 16: 16–21).

555.18 *Pikes clash on cuirasses*: as in the 1798 Rebellion, where the Irish were armed with pikes, the English cavalry protected by cuirasses (armour of linked breastplate and backplate).

555.22 *The midnight sun is darkened*: the (one presumes *not* 'midnight') sun was darkened at Jesus's crucifixion (Luke 23: 44–5).

555.22–3 *The earth trembles ... arise*: according to Matt. 27: 51–2, after the crucifixion, 'the earth did quake, and the rocks rent; | And the graves were opened; and many bodies of the saints which slept arose'; earlier (Matt. 25: 32), Jesus had predicted that the Last Judgement would separate the sheep from the goats.

555.31–2 *Laughing witches ... broomsticks*: as Tam O'Shanter witnesses in Robert Burns's (1791) poem of that name.

555.32 *It rains dragon's teeth*: 'to sow dragon's teeth' is to 'stir up strife or war; especially to do something which is intended to put an end to strife but which brings it about' (Brewer); after the tale of Cadmus, legendary founder of Thebes, whom Athena advised to sow the teeth of the dragon he had just slain; he did so and armed men sprang up and fought one another until only five remained; with these five Cadmus founded Thebes.

556.2 *Wolfe Tome*: should read '*Wolfe Tone*'.

556.3 *Michael Davitt*: (1846–1906), Irish nationalist, founder of the Land League (1879), MP, Parnell's colleague, helped form the policies uniting the issues of land reform and Home Rule, parted with Parnell and was elected MP on an anti-Parnellite ticket (1892).

556.4 *John Redmond*: (1856–1918), Irish nationalist, MP, strong force in the Irish Parliamentary Party, led the Parnellite minority of that Party (1891) and reunited the Party in 1900, secured introduction of the third Home Rule Bill (1912), shattered by the events of the Easter uprising (1916).

556.4 *John O'Leary*: (1830–1907), Irish nationalist prominent in the Irish literary revival, edited the Fenian *Irish People* (1863), imprisoned (1865–74), released and went to Paris, returned under 1885 Amnesty Act; mentor of Yeats and Maud Gonne.

556.8–12 *Black candles ... her swollen belly*: this parodies a Black Mass (an inversion of the Mass in which Satan is worshipped rather than Christ); often the body of a naked woman forms the altar; note the back-to-front aspect employed throughout.

556.18 *Introibo ad altare diaboli*: Latin: 'I will go unto the altar of Satan [the devil]'; inversion of the Introit chanted by Mulligan on the opening page of *Ulysses* (3.5 n.).

556.22 *blooddripping host*: literal, not figurative ('wine'), blood is used in the Black Mass.

556.22 *Corpus meum*: Latin: 'My body'.

556.27 *Htengier ... Aiulella!*: should read 'Tnetopinmo'; reversal of 'Alleluia, for the Lord God omnipotent reigneth' (Rev. 19: 6).

556.30 *Dooooooooooog!*: reversal of 'goooooooooood!', i.e. 'god'.

557.11–14 OLD GUMMY GRANNY ... *O good God, take him!*: should be moved to follow (as new lines) 'pure reason.' (557.27).

557.22 *Exit Judas. Et laqueo se suspendit*: Latin: 'Judas left. And went and hanged himself' (after Matt. 27: 5).

558.15 *(The retriever, ... barks noisily)*: should be moved to follow (as new lines) 'blasted fucking windpipe!' (557.10).

564.17–18 *Who ... drive ... wood's woven shade?*: Stephen's mumbled repetition of Yeats's song 'Who Goes with Fergus' which earlier in the day he recalled having sung at his mother's deathbed (see 9.21–3 n.).

565.2–3 *In the shady wood ... Ferguson*: Bloom's failure to hear (or to comprehend) Stephen's words leads him to misconstrue.

565.4–5 *swear that I will ... art or arts*: version of the oath of secrecy sworn by Freemasons.

565.12–13 *He reads from right ... kissing the page*: Rudy as devout Hebrew scholar.

565.20 *lambskin*: should read '*lambkin*'.

EUMAEUS

Location: The cabmen's shelter under Loopline railway bridge (just west of the Custom House, near Butt Bridge (F4)). Stephen and Bloom walk from nighttown by way of Beaver, Montgomery, and Amiens Streets (F3), then pass behind the Custom House and under Loopline Bridge to the shelter.

Time: 1 a.m. (*L*: 12–1; *G*: 1 a.m.)

Homer: After leaving Phaecia and the palace of King Alcinous with food, rich gifts, and oarsmen, Odysseus finally arrives in Ithaca to be met by Athena in the guise of a shepherd. She has shrouded him in mist, and he fails to recognize either her or the land as Ithaca. Faced with a stranger, he lies about who he is. Athena reveals herself and tells him that this is Ithaca. Overwhelmed with joy, Odysseus 'kissed the grain-giving soil' (162). Athena disguises him as a foul and hideous beggar so that none will know him, and advises him to seek his loyal swineherd, Eumaeus. Meanwhile, she will find Telemachus and set him on his journey home. Odysseus finds Eumaeus, who pities him, feeds him, provides him with a goatskin to cover him in sleep. Still wary, Odysseus fabricates stories about his identity and adventures, and Eumaeus responds, 'some of your words ... were wide of the truth' (173). In return for a fine tale, Eumaeus provides Odysseus with a comfortable bed of goatskins. From Eumaeus, Odysseus hears the stories of his parents' and family's hardships in his absence. From this point until the end of the *Odyssey*, Eumaeus helps Odysseus as he returns to his palace in disguise, challenges the suitors to the contest of the bow (during which Odysseus reveals himself to Eumaeus), slays them, and makes peace with his subjects. Throughout it all, Eumaeus faithfully serves and aids him. By contrast, another servant, the goatherd Melanthius, proves utterly disloyal: he taunts the disguised Odysseus, tries to chase him from the palace, and helps the suitors in their battle with Odysseus, by retrieving the arms Telemachus has hidden in the storeroom. In retaliation, Odysseus demands that his arms and legs be bound behind and that he be hoisted to the rafters and left hanging. Once Odysseus has triumphed, Melanthius is executed by having his nose, ears, hands, and feet cut off and his entrails torn out and fed to the dogs. (Books XIV–XXII)

Schemata: In addition to Eumaeus, Ulysses, Telemachus, and the Bad Goatherd [Melanthius], *L* lists Ulysses Pseudangelos among the personae. The latter, 'Ulysses the False Messenger', is the title of a now lost Greek play cited by Aristotle. The significance here undoubtedly lies in the name itself as *G* gives 'The Sailor' as correspondence for him. *G*'s other correspondences are Eumaeus, Skin-the-Goat; Melanthius, Corley.

L and *G* agree on Organ (Nerves) and Colour (none), but differ on Technic (*L*: Relaxed Prose; *G*: Narrative (old)), Art (*L*: none; *G*: Navigation) and Symbol (*L*: none; *G*: Sailors). *L*'s Sense is 'The Ambush on Home Ground'.

'Preparatory to anything else' *Eumaeus* begins: begins itself and claims its power to begin *Ulysses* all over again. By now we have become used to the fact that the fundamental narrative unit of this book is the episode: each discretely devotes itself to a single hour, a single organ, a single Homeric episode; each increasingly stylistically segregates itself from its cohorts; each (whether quietly or deafeningly) demands an adjustment of our prior reading habits. In this sense, then *Eumaeus*'s opening words are true: they are 'preparatory to anything else' in the episode and symptomatic of the pleasure the text takes in slyly drawing our attention to its ability constantly to revise itself. But these words also lie about their 'preparatory' status, coming as they do, so late in *Ulysses*. Further, the seemingly empty phrase tempts us into impatience, for it appears to signify nothing but its own temporal position: the first words in a sentence are *always* 'preparatory to anything else'. So *Eumaeus* begins with words that are both false and true, significant and empty. *Caveat lector*: things are not always what they seem here.

Or rather, things are always what they seem and something other at the same time. For example, situated as it is between the two excessively formally aberrant episodes *Circe* and *Ithaca*, *Eumaeus* appears (thankfully) narratively 'normal'. Everything proceeds from the perspective of a third-person narrator: 'Stephen repeatedly yawned'; 'Mr Bloom brushed off the greater bulk of the shavings'. In this, *Eumaeus* passes for a narrative related by an omniscient narrator. Very quickly we learn differently: Stephen expresses thirst, Bloom suggests they might find something to drink at the cabman's shelter, but how to get there? '[H]e pondered suitable ways and means during which Stephen repeatedly yawned. So far as he could see he was rather pale in the face so that it occurred to him as highly advisable to get a conveyance of some description which would answer in their then condition.' Our omniscient narrator seems to be nodding at the wheel of this narrative 'conveyance'. In the second sentence, the first 'he' is Bloom, the second 'he' Stephen; then comes a 'him' which can only be Bloom (or could it be Stephen?); the final pronoun ('their') possessively links them in a mutual 'condition'. And that condition? An episode later, *Ithaca* will 'substitut[e] Stephen for Bloom Stoom' and 'Bloom for Stephen Blephen' (635). 'Preparatory to anything else' *Eumaeus* has already done so.

Nor is it only Blephen and Stoom who are often indistinguishable here. In *Eumaeus* determining whose consciousness informs the narrative at a given moment often exceeds the abilities of even the wariest reader. Turn back to the 'Introduction', p. xxxv, and try to sort out whose consciousness is driving *those* sentences. Omniscient (authorial) narrator, Stephen, Bloom dissolve and merge in an indirect discourse so free as to be virtually unattributable. And, while the language of the characters is absorbed by the narrative, everything is infected with a tendency to an exhausted, verbose, constantly misfiring, sententious, logorrhoeic, never-use-one-word-when-thirty-will-do kind of prolixity. All this prompts a desperate desire to sort things out. Frantically, we assign one part of a sentence to Stephen, another to Bloom, a third to a narrator, but drawing the lines between them is unnervingly difficult and logically perverse. Such a desire to delineate derives from our own anxiety at so obvious a dissolution of boundaries. For we are like Bloom, who will 'never [go] beyond a certain point where he invariably drew the line as it simply led to trouble all round to say nothing of your being at the tender mercy of others practically'. Ulysses's wary watchfulness attends him while the text (previously so acutely aware of its own capacities to define, discriminate, erect, nominate, undo, recirculate) proceeds seemingly unregarding. But no matter how much Bloom busies himself 'Sherlockholmesing' the situation, he cannot prevent his sudden, unexpected, nettling and unsettling transformation into 'L. Boom' (a misnomer which the narrative happily appropriates to its own ends). Through its casual disregard of territorial boundaries (whether those of linguistic, narratorial, or epistemological propriety) and its continual assertion that 'quite possibly there was not one vestige of truth in' it, *Eumaeus* prompts our vigilance and scepticism. But no matter how vigilant or sceptical, we may never be able wholly to separate truth from falsity for 'it was quite within the bounds of possibility that it was not an entire fabrication though at first blush there was not much inherent probability in all the spoof'. And this, despite our desire for discrimination, segregation, delineation, provokes the admission that we—like Blephen, Stoom, and 'the doughty narrator'—are all 'at the tender mercy of others practically'.

569.3 *orthodox Samaritan fashion*: an oxymoron: the good Samaritan (Luke 10: 30–7) was anything but 'orthodox'; it was the 'orthodox' Jews—the priest and the Levite—who failed to help the man who had fallen among thieves.

569.15–16 *e.d.ed*: slang: 'finished'.

569.17 *preliminaries, as, in spite*: should read 'preliminaries as brushing, in spite'.

569.19 *shaving line, brushing they*: should read 'shaving line, they'.
569.24 *Jehu*: slang: 'cabdriver' after 2 Kgs. 9: 20: 'Jehu . . . driveth furiously'.
570.10 *Jupiter Pluvius*: Latin: 'Jupiter the Rainmaker'.
570.20–2 *Stephen thought to think of Ibsen . . . in Talbot place*: here Stephen remakes a connection he had earlier made in *Portrait*: 'as he went by Baird's stonecutting works in Talbot Place the spirit of Ibsen would blow through him like a keen wind' (ch. 5, p. 176); Henrik Ibsen (1828–1906), Norwegian dramatist whom the young Joyce admired immensely (see esp. his 1900 essay, 'Ibsen's New Drama', *CW* 47–67). The association probably arises through the connection of the stonecutter's with Rubek, the sculptor in Ibsen's *When We Dead Awaken* (1900).
570.26–7 *O tell me where is fancy bread*: the bad advertising pun derives from the opening line of Portia's song in *The Merchant of Venice*, III. ii. 63–4: 'Tell me where is fancy bred, | Or in the heart or in the head?'
571.1 *that man in the gap*: P. W. Joyce explains this as colloquial for a 'man who courageously and successfully defends any cause or any position', after the Irish king's man posted at dangerous passes at times of threatened invasion (182); see 285.2.
571.7–8 *unscrupulous in the service of the Crown*: common complaint: the Dublin Metropolitan Police, while Irish, were popularly perceived as instruments of English policy and English power.
571.19–20 *the much vexed question of stimulants*: the vociferous Temperance debate.
572.20 *Lord John Corley*: one of *Dubliners*'s 'Two Gallants'.
572.28 *some relative had enjoyed*: should read 'some relative, a woman, as the tale went, of extreme beauty, had'.
572.35 *sprinkling of other*: should read 'sprinkling of a number of other'.
573.18–19 *the Brazen Head . . . the friar Bacon*: the Brazen Head Hotel reminds Stephen of Friar Bacon in the play *The Honourable History of Friar Bacon and Friar Bungay* (*c.*1589–92) by Robert Greene (1558–92), English poet and dramatist; in it Friar Bacon, a necromancer, creates what should be a magical brazen head, but, inevitably, things go wrong (*G*).
573.24 *haud ignarus malorum miseris succurrere disco*: Latin: 'by no means unacquainted with evils, I know how to aid the wretched'; an adaptation of *Non ignara mali, miseris succerrere disco* (Latin: 'Not unacquainted with ill, I know how to aid the wretched'), Virgil, *Aeneid*, I. 630.
573.34 *invetiongstia*: should read 'investigation'.
574.13 *The Carl Rosa*: popular English opera company (est. 1873) named after its founder, the German violinist Carl Rosa (1842–89).
574.32 *chronic impecuniosity. Probably*: should read 'chronic impecuniosity. Palpably'.
574.36 *rara avis*: Latin: 'rare bird'.
575.21 *Everyone according to . . . to his deeds*: Bloomian adaptation of Karl Marx's maxim: 'From each according to his ability, to each according to his needs'.

576.4 *in the confusion*: should read 'in the confusion, which they did.'.

576.13 *the third precept of the church*: 'To observe the fasts on the days during the seasons appointed' (*T*).

576.14 *quarter tense or, if not, ember days*: they are the same thing: 'quarter tense' (from the Latin *quattuor tempora* ('four times')) being the Middle English term for 'ember days': the days of fast set aside at the beginning of each of the four religious 'seasons' (*T*).

577.12–15 *Putanna madonna . . . Mortacci sui!*: two lines have mistakenly dropped out: after '*—Dice lui, però*' insert as new ¶ '*—Mezzo.*'; after '*—Farabutto! Mortacci sui!*' insert as new ¶ '*—Ma ascolta! Cinque la testa più . . .*'; '*Putanna*' should read '*Puttana*'. Translated (from the slang Italian) the lines now read:

—Whore of the Blessed Virgin, he must give us money! I'm right? Busted arsehole!

—Let's get this clear. Half a sovereign more . . .

—So that's what he says, but.

—Half.

—Crook! His filthy dead!

—But listen! Five more per head . . .

577.19 *Skin-the-Goat, Fitzharris, the invincible*: see 131.5–6 n.; James Fitzharris was released in 1902 from his life sentence (as an accessory in the Phoenix Park murders), but Joyce, not history, places him in the cabman's shelter.

578.4 *Bella Poetria!*: Bloom's attempt at (the Italian) *Bella Poesia*: 'Beautiful Poetry'.

578.5 *Belladonna voglio*: should read '*Belladonna. Voglio.*'; again, Bloom Italian: 'Beautiful woman. I want', but *belladonna* is also the name of the poisonous plant 'deadly nightshade'.

578.21–2 *Cicero, Podmore . . . What's in a name?*: Adams points out that the first three pairs of names suggest a word-association puzzle, though the associations suggested are pretty far-fetched: 'Cicero' (Latin: *cicera*: 'chickpea') leads in English to 'Podmore'; 'Napoleon': Buonaparte (French: 'good part'): 'Goodbody'; 'Jesus': Christ: Anointed: Oil: 'Doyle' (Adams, 223); Shakespeare was not a common name, but William was by no means its sole possessor; the final phrase is Juliet's on her discovery that Romeo's last name is that of her family's enemy (*Romeo and Juliet*, II. ii. 43).

578.24–5 *Buffalo Bill*: William Frederick Cody (1846–1917), American frontiersman, sharpshooter, and founder of Buffalo Bill's Wild West Show.

579.36–7 *W. B. Murphy, of Carrigaloe*: in *RM* Joyce wrote, not 'W.B.', but 'D.B.'.

580.3 *I hails from. My little*: should read 'I hails from. I belongs there. That's where I hails from. My little'.

580.9 *Alice Ben Bolt*: from popular song 'Ben Bolt' by Thomas Dunn English and Nelson Kneass; Ben Bolt, a sailor, returns home after twenty years' absence to discover his wife, Alice, has died.

580.9 *Enoch Arden*: poem (1864) by Tennyson about a sailor who, having married his sweetheart Annie Lee, sails to China, is shipwrecked, returns home years later to discover that Annie Lee, having presumed him dead, has remarried; Enoch keeps his secret and dies 'a strong heroic soul' but broken-hearted.

580.10 *Caoc O'Leary*: 'Caoc': Gaelic: *caoch*: 'one-eyed'; 'Caoch the Piper', a ballad by John Keegan (1809–49) of a piper (Caoch O'Leary) who returns after twenty years, asks 'Does anybody hereabouts | Remember Caoch the Piper?', and dies.

580.11 *poor John Casey*: Bloom confuses John Keegan (580.10n.) with John Keegan Casey (1846–70), Fenian and balladeer who died in prison.

581.5 *South America. I seen*: should read 'South America. We was chased by pirates one voyage. I seen'.

581.7 *Gospodi pomilooy*: should read '*pomilyou*'; Old Church Slavonic: 'God have mercy on you' (*G*).

581.19 *Choza de Indios. Beni, Bolivia*: Spanish: 'Indian huts'; 'Beni' is a north-eastern inland Bolivian province.

581.29 *genially*: should read 'generally'.

581.34 *Tarjeta Postal . . . Chile*: Spanish: 'Postcard. Mr A. Boudin [French: 'black pudding'], Becchi [Italian: *becchino*: 'gravedigger'] Gallery, Santiago, Chile'.

581.37 *William Tell*: legendary (15th-c.) Swiss hero; sentenced to death by the Austrians, he can go free if he can shoot an apple off his son's head (which, of course, he does).

581.37–582.1 *the Lazarillo-Don Cesar . . . depicted in Maritana*: Don Cesar, hero of *Maritana* (see 83.18–19n.), escapes the villain Don Juan's (second) attempt on his life when Don Juan's musket-ball lodges in Don Cesar's hat.

582.4 *boxed the compass*: literally: name the 32 points of the compass in order; figuratively: do an about-face.

582.33 *Moody-Manners*: at the time, the largest English opera company in the world, founded by the Irish Charles Manners (1857–1935) and his English wife, the soprano Madame Fanny Moody.

583.4 *tapis*: French: 'carpet'.

583.4 *the circumlocution departments*: cliché for governmental departments, from Dickens's *Little Dorrit* (1857), ch. 10.

583.21 *farther away from the madding crowd*: after the title of Thomas Hardy's novel (1874) *Far from the Madding Crowd*, which in turn takes its title from Thomas Gray's 'Elegy Written in a Country Church-Yard' (1751), stanza 19: 'Far from the madding crowd's ignoble strife Their sober wishes never learned to stray'.

583.24 *coup d'œil*: French: 'glance'.

583.28 *Grace O'Malley*: see 316.13n.; legend holds that Lord Howth refused her hospitality, so she kidnapped his son to demand it.

583.28 *George IV*: (1762–1830), King of England (1820–30), made a state visit to Ireland, Aug. 1821, landing at Howth; first visit to Ireland by an English king since William III.

583.29–30 *in the spring when young men's fancy*: after Tennyson's 'Locksley Hall' (1842), l. 20: 'In the spring a young man's fancy lightly turns to thoughts of love'.

584.4 *Chinese*: should read 'Chinks'.

584.24 *where ignorance is bliss*: now proverbial, but from Thomas Gray's 'Ode on a Distant Prospect of Eton College' (1742) ll, 99–100: 'Where ignorance is bliss, 'Tis folly to be wise'.

585.1–2 *eightyone ... turned fifteen*: no: 6 May 1882, and Bloom (whose exact birthday we do not know, but whose birth year is 1866) could not have 'just turned fifteen'.

585.11 *Mr Bloom interpolated.*: should read 'Mr B. interrogated.'.

585.14 *I'm tired of all them rocks in the sea*: Murphy seems not to know Gibraltar, which casts doubts on his whole tale as he would have had to stop at, or at least pass, it to get to many of his claimed destinations.

585.23–4 *staring quite obviously*: should read 'staring quite obliviously'.

585.24 *dreaming of fresh woods and pastures new*: from Milton's 'Lycidas' (see 26.1–3, 15 n.), l. 193: 'Tomorrow to fresh Woods, and Pastures new'.

586.19 *Skibereen father*: from 'Old Skibbereen', an anonymous ballad about the famine, in which a father explains to his son that he was forced to leave Ireland because, having joined 'with Erin's boys', he was hunted as a traitor.

588.14–15 *Fear not them that ... to buy the soul*: after Matt. 10: 28: 'Fear not them which kill the body, but are not able to kill the soul'.

588.33–7 *it is a simple substance ... curruptio per accidens*: St Thomas Aquinas, *Summa Theologica*, Part I(I), question LXXV, art. 6: 'We must assert that the intellectual principle which we call the human soul is incorruptible. For a thing may be corrupted in two ways—of itself [*corruptio per se*], and accidentally [*per accidens*]'. He goes on to argue that the soul, being 'simple', cannot be corrupted, for 'corruption is found only where there is contrariety'.

589.3 *a demurrer*: at law, either one of two pleas: (1) that were the facts presented true, they would still be insufficient to sustain the claim made, or (2) that a defect exists on the face of the complaint rendering the action untenable.

589.7 *Röngten*: should read 'Röntgen'; see 171.6–7 n.

589.7 *Edison*: Thomas Alva Edison (1847–1931), inventor of, among other things, the electric light and the phonograph, but *not* the telescope.

589.8 *Galileo*: (1564–1642), Italian astronomer, *not* the inventor of the telescope, despite legend, but one who clearly demonstrated its usefulness.

589.22 *our national poet*: Shakespeare would not incontestably be admitted to be an Irishman's 'national poet'; the epithet is more usually attached (by the English, of Ireland's poets) to Thomas Moore (see 155.5–6 n.); but see *Portrait*, ch. 5, p. 180.

589.31 *Coffee Palace*: the Dublin Temperance Institute and Coffee Booths and Restaurant, run by the Dublin Total Abstinence Society.

590.3 *Sulphate of copper poison, S O_4*: copper sulphate would be $CuSO_4$.

590.11 *puddle—it clopped out of it when taken up—by*: should read 'puddle it clopped out of when taken up by'.

590.18 *knife ... reminds me of Roman history*: probably of Julius Caesar's stabbing (see 25.21–2 and n.).

590.37 *the oakum and treadmill fraternity*: those who picked oakum and walked treadmills as punishment: English prisoners.

591.4–5 *Antonio ... pen of our national poet*: the best-known of Shakespeare's Antonios is the eponymous hero of *The Merchant of Venice*.

591.9–10 *any ancient mariner ... Hesperus*: to 'draw the long bow': tell a tall tale, as does Coleridge's Ancient Mariner in *The Rime of the Ancient Mariner* (1798); but Odysseus, too, draws the long bow (see headnote to *Penelope*); 'Hesperus' (after the evening star): the fated ship in Longfellow's poem 'The Wreck of the Hesperus' (1840).

591.16 *Aztecs ... sitting bowlegged*: Bloom probably means 'ascetics' rather than 'Aztecs', who did not sit bowlegged in worship.

591.22 *Sinbad*: sailor (an Odysseus figure) in the *Arabian Nights* (see 613.9 n.), but also the eponymous hero of *Sinbad the Sailor* in the very popular pantomime of that name (see 631.20 n.).

591.23 *Ludwig, alias Ledwidge*: William Ledwidge (1847–1923), Dublin baritone with the stage name 'Ludwig', who played the Flying Dutchman in the musical version of *Vanderdecken: or, The Flying Dutchman* (G).

591.32 *little Italy there, near the Coombe*: small Italian community in Dublin (D5).

591.33–4 *the harmless necessary animal of the feline persuasion*: cliché from Shylock's phrase in *The Merchant of Venice*, IV. i. 55: 'a harmless necessary cat'.

591.35 *tuckink*: should read 'tuckin': 'a large meal'.

592.2 *quietus*: 'release from life'; cf. *Hamlet*, III. i. 74–5: 'he himself might his quietus make | With a bare bodkin'.

592.10 *Roberto ruba roba sua*: Italian: 'Roberto stole his things'.

592.13–14 *the impetuosity of Dante ... fell in love with*: according to Boccaccio, Dante Alighieri's (1265–1321) 'Beatrice' (the image of ideal love in the *Divine Comedy*) was modelled on Beatrice Portinari (1266–90), a Florentine woman with whom he fell in love, though she was already married to Simone de Bardi; hence the 'triangle'.

592.14 *Leonardo*: Leonardo da Vinci (1452–1519), painter, sculptor, inventor; da Vinci's *Mona Lisa* has repeatedly been linked with Dante's Beatrice.

592.14–15 *san Tommaso Mastino*: Italian: 'St Thomas the Mastiff' (i.e. bulldog), so St Thomas Aquinas (see 17.33–4 n.); Dante relied heavily on Aquinas's philosophies.

592.33–593.2 *the wreck of Daunt's rock ... petrified with horror*: should read 'wreck off Daunt's rock': a *Finnish* ship *Palme* went aground on Booterstown Strand, Dublin Bay (*not* 'off Daunt's rock', which is in Cork harbour), 24 Dec. 1895; one lifeboat capsized in the attempted rescue (15 dead); Albert William Quill published a verse 'The Storm of Christmas Eve, 1895' (a masterpiece of doggerel) in the *Irish Times* (16 Jan. 1896) (*T* and *G*).

593.3–7 *the case of the s.s. Lady Cairns . . . her hold*: shipwreck in which the English *Lady Cairns* was rammed by the German *Mona* (Mar. 1904); the former sank virtually immediately; all lost; the *Mona* was found to have had right-of-way and not to have been negligent (*T*).

593.33 *corporation, who,*: should read 'corporation stones, who,'.

593.35 *on the parish rates*: the poor.

593.37–594.1 *in the arms of Morpheus*: in Greek and Roman mythology, the god of dreams; see 614.18 for a more truly Bloomian version of this adage.

594.6 *stiver*: from Dutch coin, slang for a coin of very small denomination, e.g. English penny.

594.16–20 *why that ship ran bang against . . . Leverline*: for Galway harbour, see 33.3 n.; the case referred to here is that of a ship, *Indian Empire* (owned by John Orell Lever, founder of the company funding the Galway scheme, not a captain), which—in broad daylight, entering the 9-mile-wide Galway channel—managed to run into the only rock in the harbour; sabotage was suspected but it seems rather that bad luck (which continued for years) was to blame. (See *T*.)

594.31–4 *The biscuits was as hard as brass . . . Johnny Lever, O!*: adaptation of English sea shanty 'Leave Her, Johnny, Leave Her!' (The pun is obvious; see 594.16–20 n.)

595.7 *coal in large quantities*: Skin-the-Goat's claims for Ireland's natural resources are significantly hyperbolic (see *G*).

595.13–14 *Colonel Everard . . . growing tobacco*: should read 'Navan' not 'Cavan'; an article in the *Irish Homestead* (9 July 1904) reports that Colonel N. T. Everard was growing tobacco near Navan in County Meath (*T*).

595.18–19 *The Germans and the Japs . . . lookin*: i.e. the apparent German and Japanese expansionist policies might pose a threat to England's parallel policies.

595.19 *The Boers were the beginning of the end*: while the Boers lost the Boer War, they succeeded in demonstrating how tenuous was the hold Britain had on her empire.

595.20–1 *Ireland, her Achilles heel*: phrase from George Bernard Shaw's 'Preface' to *John Bull's Other Island* (1906): 'The Irish coast is for the English invasion-scaremonger the heel of Achilles'; Achilles's heel was, of course, his weak spot: when his mother, Thetis, dipped him into the River Styx (to make him invincible), she held him by (and so prevented the water from reaching) his heel.

595.25–6 *Ireland, Parnell said . . . sons*: the sentiment may be typical of Parnell, but the source remains unidentified.

596.2 *Jem Mullins*: the archetypal 'self-made man': James Mullin (1846–1920), born into a peasant family, taught himself, eventually became a physician.

596.32 *felonsetting*: 'betraying rebels by publicizing their whereabouts' (*G*).

596.32 *Dannyman*: 'an informer'; from Danny Mann, character in Gerald Griffin's (1803–40) novel *The Collegians* (1829) and, later, in Boucicault's *The Colleen Bawn* (see 89.9 n.).

597.8–9 *Fitz, nicknamed Skin-the-Goat, merely . . . perpetrators*: should read 'Skin-the, merely'; he did not; he merely drove the decoy cab (see 131.5–6 n.; 131.33).

597.11 *the plea some legal luminary saved his skin on*: at his first trial (for murder), Fitzharris was acquitted; at his second (for being an accessory), he was found guilty; his counsel: Richard 'Dick' Adams (see 132.10–11).

597.33–5 *Ex quibus . . . secundum carnem*: th phrase Stephen quotes reads, in its entirety in the Vulgate Bible, *et ex quibus est Christus secundum carnem*; Latin: 'and of that race is Christ according to the flesh' (Vulgate Rom. 9: 5); Stephen deletes 'is Christ'.

598.9–10 *Memorable bloody bridge battle and seven minutes' war*: for 'bloody bridge battle', see 242.10 n.; 'Skinner's alley' and 'Ormond market' were Dublin neighbourhoods lying either side of the Liffey (across Richmond Bridge (E4) from one another); the bridge was the site of various 18th-c. fights between the competing Dublin 'gangs' from the two districts (*G*); the skirmish's name—'seven minutes' war'—is probably Stephen's joke after the Seven Years War (1756–63) which involved most of Europe.

598.26–7 *Spain decayed . . . jews out*: the Jews were expelled from Spain in 1492 by Ferdinand V; Spain's fortunes did begin a decline, though not through any apparently connected cause (*G*).

598.27–9 *England prospered when Cromwell . . . imported them*: the Jews were expelled from England in 1290 (reign of Edward I); Oliver Cromwell (1599–1658) did push for the right to readmission for a select number of prosperous Jewish families; stretching it, one could say that England prospered as a result, as they brought with them wealth and expertise which helped to stabilize the economy left shaky by the Civil War (*G*).

598.29 *they are practical*: should read 'they are imbued with the proper spirit. They are practical'.

598.32–3 *Spain again . . . goahead America*: the United States easily defeated the Spanish in the Spanish–American war (23 Apr.–12 Aug. 1898) and emerged from the victory a significant world power; Spain's empire was severely diminished by the treaty which ended the war.

598.33–5 *Turks, it's in the dogma . . . better*: Bloom attributes Turkish poverty to their (Muslim) belief that death in a holy war guaranteed salvation (and so removed the impulse to improve living conditions).

598.35–6 *That's the juggle . . . false pretenses*: the suggestion is that Catholic priests ('p.p.': 'parish priest') get money by false pretences: that they hold sole right of access (through Catholic theology) to heaven.

599.5–6 *Ubi patria . . . vita beni*: should read '*bene*'; Bloom's ill-remembered Latin: *Ubi patria vita bene*: 'where my country [is, there is] the good life'; a free adaptation of Cicero's *Ubi bene, ibi patria*: 'where I am well off, there is my country'.

599.28 *faubourg Saint-Patrice called Ireland for short*: French: 'St Patrick's suburb'; i.e. Ireland as dominated by St Patrick or Catholicism.

600.22–3 *section two of the Criminal Law Amendment Act*: section II of the Criminal Law Amendment Act (1885) prohibited the solicitation or procurement of women for illicit sexual practices (i.e. prostitution); *T* suggests Bloom may be confusing section II with section XI which prohibited homosexual acts (and was Oscar Wilde's undoing).

600.26–30 *the tattoo which was all . . . the head of state*: tattoos were fashionable among the nobility at the turn of the century: not only Edward VII, but George V, Tsar Nicholas II, and King Alphonso XII of Spain all sported them; those in high society ('the upper ten [percent]') followed suit.

600.32 *the Cornwall case*: either of two cases may be alluded to here: (1) an 1870 divorce case in which Edward VII (then Duke of Cornwall) was called as a witness when two friends were named as correspondents by Sir Charles Mordaunt; (2) an 1883 public scandal when two Dublin Castle officials, Cornwall and French, were involved in an extensive homosexual circle (*G*).

600.33 *Mrs Grundy*: the quintessential voice of middle-class mores, from Thomas Moxton's (*c.*1764–1838) play *Speed the Plough* (1798): 'What will Mrs Grundy say?'

601.19 *the submerged tenth*: phrase coined by General William Booth (1829–1912), founder of the Salvation Army, to describe that percentage of the population in England which lived in abject poverty (in *In Darkest England; and the Way Out* (1890)).

601.25 *The pink edition . . . Telegraph*: the latest edition of any Dublin daily newspaper, so containing extra coverage of the day's sporting events. Most of the stories Bloom reads are Joyce's adaptations of actual articles in the *Evening Telegraph*, 16 June 1904. *G* gives full accounts.

601.35 *Ascot Throwaway*: should read 'Ascot meeting, the Gold Cup. Victory of outsider *Throwaway*'.

602.30–1 *third event at Ascot on page three, his side-value 1,000 sovs*: should read 'third event at Ascot on page three, his side. Value 1,000 sovs.', i.e. the article about Ascot is on Bloom's side (as opposed to Stephen's side) of the paper: Stephen sits on Bloom's left, Bloom on Stephen's right (since Stephen is reading page two (602.27)).

602.32–3 *by Rightaway, 5 yrs, 9 st 4 lbs, Thrale (W. Lane)*: should read 'by *Rightaway—Thrale*, 5 yrs, 9 st 4 lbs, (W. Lane)'.

603.2 *300*: should read '3,000'.

603.13 ff. *Return of Parnell . . .*: what follow regarding Parnell are tales typical of those which circulated for years after his death—particularly that he had not died (the coffin was filled with stones) but had escaped to South Africa. Bloom's 'memories' combine fact with mistake: Parnell died 6 Oct. 1891 (nearly thirteen—not 'twenty odd'—years previously); the Catholic hierarchy stayed out of the controversy until late Nov. 1890, when they urged his retirement on 'moral' grounds, to which Parnell responded that the Church ought to stay out of political matters; the Irish populace *was* strongly anti-Parnellite at the end (and he *was* burned in effigy); the stated cause of his death was vague: rheumatic fever and a weak heart; his liaison with Katherine O'Shea was an open secret; his 'political arrangements' were in chaos, *not* 'nearing completion' at his death; only 45 of the 72 (including Parnell) present in Committee Room 15 (site of the split on 6 December 1890 in the Irish Parliamentary Party) 'rounded on' Parnell (leaving him leading an emasculated party of 26); the *United Ireland* was Parnell's paper (taken over by anti-Parnellites, retaken by Parnell by force, returned to anti-Parnellism shortly thereafter), the *Insuppressible* the anti-Parnellite organ (founded when the *United Ireland* was reclaimed by Parnell).

604.14 *expression*: should read 'exterior'.

604.20–3 *the claimant in the Tichborne case . . . Lord Bellew*: one Arthur Orton (1834–98), an Australian, claimed to be Robert Charles Tichborne (1829–54), the heir (lost at sea on a ship called *Bella*) to a title and a huge fortune; at trial (1871), Lord Bellow, who had been at school with the lost heir, testified that Tichborne had a tattoo which Orton did not have; Orton lost and was successfully prosecuted for perjury (*G*).

604.29 *That bitch, that English whore*: the misogynistic comments about Katherine O'Shea, Parnell's partner (then wife), are also typical of contemporary rumours and similarly mistaken: there is no evidence she was promiscuous; her relationship with Parnell was a *de facto* marriage known to her husband Captain William Henry O'Shea; nor, incidentally, was she half Spanish. Parnell's refusal to testify at the trial left many of the rumours unchallenged.

604.32 *plenty of her. I seen*: should read 'plenty of her. She loosened many a man's thighs. I seen'.

605.7 *encouraging . . . downfal*: should read 'encompassing . . . downfall'.

605.29 *farewell, my gallant captain*: song at end of Act I of *Maritana* (see 83.18–19n.); Don Cesar to the Captain of the Guard on challenging him to a duel.

606.13 *Stephen. And,*: should read 'Stephen, about blood and the sun. And,'.

606.14–17 *The king of Spain's daughter . . . so and so many*: Stephen alludes first to the nursery rhyme: 'The king of Spain's daughter | Came to visit me, | And all for the sake | Of my little nut tree' (see 552.29); then to an anonymous sea ballad 'Spanish Ladies': *G* quotes in full; Stephen mumbles the first lines of the first and third stanzas and the final line of the chorus; (in order mentioned): 'Farewell and adieu to you, gay Spanish ladies'; 'Now the first land we made it is called the Deadman | Then, Ramshead . . .'; 'From Ushant to Scilly is thirty-five leagues'.

606.23 *contents rapidly,*: should read 'contents it contained rapidly,'.

607.13–14 *All the rest, yes, Puritanism. It does though, St Joseph's sovereign . . . whereas no photograph could*: should read 'All the rest. Yes, puritanisme, it does though Saint Joseph's sovereign thievery alors (Bandez!) Figne toi trop. Whereas no photograph could'. Not that this renders the passage less obscure. The French reads: 'puritanism . . . o.k. (Get a hard on!) Bugger yourself completely'. 'Saint Joseph's sovereign thievery' undoubtedly refers to Joseph's usurpation of God's role in relation to Mary. The sentences ('Yes . . . trop') are characteristically Stephen, not Bloom, and may therefore be Stephen's thoughts interjected into the narrative stream of Bloom's rambling (though if the curses are directed at Bloom they are more hostile than Stephen's other recorded attitudes to him; they are more characteristic of his silent comments to himself when he recognizes that his theorizing is going over the top). Beyond this, you are on your own. (See *RM*, *Eumaeus*, fol. 39.)

607.33–4 *with apologies to Lindley Murray*: Lindley Murray (1745–1826), English grammarian, author of *Grammar of the English Language* (1795) and other standard textbooks.

608.12–13 *Then the decree nisi . . . absolute*: the usual procedure for the granting of a divorce in England: a provisional divorce is granted (a 'decree *nisi*' (Latin: 'unless')) which will become 'absolute' unless some substantial change to the known facts occurs; the king's proctor could ask for such further evidence to be presented (especially if one party claimed to have new evidence or not to have been fairly heard); if no substantial alteration is shown, the decree *nisi* becomes absolute.

608.25 *the O'Brienite scribes*: William O'Brien (1852–1928), editor of *United Ireland* at the time of its move to anti-Parnellism, though he was in America at the time; thus, the paper was in the hands of his 'scribes', particularly Matthew Bodkin, acting editor responsible for the shift.

609.10 *after the burial . . . left him alone in his glory*: from the public schoolboys' favourite verse, 'The Burial of Sir John Moore at Corunna' (1817), by the Irish poet Revd Charles Wolfe (1791–1823): 'We carved not a line, and we raised not a stone— | But we left him alone with his glory' (ll. 31–2).

609.17 *the usual boy Jones*: the usual informer, after one 'Jones', Trinity College student who supposedly informed on Robert Emmet (see 110.5–6 n.). (See *G*.)

610.3 *conditio sine qua non*: Latin: literally: 'the condition without which not', i.e. 'the indispensable condition'.

610.26 *Buckshot Foster*: William Edward ('Buckshot') Forster (1818–86), Irish Chief Secretary (1880–2), introduced Coercion Bill in Parliament (1881), acquired nickname because he reputedly authorized the use of buckshot to disperse crowds.

610.29 *the evicted tenants question*: the eviction of the very poor Irish peasants from their lands from the mid-19th c. on; resulted in the political movement (espoused by the Land League) to guarantee tenants' ownership of the land.

610.35–6 *Michael Davitt . . . backtothelander*: Davitt (see 556.3 n.) urged the purchase of lands with public funds; Bloom advocates communal working and ownership of the land (*G*).

613.9 *The Arabian Nights Entertainment*: an Arabic narrative cycle dating from *c.*1100; the first complete English translation was Sir Richard Burton's (1821–90) edition *The Thousand Nights and a Night* (1885–8).

613.9–10 *Red as a Rose is She*: sentimental novel (1870) by Rhoda Broughton (1840–1920).

613.20 *feet*: should read 'seat'.

613.25 *literally the last of the Mohicans*: *The Last of the Mohicans* (1826), a novel in James Fenimore Cooper's (1789–1851) *Leatherstocking Tales*; figuratively (not 'literally') here, the last pennies.

614.4 *around nimbly, considering frankly, at*: should read 'around, nimbly considering, frankly at'.

614.20–1 *in fact a stoning to death ... time of the split*: again, Bloom's figures are mistaken; Parnellites held 86 (of the 103) Parliamentary seats for Ireland; 72 (of the 86) were present at the famous meeting (6 Dec. 1890); 45 split from Parnell; 26 remained loyal, though some of these left during 1891. Again, the 'stoning' would be figurative, not 'in fact' (stoning being the biblical punishment for adultery).

614.28 *Mercadante's Huguenots ... Words on the Cross*: Bloom's persistent confusion: Mercadante composed *Seven Last Words* (see 79.10n.); Meyerbeer, *Huguenots* (see 160.21–3n.).

614.33 *Bid me to live ... protestant to be*: ll. 1–2 of Robert Herrick's (1591–1674) 'To Anthea, Who May Command Him Anything', in *Hesperides* (1648); 'protestant' is a pun in the poem, which is a love lyric, not a Protestant hymn.

615.6 *light opera of the Don Giovanni description*: Mozart's opera is hardly 'light', nor is Mendelssohn's style (615.8) of a 'severe classical school'.

615.15 *Shakespeare's songs, at least of in or about that period*: the music to which the songs were set was not Shakespeare's but, rather, 'of the period'.

615.16–17 *lutenist Dowland ... Doulandus*: in the original: *annos ludendo hausi* (an anagram of *Iohannes Doulandus*); Latin: 'I have consumed years in playing'; 'John Dowland': (1563–1626), English lutenist and composer, whose emblem was underwritten by the Latin motto.

615.18 *Mr Arnold Dolmetsch*: early 20th-c. London musician and instrument maker who made a psaltery for Yeats (*JJ* 154–5).

615.19–20 *Farnaby and son with their dux and comes conceits*: Giles (*c.*1565–1640) and Richard (b. 1590) Farnaby, father and son; Giles was a composer of songs; *dux*: Latin: 'leader'; *comes*: 'companion': the subject and response in Farnaby's canons.

615.20–1 *Byrd (William), who played the virginals ... Queen's Chapel*: William Byrd (1543–1623), composer and Elizabeth I's organist.

615.21–2 *one Tomkins ... and John Bull*: probably Thomas Tomkins (1572–1656), organist and composer; Dr John Bull (?1563–1628), composer, singer, organist, professor of music, not to be confused (as Bloom nearly does at 615.27–8) with John Bull the personification of England (from Dr John Arbuthnot's (1667–1735) *History of John Bull* (1712)).

616.15–16 *in medias res*: Latin: 'in the midst of things'; how all good epics begin.

616.25–6 *Youth here has End by Jans Pieter Sweelinck*: Jan Pieterszoon Sweelinck (1562–1621), Dutch organist and composer of 'Mein junges Leben hat ein End' (German: 'My young life has an end').

616.29–30 *Von der Sirenen . . . die Poeten dichten*: German: 'From the Sirens' craftiness | Poets make poems'; opening lines of the German composer Johannes Jeep's (c.1582–1644) song '*Dulcia dum loquitur cogitat insidias*' (1614) (Latin: 'The charm while they are talking is thought insidious'). The first verse: 'Von der Sirenen Listigkeit | tun die Poeten dichten | daß sie mit ihrer Lieblichkeit | viel Leut im Meer hinrichten. | Dann ihr Gesang so süß erklingt | daß die Schiffleut entschlafen, | welches das Schiff in Unglück bringt | und tut alls Übel schaffen' (German: 'From the sirens' craftiness | Poets make poems, | That they with their loveliness | Do to death many people in the sea. | For their song sounds so sweet, | That the sailors fall asleep, | Which brings misfortune to the ship | And brings about all evil').

617.30 *genus omne*: Latin: 'all the kind'.

618.25 *Und alle Schiffe brücken*: German: literally, 'And all ships bridge'; *not*, as Stephen implies, a line from Johannes Jeep's 'ballad', but a garbled version of the last two lines (see 616.29–30n.). It's as though Stephen mistakenly thinks *brücken* means 'are broken'.

ITHACA

Location: 7 Eccles Street, home of Leopold and Molly Bloom (E2). Stephen and Bloom, leaving the cabman's shelter and travelling 'at normal walking pace', follow, in order, Beresford Place (F2), Lower and Middle Gardiner Streets, Mountjoy Square West, Gardiner's Place (F3), Temple Street North (E3), the circus in front of St George's Church, and finally enter Eccles Street.

Time: 2 a.m. (*L*: 1–2; *G*: 2 a.m.)

Homer: Ithaca is Odysseus's homeland, toward which he strives through much of the narrative. When he finally does get home, he kisses the soil in grateful relief and recognition. With the help of Telemachus, Eumaeus, and Philoetius (a loyal herdsman), Odysseus first bests, then slays Penelope's suitors and reclaims his land. Through the contest of the bow, Odysseus triumphs and reveals himself as the true king. The bow (given to Odysseus by Iphitus, who was later slain by Hercules) has been kept safe by Penelope for her husband's return. In the contest, the man who can most quickly and easily string the bow, then shoot an arrow straightest through the handles of twelve standing axes, will win the hand of Penelope. Telemachus attempts the feat, but cannot string the bow. Nor can

Leodes (a suitor who claims to be faithful, but whom Odysseus does not spare) nor Eurymachus. Antinous makes the excuse that it is a feast day and no time for contests. Odysseus, still disguised as a filthy beggar, takes, tests, and strings the bow, then shoots an arrow straight through the axe handles. In the meantime, the doors have been barred by Eumaeus, Philoetius, and Eurycleia (Odysseus's faithful nurse who had already recognized him when, in bathing him, she saw the scar on his thigh made by the boar's tusk when he went to Parnassus to find his grandfather, Autolycus). Odysseus, Telemachus, Eumaeus, and Philoetius then slay the suitors. (Books XIII–XXIV)

Schemata: *L* lists as personae Ulysses, Telemachus, Eurycleia, and the Suitors, while *G* provides the correspondences: Suitors, scruples; Eurymachus, Boylan; the Bow, reason. *L* and *G* disagree completely: Colour (*L*: 'starry milky'; *G*: none), Art (*L*: none; *G*: Science), Organ (*L*: Juices; *G*: Skeleton), Symbol (*L*: none, *G*: Comets), Technic (*L*: Dialogue, Pacified style, Fusion; *G*: Catechism (impersonal)). *L*'s Sense is 'Armed Hope'.

Joyce's Hints: While writing *Ithaca*, Joyce wrote to Frank Budgen: 'I am writing *Ithaca* in the form of a mathematical catechism. All events are resolved into their cosmic physical, psychical etc. equivalents, e.g. Bloom jumping down the area, drawing water from the tap, the micturition in the garden, the cone of incense, lighted candle and statue so that not only will the reader know everything and know it in the baldest coldest way, but Bloom and Stephen thereby become heavenly bodies, wanderers like the stars at which they gaze' (*LI* 159–60; 2/21). To Claud Sykes, he commented that he was 'struggling with the aridities of Ithaca—a mathematico-astronomico-physico-mechanico-geometrico-chemico sublimation of Bloom and Stephen (devil take 'em both) to prepare for the final amplitudinously curvilinear episode *Penelope*' (*LI* 164; n.d., ?Spring 1921).

If *Circe* seemed formally to announce its escape from narrative fiction into drama, *Ithaca* appears formally to take leave of literature altogether. What we see on the page—questions and answers—bears little resemblance to any literary genre previously experienced. Here most explicitly the text plays at being an encyclopaedia, though an oddly catechitical one. We acquire more 'factual' information over the course of its pages than in any one other episode, probably more than in all the other episodes combined. We learn Bloom's height, his weight, the contents of his bookshelves, what he spent during the day (with a notable exception), the dimensions of his dream house, an assortment of astronomical facts, the path that water follows in its progress from rain to tap-water, the cat's progress during Bloom's and Stephen's procession to the back garden for an intimately detailed 'simultaneous urination'. In a language which is at once impersonal, nominative, 'arid', and self-generating, the text propels itself forward, apparently driven by an accelerating impulse to name and describe with increasing specificity increasingly irrelevant phenomena. So, Bloom unlocks and opens the door 'By inserting the barrel of an arruginated male key in the hole of an unstable female lock, obtaining a purchase on the bow of the key and turning its wards from right to left, withdrawing a bolt from its staple, pulling inward spasmodically an obsolescent unhinged door and revealing an aperture for free egress and free ingress'. Action, so precisely delineated, broken down into such minute constituent movements, applied to such exactly named physical phenomena, virtually ceases to be action. Narrative nearly disappears beneath the weight of such nominative proliferation (dialogue, the illusion of the human voice engaged in conversation, does). Not to mention the actual triviality of the action itself. Other narratives would more usually content themselves with statements in the order of 'Bloom unlocked the door to let Stephen out'. No logic beyond the stochastic (the random or merely probable) can be detected behind the selection of facts to be related. The text appears both voracious and distracted: hungry to name everything, so frantic to do so that it turns its attention now here, now there with no apparent rhyme or reason.

Driven by the need to name the physical world, *Ithaca* obsessively asks 'What?' There are eight times as many 'whats' as 'whys' in this episode, little interested as it is in motivation, and so hugely concerned with nomination. Such a drive to name, to propagate facts corresponds, at least superficially, to the hard rocks, the solidity and permanence of Ithaca. The compulsive urge to know the 'whats' in precise, unmistakable detail correlates with the anxiety of Odysseus in his initial failure to recognize his homeland. Further, though, such precise, 'scientific', denotative language deceives us into thinking it is value free, capable of avoiding the corrupting influence of figurative language, of metaphor. But a central irony of *Ithaca* is that such 'scientific' denotation reveals its own indebtedness to metaphor: note the 'male barrel', the 'unstable female lock', the 'purchase' obtained. Scientific discourse swerves into figurative trope (Greek *τρόπος*: 'to turn') and literature enters through the back door (which is, after all, an 'aperture for free egress and free ingress'). Just as narrative persists beneath the relentless drive nominally to displace it (events *do* happen here). *Ithaca* is literature after all. Joyce confessed to Budgen that *Ithaca* was his favourite episode and declared it 'the ugly duckling of the book' (Budgen, *James Joyce and the Making of 'Ulysses'*, 258). The thing about ugly ducklings is that they have an uncanny ability to turn into swans.

619.13 *paraheliotropic*: botany: 'of leaves: turning their edges in the direction of incident light' (*OED*).

620.5–10 *the anachronism . . . Rossnaree*: King Cormac Mac Art (r. *c.*254–77 (or 266 according to *The Annals of the Four Masters* (see 318.8–11 n.)), legendary convert to Christianity, which did not arrive in Ireland until St Patrick brought it in *c.*432; the *Annals* describes Cormac as dying as the result of choking on a salmon bone; Patrick's genealogy is similarly adapted from the *Annals* (*T*).

620.14–16 *a matutinal cloud . . . woman's hand*: 'matutinal' because Bloom and

Stephen have seen it in the morning; 'no bigger than a woman's hand': after the cloud Elijah sees as answer to his prayer to end the drought he has brought against Ahab: 'a little cloud out of the sea, like a man's hand' (1 Kgs. 18: 44).

620.31 *Julius Mastiansky*: should read 'Julius (Juda) Mastiansky'.

621.24–5 *five feet nine inches and a half*: the average height of Irish men recruited to British service in 1901 was 5′ 4½″, 5″ shorter than Bloom.

621.32–622.1 *the last feast of the Ascension ... christian era*: the Feast of the Ascension: fortieth day after Easter (in 1904, 12 May); the datings from other calendars described here are listed in *Thom's Dublin Directory* (1904), p. 1 (*T*).

622.15–16 *candle, a*: should read 'candle of 1 CP, a'.

622.17 *candle of 1 CP*: should read 'candle'.

623.11 *Island: of*: should read 'Island: of his aunt Sara, wife of Richie (Richard) Goulding, in the kitchen of their lodgings at 62 Clanbrassil street: of'.

623.13 *feast of Saint Francis-Xavier 1898*: St Francis Xavier (1506–52), Spanish Jesuit, missionary; his feast: 3 Dec.; see *Portrait*, ch. 3, where the retreat is held during the three days leading up to St Francis's Feast Day, the day itself marking Stephen's repentance and release from guilt.

623.32–624.5 *From Roundwood reservoir . . . Leeson street*: Joyce gets his description of the Dublin waterworks from *Thom's* (1904), 'Dublin Annals' (section for 1868, the year of their completion) (*T*).

624.21 *Mercator's projection*: Gerardus Mercator (1512–94), Flemish geographer, projected the map of the world from the three-dimensional sphere to a two-dimensional map; in the result the oceans are disproportionately large (as are the land masses near the two poles).

624.30 *multisecular*: 'lasting over many centuries'.

624.31 *luteosfulvous*: should read 'luteofulvous': 'of a tawny yellow colour' (*OED*).

624.33 *peninsulas and downwardtrending*: should read 'peninsulas and islands, its persistent formation of homothetic islands, peninsulas and downwardtrending'.

625.7 *rhabdomantic*: 'rhabdomancy': 'the art of discovering springs of water in the earth by means of a divining rod' (*OED*).

625.7 *hygrometric*: 'measuring the degree of humidity in the atmosphere' (*OED*).

625.24 *lacustrine*: 'of or pertaining to lakes'.

626.25 *luminiferous diathermanous*: 'luminiferous': 'producing or emitting light'; 'diathermanous': 'having the property of freely transmitting radiant heat' (*OED*).

626.31–2 *72 thermal units . . . 50° to 212° Fahrenheit*: no; since a 'British thermal unit' is the amount of heat necessary to raise one pound of water one degree Fahrenheit, 162 BTUs would be needed, not 72.

627.2 *falciform*: 'sickle-shaped'.

627.15 *humected*: rare: 'moistened'.

627.24 *heliotherapy, psychophysicotherapeutics, osteopathic surgery*: all (in 1904) relatively recently developed 'alternative' medical treatments: 'heliotherapy':

'sun therapy'; 'psycho-physics': 'the investigation of the relations between physical stimuli and psychic action in the production of sensations' (1879); 'osteopathy': 'a theory of disease and method of cure which assumes that deformation of the skeleton and consequent interference with the adjacent nerves and blood-vessels are the cause of most diseases' (1897) (*OED*).

628.28 *Elijah, restorer of the church of Zion*: i.e. Dr John Alexander Dowie (see 144.13 n. and 406.37 n.).

628.34–629.2 *with the light of inspiration ... prediction*: Bloom, described in the terms of John F. Taylor's earlier description of Moses (in *Aeolus*, 137.21–4).

629.13 *Light to the gentiles*: Isaiah's description of the yet-to-come Messiah: 'a light to the Gentiles' (Isa. 49: 6); but see, too, 319.15 where Bloom is derogatorily referred to as 'a new apostle to the gentiles'.

629.29–30 *Epps's massproduct, the creature cocoa*: note the 'transubstantiation' of the '*creature* cocoa' into '*mass*product'.

631.7 *kinetic poet*: in *Portrait*, Stephen remarks: 'The feelings excited by improper art are kinetic, desire or loathing. Desire urges us to possess, to go to something; loathing urges us to abandon, to go from something. These are kinetic emotions. The arts which excite them, pornographical or didactic, are therefore improper arts' (ch. 5, p. 205). Here, Bloom clearly intended to excite Molly's desire.

631.8 *Marion Tweedy*: should read 'Marion (Molly) Tweedy'.

631.16 *If Brian Boru ... Dublin now*: for Brian Boru (Boroimhe), see 96.9 n.

631.20 *Sinbad the Sailor*: an immensely popular pantomime in Dublin which went through numerous 'editions'—the first, 26 Dec. 1892; the second, 30 Jan. 1893; the details that follow are accurate *except* that it was written by Greenleaf Withers *not* by the American poet John Greenleaf Whittier (1807–92); similarly 'Nelly Bouverist' combines Kate Neverist and Nellie Bouverie (see Adams, 76–82).

631.26 *diamond jubilee of Queen Victoria*: the diamond jubilee (60th anniversary of the accession) of Queen Victoria: 22 June 1897; the opening of the Dublin Fishmarket: 11 May 1897.

632.18 *maximum postdiluvian age of 70*: 'The days of our years are threescore years and ten' (Ps. 90: 10); 'postdiluvian': after Noah's Flood; 'antediluvian' ages recorded in the Bible were much greater, e.g. Methuselah reached 'nine hundred sixty and nine years' (Gen. 5: 27).

632.18–23 *Bloom, being 1190 ... 81,396 B.C.*: is Joyce or Bloom the bad arithmetician? Three mistakes occur here; *G* explains what they are and how they happened.

633.7 *Mrs Riordan*: should read 'Mrs Riordan (Dante)'; as should now be obvious, Mrs Riordan is 'Dante' from *Portrait*, ch. 1.

634.1–2 *green and maroon ... Davitt, her tissue papers*: again, *Portrait*: 'Dante had two brushes in her press. The brush with the maroon velvet back was for Michael Davitt and the brush with the green velvet back was for Parnell. Dante gave him a cachou every time he brought her a piece of tissue paper' (ch. 1, p. 7).

634.11 *pleasant relaxation*: should read 'pleasant rigidity, a more pleasant relaxation'.

634.11 *repristination*: rare: 'restoration to original condition'.

634.19–21 *were Bloom's thoughts . . . about Stephen*: see ERRATA to make sense of this.

634.26, 29–30 *transubstantial heir*; *consubstantial heir*: aside from their place in Stephen's recurrent thoughts concerning fatherhood (see 38.24–5 n. and 374.8–9 n.), the two phrases here signify the facts of Bloom's father being dead, Stephen's alive.

635.14 *royal university*: an examination board and degree-granting institution, not a residential university.

636.1 *orreries*: machines devised to show by clockwork the motions of the planets about the sun.

636.9 *monoideal*: a Joyce coinage: probably from *monoïdeism*: 'concentration of the mind upon one idea; especially as a form of monomania' (*OED*).

637.15–16 *Queen's hotel, Queen's hotel Queen's Ho . . .*: should read 'Queen's Hotel, Queen's Hotel, Queen's Hotel, Queen's Ho . . .'.

638.6 *My Favourite Hero*: title of essay the schoolboy Joyce wrote on Ulysses (*JJ* 46).

638.16–17 *the summer solstice . . . 8.29 p.m.*: the facts are correct and probably come from *Thom's*; St Aloysius Gonzaga (1568–91), Jesuit, patron of youth, renowned for his piety and purity, died from plague contracted nursing its victims; 'Aloysius' was Joyce's saint's name.

639.11–12 *alias (a mendacious person mentioned in sacred Scripture)*: a 'Mollypropism' for 'Ananias' who lied to Peter and died (Acts 5: 1–11).

640.3–4 *Moses Maimonides, author of the More Nebukim*: for Maimonides, see 28.25 n. *Moreh Nebukim* (Hebrew: 'Guide for the Perplexed'): his attempt to reconcile Hebraic thought with Aristotelian principles.

640.8–10 *Aristotle . . . rabbinical philosopher*: a legend, utterly unsubstantiated.

640.15 *Mendoza (pugilist)*: Daniel Mendoza (1763–1836), nicknamed 'Star of Israel', an English Jewish boxer, champion of England (1792–5).

640.15 *Ferdinand Lassalle*: (1825–64), German Jewish Socialist political reformer who worked to found a workers' party in Germany.

640.19 *suil, suil, suil . . . suil go cuin*: Gaelic: *siúl, siúl, siúl a rún, siúl go socair agus siúl go ciúin*: 'walk, walk, walk my dear, walk safely and walk calmly'; first two lines of the chorus of the ballad 'Shule Aroon' (Gaelic: *Siúl a rún*).

640.21 *Kifeloch, harimon . . . l'zamatejch*: Hebrew of S. of S. 4: 3: 'thy temples are like a piece of a pomegranate within thy locks'.

640.25 *On the penultimate*: should read 'By juxtaposition. On the penultimate'.

640.28–9 *Irish characters . . . modified*: the Gaelic characters (corresponding to the English letters *g, e, d, m*; the seventh, fifth, fourth, and eleventh letters respectively): 'simple': ᵹ, e, ꝺ, m; 'modified': ᵹ̇, ė, ꝺ̇, ṁ.

640.29–31 *Hebrew characters ... 100*: 'goph' should read 'qoph'; the Hebrew characters: 'gimel': ג (*g*; third); 'aleph': א (*a*; first); 'daleth': ד (*d*; fourth); 'mem': מ (*m*; thirteenth); 'qoph': ק (*q*; nineteenth); numerical values, respectively: 3, 1, 4, 40, 100.

641.2 *the extinct and the revived*: biblical Hebrew, like classical Greek, is considered a 'dead' language because it is a written, studied, but not 'spoken' language. The Hebrew spoken by Jews has been modified by Aramaic and Latin. In 1904 common use of Gaelic in Ireland had virtually disappeared (except in the West) though efforts were being made to revive it.

641.7–8 *epenthetic and servile letters*: respectively, 'letters inserted in the middle of words' and 'letters not belonging to the root of the words in which they occur' (*OED*).

641.8–11 *both having been taught ... Ireland*: a legend propagated by Geoffrey Keating (*c.*1570–*c.*1644), in his *Foras Feasa ar Éirinn* ('History of Ireland') (*c.*1629), Bk. I, sect. xv: he construes a genealogy for the Milesians Heber and Heremon which includes as their ancestor Fenius Farsaigh (a supposed descendant of Noah), who, Keating claims, founded a school of languages on the plain of Shinar, 242 years after the Flood, 60 years after the Tower of Babel (see Adams, 136–7).

641.13 *Torah*: strictly, the Pentateuch, or first five books of the Old Testament (supposedly written by Moses): Genesis, Exodus, Leviticus, Numbers, Deuteronomy; but also the Oral Law and its Talmudic commentaries.

641.13–14 *Talmud (Mischna and Ghemara)*: Jewish civil and ceremonial law; 'Mishna': the law elaborated from the Pentateuch; 'Gemara': commentary on the Mishna.

641.14 *Massor*: the 'Masora': a system of pronunciation for biblical Hebrew including textual information about the Hebrew Bible.

641.14 *Book of the Dun Cow*: Gaelic: *Leabhar na hUidre*: earliest transcription of Irish legends, compiled by Mailmur Mac Kelleher (d. 1106).

641.14–15 *Book of Ballymote*: see 318.4–5 n.

641.15 *Garland of Howth*: 8th- or 9th-c. illuminated Latin manuscript of the four Gospels.

641.15 *Book of Kells*: *c.*8th-c. illuminated manuscript of the four Gospels; Ireland's most famous illuminated manuscript and, Joyce maintained, an inspiration for *Finnegans Wake*.

641.15 *their dispersal*: history records numerous Jewish dispersals (or 'Diaspora'); principal among them: the Babylonian captivity (597–538 BC); the expulsion from (the now) Israel by the Romans (*c.*70 AD); the expulsion from Spain (1492); expulsion from Eastern Europe in the 19th c. The Irish similarly: Flight of the Earls (1607); after the Treaty of Limerick (1691); during the Great Famine (1840s).

641.16–17 *ecclesiastical rites ... Eve's tavern*: for 'S. Marys abbey', see 221.10–12 n. Catholic worship survived during English attempts to suppress it in the 16th and 17th cs., partly through the wiles of the Franciscans, who in 1618 established an underground church in Rosemary Lane, off Merchant's Quay (D4); the entrance was in a lane on which a tavern named 'Adam and Eve's' was also located, so church attenders could appear to be going to the pub; the church became known colloquially as Adam and Eve's (see the opening line of *Finnegans Wake*).

641.18 *proscription of... jewish dress acts*: laws enacted after the Treaty of Limerick (1691) were expressly aimed at the suppression of Catholicism, and, in legend, the 'wearin' o' the green' was prohibited (see 44.6 n.); the history of Judaism is rife with acts suppressing the wearing of Jewish religious dress.

641.19 *restoration in Chanan David of Zion*: should read 'Chanah'; i.e. the restoration of 'Zion' (a Jewish homeland) in King David's land, Canaan; the purchase of Palestine from the sultan of Turkey for such a purpose was proposed by Theodore Herzel (1896) (see *G*).

641.23–4 *Kolod balejwaw ... homijah*: the opening lines of the Austrian Hebrew Naphtali Herz Imber's (1856–1909) 'Hatikvah' (Hebrew: 'Hope'), which later became Israel's national anthem; loose translation: 'As long as deep within the heart | The soul of Judea is turbulent and strong' (*T* and *G*).

641.32 *cuneiform*: ancient writing of the Near East using wedge-shaped characters.

641.33 *virgular*: with sloping lines.

641.33 *quinquecostate*: Latin: 'five ribbed'.

641.33 *ogham*: ancient Irish and British 20-character alphabet: uses parallel strokes on either side of or across a continuous line (*OEED*).

642.11 *The traditional figure of hypostasis*: i.e. what Jesus the man looked like; 'hypostasis': the whole nature of Christ as god and man combined.

642.12 *Johannes Damascenus, Lentulus Romanus and Epiphanius Monachus*: all commentators on the physical characteristics of Jesus; in order: St John Damascene (*c.*700–*c.*754), Doctor of the Church, described Jesus as 'tall' and 'of a pale complexion, olive-tinted, and of the colour of wheat'; Lentulus Romanus, a fictional Roman governor of Judea before Pontius Pilate and supposed composer of a letter describing Jesus as 'a man of tall stature' whose hair was 'somewhat wine-coloured'; St Epiphanius the Monk (*c.*315–403), Father of the Eastern Church, described Jesus much as St John Damascene was later to do.

642.13 *leucodermic, sesquipedalian*: respectively: 'white-skinned'; literally, 'a foot and a half in height', figuratively, 'lengthy'. On the latter: Stephen may mistakenly think that the prefix 'sesqui' ('one and a half') means 'six', so 'sesquipedalian': 'six-footed', i.e. 'six feet tall'; according to tradition, Jesus was the only man ever to be exactly six feet tall. See *Stephen Hero*: 'I don't believe . . . that Jesus was the only man that ever had pure auburn hair . . . nor that he was the only man that was exactly six feet high, neither more nor less' (122).

643.2–644.17 *Little Harry Hughes . . . lies among the dead*: 'it ow'er the je's' should read 'it o'er the jew's'; variant of actual ballad derived from the story of the boy, Hugh of Lincoln, supposedly crucified by Jews (*c.*1255).

645.15 *veridicity*: 'truthfulness in speech'.

646.10 *distant intervals to its*: should read 'distant intervals to more distant intervals to its'.

647.17 *imbalsamation*: rare: 'balsamation': 'embalming'.

648.19 *Mrs Emily Sinico*: her death occurs in 'A Painful Case' in *Dubliners.*

649.19 *imprevidibility*: Joyce's Latinate coinage: *im-* ('un') *pre-* ('fore') *vid-* ('see'; from Latin: *videre*, 'to see'), so 'unforeseeability'.

649.21 *reagent*: 'reactive substance'.

650.22–3 *ineluctably constructed upon the incertitude of the void*: see 199.4–10.

650.29–30 *In what order of precedence . . . inhabitation effected?*: in the manner of the ceremonial celebration of Passover (which marks the Jewish exodus from Egypt to the wilderness) in which the head of the house takes precedence.

650.33 *Diaconal*: 'of or belonging to a deacon'.

651.1 *secreto*: Latin: 'set apart'; prayers spoken in a low voice which immediately precede the preface in the Mass.

651.2–3 *The 113 th. modus peregrinus . . . barbaro*: Latin: 'mode of going abroad'; then Ps. 113: 1 (Vulgate; 114: 1 AV): 'When Israel went out of Egypt, the house of Jacob from a people of strange language'; the verse is used in the celebration of Passover.

651.15–18 *the infinite lattiginous . . . centre of the earth*: 'lattiginous': 'of the nature of a lattice'; it is a commonplace that stars invisible in daylight can be seen during the day from the bottom of a hole 'sufficiently deep'; as of yet, 'sufficiently deep' has not been reached.

651.18 *Sirius (alpha in Canis Maior)*: Bloom's facts here were all correct in terms of 1904 astronomical understanding, though his estimates are inevitably low (at times very low) or slow (*G*).

651.23–4 *of the parallax . . . evermoving*: 'parallactic drift': the distance a star appears to move that really results from the movement of the earth; stars do move, but they appear to move more than they do because of parallactic drift.

651.24 *evermoving from*: should read 'evermoving wanderers from'.

652.9–18 *the existence of a number computed . . . any of its powers*: Kenner asserts that Bloom's number, 9^9 to the ninth power ($9^9 \times 9^9 \times 9^9 \ldots$), 'will commence with 4 and boast 369,693,099 additional digits' and that Bloom's stated need for '33 closely printed volumes of 1000 pages each' to reproduce the number is 'in the ballpark' (167–8).

652.26 *statosphere*: should read 'stratosphere'.

652.34–5 *to vanities . . . all that is vanity*; Eccles. 1: 2: 'Vanity of vanities, saith the Preacher, vanity of vanities, all is vanity'.

653.1–2 *and the problem of possible redemption? . . . major*: Bloom's problem: (major premiss) if life exists elsewhere it is human and therefore subject to human frailties ('vanity'), so (minor premiss), since if life exists elsewhere it will be vain, redemption is improbable.

653.4–34 *The various colours . . . pallor of human beings*: a representative catalogue of astronomical knowledge available as of 1904 (*G* provides detailed glosses): stars 'up to and including the 7th' brilliancy could be seen by the naked eye (if one were keen-sighted); 'Walsingham way': the Milky Way as referred to in *Piers Plowman* (14th c.); 'Gallileo . . . Galle': all discovered (or confirmed the existence of) various moons, asteroids, or planets; Bode and Kepler: numerically calculated distances between planets (Bode) or the ratios of distances from the sun to rotation times (Kepler); 'hirsute': 'hairy' (because of comets' long tails); 'perihelion': of an orbit, the point nearest the sun; 'aphelion': of an orbit, the point farthest from the sun; what were believed to be the 'Libyan [area of Mars] floods' occurred in 1894 (12 years after Stephen was born); a new star did appear above delta in Cassiopeia eight years after Shakespeare was born (see 201.22–7); new stars were being discovered constantly ('Corona Septentrionalis' in May 1866, Bloom's birth year; 'S. Andromedae' in 1885, three years after Stephen's birth), so Bloom's guess about the coincidences of the births of stars and individuals will be right (if one allows a sufficient time lag one way or the other for the 'coincidence').

654.4 *Utopia*: after Sir Thomas More's (?1477–1535) political essay *Utopia* (1516); 'Utopia' (meaning 'no place') is More's 'New Latin' coinage.

654.6 *probable*: should be moved to follow 'its' at 654.9.

654.17 *selenographical*: of a map of the moon's surface.

654.22 *tellurian*: of earth dwellers.

655.7 *invisible person*: should read 'invisible attractive person'.

655.22 *irruent*: rushing into.

655.31 *pelosity*: hairiness.

655.31–656.1 *the problem of the sacerdotal . . . unnecessary servile work)*: problem: if Jesus was born with perfect complete body, why was he circumcised and what was its effect? Was he 'changed' thereby? The Catholic theological position is 'no' (see Rom. 4); Jesus's circumcision is fêted on 1 Jan. under the auspices of the Octave of the Nativity (in 1904 Ireland, a holy day).

656.1–5 *problem as to whether . . . hair and toenails*: problem: was the excised prepuce of Jesus (now a relic resting in Calcata outside Rome) to be worshipped as the body of God (with the supreme worship: 'latria') or as human (with 'hyperdulia', the veneration accorded the Virgin Mary)?

656.7–9 *A star precipitated . . . sign of Leo*: the shooting star moves from the Lyre (Orpheus's lyre, symbol of the poet), past the Coma Berenices ('Tress of Berenice'; named for Berenice, wife of Ptolemy III, who vowed she would sacrifice her hair to Aphrodite if her husband returned safely from war; he did; she did; it became a constellation) towards Leo (the Lion, an obvious analogue of Leopold).

656.26–7 *Liliata rutilantium . . . Chorus excipiat*: Stephen changes the original punctuation and phrasing here (see 10.21–2 n.): Latin: 'Bright as lilies. A throng gathers about you. Jubilant you of virgins. Chorus rescues.'

657.28–9 *his gaze turned . . . east*: 'Mizrach': Hebrew: ' the east'; Bloom's turning to the east parallels the posture in prayer of devout Jews when west of Jerusalem.

660.16 *ipsorelative . . . aliorelative*: 'ipsorelative': with relation to the self (Latin: *ipse*: 'self'); 'aliorelative': with relation to others (Latin: *alius*: 'other').

660.28 *Catalogue these books*: in the list that follows, one book has dropped out: add '*The Beauties of Killarney* (wrappers).' after '*The Child's Guide* (blue cloth).' Most are actual books, only five are untraceable: *The Beauties of Killarney*, *Thoughts from Spinoza*, *Philosophy of the Talmud*, *A Handbook of Astronomy* (all of these being 'generic books') and *The Hidden Life of Christ* (appropriately unknown). *G* and *T* provide glosses.

663.5 *Narcissus*: in Greek myth: a handsome youth who despised love; Echo fell in love with him and, when spurned, pined away until only her voice remained; Nemesis arranged for him to catch a glimpse of himself in a stream; he fell in love with his own reflection which he henceforth watched incessantly; eventually, trying to make out his features in the river Styx, he died; on that spot flowers bearing his name sprang up. His name has come to be synonymous with self-love. (See 508.13–14 and 725.27–32.)

663.29 *occasion* (*10 October*: should read 'occasion (17 October'.

664.2–24 *Debit . . . BALANCE . . . 0.16.6*: ERRATA emends Bloom's balance to the arithmetically correct sum: '0.17.5'; but absent from the 'Debit' column is the eleven shillings he spent at Bella Cohen's.

664.37 *unguial*: should read 'unguical' (and at 665.3): 'of a nail or claw'.

665.12 *Rus in Urbe*: Latin: ' the Country in the City'.

665.12–13 *Qui Si Sana*: Latin: 'Here One is Healthy'.

665.24 *5 minutes*: should read '15 minutes'.

665.27 *messuage*: dwelling-house, its outbuildings, and adjacent land.

666.34 *haytedder*: machine for spreading damp hay so it can dry.

667.11 *solidungular*: of an animal, having uncloven hooves.

667.13 *erigible*: capable of being erected.

667.29 *estivation*: summer retreat.

667.29 *vespertinal*: occurring in the evening.

668.12 *(Semper paratus)*: Latin: 'Always ready'.

668.28 *covin*: arch.: fraud, deceit, but also 'a privy agreement between two or more to the prejudice of another' (*OED*).

668.29 *venville rights*: common rights to use of forests (for pasture, fuel, and natural materials for building) held by tenants of certain lands (specifically those adjoining Dartmoor).

669.11 *Charles Darwin*: (1809–82), English biologist and evolutionist, author of *On the Origin of Species* (1859) and *The Descent of Man and Selection in Relation to Sex* (1871).

669.13–14 *James Fintan Lalor*: (1807–49), Irish political journalist, supporter of radical land reform (nationalization) and the use of physical force to secure Irish independence; a Young Irelander (splinter group of the Repeal Movement, grouped around the *Nation*, for which Lalor wrote (founded by Thomas Osborne Davis (1814–45), John Blake Dillon (1816–66), and Charles Gavan Duffy (1816–1903)), and the *United Irishman* (see 669.14n.) and devoted to romantic and cultural nationalism).

669.14 *John Fisher Murray*: (1811–65), Irish political satirist and Young Irelander.

669.14 *John Mitchel*: (1815–75), Irish radical journalist, Young Irelander, wrote for *Nation*, founded *United Irishman* (1848), 'in which he advocated a "holy war" to sweep English influence from Ireland' (Foster, 314 n. xxiii), imprisoned, escaped to America (1853), returned (1872), elected MP (1875) eight days before dying.

669.14 *J. F. X. O'Brien*: (1828–1905), American Fenian and doctor, served as medical officer in the Union Army of the US Civil War, moved to Ireland, involved in Fenian uprising in Cork (1867), convicted and sentenced to death, commuted, released (1869), MP (1885–1905), Parnellite until the 1891 split, advocate of economic and political independence for Ireland (*G*).

669.22 *the marquess of Ripon*: George Frederick Samuel Robinson (1827–1909), first marquess of Ripon, Catholic convert and supporter of Gladstone's Irish policies for Home Rule and land reform.

669.23 *John Morley*: should read '(honest) John Morley'; (1838–1923), English statesman, outspoken in his opposition to England's policy of coercion in Ireland, pro-Home Rule; briefly Chief Secretary for Ireland (1886).

670.23 *on delivery at*: should read 'on delivery per delivery at'.

672.5–6 *Blum Pascha . . . Rockefeller*: all eminent, most Jewish, financiers (*G*).

672.9 *eventually*: should read 'eventuality'.

673.8 *Mizpah*: Hebrew: 'Watchtower'; used as a greeting, prayer, or blessing in Hebrew (see Gen. 31: 49).

673.16 *William Ewart Gladstone's . . . (never passed into law)*: the bill (the 'first Home Rule bill'), proposed in 1886 by Gladstone's coalition government (in which the Parnellites held the exact balance), defeated 343 to 313 on 8 June 1886 (leading to the collapse of Gladstone's government); the second Home Rule bill, also proposed by Gladstone (Feb. 1893), passed the House of Commons but was resoundingly defeated in the House of Lords (Sep. 1893).

673.21 *deceased: 3 typewritten*: should read 'deceased: a cameo scarfpin, property of Rudolph Bloom (born Virag), deceased: 3 typewritten'.

673.24 *boustrephodontic*: more commonly 'boustrophedonic': of a writing which follows alternately from right to left then left to right, like the course of the plough (*OED*); Bloom's code: write out the alphabet, directly beneath write it again *in reverse*, assigning A to Z, B to Y, C to X, etc.; this makes the encoded message read when decoded: M.RTH./DR.FF.LC/D.LPH.NS/B.RN ('vowels suppressed'); note that the last 'line' ('Y.IM': 'B.RN') does not follow in 'boustrophedonic' fashion.

673.33 *buccal*: of or pertaining to the cheeks (here, the cheeks of the buttocks).

674.11 *thaumaturgic*: wonder-working.

675.2–3 *the most immediate*: should read 'the not immediate'.

675.7 *Paula*: feminine of 'Paul' (Joyce's middle name, Augustine, was entered on his baptismal certificate as 'Augusta' (Gorman, 6)).

675.30–1 *the passage of thanksgiving... Pessach (Passover)*: a prayer in which thanks are given for the deliverance of the Jews from Egypt, for the Torah and laws of Judaism, and for the plentiful food about to be eaten.

676.5–6 *das Herz... Gott... dein*: German: 'the heart'; 'God'; 'your'.

676.18 *hebdomadary*: every seven days; weekly.

676.20–1 *ineffability of the tetragrammation*: should read 'tetragrammaton'; 'ineffability': 'unutterability'; 'tetragrammaton': the four consonants of the Hebrew name of God (not to be spoken): JHVH or JHWH or YHVH or YHWH, usually expanded to 'Yahweh' (or 'Jehovah').

676.29 *Maria Theresia, empress of Austria*: (1717–80), married to Holy Roman Emperor Francis I, daughter of Holy Roman Emperor Charles VI.

677.23 *helotic*: of or pertaining to a serf.

677.25 *Mendicancy*: beggary or begging.

678.27 *the cliffs of Moher*: the list includes, as would be expected, the noted 'beauty spots' of Ireland; the subsequent list includes a rather more idiosyncratic grouping of world sites.

679.14 *septentrional*: after *Septentriones* (Latin: *septem*: 'seven'; *triones*: 'ploughing oxen'), the Roman name for the seven stars forming the constellation Ursa Major ('the Plough' or 'Big Dipper').

679.29 *Everyman*: Morality play (*c.*1509–19) in which Everyman faces death accompanied only by Good Deeds; Joyce parodies its style in *Oxen*, 368.37–369.14.

679.29 *Noman*: the name Odysseus provides when asked his name by Polyphemus the Cyclops (see *Cyclops* headnote).

680.5 *hea would her*: should read 'he would hear'.

680.6 *summons or recall*: see Gilbert schema. In the *Odyssey*, Hermes's message to Calypso (and through her to Odysseus) that Odysseus is to be freed to return to Ithaca.

680.9–10 *an estranged avenger... dark crusader*: after Odysseus's behaviour on his return to Ithaca.

680.31–681.11 *breakfast (burnt offering) ... (atonement)*: a Jewish liturgical recapitulation of Bloom's day (parallel to the parodic Catholic litany in *Circe*, 470.8–19). See *G* for full glosses.

680.33–681.1 *Urim and Thummim*: two objects whose precise nature is unknown, worn in or attached to the breastplate of the Jewish high priest whereby he came to know the will of Jehovah (see Exod. 28: 29–30).

681.3 *Simchath Torah*: Hebrew: 'Rejoice in the Law'; last day of the Feast of Tabernacles (see 58.30n.) when the reading of the Torah is completed and re-begun.

681.4 *Shira Shirim*: Hebrew: 'Song of Songs' (Song of Solomon).

681.23 *walking, silently,*: should read 'walking, charged with collected articles of recently disvested male wearing apparel, silently'.

683.19 *Assuming Mulvey to be the first term*: this list, hyperbolic in the extreme if anything remotely resembling sufficient definitions of adultery are taken into account, has proven the stumbling block of many an unwitting Joycean. Proceed with care.

684.33 *natured nature*: translation of the medieval Latin *natura naturata*: the world as an effect of material causes.

685.11 *altered*: should read 'parallel'.

685.25 *impossibly. If any,*: should read 'impossibly. Hushmoney by moral influence, possibly. If any,'.

685.32–3 *the presupposed intangibility of the thing in itself*: perhaps parodic of Immanuel Kant (1724–1804), German philosopher, who argued that reality exists on two levels, the 'phenomenal' (the surface of things, knowable and capable of demonstration) and the 'noumenal' (the *Ding an Sich* or 'thing-in-itself', only capable of postulation, not demonstration).

686.3–8 *an aorist preterite proposition . . . passive voice*: after Greek grammar: 'aorist': verb expressing the simple past tense; 'preterite': a completed past action. The two ('active' and 'passive' voice) 'correlative propositions': 'He fucked her'; 'She was fucked by him'.

686.15–17 *(the land of the midnight sun . . land of promise)*: all places of (actual or metaphorical) endless sun: lands of immortality or blessedness.

686.17 *adipose posterior*: should read 'adipose anterior and posterior'.

687.10 *peccaminous*: 'sinful'.

687.12 *postcenal*: 'after dinner'; from Latin *cena*: 'dinner'; but in medieval Latin, *cena* refers specifically to the Lord's Supper.

687.31 *January 1895, aged*: should read 'January 1894, aged'.

688.3 *catamenic hemorrhage*: more usually 'catamenial': 'of menstrual discharge'; so menstrual bleeding.

688.29 *Gea-Tellus*: conflation of Greek goddess of the earth, Gaea, and Roman goddess of the earth, Tellus Mater.

689.10–11 *a square round . . . roc's auk's egg*: 'square round' as in the circle squared (see 484.5 n.); the roc: a huge, mythical bird capable of carrying elephants off; Sinbad finds a roc's egg in *Arabian Nights*; the auk: an extinct flightless bird which laid only one egg at each sitting.

PENELOPE

Location: Bedroom, upstairs, 7 Eccles Street, home of Leopold and Molly Bloom (E2).

Time: ∞

Homer: Penelope, Odysseus's faithful wife, increasingly hopelessly waits at home in Ithaca for the return of her husband whom she has not seen since his departure for the Trojan War ten years earlier. When leaving, he warned her that he might not return and bade her, 'when you see this son of ours grown to bearded manhood, then leave your own palace and marry whom you will' (223). Telemachus having now reached adulthood, Penelope begins to despair. Until now, she has been able to hold off the suitors (who would have her hand and thus gain Odysseus's lands and wealth): 'I spin them out a thread of stratagems' (231). Most famously, she declared that she would choose one from among the suitors when she had finished weaving a fitting burial robe for her father-in-law Laertes. Then she set about weaving during the day, only to delay finishing by unravelling it at night. She succeeds with the subterfuge for three years until, betrayed by one of her serving women, she is discovered at her deceit by the suitors. Declaring that her true beauty was taken away with Odysseus's departure (and that it would only return with her noble husband), she now despairs. By the time Odysseus does return in disguise, she willingly sets one last test for the suitors: the contest of the bow. (See *Ithaca* above.) After Odysseus succeeds at the contest and slays the suitors (during which time Penelope remains in her chamber upstairs), Eurycleia (his faithful nurse) tells Penelope Odysseus has returned, but Penelope refuses to believe her. Odysseus, having bathed and had his own stature restored by Athena, addresses her: 'No other wife would be heartless enough to keep aloof from her husband so' (280). Penelope responds with her final stratagem, telling Eurycleia to fetch a bedstead and make a bed for him in the bridal chamber he built himself. Odysseus passes the test by asking who had succeeded in removing the bed he had made himself, using as bedpost the living olive tree around which he had built the chamber. Penelope at last recognizes him and begs to be forgiven for her suspicion. They retire to bed, where 'Penelope listened to him enraptured, and sleep did not fall upon her eyelids till he had told his tale to the end' (284). (Her presence is felt in virtually every Book of the *Odyssey*; the recognition/reconciliation scene occurs in Book XXIII.)

Schemata: *L* lists as personae Laertes, Ulysses, Penelope. *G*'s correspondences 'dehumanize' Penelope by making her 'Earth' and her Web 'Movement'. *L* and *G* agree only on the Art (both have none) and, in part, on the Technic (*L*: Monologue, Resigned style; *G*: Monologue (female)). On all else they differ. Colour (*L*: 'starry milky *then* new dawn'; *G*: none), Organ (*L*: Fat; *G*: Flesh), Symbol (*L*: none; *G*: Earth). *L*'s Sense is 'The Past Sleeps'.

Joyce's Hints: To Frank Budgen Joyce wrote of the final episode: '*Penelope* is the clou of the book. The first sentence contains 2500 words. There are eight sentences in the episode. It begins and ends with the female word *yes*. It turns like the huge earth ball slowly surely and evenly round and round spinning, its four cardinal points being the female breasts, arse, womb and cunt expressed by the words *because*, *bottom* (in all senses bottom button, bottom of the class, bottom of the sea, bottom of his heart), *woman*, *yes*. Though probably more obscene than any preceding episode it seems to me to be perfectly sane full amoral fertilisable untrustworthy engaging shrewd limited prudent indifferent *Weib. Ich bin der* [*sic*] *Fleisch der stets bejaht*' (*SL* 285; 16/8/21). To Harriet Weaver he commented, first, that '*Penelope* has no beginning, middle or end' (*LI* 172; 7/10/21) and, later, that he had 'rejected the usual interpretation of her as a human apparition—that aspect being better represented by Calypso, Nausikaa and Circe, to say nothing of the pseudo Homeric figures. In conception and technique I tried to depict the earth which is prehuman and presumably posthuman' (*LI* 180; 8/2/22). Though note that a year earlier he had written to Budgen: 'The last word (human, all too human) is left to Penelope. This is the indispensable countersign to Bloom's passport to eternity. I mean the last episode *Penelope*' (*LI* 160; 2/21).

'they all write about some woman in their poetry' thinks Molly, casually dismissing the traditional male impulse to 'write women' into their texts. Similarly, she pronounces Bloom's proffered reading matter inadequate, for 'theres nothing for a woman in that all invention made up'. When with equal disregard she thinks 'I dont like books with a Molly in them', her general suspicion of men's notions of how to write (or write *for*) women has narrowed to an implied rejection of *Ulysses* itself. Now, in one sense, none of this is new: we have by now become used to *Ulysses*'s self-reflexive capacity, its ability to comment upon its own signifying procedures, its inclination critically to scrutinize its own pretensions to meaning. The newness comes in the specific gendering of these dismissals, that is, in their perspectival shift from the masculine to the feminine (however much the fact of their being written by a man may be thought to diminish the degree of shift). Or, put slightly differently, the capacity to change perspective—to see and be seen, to embrace and criticize, to distinguish through particularity and unite through commonality, to inhabit both body and mind, memory and immediacy—is precisely what constitutes 'femininity' in *Penelope*.

Molly repeatedly imagines herself in the place of others as she continually identifies across a range of positions: 'I wouldnt mind being a man and get up on a lovely woman', 'I know what boys feel with that down on their cheek', 'just imagine having to get into bed with a thing like that that might murder you any moment', 'Im a little like that dirty bitch in that Spanish photo he has'. (It is, of course, his equivalent ability which distinguishes Bloom from other men in Molly's mind: 'that was why I liked him because I saw he understood or felt what a woman is'.) Similarly, she can by turns be the desiring subject ('I made him blush a little when I got over him'; 'I had the devils own job to get it out of him') or the desired object ('they [her breasts] were so plump and tempting ... they excite myself sometimes'). She can appreciate one moment ('itd be much better for the world to be governed by the women in it') and criticize the next ('we are a dreadful lot of bitches'). Or individually distinguish on the basis of idiosyncrasy ('theyre all so different'; 'I never in all my life felt anyone had one the size of that to make you feel full up'; 'Poldy has more spunk in him') and generically unite on the grounds of similarity ('they want to do everything too quick take all the pleasure out of it').

If Molly's text is the most overtly libidinal (no one else concerns *himself* quite so much with sex), it is also the most strictly mentally contained—this is the only episode narrated *entirely* in interior monologue, that textual analogue of thought. Her mental terrain is memory. This land she inhabits with neither regret at its passing nor longing for its return. For Molly's memory serves her present pleasure: she openly acknowledges its actual pastness' ('I suppose theyre all dead and rotten long ago'), yet freely brings it into the present to meet the ends of immediate satisfaction ('first I put my arms around him yes and drew him down to me so he could feel my breasts all perfume yes and his heart was going like mad and yes I said yes I will Yes').

In this seemingly endless recirculation of the past, *Penelope* embodies *Ulysses*'s ostensibly limitless capacity to textually recycle itself. And despite Joyce's declaration that '*Penelope* has no beginning, middle or end', it is paradoxically she who can bring *Ulysses* to an (affirmative) end. Perhaps, as Molly knows, this is 'because a woman whatever she does knows where to stop'.

691.12 *Pooles Myriorana*: should read 'Myriorama'; a 'myriorama': a large picture composed of several smaller pictures which can be rearranged to form a new picture; Pooles' was a travelling show (usually a travelogue with commentary) which appeared in Dublin about once every year.

692.34 *anyhow its done now once and for all*: if 'it' refers to 'having extramarital sexual relations' generally, Molly's thought casts light on Bloom's list of suspected rivals (683.19–27).

693.18 *give something to H H the pope for a penance*: 'H[is] H[oliness] the Pope' would have differing views, since Catholic doctrine specifies that it is an even greater sin to commit adultery with a priest than with a layman.

693.30–3 *that thunder woke me up . . . awful thunderbolts*: Stephen (and Joyce) share Molly's feelings about thunderstorms (*JJ* 25; *Portrait*: 'I fear many things: dogs, horses, firearms, the sea, thunderstorms, machinery, the country roads at night. . . . I imagine, Stephen said, that there is a malevolent reality behind those things I say I fear' (ch. 5, p. 243)).

694.30 *about Our Lord being a carpenter*: he was, according to Mark 6: 2–3.

694.32–3 *the first socialist he said He was*: after Matt. 19: 21: 'Jesus said unto him, If thou wilt be perfect, go and sell that thou hast, and give to the poor, and thou shalt have treasure in heaven: and come and follow me'.

695.1–4 *mass or meeting . . . was going to*: these lines should appear as the first four lines of 694, not 695.

695.16 *plabbery*: Gaelic: *plabar*: 'anything pasty, viscous, or slushy'; also *plabaíre*: 'fleshy-faced person with thick indistinct speech'.

695.16 *to her*: should follow 'declaration' at 695.15.

695.24 *glauming*: Gaelic: *glám*: 'grasp clutch'.
695.34 *grigged*: Gaelic: *griog*: 'excite desire, tantalize'.
696.12 *up up*: should read 'U p up'.
696.12 *O Sweetheart May*: (1895) song in which child May asks singer to marry her but when he returns (after she's grown) she is already betrothed to another.
696.17–27 *Mrs Maybrick that poisoned her husband . . . hang a woman*: Mrs Florence Elizabeth Chandler Maybrick (1862–1941) was accused of murdering her husband, James (1839–89), by arsenic poisoning (11 May 1889); convicted; sentenced to death; sentence commuted (22 Aug. 1889); released (25 Jan. 1904).
697.6 *mouth*: should read 'month'. The stone for Molly's month, Sept., is chrysolite, not aquamarine (Oct.'s stone).
697.14 *Katty Lanner*: Katti Lanner (1831–1915), ballet mistress and choreographer of English Theatre of Varieties, London; daughter of Joseph Lanner (1801–43), Austrian composer, and creator of the Viennese waltz. (See 535.22 and *G*.)
697.18 *Bartell dArcy*: it is Bartell d'Arcy's singing of 'The Lass of Aughrim' which affects Gretta Conroy so strongly in 'The Dead'.
697.19 *Gounods Ave Maria*: Charles François Gounod (1818–93), French composer, set the 'Hail Mary' (*Ave Maria*) (1859) to a Bach melody.
697.19–20 *what are we waiting . . . the brow and part*: from a song 'Good-bye' by G. J. Whyte-Melville and F. Paolo Tosti; third verse: 'What are we waiting for? Oh? My Heart! | Kiss me straight on the brows, and part! | Again, again! My Heart! My Heart! | What are we waiting for, you and I? | A pleading look, a stifled cry, | Good-bye, Forever, Good-bye'.
697.35 *skeezing*: covert staring.
698.4 *Zingari colours*: gypsy colours; from Italian *zingari*: 'gypsies'.
698.14–15 *O Maria Santisima*: Italian: 'O Mary Most Holy'.
698.15: *dreeping*: drooping or walking very slowly (*G*).
699.17 *for England home and beauty*: see 216.9, 12 n.
699.18 *there is a charming girl I love*: after 'It is a Charming Girl I Love', song in Act I of *The Lily of Killarney* (see 89.9 n.).
700.9 *Kathleen Kearney*: daughter of 'A Mother' in *Dubliners*.
700.13 *Stabat Mater*: see 79.4 n.
700.14: *Lead Kindly Light*: song by John Henry (Cardinal) Newman (1801–80), properly titled 'The Pillar of Cloud' (1833).
700.17 *Sinner Fein*: Molly-propism for Sinn Féin (see 7.31 n.).
700.19 *Griffith*: should read 'Griffiths', hence Molly's misremembered version of (Arthur) Griffith (see 43.11–12 n.).
700.21 *Pretoria*: capital of the Boer republic of Transvaal in South Africa; no battle of the Boer War was fought here, though there were battles at Ladysmith and Bloemfontein (see 434.10 n. and 457.10 n.).
700.27–8 *oom Paul and the rest of the old Krugers*: 'oom [uncle] Paul': Stephanus Johannes Paulus Kruger (1825–1904), president of Transvaal (1883–1900), opposed to English dominion.

700.35 *the Dublins that won Tugela*: a costly Boer War campaign for the English was fought in the Tugela River valley; they (including a battalion of Royal Dublin Fusiliers) crossed the river and stormed Spion Kop (key Boer position) but were caught in crossfire and had to retreat having suffered heavy casualties.

701.37 *Manola*: Spanish: a 'Manola' is a female Madrilenian of low class; hence, a street song sung by such a one (?).

702.5 *the Gentlewoman*: London sixpenny weekly 'ladies'' magazine.

702.34 *Ill be 33 in September*: no, she'll be 34 (see 687.25–6).

702.37 *Kitty OShea in Grantham street*: not to be confused with the more famous 'Kitty O'Shea', wife of Charles Stewart Parnell.

703.2–3 *Mrs Langtry the Jersey Lily the prince of Wales was in love with*: Lillie Langtry (1852–1929), 'the Jersey Lily'; daughter of a Jersey vicar; married wealthy Irish widower Edward Langtry; had an affair with the Prince of Wales; left her husband; became a successful (if, reputedly, untalented) actress.

703.9–11 *the works of Master Francois . . . bumgut fell out*: François Rabelais (*c.* 1490–1553), French satirical novelist, Franciscan then Benedictine monk, in his *The Histories of Gargantua and Pantagruel* (1534); Gargantua's mother Gargamelle thinks she's giving birth only to discover that 'her right intestine–which you call the bum-gut' is slipping out owing to her having eaten too much tripe; a midwife gives her an astringent which tightens everything so much that Gargantua can only get out by entering 'the hollow vein . . . climbing through the diaphragm to a point above the shoulders where this vein divides in two . . . [taking] the left fork and [coming] out by the left ear' (trans. J. M. Cohen (Harmondsworth: Penguin, 1955), i. 6. 52).

703.17 *after the ball was over*: from the song 'After the Ball' (1892) by Charles Harris.

703.17–18 *like the infant Jesus . . . arms*: the nativity shrine Molly recalls is at the Church of Oblate Fathers of Mary Immaculate, Inchicore, Dublin, to which, according to Stanislaus Joyce, Dante used to take the Joyce children (*My Brother's Keeper*, 9–10).

703.21–2 *H.R.H. . . . the year I was born*: the Prince of Wales apparently did not visit Gibraltar in 1870 (Molly's birth year), though he did in 1859 and 1876.

703.28 *plottering*: dawdling.

703.33 *mirada*: Spanish: 'look'.

704.4 *mathering*: mothering.

704.34 *I asked him*: should read 'I asked him about her'.

704.34–705.12 *that disgusting Cameron . . . something there*: should follow 'cabbage-leaf' at 704.28.

705.5–6 *coming home with . . . coming home with*: the repeated phrase 'of those rotten places the night coming home with' should be deleted.

705.8 *93 the canal was frozen*: both the Royal and Grand Canals froze over in 1893.

705.10 *meadero*: Spanish: 'urinal'.

705.12–13 *met something with hoses in it*: of course, 'met him pike hoses' (see 147.11) or 'metempsychosis' (see 62.4–13).

706.7 *Loves old sweet sonnnng*: should read 'Loves old sweeeetsonnnng'. See 61.20 n.

706.21 *Mrs Stanhope*: after Lady Hester Stanhope (1776–1839), niece and private secretary of William Pitt 'the Younger' (1759–1806); later, settled in Syria, where she evolved her own religion, and founded a monastery (on Mount Lebanon).

706.25 *wogger*: crude slang for dark-skinned person.

706.26 *in old Madrid . . . Waiting*: for the two songs, 'In Old Madrid' (to which Molly returns at 709.28–9 and 725.13–14, 17, 18–19) and 'Waiting' (to which she returns at 708.9–10); see, respectively, 264.20 n. and 264.17 n.

706.26 *Concone is the name . . . exercises*: Giuseppe Concone (1801–61), Italian voice teacher famous for his vocal exercises.

706.31–2 *love yes affly xxxxx*: should read 'love yrs affly Hester xxxxx'.

707.19 *after the change*: after this phrase, add: 'he was attractive to a girl in spite of being bald intelligent looking disappointed and gay at the same time he was like Thomas in the shadow of Ashlydyat'; *The Shadow of Ashlydyat* (1863), a novel by Mrs Henry Wood (1814–87); Thomas is the elder (greyer, less demonstrative, more long-suffering) brother of George (who is 'gay' but dishonest).

707.21–2 *the Moonstone . . . Wilkie Collins*: *The Moonstone* (1868), a novel by Wilkie Collins (1824–89), with *The Woman in White* (1860), generally considered the first full-length detective novels in English.

707.22 *East Lynne*: *East Lynne, Or the Earl's Daughter* (1861), another enormously popular novel by Mrs Henry Wood (see 707.19 n.).

707.23 *Henry Dunbar*: novel (1864) by Mary Elizabeth Braddon (1835–1915).

707.25 *Lord Lytton Eugene Aram*: *The Trial and Life of Eugene Aram* (1832) by Edward Bulwer-Lytton, Baron Lytton (1803–73), a crime novel written to expose the social injustices attendant on poverty.

707.25–6 *Molly bawn . . . Mrs Hungerford*: *Molly Bawn* (1878), a novel by Margaret Wolfe Hungerford (?1855–97) (pseudonym 'The Duchess'); title taken from Irish ballad that begins 'Oh! Molly Bawn! Why leave me pining?'; 'bawn': Gaelic: *bán*: 'white, pretty'.

707.27 *the one from Flanders*: of course, Moll Flanders in Daniel Defoe's *The Fortunes and Misfortunes of the Famous Moll Flanders* (1722).

708.1 *the swell of the ship*: should read 'the smell of ship'.

708.9–10 *waiting always waiting . . . flying feet*: from 'Waiting' (see 264.17 n.).

708.12–13 *when general Ulysses Grant . . . off the ship*: Grant (1822–85), US Civil War general and US President (1869–77), visited Gibraltar on 17 Nov. 1878; 'old Sprague the codsul' (should read 'consul'): Horatio Jones Sprague, US consul to Gibraltar (*c.*1873–1902) (G).

708.18 *jellibees*: Arabic: *jalab*: 'long hooded cloak'.

708.18 *levites assembly*: Levites: Jewish tribe, members of which traditionally served as attendants to the high priests.

709.12 *to write after*: should read 'to write from Canada after'.

709.12–13 *pisto madrileno*: Spanish: a dish of tomatoes and red peppers.

709.19 *pneumonia*: should read 'neumonia'.

709.20 *mine its a bother*: should read 'mine poor Nancy its a bother'.

709.22–3 *bereavement symphathy . . . newphew with*: should read: 'bereavement symp~~h~~athy . . . ne~~w~~phew with'.

709.34 *the ladies letterwriter*: *The Ladies' and Gentlemen's Model Letter Writer (a complete guide to correspondences on all subjects)* (1871).

710.6 *horquilla*: Spanish: 'hairpin'.

710.11 *4 drunken English sailors took all the rock from them*: Gibraltar was taken from the Spanish by a Dutch–English force of *c.* 1,800, 24 July 1704, during the War of the Spanish Succession (1700–14); the English then claimed it for themselves.

710.15–16 *when the priest was going . . . the vatican to the dying*: 'vatican': a Mollypropism for *viaticum* (Latin: 'travelling money; provisions for a journey'), the Eucharist given to a dying or seriously ill person.

710.21–2 *the language of stamps*: the position of the stamp on a letter was thought to convey a secret, perhaps unconscious, meaning, e.g. if it were at the top centre, the answer was 'yes'.

710.22 *shall I wear a white rose*: song 'Shall I Wear a White Rose?' by H. S. Clarke and E. B. Farmer.

710.24 *the Moorish wall*: long wall crossing the upper plateau of the Rock of Gibraltar.

710.24 *my sweetheart when a boy*: song by Wilford Morgan and 'Enoch'.

710.28 *de la Flora*: Spanish: 'of the flower'.

710.29 *there is a flower that bloometh*: see 486.21–2 n.

710.33 *the pesetas and the perragordas*: small-denomination Spanish coins.

710.35 *May when the infant king of Spain was born*: Alfonso XIII (d. 1941) was born 17 May 1886 and, his father having died in 1885, was 'infant king'.

711.2 *rock scorpion*: slang for a Gibraltar-born Spaniard.

711.18 *embarazada*: Spanish: 'pregnant'.

711.30 *morning*: should read 'moaning'.

711.33 *Molly darling*: song (1871) by Will S. Hays.

712.16 *womans higher functions*: often appealed to by anti-suffragist campaigners.

712.17 *the new woman bloomers*: women's underpants designed by Elizabeth Smith Miller and advocated as sensible and hygienic by (and so named after) Amelia Jenks Bloomer (1818–94), suffragist, temperance reformer, feminist editor.

712.17–18 *God send him sense and me more money*: proverbial, after a line in Swift's *Polite Conversation* (1738), conversation III; Lady Answerall: 'Well, God send him more Wit, and me more Money'.

712.26 *Europe*: should read 'Europa'.
713.5 *peau despagne*: 'peau d'Espagne': French: 'Spanish skin'.
713.7 *Claddagh ring*: traditional Galway wedding ring; 'Claddagh': a district in city Galway; the ring shows two hands holding a heart.
713.10 *pure 16 carat gold*: should read 'pure 18 carrot gold'.
713.10 *it was very heavy*: after this phrase add: 'but what could you get in a place like that the sandfrog shower from Africa and that derelict ship that came up the harbour Marie the Marie whatyoucallit no he hadnt a moustache that was Gardiner yes'; Molly is reaching for 'Marie Celeste': Arthur Conan Doyle's account (*Cornhill Magazine*, Jan. 1884) of the ship *Mary Celeste*, found abandoned under full sail off the coast of Portugal (4 Dec. 1872) and towed into Gibraltar.
713.12–14 *once in the dear deaead days beyondre call . . . loves sweet ssoooooong*: lines from 'Love's Old Sweet Song' (see 61.20 n.).
713.16 *skitting*: 'Laughing and giggling in a silly way' (P. W. Joyce, 325).
713.34–5 *My Ladys Bower . . . vaunted rooms*: song by F. E. Weatherly and Hope Temple which begins 'Thro' the moated Grange at twilight, | My love and I we went, | By empty rooms and lonely stairs, | In lovers' sweet content | . . . | But the place we lov'd best of all | Was called "my Lady's bower"' (*G*).
714.35 *lecking*: moistening.
715.17–18 *the steeplechase for the gold cup*: if Molly is thinking of the Ascot Gold Cup, it was a flat race, not a steeplechase.
715.31 *Mr de Kock*: Molly is mistaken about his name being a nickname (see 62.27 n.).
717.5–6 *and helping her . . . not him*: should follow 'fact' at 717.7.
717.16–17 *the last plumpudding too split in 2 halves*: a superstition, that a cake or 'pudding' which breaks in half on being removed from the pan portends a broken marriage, a separation or parting.
717.22–3 *the Only Way in the Theatre royal*: *The Only Way* (1899), play by Freeman Crofts Wills (*c.*1849–1913) and Frederick Langbridge; a sentimental adaptation of Charles Dickens's *A Tale of Two Cities* (1859).
717.26 *Beerbohm Tree in Trilby*: Sir Herbert Beerbohm Tree (1853–1917), English actor, played Svengali in a production of *Trilby* (see 494.6 n.) at the Gaiety Theatre in Dublin, 10–11 Oct. 1895 (*G*).
718.1–2 *Martin Harvey*: see 342.8 n.; Martin-Harvey's first success as an actor came in his role as Sydney Carton in *The Only Way* in 1899.
718.2–3 *it must be real love . . . for nothing*: in *The Only Way* (as in Dickens's *Tale*), Sydney Carton assumes the place of the Marquis St Evrémonde and dies at the guillotine, so that Evrémonde can stay with his wife Lucie (with whom Carton is himself in love) (*T*).
719.13 *that thing has come on me*: Molly has, of course, started her menstrual period.
719.25 *wife of Scarli*: *The Wife of Scarli* (1897) by G. A. Greene, English version of

Italian play *Tristi amori* ('sorrows of love'), by Giuseppe Giacosa, performed in Dublin, 22 Oct. 1897 (*G*).

719.32 *the clean sheets the clean linen*: should read 'the clean sheets I just put on I suppose the clean linen'.

720.12 *scout*: 'to squirt'.

720.18 *O how the waters come down at Lahore*: Molly's version of Robert Southey's (1774–1843) lines '"How does the water | Come down at Lodore?"' from 'The Cataract of Lodore' (1823); an onomatopoeic poem describing (for 120 lines) the water's fall in the Cumberland cataract; 'Lahore': in 1904, the capital of the Punjab, India.

721.1 *frequent omissions*: Molly-propism for 'frequent emissions'.

721.6 *strap*: 'A bold forward girl or woman' (P. W. Joyce, 336).

721.9 *a thing of beauty and of joy for ever*: Molly's adaptation of the first line of Keats's *Endymion* (see 479.26 n.).

721.17 *sloothering*: slobbering.

721.19 *blather*: Gaelic: *bladar*: 'coaxing, flattery'.

721.19 *strool*: Gaelic: *struille*: 'anything untidy or confused'; but also *srúill*: 'stream, channel'.

721.20–1 *O beau pays de la Touraine*: French: 'O beautiful country of La Touraine'; aria sung by Queen Marguerite de Valois in Act II of Meyerbeer's *Les Huguenots* (see 160.21–3 n.).

722.7 *Lord Napier*: Robert Cornelis, Lord Napier (1810–90), Field Marshal, Commander-in-Chief in India (1869–75) and Governor of Gibraltar (1876–83).

722.31–2 *the Aristocrats Masterpiece*: i.e. *Aristotle's Masterpiece*, for which see 226.2 n.

723.6 *wethen*: perhaps, a contraction of 'why then?'—an expostulatory reply (*G*).

723.19–21 *Tom Kernan . . . W C drunk*: the principal action of 'Grace' in *Dubliners*.

723.37–724.1 *Bill Bailey . . . come home*: song (1902) by Hughie Cannon.

724.8 *him and*: should read 'him trotting off in his trowlers and'.

724.11 *Maritana*: for *Maritana*, see 83.18–19 n.; at 724.14–15, Molly recalls singing 'O Maritana! Wildwood Flower', a duet sung by Don Cesar and Maritana in Act III of the opera.

724.12 *Phoebe dearest*: song, 'Phoebe Dearest, Tell O Tell Me', by Claxon Bellamy and J. L. Hatton.

724.12–13 *goodbye sweetheart . . . sweet tart goodbye*: 'goodbye *sweet*heart' should read 'goodbye sweetheart *sweet*heart'; song, 'Goodbye, Sweetheart, Goodbye', by Jane Williams and John L. Hatton (see 253.23 n. and 255.24, 30 n.).

724.25 *one thing nor the other of*: should read 'one thing nor the other the first cry was enough for me I heard the deathwatch too ticking in the wall of'; 'deathwatch': deathwatch beetle.

726.34 *coronado*: Spanish: 'tonsured'; though Molly may mean *cornudo*: Spanish: 'horned, cuckolded' (*G*).

728.29 *father Vial plana*: should read 'father Vilaplana'.

728.29–30 *Rosales y O'Reilly in the Calle las Siete Revueltas*: Spanish: 'Rosie O'Reilly in the Street of Seven Turnings' (the latter being a street known as 'City Mill Lane' to English-speaking Gibraltarians).

728.36 *como esta usted muy bien gracias y usted*: Spanish: 'how are you very well thank you and you?'.

729.2 *Valera*: Juan Valera Y Alcalá Galiano (1824–1905), Spanish novelist, poet, politician.

729.2 *the questions in it all upside down the two ways*: i.e. because of the punctuation marking a question in Spanish: '¿ sentence ?'.

729.10 *criada*: Spanish: 'maid'.

729.13–14 *dos huevos estrellados senor*: Spanish: 'two fried eggs sir'.

729.20 *gesabo*: see 357.3 and n.

729.34–5 *mi fa pieta Masetto ... presto non son più forte*: Italian: 'I'm sorry for Masetto! Quick, my strength is failing!' Zerlina in response to Don Giovanni's promptings in *Don Giovanni*, I. iii (see 61.20 n.).

730.7 *this vale of tears*: proverbial to the point of cliché for 'this life'.

731.35 *all birds fly*: children's game.

731.35 *I say stoop*: children's game.

732.9 *posadas glancing*: should read 'posadas 2 glancing'; 'posadas': Spanish: 'inns or town houses'.